AF378762

The Bristol and Gloucestershire Archaeological Society
Gloucestershire Record Series

Hon. General Editor

David J.H. Smith, M.A., F.S.A.
County and Diocesan Archivist of Gloucestershire

Hon. Editorial Advisors

Christopher Elrington, M.A., F.S.A., F.R.Hist.S.
General Editor of the
Victoria History of the Counties of England

Brian S. Smith, M.A., F.S.A., F.R.Hist.S.
Secretary to the
Royal Commission on Historical Manuscripts

Volume 3

Ralph Bigland
Historical Monumental and Genealogical Collections
Relative to the County of Gloucester

Part 2: Daglingworth–Moreton Valence

RALPH BIGLAND
HISTORICAL, MONUMENTAL AND GENEALOGICAL COLLECTIONS RELATIVE TO THE COUNTY OF GLOUCESTER

PART TWO:
DAGLINGWORTH–MORETON VALENCE

Edited by Brian Frith

The Bristol and Gloucestershire Archaeological Society

1990

The Bristol and Gloucestershire Archaeological Society
Gloucestershire Record Series

© The Bristol and Gloucestershire Archaeological Society

ISBN 0 900197 30 7

Produced for the Society by
Alan Sutton Publishing Ltd., Phoenix Mill, Far Thrupp, Stroud, Glos. GL5 2BU
Printed in Great Britain

CONTENTS

Page

LIST OF PLATES

FOREWORD

This second part of Ralph Bigland's *Historical, Monumental and Genealogical Collections, relative to the County of Gloucester*, completes the parishes which appeared in his original Volume I which ended with Guiting Temple (or Temple Guiting) and continues with those included in Volume II up to Moreton Valence.

Some of the information in the Foreword to Part 1 of the present edition also applies to this part. In particular, the spelling of some parish names differs from those normally met with today, so such places as Dean Michel and Dene Parva appear to be out of sequence by modern spelling. Bigland also uses unfamiliar names such as Hampton Monialium, though the subsequent pages are headed in the more usual form of Minchin Hampton. Littleton (or West Littleton) usually appearing in association with Tormarton, is also to be found in the present volume, not to be confused with Littleton-on-Severn which it precedes. The City of Gloucester was never included in Bigland's *Collections* but his notes were added to and used by the Rev. Thomas Fosbrooke who published them in 1819 as a completely separate work. As this has been re-printed it is not included here. The new pagination has been continued consecutively and the numbering of the parishes, as used by Bigland, should be ignored. Some of the plates were published slightly out of their natural sequence. Bigland's intention to include armorial bearings of the principal families in parish order was not sustained beyond the first volume of the original edition; those for Deerhurst–Guiting are included at the end of this part.

In the section on Minchin Hampton will be found notes on the fossils and botany of that area, whilst Henbury contains details of Roman coins found there in 1708, 1712 and 1768, as well as an interesting list of family portraits by eminent artists in Kingsweston House in that parish. Also in this part is a section for the Forest of Dean, with a useful description of that large extraparochial area, its history, and details of its customs and industries. Needless to say, being extraparochial, no monumental inscriptions are included.

The reader's attention is again drawn to the fact that any errors in the original printing have not been altered, and that some of the blemishes, not removable, still appear, though every effort has been made to eliminate them.

Comprehensive indexes to the whole work will appear in the final part.

Brian Frith
January, 1990

HISTORICAL, MONUMENTAL

AND

GENEALOGICAL COLLECTIONS,

RELATIVE TO THE COUNTY OF

GLOUCESTER;

PRINTED FROM THE ORIGINAL PAPERS

OF THE LATE

RALPH BIGLAND, Esq.

GARTER PRINCIPAL KING OF ARMS.

L O N D O N:

Printed by JOHN NICHOLS,

For RICHARD BIGLAND, of FROCESTER, in the County of GLOUCESTER, Efq.
Son of the late RALPH BIGLAND, Efq.

" IT is the prevailing Opinion of the World, that thefe Performances are folely
" fabricated by the petty Diligence of thofe unafpiring Antiquaries who employ
" their Time in collecting Coats of Arms, poring over Parifh Regifters, and
" tranfcribing Tombftones.—But HISTORIES of COUNTIES, if properly written,
" become Works of Entertainment, of Importance, and Univerfality.

" They may be made the Vehicles of much general Information, and fuch
" as is interefting to every Reader of a liberal Curiofity.

" What is local is often national."
WARTON.

LIES in the Hundred of *Crowthorne* and *Minety*, in the *Cotefwold* Divifion, three Miles North-weft-ward from *Cirencefter*, and fixteen in the precifely oppofite Direction from GLOUCESTER. The Soil is in general light and ftony, applied to Tillage, with a fmall Exception of Pafture and Woodland, within a Boundary of nearly fix Miles. To afcertain the Derivation of this fingular Name, is left to more experienced Etymologifts.

The Living, which is a Rectory in the Deanery of *Cirencefter*, was in 1499 in the Prefentation of the Abbefs of *Godftowe*, co. *Oxon*; and at the Suppreffion was referved to the Crown. It appears that the Church, which is a plain Structure of a Nave only, with a low embattled Tower, was erected at the Expence of the Nunnery.

In *Domefday* Book nothing is faid of this Manor; but in the Efcheator's Return of Vills in the Hundred of *Cirencefter* in 1281, 9 EDW. I. it occurs as including the contiguous Parifh of *Stratton*. RALPH DE BLOET obtained a Grant of free Warren of this Manor at that Time, ftating that it had been held by his Anceftor in the Reign of HENRY the Second. LIONEL Duke of CLARENCE * held it in the 14th Century. The Family of BLOET regained the Poffeffion at his Death, and it paffed by Marriage in 1378, 2 RICH. II. to JAMES, afterwards Baron BERKELEY. In that Barony it continued till 1601, 44 ELIZ. when it was fold by HENRY Lord BERKELEY, to Sir HENRY POOLE, of *Saperton*, for the Sum of 1320*l.* With fome of the adjoining Eftates of POOLE and ATKINS, it was purchafed early in this Century by ALLEN Lord BATHURST. The Demefnes are not extenfive; the principal Proprietors of Eftates are the Families of HAYNES and HINTON.

The *Irmin Street* (*Via Militaris*), or great Confular Road from GLOUCESTER to *Cirencefter*, paffes through this Parifh. This is one of the moft perfect public Works of the *Romans*, and ftill ferves its original Purpofe. Sufficient Veftiges of an advanced Poft from the grand Station at *Cirencefter* are difcovered in a Field near the Village.

Upon the Eaft Side of this Road is a fpacious Plain called *Dagham* Down, remarkable for a fingular Kind of Stone. It is found very near the Surface, upon a Bed of fine black Earth, in detached Blocks of the moft grotefque Formation, with abundant circular Perforations of feveral Inches diameter, and delicately fmooth. The Confiftence of thefe is fo firm as to refift the Effects of Weather, and they are frequently of a large Size. When ufed as ornamental in ruftic Buildings, they feem to anfwer the leading Idea of that Order, in a Manner not to be attained by anything artificial. On the fame Down is a Stone of a very clofe Grain, full of Petrifactions, and refembling the Marbles of *Derbyfhire*, when polifhed.

B E N E F A C T I O N S.

JEREMIAH HANCOCK, by Will, 1730, gave 100*l.* and WILLIAM BELITHA, Efq. 35*l.* for the religious Inftruction of the Poor; the annual Produce of both which now is 4*l.* 10*s.*
RICHARD SANDERS gave 5*l.* for the Ufe of the Poor for ever.
GILES HANCOCK, 1639, gave 5*l.* for the fame Purpofe.
EDMOND HINTON, 1773, likewife bequeathed 5*l.* for the Ufe of the Poor.
Other Donations, to the Amount of 20*l.* were given; the Intereft of which is alfo applied for the Ufe of the Poor.

INCUMBENTS.	PATRONS.	INCUMBENTS.	PATRONS.
1499 —————,	Abbefs of Godftowe.	1723 James Kilner, M. A.	King George I.
——— Richard Sanders,	—————.	1729 Jofeph Harrifon, M. A.	King George II.
1617 Anthony Haviland,	King James I.	1753 Jofeph Chapman, M.A.	King George II.
——— ——— Humphrys,	—————.	1776 Jofeph Chapman, D.D.	King George III.
1675 Nathaniel Gwyn,	King Charles II.		

* " ELIZA, Uxor BARTHOLOMÆI PYCOTT, Filia & Hæres JOHANNIS BLOET, de *Dagelinworth* & *Ragland*, conceffit LIONELLO
" Duci CLARENC', Manerium de *Dagelinworth* co GLOUCEST." Clauf. Rot. 42. m. 23.

5 Z

PRESENT

PRESENT LORD OF THE MANOR,
The Right Honourable HENRY Earl BATHURST.

The Perfons fummoned from this Place by the Heralds in 1682 and 1683 were
Giles Hancock, Gent. and Nathaniel Gwynne, Clerk.

At the Election in 1776, Seven Freeholders polled from this Parifh.

The Regifter commences in 1561.

ANNUAL ACCOUNT OF MARRIAGES, BIRTHS, AND BURIALS, IN THIS PARISH.

A.D.	Mar.	Bir.	Bur.	A.D.	Mar.	Bir.	Bur.	A.D.	Mar.	Bir.	Bur.	A.D.	Mar.	Bir.	Bur.
1781	1	10	4	1786	—	6	9	1791				1796			
1782	2	8	7	1787	3	9	6	1792				1797			
1783	—	4	6	1788	3	6	4	1793				1798			
1784	4	11	5	1789				1794				1799			
1785	2	6	4	1790				1795				1800			

INSCRIPTIONS IN THE CHURCH.

ON MONUMENTS.

Arms ; a Lion rampant ducally crowned, between three crofs Crofslets for KING.

Erected by MARY WEBB, Widow, 1731, in Teftimony of her filial, conjugal, and parental, Affection,
To the Memory of
Mr. THOMAS KING her Father, who died Anno Dom. 1710.

Mrs. ELIZABETH KING her Mother, who died Anno Dom. 1719.

NATHANIEL WEBB her Hufband, who died Anno Dom. 1728.

THOMAS WEBB her Son, who died Anno Dom. 1708.

KING WEBB her Son, who died Anno Dom. 1724.

ELEANOR CHEEKER her Sifter, who died Anno Dom. 1717.

ANNE HAINES her Grand-daughter, who died Anno Dom. 1729.

ANNE HINTON her Grand-daughter, who died Anno Dom. 1739.

To the Remains of thefe were added thofe of MARY herfelf, a Widow indeed, 1750, aged 82.

Arms ; three Crefcents counterchanged for HAYNES ;—impaling, a Lion rampant, for EDWARDS.

Erected by SARAH, the Widow of GILES HAYNES, of this Parifh, To the Memory of him, her loving and beloved Hufband, who died May 3, 1743, aged 85 Years.

The Soul of the abovenamed SARAH took its Flight from King Stanley to the Heavenly Manfions, and her Body was brought here to be interr'd Sept. 4, 1751, aged 87.

ON FLAT STONES.

M. S.
NATHANIELIS GWYNNE,
Ecclefiæ hujus per annos prope 48 Rectoris, qui poft longam
Valetudinem placide
in Domino obdormivit
Maii 30,
Anno { Domini 1723.
{ Ætat. 83.

H. I.
JANÆ,
JOSEPHI CHAPMAN,
Ecclefiæ hujus Rectoris,
Uxor,
Ob. 24 Junii, 1773, æt. 52.

IN THE CHURCH PORCH.

Mr. GILES HANCOCK,
ætatis fuæ 71,
April 17, 1684.

The Diffection and Diftribution of
GILES HANDCOX,
Who to Earth bequeaths to Earth, to Heaven his Soule,
To Friends his Love, to the Poore a five Pound Dole ;
To remain for ever, and be employed for their beft Advantage and Relief in Daglingworth,
April the 9th, 1638.

IN THE CHURCH YARD.

TIMOTHY WEBB, fenior, died Sept. 2, 1721, in the 82d Year of his Age.

DOROTHY his Wife died Sept. 8, 1687.

DANIEL WEBB died March 26, 1715, aged 35.

TIMOTHY, Son of DANIEL and SARAH WEBB, died Jan. 6, 1748, aged 42.

ELIZABETH, Wife of TIMOTHY WEBB, died June 10, 1757, aged 57.

ELIZABETH, Wife of WILLIAM WEBB, and Daughter of DANIEL and EAMEY DAVIS, of Cirencefter, died Nov. 27, 1780, aged 29.

ON TOMBS.

DANIEL and ELIZABETH their Children died Infants.

THOMAS SMITH, died March 11, 1766, aged 82.

SARAH his Wife, died April 23, 1765, aged 80.

ON FLAT AND HEAD STONES.

	Died	Aged
John Evans, fenior -	8 Sept. 1758	54
Jacob, Son of John and Ann Evans	9 Apr. 1766	27
Thomas, Son of John Sadler, of Brimpsfield - -	26 Feb. 1730	31
Hannah Sadler - -	30 Apr. 1731	14
Richard Window -	20 May, 1771	82
Anne his Wife - -	18 Jan. 1762	71
William Cowley -	8 Nov. 1735	66
Martha, Wife of William Cowley	19 Oct. 1728	55
Sarah, Wife of Giles Haynes	— Sept. 1751	87
John, Son of John and Ann Haynes	29 Nov. 1757	13
Jane their Daughter -	18 Nov. 1758	21
Sarah, Daughter of John and Ann Haynes - -	3 Apr. 1778	44
Elizabeth their Grand-daughter	23 Apr. 1779	27
	Died	Aged
Mary, Wife of William Hewlings, of Cirencefter -	15 Nov. 1776	26
John Haynes - -	8 Dec. 1771	71
Anne, Wife of John Haynes	10 Oct. 1778	66
John Afhmead - -	10 June, 1758	—
Ann his Wife - -	24 June, 1760	—
John Afhmead, of Baret's Brook	14 May, 1741	36
Richard Harris -	7 Dec. 1772	60
Thomas Richardfon, Maltfter, of this Parifh - -	28 Dec. 1771	67
Ann his Wife - -	28 Nov. 1781	67
Mary their Daughter -	21 Mar. 1757	17
Elizabeth, Relict of Thomas Webb, of Minchinhampton -	21 Dec. 1725	—
William Champion -	24 Dec. 1727	32

XC. DEAN

XC. DEAN MICHEL, or DENE MAGNA.

THOUGH the additional Name be generally fuppofed to have been given by the Tutelar *St. Michael*, it will be found to be of *Saxon* original, from the Word micl, or *great*, in Diftinction from the contiguous Parifh of *Little Dean*. This Conjecture is confirmed by its Application in other Parts of the County.

Michel Dean is a fmall Market Town, confifting of three narrow Streets very irregularly built, two of them diverging from the Extremity of the other, in the Form of a *Roman* Y. Late in the Reign of HENRY VI. the prefent Charter was granted for a weekly Market on Monday, and two annual Fairs, on Eafter Monday, and the 10th of October. Thefe are now well frequented, and the Adjuftment of Weights and Meafures is fettled by the Arbitration of an Officer, appointed by the Lord of the Manor, to whom certain Tolls are due. The Town, evidently more confiderable in former Times, is fituate in a very deep Dell, furrounded, excepting on the North-eaft, by wooded Hills, on the great Road from GLOUCESTER to *Monmouth*, about eleven Miles on the Weft.

The Form of the Parifh is an irregular Circle nearly four Miles acrofs in the wideft Part. Two thirds of the inclofed Lands are Pafture. Being a Member of the Hundred of *St. Briavel*, the Inhabitants are entitled to all the Immunities and Privileges of the Foreft. The Soil is moft commonly of a deep red Clay. Large Quantities of the *Scoria*, or Iron Cinders, are eafily collected and fold. It is long fince the Manufacture of Pins flourifhed in the Town, and gave Place to that of Leather, which is now carried on to fome Extent. It is faid that coarfe Cloth was formerly made here.

The Benefice is a Rectory in the *Foreft* Deanery *, the Patronage of which has ever been connected with the Manor.

* The *Foreft* Deanery was originally Part of the Diocefe of *Hereford*, till the Erection of the See of GLOUCESTER. The Archdeacon of *Hereford* vifits every Summer, and the Chancellor of GLOUCESTER the other Part of the Year.

The

The Ground Plot of the Church, dedicated to *St. Michael*, is of a quadrangular Form, nearly equilateral, and confifts of a Nave, two Aifles on the North, and one on the South, to which adjoins the Tower, not embattled, but finifhed by a Spire 156 Feet from the Foundation, extremely light, and of truly beautiful Gothic Proportions. Early in this Century it received confiderable Reparations. In the Eaft Window of the farther North Aifle are fome perfect Remains of painted Glafs, with which the Church was profufely de corated. In the higher Compartments is an Affemblage of female Figures with mufical Inftruments, and, difperfed in other Panes, the Heads of Nobles and Ecclefiaftics of either Sex, delicately wrought. The whole Roof is of Oak Frame, and ftudded with Rofes and other Devices, of exquifite Carving. Dr. Parsons fpeaks of Arms in the Chancel Window, " On a Fefs Gules, between three Birds, three Rofes Argent, " for . . . . . ." And in the great Weft Window, " Azure, on a Chief Argent, two Mullets Gules, for " . . . . ;—impaling Gules, a Chevron between three Bulls Heads affrontè, for Baynham."

Of the many mutilated Slabs *, once ornamented with fplendid Braffes, an imperfect one only re- mains; it is of Thomas Baynham, who died in 1444, the Founder of a Chantry dedicated to the *Holy Trinity* (the laft Incumbent of which was Henry Hooper), and moft probably a very munificent Bene- factor to the whole Fabric. The two North Aifles are moft clearly of the Style of his Day.

The Manor, foon after the Conqueft, was held by the Family of De Laci, but with fome fubfequent Alienations to the Abbies of Gloucester and *Porchefter*, alias *Southwyke* in *Hampfhire*. To Perfons of the Names of De Dene and Abbenhall, the Family of Greyndour fucceeded, foon after the Com- mencement of the 14th Century. Sir John Greyndour, who was Lord of this Manor † in the Reign of Henry IV, was Sheriff of the County in 1405 and 1409, whofe official Seal was lately difcovered in a Field near *Durfley*. The Defcent of the Manor after this Period has been hitherto imperfectly defcribed. John Tiptoft, the accomplifhed and unfortunate Earl of *Worcefter*, having married Elizabeth, Daugh- ter of Robert, only Son of Sir John Greyndour, became poffeffed of this Manor. Upon his Attainder and Death in 1471 it reverted to Alice the fecond Wife of Thomas Baynham already mentioned, and Daughter of William Walweyne, the Grandfon of Sir John Greyndour. In the Defcendants of

---

* Monuments of Brafs in our Churches, notwithftanding the boafted proverbial Durability of fuch Memorials, have proved far more perifhable than thofe of Stone. But thefe Loffes are not fo much owing to Time, as to Fanaticifm, a more powerful, at leaft a more furious Deftroyer. Warton's *Kiddington*, p. 7.

† Now in the Poffeffion of Mr. Shrapnell, of *Durfley*. It is of a compofed Metal, chiefly Brafs. Its Form is octangu- lar, and the Legend, " S. (*Sigillum*) JOHANNI' GREYNDOUR;" and on a quatrefoil, " S. D. H. R. *Sigillum Domini* Henrici " *Regis.*" See the Plate.

Thomas

Thomas Baynham it remained till about 1600, when it was fold to Sir Robert Woodruff. From the Commencement of this Century it has been held by the Family of Colchester. The principal Estates are that annexed to the Manor, and one belonging to Joseph Pyrke, Esq.

In a Wood upon a Hill about half a Mile from the Town is a subterraneous Passage communicating with the Church, concerning which many legendary Stories are told, but asserted with probability to have been in Feudal Times the Retreat of Outlaws who sought Sanctuary.

B E N E F A C T I O N S.

Jonathan Parker bequeathed 200l. to be laid out in Lands, the Profits of which to be applied in cloathing and apprenticeing some, or one Child yearly; the Produce is now 12l. 10s. a Year.

Richard Walwin left 20l.; the annual Produce thereof 1l. to be given to such Poor as are not on the Parish Book, on the Feast of St. John the Evangelist.

William Morse by his Will gave 100l. with which Land has been purchased; the yearly Profits 6l. 10s. to be given to the Poor on Christmas Day for ever.

Walter Little devised 15l.; the annual Produce, 15s. to be distributed amongst the Poor on the Feast of St. John the Evangelist.

Andrew Crew likewise gave 10l.; the Produce of which, 14s. a Year, to be applied to the same Purpose.

Robert Stanton bequeathed 6s. 8d. a Year, payable out of a Messuage, to be given to the Poor on the Feast aforesaid.

Jane Walter, 1760, left 20l.; the Interest of which, 1l. to buy Bibles for the Poor Inhabitants being Parishioners.

Within these few Years a Charity School hath been established in this Town by voluntary Subscription, wherein upwards of fifty Children have been taught to read and write, which by a laudable Exertion of its Promoters, has produced a wonderful Reformation in the Morals of the rising Generation.

Incumbents.	Patrons.	Incumbents.	Patrons.
—— William Austyn,	——————.	1674 Thomas Andrews, M.A.	William Collins.
1552 Edward Blennerhaffet,	——————.	1679 Richard Hall, M. A.	Robert Pawling.
1574 Richard Petty,	Thomas Horn.	1723 John White,	Maynard Colchester, Esq.
1587 Richard Petty,	Q. Elizabeth.	1727 Richard Roberts,	The same.
1592 Hugh Griffiths,	Thomas Bayntun.	1770 William Parry,	The same.
1623 Richard Stringer, M.A.	——————.	1773 John Harris, B. A.	The same.

Present Lord of the Manor;

John Colchester, Esq.

The Persons summoned from this Parish by the Heralds in 1682 and 1683, were

—— Nash, Gent.
—— Morse, Gent.
Thomas Rudge, Gent.
Richard Pyrke, Gent.

Charles Warner, Gent.
Thomas Wade, Gent.
Thomas Gottenvy, Gent.
William Merrick, Gent.

Giles Tower, Gent.
George Tower, Gent.
Thomas Wintell, Gent.
Christopher Hathaway, Gent.

At the Election in 1776 Thirty-four Freeholders polled from this Parish.

The Register commences with an Entry in 1680.

Annual Account of Marriages, Births, and Burials, in this Parish.

A.D.	Mar.	Bir.	Bur.	A.D.	Mar.	Bir.	Bur.	A.D.	Mar.	Bir.	Bur.	A.D.	Mar.	Bir.	Bur.
1781	5	15	13	1786	4	20	9	1791				1796			
1782	3	23	7	1787	5	18	8	1792				1797			
1783	5	17	11	1788	8	27	6	1793				1798			
1784	6	16	10	1789				1794				1799			
1785	2	21	7	1790				1795				1800			

6 A   I N

IN THE FARTHER NORTH AISLE.

A large blue Slab, the Effigies in Brafs of a Man between his two Wives in different Dreffes, that on the left with a very fingular Coif and Gloves.   Over the Man's Head an Efcutcheon (*gone*) with a Mantle and Creft.   Four corner Efcutcheons, three remaining; 1. Gules, a Chevron between three Bulls Heads cabofhed Argent, for BAYNHAM; 2. a Fefs furmounted of another indented, for HODYE; 3. Quarterly, 1ft and 4th, BAYNHAM; 2d and 3d, on a Chief three Mullets;—impaling, Per Pale Or and Vert, twelve Guttès counterchanged, for GREYNDOUR, and Crufuly a Fefs, for . . . .*.

INSCRIPTIONS IN THE CHURCH.

ON A STONE AGAINST THE EAST WALL IN
THE CHANCEL :

Hic conditur fub terrâ RICHARDUS STRINGER,
Filius RICHARDI STRINGER, hujus Ecclefiæ Rectoris;
et ELIZABETHÆ uxoris, natus Deane Magnæ,
educatus fcholæ Collegialis Gloceftrenfis,
necnon morte peremptus, Aprilis 12,
Anno Salutis 1647, ætatis fuæ 15.

ON A MONUMENT AGAINST THE SAME WALL :

Ut fciant Pofteri
Infra recondi caducum quod fuit
Venerabilis Viri RICHARDI HALL,
Hujus Ecclefiæ per Annos 44,
Et Ecclefiæ Abinghall Anno 37.
Paftoris probatiffimi
Uxores duxerat JOANNEM & SARAM ;
Quarum
Illa prope maritum hic fepulta jacet;
Hæc autem fuperftes amiffum dolet.
Obiit
Anno { Domini 1722.
       { Ætatis 72.

In Memoriam etiam THOMÆ WORGAN,
Generofi, qui hoc Monumentum
Erexit, & obiit Julii decimo die, 1726,
ætatis fuæ 40.

Alfo SARAH, Wife of Mr. RICHARD HALL,
deceafed in the Year 1729.

Alfo MARY, Wife of Mr. THOMAS WORGAN,
departed this Life Feb. 11, 1746, æt. 59.

ON FLAT STONES
IN THE CHANCEL.

To the Memory of the painful
and faithful Preacher of God's Word,
both by Life and Doctrine,
Mr. RICHARD STRINGER,
Mafter of Arts, and Rector of this Church
fifty-two Years, who went to be with
the Lord JESUS the 4th of February 1674,
in the 77th Year of his Age.

Labor in viâ, in Patriâ quies.

JOAN, Wife of RICHARD HALL,
Rector of this Parifh, was buried
March 5, 1698, in the 42d Year of her Age.

Mrs. AMY HALL
died Jan. 18, 1706-7, in the 92d Year of her Age.

THOMAS WORGAN, 1679.

WILLIAM CALLOW, late of Deane Magna, Gent.
departed this Life Nov. 28, 1677, aged 61.

MARY BARRETT, 1769.

ISABEL, Wife of WILLIAM CALLOW, Gent.
died Dec. 31, 1677, æt. 74.

Hic jacet Mortale quod fuit
FRANCISCI ASHMEADE, qui obiit
15 Die menfis Februarii, A. D. 1729,
ætatis fuæ 55.

SUSANNAH, Daughter of
FRANCIS ASHMEAD, Surgeon,
departed this Life April 30, 1743, aged 39.

HENRY PLATT, of this Town,
died June 17, 1762, aged 45.

ON A MONUMENT IN THE NAVE :

Arms; a Chevron between three Palmer's Scrips.

Underneath this Place are depofited
the Remains of Mr. JOHN PALMER,
Joiner and Citizen of London,
late of this Town, who died the
18th of June, 1782, æt. 68.
He was an affectionate Hufband and fincere Friend.

ON FLAT STONES.

WILLIAM HUGHES, of this Parifh, Gent.
deceafed Feb. 14, 1722, in the 46th Year of his Age.

WILLIAM, Son of WILLIAM and ANN HUGHES,
died June 8, 1712, aged 6.

---

* This Memorial was for THOMAS BAYNHAM, Efq. who died in 1444, whofe firft Wife was MARGERY, Daughter of Sir RICHARD HODYE, Knight, and his fecond ALICE, Daughter of WILLIAM WALWYN.

Hic

Hic jacet Corpus EDVARDI PARTRIDGE, fen.
qui obiit decimo Die Jan. Anno Dom. 1691,
ætatis fuæ 82.

Here lieth the Bodies of
DEBORAH and DEBORAH, the Daughters of
EDWARD MORSE, of this Town,
the eldeft departed this Life
the 14th, the youngeft the 18th,
of May, 1661.

MARGARET, Daughter of EDWARD MORSE,
died April 9, 1680.

Subter hunc
Lapidem reconduntur exuviæ ANNÆ, filiæ
JOHANNIS JELF, Rectori de Blayfdon, Comitatu
Glouceftrienfi, per MARIAM
Uxorem. Sponfa fuit
THOMÆ SARGEAUNT, de
Mitchel Deane, Comitatu prædicto;
Conjux amantiffima & felectiffima;
Fœmina pia & prudens;
Amicis fidelis,
Indigentibus liberalis;
Quæ poft vitam viginti & quatuor
Annorum animam efflavit
Vicefimo fexto die Septembris,
Anno Salutis 1755.

THOMAS RUDGE, of this Town,
departed this Life July 6, 1714, aged 28.

SARAH, Daughter of JOHN and JOANNAH RUDGE,
died Aug. 14, 1752, aged 40.

SARAH, Wife of THOMAS RUDGE,
died Oct. 13, 1711, aged 25.

ROBERT BROOKES, of this Town, Mercer,
died Feb. 27, 1747, aged 54.

ELIZABETH, the Wife of Mr. WALTER RUDGE,
of this Town, Mercer, died Feb. 4, 1675.

Mr. WALTER RUDGE
departed this Life Oct. 4, 1689.

Mr. NATHANIEL RUDGE their Son
died Aug. 30, 1725, aged 61.

MARGARET, the Wife of SAMUEL BROOKES,
of this Town, Mercer, eldeft Daughter of
Mr. NATHANIEL RUDGE,
died Oct. 2, 1724, aged 33.

ROBERT their Son
died Sept. 28, 1724.

WILLIAM RIDER, of this Town,
died in October 1714.

JOAN his Wife
was buried Dec. 23, 1679.

SAMUEL DICKES
died Aug. 14, 1752, aged 42.

SAMUEL his Son, by JANE his Wife,
died Auguft 19, 1752, aged 11.

ROBERT, Son of ROBERT RUSSELL,
died Dec. 30, 1759, aged 31.

SARAH, Daughter of JOHN and SARAH VOICE,
died April 15, 1757, aged 11.

ON A MONUMENT IN THE SOUTH AISLE:

Arms; Gules, a Crofs Argent between four
Swords erect of the fecond, hilted Or, for HOLMES

This Monument was erected in
Memory of ELIZABETH, the Daughter of
THOMAS and MARY HOLMES, of the Parifh of
Llangarran, who departed this Life
the 5th of February, 1758,
aged 21 Years.

In Memory of MARY HOLMES,
who departed this Life the 15th of March, 1765,
aged 61 Years.

ON FLAT STONES
IN THE SOUTH AISLE.

THOMAS BURGUM
departed this Life Sept. 3, 1748, aged 35.

ROGER APPLETREE, of this Town, Cooper,
died July 5, 1773, aged 56.

SARAH EDWARDS, of this Town,
was buried Aug. 7, 1722, aged 69.

IN THE BELLFRY.

THOMAS MORGAN, of this Town, Sadler,
died May 21, 1769, aged 32.

THOMAS HUGHES
departed this Life May 27, 1755, aged 43.

JOHN LANE
died the 20th of January, 1644.

IN THE NORTH AISLES.
ON MONUMENTS.

To the Memory of BETTY, Wife of
FRANCIS LEWIS,
who died May 31, 1768, aged 38.

Near this Place lie the Remains of
JOHN STEPHENS, who departed this Life
the 23d April, 1767, aged 58.

Alfo the Remains of TACY his Wife,
who died Jan. 7, 1773, aged 70.

Near this Place alfo lie the Remains of
SARAH, the Wife of JOHN STEPHENS,
of this Town, Currier,
who departed this Life Dec. 26, 1779, aged 43.

Near

Near this Place lie the Remains of
WILLIAM CROSS, of this Town, Mercer,
who departed this Life Feb. 8, 1734, aged 38.

Alſo ELIZABETH his Wife.
She departed her Life May 27, 1754, aged 64.

SOPHIA, the Daughter of
WILLIAM and ELIZABETH CROSS,
died in her Infancy.

Alſo ELIZABETH, the Wife of WILLIAM CROSS,
of this Town, Mercer,
departed this Life, with her Son,
July 27, 1776, aged 35.

———

Arms; Per Pale, three Saltires, for LANE;—
impaling, on a Feſs three Cheſſrooks and in Chief
three Martlets, for BROWNE.

Near this Place
lie the Remains of WILLIAM LANE, Gent.
who died May 7, 1748,
aged 63.

Alſo of ELIZABETH his Wife,
who died April the 1ſt, 1753,
aged 66.

They reſigned this Life,
with well grounded Hopes for a better,
having given to the World ſuch well known
Examples of the conſcientious Diſcharge
of the Duties reſpectively incumbent upon them,
as need not Praiſes,
but deſerve Imitation.

———

Arms; Argent, a Chevron between three Dolphins embowed Sable, for SARGEAUNT;—impaling,
on a Feſs three Mullets and a Canton, for PYRKE.

In Memory of EDWARD SARGEAUNT, of
Hart Barn in the Pariſh of Longhope
in this County, Gent.
who deceaſed July 24, 1698,
aged 92 Years.

Alſo of ANNE his Wife,
who deceaſed June the 21ſt, 1653.

Alſo JOHN, Son of EDWARD SARGEAUNT, Gent.
who died April 19, 1720, aged 80 Years.

Alſo ANNE his Wife, Daughter of
THOMAS PURY, of Tainton, Gent.
died March 20, 1727, aged 83 Years.

———

ELIZABETH, Wife of HENRY YEARSLEY,
departed this Life Feb. 15, 1754, aged 70.

Likewiſe WILLIAM BARRON,
Apothecary and Surgeon of this Town,
died April 20, 1767, aged 44.

HENRY YEARSLEY, of this Town,
died the 30th of October, 1767, aged 77.

ON FLAT STONES.

MARY, the Widow of JOHN SARGEAUNT, Gent.
deceaſed in the Year of our Lord GOD 1671.

Alſo EDWARD, Son of JOHN SARGEAUNT, Gent.
died Oct. 14, 1690, aged 30.

Mr. SAMUEL SARGEAUNT, Son of
JOHN and ANN SARGEAUNT, Gent.
died April 1, 1757, aged 72.

———

ELIZABETH, the Wife of ROBERT SARGEAUNT,
of this Town, Gent. paid the Debt of Nature,
Feb. 22, 1721, aged 41.

ISABEL, Wife of EDWARD SARGEAUNT,
died April the 3d, 1753.

ELIZABETH, Daughter of the ſaid EDWARD,
died May the 10th, 1753.

———

WILLIAM, Son of JOHN SARGEAUNT,
of Hart Barn, Gent. and ANNE his Wife,
died March 23, 1734.

RICHARD, another Son,
died Dec. 6, 1738.

ANNE their Daughter
died Dec. 8, 1738; Infants.

———

MARY, Relict of WILLIAM SARGEAUNT,
of Hart Barn, Gent. departed thie Life
Dec. 7, 1735, aged 59 Years.

WILLIAM SARGEAUNT, of Hart Barn
in the Pariſh of Longhope,
died May 3, 1752, aged 33.

ELIZABETH, Wife of THOMAS BOWER, Gent.
deceaſed October 3, 1639.

ROBERT SARGEAUNT, of Hart's Barn
in this County, Gent.
died Jan. 19, 1732, aged 55.

MARY, Widow and Relict of
the above ROBERT SARGEAUNT, Gent.
died Jan. 3, 1776, aged 78.

———

THOMAS TOMKINS, Gent.
departed this Life the 5th of June, 1711.

Alſo ELIZABETH, the Wife of
THOMAS TOMKINS, Gent.
Daughter of EDWARD MACHEN, Eſq.
died the 19th of Dec. 1712.

———

EDWARD MACHEN, Eſq.
died May 2, 1708.

ANN TOMKINS, Grand Daughter of
EDWARD MACHEN, Eſq.
died April 19, 1708.

———

HENRY HAWKINS, of Engliſh Bicknor,
died Feb. 27, 1745, aged 28.

SUSANNA

Susanna, Wife of Thomas Butcher,
died July 5, 1706, aged 24.

John, the Son of John Green,
of this Town, by Elizabeth his Wife,
died June 22, 1735.

Alfo John Green, fenior,
died Feb. 7, 1750, aged 44.

Mary their Daughter
died Jan. 8, 1737.

John Butcher, of this Town,
died July 21, 1714, in the 36th Year of his Age.

Mary Morgan, Widow,
died Sept. 25, 1708, aged 79.

Timothy Morgan
died Aug. 15, 1746, aged 76.

Charles, Son of John Collins,
by Sarah his Wife,
died Jan. 11, 1751, aged 8.

Mary, Wife of Giles Tower,
died Nov. 10, 1682, aged 31.

Elizabeth, Wife of Giles Tower, junior,
died Nov. 28, 1711, aged 35.

Giles Tower
died June 28, 1719, aged 73.

Giles Tower, junior,
died June 15, 1755, aged 77.

Sarah, Wife of James Rudge,
and Daughter of Giles and Elizabeth Tower,
died March 2, 1765, aged 58.

Elizabeth, Wife of Thomas Perkins, fenior,
late of the Hay in the Parifh of Afton Ingham,
and Daughter of Giles and Elizabeth Tower,
died Nov. 6, 1779, aged 75.

Elizabeth, Wife of Henry Yearsley,
was interred Feb. 17, 1754.

Henry Yearsley, of this Town,
died Oct. 30, 1767, aged 77.

Ann, Relict of John Aldridge,
died May 9, 1776, aged 40.

Nancy, Relict of the above John Aldridge,
was buried Nov. 17, 1781, aged 33.

John their Son died an Infant.

John Barrow
died Feb. 28, 1750, aged 43.

John Morgan, of this Town, Sadler,
died July 27, 1766, aged 62.

Anne his Wife
died March 30, 1785, aged 84.

Susanna, Wife of William Meyrick,
died April the 13th, 1678.

William Meyrick
died July 6, 1697.

Susanna their Daughter
died Dec. 26, 1702.

Robert Gabbett
died March 24, 1646.

Elizabeth his Wife
died Oct. 26, 1659.

Hannah, Wife of Dr. Powell,
departed this Life Dec. 25, 1711, aged 70.

Sarah, Wife of William Pearce,
died Auguft 14, 1746, aged 23.

John, Son of William Pearce,
died Dec. 20, 1726.

Here lieth the Body of
Richard Pyrke, of the Dunftan, Gent.
Son of Robert, who lyeth with his
Father in Abbinghall Chancel.
The faid Richard left Iffue,
Richard, Jonathan, Lazarus, Anna, and
Elizabeth.

Here alfo lyeth Mary his Daughter,
who married with Thomas Wilkins, Gent.
and died March 3, 1722.

Thomas Wallin, junior,
died January 1, 1698.

William Gibbs
was buried March 1, 1728-9,
aged 59.

Elizabeth his Wife
was buried April 6, 1729, aged 61.

Pyrke Nathaniel Lloyd,
died Feb. 2, 1739, aged 3.

James Lloyd
was buried Auguft 28, 1752, aged 22.

James Lloyd, fenior,
died Dec. 26, 1770, aged 74.

Mary, the Daughter of
Henry and Elizabeth Lewis,
Surgeon of this Town,
died Dec. 16, 1739.

Anne their Daughter died March 10, 1739.

Mrs. Anne Huntridge, Grandmother of the
aforefaid Mary and Ann Lewis,
who departed this Life June 7, 1740, aged 69.

Thomas Turbervile
died April 14, 1728.

Thomas Bradley
died Jan. 11, 1693, aged 59.

William

WILLIAM COXE
died Auguſt 14, 1657.

ELIZABETH, Wife of **THOMAS RUDGE**,
died February 4, 1675.

THOMAS WALLIN
died Oct. 29, 1695, aged 64.

ELIZABETH, Daughter of
GEORGE and **CATHARINE GIBBS**,
died Auguſt 4, 1751.

ELIZABETH LANE, Widow,
died January 26, 1692.

REBECKAH LANE her Daughter
died Nov. 17, 1694.

THOMAS, Son of **THOMAS MERRITT**,
of this Town, Baker,
died April 24, 1739, aged 28.

JONATHAN, Son of **JONATHAN RUDGE**,
by **CATHARINE** his Wife,
was buried Dec. 19, 1726, aged 31.

ON FLAT STONES
AT THE WEST END.

WILLIAM BANNISTER,
of this Town, Yeoman,
died March 31, 1716, aged near 64.

THOMAS PACEY
died April 5, 1731, aged 44.

MARY PACEY
died July 19, 1755, aged 64.

THOMAS PACEY, of this Town, Blackſmith,
died Sept. 7, 1724, aged 70.

WALTER PACEY
died May 17, 1762, aged 76.

JANE PACEY
died March 17, 1729, aged 77.

SARAH PACEY
died Feb. 6, 1749, aged 56.

IN THE CHURCH PORCH.

ANN, Wife of **ROBERT PEARCE**,
Relict of **WILLIAM BOSSOM**,
died May 17, 1780, aged 68.

THOMAS BARNARD, junior,
died May 15, 1774, aged 26.

SARAH his Wife
died April 15, 1772, aged 33.

IN THE CHURCH YARD, ON TOMBS.

DANIEL PLATT, of this Town, Glover,
died July 6, 1737.

CHARLES GIBBONS, ſenior,
died April 7, 1741, aged 54.

SUSAN his Wife
died March 4, 1760, aged 77.

WILLIAM, Son of
WILLIAM and **ELIZABETH LODGE**,
died June 6, 1758, aged 20.

THOMAS BOSSOM, of this Town,
died Nov. 30, 1749, aged 79.

EDWARD, Son of
MARGARET WILLIAMS,
died March 7, 1762, aged 19.

JAMES BULLOCK,
late of this Town, Butcher,
died October 5, 1776, aged 59.

MARY, Daughter of
JOHN BULLOCK,
by **SARAH** his Wife,
of the Pariſh of Minſterworth,
died Oct. 7, 1764, aged 13.

ON FLAT AND HEAD STONES.

	Died	Aged
Sybil Edwards -	28 Aug. 1762	51
Thomas Mitchell -	15 Jan. 1705	70
John Knight, of the Pariſh of Abbinghall - -	17 Mar. 1763	62
Mary his Wife -	9 Nov. 1778	78
Mary, Wife of John Leonard	14 Apr. 1784	—
Thomas their Son -	23 Dec. 1775	37
Mary, Wife of John Harding, Daughter of John and Mary Leonard	19 Oct. 1782	37
Betty, Wife of Henry Hartley, Daughter of John and Mary Leonard	11 Sept. 1787	38
John Morgan - -	27 Mar. 1755	58
Mary, Wife of John Morgan	22 Dec. 1755	75
Sarah Andrews Hartland, Daughter of Miles and Beata Hartland	26 Jan. 1779	7
Benjamina their Daughter -	1 Jan. 1782	3
Aneriſt, Wife of Benjamin James	26 Feb. 1743	—
Jane, Wife of Thomas Griffiths	23 Jan. 1786	57
John Griffiths - -	—— —— 1750	44
Elizabeth his Wife -	—— —— 1766	60
Mary Griffiths -	7 Nov. 1751	82

	Died	Aged
Thomas Walden -	11 Jan. 1747	—
Mary his Wife -	31 May, 1728	—
Mary Rudge, Widow -	3 Apr. 1730	74
Thomas Boſſom - -	—— —— 1706	—
Sarah, Wife of James Baldwin	8 May, 1773	87
Thomas Roberts -	4 Apr. 1712	—
Thomas Roberts -	22 Apr. 1740	43
Mary, Wife of Thomas Roberts	24 Jan. 1747	52
Jane Meek, Widow -	20 Jan. 1751	82
John Leonard, of this Town	22 May, 1784	76
Charles Walden -	15 Dec. 1755	48
Margaret his Wife, late Wife of Richard Knight -	12 Jan. 1759	54
Thomas Lane -	12 Feb. 1708	—
Jane his Wife, afterwards Wife of Iſaac Caſtle -	28 Jan. 1750	82
Henry Hartley -	12 Mar. 1771	62
Sarah his Wife - -	25 June, 1782	62
James Dowle - -	20 Dec. 1758	78
Sarah, Wife of James Dowle	21 Sept. 1767	73

XCI. DENE

XCI. DENE PARVA, or LITTLE DEAN.

OF this Parish the early Records are exactly the fame, as of its adjoining, *Michel Dean*, from which it was originally feparated. It is of an oval Form, one Mile in Breadth, and one Mile and a half in Length, of a deep fertile Soil, chiefly Pafture; three Miles South from *Michel Dean*, and twelve from GLOUCESTER on the Weft.

The Village is large and well peopled; the poorer Inhabitants are employed in a Manufacture of Nails. In the midft of it is a very curious Market Crofs, around the Shaft of which is a low octangular Roof, which is then finifhed by a Pinnacle of fine Gothic Workmanfhip, with Niches and Effigies, on a fmall Scale. There are two annual Fairs.

The Living is an Impropriation annexed to *Newnham*, given to the Hofpital of *St. Bartholomew* in GLOUCESTER, and now held by the Mayor and Burgeffes as Truftees. It is leafed to the Incumbent for 8*l.* a Year, to whom all other Tythes are due.

The Church, dedicated to *St. Ethelbert*, confifts of a Nave and North Aifle, with a Chantry parallel to the Chancel, and a Spire of exact and elegant Proportions. The Windows of the North Aifle and Chantry exhibit very rich Remains of painted Glafs. Twice repeated are, " Or, a Fefs between fix Rofes " Gules," the augmented Bearing of the Family of ABBENHALL, by one of whom this Chantry was founded in 1412, 13 HEN. IV. GEORGE POMEROY, the laft Prieft, retired with a Penfion of 4*l.* The ancient facerdotal Veftments of Velvet, embroidered with the Portraits of Saints, are now ufed as a Covering for the Reading Defk.

In *Domefday* Book no mention is made of the Manor, and it appears for the moft Part to have been held with *Michel Dean.* Yet, a diftinct Manor was granted to the Abbey of *Flaxley*, and confirmed to Sir ANTHONY KINGSTONE at the Suppreffion 1545. RICHARD BRAIN purchafed the principal Eftate in 1573, 15 ELIZ. and in the next Century it was transferred to the Family of BRIDGEMAN. Upon their Removal to *Prinknafh*, it was fold to the Anceftor of the prefent Proprietor, JOSEPH PYRKE, Efq. The chief Manor* was vefted in the Family of HEANE in 1610, 8 JAC. of whom it was purchafed in 1676, 2 CAR. 11. by JOHN PARKER, Gent. of *Hasfield* whofe Daughters and Coheirs, in 1700, re-fold it to MAYNARD COLCHESTER, Efq. an Anceftor of the prefent Poffeffor. The Families of ABRAHALL and SKIPP are poffeffed of other Eftates.

In this Village was a very memorable Skirmifh during the Civil Wars †.

The Houfe of Correction, now erecting here in purfuance of an Act paffed in 1784, for the *Foreft* Divifion, is built in a Style of fingular Propriety, and evinces the fuperior Skill of the Architect.

B E N E F A C T I O N S.

THOMAS BARTLEM, 1714, gave by Will a Houfe and Garden, value 1*l.* 5*s.* a Year, to be diftributed in Bread to the Poor.

EUSTACE HARDWICK bequeathed two Clofes of Land; the annual Produce of which, 9*l.* to be applied in cloathing the Poor (after deducting 10*s.* for a Sermon, and the Expences of repairing her Tomb).

JANE WALTERS, 1760, gave 20*l.* for Bibles, for the Poor of this Parifh.

---

* THOMAS MARSHALL, Rector of *Lincoln College, Oxford,* endowed certain Scholarfhips with a Rent Charge of 12*l.* per Annum, iffuing from the Manor of *Little Dean.* WOOD's Ath. vol. II. p. 592. Antiq. Oxon. p. 249.

† " The Enemy had another Guard at *Little Deane*, wither the Governor commanded a Party of Horfe, to give them Alarms " whilft he fell upon *Weftbury.* Thefe Horfe found the Enemy ftraggling in the Towne; and upon the Difcovery of their Ap- " proach fhuffling towards the Garrifon, which the Troopers obferving, alighted and ran together with them into the Houfe, " where they tooke about twenty Men. Neere unto which Guard, Lieutenant Colonel CONGRAVE, Governor of *Newnham,* " and one Captain WIGMORE, with a few private Soldiers, were furrounded, in fome Houfes by the Refidue of our Horfe. " Thefe had accepted Quarter, ready to furrender themfelves, when one of their Company from the Houfe kils a Trooper; " which fo enraged the reft, that they broke in upon them, and put them all to the Sword; in which Accident this Paffage was " not to be forgotten, that expreffed in one Place an extreme Contrariety in the Spirits of Men under the Stroke of Death. " CONGRAVE died with thefe Words, ' Lord receive my Soul!' but WIGMORE crying nothing but ' Dam me more, dame me " more!' defperately requiring at the laft Stroke, as enraged at Divine Revenge."

CORBET's Military Government of GLOUCESTER, pp. 67. 68.

DOROTHY

Dorothy Pyrke, 1760, left 200*l.* the Intereſt of which to be diſtributed as follows, viz. 4*l.* 10*s.* for a School and Books, 1*l.* 1*s.* for a Sermon on Good Friday, and the Remainder for Linen Garments for the Poor ; the annual Produce now is 7*l.*

Preſent Officiating Miniſter, Benjamin Webb, Clerk.

The former Series will be inſerted under *NEWNHAM,* to which the Curacy is annexed.

PRESENT PROPRIETORS OF THE MANORS,

Of Part lying towards the Foreſt,	Of the Chief Manor,
Sir Thomas Crawley Boevey, Bart.	John Colchester, Eſq.

The Perſons ſummoned from this Pariſh by the Heralds, in 1682 and 1683, were

Thomas Pyrke, Gent.	William Braine, Gent.
Chriſtopher Braine, Gent.	John Braine, Gent.
Euſeby Hardwick, Gent.	Miles White, Gent.

At the Election in 1776 Twenty-nine Freeholders polled from this Pariſh.

The firſt Entry in the Regiſter bears Date 1684.

ANNUAL ACCOUNT OF MARRIAGES, BIRTHS, AND BURIALS, IN THIS PARISH.

A.D.	Mar.	Bir.	Bur.	A.D.	Mar.	Bir.	Bur.	A.D.	Mar.	Bir.	Bur.	A.D.	Mar.	Bir.	Bur.
1781	4	22	12	1786	4	26	9	1791				1796			
1782	—	20	8	1787	7	20	26	1792				1797			
1783	2	17	12	1788	4	23	13	1793				1798			
1784	4	20	10	1789				1794				1799			
1785	7	18	11	1790				1795				1800			

INSCRIPTIONS IN THE CHURCH.

THE FOLLOWING ARMS AND INSCRIPTION WERE ON A MONUMENT ON THE SOUTH SIDE THE CHANCEL, NOW ENTIRELY DEMOLISHED :

On a Feſs three Mulletts and a Canton, for Pyrke;—impaling, a Croſs, and in the dexter chief Point a Roſe.

Ad poſteros ſuos.
Vanus honor tituli, nec opum poſſeſſio certa,
Virtus ſola decus, mens bona divitiæ.
O quicunque domum cupias nomenque tueri,
Nomen amare pius diſce domumque Dei.
H. S. I.
Thomas Pyrke, Armiger,
Qui
Uſque adeo in verbis fidem,
in poculis ſobrietatem,
Et in hoc comitatu juſticiarius,
Pacem publicam conſervavit,
Ut tandem ævi ſatur
Ann. ætat. LXXII, April IX, A. D. MDCCII.
In pace deceſſit.
Uxore Debora tribuſque filiis diu antea
Præmiſſis, & in ecclefia de Abbenhall, una
Cum progenitorum ſtirpe ſepultis.
Ejus Memoriæ
Nathaniel, filius hæreſque,
Hoc monumentum gratus parentavit.

ON A NEAT MONUMENT OF VARIEGATED MARBLE, WITH A SARCOPHAGUS AND URN :

Arms ; Pyrke as before ;—impaling, Azure, a Feſs, and in chief two Mullets Or, for Yate.

Here lie the Remains of
Thomas Pyrke, Eſq.
one of his Majeſty's Juſtices of the Peace,
a Verdurer of the Foreſt of Dean,
and Deputy Conſtable of the Caſtle of St. Breeval ;
all which Offices he diſcharged with
Honour and Integrity.
He married Dorothy, Daughter of
Richard Yate, of Arlingham, Eſq.
By whom he had four Sons
and two Daughters ;
Thomas and Charles, two of his Sons,
are interred in this Church ;
Nathaniel and Maynard,
Bridget and Dorothy,
in the Pariſh Church of Abbinhall.
He died March 2, 1752, aged 65.

Mrs. Pyrke cauſed this Monument
to be erected, out of her great Affection
and Regard to the Memory of
ſo good an Huſband.

ON

ON FLAT STONES IN THE CHANCEL.

ELIZABETH, the Wife of THOMAS PYRKE, Efq.
departed this Life Oct. 12, 1679.

After many fore and heavy Afflictions
for the Lofs of her Hufband and fix Children,
Here refts, in hopes of a glorious Refurrection,
the Body of DOROTHY PYRKE, Wife of
THOMAS PYRKE, Efq.
of this Parifh, and fecond Daughter of
RICHARD YATE, Efq.
of Arlingham in this County.
She deceafed the 24th of January, 1762,
aged 76 Years.

ELIZABETH, Wife of DUNCOMBE PYRKE, Gent.
who died October the 16th, 1729.

MARY YOUNG, late of the Grange
in the Parifh of Flaxley,
in the County of Gloucefter, Widow
of JOHN YOUNG, of
Lay in the Parifh of Weftbury, Gent.
and Daughter of THOMAS PYRKE,
of Little Dean, Efq.
who departed this Life Feb. 7, 1741, aged 78.

MARY, Mother of the faid MARY YOUNG,
and Wife of the faid THOMAS PYRKE,
who departed this Life May 17, 1668.

Mr. CHARLES PYRKE,
Son of THOMAS PYRKE, of this Parifh, Efq.
by DOROTHY his Wife,
died the 19th of April, 1744, aged 23.

ROWLAND HEANE
departed this Life the 23d of October, 1610.

Hic requiefcit DEBORAH,
Uxor THOMÆ ROD, de Newnton prope
Hereford, Gen. & filia GULIELMI ROWLES,
de Cockfhoote in Newnham, Gen.
Obiit III die
Augufti, { A. D. 1687.
          { Ætatis XXVII.

Hic pace . . . . . . MARIA, uxor
GULIELMI ROWLES, de Cockfhoote in
. . . . . . cui peperit quatuor
. . . . . MARIAM, uxorem
. . . . . . Stapleton prope Briftol, Gen.
ELIZABETHAM, uxorem GULIELMI
SCUDAMORE, de Glouc. Gen. &
DEBORA, nuper uxorem THOMÆ ROD,
de Newton prope Hereford,
Gen. obiit XXVIto
Die Octob. Anno { Domini 1687.
                  { Ætatis 62.

Here lyeth alfo the Body of
WILLIAM ROWLES, of the Cockfhoote,
late the Hufband of the aforefaid
MARY, who departed this Life
the . . Day of Auguft, A. D. 1694,
ætatis fuæ 71.

JOHN HAWKINS, Gent.
deceafed February 16, 1673.

In Memoria æterna erit juftus.
JOHANNES WILSE,
Hujus ecclefiæ per annos 21 minifter,
Vir pius, probus, integer, pacificus,
Pauperibus ultra facultatem benignus,
Satur dierum pene octogenarius.
Hic obdormiffit.
JOANNA pariter
Uxor ipfius amantiffima caftiffimaque,
Matrona moribus optimis & illibatis,
Quæ tres ipfi liberos peperit & educavit,
JOHANNEM, MARGARETAM, & MARIAM,
recumbit a latere :
Uterque tubæ noviffimæ fonitum expectans.
Abi tu, lector, & fpira æternitatem.
Ob. { Ille Dec. 19, 1636, } ætatis { 79.
     { Illa Aug. 12, 1639, }   { 59.
Filius JOHANNES, ecclefiæ de Newent vicarius,
Pietatis ergo, & in fati folatium pofuit.

H. S. E.
EUSTATIUS HARDWICK,
de Dean Parva in com. Glouc. Gen.
Filius JOHANNIS, de Hardwick
prope Bromiard comit. Hereford, Gen.
qui obiit 20° Mart. 1703,
circa centefimum ætatis annum.

Hic jacet
MARIA,
Filia EUSTATII HARDWICK, Gen.
per MARIAM conjugem ejus,
Filiam Domini GEORGII PRATT,
de Colefhill, com. Berc. Baron.
per MARGARETTAM, filiam
Domini HUMFREDI FORSTER,
de Aldermafton, eom. Berc. Baron.
Quæ obiit
1 Augufti, Anno Dom. 1694,
ætatis 12.

THE FOLLOWING ARMS AND INSCRIPTION WERE
IN THE NAVE AGAINST THE SOUTH WALL, BUT
ARE NOW UTTERLY DESTROYED :

Sable, ten Bezants, 4, 3, 2, 1, and on a Chief
Argent, a Lion paffant Sable, for BRIDGMAN.

Here refteth the Body of
CHARLES BRIDGMAN, Efq.
and Juftice of the Peace,
who died the 27th of December,
1643.

ON FLAT STONES.

THOMAS MORSE
deceafed the 14th Day of June,
Anno Domini 1614.

JOAN, Wife of THOMAS MORSE,
deceafed the 1ft Day of June,
A. D. 1615.

In Memory of JAMES HARRIS, Gent.
Keeper of Latimer Walk, in his Majesty's
Foreft of Dean in the County of Gloucefter,
which Office he held upwards of thirty Years,
and executed it with Honour and Integrity.
He departed this Life
the 10th of January, 1761;
aged 60 Years.

Alfo in Memory of
CATHARINE his Wife,
who departed this Life March 2, 1747-8,
aged 47.

ON FLAT STONES IN THE NORTH AISLE.

Arms; a Mullet, and in Chief two Crefcents.

GEORGE BARRON, Clothier,
departed this Life Auguft 3,
Anno Dom. 1707.

Alfo the Body of NICHOLAS,
the Son of GEORGE BARRON, Gent.
who departed this Life Feb. 14, 1702.

Alfo MARGERY, Daughter of
GEORGE BARRON,
who deceafed May 24, 1705.

Here refteth the Body of
. . . . . . PEMBRUGE, of
. . . . . in the County of Hereford,
who departed this Life the 26th of May, 1688,
ætat. fuæ 87.

FRANCES, the Wife of
RICHARD STAFFORD, Daughter of
THOMAS DAVIS, of the Bourne
in the Parifh of Stroud, Clothier,
deceafed the 19th Day of June,
A. D. 1656.

JOHN CHANNAN, Gent.
departed this Life June 12, 1775,
aged 79 Years, 5 Months, and 24 Days.

Arms; Azure, on a Fefs, between three Bugle
Horns ftringed Argent, a Hemp Hackle Gules.

KITFORD BRAINE, fenior,
departed this Life Dec. 5, 1705.

IN THE CHURCH YARD, ON TOMBS.

PHILIP ROBINSON, fenior,
died April 16, 1712, aged 66.

HENRY, Son of
PHILIP ROBINSON,
died Dec. 12, 1712.

SARAH, Wife of the above
PHILIP ROBINSON,
departed this Life Sept. 15, 1730,
aged 94.

JOHN ROBINSON,
Son of the above
PHILIP and SARAH ROBINSON,
died Sept. 14, 1767, aged 89.

JANE, Wife of
JOHN ROBINSON,
died May 17, 1768, aged 53.

PHILIP ROBINSON
died Dec. 9, 1711, aged 37.

MARY his Wife
died January 27, 1691.

JANE, Wife of
JOHN ROBINSON,
of Little Dean's Crofs, Gent.
died May 17, 1768, aged 53.

JOHN ROBINSON,
of Little Dean's Crofs, Gent.
died Feb. 21, 1784, aged 72.

PHILIP ROBINSON, Gent.
died Feb. 23, 1776, aged 74.

JOHN ROBINSON his Brother
died Sept. 4, 1785, aged 76.

MARY, Wife of
THOMAS TAYLOR,
of this Parifh, and
Daughter of RICHARD LONGSTRETH,
of Frampton upon Severn,
died Sept. 26, 1741, aged 35.

THOMAS TAYLOR,
of this Parifh,
died Oct. 18, 1784, aged near 76.

EMY, Wife of
THOMAS HOBBS,
died April 4, 1772, aged 38.

NATHANIEL MAULE,
Father of the above EMY HOBBS,
died Feb. 18, 1774, aged 73.

THOMAS HOBBS
died April 24, 1787, aged 57.

WILLIAM JAMES
died June 12, 1782, aged 90.
He was Clerk of this Parifh forty-feven
Years.

ANN, Wife of
WILLIAM JAMES,
was buried May 4, 1760, aged 68.

THOMAS PACKER,
of this Parifh,
died Dec. 22, 1779, aged 73.

WILLIAM PACKER
died Aug. 1, 1786, aged 82.

SAMUEL STEEL,
of this Parifh, Surgeon,
died March 29, 1747, aged 89.

MARY, Wife of
JOHN STEEL, Carpenter,
was buried Nov. 13, 1741, aged 35.

SUSANNA, Daughter of
JOHN STEEL and MARY his Wife,
died in Auguft 1755, aged 15.

JOHN STEEL
died Nov. 5, 1757, aged 64.

LUCY, Wife of
JOHN BRETT,
of Little Dean Lodge,
died June 10, 1767, aged 34.

SARAH, Wife of
JAMES TINGEL,
was buried July 6, 1764, aged 38.

ANN MORGAN
died May 24, 1761, aged 70.

S

Mrs.

Mrs. SARAH ARTHUR
died Feb. 21, 1726-7, aged 72.

Mr. RICHARD BROWNING her Nephew
died May 17, 1739, aged 55.

WILLIAM ABRAHALL
died May 7, 1724.

DOROTHY his Wife
died Jan. 1, 1742, aged 80.

ISABELL, Wife of
AARON WICKS, of the
Parish of Hamton,
Daughter of
THOMAS and ELIZABETH ABRAHALL,
of this Parish.
died Dec. 7, 1771, aged 41.

ELIZABETH, Wife of
THOMAS ABRAHALL,
of this Parish,
died May 26, 1766, aged 65.

THOMAS ABRAHALL
died Jan. 10, 1779, aged 81.

MARKEY ABRAHALL, junior,
died April 3, 1775, aged 42.

MARKEY ABRAHALL, senior,
died Oct. 24, 1775, aged 73.

MARY his Wife
died Jan. 23, 1771, aged 71.

JOHN BROBEN,
of the Parish of Newnham,
died Nov. 16, 1767, aged 62.

SARAH, Wife of
JOSEPH BROBEN,
died Feb. 12, 1787, aged 63.

JOHN their Son
died Dec. 31, 1786, aged 29.

ROBERT PYRKE,
late of Newnham, Gent.
died May 13, 1780,
in the 44th Year of his Age.

JOHN PYRKE, Gent.
Brother of the above
ROBERT PYRKE,
died Sept. 2, 1772,
in the 31st Year of his Age.

Arms; six Lions rampant 3, 2, 1,
for SAVAGE.

Here are deposited
the Remains of
ELIZABETH SAVAGE,
Wife of Lieutenant and
Quarter-master HENRY SAVAGE,
late of the
Hon. East India Company Military,
died Aug. 17, 1787, aged 35.

THOMAS WILMOT,
of this Parish,
died July 2, 1780, aged 58.

WILLIAM OKEY
died March 25, 1774, aged 72.

ELIZABETH his Wife
died May 10, 1775, aged 81.

Mrs. MARY, Widow of
Mr. SAMUEL KEYNTON,
of London, Merchant,
died July 22, 1763, aged 73.

Mrs. KATHERINE SKIPP,
Daughter of
SAMUEL and MARY KEYNTON,
and Wife of
GEORGE SKIPP, Gent.
of the Grange
in the Parish of Flaxley,
departed this Life Dec. 8, 1772,
aged 50.

GEORGE SKIPP, Esq.
of the Grange
in the Parish of Flaxley,
of a very ancient
Family of that Name
in the County of Hereford,
and lineally descended from the
Right Rev. JOHN SKIPP,
Lord Bishop of Hereford,
in the Reign of
King EDWARD the Sixth,
Son of
RICHARD SKIPP,
of Donnington Hall
in the County of Hereford, Esq.
and of MARY his Wife,
Daughter of
THOMAS PYRKE, Esq.
of this Parish.
He died May 3, 1783, aged 83.

ON HEAD STONES.

	Died	Aged		Died	Aged
William Pearce	12 Sept. 1769	47	Elizabeth his Daughter	14 Apr. 1771	14
Elizabeth, Wife of William Phillips	19 Aug. 1759	63	Sarah, Wife of James Bennett, Daughter of Richard Stiles	20 Apr. 1734	33
Ann, Wife of William Baldwin	14 Aug. 1772	57	James Bennett	24 July, 1765	57
Henry Robinson	17 Nov. 1707	—	Ann Harvey	21 Dec. 1754	58
Henry Robinson	21 Jan. 1715	56	Thomas Hobbs	2 July, 1752	65
Alice, Wife of James Drew	2 Apr. 1788	59	Frances his Wife	3 July, 1752	56
James Drew	26 Mar. 1747	62	Abigail Adams	3 July, 1741	82
George his Son	1 Mar. 1747	27	William Trigg	8 Sept. 1743	55
Thomas Ward	16 Jan. 1750	54	Frances, Wife of Joseph Williams	25 June, 1787	64
Elizabeth his Wife	6 May, 1750	58	Samuel Trigg	8 Jan. 1747	57
John Ward	27 Dec. 1711	—	John Trigg, senior	14 Jan. 1728	80
Elizabeth, Wife of John Trigg	23 May, 1787	60	Abigail his Wife	31 Mar. 1732	80
Anthony Ward	16 Mar. 1751	21	Hannah, Wife of Thomas Wood	5 Dec. 1760	37
John Guest	23 Feb. 1727	65	Ann his second Wife	31 May, 1781	47
Elizabeth his Wife	8 Mar. 1736	65	James Ovard	27 May, 1744	43
Sarah, Wife of Richard Guest	12 Dec. 1746	45	Ann his Wife	3 Dec. 1780	76
Elizabeth, Wife of William Packer	2 Apr. 1769	35	James Morgan	— 1714	52
John Guest	1 Aug. 1764	72	Ann, Wife of James Morgan	10 Apr. 1757	82
Mary his Wife	21 Aug. 1750	62	Thomas, Son of James and Mary Morgan	17 May, 1760	17
Ann their Daughter	7 Oct. 1741	15	James Morgan, senior	7 June, 1772	77
Robert Tingle	14 Jan. 1789	76	Ann his Wife	21 Apr. 1776	76
Joan his Wife	22 Apr. 1784	78	George Morgan	5 June, 1746	33
Elizabeth, Wife of Anthony Brain	26 Nov. 1787	45	James Very	10 Jan. 1756	34
Richard Wood, junior	3 Nov. 1711	—	Elizabeth, Wife of Thomas Baynham, of the Parish of Flaxley	27 Mar. 1783	80
Ann, Wife of Richard Stiles	23 Sept. 1727	55			
William Mayfield	18 Mar. 1745	53			
William Williams	1 June, 1780	55			

O N

O N   H E A D   S T O N E S.

	Died	Aged
John Thomas - -	13 Oct. 1757	47
Esther, Daughter of John and Elizabeth Thomas -	22 Jan. 1766	22
William Trigg - -	8 Oct. 1782	65
Mary his Wife -	2 Jan. 1763	58
Sarah his second Wife -	10 May, 1782	72
William Whetstone -	14 Apr. 1748	65
Mary, Wife of Thomas Wood, Daughter of William Whetstone - -	18 Dec. 1757	27
John Charles - -	9 May, 1755	62
Anthony Rickett -	30 Oct. 1747	66
Thomas Moore -	27 May, 1781	62
John Morgan -	28 July, 1781	61
William, Son of William and Mary Fowle, of Longhope -	23 Apr. 1759	33
Ann Stephens -	23 Feb. 1769	73
Mary, Wife of Joseph Wooley	17 Feb. 1745	25
Giles Clarke - -	5 Jan. 1723	—
Mary his Daughter -	6 July, 1727	—
Jonathan Packer -	1 July, 1735	67
Gabriel Packer -	14 Mar. 1739	73
Margaret his Wife -	8 Mar. 1759	88
Mary their Daughter -	20 Mar. 1759	50
Samuel Packer -	20 Mar. 1746	32
Margaret Packer -	7 May, 1767	65

	Died	Aged
David Price - -	9 May, 1752	64
Sarah Steel - -	1 June, 1768	20
William Smith - -	5 Mar. 1786	34
Jacob Broben -	19 Oct. 1748	52
Mary Broben, of Newnham	8 Apr. 1751	46
John Broben - -	8 Jan. 1759	70
John Reynolds, one of the Keepers of the Forest of Dean -	in May, 1740	47
Ann his Wife, Daughter of Desborough Bridger, of Slimbridge, Gent. - -	17 Oct. 1756	68
Thomas Jones -	27 Nov. 1766	80
Ann his Wife - -	24 Dec. 1755	62
Thomas Webb -	19 Jan. 1781	71
Rebeckah his Wife -	4 Sept. 1757	57
William Howell -	3 Aug. 1765	60
Samuel Young -	11 Jan. 1787	73
Elizabeth his Wife -	22 Jan. 1761	61
Jane Hale - -	10 Oct. 1763	67
Audrey, Wife of William Brooke	30 Aug. 1746	53
Richard Brooks -	15 Jan. 1756	23
William Moore - -	25 Apr. 1762	57
Elizabeth his Wife -	2 July, 1781	75
Thomas, Son of William and Elizabeth Moore -	6 Dec. 1780	16
Beata Mountjoy -	19 Nov. 1745	80

FOREST

FOREST OF DEAN.

THE Origin of Forefts in *England*, as an Appendage to the Crown, was certainly prior to the Conqueft. Canute, in the firft Year of his Reign, iffued an Edict * prohibiting his Subjects from interfering with the Royal Inclofures. It is therefore probable that William the Conqueror found many in his new Dominions †, and was more jealous of this than of any of his Prerogatives, and more ambitious to extend it. His Succeffors, Henry II, Richard, and John, depopulated whole Countries to enlarge their Forefts. Thefe Boundaries were in 1300, 28 Edw. I. reduced to their ancient Limitation, as afcertained by Perambulations. New Laws for Foreft Government were enacted, and confirmed by Parliament in the celebrated "*Charta de Forefta.*"

The Foreft of *Dean* ‡ is fituate in the weftern Part of the County, between the navigable Rivers *Severn* and *Wye*. The Quantity of Land belonging to the Crown, within the laft Perambulation, is about 23015 Acres, exclufive of Freehold Property. In different Parts are 589 Cottages, containing about 2000 Inhabitants, and 1798 fmall Inclofures, amounting to 1385 Acres, belonging to the Foreft, but occupied by Cottagers. As the whole Foreft is extra-parochial, thefe are exempted from Rates and Taxes, have unlimited Right of Pafturage, befide the Accefs to the Wood and Timber, and the Privilege of finking Mines.

The early Records abound in Accounts of Perambulations. In 1225, 9 Hen. III. one was made on the Petition of the Monks of *Flaxley* §, including the Additions made in former Reigns, which in 1300, 28 Edw. I. were difafforefted, and called *Purlieus*. This Settlement was confirmed by Parliament in 1326, 1 Edw. III.

Although numerous Grants are ftill extant of Lands and Immunities within the Verge of the Foreft, they feem not to belong to our prefent Purpofe, as being chiefly of the Mines, Forges, or of Lands reftored. No Subject had obtained a Leafe from the Crown of the Royalties prior to 1611, 9 Jac. I. who granted to William Herbert, Earl of *Pembroke*, the whole Foreft, at the annual Rent of 2433*l.* 6*s.* 8*d.* for 21 Years. In 1623 the Limits were again afcertained, on Complaint of William Wyntour and William Bell, who became the Leffees, in Confideration of 1074*l.* 8*s.* (June 30, 1619), and who then covenanted that their Lands fhould remain in the Jurifdiction of Foreft Law. King Charles, upon his Acceffion in 1625, transferred the Leafe to Sir Edward Villiers, for a Confideration not fpecified, in the 10th of whofe Reign (July 10, 1634) a Juftice Seat was held at Gloucester, and a Report made concerning the Metes and Bounds ‖. About three Years afterwards, Sir John Wyntour, of *Lidney*, offering to become the Purchafer, an accurate Survey was returned by the Commiffioners, ftating that the Foreft contained 23521 Acres. After difafforefting the whole, the King ratified the Purchafe by his Letters Patent, dated March 31, 1641, for the Sum of 106,000*l.* to be paid by Inftal-

---

* " Volo, ut omnis liber Homo pro libito fuo habeat venerem & viridem in planis fuis, fuper terras fuas, fine Chaceâ tamen, " & *devitent* omnes *meam* ubicunque eam habere voluero." Treatife of Foreft Laws, by John Manwood, 4to, 1589, p. 12.

† " The neweft Foreft that is in *England* at this Day is the *Newe Foreft* in *Hampfhire*, made in William the Conqueror's " Time. But there is no other Foreft in *England* whereof the beginning can be fhewed, neyther by the Chronicles, Hiftorie, nor " Records, fo auncient are all other Foreftes in the Land. And as auncient are the Foreft Laws, faving fome fewe of them " that are altered, and are made more favourable than they were, by the " *Charta de Forefta*," and other later Statutes." Ib. p. 5.
 Peramb. Foreftæ de *Dene*, co. Glouc. ex Rotulis de Anno 28 Edwardi Primi. Turr. *Lond.*

‡ " The ancient Brittaines, fayth Speed, attribute the Name of *Arden* to Foreftes and Woods, but Gyraldus Cambren- " sis gives it the Name of " *Danutia*," or *Danica Sylva*," or the Danes Woods, who did lurk and fhelter themfelves in thefe " fhady Places. But long before the Time of the *Danes*, thefe Woods were poffeffed by the *Silures*, a fierce and warlike People " which overrun *Monmouthfhire* and *Herefordfhire*." MSS. Parsons.
 " ———— Queen of Forefts all, that Weft of *Severn* lie,
 " Her broad and bufhy Top, *Dean*, holdeth up fo high,
 " The leffer are not feen, fhe is fo tall and large." Drayton's Poly-Olbion, Song 7.

§ Stating it to contain ten Bailiwicks, on the Oaths of twelve Regarders; the Terrier is now preferved in the Record Office at *Weftminfter.*

‖ Report of the Grand Jury : " We agree that the Metes and Bounds of the Foreft of *Dene* ought to be according to Peram- " bulation made 12 Hen. III. and 10 Edw. I. becaufe we find the Perambulation of 28 Edw. I. to be granted by Patent 20 " Edw. I. and becaufe of the Act of Parliament in 10 Edw. III. and a Poffeffion of 300 and odd Years concurring therewithal. " We therefore refer it to the Judgement of this honourable Court, whether the Perambulation of 28 Edw. I. ought to ftand in " Force. Whereupon the King's Council moved the Judges to deliver their Opinion for the Matter in Law, which they all " agreed on as before, and then the King's Council moved the Jury, fince when the Verdict in Law was fatisfied by the " Judges, that they would agree to leave out the latter Part of the Verdict, and let the firft Part ftand only for the Verdict. We " therefore agree, that the Metes and Bounds of the Foreft of *Dean* ought to be according to the Perambulation made 12 " Hen. III. and 10 Edw. I. to which the Grand Jury, and the Officers of the Foreft, and the Fairemen, and Reeve, fubfcribed " their Names." Report of the Surveyor, John Pitt, Efq. 1788.

6 D

ments,

ments, and a Fee-farm Rent of 1950*l*. 12*s.* 8*d.* for ever,   The Coal Mines and Quarries of Grindſtone only were excepted, having been leaſed for 31 Years to Edward Tyringham in 1637 at 30*l.* a Year *.

In 1656, Cromwell, in his Military Parliament, declared the Patent of Sir John Wyntour, who had been a zealous Royaliſt, null and void.   He re-afforeſted 18000 Acres, and expelled and deſtroyed the Cabins of 400 beggarly People, who ſubſiſted by the Waſte of the Timber.

Upon the Reſtoration of Charles II, 1660, Sir John Wyntour regained his Patent, and entered on Poſſeſſion ; and upon Surrender of his former Charter a new Agreement was made, and he was indemnified by a Grant of 30,000*l.* from the Treaſury.   It appears that he took undue Advantage of his Privileges, as a Complaint was laid before the Council in 1663, " that Sir John Wyntour had 500 Cutters " of Wood employed in *Dean* Foreſt."   An Order of Council, dated July 20, was accordingly iſſued to prohibit a farther Devaſtation.

Sir Charles Harbord, a very active Surveyor of the Crown Lands, procured an Act of Parliament to be paſſed in 1668, 20 Car. II. by which it was ordained that " 11000 Acres ſhould be encloſed and " ſet apart as a Nurſery for Timber, that 12888 Acres are in private Eſtates or Commons, and that the " uncloſed ſhould be commonable to the adjoining Pariſhes, the Crown having no Right to keep " more than 800 Head of Deer at one Time.   Tyringham's Leaſe of the Mines was renewed for 31 " Years, and it was reſolved that the Crown could not grant for a longer Term."   The ſame Year, under the Direction of Henry Marquis of Worcester, Lord Warden, 8487 Acres were incloſed and planted, and the remaining 2513 ſoon afterward.   The Income to the Crown was then 5390*l.* a Year.

In 1691, 3 Will. and Mary, a Commiſſion was directed to Henry Duke of Beaufort, Lord Warden, who returned that the Number of incloſed Acres were 9025, and the Value of the Timber, beſide Oak, 148,745*l.* 16*s.* 8*d.*   About the Year 1705 Edward Wilcox, Surveyor, propoſed to the Council, that " if 11000 Acres, planted and incloſed, be divided into ſixteen Parts ; and one ſixteenth, " being 700 Acres, be annually felled, leaving Standards of Oak and Beech, each Cutting would yield " 3500*l.* and the other Parts would grow to Perfection."   To this Plan Lord Treaſurer Godolphin acceded, and a Warrant was iſſued for the immediate Performance.   It is conjectured that the Foreſt was about this Period in its beſt State, for though the Foreſt Courts had not been ſo regularly held as before the Revolution, yet the greateſt Attention was paid by the Servants of the Crown.   Different Commiſſioners were ſent by the Treaſury to view the Foreſt, who made the moſt minute Returns ; and as the Cottages were pulled down, it is probable that every Incroachment was reclaimed.   But Abuſes have ſince gradually prevailed, and have been ſuffered to increaſe, to a Degree that ſufficiently accounts for the preſent unprofitable State of the Foreſt.   Competent Judges have aſſerted that the Decreaſe of Timber is more than in a Proportion of four-fifths.

In 1758 a Propoſal was made by John Pitt, Eſq. Surveyor, for incloſing 2000 Acres more, and ordered accordingly.   In the next Year 9200 Feet of Timber were granted by Warrant towards building the Infirmary at Gloucester.   An additional Incloſure of 2000 Acres was completed in 1771, at the Expence of 2077*l.* 18*s.* 10*d.*

When the Act for erecting the new Priſons in this County paſſed, an Order (dated 26 April, 1786) was iſſued from the Treaſury for the clear Amount of 2000*l.* to be raiſed by *Sale of Timber,* and applied to that Purpoſe.

A Return of Timber felled for the Navy from 1761 to 1786, both incluſive :

Receipts.		Loads.	Feet.	Value.	£.	s.	d.
Total felled.	Of Oak, ——	16573	14	——	} 30573	14	4
	Of Beech ——	871	41	——			
	Cord Wood, —	22430		——————	6955	7	1
	Stakes, —————			—————	12	3	10½
	Bark, ——	1510 Tons,		—	2650	1	5
				Total,	41319	13	7½
				Diſburſed,	13619	13	7½
				Balance,	27719	6	8½

In the Foreſt Diſtrict are 2077 exempted Acres, in *Hudnall's* and *Abbot's* Woods, which are commonable to the Natives of the Hundred and Pariſh of *St. Briavel's* †.

The Site of the Foreſt exhibits a great Variety of Ground.   It breaks into numberleſs deep and narrow Vallies, the Acclivities of which are clothed with the impenetrable and matted Foliage of the

* Extract from an Indenture made under the Great Seal between the King and Sir John Wyntour, Knight, dated 20 Feb. 15 Car. I.
† Report of the Commiſſioners of Foreſts and Crown Lands, 1788.

Birch

Birch Tree, Hawthorn, and other low Wood, interfperfed with venerable Oaks. In moft of thefe are Springs, but not copious, of a very dark ferruginous Colour, and very ftrongly impregnated with Steel. The high Lands fpread into Plains, which are fhaded by Foreft Trees of almoft every Defcription, and not unufually of fingular Size and Beauty. The Timber moft natural to this Soil is of Oak and Beech; and in the cultivated Parts are Apple Trees peculiar to it, called the *Styre*, of which a Kind of Cyder is made of remarkable Strength and Flavour, and of a very perceptible chalybeate Tafte.

Moft of the ufeful foffile Productions are found here in great Quantities and Perfection; Iron Ore *, Coal †, Ochre, and Stone.

We collect from very early Records, that the Iron Ore was difcovered and made into Bars. The Abbot of *Flaxley* was poffeffed of a Forge by royal Grant, foon after the Foundation of the Abbey in the Reign of HENRY II. and was allowed two Oaks weekly for the Supply of it, a Privilege commuted in 1258, 42 HEN. III. for *Abbot's* Wood of 872 Acres held by the Abbey till the Diffolution.

In the next Reign were many fmelting Kilns, which were called "*Forgeæ errantes* ‡;" but all paid an annual Rent, or were referved to the Crown. Large Furnaces now in Ufe were erected in 1617. It appears from the immenfe Quantities of Iron Cinders imperfectly wrought, which are difcovered near the Surface, that the Art of fmelting the Ore was in the early Ages very uncertainly known or practifed. The Coal is found at a comparatively flight Depth, and produces a very intenfe Heat, which renders it the better adapted to the Ufe of the Forges. The Stone is compofed of a deep red Grit, acquires Hardnefs by being expofed to the Air, and is ferviceable in Buildings of all Kinds. The Arable Lands are comparatively very few.

The Procefs ufed in fmelting and preparing the Ore varies at prefent but little from that defcribed in the MSS. of Dr. PARSONS, written about a Century ago; his full Account is therefore fubjoined §.

MANWOOD

---

* " *Minera ferri chryftallizata*," the more common Sort, not much attracted by the Magnet. " *Minera ferri nigricans Magneti amica*," of a darker Colour and better Quality, called by the Miners " Erufh Ore." It has an infinite Variety of Forms, ftriated, radiated, and teffarated, or broken into Dice, very ftrongly attracted by the Magnet. The Pipe Ore is a Collection of fmall cylindrical Columns, occafioned by the Metal falling like Icicles in a State of Fufion from the Mafs to which the Pipes are affixed.

† The Coal has a fhining and gloffy Appearance, crackles much when thrown on the Fire, but is neither fo bitumiuous nor lafting as fome other Sorts.

‡ " Si Dom. Rex habet unam Forgeam errantem prædicti Operatores invenient ei Mineam ad fuftentationem prædictæ Forgeæ. " Et Dom. Rex dabit eis pro quali fummâ 1 den. Item, Dom. Rex habebit de quâlibet fummâ Mineæ quæ ducetur extra Foreftâ " un. ob. & omnia quæ Dominus Rex capit de Minea ponuntur ad firmam pro XLVI lib."

MSS. HALE, in the Library of *Lincoln's Inn*.

From the fame MSS. it appears that in 1282, 10 EDW. I. feventy-two Forges were leafed from the Crown, " Et quælibet " Forgea per Annum dabit Dom. Regi VII fol. & forgea operans per dimid. anni dabit III fol. VI den."

§ "D E A N   F O R R E S T.

" The Forreft of *Dean* comprehendeth that Part of *Glouceftershire* that lyeth between the two Rivers *Wye* and *Severn*, containing " at leaft 20000 Acres, befides the *Lea Bayley*, which is 4000 Acres more, and all the wafte and mean Lands thereunto belong- " ing, and appertaining to the Poor, were meafured likewife, and found to amount to 33000 Acres more; fo that the whole " Dimenfions of the Foreft containeth at leaft 57000 Acres, whofe Soil is generally of a ftiff Clay, and in the Winter deep and " miry, but in the Summer dry and parching. Vid. Phil. Tranf. No. 137. p. 951.

" The Springes of the Forreft are for the moft Part of a brownifh Colour, or Umber Colour, occafioned by their Paffages " through the Veyns of Oker, of which there is a great plenty, or elfe through the rufhy Tincture of the Mineralls of the " Ore, which fuperabound in the Forreft.

" The Ground of the Forreft is more inclined to Wood and Cole then Corne, yet they have enough of it too.

" The Inhabitants are fome of them a Sort of robuftic wild People, that muft be civilized by good Difcipline and Govern- " ment.

" The Ore and Cinder, wherewith they make their Iron (which is the great Imployment of the poorer Sort of Inhabi- " tants); 'tis dug in moft Parts of the Forreft, one in the Bowells, and the other towards the Surface of the Earth.

" But whether it be by virtue of the Forreft Laws, or other Cuftome, the head Gaviler of the Forreft, or others deputed by " him, provided they are born in the Hundred of *St. Briavel's*, may go into any Man's Ground whatfoever, within the Limita- " tion of the Forreft, and dig or delve for Ore and Cinders without any Moleftation.

" There are two Sorts of Ore: the beft Ore is your Brufh Ore, of a blewifh Colour, very ponderous, and full of fhining " Specks, like Grains of Silver; this affordeth the greateft Quantity of Iron, but being melted alone, produceth a mettal very " fhort and brittle. To remedy this Inconvenience they make Ufe of another Material, which they call Cinder, it being nothing " elfe but the Refufe of the Ore, after the melting hath been extracted; which being melted with the other in due Quantity, " gives it that excellent Temper of toughnefs, for which this Iron is preferred before any other that is brought from foreign " Parts.

" But it is to be noted, that in former Times, when their Works were few, and their Vent fmall, they made Ufe of no other " Bellows but fuch as were moved by the Strength of Men. by Reafon whereof their Fires were much lefs intenfe than in the " Furnaces they now employ; fo that having in them only melted downe the principal Part of the Ore, they rejected the " reft as ufelefs, and not worth their Charge; this they call their Cinder, and is now found in an unexhauftable Quantity " throughout all the Parts of the Country where any Glomerery's formerly ftood, for fo were they then called.

" After they have provided their Ore, their firft Work is to calcine it, which is done in Kilns, much after the Fafhion of our " ordinary Lime Kilns; thefe they fill up to the Top with Coal and Ore untill it be full, and fo putting Fire to the Bottom, " they let it burn till the Coal be wafted, and then renew the Kilnes with frefh Ore and Coal: this is done without any Infu- " fion of Mettal; and ferves to confume the more droffy Part of the Ore, and to make it fryable, fupplying the beating and " wafhing, which are to no other Mettals; from hence they carry it to their Furnaces, which are built of Brick and Stone, " about twenty-four Foot fquare on the outfide, and near thirty Foot in height within, and not above eight or ten Foot over, " where it is wideft, which is about the Middle, the Top and Bottom having a narrow Compafs, much like the Form of an

" Egg.

3

Manwood (cap. I. p. 6.) ftates that certain Officers are neceffary to the Conftitution of all Forefts to hold the Courts for the due Execution of the Foreft Laws. Thefe have been in immemorial Ufage in the Foreft of *Dean*; and peculiar to it is a Court of *Free Miners*, who exercife an independent Jurif-diction.

The great Officer is the Lord Warden, by Patent, during the King's Pleafure. He is the Keeper of the Deer only, and has for himfelf no Salary, but receives 210*l.* a Year from the Treafury, for the Wages of the Confervators. To this Office is annexed the Conftablefhip of the Caftle and Hundred of *St. Briavel*, from which arifes a rent Charge of 40*l.* a Year, which is allowed to the Keepers.

Six Deputy Wardens, who prefide alternately at the Court of Free Miners.

Four Verdurers, whofe Duty it is to preferve the Vert * and Venifon of the Foreft, to prevent Pur-prefture, Wafte, and Affart, and to inflict Penalties where committed. Elected by the Freeholders of the County at large. They have each an annual Claim of two Fee Deer.

Conservator,

" Egg. Behind the Furnace are placed two high Pair of Bellows, whofe Nofes meet at a little Hole near the Bottom : thefe are
" compreffed together by certain Buttons placed on the Axis of a very large Wheel, which is turned about with Water, in the
" Manner of an overfhot Mill. As foon as thefe Buttons are flid off, the Bellows are raifed again by a Counterpoife of Weights,
" whereby they are made to play alternately, the one giving its Blaft whilft the other is rifing.

" At firft they fill thefe Furnaces with Ore and Cinder intermixt with Fuel, which in thefe Works is always Charcoal, laying
" them hollow at the Bottom, that they may the more eafily take Fire, but after they are once kindled, the Materials run to-
" gether into an hard Cake or Lump, which is fuftained by the Furnace, and thorough this the Mettal as it runs trickles down
" the Receivers, which are placed at the Bottom, where there is a paffage open, by which they take away the Scum and Drofs,
" and let out their Mettal as they fee Occafion.

" Before the Mouth of the Furnace lyeth a great Bed of Sand, where they make Furrows of the Fafhion they defire to caft
" their Iron into thefe, when the Receivers are full, they let in their Mettal, which is made fo very fluid by the Violence of
" the Fire, that it not only runs to a confiderable Diftance, but ftands afterwards boiling a great while.

" After thefe Furnaces are once at Work, they keep them conftantly employed for many Months together, never fuffering
" the Fire to flacken Night or Day, but ftill fupplying the wafte of Fuel and other Materials with frefh, poured in at the
" Top.

" Several Attempts have been made to bring in the Ufe of the Sea Coal in thefe Works inftead of Charcoal ; the former
" being to be had at an eafy Rate, the latter not without a great Expence ; but hitherto they have proved ineffectual, the
" Workmen finding by Experience that a Sea Coal Fire, how vehement foever, will not penetrate the moft fixed Parts of the
" Ore, by which Means they leave much of the Mettal behind them unmelted.

" From thefe Furnaces they bring the Sows and Piggs of Iron, as they call them, to their Forges ; thefe are two Sorts,
" though they ftood together under the fame Roof; one they call their Finery, and the other Chafers : both of them are upon
" Hearths, upon which they place great Heaps of Sea Coal, and behind them Bellows like thofe of the Furnaces, but nothing
" near fo large.

" In their Finerys they firft put their Peggs of Iron, placing three or four of them together, behind the Fire, with a little
" of one End thruft into it, where, foftening by Degrees, they ftir and work them with long Barrs of Iron, till the Mettal runs
" together in a round Maffe or Lump, which they call an Half Bloome ; this they take out, and giving it a few Strokes with
" their Sledges, they carry it to a great weighty Hammer, raifed likewife by the Motion of a Water Wheel, where applying it
" dexteroufly to the Blows, they prefently beat it into a thick fhort fquare ; this they put into the Finery again, and heating it
" red hot, they work it under the fame Hammer till it comes to the Shape of a Bar in the Middle, with two fquare Knobs in
" the Ends ; laft of all they give it other Heatings in the Chaffens, and more Workings under the Hammer, till they have
" brought their Iron into Barrs of feveral Shapes, in which Fafhion they expofe them to fale.

" All their principal Iron undergoes the aforementioned Preparations, yet for feveral other Purpofes, as for Backs of Chim-
" neys, Hearths, of Ovens, and the like ; they have a Sort of caft Iron, which they take out of the Receivers of the Furnace,
" fo foon as it is melted in great Ladles, and pour it into the Moulds of fine Sand in like Manner as they do caft Brafs and
" and fofter Mettals, but this Sort of Iron is fo very brittle, that being heated, with one Blow of a Hammer it breaks all to
" Pieces.

" Now, although this Fault be moft found in this Sort of Iron, yet if in the Working the beft Sort of Iron they omit any
" one Procefs, it will be fure to want fome Part of its toughnefs, which they efteem its Perfection.

" Of the Oak in the Forreft of *Dean*, fee Fuller's Worthies, p. 349.

" Mr. Evelyn alfo, in his Book of Planting, faith, that in the Reign of Queen Elizabeth, *Spain* fent over an Ambaffador,
" on purpofe to have (by private Practifes) this Wood deftroyed, but what was not done by thefe Means, was by the late Re-
" bellion in Charles I's Days, being expofed to Sale for Fuel and other Ufes.

" There is great plenty of red, blue, and yellow Ochre, the chiefeft of which Pitts are at *Yellow Craft* in *Little Dean*.
" In feveral Parts of the Forreft there are Quarries of Mill-ftones, Grind-ftones, and Wheel-ftones ; they are about *Stanton*,
" Q. *Worden ?*

" In the Days of King Charles I. there was a Lord High Conftable of the Forreft, a Lord Chief Juftice in Eyre, with other
" Officers, for which there are fix feveral Lodges, *viz.*

" 1. The *Speech Houfe*, in the Centre of the Forreft, between *Daniel's More* and *Kenftoe Hill*.
" 2. *York Lodge*, which ftandeth at the upper End of *Lumbard's Marfh*, near the Park End Furnace.
" 3. *Worcefter Lodge*, it ftandeth on *Wimberley Hill*.
" 4. *Ruerdean's Lodge*.
" 5. *Danby Lodge*, which ftandeth upon the *Old Bayley Hill*, near *Lidney*.
" 6. *Latimore Lodge*, it ftandeth on *Dean Mill Hill*, not far from the Beacon.

" Three Streams, or Brooks, *viz.*

" 1. The *Dean Stream*.
" 2. *Anderford Brook*.
" 3. *Black Poole Stream.*"   MSS. Parsons, Bodl. Lib. Oxon.

* " The *Vert* is the greene Wodes that are Covertes. The *Venifon* is every Beafte of the Forefte and Chafe, by a general
" Woorde ufed for them all." Manwood, p. 6.

" Purprefture,

CONSERVATOR, appointed by the Lords of the Treafury, with a Salary of 64*l.* 16*s.* a Year. His Office is to infpect and preferve the Timber; he employs fix Keepers *, who have their diftinct Walks or Diftricts.

In the Foreft are feven WOODWARDSHIPS, which are held by hereditary Grants. Of, 1. *Stanton* and *Bicknor*; 2. *The Bearfe*; 3. *Magna Dene* and *Lea Bayley*; 4. *Blakeney*; 5. *Ruar Dene*; 6. *Abbenhall*; 7. *Blyth's Bayley.* The Perquifites of thefe are the Lop and Top of all felled Timber, and all windfall and dotard Trees (*ficca & vento proftrata*) within their refpective Bailywicks.

The CHIEF and eight FORESTERS IN FEE.

The CHIEF FORESTER is Bow-bearer to the King. He has no Salary, but claims to be entitled to ten Bucks and ten Does in each Seafon, and to the right Shoulder of every Deer killed in the Foreft. As Bow-bearer, to attend the King, with a Bow and Arrow, and fix ftout Bowmen cloathed in green, when-ever he hunts within the Foreft, and has an unlimited Right of Hunting, Hawking, and Fifhing.

The GAVELLER †, or Keeper of the King's Gawles, to whom a Fee of 5*s.* is due from every free Miner on the opening of new Mines. Appointed by the Lords of the Treafury.

PRESENT OFFICERS OF THE FOREST OF Dean.

Lord Warden and Conftable of St. Briavel's,

Right Hon. Frederick Auguftus Earl of Berkeley.

Deputy Wardens,

Sir John Guife, Bart.
Sir Thomas Crawley Boevey, Bart.
John Colchefter, Efq.
Edmund Probyn, Efq.
Roynon Jones, Efq.
Jofeph Pyrke, Efq.

Verdurers,

Sir John Guife, Bart.
Edmund Probyn,
Roynon Jones,
Jofeph Pyrke, Efqrs.

Conſervator,

Roynon Jones, Efq.

Woodwards,

William Hall, Lord Vifcount Gage,
Charles Edwyn, Efq.
John Colchefter, Efq.

George Savage, Efq.
Mary and Jane Clarke, Spinfters,
Edmund Probyn, Efq.
John Beale, Gent.

Chief Forefter in Fee and Bow-bearer,

Charles Edwyn, Efq.

Forefters in Fee,

Mayor and Burgeffes of the City of *Gloucefter,*
Mary and Jane Clarke, Spinfters, of the *Hill Common,*
Thomas Foley, Efq.
Heirs of Ralph Colfter,
Heirs of Thomas Williams,
Heirs of John Ayres,
Heirs of Sir Robert Gunning, Knight,
Heirs of Henry Yearfley.

Gaveller,

George Cæfar Hopkinfon, Efq.

Steward of the Swannimote,

John Mathews, Attorney at Law.

Three Courts are neceffarily held for the Government of all Forefts, *viz.*

1. The Court of *Attachment,* who take Cognizance in all Caufes " *de viridi & venatione,*" Vert and Venifon; enroll the Offenders, in order to prefent them at the Juftice Seat. They have a power of En-quiry, but not of Conviction, and are required to meet once in forty Days.

2. The Court of *Swannimote* ‡; held likewife before the Verdurers, by the Steward of the *Swannimote* thrice in the Year. Here the Freeholders are fummoned to make Inquefts and empannel Juries.

" *Purpreſture,* from the Norman " *pourpris,*" *conſeptum,* an Inclofure, but more properly an Incroachment."
See MANWOOD, cap. X.
Aſſart. " Verelie when that the pleafant Woods of the Forefte, or thicke bufhie Places, meete for the fecret feeding of
" wild Beaftes, be cutte down, deftroyed, or plucked uppe by the Rotes, and the fame Ground be made a Plaine, and turned
" into arable Land. This by the Lawes of the Forefte is properly faid to be an Affart, or Land affarted.
" *Waſte* is a Worde chieflie in Ufe amongft Lawyers, and was brought into this Lande by the Normans, being derived from
" the French Verbe ' gafter,' i. e. vaftare to lay wafte." Ibid. cap. IX. pp. 47. 49.

* Thefe inhabit fix Lodges, the *King's, York, Worcefter, Danby, Herbert, Latimer,* with a Salary each of 15*l.* a Year.
† From " Gaƥol," in Anglo-Saxon, a Tribute; though ftated to have been an ancient Office, none upon Record prior to 1660.
‡ This Term is derived by Lord COKE from the Saxon " Speȝn," Servant, and " Ɱoꞇe, or Ꝑemoꞇe," a Court; alluding to its being a Court of the Officers of the Foreft, and preparatory to the Juftice Seat.

6 E
3. The

3. The *Juſtice Seat*, ſummoned by the Chief Juſtice in Eyre South of *Trent*, once only in three **Years**. Before this Court are heard and determined all Cauſes which reſpect the Franchiſes and Privileges of the Foreſt, and the Treſpaſſes againſt them.   Prior to which, the Regarders, or Commiſſioners, muſt inſpect and review the whole Foreſt, in order to make due Preſentments.

All which Courts uſually aſſemble at the King's Lodge, more commonly called the " *Speech Houſe*," ſituate nearly in the Centre of the Foreſt.

Beſide theſe are two others, peculiar to the Foreſt of *Dean*, *viz.* the Court of *Record* for the Hundred of *St. Briavel's* (already mentioned in the Account of the Caſtle) and that of the *Free Miners*.

The *Mine Law* Court, however ancient, has not been recorded in the Archives of the Foreſt before 1635, 10 CAR. I. when PHILIP Earl of PEMBROKE, as Conſtable of *St. Briavel's*, claimed to preſide. It conſiſts of the Gaveller and a Jury of forty-eight Free Miners, who muſt be Natives of the Hundred, and have been employed in a Mine at leaſt for the Space of a Year and a Day.   Their Privileges are to enact and enforce Bye Laws in remedy of Grievances, or for Accommodation, with the unanimous Conſent of the Jury; and to cut *Wood, but not Timber*, excepting for ſinking the Mines, as well in the Lands of private Perſons, as in the King's Soil, and to ſearch for Ore.   It has been computed that not leſs than 100 Tons of Wood are conſumed yearly.   From a late Report of the Gaveller, made to the Commiſſioners for enquiring into the State of the Foreſt, it appears that " there is at preſent no Iron Mine regularly " worked; that 121 Coal Pits produce weekly 1816 Tons; and that the Compoſitions of 662 Free Miners " amount to 215*l.* 8*s. per Annum.*"   This laſt Circumſtance is occaſioned by the frequency of opening new Mines, which is done as ſoon as they are prevented by Water, which commonly happens at a ſhallow Depth.   As yet, they have not erected Engines of modern Invention, ſo uſeful in other Collieries, and oppoſe every Innovation, as perhaps eventually ſubverſive of their ancient and eſtabliſhed Rights.

XCII. DEERHURST,

XCII. DEERHURST, OR DEORHURST.

AT *Deorhyrſte* in the firſt Periods of the *Saxon* Heptarchy a Cell for Religious was eſtabliſhed by Dodo, a tributary Prince of the Kingdom of *Mercia,* and much may be collected from the early Chroniclers both of its ecclefiaſtical and military Hiſtory.

The Pariſh of *Deerhurſt* is nearly of a circular Form, the chief of its own Hundred *, and of large Extent. It is diſtant three Miles South from *Tewkeſbury,* and eight from Gloucester on the North. The Soil near the River *Severn* is of a deep Clay, applied more generally to Paſture, and ſubject to frequent Inundations, but it varies on the higher Grounds †. Upon the Banks of the *Severn* a Tract of Commonable Lands extends for four Miles. A few Years fince, the Inhabitants of the adjoining Pariſh of *Leigh* ſunk a Ditch to divide the Commons; but, on being ſued, were obliged to relinquiſh their Plan.

The Æra of the Foundation ‡ of the Priory of *Deerhurſt* is placed about 750, when Dodo, already the Founder of *Tewkeſbury,* in refpect to the Memory of his Brother Almarick, who had lived and was interred here, erected over his Grave a ſtately Chapel, and eſtabliſhed a Fraternity of Prieſts. Thefe were ſoon difperfed, and the Structure demoliſhed by the Ravages of the *Danes,* but re-built in 980; though it remained in an unflouriſhing State till it was given by Edward the Confessor (1056) to the Abbey of *St. Dennis* in *France,* to which it became a Cell of *Benedictine* Monks, and was confirmed to them in 1069 by William the Conqueror. It poſſeſſed eight Lordſhips, and was accounted worth 300 Marks a Year, when it was ſold by the Abbot and Convent of *St. Dennis* to Richard Earl of Cornwall in 1250. In 1388, 11 Ric. II. ſome Pretence was found for ſeizing their Lands, and they were granted to John de Beauchamp, of *Holte.* It does not appear that they were inherited by that Family, for in 1418, 2 Hen. V. when the Alien Priories were diſſolved, this was ſtated to be " Prioratus Indigena," and confequently not ſubject to that Statute. In the firſt Year of the next Reign, on the Petition of the Convent and Hugh Magason the laſt Prior Alien, the Monaſtery of *St. Dennis* was diveſted of its Right, and the Nomination of the Prior conferred on the Convent, the Patronage of which was given to the Abbey of *Tewkeſbury.* Yet, in the 19th of his Reign, King Henry VI. endowed his College at *Eaton* with Parcel of their Revenues. The Denization was however revoked by Edward the Fourth, who firſt detatched thefe Lands from *Eaton,* and ſettled them on the College of *Fotheringhey;* then reſtored them to *Eaton,* and laſtly to *Tewkeſbury.* Continued Law-ſuits were carried on between thefe Eccleſiaſtics till the Reign of Henry the Seventh, when the laſt mentioned obtained the entire Poſſeſſion of *Deerhurſt.* At the Diſſolution in 1543, 34 Hen. VIII. it was purchafed as Parcel of *Tewkeſbury* by William Throckmorton, and had a yearly Rental, which in the Valuations was included in that of *Tewkeſbury.* To John Bromsgrove, the laſt Prior, a Penfion was aſſigned of 13*l.* 6*s.* 8*d.* annually. The Site, and an Eſtate confequently exempt from Tythes, was purchafed in the laſt Century by the noble

---

* " At the Time of the *Norman* Survey there were more Hundreds than at prefent; confequently thofe which now remain do " not always contain the fame Places as at that Time; nor do the *Norman* Hundreds always contain 100 Villages. This has " introduced ſtill greater Confuſion into Domefday Book." Warton's *Kiddington,* p. 31. n.

† " The riſing Grounds of *Deerhurſt* are covered with a red Loam, a remarkable Species of Soil, common to the Hillocks " of the over *Severn* Diſtrict, and to the inferior Hills of *Herefordſhire.* It is here called ' Red Land,' and refembles much the " Red Hills of *Nottinghamſhire.*" Marshall's Rur. Econ. of Glouc. vol. I. p. 66.

‡ " DEIRHURSTE in GLOCESTERSHIR.

" It ſtandith as *Severne* Ryver cummithe downe *in læva ripa* a Mile beneth *Theokeſbyri.* The Site of the Towne, as it is now, " is in a Manner of a Medow. So that when *Severne* much riſith the Water cummith almoſte about the Towne. It is to be ſup" poſed, that it was of olde Tyme leſſe ſubjecte to Waters, and that the Bottom of *Severne* then deeper without chokıng of Sandes " dyd at Flouddes leſte Hurte. It is now but a poore Village, and the Lordſhip longged a late partely to the Abbate of *Tewkes-* " *buri.* Such Parte as *Weſtminſtre* had, was longging to *Perſore* Abbay, tyl William Conqueror gave it away. *Derehurſte* Abbay " had the Reſidew, afore that the Houſe of *Derehurſte* was alienatid from the Monaſterie of *St. Dionife* by *Parife,* to the which it was " a Celle, and one Hugh Magason, a Monk of *St. Dionife,* was the laſt Priour aliene there yn Edwarde IV. Dayes, and about " that Tyme it was diſſolvid, and moſte of the Landes of it given *Fotheringey,* and *Eton* College, as it is ſaid, had ſum Title. After " Sute betwixte the Colleges and the Abbay of *Theokeſbyri,* Debatinges was, and after longe Tracte, a final Ende made in Henrie " the 7 Dayes, that the Priourie of *Goldcliffe* longgin then newly to *Teokeſbyri,* ſhould go with the Landes to *Fothering y* College, " and *Dehorhurſte* unto *Theokeſbyri.* Bede makith mention that yn his Tyme there was a notable Abbay at *Derelyrſte.* It was de" ſtroyed by the *Danes.* Werstannus fledde thens, as it is ſaid, to *Malverne.* The *Frenche* Order was an Erection fyns the " Conqueſt. The old Priory ſtode Eſt from *Severne* a Bow Shotte, and North of the Towne. There remayne yet dyverfe " Names of Streates as *Fiſſchar* Strete, and other. But the Buildings of them be gone. There be yet 2 Fayies kept, one at " eche Day, ' in inventione & exaltatione Crucis." Leland's Itin. vol. VI. pp. 78. 79.

Family

Family of COVENTRY *. GEORGE Earl of COVENTRY was created Vifcount DEERHURST, by Patent, bearing Date April 26, 1697, 9 WILL. III. †

The Church of *Deerburft* exercifes a peculiar Jurifdiction over the following Parifhes: " *Corfe, Forthampton, Hasfield, Leigh, Staverton, Bodington,* and *Tirley.*" Thefe claim archidiaconal Vifitation at their Mother Church, and had no Right of Sepulture in their own Cemeteries till confirmed by the Priors. The Benefice is unufually fmall, being only a ftipendiary Curacy of 6*l.* 13*s.* 4*d.* a Year, due from the Impropriation; it has been twice augmented by Queen ANNE's Bounty. The Family of THROGMORTON continued the Impropriators for feveral Defcents, of whom it was held by the FERMORS. Sir JOHN POWELL, Knight, a Juftice of the King's Bench in the beginning of the prefent Century, be-came the Poffeffor, and dying in 1713 bequeathed it with other confiderable Eftates to JOHN SNELL, Efq. his Nephew, whofe Reprefentative is POWELL SNELL, Efq. of *Guiting Grange.*

Of the Structure of the Church, dedicated to the *Holy Trinity* and *St. Dennis,* the prefent dilapidated State leaves much room for Conjecture. It has a very lofty Nave and Chancel, with two low Aifles, and a Tower at the Weft End, upon which was a Spire, blown down in 1666.

Here was certainly a more ancient Building, with which this is connected. Circular *Saxon* Arches are incorporated into the Walls, but the Arches now feen are pointed, the capitals of the Pillars foliated, and the Windows fquare, a Style of the later Gothic. Adjoining, and communicating with the Chancel, are Remains of the Priory, now modernized. The old Inhabitants of the Village defcribe a very fpa-cious Hall and other Apartments, which formed the Quadrangle, at this Time almoft in Ruins.

Prior to the Conqueft the Manor was held by the Abbey of *Perfhore* in *Worcefterfhire,* from which it was at that Time forcibly taken and given to the Monks of *Weftminfter.* Their Right was interrupted by ROBERT FITZ HAMAN, but recovered by Law in the Reign of HENRY the Second. From that Period till the Diffolution it formed a Part of their Revenues, which were granted to the See of *Weftminfter* by HENRY the Eighth, and confirmed to the Dean and Chapter by Queen ELIZABETH,

In this Parifh are four Hamlets, *viz.*

1. *Aperley*; anciently belonging to the Abbey of *Weftminfter.* A confiderable Eftate, long vefted in the Family of LANE, was bequeathed by the laft of them to CAPEL PAYNE, Efq. in 1755 ‡. A reputed and diftinct Manor in *Aperley,* with a capital Meffuage, and 400 Acres of Land, were held by EDWARD BRUGES in the Reign of HENRY the Sixth. He was fucceeded by the Family of THROCKMORTON, from whom it came to POWELL and SNELL.

2. *Wightfield.* From GILBERT LE DESPENCER this Eftate paffed to Sir JOHN CASSEY, Knight, Chief Baron of the Exchequer, who died in 1400, 1 HEN. IV. In 1468, 9 EDW. IV. JOHN CASSEY, Efq. was Sheriff of this County. This Family retained it till the beginning of the laft Century, which is now inherited from Judge POWELL by POWELL SNELL, Efq.

3. *Walton.* A Manor held likewife under the Church at *Weftminfter,* which includes, 4. *Hardwick,* of the fame Defcription; which were held by many Defcents of the Family of HARRIS, afterward refi-dent in GLOUCESTER.

THOMAS DOWDESWELL, of *Pull Court,* as Leffee, holds Courts for *Plaiftowe* in this Parifh, which have Jurifdiction over all the Manors in the lower Divifion of the Hundred of *Weftminfter.* In this Diftrict all the abovementioned Hamlets are contained; the Convent having procured moft of their Pof-feffions in this County to be thus incorporated.

The chief Eftates in this Parifh are vefted in the Right Honourable GEORGE Earl of COVENTRY, and the Families of SNELL, PAYNE, and HYETT, of *Painfwick.*

* See TANNER's Notitia Monaftica, GLOUCESTERSH. No. 10. edit. NASMITH. DUGDALE's Monafticon, tom. I. pp. 127. 547. tom. II p 965. FELIBIEN, l'Hiftoire de l'Abb. Royal de *S. Denys à Paris,* Append. n. cxv. In ATKINS's GLOUCESTER-SHIRE, pp. 125. 365. 368. 371. 386. 429. 430. 460. 492. 537. 608. 687. 788. 797. and 847. concerning Manors, Impropriations, and Eftates, belonging to this Priory, at GLOUCESTER, *Colne St. Dennis, Compton Parva, Corfe, Deerhurft, Eaftleche Turville, Hockington, Hasfield, Welford, Leygh, Staverton, Prefton, Haw, Welford,* and *Woolftone,* in this County. In NASH's *Worcefterfhire,* vol. I. p. 337. of the Advowfon of *Droitwich.* In STEVENS's Supplement, vol. I. p. 273. Cart. 12 EDW. II. n. 17. pro 2 Feriis apud *Dereburft,* &c. FULLER's Church Hift. book VI. p. 303. COLLINS, Tit. *Coventry.*

† ATKINS relates that the following Infcription was placed over the Gate:

" Hanc Aulam DODO Dux confecrari fecit in Ecclefiam, ad Honorem Beatæ MARIÆ Virginis ob amorem fratris fui ALMARICI."

And in the Year 1675 a Stone was difcovered, which was thus infcribed:

" ODDA Dux juffit hanc Aulam regiam conftrui atque dedicari in honorem *S. Trinitatis* pro Anima Germani fui ELFRICI quæ " de hoc loco affumpta eft. EALDREDUS vero Epifcopus qui eandem dedicavit 11 id. Aprilis, XIV autem anno Regni S. ED-" WARDI Regis *Angiorum.*"

‡ WILLIAM DE LA MARE made a Deed of Gift to the Hofpital of *St. Bartholomew* in GLOUCESTER of two Carroes of Wheat (16 Bufhels), to be paid yearly, from his Barn at *Apperley,* alias *Haperlez.*

In

In the Year 1016 a very memorable Treaty was propofed at *Deorhyrft*, where the Armes of Ed-mund Ironside and Canute the *Dane* * were drawn up in order of Battle on either Side the *Severn.* The Divifion of the Kingdom was ratified between them in a fmall Ifland called Oalni3, or *Olney*, but as there is another of the fame Name near Glocester, Hiftorians are not agreed; they are however unanimous in afferting that the Truce was completed at *Deorhurft.*

B E N E F A C T I O N S.

Dr. Robert Huntington, Bifhop of *Raphoe* in *Ireland*, gave a Rent Charge of 2*l.* a Year, payable out of Lands, for the apprenticing poor Boys alternately with the Parifh of *Leigh*.

Sarah Roberts left Lands, the annual Produce of which now is 2*l.* to be diftributed in Bread, on *St. Thomas's Day*, amongft fuch Poor as do not receive weekly pay.

Curates.	Patrons.	Curates.	Patrons.
1682 George Styles,	—— Farmor, Efq.	1746 Will. Palmer, B.A.	Bifhop of Gloucester.
1711 * * * * *	* * * * * * *	1750 Charles Bifhop, B. A.	The fame.
1736 Rich. Braffington,	Bifhop of Gloucester.	1773 Will. Davies, Clerk,	The fame.

Present Lord of the Manors,
Of *Deerhurft* and *Plaiftow*,
Thomas Dowdeswell, Esq.

The Perfons fummoned from this Place and his Hamlets by the Heralds, in 1682 and 1683, were

Edward Harris, Gent. of *Walton.*
Edward Smith, Gent.
Roger Mortimer, Gent.

William Lane, Gent. of *Aperley.*
George Banifter, Gent.

At the Election in 1776, Thirty-two Freeholders polled from this Parifh.

The Regifter begins in 1558, and in 1698 has the following Entry :

" The King's Dues upon Marriages, Births, and Burials, were paid untill the 20th of October, " 1698, and likewife Batchelors and Widowers ;" which proves that Tax to be no new Expedient for the Supply of Government.

Annual Account of Marriages, Births, and Burials, in this Parish.

A.D.	Mar.	Bir.	Bur.	A.D.	Mar.	Bir.	Bur.	A.D.	Mar.	Bir.	Bur.	A.D.	Mar.	Bir.	Bur.
1781	3	23	16	1786	2	18	17	1791				1796			
1782	4	26	16	1787	2	11	11	1792				1797			
1783	1	18	10	1788	5	10	6	1793				1798			
1784	3	13	15	1789				1794				1799			
1785	6	15	31	1790				1795				1800			

INSCRIPTIONS IN THE CHURCH.

On a large grey Marble, the Effigies of a Man in his Judge's Robes, at his Feet a Lion. A Woman in the Dress of the Times, at her Feet a Greyhound. Over their Heads the Figures of Christ and St. Anne instructing the Virgin. Four corner Escutcheons, two remaining † :

1. Argent, a Chevron between three Falcon's Heads erafed Gules, for Cassey. 2. Three Lions paffant in Pale.

Hic jacet Joh'es Caffey, Miles, quondam capitalis Baro' Ss'carij D'm'i Regis, qui obiit XXIII die Maii, Anno D'ni MCCCC, & Alicia uxor ejus, quor' a'i'bus p'piciet' Deus. Amen.

* Ambo reges ad locum qui *Deorhirfte* nominatur in unum convenerunt. Eadmundus cum fuis in Occidentali ripâ *Sabrinæ* " Canutus vero in Orientali cum fuis. Deinde uterque Rex in infulam quæ *Olanege* appellatur, & eft in medio fluvii fita, " trabariis advehitur. Ubi Pace & Fraternitate Sacramentis confirmatâ, dein armis & veftibus mutuatis, tributoque quod " claff"icæ manui penderetur ftatuto, invicem dicefferunt. Sunt qui feribunt duellum commiffum fuiffe in *Olaneg* inter Ead-" mundum & Canutum." Leland's Collectanea, vol. III. p. 354.
This Event is alfo mentioned by Holinshed, vol. I. p. 255. Milton's Hiftory of *Britain*, book VI. p. 265. Speed's Hift. pp. 371. 1056. Camden's Britannia, edit. Gibson, vol. I. p. 272. Strutt's Saxon Chronicle, vol. II. pp. 103. &c.
† " Sir John Cassey was appointed Chief Baron of the Exchequer, 12 Ric. II. 1389; and again, 1 Hen. IV. 1399." Dugdale's Orig. Jud. Chron. Series.

On

On a flat blue Stone inlaid with Brass, the Figure of a Woman in the Dress of the Times. Four corner Escutcheons, one only remaining :

Quarterly, 1. and 4. Argent, a Crofs Sable, charged with a Leopard's Face in the Centre Or; Bruges. 2. De Chandos. 3. Berkeley, of *Coberley*.

Here lyethe Elyzabethe Rowdon, funetyme Wyffe to Wyll'm Caffey, of Whyghtfylde, Efquyer, after the Dethe of the fayde Wyll'm was marryed to Walter Rowdon, Efquyer, and was Doughtyr to Thomas Bruges, of Coverle, Efquyer, which Elizabethe dyed the XXIIJ Day of Januarie, Anno D'ni MDXXII, for whofe Soule of your Charitie fay a Pater Nofter.

ON FLAT STONES IN THE CHANCEL.

Arms ; Argent, a Fefs Sable, between three Lions Heads erafed Gules, for Fremor;—impaling, Argent, three Bars Sable, and in chief three Martletts of the fecond, for Carill.

Hic jacet Elizabetha, uxor
Petri Fermor, Armigeri,
toparchæ hujus Manerii,
Filia Joannis Carill,
de Langley Surria, Armigeri,
& ex nobiliffima profapia comitum
Kingfordiæ, oriunda
piiffime obiit ficut
vixit 11 Junii, Anno 1677.

Here lyeth the Body of
Peter Fermor, fecond Son to
Henry Fermor, Efq.
of Tufmore in Oxfordfhire.
He dyed on the 16th Day of December,
Anno Domini 1691.

Arms ; Barry of fix Or and Azure, an Inefcutcheon Ermine, on a Chief of the firft, three Palletts between two Gyronnies of the fecond, for Mortimer ;—impaling, Barry of ten Argent and Azure, over all a Lion rampant Gules, for Stratford.

Here lyeth the Body of
Elizabeth, the Wife of Roger Mortimer, Gent.
who departed this Life the 17th Day of January,
Anno Domini 1682.

Here alfo lyeth the Body of
Roger Mortimer, Gent.
who departed this Life the
25th Day of June, Anno Dom. 1683.

ON A MONUMENT IN THE NORTH AISLE:

Arms; Per Pale Azure and Gules, three Saltires Or, in the Centre a Mullett of the laft, for Lane.

Near this Place
lie the Remains of William Lane, Efq.
late of Apperley in this Parifh,
who departed this Life
Auguft 2, 1755, aged 65 Years.

ON FLAT STONES.

Arms; on three Efcutcheons ; 1ft, Parti Per Pale Gules and Azure, three Lions rampant Or, for Powell. 2d, Per Pale Argent and Gules, a Lion rampant Sable for Roberts. 3d, Azure, three Lozenges in Fefs Or, for Freeman.

Margaret, the Wife of
James Powell, Efq. Daughter of
John Roberts, of Fiddington, Gent.
deceafed Sept. 5, 1656.
M. D. Q. P.
Kemmet Freeman.

Thomas Clutterbook,
of Leonard Stanley, Gent.
died the 23d of February, 1656.

Here lyeth the Body of
John Powell, of the City of Gloucefter, Efq.
who departed this Life the .. Day of Nov. 1666.

Here lieth the Body of
Edward Guye, Gent. who married
Frances, the eldeft Daughter of
John Cotheridge, Efq. and had by her
fix Sonnes and one Daughter, and was
here buried the fixth Day of
December, Anno 1612.

Arms ; Mortimer as before ;—impaling, Ermine, on a Bend Gules, three Eagles difplayed Or, for Baghott.

Elizabeth, the Wife of
Edmund Mortimer, died the 12th Day of
November, Anno Dom. 1680.

Joseph, Son of Joseph and Ann Wintle,
of Plaiftow,
died Auguft 8, 1753, aged 12.

Alfo Anne, Wife of Joseph Wintle,
died July 20, 1754, aged 48.

Joseph Wintle, of Plaiftow,
died Oct. 30, 1770, aged 57.

William Dipper, late of Plaiftow,
departed this Life the 25th Day of
January, 1709, aged 47.

William, Son of
William and Ann Dipper,
died an Infant.

Alfo Mrs. Ann Dipper,
Relict of Thomas Wintle, of Plaiftow,
and late Wife of Mr. William Dipper,
died Jan. 27, 1745, in the 67th Year of her Age.

John

JOHN HERRING
died June 17, 1704, aged 56.

PARRY, the Son of JOHN and JOYCE HERRING,
departed this Life the 4th of June, 1689.

JOYCE, Wife of RICHARD SCANDRETT,
died Auguſt 13, 1694, aged 68.

RICHARD, Son of JOHN and JOYCE HERRING,
died an Infant.

Hic inhumatur Corpus GEORGII STILES,
hujus Parochiæ Clericus
Viginti & novem Annis.
Obiit trigeſimo die Septembris,
Anno Salutis 1711, ætatis 67.

ON FLAT STONES IN THE NAVE.

THOMAS COX, of this Place,
departed this Life the 10th Day of March, 1736,
aged 60.

MARY, the Daughter of
THOMAS and SUSANNA COX,
departed this Life the 31ſt of Auguſt, 1738,
aged 19.

SUSANNA, Wife of the abovenamed
THOMAS COX, departed this Life
January the 31ſt, 1739, aged 61.

MARY, Wife of THOMAS COX,
died November the 17th, 1746, aged 24.

GEORGE their Son
died Jan. 23, 1747-8, an Infant.

THOMAS COX, late of Apperley, Gent.
died the 24th of May, 1763, aged 48.

JOHN FLUCK, of Apperley,
was buried the 7th of January, 1685, aged 67.

SUSANNA his Wife
was buried March the 20th, 1703-4,
aged 78 Years.

Alſo SARAH TULLY her Daughter,
Relict of ARTHUR TULLY, of
Kencheſter in com. Hereford, Gent.
was buried December 17, 1723, aged 68.

Alſo three Grandchildren.

MARY, Daughter of JOHN and MARY COX,
died July 7, 1715, aged 8.

Here lyeth, by his own expreſs Deſire,
the Body of THOMAS CHURCH,
late of the City of Worceſter, Baker,
who departed this Life July 26, 1766,
in the 33d Year of his Age.

IN THE CHURCH YARD, ON TOMBS.

WILLIAM POPE,
late of the Lye,
died Oct. 29, 1750, aged 43.

SAMUEL HEALING, of Apperley in this Pariſh,
died March 10, 1782, aged 72.

JOHN HEALING, of Whitefield in this Pariſh,
died Feb. 14, 1782, aged 33.

ON HEAD STONES.

	Died	Aged
Lawrence Cox, Yeoman -	19 Jan. 1741	52
Mary his Wife -	1 Feb. 1771	72
Anne, Wife of Thomas Cox	4 Jan. 1729	84
Charles Cox, Gent. late of Tewkeſbury - -	16 Jan. 1762	32
Catharina, the Wife of John Cox, Mercer, of Tewkeſbury, and Daughter of George Whitmore, of Cann Hall in the County of Salop, Eſq. - -	26 Jan. 1763	32
Sarah, Wife of Thomas Cox, of this Pariſh, and late Widow of Giles Surman - -	3 Mar. 1766	71
Thomas Cox - -	12 July, 1768	72
Giles Surman -	7 Apr. 1742	50
Giles Surman - -	25 Aug. 1768	53
William Cox, of this Pariſh, Daughter of Thomas and Mary Cox, of Dumbleton -	9 Oct. 1758	25
John Cox - -	11 Apr. 1739	69
Mary his Wife - -	24 Aug. 1738	65
John, Son of John and Ann Cox	28 Dec. 1759	25
Sarah, Wife of William Cox	17 Feb. 1758	32
Edmund Locett, of this Pariſh	24 Jan. 1743	77
Margaret his Wife -	18 July, 1755	80
John Brown - -	20 Oct. 1757	32
Sarah his Wife -	8 Oct. 1757	44
William, Son of John and Sarah Brown - -	27 Feb. 1760	20
William Fluck, of the Oak -	9 July, 1710	84
Elizabeth, Wife of John Fluck, of the Oak - -	27 Aug. 1697	34
John Fluck, of the Oak, ſenior	12 June, 1725	68
Giles Fluck, of this Pariſh, Yeoman	27 Jan. 1737	62
Eleanor his Wife - -	3 May, 1740	60
John their Son - -	8 Feb. 1740	27
John Fluck, of the Oak -	30 Mar. 1760	62
Suſannah his Wife -	6 June, 1758	57
William Fluck -	8 Apr. 1682	48
Edith his Wife -	19 May, 1673	43
Edward Fluck - -	25 Oct. 1706	84
Joſeph, Son of John and Suſanna Fluck, of the Oak -	2 Nov. 1764	38
Sarah his Wife -	6 Feb. 1762	23
William Stiles, ſenior -	5 Apr. 1729	58
Mary his Wife -	2 May, 1743	64
Thomas Stiles - -	30 Mar. 1766	66
Elizabeth his Wife -	12 Feb. 1761	57
John their Son -	2 Feb. 1760	18
William Stiles, Son of Thomas Stiles, ſenior, by Elizabeth his Wife, late of Comberwood in the Pariſh of Tirley, Yeoman -	4 June, 1766	28
William Haling -	26 Feb. 1711	36
Elizabeth, Wife of John Haling, junior - -	24 July, 1723	5
John Haling - -	15 Apr. 1729	43
Elizabeth, Wife of William Herbert of Hatherley, Daughter of John Haling - -	— June, 1737	20

O N

ON HEAD STONES.

	Died	Aged
John Haling -	31 July, 1702	77
Judith, Daughter of Samuel and Judith Haling -	13 Aug. 1762	13
Richard Piff, Yeoman -	14 Feb. 1758	65
Elizabeth his Wife -	10 Oct. 1753	74
Isabel, Wife of William Eagles	18 Aug. 1728	39
William Eagles - -	2 Jan. 1742	52
William Haling -	4 May, 1782	71
Mary, Wife of William White	5 Mar. 1754	50
Mary, Wife of Joseph Sheppard	4 Aug. 1750	47
John Creswell -	28 Jan. 1733	70
Mary his Wife - -	20 Apr. 1736	60
Capel Colchester -	11 Apr. 1718	54
Anna his Wife -	20 Apr. 1698	32
William Fewster -	20 Sept. 1720	86
Mary his Wife - -	27 July, ——	70
Thomas Hampton -	7 Mar. 1684	30
Elizabeth his Wife -	2 Feb. 1689	28
Thomas Hampton -	17 Oct. 1701	76
Margaret his Wife -	9 Dec. 1682	—
Edmund Hampton -	12 Dec. 1709	76
Mary his Wife -	23 Dec. 1704	64
John Hampton, of this Parish	20 Jan. 1771	30
William Haynes - -	28 Oct. 1698	65
Dinah, Wife of Stephen Lun	11 Jan. 1741	63
Giles Hawker - -	29 July, 1685	67
Alice his Wife -	22 Mar. 1688	—
Francis, Son of the Rev. Francis Lamb - -	13 Oct. 1755	27
Elizabeth Marshall -	— Apr. 1743	23
Ann, Wife of Samuel Fox, of Bourton on the Water -	16 Oct. 1742	73
William Stone -	12 Apr. 1761	58
Elizabeth his Wife -	3 May, 1779	73
Elizabeth, Wife of Joseph Barnard	2 July, 1734	42
William Barnard -	14 Oct. 1786	70
Sarah, Wife of William Thurston, and late Wife of William Barnard, of Handby Castle -	12 Feb. 1779	66
Jerard Pope - -	18 Mar. 1696	68
Margaret his Wife -	21 Jan. 1687	59
Mary, Wife of William Allen	25 Mar. 1749	32
Benjamin, Son of William and Mary Barnes - -	5 May, 1727	25
Richard Smith, Yeoman -	6 Feb. 1715	65
Joan, Wife of John Wintle	19 Nov. 1761	59
Philippa Greenway -	9 Dec. 1716	93
Richard Beale - -	28 Nov. 1702	67
Joan, Wife of Richard Beale, and late Wife of John Ashley	25 Apr. 1711	61
Robert Evenis -	15 June, 1743	70
Sarah his Wife -	3 Nov. 1734	61
Thomas Evenis - -	18 Oct. 1763	75
Mary his Wife -	27 Jan. 1771	70

	Died	Aged
William Farmer - -	14 Apr. 1682	—
William Farmer -	28 Oct. 1707	48
Elizabeth, Wife of Charles Andrews	11 Sept. 1768	33
James Gamon -	1 Nov. 1737	58
Ann, Wife of James Gamon	24 June, 1778	83
William Brooks, of Deerhurst Walton	3 Feb. 1764	48
Joseph Gregory, of this Parish	1 Mar. 1770	59
Elizabeth his Wife -	3 Jan. 1753	26
Christopher Shayle, senior	22 Jan. 1765	72
Thomas his Son -	25 July, 1763	35
Henry, Son of Thomas and Elizabeth Shayle - -	6 July, 1755	42
Thomas Shayle -	10 Apr. 1756	87
William, Son of Henry and Jane Shayle - -	12 June, 1769	26
Elizabeth, Wife of Christopher Shayle - -	28 July, 1761	80
Mary, Wife of John Sollars -	4 Oct. 1715	60
Thomas Newman -	4 Dec. 1784	53
Martha, Wife of William Newman, of Apperley - -	21 Dec. 1767	56
William Newman, of Apperley	2 July, 1781	65
Thomas Butt - -	6 Nov. 1689	53
Robert, Son of Thomas and Margaret Butt - -	9 Oct. 1690	28
Edward Mann -	6 Dec. 1785	55
Elizabeth, Wife of Edward Mann	8 Jan. 1774	40
Edward their Son -	8 Jan. 1784	17
William Windows -	1 Nov. 1750	46
Sarah his Wife, and late Wife of Thomas Fluck -	26 Oct. 1781	71
Elizabeth Lane -	30 Dec. 1709	28
Sarah, Wife of William Clarkson	28 Sept. 1709	28
William Whithorne -	17 May, 1741	72
Mary his Wife -	2 July, 1785	84
William Brooks -	3 Feb. 1764	48
Sarah, Wife of William Wells	28 Oct. 1770	36
Mary, Wife of William Price	12 Aug. 1766	21
Philippa, Wife of Thomas Dipper	25 Apr. 1738	47
William Dipper, senior -	30 Sept. 1716	59
Hannah, Wife of William Dipper, late of Apperley -	5 Nov. 1776	72
William Dipper, Yeoman -	24 May, 1769	80
Mary, Wife of Robert Watts, first the Wife of Thomas Evenis	5 Feb. 1722	63
Isaac Pearce - -	26 Apr. 1748	88
Thomas Etheridge, senior -	13 Mar. 1715	66
Thomas Etheridge, junior -	7 Mar. 1715	37
Thomas Dovey - -	19 June, 1748	58
Richard Nelms - -	8 Nov. 1781	70
Esther his Wife -	11 Dec. 1763	43
Richard their Son -	21 Dec. 1770	21
Richard Jones - -	11 June, 1729	45
Mary his Wife - -	2 Nov. 1741	65

XCIII. DEINTON,

MORE anciently *DONNINGTUNE*, though fubfequently to the *Domefday* Survey, in which it does not occur, but as *DIDINTONE*.

The Parifh of *Deynton* conftitutes a Part of the united Hundreds of *Langley* and *Swinefhead*, is nearly three Miles long and two broad, fix Miles from *Sodbury* on the South, four from *Marfhfield* on the Weft, and thirty-five in a foutherly Direction from GLOUCESTER. The Soil is light and loamy, chiefly Pafturage, with an inconfiderable Proportion of arable Lands. At *Bitton* the River *Boyd* interfecting this Parifh runs in Confluence with the *Avon*.

The Benefice is rectorial, with an extenfive Glebe, in the Patronage of the Crown, and comprifed within the Deanery of *Hawkefbury*.

The Church, dedicated to the *Holy Trinity*, is conftructed with a Nave, North Aifle, and a low embattled Tower. The dividing Arches are maffy and pointed, of early Architecture. THOMAS COKER, M. A. Rector, re-built the Chancel in 1767, and the Nave was lengthened and modernized about two Years fince. By the fame Incumbent the Rectory Houfe was erected in a commodious and elegant Style.

The Manor was Parcel of the Honour of GLOUCESTER, and held in Fee for many Generations under the DE CLARES by a Family to which it gave Name. In 1278, 6 EDW. I. JOHN DE TRACI purchafed it of THOMAS DE DEYNTON, in whofe Defcendants it remained till the Reign of Queen ELIZABETH, when it was transferred to ARTHUR PLAYER, Efq. and others. Early in the prefent Century it belonged to the Family of LANGTON. The principal Eftate is vefted in WILLIAM GORE LANGTON, Efq. which Name he affumed on his Marriage with the Heir.

An exempted Manor, called the *Bury*, paffed from the STILLS to the HILLMANS, who now poffefs it. *Tracy Park* Lodge was long the Eftate and Refidence of the Family of RIDLEY, and by many fubfequent Purchafes is now of ——— BUSH, Efq. It pays a Mark only, yearly, in Lieu of Tythes. There was anciently a free Chapel adjoining to the Manor Houfe, for the Site of which 5*s*. 4*d*. is ftill due as an Audit to the Crown.

The Courfe of the River *Boyd* is through a very deep Channel of Rocks, rifing almoft in a perpendicular Direction, upon either Side of which are very diftinct Vallations for advanced Pofts, probably communicating with the Military Way from *Aquæ Solis* to the *Trajectus*.

Lead Ore is found, but not of fufficient Quality to encourage the Eftablifhment of Works. Many of the poorer Inhabitants are employed in calcining the Rock Stone, which produces Lime of remarkable Strength and Whitenefs.

BENEFACTIONS.

WILLIAM TRACY, Efq. by Deed, 1530, gave Land for the Erection of a Poor Houfe.

JOHN LANGTON, Efq. 1660, gave 20*l*. which Sum has been laid out in Land; the annual Produce is 16*s*.

The Rev. WILLIAM LANGTON, 1668, bequeathed 200*l*. for the Endowment of a School and apprenticing poor Children; this Sum has likewife been laid out in Land; the yearly Profits of which are 7*l*.

Mr. ATWELL gave 100*l*. the Intereft of which, 3*l*. 10*s*. to put out poor Children Apprentices.

PHILIPPA STILL gave 10*l*. for the Relief of the Poor; the annual Produce of which is 10*s*.

Mr. SAMUEL PARKER, 1759, devifed 20*l*. for apprenticing poor Children; the annual Profit of which is 16*s*.

6 G

INCUMBENTS.

INCUMBENTS.	PATRONS.	INCUMBENTS.	PATRONS.
1278 ——————,	Thomas de Deynton.	1678 Jofeph Jackfon,	King Charles II.
—— Arthur Saul,	Queen Elizabeth.	* * * * * * * * * * * * * *	
1586 William Dyke,	——————.	1720 Rich. Furney, M. A.	King George I.
1588 Thomas Cooley,	Sir John Tracey, Knt.	1727 James Howe, M. A.	The fame.
1593 Thomas Cozen,	——————.	1728 David Duncan, M. A.	King George II.
1613 William Beeley,	King James I.	1745 Tho. Coker, M.A. (refigned)	The fame.
1615 George Beeley,	The fame.	1783 Peter Gunning, M. A.	King George III.
1640 Robert Wilkes,	King Charles I.		

PRESENT PROPRIETORS OF THE MANORS,

Of *Deinton,*

WILLIAM GORE LANGTON, ESQ.

Of the *Bury,*

HENRY HILLMAN, ESQ.

The Perfons fummoned from this Place by the Heralds in 1682 and 1683, were

Henry Still, Efq.
John Parker, Gent.
—— Ridley, Gent.

At the Election in 1776 Twenty-three Freeholders polled from this Parifh.

The oldeft Regifter bears Date in 1566.

ANNUAL ACCOUNT OF MARRIAGES, BIRTHS, AND BURIALS, IN THIS PARISH.

A.D.	Mar.	Bir.	Bur.	A.D.	Mar.	Bir.	Bur.	A.D.	Mar.	Bir.	Bur.	A.D.	Mar.	Bir.	Bur.
1781	1	13	8	1786	3	15	7	1791				1796			
1782	3	7	12	1787	3	7	6	1792				1797			
1783	1	7	6	1788	2	12	8	1793				1798			
1784	4	12	9	1789				1794				1799			
1785	3	7	4	1790				1795				1800			

INSCRIPTIONS IN THE CHURCH.

ON A NEAT MONUMENT OF WHITE AND VARIEGATED MARBLE IN THE NAVE :

Arms ; Quarterly, Gules and Or, a Bend Argent, for LANGTON ;—impaling, Argent, a Crofs Sable, charged in the Centre with a Leopard's Face Or, for BRIDGES.

M. S.
ELIZABETHÆ LANGTON,
Filiæ
EDWARDI BRIDGES, de Cainfham,
in Com. Somerfet. Arm.
Uxoris
JOHANNIS LANGTON, de Deinton,
in Com. Gloceft. Gen.
a cujus morte
Vidua vixit annos ultra
quadraginta,
ut Charitati in Pauperes,
Benignitati in fuos,
Pietate in Deum,
Curis foluta
fefe devoveret,
ætat. 83°, died 33°,
falut. 24 Mar. 1702-3.
Sancta Matrona
fuas exuvias juxta
illuftrium Majorum cineres
in Ecclefia de Cainfham

recondi juffit,
fed cum inter multifaria
numerofæ familiæ
marmora
in Anguftis iftius cancellis,
Monumento defuerit locus
in hujus Parochiæ Ecclefiam,
in qua
longam bonis operibus
peragandis
Viduitatem confumpfit,
CAROLUS, SYMES, & AMY MEREDITH,
Nepotes & Executores,
Marmor hoc gratitudinis ergo
pofuerunt.

ON A PLAIN TABLET :

Underneath lyeth the Body of MARY, the Wife of EDMUND CHAPP, who departed this Life the 18th Day of September, Anno Domini 1695, ætatis fuæ 32.

On

ON A MONUMENT ON THE NORTH SIDE THE
CHANCEL :

JOSEPH JACKSON, M. A.
the faithful Vicar of this Church
41 Years,
died Jan. 12, 1719.
He was an eminent Pattern
of primitive Piety,
and the perfecting Difcipline of the Crofs;
found and zealous
in the Faith ;
conftant and diligent
in his Miniftry,
as a true Prieft of GOD
and Difciple of CHRIST.

ELIZABETH his Wife,
an holy and godly Matron,
imitating her Hufband's Vertues,
died Feb. 12, 1721.

The Memory of the Juft is bleffed.

ON A PLAIN TABLET :

Near this Place lieth the Body of
SAMUEL PACKER, of this Parifh, Yeoman,
who departed this Life the
6th of September, 1751, aged 64 Years.

The Body of
JOHN PACKER, of this Parifh, Yeoman,
lies near this Place, who departed this Life
the 27th of November, 1760,
aged 90 Years.

ON ANOTHER TABLET AT THE WEST END :

Near this Place was interred the Body of
PHILIP, Son of ROBERT PALMER,
by ANN his Wife.
He died Sept. 26, 1748,
aged 1 Year and 6 Months.

Alfo
PHILIP, a fecond Son of that Name,
died October 13, 1759,
aged 8 Years and 6 Months.

Alfo
BETTY, Daughter of ROBERT and ANN PALMER,
died June 29, 1771, in the 18th Year of her Age.

ON FLAT STONES IN THE NAVE.

ON A BRASS PLATE :

M. S.
Conjugis fui chariffimi GEORGII WEARE,
de hac Parochia, Generofi,
Filii HENRICI WEARE, de Henton,
& PENELOPES uxoris ejus,
qui quidem GEORGIUS, placide in
Domine obdormivit 17, & hic fepultus fuit
21 die Januarii, Anno Domini 1686,
ætatis fuæ 41.

Chriftus mihi vita, Mors mihi lucrum.
ANNA uxor ejus mœftiffima L. P.

JOHN ROBINSON
departed this Life May 4, 1670,
aged 38.

ELIZABETH his Daughter
died March 8, 1719,
aged 57 Years and 2 Months.

SAMUEL PACKER
departed this Life Jan. 14, 1712,
aged 62 Years and 6 Months.

SARAH, the Wife of
the abovefaid SAMUEL PACKER,
died May 12, 1743, aged 83.

SARAH, Daughter of
SAMUEL and SARAH PACKER,
departed this Life Sept. 1, 1747, aged 41.

WILLIAM their Son
died Sept. 3, 172 .. aged 41.

MARGARET, Daughter of
RICHARD and ANN DAVIS,
died October 23, 1713,
aged 43 Years and 8 Months.

ANN, the Wife of RICHARD DAVIS,
Mother of the abovefaid MARGARET,
died Auguft 14, 1735,
in the 97th Year of her Age.

KATHERINE, Wife of THOMAS LEWEN,
died the 8th of June, 1754,
in the 88th Year of her Age.

JOHN DAVIS, of the City of Briftol,
departed this Life June 3, 1757,
in the 85th Year of his Age.

MARY, the Wife of THOMAS FARR,
of the City of Briftol, and Daughter of
SAMUEL PACKER, of
the Parifh of Wefterleigh,
departed this Life February 7, 1717,
in the 38th Year of her Age.

ON FLAT STONES IN THE
NORTH AISLE.

MARGARET, the Daughter of
ARTHUR and DOROTHE PLAYER,
died 22 June, Anno Dom. 1596.

THOMAS BROWNE
departed this Life April ... Anno Dom. 1610.

ELNER RODBOURNE
was buried the laft Day of July, A. D. 1614.

RICHARD RIDLEY,
of Well Houfe in this Parifh,
died Auguft 25, 1625.

ELIZABETH,

ELIZABETH, the Wife of RICHARD RIDLEY,
deceafed the 1ft Day of January, Anno Dom. 1627.

THOMAS RIDLEY, Gent.
was buried Auguft 12, 1662.

RICHARD RIDLEY, Gent.
eldeft Son of the faid THOMAS RIDLEY,
died April 17, 1690, aged 62.

HESTER RIDLEY
was buried September the . . 1671.

ALICE, Wife of THOMAS RIDLEY,
departed this Life the 24th of Oftober, 1678.

JEANE, the Daughter of
RICHARD and SARAH RIDLEY,
departed this Life Auguft 7, A. D. 1686.

Here refteth the Body of
THOMAS and PRESCILLA,
Son and Daughter of JOHN ATWOOD,
who did depart this Life;
THOMAS,
the 12th of Sept. Anno Domini 1647;
and PRESCILLA,
the 18th of May, Anno Dom. 1659.

IN THE CHURCH YARD, ON TOMBS.

The Rev. Mr. ROBERT WILKES,
Reftor of this Parifh,
was buried November . . 1677.

REBECKAH his Wife
was buried the 9th of December, 1699.

REBECKAH their Daughter
was buried June 15, 1680, aged 14.

ANN their Daughter
died January . . . . . . aged 28.

Within this Tomb lies the Body of
the Rev. Mr. FRANCIS WILKES,
who departed this Life the
21ft Day of April, 1744, aged 79 Years.
He was many Years the faithful
Minifter of Rowbarrow and Burrington
in the County of Somerfet,
upwards of Fifty-two Years,
and Son of
the Reverend Mr. ROBERT WILKES,
formerly Minifter of this Parifh.

Here alfo lies interred . . . . the well-beloved
Wife of the faid Mr. FRANCIS WILKES,
who died the 20th Day of Oftober, 1738,
aged 78 Years.

RICHARD, Son of
WILLIAM and HANNAH BUTLER,
died May 8, 1763, aged 22.

WILLIAM BUTLER, Yeoman,
died June 2, 1763, aged 52.

SARAH, Daughter of
WILLIAM and HANNAH BUTLER,
died June 11, 1770, aged 21.

HANNAH, Wife of JOHN BRYAN, fenior,
died Nov. 25, 1737, aged 52.

JOHN BRYAN, fenior,
died Sept. 25, 1760, aged 84.

JOHN BRYAN, junior,
died Feb. 25, 1758, aged 53.

BETTY his Wife
died May 11, 1735, aged 22.

WILLIAM NICHOLLS
died March 18, 1713, aged 40.

SAMUEL his Son
died Auguft 30;

And MARY his Daughter,
May the 10th, 1700.

GEORGE, the Son of
WILLIAM and MARY NICHOLLS,
was buried May 30, 1722, aged 26.

JAMES, the Son of
WILLIAM and MARY NICHOLLS,
died March 25, 1740, aged 20.

MARY, Wife of WILLIAM NICHOLLS,
died September 15, 1742, aged 71.

WILLIAM NICHOLLS
died February 4, 1769, in the
68th Year of his Age.

ELIZABETH, Wife of WILLIAM NICHOLLS,
died April 5, 1775, aged 60.

MARY their Daughter died in her Infancy.

WILLIAM DAVIS, Yeoman,
died Oftober 7, 1778, aged 67.

HANNAH, Wife of EDWARD DAVIS,
died March 26, 1751, aged 62.

EDWARD

EDWARD DAVIS
died June 14, 1749, in the 66th Year of his Age.

ELIZABETH, Wife of
EDWARD DAVIS, Daughter of
WILLIAM and ELIZABETH SAUNDERS,
died the 20th of March, 1722, aged 39.

ELIZABETH, Wife of JACOB AMOS,
Daughter of EDWARD and ELIZABETH DAVIS,
died October 18, 1748, aged 28.

Also two Sons and one Daughter of
EDWARD and ELIZABETH DAVIS, died as follows:

SAMUEL died May 3, 1720.

JAMES died Feb. 5, 1721.

MARY died Jan. 17, 1713.

ANN, Wife of MOSES TOGHILL,
Daughter of EDWARD and ELIZABETH DAVIS,
died October 19, 1781, aged 71.

RICHARD NEALE
died April 11, 1736, aged 77.

JANE, Wife of RICHARD NEALE,
died Feb. 17, 1704, aged 44.

LUCY, Wife of GEORGE TOGHILL,
died Aug. 15, 1754, aged 21.

JANE, Wife of WILLIAM JONES,
died April 5, 1738, aged 49.

WILLIAM JONES
died March 16, 1767, aged about 80.

SAMUEL, Son of WILLIAM and JANE JONES,
died Feb. 13, 1777, aged 56.

SARAH, Wife of GILES BROWNING,
died April 19, 1746, aged 52.

GILES BROWNING
died Jan. 14, 1772, in the 77th Year of his Age.

WILLIAM BROWNING
died May 29, 1783, aged 62.

MARY, Wife of RICHARD BENNETT,
and Daughter of TOBIAS LUTON,
died in July 1710, aged 26.

THOMAS CREW
died April 24, 1747, aged 52.

MARY his Wife
died March 20, 1727, aged 34.

SARAH, Wife of MATTHEW SNAILUM,
died April 24, 1775, aged 87.

THOMAS their Son
died Oct. 21, 1752, aged 32.

MATTHEW SNAILUM
died in November 1733, aged 49.

SAMUEL MANNINGS, senior,
died April 18, 1712,
aged 53 Years and 10 Months.

SARAH his Wife
died the 6th of May, 1742, aged 82.

WILLIAM, Son of
SAMUEL and HANNAH MANNINGS,
died March 19, 1737, aged 17.

SAMUEL MANNINGS, Yeoman,
died May 7, 1731, aged 40.

HANNAH, Wife of SAMUEL MANNINGS,
died Feb. 21, 1761, aged 72.

O N   H E A D   S T O N E S.

	Died	Aged
Sarah, Wife of Thomas Gay	5 June, 1741	28
Grace, Wife of Thomas Mannings	15 Nov. 1761	31
Isaac Mannings	26 Mar. 1751	31
Thomas Godard	17 Apr. 1766	36
Ann, Wife of Robert Bolwell	19 Mar. 1740	38
Hugh, Son of Robert and Mary Bolwell	5 June, 1742	14
Mary their Daughter	10 Aug. 1743	18
Mary, Wife of Samuel Francom	21 May, 1750	56
Sarah their Daughter	—— 1731	18
Esther their Daughter	—— 1731	5
Elizabeth, Daughter of Richard and Margaret Strange	19 July, 1749	20
Ann, Wife of Robert Razey, Daughter of Richard and Margaret Strange, of Wick and Abson	25 Mar. 1756	33
Jane, Daughter of Richard and Mary Strange	27 Dec. 1758	34
Richard Strange, of Wick and Abson	27 Sept. 1761	71
William Elmes	12 May, 1764	33
John Simmonds	23 May, 1766	37
Ann his Wife	7 Aug. 1776	57
Mary, second Wife of John Ragles	24 Aug. 1720	65
Mary, Wife of William Nicholls	15 Sept. 1742	71

6 H

O N

ON HEAD STONES.

	Died	Aged
James, Son of William and Elizabeth Nicholls	29 Jan. 1767	27
Elizabeth, Wife of James England	29 May, 1781	56
Thomas Gunning	14 Feb. 1780	62
Hannah, Wife of Thomas Gunning,	19 Jan. 1779	66
Thomas Pinker	2 Feb. 1784	60
Hannah, Wife of Thomas Pinker	19 Jan. 1767	38
George Davis	15 Dec. 1750	34
George, Son of Thomas and Elizabeth Gunning	21 Jan. 1764	38
William their Son	8 June, 1763	35
Mary, Wife of Peter Vines, of Dirham	18 May, 1775	48
Charles Thomas	10 Nov. 1770	38
John, Son of William and Elizabeth Nicholls	11 Mar. 1777	28
Doctor their Son	4 Feb. 1780	26
Edward Weſt	2 Oct. 1768	58
Ann his Wife	31 Dec. 1774	63
John Nicholls	13 Dec. 1766	68
Sarah Gunning	14 Oct. 1779	47
Elizabeth Stilman, Daughter of John and Mary Gunning	25 Aug. 1778	35
Mary, Wife of John Gunning	1 Oct. 1774	59
George, Ann, and Sarah, their Children, died young.		
Joſeph England	29 Aug. 1771	80
Sarah, Wife of Joſeph England	19 Dec. 1756	59
George England	23 Dec. 1776	51
Mary, Wife of Tobias Luton	in Dec. 1722	70
Mary Luton, Spinſter, Grand-daughter of the above	17 May, 1782	66
John Francombe, upwards of 40 Years Clerk of this Pariſh	9 Mar. 1764	76
Edward Fox	3 Jan. 1769	49
Jane his Wife	9 Dec. 1772	47
Edith their Daughter	2 Dec. 1768	22
Margaret, Wife of Joſeph England	26 Apr. 1722	25
Joſeph England, ſenior	31 Aug. 1733	79

XCIV.

L IES in the Hundred of *Kiftefgate*, three Miles diftant from *Winchcombe* on the North, eight Miles Weft from *Campden*, and more than eighteen North-eaft from the City of GLOUCESTER. Of the Soil, which is a light Clay, nearly equal Portions are Pafture and Tillage, within a Circuit of ten Miles interfected by the Rivulet *Ifbourn*, which joins the *Avon* near *Evefham*.

The Living, which is a Vicarage in the Deanery of *Campden*, became a Stipendiary of the Abbey of *Hayles* in 1270, with a Penfion of ten Marks a Year, which is now received from the Impropriation. It was at the Diffolution included in the Grant then made to Sir EDWARD SEYMOUR, and fince transferred to the noble Family of TRACEY. In 1738, this Vicarage, with the Rectory of *Pynock* and the Chapelry of *Hayles*, were confolidated into one Prefentation by Confent of Dr. MARTIN BENSON, the Diocefan, the Patron, and Incumbent.

The Church, dedicated to *St. George*, has a Nave only, with a light embattled Tower at the Weft End. It was built at the fole Expence of WILLIAM WHYTCHYRCHE, Abbot of *Hayles*, between the Years 1470 and 1479. After the fatal Battle of *Tewkefbury* in 1472, it is traditionally faid that fome of the *Lancaftrians*, who had fled to the Church of *Didbroke* for Sanctuary, were there bafely put to Death, and that after fuch Pollution, it was re-built by the Abbot. Several Portraits in painted Glafs were perfect in the beginning of this Century, which are now mutilated or removed by modern Reparations. In the great Eaft Window were the Figures of two female Saints, and that of the Founder, with thefe Arms and Infcription : " Argent, a Lion rampant Gules, within a Bordure bezantee." 2. " Or, a " Spread Eagle Sable ;" Abbey of *Hayles*. " 𝔒rate pro a'i'a 𝔚yll'i 𝔚ytchyrche, qui hoc templum fun= " dabit cum Cancello." And in the Window of the Belfry, the Effigies of the tutelar Saint GEORGE and Pope SILVESTER. The Sarcophagus, or raifed Tomb in which the Founder is buried, is compofed of blue Marble beneath a Niche on the North Side of the Nave. Upon the Lid was a Crofs florettè, on one Side a Chalice, on the other a Mafs Book, but fince defaced.

When the Abbey of *Hayles* was eftablifhed and endowed by RICHARD the titular King of the *Romans* in 1246, this Manor was included in their Rental. At the Suppreffion it was granted to the Progenitor of the prefent Proprietor, and has the principal Eftate annexed.

The Tything of *Cofcombe* contains the rifing Grounds on the North-eaft. The ancient Houfe, one of the Refidences of the Abbots of *Hayles*, was re-built by Judge TRACEY early in this Century. It has fince paffed with a competent Eftate to his Grandfon ROBERT TRACEY, Efq. from whom to ROBERT PRATT, Efq. whofe Relict has re-married with STEYNER HOLFORD, Efq. the prefent Poffeffor. The Chapel mentioned by ATKYNS is no longer applied to facred Ufes.

Wormington Grange, Parcel of the Abbey Eftates, was granted to ROBERT ACTON 1541. From the Family of JEFFERIES it is now held by —— GUEST, Efq. Other Lands have been long vefted in the Family of JAMES. The Intrenchments of fome early Period abound on the Hills.

No Benefactions to the Poor.

INCUMBENTS.	PATRONS.	INCUMBENTS.	PATRONS.
—— Meredith Evans,	——————.	1737 William Winde,	——————.
1586 William Crumpe,	Antony Hodgkyns.	1745 John Holbroke, M. A.	——————.
* * * * * *	* * * * * *	1765 John Tracey, D. D.	——————.
—— —— Winde,	Lord Tracey.	1769 John Tracey, D. D.	——————.

PRESENT LORD OF THE MANOR,

The Right Honourable CHARLES Lord Vifcount TRACEY, of *Rathcoole* in the Kingdom of *Ireland*.

The Perfons fummoned from this Parifh by the Heralds, in 1682 and 1683, were

Richard Fletcher, Gent. and Edward Workman, Gent.

At the Election in 1776 Two Freeholders polled from this Parifh.

The

The Date of the oldeſt Regiſter cannot be aſcertained.

ANNUAL ACCOUNT OF MARRIAGES, BIRTHS, AND BURIALS, IN THIS PARISH.

A.D.	Mar.	Bir.	Bur.	A.D.	Mar.	Bir.	Bur.	A.D.	Mar.	Bir.	Bur.	A.D.	Mar.	Bir.	Bur.
1781	3	7	6	1786	5	11	4	1791				1796			
1782	2	11	5	1787	4	9	9	1792				1797			
1783	4	6	4	1788	3	5	5	1793				1798			
1784	1	13	6	1789				1794				1799			
1785	1	7	4	1790				1795				1800			

This Regiſter includes the Inhabitants of *Hayles and Pynnock*.

INSCRIPTIONS IN THE CHURCH.

ON A NEAT MONUMENT OF WHITE AND VARIEGATED MARBLE IN THE CHANCEL :

Arms ; Or, between two Bendlets Gules, an Eſcallop in the dexter Chief Point Sable, for TRACEY ;—impaling, Or, a Feſs wavy between ſix Billets Sable, for DOWDESWELL.

Near this Place
lies interred the Body
of the Honourable ROBERT TRACY, Eſq.
Son of the Right Honourable ROBERT, late
Lord Viſcount TRACY, of Todington.
He was Judge twenty-ſix Years
in the Courts of Weſtminſter ;
but being ſtruck with the Palſy
in the Year 1726, reſigned a Commiſſion
which he had ſo long executed
with the greateſt Knowledge,

Moderation, and Integrity,
to the Honour of his Prince,
and univerſal Satisfaction
of his Fellow Subjects.
Obiit 11 Sept. Anno 1735,
ætat. 80.

Benefacere magis quam conſpici.

ON A FLAT STONE.

In Memory of MARGERY,
Wife of WILLIAM BAYLIS,
of this Town, who died
in September 1742, aged 40.

WILLIAM BAYLIS aforeſaid
died Aug. 23, 1757, aged 59.

IN THE CHURCH YARD, ON A TOMB.

JAMES HAYES
died the 23d Day of July, 1718, aged 71.

ON HEAD STONES.

	Died	Aged
Thomas Agg －	26 June, 1752	63
Ann his wife － －	13 Nov. 1776	77
Benjamin Clare － －	20 Jan. 1758	52
Julyana his Wife －	29 Jan. 1768	64
John their Son － －	1 Sept. 1786	49
Leigh James the elder －	6 Feb. 1744	80
Heſter his Wife －	10 July, 1764	80
Margery James － －	25 Sept. 1714	69
Ann, Wife of Thomas James	2 July, 1744	69
Thomas James －	24 Oct. 1751	76
Richard Greening, ſenior －	12 June, 1682	—
Anne. Wife of Richard Greening	12 Mar. 1738	90
John Gibbons － －	8 Oct. 1746	74
Anthony Baylis －	20 Sept. 1728	55

	Died	Aged
John Reeve, ſenior －	25 Mar. 17.6	79
Ann, Wife of John Reeve －	21 May, 1747	72
Richard Baker －	26 Feb. 1787	80
Elizabeth, Wife of James Agg	27 Nov. 1723	71
Ann, Wife of John Buts －	11 Nov. 1788	58
Ann, Wife of Thomas Tiff, ſenior	21 Aug. 1735	54
Thomas Tiff, ſenior －	7 Nov. 1750	78
Anna, Wife of Thomas Tiff, of Southam － －	12 Feb. 1759	59
Thomas Tiff, of Southam in the Pariſh of Biſhop's Cleeve －	12 Dec. 1784	74
Anna, Daughter of Thomas and Ann Tiff － －	10 Nov. 1775	33

XCV. DIDMARTON

I S fituate in the Hundred of *Grumbald's Afh*, upon the Extremity of the lower *Cotefwold*, bounded by the County of *Wilts*. It is fix Miles diftant from *Tetbury* on the South-weft, eight South from *Wootton Under Edge*, and nearly twenty-two in the fame Direction from GLOUCESTER. The Circumference of the Parifh is from feven to eight Miles, including a light Soil, tilled, with very fmall Exception. The Village lies on the great Road from *Oxford* to *Bath* and BRISTOL.

The Living is a Rectory in the Deanery of *Hawkefbury*, endowed with 52 Acres of Glebe. In 1735 it was united in the fame Prefentation with *Oldbury on the Hill*. The Church, dedicated to *St. Law-rence*, is inconfiderable ; it has an Aifle projecting from the End of the Nave. Sir R. ATKYNS affigns the fame Reafon for this Form that induced PHILIP of *Spain* to build the *Efcurial*, with a Reference to the Initial of the Tutelary Saint.

In the oldeft Records we find the manerial Territory extending over the whole Parifh, and fuccefively enjoyed by the Families of DE SYWARD, WROSTON, and WROUGHTON. In 1571, 13 ELIZ. SIMON CO-DRINGTON, of *Codrington*, married GRISEL, the Co-heir of RICHARD SECOLE, Efq. and received this Eftate in Dower. Of the lineal Defcendants of this Marriage it was purchafed in 17 .. by CHARLES NOEL, fourth Duke of BEAUFORT. The Manor-houfe was built by the CODRINGTONS foon after their Succeffion.

Tumuli, or Barrows, the fuppofed Repofitories of Military Antiquities, are fhewn within the Limits of this Parifh.

B E N E F A C T I O N S.

NICHOLAS IDDOLS devifed by Will, 1687, Lands, the annual Produce of which is 1*l.* 10s. for the Relief and Maintenance of the Poor.

INCUMBENTS.	PATRONS.	INCUMBENTS.	PATRONS.
—— George Longford,	——————.	1735 Thomas Heather, M.A.	——————.
1607 Marmaduke Chapman,	Simon Codrington.	1753 William Cooke, M. A.	Charles Noel Duke of Beaufort.
1673 Thomas Byrton,	Robert Codrington.		
1680 —— Blifs,	——————.	1780 Edward Eftcourt, LL..D.	Henry Duke of Beaufort.
1724 William Skinner, M. A.	———————		

PRESENT LORD OF THE MANOR,

His Grace HENRY Duke of BEAUFORT.

The Perfons fummoned from this Parifh by the Heralds in 1682 and 1683, were

Robert Codrington, Efq. and —— Blifs, Clerk.

It does not appear that any Freeholder polled from this Parifh at the Election in 1776.

The Regifter commences in 1675, and is very imperfect.

ANNUAL ACCOUNT OF MARRIAGES, BIRTHS, AND BURIALS, IN THIS PARISH.

A.D.	Mar.	Bir.	Bur.	A.D.	Mar.	Bir.	Bur.	A.D.	Mar.	Bir.	Bur.	A.D.	Mar.	Bir.	Bur.
1781	—	4	—	1786	—	4	—	1791				1796			
1782	—	2	—	1787	1	2	—	1792				1797			
1783	—	3	—	1788	1	3	2	1793				1798			
1784	—	1	1	1789	2	4	1	1794				1799			
1785	1	3	3	1790				1795				1800			

INSCRIPTIONS

INSCRIPTIONS IN THE CHURCH.

IN THE CHANCEL.

ON MONUMENTS.

Arms; Argent, a Fefs embattled Sable, between three Lions paffant Gules, for CODRINGTON;——impaling, Lozengy Gules and vairè.

Under this Marble lyeth the Bodies of two Sonnes and three Daughters of JOHN and FRANCIS CODRINGTON, that were ftill born.

Here lieth the Bodies of FRANCES the eldeft Daughter, and CHRISTOPHER the fourth Son, of ROBERT CODRINGTON, Efq. and AGNES his Wife, who died in the Year of our Lord 1686.

ON A NEAT MONUMENT OF VARIEGATED MARBLE:

Arms, on three Efcutcheons; 1. Quarterly, 1ft and 4th, Argent, three Bugle Horns Sable, for FORRESTER; 2d and 3d, Azure, nine Mulletts Or, for . 2. Argent, two Chevronels Azure within a Bordure engrailed Gules, for TYRRELL;—impaling, Argent, a Fefs embattled Sable, between three Lions paffant Gules, for CODRINGTON. 3. FORRESTER;—impaling, TYRRELL, as before.

In Memory of ELIZABETH TYRRELL, Widow of CHAS. TYRRELL, Efq. fecond Son of Sir THOMAS TYRRELL, of Thornton in the County of Bucks, Bart. and one of the Daughters of ROBERT CODRINGTON, Efq. and AGNES his Wife, who died the 30th of July, 1745, aged 76 Years.

Alfo of WILLIAM Lord FORRESTER, of Coftorphin in Mid Lothian, who died Oct. 16, 1763.

Alfo of ELIZABETH FORRESTER, the Widow of JOHN FORRESTER, Efq. Captain in his Majefty's Navy, and Daughter of the faid CHARLES and ELIZABETH TYRRELL, who died Oct. 24, 1776.

Erected by Order of the faid ELIZABETH FORRESTER, to the Memory of her Mother and Son abovenamed.

ON FLAT STONES.

Here lieth the Body of AGNES CODRINGTON, the Wife of SIMON CODRINGTON, who deceafed the 12th of January, Anno Dom. 1618.

Here alfo lieth the Body of ROBERT CODRINGTON, Efq. who departed this Life the 11th Day of June, Anno Dom. 1717, ætatis fuæ 68.

F. C.

Here lieth the Body of AGNES CODRINGTON, late Wife of ROBERT CODRINGTON, Efq. who departed this Life the 25th Day of October, Anno Domini 1717, ætatis fuæ 63.

RICHARD CODRINGTON, Son of ROBERT CODRINGTON, Efq. and AGNES his Wife, was interred September 23, A. D. 1691.

R. C.

Here lieth the Body of RACHEL, the fifth Daughter of ROBERT CODRINGTON, Efq. and AGNES his Wife, who departed this Life September the 7th, in the 16th Year of her Age, A. D. 1699.

F. C.

Here alfo lieth the Body of FRANCES, the eighth Daughter of ROBERT CODRINGTON, Efq. and AGNES his Wife. Ob. Mar. 8, A. D. 1721.

ON A NEAT MARBLE MONUMENT IN THE NAVE:

In Memory of CORNELIUS ROBBINS, of this Parifh, Gent. who died Feb. 1, 1775, aged 44.

And of MARY his Wife, who died Sept. 24, 1762, aged 32.

Alfo MARY their Daughter, Wife of JOSEPH PITT, of Cirencefter, Gent. She died April 2, 1788, aged 27.

ON A SQUARE MARBLE TABLET:

Near this Place lieth interred the Body of ROBERT CROUCHER, Gent. of this Parifh, who departed this Life Dec. 19, 1785, in the 82d Year of his Age. He was Servant 55 Years to HENRY 3d Duke of BEAUFORT, to CHARLES NOEL 4th Duke of BEAUFORT, and to HENRY 5th Duke of BEAUFORT; 45 Years of which Time he ferved the Office of Steward, on their feveral Eftates in the Counties of Gloucefter and Wilts. HENRY 5th Duke of BEAUFORT has caufed this Stone to be erected to his Memory, in Teftimony of his Fidelity, Honefty, and Integrity.

ON FLAT STONES IN THE NORTH AISLE.

Here lyeth the Body of HANNAH DEVERELL, Daughter of DANIEL DEVERELL, of Wapley, and late fervant to ROBERT CODRINGTON, Efq. who departed this Life the 3d Day of October, 1682, æt. 27.

Here lyeth the Body of THOMAS OLDHAM, Gent. who departed this Life the 1ft Day of June, 1694, ætatis fuæ 70.

IN THE CHURCH YARD, ON TOMBS.

THOMAS HOLBOROW, of this Parifh, Yeoman, was buried June 14, 1681.

ELIZABETH his Wife was buried May 4, 1676.

And JOAN their Daughter was buried in 1682.

WILLIAM HOLBOROW, 1701.

SAMUEL HOLBOROW, Yeoman, departed this Life Oct. 6, 1732.

WILLIAM HAYARD died Sept. 26, 1779, aged 48.

SARAH, Wife of JOHN PAYNE, of Selwood, and Daughter of JOHN AYLET and PHILOPONE his Wife, of the Parifh of Uley, was buried Nov. 14, 1672, aged 34.

MARY EYILS, of Atford in the Parifh of Bradford, died Oct. 2, 1768, aged 68.

WILLIAM ROBBINS, of this Parifh, died Feb. 25, 1763, aged 74.

MARY his fecond Wife died March 25, 1738, in the 38th Year of her Age.

ANNE his third Wife died May 15, 1740, aged 60.

Hannah, Wife of GABRIEL ROBBINS, late of Woodfha, died May 27, 1738, aged 71.

GABRIEL ROBBINS died Feb. 1, 1775, aged 45.

GEORGE WATTS died Dec. 30, 1783, aged 86.

ON FLAT AND HEAD STONES.

	Died	Aged
Mary, Daughter of Robert and Mary Croucher - -	19 Feb. 1742	6 m
Mrs. Mary Hatcham -	12 Feb. 1755	84
Robert Croucher, Son of Richard-David and Jane Croucher, died Feb. 19, 1780, aged 1 Year, 8 Months, and 25 Days.		
William Melhuifh, Son of John and Hannah Melhuifh -	20 Nov. 1751	15
Hannah Melhuifh -	12 July, 1785	79
Sarah Denning - -	22 June, 1752	80
Mary her Daughter, Wife of Jofeph Chappel - -	26 Apr. 1760	60
Thomas Minty, fenior -	28 Nov. 1759	64
Margery, Wife of Thomas Minty	24 Nov. 1759	75
Nathaniel Watts -	3 Feb. 1732	63
Edith, Wife of Nathaniel Watts	—— 1758	89
Maurice, Son of Nathaniel Watts	5 July, 1753	54
Ann, Wife of George Watts	2 July, 1741	44

XCVI.

XCVI. DODINGTON

IS a Parifh in the lower Divifion of the Hundred of *Grumbald's Afh*, diftant from *Sodbury* three Miles on the South eaft, five from *Marfhfield* on the North, and twenty-eight from the City of Gloucester in a foutherly Direction.

The Boundary is of an oval Form, two Miles in the wideft Part, and three in length, of a Soil deep in the Vale, but becoming gradually lighter on the Bafes of the Hills which furround it on the Eaft and North Sides. Sixty Acres only are tilled in the whole Parifh.

The Benefice is rectorial, in the Deanery of *Hawkefbury*. It appears that certain Tythes were claimed by the Prior of *Stanley St. Leonard* in 1277, 4 Edw. I. and that the Abbey of *Keynfham*, co. *Somerfet*, held what was then ftyled the Rectory

No Marks of Antiquity remain in the Church, which is dedicated to the *Holy Virgin* ; it is of fmall Dimenfions with a low Tower at the Weft End.

William the Conqueror gave the Manor to the Bifhop of *Conftance*, and it was held under him for many Centuries by the Defcendants of Roger de Berkeley, of *Durfley*, as Parcel of the Eftate of that Family *. The Heir in 1403 carried it into the Name of De Cantilupe by Marriage, and in 1473 it paffed by the fame Circumftance to Thomas Wekys. In the Reign of Queen Elizabeth it was purchafed by Giles Codrington, whofe lineal Defcendant Samuel Codrington †, re-fold it to the celebrated Christopher Codrington ‡, Governor of the *Leeward Iflands*, who returned it by his Will, dated 1702, to his relative William Codrington, created a Baronet April 21, 1721, the Father of the prefent Poffeffor.

The Demefnes extend over the greater Part of the Parifh, excepting the Eftate of Walter Long, Efq.

The ancient Manor-houfe owes its Erection to Robert Wekys in 1557. The Front is a fubfequent Addition in the beft Style of James the Firft's Reign, and is very fpacious, fituate on an eafy Elevation of delightful Lawn; above the Houfe are two very beautiful Sheets of Water formed from the Source of the River *Froom*, and one below it. Much picturefque Scenery is found in the Park, the Ground being broken into many Knowls and Ridges extremely fteep, which are relieved by Trees of great Age and Beauty, and Clumps very judicioufly planted. The Refult of the whole is fuch as characterizes the moft admired ancient Refidences of the *Englifh* Gentry. It is very advantageoufly feen through an Avenue near the great Road leading to *Bath*.

Upon the Summits of the furrounding Hills are the Veftiges of a Chain of " *Caftra exploratorum*," and more advanced on the Plain indubitable Traces of a larger Camp.

Leland relates, that " a Glaffe with Bones yn a Sepulchre found by *Dodington* Chirche yn the high " Way. Pottes exceding finely nelyd and florifhed in the *Roman's* Tymes, diggid out of the Groundes " in the Feldes at *Dodington* §." Thefe Vallations were afterwards occupied by the *Saxons*, when they repelled the *Danes*' landing at Bristol.

Holinshed fays that King Edward the Fourth refted his Army here fome Days, when on his March toward *Tewkefbury*, where he totally deftroyed the remaining Forces of the *Lancaftrian* Party.

---

* " *Dodington* longed to the Barkeleys. Mr. Wekys, of *Dodington*, contendith by fum Reafons that the Berkeleys, of " *Durflege*, wher of as olde an Houfe, or older than the Berkeleys, of *Berkeley*. But the Name of Berkeley Towne and " Lordfhip, of whom the Berkeleys wher caullid, foundeth to the contrarie." Leland's Itin. vol. VI. p. 74.

† Robert Codrington is noticed in Wood's Athenæ, vol. II. p. 243, as being of this Family, and a Native of this County. He was a Demy of *Magdalen College, Oxford*; and wrote, befide many Tranflations, the Life of Robert Earl of Essex, 1646, 4to. He died of the Plague, in *London*, in 1665.

‡ Christopher Codrington was born in the Ifland of *Barbadoes* in 1668; admitted Fellow of *All Souls College*, 1689. Quitting the Univerfity, but retaining his Fellowfhip, he entered into the Army, and foon obtained Promotion from King William. On the Conclufion of the Peace at *Rhyfwick* he was appointed Captain General and Governor in Chief of the *Leeward Caribee* Iflands. In 1701 Articles of Impeachment were brought againft him before the Commons of *England*, by whom he was honourably acquitted. Some Time previous to his Death he refigned his Government, and retired to the Enjoyment of a ftudious Life. He died in *Barbadoes* in 1710. He bequeathed 10,000*l.* to *All Souls College*, to found and furnifh a magnificent Library, in which is a Statue of him, in a *Roman* Garb, by Sir H. Cheere, and a Buft by Rysbrack. His other Bequefts were equally judicious and munificent. See Biog. Brit. vol. III. p. 674. edit. Kippis.

§ Itin. vol. VI. p. 72.

I

No

No Benefactions to the Poor.

Incumbents.	Patrons.	Incumbents.	Patrons.
1500 ——————,	Abbot of Gloucester.	1675 Samuel Hieron,	Samuel Codrington, Efq.
1559 Henry Townfhend,	——————.	1693 Richard Codrington,	The fame.
1578 Thomas Wilfie,	——————.	1732 Lingen Unett, Clerk,	——————.
1593 John Coyde,	Sir John Poyntz.	1738 Thomas Bennet, D. D.	——————.
1597 Hugh Clunn,	William Herbert, Efq.	1750 William Hughes, LL.B.	Sir W. Codrington.
1622 Robert Greenhill, or Greenald.	——————.	1769 Philip Blifs, M. A.	Sir W. Codrington.
1661 Thomas Codrington,	——————.	1775 Philip Blifs, M. A.	The fame.

Present Lord of the Manor,

Sir William Codrington, Bart.

The only Perfon fummoned from this Place by the Heralds in 1682 and 1683, was
Samuel Codrington, Efq.

It does not appear that any Perfon polled from this Parifh at the Election in 1776.

The earlieft Date in the Regifter occurs in 1575.

Annual Account of Marriages, Births, and Burials, in this Parish.

A.D.	Mar.	Bir.	Bur.	A.D.	Mar.	Bir.	Bur.	A.D.	Mar.	Bir.	Bur.	A.D.	Mar.	Bir	Bur.
1781	—	5	1	1786	—	2	—	1791				1796			
1782	—	4	1	1787	1	5	—	1792				1797			
1783	1	4	—	1788	—	1	2	1793				1798			
1784	—	—	3	1789	1	3	—	1794				1799			
1785	1	6	6	1790				1795				1800			

INSCRIPTIONS IN THE CHURCH.

On a Monument against the South Wall in
the Chancel :

P. M.
Roberti Greenaldi, hujus Ecclefiæ
Paftoris An. 38, qui obiit 8°
die Jan. 1660,
æt. 83.

On a Monument on the North Side :

Arms; Per Fefs three Squirrels counterchanged,
for Horler ;—impaling, Argent, a Fefs embattled
Sable, between three Lions paffant Gules, for Codrington.

P. M.
Quod reliquum eft
Joannæ filiæ Ricardi Codrington,
Gen. Uxoris Chariffimæ Jeremiæ
Horler, Rectoris de Sodbury
Parva, quæ obiit tertio die Martii,
Anno Dom. 1721.

Depofitum etiam Jeremiæ
Horler prædict. qui obiit
primo die Martii, 1723-4.

Ricardi Codrington, A. M.
Hujus Ecclefiæ Rectoris.
Obiit 1 Feb. 1732.

On a flat Stone in the Chancel :

Within this Vault, under this Stone,
lieth Mr. Thomas Codrington,
Lord and Rector of this Place,
who died in the Year of our Lord 1675,
September 13, æt. fuæ 44.

On a flat Stone in the Nave :

Arms ; Quarterly, 1ft and 4th, Codrington, as
before ; 2d and 3d, on a Bend three Rofes ;—impaling, on a Chevron between three Boars Heads
couped, an Eftoile, for Chapman.

Here lieth the Body of
Mrs. Dorothy Chapman,
Sifter to the Honourable
William Codringion, Efq.
who departed this Life June 25,
Anno Dom. 1712.

Alfo the Body of William, the Son of
the faid William Codrington
and Elizabeth his Wife,
who departed this Life November the 26th,
Anno Dom. 1718, aged 12 Days.

I N

IN THE CHURCH YARD, ON TOMBS.

ELIZABETH CODRINGTON, the Wife of
SAMUEL CODRINGTON, Efq.
changed Mortality to Immortality,
the 22d Day of February, 1687, aged 82.

This Monument was repaired and beautified
by the Executor of SAMUEL CODRINGTON, Efq.
Anno Domini 1717, to preferve the Memory of
the Piety, Charity, and other great Virtues
of the faid Mrs. CODRINGTON.

ARTHUR PARKER
died Dec. 16, 1769, aged 66.

REBECCA his Wife
died May 31, 1784, aged 78.

MARY, Wife of RICHARD EXEL,
and Daughter of
ARTHUR and REBECCA PARKER,
died Feb. 2, 1769, aged 30.

JOHN, Son of
ARTHUR and REBECCA PARKER,
died Eeb. 20, 1784, aged 32.

JANE, Wife of
JOHN SARGEAUNT, Daughter of
ARTHUR and REBECCA PARKER,
died Feb. 20, 1784, aged 44.

ON A FLAT STONE:

JOHANNES BATTIN ob. 1682.

MARIÆ, uxoris JOHANNIS BATTIN,
quinque liberorum matris, quæ
75 annos nata . . . . . . nuper denata
fuit, anno Domini 1685.

JOHANNES BATTIN.
Obiit die . . . anno Dom. 168 . .
ætatis fuæ 86.

ON HEAD STONES.

	Died		Aged
John Naifh	15 Sept.	1773	52
William Young	30 Nov.	1785	77
Elizabeth, Wife of William Ship	20 Apr.	1785	35
John, Son of William and Elizabeth Glafkodine	15 Oct.	1773	25
Francis Clark	19 July,	1774	81
Sarah his Wife	17 Dec.	1755	80
Samuel Greenald	12 Aug.	1715	22
Elizabeth, Daughter of Robert and Elizabeth Holway	19 Jan.	1718	12
Robert Holway	10 Nov.	1735	73
Elizabeth his Wife	6 Oct.	1743	67

6 K   XCVII. DORSINGTON.

IN the Courfe of Topographic Refearches, many Places neceffarily occur, which afford no Materials of curious Inveftigation. Of this Defcription particularly is *Dorfington*, a very fmall Parifh of the Hundred of *Kiftefgate*, fix Miles North from *Campden*, feven South-weft from *Stratford upon Avon*, and thirty-three computed Miles from GLOUCESTER on the North-eaft. The Terrier of the whole Parifh does not exceed 1000 Acres, tilled and Pafture in nearly equal Portions, of a very heavy and fertile Soil.

The Rectory is endowed with a confiderable Glebe, and is in the Deanery of *Campden*.

The Church is defcribed by Sir R. ATKINS to have been a very inconfiderable Structure, previous to the Conflagration 1754, by which, with a great Part of the Village, it was deftroyed. It was re-built with Brick on a fmall modern Plan, and confifts of a Nave only.

Of the Manor the fole Poffeffors were the DE NEWBURGHS and BEAUCHAMPS, Earls of WARWICK, for feveral Centuries after the Conqueft. Afterward the Family of DE DRAYTON, from whom, with intermediate Purchafers of fhort Continuance, it paffed to THOMAS RAWLINS, Serjeant at Law, in the Reign of JAMES the Firft, and with it the Property of the whole Parifh, which has been tranfmitted to the prefent Poffeffor.

No Benefactions to the Poor.

INCUMBENTS.	PATRONS.	INCUMBENTS.	PATRONS.
—— Richard Phelps,	——————.	1681 Thomas Yeate, M. A.	The fame.
1571 Thomas Phelps,	——————.	1713 William Yeate, M. A.	——————.
—— Thomas Turner, D.D.	——————.	1735 William Bell, M. A.	——————.
1593 John Rutter,	Chriftopher Turner.	1739 Wm. Gelfthorpe, B.A.	——————.
1633 Ferryman Rutter,	——————.	1777 Edmund Rawlins, M.A.	Wm. Rawlins, Efq.
1668 John Ward, D. D.	Thomas Rawlins, Efq.		

PRESENT LORD OF THE MANOR,

WILLIAM RAWLINS, Efq.

No Perfon appears to have been fummoned by the Heralds, in 1682 and 1683.

At the Election in 1776 Three Freeholders polled from this Parifh.

The oldeft Regifter bears Date in 1591.

ANNUAL ACCOUNT OF MARRIAGES, BIRTHS, AND BURIALS, IN THIS PARISH.

A.D.	Mar.	Bir.	Bur.	A.D.	Mar.	Bir.	Bur.	A.D.	Mar.	Bir.	Bur.	A.D.	Mar.	Bir.	Bur.
1781	1	3	4	1786	2	3	2	1791				1796			
1782	—	4	2	1787	1	2	3	1792				1797			
1783	2	2	3	1788	—	3	1	1793				1798			
1784	1	5	5	1789	1	2	4	1794				1799			
1785	—	3	2	1790				1795				1800			

INSCRIPTIONS

INSCRIPTIONS IN THE CHURCH.

ON FLAT STONES.

M. S.
THOMÆ YEATE, M. A.
hujus Ecclefiæ per xxxii annos Rectoris,
Qui obiit 9 die Novembris,
Anno { Salutis 1713.
{ Ætatis 55.

Depofitum
A. YEATE THOMÆ Conjugis,
Quæ obiit Jan. 30,
Anno Dom. 1742,
ætatis 81.

Hic jacet
GULIELMUS YEATE, A. M.
Vir Literarum amore morum probitate,
Animo hofpitali,
Perquam infignis;
In Deum, in patriam, in propinquos pietatis,
In amicos fidei,
Religiofus cultor;
Cunctis ergo bonis flebilis occidit,
utpote cui una cura & ftudium fuit
Comitate & beneficiis
De cunctis bene mereri.
Obiit 4° die Martii, Anno Dom. 1734,
ætatis fuæ 48.

BARBARA, Wife of THOMAS YEATE, Gent.
died June 25, 1765, aged 45.
She was the eldeft Daughter of the
Rev. THOMAS WARD,
Rector of Bliffworth in the County of
Northampton, and of Bygrave in the
County of Hertford.

Depofitum
JOHANNES GELSTHROPE,
Qui obiit decimo die Julii,
Anno { Ætatis 43.
{ Salutis 1718.

M. S.
Fœminæ intergerrimæ femper
Colendæ ALICIÆ RAWLINS,
Quæ hac in parœcia nata 1684.

Patre THOMÂ YEATE, Rectore,
Hic etiam viri fui inter prioris cineres
Exuvias mortales fuas pro amore
Deponi voluit.
Obiit 25 die Aprilis, anno Dom. 1770,
ætatis 86.

Here lyeth the Body of
THOMAS GELSTHROPE, Gent.
who departed this Life
Auguft 31, Anno Dom. 1735,
aged 22.

In hopes of joyful Refurrection,
here lieth the Body of
WILLIAM GELSTHROPE, A. B.
38 Years Rector of this Parifh.
He died Auguft 19, 1777,
in the 63d Year of his Age;
of whom it may truly be faid,
that he lived in an uniform and
conftant Obedience to thofe
two great Commandments on which
hang all the Law and the Prophets.

IN THE CHURCH YARD.

ON HEAD STONES.

	Died	Aged
Richard Dennis	12 Mar. 1727	73
Mary, Wife of John Holtham	5 Sept. 1776	57
Thomas Ofborne	2 Mar. 1764	50
Martha, Wife of John Heming	20 May, 1757	40
Anne, Daughter of William Durham and Elizabeth his Wife	1 May, 1743	20
William Holtham	6 Nov. 1779	70
Mary his Wife	26 Oct. 1780	80
Richard Marriott	2 Jan. 1779	43
Mary Marriott	28 Feb. 1780	70

XCVII. DOWDESWELL,

XCVIII. D O W D E S W E L L,
O R
D O L S W E L L E,

I S one of the Parishes of which the Hundred of *Bradley* is composed, four Miles distant from *Cheltenham* on the East, seven South from *Winchcombe*, and twelve North-east from GLOUCESTER.

The Boundaries inclose a Tract of a long Form, two Miles in the widest Part, three in Length, and very narrow toward the Extremity. Of the Soil the nature varies from deep Clay to Gravel; the greater Portion is applied to Pasture; besides which there are 200 Acres of Woodland.

The Living is a Rectory in the Deanery of *Winchcombe*; the Patronage of which has been vested, with temporary Alienations only, in the Family of ROGERS since the Reign of Queen ELIZABETH. That the ancient Church has been re-built is sufficiently evident from the Style of the present, which consists of a Transept of equal Height and Dimensions. The low and massy Spire in the Centre is said to have been completed at the joint Expence of RICHARD HABINGTON and RICHARD ROGERS, as late as 1577. In the Chancel remains, without Arms or Inscription, the brass Effigy of a Man, in a Robe diapered, with Roses and Fleurs de Lis inserted in the Interstices, but no Mullets, as it has been said. The Head is tonsured; and the ingenious Mr. GOUGH * asserts it to be the exact Counterpart of that of RO-BERT EGLESFIELD, Founder of *Queen's College, Oxford*, only smaller, who died in 1349.

Bishop TANNER, in his Catalogue of the Abbots of *Hayles*, mentions that ROBERT, an Abbot, elected in 1380, retired in 1402, and died in 1420. Tradition affirms this to have been a Memorial for one of the Abbots; and the Time, and comparative Circumstances, determine it in some Measure to be the Person abovementioned.

In the Church Yard is a Yew Tree of primæval Date, and in a State of very flourishing Vegetation †.

The Rectory-house has great Advantages of Situation, commanding a very beautiful Point of View. On either Side a Ridge of Hills, one covered with low Wood, the other breaking into a bare Rock, forming a bold Vista, which is terminated by the grotesque Hill of *Churchdown* in the Centre, and the Landscape closed by the Mountains of *Hatterel*, which beautifully blend with the Horizon. Of modern Improvements those most eligible have been adopted by the present Incumbent, and with no sparing Hand.

The Church of *Worcester*, according to the first Records, possessed the chief Manor, held as of *Whithington*. King HENRY the Third, by Detachment, gave it to the Knights Templars, at whose Suppression it passed to the College of *Westbury upon Trim*. Sir RALPH SADLER afterward obtained it, from whom it was transferred by Purchase to the Ancestor of the present Possessor. It then owed Service to the Manor of *Guiting*. *Upper Dowdeswell* belonged in the Reign of HENRY VII. to Sir EDMOND TAME, whose Son sold it to NICHOLAS HABINGTON, of a very ancient Family seated in *Worcestershire*. They retained it for several Generations. ANTONY HABINGTON, or ABYNGTON, was of the Court of Prince HENRY, Son of JAMES I. and JOHN his Descendant, was fain to compound with the Commissioners of Parliament for this Estate, for 364*l.* Sir EDWARD RICH succeeded by Purchase, of whose Heir-general it was bought by CHARLES VAN NOTTEN, Esq. who has since assumed the Surname of POLE.

Sandiwell originally was in the great Lordship of GLOUCESTER; but in the Beginning of the last Century was purchased by WILLIAM ROGERS, who bequeathed it to JOHN ROGERS, his youngest Son. Of his Descendant it was bought by HENRY BRETT, Esq. in 1680, who began the present Mansion House, which was sold by his Son to HENRY Lord CONWAY of the Kingdom of *Ireland*. His Successor the Earl of HERTFORD re-sold it to the late THOMAS TRACEY, Esq. Knight of the Shire for this

---

* Sepulchral Monuments, p. 157.

† Antiquaries seem much at a Loss how to determine about what Period Yew Trees first obtained a Place in Church Yards. A Statute passed in 35 EDW. I. the Title of which is " Ne Rector Arbores prosternat in Cœmiterio." As we seldom see other Trees planted in Church Yards, this Statute must have most probably related to Yew Trees, and consequently their being planted there is of much more ancient Date than 1307. WHITE's History of *Selbourne*.

County,

County, and it is the prefent Refidence of his Relict, Daughter and fole Heir of Sir WILLIAM DODWELL, Bart. of *Sevenhampton* in this County. The Houfe is a handfome modern Edifice, inclofed in a Park of lefs than a Hundred Acres in Extent. When the Foundations were making, Coffins of Lead were difcovered near the Surface, fuppofed to be of the *Romans*, after the Introduction of Chriftianity.

Pegglefworth lies on one of the higheft Summits of *Cotefwold*; the principal Share of it is vefted in JOHN WADE, Efq. of *Woodchefter*, and confifts almoft entirely of arable Inclofures.

The great Road from GLOUCESTER to *London* has been lately formed, and brought in a new Direction from *Cheltenham*, through this Parifh to *Frogmill*, whereby the Afcent is rendered much more eafy than by the former Courfe up *Crickley Hill*.

Near to *Andover's Ford* a very fharp Encounter happened between the Parties during the Civil War[*].

No Benefactions to the Poor.

INCUMBENTS.	PATRONS.	INCUMBENTS.	PATRONS.
—— Roger Green,	——————.	1670 Jofeph Sterne,	——————.
1575 Thomas Childes,	William Rogers, Efq.	1701 Charles Neville, Efq.	W. Rogers, Efq.
1597 Robert Temple,	Queen Elizabeth.	1717 John Rogers,	The fame.
1612 John Crowther,	——————.	1768 John Arnold, LL. B.	——————.
1623 William Driver,	——————.	1778 William Baker, LL. B.	John Read, Efq.
—— ——————,	W. Rogers, Efq.		

PRESENT PROPRIETORS OF THE MANORS,

Of *Lower Dowdefwell* and *Rofley*.   Of *Upper Dowdefwell*.
EDWARD ROGERS, ESQ.   CHARLES POLE, ESQ.

Of *Pegglefworth*.
JOHN WADE, ESQ.

The Perfons fummoned from this Place by the Heralds in 1682 and 1683, were

The Heirs of Sir Edward Rich,   Sir Thomas Earle, Knight,
William Rogers, Efq.   Paul Dodwell, Gent.

At the Election in 1776 Three Freeholders polled from this Parifh.

ANNUAL ACCOUNT OF MARRIAGES, BIRTHS, AND BURIALS, IN THIS PARISH.

A.D.	Mar.	Bir.	Bur.	A.D.	Mar.	Bir.	Bur.	A.D.	Mar.	Bir.	Bur.	A.D.	Mar.	Bir.	Bur.
1781	1	11	2	1786	1	5	3	1791				1796			
1782	2	3	2	1787	3	3	2	1792				1797			
1783	1	5	3	1788	3	9	2	1793				1798			
1784	—	6	5	1789				1794				1799			
1785	3	3	4	1790				1795				1800			

INSCRIPTIONS IN THE CHURCH.

ON A TABLET ON THE SOUTH SIDE OF THE CHANCEL :

Arms ; Argent, a Mullet Sable, and on a Chief Gules, a Fleur de lis Or, for ROGERS.

Parcite cœlicolæ lachrymis, hi morte quiefcunt
Funebris hæc requies funera mortis erit.
Vincula diffolvit CHRISTUS, Domino remeantur,
Confortes thalamis fic rediere fuis.

Upon the Death of WILLIAM ROGERS, Gent.
buried June 2, 1549.

And of HELLEN his Wife
interred February the firft, 1648.

ON A MONUMENT AGAINST THE SAME WALL :

Arms ; ROGERS as before ;—impaling, Argent, a Crofs raguly Gules, for LAWRENCE.

To the Memory of WILLIAM ROGERS,
of Sandiwell in this Parifh of Dowdfwell, Gent.
who departed this Life the 11th Day of January,
1663, in the 67th Year of his Age.

To the Memory of
ELIZABETH ROGERS, Widow,
late Wife of WILLIAM ROGERS,
of Sandiwell, Gent.
deceafed the 22d of July, 1670.

[*] CORBET's Military Government of GLOUCESTER, p. 37.

On a handsome Monument supported by
Columns of variegated Marble, with the
Bust of William Rogers, Esq.

Arms ; Rogers as before.

Hic prope jacet
Gulielmus Rogers, Armiger,
Magistrorum Curiæ Cancellariæ nuper primus.
Obiit nono die Aprilis, Anno Domini 1734,
ætatis suæ 76.
Christianæ Religionis veritatem firmiter credens,
Omnem superstitionem vehementer abhorrens,
Dei unitatem religiose colens,
Christi Redemptionem strenue expectans,
Justum & honestum utili anteferens.

On a brass Plate :

Here lyeth the Body of
John Crowther, Master of Arts,
and some time Parson of this Parish,
who departed this Life the 14th day of Sept.
in the Yeare of our Lord 1623.

Ætas an virtus (licet ambas sat scio magnas)
Qui novit, dicat quæ tibi major erat ;
Anni comperti quatuor bis bisque triginta ;
At quis virtutes enumerare potest ?
Tum bene, tumque diu vita tum morte beatus,
Vixit sic vivam, sic moriarque precor.

O N   F L A T   S T O N E S
I N   T H E   C H A N C E L.

Jane, the Daughter of William Driver,
was buried Feb. 25, 1650.

Under this Stone lies the Body of
John Rogers, Esq.
who died Dec. 2, 1760,
aged 26 Years.

The Rev. John Arnold, B. L.
Rector of this Parish and Cobberley,
who died July 17, 1778, aged 46 Years.

Underneath lie the Remains of
the late Rev. Richard Rogers, LL. B.
of Charlton Kings.
He died March 10, 1780, aged 46 Years.

In Memory of John Applegarth, Gent.
who died Nov. 6, 1753, aged 78.

O N   F L A T   S T O N E S
I N   T H E   N O R T H   A I S L E.

In Memoriam Gulielmi Rogers, Arm.
Obiit Aug. 31, 1678, ætatis suæ 51.

In Memory of Anne Rogers,
Wife of William Rogers, Esq.
who died March 15, 1776, aged 35.

Anne, Daughter of
William and Anne Rogers,
died February 6, 1773,
aged 10 Months and 14 Days.

IN THE SOUTH AISLE.

On a neat Monument :

Arms ; Per Pale Sable and Gules, a Cross bot-
tonè fitchée between four Fleurs de lis Or, for Rich ;
—impaling, Azure, on a Chevron Argent, three
Roses Gules, for Gilbert.

In Memory of
Baily Rich, eldest Son of
Lionel Rich, of Upper Dowdeswell, Esq.
He married the only Daughter and Heir of
John Gilbert, of Swindon,
in the County of Wilts, Gent.
by whom he had one Son,
born Feb. 15, 1688;
buried April 18, 1723.

Elizabeth, Daughter of
Edward Gilbert Rich, Esq.
and Mary his Wife,
born Aug. 10, 1740;
buried April 19, 1741.

Here likewise are reposed the Remains of
Mary his Daughter, the beloved Wife of
Robert Lawrence, Esq,
whose Mind was a sweet Assemblage
of every social and benevolent Affection,
eminently displayed by the warm Exertions of
Friendship ; the endearing Sympathy of
connubial Love ;
and by Meekness and Humility,
and the regular Practice of all those Duties
which are the Result of a truly Christian Faith.
Thus fitted for a better State,
she calmly resigned her Soul into the
Hands of her blessed Redeemer,
on the 21st Day of January,
in the Year of our Lord 1761, aged 22.

Elizabeth their Daughter died an Infant.

On another neat Monument :

Arms ; Rich as before ;—impaling, Argent, on
a Chevron Azure, between three Lozenges Sable,
three Bucks Heads caboled Or, for

In Memory of Edward Rich,
of Upper Dowdeswell, Esquire,
Bencher and Barrister at Law, of the
Honourable Society of Lincoln's Inne,
who deceased the 5th Day of February, A. D. 1680,
aged 78 Years.

Mary, Wife of Lionel Rich, Esq.
buried the 7th of February, 1734,
aged 69 Years.

Lionel Rich, Esq.
buried April 26, 1736,
aged 71 Years.

O N

O N   F L A T   S T O N E S.

Here lieth the Body of
ELIZABETH ABBINGTON,
Widow and Relict of ANTHONY ABBINGTON,
of Dowdefwell,
who moft religioufiy departed this Life
27 Dec. 1640.

Here lieth the Body of
MARTHA, the Widow and Relict of
EDWARD RICH, Efq.
who died March 30, 1684, aged 73.

I N   T H E   C H U R C H   Y A R D.

ON A TABLET AGAINST THE CHURCH:

In Memory of
ROBERT ROGERS, Gent.
who departed this Life
Jan. 27, 1777, aged 62 Years.

SARAH, Wife of
NATHANIEL OKEY,
died March 13, 1717, aged 22.

JOHN OKEY, Son of
NATHANIEL and SARAH OKEY,
died January 29, 1769, aged 52.

NATHANIEL OKEY
died Feb. 12, 1771, aged 84.

O N   T O M B S.

THOMAS ROGERS,
of the Lower Houfe in this Parifh, Gent.
died Oct. 18, 1731, aged 76.

WILLIAM MAJOR
died April 2, 1729, aged 77.

JANE his Wife
was buried June 2, 1726,
aged 86.

WILLIAM ROGERS,
of the Lower Houfe, Gent.
died Feb. 14, 1774, aged 66.

ELIZABETH his Wife
died Auguft 3, 1773, aged 67.

WILLIAM their Son
died July 1, 1754,
in the 14th Year of his Age.

REBECKAH, Wife of
THOMAS NEALE, and Daughter of
ANTHONY LAWRENCE, Gent.
died the 8th Day of May, 1743,
aged 28.

Mrs. MARGARET PERRY,
Wife of ROGER PERRY,
died Auguft 27, 1731, aged 52.

This Tomb was erected
by Order of her Son
PETER PERRY, Efq.
in Memory of the beft of
Wives, Mothers, and Women.

O N   H E A D   S T O N E S.

	Died	Aged
Edward Land	21 Mar. 1773	51
William, Son of James and Parthenia Emes	5 Oct. 1776	20
Edward their Son	19 May, 1777	32
John Robbins	14 Nov. 1783	36
Richard Venfield	29 Mar. 1785	76
Ann, Wife of Nathaniel Okey	26 Jan. 1771	84
Francis Ingram	23 Oct. 1724	87
Frances his Wife	—— 1672	—
John Joynes	10 Sept. 1727	36
Mary, Wife of Thomas Caudle	27 Feb. 1781	52

4

ON

O N   H E A D   S T O N E S.

	Died	Aged
Elizabeth, Wife of John Cull	9 Aug. 1693	—
John Goodall	31 Aug. 1779	59
John, Son of John and Mary Goodall	8 Jan. 1771	10
Jofeph Bunce	8 Feb. 1745	45
Frances, Wife of James Stanley	1 Oct. 1759	53
James Stanley	26 Mar. 1765	—
John Chappel	29 Aug. 1785	79
John Hathaway, fenior	26 Feb. 1712	72
Eleanor, Wife of James Cooper	9 Nov. 1680	94
Jofeph Williams	7 Oct. 1764	57
Thomas Mofen	25 Jan. 1771	72
Ann Mary his Wife	6 Dec. 1768	67
William Mofen	25 Aug. 1718	29
Ann Mofen	1 June, 1787	78
James Mofen	10 Feb. 1736	76
Sarah his Wife	24 Oct. 1740	77
James Batt	30 May, 1786	17

XCIX. DOWNE

XCIX. DOWNE AMPNEY.

U NDER the general Denomination, *Omeney* in *Domefday* Book, four Parifhes are defcribed, fituate on a Rivulet which is not otherwife diftinguifhed than as *Ampney* Brook.

Down Ampney, or *Ampney Inferior*, lies on the Eaftern Confines of the County adjoining *Wiltfhire*, in the Hundred of *Crowthorne* and *Minety*, diftant from *Cirencefter* fix Miles on the South, two from *Cricklade*, *Wilts*, on the South, and twenty-three in a fimilar Direction from the City of GLOUCESTER. The Soil, confifting of 2500 Acres, varies from Loam to Gravel, and is equally applied to Pafture and Tillage, the Rivulet interfecting the whole in its courfe to the *Ifis*.

The Living is vicarial, the Impropriate Tythes of which were given by King EDWARD I. to the Knights Templars, of whom was NICHOLAS DE VILLARS 1268, who probably procured the Donation. In 1315, EDW. II. when the Templars were fuppreffed, they paffed to the Abbey of *Cirencefter*, where they remained till 1544, when they were granted to the College of *Chrift Church* in *Oxford*, who now prefent to the Vicarage *.

Of the Church, dedicated to *All Hallows*, the Conftruction is evidently complete and of the fame Period, of the latter part of the 13th Century. It has a Nave fupported by four pointed Arches, with two Aifles, a Tranfept and a Tower embattled and finifhed by an ornamented Spire. In the Chancel under a plain Arcade, is a Sarcophagus with a Crofs Florettèe, and encircled with a Laurel-wreath. In the South Tranfept under a Niche of Quaterfoils, is a female Figure in Free Stone, fupplicating; near it, on a Table of black Marble, a Knight Templar, in reticulated Armour, crofs-legged with a Talbot at the Feet and drawing his Sword, the Scabbard of which he holds in his left Hand. The Shield is of the Heater-fhape, and bears a Crofs charged with five Efcalops †. Adjoining to it is a Slab infcribed with Saxon Characters round the Margin, but totally illegible.

The Fraternity of Knights Templars certainly founded the prefent Church, in which pious Work they were affifted by NICHOLAS DE VILLARS about the year 1260.

During the firft Century after the Conqueft, the Manor was annexed to the Crown. In 1250, 46 HEN. III. EDWARD CROUCHBACK, Earl of *Lancafter*, his fecond Son, granted it in Fee to NICHOLAS DE VILLERS, whofe Family retained it till 1363, 35 EDW. III. About the beginning of the reign of RICHARD II. Sir THOMAS HUNGERFORD ‡ purchafed it, and it became the refidence of his lineal Defcendants to Sir ANTHONY HUNGERFORD, Knt. whofe Daughter and fole Heir, upon his death in 1645, transferred it to EDMUND DUNCH §, Efq. by marriage. JAMES CRAGGS ||, Efq. Secretary of State to King GEORGE I. having bought the manerial Eftate, bequeathed it to his natural Daughters and Coheirs; ANN, firft married to JOHN KNIGHT, Efq. of *Gosfield Hall*, Co. *Effex* : fecondly, to ROBERT NUGENT **, Lord Vifcount CLARE of the Kingdom of *Ireland*, who affumed the Name of CRAGGS, and died in 1788; and HARRIOT †† the Wife of RICHARD ELIOT, of *Port Eliot*, Co. *Cornwall*, whofe Son upon the Death of

---

* " In thofe times Vicars fignified no more than Curates, and were removeable at the Will of the Rector. But when Churches " were appropriated to Monafteries, and the Religious were forced to fet out a Portion of the Glebe and Tythes for the mainte- " nance of a Vicar, fuch a one is called a Perpetual Vicar made prefentative and inftitutive." BLOMEFIELD's Norfolk, v. I. p. 13.

† NICHOLAS DE VELERES is recorded in an old Roll of Arms bearing Argente, une Croife Goulis, & cinque Efchalops d'Or. COLLINGS Tit. *Jerfey*, v. IV. p. 155. fays, that NICHOLAS DE VYLERS, fon of ALEXANDER DE VYLERS, of *Brokefby*, Co. *Leic.* charged for this, his paternal Coat, Sable, three Cinquefoils, Argent, in 1266. *Mr.* GOUGH *(Sep. Mon. Cent.* 13. p. 96.) notices this Figure, which is very refemblant of thofe in the *Temple* Church, which are engraven in his acurate and fumptuous Work.

‡ Sir THOMAS HUNGERFORD, Knight, was elected and conftituted the firft ftanding Speaker of the Houfe of Commons in 1376, 51 EDWARD III. " The Duke of LANCASTER taught hym to demaund two tenths in one Yere. The Knightes of Parlimente, whom the Duke hadde made at hys pleafure defyred refpite, that they might deliberately anfwer hym ; for all the other Knightes in the laft Parlement, who had ftoutlie ftode with the Commonaulty, he had caufed to be moved, except twelve whom hee could not remove. Of the greater Part Mafter HUNGERFORD was elected to delivre their Aunfwere, who was a Knight very familiar with the Duke, and was hys Stewarde." STOWE's Annals, p. 273.

§ " EDMUND DUNCH, Efq. of *Little Wittenham*, Co. *Berks*, married BRIDGET, Daughter and fole Heir of Sir ANTONY HUN- " GERFORD, Knt. of *Downe Ampney*, which Manor was part of her large Fortune, £60,000 at leaft ; a prodigious fum in thofe " days. By the Protector, OLIVER CROMWELL, he was created Baron BURNEL of *Eaft Wittenham* by Patent, bearing Date April " 26, 1658." A *Fac fimile* of his Patent is engraven in the laft Edition of NOBLE's Memoirs of CROMWELL, v. II. p. 162.

|| JAMES CRAGGS, Efq. joint Secretary of State with Earl STANHOPE, died February 16, 1720.

** COLLINS's Supplement, p. 299.

† ALMON's Peerage of *Ireland*, v. II. p. 128.

6 M

his

his Mother and Aunt, became fole Proprietor.   He was created a Baron by Patent, January 30, 1784, 24 George III. by the Title of Lord *Eliot* of *St. German's* in the County of *Cornwall*.

Of the great Manor Houfe, feveral Parts exhibit much higher Antiquity than the Reign of King Henry VIII. particularly the Porch, the Arch of which is of quarterfoils, and which with the Hall compofes the chief Front.   The Arms of Hungerford, " Sable two Bars Agent, and in chief three Plates," are very frequently difperfed, particularly on the Bafe of a very fingular Chimney, a Column ornamented with Tracery.   A Range of Buildings which connected the great Gateway, and is now deftroyed, completed three fides of the Quadrangle *.   The Portal, or grand Entrance, is flanked by two octangular Turrets, embattled, and embellifhed with the Arms of Hungerford, their Cognizance (a Garb between two Sickles,) and the Cypher of the Builder, Sir Antony Hungerford.   Over the Arch, upon a large Efcocheon, Hungerford ;—impaling quarterly, 1. Argent, on a Bend Guiles, three Martlets Or, for Danvers ; 2. Gules, two Bars, and in Chief two Bucks Heads caboffed Or, for Popham ; 3. Barry, nebulè Gules and Or, for Dantesey ; 4th as 1ft.   The Hall is very lofty and fpacious, with a Roof of timber Frame, which is fupported by Cherubs holding Efcocheons charged with Arms, Cognizance and Cypher A. H.   In the Windows are, Quarterly, 1ft and 4th, Hungerford; 2d and 3d, Per Pale, indented Vert and Gules a Cheveron Or, for De Heytesbury ;—impaling, Paly wavy of fix Or and Gules, for Moleyns.   Upon the Wainfcot, which is of fmall Compartments filled with Mantles, are many grotefque Mouldings and a date, 1537.

We have been the more minute in this Defcription, as there are few fo perfect Specimens of the Architecture of that Age now remaining in this County.

No Benefactions to the Poor.

Incumbents.	Patrons.	Incumbents.	Patrons.
1530	Abbey of Cirencefter.	1681 Jofeph Richards, M. A.	——————— .
—15 Bartholemew Ferrars,	———————	1687 Michael Bingley, B. A.	———————
1585 Simon Preffe,	Anthony Hungerford.	1746 Thomas Smith, M. A.	———————
1590 Henry Bifhop,	John Hungerford.	1785 John Morgan, M. A.	——————
1603 Robert Alford,	R. James.	1788 Andrew Price, M. A.	———————
1679 Henry Green, M. A. Ch. Ch. College, Oxford.			

Present Lord of the Manor,

The Right Honourable Edward Craggs Eliot Lord Eliot.

The Perfons fummoned from this Place by the Heralds in 1682 and 1683 were,

The Heirs of Hungerford Dunch, Efq. and Henry Fletcher, Gent.

At the Election in 1776, Two Freeholders polled from this Parifh.

The oldeft Regifter bears Date 1603, and is written in Latin to 1641.

Annual Account of Marriages, Births, and Burials, in this Parish.

A.D.	Mar.	Bir.	Bur.	A.D.	Mar.	Bir.	Bur.	A.D.	Mar.	Bir.	Bur.	A.D.	Mar.	Bir.	Bur.
1781	4	11	5	1786	2	6	9	1791				1796			
1782	3	7	6	1787	1	10	6	1792				1797			
1783	3	11	4	1788	3	9	7	1793				1798			
1784	4	7	3	1789	2	8	7	1794				1799			
1785	1	4	6	1790				1795				1800			

* Gateways of this kind became a very fafhionable Appendage to the moft magnificent Refidences in the beginning of the Sixteenth Century.   They were introduced by Holbein, who defigned that at *Whitehall*.   Similar Edifices are at *Derry Hall*, Co. *Wilts*, built by Sir Andrew Bayntun ; at *Coughton*, Co. *Warwick*, by Sir Robert Throcmorton and others.   Sir Antony Hungerford was Knight of the Shire for this County in the firft Parliament of Queen Mary, 1553.   He finifhed this building after his marriage with his fecond Wife Elizabeth, Daughter of Sir John Danvers, of *Dantefey*, Co. *Wilts*.   " *Ampney Brook*, " (fays Leland, Itin. v. II. p. 23.) rifeth a little above *Ampney* Town, out of a Rok by North, and goeth a 3 Miles or more of, to " *Down Ampney*, wher Syr Antony Hungerford hath a fayr Houfe of Stone *ripâ ulteriori*. *Ampney* goith into *Ifis*, a Mile beneth " *Down Ampney*, again *Nunne Eiton* in *Wilfhir*."

INSCRIPTIONS

INSCRIPTIONS IN THE CHURCH.

On Tablets in the Chancel.

In Memory of
CESAR CHANDLER, Gent.
who departed this Life Dec. 6, 1754.

In Memory of
ANN, the Wife of
CESAR CHANDLER, Gent.
who departed this Life Oct. 26, 1752,
aged 65.

A MURAL MONUMENT OF ALABAS-
TER, UNDER A DOUBLE ARCADE,
TWO FIGURES OF MEN KNEELING IN
ARMOUR; A DESK BETWEEN THEM.
THE PEDIMENT FINISHED WITH EM-
BLEMS AND DEVICES; UPON THE
ARCHITRAVE, ON SEPARATE ES-
CUTCHEONS,

1ft. Gules a Cheveron Ermine, be-
tween ten Crosses patée Argent for
BERKELEY, of *Stoke*; 2. three Eagles
displayed, for EARNLEY; 3. Gules, a
Cheveron vairy between three Crescents
Or, for GODDARD; 4. Gules, three
Luciers haurient Argent, femée Crosses
Crollets Or for LUCIE. In the Centre,
HUNGERFORD; Quartering, 1. HUN-
GERFORD; 2. DE HEYTESBURY; 3.
Azure, three Garbs and a Chief Or, for
PEVEREL; 4. Argent, three Toads erect
Sable, for BOTTREAUX; 5. Argent,
two Bars Gules, in Chief three Tor-
teaxes, for MOELS; 6. Ermine, within
a Bordure Sable, bezantée, a Lion ram-
pant Gules, for CORNWALL; 8. Or, three
Torteauxes, in Chief a Label of three
Points, charged with three Fleurs de lis
each, for COURTENAY; 9. Barry of
fix Ermine and Gules, for HUSSEY;
10. Argent, a Gryphon fegreant Gules,
for BOTREAUX; 11. MOLEYNS; 12. Sable, on a Chief Argent, three Lozenges
Gules, for MOLYNS; 13. Argent, a
Bend Sable, and a Label of three Points,
for SAINTLOE; 14. Or, a Lion rampant
crowned Azure; 15. Azure, three Pales
dancettè Or, for MAUDUIT; 16. HUN-
GERFORD, as before.

In this Chapel lieth the Body of
Sir JOHN HUNGERFORD, Knight,
lineally descended from
WALTER Lord HUNGERFORD,
Knight of the Noble Order of the Garter,
who was Honourable in his Life,
ferviceable to his King and Country,
liberal to his Friends, charitable

to the Poor, and courteous to all.
He first married MARY,
the Daughter of
Sir RICHARD BARKLY, Knight,
by whom he had three Sonnes
and fower Daughters,
and afterwards ANNA, the Daughter of
EDWARD GODDARD, Esq.
He died the XVIII. Day of March,
in the LXIX. Year of his Age,
Anno R. R. CAROLI Decimo,
Annoque Domini 1634.

Chriftus Mihi Vita.

Sir ANTHONY HUNGERFORD, Knight,
now living (eldeft fon to this
Sir JOHN HUNGERFORD, Knight),
was first married to ELIZABETH LUCY,
Daughter to Sir THOMAS LUCY, Knt.
by whom he had two Daughters,
(one died young, BRIDGET furvived,
and was married to
EDMUND DUNCH, Esq.);
and afterwards, the faid Sir ANTONY
Married JANE EARNLY,
Daughter of MICHAEL EARNLY, Esq.
by SUSAN HUNGERFORD,
Daughter and one of the Coheirs of
Sir WALTER HUNGERFORD,
of Farley, Knight.
He erected this Monument in the
LIId. Year of his Age,
for the Honour of his dear Father,
and in Remembrace of his own Mortality,
Sept. 30, Ann. R. R. CAROLI XIII.
Anno Domini 1637.

On a Brass Plate:

CHRISTUS eft refurrectio mortuorum.
Hic jacet MARIA Domina HUNGERFORD,
nuper uxoris JOHANNIS HUNGERFORD,
de Downe Ampney, Militis,
(Fuliaque RICHARDI BARKLEY,
Militis qui a MAURICIO Domino
BARKLEY, per Dominam ISABELLAM
Uxorem ejus, Filiam RICHARDI
PLANTAGENET, comitis Cornubiæ,
ac regis Romanorum, filii Johannis
Regis Angliæ, linealiter defcendebat),
quæ fuit veræ pietatis rarum exemplum,
Bonarum literarum valde ftudiofa,
exquifitæ pudicitiæ obfervantiffima
marito fuo chara, et amantiffima liberi
cognatis et amicis fuis plena
Charitatis et Bonorum operum.
Vixit cum marito fuo conjunctiffime

Quadraginta et quatuor annos.
Apoftema in pectore vitam ejus
Finivit decimo octavo die Julij,
vefperi circa horam feptimam,
Anno ætatis fuæ fexageffimo quinto,
Annoque Domini computatione Angliæ
1628 { ficut vita finis ita.
     { Vivit poft funera virtus.
Ultimum officii et Amoris mei erga
Eandam MARIAM Dominam
HUNGERFORD et verum
Teftimonium, WILLIELMUS PLATT,

On a Tablet.

Here lieth JOHN, the fecond Son of
Sir JOHN HUNGERFORD, Knt.
who was buried the 5th Day of March,
Anno Dom. 1643.

On Flat Stones in the Nave.

ANTHONY KING
died May 18, 1662.

ALICE his Wife,
died Jan. 22, 16 .. 8.

RICHARD BENNETT
was buried Auguft 30, 1675.

MARY, Wife of HENRY FLETCHER,
died Auguft 11, 1707.

ANNE, the Wife of
THOMAS HOUSE, of this Parifh,
departed this Life May 9, 1764,
aged 72.

IN THE CHURCH YARD.   ON TOMBS.

EDMUND HILLIER
died March 15, 1726, aged 70.

Alfo JOHN and ELIZABETH HILLIER,
Father and Mother of the faid
EDMUND HILLIER;
and JOHN his elder Brother.

———

THOMAS KING
died July 25, 1767, aged 72.

MARY his Wife
died Jan. 19, 1771, aged 73.

THOMAS, CHRISTOPHER, and JANE,
their Children, died young.

———

EDWARD KIMBER
died April 27, 1766, aged 69.

ELIZABETH his Wife
died Feb. 2, 1742, aged 55.

EDWARD their Son
died Nov. 14, 1762, aged 45.

THOMAS, Son of EDWARD and
ELIZABETH KIMBER,
died March 27, 1779, aged 52.

WILLIAM KIMBER, fenior,
died Auguft 4, 1782, aged 66.

HESTER his Wife
died Auguft 11, 1786, aged 74.

———

LAWRENCE BURGESS
died July 11, 1775, aged 87.

ELIZABETH, Wife of CHRISTOPHER
SAUNDERS, of CRICKLADE,
Daughter of Mr. LAWRENCE BURGESS
ELIZABETH and his Wife,
died Oct. 2, 1719,
aged 27 Years 7 Months.

———

HARRY BURGESS, Gent.
died April 2, 1725, aged 37.

MARY, Wife of JOHN GINGELL,
died April 15, 1725, aged 33.

MARY, their Daughter,
died Oct. 8, 1754, aged 30.

———

CATHARINE, Wife of
LAWRENCE BURGESS, fenior,
died Oct. 18, 1777, aged 85.

LAWRENCE BURGESS, junior,
Son of LAWRENCE and
CATHARINE BURGESS,
died Jan. 18, 1786, aged 58.

———

JOHN GINGELL
died April 9, 1767, aged 54.

ON   H E A D   S T O N E S.

	Died	Aged
John Golding, of the Ley	4 Feb. 1776	65
Ann his Wife	19 June, 1776	57
Edward Hayward	9 Apr. 1752	69
Anne his Wife	27 June, 1767	70
John Howfe, fenior	30 July, 1745	95
Mary his Wife	17 Nov. 1732	80
John Howfe	31 May, 1786	73
John, Son of Thomas and Sarah Golding	12 June, 1787	17
Sarah, Wife of Thomas Golding	19 Nov. 1782	44
Robert Archer	23 June, 1740	75
Ann his Wife	29 —— 1755	60
John, Son of John and Mary Hewer	30 May, 1730	17
Mary his Mother	2 Jan. 1766	91
Henry Hewer	9 Feb. 1749	74
Mary, Wife of Richard Hewer	15 June, 1742	26
Betty, Wife of Giles Hewer	22 Dec. 1777	48
John Hodges	26 Sept. 1750	82
Amy, Wife of David Archer	24 Nov. 1769	31
Margaret, Wife of John Archer	2 Sept. 1747	77
John Archer	7 Mar. 1730	61
John, Son of John and Margaret Archer	22 July, 1761	62
John Archer	24 Feb. 1716	66
Robert their Son	19 Dec. 1760	77
John Archer	3 June. 1687	35
David, Son of John and Jane Archer	11 June, 1749	63
Mary, Wife of Richard Archer	6 Aug. 1708	29
Richard Archer	14 Mar. 1737	63
William Mealling	14 Feb. 1698	35
Ann, Wife of William Mealling	17 Oct. 1727	29
Ann, Daughter of John and Elizabeth Archer	13 Feb. 1752	57
John Creed	16 Jan. 1732	72
Elizabeth Creed	21 Nov. 1754	80
Anthony Creed	6 Dec, 1694	—
Elizabeth his Wife	5 Oct. 1704	82
Thomas, Son of Thomas and Elizabeth Adams	18 Feb. 1752	45

	Died	Aged
William Kimber	23 Dec. 1760	69
Mary his Wife	13 Aug. 1762	54
Mary, Wife of Anthony King	22 Apr. 1771	84
Jane, their Daughter	25 Mar. 1756	33
Anthony King	30 May, 1755	44
Elizabeth his Wife	9 July, 1 45	34
Alice, Daughter of Chriftopher and Elizabeth King	12 Nov. 1785	48
Chriftopher King	15 June, 1740	54
Francis, Wife of Thomas King	15 June, 1729	81
Thomas King, fenior	1 Jan. 1733	85
Sarah, Wife of Henry Hathaway	2 Feb. 1780	53
John, Son of Henry and Mary Smith	1 July, 1781	46
Sarah, Wife of John Smith,	9 Oct. 1782	49
John Kimber	30 Dec. 1744	50
Robert, Son of William and Ann Mealing	18 Aug. 1753	49
Alice, Daughter of William and Ann Mealling	12 Oct. 1766	77
Thomas Trinder	6 Nov. 1759	72
Margaret his Wife	4 Oct. 1758	68
Edmund, Son of Edmund and Prifcilla Trinder	29 Nov. 1780	24
Prifcilla, Wife of Richard Harrifon, Daughter of Edmund and Prifcilla Trinder	1 July, 1785	21
Edmund Betterton	14 June, 1767	63
Mary, Wife of Walter Betterton	5 —— 1754	77
John, Son of Lawrence and Catharine Burgefs	18 Mar. 1663	31
Harry their Son	18 Mar. 1763	31
Deborah, Wife of Philip Lidiard	11 June, 1765	64
Edward, Son of Thomas and Edith Pitts	8 Dec. 1726	76
Margaret Pitts	24 Aug. 1746	77
Thomas, Son of Lawrence and Catharine Burgefs	31 Jan. 1765	35
Thomas Matthews	19 Apr. 1739	69
Ann his Wife	19 Feb. 1759	65

C.

C. DOWNE-HATHERLEY

IS a Parifh of fmall extent, in the Hundred of *Dudftone* and *King's Barton*, fituate in the great Vale of GLOUCESTER, from which City it is diftant four Miles on the North-eaft, fix from *Tewkefbury* in the oppofite Direction, and an equal Diftance from *Cheltenham* on the Weft. Of the Soil an exact Defcription is fubjoined *; it is chiefly in Tillage. The Terrier contains nearly 700 Acres; including a common Meadow of more than Sixty.

The Benefice is a Vicarage in the Deanery of *Winchcombe*, and the Church dedicated to *St. Mary*, and *Corpus Chrifti*, a fmall unornamented Building, with no interefting Veftige of Antiquity.

Domefday Book records this Manor, under the Title of " *Terra Regis* ;" it was, on the Creation of the Barony of GIFFARD of *Brimpsfield*, annexed to it ; and held by Knight's Service in 1311, 4 EDW. II. by Sir JOHN DE WYLLINTON. Sir THOMAS BROKE in 1389, 12 RICH. II. having married the Heir of his Defcendant, levied a Fine. With the large Eftates of that Family it paffed by Inheritance to the gallant and learned Sir FULK GREVILLE, created Baron BROKE, of *Beauchamp Court* in 1620, and of whom in 157., 14 ELIZ. NICHOLAS NORWOOD, Efq. (of the Family, fettled at *Leckhampton*,) purchafed the manerial Eftate ; from which laft it was transferred to that of GWINNETT, of *Badgeworth*. The prefent Reprefentative of which Family is WILLIAM CATCHMAY, Efq. who affumed the Surname and Arms of GWINNETT by royal Sign manual. But the Property of the largeft Eftate was vefted in 1368, 41 EDW. III. in JOHN-AT-YATE, from whom it paffed to the BERKELEY's, of *Beverftone*. Early in the laft Century the Family of BRETT was eftablifhed at *Hatherly* : they were fucceeded by that of GIBBES, about the Year 1720 ; and by WILLIAM GIBBES, Efq. who died in 1784, this principal Eftate was bequeathed to RICHARD SUTTON, of *Norwood Park*, co. *Notts*, who was created a Baronet, by Patent, dated 25 Sept. 1772, 12 GEO. III.

The Parifh does not afford any other Subject of Remark.

BENEFACTIONS.

WILLIAM DRINKWATER, by Will, 1613, left 10s. a Year, to be given to the Poor at Chriftmas ; payable out of an Eftate.
—— COX, 1654, gave 20s. a Year, payable out of an Eftate at *Upton St. Leonards,* to be diftributed amongft fuch Poor as do not receive Alms at Chriftmas.
HENRY BRETT, Efq. 1711, gave a Cottage, and three Acres of Arable Land ; the Annual Produce of which now is 1l. 8s.

INCUMBENTS.	PATRONS.	INCUMBENTS.	PATRONS.
1305 ————	Priory of St. Ofwald in GLOUCESTER.	—— Anthony Robertfon,	————
———— ————	Priory of Ufk.	1660 John Fox,	Charles Norwood, Efq.
1500 ————	Abbey of St. Peter in GLOUCESTER.	—— Humphrey Randal,	K. Charles II.
		1671 Samuel Broad, M. A.	——
—— James Wylliams,	————.	1707 Thomas Pugh,	Q. Anne.
1563 Henry Aifgill, M. A.	Q. Eliz.	1727 Samuel Gwinnett, M.A.	K. George I.
1622 Jofhua Aifgill, D.D.	King James I.	1775 Martin Barry, LL. B.	K. George III.

* " On examining the Soil of a Ground which is defervedly efteemed the beft Piece of Land in the Parifh of *Downe-Hatherley*,
" and which though a rifing Ground bears no Veftige of the Plow, I found as follows.—The firft fix Inches, a ftrong Loam
" (a Mixture of Clay and Sand) free from calcarious Matter ; from 6 to 9 Inches a dark-brown Clay, very weakly calcarious ; at
" 12 a fimilar Soil, but fomewhat more calcarious ; from 15 to 18 Inches a ftronger bluifh Clay ftill more ftrongly calcarious.
" The firft fix Inches I found thickly interwoven with Fibres, which leffened in Number as the Depth increafed, but ever at 18
" Inches the Soil appeared to be full of them. Hence appears the Value of a rich Subfoil to Grafs Land. The Piece has never
" been plowed, becaufe perhaps it never required Plowing ; its Sward never failed it, continuing in full Vigour through fuccef-
" five Generations. It is obfervable, however, that the Ground under Notice, does not fhoot early in Spring, but its Sap once
" in Motion its Growth is uncommonly rapid." MARSHAL's Rur. Œcon. of GLOCESTERSH. Vol. I. p. 181.

6 N

PRESENT

PRESENT LORD OF THE MANOR,

WILLIAM CATCHMAY GWINNETT, ESQ.

The Perfons fummoned from this Place by the Heralds in 1682 and 1683, were Samuel Broad, Vicar, and Richard Bifley, Gent.

At the Election in 1776 Ten Freeholders polled from this Parifh.

The Regifter has its firft Date in 1563; and is chiefly written in Latin.

ANNUAL ACCOUNT OF MARRIAGES, BIRTHS, AND BURIALS, IN THIS PARISH.

A.D.	Mar.	Bir.	Bur.	A.D.	Mar.	Bir.	Bur.	A.D.	Mar.	Bir.	Bur.	A.D.	Mar.	Bir.	Bur.
1781	2	5	2	1786	—	3	3	1791				1796			
1782	2	5	5	1787	—	1	4	1792				1797			
1783	1	5	—	1788	—	—	3	1793				1798			
1784	3	—	—	1789	4	2	5	1794				1799			
1785	—	4	11	1790				1795				1800			

INSCRIPTIONS IN THE CHURCH.

ON A COARSE STONE AGAINST THE WALL IN THE CHANCEL :

Arms; Checquy, Argent and Sable, on a Bend Gules, three Efcallops Or.

Vita fumo fugacior.

Here lyeth buried the Body of WILLYAM PARTEREDGE, Efquier, who departed this Life the 15th of Aprill, 1609.

Memento quam fis brevis evi.

ON A MONUMENT ON THE SOUTH SIDE :

Arms; on threee Efcutcheons; 1. Gules, a Fefs dancettè Argent, between 11 Billets Or, for BRETT. 2. BRETT;—impaling, Or, on a Fefs Sable three Bezants, and in chief a Greyhound current of the fecond, for EVANS. 3. Or, a Saltire engrailed, between four crofs Crofslets Sable.

To the pious Memory of HESTER, the beautiful Daughter of RICHARD and MARGARET EVANS, of Enftone in Oxfordfhire, Gent. The virtuous Wife of HENRY BRETT, of Hatherley, Efq. who died June 7, Anno æt. 38. Sal. 1696.

Alfo to the pious Memory of GEORGE BRETT, Efq. and JOYCE his Wife, Father and Mother of HENRY, who were here buried;

GEORGE, Anno æt. 47. Sal. 1667.

JOYCE, Anno æt... Sal. 1662.

ON FLAT STONES

IN THE CHANCEL.

ANNE BRETT, the Daughter of GEORGE BRETT, Efq. and of JOYCE his Wife, was buried the 10th Day of July, A. D. 1662.

ROBERT, Son of HENRY BRETT, Efq. and HESTER his Wife, deceafed June .. Anno 16 .. aged 6 Months.

HESTER, Wife of HENRY BRETT, Efq. departed this Life the 7th Day of June, in the Year of our Lord 1696, aged 38.

ARTHUR BRETT, Son of GEORGE BRETT, Efq. and JOYCE his Wife, was buried March 20, 1661.

HENRY BRETT, Son of GEORGE BRETT, Efq. and JOYCE his Wife, was buried July 2, 1656.

HESTER, Relict of JOSHUA AISGILL, Doctor in Divinity, died May 27, 1690, aged 90.

The

The Rev. THOMAS PUGH,
Vicar of this Church twenty Years,
died Auguft 13, 1727, aged 57.

SARAH WILLIAMS, his Sifter
in Law, lies near this Place, 1726.

In Memory of SUSANNAH,
the Wife of MARTIN BARRY, Vicar of this Parifh,
Daughter of GABRIEL HARRIS,
Alderman of Gloucefter,
who departed this Life Nov. 2, 1779, aged 31.

Alfo of SUSANNAH his Wife,
Daughter of DANIEL ELLIS, of Minfterworth,
who died Jan. 9, 1784, aged 34.

Alfo of BARBARA his Wife,
Daughter of JAMES ROOKE, Efq.
of Bigfware, in the Parifh of St. Briavel's,
who died May 12, 1788, aged . . . .

ON A NEAT MONUMENT OF WHITE AND VARIEGATED
MARBLE, IN THE NAVE :

Arms ; Argent, three Battle-axes Sable, for GIBBES.

To the Memory of
WROUGHTON GIBBES, Efquire, and
ELIZABETH-BATHURST GIBBES,
This Monument was erected, agreeable
to the Direction of the laft Will of the late
WILLIAM GIBBES, Efq. of this Place,
as a Teftimony of his Regard and Efteem,
A. D. 1785.

WROUGHTON GIBBES,
ob. 9 May, 1728, æt. 32.

ELIZABETH-BATHURST GIBBES,
ob. Mar. 15, 1763, æt. 72.

IN THE CHURCH YARD, ON TOMBS.

Arms ; on three Efcutcheons ; 1. Chequy, for
AISGILL. 2. on a Fefs three Croffes patée fitchy,
and on a Canton a Fleur de Lis. 3. On a Crofs
five Cinquefoils, for VILLIERS.

Hic jacet fepultus venerabilis
Vir HENRICUS AISGILL, Ecclefiæ
Cathedralis Menevenfis Cancellarius,
Gloceftrenfis Prebendarius, necnon
hujus Parochiæ Vicarius,
qui obiit in Domino Junii 18,
Anno Dom. 1622.

WILLIAM DRINKWATER
was buried the 29th of January, 1615,
who (in Zeal to the Worde)
gave Forty Shillings yearly for ever, towarde
the Maintainance of a Preacher in Gloucefter,
and Ten Shillings in Charity, Ten Shillings
yearly to the Poor of Hatherly for ever.

ON A RAISED CIRCULAR TOMB :

Arms, on two Efcutcheons; 1. a Chevron between
three Spears Heads, for GWINNETT. 2. On a Fefs
a Lion iffuant.

Hæc urna colligit caftè
& amplectitur
quod eft mortale ANNÆ GWINNETT,
cujus formam mentemque honeftârunt
gratia venerefque ;
& in fœminâ verè patuit & eluxit

Socratica virtus καλοκαγαθια ;
fic moribus & elegantiis ornata
fuis, amicis, notis,
vixit chara,
& omnibus vitæ partibus bene peractis
deceffit plorata.
Anno { ÆÆtatis 74.
{ Salutis 1768.

Hos cineres
nec mitrata violet infolentia,
nec mitrata lædat aut malitia,
heu ! fordidæ tenuifque mentis vitium,
& literis ingenioque prorfus alienæ !
Nec polluant artes infimorum pravæ,
quippe has fœces olim ingurgitarunt
mors & infamia.
Sunt SAMUELIS GWINNETT, paftoris fidi,
nec verbum adulterantis, nec parcè cauponantis,
at in hujus Ecclefiæ muniis obeundis
largi, fimplicis, finceri, inftantis ;
fubfecivas horas dedit academiæ,
at inter hafce feveriores difciplinas
nec inurbanus, nec inficetus ;
denique per vitam honeftam & decoram
homo vere philofophicus ftuduit,
civilis excoluit.
Anno { Vicariatûs 48.
{ ÆÆtatis 75.
{ Salutis 1775.

ON THE BASE :

Filius hunc lapidem parentibus
pofuit piè,
& lachrymis facieque averfâ
charitatis extrema ritè perfolvit.

ON

O N H E A D S T O N E S.

	Died	Aged
George Piffe, fenior,	25 June, 1732	50
Betty, Wife of George Piffe	3 Feb. 1766	26
John Betty	24 June, 1757	50
Anne his Wife	11 Apr. 1744	48
Thomas Butt, fenior	28 May, 1752	86
Mary his Wife	16 Feb. 1756	64
Thomas Butt, junior	24 Aug. 1757	51
Sarah, Wife of Thomas Holder, of Churchdown	2 Dec. 1714	60
Thomas their Son	11 Feb. 1714	27
Adam Jackfon, of Longford in the Parifh of St. Mary de Load	14 Feb. 1766	101
Efther his Wife	6 Sept. 1759	73
John Martin	20 Nov. 1693	32
Anne his Wife	13 Sept. 1708	—
David their Son	11 Apr. 1712	21
Thomas Thayer, of the Hamlet of Twigworth	11 Sept. 1700	80
William Thayer	2 Dec. 1714	22
John Lett	11 Nov. 1762	80
Mary his Wife	2 Apr. 1754	66
Mary, Wife of Francis Lett	31 Oct. 1761	21
John, Son of Edward and Jane Prefton, of the Hamlet of Twigworth	15 Oct. 1776	24
Jane their Daughter	5 May, 1786	24
Elizabeth, Wife of William Prefton	16 May, 1786	21
Edward Roane	25 Feb. 1675	52
Joan his Wife	16 Apr. 1695	60
James their Son	3 Jan. 1689	24
Giles Edwards, of Twigworth	12 Mar. 1701	57
John Edwards, of Twigworth	25 Jan. 1684	69
Emmanuel Lane, Gent.	29 July, 1698	—
Ann, Relict of William Randall, Gent.	18 May, 1699	—
Jane, Wife of Emmanuel Lane, Gent.	2 Nov. 1694	55
Sarah, Wife of John Vernon	22 Aug. 1714	54

CI. DRIFFIELD,

CI. DRIFFIELD, OR DRYFFELDE.

THIS Parifh is included in the Hundred of *Crowthorne* and *Minety*, four Miles diftant from *Ciren-cefter* South-eaftward, three in the oppofite Direction from *Cricklade* in *Wiltſhire*, and twenty-one from GLOUCESTER. Within the Boundaries about a thoufand Acres are included; the Grafs Lands are cold and unproductive; thofe tilled are of a light Soil, yet not unfertile. The Common Fields are hitherto uninclofed.

All the impropriate Tythes have been allotted to the Vicarage fince the Suppreffion of the Abbey of *Cirencefter*, who held them with the Advowfon; and forty-one Acres of Glebe were then added. It belongs to the Deanery of *Cirencefter*.

The Church, dedicated to *St. Mary*, was re-built about thirty Years fince, at the fole Expence of GABRIEL HANGER, Lord COLERAINE. It is an Edifice in the modern Style, of great Symmetry and Neatnefs; efpecially in the internal Decorations. Sir R. ATKYNS remarks of the old Church, that " it " was a ftrong Building with a Tower at the Weft End, and that there was an Infcription in the Chan- " cell for Sir JOHN PRETTYMAN, Knight, Lord of the Manor, who died in 1638." Now deftroyed.

Amongft the Poffeffions of REMBALD the Prieft, the Manor of " *Dryffelle*" was enrolled, and given to the Abbey of *Auguſtine* Canons at *Cirencefter* by King HENRY I. By the Charter of Confirmation granted by EDWARD III. they poffeffed here eight Hides of Land. In 1546 thefe Lands were given in Exchange for others at *Waltham*, co. *Effex*, to HUMPHRY and GEORGE BROWNE; by MARY, the elder Coheir of Sir HUMPHRY BROWNE, Knight, of *Ridley Hall*, co. *Effex*, and one of the Juftices of the Common Pleas; they paffed in Marriage Settlement to THOMAS WILFORD, Efq. prior to 1608, to whom fucceeded Sir JOHN PRETTYMAN. JOHN D'AUNGIER, or HANGER, a Merchant in *London* in the Reign of CHARLES I. purchafed the manerial Eftate extending over the whole Parifh. His Defcendant GABRIEL HANGER was created Baron COLERAINE, of *Coleraine*, in the County of *Londonderry*, in *Ireland*, Dec. 1, 1762, 2 GEO. III.

Upon the Site of the Manor-houfe, modernized and improved by its later Poffeffors, was a country Refidence of the Abbots of *Cirencefter*. To this Place, at the Difperfion of their other Property, JOHN BLAKE, the laft Abbot, was permitted to retire with a Penfion of 200*l*. a Year, and fpent feveral Years in Acts of religious Retirement. He was buried in the Chancel under an uninfcribed Stone, nor can the Date of his Death be afcertained by any authentic Document. Parts of the prefent Houfe are of the Style of the Commencement of the laft Century; others more modern.

B E N E F A C T I O N S.

Five Pounds a Year are given by the Society for the Encouragement of Sunday Schools, to teach forty poor Children to read.

INCUMBENTS.	PATRONS.	INCUMBENTS.	PATRONS.
To 1539	Abbey of Cirencefter.	1674 Ric. Parfons*, LL.B.	Bifhop of GLOUCESTER.
——— John Adams,	William Adams.	1725 Thomas Edwards,	Robert Vefey, Gent.
1583 Henry Hall,	———————.	1732 Richard Arthur, B. A.	Thomas Humphrys.
——— Samuel Mitchel,	Sir John Prettyman.	1736 Thos. Humphrys, Clerk,	———————.
1665 Sam. Rich, D.D. } in dif-	{ Wm. Prettyman.	1748 Thomas Bray, B. D.	Gab. Hanger, Efq.
1666 Sam. Rich, D.D. } pute.	{ Bp. of GLOUCESTER.	1777 Richard Denifon Cum-	
1673 Thomas Mole,	——— Griffin, Gent.	berland, LL.B.	Thomas Smith, Efq.

* RICHARD PARSONS was born in 1643: Fellow of *New College, Oxford*; LL. B. 1665; appointed Chancellor of the Diocefe of GLOUCESTER 1677; LL. D 1687. He died 1711, aged 68.
" Dr. RICHARD PARSONS, whofe Office, as Chancellor of this Diocefe, gave him great Opportunities for fuch a Work, un- " dertook a Hiftory of the Cathedral and Diocefe at the Requeft of Mr. WHARTON, who intended to have publifhed it in another " Volume of his " Anglia Sacra." Bifhop NICOLSON fays, he collected two Volumes, which were digefted into fo good a " Method, that they well deferved the Title of a complete Hiftory. The firft was intituled, " Memoires of the ancient Abbey " and prefent Cathedral of GLOUCESTER;" the other, " A parochial Vifitation of the Diocefe." This laft was in LE NEVE's " Catalogue; the other in the Bodleian Library, *Oxford*. Whatever his Plan was, he put a Stop to it, as his ill State of Health " had prevented his digefting his Collections." GOUGH's Britifh Topography.

6 O

PRESENT

PRESENT LORD OF THE MANOR,

The Right Honourable JOHN HANGER Lord COLERAINE.

The only Perſon ſummoned from this Place by the Heralds in 1682 and 1683, was George Hanger, Eſq.

At the Election in 1776, only One Freeholder polled from this Pariſh.

The Regiſter commences with the Year 1560.

ANNUAL ACCOUNT OF MARRIAGES, BIRTHS, AND BURIALS, IN THIS PARISH.

A.D.	Mar.	Bir.	Bur.	A.D.	Mar.	Bir.	Bur.	A.D.	Mar.	Bir.	Bur.	A.D.	Mar.	Bir.	Bur.
1781	2	3	2	1786	1	6	2	1791				1796			
1782	—	3	1	1787	2	3	1	1792				1797			
1783	1	4	2	1788	1	2	—	1793				1798			
1784	—	3	6	1789	1	1	4	1794				1799			
1785	1	2	1	1790				1795				1800			

INSCRIPTIONS IN THE CHURCH.

ON A TABLET IN THE CHANCEL:

Arms; a Griffin ſalient per Feſs for HANGER.

Near this Place lies interred the Body of
GEORGE HANGER, Eſq.
who departed this Life, the 30th of May,
Anno Dom. 1688, in the 74th Year of his Age.

Arms; on a Lozenge a Lion rampant regardant.

Near this Place lies interred the Body of
Mrs. ANNE HAINGER, late Wife of
GEORGE HAINGER, Eſq. deceaſed,
who departed this Life the 22d Day of July,
Anno Dom. 1698, in the 70th Year of her Age.

ON A NEAT MARBLE MONUMENT:

Arms; HANGER as before.

Near this Place
lies the Body of Sir GEORGE HANGER, Knight,
who departed this Life the 24th Day of Nov. 1731,
aged 80 Years.

Near this Place
lieth the Body of Dame ANN HANGER,
Relict of Sir GEORGE HANGER, Knight.
She was Daughter and Coheireſs of
Sir JOHN BEALE, of Farringham
in the County of Kent, Bart.
and departed this Life the 13th Day of November,
1742, aged 73.

ON ANOTHER NEAT MARBLE TABLET:

Near this Place
lieth the Body of Mrs. JANE HANGER,
Daughter of Sir GEORGE HANGER,
who departed this Life the 17th Day of January,
Anno Dom. 1764, aged 70.
Relations and Friends reſerve her Memory,
for ſhe had many Virtues! and,
above all, a thorough Senſe of Religion;
ſo died in full Hopes of a bleſſed Reſurrection!

ON ANOTHER TABLET NEAR THE FORMER:

Here reſteth the Body of
Mrs. MARY HANGER,
Daughter of Sir GEORGE HANGER, Knight,
who departed this Life the 17th Day of June,
Anno Dom. 1722.
She was pious, virtuous, and charitable;
and endued with
all thoſe amiable Qualifications
that could make her Life deſirable,
and her Change happy.

ON AN ELEGANT MARBLE MONUMENT:

Arms; Quarterly, 1ſt and 4th, HANGER as before; 2d and 3d, Sable, on a Chevron Or, between three Griffin's Heads eraſed Argent, three Eſtoiles Gules, for BEATE. On an Eſcutcheon of Pretence, quarterly, 1ſt and 4th, Argent, a Chevron Azure, between three Demi Lions rampant Gules, for BOND; 2d and 3d, Sable, a Chevron between three Boys Heads couped at the Shoulders Argent, for VAUGHAN. Motto, *Artes Honorabit.*

Here lieth
in Expectation of the laſt Day,
GABRIEL HANGER, Lord COLERAINE;
what manner of Man he was
that Day will diſcover.
He died Jan. 24, 1773, aged 75.

Here alſo,
in hope of a joyful Reſurrection,
lieth buried with her Lord,
ELIZABETH Lady COLERAINE,
Daughter and Heireſs of
RICHARD BOND, Eſq. of Cowbury
in the County of Hereford.
She died Dec. 19, 1780,
aged 65.

ON

ON FLAT STONES.

Under this Stone lyeth the Body of
GABRIEL HANGER, Son of
GABRIEL HANGER, Efq. of Dryffield,
who died the 28th Day of July,
Anno Dom. 1747, aged 9 Years.

Here lieth interred the Bodie of
JOHN HANGER, of London, Merchant,
deceafed the 16th Day of May, 1654.

Alfo of Mrs. MARTHA TROTT,
the Daughter of the faid JOHN HANGER,
who deceafed October the 10th, 1688.

IN THE CHURCH YARD, ON TOMBS.

FRANCIS RADWAY
died April 22, 1761, aged 76.

ANNE his Wife
died Dec. 10, 1748, aged 76.

ANNE their Daughter
died Auguft 9, 1715, aged 6.

RICHARD HOWES, fenior,
died May 5, 1730, aged 68.

ANNE his Wife
died Feb. 5, 1757, aged 99.

ELIZABETH SOUDLEY, of this Parifh,
Wife of JOHN JONES, RICHARD CRAFTS, and
OBADIAH BLAGROVE,
all Citizens and Stationers of London,
departed this Life the 22d Day of Oct. 1709,
aged 83 Years.

ELIZABETH, Wife of JOHN FORSHEW,
died March 23, 1739, aged 72.

ANNE FORSHEW
died the 24 May, 1729, aged 31.

THOMAS HAYWARD,
Clerk of this Parifh,
died July 1, 1731, aged 74.

ELIZABETH his Wife
died Oct. 18, 1691, aged 44.

JANE his fecond Wife
died Oct. 5, 1720, aged 61.

ANNE, Daughter of
THOMAS and ELIZABETH HAYWARD,
died Dec. 25, 1756, aged 72.

JOHN HAYWARD
died Dec. 10, 1739, aged 45.

ON HEAD STONES.

	Died	Aged
Henry Adams	6 Apr. 1746	77
Mary his Wife	30 Mar. 1753	77
Michael Dubber	18 Jan. 1728	—
Sarah his Wife	18 Sept. 1733	66
John Adams	27 Apr. 1729	65
Rebecca his Wife	30 Jan. 1739	63
Thomas Kilby	4 Oct. 1752	90
Margaret, Wife of Thomas Kilby	1 Apr. 1739	67
John Kilby	9 Jan. 1749	56
John Lane	30 Nov. 1747	74
Jane, Wife of John Ficketts	10 Feb. 1749	41
Peter Wakefield	28 Apr. 1754	86
William Eldridge, fenior	31 Dec. 1736	81
Mary his Wife	20 Sept. 1741	75
Elizabeth, Wife of John Weekes	23 Dec. 1753	62
Jane, Wife of William Brufh	22 Dec. 1783	40
Michael True	19 May, 1750	51
Sarah Wakefield	2 Apr. 1784	77
Katharine, Wife of William Goodrick	4 Dec. 1779	94
William, Son of John Lane	22 May, 1774	65
Joan, Wife of John Kilby	28 May, 1774	78
William Ayliffe	20 July, 1748	52

CII. DUMBLETON.

 # D U M B L E T O N.

THE Diſtance of this Pariſh, which lies in the Hundred of *Kifteſgate*, from *Eveſham* in *Worceſterſhire*, is ſix Miles on the South, four North from *Winchcombe*, and eighteen North-eaſtward from the City of GLOUCESTER. Two thouſand five Hundred Acres are deſcribed in its Terrier; one fourth only of which is in Tillage, of a ſtrong Clay Soil; and ſingularly fertile, near the Rivulet *Iſbourne*.

The Benefice is rectorial, in the Deanery of *Campden*, charged with 10*s.* a Year to *Trinity College, Oxford*, which is inveſted with certain impropriate Tythes, of the yearly Value of 10*l.*; and with the Remainder and Glebe of eighty Acres, the Vicarage is endowed *.

There are good Reaſons for Conjecture, that the Church, dedicated to *St. Peter*, was erected at the Charge of the Abbey of *Abingdon*, co. *Berks*, in the 13th Century, who bound themſelves to the Repairs of it, an Expence from which the Pariſhioners are ſtill exempted. It conſiſts of a Nave, a low South Aiſle, and a ſepulchral Chapel, projecting as a Semi-tranſept from the North Side, with a maſſive embattled Tower. This Dormitory may have been co-eval with the other Building; it was erected by ROBERT DASTYN, or DASTON. Around the Margins of Slabs are theſe mutilated Inſcriptions, in the *Norman* Language, and partly *Saxon* Character: " ROBERT DASTYN FVNDVR : D . . . . " DEV DEL : ALꟿE EYT ꟿERLI." Upon the other, " ꟿARᴌERIE DASTIN ᴌIST ILL : " DEV : DEL ALꟿE." Such Memorials were not unfrequent as late as the Reigns of the three EDWARDS †. *Jeſus College, Oxford*, as holding the former Property of this Family, is liable to Repairs of this Part only.

King ATHELSTAN ‡, in 931, included this Manor, taxed at ſeven Hides and a Half (750 Acres) in his Charter of Foundation of the Abbey of *Abingdon*, and in 15 EDW. I. 1287, the Abbot proved his Right of free Warren, &c. When that Houſe was diſſolved in 1543, the Manor and Advowſon were granted to THOMAS TOUCHET Lord AUDLEY, and Sir THOMAS POPE, Knight, in Exchange for *Layer Marney*, co. *Eſſex*, but confirmed to the latter two Years afterward. He bequeathed this manerial Eſtate to EDMUND HUTCHINS §, by his Will, dated 1556, the Son of his ſecond Siſter ELIZABETH, who had married RICHARD HUTCHINS, of *Chipping Norton*, co. *Oxford*. Dying without Iſſue he gave it to his Wife DOROTHY, Daughter of THOMAS COCKS, of *Cleeve*, who ſettled it on her Brother CHARLES COCKS and his Heirs in 1646, the Progenitor of the preſent Proprietor. Upon the Demiſe of Sir ROBERT COCKS in 1765, the fourth in Deſcent from RICHARD COCKS, created a Baronet in 1666, it lapſed to the Heir General CHARLES COCKS, of *Caſtle Ditch*, co. *Hereford*, who was created a Baronet Sept. 19, 1772, and a Baron May 7, 1784, 24 GEO. III. by the Title of Lord SOMERS, Baron of EVESHAM.

The Manor-houſe is now partly taken down and refitted as a Farm : it was large and commodious, and the conſtant Reſidence of the Family.

---

* A Portion of Diviſion of the rectorial Tythes of this extenſive Pariſh (together with a Penſion of 10*s.* charged on the Vicarage) formerly belonging to the Abbey of *Abingdon*, was given to *Trinity College, Oxford*, by the Founder Sir THOMAS POPE, about 1557. This Eſtate, as early as the Beginning of the Reign of JAMES I. paid annually to the College 4*l.* 9*s.* in Money-rent, and in Corn-rent five Quarters of Wheat, and one of Malt, with a Fine in Proportion at ſtated Periods. Under CROMWELL's Protectorate, Dr. ROB. HARRIS, the uſurping Preſident of the College, with his Fellows, foreſeeing the uncertainty of their Eſtabliſhment, took an exorbitant Fine for this Eſtate. At the Reſtoration, the re-inſtated Preſident and Fellows applying to the Leſſee for a Renewal, the Caſe was referred to the Lord Chancellor; who was of Opinion, that the College, by the Exorbitancy of their laſt Fine, had ſold out almoſt their whole preſent and reverſionary Intereſt in this Property; and therefore decreed, that the original Fine ſhould be converted into a fixed annual Payment to the College of 1*cl.*; the Penſion of 10*s.* remaining as at firſt. The Claims of this Pariſh, with thoſe of *Compton Parva*, reſpecting the Foundation of *Trinity College*, were erroneouſly ſtated in a Note (p. 421). The Founder recommends only the Natives of his Manors to the Society, pre-ſuppoſing them to poſſeſs the requiſite Qualifications ſpecified in the Statutes. The Preference is therefore conditional, nor has any ſubſequent viſitorial Injunction affected this particular Privilege. We are ever willing to avail ourſelves of Information, or to adopt Corrections when ſo candidly offered; eſpecially if what has been aſſerted can poſſibly convey Prejudice, or give Offence.
See GUTCH, Hiſt. Univ. *Oxon.* p. 523.

† GOUGH's Sep. Mon. Introd. p. cxvii.

‡ TANNER's Not. *Berks*, N° 1. STEVENS's Suppl. vol. I. p. 507. Placit. 15 EDW. I. Quo Warranto de Libertatibus in *Dumbleton*.

§ EDMUND HUTCHINS was one of the Scholars of *Trinity College, Oxford*, appointed by the Founder, and admitted in 1556, æt, 22, which he quitted in 1558. By his Will, dated Jan. 28, 1602, he left to the Society the Advowſon of the Church of *Dumbleton*, and Lands worth 33*l.* 6*s.* 8*d.* a Year, partly to be applied to charitable Uſes, and the Reſidue to them. But his four Siſters and Co-heirs claiming the Premiſſes, the Benefaction was annulled by a Decree in Chancery. Upon a Buttreſs in the College, the following Memorial remains of him cut in the Stone, " 𝕵𝖊𝖘𝖚 𝖍𝖆𝖛𝖊 𝕸 𝕯. 𝕲 𝕳𝖚𝖙𝖈𝖍𝖎𝖓𝖘 ;" i. e. " JESUS have Mercy " on E. HUTCHINS." WARTON's Life of Sir T. POPE, p. 395.

2

Another

Another confiderable Eftate is attributed in *Domefday* Book to WILLIAM GOIZENBODED, which, in the early fucceeding Centuries was transferred to the Family of DASTON. Parcel of this Eftate was purchafed in 1629 by the Executors of Sir THOMAS WYNNE, Knight, and the Principal and Fellows of *Jefus College, Oxford,* were enfeoffed of it, for the Maintenance of one Scholar on their Foundation, and other Purpofes *.

Such is the Hiftory of the Property of this Parifh, which furnifhes no botanical Rarity, nor would enrich with its Productions the Claffes of the Foffilift.

B E N E F A C T I O N S.

JOHN COCKS, Efq. 1723, bequeathed Land, the Yearly Rent of which, now is 23*l.* 4*s.* five of which, to place out fome Boy or Girl Yearly, or at two or three Years, as his Executors fhall think fit; the remaining Part to be diftributed amongft fuch Poor as do not receive Alms.

INCUMBENTS.	PATRONS.	INCUMBENTS.	PATRONS.
To 1543,	Abbey of Abingdon.	1733 William Cockes, B. A.	——————.
1581 Oliver Dafton,	Edmund Hutchins, Efq.	1734 Kynard Baghott, B. A.	Will. Baghott, Efq.
1615 Michael Wallington,	William Dobyns.	1735 Thomas Baghott, M. A.	The fame.
1640 Tho. Wafhbourne, B.D.	——————.	1762 John Baghott De la Bere,	William Baghott De la Bere.
1687 Charles Cockes, M. A.	Sir Ric. Cockes, Bart.		

PRESENT LORD OF THE MANOR,

The Right Honourable CHARLES Lord SOMERS, Baron of EVESHAM.

The only Perfon fummoned from this Parifh by the Heralds in 1682 and 1683, was
Sir Richard Cockes, Bart.

At the Election in 1776 Two Freeholders polled from this Parifh.

ANNUAL ACCOUNT OF MARRIAGES, BIRTHS, AND BURIALS, IN THIS PARISH.

A.D.	Mar.	Bir.	Bur.	A.D.	Mar.	Bir.	Bur.	A.D.	Mar.	Bir.	Bur.	A.D.	Mar.	Bir.	Bur.
1781	2	8	4	1786	1	6	4	1791				1796			
1782	2	11	6	1787	3	6	4	1792				1797			
1783	4	11	4	1788	5	6	4	1793				1798			
1784	—	12	12	1789				1794				1799			
1785	1	7	10	1790				1795				1800			

INSCRIPTIONS IN THE CHURCH,

UNDER AN ARCADE, TWO FIGURES KNEELING,
IN THE DRESS AND STYLE OF THE TIMES.

Arms; On Efcutcheons, quarterly, Or, a Lion rampant Azure, for PERCYE; 2d and 3d, Gules, three Lucies haurient proper, for LUCIE ;—impaling, Sable, a Chevron between three Stags' Attires, Argent for COCKES.

Here lye the Bodies of Sir CHARLES PERCYE, Knt. 3d Son of the Earle of Northumberland, and of Dame DOROTHY his Wife, the Daughter of THOMAS COCKS, of Cleeve, Efq. and of ANNE their Daughter. Sir CHARLES was buried the 9th Day of July, Anno Domini 1628. Dame DOROTHY, the 28th of June, Anno Domini 1646.

ON A HANDSOME MARBLE TABLET;

Arms; COCKES as before.

Memoriæ Sacrum
CAROLI COCKS, Armigeri, Filii quarti
THOMÆ COCKS, de Cleeve, in Agro Glouceftrienfi,
Armigeri, qui obiit decimo quinto die Augufti,
Anno ætatis fuæ octogeffimo tertio,
Annoque Domini MDCLIV.

RICHARDUS COCKS, Baronettus, nepos ejufdem
CAROLI & cui maxima Hereditatis fuæ partem legavit
CAROLUS hoc Monumentum Amoris
& Gratitudinis ergo
extruxit.

---

* WOOD's Antiq. *Oxon.* edit. GUTCH, p. 373.

Upon a large Monument :

Arms ; Cockes ;—impaling, Paly of fix Or and Gules, on a Bend Sable three Mullets of the Field, for Elton.

In Memory of
Sir Richard Cocks, Baronet, and of Dame Susanna his Wife.　He was the fecond Son of Richard Cocks, of Caftle Ditch in the County of Hereford, Efq. and of Judith his Wife,
Daughter and Coheir of John Elliott, Efq.
She was the 5th Daughter of Ambrose Elton, of the Hafle in the County of Hereford, Efq.
and of Anne his Wife, Daughter of
Sir Edward Aston, of Tixall in the County of Stafford.　He, in his younger Days, accompanied his Uncle Christopher Cocks, who was honoured by King James the Firft, with a public Character into Mufcovy ; and after his Return he retired into the Country, and was concerned with no publick Matters, more than the Offices of Juftice of the Peace and High Sheriff.　She was a Lady diftinguifhed by very great Ornaments of Mind and Body ; the vifible Remains of which continued with her to her laft Hour.
They kept good Hofpitality, loved their Tenants and Neighbours, and on all Occafions did them all the Service they could.　He lived peaceably with them, and kept them in Peace one with another.
He was a great Sufferer for his Love to the Royal Family, and for his Zeale for the Laws and Eftablifhed Religion of his Country.
They were indulgent Parents, good to their Servants, and charitable to the Poor.
They gave their Children good Fortunes, and liberal Education.
They had three Sons, Richard, Charles, and John ; and two Daughters, Judith and Elizabeth.
But John the younger, and Elizabeth, the Relict of Sir John Fust, of Hill in this County, Baronet, only furvived them ; fhe, out of a juft Remembrance, and Gratitude to fo good Parents, and believing the Memory of them would be grateful to their Neighbours, ordered her Brother John Cocks to erect this Monument for them.
He died September 16, A. D. 1684, aged 82.
She died March 10, A. D. 1689, aged 84.

Against the South Wall in the Chancel, on a square Marble Tablet :

To the happy Memory of Mrs. Dorothy Cocks.
She died the 29th Day of October, 1714,
in the 58th Year of her Age, and lies interred in the Chancel near the Communion Table.
She was eldeft Child of Richard Cocks, Efq. and of Mary his Wife, the youngeft Daughter of Sir Robert Cooke, of Hynam, by his firft Wife ; her Father and her Mother both died when fhe was about 14 Years old.　She was of a middle Stature, endowed with great Ornaments of Body, and with far greater of the Mind.　She was a Woman of a very good and compaffionate Nature, of a great Underftanding, and made a very good Ufe of it ;
fhe chofe rather to be a Mother to her younger Sifters, than to be engaged in another Family ;
and by her Care and good Inftructions,
fhe helped to breed them up in Piety and Religion,

and other neceffary Knowledge.
Envy itfelf cannot charge her with an unbecoming Action, or Expreffion, in her whole Life.
She was a Woman of great Piety, Patience, and Humanity ; fhe fpent great Part of her Life in her Devotions and Prayers, for herfelf, her Friends, and her Country ; fhe bore a tedious Sicknefs, and other Misfortunes that attended her infirm Body with all Chearfulnefs and Refignation ;
fhe made Ufe of her Time and Fortune, not only to ferve Friends and Relations, but even Strangers that were diftreffed.　Therefore Sir Richard Cocks, her eldeft Brother, out of a grateful Remembrance of thefe Virtues, has chofe rather to fet up this true and juft Epitaph, than a magnificent Monument, with an Intention to make her Family blufh, when they deviate from fuch a Precedent ; and that they and others may imitate her Example in this World, and be happy wirh her in the next.

IN　THE　NAVE.

On a large Marble Monument :

Arms ; Cocks as before ;—impaling, Gules, a Saltire Argent, charged in the Centre with a Rofe of the firft, for Neville.

To the facred Memory of Frances Lady Cocks, dearly and defervedly beloved Wife of Sir Richard Cocks, of Dumbleton in the County of Gloucefter, Bart.　She was the fifth, and youngeft Daughter of Colonel Richard Neville, of Billingfbear in the County of Berks, who was defcended from a younger Son of Lord Abergavenny and of Anne his Wife, one of the Daughters of Sir Christopher Heydon, of Bocanfthrop in the County of Norfolk. She was a Lady endowed with all the Accomplifhments Nature or Education would beftow upon or form in her ; fhe was eminently pious and zealous for the eftablifhed Government and Religion, which was demonftrated by the many Hours fhe daily fpent in her private Devotions, and her conftant Attendance, even to the Hazard of her Health, upon the Service of the Church.　She was an Ornament to the Honourable Family from which fhe defcended, and was efteemed an Honour and a Bleffing to the Family fhe came into.　She was an obliging good Neighbour to the Rich, charitable to the Poor, the kindeft Miftrefs, and the beft of Wives.　She lived more than 35 Years in Praife, Harmony, and Tranquillity with her Hufband, as far as human Imbecillities common to the beft of Mortals would permit ; fhe continued, in defpight of, and the Infirmities incident to, Mortality, chearful and comely to the laft Minute of her Life.　She died, after a fhort Indifpofition, of a Fever, and upon a Cold, the 1ft of Feb. Anno Dom. 1723, in the fixtieth Year of her Age.　Her Hufband therefore expreffeth his Gratitude to Heaven for his folong enjoying fo great a Bleffing and Comfort; and leaft the Remembrance of her fhould perifh with the Memory of this Generation, to perpetuate, as far as in him lies, the Virtues of fo excellent a Perfon, has ordered this Monument to be erected.

On

ON A NEAT TABLET OF WAITE MARBLE :

In Memory of Sir ROBERT COCKS, Bart.
who, after fuftaining with Chriftian Fortitude
and Refignation, the moft affecting Lofs of
an amiable Wife and three Children
in the courfe of a few Days, by a cruel
Diftemper which attaked his Family,
had the Misfortune to lofe his own
Life, by a Fall from his Horfe in April 1765,
and lies buried near this Place.

IN THE SOUTH AISLE.

ON A MARBLE MONUMENT, WITH ELEGANT
SCULPTURE AND DEVICES :

ELIZABETH,
Wife of Sir ROBERT COCKS, Bart.
and Daughter of JAMES CHOLMELEY, Efq.
of Eafton in the County of Lincoln,
with three of her Children,
CHARLES, ANN, and CATHERINE,
were carried fucceffively, by the fame fatal Sicknefs,
a Fever and a fore Throat,
to the Grave
in a few Days.
A moft excellent and amiable Mother,
the two youngeft in the brighteft Dawn of Hope,
the eldeft in the fweeteft Bloom of Virtue,
growing up like the faireft Flowers,
like the faireft Flowers
were cut down.
This Place where they fleep
is marked out by the unfeigned Grief of a Hufband,
mixed with the Tears and unflattering
Praife of furviving Friends,
unhappy in being Survivors,
unlefs they tread in the fame blamelefs Steps ;
happy could they, by keeping her in Remembrance,
reach the fame fhining Heights
of Lovelinefs, Virtue, and Religion.

CHARLES,	died Jan. 21, aged	3	Years,
ANNE,	Jan. 28,	8,	
ELIZABETH,	Jan. 30,	39,	
CATHERINE,	Feb. 7,	16,	
	A. D. 1749.		

Alfo three other Children,

CHUBB,	died April 3, 1735, aged	1 Year 8 Mo.
ELIZABETH,	July 2, 1738,	9 Months.
ROBERT,	Sept. 27, 1740,	10 Years.

ON ANOTHER ELEGANT MARBLE MONUMENT :

Arms ; COCKS as before.

To the Memory of
Mifs DOROTHY COCKS,
the youngeft and only furviving Child
of Sir ROBERT COCKS, of Dumbleton, Bart.
who died, April 24, 1767, aged 18 Years,
much lamented by all who knew her ;
A fair Flower
cut off in the Bloffom of Life,
amiable in her Perfon,
fenfible and prudent in all her Actions,
untainted with the Follies
and Difipation of the Age
in which fhe lived.
This little Monument, in Teftimony
of her great Love and Affection,
is erected by her Aunt
Mrs. SARAH COCKS.

ON FLAT STONES IN THE NAVE.

Here lieth the Body of
ANTHONY, the Son of ANTHONY BEST, Gent.
He lived in the Parifh of St. Clement, London,
and laid here to reft, in Hope of a joyful
Refurrection.
A Man faithful to his Friend,
and loving to the Poor.
He gave to this Parifh twenty Pounds at his Death.
He was buried the 14th of Sept. 1687,
ætatis fuæ 41.

Mr. ANTHONY BEST the elder
departed this Life the laft Day of Auguft,
in the Year 1685, ætat. fuæ 75.

Alfo ANNE his Wife
died Jan. 15, 1699.

In Memory of Mrs. ELIZABETH KEEN,
who was twenty Years Houfekeeper to
Sir ROBERT COCKS, Baronet.
She departed this Life June 11, 1753,
aged 51 Years.

IN THE NORTH AISLE.

ON A FLAT STONE WERE THE FIGURES OF A MAN
AND WOMAN IN BRASS, AND AT THEIR FEET THIS
INSCRIPTION ; ALL OF WHICH ARE NOW ENTIRELY
DEMOLISHED :

Orate p' a'i'bus Will'i Dafton, filii Joh'is Dafton
et Annæ uxoris ejus, qui quidem Will'us, obiit
Anno Domini Mill'imo CCCCC°XIII°. quor'
a'i'ab' p'picietur Deus.

IN THE CHURCH YARD, ON TOMBS.

John Inglis
died . . . . . 1647.

John State, Yeoman,
died Aug. 1, 1728, aged 59.

Ann his Wife
died Jan. 6, 1721-2, aged 44.

John Agge
died April 8, 1705, aged 62.

John his Son, by Sarah his Wife,
was buried Dec. 11, 1677, aged 8 Months.

Sarah, Wife of John Agge,
died May 7, 1729, aged 77.

Hannah, Wife of Job Stock,
died May 17, 1730, aged 39.

O N   H E A D   S T O N E S.

	Died	Aged
Mary, Wife of John Timbrell	20 Sept. 1776	89
John Timbrell	15 Dec. 1780	80
Mary, Daughter of John and Mary Cowles	20 Feb. 1757	40
Mary, Wife of John Field	14 Feb. 1773	72
Richard James	3 Aug. 1775	67
Mary, Wife of Robert Staite	5 Sept. 1779	46
Thomas Pilman	8 Nov. 1720	63
Elizabeth his Wife	30 Aug. 1771	79
Richard Dobbins	18 May, 1784	53
John Harris	18 Sept. 1782	85
Mary, Wife of James Dunn	6 Sept. 1763	49
Joseph Wheeler	2 Dec. 1752	85
Mary his Wife	8 —— 1747	77
Richard Baker	9 Mar. 1742	65
John Andrews	5 July, 1744	81
Elizabeth his Wife	25 Mar. 1729	54
David Phillips	22 Dec. 1766	37
Francis Dunn	15 Feb. 1776	89
James Dunn	18 Feb. 1784	64
Elizabeth, Wife of Richard James	16 Oct. 1745	31
Richard James	3 Aug. 1775	67
John his Son	2 July, 1774	36
Edward Foort	10 June, 1750	47
Elizabeth, Wife of Edward Clayton	4 Sept. 1729	36
Henry Clayton	27 Jan. 1743	52
Ann his Wife	1 Dec. 1753	62
Sarah, Wife of John Cullabine	13 Mar. 1754	40
John Cullabine	8 June, 1782	67
Mary, Wife of John Baylis	15 Feb. 1781	30

CIII.

CIII. DUNTESBORNE ABBATIS,

OR

UPPER DUNTESBORNE,

A PARISH fituate on the South-weft fide of the *Irmin-ftreet*, or *Fofs* Road, from *Cirencefter* to Gloucester, from which it is diftant twelve Miles South-eaftward, and from the former Place five, in the precifely oppofite Direction. The Soil is chiefly light, and in Tillage, by a proportion of three-fourths; of confiderable Extent, and divided between the Hundreds of *Crowthorne* and *Minety*, and *Rapfgate*.

Of the Benefice, a Rectory in the Deanery of *Cirencefter*; the Advowfon originally annexed to the Manor, is faid to have been obtained from the Crown by Esme Stuart, Duke of *Richmond*, in 1611, 8 James I; but it does not appear, that he prefented. From the Family of Estcourt, and others, who have been Patrons fince 1583, it was transferred to the laft, and is now vefted in the Family of the prefent Incumbent *.

The Church, dedicated to *St. Peter* (the Tutelar of its Patron Monaftery at Gloucester), is an inconfiderable Structure, with a low flated Tower at the Weft end. It is a Member of the Deanery of *Cirencefter*.

When *Domefday* was compiled, a noble Houfe of the *Normans* held the greater Divifion of *Duntefborne*, but various Property is fpecified, and in divers Portions. The Vill and Manerial Rights, confifting of 5 Hides (nearly 600 cultivated Acres), were granted to the Abbey of *St. Peter* in Gloucester, by Emmeline, Relict of Walter de Laci, upon his fudden Death in 1085; and, in 1100, Gilbert de Eskotte added other Lands. Thefe Eftates were purchafed out of the Court of Augmentations in 1558, 1 Eliz. by William Morgan and James Dolle, in the Defcendants of which laft they remained, to Oliver Dolle in 1660, though with confiderable diminutions. The Family of Pleydell, of Coleshill, co. *Berks*, long after their Poffeffion of other Eftates in this Parifh, purchafed the Manor. Sir Mark Stuart Pleydell, Baronet, about thirty Years fince built a Houfe, on a fingular Plan, on an Eminence in this Parifh, which he felected for the very beautiful rural Scenery which it prefents; and to which he frequently retired. Upon his Death, in 1770, he devifed this Manor and Eftate to the prefent Earl of Radnor, Son of William Bouverie, Vifcount *Folkeftone* (created Earl of *Radnor* Oct. 31, 1765, 5 Geo. III.), by Harriot his Wife, fole Daughter and Heir, then deceafed. One Hide, given by Richard Murdac, in 1499, to the Priory of *Llanthoni*, paffed in 1544, to Richard Andrews and Richard Temple †.

The only Hamlet is *Duntefborne Lear*, or *de Lyra*, which is a part of the Hundred of *Rapfgate*, held at the Conqueft by the Abbey of *Lyra*, in *Normandy* ‡, and transferred at the Suppreffion of Alien Priories, to the *Auguftine's* of *Cirencefter* in 1416, 2 Hen. V. In 1575, 17 Eliz. it was bought by John Pleydell, of *Wefton*, co. *Berks*, and is now incorporated with the Manerial Eftate. It was anciently recorded as a feparate Manor, and included *Nutbean Farm*.

Other Property, exclufive of the principal, is vefted in the Families of Chapman, Field, and Harding.

BENEFACTIONS.

Thomas Muggleton, 1659, gave by Will a Freehold Pafture Ground in this Parifh, now let at 4l. 4s. per Annum, to be given to the Poor of the Parifh of *Dunfborne Abbotts*, *Miferden*, *Winfton*, and *Side*, in the following Proportions, viz. 15s. per Annum to each of the four Parifhes, and the produce of a Coppice Wood growing thereon (cut every 14 Years); after all Expences are difcharged, to be divided between the four Parifhes, deducting 15s. for Repairs, 5s. being paid to the Overfeers of *Dunfborne Abbotts* for their Trouble.

William Harding, 1785, by Will gave Twenty Pounds, the Intereft thereof for inftructing as many Poor Children as the Officers think proper.

A School Houfe has alfo been built by the Parifhioners.

---

* The whole Parifh, though once vefted in the Church, is fubject to Tythes ; and the Feaft, or Refection, formerly given by the Rector to his Parifhioners on Palm Sunday, was commuted for 20s. to be diftributed amongft the Poor, with confent of the Diocefan, in 1681.

† Dugdale's Monaft. vol. II. p. 72.

‡ Ibid. vol. II. p. 985.

6 Q

523

Incumbents.	Patrons.	Incumbents.	Patrons.
1541 ——————,	Abbey of Gloucester.	1620 William Poole,	The fame.
1573 James Ballard,	Bifhop of Gloucester.	1661 Thomas Phipps,	Wm. Morfe and J. Lord.
1575 Hugh Humphrys,	Anthony Herbert.	1714 William Phipps,	Jofeph Jones, Gent.
1583 Thomas Knight,	Thomas Eftcourt, Efq.	1733 Tho. Davies, B. A.	Edmund Davies, Gent.
1594 Giles Dymoke,	The fame.	1772 Jof. Chapman, B. A.	James Clutterbuck, Efq.
1613 Thomas Cole,	Sir Thomas Eftcourt.		

Present Lord of the Manor of *Duntefborne Abbatis* and *De Lyra*.

The Right Honourable Jacob Pleydell Bouverie Earl of Radnor.

The Perfons fummoned from this Place by the Heralds in 1682 and 1683 were,

William Phipps, Rector, and Oliver Dolle, Gent.

At the Election in 1776, Fourteen Freeholders polled from this Parifh, and the Hamlet of *Duntefborne Lear*.

The oldeft Regifter bears Date 1683.

Annual Account of Marriages, Births, and Burials, in this Parish.

A.D.	Mar.	Bir.	Bur.	A.D.	Mar.	Bir.	Bur.	A.D.	Mar.	Bir.	Bur.	A.D.	Mar.	Bir.	Bur.
1781	2	7	2	1786	2	8	5	1791				1796			
1782	2	17	2	1787	1	9	8	1792				1797			
1783	2	8	4	1788	—	12	7	1793				1798			
1784	1	13	5	1789				1794				1799			
1785	3	9	14	1790				1795				1800			

I N S C R I P T I O N S   I N   T H E   C H U R C H.

ON FLAT STONES IN THE CHANCEL.

In Memoriam
Mariæ uxoris Thomæ Phipps,
Rectoris hujus Ecclefiæ, quæ
fepulta fuit decimo die Januarii,
Anno Salutis 1694.

Mr. William Phipps,
Rector of this Church,
was buried Dec. 17, 1732, aged 71.

Ann, the Daughter of

John Partridge,

and Wife of

Thomas Phipps,

Rector of this Church,

was here buried

. . . .

Here refteth the Body of
Oliver Dolle, Gentleman,
who departed this Life
the 2d Day of September,
Anno Domini 1660.

Here lieth the Body of
Anne, the Wife of Thomas Limbrick.
She died the 15th Day of April, 1754,
aged 82.

I N   T H E   C H U R C H   Y A R D.

Against the Porch:

Beneath this Place lieth Anthony Sly,
of this Parifh.
He died the 9th Day of July, 1736,
aged 93 Years.

On a Tomb:

William Freeman, of this Parifh,
died March 13, 1769, aged 69.

Mary his Wife
died Oct. 9, 1765, aged 56.

O N   F L A T   A N D   H E A D   S T O N E S.

	Died	Aged		Died	Aged
Jofeph Sayer, fenior, of Dunfborn Roufe - -	1 June, 1729	43	William Beams -	23 Jan. 1780	49
Jofeph Sayer, junior, -	14 June, 1729	18	John, Son of John and Mary Tayler	3 July, 1763	39
Joan, Wife of Jofeph Sayer	6 May, 1720	—	Sarah, Wife of James Hobbs	21 Mar. 1761	40
Richard, Son of William and Mary Freeman - -	6 Dec. 1748	7	John, Son of Thomas and Mary Harding - -	6 July, 1715	27
Thomas Field, - -	5 Aug. 1765	36	Thomas Harding -	10 Jan. 1753	67
John Field - -	24 Oct. 1751	57	Mary his Wife -	28 May, 1774	88
William Field - -	— June, 1775	60	William Harding -	30 June, 1785	64
Edward Field -	— Aug. 1778	58	Thomas, the firft Son of Thomas and Mary Harding	18 May, 1755	88
Thomas Field - -	7 July, 1744	47	Mary, Wife of Anthony Sly	29 Jan. 1732	70
Henry Field, fourth Son of Thomas and Ann Field	15 Dec. 1724	27	Mary, Wife of John Hill -	22 Jan. 1733	71
Mary, Wife of Thomas Clark, and Daughter of Edward and Sarah Dolle - -	17 Jan. 1737	28	Elizabeth, Wife of William Paifh	3 June, 1743	47
Mary, Wife of John Tayler -	9 June, 1763	70	Sarah, Wife of William Eldridge	8 Feb. 1746	56
			Thomas Truftum -	27 July, 1690	—
			Elianor, Wife of Thomas Truftum	10 Oct. 1730	53
			Jeremiah Griffith -	— —— 1729	—

CIV. DUNTESBORNE

CIV. DUNTESBORNE MILITIS RUFI,
OR
L E R O U S.

IT was cuftomary, with the *Norman* Followers of the Conqueror, to apply their Surnames from any Perfonal Singularity; and amongft many other Inftances, Rufus, Blondus, and Nigellus, were the Progenitors of the modern Families of Rous, Blount, and Neale. The former were the early Pofleffors of this Parifh, called likewife *Lower Duntefborne*, with a Reference to its Situation on the Bourn or Rivulet, and its Vicinity to *Cirencefter*, about four Miles on the North-eaft. It lies in the Hundred of *Crowthorne* and *Minety*, of a light Soil moftly tilled, forming a Terrier of 1800 Acres, one Hundred of which are Woodland.

The Living, which is a Rectory in the Deanery of *Cirencefter*, is charged with the annual Payment of a Mark to the Crown; formerly due to the Knights Hofpitallers of *St. John* of *Jerufalem*, who were Patrons. It is evident that the Advowfon was detached from the Manor, as we find it purchafed by Dr. Robert Morwent, the fecond Prefident of *Corpus Chrifti College Oxford*, who, on his Demife in 1557, bequeathed it to that Society.

In the Church, dedicated to *St. Michael*, nothing occurs worthy notice. The dimenfions are very fmall. Under the Chancel is an Arched Vault communicating with the Church, probably not fepulchral, but ufed in certain Ceremonies of the Romifh Worfhip.

King William, foon after the Conqueft, gave this Manor to his Coufin William de Owe, afterward to John Rufus Miles, or Le Rous, the laft of whofe race was attainted for Rebellion with John Giffard, Baron of *Brimpsfield*, in 1322, and his Lands confifcated. By the Family of Mull, or Milles, it was likewife forfeited for their Attachment to the *Lancaftrian* Caufe, and granted by Edward IV. in 1465, to Thomas Herbert; and, in 1474 to Sir Richard Beauchamp. Dr. Richard Fox, Bifhop of *Winton*, obtaining this Manor, fettled it upon *Corpus ChriftiCollege Oxford*, by his Charter of Foundation in 1517, who have been the fubfequent Proprietors.

The Ancient Manor and Park of *Pinbury*, chiefly in this Parifh, was given by the Conqueror to the Nuns of *Caen**, in *Normandy*, and then taxed at five Hides. In 1416, 2 Hen. V. it was transferred, with *Minchin-Hampton*, and *Avening*, parcel of the fame Eftate, to the Nunnery of *Syon*, in *Middlefex* who had a Cell here; and upon the general Suppreffion, granted in 1543 to Andrew Lord Windsor, in exchange for *Stanwell*, co. *Middlefex*. It next paffed by Purchafe to Sir Henry Poole, of *Saperton*, in 1600; from that Family to Sir Robert Atkyns, fen. (1660), whofe Son Sir Robert built the prefent dilapidated Manfion Houfe, and made it his refidence till the Death of his Father in 1709. Edward Atkyns, Efq. of *Eaft Sheen*, co. *Surrey*, the Heir-general, fold this Manor and Eftate in 1786 to the Right Honourable Henry Bathurst, Lord Apsley. The Site confifts of deep Glens, through which is the winding Courfe of the Rivulet *Froome*, pleafingly diverfified with Beech Woods.

Part of Earl Bathurst's Eftate at *Oakley* is within the Boundary of this Parifh.

No Benefactions to the Poor.

Incumbents.	Patrons.	Incumbents.	Patrons.
1537 Robert Morwent, B. D. †	———————	1679 James Seffions, B. D.	Corpus Chr. Col. Oxford.
1558 Richard Woodward, B. D.	Corpus Chr. Col. Oxford.	1695 Jofias Dockwray, B. D.	The fame.
1561 William Bocher, B. D. ‡	The fame.	1738 William Marfhall, M. A.	The fame.
* * * * * * * *	* * * * *	1745 Edward Ford, B. D.	The fame.
1623 John Hampton, B. D.	The fame.	1762 Thomas Pettener, M. A.	The fame.
1654 William Symmes, B. D.	The fame.	1771 William Finden, B. D.	The fame.

" * *Caen* is the Capital of Lower *Normandy*, in the Diocefe of *Bayeaux*, in which City are two famous *Benedictine* Abbies, one
" for Monks, and the other for Nuns. The Nunnery of the *Holy Trinity* was founded about the Year, 1064, by Matilda,
" Wife of William the Conqueror, where her Monument remains at this Day."
   Kelham's *Domefday*, p. 57. Tanner's Not. Mon. *Middlefex*, N° VII. Dugdale's Monaft. vol. II. p. 958.
† Wood's Fafti *Oxon.* Vol. I. p. 661. Antiq. Univ. *Oxon.* edit Gutch; p. 395.
‡ William Bocher, B. D. Prefident of *Corpus Chrifti College*, 1561, which he foon after quitted, being " in animo Catho-
" licus;" and, retiring to his fmall cure at *Duntfborne Militis*, near *Cirencefter*, in *Gloucefterfhire*, lived there obfcurely many Years.
At length giving way to Fate, was buried in the Church there, Nov. 1, 1585." Wood's Fafti, Vol. I. p. 717, and Antiq. Univ.
Oxon. p. 396. Edit. Gutch.

Present

DUNTESBORNE MILITIS RUFI.

PRESENT PROPRIETORS OF THE MANORS,

Of *Duntesborne,*

The Prefident, Fellows, and Scholars of *Corpus Chrifti College, Oxford.*

Of *Pinbury,*

The Right Honourable HENRY Lord APSLEY.

The only Perfon fummoned by the Heralds, in 1682 and 1683, was
Thomas King, Gent.

It does not appear that any Perfon polled from this Parifh at the Election in 1776.

The earlieft Date in the Regifter occurs in 1545.

ANNUAL ACCOUNT OF MARRIAGES, BIRTHS, AND BURIALS, IN THIS PARISH.

A.D.	Mar.	Bir.	Bur.	A.D.	Mar.	Bir.	Bur.	A.D.	Mar.	Bir.	Bur.	A.D.	Mar.	Bir.	Bur.
1781	—	3	2	1786	—	1	2	1791				1796			
1782	—	1	2	1787	2	—	1	1792				1797			
1783	—	1	2	1788	1	5	3	1793				1798			
1784	—	1	3	1789				1794				1799			
1785	2	5	3	1790				1795				1800			

INSCRIPTIONS IN THE CHURCH.

ON FLAT STONES IN THE CHANCEL.

JACOBUS SESSIONS,
Hujus Ecclefiæ Rector,
infra jacet fepultus.
Obiit Augufti XXVI.
Anno Domini 1695.
A cœna Domini
ad cœnam Agni.

Filius natu minor
JACOBI & ELIZ. SESSIONS,
Natus fuit tertio,
Denatus 10 Sept. 1687.

Gloria Deo opt. max.
qui repetit
Animam JOSIÆ Filii natu max.
JOSIÆ DOCKWRAY,
VII. Id. Nov.

Anno { Ætatis fuæ 12. { Salutis 1709.

Prope jacent offa REBECCÆ Matris,
co juventis
Depofita VI. Julii, 1700.

ON A BRASS PLATE AGAINST THE SOUTH WALL IN THE CHANCEL:

Underneath are the
Remains of the
Rev. THOMAS PETTENER,
formerly Fellow of
Chrifti College, Oxon,
and late Rector of this Parifh,
who departed this Life
the 20th Day of April, 1771,
in the 37th Year of his Age.

IN THE CHURCH YARD, ON TOMBS.

JOHN JEFFERIS, of Dunfburne,
deceafed the 12th Day of Sept. 1611
(this JOHN JEFFERIS, deceafed was the
youngeft Son of his Father,
RICHARD JEFFERIS, of Dunfburne).

By ELIZABETH his Wife he had eight
Children; four Sons and four Daughters.

JOHN,	ELIZABETH,
GEORGE,	ANNE,
THOMAS,	SUSANNA,
JOHN,	ELIZABETH.

THOMAS, youngeft Son of
THOMAS JEFFERIS, Gent.
died February 10, Anno Domini 1696.

MARGARET, firft Wife of
THOMAS JEFFERIS, Gent.
fecondly, the Wife of
WILLIAM MARSHALL, Gent.
died Jan. 7, 1722, aged 75.

CATHARINE JEFFERIS,
Daughter of RICHARD JEFFERIS,
departed this Life the .. Day of
Dec. 1680.

ANN, Widow of PAUL JEFFERIS,
was buried May 16, 1682.

RICHARD HOWES
died June 29, 1695.

ANN his Wife
died May 12, 1696.

MARY, Wife of JOHN HAYNES,
of this Parifh, Yeoman,
died the 12th Day of Oct. 1724, aged 27.

RICHARD, Son of
JOHN HAYNES, Yeoman,
was buried Dec. 1, 1724, aged 3 Months.

ELIZABETH, fecond Wife of
JOHN HAYNES, of this Parifh, Yeoman,
deceafed the 8th Day of Auguft, 1760,
aged 66 Years.

M. S.
EDVARDI FORD, S. T. B.
C. C. C. apud Oxonienfes, nuper foc.
huic tandem Ecclefiæ præefle.
Evocati.
Qualis erat,
In excolendis Tyronum ingeniis
Publica apud Virginienfes ichola
Teftatur fatis;
nec laus fuæ
In alumnis Domi inftituendis
apud omnes præcipuè Academicos
Vigeat minus.
Tam defideratiffimo marito ac parenti
Voluit hocce faxum infcribi
Mœrens vidua.
Obiit 9 Octobris die, 1761,
ætat. 45.

ELIZABETH his Wife
was alfo buried near him
Dec. 19, 1763.

ON FLAT AND HEAD STONES.

	Died	Aged
Richard Howes -	22 Dec. 1724	79
Richard Smart, Efq. -	20 Feb. 1776	67
John Cox - -	29 Jan. 1746	82
Thomas Tombs -	11 Mar. 1733	51
Thomas Tombs -	21 June, 1780	69
Giles Tombs, junior -	— Jan. 1715	—
Mary, Wife of William Tombs	25 Dec. 1740	34
Stephen Price - -	12 July, 1736	33
Catharine his Wife -	8 May, 1736	30
Thomas Howes, Yeoman -	14 Apr. 1709	91
Anne, Wife of Thomas Howes, Yeoman - -	21 Dec. 1718	91
Giles Haynes - -	— Sept. 1708	—
Mary his Wife -	— May, 1680	—

4

CV.   D U R S L E Y;

C ONCERNING which, the following very minute and authentic Account is given in the Collecti
ons of JOHN SMYTH, Efq. preferved amongft the Archives in *Berkeley Caftle*:

“ *Durfeley*, in *Domefdei* Book written *Derfilege*, and foone after *Dureflega*; wherein WILLIAM the
“ CONQUEROR had three Hides of Land in Demefne, as that Booke fhewethe, which with one other Hide
“ of Land, the old Inheritance of the *Berkeleis*, were late the Inheritance of Sir THOMAS ESTCOURTE,
“ Knight, who dyed without Iffue in 22 Jac. Regis, and nowe of THOMAS ESTCOURTE, Efquior, Son
“ of EDMOND, Brother of the faid Sir THOMAS, all holden of the Kinge, by Tenure of Knightes Ser-
“ vice in *Capite*. The Name of this ancient Towne, I conceive to come from the Britifh Word *Dwr*,
“ which fignifieth Water, which plentifully arifeth by, and runneth through the fame; and the *Saxon*
“ Word LÉEÆ, LELE, or LEY, which, being all one, doe fometimes fignifie Water, and fometimes
“ Place; the Water running through this Towne, is at this Day *Ewelme*. The Towne gives Name to
“ one of the Deaneries of this County, wherein are the Churches of *Berkelei*, of *Slymbridge*, of *Couley*,
“ of *Camme*, of *Frampton*, of *Durfeley*, of *Iweley*, of *Newinton*, of *Beverflon*, and of *Wotton*; as by
“ the ancient Roll of Taxation, in 20 EDW. I. in the Tower of *London* appeareth. The Rectory of
“ *Durfeley* is accompted the Corps or Body of the Arch Deaconry of this County of GLOUCESTER, and
“ is of Cuftom and Right the Incumbency of him, that is, for the Time “ Oculus Epifcopi,” the Arch-
“ Deacon, which is at this time HUGH ROBINSON, Doctor in Divinitie.

“ The forefaid Hide of Lande was the old Habitation of the ancient Familie of the BERKELIES,
“ called of DURSELEY *, in a Caftle by them built, before the Conqueft (the ruins whereof are now fruite-
“ full, with Barley and Wode there growinge), and they afterward alfoe held from EDWARDE CONFESSOR,
“ and from WILLIAM the CONQUEROR, and from his two Sons WILLIAM RUFUS and HENRIE I, and
“ alfoe halfe the Raigne of K. STEPHEN : the firft mentioned three hides in *Domefdei* Booke, with the
“ whole Manor of *Berkelai* (in effect) and all *Berkeley Herneffe*, whereof *Durfley* was an Hamlet or
“ Parcell (of thofe Kings) in Fee Farme, at the Yearlie Rent of 500*l*. 17*s*. 2*d*. as the great Roll of the
“ Pipe, in the firft Yeere of the Raigne of K. HENRY II. doth fhew. The firft of which Family,
“ whofe Name I can certainlie faften upon, is ROGER BERKELEI, mentioned in the faid Book of *Do-*
“ *mefdei*, who alfo lived in the Reign of EDWARD CONFESSOR, and was Father of WILLIAM BERKELEY,
“ who, in the Rign of K. HENRY I. founded the Abbey of *Kingfwood*, by *Wotton Under Edge*, in that
“ time, and after, called the Manor of *Acholt*; as, amongft many other Proofes, the confirmation of K.
“ HENRY the fecond made in the eleventh Year of his Raigne to the Abbott of that Monaftery, for ten
“ Marks Fine, fpeaketh, fpecified in the great Pipe Roll in the Exchequer for that Yeare. Which
“ WILLIAM BERKELEY was father of ROGER BERKELEY, who lived in the time of K. STEPHEN ; who,
“ by HAVISIA his Wife, was Father of ROBERT; who, by HELENA his Wife, Daughter of the Lord
“ ROBERT Sonne of HARDING, firft Lord of BERKELEY, had from her Father's Gift the Manor of
“ *Durfley*, in Fee Simple, for her Marriage Portion. Between whom was Iffue ROGER ; who, by
“ HAVISIA his firft Wife, had Iffue, HENRY; which HENRY, by AGNES his Wife, had Iffue, JOHN;
“ which JOHN, by SIBELL his Wife, had Iffue HENRY; which HENRY, by JOANE his Wife, had Iffue
“ WILLIAM, JOHN, and HENRY; which WILLIAM and JOHN, dying without Iffue, left the Manor to
“ defcend upon the faid HENRY their Brother; which HENRY had Iffue JOHN, who, by HAVISIA his
“ Wife, left Iffue, NICHOLAS and MAUD. Which NICHOLAS marryed CICELEY, Sifter and Heire of
“ Sir JOHN DE LA MORE of *Bitton*, but died without Iffue, 6 RICH. II. 1382; whereby this Manor de-
“ fcended to the faid MAUD his Sifter, who was married to ROBERT DE CANTILUPO, and died in the 4th
“ HENRY IV. by whom fhe left Iffue ROBERT, who died in 14 . . , leaving Iffue ELIZABETH, his
“ only Daughter and Heire, married to RICHARD CHEDDER; which RICHARD and ELIZABETH his Wife
“ were they who, in 13 HENRY IV. fold by a Fine then levyed, the Advowfon of the faid Abbey of

* *Dereflega* alias *Drifelega*. It was once in the Foreft (of *Kingfwood*) a Quarry of Tophe Stone by *Drifalege*, whereof much
of the Caftell was builded   Part of *Drifeley* Caftell brought to make the new Houfe at *Dodington*. LELAND's Itin. V. 6. f. 75.
“ *Dourfeley* is a praty clothinge Town, ftanding on a Pece of the clyving of a Hill, priveleged at 9 Yeres fins with a Market;
ther is in the Townes felf a goodlie Springe, and is as the principal Hedd of the Brooke, fervynge the Tukking Mills about the
Towne. The Water refortith into *Severne*, that is about four Myles of, touching by the way fume other villagis. This Towne
hadd a Caftell in it fum tyme longynge to the BERKELEY's, fins to the WIKYS, fins fell to Decay; and is clene taken downe. It
had a metelie good Ditch about yt, and was for the moft Parte, made of towfe Stone, full of Pores and Holes lyke a Punice.
There is a Quary of this Stone about *Dourfley*, and it will laft very longe.” LELAND's Itin. V. 7, p. 2, f. 73.
This Species of Stone is called “ *Tophus*,” by Foffilifts, and, for its fpecific Lightnefs and extreme durability, was frequently
ufed in vaulting Cielings, fet between the Ribs of the fpringing Arches. The High Choir of the Cathedral at GLOUCESTER is
a fine Specimen of this application of it. It is noticed in HARRISON's Introduction to HOLINSHED's Hiftory of *England*, p. 114.
In *Durfeley* and the adjacent Parifhes thefe Foffils are to be difcovered: “ Nautili, Ammonoidæ, Cochleæ, and Belemnites.
“ Likewife Oftracites, Mytili, and Pinnæ Marinæ, befide Afteriæ Columnaris, found in fome of the running Streams, but rather
“ fcarce. With petrified Wood, and Impreffions of Leaves, particularly in the Toph Stone.”

6 R

“ Kingswood

D U R S L E Y.

TOMB,
IN DURSLEY CHURCH.

" *Kingswood* to Thomas, then Lord Berkeley, the fourth of that Name; whereof William Berke-
" ley, in the time of K. Henry I. was Founder.   After the Death of which Richard Chedder and
" Elizabeth, in the time of Kinge Henry VI. the Manor of *Dursley* came to Thomas Wike alias
" Wekys, in 1464, leaving Issue John Wekys, who died in the 1 Hen. VII. and was Father of
" Edmund Wykes, who died in the 6th of Henry VIII. Father of Nicholas Wykes, who died 4th
" Phil. and Mar. whose Sonne John Wykes died in the Life-time of his Father, leaving Issue
" Robert Wykes, who, in the 9th of Elizabeth, sold the Manor of *Dursley*, to Richard
" Byrde and his Heires; and he shortlie after to Edmond Woolworth alias Webbe, who died,
" leaving Issue, William; who, in 9 Eliz. sold the same to Thomas Escourte, Esq. who died in
" — Eliz. leaving Issue, Sir Thomas Estcourte, Knt. who, dying in 22 James I. left the same to
" Thomas Escourte, his Brother Edmond's Sonne, as is aforesaid.   Howbeit, Richard Webbe alias
" Woolworth, Son and Heir of the said William, to this Day receiveth 20*l.* per Ann out of the
" Manor for his Life, from the Heir of the said Richard Bird.

" It can not be unpleasinge to *you*, delighting in such reverend Antiquities, to reade out of that vene-
" rable Booke, called the red Booke, in the Office of Kinge's Remembrancer in the Exchequer; the
" Certificate of the said Roger Berkeley, made to K. Henry II. in the 13th Yeere of his Raigne; in
" the original wordes thus, " Carta Rogeride Berkelay." Sciat Dñs Rex quod habeo duos Milites
" & Dimid. Feofatos de veteri Feofamento, unde Hugo de Planca tenet dimidiam Hidam. Et de istis
" integrum militem habetis ad dimid. faciend. Tenent. viz. Radulphus de Ywelege dimid. hidam;
" Fæmina Radulphi Canteleni dimid. hidam. Rogerus de Alba Maria unam Virgatam; Simon
" de Couelege unam Virgatam; et sic habetis dimid. militem. Ad alterum Militem faciend. Walte-
" rus de Holcombe tenet tres hidas & dimid. Reginaldus de Alba Mara tres hidas. Et ita tenent
" isti tres decem Hidas, unde nolunt michi facere Servicium, nisi de tribus virgatis scil. unusquisque de
" una virgatâ. Et ita habetis duos Milites & dimid. Feodatos, & nullum habes Feofatum de novo, de
" meo tempore. Si vobis in antea de Dominio meo placet audire. In manerio meo de *Coberley*, habeo
" Feodum duorum Militum; apud *Stanley* Feodum unus Militis cum unâ hidâ de *Chedrington*. In *New-*
" *inton* habeo Feodum unius Militis. In *Dureslege* unam hidam; *Osleword* dimid. hidam. In *Dockingiune*
" tres hidas & dimid. In *Slimbrugge* tres hidas, quas Ego assensû vestro, dedi Mauricio filio Roberti,
" unde nullum habeo Servicium. *Kingeswodum* tenent *Albi Monachi* ex dono Wil'li de Berkelai,
" unde vobis integrum Militem facio; quare ipsi michi nullum servicium reddere volunt*." Thus that
" Certificate. And upon his Hide of Land in *Dursley*, doubtless was his dwelling Place in his Castell,
" ancientlie bnilt thereon; which was an olde Freehold of itselfe, and not Parcell of the Manor, either
" of *Berkeley*, or *Dursley*.

" An ancient Booke of Knightes Fees in the time of Edw. 1. in the Exchequer, with the Remembran-
" cer to the Lord Treasurer, thus " Henricus de Berkelay tenet *Durselege* & *Newintune* de rege in
" *Capite*, per Servicium duorum Militum." An Inquisition in the Tower, in 15 Edw. N° 18, findeth
" that Henry Berkeley dyed, seized (inter alia) of the Manor of *Stanley St. Leonard*, quod pertinet
" ad Baronium de *Dersilege*; and that William was his Son and Heire, 15 Yeeres old. The *Pat. Roll.*
" Members 2 and 6, 38 Henry III. shews that the King granted Liberty to William Berkelei of
" *Dourfley*, for terme of Life to hunt the Fox, Wolfe, Hare, Wild-Cat, Badger, &c. and that he should
" not be returned upon any Jury, nor be made Sheriffe, Coroner, &c. against his Will. And by the
" *Pat. Roll*, 39 Henry III. Pag. 2, this W. de Berkeley was Valettus regis, one that waits on
" the King in his Bedchamber; and, by *Pat. Rot.* 53 Hen. III. This W. de B. was pardoned by
" the King, his partakinge with Roger de Clifford, his Rebellion and Stirres against the Kinge;
" because he would not keep the Statutes and Provision of the Parliament made at *Oxford*. This Henry
" de Berkeley Lord of *Dursley* had, in the 9th Edw. I. a tryall with Thomas Lord Berkeley, the
" second of that Name, for the Liberties thereof. And in the said 9th and 13th of the same, hee as it
" seems, put forward two Writs of *Quo Warranto* against the said Thomas Lord Berkeley; which,
" coming to a Tryal at Glocester, the Jury found that the Ancestors of the said Lord Thomas, in the
" Reigns of Henry II. and King John, used, that if any Thieves, either in the Courte or in the Towne
" of *Dursley*, to bring them the same Day to the Castell at *Berkeley*, if the Day sufficed; and they were
" accustomed to receive their Judgement, and to have Justice executed upon them. The Book in the
" Exchequer called the " Nomina Villarum," compiled in 9 Edw. II. sayeth, that in the Hundred of
" *Berkeley*, are two Burrowe Townes, viz. *Berkeley*, whereof Thomas Lord Berkeley is Lord; and
" *Dursley*, whereof John Son of William Berkeley is Lord. The said John Sonne of William
" Berkrley, taking Advantage in the 1ft Edw. III. while Thomas Lord Berkeley, Granchilde and
" Heire to the last mentioned, was in tryall by Parlement about his Life and Fortunes, about the Murder
" of K. Edw. II. in *Berkeley Castell*; exhibits his Petition in that Parliament, settinge forthe, " Howe
" himself holds the Manors of *Newinton* and *Dursley* of the King, by Knightes Service in Capite.
" And, that the said Thomas Lord Berkeley being one of the Guardians of the Peace there, hath,
" by his Seignory and Office, often wrongfully distreined him by his Plow Cattle, and that no deliverance
" would be made of them by the Sheriff, nor by his Bayly, nor other Minister; for that they are all of
" his Fee and Livery, or of his household Servants; and soe, by his Seignory, and by Duresse, and by
" colour of a newe Purchase, that hee hath made; and by the Aid of Roger Mortimer, late one of the
" Kinge's Counsaillers; to have Returne of Writs and all other royal Franchises, within his Hundred of

---

* These Possessions are more minutely specified, and with some Variation, in the " Liber Niger Scaccarii," published by
Hearne, vol. I. p. 166.

2   " *Berkeley;*

" *Berkeley;* which before was guildable, would encroach to him the Attendance and Seignory of him
" the faid JOHN, to his Difinherifon, and the Damage of the Kinge, wherof hee now praies Remedy
" in this High Court of Parliament, wherto the Aunfwer was, that the Rolles of the Chancery, fhould
" be viewed; and more, I thinke, followed not hereupon.

" In this Towne is a Markett each Thurfday, and two Fayre Days; the one on the 25th of April *,
" called *St. Mark's* Day, the other on the 25th of November, called *St. Clement's* Day; but when, or by
" what Kinge granted to the Lord hereof, I have not obferved. The Governmente of this Towne is by
" a Magiftrate called a Bayliffe, yeerelie chofen by the Lord's Steward, and the Jury at the Leete, or
" Law Day, holden within a Month after Michaelmas.

" In this Towne is a Rock of ftrange Stone, called a Puff-ftone, or, as fome pronounce, a Toufe-
" ftone, wherin is no Chink, Cracke, Chop, or Lifne, at all, like a Sponge; of an incredible Durance,
" as the Walls of *Berkeley* Caftell, made of Ruines of the Nunnerye there, demolifhed neere 700 Yeeres
" agoe, may witnefs; very eafy to be cut, and foft. Through which Rocke, divers Vaultes, Houfes,
" Cellars, Milles, and Water-courfes, in the Towne are cutt and runne, the like is faid not to be elf-
" where found; and by it, and through Parte of it runneth the Streame from the fayre Fountain, called
" *Ewelme,* ancientlie in the Time of HENRY III, and afore written *Hewelme* in divers Deedes.

" To have vifited an ancient Hermitage, feated in the Midft of the Defart Woodes, hanging over
" this Towne, may feeme in Daies of fuch Belief to have been an Expiatorie, or meritorious Worke;
" through the pains-takeing in the uneafy and dangerous Clyming and Accefs to the Hermite's Celle;
" up and downe the craggy Hills leading therto. The laft Time I finde Mention of Heremite, or
" Hermitage, is in the Court-roll of the Manor of *Hamme,* in 8 HENRY VIII, when hee was awarded
" at that Courte (*bina manu*), with two Handes, to prove that the Horfe, which had hither ftrayed, and
" there taken up, was not thence ftolen by him; but his owne proper Goodes; but though hee had
" Reftitution, yet doubtlefs moft of them were hipocriticall Knaves."

The Town of *Durfley* is fituate at the Bafe of a fteep Hill, covered with hanging Beech Woods, four
Miles on the North from *Wotton Under Edge,* and fifteen fouthward from GLOUCESTER. The Streets are
planned irregularly, and of no great Extent, with many refpectable Buildings unfavourably placed †.
In Dr. PARSONS's MSS. it is faid that the firft Charter for the Market and Fairs was obtained in 1471,
11 EDW. IV. by WILLIAM Lord BERKELEY, and renewed, in 1612, on the Petition of Sir THOMAS
ESTCOURT, Knight. The old Crofs, which was an open Arcade, falling to decay, the prefent very commodious Market-houfe was erected in 1738 at the fole Expence of the Lord of the Manor. The Office
of Bailiff is certainly of very ancient Eftablifhment, though no Evidences fupplying a Catalogue of
them prior to 1567 have reached us. Their prefent Office is to fuperintend the Police of the Town,
and adjuft annually the Weights and Meafures; in early Times, it is probable, they exercifed more
extenfive Jurifdiction.

PRÆPOSITI, OR BAILIFFS.

A. D.			A. D.	
1567	James Smallwood.		1589	John Plomer.
1568	Roger Pytt.		1590	Thomas Auftyn.
1569	Chriftoph. Webbe, alias Woolworth.		1591	Richard Martin.
1570	William Berry.		1592	Richard Browninge.
1571	Richard Berry.		1593	. . . .
1572	William Webbe, alias Woolworth.		1594	. . . .
1573	. . . .		1595	. . . .
1574	. . . .		1596	. . . .
1574	. . . .		1597	. . . .
1575	. . . .		1598	. . . .
1576	. . . .		1599	. . . .
1577	. . . .		1600	. . . .
1578	. . . .		1601	. . . .
1579	Richard Maxtone.		1602	. . . .
1580	William Trotman.		1603	John Plomer.
1581	. . . .		1604	. . . .
1582	Alexander Burton.		1605	. . . .
1583	Thomas Trotman.		1606	. . . .
1584	Thomas Parker.		1607	. . . .
1585	John Tyler.		1608	. . . .
1586	Richard Maxtone.		1609	. . . .
1587	William Purnell.		1610	. . . .
1588	Thomas Trotman.		1611	Maurice Tyler.

* By the alteration of Style, thefe are now held on the 6th of May, and the 4th of December.
† There are feveral very old Dwelling-houfes in this Town; one of which has an external Date 1520; within, a Chamber
of Oak Wainfcot, and arched Roof of Timber Frame, the Beams highly carved and ornamented with a Cypher, E. W. 1539.
It might have belonged to the WEBBES, alias WOOLWORTH, or the WEKYS's.

6 R 2   A. D. 1612

A. D.		A. D.	
1612	Arthur Vizar.	1681	William Tippetts.
1613	Richard Tippetts.	1682	Samuel King.
1614	John Martin.	1683	Richard Tippetts.
1615	. . . .	1684	Walter Maye.
1616	William Harding.	1685	Jacob Wallington.
1617	Ifaac Smith.	1686	John Williams.
1618	. . . .	1687	Ifaac Smyth.
1619	. . . .	1688	William Lytton.
1620	Richard Tippetts.	1689	Thomas Purnell.
1621	Henry Trotman.	1690	John Partridge.
1622	. . . .	1691	John Purnell.
1623	. . . .	1692	Benjamin Symonds.
1624	William Harding.	1693	Samuel Clarke.
1625	Thomas Hyett.	1694	John Webb.
1626	Thomas Smyth.	1695	Robert Whateley.
1627	Richard Merick.	1696	Richard Merrick.
1628	Philip Biggs.	1697	Thomas King.
1629	Richard Browninge.	1698	Jofeph Pulley.
1630	Ifaac Smith.	1699	Maurice Philips.
1631	Richard Oliver.	1700	Samuel King.
1632	John Tyler.	1701	Richard Tippetts.
1633	. . . .	1702	James Bayley.
1634	Nicholas Dangerfield.	1703	William Purnell.
1635	George Grace.	1704	Jacob Wellington.
1636	Thomas Watkyns.	1705	Ifaac Smyth.
1637	John Browninge.	1706	Ifaac Smyth.
1638	Samuel Harding.	1707	John Philips.
1939	William Hill.	1708	Maurice Smith.
1640	Henry Smith.	1709	. . . .
1641	John Tucker.	1710	. . . .
1642	Nicholas Dangerfield.	1711	. . . .
1643	William Pitt.	1712	Roger Whateley.
1644	. . . .	1713	William Symondes.
1645	John Hodges.	1714	Jofiah Arundell.
1646	. . . .	1715	. . . .
1647	John Philips.	1716	. . . .
1648	Auguftin Philips.	1717	. . . .
3649	George Martin.	1718	. . . .
1650	William Tippets.	1719	. . . .
1651	Henry Adey.	1720	. . . .
1652	John Arundel.	1721	. . . .
1653	Ifaac Smith.	1722	. . . .
1654	John Purnell.	1723	. . . .
1655	Obadiah Webb.	1724	. . . .
1656	William Purnell.	1725	. . . .
1657	John Watkins.	1726	. . . .
1658	John Arundell.	1727	. . . .
1656	John Oliver.	1728	. . . .
1660	John Till-Adams.	1729	. . . .
1661	William Partridge.	1730	Selwyn James.
1662	Edmond Perrott.	1731	Giles Hodges.
1663	John Tucker.	1732	John Purnell.
1664	William Tippetts.	1733	Richard Oliver.
1665	Thomas Everett.	1737	James Nicholas.
1666	Henry Smith.	1735	Samuel Wallington.
1667	Samuel Symonds.	1736	Thomas Morfe.
1668	John Arundell.	1737	Timothy Wallington.
1669	William Smith.	1738	Samuel Clarke.
1670	William Lytton.	1739	Richard Cooper.
1671	John Purnell.	1740	Jacob Stiff.
1672	Arthur Crew.	1741	Thomas Purnell.
1673	William Powell.	1742	Jofias Clarke.
1674	John Oliver.	1745	Thomas Wallington.
1675	William Merrick.	1744	William Browning.
1676	. . . .	1745	John Moodey.
1677	William Partridge.	1746	John Gethen.
1678	Daniel Knight.	1747	George Faithorne.
1679	Thomas King.	1748	Nathaniel Lawfon.
1680	Thomas King.	1749	Jofeph Till-Adam.

A. D. 1750

A. D.			A. D.	
1750	Richard Tippetts.		1770	Benjamin Millard.
1751	Maurice Smith.		1771	Richard Williams.
1752	John Plomer.		1772	Ifaac Danford.
1753	Lewis Hofkins.		1773	Ifaac Jones.
1754	William Long.		1774	John Ball.
1755	Jofeph Faithorne.		1775	William Roach.
1756	William Heaven.		1776	William Drew.
1757	John King.		1777	Samuel Griffin.
1758	William Plomer.		1778	William King.
1759	William Blake.		1779	Thomas Lewton.
1760	Samuel Lewton.		1780	Benjamin Millard, junior.
1761	Thomas Cam.		1781	Daniel Dimorey.
1762	Jofiah Tippetts.		1782	William Jackfon.
1763	Samuel Phillimore.		1783	John Wallington.
1764	Morgan Pulley.		1784	James Wheeler.
1765	Hugh Everett, fenior.		1785	Nathaniel Blackwell.
1766	Thomas Morfe, junior.		1786	Richard Williams, junior.
1767	Thomas Tippetts.		1787	Jonathan Hitchins.
1768	Benjamin Smith.		1788	Thomas Moore.
1769	Samuel Wallington.		1789	John Long.

The Boundaries of the Parifh are found by the laft Perambulation to exceed eight Miles, of a Soil light and gravelly, moftly in Pafture, with 2000 Acres of Woodland. Exclufive of the manerial Eftate, the chief Property is held by the Families of PHELPS, the two diftinct Families of PURNELL, the Mayor, Aldermen, and Burgeffes of the City of *Briftol,* and the Families of TIPPETTS, VIZARD, ADEY, WAL-LINGTON, and BLACKWELL.

Of the Manor fo accurate an Account has been given, as to preclude the Neceffity of adding more than that it ftill is vefted in the laft mentioned Name and Family.

As early as HENRY the VIIIth's Reign, the Caftle was become a mere Ruin; it was a Baronial Refi-dence only, for the Site is fo commanded by furrounding Hills as to render it ineffectual to any military Purpofe, even upon the ancient Syftem of War. It has been ftyled the Barony of *Durfley,* although none of this Houfe of BERKELEY have ever received Summons to Parliament; but in 1679, 31 CAR. II. GEORGE Baron BERKELEY was created Vifcount DURSLEY by Patent *.

The Manufacture of Cloth was eftablifhed in this Town and Parifh foon after its more general Introduc-tion from *Flanders,* and has enriched many Families. It ftill employs the poorer Inhabitants, and is conducted with Reputation and Succefs.

The Benefice is a Rectory, anciently charged with a Payment of 1*l*. 6*s*. 8*d*. to the Priory of *Stanley St. Leonard,* and in the Patronage of the Abbot of GLOUCESTER, who in 1475, at the Inftance of JOHN CARPENTER Bifhop of *Worcefter,* exchanged this Rectory for the Houfe of the Archdeacon in GLOUCESTER, to which Dignity it was then appropriated, and has fince continued to be annexed.

It is the Chief of its own Deanery.

The Church, dedicated to *St. James,* confifts of a fpacious Nave, two Aifles, a Tower of *modern* Gothic, and a very handfome Portal. The dividing Arches are light; carved on the Timber frame Roof, are the Arms of BERKELEY † and FITZALAN, and the Device of THOMAS TANNER ‡; who, in the Reign of HENRY the VIth, erected a Chapel at the End of the South Aifle, for the Reception of a Chan-try, in which is the Figure of a Skeleton beneath a Canopy, intended as a Memorial of him. It is probable that he contributed to the external Embellifhment of the whole South Side of the Church, which is in the beft Style of that Age. The old Spire fell in 1699, whilft the Bells were ringing; by which Accident feveral Lives were loft. It was rebuilt and finifhed in 1709, at the Expence of 1000*l*. The Chancel was likewife re-erected in 1738, and neatly fitted up.

---

* COLLINS's Peerage, vol. III. Title BERKELEY.

† Not BERKELEY of *Durfley,* who bore " Argent, a Fefs between three Martlets Sable—as in the Church at *Coberley,* p. 405.

‡ Amongft the Names of Gentry returned by the Commiffioners in 1433, 12 HENRY VI. for the better Prefervation of the Peace, was " THOMAS TANNER, of *Dourfeley*." FULLER's Worthies, *Glouc.* p. 363. About this Period, when the legitimate Bearers of Arms were fo jealous of their Paternal Efcutcheon, it was cuftomary for many, who were not entitled to Coat Armour, to invent and ufe certain Symbols, or Marks of no heraldic Adaptation. Many Specimens of thefe are found on Braffes intended for wealthy Citizens, and as frequently carved on Wood or Stone, where they had contributed to any public Edifice.

Mr. GOUGH, Sep. Mon. p. cx. remarks, " I fhall only mention one Monument more, which is fomewhat peculiar, I mean the " Reprefentation of a Skeleton in a Shroud lying either under or on a Table Tomb. I obferved one of this make in almoft all " the Conventual and Cathedral Churches throughout *England,* but fcarcely ever more than one ; but what Age to attribute the " unknown ones to, I find no Date to guefs by, fince there is one at *York* as ancient as 1241, and in *Briftol* Cathedral for PAUL " BUSH as late as 1558, who is reprefented in the fame Manner ; and I have obferved fome of every Age between."

6 S

A fmall

A fmall Turret, which contained the Saints Bell [*], ftill remains; and a Shrine at the end of the North Aifle, where was the other Chantry, of which RICHARD BREIC was the laft Incumbent.

With *Woodmancote*, the only Hamlet in this Parifh, Mr. SMYTH proceeds with his ufual Accuracy and Minutenefs :

" *Woodmancote*, anciently written *Wodemancote*, is an ancient Manor, with the Parifh of *Durfley*,
" holden of GEORGE Lord BERKELEY of his Manor of *Berkeley*, by half a Knighte's Fee, and Sute to
" his Hundred Courte, and before the charteringe thereof, by feveral Sales.　The Scituation of the ca-
" pitall Meffuage, and Manor-houfe of this Village or Townfhip of *Woodmancote* affureth us from
" whence the Name is derived, as that it was the Cote or Dwelling-houfe of the Woodman or Wood-
" ward, wholly inclofed almoft with the Woods of that Manor, and of the Manor of *Durfley*, lying
" togeather, as alfoe did fpacious Woods of other Manors therto adjoininge.　For the ancient Owners
" of this *Woodmancott* from the Time of WILLIAM the CONQUEROR, or before, untill the Tyme of
" HENRY IIId, I referre you to what I have formerlie written of *Nybley*.　And in that Kinge's Reign
" it was the Land of OTTO, alias OTHO, the Sonne of WILLIAM, and of WILLIAM, the Sonne of
" OTHO; I fuppofe that two of that Name fucceeded the one the other; and after of THOMAS, Sonne of
" OTTO, who dying, 2 EDW. I. lefte it to OTTO his Sonne, then but 9 Years olde, as an Inquifition
" fhewith.　From whom it came to ROBERT DE SWYNEBORNE, who dying in 19 EDW. II. left the
" fame to his Son THOMAS DE SWYNEBORNE, and after it came to MARGERY DE SWINEBORN, upon whofe
" Death, in 16 EDW. III. controverfie arofe about this Manor, and WARREN FITZWARREN (who
" dwelte where I now doe) crept into the Poffeffion therof, who after, with THOMAS his Brother, and
" CATHERINE their Sifter, in 25 EDW. III. releafed all their Intereft to another ROBERT DE SWYNE-
" BOURNE and his Heires, from whom, by his Deede inrolled in the Court of Common Pleas (the faid
" 25 EDW. III. Rot. 2.), it came to WILLIAM DE CHELTENHAM and WILLIAM DE WESTAL and
" theyr Heires, who beinge Servants in the Houfe of THOMAS Lord BERKELEY, the third of that
" Name, according to the Truft in them repofed, conveyed the fame to the Lady KATHERINE,
" the fecond Wife of him the faid Lord BERKELEY, and to MAURICE their Sonne (then very
" younge), and to the Heires Males of his Body, with divers other Remainders over, as by the
" Deede in *Berkeley* Caftle appears, by which Purchace and Entayle this Manor came unto, to, and
" fettled in, Sir JOHN BERKELEY, Brother and Heire Male of the faid MAURICE, for that the faid
" MAURICE in his Minority dyed without Iffue.　Which Sir JOHN BERKELEY, after the Death of the
" faid Lady CATHERINE, who died 9 RICHARD IId. held this Manor, and died feifed thereof, to him
" and the Heirs Males of his Bodie in 6 HEN. VI. leaving Iffue MAURICE BERKELEY, Father of
" MAURICE and EDWARD; which MAURICE had Iffue WILLIAM, which WILLIAM died without Iffue
" Male, and the faid EDWARD was his Unkle and Heire Male, by Force of the faid Entayle, which
" EDWARD had Iffue THOMAS and WILLIAM, the faid THOMAS had Iffue JOHN, who died without Iffue
" Male of his Body, and the faid WILLIAM was his Unkle and Heire, which WILLIAM died, 5 EDW. VI.
" having Iffue JOHN BERKELEY, who in Eafter Term, 9 ELIZ. fold this Manor of *Woodmancott* to
" RICHARD LAMBERT, a Merchant in *London*, by whofe Death, in 30 ELIZ. it defcended to WINEFRID
" his Daughter and Heire, whofe Mother was re-married to Sir HENRY WINSTON, Knight, and the
" faid WINEFRID was in Ward for this Manor to HENRY Lord BERKELEY, who dying in her Minority
" without Iffue, the fame defcended to her Unkle EDMOND LAMBERT (afterward written EDWARD),
" Brother of the faid RICHARD the Purchacer; which EDWARD, after in his Life Time, in the Tyme
" of King JAMES, and his Feoffees in Truft after his Death, in 7 JAC. I. for raifinge of Portions for his
" Daughters, foe fcattered almoft all the Lands of the Manor by theyr feveral Sales, in temp. JAC. I.
" to particular Men, that it is now in 1639, 15 CAROLI I. the Inheritance of 38 Freeholders.

" But fith this Manor is not named in the Booke of *Domefday*, either as a Member of the Manor
" and Barony of *Berkeley*, or as a Parcell of the ancient Poffeffions of the BERKELEYS, of *Durfley*,
" wherin all Landes in this Countie are fet downe, nor in the Certificate of ROGER BERKELEY, made to
" Kinge HENRY IId, of all the Landes that hee or his Anceftors held; I cannot refolve otherwife, but
" that it was a Freehold in the Hand of one ancient *Saxon* or other, holden of the Lady Abbeffe and
" Nunnes of *Berkeley*, unleffe I fhould fay, it is in *Domefday* Boke comprehended under the Manor of
" *Came*, whereof fome Inquifitions finde it to be holden of the Manor and an Hamblet therof, wherunto
" I doe enclyne.　Though the Inhabitants of this Manor claim to have a Leet or Lawe Day amongft
" themfelves, yet the Tythingman thereof, with fome of this Manor or Tything of *Woodmancote*, appear
" twice in the Year at the Leete holden at *Berkeley*, for the Hundred of *Berkeley*, and prefent as to that
" Court appertaineth.　In the Time of HENRY VI. arofe a Queftion between the Inhabitants of *Wood-*
" *mancote*, and fuch of the Inhabitants of *Nybley* as are called *Warren's* Tenants, about paying the fif-
" teene, or King's Silver.　Here are dyvers Lands and Tenements called *Clifford's* Landes, fometime
" the Land of *Fontes*, in fome Recordes and Evidences called a Manor, holden of this Manor of *Wood-*
" *mancote*, now the Inheritance of certaine Feoffees to the Ufe of the Citie of BRISTOL, whoe by their
" Attorney doe Suite at the Court of the Hundred of *Berkeley*, and pay the yearlie Rent of 4*d.* to the

---

[*] A *Saint's* Bell is fo called becaufe it was rung when the Prieft came to thofe Words of the Mafs " *Sancte! Sancte! Sancte! Deus*
" *Sabaoth!*" that all Perfons who were abfent might fall on their Knees in Reverence of the Holy Office then going on in the Church.
Of this is the following curious Notice in the Regifter.　" *Mem* 1647, It is agreed that JOHN TILL ADAMS and EDWARD PER-
" KOT do keepe the Sainte's Bell, till they be payde 1*l.* 6*s.* 9*d.* which they have laid out in their Office of Churchwardens."

" Lord

" Lord BERKELEY's Manor of *Came*. Touchinge which Land are feveral Inquifitions, after the Death
" of ALEXANDER BRADWAY, in 19 HEN. VII. and another after the Death of JAMES CLIFFORD, 37
" HEN. VIII. and another after the Death of HENRY CLIFFORD in 1 ELIZ. who left Iffue JAMES, who in
" .. ELIZ. alienated the fame, and mentioned therin to be 8 Meffuages, and 192 Acres of Land, holden
" of the Manor of *Durfley* by 17*s.* Rente."

From other equally authentic Evidences, with which we have been favoured, it appears, that in 1670,
22 CHARLES II. it was transferred by Purchafe from WILLIAM LUDEN and ELIZABETH his Wife, Sifter
of ARTHUR BROMWICH, Efq. to JOHN ARUNDELL. In 1762 it was fold by the Coheirs of JOHN ARUN-
DELL, Gent. to JOHN DE LA FIELD PHELPS, Efq. the Father of the prefent Poffeffor. The Homage
paid twice a Year to the Court at *Berkeley*, is a Thong of blue Leather, tagged with Tin at each End.

The Village of *Woodmancot* contains many Houfes, and adjoins the Town of *Durfley.*

EDWARD FOX *, Bifhop of *Hereford*, a very ftrenuous Promoter of the Reformation, was a Native of
this Place.

B E N E F A C T I O N S.

A Tenement, now called the Church Houfe, and a Piece of Land called the Torch Acre, to Feoffees
for ever, for repairing the Church ✝.

The Houfes, now called the Alms-houfes, to Feoffees for ever, for the Benefit of the Poor.

Mr. SPILMAN, by Deed, gave to Truftees, an Eftate for ever, in the Parifh of *Standifh*, of the yearly
Value of 4*l.* for the Ufe of the Poor.

Mr. HENRY STUBBS gave 10*s.* yearly, to buy Books for poor Children.

Mr. HUGH SMITH, of *Durfley*, by Will, Jan. 1, 1637, gave two Tenements at the Broad Well, for
repairing the Church.

Sir THOMAS ESTCOURT, by Will, Aug. 10, 1642, gave a Moiety of the clear yearly Rents of his
Tenements in *Tetbury*, after deducting 40*s.* a Year for the Relief of the Poor, now fettled at 10*l.* a Year.

Mr. THROGMORTON TROTMAN, of *London*, by Will, Oct. 30, 1663, gave 15*l.* a Year for ever, for a
Lecture to be preached every Thurfday.

Mr. JOHN ARUNDELL, of *Durfley*, by Will, May 19, 1703, gave an Acre of Ground, in the Parifh
of *Cam*, to Truftees, for ever, for buying Books, and teaching poor Children to read.

JOSIAH SHEPHARD, by Will, in 1726, bequeathed 100*l.* for the Support of a School ; 260*l.* more were
added by Subfcription, the Income of which is 24*l.*

Mrs. ANN PURNELL, of *Durfley*, Widow, by Will, Dec. 21, 1759, gave to Truftees 100*l.* for purchafing Lands, the Income of which to be applied as followeth : 10*s.* to the officiating Minifter to preach
every Good Friday in the Afternoon ; the Remainder for teaching poor Children to read. And alfo 60*l.*
to be laid out as followeth : 10*l.* to the officiating Minifter for preaching a Sermon on New Year's Day
in the Morning for ever, and the Remainder to be equally divided amongft Forty poor Widows of the Parifh.

NATHANIEL LAWSON, Gent. in 1766, left 2*l.* 5*s.* 7*d.* to be diftributed in Bread, yearly, amongft the Poor.

JACOB STIFF, Gent. bequeathed, in 1769, 1*l.* 10*s.* to be annually applied to the fame Purpofe.

INCUMBENTS.	PATRONS.	INCUMBENTS.	PATRONS.
1541 Nich. Wootton, LL.D.	Bp. of GLOUCESTER.	1662 Edward Pope, M. A.	Bp. of GLOUCESTER.
1553 John Williams, LL. D.	The fame.	1671 John Gregory, M. A.	The fame.
1558 Guy Eaton, B. D.	The fame.	1678 Thomas Hyde, M. A.	The fame.
1574 George Savage, LL. D.	The fame.	1702 Robert Parfons, M. A.	The fame.
1602 Robert Hill, B. D.	The fame.	1714 Nathaniel Lye, D. D.	The fame.
1606 Samuel Burton, M. A.	The fame.	1737 William Geekie, D. D.	The fame.
1634 Hugh Robinfon, D. D.	The fame.	1767 Richard Hurd, B. D.	The fame.
———— ————,	The fame.	1774 James Webfter, LL.B.	The fame.
1660 John Middleton,	The fame.		

* EDWARD FOX, a Cantabrigian, had the Temporalities of the See of *Hereford* reftored to him in 1535. He was an eminent
Scholar of his Time, and was born at *Durfley*, in *Gloucefterfhire*, educated at *Eaton* School, neere *Windfor*, admitted Scholar of
King's College, *Cambridge*, March 15, 1512, became Provoft of it Dec. 27, 1528, and afterward the King's Almoner, one of his
Privy Council, and a great Promoter of his Divorce from Queen KATHERINE, particularly in the Univerfity of *Cambridge*, where
he and Dr. STEPHEN GARDINER procured, with much Difficulty, and earneft engaging of themfelves, the Teftimony of the
Univerfity for the King's Divorce 1530. In September 1531 he was inftalled Archdeacon of *Leicefter*, and in November 1533 he
was made Archdeacon of *Dorfet* ; about which Time he had been Embaffador into *France* and *Germany* many Times, and afterwards was fecretly a Favorer of the reformed Religion, infomuch that MARTIN BUCER dedicated his Commentary on the Evangelifts to him. By his laft Will, dated May 8, 1538, it appears that he bequeathed his Body to be buried in the Church of *St.
Mary Hault*, in *London*, the Patronage of which belongs to the Bifhop of *Hereford*. WOOD's Ath. vol. I. p. 559.
    FULLER, in his Worthies, p. 355, adds, " that he firft brought CRANMER to the Knowledge of the King, which Doctor firft
" brought the King to Knowledge of himfelf, refpecting his Marriage with the Widow of his Brother. He was the principal
" Pillar of the Reformation, as to the politick and prudential Part thereof ; being of more Activity, and of no leffe Ability,
" than CRANMER himfelf." Defcanting, in p. 353, upon the Proverb, " You are a Man of *Durflev*," he obferves, " Thus fure
" I am that there was a Man of *Durfley*, a Man of Men, EDWARD FOX by Name, a right goodly and gracious Prelate." See
farther. LLOYD's State Worthies, p 86. New Biographical Dictionary, vol. II. p. 144.
    ✝ The oldeft Deed extant of the Church Houfe and Torch Acre, is dated the 4th of September, 28 HEN. VIII. Tradition
reports it to have been the Gift of TANNER ; the original Deeds were probably conveyed away at the Diffolution of Monafteries.

5

PRESENT PROPRIETORS OF THE MANORS,

Of *Durfley*,   Of *Woodmancote*,
THOMAS ESTCOURT, ESQ.   JOHN DE LA FIELD PHELPS, ESQ.

The Perfons fummoned from this Place by the Heralds in 1682 and 1683 were

William Purnell, Efq.   Francis Whitney, Gent.
John Arundell, Efq.   Thomas Bailey, Gent.
William Smyth, Gent.

At the Election in 1776, Thirty-nine Freeholders polled from this Parifh.

The Regifter commences in 1640; one prior to it has been deftroyed, bearing Date 1556.

ANNUAL ACCOUNT OF MARRIAGES, BIRTHS, AND BURIALS, IN THIS PARISH.

A.D.	Mar.	Bir.	Bur.	A.D.	Mar.	Bir.	Bur.	A.D.	Mar.	Bir.	Bur.	A.D.	Mar.	Bir.	Bur.
1781	13	43	27	1786	11	59	45	1791				1796			
1782	16	54	21	1787	18	62	52	1792				1797			
1783	28	46	25	1788	15	61	37	1793				1798			
1784	14	66	39	1789				1794				1799			
1785	18	51	44	1790				1795				1800			

INSCRIPTIONS IN THE CHURCH.

ON MONUMENTS IN THE CHANCEL.

Arms; Vert, a Chevron between three Lions Heads erafed Or, for PLOMER.

To the Memory of
WILLIAM PLOMER, of the City of
Briftol; and alfo of
HANNAH his Wife,
Daughter of SAMUEL CLARK,
of this Town, Mercer, who died, viz.
he April 2, 1731, aged 33;
and fhe July 1, 1734, aged 41.

Near this Place lies the Body of
JOHN PLOMER, of this Town, Mercer,
Son of the faid WILLIAM and HANNAH,
who died November 23, 1757, aged 30.

Arms; Per Pale a Wolf falient, between fix Croffes Crofslets, for PHELPS;
—impaling, quarterly, Azure and Or in the firft Quarter, a Hawk's Lure of the fecond, for FOWLER.

To the Memory of JOHN PHELPS, Efq.
who died June 16, 1755,
in the 44th Year of his Age.
This Monument was erected by
his eldeft Son
JOHN DE LA FIELD PHELPS.

Near this Place lies interred
JOHN DE LA FIELD PHELPS, Efq.
who died April 21, 1771,
in the 37th Year of his Age.
He was many Years in the
Commiffion of the Peace, and ferved
High Sheriff in the Year 1761.

Alfo ESTHER his Daughter,
who died April 8, 1767,
in the 5th Year of her Age.

In this Chancel (with the Family)
lieth Mr. WILL. PURNELL, Merchant,
Son of JOHN PURNELL, Gent.
Obiit 18 June, 1715, æt. 59.

Arms; on a Fefs between three Lozenges, three Cinquefoils, for PURNELL;
—impaling, on a Bend three Rofes, in the finifter chief Point a Cheffrook, for SMALL.

H. S. E.

THOMAS PURNELL, de Kingfhill, Arm.
Vir ingenio admodum humanus,
moribus gravis, vitæ integerrimus,
qui cum patriæ diu inferviffet,
amicis pariter ac familiaribus carus,
annis tandem & honore gravis,
animam Deo reddidit die Octob. XXIX.
A. D. MDCCXXIX. ætatis fuæ LXXII.
Non procul ab hoc marmore jacet
filius natu minimus NATHANAEL,
optimæ fpei adolefcentulus.
Obiit X. Oct. MDCCXVIII.
Anno ætatis XVII.

Et ANNA, uxor THOMÆ PURNELL, Arm.
quæ hanc vitam difceffit vicefimo
die Februarii MDCCXXXV.
ætatis fuo octogeffimo anno.

Et GULIELMUS PURNELL, Generofus,
filius prædicti THOMÆ fecundus,
qui poftquam inter Rutinos honefto
Mercatoris officio, intentus patriæ fuæ,
diu inferviffet, commodo in peregre
reverfus in placido apud Tilfdown,
receffu vitam confummavit
XXIV. die Octobris,
A. D. MDCCLI. ætat. LVII.

Near this Place lieth the Body of
WILLIAM LITTON, Clothier,
who departed this Life the
3d Day of June, in the Year of our Lord
1705, aged 61 Years.

Alfo the Body of
ANNE, Daughter of
ROBERT CLARKE, Gent.
firft Wife of the abovenamed
WILLIAM LITTON; and, after, Wife of
JOHN HYETT, Efq. deceafed,
late Mayor, and one of the Aldermen,
of the City of Gloucefter,
who departed this Life in the Year 1730,
aged 67 Years.

Arms; on a Bend between two Roundlets, three Swans, for CLARKE.

Near this Place was interred
SAMUEL CLARKE,
of this Town, Mercer;
and alfo HANNAH his Wife.
He died Dec. 18, 1737, in the
73d Year of his Age;
and fhe Sept. 8, 1729, aged 65.

Alfo near this Place refteth the Body of
SAMUEL CLARKE, Mercer,
Son of the aforefaid
SAMUEL and HANNAH CLARKE,
who departed this Life Dec. 21, 1747,
in the 56th Year of his Age.

Likewife near this Place refteth
the Body of WILLIAM, Son of the
aforefaid SAMUEL and
HANNAH CLARKE,
who departed this Life April 28, 1749,
in the 56th Year of his Age.

Alfo near this Place refteth the
Body of JOSIAH CLARKE, Mercer,
Son of the faid SAMUEL and HANNAH,
who died May 13, 1754,
in the 54th Year of his Age.

ON FLAT STONES.

WITHIN THE RAILS ARE THREE
LOZENGE-SHAPED BRASS PLATES, WITH
THIS INSCRIPTION ON ONE:

To the Memory of
Mrs. FRANCES WARBURTON,
Sifter of WILLIAM WARBURTON, D. D.
Bifhop of Gloucefter;
a Woman of an excellent Underftanding,
with a benevolent and compaffionate
Heart.
She was born at Newark upon Trent
Nov. 3, 1704;
died at the Parfonage in this Town
Aug. 1, 1780;
and was buried
near this Place.

O::

On the second :

To the Memory of
Elizabeth Webster, eldeft
Daughter of James Webster, LL.B.
Archdeacon of Gloucefter,
and of Sarah his Wife.
Her Days were few, innocent, and
without reproach.
She was born at Brant.Broughton,
Lincolnfhire,
Jan. 15, 1762 ;
died at the Parfonage in this Town
June 2, 1780 ;
and was interred
near this Place.

On the third :

To the Memory of
Frances Webster, the third
Daughter of James Webster, LL. B.
Archdeacon of Gloucefter,
and of Sarah his Wife.
Her Perfon was amiable, and her Life
blamelefs.
She was born at Brant Broughton,
Lincolnfhire,
June 16, 1764 ;
died at Taunton, Somerfetfhire,
Dec. 19, 1785 ;
and was buried
near this Place.

Here lyeth the Body of
Elizabeth, Wife of
Henry Arundell, Clothier,
who departed this Life the
26th Day of . . . . 16 .. aged ..

Here refteth the Body of
Josiah Arundell,
of this Parifh, Gent.
who died April 21, 1756,
aged 72 Years.

Here refteth the Body of
Anne, Daughter of John Arundell.

In Memory of
Nathaniel Webb, of this Town,
who departed this Life April 2, 1739,
aged 76.

Alfo of Margaret his Relict,
and Daughter of
Edmund Yeme, of Howlfhill,
in the Parifh of Walford,
in the County of Hereford. Gent.
who departed this Life
the 29th Day of November, 1741,
aged 66.

Here refteth the Body of
Anne, Wife of Thomas Nicholas,
of Wanfwell, in the Parifh of Berkeley,
who departed this Life June 21, 1746,
aged 78.

Alfo the Body of
Mr. James Nicholas,
of this Town, Clothier,
who departed this Life Feb. 7, 1757,
aged 48 Years.

Alfo the Body of
Ann, the Wife of James Nicholas,
Clothier,
who departed this Life July 9, 1735,
aged 29.

Here lyeth the Body of
William Purnell, Clothier,
who departed this Life October 29, 1633,
ætatis fuæ 54.

In Memory of
Thomas Purnell, of Kingfhill, Efq.
Son of William Purnell,
of this Town,
who died October 29, 1729,
aged 72.

Alfo Anne, Wife of
Thomas Purnell, Efq.
departed this Life in February 1745,
in the 80th Year of her Age.

And alfo William Purnell,
of Tillfdown, Gent.
Son of the faid Thomas and Anne,
who died the 2 . . . . aged ..

Here lyeth the Body of
John, the Son of John Purnell,
Clothier,
who died June 30, 1712,
aged 21 Years.

Here lyeth the Body of
Anne, the Wife of John Purnell,
who departed this Life the 28th Day of
September, 1699, æt. fuæ 71.

Alfo the Body of
John Purnell, Clothier,
who departed this Life the 13th Day of
June, 1714, aged 51 Years.

In Memory of
Ann Purnell, eldeft Daughter of
John Purnell, of this Town, Gent.
who died Auguft 28, 1729, aged 79.

John Purnell, fenior, Clothier,
was here buried the 23d Day of
February, 1686.

Here lyeth the Body of
Ann, the Daughter of
John Purnell, Clothier,
who departed this Life the 25th Day of
September, 1710, aged 17 Years.

Here lyeth the Body of
Anne Hunt, eldeft Daughter of
Thomas Purnell, Efq.
who died April 13, 1762, aged 74.

Richard, the Son of
Richard Morgan, Gent.
died the 28th Day of Dec. 1742,
aged 2 Months.

On a Marble Tablet :

In Memory of Thomas Purnell, Efq.
and Susan his Wife,
who departed this Life ;
he April .. 1743, aged 51 ;
and fhe May 23, 1760, aged 71.

Alfo John their Son
departed this Life May 26, 1752,
aged 34.

And alfo William Jones, Gent.
was buried here Nov. 26, 1755, aged 39.

In Memory of
Martha, the Wife of Thomas Bayly,
and Daughter of John Purnell, fenior,
of this Town, Gent.
who departed this Life the 12th Day of
May, 1731, in the 71ft Year of her Age.

Here lieth the Body of
Esther, the Widow of
Thomas Fryer, of this Parifh,
Clothier.
She was the Daughter of
Thomas Tyndal, of Stinchcomb,
Gent. and was firft married to
John Elliott, Clerk,
fome time Curate of this Parifh, and
afterwards Rector of Edgworth,
in this County.
She died April the 30th, 1743,
in the 82nd Year of her Age.

Alfo Hannah, Daughter of
the faid John and Esther Elliott,
who died Sept 16, 1698,
in the 4th Year of her Age.

Alfo Elizabeth their Daughter,
and Widow of Samuel Yeates,
of the Parifh of Minchinghampton, Dyer.
She died July the 26th, 1756,
in the 64th Year of her Age.

Alfo of Onesiphorus Elliott, Clothier,
youngeft Son of the faid
John and Esther,
who died April 19, 1766,
in the 65th Year of his Age.

Here lyeth the Body of
Mary, Wife of
George Faithorn, Clothier,
who died Sept. 18, 1748,
aged 23 Years.

Alfo the faid George Faithorn,
died Sept. 29, 1751, aged 29 Years.

Here refteth the Body of
John Purnell, fenior,
Clothier, in Durfley,
who departed this Life the 12th of May,
1692.

Alfo the Body of
Margaret, the Wife of
John Purnell, fenior, Clothier,
who died the 10th Day of January, 1712,
aged 73.

And Joseph their Son
departed this Life January 14, 1732,
in the 63d Year of his Age.

And Mary his Wife,
aged 56, 1743.

IN THE NAVE.

On a Marble Monument fixed
against a Pillar :

Near this Place lieth the Body of
Frances, Wife of John A Wood,
Gent. and Relict of John Phillips.
She died Jan. 27, A. D. 1728,
ætat. fuæ 72.

Alfo of John Phillips,
Son of the faid Frances,
by her former Husband.
He died Jan. 19 Anno Dom. 1709,
æt. fuæ 28.

Alfo two Sons and one Daughter of
William Purnell and Ann his Wife,
Daughter of the faid Frances ;
they died in their Childhood.

On

On a neat Marble Tablet.

To the Memory of
WILLIAM MOORE, a Captain in the
45th Regiment of Foot,
who died October 19, 1784,
aged 66 Years,
after a service in the Army of Thirty
Years.

Here lieth the Body of
THOMAS WALLINGTON, of this Town,
Gent. who died September 14, 1753,
aged 57 Years.

On a Marble Tablet.

Underneath lye the Bodys of 9
Children of JOHN PURNELL, Esq.
and ANNE his Wife.

On a Marble Tablet against a
Pillar in the Nave.

To the Memory of JAMES SHRAPNELL,
a Midshipman in the Royal Navy,
Son of JAMES SHRAPNELL of this Town,
Gent. by MARY, only Daughter of
JOSEPH TILY, Esq. of Chelsea, in the
County of Middlesex, and Grandaughter
of Sir JOSEPH TILY, Knt. he was born
at Trowbridge in the County of Wilts,
June 30, 1755, died at Sea, Oct. 11, 1780.

MOSES KNIGHT, of this Town,
who died November 10, 1750,
aged 34 Years.

Also of THOMAS his Son, who
died February 14, 1773, aged 23 Years.

In Memory of JAMES PAXTON,
who died March 28, 1781,
aged 29 Years.

WILLIAM PERRET, who died the
first day of January, 1700, aged 68.

JOHN LAWSON, who departed this
Life March 19, 17.., aged ...

EDRUS MORSE, jun. obiit.
Julii 1, 1724, ætatis suæ 50.

FLO.. the Wife of
EDWARD MORSE, jun.

NICHUS MORSE, fius Edri,
February   , Anno 17 ,

Hanna, ux. EDRI MORSE,
obiit 9 die Augusti, 1698.

In Memory of HANNAH, the Wife of
JOHN CROOME, and Daughter of
EDWARD MORSE, of this Town, Gent.
who died July 20, 1741, aged 39 Years.

On a plain Marble:

JOHN ARUNDELL, Esq.
died April 28, 1722, aged 45,

JOHN his Son, March 18, 1743, aged 43.

JOHN his Grandson, August 8, 1737,
aged 3.

ANN, Relict of the second named JOHN,
June 12, 1756, aged 50.

Arms; Ermine 3 Bars wavy Sable,
on a Chief Gules a Saltire Or; for
WALLINGTON;—impaling, Argent, on
a Fess Sable, between three Lozenges
Gules, three Cinque foils of the Field,
for PURNELL.

To the Memory of
WILLIAM PURNELL, Gent.
who died December 20, 1765
aged 65.

Also of CHARLES WALLINGTON,
Vicar of Frampton, and Curate of
Dursley,
who died March 1, 1765, aged 66,

and MARY his Wife,
who died March 9, 1738, aged 38.

UNDER THIS ON AN OLD STONE:

Here lyeth the body of
ANN, the Daughter of JOHN ARUNDELL,
Clothier,
who was buried the 2nd day of July,
1699, aged 7 Yeeres.

And also of ANNE his Daughter,
who was buried on August 1, 1702,
aged 22 Yeeres.

And also of ELIZABETH his Daughter,
who was buried September 11, 1703,
aged 17 Weeks and 4 Dayes.

And also MARY his Daughter,
who was buried the tenth of March, 17..,
aged .. Weekes.

ANN MELCHER, Daughter of
ROBERT and MARY MELCHER,
of Sutton Bangor in the County of Wilts,
was here interred,
April 11, 1729, æt. 30.

Under the adjoining Pew
lyeth the Body of MARY SMITH,
Wife of BENJ. SMITH,
and Daughter of Mr. GEORGE LAWRENCE,
of Slimbridge;
who died April 8, 1780, aged 27.

In Memory of
MAURICE SMITH of this Town, Mercer,
who departed this Life March 13, 1763,
aged 43 Years.

Also of ELIZABETH his Wife,
who departed this Life August 26, 1753,
aged 30 Years.

In Memory of
Mr. JOHN SMITH of this Town, Clothier,
who died November 19, 1774,
aged 57 Years.

Also of DEBORAH his Wife,
who died December 17, 1778,
aged 52 Years.

Here lieth
the Body of REBECKAH TIPPETTS,
Daughter of JOHN TIPPETTS, of the
New Mills, Clothier,
who departed this Life June 18, 1747,
aged 54 Years.

Also of SARAH,
the Wife of Mr. THOMAS KING of
this Town, who died February 23, 1774,
aged 83 Years,

SARAH, Wife of WILLIAM HEAVEN
of this Town, Clothier,
departed this Life April 21, 1734,
in the 37th Year of her Age,

SARAH their Daughter, in 1734,
an Infant.

WILLIAM HEAVEN, of this Town,
Clothier,
departed this Life Feb. 15, 1762,
aged 68.

ELIZABETH his Daughter
departed this Life Nov. 20, 1753,
aged 23.

In Memory of NATHANIEL PARRY,
and SARAH his Wife,
He died November 24, 1770,
aged 75 Years.
She died December 10, 1770,
aged 71 Years.

MAURICE PHILLIPS departed this Life
May 8, 1744, aged 74.

MARY his Wife
died December 20, 1755, aged 82 Years.

Here lieth the Body of WILLIAM, Son
of WILLIAM PURNELL, Mercer,
who died November 28, 1704,
aged 2 Years and 1 Month.

Also MARY, Daughter of JOHN PURNELL,
with several more Children, who all
died in Infancy.

GODDARD, who died June 21, 1701

JAMES SEABORN died
December 23, 1727,
in the 40th Year of his Age,

WILLIAM PEARCE
was buried February 14, 1727,
in the 30th Year of his Age.

Here resteth the Body of
JOHN PARTRIDGE, who departed this
Life December 7, Anno Dom. 1712,
aged 48 Years.

Here resteth the Body
of JAMES WORKMAN, of Dursley,
Victualler, who was buried
the 18th day of May, Anno Dom. 1706.

Also the Body
of JOHN VIZARD, late of Bristol,
Tobacconist, who died Jan. 17, 1736,
aged 59 Years.

In Memory of E. DURFORD, Widow,
who was buried here January , 1770,
aged 85 Years.

In Memory of ANNA PHELPS,
who died July 6, 1724, aged 45 Years,

Also of JOSEPH PHELPS,
who died December 20, 1737, aged 50.

Also of JOSEPH PHELPS,
son of the above JOSEPH and ANNA
PHELPS, who died July 10, 1786,
aged 68 Years.

Likewise of ANN his Wife,
who died February 11, 1776,
aged 70 Years.

Also two of their Daughters,

MARY died January 6, 1747,
aged 6 Months.

ANN died September 29, 1748,
aged 7 Years.

JOHN MOODY of this Town, Clothier,
died April 16, 1656, aged 55 Years.

ON

ON MONUMENTS IN THE
NORTH AISLE.

Arms ; on a Chevron between three
Dolphins embowed, three Crofles formée,
for TIPPETTS.

In Memory of WILLIAM TIPPETTS,
of this Town, Clothier,
and HANNAH his Wife.
He died March 25, 1725, aged 51.
She December 11, 1757, aged 51 alfo.

Alfo SARAH, Wife of
THOMAS TIPPETTS, their Son,
who died November 12, 1753, aged 31.

Likewife HANNAH CORNWALL,
Daughter of the above
WILLIAM and HANNAH,
died Feb. 26, 1777, aged 56.

Alfo the faid THOMAS TIPPETTS,
died April 5, 1789, æt. 60.

Arms; on a Bend Sable three Leopards
Faces of the Field, for ADEY.

M. S.
HENRY ADEY, Clothier,
died Jan. 7, 1734, aged 44 Years.

CHRISTIAN his Wife
died July 30, 1764, aged 15 Years.

Their Children:
WILLIAM
died Feb. 19, 1731, aged 9 Months.

ANN
died Dec. 23, 1742, aged 29 Years.

MARTHA
died May 17, 1762, aged 29 Years.

HENRY
died Aug. 13, 1766, aged 45 Years.

Alfo JUDITH, Wife of
HENRY ADEY, jun.
died July 10, 1755, aged 30 Years.

Arms; PULLEY, impaling HAYWARD.

Memento Mori.
In this Ifle
are depofited the Remains of
JOSEPH PULLEY, fen. and MARY his
Wife.
He departed this Life July 27, 1730,
aged 67 Years.
She was interred Feb. 2, 1748, aged 64.

Here alfo lieth ANN,
the beloved Daughter of the faid
JOSEPH and MARY PULLEY,
who died November 25, 1757,
aged 38 Years.

Here is depofited the Body of
THOMAS LEWTON, of this Town,
who departed this Life Dec. 24, 1760,
ætat. 60.

Alfo ANN his Daughter,
Wife of JAMES GETHEN, jun.
departed this Life March 7, 1762,
ætat. 32.
Alfo the Body of SAMUEL LEWTON,
Son of the above THOMAS LEWTON,
who departed this Life Feb. 10, 1764,
in the 38th Year of his Age.

Alfo here lieth the Body of
ANN LEWTON, Wife of the faid
THOMAS LEWTON,
who died March 14, 1776, aged ...

In this Aifle is an Atchievement,
bearing the Arms of WALLINGTON ;—
impaling, Per Pale, three Doves, for
THOMAS. Creft, a Dove, Wings difplayed, between two Spears erect.

SARAH, Daughter of
GILES and SARAH HODGES,
was buried here April 19, 1735,
aged 3 Years.

ANN, the Daughter of
RICHARD HODGES, Clothier, of Durfley,
died Jan. 17, 1704.

Here lyeth the Body of
RICHARD HODGES,
who departed this Life the .. Day of
Auguft, Anno 1711, aged 49 Years.

ANN, the Wife of RICHARD HODGES,
died the 23d Day of May, 1743,
aged 60 Years.

Here refteth the Body of
ANN, Relict of CHARLES PURNELL,
Gent. of North Nibley,
who died May 12, 1759, æt. 73.

Here refteth the Body of
MARY, Wife of ABRAHAM DANFORD,
who departed this Life
April 27, 1747, aged 70 Years.

Alfo EDMUND PERRATT, fenior,
died Anno Domini 1666.

Alfo EDMUND PERRATT, junior,
died Anno Domini 1723.

Likewife SAMUEL CHAMBERLAIN
died Sept. 27, 1729, aged 3 Years.

In Memory of
NICHOLAS NEALE, Clothier,
who died Dec. 20, 1756, aged 85.

Alfo of REBECCA his Wife,
who died Oct. 21, 1728, aged 35.

And of
two of their Sons, who died Infants.

Here refteth the Body of
THOMAS FRYER, of this Parifh, Clothier,
who departed this Life the 16th Day of
July, 1716, aged 50 Years.

Alfo of SARAH, Wife of
ISAAC OLIVER, fenior,
died the 16th Day of May, 1707.

SAMUEL MOODY, of this Town, Clothier,
died June 27, 17.. aged 58.

Here refteth the Body of
JOHN PURNELL, jun.
who departed this Life
the 8th Day of ...... 1696.

ESTHER, Wife of THOMAS BRUGE,
died Aug. 29, 17 ...

Alfo MOSES, Son of
MOSES and LYDIA Knight,
who died, 1746, an Infant.

Here refteth the Body of
ROBERT RENFREW, Chapn
who died July 14, 1738, aged 28 Years.

MARY HODGES,
Daughter of CHRISTIAN ADEY,
died Dec. 8, 1775, aged 82 Years.

To the Memory of the
Family of ADEY,
as defcribed in their Monument.

In Memory of HANNAH TIPPETTS,
who died Dec. 11, 1747,
aged 51 Years.

Alfo SARAH, Wife of
THOMAS TIPPETTS,
died Nov. 12, 1752, aged 31 Years.

Here refteth the Body of
RICHARD TIPPETTS,
of this Town, Clothier,
who died Feb. 16, 1730,
aged 41 Years.

In Memory of JOHN WATKINS,
who died March 24, 1781,
aged 61 Years.

In Memory of ESTHER,
the Wife of JOHN WATKINS,
of this Town,
who died Oct. 24, 1776,
aged 70 Years.

In Memory of JAMES GETHAN,
of this Town, fenior,
who died Auguft 9, 1781.
aged 78 Years.

Alfo ELIZABETH his Wife,
who died December 11, 1776,
aged 83 Years.

And alfo of their Son JOHN GETHAN,
of this Town, Cardmaker,
who died March 2, 1784,
aged 49 Years.

Alfo two Sons of
JOHN and MARY GETHAN,
who died, viz.
WILLIAM,
Sept. 3, 1770, aged 1 Year.
RICHARD,
March 25, 1778, aged 7 Years.

ON MONUMENTS IN THE
SOUTH AISLE.

Arms ; Per Cheveron embattled, in
Chief, two Eftoils in Bafe, two Spears
in Saltire,—for STIFF.

In Memory of
ELIZABETH, the Wife of JACOB STIFF,
who departed this Life Feb. 25, 1760,
in the 45th Year of her Age.

Alfo of Mr. JACOB STIFF,
who died Dec. 26, 1769,
aged 56 Years.

Near this Place lies interred
the Body of JOHN A WOOD,
of Durfley, Gent.
who died Auguft 4, 1740,
aged 68 Years.

T*

To the Memory of
Ann Barnes, Relict of John Barnes,
Surgeon, and only Sister of
Nathaniel Hickes, of Weftend,
in this County, Efq.
She died the 9th of April, 1768,
ætat. 57.

ON FLAT STONES.

Under this Stone is depofited
the Body of John Barnes, Gent.
eldeft Son of John Barnes,
of Gannerew, near Monmouth,
in the County of Hereford, Gent.
who departed this Life the firft Day of
July, in the Year of our Lord 1761,
in the 55th Year of his Age.

Brett Randolph, Efq.
late of Warwick, of James River,
Virginia,
born Sept. 4, 1732,
died Sept. 4, 1759.

Alfo Mary, Relict of
the faid Brett Randolph,
died Nov. 24, 1779, aged 49 Years.

Memoria Gulielmi Smith, Generofi,
qui mortem obiit vicefimo tertio die
Julii, A. D. 1733, ætatis 34.

In Memory of Daniel White,
who died Jan. 31, 1744, aged 53.

Elizabeth, Wife of
John Lawson,
died March 29, 1756.

Alfo Ann their Daughter
died . . . .

ON MONUMENTS AGAINST
THE BELFRY.

North Side.

Arms ; Checquy Or and Azure, on a
Fefs Gules three Lozenges Argent, for
Capel. Creft, three Oftrich Feathers
Argent.

Near this Place lyeth the Body of
Daniel Capel,
Vicar of Cam, and Curate of Durfley,
who departed this Life May 1,
A. D. 1737, aged 68 Years.

South Side.

Arms ; Argent, on a Fefs Sable, between three Lozenges Gules, three
Cinquefoils of the Field, for Purnell;
—impaling, Argent, a Chevron Azure,
between three Falcons rifing proper, for
Philipps.

In Memory of
William Purnell, Gent.
who departed this Life Jan. 4, 1743,
aged 69.

And of Ann his Wife,
who died May 11, 1760, aged 76.

And of their Son
John Purnell, of Newhoufe, Efq.
who, adorned with every focial
and Chriftian Virtue,
as a Son, a Hufband, a Father, and
a Friend,
drew his laft Breath without a Groan,
and crown'd a Life of Piety
by a Death of Peace.
He marryed Anna, Daughter of
John Phelps, Efq.
by Mary, Daughter of
John Arundell, Efq.
whofe congenial Benevolence, and
amiable Conduct in the
female Duties of domeftic Life,
rendered her Death feverely felt,
and fincerely lamented.
She died March 18, 1765, aged 58.
He died October 31, 1782, aged 78.

IN THE CHURCH YARD, ON TOMBS.

William May
was buried June 27, 1685.

Two Daughters of
John and Mary King.

Ann died 18 December, 1685.

Elizabeth died 6 January, 1686.

Thomas King, of this Town,
who died the 8th of January, 1689,
aged 74.

Thomas King,
of this Town, fenior, Baker,
died March 30, 1722, aged 85 Years.

Mary his Wife
died April 24, 1717, aged 84 Years.

Henry their Son
died April 15, 1733, aged 60 Years.

Thomas their Son
died Oct. 25, 1746, aged 19.

Ann their Daughter
died Dec. 20, 1759, aged 30 Years.

Mary, Wife of
Richard Roe, of this Town, fenior,
died Jan. 2, 1760, aged 75.

Alfo Edward and William their Sons
were buried here.

Alfo the faid Richard Roe
died April 17, 1770, aged 85 Years.

Elizabeth and Ann,
Daughters of Richard Roe,
were buried here.

Judith, Wife of Thomas King,
died Feb. 14, 1734, aged 35 Years.

Elizabeth her Daughter
died Dec. 11, 1734, aged 3.

Thomas Taylor,
of this Town, Baker,
died Aug. 13, 1752, aged 33.

Two of his Children by Mary his Wife
are buried here.

Thomas, Son of
William and Mary Taylor,
died Nov. 3, 1710, aged 9 Months.

Mary Jenkins, Daughter of
William and Mary Taylor,
died June 14, 1780, aged 71.

Hannah her Daughter
died Oct. 4, 1779, aged 32.

Sarah, Wife of William Taylor,
died May 9, 1751, aged 69.

Alfo five of her Children.

Four died in their Infancy.

Hannah died in the 15th Year of her
Age.

Sarah, Daughter of
John and Eliz. Everett,
died Sept. 12, 1747, aged 22.

Elizabeth, Wife of
John Everett,
died Aug. 6, 1767, aged 68.

Mary, Wife of
Thomas Collier, fen.
died Oct. 8, 1780, aged 66 Years.

Hester their Daughter
died March 13, 1748, aged 4 Years.

Thomas Collier, jun.
died Jan. 8, 1785, aged 36.

Here refteth the Body of
John Hallows, late Clark of this
Parifh,
who died Jan. 7, 1745,
in the 61ft Year of his Age.

Alfo Joan, Wife of
the faid John Hallows.

Joseph Hallows
died May 23, 1787, aged 64 Years.

Jane, Wife of James Gethen of this
Town, Baker.

Alfo four of their Children.

Under this Tomb lie the Bodies of
Thomas Gethen, and Mary his Wife.

Thomas their Son
died Dec. 8, 1787, aged 67.

Ann, Wife of John Gethen, and
Daughter of Robert Bennett of
Wotton Under Edge, Writing Mafter,
died March 5, 1749, aged 48 Years.

John Gethen died Dec. 7, 1781,
aged 79 Years.

Thomas

THOMAS and WILLIAM,
Sons of JOHN and MARY,
were buried here Infants.

MARY, Daughter of THOMAS and
MARY BALL, died Sep. 14, 1746,
aged 10 Years.

MARY, Wife of JOHN BALL, Baker,
died Nov. 5, 1741, aged 33.

SARAH, his Second Wife
died Jan. 11, 1784, aged 78.

SUSANNA, Daughter of
FRANCIS WHITNEY,
died Nov. 6, 1773, aged 29.

FRANCIS WHITNEY, of this Town,
Clothier, died April 4, 1763, aged 63.

MARY, Wife of JAMES NICHOLAS,
died Nov. 18, 1773, aged 31.

JAMES, their Son died Jan. 10, 1774,
aged 4 Years.

MARY, their Daughter died April 14,
1774, aged 1 Year.

MARY, Wife of FRANCIS WHITNEY,
died Jan. 26, 1737, aged 36.

Four Children died in their Infancy.

FRANCIS WHITNEY
died Oct. 18, 1702, aged 72 Years.

MARY, Wife of FRANCIS WHITNEY,
died Aug. 6, 1699.

Also here lyeth ROBERT WHITNEY,
their Son.

CHARLES WHITNEY, Clothier,
died Jan. 6, 1733, aged 59.

MARY, their Daughter, was buried
Dec. 2, 1734, aged 36.

MARY, Wife of THOMAS HILL, jun.
died Nov. 9, 1765, aged 48 Years.

THOMAS HILL, jun.
died May, 20, 1772, aged 61.

EDWARD FRIEND
died April 28, 1774, aged 49.

ELIZABETH, his Wife, Daughter of
THOMAS HILL,
died Jan. 20, 1765, aged 43.

EDWARD their Son, Aug. 3, 1755,
aged 2 Years.

THOMAS HILL
died June 10, 1758, aged 73 Years.

ELIZABETH, Wife of THOMAS HILL,
died June 19, 1762, aged 77.

WILLIAM FAITHORN
died Sep. 12, 1758, aged 26.

Two of his Children, viz.

MARY,
died March 1, 1757, aged 1 Year.

NATHANIEL,
died March 2, 1757, aged 5 Years.

HESTER, his Wife,
died April 24, 1785, aged 60.

JOSEPH FAITHORN, jun. of this Town,
Brazier, died July 21, 1742, aged 58.

MARTHA, Wife of
JOSEPH FAITHORN, jun.
died Feb. 8, 1718, aged 23.

THOMAS TILLADAM, Cardmaker,
Dec. 18, 1743, aged 58.

JOSEPH, Son of THOMAS TILLADAM,
died Oct. 8, 1769, aged 49 Years.

ELIZABETH his Daughter
died June 20, 1772, aged 19 Years.

THOMAS TILLADAM
died July 23, 1761, aged 48 Years.

DEBORAH, Wife of
THOMAS TILLADAM, Cardmaker,
died April 2, 1731, aged 39.

Also Six Children.

MARY, Wife of
THOMAS TILLADAM, jun.
died Oct. 29, 1748, aged 31.

JOHN their Son, April 5, 1742,
aged 6 Months.

MARTHA, Wife of
JOSEPH TILLADAM,
died May 15, 1767, aged 39 Years.

Hic jacent Reliquiæ
SAMUELIS ROGERS . . . . . .

Hic jacet Corpus JACOBI BAYLEY,
de Londino, Gent.
Obiit die Novembris 2, 1731.

OBADIAH WEBB, Mercer,
once Bayliff of this Town,
buried Oct. 29, 1669, aged 49.

ELIZABETH his Wife,
Oct. 17, 1692, aged 72.

ROBERT their Son
died Jan. 21, 1666, aged 19.

SAMUEL their Son
died July 20, 1667, aged 17.

MARY, Feb. 2, 1670, aged 10.

MARY HICKS was buried
Sep 16, 1742, aged 40.

JOHN WEBB, Mercer,
died June 30, 1722, aged 64.

ELIZABETH his Daughter
died Feb. 3, 1690, aged 4 Years.

SARAH his Wife
died Jan. 31, 1732, aged 68.

ARTHUR VIZAR, of this Town, Gent.
died Jan 6, 1663, aged 71 Years.

JOHN VIZARD, of this Town, Clothier,
his Kinsman, and HANNAH his Wife,
who died, viz.

He, April 5, 1731, aged 65 Years;
She, Feb. 15, 1733, aged 69 Years.

HANNAH their Daughter, Wife of
WILLIAM ROACH,
died Sept. 30, 1756, aged 55 Years.

MARY, Wife of GEORGE WHITNEY,
and Daughter of JOHN and
HANNAH VIZARD,
died July 12, 1757, aged 50.

MARTHA VIZARD,
another of their Daughters,
died March 12, 1786, aged 67.

HANNAH ROACH,
died May 6, 1787, aged 42 Years.

MAURICE BUTCHER, Native of Cam,
died Jan. 18, 1771, aged 77 Years.

SARAH his Wife, Daughter of
ROBERT and SARAH WEIGHT,
died Oct. 4, 1770, aged 73.

ROBERT WEIGHT
died Jan. 9, 1741, aged 75 Years.

SARAH his Wife
died May 22, 1741, aged 76 Years.

PETER their Son was buried here.

MAURICE BUTCHER,
of this Town, Cardmaker,
died April 22, 1778, aged 44 Years.

ANN SMITH, Relict of
SAMUEL SMITH, and Daughter of
JOHN and ALICE LAMB,
died Nov. 25, 1775, aged 74.

CHARLES EGGBY
died July 10, 1744, aged 47 Years.

HESTER his Wife
died June 27, 1767, aged 73 Years.

JOHN, CHARLES, and WILLIAM,
their Sons, died Young.

DANIEL their Brother
died Dec. 10, 1781, aged 49.

MARY, Wife of WILLIAM DREW,
died Oct. 2, 1774, aged 49 Years.

ELIZABETH WORKMAN,
died March 10, 1779, aged 73.

Here lyeth the Body of
HENRY ADEY,
who departed this Life,
August 19, 1664.

MARTHA, the Wife of HENRY ADEY,
was buried Feb. 26, 1745, aged 68.

Here lieth the Body of JOHN TUCKER,
who died May 12, 1637, aged 88.

Here resteth the Body of
HENRY ADEY, of Durfley, Clothier,
who departed this Life the 11th day of
May, Anno Dom. 1704, ætatis suæ 51.

Here resteth the Body of
JOHN ADEY,
who died May 4, 1743, aged 79 Years.

DANIEL ADEY, Son of
JOHN ADEY, Clothier,
died Jan. 9, 1729, aged 39 Years.

JOHN ADEY, Son of
JOHN ADEY, Clothier,
died Nov. 6, 1761, aged 67 Years.

LYDIA WASHBOURNE, Daughter of
JOHN ADEY,
died July 27, 1765, aged 64 Years.

HESTER, Daughter of JOHN ADEY,
died June 12, 1770, aged 81 Years.

JOANNA, Wife of JOHN HURLSTONE,
died Oct. 15, 1774, aged 51 Years.

JOHN HURLSTONE
died Dec. 17, 1778, aged 62 Years.

JOYCE,

Joyce, the Daughter of
John and Joanna Hurlstone,
died April 21, 1777, aged 30.

Elizabeth, the Wife of
Samuel Trotman, Daughter of
Richard and Sarah Merrick,
died March 16, 1771, aged 63.

Richard Merrick, sen. Mercer,
died May 10, 1714, aged 45.

William Merrick, Mercer,
was buried Aug. 20, ...

Daniel, Son of William Merrick,
died . . . . day of January.

Isaac Smyth,
of this Parish, Clothier,
died May 17, 1726, aged 71.

H. I. E.
Annæ, Filiæ plurimum dilectæ,
Johannis Berriman, hujus Parochiæ,
Pharmacopolæ, quæ deceſſit
16 die Augusti, Anno 1725,
Ætatis suæ decimo quinto.

Eliz. Filia Johannis &
Johannæ Barnes, e vitâ migravit
Maii 16, 1742, & Anno Ætatis suæ . . . .

Johanna, Uxor Johannis Barnes,
obiit 28 Augusti Annoque Dom. 1747,
Ætatis suæ 40.

Here lieth the Body of
Woolvin Barnes,
who died Aug. 11, 1760,
Ætatis suæ . . . .

John Tippetts, sen.
of the New Mills, Clothier,
departed this Life, May 31, 1706,
aged 55.

Mary his Wife,
died Nov. 4, 1727, aged 67.

Mary and Rebecca,
Daughters of the faid John and Mary,
interred here.

John Tippetts,
of the New Mills, in this Parish Clothier,
died July 17, 1736, aged 41.

John, the Son of
John and Ann Tippetts,
died Jan. 17, 1736, aged 6 Years.

Ann, Relict of
John Tippetts, Clothier,
died Sept. 8, 1758, aged 57.

Mary, Wife of Joseph Slucock,
Daughter of John and Eliz. Phillips,
died April 8, 1729, aged 47.

Hic Jacet
Johannis Berriman,
hujus oppidi,
Pharmacopola celeberrimus,
qui obiit decimo quarto die
Menſis Aprilis, Anno Domini 1748,
Ætatis suæ 74.
Deo fretus, Amicis blandus,
Germanis munificus,
omnibus carus ;
multis ille bonis
flebilis occidit.

Mr. James Berriman Tippetts,
of this Town, Apothecary,
Nephew to the above John Berriman,
died June 20, 1782.

William Partridge, Mercer,
died Feb. 2, 1682, aged 54.

Eliz. Wife of
William Partridge, Mercer,
died Oct. 12, 1721, aged 75.

William, Son of
William Partridge,
died Nov. 1, 1663, aged 2 Years,

Ann Davis
died April 15, 1754, aged 75.
Samuel, Son of Benjamin and
Elizabeth Hill,
died Feb. 28, 1759, aged 7 Years.

William Partridge,
of Durſley, Clothier,
died the laſt day of Feb. 1690,
aged 20 Years.

John, Son of Giles and
Ann Workman,
died Sep. 23, 1748, aged 28.

Eliz. Relict of John Workman,
and Wife of Samuel Gardner,
died April 19, 1744, aged 62.

Maurice Smith
died Dec. 4, 1736, aged 60.

Elizabeth, Wife of
Maurice Smith,
died Nov. 29, 1738, aged 54 Years.

Three Children of
Maurice and Elizabeth Smith
died young.

Ann Watkins,
Wife of John Watkins, Mercer,
who deceaſed Feb. 15, 1660,
being aged 50 Years.

John Watkins, of Durſley, Mercer,
died Oct. 6, 1691.

Elizabeth, Wife of
Samuel King, Daughter of
John Watkins,
buried here Dec. 5, 1704.

Nathaniel, Son of Samuel King,
died Oct. 22, 1704.

Elizabeth, Wife of
Maurice Smith, Daughter of
Samuel King,
died Dec. 2, 1704.

Alſo Samuel King, Mercer,
died Oct. 2, 1708.

Maurice Phillips,
of this Town, Clothier,
died March 5, 1720, aged 86.

Elizabeth, Wife of
Maurice Phillips,
died Oct. 1, 1730, aged 95.

They lived in Wedlock 65 Years.

Samuel and Elizabeth Elliot.
He died Feb. 6, 1774,
aged 84 Years.
She died Dec. 14, 1727.

John their Son
died May 12, 1743, aged 22.

William
July 1, 1770, aged 30.

Judith, Daughter of
Samuel Elliott, by Elizabeth
his ſecond Wife,
died Aug. 12, 1775, aged 26 Years.

Henry Williams
died Dec. 16. 1694.

Edmund, Son of
Edmund and Jane Hort,
died May 20, 1735, aged 22.

Thomas their Son
died Jan. 29, 1738, aged 23 Years.

Four more of their Children buried here.

Nathaniel
died May 29, 1723, aged 5 Years.

Jane
died Sept. 12, 1728, aged 2 Years.

John
died May 30, 1733, aged 3 Years.

Alice
died Jan. 12, 1773, aged 22.

Edmund Hort, of Durſley,
died Aug. 4, 1738, aged 57.

Jane his Wife
died Jan. 13, 17 . . .

Sarah, Wife of Richard Cooper,
died April 5, 1744, aged 59.

Martha their Daughter
died Aug. 20, 1736, aged 13 Years.

Richard Cooper
died Jan. 19, 1749, aged 64 Years.

Maurice Andrews
died Sept. 22, 1749, aged 29.

Maurice, Son of John Andrews,
died May 12, 1712, aged 34.

John, Son of the ſaid
Maurice Andrews.

Eliz. Wife of Maurice Andrews,
died Sept. 14, 1759, aged 80.

John Andrews
died March 26, 1752, aged 72.

Nathaniel Went
died March 29, 1759, aged 84.

Hannah Went
died Aug. 15, 1744, aged 42.

John Went
died Oct. 9, 1772. aged 62.

Hannah Blackwell,
died Aug. 16, 1744, aged 42.

Ann George
died Jan. 15, 1782, aged 81.

Jacob Wallington, Eſq.
was buried March 31, 1740,
aged 28 Years.

Nicholas Neale, Clothier,
was buried Oct. 26, 1702, aged 63.

Alice his Wife
died Jan. 14, 1734, aged 80.

Thomas Neale,
of this Town, Clothier,
died March 28, 1754, aged 71.

Esther, Daughter of John Neale,
of this Town,
died May 25, 1759, aged 36.

Mary, Daughter of Thomas Neale,
died Feb. 27, 1755, aged 36 Years.

William

WILLIAM SANIGEAR,
of this Town,
died Feb. 4, 1771, aged 70.

MARTHA his Wife
died March 9, 1753, aged 55.

MARY, Daughter of
WILLIAM SANIGEAR, jun.
died Feb. 24, 1759, aged 2 Years.

SARAH, Wife of ABRAHAM SANIGEAR,
Daughter of
THOMAS and ANN LEWTON,
died June 14, 1770, aged 34 Years.

WILLIAM their Son
died July 14, 1760, aged 7 Years.

JOSEPH JONES,
died May 2, 1735, aged 42.

LUCAS his Son
died June 25, 1763, aged 35.

JOSEPH, Son of JOSEPH JONES,
died July 23, 1769, aged 39 Years.

ELIZABETH, Wife of
JOSEPH JONES, junior,
died May 3, 1770, aged 39 Years.

JACOB STIFF,
died Nov. 18, 1735, aged 56 Years.

ANN, Daughter of
JACOB and ELIZ. STIFF,
died May 24, 1735, aged 17.
Three more of their Children were
buried here.

MARY, Wife of JOSEPH CARTER,
died April 18, 1722, aged 31.

Three Children dyed young.

JOSEPH CARTER
dyed June 20, 1780, aged 49.

Four Children of
THOMAS and MARY SMITH.

THOMAS SMITH
died April 19, 1768, aged 58 Years.

ON FLAT AND HEAD STONES.

	Died	Aged
James Griffin, Baker	22 Apr. 1764	28
John Griffin, Baker	18 July, 1755	53
John his Son	10 Aug. 1746	11
Christopher Pincott	29 Oct. 1782	88
Elizabeth his Daughter	25 June, 1733	12
James Pincott	15 Sept. 1748	20
Daniel Pincott	7 Mar. 1772	72
Mary his Wife	14 Jan. 1757	60
Ann, Wife of Thomas Williams	4 May, 1776	37
Two Children of Robert and Christian Thurston	in Infancy.	
Richard, Son of John Pingrey, of Acton, in Worcestershire	19 June, 1753	56
Joseph Weaver	21 Jan. 1730	45
Three Children of Joseph and Sarah Stephens	—— 1717	—
Henry, Son of Daniel and Ann Budding	9 Jan. 1715	—
Robert How	30 Oct. 1723	60
Nathaniel Newth	5 July, 1763	61
Ann his Wife	20 Oct. 1748	49
John, Wife of John Vizard, sen.	—— 1718	—
William Hallowes and } He	21 July, 1718	—
Ann his Wife } She	20 Oct. 1723	—
Samuel, Son of the said William and Ann	24 July, 1734	21
Sarah Hallowes, Widow	23 Mar. 1723	87
James Barnfield	24 Jan. 1721	77
Robert Belcher	15 May, 1727	22
Ann, Daughter of John and Elizabeth Belcher	15 July, 1718	—
Samuel Belcher, Joiner	2 Sept. 1761	52
Mary, Wife of Thomas Everett	19 Aug. 1762	83
Thomas Everett	11 Sept. 1764	76
Martha, Wife of John Hickes, Surgeon	17 Apr. 1709	58
Thomas Hickes, Surgeon, Son of John and Martha	7 May, 1732	42
Sarah, Daughter of Joseph and Sarah Weaver	18 May, 1723	1
John Hart	20 Feb. 1774	37
Joan his Wife	18 Feb. 1769	29
Mary, Wife of Joseph Williams	2 Feb. 1745	68
Three of his Wives and two Children	——	—
Benjamin Hallows	7 May, 1734	68
Sarah his Wife	7 Apr. 1728	52
William Stevens, Mason	26 Aug. 1739	60
Mary, Wife of Thomas Curtis	22 Mar. 1747	56
Thomas, Son of Thomas and Sarah Nichols	18 May, 1769	13
Thomas Nichols	16 Dec. 1771	72
Richard, Son of James Trull	— Jan. 1722	25
Ann Pullin	5 May, 1735	70
John Pullin	12 June, 1735	24
Mary, Wife of Jonathan Lamb	6 June, 1741	39
Margaret her Daughter	29 Jan. 1728	7
Hugh Everett	26 Oct. 1781	52
Joseph his Son	11 Oct. 1770	6

	Died	Aged
Mary, Wife of Thomas Green	6 Feb. 1757	54
Thomas Green	25 Feb. 1758	54
William Wood	8 Sept. 1760	59
Judith his Wife	13 Mar. 1777	81
Elizabeth, Wife of Jacob Clark	8 Mar. 1745	25
Mary his second Wife	17 Nov. 1770	52
John Higgins	20 Sept. 1778	81
Mary his Wife	— Nov. 1770	70
Joseph Sanfum	2 Dec. 1783	37
Arthur Vizard	26 Sept. 1784	77
Mary, Wife of Jacob Willey, Basket-maker	30 July, 1765	72
Arthur Perry	1 Dec. 1747	—
Mary his Wife	— May, 1743	—
Thomas Gibbs	26 May, 1745	37
Sarah his Wife	——	—
Nicholas Neale, of this Town, jun.	4 Nov. 1770	52
Ann his Wife	2 Sept. 1781	65
John Morgan	——	—
Sarah, Wife of James Morgan	22 Mar. 1767	—
Joseph Oliver, Clothdrawer	— Nov. ——	43
Abraham, Son of Thomas and Esther Stiff	10 Sept. 1738	—
Elizabeth, Wife of Thomas Oldland	20 May, 1752	39
Elizabeth Harrold	16 Feb. 1784	82
Elizabeth her Daughter	21 Apr. 1762	10
John Lance	10 Mar. 1784	45
Frances Elder	1 June, 1762	—
Martha, Daughter of John and Susanna Dando	12 Mar. 1759	2
Stephen, Son of the said John and Susanna	4 May, 1759	—
Thomas Browning, Wheelwright	9 Sept. 1752	—
William, Son of John Collins	——	—
Timothy Trotman, Baker	12 Sept. 1773	60
Mary his Wife	23 Oct. 1773	61
Christiana, Daughter of Robert and Ann Smith	8 Apr. 1779	3
Richard Cornock	7 Nov. 1762	27
Mary, Wife of Thomas Smith, jun.	4 Jan. 1772	58
Ann, Daughter of John Craig	9 May, 1767	31
Sarah, Wife of Thomas Hughes	4 Feb. 1734	38
Elizabeth, Wife of Benjamin Millard, senior	16 Oct. 1735	42
Three of their Children	——	—
Sarah, Wife of John Wilkes	11 Feb. 1770	39
Ann her Daughter	22 Sept. 1770	2
William, Son of William and Hannah Wood	6 Mar. 1759	3
John Wood	2 Apr. 1762	73
Sarah his Wife	25 Apr. 1762	78
Samuel Smith, Butcher	12 Sept. 1757	50
Samuel his Son	10 Sept. 1766	31
John Ireland, senior	14 Apr. 1691	56
Rebecca his Wife	27 Feb. 1715	78
William his Son	21 June, 1686	18
Francis Curtis	2 Apr. 1716	77
Katharine his Wife	2 Feb. 1747	88

C N

ON FLAT AND HEAD STONES.

	Died	Aged
Francis Curtis, Clothier -	8 Mar. 1759	66
Elizabeth his Daughter -	— — —	—
Thomas Curtis, Carpenter -	9 Sept. 17‚6	65
Mary, Wife of Thomas Grace	1 Jan. 1767	38
Edmund Lewis, of the City of Bristol, Blacksmith -	24 Aug. 1752	—
Judith, Wife of John Smith, Cardmaker - -	30 Apr. 1757	60
The said John Smith -	1 May, 1760	84
Mary, Wife of Thomas Wyman	6 Apr. 1770	50
Elizabeth their Daughter -	17 Aug. 1764	18
William, Son of William and Sarah Blake - -	8 Feb. 1784	—
William Blake, senior -	22 Apr. 1786	59
Daniel Cull - -	4 Mar. 1785	63
Mary, Daughter of John and Mary Cull - -	17 June, 1786	23
Edward Wells - -	17 May, 1754	72
Sarah his Wife -	12 Dec. 1747	80
John Harding, Cardmaker	23 Dec. 1761	60
Elizabeth his Wife -	29 Aug. 1767	64
Elizabeth, Wife of Thomas Brothers	9 May, 1722	48
Thomas Brothers -	11 June, 1728	62
Joseph Keiching, Cordwainer	9 Dec. 1736	73
Elizabeth his Wife -	— — —	67
Joseph their Son -	3 Dec. 1759	61
Daniel, Son of Daniel and Sarah Workman - -	14 Sept. 1758	3
Robert Workman -	— Dec. 1748	65
Sarah his Wife - -	11 Aug. 1735	42
Elizabeth, Wife of Samuel Hill	6 Mar. 1737	54
William Holder -	23 Sept. 1767	66
Hester his Wife - -	6 Dec. 1746	57
William their Son -	31 Apr. 1732	27
Elizabeth their Daughter -	8 Oct. 1768	32
Robert Clark - -	8 May, 1721	75
Robert Collier - -	2 Aug. 1764	65
Martha his Wife -	2 Feb. 1747	47
Nathaniel their Son -	14 Oct. 1742	16
Thomas their Son -	20 June, 1764	22
Nathaniel Pitt -	12 Aug. 1723	72
Mary his Wife - -	23 Dec. 1741	79
Daniel Egby - -	15 Feb. 1737	65
Sarah his Wife -	17 Jan. 1756	84
Daniel their Son -	18 Dec. 1778	62
Sarah his Wife, Daughter of William and Sarah Taylor -	14 Oct. 1780	64
William Roach -	31 July, 1703	76
Hannah his Wife -	7 May, 1709	—
Josiah Roach, of Cam, their Son	5 Oct. 1753	74
Ann, Wife of Benjamin King	22 Mar. 1712	37
John Lamb - -	23 Aug. 1731	71
Sarah Rogers - -	7 Oct. 1740	—

	Died	Aged
Two Sons and two Daughters of Joseph and Hannah Williams	— — —	—
John Weight - -	— — —	—
John Millard - -	6 Jan. 1756	66
John his Son - -	— — —	—
Elizabeth his Wife -	17 Jan. 1757	81
Esther, Wife of John Phelps	22 Jan. 1757	28
Richard Wyman Fuller -	1 Dec. 1743	45
Mary his Daughter -	15 Apr. 1730	2
Two Children of Thomas and Elizabeth Harman -	— — —	—
Ann, Wife of Samuel Stockwell	7 May, 1746	17
William Browning -	25 Dec. 1745	60
Elizabeth his Wife -	11 Apr. 1725	41
Daniel their Son -	22 Dec. 1715	11
Martha, Wife of Thomas Heath	18 Apr. 1733	95
Sarah their Daughter -	21 Sept. 1734	55
Elizabeth, Daughter of Thomas and Elizabeth Dawes, of North Nibley	8 Apr. 1755	39
Thomas Daw - -	25 May, 1771	89
Thomas Cook, Glover -	12 Sept. 1756	62
Samuel Morgan - -	11 Dec. 1777	80
Mary his Wife - -	23 July, 1768	60
Three of their Children died young.		
Jacob Clark, senior -	6 Apr. 1763	73
Esther his Wife - -	16 Apr. 1762	73
William their Son -	11 Feb. 1757	9
James Gethen, Cardmaker -	26 May, 1736	88
Lois his Wife - -	3 Oct. 1738	69
Betty, Wife of Nathaniel Young	19 Feb. 1753	35
Daniel Young -	22 July, 1746	67
Sampson Browning -	16 Aug. 1748	42
Elizabeth, Wife of Sampson Browning, senior - -	— July, 1727	—
Mary, Wife of Thomas Wyman	6 July, 1770	—
Thomas Wyman, junior -	16 June, 1772	23
Daniel Ricketts -	— Sept. 1727	57
William Trotman -	9 July, 1729	32
Edward and Mary, Son and Daughter of ——Seaborn -	— — —	—
John Grace - -	31 Jan. 1672	—
John Damzel - -	27 May, 1730	51
Margery his Wife -	27 Oct. 1758	82
Joan, Wife of Daniel Webb	13 Aug. 1708	62
James Vinton - -	13 Oct. 1733	69
Thomas his Son -	29 Jan. 1727	19
Elizabeth, Wife of Thomas Jenkins	10 Feb. 1720	74
Sarah, Wife of Thomas Jenkins, jun.	31 Dec. 1785	—
Richard Hitchins -	26 Oct. 1787	61
Mary his Wife - -	27 Apr. 1788	64
Mary their Daughter, Wife of John Harding - -	4 Oct. 1789	29

CVI. DYMOCK

CVI.   D Y M O C K

IS a very large Parifh, in the Hundred of *Botloe*, contiguous to the County of *Hereford*, three Miles and a half diftant from *Newent*, eleven Miles North from *Michel Dean*, and feventeen North-weft from the City of GLOUCESTER. Its Extent is nearly fix Miles each Way, being of a circular Form; the Soil, one Part in feven, light and fandy, and the Remainder Clay, peculiarly favourable to the Growth of Oak Timber, and very numerous Orchards, as the Fruit Trees are frequently planted in the arable Fields *.

The Living is a Vicarage, endowed with Tythes, though of late Years ftipendiary only from the Impropriation †. It was confirmed in 1242 by the Bull of Pope ALEXANDER III. to the *Benedictine* Abbey of *Cormeilles*, in *Normandy*, " Ecclefiam de *Dimoc*, cum omnibus pertinentiis fuis, & decimis apud *Di-* " *moc* 40 Solid. decimam de toto Dominio, & unam virgatam terræ in eâdem villâ ‡ ;" which was transferred to the Mafter and Fellows of the College of *Fotheringhey*, co. *Northampton*, when founded by King HENRY IV. §   At the final Suppreffion of Monafteries, the faid Mafter and Fellows furrendered the Impropriation, by Deed of Exchange, to King HENRY VIII. in the 38th of his Reign, 1547; and in the 1ft of EDW. VI. Sir RICHARD LEE, Knight, procured a Grant of it in Fee, at the yearly Rent of 40s. The Family of WYNTER, eminent for their Attachment to the STUARTS, afterwards held the Rectory, with the Advowfon, which in 1652 (the Eftates of Sir JOHN WYNTER being confifcated by the Parliament) was fold to DANIEL WYCHERLEY and THOMAS MILWARD, Efqrs. Of Sir ORLANDO HUMPHREYS it was purchafed by GEORGE PRITCHARD, Efq. whofe Daughter and fole Heir, deceafed, was the Wife of HENRY LAMBERT, Efq. by whom fhe left one Daughter, SUSAN LAMBERT PRIICHARD, whofe Property it now is.

The Church is dedicated to *St. Mary*, and is included in the *Foreft* Deanery. The Nave is long and fpacious, with a Tranfept of unequal Height, and not oppofite. In the North is a Gothic Arcade, which contained the Image of the *Virgin*; the laft Chaplain of the Chantry dedicated to her was JOHN WOOD. Againft the Tower, which is maffy, with a very obtufe Spire, are, two Efcocheons, bearing, 1. Three Pheons, for FORSTER; 2. Two Bendlets, charged with Barrs dancettè. In the Veftry is an old mural Monument, intended for the Family of BRYDGES, to which Braffes were once affixed. The original Form of the Building is much altered by frequent and modern Repairs.

It appears, that the Village of *Dymock* was in early Times privileged with a Market and Fairs, that it was of greater Extent and more populous; and that the Inhabitants were exempted from certain County Rates, by King HENRY the Third. To the Collectors of the King's Tenths and Fifteenths it then paid 8*l.* 16*s.* 6*d.* from which 2*l.* 16*s.* 6*d.* were deducted.

What Accounts of the Defcent of the Manor have been tranfmitted to us are vague and uncertain, for it has been divided, and the Portions inaccurately fpecified. By the Crown it was given and annexed to the Earldom of *Hereford*; it is afterward faid to have belonged to the Families of CLIFFORD and GRANDISON. In 32 HEN. VI. Sir WALTER DEVEREUX and ELIZABETH his Wife, claimed four Parts of the Manor, which were vefted in 1565, 7 ELIZ. in WALTER Vifcount HEREFORD, by whom they were fettled in Jointure on LETICE his Wife (re-married to ROBERT DUDLEY, Earl of *Leicefter*),

---

* " In the deep-foiled Diftrict about *Dymock*, where the whole Country may be faid to be a Foreft of Fruit Trees, the Occupiers " of Fruit Grounds, experiencing the Evil of Trees in arable Lands, are planting in their Grafs Grounds. This, however, appears " to be a wrong Principle. Let them lay their old Orchards to Grafs, and if they plant break up their young Orchards to " Arable; this will be changing the Courfe of Hufbandry, and be at once beneficial to the Land and the Trees."
                                                     MARSHALL's Rur. Œc. vol. II. p. 287.

† " Vicarage. Decim' ibidem. Abb. *Flaxley*, olim Imp. 9*l.* 13*s.* 4*d.* BACON's Lib. Reg. p. 333.

‡ DUGDALE's Mon. vol. II. pp. 663. 964.   " Valor annuus Ecclefiarum De *Newent Beckford* & *Dymoc*, quæ funt Poffeffiones " Spirituales ad Prioratum de *Newent* fpectantes, pro quibus JOHANNES CHEYNE, Chivaler, & THOMAS HORSTON, Cler. nuper " Firmarii earandarum 150 Marcas annuatim nobis per literas prefentes reddere tenebantur."

§ 67*l.* 6*s.* 8*d.* quandam annuam Firmam quam JOHANNES CHEIGNE, Chivaler, reddere tenetur annuatim pro cuftodiâ Maneriorum temporalium de *Newent*, &c. Ibid. vol. I. p. 159.
The Vicar for many Years paft has received an annual Stipend from the Impropriation of 40*l.* and lately of 60*l.* But it appears by the Return made to the Commiffion to afcertain the Firft Fruits due to the Crown, under the Statute of 26 HEN. VIII. that the Vicar was then entitled to vicarial Tythes, and by the Charters of *Fotheringhey*, temp. EDW. IV. and RICH. III. that fuch were of the whole Parifh, excepting thofe of Corn and Grain.

6 X

and

and whofe Right was proved in 1581 *.   Giles Forster, Efq. was the Proprietor in 1608, and foon
after

* The Cuftoms of *Dymock* were inveftigated by the Committee of the Houfe of Commons for fcrutinizing the Votes
at the contefted Election in 1776, when the Tenants of the Manor were declared to have given legal Suffrages.

A Schedule indented, of the old and ancient Cuftom of the Manor of *Dymock*, in the County of Gloucester, made and enrolled
the fifth Day of Aprill, in the feventh Year of the Reign of Queen Elizabeth, ufed within the faid Manor, by the Cuftom
and ancient Demeyne Tennants of the faid Manor Time out of Mind, or the Remhmbrance of any Man, between the Right
Hon. Walter Vicount Hereford, Lord Ferrers of Chartley, and Lord of the faid Manor of *Dymock*, of the one Part,
and the ancient Demeyne Tennants of the Manor aforefaid of the other Part, as hereafter be expreffed.

1. Imprimis, The Cuftom of the faid Manor of *Dymock* is, and always has been for the Time aforefaid, that the cuftomary and
ancient Demeyne Tennants of the faid Manor as aforefaid, do hold their Lands to them and to the Heirs of their Bodys lawfully
begotten ; the Reverfion and Remainder thereof, in Fee, to the Lord of the faid Manor as aforefaid.

Item 2d, That they have ufed always, all the Time aforefaid, when they be difpofed to will, fell, give, grant, or alienate their
Lands or Tenements to any Perfon or Perfons whatfoever, to make Eftate thereof by free Deed indented or poll Deed, to fuch
Perfons whatfoever, to have and to hold to them and to the Heirs of their Bodys lawfully begotten, the Remainder thereof to
the Lord of the faid Manor and his Heirs for ever, with Lycence of the Lord of theManor in that Behalf obtained.

Item 3d, The Cuftom is, that the Lord of the Manor, for the Time being, have always ufed for the Time aforefaid, to give
and grant in the Court or Court Baron there, within the faid Manor, upon Requeft of any Tennant or Tennants difpofed to
make Alienation, as is aforefaid, fuch Lycence to do the fame, and the Lycence to be enrolled in the Court Rolls of the faid
Manor, by the Steward of the Lord for the Time being.

Item 4th, That the Tennants aforefaid, for fuch Lycences and Alienation as is aforefaid, have ufed to pay to the Lord of the
Manor one Year's Rent, by the Name of a Relief, and to the Steward for the Copy of the faid Lycence Two Shillings.

Item 5th, The Cuftom is, that the Lord of the Manor fhall yearly, Two Times in the Year, keep his Law Days and Court
Barons in Maner and Form following ; that is to fay, one within a Month next after the Feaft of Saint Michael the Archangell,
and the other within a Month next Hock Tuefday.

Item 6th, The Cuftom is, that all and every fuch Alienation made of Lands or Tenements, with Lycence as aforefaid, fhall
be Barrs for ever, by Cuftom of the faid Manor, to the Heir or Heirs of fuch Tenant or Tenants, and allfo to the Lord of the
faid Manor and his Heirs, to demand or claim any of the Lands and Tenements fo alienated, as is aforefaid ; and in default of
Iffue of the Body of the Tenant that alienateth, and that no Writts of Forme, donne en defcendre for the Heir, nor Remainder
for the Lord, hath been ufed to be commenced, or brought within the faid Manor, or at Common Law, by any Heir or Heirs
of the Tenants aforefaid, or by the Lord or his Heirs, for the Lands alienated, with Licence as is aforefaid, for that every fuch
Tenant may alienate, as is aforefaid, by the Cuftom of the faid Manor.

Item 7th, The Cuftom is, that every Tenant aforefaid fhall pay to the Lord and his Heirs at their Deaths his beft Beaft, that
in Value fhall be the beft, for Herriotts and Relief, which is one Year's Rent, for every Meafe whereof every fuch Tenant fhall
dye feized, not otherwife, except it be fpecially referved upon their Grants heretofore made ; if the Tenant that deceafed
having no Cattle of his own, then to pay his beft Implement of Houfehold Stuff for the Herriot, and for his Relief a Year's
Rent.

Item 8th, The Cuftom is, to have a Three-week's Court, if there be any Plaints of Debts, Trefpafs, or otherwife, according
to the Cuftom of the faid Manor, affirmed by any Perfon within the fame Manor, till the fame be ended and tryed ; and that all
the Cuftom, Lands, and Tenements, within the faid Manor, be pleadable within the faid Manor, by Writt of Right of Clofe,
and not at Common Law.

Item 9th, The Cuftom of the faid Manor is, that if any do demand any Cuftomary Lands within the faid Manor, by Writt of
Right of Clofe, againft any Tenant within the Manor aforefaid, there to be brought according to the faid Cuftom of the faid
Manor, that upon fufficient Warning to be given unto the Lord or his Steward of the faid Manor, they are allways to have a
Three-weeks Court, untill the Matter in contreverfe be tryed.

Item 10th, The Cuftom is, that if a Writt of Right of Clofe, according to the Cuftom of the faid Manor, by him that has
Caufe to demand cuftomary Lands therein, that he that purchafe or bring fuch Writt fhall, at the Law Day or Court Baron,
deliver the fame Writt unto the Steward in the Prefence of the Court, and the Steward to break the fame Writt in the Face of
the Court, and to read the fame, and to have Six Shillings and Eight Pence for breaking the Writt, and the Bailiff Three Shillings
and Four Pence.

And then always after, the Steward or his fufficient Deputy every Three Weeks to keep the Lord's Court within the faid Manor,
untill the Matter be tryed, according to the Cuftom of the faid Manor, or otherwife made a End off, by any Ways whatfoever,
fo that he that brings the Writt fhall bear the Steward Charges.

Item 11th, The Cuftom is, that the Lord to have a Steward certain of the faid Manor, who fhall always keep his Courts by
fufficient Warrant from the Lord of the faid Manor, under his Hand and Seal of Arms, and the Warrant of the faid Steward
always at every Court, upon Demand, to be read in open Court for the true Knowledge of the Tenants, who is Steward of the
faid Court, if it be required, and the fame Warrant to be immediatelv after delivered unto the Tenants aforefaid, according to
the Cuftom of the faid Manor ; fo it be no Patent for the faid Stewardfhip.

Item 12th, The Cuftom of the faid Manor, for the Time aforefaid, have been, that all the Tenants of the faid Manor that do
any Service in the Homage, charged, or any other, being in any Office, that Day of the faid Two Generall Courts to be twice
holden by the Year as aforefaid, to have their Dinners at the Lord's Expence.

Item 13th, That the Cuftom is, that the Lord, or his Steward, for the Time being, at every his faid Two Courts as is aforefaid, fhall chofe one of his Free Benchers, or Free Suiters of the Court, and the Tenants to chofe another, and that they do for
that Time elect and chofe the Twelve Men every their Court Days for the Lord's Homage ; if they cannot agree, then the
Steward of the Lord fhall chofe and elect the Twelve Men indeferently between the Lord and Tenants aforefaid.

Item 14th, The Cuftom is, that if any of the Lord's Tenants do commit any Felony, and thereof be attainted by Law by
any Means whatfoever, that then the faid Lord of the faid Manor fhall not have his Lands holden by Efcheat, nor the King's
Majefty the Day, Year, and Waft, but the next Heire immediately muft have the fame, for that the Father ought to goe to the
Bough, and the Son to the Plow.

Item 15th, The Cuftom is, that no Tenant may alienate, give, nor grant his Lands or Tenements, or Parcell thereof, otherwife than is aforefaid, without the Lycence of the Lord, upon Pain of Forfeiture of his Lands and Tenements, but only for
Twenty-one Years in Poffeffion, or under, by Leafe, upon reafonable Suit and Requeft.

Item 16th, The Cuftom is, that every Court thereto to be holden within the faid Manor there muft be Three Benchers of the
Free Suiters to the Court at the leaft, or elfe no Court to be holden within the faid Manor, and the Benchers to be amerced by
the Steward's Directions.

Item 17th, The Cuftom of the faid Manor is, that the Lord's Steward may at any of the faid Two Days demand the Sight
of fuch Evidence as any Tenant within the faid Manor holdeth his Lands by, and if they or any of them refufe to fhew the
fame to the Steward at the next Law Day, to the End it may be enrolled, and no fufficient Caufe by burning of the Evidences,
Embezzlements, or fuch like, why the fame cannot be fhewed, then the Lord fhall feize the Lands till the Evidence be
fhewed.

Item 18th, The Cuftom is, that if any Tenant hereafter have any Deed of Intail made to him by Lycence as is aforefaid,
fhall, within one Year next after the Date of the faid Deed of Intail, bring the fame to the Steward to be enrolled, upon
Pain of Forfeiture, fo much as he paid for his Lycence.

Item 19th, The Cuftom is, that every Tenant which fhall have Lycence granted to alienate, fhall execute the fame within a
Twelvemonth and one Day next from the Date, elfe the Lycence to be void.

Item

after Sir JOHN WYNTER, of *Lydney*, and having been fold by Parliament, as the Impropriation had been, it paffed in 1657 to EVAN SEYS, Serjeant at Law, who re-fold it to EDWARD PYE, Merchant.   EDWARD PYE CHAMBERLAYNE, Efq. received it from the laft mentioned by Will in 1712; and his Son transferred the Manfion-houfe called the *Boyce*, with the manerial Eftate, to ANN CAM, Spinfter, by Purchafe; upon her Death, in 1790, fhe was fucceeded by JOHN MOGGRIDGE, Efq. of *Bradford*, co. *Wilts*, in the Eftate, and by JOHN THACKWELL, Efq. of *Berrow*, co. *Worcefter*, in the Manor.

In this Parifh are five Tythings; thus divided.   In *Wood End* Divifion, the Tythings of *Flaxley* and *Gamage Hall*.   Thefe, by long Ufage, are now called the Manor of *Little Dymock*.   The Abbey of *Flaxley*, by Charter of HENRY Duke of NORMANDY, poffeffed " all the Demefnes in *Dymock*, and half " the Wood there," and by a fubfequent Charter after his Succeffion as K. HENRY II. " All the Demefnes " at *Dymoc*, and five Yard Lands and a Half, befide the Demefnes, and half the Wood *."   Sir ANTONY KINGSTONE procured a Grant of this Eftate at the Suppreffion, which is confequently exempt from Tythes.   In 1582 THOMAS WENMAN purchafed it; and from the WENMANS it defcended to WENMAN WYNNIATT, Efq. and it is now vefted in the Rev. REGINALD WYNNIATT, M. A. of *Staunton*.   *Gamage Hall*, is the Manor-houfe detached by Sale from the Eftate about 60 Years fince, when the Privilege of holding Courts there was referved; it is now the Property of RICHARD SARGEANT, Gent.   In former Centuries, it was held by the Families of DE GAMAGE, PEMBRUGE, and MORETON, and exercifes the fame Jurifdiction within itfelf as the greater Manor.   By the Family of HILL, feveral good Eftates in this Tything have been poffeffed for many Generations.

Ryeland Divifion contains the Tythings of *Ryton* and *Ockington*.   An Eftate called *Crowfield* was purchafed by MATTHEW PAULL, Gent. of a Branch of the Family of HILL; and another called *Pit Leafow* is now held by GEORGE HAYWARD, M. A. of *Frocefter*.

The *Ketford* Eftate in 1456, 36. HEN. VI. was vefted in the Family of HANDBOROUGH.   THOMAS BRYDGES (of the CHANDOS Family) received it in Dower with MA·D his Wife, Daughter of THOMAS HANDBOROUGH.   Sir JOHN BRYDGES, Lord Mayor of *London* in 1521, 12 HEN. VIII. was their Son, and a Native of *Dymock*.   It includes two large Farms, *Great Ketford*, bought in 1670 of WILLIAM GROVE, Gent. by THOMAS WALL, Efq. in Truft for his Son-in-law RICE YATE, of *Bromefberrow*; the other called *Hill Place*, purchafed in 1732, by Colonel WALTER YATE, of the Relict of CHRISTOPHER WOODWARD, Gent. of *Newent*, in whofe Family it had been vefted fince 1598, 40 ELIZ. then transferred by Sale from HUMPHRY FORSTER, Efq. of the *Boyce*.

The capital Meffuage called the *Callow*, was purchafed in 1687 by RICE YATE, Efq. of the Family of SHEYLE; and another Eftate called *Cutt Mill*, was bequeathed in 1664 to CATHERINE his Wife, by her Father THOMAS WALL, Efq. of *Lintridge*; all which Property is now inherited by WALTER HONYWOOD YATE, a Minor, eldeft Son of the late ROBERT GORGES DOBYNS YATE, Efq. deceafed.   *Great Lintridge* was long the Refidence of the WALLS, an ancient and opulent Houfe; from them it paffed to GEORGE PRITCHARD, Efq. from whom, with the Impropriation, to HENRY LAMBERT, Efq. *Ockington* was the Eftate of the Family of WEALE; now of BAYLISS, by Purchafe.

In *Ledington* Divifion, the Tything of *Leadington*, fituate near the Rivulet *Leaden*, a competent Eftate, now belonging to THOMAS HANKINS, Gent. has been the Refidence of his Progenitors for many Centuries. JOHN CAM, M. D. of *Hereford*, has other Property in this Tything.

During the Civil War a Garrifon was fupported at *Dymock* for the King, by his ftrenuous Partizan Sir JOHN WYNTER †.

ROGER DIMOC, a learned *Dominican*, who died in 1390, is faid to have been born here; and ROBERT BURHILL, D. D. in the laft Century ‡.

Item 20th, The Cuftom is, that if any Tenant dye feized without Iffue of his Body, that then the Lord fhall have the Land to him and his Heirs, to be difpofed off at his and their Will and Pleafure, after fuch Eftate expired, as where made by the Lycence of the Lord by the fame Tennant that died.

Item 21ft, The Cuftom is, that the Wife of every Tennant that dyeth feized fhall have the third Part for her Dower, as well againft the Heir as the Lord.

Item 22d, It is agreed, that the Tennants fhall from Time to Time do fuch Service in Time of War as have heretofore been accuftomed.

The 2d Day of June, in the faid Year of Queen ELIZABETH, this Indenture was acknowledged in Chancery by the faid Vifcount, and was exemplified at the Requeft of EVAN SEYS, Sargeant at Law, under the Great Seal, the 2d Day of December, 1657.

LENTHALL, Cancellarius.

Examined by us, NATTABER,
WM. HARRINGTON, } Mafters in Chancery.

* ATKYNS's *Gloucefterfhire*, p. 438.   DUGDALE's Monaft. vol. I. p. 884.
† CORBET's Military Government of *Gloucefter*, p. 64.
‡ Of whom fee WOOD's Athenæ, vol. II. p. 4.

BENEFACTIONS.

B E N E F A C T I O N S.

1650. WILLIAM SKINNER, LL. D. gave Land for the Benefit of the Poor, which now produces 4*s.* a Year.

WILLIAM WALL, Efq. gave Land, Seventy-two Yards in Length, and Eleven in Breadth, to poor Cottagers.

1717. ROBERT WYNTER, Gent. bequeathed Lands, the annual Produce of which is 30*l.* to cloath Twenty poor People.

1719. WILLIAM WEALE, Citizen of *London*, gave 100*l.* the Intereft of which to be laid out in Bread, yearly, at Chriftmas.

1734. WILLIAM HOOPER, Gent. left a Rent Charge of 3*l.* a Year for inftructing poor Children.

THOMAS MURREL gave 10*s.* yearly, to be given to Ten poor Widows, and 10*s.* to the Minifter of the Parifh for a Sermon recommending Charity, upon Candlemas Day.

In the Year 1785 certain Premifes were purchafed and fitted for the Reception of a School, by a Subfcription of 140*l.* raifed by the Parifhioners, for educating the Children of the induftrious Poor on Sundays, agreeably to the late Inftitution.

INCUMBENTS.	PATRONS.	INCUMBENTS.	PATRONS.
1577 Walter Coulfey,	Bp. of Gloucefter.	1667 Grindal Wilfon,	John Sheyle, Gent.
1588 James Thomas,	Queen Elizabeth.	1720 Samuel Savage,	Sir W. Humphreys.
1625 William Morgan,	Wm. Wynter, Efq.	1761 Wm. Hayward, M.A.	Geo. Pritchard, Gent.
* * * * * * * * * * * * * *	1787 Jof. Symondes,	Henry Lambert, Efq.
1664 Thomas Eaton,	Wm. Wynter, Efq.		

PRESENT PROPRIETORS OF THE MANORS,

Of *Great Dymock*,	Of *Little Dymock*,
JOHN THACKWELL, ESQ.	REGINALD WYNNIATT, M. A.

The Perfons fummoned by the Heralds, in 1682 and 1683, were

William Wynter, Efq.	William Wall, Efq.
Edward Pye, Efq.	John Camm, Gent.
Grindal Wilfon, Vicar,	John Holmes, Gent.

At the Election in 1776, Thirty-four Freeholders polled from this Parifh and its Hamlets.

The earlieft Date in the Regifter occurs in 1538.

ANNUAL ACCOUNT OF MARRIAGES, BIRTHS, AND BURIALS, IN THIS PARISH.

A.D.	Mar.	Bir.	Bur.	A.D.	Mar.	Bir.	Bur.	A.D.	Mar.	Bir.	Bur.	A.D.	Mar.	Bir.	Bur.
1781	6	39	23	1786	—	38	10	1791				1796			
1782	5	33	16	1787	7	37	19	1792				1797			
1783	5	28	29	1788	4	34	16	1793				1798			
1784	7	39	14	1789	6	41	9	1794				1799			
1785	2	35	37	1790				1795				1800			

I N S C R I P T I O N S   I N   T H E   C H U R C H.

ON MARBLE MONUMENTS IN THE CHANCEL.

Arms; Quarterly, 1ft and 4th, a Crofs, for WALL; 2d and 3d, Checquy Or and Azure, on a Fefs Gules, three Lozenges Argent, for CAPEL;—impaling, Gules, an Inefcutcheon Argent, within an Orle of Mullets Or, for CHAMBERLAYNE.

To the pious Memory of THOMAS WALL, Efq. a Graduate of the Univerfity of Oxford, who departed this Life the 15th of March, A. D. 1664, aged 64.

And alfo of DOROTHY his Wife, defcended from the Family of the BERKELIES, in the Countie of Worcefter, who departed this Life the 4th of May, A. D. 1672, aged 66.

And to the pious Memory of WILLIAM WALL, Efq. only Son of the faid THOMAS and DOROTHY, Vic. Com. Glouc. A. D. 1682.

And alfo of DOROTHY his Wife, defcended from the Family of CAPELS, in the County of Hereford.

And likewife to the pious Memory of THOMAS WALL, Efq. Son and Heir of the faid WILLIAM, defcended from the Family of CHAMBERLAIN, in the County of Warwick. He died Nov. 9, 1694.

Arms;

Arms; Sable, a Fefs Ermine, a Mullet for Difference. **Wynter.**

Here lies interred the
Body of Robert Wintour,
of the Inner Temple, London, Gent.
Son of William Wintour,
of Dymock, Efq.
the laft of the Heirs Male
defcended from that ancient and
honourable Family,
who departed this Life
the 21ft Day of February, 1718,
aged 61 Years,
and was a good Benefactor
to the Poor of this Parifh.

ON FLAT STONES.

Arms; Wynter;—impaling, a Fefs
between three Lions Heads erafed, for
Farmer.

Here lyeth the Body of
Captain William Wintour, Gent.
who departed this Life Jan. 20,
A. D. 1666.

Here lyeth the Body of
Margaret Wintour,
late Wife of
Captain William Wintour, Gent.
who departed this Life
the 8th Day of January, A. D. 1674.

Underneath this Stone lies the Body of
Robert Wintour,
of the Inner Temple, London, Gent.

Here lyeth Hester,
the Daughter of Will. Wintour, Efq.
and of Hester his Wife,
who died the 1ft Day of September,
. . . .

IN THE NAVE.

On a Marble Monument:

Arms; Ermine, a Bend lozengy Gules,
for Pye. Creft, a Crofs fitchy, between
two Wings.

In Memory of
Edward Pye Chamberlain, Efq.
of the Boyce, in this Parifh,
who died April 20, 1729,
aged 38 Years.

Likewife of
Elizabeth his Wife,
who died Nov. 19, 1775,
aged 76.

And alfo of four of their Children
who died Infants.

This Monument was erected by
Edward Pye Chamberlayne, Efq.
in Duty to his worthy and deceafed
Parents.

Against the North Wall, upon a handsome marble Monument:

Arms; a Crofs engrailed, for Cam.

Near this Place lies interred
Joseph Cam, Son of Joseph Cam,
Citizen of London.
Died Oct. 20, 1719, aged 12.

Mary Parsons,
Mother of Mary Cam,
Wife of Joseph Cam, fenior,
died May 24, 1724, aged 80.

Joseph Cam, Citizen of London,
died Aug. 5, 1720, aged 65.

Ann Cam, Daughter of
the faid Joseph,
died Sept. 22, 1734, aged 21.

Mary Cam, Wife of
the faid Joseph,
died Oct. 8, 1752, aged 71.

Joseph Cam, Son of
William and Mary Cam,
Citizen of London,
died Oct. 3, 1753, aged 26.

Mary Cam, Wife of
William Cam,
died June 3, 1774, aged 72.

Alfo two Infants,
the Children of the faid
William and Mary Cam.

ON FLAT STONES.

In Memory of
Thomas Wall, Efq.
who died Nov. 9, 1694, aged 33 Years.

Near this Place lyeth
Peneloph, the Daughter of
William Wall of the Park,
in the County of Hereford, Efq.
by Katharine his Wife.
She departed this Life January 5, 1719,
aged 1 Year and 6 Months.

Here lyeth the Body of
Mary Chamberlain, Widow,
and Relict of Thomas Wall,
of Lintridge, in this Parifh, Efq.
of the Family of Edward Pye, Efq.
Lord of the Mannour of Great Dymock,
and had by her faid Hufband
one Son and two Daughters,
Dorothy, William, and
Elizabeth Pye.
She departed this Life May 2, 1707,
in Hopes of a bleffed Refurrection to
eternal Life.

Here lyeth the Body of
Edward Pye, of Boyce, Efq.
who departed this Life,
in Hopes of a better,
the 31ft of Auguft, 1692,
in the eightieth Year of his Age.

IN THE NORTH TRANSEPT.

Arms; on a Fefs between three Anchors
a Griffin paffant, for Wynniatt.

Jufta hoc marmor,
Johannes Wynniatt, Gener,
Vir pius & probus, liberalis in omnes,
Pauperibus largâ manu beneficus
exuvias depofuit 15 Octob. 1670.

Richardus Winniatt, Filius,
Pietatis ergô pofuit.

Arms; two Bars, in chief a Lion
paffant.

In Memory of
Richard Hill, of Edulus Place,
who departed this Life
June 13, 1772, aged 57.

Alfo Mary his Relict,
who departed this Life
April 1776, aged 73.

Alfo Thomas Rooke Moore,
Son of the above
Richard and Mary Hill,
who departed this Life
July 18, 1746, aged near 6 Months.

Arms; Barry, wavy of fix, in Bafe, a
Lion paffant, in Fefs, and in Chief, three
Roundlets.

Near this Place is interred
the Body of William Hankins, Efq.
late of the Greenhoufe, in this Parifh,
who departed this Life,
Nov. 9, 1771, aged 54.

Alfo John, Son of
William Hankins, Efq.
by Mary his Wife,
who departed this Life
Feb. 15, 1775, aged 36.

ON FLAT STONES.

Here lyeth the Body of
Elizabeth, the former Wife of
John Hankins.

Alfo Ursula, the Wife of
William Swayne, of the
Parifh of Newnham, Daughter of
John Hankins, fen.
of the Greenhoufe.
She died Oct. 7, 1742, aged 50.

Here lyeth the Body of
John Hankins, jun.
of the Greenhoufe,
who departed this Life
Sept. 10, 1728, aged 39.
He was a loving Hufband,
a tender Father, and a faithful Friend.

Alfo in Memory of
Ann, the Wife of
Thomas Shailes, of Woodfields,
and Daughter of
John Hankins abovementioned
by Ann his Wife.
She died Oct. 21, 1780, aged 69.
She was a loving Wife,
a good Chriftian, and a fincere Friend.

In Memory of
ANN HANKINS, Wife of
JOHN HANKINS,
of the Greenhouse, senior.
She died the 14th Day of December,
1776, aged 86 Years.
She was a good Wife.
a tender Mother and Grandmother.

ON A TOMB IN THE VESTRY:

Arms; Quarterly, 1st and 4th, Gules,
a Chevron vairy, between three Pelicans
Heads erased Sable, for MACHEN ; 2d
and 3d, three Holly Leaves.

Here lyeth the Body of
Mr. JAMES MACHEN, senior,
who died March 10, 1760, aged 58.

Here also lyeth the Body of
Mrs. SARAH, the Wife of
the above Mr. JAMES MACHEN.
She departed this Life
July 23, 1763, aged 67.

ON A MONUMENT AGAINST THE
CHURCH :

Near
this Stone are the Remains
of HANNAH,
late Wife of JAMES AMOTT
(Officer of Excise).
She was born at Uttoxeter,
in Staffordshire,
and died March 21, 1770,
aged 24 Years.

IN THE CHURCH YARD, ON TOMBS.

THOMAS COMMINS
died May 20, 1780, aged 78.

ANN his Wife
died July 21, 1761, aged 62.

WILLIAM SMITH
died Dec. 13, 1716, aged 74.

JONE his Wife
died Aug. 1, 1723, aged ...

Father and Mother to the above
ANN COMMINS.

JOHN CAM
died Jan. 10, 1679, aged 60.

ANN his Wife
died Sept. 11, 1701, aged 75.

JOHN their Son
died June 10, 1707, aged 56.

ANN his Wife
died April 12, 1742, aged 88.

JOHN, Son of
the latter JOHN,
died Sept. 11, 1739, aged 60.

WILLIAM CAM, Esq.
died April 22, 1767, aged 85.

JOHN CAM, Esq. his Son,
died June 11, 1767, aged 32.

JOHN CAM
died Nov. 5, 1753, aged 75.

ANN his Wife
died Sept. 24, 1754, aged 80.

ROBERT CAM
died Nov. 30, 1683, aged 32.

DORCAS his Wife
died Sept. 15, 1712, aged 60.

THOMAS GREENE
died Feb. 22, 1707, aged 86.

WILLIAM LOVERIDG
died .... 17, 1709, aged 66.

MARY his Daughter
died May .. 1677, ...

RICHARD SKIPP
died Aug. 1, 1785, aged 40.

ROBERT his Son
died March 12, 1781, aged 6 Weeks.

ROBERT, another of his Sons,
died Dec. 28, 1783, aged 1 Year.

RICHARD HILL
was interred May 27, 1756, aged 43.

RICHARD HILL, jun.
died June 26, 1765, aged 28.

HESTER, Relict of
WILLIAM MANN,
died Oct. 3, 1720, aged 60.

RICHARD HILL
died Sept. 13, 1729, aged 66.

SUSANNAH his Wife
died July 14, 1730, aged 52.

RICHARD HILL
died March 5, 171.. aged 79.

JANE his Wife
died June 1, 1715, aged 72.

SARAH, the Wife of
RICHARD HALL,
died Nov. 17, 1760, aged 42.

RICHARD HALL
died Feb. 26, 1780, aged 69.

ROBERT HALL
died March 17, 1715, aged 45.

ROBERT his Son
died Aug. 27, 1711, aged 3.

PROFET NASH
died Nov. 12, 1785.

WILLIAM WEALE, Gent.
died Jan. 1, 1721, aged 74.

WILLIAM his Son
died in his Infancy.

MARGERY his Wife
died Dec. 31, 1731, aged 83.

WILLIAM his Son
died Jan. 6, 1735, aged 45.

JOHN WEALE
died Sept. 12, 1759, aged 83.

JOSEPH WEALE
died April 29, 1757, aged 72.

HESTER his Wife
died Dec. 3, 1735, aged 45.

ANN their Daughter
died May 20, 1740, aged 22.

ON

ON FLAT AND HEAD STONES.

Name	Died	Aged
Ann, the Wife of Edward Smith	18 Jan. 1758	22
William Hodges	22 Sept. 1733	52
Judith his Wife	15 Sept. 1729	51
Richard, the Son of William and Hannah Hodges	11 June, 1758	4
Richard, another of their Sons	23 Mar. 1766	6
Thomas their Son	26 Oct. 1775	30
John their Son	3 Jan. 1777	29
John, the Son of Jonas Powell	26 Dec. 1764	47
Jonas Powell - buried	20 Dec. 1755	57
Younger Son of William and Sarah Hooper	12 Dec. 1775	44
Sarah Hooper	15 Apr. 1751	31
Mary, Wife of Richard Jenkins	6 May, 1733	76
Mary, Daughter of Benjamin Banks, buried in the 22d Year of her Age.		
Mary, Wife of Richard Willliams	17 Aug. 1735	65
Richard Williams	4 June, 1734	62
Joseph Taler,	14 Aug. 1738	29
William, Son of Joseph Dobbs	14 Aug. 1785	25
Sarah, Wife of William Stone	16 Mar. 1700	50
Samuel, Son of William Stone	12 Feb. 1712	19
William Stone	11 June, 1733	78
Margaret, the Wife of Philip Mail	22 Aug. 1766	63
Ann Roberson, Widow	23 May, 1729	71
Henry Roberson	13 Mar. ——	—
William Powell	24 Aug. 1712	80
Benjamin Phillips	13 Sept. 1734	24
Richard Wintour	11 July, 1732	—
Jof. Webb	26 Dec. 1783	49
Daniel his Son	31 Dec. 1779	5
Joseph Robinson } both buried	8 Apr. 1726	36
and Mary his Wife		48
Jonathan Drew	9 Mar. 1737	30
Thomas Drew	15 Mar. 1780	37
Edward Tyler	19 Jan. 1789	82
Mary, Wife of John Hodges	9 Dec. 1745	26
John Pimbley	19 Mar. 1782	44
Nancy, the Daughter of Daniel and Mary Woore	26 Oct. 1769	7
Elizabeth, Wife of John Burgom	27 Apr. 1729	56
John Burgom	25 Mar. 1733	52
George Hankins	11 June, 1774	62
Ann his Daughter	14 May, 1785	27
Elizabeth, Wife of John Puckmore	27 May, 1731	29
John Puckmore	15 Oct. 1747	62
John his Son died young.		
Mary, Wife of William Puckmore	9 June, 1762	56
Elizabeth, Wife of Robert Millard	— Sept. ——	64
Jane, Daughter of Thomas Gardiner	20 Mar. 1768	51
Elizabeth, Wife of John Bofwood	15 May, 1771	67
John Wigmore	17 Sept. 1782	52
William his Son	10 July, 1770	—
Elizabeth, Wife of John Hill	14 July, 1732	—
Sarah, Wife of John Hill	—— ——	—
Hannah, Wife of Thomas Hill	30 Dec. 1751	60
Thomas Hill	27 Sept. 1756	69
Sarah his Daughter	—— ——	—
Ann, Daughter of John Hill	14 June, 1785	2
John Hill	20 Dec. 1760	59
Ann Hill - buried	20 Mar. 1720	68
John Hill - buried	11 Sept. 1744	71
Richard, Son of William Thurston	8 Sept. 1779	2
William, Son of James Wingod buried	16 Jan. 1741	34
Jane, Wife of Thomas Stephens	29 Apr. 1761	67
Thomas Stephens	10 Feb. 1767	76
Hannah, Wife of Thomas Stallard	18 Dec. 1733	35
Elizabeth, Wife of Jonathan Landon	31 Aug. 1729	74
Mary, Daughter of James Barnes	30 Mar. 1770	12
James Barnes	26 Jan 1782	59
Richard, Son of John Williams	23 Dec. 1745	19
William Morton	3 July, 1753	54
Anna his Wife	24 June, 1776	74
George Sier, Mason	14 Oct. 1778	38
Susannah, Wife of William Davis	4 Feb. 1758	58
John Davis - buried	10 Apr. 1727	70
Ann, Wife of Benjamin Parsons	10 May, 1733	40
William Jones	25 Aug. 1766	58
Mary his Wife	18 June, 1787	74
Edward their Son	21 Jan. 1766	12
Betty their Daughter	11 Nov. 1780	39
Mary their Daughter	20 May, 1777	31
John Jones	2 July, 1766	29
Three of his Children died young.		
William Handman	7 Dec. 1773	71
George Price	3 Oct. 1720	42
Abigail his Wife	21 Dec. 1724	37
Mary, Wife of William Bosworth	21 Oct. 1762	77
Thomas, Son of William Smith	5 June, 1726	25
Margaret, Wife of William Williams	30 Mar. 1733	36
Margaret Powell	6 Nov. 1748	62
Betty, Wife of John Pewtrifs	10 Mar. 1738	39
Daniel Packer	2 Nov. 1743	52
John Selwyn	23 July, 1695	—
William Selwyn	8 Oct. 1781	77
John, the Son of Thomas Gunter	4 Aug. 1733	33
John Walker	10 Jan. 1738	31
Hannah his Wife	11 Aug. 1737	32
Thomas Gunter	8 Sept. 1722	60
William Hope	1 Nov. 1770	65
Mary his Wife	7 Mar. 1782	83
Jonathan Williams	2 May, 1770	61
Sarah his Wife	21 Nov. 1758	49
Sarah, Wife of William Davis	29 Mar. 1729	47
Comfort, another Wife to the above	14 June, 1775	78
Comfort their Daughter	9 Feb. 1760	24
Two more of their Children died young.		
Lydia, Wife of Edward Grundy	22 Nov. 1779	54
Ann their Daughter	26 Mar. 1766	10
Ann, the Wife of Edward Grundy	15 Mar. 1754	60
James Cooper, fenior	13 June, 1746	74
Sibil his Wife	8 Jan. 1758	84
Elizabeth their Daughter	14 July, 1747	4
Jane, Daughter of James Cooper, junior	14 Mar. 1765	2
James his Son	19 Mar. 1765	—
James Cooper	6 Mar. 1777	65
Elizabeth, Wife of John Evans	13 Feb. 1766	75
Thomas Adams	1 Apr. 1758	70
Walter Chambers, fenior	11 Mar. 1788	66
Walter Chambers, junior	16 May, 1788	32
Richard Phelpotts	30 Apr. 1719	—
Jane, Wife of Charles Rook	21 Dec. 1784	84
Mary Eaton	8 Dec. 1785	27
Elizabeth Murrell - buried	23 May, 1733	62
John Moyle	17 Apr. 1786	69
Richard Turner	22 Feb. 1761	66
Elizabeth his Wife	7 Sept. 1757	55
Thomas Attwood died in his infancy.		
John Moyle	6 Aug. 1732	44
Elizabeth, Wife of Joseph Cummins	22 Feb. 1758	82
Lucy, Relict of Thomas Haines	14 Dec. 1741	60

CVII. DYRHAM,

CVII. DYRHAM, or DEREHAM.

THIS Parifh lies in the Hundred of *Grumbald's Afh*, Four Miles Weft of *Marfhfield*, Five South from *Chipping Sodbury*, Eight Northward from *Bath*, and Thirty-one Southward from the City of GLOUCESTER. It is nearly Eight Miles in Extent, of a rich Soil, chiefly applied to Pafture. In the Two common Fields are Seven Hundred Acres, exclufive of the inclofed Arable Land. The Village is fituate on the Bafe of a very narrow Amphitheatre formed by fteep Acclivities, from which iffue many fmall Springs, the Source of the River *Boyd*.

Of the Benefice, which is a Rectory in the Deanery of *Hawkefbury*, the Advowfon has never been alienated from the Manor. The Glebe exceeds Eighty Acres.

It is traditionally afferted, that the Church, dedicated to *St. Peter*, was built by Sir MAURICE RUSSEL, Knight, before the Year 1401. The Style of Architecture is evidently of that Age ; a Nave, Two Aifles, and embattled Tower, of regular Gothic. In 1520, Sir WILLIAM DENYS and ANNE his Wife founded a Chantry Gild, and erected, or prepared, the South Aifle for the Reception of its Service*.

The

---

* Sir WILLIAM DENNIS and others founded a Gild in this Church, 1520. The Method of its Foundation, and the Statutes, are ftill preferved, and are here inferted, which may fhew the Nature of Gilds in general.

Memorandum, In the Year of our Lord 1520, October the firft, in the twelfth Year of King HENRY the Eighth, Sir WILLIAM DENNIS, Knight, Dame ANNE his Wife, ROBERT LLEN, Parfon of the Church of *Dyrham*, THOMAS LLEN, and WILLIAM WERE, who were Servants to the faid Sir WILLIAM and Dame ANNE, founded firft a Prieft to fing Mafs dayley within the Parifh Church of *Dyrham*, within the Chapel of *St. Denys*, to pray for the Founders of the faid Mafs, and for all thofe that will become Brothers and Sifters, or any thing helping for the Maintenance of the faid Fraternity or Gild.

Item, The faid Prieft fhall, or may fignify before he begin his Mafs, pray in general for the good State of the Founders, and Brothers, and Sifters, and for all Benefactors to the faid Gild.

Item, The faid Prieft, at his coming to the Savetory, fhall fay for the Souls of the faid Founders, Brethren, and Sifters, which be Dead *De Profundis*.

Item, The Proctor of the faid Gild, for the Time being, fhall caufe four folemn Dirges and Maffes, according to Note, to be fung at four Times within the Year, which Times fhall appear following thefe words : " Let us Pray."

Item, The Dirge and Mafs to be kept upon *St. Denys* Eve, and the Mafs upon the Day, which fhall be the ninth Day of October.

Item, The fecond Dirge and Mafs to be kept the eighth and ninth Day of January.

Item, The third Dirge and Mafs to be kept the twenty-ninth and thirtieth Day of March.

Item, The fourth Dirge and Mafs to be kept the twenty-feventh and twenty-eighth Day of June.

Item, The faid Prieft before he goeth to the Quarter Mafs fhall pray for the State of the Founders, Brothers, and Sifters, and for the Souls of them that be dead, generally, or efpecially, as he hath Time.

Item, The Proctor of the faid Gild fhall caufe, at every Quarter of the Year, to be at that folemn Mafs, the Parfon of the Church, or his Prieft in his Abfence, with four other honeft Priefts to help to fing the Dirge, and to fing Mafs on the Morrow.

Item, The Proctor of the faid Gild fhall, of the Stock of the faid Gild, pay every Prieft for his coming, and for his Devout Doing, 6d ; and to the Ringers 4d.

Item, Such Perfons as fhall be named and chofen to be Proctors of the faid Gild, fhall be every Year named and chofen the firft Day of February.

Item, The faid Proctors fhall make their Account every Year upon the firft Day of February.

Item, The faid Proctors fhall make their Account upon the faid Day within the Church of *Dyrham*, within the Trinity Chapel, and to lay down the Money of their Collections upon the Altar there.

Item, The Account fhall be made before the Lord of the Lordfhip, or the Lord's Bayliff in his Abfence, the Parfon of the Church, or his Prieft in his Abfence, and two of the eldeft Brethren within the Parifh, and all the Brethren within the faid Parifh, if they will be at it.

Item, At the Account, the old Proctors before they be difcharged fhall name to the faid Lord, or to his Bayliff, the Parfon, or his Prieft, fuch as fhall take the Account, fix Perfons, of the which fix, the faid Lord, or his Bayliff, the Parfon, or his Prieft, that taketh the Accounts, fhall name two to be Collectors, and there, openly, the faid Lord, or Bayliff, Parfon, or Prieft, which taketh the Account fhall deliver the faid Money to the new Proctors.

Memorandum, That WILLIAM WERE hath given to *St. Denys's* Chapel a Challice of Silver.

Memorandum, That where Sir WILLIAM DENNIS and Dame ANNE his Wife, and ROBERT LLEN, Parfon of the Church of *Dyrham*, THOMAS LLEN, and WILLIAM WERE, having conftituted and ordained a Prieft to fing dayly in *St. Denys* Chapel, within the Church of *Dyrham*, for the Maintenance of the faid Prieft; Sir WILLIAM DENNIS hath promifed to give to the Proctors and their Succeffors of the Gild of *St. Denys*, for the forefaid Maintenance of the faid Prieft, 16 Kine.

Item, The faid Dame ANNE, by the Licence of the faid Sir WILLIAM her Hufband, hath promifed to give 8 Kine.

Item, ROBERT LLEN, Parfon of the aforefaid Church, hath promifed to give 100 Sheep.

Item, THOMAS LLEN 50 Sheep.

Item, WILLIAM WERE in Oxen and Kine 16.

Item, There is let to JOHN FORD, of *Pucclechurch*, 8 Kine of *St. Nicholas* Stock, paying by the Year, for every Cow ,22d.

Item, In like Manner to HUMPHREY LLEN, of *St. Nicholas* Stock, 4 Kine.

Item, To JOHN WARD, of *St. Nicholas* Stock, 4 Kine.

Item, The Proctors of *St. Denys* Gild fhall pay, quarterly, to the Prieft that fingeth in the faid Chapel, for his Salary, 33s. 4d.

Item,

The Manor was once a Barony. Soon after the Conqueſt it paſſed to the Family of NEWMARCH (DE NOVO MERCATŨ), and JAMES, ſtyled Baron of *Newmarch* and *Dereham* *, dying in 1199, 17 JOHN, bequeathed this Eſtate to ISABEL his Coheir, the Wife of RALPH DE RUSSEL. In this knightly Family (the Anceſtors of the Duke of BEDFORD, and GORGES, of *Somerſetſhire* and *Herefordſhire*) it deſcended to Sir MAURICE RUSSEL, who died in 1401, then Sheriff of this County, which Office he had before borne in the Year 1396. He left this Manor in Moiety, between his Coheirs MARGARET, the Wife of Sir GILBERT DENYS, and ISABEL, married to Sir JOHN DRAYTON, who were jointly ſeiſed of it in 1415, 3 HEN. V.; In 1422 the former died poſſeſſed of the whole Eſtate, the Moiety of which he had purchaſed †. Sir WALTER DENNIS was the laſt Poſſeſſor of that Name, for, joining with RICHARD DENNIS, Eſq. his Son, he transferred it to GEORGE WYNTER, Eſq. Brother of Sir WILLIAM WYNTER, of *Lydney*, by Deed, bearing Date 1571, 13 ELIZ. Here they reſided in Splendour till the Death of JOHN WYNTER, Eſq. in 1668, whoſe only Daughter and Heir had married WILLIAM BLATHWAYTE ‡, Eſq. of a Family ſettled in *Cumberland*; and whoſe lineal Deſcendant is the preſent Proprietor of the manerial Eſtate, which includes the greater Part of the Pariſh.

LELAND ſpeaks very copiouſly of *Dyrham*, " wher Maſtar DIONISE dwellithe, havinge a faire Howſe " of achelie Stones, and a Parke. *Dereham* Village is a 2 Mils from *Tormerton*. Ther is a fayr Manor- " place longinge to Maſtar DIONISE. The Lordſhippe of auncient Time longid to the RUSSELS. One " JOHN RUSSEL and ELIZABETHE hys Wife lyethe buryed in the Paroche Churche, but they had but " a meane Houſe there. From them it cam by Heyre-general onto the DIONISIES, of whom one " GILBERT DENYS was accountid, as one of the firſt that ther poſſeſſyd. Then cam MAURICE, and " hee ther buyldid a new Courte. And Ser GULIAM DIONYS buildid annother Courte of late Yeres. " The DIONISIS hathe here a fayr Parke, and alſo a fair Lordſhippe §."

Upon the ſame Spot, the preſent very ſumptuous Manſion was erected by WILLIAM BLATHWAYTE, Eſq. Secretary at War and of State in the Reign of King WILLIAM III. It has an Air of great Magnificence on its firſt breaking on the Sight; but the Elevation is neceſſarily unfavourable, from the Confinement of the Hills, which, excepting on the South-weſt, riſe almoſt perpendicularly above it. The Building was completed in 1698, from a Deſign of WILLIAM TALMAN ||, who conducted the whole at an immenſe Coſt. An Elevation of it is publiſhed in CAMPBELL's " Vitruvius Britannicus," vol. II. p. 94. and another in Sir R. ATKINS's Hiſtory, by KIP, with more than his uſual Fidelity. His Delineation is the more valuable, as exhibiting a Bird's Eye View of the Pleaſure Grounds, now reconciled to modern Taſte, which were deſigned by LE NAUTRE, and were the firſt Specimen in that Day, of Caſcades and Jets d'Eau carried to the very Summit of the Hill. Every Caprice of the *Dutch* Style, which could be effected by Art, abounded at *Dyrham*, where ſuch Ornaments were ſo numerous and ſumptuous as to defy both Expence and Imitation. The Houſe conſiſts of Two Fronts, the principal of which extends 130 Feet. There are beſide, Two Wings and a Quadrangle of Offices. The Baſe is of ruſtic, and the firſt Floor contains a Suite of many excellent Apartments. The Windows are decorated with alternate Pediments, and the Cornice finiſhed with Trophies, Urns, and a Profuſion of Ornament. The Park is extenſive and well planted, firſt incloſed by Sir WILLIAM DENNIS, one of the Eſquires of the Body to King HENRY the Eighth, from whom in 1512 he obtained Licence " to impark 500 Acres within his " Manor of *Dereham* **."

Item, The Proctors ſhall receive the Money for the Payment of the ſaid Prieſt, as followeth:

	s.	d.
Of Sir WILLIAM DENNIS, quarterly, till the ſaid 16 Kine be delivered to the Proctors of the ſaid Gild, for the Time being,	6	8
Of Dame ANNE DENNIS	3	4
Of Mr. ROBERT LLEN, Parſon of the ſaid Church	6	8
Of THOMAS LLEN,	3	4
Of WILLIAM WERE,	6	8
Of JOHN FORD,	3	4
Of HUMPHRY LLEN,	1	8
Of JOHN WARD,	1	8
	33	4

Memorandum, The ſaid Prieſt ſhall find himſelf for to ſing at the ſaid Altar, Bread, Wine, and Wax.

Many were the Brethren and Siſters of this Gild, who were prevailed upon to contribute towards its Maintenance; which Perſons lived in 50 ſeveral Pariſhes at leaſt, in *Briſtol, Bath, Somerſetſhire,* and *Glouceſterſhire*, and might amount in Number to 300 Perſons. The uſual pay from each Perſon was 10 or 20d quarterly.

* COLLINS, Tit. BEDFORD, vol. I. p. 244.

† It is probable that the following armorial Enſigns, (mentioned in a MS. of JOHN SMYTH, Eſq. of *North Nibley* in 1607, and now in the *College of Arms, London*.) were by him emblazoned in the Windows of the Church. 1. Gules, a Bend engrailed Azure, between three Leopard's Faces jeſſant, Or; DENNYS; quartering, Argent, a Chevaron Gules, between three Roundlets Azure; BASKERVILLE; 2. quarterly, 1. DENNIS; 2. Argent, on a Chief Gules three Bezants; RUSSEL; 3. Lozengy, Or and Azure, a Chevron Gules; GORGES; 4. Azure, a Croſs moline Or; MOLINEUX. 3. Quarterly, 1ſt and 4th, DENNYS; 2d and 3d, D'ANVERS;—impaling, BERKELEY, MOWBRAY, BROTHERTON, and WARREN, quarterly. 4. Argent, three Lozenges conjoined, in Feſs Gules; MONTAGU. 5. Or, three Torteauxes and a Label Azure; COURTENAY. 6. Vairè Or and Gules; FERRARS. 7. Azure, two Chevronels Gules, and a Label Azure; ST. MAUR; quartering, Or, a Lion rampant Azure; PERCIE. 8. Argent, a Griffin ſegreant Gules; BOTREAUX. 9. Gules, four Lozenges Argent, each charged with an Eſcallop Azure; CHEYNEY. 10. MOLEYNEUX, or MOLEYNS. 11. GORGES. 12. Lozengy, Gules and Ermine, BOTFLYE. 13. DENNYS. 14. RUSSEL, quartering, GORGES. 15. Azure, two Barrs dancettè Or; DE LA RIVIERE;—impaling, RUSSEL and GORGES quarterly. 16. COURTENAY. 17. HEYTESBURY, quartering HUNGERFORD, as at *Downe Ampney*.

‡ WOOD's Faſti, vol. II. p. 832. ATKYNS's *Glonc.* p. 414.

§ Itin. vol. VII. pp. 72. 74.

|| WALPOLE's Anecdotes of Painting, vol. III. p. 263.

** " GULIELMUS DENNYS, unus Armig. pro corpore Regis, 5 Junii, 3 HEN. VIII. habet licentiam imparcandi 500 acras " terræ apud *Le Worthy*, infra manerium ſuum de *Dereham*, co. *Glouc.* cum liberâ warennâ." Bill. ſign. 1, 2, HEN. VIII.

6 Z

Hinton,

Hinton, or *Henton*, is the only Hamlet, originally a diftinct Manor held by the Family of DE LA RIVERE, or DE RIPARIIS; of whom, having been purchafed by the RUSSELS, it was confolidated witn the Demefnes. The Coheirs of Sir MAURICE RUSSEL detached the chief Eftate by Sale to THOMAS WHITE, Efq. who was Mayor of *Briftol* in 1530, 21 HEN. VIII. and which, then producing 22*l.* 12*s.* per Annum, he gave by Deed, Jan. 14, 1541, to exempt the *Severn* Veffels from the Cuftoms of the Port of *Briftol*, and other charitable Purpofes *.

In the very remote Æra of the *Britifh* and *Saxon* Wars, *Dyrham* was the Scene of many military Tranfactions. In an ancient Map of the *Saxon* Heptarchy "Deopham" is defcribed as a Place of Confe-quence †. LELAND, enumerating the Encampments which are to be traced on this Chain of Hills, fpeaks of three " by *Derham.* Maftar DIONISE's Houfe, and all towchinge on one Hilly Creafte."

The Camp on *Hinton Hill* inclofes at leaft Twenty Acres of Ground, and is fuppofed to have been occupied by the *Saxons* in 599, when they gained a fignal Victory over the *Britons*, flew three of their Princes, and took the Cities of *Cirencefter*, *Gloucefter*, and *Bath* ‡.

B E N E F A C T I O N S.

Mr. WILLIAM LANGTON, formerly Rector of this Parifh, left by Will, dated July 20, 1668, 600*l.* for the Ufe of the Poor of the Parifhes of *Dyrham* and *Deynton*, in the County of *Gloucefter*, which Sum he bequeathed to twelve Perfons therein named, in Truft, for the Intent and Purpofe of purchafing Land in Fee Simple, the Profits, or Rents thereof to be laid out thus : 10*s.* a Year to be paid to the Minifter of this Parifh, or his Reprefentative, for ever, to preach a Sermon every Year on Eafter Mon-day; the Refidue of the Rent to be divided into three Parts, two thirds to be paid to the Churchwardens, or Overfeers of the Poor of this Parifh for ever, to be employed by them with the Difcretion and Con-fent of the Minifter, and fome of the Truftees, or chiefeft of the Parifhioners, for the educating or teaching any poor Children whatfoever, and for binding Apprentices of fuch poor Men's Children as re-ceive no Alms of the Parifh; the other third Part of the Rent to be paid to the Churchwardens, or Over-feers of the Parifh of *Deynton* for ever, to be employed by them in the Manner prefcribed to the Church-wardens and Overfeers of this Parifh; when fix of the Truftees are dead, the furviving Truftees are di-rected to convey the Land to twelve other Perfons, to be fucceffively chofen by the Minifters of the Parifhes of *Dyrham* and *Deynton*, together with the Churchwardens and Overfeers of the Poor, and moft fubftantial Inhabitants of thefe Parifhes for the Time being; the annual Produce of thefe Lands now are 35*l.*

On the firft of February, 1774, Mr. PETER GRAND, the prefent Rector of *Dyrham*, did purchafe in the public Funds, out of feveral Years' Savings, proceeding chiefly from a Coal Mine, 100*l.* Stock in the Confolidated 3 per Cent Annuities, in his Name, and for the fole Ufe of, and Benefit of that Part of Mr. LANGTON's Charity, which is now, or may hereafter be due to this Parifh.

A School Houfe was alfo built by Mr. GRAND, at his own Expence, 1770.

INCUMBENTS.	PATRONS.	INCUMBENTS.	PATRONS.
1520 Robert Llen,	Sir William Dennys.	1638 Wm. Langton, M.A.	Sir George Wynter.
* * * * * * *	* * * * * * *	1668 Henry Hofkins,	John Wynter, Efq.
1570 Walter Dennys,	Edward Dennys, Efq.	1680 Sam. Trewman, B.D.	The fame.
1577 John Hall,	George Wynter, Efq.	1699 Mervin Perry,	Wm. Blathwayte, Efq.
1587 John Hawling,	Queen Elizabeth.	1753 Peter Grand, M.A.	Wm. Blathwayte, Efq.

PRESENT LORD OF THE MANOR,

WILLIAM BLATHWAYTE, ESQ.

The Perfons fummoned from this Place by the Heralds in 1682 and 1683 were

John Wynter, Efq. and Thomas Weare, Gent.

At the Election in 1776, Two Freeholders polled from this Parifh.

The Regifter has its firft Date in 1567.

ANNUAL ACCOUNT OF MARRIAGES, BIRTHS, AND BURIALS, IN THIS PARISH.

A.D.	Mar.	Bir.	Bur.	A.D.	Mar.	Bir.	Bur.	A.D.	Mar.	Bir.	Bur.	A.D.	Mar.	Bir.	Bur.
1781	2	11	6	1786	2	11	6	1791				1796			
1782	3	7	5	1787	3	12	10	1792				1797			
1783	—	14	5	1788	3	11	5	1793				1798			
1784	1	9	7	1789				1794				1799			
1785	2	9	8	1790				1795				1800			

* BARRET's Hiftory of *Briftol*, pp. 135. 613.

† STRUTT's *Saxon* Chronicle, vol. II. Append. Plate XX. p. 277. CAMDEN's Britannia, &c.

‡ " Anno 599, Rex *Occidental. Sax.* CEAULIN, & filius ejus CUTHWINE, in loco qui vocatur *Deorham*, cum *Britonibus* pugna-" vère, & eorum tres Reges CONMAIEL, CONDIDAN, & FARNMEIL, cum multis aliis, trucidavêre: illifque tres civitates, vide-" licet, *Gloaucefter*, *Cyrenceafter*, & *Bathanceafter*, abftulerunt."

LELAND, Collect. vol. II. pp. 277. 294. CAMDEN's Britannia, vol. I. p. 280. HOLINSHED, p. 142. &c.

INSCRIPTIONS

INSCRIPTIONS IN THE CHURCH.

Upon a Marble Slab, inlaid with the Figures of a Knight and his Lady for Sir Maurice Russel and Dame Isabel his Wife, these Verses in the Gothic Character.

Miles pribatus bita, jacet hic tumulatus
Sub petra ſtratus, Maurice Ruſſel
bocitatus
Iſabel ſponſa fuit hujus militis iſta
Quae jacet abſconſa ſub marmoreo
mobo alto
Coeli ſolamen Trinitas eis conferat,
Amen
Qui fuit, eſt, et erit, concita marte
perit.

On a large Freestone Monument in the Chancel:

Arms; Quarterly Gules and Or, a Bend Argent, for Langton.

M. S.
Gulielmi Langton, A. M.
hujus Eccleſiæ
Paſtoris nuper vigilantiſſimi,
de grege ſuo multiſq. aliis,
optime merentis;
Qui quum ad uſus tum pietatis
tum charitatis,
800 *l*, non minus
dediſſet,
Poſt laudabilis vitæ
(Annorum fer. 59) ſtadium
Ad Patriam cœleſtem evocatus,
Quod mortale in eo fuit
hoc pulvere
Deponendum
curavit.

Obiit ⎱ Aug. ⎰ 7 ⎰ 1668.
Sepultus ⎰ 　　⎰ 17 ⎰

Amoris gratitudinis ergò,
poſuit Johannes Meredith, Armiger.

On a painted Board against the South Wall of the Chancel,

Near this Place lieth the Body of
The Rev. Mr. Mervin Perry,
who, after being Rector of this Pariſh
53 Years, died much lamented
by all his Pariſhioners
Dec. 17, 1753, ætat. fuæ 88.

Alſo of Elizabeth his Wife,
who died March 6, 1752, æt. fuæ 73.

ON FLAT STONES IN THE CHANCEL.

In ſpem
Glorioſæ Reſurrectionis
Exuviæ his reponuntur
Gulielmi Langton,
Fideliſſimi hujus Eccleſiæ
Paſtoris,
Qui poſt annorum ferme 30,
labores indefeſſos ibidem
Exantlatos,
Mortilatem exeuns,
in Chriſto placidiſſime
requievit,
Auguſti ſeptimo
Æræ Chriſtianæ 1668,
Ætatis fuæ 59.

Here lieth the Body of Amii,
late Wife of Samuel Trewman,
Rector of this Pariſh, and
Daughter of Thomas Symes,
late of Winterburne, Eſq.
who departed this Life
Oct. 29, 1677, aged 26 Years.

Samuel Trewman, S. T. B.
hujus Eccleſiæ Rector,
obiit XXX. Dec. Anno Domini
MDCLXXXVIII.

IN THE SOUTH AISLE.

Under a Canopy, supported by Pillars of the Corinthian Order, the Cumbent Figures of a Man in Armour and his Wife, Supplicating:

Arms; Sable, a Feſs Ermine, for Wynter;—impaling quarterly, firſt and fourth, Sable, on a Feſs, between three Bugles, Argent, a Hemp-brake, Gules, for Brain; 2. a Croſs raguly; 3. Sable, ten Plates, on a Chief of the 2d, a Lion paſſant of the 1ſt, Bridgeman.

Georgio Wynter,
Armigero (qui animam efflavit XXIX die Novembris, anno Domini 1581), Anna Wvnter uxor pia charo conjugi hoc Monumentum poſuit, ſtatuens cum et ipſa Dei juſſu vitæ hujus ſtationem peregerit, hic juxta mariti funus ſuum quoque reponi, ut quibus vivis unus erat animus, eiſdem et mortuis unus eſſet corporum quieſcendi locus, ſub ſpe futuræ Reſurrectionis.

Mole ſub hac placidem capiunt en Membra Georgi Wynteri Requiem, duos perſæpe labores, qui ſolida in terram fluctivantibus undis et pace innocuâ ſimul, et pugnacibus armis ſuſtinuit Patriæ dum publica munia ceſſit.

Anna fuit quondam hæc illi fidiſſima conjux,
Undenas, thalami, ſobole tulit iſta viriles
Quatuor, et ſeptem generoſo ſtemmate natas.

On a very elegant Monument of variegated Marble:

Arms; Two Bendlets engrailed; Blathwayte, quartering Wynter as before; Blathwayte;—impaling, Argent, on a Bend engrailed Gules, a Bezant between two Swans Argent.

D. O. M.
Trino et uni,
In piam Memoriam
Johannis et Franciscæ Wynter,
Necnon Mariæ obſequentiſſimæ
Ipſorum Filiæ et Hæredis,
Piè Anteceſſoribus Seſe et Poſteris
Tabulam hanc cum conditorio
quæ prius deſtinata,
nunc perfecta,
Gulielmus Blathwayt,
Mariæ
Chariſſimus et amantiſſimus
Conjux.
D. D.　D. D.　C. C.
Anno Salutis
MDCCXI.

ON FLAT STONES IN THE SOUTH AISLE.

Frances, Wife of
John Wynter, Eſq.
departed this Life, Nov. 20, 1691.

Ann the Daughter of John Winter,
of Dirham, in the County of
Gloceſter, Eſq
departed this Life, Jan. 30, 1684.

Joseph Blathwayt, Son of
William Blathwayt, Eſq.
and Thomasine his Wife,
died Jan. 18, 1741, aged 15.
William Blathwayt, Eſq.
died March 24, 1742, aged 56.
Alſo Mrs. Thomasine Blathwayt,
died Feb. 4, 1774, aged 79.

Elizabeth, Relict of James Burton,
of the City of Bath, Mercer,
died Feb. 28, 1725, aged 82.

ON MONUMENTS IN THE NORTH AISLE.

Near this Place, lieth the Body of
Isaac Tyler,
who departed this Life, Dec. 11, 1693,
Aged 65 Years.
Likewiſe Edith, the Wife
of the ſaid Isaac Tyler,
who died Feb. 12, 1715.
Near this Place lyeth the Body of
Ann, the Wife of Isaac Tyler,
who departed this Life Jan. 29, 1682-3,
Aged 40 Years.

Arms; three Lozenges, for Freeman;
—impaling on a Feſs, between two Leopards, Paſſant Guardant, three Creſcents for Tyler.

In Memory of Francis Freeman,
of Norton-malereward, in the
County of Somerſet, Eſq.
He died Oct. 18, 1757, aged 70,
and lies interred in a Vault near this Place.

Alſo of Mary his beloved Wife,
Daughter and Heireſs of Isaac Tyler,
formerly of this Pariſh, Gent.
She died Dec. 28, 1754, aged 67,
and lies interred in the ſame Vault.

ON FLAT STONES.

Mary, late Wife of Henry Weare,
died Apr. 12, 1639, aged 24.
Thomas Weare, of this Pariſh, Gent.
died Oct. 26, 1697, in the 60th Year
of his Age.

Penelope, late the Wife of
Henry Weare,
died Aug. 14, 1669, Aged 65.

William Weare, of this Pariſh, Gent.
died June 29, 1697, in the 58th Year
of his Age.

William Neale
departed this Life, the 25th Day of
January, Anno Domini 1654.
Michael Neale,
died June 17, 1652.

John

John Neale, junior,
died Oct. 27, Anno Dom. 1671.

Jane, the Wife of Thomas Hurnall,
departed this Life Sept. 25, 1702,
Ætatis suæ 32.

Also Elizabeth their Daughter.

Elizabeth, Wife of
John Hurnall, Yeoman,
departed this Life, Aug. 10, 1674.

Here resteth the Bodie
of Richard Codrington,
of . . . . Esq.
who departed this Life, May 20, 1635.

Here lies interred the remains of
Walter Tyler of this Parish, Gent.
who died Jan. 19, 1755, aged 78.

Also Elizabeth his Wife,
died Feb. 15, 1766, aged 73.

Also of William and John, their Sons.

IN THE CHURCH YARD, ON TOMBS.

Richard Bolwell of the Parish of
Walcot, near Bath, Son of
Hugh and Grace Bolwell,
of the Parish of Coldashton,
died Dec. 19, 1750, aged 53.

Moses Butler, Yeoman,
died June 18, 1761, aged 60.

John Tyler, Yeoman,
died Dec. 25, 1705.

Frances his Wife,
died Aug. 17, 1699, aged 68.

John their Son,
died Feb. 1725, aged 49.

William, Son of William Tiler,
died Dec. 18, 1716.

Mary, Wife of Philip West,
died Aug. 22, 1745, aged 26.

John, Son of Philip and
Elizabeth West,
died March 7, 1726, aged 25.

Jane, their Daughter,
died July 14, 1730, aged 22.

Philip West, the Elder,
died May 11, 1738, aged 69.

Elizabeth his Wife,
died April 10, 1744, aged 71.

Roger Hawkins,
late Servant to
William Blathwayt, Esq,
died Nov. 15, 1761, aged 52.

Edward Toghill, sen.
died Sept. 24. 1747.

Martha, Wife of Stephen Toghill,
died Jan. 23, 1784, Aged 42.

Mary Crew,
died May 5, 1776, aged 72.

Thomas Crew her Husband, aged 52,
was buried at Doynton.

John, the Son of
Jeremiah and Mary North,
died Nov. 5, 1727, aged 21.

Jeremiah their Son,
died Feb. 28, 1722, aged 9.

Jeremiah North,
died Sept. 23, 1731, aged 55.

Mary, Wife of Jeremiah North,
died Dec. 21, 1776, aged 88.

Samuel North,
died Nov. 27, 1787, aged 65.

ON HEAD STONES.

	Died	Aged
William Bryan	3 Apr. 1767	65
Mary his Wife	2 Apr. 1745	45
Hannah their Daughter	25 Nov. 1745	4
Edward, Son of Guy and Mary Bryan	28 Oct. 1745	4
Betty their Daughter	1 Jan. 1766	30
Francis Hathaway	29 June, 1768	90
Elizabeth, Wife of Francis Hathaway, of Pucklechurch	2 May, 1747	57
Edmund Matthews	25 Mar. 1757	49
Jane his Wife	14 Aug. 1749	46
George, Son of George and Sarah Butler	30 Apr. 1763	24
William their Son	6 Jan. 1755	3
Richard their Son	3 Sept. 1751	7
David West	— Dec. 1742	26
Jane, Daughter of George and Martha Anstee	11 Dec. 1771	24
John their Son	21 Nov. 1771	33
George their Son	16 May, 1770	29
Robert their Son	16 July, 1762	13
Anne, Wife of Robert Anstee	5 Oct. 1761	82
Robert Anstee	5 Apr. 1762	79
Mary, Wife of Robert Anstee	28 June, 1723	34
John their Son, died Young		
Robert Anstee	20 Dec. 1772	85
Selah, Daughter of Richard and Diana Collins	5 Nov. 1752	11
Richard Collins	6 Feb. 1748	42
Richard Son of Richard and Diana Collins		35
	5 Aug. 1780	
Hannah their Daughter	22 May, 1781	34
Abraham, Son of William and Rebecca Collins	21 Jan. 1779	10
Mary, Wife of William Newman	6 Mar. 1787	51
Joanna, Wife of Robert Brimble	1 Dec. 1775	42

	Died	Aged
Ann, Wife of John Brimble	28 June, 1749	23
Benjamin Smith	4 Nov. 1779	80
Ann his Wife	22 Mar. 1770	70
Edward Millard	27 Oct. 1773	77
Ann his Wife	12 Feb. 1780	84
William, Son of William and Mary Looker	28 Aug. 1776	20
James Adams	25 Feb. 1754	36
Philip Harding	22 Sept. 1758	41
Hannah, Relict of the above, and late Wife of William May	25 July, 1773	61
James Hill	7 June, 1740	60
Nathaniel Hill, of Mangotsfield	6 Apr. 1789	78
Edward Camborne	17 Sept. 1749	50
Ann Summers, Widow	25 Dec. 1741	73
Robert May	1 Aug. 1758	60
Sarah his Wife	20 Sept. 1768	87
Edward Cemery	15 Oct. 1770	64
Patience his Wife	6 Mar. 1772	67
Ann Cemery	22 June, 1749	85
John Lamb, of the City of Bristol	13 Jan. 1765	44
Elizabeth, Wife of Francis Papps of the City of Bristol	19 July, 1779	59
Richard Sommers	1 Dec. 1753	38
Mary, Wife of Richard Sommers	23 June, 1752	51
William, Son of Guy and Mary Bryan	24 June, 1758	7
Edward their Son	25 June, 1758	10
Ruth their Daughter	5 Mar. 1782	39
Melior, Wife of Thomas Sloper, Daughter of Charles and Ann Snell, of this Parish	29 Mar. 1777	77
Thomas Sloper, Son of Thomas Sloper of Acton Turville, in this County, and late of this Parish, by Sarah his Wife, Daughter of John Neale, of this Parish	11 Jan. 1771	76

CVIII. EASTINGTON.

CVIII. EASTINGTON.

O F this Parifh no feparate Account is given in *Domefday* Book ; and it is conjectured to have been then included in the adjoining Lordfhip of *Frampton*.

The Village of *Eaftington* is fituate in the lower Part of the Vale of *Stroudwater*, in the Hundred of *Whitftone*, upon the River *Froom*, by different Branches of which the Parifh is interfected. It is diftant from *Stroud* fix Miles weftward, fix North from *Durfley*, and from Gloucester ten on the South. About 2000 Acres are defcribed in the Terrier, of a Soil varying from Gravel to Clay, chiefly Meadow and Pafture, in a Proportion of three fourths. The Inhabitants occupying Lands have a Privilege of Common in a Meadow of 70 Acres, reftricted to certain Seafons of the Year.

The Benefice, which is Rectorial *, is a Member of the Deanery of *Stonehoufe*, and is endowed with an extenfive Glebe. Sir R. Atkins, in afferting that the Advowfon belonged to the Benedictine Nuns of *Clerkenwell*, in the County of *Middlefex*, has miftaken this Parifh for that of *Eaftington* or *Ampney St. Peter*, in this County, for it certainly was never detached from the Manor. In the Church, dedicated to *St. Michael*, there is ample Room for Inveftigation. It has a Nave and North Aifle, with a plain embattled Tower at the Weft End. Whatever be the Date of the firft Structure, indubitable Proofs remain of its having been internally decorated, and the Aifle probably built, by the munificent and unfortunate Edward Stafford, the laft Duke of *Buckingham* of that Family. The whole Roof is of Oak, very neatly framed, and jointed with Rofettes. Upon the Architrave of the South Door, intermixed with Foliage, are the Gothic Letters 𝕊. 𝔹. (Stafford and Buckingham) and between them a ducal Coronet, charged with the Roman Letter W. Thefe appear likewife in painted Glafs in the Nave, with the Addition of a Gothic 𝔻 inclofing a 𝔟. for *Dux Buckingamenfis*, the ufual Cypher and Cognizance of that Nobleman †. Upon other Panes were the Arms of Clara and De Audley, Earls of Gloucester. The Font is very ancient, a fingle Column with Sculpture in a peculiar Style.

Preferved in a Window of the Rectory Houfe (of feveral Centuries ftanding) is a Series of Compartments of ftained Glafs, exhibiting the Arms of Queen Elizabeth, and nine others of Soldiers performing different military Exercifes ; they are by fome *Flemifh* Hand, and very delicately and correctly finifhed.

The Hiftory of the Defcent of the Manor may be accurately ftated ; although the Name does not appear in the *Domefday* Survey, we collect that Winebald de Balun or Baladon, a *Norman* Knight, received it from the Conqueror. In 1319, 12 Edw. II. Hugh de Audley married Isolda de Balun, the fole Heir of that Family ; and in the next Reign it paffed in Dower to Ralph Baron Stafford with Margaret Audley. Being annexed to the immenfe Eftates of the Staffords, it remained with them 'till the Attainder and Death of Edward Duke of Buckingham in 1522, 13 Hen. VIII. when a Life Intereft was granted to Thomas Heneage, Efq. and Catherine his Wife. By their Deceafe in 1532 the Manor reverted to Henry Lord Stafford, whofe Son Edward fold it to Edward Stephens, Efq. in 1573, 15 Eliz. in whofe lineal Defcendant it is now vefted. He was the Anceftor of the four very opulent and refpectable Families of Stephens, fettled at *Eaftington* and *Chavenage*, *Lypiate*, *Little Sodbury*, and *Cherington*, all at one Time refident in this County, which they have frequently reprefented in Parliament. Nathaniel Stephens, Efq. who died in 1660, very feduloufly promoted the republican Intereft, and exerted his local Influence to that Effect with great Succefs. He was an active Commiffioner in all the Tranfactions of that Party ‡.

The Manor Houfe, which was during thofe Commotions ufed as a Garrifon, was built by Edward Stephens, Efq. in 1578. It was remarkably fpacious, and in the beft Style of that Day, with a Front of very curious and expenfive Mafonry. It was levelled with the Ground in 1778, and the Materials difperfed and fold.

---

* " A Portion of Tythes in *Eaftington*, was granted to the Monks of *Bermondfey*, in *Surrey*, by W. de Balun, 1088."

Sir R. Atkins.

" Penf. 20s. Vicario de *Frocefter*." Bacon's Lib. Reg. p. 343.
Advowfon of *Eaftington* (or *Ampney St. Peter*) granted to the Nuns of *Clerkenwell*, Dugdale's Mon. vol. I. p. 418. Newcourt Dioc. Lond. vol. I. p. 657. Tanner's Not. Mon. N° V. *Middlefex*.

† " Arms, Argent a File of five Lambeaux azure, anciently fet up in the Church of *Eaftington*, co. Glouc. and is borne by " Henlinton." Guillim's Heraldry, fect. I. p. 22. Edit. 1679.

‡ Wood's Athen. vol. II. p. 491. Corbet, &c.

7 A

Here

556

Eastington.

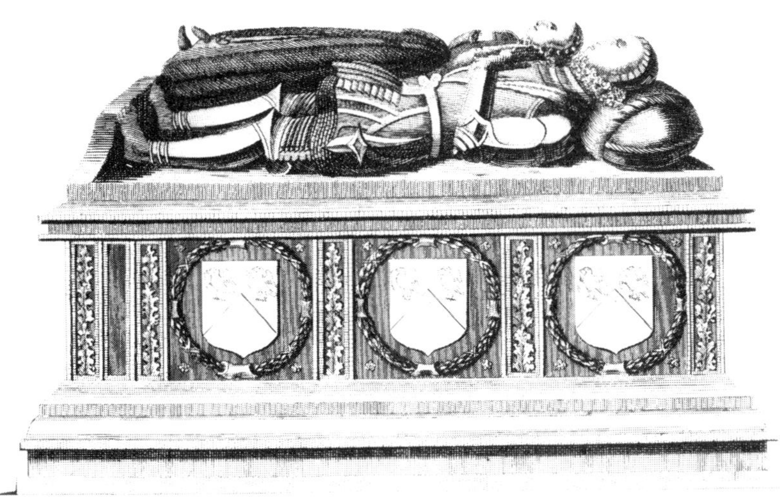

Tomb of EDWARD STEPHENS Esquire
and JOAN his WIFE, 1587.

Here are feveral confiderable Eftates, called corruptedly *Mill-End*, *Nup-End*, *Naft-End*; the two latter mean the Upper and Eaft End of the Parifh. Thefe, though once perhaps annexed to the Manor, were in the Tenure of *Walter Clutterbuck*, Gent. foon after the Year 1557, 2d MARY. His Sons, RICHARD, PETER, and FABIAN, were Progenitors of three diftinct Families of good Repute, each fettled on their own Eftate *.

Millend-Houfe, built by his eldeft Son, is the ancient Refidence, and now belongs to WILLIAM FRYER, Efq. in Right of his Wife, the Relict of RICHARD CLUTTERBUCK, Efq. the laft Heir Male of that Branch.

Another principal Eftate was held by NATHANIEL CLUTTERBUCK, Gent. who married MARY the eldeft Coheir of JOHN CLIFFORD, Efq. of *Frampton* upon *Severn*, and is now inherited by ELIZABETH PHILIPS, Relict of EDMUND PHILIPS, Gent. of the City of GLOUCESTER.

Nup-End, now vefted in the Family of PURNELL, was purchafed of the CLUTTERBUCKS by JOSEPH ELLIS, Efq. by whom it was refold in 1768.

Framilode Mills, within the Limits of this Parifh, were once the Property of Ecclefiafticks. In the Charter of Foundation of the Abbey of *St. Peter* in GLOUCESTER is recited " Molendinum de Framilodâ " quod *Winebaldus de Baladonâ* reddidit Ecclefiæ †," and in a Terrier of their Poffeffions dated 1575, two Mills at *Framelode* are fpecified. The Abbey of *Winchecombe* were Proprietors " de Medietate Gurgitis de *Framelode* in aquâ *Sabrinæ*."

The only Hamlet, or Tything, is *Alkerton*, or *Alcrinton*, which, though a diftinct Manor, has been jointly held for many Ages.

Neale's Place, the chief Eftate in this Divifion, was purchafed early in the prefent Century by JOHN KING, Gent. (who was of an ancient Family, fettled at *Blackhall* in the Parifh of *King's Peon* in *Herefordfhire*), and is inherited by his Grandfon, RICHARD KING, Efq.

Near the Manfion Houfe, a Spring of Medicinal Water was difcovered by finking a Well about thirty Years fince, which has very ftrong cathartic Qualities ‡.

Other Lands formerly the Property of HORTON, of *Wootton*, are now feverally vefted in the Families of FORD, BIGLAND, TALBOYS, and KNOWLES; and the Eftate, called *Puddle Wharf*, is held by the Relict of SAMUEL SHEPPARD, Efq. of *Minchin-Hampton*.

The Prior of *Stanley St. Leonard*, prefented to the Chantry of *Alkerton*, in the Church of *Eaftington*; and, in 1339, procured an Inhibition that the Inhabitants fhould attend divine Service in no other Church.

The Navigable Canal from *Walbridge* to *Framilode*, which was completed in 1779, extends two Miles through this Parifh.

B E N E F A C T I O N S.

RICHARD CLUTTERBUCK, of *Nup-End*, Gent. by Will, 1735, gave 15s. to the Minifter, and 5s. to the Clerk of this Parifh, to be paid every Year, for a Sermon preached yearly on Afcenfion Day.

He alfo gave another Sum of 2l. to be paid Yearly on Chriftmas Day to poor Houfekeepers, and charged his Eftate in the faid Parifh with the Payment of the aforementioned Sums to the Minifter, Clerk, and poor Houfekeepers, for ever.

Dec. 20, 1764, the Sum of 537l. 5s. 11d. was fubfcribed by RICHARD STEPHENS, Efq. ROBERT STEPHENS, M. A. Clerk, PHILIP SHEPPARD, M. A. Clerk, SAMUEL GLASSE, M. A. Clerk, WILLIAM KNIGHT, JOSEPH ELLIS, RICHARD CLUTTERBUCK, and ONESIPHORUS ELLIOT, Gent. vefted in Truftees, the annual Produce of which is 16l. 2s. 4d. for teaching poor Children to read.

1782, JOHN BLANCH, Gent. left by Will 100l. which, being laid out in the South Sea Stock, produces 5l. 4s. 8d. which is divided between ten poor Houfekeepers on Michaelmas Day.

---

* " WALTER CLUTTERBUCK, ob. 30 ELIZ. entailed Eftates on his Sons, RICHARD, PETER, and FABIAN."

MSS. SNELL.

† DUGDALE's Mon. vol. III. p. 8. Pat. 14 EDW. II. M. 2. p. 11. TANNER's Mon. N° 33.

‡ This Water is found by Analyfis to confift of a large Quantity of *Epfom* Salt, calcareous Earth, and a very fmall Portion of Sea Salt. See BERKENHOUT, vol. III. p. 63. MONRO, Vol. I. p. 148, defines it to be " a purgative Water, which upon " Evaporation produced feven hundred and fifty-two Grains from a Gallon, fixty-four of which were a calcareous Earth, fix " hundred and eighty-eight Grains a faline Matter, moftly a calcareous glauber Salt, but with a fmall Mixture of Sea Salt." This Analyfis was made by Dr. SHORT.

INCUMBENTS.

INCUMBENTS.	PATRONS.	INCUMBENTS.	PATRONS.
1319 ——————	Hugh and Ifolda de Audley.	1635 William Mew,	Nathan. Stephens, Efq.
1343 ——————	Hugh Baron Stafford.	1665 Samuel Mew, B. D.	Richard Stephens, Efq.
* * * * * * * * * * * *		1707 Wm. Dighton, M. A.	Nathan. Stephens, Efq.
1571 Richard Syrrel,	G. Fettiplace, and others.	1760 Rob. Stephens, M. A.	——————
1581 Robert Ball,	——————	1776 Wm. Davies, M. A.	R. Stephens, M. A.
1613 R. Capel *, M. A.	Nathan. Stephens, Efq.		

PRESENT LORD OF THE MANOR,

HENRY STEPHENS, Efq. who holds Court Baron for the Hundred of *Whitftone.*

The Perfons fummoned from this Place by the Heralds in 1682 and 1683 were,

Nathaniel Stephens, Efq.
Richard Stephens, Efq.

Nathaniel Clutterbuck, Gent.
William Clutterbuck, Gent. of *Alkerton.*
Samuel Mew, Rector.

At the Election in 1776, Nineteen Freeholders polled from this Parifh.

The firft Date of the Regifter is in 1558.

ANNUAL ACCOUNT OF MARRIAGES, BIRTHS, AND BURIALS, IN THIS PARISH.

A.D.	Mar.	Bir.	Bur.	A.D.	Mar.	Bir.	Bur.	A.D.	Mar.	Bir.	Bur.	A.D.	Mar.	Bir.	Bur.
1781	5	19	16	1786	8	20	18	1791				1796			
1782	8	24	15	1787	3	43	12	1792				1797			
1783	2	16	22	1788	6	23	17	1793				1798			
1784	5	14	14	1789				1794				1799			
1785	9	24	18	1790				1795				1800			

INSCRIPTIONS IN THE CHURCH.

IN THE CHANCEL.

Upon a raifed Altar Tomb of Free-ftone, the cumbent Figure of a Man and Woman in the Drefs of the Times. Repeated on different Compartments, Parti per Chevron Azure and Argent, two Falcons rifing Or, for STEPHENS. On an Efcocheon fixed to the Wall, STEPHENS;—impaling, quarterly, 1ft and 4th, a Cinquefoil, and in Chief a Lion paffant, for FOWLER; 2d and 3d, on a Bend three Crofs Crofslets.

On a blue Marble Slab, the Effigy in Brafs of a Woman in a Mantle, bearing the following Arms: Quarterly, 1. Argent, a Bend Sable, within a Bordure engrailed Azure, KNEVET; 2. Argent, a Bend Azure, and Chief Gules, CROMWELL; 3. Chequy Or and Gules, a Chief Ermine, TATSHALL; 4. Chequy Or and Gules, a Bend Ermine, DE CAILLI, or CLIFTON; 5. Paly of fix within a Bordure bezanté; 6. Bendy of fix a Canton. Four corner Efcocheons; 1. as before, 2. on a Lozenge, Quarterly, 1. KNEVET; 2. CROMWELL; 3. TATSHAL; 4. CAILLI; 5. DE

WOODSTOCK; 6. Paly of fix within a Bordure, bezante; 7. Bendy of fix a Canton; 8. Or, a Cheveron Gules, STAFFORD; 9. Azure, a Bend cottifed, between fix Lioncels rampant, Or. DE BOHUN. The others effaced.

Infcription round the Verge.

"𝕳ere lyeth 𝕰lizabeth 𝕶nevet † 𝕯aughter of 𝕾ir 𝖂ill 𝕶nevet, 𝕶night, whiche 𝕰lizabethe deceffed the firft 𝕯ay of 𝕹ovembre, in the 𝖄ere of our 𝕷ord 𝕲od, 𝕸. 𝕯. and 𝖝𝖆𝖏𝖏𝖏. 𝕺n whofe 𝕾oule 𝕵efu have 𝕸ercy." 𝕬men.

* " RICHARD CAPEL was born of good Parentage, within the City of GLOUCESTER, educated in Grammar Learning there,
" became a Commoner of *St. Alban Hall* in 1601, æt. 17, elected Demy of *Magdalene College* foon after, and, in 1609, made Fellow
" of that Houfe, being then M. A. which was the higheft Degree he took in this Univerfity. While he continued there, his
" Eminency was great, was reforted to by noted Men, efpecially of the Calvinian Party, had many Pupils put to his Charge, of
" whom divers afterward became noted for their Learning, as ACCEPTED FREWEN, Archbifhop of York, W. PEMBLE, and
" others. Afterward, leaving the College upon obtaining the Rectory of *Eaftington* in his own County, became eminent there
" among the Puritanical Party, for his painful and practical Way of preaching, his exemplary Life and Converfation, and in
" doing many good Offices for thofe of his Function. When the Book concerning Sports on the Lord's Day was ordained to be
" read in all Churches in 1633, he refufed to do it, and thereupon willingly refigning his Rectory, obtained Licence to practice
" Phyfick from the Bifhop of GLOUCESTER, fo that fettling at *Pitchcombe* near to *Stroud,* in the faid County (where he had a
" a temporal Eftate) was reforted to, efpecially by thofe of his Opinion for his Succefs in that Faculty. In the Beginning of
" the grand Rebellion he clofed with the Prefbyterians, was made one of the Affembly of Divines, but refufed to fit among
" them, and was, as I conceive, reftored to his Benefice, or elfe had a better conferred upon him. He paid his laft Debt to
" Nature at *Pitchcombe, Sept.* 21, 1656, and was buried within the Precincts of the Church there. His Father's Name was
" CHRISTOPHER CAPEL, a ftout Alderman of GLOUCESTER, and a good Friend to fuch Minifters as had fuffered for Non-
" conformity." WOOD's Athen. vol. II. p. 128.
Of his Tracts, which were many, " The Tentations" are the moft efteemed.
"WILLIAM PEMBLE, born in *Kent,* was fent to *Magdalene College,* aged 18, and continued a fevere Student under R. CAPEL,
" became a noted Tutor, a famous Preacher, a fkilful Linguift, and an Ornament to the Society in which he lived. All which
" Accomplifhments were knit together, in a Body of about 32 Years of Age; which, had it lived to Maturity, would have been
" a Prodigy of Learning. At length, retiring to the Houfe of RICHARD CAPEL, at *Eaftington,* he died of a burning Fever
" in the Year 1623, and was buried in the Yard, under the great Yew Tree, on the North Side of *Eaftington* Church."
WOOD's Athenæ, vol. I. p. 405.

† She was the Daughter of Sir WILLIAM KNEVET. Knt. of *Buckenham* Caftle, in the County of *Norfolk,* by JOAN his fecond Wife, Sifter of EDWARD Duke of BUCKINGHAM, commonly ftyled Lady BEAUMONT. BLOMEFIELD's Norfolk, vol. I. p. 257.
On

ON A HANDSOME MARBLE
MONUMENT:

Arms; Per Chevron Azure and
Argent, in Chief two Falcons rifing
Or, for STEPHENS;—impaling, two
Helmets in Chief, and a Garb in Bafe,
for CHOLMLEY.

To the Memory of
RICHARD STEPHENS, Grandfon of
RICHARD, and Son of
NATHANIEL STEPHENS, Efqrs.
Lords of this Mannor,
Perfons of great Worth, and ufeful
in their Times.

NATHANIEL dyed May 22. 1660,
aged 71 Years.

His Son RICHARD dyed March 4, 1768,
aged 58 Years.
Hee married ANN, Daughter to
Sir HUGH CHOLMELEY,
of Whitby, in Yorkfhire,
Kt. and Baronet,
and had by her five Sons and three
Daughters, all living at the Time of
his Death, who in his Life gave
fignall Proofs of his Piety,
Wifdome, and Patience;
of a generous Spirit,
joyned with an humble Minde.

Arms; STEPHENS, as above.

To the Memory of
ROBERT STEPHENS, of the
Middle Temple,
Serjeant at Law, Son of
NATHANIEL STEPHENS,
Brother of RICHARD STEPHENS,
of this Place, Efqrs.
Lords of this Mannor,
borne July 25, 1622, died Nov. 4, 1675,
aged 53.
He was exquifitely knowing in the
Lawes of this Kingdome, and in
all other reall and folid Learning,
a publique Loffe to his Country and
Age in which he lived.

ON A MONUMENT AGAINST ONE
OF THE PILLARS:

Arms; Sable, a Chevron between
three Griffins Heads erafed Or, charged
with three Mullets of the Field, for
BEALE ;—impaling, Chequy, Or and
Sable, for ST. BARB.

Memoriæ Sacrum
Dominæ EDITHÆ BEALE,
Uxoris et Viduæ ROBERTI BEALE,
de Priors Marfton, in com. Warwick,
Arm. regnante ELIZABETHA
Confilio Regio et Epiftolii,
& in Borealibus Angliæ partibus
Secretarii (qui diem claufit extremum
27 Maii, An. D. 1602),
& Filiæ HENRICI SAINTBARB,
ex antiquiffima SAINTBARBORUM,
de Afhington, in com. Somerfet, Arm.
Familia, & ELEONORÆ LEWKENOR,
de Trotten, in com. Suffex,
quem pulcherrimâ prole ditavit
Filios habuit duos FRANCISCUM &
ROBERTUM, et 9 filias FRANCISCAM
URSULAMBRIDGETTAMMARGERETTAM
(nuptam HENRICO YELVERTONO, Mil.)
Un. Juft. de Communi Banco
(ELIZABETHAM nuptam
WILLIMO SMITH de Elmfett in
Com. Suff. Arm.)

MAGDELENAM, CATHERINAM,
(Nuptam NATH. STEPHENS)
de Eaftington, in Com. GLOUCE.
Arm. ANNAM, et AMIAM.
Fœminæ piiffimæ, prudentiffimæ,
pudiciffimæ, et erga egenos
munificentiffimæ, cujus beata Anima
è terreftri carcere emigravit
11 Julii, A. D. 1628, Ætat 75,
et Corpus in his STEPHANORUM,
de Eaftington, fepulchris requiefcit
reconditum in certiffimam gloriofæ
Refurrectionis fpem.

ON A BRASS PLATE IN THE OLD TEXT.

Arms; STEPHENS; Creft a Demi-
Eagle.

Here underneath lye buried the Bodies
of Edward Stephens, Gentleman, and
Joan his Wife, which both feared God,
hated Evil, were helpeful to the Poore, of
good Report, and toward their later Dayes,
having heere fettled he was Patron of this
Church, the Myniftery of the Word; they
were diligent Hearers and Embracers of the
Truthe. He dyed 22 of Octob. 1587, 29
Regine Elizabethe. beinge about 61
Yeares of Age, and fhe 5 of Auguft in the
fame Yeare, aged about 63 Yeares, leaving
behind them 3 Sonnes and 2 Daughters
living.

ON FLAT STONES.

Here refteth the Body of
JAMES STEPHENS, Clothier,
the Sonne of
EDWARD STEPHENS, Gentleman.
Waiting for a Refurrection to Glorie,
he deceafed on the 19th Day of
Februarie 1590.

Here lieth the Body of ELIZA,
the Daughter of JAMES STEPHENS;
fhe died 27 June, aged fix Years
and feven Months, 1636.

Here lyes the Body of RICHARD,
fon of WILLIAM CLUTTERBUCK,
of this Parifh, Clothier,
who died June 26, 1714,
in the 64th Year of his Age.
Here alfo lies the Body of
HANNAH, the Wife of
RICHARD CLUTTERBUCK,
and Daughter of GILES NASH,
of Stonehoufe, who died July 28, 1746,
in the 87th Year of her Age.

Here lieth the Body of
REBEKAH, the Wife of
WILLIAM CLUTTERBUCK,
Daughter of THO. PERRIE,
of Wotton under Edge, Gent.
who died 4 April, 1706.

Here lieth the Body of
WILLIAM, Son of
RICHARD CLUTTERBUCK, Clothier,
who died the 20th of July, 1705,
in the 84th Yeare of his Age.

Alfo
Here refteth the Body of
GILES CLTTERBUCK, Gent.
Son of RICHARD and HANNAH
CLUTTERBUCK.
He was born May 7, 1693,
died January 23, 1760.

Here lieth the Body of
Mrs. ANN CLUTTERBUCK,
Relict of Mr. GILES CLUTTERBUCK,
who departed this Life
Nov. 19, 1771, aged 67 Years.

Here lieth the Body of
. . . . . the laft Wife of
WILLIAM MEW, M. A.
Rector of this Church,
formerly the Widow of
WM. CLUTTERBUCK, of this Parifh,
Clothier, who departed
this Life .. April, 1642,
. . . . of her Age 79.

Here refteth the Body of
RICHARD CLUTTERBUCK,
the Sonne of
WILLIAM CLUTTERBUCK, Clothier,
Waiting for a full Refurrection to Glory.
He fell on Sleep the 3d Day of June,
Anno 1652.

Here lieth ANNA, Daughter of
DANIEL FOWLER of Stonehoufe,
Gent. and Wife of
RICHARD CLUTTERBUCK
of this Parifh, Clothier,
buried Oct. 4, 1677.

Here lieth the Body of
RICHARD CLUTTERBUCK, Efq.
late of Millend in this Parifh,
who died fuddenly,
as he was returning from the public
Worfhip of GOD,
which he conftantly attended
during the whole Courfe of his Life.
May the ferious Confideration
of that awful Act of Providence,
which removed him to a better World,
incline our Hearts to imitate his Piety,
and to fay,
" Thy Will be done !" Matt. xxiv. 17.
He died September 27, 1778,
aged 52.

Arms; STEPHENS;—impaling, Argent, on a Bend Sable, three Annulets
Or, a Label Azure, for ST. LOE.

MARGARET, late Wife of
RICHARD STEPHENS, Efquier,
and one of the Daughters of
EDWARD SAINTLOO, Efquier,
and MARGARET his Wife,
refteth in this Bedde.
As her Life was blamelefs and holy,
fo her End was full of Peace.
She fell on Sleep March 4, 1591,
leaving one Sonne and three
Daughters.

How long, O Lord ! Holy and True !

Hic

Hic jacet quod mortale fuit
HANNÆ ux. GUALT. MARSHALL,
filiæ GULIELMI CLUTTERBUCK,
quæ obiit 12 die Septembris,
anno Domini 1683, ætat. fuæ 27°.
Etiam GUALT. MARSHALL, Gen.
qui obiit Apr. 6°,
A. D. 1732, ætat. fuæ. 78
Etiam MARGARETTÆ
GUALT. MARSHALL, Gen. Uxoris
JOSEPHI AYLOFFE,
è Gray's-Inn, Armigr. filiæ,
quæ obiit die Julii 15°,
Anno Dom. 1758, ætatis fuæ 88.
Ac etiam ANNÆ, filiæ
NATH'IS POOLE, quæ obiit,
18 die Octob. anno Dom. 1717.

Arms ; STEPHENS impaling BEALE.

Here refteth the Body of
CATHARINE, the Wife of
NATHANIEL STEPHENS, Efq.
the Daughter of
ROBERT BEALE, Efq.
Clerk of the Councell to Queen ELIZ.
who lived in Honour, and dyed in the
Faith of our Lord Jefus,
Feb. 22, an. 1632,
She left behind her in this Vale of
Teares 3 Sons, HENRY, RICHARD,
and ROBERT, and 5 Daughters,
MARGARET, CATHARINE, SARAH,
HANNA and ABIGAIL,
expecting a joyful Refurrection, and
an immortal Crown of Glory at the
laft Day.

Here lieth the Body of
EDITH STEPHENS,
fecond Daughter of
NATHANIEL STEPHENS,
of Eaftington, Efquier,
who died the 6th Day of
September, an. D. 1632.
being 14 Yeares old.

Here lyeth the Body of
FRANCIS, Son of
NATHANIEL STEPHENS, Efq.
who died the 31 Day of March, 1701,
aged near ten Months.

Alfo FRANCES, his Daughter,
who died the 10th Day of March,
aged 1 Year and . . . Months.

IN THE NORTH AISLE.

FLAT STONES, ON BRASS PLATES.

Here lyeth the Body of
KATHARINE, the Wife of
EDWARD STEPHENS,
of this Parifh, Gent. Daughter of
SAMUEL TREWMAN,
Rector of Dyrham in this County,
who departed this Life the
23d Day of April, An. Dom. 1705,
Ætatis fuæ 27.

Here lyeth the Body of
EDWARD STEPHENS, Gent.
of this Parifh of Eaftington,
who departed this Life
the 9th of September, 1734,
in the 62d Year of his Age.

IN THE SOUTH AISLE.

To the Pious Memory of
SARAH, the Daughter of
JOHN KING, Gent. and Wife of
NATHANIEL STEPHENS, Gent.
who died the 13th of December,
1736, aged 54 Years.

Near this Place lie the Bodies of
RICHARD and CATHARINE,
Son and Daughter of
NATH. STEPHENS.   RICHARD died the
1ft of June, 1742, in the
29th Year of his Age.
CATHARINE died March 29, 1741,
aged 26 Years.

Alfo of NATHANIEL STEPHENS, Gent.
who died Aug. 8, 1744.
aged 67 Years.

ANNE, Wife of ELLIS JAMES,
of this Parifh, Gent.
and Daughter of
EDWARD STEPHENS, Gent.
and CATHARINE his Wife,
died 15 Dec. 1766, aged 52.

ELLIS JAMES, their Son,
died 22nd Dec. 1774, aged 27.

MARY their Daughter
died 26 Oct. 1782, aged 38.

The above mentioned Mr. ELLIS JAMES
died 17 March, 1790, aged 80.

IN THE CHURCH YARD.

WILLIAM PEMBLE, Mafter of Arts,
and Preacher, which was here buried
September 23d 1623.

ON MONUMENTS AGAINST

THE EAST END OF THE

CHURCH.

Arms ; Azure, a Lion rampant, and
in Chief three Efcallops Argent, for
CLUTTERBUCK, on an Efcocheon of
Pretence Chequy Or and Azure, on a
Bend Gules three Lions paffant of the
Firft for CLIFFORD.

In Memoriam
NATH'IS CLUTTERBUCK, Gen.
qui obiit 13 die Oct'ris, 1680,
Pronepotis GULIELMI, fen.
Nepotis RICHARDI,   } CLUTTER-
Filii GULIELMI jun. }   BUCK.
Qui omnes olim habitaverunt
Naftend in hâc Parochiâ.
Et Mariæ uxoris ejus 2dæ filiæ natu
maximæ, et unius Coheredum
JOH'IS CLIFFORD, Gen. de Frampton,
fup. Sabrina ; quæ obiit
7 die Octob. 1680,
GULIELMUS FILIUS, natu maximus
ipfor' NATH'IS & MARIÆ, ex pietate
erga Parentes majorefque fuos,
hoc pofuit.

In Memory of
JUDITH HICKS, Widow,
who died the 16th of Feb. 1760,
aged 80 Years.

Near this Place lieth the Body of
WILLIAM, Son of
GILES CLUTTERBUCK, Gent.
by ANN his Wife, born Nov. 23, 1724,
died May 19, 1725.

Alfo of CATHARINE, their Daughter.
She was born Dec. 11, 1727,
died Aug. 14, 1728.

ON A NEAT RAISED TOMB.

Arms ; STEPHENS impaling CHOLM-
LEY as before.

ROBERT STEPHENS *, Efq.
Fourth Son of
RICHARD STEPHENS, Efq.
Lord of this Manor,
died 12 Nov. 1732, aged 67.
He was Barrifter at Law of the
Middle Temple,
and Soficitor of the Cuftoms to their
late Majefties Queen ANNE and
King GEORGE the Firft.
In his voluntary Refignation of which,
he was for a Teftimony of his Fidelity
made Hiftoriographer.
A Gentleman for his Skill in the Law,
Antiquity, and Polite Learning,

and for his Juftice and Integrity
in all his Actions,
worthy to be remembered.
He married MARY, Daughter of
Sir HUGH CHOLMLEY, Bart.
of Whitby in the County of York,
and Relict of NATH. CHOLMLEY,
of Leicefterfhire, Efq.
who, furviving, erected this Monument.

HANNAH, Wife of
WILLIAM DEIGHTON,
Minifter of this Parifh,
and Daughter of THOMAS TYNDALL,
of Stinchcomb, Gent.
died Dec. 13, 1738,
in the 73d Year of her Age.

Alfo WILLIAM DEIGHTON,
who was Minifter of
this Parifh 53 Years,
died Feb. 19, 1760,
in the 93d Year of his Age.

ROBERT BALL, who was Paftor
of this Church 32 Years,
died July 21, anno 1613, ætatis fuæ 63.

Of whom fee a very excellent Character in the New Biographical Dictionary, vol. XI. p. 577.

7 B

DOROTHY,

Dorothy, Wife of
Richard Capel, Preacher,
and Daughter of
Illiam Plumstead of Plumstead,
in Norfolk, Esq.
died Sept. 14, 1622, ætatis 28.

Richard Clutterbuck, Gent.
died Nov. 25, 1735, aged 80 Years.

Grace his Wife (and Daughter of
Maurice and Grace Dyer, late of
Redwick in the Parish of Henbury)
died June 29, 1720,
in the 60th Year of her Age.

Charles Clutterbuck, Gent.
died the 28th Day of May, 1744.
aged 48 Years.

Sarah, Wife of Edward Cox,
and Sister of
Charles Clutterbuck, Gent.
died Sept. 28, 1758, aged 58.

In Memory of
Josiah Clutterbuck of this Parish,
who died Feb. 26, A. D. 1741,
in the 81st Year of his Age.

Also Anne his Wife,
who died Feb. 14, A. D. 1730,
in the 69th Year of her Age.

Mary, Relict of Daniel Partridge,
and Wife of John Pitt, of Stonehouse,
died March 13, 1777, aged 83.

Hic et contiguæ reconduntur cineres
Nathan. Clutterbucke, Gen.
qui obijt 13 die Octob. 1680 ;
Margaretæ uxoris ejus primæ,
quæ obijt 8 Maii 1657.
Ipsa fuit filia
Johannis Clutterbucke,
Neptis Fabiani Clutterbucke,
de Nupend, Proneptis
Willielmi Clutterbucke,
de Natiend.
Et Nathanielis filii ipsorum,
qui obiit 18 Julii, 1656,
ac etiam Mariæ, uxoris ejus secundæ,
quæ ob. 7 Octobris, 1680.
Mariæ Filiæ, quæ obiit 27 Julii, 1670.
Hic ibique Filii natu minimi, sepult.
21 Octobris 1680,
ipsorum Nathanielis & Mariæ.
Nec non
Mariæ, infantulæ
Guil. Clutterbucke,
Generosi, Neptis Nath's & Mariæ
supra dict. quæ obiit 12 Sept. 1683.

William Clutterbuck,
of Nupend, Gent.
died June 11, 1700,
in the 74th Year of his Age.

Also three of his Children, viz.

John, died Nov. 5. 1690, aged 35.

Henry, died Jan. 26, 1689, aged 28.

Martha, died June 24, 1688,
aged 24.

Martha his Wife, and Daughter of
Richard Clutterbuck of Mill End,
Clothier,
died April 12, 1722, aged 90 Years.

Also William and . . . . . Son and
Daughter of William Clutterbuck.
William died March 1, 1707,
aged 39,

. . . . died Sept. 6, 1713, aged 60.
She was the Wife of John Pope of Cam,
Clothier.

Also John Clutterbuck, sen.
died Oct. 21, 1664.

Also Ann his Wife,
Daughter of Henry Fowler, Gent.
who was buried Oct. 6, 1633.

James Budding, of this Parish,
died Sept. 13, 1732, aged 72 Years.

Also George Budding,
August 16, 1613.

Also George Budding,
Feb. 18, 1694, aged 73.

William Budding, of Nupend,
died Feb. 26, 1735, aged 54 Years.

Also Mary his Wife
died Dec. 12, 1741, aged 57 Years.

Elizabeth, Daughter of
William Blanch,
died April 28, 1686.

Elizabeth, Wife of Thomas Blanch,
Nov. 10, 1701, aged 41.

Thomas Blanch,
Feb. 24, 1706, in the
61st Year of his Age.

Mary his first Wife
died March 20, 1673.

Ad Memoriam Felicem Mariæ,
uxoris Charissimæ
Johannis Blanch, Filiæ
Ridhardi Cambridge,
quæ obiit 11 Junii, anno 1686,
Ætatis 25.

Richard Blanch,
December 19, 1736.

Catharine, Daughter of
Thomas Blanch,
June 29, 1740, aged 44.

Hannah, Wife of
Thomas Southerland of London,
June 24, 1720,
in the 73d Year of her Age.

Elizabeth, Wife of
William Blanch, May 3, 1641.

Mary, Wife of Thomas Crew,
and Daughter of Thomas Blanch,
dyed May 15, 17 . .
Ætatis suæ 28.

Rebecca their Daughter,
Jan. 22, 1700, aged 2 Days.

Susannah Bishopp,
July 31, 1722, aged 62.

John King, buried Sept. 2, 1721,
aged 66 Years.

Also Catharine his Wife
buried Oct. 16, 1704, aged 43 Years.

Also five of his Children, viz.
John, buried Oct. 6, 1704,
aged 20 Years.

Elizabeth, buried April 2, 1716,
aged 30 Years.

Richard, buried Sept. 26, 1694,
aged 5 Years.

Catharine, buried Oct. 9, 1694,
aged 3 Years.

Esther, buried Sept. 1, 1701,
aged 3 Months.

Richard, Son of John King,
January 28, 1747, aged 51.

Elizabeth his Daughter,
May 7, 1745, an Infant.

Elizabeth, Wife of the above
Richard, April 18, 1782,
aged near 72.

Also Catharine, Daughter of
Richard and Elizabeth,
Dec. 2, 1773, aged 36.

Samuel Knight,
Dec. 19, 1687, aged 86.

Joseph his Son, March 11, 1712,
in the 80th Year of his Age.
Mary, Relict of Mr. Edward Smith,
Vicar of Frocester,
formerly Relict of Mr Joseph Knight,
buried March 27, 1735,
aged 68 Years.

Nathaniel Body,
Son of Nathaniel Body of Tetbury,
July 30, 1717, aged 23 Years.

Jonathan Bishop, Son of
Walter Bishop, Clerk,
March 19, 1717, aged 17 Years.

John Highway, died Jan. 22, 1735,
aged 45 Years.

Sarah, Relict of John Highway,
and Wife of William Heard,
died Feb. 7, 1754, aged 58 Years.

Ezekiah his Son, Nov. 5, 1744,
aged 19 Years.

Martha his Daughter,
April 20, 1732, aged 5 Years.

On a Brass Plate.

John Warner, Jan. 30, 1782,
aged 52 Years.

Four of his Children, viz.
William, died Feb. 13, 1767,
aged 13 Weeks.

Mary, died April 18, 1770,
aged 2 Years.

Christian, June 26, 1770,
aged 6 Years.

Ann, Oct. 2, 1774, aged 14 Years.

ON

ON FLAT AND HEAD STONES.

	Died	Aged
Dorothy, Wife of William Stone	2 Mar. 1727	50
John Wilkins, Clerk of this Parish 33 Years	13 Sept. 1786	79
Abigail his Wife	9 Oct. 1748	49
Elizabeth his second Wife	12 May, 1771	75
John, Son of John and Abigail Wilkins	18 May, 1736	—
Sarah their Daughter	7 Apr. 1739	6
John Peglar,	2 Nov. 1772	70
Elizabeth his Wife	21 Apr. 1773	68
John their Son	11 Apr. 1777	—
Hannah, Wife of Nath. Perkins	13 Sept. 1700	—
Nathaniel their Son	2 Oct. 1722	—
Ann, Daughter of Joseph Peglar	28 Apr. 1734	1
Nath. Pitt	12 May, 1689	—
Thomas, Son of Thomas Bird	13 Dec. 1782	17
Richard Smith	18 Apr. 1712	77
Joshua Palmer	23 Nov. 1772	72
Sarah his Wife	10 Nov. 1764	65
Martha, Wife of William Freeman	14 June, 1760	53
Sarah, Wife of Abraham Pritchard	. . . . . .	
Mary, Wife of Samuel Beard	.. Apr. 1701	—
William Goodwin	13 June, 1722	77
Abigail his Wife	15 Nov. 1720	76
Jane, Wife of Richard Smith,	7 Feb. 1685	52
Nathaniel Miles, Junior	13 Feb. 173	32
Elizabeth his Wife	—	—
Joseph Miles	5 Nov. 1770	68
Hannah his Wife	13 Aug. 1778	72
Hannah, Wife of William Mower	23 May, 1729	35
Elizabeth, Daughter of Will. King	18 May, 1701	—
Mary, Wife of Nathaniel King	25 May, 1706	—
Richard Eagles	4 May, 1728	67
Mary his Wife	22 Mar. 1695	53
Hester Browning	27 Oct. 1722	15
Thomas Browning, an Infant	29 Mar. 1719	—
Richard their Father	17 Nov. 1729	50
Thomas Evans	6 July, 1769	66
Sarah his Wife	8 July, 1752	48
Sarah, Wife of William Evans	2 Sept. 1708	32
John and Sarah their Children	—— 1708	—
Catharine his Wife	25 Oct. 1740	—
William Evans	15 Mar. 174⅞	75
Mary his Wife	15 Apr. 1715	42
Edward Evans, buried	13 Dec. 1730	54
John, Son of William Evans,	24 Mar. 1762	48
Sarah, Daughter of John Evans	30 July, 1755	4
Ann, Daughter of James and Margarett Hyatt	21 Aug. 1728	8
James Wetmore	9 Jan. 1772	80
Sarah his Wife	11 June, 1781	80
Sarah, Mary, and Elizabeth their Children		
James Hyatt	6 Apr. 1742	62
William Hyatt	12 Nov. 1761	50
Elizabeth, Wife of Samuel King	14 Mar. 1712	21
Joseph Millard	—	—
Ann Jones	—— 1714	—
Samuel Jones	—— 1726	—
George Harwood	21 July, 1707	68
Elizabeth his Wife	19 Jan. 1737	84
Thomas Clutterbuck	16 Dec. 1719	74
Sarah his Wife	24 June, 1723	—
Nathaniel Clutterbuck	8 Apr. 1748	75
Sarah his Wife	25 Jan. 1750	77
Nathaniel Hayward	21 Nov. 1774	70
Ann his Wife	8 May, 1744	39
Daniel their Son	14 Apr. 1757	19
Hester, Wife of John Hayward	25 June, 1787	51
William Heard	23 Apr. 1745	71
Sarah his Wife	22 Jan. 174⅞	71
Elizabeth, Wife of William Gabb	15 Feb. 1749	53
Mary, Wife of Thomas Underwood	12 June, 1752	30
John Clutterbuck	11 Apr. 1770	66
Elizab. Wife of Tho. Browning, bur.	15 Apr. 1740	48
Richard his Son buried	3 Apr. 1739	—

	Died	Aged
Thomas Browning	8 Mar. 1771	83
Sarah his Daughter	19 Apr. 1754	29
John, Son of Richard and Elizabeth Keasey	31 May, 1779	29
Sarah Hill	10 May, 1725	27
Benjamin Talboys	1 Oct. 1766	73
Mary his Wife	23 Dec. 1759	71
William Burley	19 Oct. 1769	52
Mary, Wife of Richard Warner	3 Apr. 1743	28
Rachael Wife of Joseph Coltow	21 June, 1764	—
Sarah, Daughter of Samuel and Elizabeth Bishop	22 July, 1742	26
Samuel Bishop	24 Jan. 1762	71
Elizabeth, Wife of John Taylor, sen.	25 Feb. 1767	74
John Taylor, sen.	24 June, 1775	82
Eliz. Simmons	9 Feb. 173¾	28
Hannah Simmons	28 May, 1754	46
Samuel Simmons	20 Aug. 1716	50
Hannah his Wife	15 Oct. 1756	87
Elizabeth, Wife of Joseph Simmons	2 Oct. 1711	—
Nathaniel Simmons	8 Nov. 1748	74
Sarah, Wife of Josiah Hael	29 May, 1728	52
Jeane his Daughter	14 Oct. 1743	14
Edward Warner	18 June, 1765	58
Joan, Wife of John Verry	22 Jan. 1729	68
Ursula, Wife of John Blanch	7 —— ——	53
Rosamond, Daughter of Samuel Legg and Wife of William Elliotts	12 Oct. 1713	28
John, son of George Knowles	6 Apr. 1727	18
Ann, Wife of Richard Willan	— Nov. 1692	—
Richard Knowles	20 Dec. 1691	57
Richard Hopton	—— —— 170	—
William Hopton	17 Dec. 1688	—
Hannah, Wife of John Davis	25 Feb. 1701	42
Daniel Craft	28 Mar. 1730	68
Elizabeth his Wife	2 Aug. 1740	60
Samuel Evans of Stroud	7 Mar. 1779	30
Edward Evans of Hardwick	25 Apr. 1771	26
John Evans, sen.	18 June, 1768	57
Elizabeth his Wife	3 Feb. 1752	37
James their Son, young	12 Mar. 1752	—
Edward Evans	1 Nov. 1770	3
John Evans	22 Nov. 1770	5
Jane, Wife of Robert Morgan	30 Oct. 1749	60
William, Son of Robert and Jane Morgan	12 Aug. 1746	30
Two of their Daughters, infants	—— ——	—
Joseph Elliott	—— ——	—
Sarah, Daughter of Joseph and Elizabeth Elliott	27 Aug. 1773	74
Joseph, Father of the said Sarah	25 Aug. 1699	—
William, Son of William Tiley	10 Oct. 1724	6
Thomas Miles	— Mar. ——	—
Elizabeth his Wife	8 July, 1708	49
Elizabeth, Wife of Daniel Clarke	9 July, 1716	62
Isaac Davis	29 June, 1787	59
Elizabeth Peglar of Cowley	23 Feb. 1765	40
John Peglar of Frampton	2 June, 1754	35
Richard Clarke of Frampton	15 Feb. 1765	75
John Michell	15 Mar. 1755	52
Sarah, Wife of Robert Stock, of Hanley, St. Leonard's	23 Mar. 1773	35
Hezekiah, Son of John and Sarah Highway	5 Nov. 1744	18
Martha their Daughter	20 Apr. 1732	4
Richard Clark	31 Mar. 1761	71
Mary his Wife, Daughter of Richard Hewes	6 Jan. 173⅚	57
Samuel, Son of William Legg	13 June, 1757	40
Samuel Legg	20 Dec. 1707	59
Ann his Wife	—— ——	—
Thomas, Son of William Legg	13 Dec. 1753	40
Ann his Wife	8 June, 1781	69
Elizabeth, Wife of William Legg	18 Jan. 1720	40
William, Son of Thomas and Sarah Legg	17 Oct. 1777	—

O N

ON FLAT AND HEAD STONES.

Name	Died	Aged	Name	Died	Aged
Elizabeth their Daughter -	6 Sept. 1778	3	Ann his Wife - -	31 Jan. 1768	62
Mary their Daughter -	8 May, 1781	1	William their Son -	15 May, 1763	19
John their Son - -	10 Apr. 1789	5	Hannah, Wife of William Stone	11 Nov. 1760	52
William Wetmore -	9 Jan. 1733	79	Abraham Watkins -	14 Sept. 1727	58
Sarah his Wife - -	15 Nov. 1731	83	Elizabeth his Relict, and Wife of		
Thomas, Son of James Wetmore	27 Oct. 1777	48	Nathaniel Simmons -	12 Feb. 1732	—
Sarah, Daughter of William and			William Peglar - -	16 June, 1729	—
Sarah Wetmore - -	21 July, 1735	10	Abigail his Wife •	24 May, 1748	85
William Wetmore - buried	14 Sept. 1765	75	Nathaniel King, sen. - buried	28 Feb. 1733	82
Richard Fennell - -	10 Nov. 1719	33	Nathaniel King, jun. -	24 Jan. 1759	69
Sarah his Wife - -	18 Oct. 1761	81	Abigail his Wife - -	27 Aug. 1729	43
Leonard Knowles - -	11 July, 1764	69	John Miles of Stonehouse -	13 May, 1744	49
Betty his Daughter -	20 June, 1734	4	Hester his Wife -	3 Dec. 1784	90
Richard Cooper, Gent. -	29 Aug. 1719	77	Thomas Miles - -	28 Nov. 1695	39
John Marshall, Gent. -	12 Aug. 1743	80	Elizabeth his Wife -	2 Aug. 1728	77
Thomas Davis -	16 Apr. 1756	64	Nathaniel Miles, sen. -	23 Oct. 1736	68
Mary his Wife - -	15 Mar. 1765	56	Ann his Wife -	—	—
Nathaniel Perkins -	30 Oct. 1768	74	Elizabeth, Wife of Nathaniel Miles	10 Feb. 1760	26
Elizabeth his Wife -	16 Apr. 1754	70	Randford Brain -	16 June, 1735	61
George Perkins - -	10 Sept. 1767	66	Ann his Wife - -	29 Dec. 1737	60

CIX. EAST

CIX. EAST LECHE ST. MARTIN,
OR
BURTHORPE.

THE Name *Leche* in *Domefday*, and other early Evidences, was applied indiſtinctly to four feveial Pariſhes; from the Rivulet on the Banks of which they are fituate *.

This Village is in the Hundred of *Brightwell's Barrow*, eight Miles from *Northleche* on the South-eaft, three Northward from *Lechlade*, and twenty-feven due Eaſt from the City of GLOUCESTER. The Pariſh is of an oval Shape, about two Miles acrofs in the wideſt Part, containing 1500 Acres, of a light ſtony Soil, three fourths of which are tilled.

DROGO FITZ PONS (the Anceſtor of the Families of POINTZ and CLIFFORD) obtained the Lordſhip of *Lecce* from the CONQUEROR, which was granted by RICHARD FITZ PONS, in the Reign of HENRY the Firſt, to the *Benedictine* Priory of *Great Malverne*, com. *Vigorn.* † His Defcendant WALTER DE CLIFFORD reclaiming it, gave it to the Abbey of *St. Peter*, in GLOUCESTER ‡. ALDRED Biſhop of WORCESTER, upon the Pretence of encreaſing Hofpitality, appropriated this and other Manors to his See, and upon his farther Promotion to *York* annexed them to that Archbiſhoprick. Thefe were afterward reſtored to the Abbey by his Succeſſor THOMAS DE BAION in 1095, with great Contrition §. In 1144, and the 9th of his Reign, King STEPHEN granted a Charter of Confirmation to the Monks of GLOUCESTER, in whofe Hands this Manor remained, till their Suppreſſion, when it was added to the Revenues of the Dean and Chapter, then about to be eſtabliſhed.

The larger Eſtate, including the Hamlet of *Fifield*, was long held by the Family of TRINDER. In the Beginning of this Century JOSEPH SMALL, Gent. became Leſſee, who built the Manor Houfe. After the Deceafe of his Son VINER SMALL, M.D. it was transferred to —— JERVIS, who was fucceeded by SLADE NASH, Efq.

Burthorpe Farm, held likewife under the Church, was firſt in Leafe to a Branch of the Family of BLOMER, of *Hatherop*, and for many Years to the DOWDESWELLS, of *Pull Court*, com. *Vigorn.* Upon the Death of the Right Honourable WILLIAM DOWDESWELL, Efq. in 1775, this Eſtate was purchaſed by TIMOTHY KIMBER, Gent. Two Freehold Eſtates, of nearly 120 Acres each, belong to the Reverend BENJAMIN BOYES, Clerk, and the Family of BUTLER, of *London*.

The Living is a Rectory, in the Deanery of *Fairford*, and in the Patronage of the Crown.

Of this Church, dedicated to *St. Martin*, and that of *Eaſt Leche Turville*, the Style of Building are exactly correfpondent, both of high Antiquity, with a Nave, femi Tranfept, and ſlated Tower. They are fituate at about 120 Yards Diſtance on either Side the River *Leche*, which is the common Boundary of both Pariſhes.

The Rectory Houfe, which is very commodious, was re-built by HENRY SMITH, D. D. a former Incumbent.

BENEFACTIONS.

Dr. HENRY SMITH, by Will, 1702, bequeathed 50*l.* the Intereſt of which to be given five Poor Perfons, on St. Thomas' Day, according to the Difcretion of the Rector.

* " Cleere *Colne* and lively *Leche* fo down from *Coteſwold's* Plaine
   " At *Lechlade* linking hands, come likewife to fupport
   " The Mother of great *Thames.*"   DRAYTON's Polyolbion, book iv. p. 233.
† DUGDALE's Mon. vol. I. p. 365. TANNER's Notitia. *Worceſterſhire*, Nº 15. Pat Rot. 20 EDW. III. m. 18. Pro Eccleſiis de *Eſt Leche*, &c. appropriandis.
‡ " Totam Terram de Manerio *Eſtleche* quam pro Manerio *Glaſherie* DE WALTERIO CLIFFORD, excambierunt."
                               DUGDALE, Addit. in vol. I. p. 9.
§ " ALDREDUS WYGORN. Epiſcopus hofpitii fui caufâ abſtulit a communi *Leche, Odynton, & Standyſch*, cum *Bertona*, retinens in " manu fuâ. Tandem in Archiepiſcopum *Ebor.* confecratur, qui ipfa maneria Ecclefiæ *Ebor.* appropriavit. Anno 1095, " THOMAS Archiepiſcopus *Ebor.* villas *Leche*, &c. reddidit *Glovernenſi* Ecclefiæ, femetipfum graviter inculpando, pectus tundendo, " genu flectendo, quia injuſtè eas tamdiu tenuerat." DUGDALE, vol. I. p. 110.

7 C   INCUMBENTS.

East Leach   S.t Martin   and East Leach Turville.

Tomb of John Guise Esq.r and Alice his Wife, in the Chancel at Elmore, 1472.

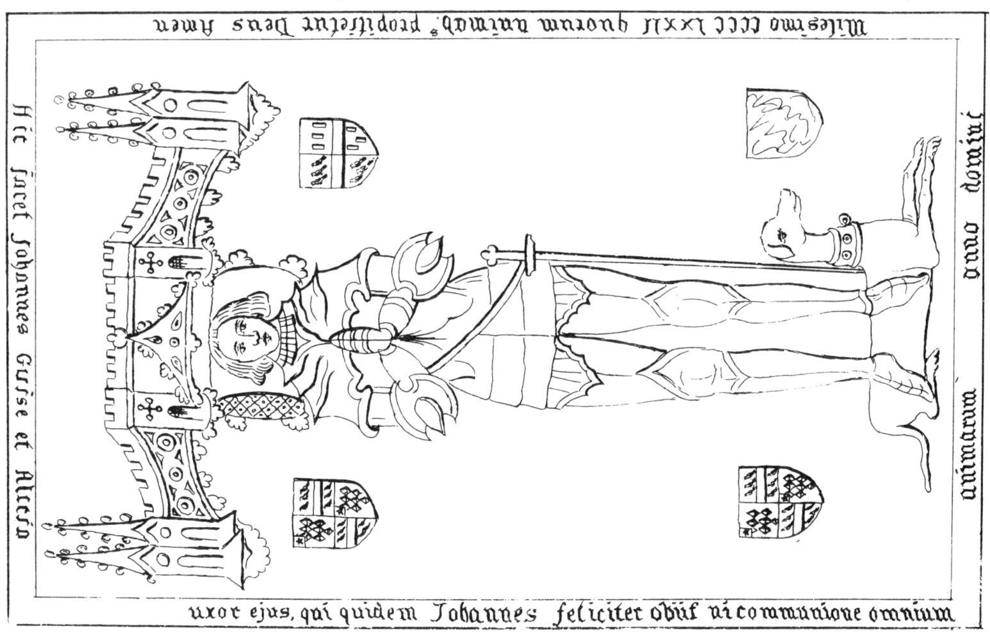

INCUMBENTS.	PATRONS.	INCUMBENTS.	PATRONS.
1578 Thomas Padwyn,	Queen Elizabeth.	1688 Henry Smith, D. D.	King James II.
1589 Simon Perrott,	————.	1702 Thomas Burton, D. D.	Queen Anne.
1600 Rowland Searchfield *,	The fame.	1720 William Afplin, M. A.	King George I.
1622 John Wall,	King James I.	1758 James Parfons, M. A.	King George II.
* * * * * * *	* * * * * *	1785 Hon. Fran. Knollys, M. A.	King George III.
—— Edward Bree,	————.		

PRESENT LESSEE OF THE MANOR,
SLADE NASH, ESQ.

There does not appear to have been any Perfon fummoned from this Place by the Heralds in 1682 and 1683.

At the Election in 1776 only One Freeholder polled from this Parifh.

The Regifter is curioufly preferved, commencing in 1538, and is continued in one Volume to the prefent Time.

ANNUAL ACCOUNT OF MARRIAGES, BIRTHS, AND BURIALS, IN THIS PARISH.

A.D.	Mar.	Bir.	Bur.	A.D.	Mar.	Bir.	Bur.	A.D.	Mar.	Bir.	Bur.	A.D.	Mar.	Bir.	Bur.
1781	1	8	3	1786	3	4	4	1791				1796			
1782	2	4	1	1787	1	6	7	1792				1797			
1783	2	2	6	1788	2	3	5	1793				1798			
1784	1	5	7	1789				1794				1799			
1785	—	2	5	1790				1795				1800			

INSCRIPTIONS IN THE CHURCH.

IN THE CHANCEL.

ON A MONUMENT FIXED IN ONE OF THE WINDOWS IN THE SOUTH WALL.

M. S.
MARIÆ, Filiæ JOHANNIS MYSTER de Hornton,
in agro Oxonienfi, generofi,
Chariffimæ vero conjug.
WILLIELMI ASPLIN, Clerici, hujus
Ecclefiæ Rectoris, quæ omnibus
Vitæ officiis probè functa animam
Deo placidè reddidit
A. D. MDCCXXXVI. æt. fuæ L.
Mortalitatis autem exuvias hic depofuit.
Maritus hic etiam eodem fub lapide,
A. D. 1758, æt. fuæ 71,
Sepultus eft, prædictus
WILLIELMUS ASPLIN, A. M.
Alkiblæ † Author, veri & æqui cultor,
pacis amator, nem' invidens;
Hanc tamen (inimicorum utpote
fuffitum) fummam fibi
Laudem duxit, quod malis ufque invifus
fuerit.
*Beatus ille qui in Domino ponit fiduciam
fuam.* Pf. xl. 5.

ON FLAT STONES.

Here lieth the Body of
ELIZABETH, the Wife of
RICHARD BLOMER, Gent.
decefed, the 17th Day of Nov.
Anno Domini 1614.

Arms; Gules, a Leopard's Face
in Centre Or, between three Croffes
patteè fitchè Argent, for PARSONS.

Beneath this Stone are depofited the
Remains of the
Rev. JAMES PARSONS, M. A.
for many Years Rector of this Parifh:
With a manly Zeal for the Caufe of
Religion and Virtue, he poffeffed that
amiable Simplicity of Manners
which engaged univerfal
Efteem and Veneration.
He died Aug. 5, 1785,
in the 67th Year of his Age.

In a Grave adjoining were interred
JANE, the Wife of the
Rev. JAMES PARSONS,
who died Oct. 14, 1780,
aged 53 Years,
and CATHARINE COLT, her Aunt,
who died Aug. 18, 1762.

Heare lyeth the Body of
RICHARD BLOMER, Gentleman,
who defefeed the xviith Day of June,
Anno Domini 1621.

Here lyeth the Body of
EDWARD BREE, Rector of this Church,
who died the 20th Day of October,
Anno Domini 1688, aged 78 Years.

IN THE CHURCH YARD.

ON A TOMB.

GEORGE BAXTER, fen.
who was buried May 23, 1727,
aged 73 Years.

Alfo of ELIZABETH, Wife of
GEORGE BAXTER,
who died Feb. 21, 1750-51.
aged 64 Years.

ON FLAT AND HEAD STONES.

	Died	Aged		Died	Aged
Elizabeth, Wife of Richard Baxter	25 Oct. 1698	81	John Curtis - -	17 Feb. 1765	52
Charles Baxter - -	3 Feb. 1700	—	Richard his Son - -	30 June, 1761	14
Richard, Son of Philip and Sarah Baxter of Bufley, Worcefterfhire	19 Sept. 1711	84	Mary, Wife of George Curtis -	2 Sept. 1768	24
Sarah, Daughter of George and Elizabeth Baxter - -	25 Feb. 1712	—	Eleanor their Daughter -	20 Jan. 1769	2
Charles their Son - -	9 Feb. 1729	20	Clara their Daughter (an Infant)	—	—
Sarah their Daughter -	27 Mar. 1740	5	Robert Greenhalf - -	28 Feb. 1784	73
Elizabeth, Wife of Richard Baxter	25 Nov. 1748	33	Jacob Stephens - -	20 Apr. 1780	82
Mary Hughes - -	15 Feb. 1691	—	Dorcas his Wife - -	18 Feb. 1772	71
William Hughes - -	5 Apr. 1713	52	Mary, Wife of John Kibble of Fifield - - -	18 Oct. 1784	75
Dorcas Hughes - -	23 Feb. 174⅚	77	Mary, Wife of Job Bifhop their Daughter - -	8 May, 1777	29
Edward, Son of Peter Newman -	14 Dec. 1709	26	William, Son of George and Mary Longford - -	29 Nov. 1781	28
James Greenhalf - -	18 Sept. 1685	—	John Freebury - -	29 Dec. 1778	46
Eleanor Greenhalf - -	5 Nov. 1708	—	Martha, Wife of Thomas Freebury	8 Apr. 1780	58
Robert Greenhalf - -	18 June, 1715⁶⁄₇	37	William, Son of John and Catharine Green - -	26 Mar. 1781	—
Sufan his Wife - -	21 Mar. 1748	62	Mary, Wife of Samuel Thomas -	20 Sept. 1780	23
Thomas Greenhalf - -	5 Aug. 1742	55	Ann, Wife of John Wheeler -	11 July, 1778	35
Anne, Wife of Thomas Harefon	28 May, 1741	41	John their Son - -	in Infancy.	
William their Son -	5 June, 1741	21			
Sufannah, Wife of Jonathan Cull	24 Feb. 1750	24			
Mary his fecond Wife -	10 Dec. 1756	40			

* Confecrated Bifhop of *Briftol* 1619, but held this Rectory in Commendam.
† Of Mr. Afplin's "Alkibla," fee Gent. Mag. vol. XLVIII. p. 221.

CX.   E A S T

cx. EAST LECHE TURVILLE.

THE Account of the preceding Parish applies likewife to this as to Diftrict, Diftance, and Soil; excepting in the Extent of the Terrier, which exceeds it by nearly a thoufand Acres. Although the additional Name be taken from the Family of *Turville*, or *Turbeville*, no Proof remains of their having poffeffed any Lands in this Parifh. A general Inclofure has been made of the Downs, upon which large Flocks were formerly fed.

The Living is a ftipendiary Curacy in the Deanery of *Fairford*, and the Impropriation was given to the Benedictine Abbey of *Tewkefbury*, by their Founder Robert Fitz Haimon, in 1100. It paffed in 20 Edw. III. 1347, to the Abbey of Gloucester, and is now held in Leafe under the Dean and Chapter, charged with 30 *l.* a Year to the Curacy *.

From the Church, dedicated to *St. Andrew*, a cumbent Figure under an Arcade, and the Portrait of John de Leche, a Prieft, in painted Glafs, are now removed. The Door-cafe has fome curious Saxon carvings. Very confiderable Repairs have been lately made.

Roger de Laci received the Manor from the Conqueror, and it defcended to the De Clares, Earls of Gloucester, from whom, through the Audleys, it was inherited by Edward Stafford, Duke of *Buckingham*, and upon his Attainder was confifcated to the Crown. Sir Edmond Tame, Knight, purchafed it of K. Henry VIII. and from one of his Co-heirs it paffed to Sir Thomas Verney, Knight, of *Compton Murdac*, co. *Warwick*. By his Defcendant it was transferred to William Blomer, Efq. before 1608, from whom, by Heirfhip, it now belongs to Sir John Webb, Bart. of *Canford*, com. *Dorfet*, and *Hatherop* in this County.

But it appears that this principal manerial Eftate was held by Tenants, or Mefne Lords, for nearly two Centuries, by the Family of Leversegge, till 1553, 6 Edw. VI. Another reputed Manor with a competent Eftate, was given by William Camerarius to the Ciftertian Monks of *Bruerne* in *Oxfordfhire*, which after their Suppreffion, was granted to John Doddington and John Jackson in 1559 †. Richard Keble (a Defcendant of Sir Henry Keble, Knt. Lord Mayor of *London* in 1510 ‡) purchafed it of them; and it was tranfmitted from him to five fucceffive Poffeffors of the fame Name, by the laft of whom it was fold to Sir John Webb, Bart. who annexed it to the whole Property of the Parifh.

Several Springs here are very ftrongly impregnated with different minerals, chiefly of a faline Quality.

B E N E F A C T I O N S.

Thomas Howes, by Will, dated April 27, 1760, gave 25 *l.* the Intereft thereof to be diftributed in Bread to the Poor on Eafter-Day.

The prefent perpetual Curate is John Chaunler, M. A. The former feries cannot be collected from the Books of the Regiftrar of this Diocefe with any precifion.

Present Lord of the Manor,
Sir John Webb, Bart.

The only Perfon fummoned from this Parifh by the Heralds in 1682 and 1683, was
Richard Keble, Efq.

It does not appear that any Freeholder polled from this Parifh at the Election in 1776.

The prefent Regifter commences in 1654.

Annual Account of Marriages, Births, and Burials, in this Parish.

A.D.	Mar.	Bir.	Bur.	A.D.	Mar.	Bir.	Bur.	A.D.	Mar.	Bir.	Bur.	A.D.	Mar.	Bir.	Bur.
1781	1	18	9	1786	3	14	2	1791				1796			
1782	7	12	6	1787	1	10	5	1792				1797			
1783	1	13	5	1788	—	9	6	1793				1798			
1784	2	11	5	1789	1	14	3	1794				1799			
1785	2	9	17	1790				1795				1800			

* Dugdale's Mon. Angl. vol. I. p. 161.
† " Conceffimus etiam eis & confirmavimus ex dono William Camerarii, ad Feodi firmam totam terram fuam de *Leche*, " cum omnibus pertinentiis fuis, &c." Carta reg. Johannis. Dugdale's Mon. vol. I. p. 835.
‡ Dugdale's Warwickshire, p. 416.

INSCRIPTIONS

INSCRIPTIONS IN THE CHURCH.

ON FLAT STONES IN THE CHANCEL.

Arms; Per Cheveron Argent, and Sable, three Elephants Heads erased counterchanged.

In Memory of ANTHONY SAUNDERS, Rector of East Leach Turvill, who died the 25th Day of March, Anno Domini, 1731, Ætat. 72.

Here lies interred the Body of ELIZABETH, Wife of ANTHONY SAUNDERS, Gent. who departed this Life, May the 9th, 1743, aged 63 Years.

Also in Memory of JOAN, Wife of WILLIAM MEALING, and Sister to the abovementioned ELIZABETH SAUNDERS, who departed this Life May 11, 1743, aged 65 Years.

Here lyeth the Body of FRANCES SAUNDERS, Wife and Relict of THOMAS SAUNDERS, Gent. deceased the 18th of January 1703, aged 75.

In Memory of JOHN SAUNDERS, Gent. who died the 27th Day of June, Anno Domini 1710, Ætat. 48.

RICHARDUS KEBLE, Gent. Natus XXXI Octobris MD.... Obiit XXV July MDCC....

Here lyeth the Body of WALTER ADDERTON, Clark, who deceased the ... Day of July ...

MARY, the Widow of RICHARD KEBLE, Gent. died January the XX. A. D. MDCCXII. Æt LXX.

Here lyeth interred the Body of JOHN PORTER, who departed this Life the 29th Day of March 1721, aged 47 Years.

Also here lyeth interred the Body of ELIZABETH, Wife of the above mentioned JOHN PORTER, who died July the 1st 1758, aged 89 Years.

IN THE NAVE.

ON A HANDSOME MARBLE MONUMENT.

1770.
SARAH ANNE, Daughter of BENJAMIN and MARY BOYES, departed this Life, July 6, aged 1 Year.

Near this are reposited the Bodies of RICHARD and DINAH BOYES. She departed this Life the 11th Nov. 1771, in the 71st Year of her Age. He the 23d of Dec. following aged 85. BENJAMIN, Son of R. E. and MARY BOYES, departed this Life Oct. 15, 1788 ....

ON FLAT STONES IN THE NORTH AISLE.

Here lies the Body of MARY, Daughter of JOSEPH TRINDER, and KATHARINE his Wife, who departed this Life, March 18, 17..

Here lies the .... of DOROTHY, Daughter of JOSEPH TRINDER, and KATHARINE his Wife, who departed this Life, August the 25th, 1696.

Here lyeth the Body of KATHARINE, Wife of JOSEPH TRINDER, who departed this Life the 25th of November 1706.

Here lyeth the Body of CECILEY, the Wife of ROBERT JONES, Yeoman, who departed this Life, August the 12th, Anno Domini 1656.

Here lyeth the Body of WILLIAM SWELL, who was buried October the 13th 1687.

IN THE CHURCH YARD, ON A TOMB.

THOMAS HOWES died 27 April 1760, aged 76 Years.

ON FLAT AND HEAD STONES.

	Died	Aged
Mary, Wife of Joseph Porter, and Daughter of John and Eleanor Newport - -	11 June, 1759	31
Richard, Son of Thomas and Frances Tuckwell - -	30 Nov. 1709	74
Sarah, Wife of Jacob Porter -	28 Dec. 1767	44
Susannah his Wife, and only Daughter of John and Mary Wakefield	29 Nov. 1728	72
Richard Tuckwell - -	29 Jan. 1755	74
John Collier - -	25 July, 1726	41
John Jones - -	16 Dec. 1762	65
Elizabeth his Wife - -	21 Aug. 1727	25
Mary his second Wife - -	—— 1770	55
John Howes - -	29 May, 1722	74
Elizabeth his Wife -	29 Aug. 1729	72
Ann their Daughter, and Wife of Richard Atterton -	5 Dec. 1750	71
John Howes - -	6 Mar. 1785	71
Thomas, Son of John and Elizabeth Porter - -	4 June, 1729	21
Samuel, Son of John and Anna Porter	11 May, 1760	24
Henry Newport buried	27 May, 1734	69
Mary his Wife - -	27 July, 1726	65
Dorothy, Wife of Richard Lapworth - -	21 Jan. 1739	70
Henry Lapworth -	19 Jan. 1741	71
William Simson - -	20 Sept. 1720	39
William Jones - -	18 Nov. 1763	81
Daniel Jones - -	21 Feb. 1741	73
Jane his Wife - -	17 Apr. 1752	84
William Dunn - -	20 Sept. 1763	66
Anne his Wife - -	26 June, 1756	73
Anne, Wife of William Iles -	29 Oct. 1766	39
William their Son - -	——	—
Sibilla, Wife of William Clark -	18 Mar. 1734	71
Idey Bradshaw -	4 May, 1738	70
Mary, Wife of Richard Browne	30 July, 1760	71
Elizabeth, Daughter of John and Elizabeth Porter -	26 Dec. 1726	19
Peter Herbert - -	5 Aug. 1768	80
Richard their Son - -	——	—
Mary Wife of John Clarke -	26 June, 1766	51
William Clark - -	12 Sept. 1788	77
Frances, Wife of Adam Clarke, and Daughter of Richard and Susannah Tuckwell - -	6 Feb. 1735	53
Jasper, Son of Adam and Frances Clarke - -	15 Apr. 1738	15
Adam Clarke - -	6 Nov. 1760	76
Ann his Wife, and Relict of John Lapworth - -	17 Oct. 1765	80
Henry Lifeley - -	27 July, 1741	—
Grace Lifeley - -	4 Nov. 1781	81
Mary Wife of John Wakefield	5 Sept. 1712	87
John Wakefield - -	4 Jan. 1721	90
John Wakefield, jun. -	29 Dec. 1729	68
Thomas Tuckwell -	26 Jan. 1745	67
Robert Richins - -	21 June, 1790	—
Catharine Richins - -	26 Jan. 1703	—
Justinian Lovesy - -	11 Dec. 1755	72
Robert Sermon, Gent. - -	3 Jan. 17$\frac{11}{87}$	46
Thomas, Son of Thomas and Elizabeth Brown - -	3 Jan. 1763	29
Sarah their Daughter - -	10 Apr. 1760	26
John Lapworth - -	11 Apr. 1741	76
Elizabeth Trinder - -	7 Mar. 1708	15
Robert Trinder - -	29 Jan. 1738	—
Hester Woodward - -	29 Aug. 1722	—

CXI. EBRINGTON,

CXI. EBRINGTON, or EBBURTON,

LIES in the Hundred of *Kiflefgate*, two Miles diftant North-eaft from *Campden*, and twenty-three in the fame Direction from the City of Gloucester.

The Boundaries of this Parifh are of an oval Shape, two Miles long, one broad, and fix in Circumference, of a Soil light and gravelly, and chiefly applied to Tillage.

The Living is a very fmall Vicarage, in the Deanery of *Campden*, the Emoluments of which arife principally from Stipends, 8*l*. per Ann. paid by the Earl of Gainsborough, in Lieu of Tythes in the Hamlet of *Charingworth*, and 10*l*. the Benefaction of Sir William Keyte, Bart. It is not in Charge. In 1377, William le Zouch, of *Charingworth*, gave Lands to the Ciftertian Abbey of *Bittlefden*, com. *Bucks*, annexing to it the Impropriation, which were granted in 1607 to Anthony and George Bonner *. The Tythes of *Charingworth* abovementioned were once held by the Abbey of *Winchcombe*.

The Church is dedicated to *St. Eadburgh*, and is fpacious and neat. It has a Nave, a femi-tranfept and low Tower. In the Chancel, which is more modern, are hiftorical Paintings in the Eaft window, from the Story of Joseph and his Brethren, with the Arms of the Donor Sir William Keyte, very well executed.

In *Domefday*, *Ebrington* is not mentioned. Some have conjectured that it is there defcribed as " *Briftentune*," the Property of William Goizenboded. In the 55th of Henry III. it was claimed by Roger de Quincy, Earl of *Winchefter*. The Family of De Bosco, or Boys, were the Poffeffors for feveral Generations, who, in 1331, 3 Edw. III. were fucceeded by Sir Roger Corbet.

Of Sir Robert Corbet it was afterwards purchafed by that great Lumiminary of the Law, Sir John Fortescue †, Lord Chancellor of *England* in the Reign of Henry Sixth. Being a zealous Lancaftrian, after the decifive Battle of *Tewkefbury*, he was attainted, and his Eftates confifcated, yet he was permitted to retire to his Manor of *Ebrington*, where he died and was interred. Upon the Death of Sir John Brugge in 1471, who had obtained this Eftate, it was reftored to the Fortescues, in which noble Family it has been without Interruption, and is ftill vefted.

The manerial Houfe is large, in the Style of the laft Century.

This Parifh comprifes three Hamlets; 1. *Ebrington*, 2. *Charingworth*, which is diftinctly fpecified in *Domefday*, belonging to Ralh de Todeni, and containing ten Hides of cultivated Land. It is a Liberty which owes Suit and Service to the King's Court, held at *Afton Subedge* ‡.

From the Turstanes the chief Eftate paffed to the Grevilles, who retained it for feveral Centuries. It has been fubfequently the Property of the Earls of Gainsborough, and the Family of Barnsley.

3. *Hidcote Bois*, or *Cote*, given in *Saxon* Times to the Benedictine Abbey of *Evefham*, com. *Vigorn*. For many Centuries the greater Part of this Tything belonged to the Keytes. Sir John Keyte was created a Baronet in 1660, in Reward of his Services to the Royal Caufe during the Rebellion. His Grandfon, Sir William Keyte, rebuilt their Refidence called " *Norton*," at a very confiderable Expence. In 1741 this Edifice was confumed by Fire, and its Poffeffor perifhed in the Flames §. Soon after this Event, the Eftate was fold by his Executors to Sir Dudley Ryder, whofe Son the Right Hon. Nathaniel Lord Harrowby has fince fucceeded.

The higher Grounds in this Parifh afford many extenfive Profpects over the Vale of *Evefham*; but of Antiquities or Natural Curiofities few fpecimens have been difcovered.

---

* W. Le Zouch, de *Charingwortb*, dedit feptem Acras terræ Abb. & Conv. de *Blethefden*, com. *Bucks*, et appropriavit Ecclefiam, anno 1377, 1 Rich. II. MSS. Parsons.

† Sir John Fortescue was the fecond Son of Sir Henry Fortescue, Lord Chief Juftice of the Common Pleas in *Ireland*. He was called to the Degree of Serjeant at Law in 1430. In 1442, he was made Lord Chief Juftice of *England*; and laftly, Lord High Chancellor to King Henry VI. After King Edward the IVth was feated on the Throne, he followed the Fortunes of the unfortunate Houfe of Lancaster, and was many Years in exile with Queen Margaret and Prince Edward her Son, previous to the Battle of *Tewkefbury*. His celebrated Book " De Laudibus Legum Angliæ" was then written, and dedicated to that ill-fated Prince. Several Editions have been publifhed in Latin and Englifh, to one of which Mr. Selden wrote Notes. His Treatife, "On the Difference between an Abfolute and a Limited Monarchy," was publifhed by John Fortescue Aland, Efq. afterwards Lord Fortescue, 8vo. 1714. Ob. æt. 90.
See Biog. Brit. Collins, vol. VII. p. 351. Granger's Biography, vol. I. p. 57, &c.

‡ MSS. Parsons, ut fup.

§ Of this fad Cataftrophe a very minute Account is given in the Gentleman's Magazine for April 1774.

7 D

BENEFACTIONS.

B E N E F A C T I O N S.

WILLIAM KEYTE, Efq. in 1635, gave by Will, the Milk of ten fufficient new Milch Kine, from the tenth of May, untill the Feaft of All Saints every Year, to be difpofed of to fuch Poor Perfons as fhould be thought fit by his Executors and Heirs and the Church-wardens for the Time being.

INCUMBENTS.	PATRONS.	INCUMBENTS.	PATRONS.
	From 1377 to 1541.	1616 Francis Hains	The fame.
	Abbey of Bittlefden.	1622 ———————	———————
1575 Thomas Sweetnam,	Queen Elizabeth.	1638 ———————	———————
—— Thomas Gyles,	The fame.	1704 Baptift Hickes,	———————
1577 Roger Williams,	Bifhop of Gloucefter.	1715 Thomas Andrews,	Queen Anne.
1610 Tnomas Hawling,	King James, or Bifhop of Briftol *.	1759 Jacob Mould, Clerk.	King George II.

PRESENT LORD OF THE MANOR,

The Right Hon. MATTHEW Earl FORTESCUE †.

The Perfons fummoned from this Place by the Heralds in 1682 and 1683 were

Sir William Keyte, Bart.   Francis Keyte, Efq.

At the Election in 1776, Four Freeholders polled from this Parifh.

The Regifter has its firft Date in 1680.

ANNUAL ACCOUNT OF MARRIAGES, BIRTHS, AND BURIALS, IN THIS PARISH.

A.D.	Mar.	Bir.	Bur.	A.D.	Mar.	Bir.	Bur.	A.D.	Mar.	Bir.	Bur.	A.D.	Mar.	Bir.	Bur.
1781	—	22	7	1786	6	16	10	1791				1796			
1782	2	13	4	1787	4	18	4	1792				1797			
1783	2	13	6	1788	7	17	13	1793				1798			
1784	1	12	5	1789	3	13	13	1794				1799			
1785	1	15	11	1790				1795				1800			

INSCRIPTIONS IN THE CHURCH.

IN THE CHANCEL.

ON MONUMENTS.

Arms; Azure, a Chevron between three Kite's heads erafed, Or, for KEYT; 2. KEYT impaling, Or, a Cheveron Sable, between three Croffes patée fitchè Gules, for RILEY; 3. KEYT; impaling, quarterly, firft and fourth, Sable, three Salmons haurient Argent, for SALMON; 2d and 3d. Argent, a Bend Azure, between a Mullet and Annulet Gules, for . . . . .

D. O. M.

In Memoriâ æternâ erit juftus.
Depofitum GULIELMI KEYT,
Armigeri, hoc fub marmore præftolatur,
Jefus donec fuus tubæ clangore
exurgere, & corruptionem
incorruptionem induere jufferit.
Comitatus Wigornienfis vicecomitis
officio functus eft:
Familia fuit fatis antiqua, ut quæ
per trecentos plus minus annos
villæ hujus primatum obtinuit.
Duxit in Uxorem EGLANTINAM
RILEY, è quâ duos filios,
JOHANNEM & GULIELMUM,
totidemque fufcepit Filias,
ANNAM nempe et ELIZABETHAM.
Infigniter erat pius:
habuitque erga pauperes
(vici præfertim hujus)
ΣΠΛΑΓΧΝΑ ΟΙΚΤΙΡΜΩΝ,
utpote qui decem vaccarum uberibus
diftentis lac, a decimo die Maii
ufque ad primum Novembris,
in perpetuum ipforum alimentum
mifericors legavit.
Amicis jucundiffimus, cunctis gratiffimus,
optimus fenex, fenio confectus,
(fummo Bonorum omnium
luctu ac defiderio)
mortalitatem cum perennitate
Placidè commutavit, idibus Octobris,
Anno Verbi Incarnati 1632,
Ætatis fuæ 78.
Jo. KEYT, filius mœftiffimus,
chariffimo parenti
Hoc pietatis ergo pofuit
ΜΝΗΜΟΣΥΝΟΝ.

UPON A TABLE TOMB, THE EFFIGY OF A MAN RECUMBENT IN A JUDGE'S ROBES.

Arms; 1. Azure, a Bend engrailed, Argent, between two Cottices, Or; FORTESCUE;—2. impaling, 1. Gules, 3. Clarions, Or. GLANVILLE, 2. Argent, three cros Croflets in Bend Sable; 2. as before; 3. FORTESCUE, 2. Or, a Raven proper, CORBET; 3. Gules, a Mullet in Chief, and a Crefcent in Bafe Argent; 4. on a Bend three Crofiers; 5. a Fefs between 6 cros Croflets; 6. FORTESCUE.

In fœlicem et immortalem Memoriam viri Domini JOHANNIS FORTESCUTI, militis grandevi, Angliæ Judicis primarii, et proceffu Temporis fub HENRICO VIto Rege et EDVARDO principe fummi Cancellarii, Confiliarii Regis prudentiffimi, Legum Angliæ peritiffimi, nec non earundem hyperafpiftis fortiffimi:
qui corporis exuvias lætam
refurrectionem expectantes hic depofuit,
Marmoreum hoc Monumentum
pofitum eft
Anno Domini MDCLXXVII.
Voto et expenfis ROBERTI FORTES-
CUTI, Armig ejufdem
Familiæ hæredis nuper defuncti.
Angligenas intra cancellos juris et æqui,
Qui tenuit cineres jam tenet urna viri.
Lex viva ille fuit, patria lux fplendida
Legis,
Forte bonis fcutum, fontibus at frutica.
Clarus erat titulis, clarus majoribus
arte,
Clarus virtute aft clarior emicuit.
Jam micat in tenebris veluti carbun-
culus orbi:
Nam Virtus radios non dare tanta ne-
quit.
Vivit adhuc FORTESCUTUS laudatus in
æva;
Vivit et in Legum Laudibus ille, fuis.

To perpetuate the Memory of that learned and excellent Man Chancellor FORTESCUE, this Monument was repaired by his Defcendant, MATTHEW Lord FORTESCUE, in the Year 1765.

* Created Baron FORTESCUE of *Caftle Hill*, July 5, 1746, 20 GEO. II. Earl FORTESCUE, and Vifcount EBRINGTON, Auguft 18, 1789, 29 GEO. III.
† See BARRET's Briftol, p. 317.

On

ON AN ELEGANT MARBLE MONU-
MENT, WITH TWO BUSTS.

Arms; 1. KEYT; 2. Sable, three Bells Argent, a Canton Ermine, PORTER; 3. SALMON; 4. Argent, a Bend Azure, between a Mullet and Annulet Gules; 5. Gules, a Fefs between fix Billets Argent, STYVELEY; 6. KEYTE;—impaling, Ermine, on a Chief indented Gules, three Efcallops Or, TAYLOR.

Dominus JOHANNES KEYT,
Jo. Fil. GUIL. Nep. Baronettus,
(Qui nuperis motibus ex parte Regis
Propriis fumptibus Hipparchus fuit)
Ex MARGARETA, GUIL. TAYLER
Armig. Hærede
fobolem fufcepit
D. GUIL. KEYT, Baronettum,
JOANNEM, THOMAM, et FRANCISCUM,
Filios;

ELIZABETHAM, Uxorem
Jo. TALBOT de Lacock, eq. aur.

MARGARETAM, Uxorem
Jo. PACKINGTON, Fil. et Hæredis
Jo. PACKINGTON, Baronetti.

Diem obiit ille 26 die Aug.
A. D. MDCLXII.

Diem obiit illa 28 die Jun.
A. D. MDCLXIX.

ON A LARGE MARBLE FLAT STONE,
WITH THE INSCRIPTION ROUND
PART OF THE VERGE.

Arms; 1. KEYTE;—impaling, Gules, a Lion Rampant within a Bordure engrailed Or, TALBOT; 3. TALBOT, on a large Efcocheon, TALBOT, with twentyfour Quarterings.

Hic requiefcit in Domino
ELIZABETHA, JOHANNIS TALEOTTI
Conjux, JOHANNIS KEYT
Armigeri primogenita; corporis
formæ exinia, animi autem dotibus
major; quæ cum peperiffet
unicum filium fibi fuperftitem
religiofiffimo exitu vitam claufit,
cujus anima in cœleftem
patriam evocata, placidè piéque
emigravit, et depofuit quod mortale
fuit, certa fpe refurgendi indutum
gloriâ; obiit primo Aprilis,
Anno Domini 1656, ætatis 21°.

ON FLAT STONES.

Arms; KEYT;—impaling, on a Fefs three Eaglets difplayed, HARRISON.

MARGARETTA,
Filia GULIELMI HARRISON,
de Caddicroft in com. Wigorn', Gen.
Uxor fecunda JOHANNIS KEYT,
de Ebbrington, in com. Glouc.
Ar. juxta quem hîc fita eft.
Diem obiit Februarii 8, A. D. 1667,
Ætatis fuæ 78.

Arms; KEYT, quatering TAYLOR, Sable, a Fefs Ermine, between three Crefcents Or, for COVENTRY.

H. S. E.
Ds. THOMAS KEYT,
Dn'i GULIELMI KEYT, Baronetti,
Et D'næ ELIZABETHÆ uxoris ejus,
Hon'bilis D'ni FRANCISCI COVENTRYE,
Armigeri, filiæ natu maximæ,
Filius natu minimus:
Summâ in Parentes obfervantiâ
nulli fecundus;
Cœlibum pudicitiam colentium
facilè primus; moribus adeo caftus,
et pudore integer,

Seculo licèt corruptiffimo,
Ut ab incontinentiæ fufpicione abeffet,
Natus XIV. cal. Sept. MDCLXXII.
Denatus IV. Cal. Jun. MDCCII.
Qui rem familiarem
Dilectiffimo Fratrino FRANCISCO KEYT
Tabellis Teftamentariis legavit.

Arms; KEYT;—impaling, PORTER, as before.

Memoriæ Sacrum
JOHANNIS KEYT, Armigeri,
GULIELMI filii primogeniti,
Qui reclinavit annofum in hoc
pulvere depofitum. Confortem tori
fideliffimam, prudentem, providam,
et pudicam, THOMÆ PORTER,
Generofi, filiam, duxit JANAM, quæ
chariffima reliquit conjugii pignora
Septem filios, et quinque filias,
Primò Wigornia, poftea Gloceftria,
Vidit Vicecomitem, Pacique præpofitum.
Regis, Reipublicæ, Religionis ergò, Dux,
Vicecomes, Irenarches, bellum fortiter,
pacem civiliter, geffit coluitque.
Nobilis ingenii, vitæ intemeratæ,
Pietatis ⎫   ⎧ Deum,
Fidelitatis ⎬ in ⎨ Principem,
Charitatis ⎭   ⎩ Proximum,
Exemplar æmulandum. Communi
procerum populique jacturâ
Fato fuccubuit Aprilis 25°,
Anno Salvatoris 1660, ætatis 76.
JOHANNES KEYT, Baronettus, filius
mœrens, pofuit.

Arms; Quarterly, KEYT, PORTER, SALMON, and TAYLOR. On an Efcocheon of Pretence, COVENTRY, as before.

H. S. E.
Cl. V. GULIELMUS KEYT, Baronettus,
Qui uxorem duxit ELIZABETHAM,
Honorabilis FRANCISCI COVENTRYE,
Filiam, et Honoratiffimi
THOMÆ BARONIS COVENTRYE,
Magni Sigilli Cuftodis, Nep'tem;
Ex quâ fufcepit quatuor filios,
JOHANNEM, ANONYMUM;
GULIELMUM, THOMAM,
(Quibus omnibus fuperftes fuit;)
Filiafque duas, MARGARETAM et
DOROTHEAM. Pauperibus et operariis
indies benevolum; Regibus, etiam
exulantibus, femper fidelem;
Hujus Ecclefiæ Paftoribus
(quibus annuatim folvenda decem
legavit libras)
In perpetuum fe præbuit munificum.
Mortiferum (quo laboravit)
morbum animo verè Chriftiano
perpeffus, tandem placidè obdormivit
S. Andreæ Fefto,
Anno Chrifti incarnati MDCCII°
Ætatis fuæ fupra LX^m VI°.

Arms; Quarterly of 6, KEYT, as before, a Label for Difference.

Fratrum altero haud ita pridem defuncto, Familiæ cladem et luctum renovavit Mors præmatura alterius, viz.
WILHELMI KEYT, Armigeri,
D'ni WILHELMI KEYT, Baronetti,
Filii natu tertii, et, fi Deus annuiffet,
Hæredis futuri.
Qui ex Generis Thalamique
Conforte fideliffimâ,
Meritoque dilectiffimâ, Agnete
D'ni JOHANNIS CLOPTON de Clopton
Equitis Aurati filia primogenitâ,
Poftquam feptem procreâffet Filios,
WILHELMUM, COVENTRIUM,
THOMAM, GILBERTUM,
JOHANNEM, FRANCISCUM,
et HASTINGIUM; et tres Filias,
ELIZABETHAM, BARBARAM, et
MARGARETAM, ab omnibus

deploratus hinc emigravit,
Fefti Omnium Sanctorum Vigiliâ,
Ad participandam Sanctorum in luce
fortem, Anno poft Chriftum natum
MDCCII°, Ætatis fuæ XXXIV.

Arms; KEYT;—impaling, Argent, on three Bars Sable fix Cinquefoils of the Field for DAYRELL.

Memoriæ Sacrum
THOMÆ KEYT de Wolford, Armigeri,
JOHANNIS filii natu minoris,
Cognatis et neceffariis amiciffimi,
Ægrotis et egenis munificentiffimi,
Omnibus humaniffimi, fato perfuncti
V° Idus Januar. Anno Salutis MDCCI.
Ætatis fuæ LXXX°.
WILHELMUS KEYT, Armiger,
Quem Hæredem ex affe inftituit
Lapidem hunc fepulchralem pofuit.

Arms; KEYT; impaling DAYRELL.

Mortis exuvias in hunc Tumulum recondidit, certâ fpe refurgendi ad vitam immortalem,
Matrona pientiffima
MARIA, GUALTERI DAYRELL
de Abendonia in agro Bercheriæ,
Armigeri, Filia, quæ fauftè et feliciter bis nupta fuit; primum, Reverendo
JOHANNI MORRIS, S. T. D.
Ædis CHRISTI apud Oxonienfes
Canonico, et Linguæ Ebrææ Profeffori
Regio; Deinde, rei militaris peritiffimo
Duci, THOMÆ KEYT,
de Wolford Magna,
In comitatu Warwici, Armigero.
Nullam poft fe reliquit fobolem;
Nomen vero melius et multo perennius,
quàm quod habere poterat a filiis
et filiabus. Poftquam annos plus
minus feptuaginta pudicè,
fanctè, piè, peregiffet,
Terrenum depofuit tabernaculum,
Ut æternum in Cœlis haberet
domicilium, nono Kalendas Novembris,
Anno Æræ Chriftianæ MDCLXXXI.

Here lyeth the Body of
WILLIAM KEYT, fecond Son to
WILLIAM KEYT, Efq.
who departed this Life March 28,
Anno Domini 1642, ætatis fuæ 57.

Arms; On a Lozenge, KEYTE.

Here lyeth the Body of
Mifs JANE KEYT, Daughter of
Mr. FRANCIS KEYT,
and ALICE his Wife, of Hitchcoate,
who departed this Life
the 30th Day of June, An. Dom. 1674,
Ætatis fuæ 2do.

Arms; KEYT;—impaling, quarterly, Argent and Gules, in the 2d and 3d, a Frett Or; over all, on a Bend Sable, three Efcallops of the 1ft, for SPENCER.

Here lies the Body of
ALICE KEYT, Daughter of
Sir WILLIAM SPENCER,
of Yardington, in the County of
Oxford; Baronet, and of
CONSTANCE his Wife, the Daughter of
Sir THOMAS LUCY, of Charlecott.
in the County of Warwick, which faid
ALICE was the late Wife of
FRANCIS KEYT, of Hithcoat, Efq.
and deceafed the 29th of May,
in the Year 1687.
A Lady dignified not only by her Birth,
but, befides her other Virtues, for her
Love and Fidelity to her Hufband.

ON

ON FLAT STONES IN THE NAVE.

Here lieth the Body of
the Rev. Mr. WILLIAM STANTON,
Minifter of this Parifh,
who departed this Life,
April 27, 1704, aged 33.
Ecclefiafticus, ch. xli. v. 13.

Here lyeth the Body of
FRANCES, the Wife of the
Rev. Mr. THOMAS ANDREWS,
Vicar of this Church,
and Daughter of MILDMAY,
Son of the Hon. W. FANE, D. D.
Sixth Son of the Right Hon.
Sir FRANCIS FANE, Earl of
WESTMORLAND. She died
March 1, 1720, aged 32.

To the Memory of the
Rev. Mr. THOMAS ANDREWS,
Vicar of this Church,
who departed this Life July 21, 1758,
aged 68.

To the Memory of DOROTHEA,
the fecond Wife of the
Rev. Mr. THOMAS ANDREWS,
Vicar of this Church,
and Daughter of
Mr. WILLIAM KEYT, of this Town,
who departed this Life
the 26th of Jan. 173¾, aged 34.

Here lyeth the Body of
WILLIAM DANIEL, Son to
ROBERT DANIEL. He married
MARGERIE, the Daughter of
WILLIAM MILWARD, of Stourton,
in com. Warwick, deceafed the
5th March, A. D. 1647, æt. fuæ 89.

Here lyeth the Body of
THOMAS BARNSLEY,
of Charringworth, Gent.
who departed this Life, Sept. 13, 1711.

IN THE SOUTH TRANSEPT.

ON A NEAT MARBLE MONUMENT.

Underneath lieth the Body of
JOHN TONGE, Efq. He died the
5th of Sept. 1786, aged 41.
From his benevolent Difpofition,
gentle Manners, and amiable Character,
he will always be remembered by
thofe who knew him with a tender
Concern. From his affectionate
Temper, fteady Friendfhip, and
honorable Principles,
his Lofs will be ever felt by a Brother
(who caufed this Stone to be placed
here in teftimony of his Virtues)
untill he himfelf mingles with the Duft.

Here lyeth the Body of
Mr. JOHN BARNSLEY,
the Son of Mr. THOMAS BARNSLEY,
of Charringworth, Gent.
who departed this Life 20 April, 1767,
aged 76 Years.

Here lieth the Body of
JOHN BARNSLEY, Gent.
of Charringworth,
who departed this Life,
Dec. 6, 1778, aged 65.

Here alfo lieth the Body of
MARY, the Daughter of
THOMAS BARNSLEY, Gent.
of Charringworth, who departed this
Life Nov. 23, 1708.

In Memory of SUSANNAH,
the Wife of Lieut. SAMUEL BARNSLEY,
of Hurft, near Reading,
in the County of Berks,
who departed this life the 8th Day of
Sept. 1776, aged   years.

On a very old Tomb are the Arms of
KEYT; impaling RILEY.

ON A FREE-STONE MONUMENT AGAINST THE WEST END OF THE CHURCH.

To the Memory of
MICHAEL WESTON and ELIZABETH
his Wife. He died March 20, 1756,
aged 55 Years, fhe died Aug. 29, 1769,
aged 65 Years.

In Memory of
MARY, Wife of JOHN MOULD
(Nephew to the Rev. Mr. MOULD)
who in a Journey from Town to fee her
Friends was arrefted by Death.
The Soul took its flight into the
invifible World, and her Remains are
configned to reft here till the Refurrection.
She died Sept. 5, 1775,
in the 29th Year of her Age.

In Memory of ELIZABETH,
Daughter of the Rev. Mr. TYRER,
and MARY his Wife,
who died July 7, 1761,
in the 25th Year of her Age.

Alfo in Memory of THOMAS,
Son of the Rev. Mr. MOULD,
and SARAH his Wife,
who died Sept. 25, 1761,
aged four Months.

ON FLAT AND HEAD STONES.

	Died	Aged
Mary, Wife of John Leeke, and Daughter of Sam. and Eliz. Keyte	19 Sept. 1704	28
William Keyte	29 Sept. 1769	50
Mary, Wife of William Whitehead	7 Jan. 1727	60
William Whitehead	.. Mar. 1730	94
Mary, Wife of John Purfer	22 Apr. 1786	67
Richard Keyte	19 Sept. 1784	70
Judith, Wife of William Whitehead	18 Mar. 1780	62
John Purfer	11 May, 1776	80
Robert Purfer	30 July, 1767	66
Hannah, Wife of John Purfer	11 Oct. 1781	75
Elizabeth their Daughter	4 Mar. 1781	38
John Purfer of Hidcoat, fen.	3 Mar. 1722	55
Jofeph Purfer	2 Jan. 1778	66
Mary, Wife of Thomas Tawney	22 June, 1729	23
William Fletcher	29 Feb. 1752	87
Eglantine his Wife	15 Mar. 1732	69
Thomas Fletcher	11 June, 1770	74
Elizabeth, Daughter of Robert and Joan Shorte	15 Dec. 1749	1
William Hobbins	19 June, 1786	67
Sarah his Wife	11 May, 1780	71
Die Unit, Son of Nathaniel and Mary Unit	22 Mar. 1777	28
Mary their Daughter	21 Feb. 1761	23
Nathaniel Unit	26 Jan. 1789	80
Mary his Wife	5 Feb. 1769	6t
John Keyte	20 Dec. 1776	36
Mary Beard	24 Aug. 1703	31
Sufannah, Wife of Richard Fletcher	2 Sept. 1721	77
Richard Fletcher	19 Nov. 1746	84
Ann, Daughter of Richard and Sarah Fletcher	20 Mar. 1762	9
Ann their Daughter	21 May, 1774	9
Jofhua their Son	20 June, 1776	—
Richard Fletcher	7 June, 1779	67
Sufannah his Daughter	27 July, 1783	—
Samuel Southam	11 Mar. 1771	66
Sarah his Wife	—— —— 1770	—
Elizabeth Daughter of Thomas and Hannah Southam	2 Sept. 1743	30
Thomas their Son	16 Apr. 1741	34
Mary and Hefter } their Daughters {	11 Nov. 1752 / 2 July, 1752	15 / 12
Hannah Southam	10 Jan. 1747	60
James Righton	14 Dec. 1755	72
Ann his Wife	13 Nov. 1737	—
Samuel Righton of Hidcoat	14 Feb. 1773	62
Thomas, fon of Thomas and Sarah Jones	6 Dec. 1760	—
Elizabeth, Wife of Richard Smith	7 Nov. 1783	52
John Hirom	11 Apr. 1768	55
Thomas Procter	15 Dec. 1746	61
Agathea his Wife	24 Sept. 1750	57
Thomas Booker	18 Mar. 1761	68
Elizabeth his Wife	— Aug. 1761	65
John Gibbs	14 Apr. 1703	30
Jane, Daughter of William and Alice Purfer	6 Feb. 1757	—
Alice Wife of William Purfer	10 Nov. 1780	85
William Purfer	9 Feb. 1765	66
Mary Parnell	1 Jan. 1764	42
Thomas Smith	23 Aug. 1784	67
Ann, Wife of Thomas Roberts	6 Apr. 1781	35
Thomas Roberts	2 Feb. 1785	78
Sarah his Wife	23 Sept. 1775	60
William Carter	28 Jan. 1751	40
Mary, Wife of Charles Ueal	18 Mar. 174	41
Samuel, Son of Wm. and Sarah Keyt	6 May, 1740	35
Elizabeth, Wife of Samuel Keyt	26 July, 1768	26

CXII.

CXII. EDGEWORTH.

A NAME defcriptive of the Situation of this Village upon feveral eafy Acclivities. It is a Parifh of no great Extent in the Hundred of *Bifley*, fix Miles Northweft from *Cirencefter*, and twelve in the precifely oppofite Direction from the City of Gloucester. The Terrier contains about 1500 Acres, including the common Fields and Woodlands; of a light Soil and chiefly in Tillage: in the Valley are fertile Meadows on the Banks of the Rivulet *l'roome*.

The Benefice, which is rectorial, is a Member of the Deanery of *Stonehoufe*, and the Church has *St. Mary* for its Patron Saint. It is conftructed with a Nave or Pace only, with a neat embattled Tower, at the Weft End, of early Norman Architecture. The few Veftiges of Antiquity it exhibits, are the Portrait of a Prieft epifcopally habited, a Lavatory and curious Subfellium, or Stone Bench, on the left Side of the Altar; with the Steps of the ancient Rood Loft. *Domefday* Books records Roger de Laci as the Proprietor of " Egefwrde," which Manor was originally connected with *Painfwick*, having been jointly inherited by Audomer de Valence, Earl of *Pembroke*, in 1324, 17 Edw. II. In the fucceeding Reign it paffed in Dower to the noble Family of Talbot, of *Godrich Caftle* in *Herefordfhire*. In 1397, 20th Rich. II. it was leafed by Richard Lord Talbot, by fervice of half a Knight's Fee to Thomas Ralegh, Efq of *Farnborough* * in the County of *Warwick*, whofe Defcendants held by Soccage as of the Manor of *Painfwick*, during a Courfe of more than 200 Years †. Sir George Ralegh, Knt. joining with Edward his Son, in 1602, 44 Eliz. conveyed it by Deed of Sale to Sir Henry Poole, Knt. of *Saperton*. About 1670, when the Property of that Family in this County was difperfed, *Edgeworth* was purchafed by Nathaniel Ridler, Efq. who built the prefent Manerial Houfe foon afterwards, and made it his Refidence. Upon the Death of Thomas Ridler, Efq. a Partition of the Eftate was made between his three Co-heirs, Elizabeth, the Wife of William Prynne, Efq. of *Charlton' Kings*, whofe Share is inherited by Dodington Hunt, Efq. and Mary, who died unmarried in 1774, and bequeathed her Share with the Manor to her Nephew, Thomas Brereton, Efq. after the Deceafe of her younger Sifter Barbara, late the Wife of the Rev. Richard Brereton, M. A. Rector, who now holds the third Portion in her Right. There is a fmall Freehold only in this Parifh, excepting a Part of *Pinbury*, defcribed under *Duntefborne Militis*. A Mill and Meadow, originally given to the Abbey of *St. Peter* in Gloucester, now belongs to the Manor. The Face of the County in this lower *Cotefwold* is well cultivated, and derives much picturefque Beauty from the numerous Woodlands and Groves of Beech, which grow fpontaneoufly, the natural Produce of the Soil.

BENEFACTIONS.

Joan Ridler, by Will, dated Aug. 27, 1714, and Mary Ridler, May 9, 1715, devifed 100*l*. the Intereft to be applied to teach poor Children to read.

Thomas Ridler, Rector in 1701, bequeathed the Intereft of 5*l*. to the Poor for ever.

John Ridler in 1724 left the Intereft of 50*l*. for the fame Purpofe.

Anne Ridler, Widow, gave by Will, April 11, 1777, 100*l*. the Intereft to be diftributed annually, according to the Difcretion of the Truftees.

—— Ward, Relict of Thomas Ward, Rector, gave 5*l*. the Intereft to be applied as the other Charities. The time of this Donation is not known.

Incumbents.	Patrons.	Incumbents.	Patrons.
1635 Henry Hayward,	————	1703 Will. Dighton, M. A.	The fame.
—— Thomas Ward.	————	1707 Edw. Loggin Gryffin,	The fame.
—— Nathaniel Capel.	Sir Henry Poole.	1729 Samuel Ridler, LL.B.	Thomas Ridler, Efq.
1684 Thomas Ridler.	Nathaniel Ridler, Efq.	1765 Rich. Brereton, M. A.	Upon his own Prefentation.
1701 John Elliot,	The fame.		

Present Lord of the Manor,

Thomas Brereton, Efq.

* See their Pedigree in Dugdale's *Warwickfhire*, p. 380.

† It appears that this Manor was not included in the Tenure of the Manor of *Painfwick*, the Articles of which were fettled at a Court Baron by Jury held in 1440 by John, afterwards Earl of Shrewfbury, and which extended to *Morton Valence* and *Whaddon*.

7 E

The

The Perfons fummoned from this Place by the Heralds in 1682 and 1683 were,

Nathaniel Ridler, Efq. and Henry Wyndowe, Efq.

At the Election in 1776, Two Freeholders polled from this Parifh.

The firft Date of the Regifter is in 1556.

ANNUAL ACCOUNT OF MARRIAGES, BIRTHS, AND BURIALS, IN THIS PARISH.

A.D.	Mar.	Bir.	Bur.	A.D.	Mar.	Bir.	Bur.	A.D.	Mar.	Bir.	Bur.	A.D.	Mar.	Bir.	Bur.
1781	—	3	3	1786	1	3	3	1791				1796			
1782	—	2	3	1787	1	4	4	1792				1797			
1783	—	3	5	1788	—	2	1	1793				1798			
1784	3	5	1	1789	—	2	1	1794				1799			
1785	1	2	3	1790				1795				1800			

INSCRIPTIONS IN THE CHURCH.

IN THE CHANCEL.

ON A MARBLE MONUMENT:

In the Church-yard adjoining
lie the Remains of
Mrs. BARBARA BRERETON,
one of the co-heireffes of
THOMAS RIDLER, Efq.
and Wife of the
Rev. RICHARD BRERETON,
Rector of this Parifh.
To her Family and near Connections
fhe was an invaluable Friend,
to the Poor a liberal Benefactrefs,
to all an Example of Sincerity,
Generofity, and unaffected Piety.
She died fuddenly, but not unprepared,
Aug. 23, 1787, Æt. 64.

ON A FLAT STONE.

In Deum pius, in uxorem et liberos
amans, in conjunctos benignus,
in omnes dum vixit officiofus,
fub hoc lapide, gloriofam expectans
refurrectionem in Domino, mortuus,
et fepultus eft, FRANCISCUS MARSHE,
Generofus, Junii, A. D. 1630.

ON FLAT STONES IN
THE NAVE.

Here lyeth the Body of
ANTHONY SADLIER, Gent.
who was charitable to the poor of
this Parifh, and lived above
One Hundred Years, who died and
was buried the 2d day of February,
Anno Domini, 1653.

On the left fide of this Stone
is interred wating to be raifed to
eternal Glory, the Body of
Mrs. ANN GODDARD, Relict of
Mr. RICHARD GODDARD, and fole
Daughter of Mr. ANTHONY SADLIER,
who lived to a good old Age,
the firft day of November, 1674.

Here lyeth the Body of
JEROME JEFFEREYS, of Weft Hood,
who died the 7th of June,
Anno Dom. 1606.

In Memory of
RICHARD GODDARD, Gent. who
was buried the 26th day of June, 1701.

IN THE CHURCH YARD, ON TOMBS.

HENRY WITTS,
buried Oct. 15, 1730, aged 83.

ANN, his Wife,
died Jan. 6, 1739-40, aged 86.

HENRY WITTS, Jun.
died Sept. 28, 1752, aged 72.

GEORGE WITTS,
died Dec. 6, 1761, aged 79.

JOHN BROWN,
died March 3, 1726,
aged 63.

MARY RIDLER, 2nd Daughter of
THOMAS RIDLER, Efq.
died Nov. 19, 1774, aged 53.
ANN, Relict of THOMAS RIDLER, Efq.
April 25, 1780, aged 79.

ON FLAT AND HEAD STONES.

	Died	Aged		Died	Aged
Charles Ballinger, fen. -	10 Aug. 1739	84	William their Son - -	20 Oct. 1725	—
Hefter Smith - -	25 Sept. 1754	34	Elizabeth their Daughter -	16 June, 1723	—
Mary Smith - -	6 Mar. 1680	—	Ann, Wife of Benjamin Dadge -	1 Oct. 1750	38
John Smith - -	12 Apr. 1735	58	Mary, Wife of James their Son	29 July, 1767	25
Jane, Wife of Henry Coal -	24 June, 1771	55	John Parfons of Dunfbourne Rous	22 Mar. 1771	86
George Blackwell - -	28 Nov. 1774	73	Elizabeth his Wife - -	20 July, 1762	67
Mary his Wife - -	3 July, 1762	71	Jane, Wife of John Brown -	18 Jan. 1745	72
Mary their Daughter -	19 Feb. 1742	11	Mary Halley - buried	18 Mar. 1742	11

CXIII. ELBERTON.

IS fituate in the lower Divifion of the Hundred of *Berkeley*, eleven Miles North from *Briftol*, and twenty-eight from GLOUCESTER on the South-weft. The Village lies in the Vale, on the Eaft-fide of the River *Severn*, the Soil is a ftrong red Clay, and produces excellent Herbage; a very fmall Portion of the Lands are in Tillage.

In Mr. SMYTH's MSS. are the fubjoined Notices:

" *Elberton*, or *Aylbertune*, *Elbrighton*, or *Eldberton* quafi, the old Barton, or Farme Place. In *Domefdie*
" Booke it is written *Eldberton*, where WILLIAM the Conquerour had five Hides of Land in Demefne.
" The Manor is now the Inheritaince of HUMPHRY HOOK, a Marchant of *Briftol*, who purchafed the
" fame of Sir ARTHUR SMYTHES, Sonne of GEORGE SMYTHES, a Goldfmith in *London*; who purchafed
" the fame of WALTER WALSH of *Sodbury*, Efq. to whom HENRY WALSH his Cozen (afterwards flaine
" in fingle Combat, by Sir EDWARD WYNTOUR) conveyed this and other Manors; which HENRY was
" the Sonne of NICHOLAS WALSH, Sonne of MAURICE WALSH (who died in 4th MARIÆ) Son of Sir
" JOHN WALSH, Sonne of Sir JOHN WALSH of *Olvefton*, and ELIZABETH his Wife, Daughter of
" RICHARD FORRISTER, als FORSTER of *Sodbury*. It is holden by Knight's Service in Capite of the
" Crowne. This Manor was Parcell of the Herneffe, viz. Nookes or Corners of the great Manor of *Berkelie*,
" and by Kinge HENRY Second in the firft Yeare of his Raigne, granted (inter alia) to ROBERT, Son
" of HARDING and his Heirs, who afterwardes, about the 12th of the faid King gave the fame to
" ROBERT his thirde Sonne and his Heires, and dyed 5 Yeares after; and by the Deth of the faid
" ROBERT, Sonne of ROBERT, in the Time of King JOHN, it defcended to MAURICE DE GANT his Son
" and Heire; by whofe Death without Iffue in 14th of HENRY III. the Manor came to ROBERT DE
" GOURNAY, Son and Heire of EVA, Sifter and Heire of the faid MAURICE, which ROBERT, dying in
" 53d HEN. III. left it by Defcent to ANSELM DE GOURNAY his Sonne, and by his Death in 14 EDW. I.
" it defcended to JOHN DE GOURNAY his Son, who dying without Iffue, five Years after his Father left
" the fame to ELIZABETH his Sifter and Heire, who was marryed to Sir JOHN AP ADAM, who died
" in 5th EDW. II. leaving Iffue, by his faid Wife, THOMAS AP ADAM, who, by a Fine and other
" Affurances in 4th EDW. III. fold this Manor with *Kingfwefton* to MAURICE BERKELEY, Knt. and his
" Heires, fecond Son of MAURICE, Lord BERKELEY, the thirde of that Name, who had Iffue, Sir
" THOMAS BERKELEY, called of *Eweley*, and died 21 EDW. III. leaving Iffue MAURICE BERKELEY,
" who died 2 HEN. IV. leaving Iffue, Sir MAURICE BERKELEY, borne after the Death of his Father,
" who dyed the 4th EDW. IV. leaving Iffue Sir MAURICE BERKELEY, Knt. to whom this Manor
" defcended, as the Inquifition, found that Yeare after his Death, fhewith. The faid Sir WILLIAM,
" then 28 Yeares old, died in 17 HEN. VII. leaving Iffue Sir ROBERT BERKELEY. But, forafmuch as
" the faid Sir WILLIAM BERKELEY was in the 1ft HEN. VII. attainted of High Treafon by Parliament,
" for partaking with Kinge RICHARD III. and this Manor granted by King HENRY VII. to JASPAR,
" Earle of *Pembroke* in Taille, though the faide Sir WILLIAM was reftored to moft of his Landes after
" Compofition made with the faid Earle and his Sonne, Sir RICHARD, after his Father's Death; yet
" fith neither of them are found to dye feized of the Manor, nor to fue Livery thereof nor any of their
" Pofteritie after them; I cannot but conceive, but that one of them fold away the fame, but when or
" to whom I have not obferved.

" In this Parifh of *Ailberton* is one ancient Freehold, created by the aforefaide ANSELM DE GOURNAY,
" by a Grant thereof made to THOMAS NORRYS and his Heires, who after fold the fame to THOMAS
" TROPYN and his Heires, and he to JOHN CHAMPNEIS and his Heires; all which feveral Aliena-
" tions are laid downe in a Pardon, dated July 18, 10 EDW. III. being made without Lycence. Yet,
" that Recorde faith that thefe Landes are holden of JOHN LYDIAN in Capite and are now (Anno 1639)
" the Inheritance of THOMAS HERYNS and of JAMES SEGAR, worth 100l. per ann', which had in the
" Name and Pofteritie of CHAMPNEIS continued in lineal Defcent till EDMOND CHAMPNEIS (that yet is),
" and his Father fold the fame of late Yeares.

" The Church of *Eldberton* is within the Deanery of Briftol, and in fome Deeds faid as alfo *Filton* to
" belong to the Mother Church of *Alkmondefbury*, as Chappels thereof *."

<hr>

* Notices relative to *Elberton* are found in the following Records:
    Inquif. 53 HEN. III. poft Mortem ROBERTI DE GOURNAY.
    ——— 14 EDW. I. poft Mort. ANSELMI DE GOURNAY.
    ——— 21 EDW. III. poft Mort. MAURICII Fil. M. DE BERKELEY.
    ——— 29 EDW. III. poft Mort. THOMÆ BERKELEY DE ULEY, Chivaler.
And of the detached Freehold:
    Inquif. 11 EDW. II. poft Mort. JOHANNIS TROPYN.
    ——— 10 EDW. III. Writ " Ad quod damnum." SMYTH, MSS.

I

To

To this accurate Account of the Property of this Parifh it remains only to be added, that the manerial Eftate paffed in Dower about the Middle of the laft Century with CECILY, Daughter of the abovementioned HUMPHRY HOOKE to Sir ROBERT CANN, Bart. and continued in that Family till the Death of the laft Baronet in 1765. Leaving no Iffue, he was fucceeded by his Nephew ROBERT CANN JEFFERIES, Efq. who died in 1773 unmarried. His Sifter, who is the Relict of the late Sir HENRY LIPPINCOTT, Bart. inherited from him. The Freehold, above defcribed, is now divided amongft feveral Proprietors, the larger Part of it has been transferred from the Families of BROWNE and VAUGHAN to the GOLDNEYS of *Clifton*. Lands in *Ailberton* once belonged to the Monaftery of *St. Auguftine* near *Briftol* " Ex dono WILLIELMI filii GREGORII, 40 folidatas Terrræ in *Ailbertune* ficut comes WILLIELMUS " eas confirmavit *."

The Living is a Vicarage, or Chapelry, in the Diocefe of *Briftol*, but in the Archdeaconry of GLOUCESTER, of the certified Value of 46l. per ann. confolidated with *Olvefton* in 1767. By the Act of Union the Dean and Chapter of *Briftol* prefent twice; and the Bifhop once; the latter has the intermediate Turn †. The Impropriation valued, at the Diffolution of *St. Auguftine's*, at 6l. has been fince given in Augmentation of the perpetual Curacy of *Horfield*.

There are grounds for Conjecture, that the Church, dedicated to *St. Mary*, was built by the Convent, in the 13th Century. It has a Nave, two Ailes, with a Tower and Spire in the Middle. The whole is now under complete Repair, having been much dilapidated from Age. No veftiges of Antiquity remain, excepting a large ftone Sarcophagus, without Arms, Ornament, or Infcription. Upon the rifing Grounds, above the Church, a Camp or Outpoft, probably *Roman*, and commanding a fine View of the River, is ftill eafily to be traced.

B E N E F A C T I O N S.

JOHN HICKS by Will bequeathed 40l. the Intereft of which to be diftributed on the 27th of December yearly in Bread and Meat.

The prefent Incumbent is JOHN CAMPLIN, D. D. prefented by the Dean and Chapter of *Briftol* in 1767.

PRESENT LADY OF THE MANOR,

Dame CATHERINE LIPPINCOTT.

It does not appear that any Perfon was fummoned from this Parifh by the Heralds in 1682 and 1683.

At the Election in 1776, Two Freeholders polled from this Parifh.

The earlieft Date in the Regifter occurs in 1653.

ANNUAL ACCOUNT OF MARRIAGES, BIRTHS, AND BURIALS, IN THIS PARISH.

A.D.	Mar.	Bir.	Bur.	A.D.	Mar.	Bir.	Bur.	A.D.	Mar.	Bir.	Bur.	A.D.	Mar.	Bir.	Bur.
1781	—	4	3	1786	—	—	1	1791				1796			
1782	3	1	5	1787	—	1	2	1792				1797			
1783	—	1	5	1788	—	3	3	1793				1798			
1784	1	—	5	1789	—	2	2	1794				1799			
1785	3	2	1	1790				1795				1800			

INSCRIPTIONS IN THE CHURCH.

IN THE NAVE.
ON FLAT STONES.

ON A BRASS PLATE.

Here lyeth the Body of
JOSEPH FRICKER, Jun. Son of
JOSEPH FRICKER, M. D. of Tockington,
Qui obiit Aug. 27, 1707.

In Memory of THOMAS, the Son of
THOMAS EDMONDS, who died
17th July, 1738, aged 7 Years.

Here lyeth the Body of
THOMAS WINFIELD, Yeoman,
buried 29th of May, A. D. 1671.

Here lyeth the Body of
JOSEPH FRICKER, late of Olveftone,
Gent. and SARAH his Wife,
who were buried,
SARAH the 29th of June, 1711,
JOSEPH the 13th of Feb. 1716.

CHRISTIAN, the Wife of
THOMAS EDMONDS of this Parifh,
and Daughter of the aforefaid
JOSEPH FRICKER, departed this Life
the 21ft Day of July, 1731,
in the 20th Year of her Age.

Here lyeth the Body of
JOHN WADE, of this Parifh, Yeoman,
who departed this Life 4th of July,
1741, aged 74 Years.

Here lyeth the Body of
BRIDGET SMITH, Widow,
who was buried May 8, 1671,
Ætatis fuæ 82.

ROUND THE VERGE.

Here lie buried the Body of
HENRY SMITH, who deceafed
October 11, 1651.

ADJOINING,
Alfo the Body of MARIAH SMITH,
Widow. She died 1 June, 1671,
Ætatis fuæ 75.

* DUGDALE's Mon. vol. II. p. 233.
Thefe LANDS were granted to PAUL BUSH and his Succeffors, Bifhops of *Briftol*, June 10, 1543, 34 HEN. VIII.
BARRET's Briftol, p. 315.

† BACON's Liber Regis, p. 108.
3

IN

IN THE CHURCH YARD, ON TOMBS.

ANN, Wife of JOHN HICKS, jun.
buried June 8, 1724, aged 53.

JOHN HICKS, fen.
died Oct. 16, 1727,
in the 89th Year of his age.

JONE his Wife, buried Nov. 11, 1688,
aged about 50.

JOHN HICKS died Sept. 10, 1733,
aged 54.

———————

JOSEPH STEPHENS, died Dec. 8, 1745,
aged 55 Years.

ELIZABETH his Wife
died July 14, 1723,
aged 40 Years.
SARAH their Daughter,
died Oct. 19, 1743, aged 26 Years.

JOSEPH and RACHAEL, their Children,
died young.

THOMAS JOHNSON, fen.
died July 1, 1766, aged 82 Years.

ELIZABETH his Wife
died April 15, 1773,
in the 88th Year of her Age.

JOHN HIGNELL, Son of
ANTHONY and ELIZABETH HIGNELL,
died Feb. 18, 1782, aged 70.

ESTHER his Wife
died Dec. 15, 1786, aged 57.

———————

JACOB MILLETT,
died Feb. 14, 1776, aged 73.

BENJAMIN his Son
died Dec. 12, 1761, aged 24.
JOSEPH his Son
died Feb. 22, 1766, aged 32.

ELEANOR and ANN his Daughters
died Young.

MARY PARTRIDGE
died March 20, 1766, aged 88.

———————

ON HEAD AND FLAT STONES.

	Died	Aged
Henry Hicks	4 Mar. 1766	80
Martha his Wife	15 Feb. 1757	52
Several of their Children died Young		
Elizabeth, Wife of John Johnfon,	27 Feb. 1762	45
Hannah their Daughter died an Infant		
William Johnfon	12 July, 1751	51
Sufannah his Wife	19 Dec. 1785	82
Ann, their Daughter, and Wife of John Cox	15 Dec. 1756	23
Mary, Wife of John Johnfon	4 May, 1739	33
John Johnfon	11 Apr. 1758	47
William Bradley	7 July, 1729	65
Mary his Widow	29 Apr. 1738	—
William Gunter	10 Oct. 1757	64
Mary his Wife	27 Dec. 1741	66
William their Son	25 Mar. 1759	40
Samuel Bayley	11 May, 1753	59
Jofeph Bayley	16 Jan. 1724	70
Mary his Wife	6 July, 1736	81
Anthony Hignell	14 Sept. 1720	52
Elizabeth his late Wife	25 July, 1748	69
Thomas, } their Sons {	25 Jan. 1729	31
Mordecai, }	23 Aug. 1748	29
Sarah their Daughter	1 Mar. 1759	42
Stephen Hignell of Cote	16 Sept. 1742	72
Dinah his Wife	11 Nov. 1737	66

	Died	Aged
Mary their Daughter	2 Nov. 1725	16
Betty, Wife of Mofes Hignell of Olvefton	23 Mar. 1745	60
William Smith	29 Apr. 1713	66
Abigail his Wife	13 Jan. 1729	84
Thomas their Son	17 Feb. 1713	27
Thomas Davies	12 Aug. 1737	70
Thomas Smith Davies	14 June, 1741	27
Mary, Wife of Thomas Davies	18 Apr. 1744	65
Elizabeth, Wife of Zachariah Jones	31 Nov. 1767	61
Mary, Wife of James Kennifon, and Daughter of Thomas and Mary Davies	23 Feb. 1750	35
James Kennifon, fen.	20 June, 1777	60
Mary and Elizabeth Daughters of Richard and Mary Weft of Weftbury, died Infants		
Mary, Daughter of Benjamin and Eleanor Hignell	15 Sept. 1740	—
Mordecai their Son	15 Feb. 1742	—
Elizabeth Smith, Spinfter,	4 Aug. 1710	60
John Pearce	4 Oct. 1721	82
Mary, Wife of John Johnfon	4 May, 1739	33
John Johnfon	11 Apr. 1758	47
Sufannah, Wife of Thomas Hignell	10 June, 1779	35

7 F

CXIV. ELKESTONE.

OR ÆLFÞESTÆNE, as denominated by the *Saxons*, is a Parish of the middle Dimensions, situate in the Hundred of *Rapsgate*, near the great Fols Road to *Cirencester*, from whence it is distant eight Miles on the North-west, seven South from *Cheltenham*, and ten Eastward from GLOUCESTER.

Fifteen Hundred Acres, by Computation, are included in the Terrier, of a dry and stony Soil, principally tilled; the Harvest, though unusually late, is very productive. The Plan of large Inclosures has been lately very generally adopted in this District.

The Living is a Rectory in the Deanery of *Stonehouse*, endowed with a Glebe of 100 Acres, and all Tythes.

Of the Church, dedicated to *St. John the Evangelist*, the original Construction is evidently as early as the *Saxon* Æra. It has a Nave only, with a Tower at the West end, sixty-six Feet high, and of plain Gothic Proportions. To the Walls are affixed four Escocheons. 1. Quarterly, over all a Bend. FITZ NICHOL. 2. Quarterly, per Fels indented ACTON. 3. Barry of eight;—POYNTZ. 4. Effaced. By these its Date is ascertained during the Reign of RICHARD II. and the probable Founder to have been Sir JOHN POYNTZ, Knt. to whom the Manor and Advowson had descended by Heirship. The Tower is connected with the Nave, by a very lofty and elegant Gothic Arch. On the outside of the whole Building, under the Roofing on either Side, is a Series of Heads and Beasts placed horizontally. They exhibit the Sculpture of a very remote Age. The Door-case is finished by a Saxon Bas relief, representing CHRIST sitting on a Throne and holding a Book, with his Symbols, a Lamb and a Dove. But the most perfect Specimen of that Style is the Inside of the Chancel, which, externally more lofty than the Nave, is not above 12 Feet in height, with a vaulted Roof of circular Arches, enriched with Scrolls of various and elaborate Sculpture *.

In the most ancient Records of the Manor, the Families of DE ACTON and POYNTZ are recited. JOHN DE ACTON held it in 1315, 8 EDW. II. In 1377, 1 RICH. II. Sir JOHN POYTZ of *Iron Acton* inherited this with the other Estates of that Family, in right of his Mother, and it continued in his Descendants for many Generations. It passed from them about the Commencement of the last Century; when, JAMES HUNTLEY, Esq. second Sir of GEORGE HUNTLEY, Knt. of *Frocester Court*, occurs as Proprietor; and about 1630, it was sold by him or his Heirs to WILLIAM, afterwards Earl CRAVEN. From that Nobleman it has been transmitted to the present Possessor, whose Patent of Creation bears Date, Dec. 11, 1665, 17th CHARLES II †.

HAMLETS. *Cockleford* situate on the Banks of the Rivulet *Churn*; 2. *Combend* lies upon an Acclivity, about a Mile eastward from the Church. It includes a very confiderable Estate, which claims the Privilege of a Manor, and became the Property of the Family of ESTCOURT, prior to 1599, 41 ELIZ.; when, THOMAS ESTCOURT, Esq. dying bequeathed it to his Son. About 1634, it was transferred by Sale to Sir JOHN HORTON, Knt. of *Broughton*, com. *Wilts*, who built or enlarged the Mansion-house, now taken down, which his Descendants made their Residence. THOMAS HORTON, Esq. died in 1727, and was succeeded in this Estate by WILLIAM BLANCH, Esq. one of his Heirs at Law. Upon his Death in 1766, he gave a Life Interest in it to his Relict, afterwards the Wife of SAMUEL WALBANK, Gent. who, joining with the Family of ROGERS of GLOUCESTER the other Claimants, conveyed it by Deed of Sale, in 1778, to SAMUEL BOWYER, Esq. the present Proprietor.

The *Roman* Antiquities discovered on this Estate were in that Part of it which extends into the Parish of *Colesbourn* ‡.

No Benefactions to the Poor.

INCUMBENTS.	PATRONS.	INCUMBENTS.	PATRONS.
—— James Huntley,	——————	1624 William Poole,	——————
1570 John Brooke,	Sir George Huntley.	1665 Samuel Rich, D. D.	William, Earl Craven.
1582 William Broad,	Q. Elizabeth.	1682 William Prior,	The same.
1594 Edward Print,	——————	1727 Humphry Lloyd, B. D.	William Lord Craven.
1611 Timothy Gate, M. A.	James and Walter Huntley, Esqrs.	1779 Charles Bishop, M. A.	William Lord Craven.
		1788 Fulwar Craven Fowle, M. A.	The same.

* " All ancient Stone Churches, built in consequence of the Converfions made by the Roman Missionaries, were built with " simple circular Arches " more & opere Romano." This Species of building, the fame in *Gothland* as in *England*, practised " down to the 10th, 11th, and 12th Centuries, has been generally referred to as *Saxon*, and commonly so called."
Archaeologia, vol. IX. p. 116.

† COLLINS's Peerage, Tit. CRAVEN, vol. VII. p. 93.

‡ Accurate Drawings and a Description of these Discoveries were communicated to the Society of Antiquaries by S. LYSONS Esq. F. A. S. and published in the Archæologia, vol. IX. p. 319.

6

PRESENT

PRESENT PROPRIETORS OF MANORS,

Of Elkeſtone,   *Of Combend.*

The Right Honourable WILLIAM Lord Craven.   SAMUEL BOWYER, Eſq.

The Perſon ſummoned from this Place by the Heralds in 1682 and 1683, was
Thomas Horton, Eſq.

At the Election in 1776, Six Freeholders polled from this Pariſh.

The earlieſt Date in the Regiſter occurs in 1592.

ANNUAL ACCOUNT OF MARRIAGES, BIRTHS, AND BURIALS, IN THIS PARISH.

A.D.	Mar.	Bir.	Bur.	A.D.	Mar.	Bir.	Bur.	A.D.	Mar.	Bir.	Bur.	A.D.	Mar.	Bir.	Bur.
1781	3	5	3	1786	—	8	8	1791				1796			
1782	4	10	4	1787	2	6	2	1792				1797			
1783	—	9	5	1788	—	7	3	1793				1798			
1784	1	5	2	1789				1794				1799			
1785	2	15	5	1790				1795				1800			

INSCRIPTIONS IN THE CHURCH.

IN THE CHANCEL.

ON A TOMB.

Here lyeth the Body of
WILLIAM POOLE, Miniſter
of this Pariſh of Elſtone
above forty Yeares, who died
the 26th Day of February
Anno Domini 1664.

ON A MARBLE MONUMENT AGAINST THE WALL, SOUTH-SIDE THE NAVE.

Arms; Sable, a Buck's Head ca-
boſſed Argent, attired Or, in Chief a
Creſcent for the ſecond for HORTON.

Over againſt this Place lies interred
THOMAS, the Son of
THOMAS HORTON, Eſq.
who whilſt living was an
example of piety and ſoberneſs
to the Gentleman Comoners of
Lincoln Colledge in Oxford,
And afterwards to thoſe of
the Middle Temple
in London,
where he died on the 21ſt of May
in the Year of our Lord 1687,
in the 25th Year of his Age.

ON A FLAT STONE.

THOMAS HORTON, Eſq.
who died Oct. 24, 1727,
aged 51 Years.

Here lyeth the Body of
JOHN, the Son of
THOMAS HORTON
of Comber ?, Eſq.
who departed this Life,
April 6, 1707,
aged eleven Weeks.

Alſo MARY his Daughter,
who departed this Life,
Feb. 23, 1708,
aged ſeven Weeks.

IN THE CHURCH YARD. ON TOMBS.

WILLIAM KENDALL,
died April 5, 1753.

REBEKAH his Wife,
Oct. 6, 1773, aged 72.

NATHANIEL POOLE,
July 16, 1692, aged 65.

MARGARET his Wife,
May 27, 1705, aged near 70.
JOSEPH their Son,
Feb. 14, 1697, aged 19.

LYDIA their Daughter,
. . . . . 1697, aged 17.

RICHARD WALKER,
Sept. 11, 1697.

JOHN FLETCHER,
May 25, 1771,
in the 55th Year of his Age.

ON HEAD AND FLAT STONES.

	Died	Aged			Died	Aged
Richard and Ann, Children of John Fletcher, Infants,			Anthony Sadler	- -	31 May, 1771	76
Ann, Wife of Anthony Sadler	22 Nov. 1744	60	Henry Bubb, ſen.	- -	9 July, 1758	55
			Henry Bubb, jun.	- -	21 Dec. 1769	39

CXV.

NO mention of this Place occurs in *Domefday* Book, neither is it known to which of the adjoining Parifhes it was annexed, nor at what Period it gained parochial Rights. It lies in the Hundred of *Dudftone* and *King's Barton*, five Miles North-eaftward from *Newnham*, and four in the oppofite Direction from the City of GLOUCESTER. Within the Boundary are comprifed about 2000 Acres, much of which is uninclofed, in fpacious Meadows on the Banks of the River *Severn*, and fubject to Inundations. The Soil is a deep Clay, of which not above one eighth Part is in Tillage ; it is peculiarly favourable to the Growth of Oak and Elm Timber, chiefly in the Hedgerows *. There are, befide, more than fixty Acres of Woodland. By the *Severn* the North-weft Termination of the Parifh is formed, excepting at " *Elmore's* " *Back* +," where a Part of *Minfterworth* extends on this fide of the River.

The impropriate Tythes were given in 1137 by MILO, Conftable of GLOUCESTER, to the Priory of *Llanthony*, and the vicarial to the Church of *St. Owen* in that City, to which they were confirmed by WALTER DE CANTILUPO, Bifhop of *Hereford*, in 1236 ‡ ; both paffed at the Diffolution to the knightly Family of GUISE. The perpetual Curacy was augmented by Lot in 1746, and the privy Tythes have been added by the Impropriator.

In the Church, confifting of a Nave and North Aifle long and fpacious, with a low embattled Tower, no ftriking veftiges of Antiquity remain, owing probably to the Repairs lately made. It is in the Deanery of GLOUCESTER, and dedicated to *St. John the Baptift*.

Of the Manor the earlieft Poffeffor upon Record was HUBERT DE BURGO, Earl of *Kent*, and chief Juftice of *England* in the Reign of HEN. III. who granted to the Monks of *Llanthony* the Tythe of Lampreys and all Fifh taken in his Gurges or Fifheries at *Elmore* §. JOHN DE BURGH, his Son, held it with Privilege of Free Warren in 1260, 44 HEN. III. and foon after gave it in Dower with one of his Kindred to NICHOLAS, Son of ROBERT GYSE, of *Afpley Gowiz*, com. *Bedford*, where they had been fettled fince the Conqueft. Sir ANSELME GYSE was confirmed in the Property of this Parifh by a farther Grant, dated 1274, 2 EDW. I. at the yearly Rent of a Clove-gilliflower, in acknowledgment of the Gift, with the Conceffion of his own Coat-armour ||. It appears, however, that the Family of GYSE were Mefne Lords only, under the Priory of *Llanthony* ; for Sir JOHN DE GYSE invefted them with the Lordfhip, referving a Fee-farm Rent, in the Reign of EDW. III. **.

It was likewife acknowledged to be Parcel of the Honour of *Hereford* in 1359 and 1373, the 23d and 46th of EDW. III., and in 1558, 5th of Q. MARY. Sir WILLIAM GYSE, Bart. the fifth in Defcent from Sir CHRISTOTOPHER GUISE, whofe Patent of Creation bears Date July 10, 1661, 13th CHARLES II. died unmarried in 1783, and bequeathed this with other Eftates to his Sifter and Heir JANE, the Wife of the Hon. and Right Rev. SHUTE BARRINGTON, Lord Bifhop of *Sarum*, after whofe Deceafe they are devifed to Sir JOHN GUISE, Bart. of *Highnam Court*.

Elmore Court, the manerial Manfion, is of very high Antiquity. It was rebuilt in the Reign of Q. ELIZ. by JOHN GUISE, Efq. with Stone brought from the Caftle of the DE BOHUNS, Earls of *Hereford* at *Harf-combe*. Over the Gateway of the Offices then erected, which include a private Chapel, are Arms ; Quarterly 1 and 4. Gules 7 Lozenges conjoined vairè, on a Canton, or a Mullet pierced Sable—GUISE ; 2 and 3 Sable a Fefs between fix Marlets, Argent—WYSHAM ++. Many Alterations and Additions have

---

* " Mr. GYSE hath, at his Manor of *Elmore* in GLOCESTERSHIR, Okes, the Rootes within the Ground, whom be convertid into very hard Stone. And ther fum fay, that ther is Ground, that if a Man cut a Piece of Wood ther and ftrike it in, it will grow." LELAND Itin. vol. III. p. 125.

+ " Back, or Bec, is an ancient Word fignifying a Ferry."

‡ Cart. *Milonis Conft*. GLOUC. " Capella de *Elmourâ* cum totâ Decimâ Dominii in omnibus ; & omnibus Decimis villanorum cum teirulâ quâdam ad colligendam Decimam." DUGDALE, Mon. Angl. vol. II. p. 70.

§ Regift. Prioratûs de *Llanthony*, 1248. Tefte RICARDO CICESTRENSI Epifcopo.

|| HUBERT DE BURGO, Earl of *Kent*, granted Lands to ANSELME DE GUISE, in the Counties of GLOUCESTER and *Buck-ingham*, whereupon the faid ANSELME bare the fame Coat with a Canton Or, charged with a Mullet of fix Points pierced Sable." CAMDEN's Remains, p. 215, 8vo.

** Priorat. de *Llanthony* pro Manerio de *Elmore*. Pat. Rot. 32 EDW. III. p. 1. m. 26. TANNER's Not. Mon. " The Manor valued at 12l. per ann. was vefted in WILLIAM HAYBARARE, ROBERT LE LITTLE, and RICHARD STOUT, Clerks in Truft for the Priory. But a Re-infeoffment was made by WILLIAM, the Prior, and the Convent, dated April 5, 1359, granting to Sir JOHN GYSE, Knt. an Annuity of 20l. for his Life, and 12 Yards of the Suit of the principal Clerks, and one Robe for his Efquire, and another for his Chamberlain. And they engage to celebrate Maffes and Requiems for the Souls of his Anceftors daily, and one folemn Anniverfary yearly for ever."

++ Several curious carved Chimney-pieces are preferved, upon which are the following Arms ;—1. GUISE quartering WYSHAM and Gules, a Fefs between 6 Billets, Or. BEAUCHAMP of *Holte*. 2. GUISE impaling, Gules three Lioncels, rampant, Or, PAUNCEFOTE. 3. GUISE impaling Gules, a Bend engrailed Azure, between three Leopard's heads, jeffant de Lys, Or, for DENNYS.

Sir JOHN GUYSE was created a Knight of the Bath at the Inftallation of ARTHUR Prince of WALES. LELAND's Collect. vol. IV. p. 252. He is likewife mentioned in HOLLINSHED's Chronicle, p. 1450, as a Knight of this County.

been

3

been subfequently made, upon a Plan which has never been completed, chiefly by Sir JOHN GUISE, about the Commencement of this Century. For many Years paft it has ceafed to be the Refidence of the Family. The Situation is advantageous, upon an eafy Acclivity, commanding a widely extended Profpect of the Vale, furrounded with the *Cotefwold* Hills; and on the oppofite Side, of the Foreft of *Dean.*

The Property independent on the Manor is inconfiderable, though there are feveral Copyhold Tenures of different Value.

Of natural Curiofities the principal is a Ridge of Rocks croffing the *Severn*, at a Place called "*Stone* "*Bench,*" about 100 Yards over, in an oblique Direction, fo near the furface at low Water as to impede Navigation. The Tide, from the fudden Contraction of the Banks of the River, gains fuch Force as to rife many Feet above the Surface, producing a very fingular and beautiful Effect.

BENEFACTIONS.

3*l.* 10*s.* a Year, vefted in Truftees, were given by Deed, the Donor and Time unknown, to repair the Severn Walls, or to repair the Church, Bridges, Highways, or to furnifh Horfe and Harnefs, &c. and for the King's Service, the Refidue for the Succour and relief of the Poor, if any remain.

Oct. 6, 1620, GILES COXE, bequeathed by Will 1*l.* 2*s.* yearly, for the Relief of the poorer Houfe-keepers, who do not receive pay from the Parifh.

INCUMBENTS.	PATRONS.	INCUMBENTS.	PATRONS.
1620 John Blanch.	———————	1716 William James,	Sir John Guife.
1625 Valentine Marfhall,	———————	1744 John Wall, B. A.	Sir John Guife.
1661 —— Lytelton, Clerk,	Sir Chriftopher Guife.	1764 John Lewis,	Sir William Guife.
—— Ben. Saunders, Clerk,	———————	1774 Jofeph Chefter, M. A.	The fame.
1701 ———————	———————		

PRESENT LORD OF THE MANOR,

The Hon. and Rt. Rev. SHUTE, Lord Bifhop of SALISBURY.

The Perfon fummoned from this Place by the Heralds in 1682 and 1683, was

Sir JOHN GUISE, Bart.

At the Election in 1776 Ten Freeholders polled from this Parifh.

The Regifter has its firft Date in 1560; but at the Conclufion of the firft Volume is a Part thus entituled, "Of Baptifme, Weddinges, and Burialls, happening at *Elmore*, out of the Worfhipfull Houfe of GUYSE, fythens the 6th Day of December 1556."

ANNUAL ACCOUNT OF MARRIAGES, BIRTHS, AND BURIALS, IN THIS PARISH.

A.D.	Mar.	Bir.	Bur.	A.D.	Mar.	Bir.	Bur.	A.D.	Mar.	Bir.	Bur.	A.D.	Mar.	Bir.	Bur.
1781	2	9	7	1786	3	17	15	1791				1796			
1782	1	16	4	1787	2	10	5	1792				1797			
1783	—	5	8	1788	7	9	4	1793				1798			
1784	1	4	5	1789	—	16	4	1794				1799			
1785	2	10	5	1790				1795				1800			

INSCRIPTIONS IN THE CHURCH.

IN THE CHANCEL.

UPON A RAISED TOMB,

The figure of a Man in Armour inlaid in a Slab of white Marble with black Lines. Four corner Efcocheons. 1. GUISE quartering fecond WYSHAM. 2. GUISE quartering WYSHAM. 3. Gules a Fefs between fix Billets, Or. BEAU-CHAMP of Holte.

Infcription in Gothic character.

Hic jacet Johannes Gyfe. & Alicia uxor ejus qui quidem Johannes feliciter obiit in cowmunione ownium animarum anno Domini Wileffmo. C C C C LXXXJE. Qnorum a i ab s. p p'icietur Deus Amen.

ON A MONUMENT OF FREESTONE.

Arms; Quarterly 1ft and 4th GUISE. 2. BEAUCHAMP. 3. WYSHAM.
This for the Worthy Memory of Sir WILLIAM GUISE, who deceafed Sept. 19, 1642.

And of WILLIAM his eldeft Son by his firft Wife, MARGARET, Daughter to Sir CHRISTOPHER KENN, Efq. who married CICELIA, Daughter of JOHN DENNIS of Pucklechurch, Efq. by whom he had four Sons and three Daughters.
He deceafed Auguft 26, 1653.

ON A MARBLE MONUMENT.

Arms; GUISE, impaling quarterly, Gules and Azure, a Crofs Flory, Or, for SNELL.

In Memory of
WILLIAM GUISE, Efq.
of the City of Gloucefter.
He was the eldeft Son of
Major HENRY GUISE, of Winterbourne
in this County, and Grandfon of
WILLIAM GUISE, Efq of this Parifh,
who departed this Life
Auguft the 28th, 1716,
in the 68th Year of his Age,

Lyeth

7 G

Lyeth here interred with William
his 4th Son. Alſo Dorothea his Wife;
departed this Life June the 12th, 1738,
aged 76;
A Lady remarkable for her ſtrict Piety,
diffuſive Charity, and engaging
Courteouſneſs of Behaviour,
flowing from the trueſt Sentiments
of Religion, Goodneſs, and Humanity.
She was the only Daughter of
John Snell *, Eſq. Lord of the Manor
of Uffeton, in the County of Warwick,
which Manour, with Lands to the
Value of near a Thouſand Pounds a
Year, he gave by Will to ſupport the
Intereſt of Epiſcopacy in Scotland;
but, this Application of his intended
Benefaction being defeated by the Union,
a Decree was obtained in the
High Court of Chancery for ſettling the
Eſtate on Baliol College, in Oxford,
for ever, to maintain, ſupport, and
educate, certain Scholars to be ſent
thither by the Univerſity of Glaſgow,
allowing to each Fifty Pounds a Year,
for Ten Years only: eight pertake at
preſent of theſe Exhibitions,
though the Eſtate may be deemed
capable of ſupporting a greater Number.
She had Iſſue three Sons and one
Daughter.

John, the eldeſt, died aged 21 Years.
He was a Gentleman of a very
extraordinary Genius, and eminently
ſtudious, having in that early
Time of Life acquired a perfect
Knowledge of all the polite Languages,
Ancient and Modern.

William, the ſecond Son died
aged 12 Years.

Henry, the third Son, is ſtill living,
and cauſed this Inſcription.

And Theodosia, the Daughter, was
married to Dennis Cooke,
of Highnam, Eſq.
and lies interred in Highnam Chapel.

ON FLAT STONES.

Arms; Guise impaling Snell;
Creſt, a Swan proper iſſuant from a
ducal Coronet.

William Guise, Gent. of Glouceſter,
Dorothea Guise, William Guise.
Depoſited in this Grave,
with their Anceſtors, are two Sons of
Henry Guise, Eſq. of Glouceſter,
or of Upton St. Leonards,
by Mary his Wife,
Daughter of Edward Cooke,
of Highnam, Eſq.
Edward and William both died
Infants, one anno 1736,
the other anno 1737.

Arms; quarterly Guise and Snell,
on an Eſcocheon of Pretence, Or, a
Cheveron chequy Gules and Azure, between three cinquefoils of the ſecond for
Cooke.

Here lyeth the Body of
Henry Guise, Eſq.
of the City of Glouceſter,
youngeſt Son of William Guise, Eſq.
who lies interred in this Chancel;
a Gentleman in his private Converſation,
well known for his engaging affability,
in publick, for his ſtrict Adminiſtration
of Juſtice. He died much lamented
the 23d of Oct, 1749, aged 51.

IN THE NORTH AISLE.

On a Flat Stone.

J. B. Bishop,
departed this Life Feb. 10, 1784,
aged 36 Years.

IN THE NAVE.

On a Neat Marble Monument.

Arms; Azure on a Feſs Argent, a
Lion paſſant Gules, between three Boars
heads couped of the 2d for Gough.

In Memory of the
Rev. Mr. William James,
late Miniſter of this Church,
and Vicar of Longney,
who died October 11, 1744, aged 59.
Alſo Mary his Wife,
Daughter of John Gough,
late of Stonehouſe in this County.
She died June 5, 1747, aged 54.
Alſo Anna, their Daughter,
who, in regard to the Memory of her
dear Parents, cauſed this
Monument to be erected.
She died Oct. 7, 1755,
aged 22 Years.

On Freestone Monuments.

In Memory of Richard Leighton,
and Susannah his Wife.
She died May 20, 1683, æt. 38,
and he Sept. 13, 1718, æt. 87.

Alſo of William Crump,
of the Pariſh of Minſterworth,
who died May 30, 1742.
Aged near 70 Years.

In Memory of Susannah, Daughter of
Daniel and Susannah Ellis,
who departed this Life
March 21, 1739.
Alſo of Elizabeth their Daughter,
who died Feb. 19, 1742,
both in their infancy.

ON A FLAT STONE.

Here reſteth the Body of the
Rev. Benjamin Saunders,
late Miniſter of this Pariſh,
who departed this Life the 17th Day of
January, anno Domini 1701.

IN THE CHURCH YARD,

Is an Arcade of four Arches, finiſhed with a Pyramid of Freeſtone, erected over the Vault of the Family of Guise.

ON TOMBS.

Here reſteth the Body of the
Reverend, Learned, eminently Pious
and painful Divine,
Mr. Valentine Marshall,
of this Place, preacher 36 Years,
and died in the 63d Year of his Age,
and was buried Oct. 3, 1661.

William Bradley,
late of Hareſfield, died July 7, 1729,
aged 66.

John Bradley died Oct. 18, 1751,
in the 63d Year of his Age.

Jane, Wife of John Bradley,
died Feb. 13, 1763, aged 69.

Henry, Son of John Bradley,
died Dec. 6, 1763, aged 33.

Elizabeth, Wife of
Arthur Knowles,
buried March 21, 1707, ætatis ſuæ 46.

Arthur Knowles, Gent.
died April 20, 1731,
aged 65 Years.

Arthur their Son,
died Nov. 19, 1707, aged 21.

Eleanor, Daughter of the
Rev. Mr. Nathaniel Hawkins,
late Miniſter of
Coln Rogers in this County,
died 18th of April 1719, aged 29 Years.

Hannah, Wife of the ſaid
Rev. Mr. Hawkins,
died 23d of Oct. 1720,
aged 61 Years.

Joseph Ellis, died Nov. 9, 1740,
aged 57.

Elizabeth his Wife
died Sept. 26, 1738, aged 50.

Phoebe their Daughter
died Oct. 16, 1744, aged 17.

John Hoskins, ſen. Mariner,
died May 7, 1696.

George Guilding
died Nov. 2, 1731, aged 72 Years.

Edward Guilding, Steward to
Sir John Guise, Bart.
died anno 1750,
in the 55th Year of his Age.

Elizabeth his Wife died 1762,
in the 72d Year of her Age.

William Astman
of the Pariſh of Hardwick,
died May 22, 1737, æt. 77.

Sarah his Wife
died March 11, 1693, æt. 31.

John Breether of Hardwick,
died March 16, 1691,
ætatis ſuæ 63.

William Astman of Hardwick,
died Jan. 25, 1763, aged 68.

Mary Wife of William Astman,
and Daughter of Henry Bradley,
buried May 17, 1734, aged 41.

Anselm Hanman died Nov. 6, 1735,
ætatis ſuæ 52.

John Hanman, of Brown's Mill,
died July 13, 1754, aged 30.

William James
died April 15, 1753, aged 68.

Richard Knowles, Gent.
died April 12, 1706, aged 73.

* See Wood's Faſti, vol. II. p. 883.

Ann

ANN, Wife of RICHARD KNOWLES,
died Feb. 20, 1692,
aged 62.

HENRY BRADLEY, fen.
died May 3, 1675, aged 56.

MARY his Wife,
died Jan. 7, 1715, aged 91.

MARY their Daughter,
died Jan. 11, 1677, aged 18.

ALICE FREEME,
Daughter of JOHN SAPTON,
late Wife to RICHARD BULLOCK,
died September 15, 1688.

HESTER, Wife of JAMES BREWER,
died Feb. 18, 1781, æt. 49 Years.

MARY, Wife of
JOHN WALL of Hardwick,
died Sept. 14, 1758, aged 71.

JOHN WALL died July 25, 1778,
aged 75.

JOHN, Son of JOHN and JANE BRADLEY,
died May 14, 1760, aged 41 Years.

ELIZABETH his Daughter
died Nov. 22, 1757, aged 4 Years.

SILVANUS VICK died June 18, 1773,
aged 56 Years.

SARAH his Wife
died July 17, 1765, aged 51 Years.

GRACE, their Daughter,
died June 2, 1765, aged 16 Years.

ANN, their Daughter,
died March 2, 1773, aged 14 Years.

MARGARET, Daughter of
RICHARD TOWNSEND,
died Dec. 15, 1681, æt. fuæ 8.

WILLIAM RANDALL
of Haresfield, Gent. died Feb. 19, 1782,
aged 56 Years.

JOYCE, Daughter of HENRY BRADLEY,
died May 18, 1757, aged 61.

HENRY, Son of HENRY BRADLEY,
buried April 18, 1730,
in the 45th Year of his Age.

HANNAH, Wife of HENRY BRADLEY,
died April 19, 1778, aged 70.

WILLIAM, Son of JOHN BRADLEY,
died March 7, 1743, aged 41 Years.

ON FLAT AND HEAD STONES.

	Died	Aged
William Jones	14 Sept. 1754	41
Hefter his Wife,	22 Sept. 1770	61
John Harber	19 Oct. 1757	33
Daniel Lane	26 July, 1746	61
Abigail his Wife	4 Jan. 1755	78
Sufannah and ⎱ their Daughters, ⎰	16 Mar. 1729	20
Efther ⎰	12 Sept. 1732	17
Daniel their Son	4 Jan. 1773	54
Henry Ockell	— Aug. 1767	79
Harry Ockell	10 Mar. 1781	57
Elizabeth his Wife	11 Oct. 1770	42
Robert James	12 Dec. 1755	56
Thomas James,	22 July, 1769	67
Elizabeth his Wife	6 Mar. 1778	80
Ann, Daughter of Silvanus and Sarah Vick	17 June, 1750	2
Sarah, Daughter of William Rowles	6 Mar. 1759	11
Betty Rowles	13 Nov. 1762	20
Sarah, Daughter of Silvanus and Sarah Vick	20 June, 1764	8
Sarah, Wife of Ephraim Smith of Saul	25 Sept. 1715	77
Silvefter, Daughter of Matthew Lane	7 May, 1731	30
Jofeph Leighton	1 Aug. 1729	42
Margaret, Daughter of Phillip Town-fend	15 Dec. 1781	8
Richard Ellis	2 Jan. 1676	—
William Ellis	20 Apr. 1683	—
Ann, Wife of Richard Leighton	24 Nov. 1704	63
Margaret, Daughter of William Ellis	20 Mar. 1668	—
William his Son	7 Feb. 1676	23
Elizabeth his Wife	12 Mar. 1711	76
Margaret, Wife of William Vick,	23 July, 1755	80
William Vick	11 May, 1761	77
Diana, Wife of Richard Ellis,	6 Apr. 1775	45
Elizabeth Ellis	29 Mar. 1770	48
Jofeph Ellis	15 Apr. 1715	—
Sarah his Wife	10 Apr. 1758	70
Daniel Ellis, fen.	6 Aug. 1764	—
Elizabeth his Wife	31 May, 1686	—
Daniel their Son	14 Dec. 1672	—
Jofeph Ellis	25 Sept. 1700	54
Richard Selly	19 Jan. 1777	74

	Died	Aged
Mary his Wife	— May, 1772	60
Sufannah, fecond Wife of Nathaniel Hawkins	23 Dec. 1738	39
William Layton	18 Nov. 1699	48
Sarah, Daughter of Phillip Wall	20 Apr. 1721	19
Thomas his Son	18 Apr. 1721	24
Mary Wall buried	17 Dec. 1729	56
Jofeph her Son ditto	15 Nov. 1720	14
Daniel Hawkins	21 Nov. 1753	31
Phillip Wall	11 Dec. 1762	67
Thomas his Son	7 June, 1752	27
Mary his Daughter	30 Jan. 1749	17
David Richards	15 Sept. 1728	71
Ann his Wife	6 Feb. 1733	62
Phillip Wall	—— —— 1712	50
William his Son	10 May, 1765	59
Elizabeth, Wife of Robert Hamlett	15 Feb. 1780	67
Robert Hamlett	19 Jan. 1786	77
Ann his Daughter, and Wife of John Griffiths	6 Aug. 1786	47
George Guilding	2 Nov. 1731	72
Mary his Daughter	10 Apr. 1732	25
John Smith	20 June, 1767	75
Sarah his Wife	7 Dec. 1751	61
Daniel, Son of Daniel and Mary Guilding	16 July, 1782	15
John Hall	12 June, 1757	60
Hannah, Wife of Jofeph James, and Daughter of James and Elizabeth Profler	16 Nov. 1769	26
Jofeph James	15 May, 1775	32
James Profler	1 Oct. 1763	60
Elizabeth his Wife	10 June, 1770	55
William Cam	27 Oct. 1768	27
Jofeph Proffer	13 Sept. 1755	51
Ann his Wife	16 Sept. 1757	59
Mary, Wife of Giles Hooper	16 Feb. 1752	55
Mary his Daughter	2 Feb. 1759	22
Mary, Wife of George Ferebury	2 Aug. 1763	62
George Ferebury	18 Jan. 1766	66
John their Son	26 May, 1741	6
Charles, Son of William and Sarah Dowell of Minfterworth	7 Mar. 1766	6

CXVI.

MORE anciently "AILMUNDESTAN," is a Parifh of the middle Size, in the Vale of GLOUCESTER, from whence it is diftant eight Miles on the North; five South-eaft from *Tewkef-bury*, and from *Cheltenham* four on the North-weft. It is divided between the Hundreds of *Weftminfter* and *Deorhurft*, containing by Computation about 1600 Acres, of a Soil varying from Clay to deep Sand, three-fourths of which are in Tillage; the whole is interfected by the Rivulet *Swilyate* in its Courfe to the *Severn*.

The Living is a Vicarage, not in Charge, in the Deanery of *Winchcombe*, of which the Impropriation and Appointment formerly belonged to the Abbey of *Tewkefbury*. In 1612, 10 JAMES I. the impropriate Tythes were purchafed of the Crown, who retained the Advowfon, by ANTONY COPE, which in 1630 were re-fold to the Principal and Fellows of *Jefus* College, *Oxford* *, under which Society the Family of GWINNETT, of *Badgeworth*, long held them, and the Leafe defcended by Heirfhip to WILLIAM CATCHMAY GWINNETT, Efq. in 1782.

Nothing worthy Remark occurs in the Church, which is dedicated to *St. Mary*; it has a Nave and South Aifle, with a ftrong embattled Tower on the Weft end.

Originally the Manor was included and defcribed as Parcel of the Manor of *Deorhurft*, and was un-juftly taken from the Monks of *Weftminfter* by ROBERT FITZ HAMAN, but reftored to them by a Suit at Law in the Reign of HEN. II. †. At the Suppreffion of the Monaftery it was confirmed to the Dean and Chapter of that Church, who are the prefent Proprietors. The Family of BUCKLE have continued Leffees fince the Reign of K. JAMES I. ‡.

H A M L E T S.

Hardwick, or *Elmftone Hardwick*, lies in the lower Part of the Hundred of *Weftminfter*, and is a diftinct Manor. In Domefday it is ftated to contain five Hides of Land, and to be a Member of *Deorhurft*. MAURICE Lord *Berkeley* died poffeffed of it in 1524, 15. HEN. VIII. From that noble Family it paffed to RICHARD LYGON, Efq. of *Arle-court* in 1567, 9 Q. ELIZ. At the Commencement of this Century RICHARD DOWDESWELL, Efq. of *Pull-court*, com. *Vigorn.*, was Lord of this Manor, which is now held in Jointure by BRIDGET, Relict of the Rt. Hon. WILLIAM DOWDESWELL, late Chancellor of the Exchequer, who died in 1775.

Uckington, is a Tything and Manor in the lower Divifion of the Hundred of *Deorhurft*, the Jurifdiction of which extends over the adjoining Parifh of *Staverton*. It has its own Conftable. In a Terrier dated in 1272, 56th of HEN. III. of the Lands transferred from the Priory of *St. Dennis* to that of *Deorhurft*, are the following Particulars, " Prior de *Deorhyrfte* habet xii bovatas terræ apud *Okintune*, et valent per " Ann. xx Sol. Item, habet ivl. xiis. iid. de redditu affifo cum auxilio rufticorum. In Villenagio " ivl ivs. ivd. Item, Manerium illud nullum poteft fuftinere Inftauramentum, quia nullum habet " Pratum, nifi tantum de quo poteft accipere unam Karratam Fœni; et redditus D'ni ROBERTI MUSGROS " dimid. Marca. Summa reddituum tam liberorum quam rufticorum cum xxii predictis boviatis " xl. iiis. iiiid. §." After the Death of EDWARD Earl of *Oxford* in 1741, it was fold by his Executors to the Family of ROGERS of *Dowdefwell*, and is now the Property of JOSEPH BERWICK, Efq, of *Worcefter*, in Right of his Wife, ANN, Daughter and fole Heir of JOHN ROGERS, Efq. A competent Eftate in this Tything belongs to JOHN BUCKLE, Gent. which has for feveral Generations been vefted in that Family.

A very valuable landed Property in this Parifh is now held by ———— HANCOCK, Efq. of *Oxfordfhire*.

In the Rental of the Abbey of *Cirencefter*, preferved by DUGDALE, one Hide of Land in *Elmondeftan* is fpecified ‖.

---

* " Several Benefactions amounting to 1350l. were laid out in 1630, by Sir EUBULE THELWALL, Knt. Principal, to pur-chafe certain Impropriations and Rent Charges in GLOUCESTERSHIRE."   WOOD's Hift. Univ. Oxon. p. 573. edit. Gutch.

† DUGDALE's Mon. Angl. vol. I. p. 61.

‡ " By Deed dated 12th Sept. 10 JAMES I. JOHN LYGON, Efq. of *Arle* conveyed the Manor of *Elmfton* to WALTER BUCKLE, " Gent. of *Uckington*."   MSS. SNELL.

§ DUGDALE's Mon. Angl. vol. I. p. 548.

‖ Ibid. vol. II. p. 89.

3

No

No Benefactions to the Poor.

INCUMBENTS.	PATRONS.	INCUMBENTS.	PATRONS.
—— Richard Mudwell,	Abbey of Tewkefbury.	1738 William Williams, B.A. The fame.	
1594 Edward Prince,	Q. Elizabeth.	1747 ——	
*　*　*　*　*　*　*	*　*　*　*　*	1763 Anthony Freeman, M.A. Geo. III.	
1694 George Styles, B. A.	William and Mary.	1789 Vacant.	
1733 Cornelius Bond,	Geo. II.		

PRESENT PROPRIETORS OF THE MANORS,

Of Elmftone,	*Of Uckington.*	*Of Elmfton Hardwick.*
JOHN BUCKLE, Gent.	JOSEPH BERWICK, Efq.	BRIDGET DOWDESWELL.

The only Perfon fummoned from this Parifh by the Heralds in 1682 and 1683, was

THOMAS WELLES, Gent. of *Uckington.*

At the Election in 1776 Six Freeholders polled from this Parifh and its Hamlets.

The prefent Regifter commences in 1564.

ANNUAL ACCOUNT OF MARRIAGES, BIRTHS, AND BURIALS, IN THIS PARISH.

A.D.	Mar.	Bir.	Bur.	A.D.	Mar.	Bir.	Bur.	A.D.	Mar.	Bir.	Bur.	A.D.	Mar.	Bir.	Bur.
1781	2	5	3	1786	3	14	7	1791				1796			
1782	5	9	6	1787	5	4	1	1792				1797			
1783	3	7	2	1788	2	7	6	1793				1798			
1784	1	8	3	1789	—	10	3	1794				1799			
1785	1	9	6	1790				1795				1800			

INSCRIPTIONS IN THE CHURCH.

ON A FLAT STONE.

Here lieth the Body of the
Rev. Mr. WILLIAM WILLIAMS,
Vicar of Elmftone and Afhchurch,
who died April 29, 1747,
aged 56 Years.

Alfo the Body of FRANCES, the Wife
of the Rev. Mr. WILLIAM WILLIAMS,
who died July 6, 1762, aged 69 Years.

ON A MONUMENT IN THE SOUTH AISLE.

In Memory of HENRY BUCKLE,
late of Milham Poft,
in the Parifh of Hayles in this County,
who departed this Life Oct. 17, 1788,
aged 35 Years.

ON FLAT STONES.

Here lieth the Body of
WALTER BUCKLE, who was buried
the 20th of Oct. A. D. 1645.

Here lieth the Body of
THOMAS BUCKLE, who departed
this Life Sept. 22, 1661.

Here lieth the Body of
ELIZABETH BUCKLE,
the Daughter of THOMAS BUCKLE,
who departed this Life the 18th of Sept.
Anno Dom. 1664.

Here lieth the Body of
ELIZABETH, the late Wife of
THOMAS BUCKLE, deceafed,
who departed this Life
the 8th of March 1668.

Here lieth the Body of
ELIZABETH, Wife of
THOMAS BUCKLE, and Daughter of
JOHN STURMY, of Swindon, Gent.
who departed this Life the
20th day of June, Anno Dom. 1709,
Anno ætatis 36.

In Memory of JOHN, eldeft Son of
THOMAS BUCKLE, who died the
1ft of March 1721, anno ætatis 26.

Near this place are alfo buried
ELIZABETH and WILLIAM, children of
the faid THOMAS BUCKLE.
ELIZABETH was buried June 24,
Anno Dom. 1702-3, æt. 3.
WILLIAM was buried March 2, 1708.
æt. 16.

In Memory of THOMAS BUCKLE,
late of this Parifh, Gent. who
departed this Life Dec. 10, A. D. 1709,
Ætatis fuæ 73.

Here lieth the Body of MARY,
Wife of the Rev. Mr. THOMAS BUCKLE,
Vicar of Stanton, who departed this
Life the 25th day of Feb. 1731,
ætatis fuæ 38.

Alfo here lieth the Body of the
Rev. Mr. THOMAS BUCKLE,
who departed this Life April 30, 1758,
ætatis fuæ 61.

In Memory of THOMAS, the Son of
WILLIAM and SARAH BUCKLE,
who died Dec. 15, A. D. 1765,
aged 7 Years.

In Memory of MARY BRISTOW,
Widow, Daughter of
Mr. THOMAS BUCKLE,
buried Dec. 14, 1714, aged 61.
ELIZABETH BURROWS, Daughter of the
Rev. Mr. BUCKLE,
obiit Oct. 18, 1777, ætat. 45.

Here lieth the Body of
EDITH, the Daughter of
THOMAS and SARAH BUCKLE,
who departed this Life April 18, 1779,
aged 13 Years.

7 H　　　　　　　　　　　　　　IN

IN THE CHURCH YARD, ON TOMBS.

JOHN GRAVES, died June 11, 1628.

MARGARET his Wife,

. . . .

GEORGE LONG, fen. of Badgworth, died Sept. 17, 1726, aged 78 Years.

ELIZABETH his Wife, died July 22, 1731, aged 69.

GEORGE LONG, jun. obiit Feb. 14, 1754, æt. 72.

ANN, Daughter of GEORGE and ISABELLA LONG, obiit April 18, 1745, æt. 16 Years.

ON FLAT AND HEAD STONES.

	Died	Aged
John Little of Boddington -	6 Feb. 1728	49
Mary his Wife, Daughter of Richard and Ann Buckle -	1 Mar. 1728	35
Thomas Little - buried	7 Dec. 1711	36
Mary his Wife - buried	7 Nov. 1711	22
Elizabeth, Daughter of Phillip Dance	31 July, 1729	17
Sufannah Little, - buried	9 Mar. 1695	61
Alice Litle, widow -	9 Jan. 1707	99
Adam Little - -	20 Apr. 1713	61
Elizabeth his Wife -	22 Mar. 1687	31
Seven of their Children, five Sons and two Daughters -		
John, Son of Phillip and Hannah Dance - -	7 June, 1743	23
Phillip Dance - -	8 Aug. 1724	48
Adam Dance - -	12 Jan. 1767	49
Betty, Daughter of John and Elizabeth Piff - -	13 June, 1738	3
Mary, Wife of William Cook, and Daughter of John Roan of Maifemore - - -	28 Apr. 1743	12
John and Mary their Children -		
Jonathan Marfhall - -	21 Jan. 1721	60
John Cook - -	13 Apr. 1780	43
Elizabeth his Wife - -	4 Dec. 1761	55
George, Son of Daniel Cook	31 May, 1739	28
John Little, jun. - -	25 Dec. 1717	20
John Butt, - -	22 Aug. 1711	48
Thomas Butt - -	1 June, 1722	24
Jane, Wife of John Cook -	18 Jan. 1739	56
John Cook - -	25 Feb. 1728	26
Daniel Cook - -	48 Dec. 1762	77
Richard Jackfons - -	5 Nov. 1743	45
Ann his Wife - -	10 July, 1745	35

	Died	Aged
Sarah, Wife of Giles Roan of Maifemore - -	25 Apr. 1735	31
William Sowle - -	7 May, 1741	36
Mary his Wife - -	2 Jan. 1749	58
Ann their Daughter - -	12 May, 1744	19
John, Son of Fereby and Ann Stait	22 May, 1754	4
Fereby Stait - -	12 Mar. 1768	58
William Fifher - buried	30 June, 1688	38
Mary his Wife - buried	28 May, 1690	44
Elizabeth, Wife of William Freeman - -	14 Aug. 1733	40
Sarah, Wife of George Marfhall	11 July, 1735	90
William their Son -	10 Feb. 1738	35
Elizabeth Kare - -	8 Feb. 1764	61
William Collins - -	3 May, 1743	53
Elizabeth, Daughter of Thomas and Elizabeth Piff - -	4 June, 1779	1
John their Son - -	10 Jan. 1771	6
Richard their Son - -		
John, Son of Thomas and Joyce Piff	25 July, 1766	31
Thomas Piff - -	10 Apr. 1750	47
William his Son - -	14 May, 1740	2
Ann his Daughter - -	14 Mar. 1761	18
Francis Tombs - -	20 Mar. 1782	72
Alice his Wife - -	25 Sept. 1771	66
Elizabeth, Wife of Samuel Pye, jun.	1 Feb. 1758	27
Elizabeth, Daughter of William and Margaret Pyff - -	4 May, 1770	14
Ann their Daughter - -	10 Mar. 1761	2
Thomas, Son of Thomas and Elizabeth Chadbourne, -	23 May, 1762	3
John Piff - -	6 May, 1754	77
John, Son of John and Mary Piff	18 Apr. 1734	35
Hannah their Daughter - buried	6 May, 1740	32

CXVII.

CXVII. F A I R F O R D.[*]

IT is acknowledged, that few Diſtricts in this County enjoy greater natural Advantages of Situation than this Pariſh, which is a Part of the Hundred of *Brightwell's Barrow*, four Miles diſtant on the Weſt from *Lechlade*, and eight eaſterly from *Cirenceſter* on the great *London* Road. From GLOUCESTER it is more than 25 Miles, inclining to the South. By Computation about 3,000 Acres lie within the Boundaries, which are four Miles in Extent, and two acroſs; of a Soil light, and intermixed with Gravel and Limeſtone, moſtly in Tillage, and productive of artificial Graſſes in great Perfection. Near the River *Colne*, which interſects the Pariſh, are many Meadows. The Woodlands do not exceed 100 Acres. In 1754 the firſt Incloſure and Allotment of the Commonable Lands were made, and completed iu 1769.

This pleaſant and ſpacious Village has been conſidered by Topographers as a Town, ſince 1668; when ANDREW BARKER, Eſq. procured a Charter for a weekly Market on Thurſday, and two annual Fairs for Cattle, now held upon the 14th of May, and the 12th of November [†].

The Plan of the Town is regular, conſiſting of two Streets neatly built; moſt of the Houſes are held by Leaſe under the Manor.

The Benefice is vicarial, and the Chief of its own Deanery, originally in the Appointment of the *Benedictine* Abbey of *Tewkeſbury*; and, ſince the Reſtoration, of the Dean and Chapter of GLOUCESTER. In 1313, 8 EDW. II. the impropriate Tythes of Corn were confirmed to that Monaſtery by Patent, having been Parcel of the Grants of their Founder ROBERT FITZ HAMAN [‡]. When the Dean and Chapter of GLOUCESTER were eſtabliſhed in 1544, they were given to them, and leaſed ſoon after to NICHOLAS OLDYSWORTH, Eſq. whoſe lineal Deſcendants have held them to the preſent Leſſee the Rev. JOHN OLDISWORTH [§], Clerk.

The Church retains many Attractions for the Virtuoſo and Antiquary. It is indeed a very finiſhed Specimen of the pureſt Gothic Architecture that prevailed about the Cloſe of the fifteenth Century. This Structure conſiſts of a lofty Nave, two Aiſles, and a Tower in the Middle; 120 Feet in length, and 55 broad. The whole is embattled; a Series of groteſque Figures ſurround the Architrave of the Tower, which is ſo low in Proportion, that it has been thought a Spire was originally intended; the Form has ſome Peculiarities; for the Buttreſſes are flattened, and gradually diminiſhed to the Top, and upon the Baſes are Effigies as large as Life, of rude Sculpture, ſo that it appears to be almoſt octangular at a ſmall Diſtance. The Parapet is ornamented with five Eſcocheons on each Side; the four larger of which bear the Arms of DE CLARE, DE SPENCER, NEWBURGH, and TAME. Others are charged with the ragged Staff and Fetterlock, the Cognizances of the Houſe of BEAUCHAMP. There are many Niches, which when filled with the highly finiſhed Images, now removed, muſt have added much to the original Beauty of this Edifice. Of its internal Form and Embelliſhments the moſt minute Deſcription we can offer, can ſcarcely be deemed ſuperfluous. The Aiſles are divided from the Nave by four Arches, the Pillars light and fluted, low enough to admit a Range of Windows above them. The Tower then intervenes. The Aiſles are continued parallel with the Chancel, with which is a Communication by two Arches of equal Height. A Skreen ſurrounding the Chancel is of very beautiful Gothic Carving in Oak, with Stalls in the ſame Style. On the left Hand of the Altar are three Niches, or Subſellia, formerly uſed by the officiating Prieſts. The upper Diviſion of either Aiſle belongs as a Chancel to the Vicar, and Lord of the Manor. The neat Pavement, and other very ſuitable Ornaments, have been at ſeveral Times given by the Family of BARKER, and their Connections. The Church owes its Re-erection to JOHN TAME, a Mer-

---

[*] The Right Honourable WILLS HILL, Earl of *Hillſborough*, was created Viſcount *Fairford*, by Patent, dated Aug. 28, 1772. He was born in the Manor Houſe.

[†] MSS. PARSONS, & Itin. ANT. A WOOD. Muſ. Aſhmol. *Oxon.*

"From *Lechlade* to *Fairford*, about a 4 Miles, al by low Ground, in a Maner in a Levell, moſt apt for Graſſe, but very ba-" rein of Woodde. It is a praty uplandiſh Towne, and moche of it longith, with the Perſonage, to *Tewkeſbyri* Abbay. *Fair-" ford* never floriſhed afore the cumming of the *Tames* onto it." LELAND, It.n. vol. II. p. 22.

" From *Lechlade* I rode to *Fairforde*, which, as LELAND ſayth, is a praty uplandiſh Towne, &c. Before the comynge of " JOHN TAME (temp. EDW. IV.), where he ſettled the Trade and Manufacture of Wool and Clothing, it never flouriſhed; " but by his Endeavours, and his Son EDMUND, there was as great Trade drove there as at *Cirenceſter*."

MS. Itin. A. WOOD, ut ſup.

[‡] DUGDALE's Mon. vol. I. p. 161. Cart. confirmat. 28 EDW. I. "Eccleſiam & Decimas de *Fairefort*." Pat. Rot. 8 EDW. II. p. 1. m. 12. "Pro Eccleſiis de *Thornbury* & *Fairford* appropriandis." TANNER's Not. Mon. No. XXI.

This Appropriation was confirmed to the Monaſtery of *Tewkeſbury* by ADAM DE ORLTON, Jan. 26, 1333, at the Inſtance of Pope BENEDICT XII. THOMAS's Survey of *Worceſter*, p. 171.

[§] Upon the general Incloſure in 1769 the Vicar had allotted to him, by Commutation, " half an Acre of Orchard adjoining " to his Houſe; 4 a. 1 r. 9 p. in the Moor; and 4 a. 2 r. in Prieſt's Hurſt of Meadow Ground; and 19 a. 39 p. of arable " Land." TERRIER.

7 I

chant,

FAIRFORD.

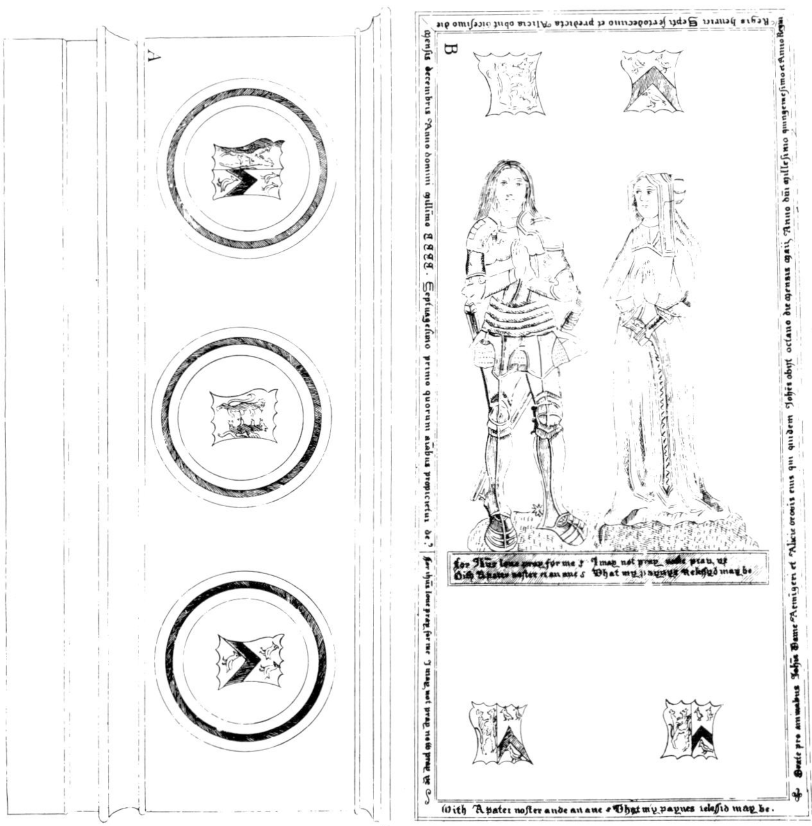

John Tame Esq.r and Alice his Wife,

chant, of a Family fettled in *London,* where feveral of them had ferved the Office of Sheriff *. About the Year 1492, foon after the Siege of *Boloigne,* a Veffel bound to the Port of *Rome,* from the *Low Countries,* and laden with painted Glafs, is faid to have been taken by him, who inftantly determined on preparing a Church here for its Reception. The Dedication of it to the *Virgin Mary* was celebrated in 1493, the probable Date of its Foundation; for the whole was not completed by JOHN TAME, who died in 1500, but remained to be finifhed by his Son Sir EDMOND TAME, Knight †. A Series of Scripture Hiftories, fo numerous and exquifitely penciled, even before the barbarous Demolition of monaftic Splendour, the whole Kingdom had not to fhow. During the Commotions in 1642, when the Republican Army were on their March towards *Cirencefter,* WILLIAM OLDYSWORTH, Efq. the Impropriator, fearing its Deftruction, caufed the whole to be taken down and concealed; and to him the Lovers of ancient Art are indebted for its prefent Exiftence, which, although mutilated in many Parts, is ftill unrivalled ‡.

In

---

* STOWE's *London,* p. 554.

† " JOHN TAME began the fair new Chirche of *Fayrford,* and EDMOND TAME finifhed it." LELAND, vol. II. p. 22.

‡ Of thefe " ftoried Windows richly dight,
    Cafting a dim religious Light,"

(for furely none can more completely anfwer the Idea of the Poet) it appears that a Defcription was engroffed on Vellum by order of Sir EDMUND TAME, and preferved in the Church Cheft. It is now loft, but a Paper Roll copied from it, falling into the Hands of Mr. MURRAY, was publifhed by HEARNE, in his Edition of ROPER's Life of Sir T. MORE, p. 273, 8vo. In 1765 another Account, collected chiefly from the Former, and popular Traditon, was printed at *Cirencefter,* of which fome Parts are rather inaccurate. There are twenty-eight Windows, with four, or more, Compartments in each; all of which deferve a minute and feparate Inveftigation, both of the Subjects, and the prefent State. If we follow the Series of Scripture Hiftories exhibited in thefe Delineations, the Account muft commence with the fifth Window, in the North Aifle, in which it may be obferved, they are in much the beft State of Prefervation.

1. Mifcellaneous, and rather imperfect. The Serpent tempting EVE. JOSHUA in Armour, kneeling. MOSES, and his Divine Legation, from the burning Bufh. The Queen of *Sheba* offering Gifts to King SOLOMON. The third and fourth Subjects are exquifitely coloured.

2. Very imperfect. The Hiftory of the Miffion of our SAVIOUR, beginning with the Marriage of ZACHARIAS and ELIZABETH; the Birth of JOHN BAPTIST; the Interview between MARY and ELIZABETH; and the Betrothing of JOSEPH and MARY.

3. Very perfect and excellent. The Salutation of the VIRGIN; Legend on a Scroll, " **Ave Maria Gra' plena Dns tecum;**" the Birth of CHRIST; the Offerings of the Wife Men; the Purification of the bleffed VIRGIN; and the Circumcifion of our LORD. In this Window it would be difficult to point out which has the greater Merit; the Air and Character of the Figures, or the perfpective View of the Infide of the Temple.

4. Perfect. The Flight into *Egypt*; the Affumption of the bleffed VIRGIN; JOSEPH and MARY feeking CHRIST after the Feaft, whom they find difputing with the Doctors in the Temple.

5. The great Eaft Window, in the moft perfect State. The triumphant Entry of JESUS into *Jerufalem*; ZACHEUS; and Figures with a Label, " **Gloria, Laus, et honor, tibi fit;**" his Agony in the Garden; JUDAS betraying him; PILATE fitting in Judgement againft him; the Jews fcourging him, and compelling him to bear his Crofs. In the upper Compartments, the Crucifixion, MARY, and the other Women, Roman Soldiers, &c. The moft ftriking Parts of this Window are, a Book covered with crimfon Velvet and gilt; the Countenances of PILATE, and of MARY, with the fuperb Caparifons upon the Horfes of the Soldiers.

6. Rather perfect. The taking down from the Crofs; JOSEPH of *Arimathea* and NICODEMUS receiving the Body, and laying it in the Sepulchre; St. MICHAEL contending with BEELZEBUB, who is overcome, and confined within a fiery Grate. The dead Body is admirably characterized.

7. Perfect, and well defigned. The Embalming of our LORD; the Angel in the Garden having rolled away the Stone; the Transfiguration, with MOSES and ELIAS. attendant Difciples, Saints PETER, JAMES, and JOHN; JESUS appearing to his Mother, with this Salutation, " **Salve fancte Parens.**" This Piece excels in perfpective; particularly a View of *Jerufalem* from the Garden, and a *Flemifh* Caftle of three Towers, to fignify the three Tabernacles.

8. CHRIST appearing to two Difciples going to *Emmaus*; manifefting himfelf to the Twelve; Unbelief of THOMAS.

9. Rather perfect. The miraculous Draught of Fifhes; the Afcenfion; and the Day of Pentecoft.

The three Succeffive Windows contain Portraits of the twelve Apoftles; over the Heads of whom, on Scrolls, are difpofed certain Sentences of the Creed. All of them in good Prefervation.

10. St. PETER. " **Credo in Deum omnipotentem Creatorem Celi et Terre.**"

St. ANDREW. " **Et in Jefum Chriftum filium ejus, unicum D'num noftrum**"

St. JAMES. " **Qui conceptus eft de Spiritu S'cto, natus ex Virgine Maria.**'

St. JOHN. " **Paffus eft fub Pontio Pilato crucifixus mortuus et fepultus.**"

11. St. THOMAS. " **Defcendit ad Inferna tertia die refurrexit a Mortuis**'

St. JAMES MINOR. " **Afcendit ad Celos fedit ad dextera' Dei Patris omnipotentis.**"

St. PHILIP. " **Inde venturus judicare vivos et mortuos.**"

St. BARTHOLOMEW. " **Credo in Spiritum S'ctum.**"

12. St. MATHIAS. " **Sanctam Ecclefiam Catholicam.**"

St. SIMON. " **Peccatorum remifhonem.**"

St. JUDE. " **Carnis refurrectionem.**"

St. MATTHEW. " **Et vitam eternam. Amen.**"

13. Imperfect. Four primitive Fathers of the Church; St. GREGORY, habited as Pope; St. JEROME, as Cardinal; St. AMBROSE and St. AUGUSTINE, as Bifhops.

14. Very imperfect. DAVID fitting in Judgement againft the *Amalekite,* for cutting off the Head of SAUL.

15. The great Weft Window; perfect; and exhibiting a View of the Laft Day; our SAVIOUR coming to Judgement, a Sword in his left Hand, " **Jufticia,**" a Palm Branch in his right, " **Mifericordia**" In the lower Compartments, St. MICHAEL in Armour, weighing Souls. The general Refurrection; an Angel conducting a Saint to Heaven; over whom. a Label, " **Omnis fpecies lauda Deum.**" St. PETER, with his Symbols, admitting the bleffed Spirits, " **Gratias ago D'no Deo pro.**" Thofe who have paffed the Gate are clothed in white Robes, and reprefent a Pope, a King, a Bifhop, and a Monk, " **Benedictus fit Deus in Donis fuis.**' On the other Side are the Infernal Regions; Devils tormenting the condemned Souls, " **Ite in Damnationem paratam vobis.**" Gothic Fancy was never more happily difplayed than in thefe Defigns, at once horrible and ludicrous. The Brilliancy of the ftrong Tints, and the Delicacy of the Drapery of the fmaller Figures, form a fingularly excellent Specimen of ancient Art.

16. Imperfect. The Judgement of SOLOMON; SAMPSON flaying the *Philiftines*; DALILAH cutting off his Hair; two Rabbinical Doctors difputing on Points of the Law. Thefe are exquifitely finifhed, the Characters of the Heads very bold, and the Drapery and facerdotal Embellifhments inimitable.

17. Imperfect. The four Evangelifts, the Head of St. MARK, very excellent.

18. Perfect.

In 1725, to prevent farther Injury, the Honourable ELIZABETH FERMOR, Daughter of WILLIAM Lord LEMPSTER, by JANE his firft Wife, Daughter of ANDREW BARKER, at the Expence of 200*l.* fecured each Window with a Lattice of Wire.

When *Domefday* was compiled, the Manor of *Fairford* was ftated to contain twenty-one Hides of Land, with thirty Plow Tillages, and was referved by the King, under the Title of " Terra Regis." In 1263, 47 HEN. III. RICHARD DE CLARE, Earl of *Gloucefter* and *Hertford*, obtained this Lordfhip, with Privilege of a Market and Fairs, which in the fucceeding Reign was confirmed to GILBERT his Son, whofe Sifter and Coheir ELIANOR, conveyed it by Marriage to HUGH LE DESPENCER the younger, in 1314. From this laft Family it defcended to the BEAUCHAMPS and NEVYLLES, Earls of *Warwick*, and was one of the hundred and fourteen Manors which were fraudulently obtained from ANNE Countefs of WARWICK * by King HENRY VII. by a Deed, dated Dec. 13, 1488. JOHN TAME aforementioned purchafed this Manor of the Crown in 1498 ; feveral Years prior to which he had been fettled here †. He was fucceeded by his Son and Grandfon, both Knights, and of the fame Name. The laft Sir EDMUND left three Sifters and Coheirs, but *Fairford* was held in Jointure by CATHARINE his Relict, twice married after his Deceafe, to Sir WALTER BUCKLER, Knight, who procured from Queen ELIZABETH a farther Confirmation of the Demefnes ‡ ; and, laftly, to ROGER LYGON, Efq. Sir THOMAS VERNEY, Knight, of *Compton Murdac*, co. *Warwick*, having married ALICE, the fecond Coheir, purchafed the Shares of the other two ; MARGARET, the Wife of Sir HUMPHRY STAFFORD, Knight, and ISABEL, the Wife of LEWIS WATKYN, Efq. fubject to the faid Jointure, by Deed of Sale, dated Feb. 26, 1547. About the Commencement of the laft Century, Sir RICHARD VERNEY, Knight, transferred this Eftate to Sir HENRY UNTON, and JOHN CROKE, Efq. who foon after re-fold it to the Family of TRACEY ; for in 1608 Sir JOHN TRACEY, Knight, occurs as Lord of the Manor.

18. Perfect ; and contains, with two others, Portraits of twelve Prophets, with Labels over the Head of each.
HOSEA.   " D mors ero tua."
AMOS.   ' Qui edificat in Celum afcenfionem."
MALACHI.   Ad vos judicio et ero teftis velor. '
JOEL.   " In valle Jofephat judicabit omnes Gentes."
19. Perfect.   EPANIAH.   " Invocabuntur omnes eum et ferbient et."
MICAH.   " Cum odium habueris dimitte."
EZEKIEL.   " Dvam vos de Sepulchris veftris Populе meus !"
OBADIAH.   ' Et erit regnum Dei.
20. Perfect.   JEREMIAH.   " Patrem invocabitis qui fecit et indidit Celos."
DAVID.   " Deus dixit en Filius meus es tu . ego hodie genui te."
ZECHARIAH.   " Sufcitabo Filios tuos "
21. The Perfecutors of the Church : DOMITIAN, TRAJAN, ADRIAN.
22. ANTONINUS, NERO, MARCUS AURELIUS.
23. HEROD, SEVERUS, MAXIMINUS.
24. DECIUS, ANANIAS, and CALEB, who bought our SAVIOUR of JUDAS.
25, 26, 27, 28. Twelve Roman Emperors, Prefervers of the Church. In the Reign of CHARLES the Firft, before their Removal, thefe Windows were infpected by Sir ANTONY VANDYKE, who, fays HEARNE, " often affirmed both to the King " and others, that many of the Figures were fo exquifitely well done, that they could not be exceeded by the beft Pencil." The Defigns are attributed to ALBERT DURER ; but it is improbable that at the Age of 20 Years he could have attained fuch Proficiency ; for he was born in 1471, and the Glafs was taken in 1492. Who was the real Artift is a Circumftance involved in fome Obfcurity. Neither LUCA VAN LEYDEN nor GOLTZIUS could have been employed, as they both flourifhed after the Church was finifhed. But for this, the extreme Refemblance of the Style of the well-known Etchings of thefe Mafters, would induce us to attribute this beautiful Work to them. May we be allowed a Conjecture, that the Defigner was FRANCESCO FRANCIA, who was born at *Bologna* in 1450, where he lived till 1518, peculiarly eminent in the Art of encauftic Painting.

In what Eftimation thefe fplendid Ornaments of our Churches were held by our pious Reformers, may be feen in HARRISON's Defcription of *England*, book II. chap. 1. p. 138. col. 2. 30. printed in 1580, and prefixed to HOLINSHED's Chronicles, where he propofes, " that white Glaffe may be provided, and fet up in their Roomes."

STRYPE, in his Annals, p. 185, fays, that Queen ELIZABETH iffued out her Proclamation, prohibiting any Perfons, under fevere Penalties, from defacing Monuments, and from breaking any Image in Glafs Windows.

---

* DUGDALE's *Warwickfhire*, p. 300.

† " Syr EDMUNDE TAME, of *Fayrford*, up by *Crekelade*, came out of the Houfe of TAME, of *Stowel*. TAME that nowe is " at *Faireford*, hath be maried a xii Yere, and hath no Childe. Wherefore be likelihode Syr HUMPHRE STAFFORD, Sun to old " STAFORD, of *Northamptonfhire*, is like to have the Landes of TAME, of *Fairеford*. For he married his Sifter ; and fo the " Name of the TAMES is like fore to Decay." LELAND, Itin. vol. VI. p. 18.
" Of this Family were the Sheriffs of this County in the Years 1505, 1519, 1523, 1536."
FULLER's Worthies, *Gloucefterfhire*, p. 367.
Sir EDMUND TAME, after finifhing the Church at *Fairford*, erected thofe at *Rendcombe* and *Barnfley*, and built feveral large Inns.
" Some thinke that the *George* Inn, in *Fairford*, was a Chauntrie Houfe, for Priefts to celebrate for the Soules of the TAMES " in the Parifh Church. There is the fame Effigies of a Man cut in Stone over the Door, as there is on the Tower of the " faid Church, perhaps of one of the TAMES.
" Note, That in the olde Houfe at the Weft End of the Church at *Cirencefter* are in every Windowe therein old Coates of " Arms. viz. of the TAMES, of *Fairford*, with the Impalements of that Family. It is an olde Houfe, built with a great deale " of Timber, known nowe by the Name of the *Swan*, in temp. HEN. VIII. by Sir E. TAME, who built *Fairford* Church."
A. WOOD's Itin. MS. ut fupra.

‡ WALTER BUCKLER, originally Fellow of *Merton* College, afterwards Canon of *Cardinal* College, was admitted B. D. June " 25, 1534, though not in prieftly Orders. This Perfon was the fecond Son of JOHN BUCKLER, of *Cawfay*, in *Dorfetfhire*, and " had been lately a Student in the Univerfity of *Paris*, was afterward promoted by the King to be a Canon of his College at " *Oxford*, founded on that of the Cardinal, and about the fame Time was fent on State Affaires to *Paris*, where he performed " with good liking to the faid King. In 1ft of EDWARD VIth, he received the Honour of Knighthood, and when Queen " ELIZABETH came to the Crown, he was made one of her Privy Council. He died at *Fairford*, in *Gloucefterfhire*, having mar" ried the Widow of Sir EDMUND TAME, Knight, Lord of that Manor, and was buried in the Church there. Over whofe " Grave, though there be no Infcription, yet his Contemporary in *Merton* College, named JOHN PARKHURST, hath perpetuated " his Memory by certain Epigrames." WOOD's Fafti, vol. I. p. 686.

2   ANDREW

ANDREW BARKER, Efq. of the very ancient Family of BARKER, alias COVERALL, of *Coverall* and *Hopton* Caftles, in the County of *Salop*, became poffeffed of this manerial Property about the Time of the Reftoration of CHARLES II. and left one Son, SAMUEL BARKER, Efq. Upon his Death in 1708, he was fucceeded by his only furviving Daughter and Heir ESTHER, married to JAMES LAMBE, Efq. of *Hackney*, co. *Middlefex*, who died without Iffue in 1761. His Relict dying in 1789, bequeathed *Fairford*, and other Eftates, to JOHN RAYMOND, Efq. who has fince affumed the Name and Arms of BARKER, by royal Sign manual, duly regiftered in the College of Arms.

There was very anciently a manerial Refidence near the Church, erected by the Earls of *Warwick*, and called *Beauchamp* and *Warwick Court* *. It appears that it was re-built by the TAMES; for LELAND obferves, " there is a fayr Manfion Place of the TAMES hard by the Chirche-yarde, builded thoroughly " by JOHN TAME and EDMUNDE TAME, the Backfide therof goithe to the very Bridg of *Fairford* †." This Houfe was taken down by ANDREW BARKER, Efq. who, with the Materials of it, built the prefent Manfion, fome Furlongs diftant; in finking the Foundations of which, Urns and Roman Coins are faid by Dr. PARSONS to have been difcovered. It is a large and commodious Edifice, and has been confiderably improved by the prefent Proprietor.

Within the Park Pale, about 200 Acres are inclofed, well planted, with an Avenue of a Mile in Length. The Pleafure Grounds were long and defervedly admired, when in that Style of Embellifhment, which diftinguifhed the Clofe of the laft Century. From the modern Art of Gardening, very judicioufly employed, they have gained additional Beauty. The River, widened for a great Diftance, with its Extremities artificially concealed, gives an Air to the Landfcape which a Situation of fewer natural Advantages could fcarcely command. The Plantations and Walks are fo difpofed as to produce that juft Combination of Nature and Art by which alone Scenes of real Tafte are made complete.

In the Reign of HENRY the Eighth, JOHN MORGAN, Efq. of the Family of *Tredegar*, com. *Monmouth*, who had been a Colonel in the Army in the preceding Reign, being connected with the Families of TAME and OLDYSWORTH ‡, fettled in this Parifh. His Eftate has been inherited by his Defcendants till 1773, when it was fold by ROBERT MORGAN, Efq. to the prefent Lord of the Manor. CHARLES TYRREL MORGAN, M. A. Barrifter at Law, now refides in the Houfe inhabited by his Anceftors, to which he has lately added many Improvements.

In this Parifh are three Tythings; 1. The *Borough*, which has its own Conftable; 2. and 3. *Eaft End*, and *Milltown End*, to each of which a Tything Man is diftinctly affigned. The Church of GLOUCESTER held two Hides of Land here in Saxon Times §. Every Eftate in the Parifh is dependent on the Jurifdiction of the Court Baron.

Fairford, as indeed all the upper Diftrict of *Cotefwold*, is very productive of extraneous Foffils.

B E N E F A C T I O N S.

Nov. ... 1632. THOMAS MORGAN, Gent. bequeathed by Will 100*l*. now vefted in the Minifter, Church Wardens, and Overfeers of the Poor; the Intereft of which to be diftributed annually on Good Friday amongft the Poor.

Dame JOAN MICO, Relict of Sir SAMUEL MICO, bequeathed by Will a Rent Charge on Lands; the annual Produce thereof is 5*l*. 4*s*. to be laid out in the purchafe of Bread, to be diftributed among the Poor on every Sunday in the Year.

She alfo bequeathed by Will 400*l*. which are laid out in Lands in the Parifh of *Leachlade*, and vefted in Feoffees, for the apprenticing of poor Boys.

MORGAN EMMOTS gave 5*l*. which are laid out in Lands in the Parifh of *Leachlade*, and vefted in Feoffees.

Mr. SMITH, of *London*, bequeathed by Will a Rent Charge on an Eftate now belonging to J. RAYMOND, Efq.; the annual Produce 1*l*. 10*s*. for teaching poor Children to read.

Hon. ELIZ. FERMOR, and MARY BARKER, Spinfter, bequeathed by Will 60*l*. yearly, laid out in Lands and vefted in Feoffees for the Eftablifhment of a Free School for teaching fixty Boys.

June 17, 1715, WILLIAM BUTCHER bequeathed by Will 40*l*. now vefted in the Minifter and Church Wardens; the annual Produce is 2*l*. to be laid out in Bread, and diftributed among the Poor in the Church every Year.

---

* CAMDEN's Britannia, ed. GIBSON, vol. II. p. 216.

† LELAND's Itin. vol. II. p. 22.

‡ THOMAS OLDYSWORTH, Efq. the feventh in lineal Defcent from Sir LANCELOT OLDYSWORTH, Knight, died in 1531, 22 HEN. VIII. He married a Daughter of JOHN MORGAN, Efq. of *Pencoed* Caftle, in the County of *Monmouth*.

MS. Pedigree.

§ " BURGHREDUS Rex *Wicciorum*, dedit Deo & Sancto Petro, Glouc. & monialibus ejus loci, duas hidas terræ apud *Fairford*, " tempore EVÆ Abbatiffæ" DUGDALE's Mon. Angl. vol. I. p. 114.

3

April

April 28, 1738. Rev. FRAMPTON HUNTINGTON bequeathed by Will 10*l.* now vested in the Minister and Church Wardens; the annual Produce, 10*s.* to be laid out in Bread, and distributed on the 22d of August in each Year, among 20 such poor Families as should constantly attend at Church, and do not receive Alms.

1770. Mr. ROBERT JENNER bequeathed by Will 10*l.* now vested in the Minister and Church Wardens; the annual Produce, 10*s.* to be distributed annually among five poor Widows.

1773. ALEXANDER COLSTON, Esq. bequeathed by Will 105*l.* now vested in the Minister and Church Wardens; the annual Produce, 5*l.* 5*s.* to be distributed on Old Candlemas Day in each Year among poor Widows.

INCUMBENTS.	PATRONS.	INCUMBENTS.	PATRONS.
1273 Ralph Hengeham,	From 1315 to 1541 Abbey of Tewkesbury.	1686 Edw. Shipman, M. A.	Dean and Chapter of GLOUCESTER.
—— William Salway,	————————.	1712 Frampton Huntington, M. A.	The same.
1585 Henry Dun,	John Jones.	1738 Joseph Atwell, D. D.	The same.
1585 Edmond James,	George Lygon, Esq.	1768 Daniel Evans, Clerk,	The same.
1617 Christoph. Nicholson,	Rob. Oldysworth, Esq.	1778 Edward Sparkes, M. A.	The same.
* * * * * * * * * * * * *		1785 James Edwards, B. D.	The same.
1657 John Shipman,	————————		

PRESENT LORD OF THE MANOR,

JOHN RAYMOND BARKER, Esq.

The Persons summoned from this Place by the Heralds in 1682 and 1683 were

Andrew Barker, Esq.   Robert Morgan, Esq.
William Oldysworth, Esq.   John Shipman, Vicar.

At the Election in 1776, Eight Freeholders polled from this Parish.

The earliest Date in the Register occurs in 1617.

ANNUAL ACCOUNT OF MARRIAGES, BIRTHS, AND BURIALS, IN THIS PARISH.

A.D.	Mar.	Bir.	Bur.	A.D.	Mar.	Bir.	Bur.	A.D.	Mar.	Bir.	Bur.	A.D.	Mar.	Bir.	Bur.
1781	6	18	10	1786	9	35	22	1791				1796			
1782	15	30	14	1787	11	35	26	1792				1797			
1783	12	22	14	1788	6	41	20	1793				1798			
1784	4	34	21	1789	8	40	11	1794				1799			
1785	17	38	14	1790				1795				1800			

ANCIENT MONUMENTS IN THE NORTH AISLE.

A Table Tomb of Italian Marble*. Upon the Slab the Effigies of a Man in Armour, and a Woman in the Dress of the Times. Four Corner Escutcheons; 1. Argent, a Lion Azure combatant, with a Griffin Vert; TAME. 2. Argent, a cheveron Gules, between three Poppinjays proper; TWYNIHOW. At their Feet TAME impaling TWYNIHOW.

Legend :   " Ffor Jesus Love pray for me,
                 " I may not pray nowe—pray ye !
                 " With a Pater Noster and Ave,
                 " That our Paynys relessid may be."

Around the Verge : " Orate pro animabus Joh'is Tame, armigeri, et Alicie uxoris ejus, qui quidem " Joh'es obiit octavo die mensis Maii, Anno D'ni Millesimo quingentesimo, et anno regni Regis Henrici " Sept'i sexto decimo. Et predicta Alicia obiit vicesimo die mensis Decembris, Anno D'ni Milesimo " CCCC septuagesimo primo quorum a'i'abus propicietur Deus."

A blue marble Slab, inlaid with the Effigies of a Man in Armour, upon his Surcoat the Arms of TAME, between two Women; upon the Mantle of the first, Sable, on a Cross, within a Bordure, both ingrailed Or, five Pellets, for GREVILLE; on the other, Or, a Saltire Sable, for TYRINGHAM. The same Arms repeated upon four corner Escutcheons. Inscription round the Verge : " Of your Charitie pray for the Soule of Edmond Tame, Knyght, heere under buried, which decessid in the Yere of our Lord God a Thousand CCCCCXXIIIJ; and for the Soule of Agnes his first Wife, which decessid the XXVIJ Day of July, Anno D'ni Milesimo CCCCCVJ; and on all Xten Soules J'hu have Mercy. Amen."

* See an Engraving annexed.

Upon

7 K

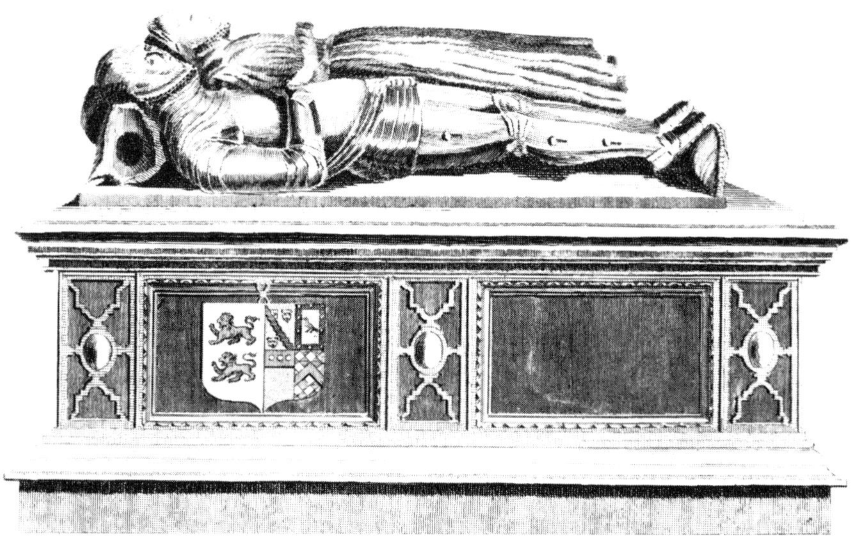

Roger Lygon Esqr & Katharine his Wife .

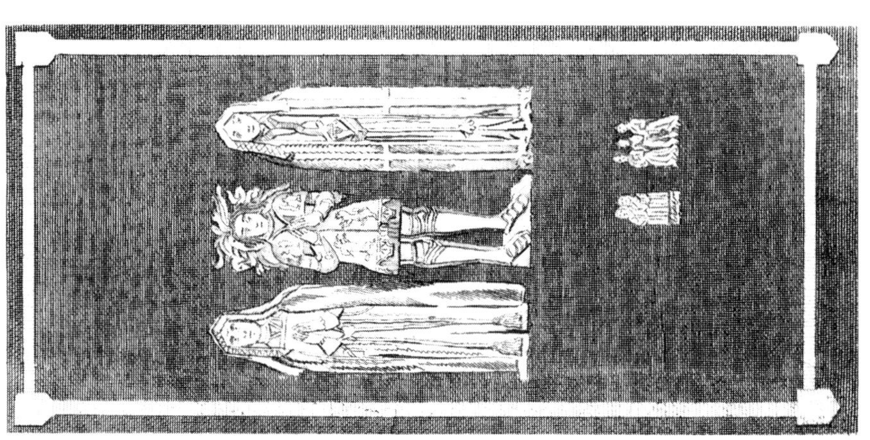

Sir Edmond Tame & his Wives.

Upon a Slab affixed to the Wall. The Effigies of the fame Perfons kneeling before Defk⁵, upon which are Books opened. Surcoats and Inefcocheons charged as before. Upon three feparate Labels, " **Jefu Lorde that made us.**" " **And with thy Blood us bought.**" " **Forgive our Trefpafs.**" Infcription at the Feet, " **Hic jacent Edmondus Dame Miles et Agnes et Elizabet uxores ejus, qui quidem Edmondus Obiit primo die Octobris Anno D'ni M. D. XXXIII. at Anno Regni Regis Henrici Octavi viceffimo ferto quorum A'iarum propicietur Deus. Amen**"

* Upon a Table Tomb, the Effigies in Freeftone of a Man in Armour recumbent, and a Woman in the Drefs of the Times. Upon Efcocheons repeated. Arms ; Argent, two Lions paffant Gules. LYGON impaling quarterly. 1. Gules a Bend engrailed Azure, between three Leopard's faces jeffant de Lys ; DENNYS. 2. Or, a Raven proper within a Bordure Gules, charged with Bezants ; CORBET. 3. Argent on a Chief Gules three Bezants ; RUSSEL. 4. Lozengy, Or, and Azure, a Cheveron Gules DE GORGES.

ON MONUMENTS.

Arms ; Topaz an Efcallop Diamond between two Bendlets ruby for TRACEY ; —impaling Argent, a Cheveron between three Efcallops Sable for LYTELTON.

Near this Place lyeth the Body of the
Lady BRIDGET TRACEY,
Wife to the
Right Hon. the Lord TRACEY.
She was buried the fifth of Nov. 1632.
She was a Lady of excellent natural
Parts ; fhe underftood the Latin Tongue
and other ufeful Parts of Learning ;
but, that which excells all,
fhe was truly pious and charitable.
Here alfo lyeth buried her eldeft
Daughter MURIAL,
who was married to
Sir WILLIAM POOLE of Saperton.
Her youngeft Daughter was married
to WILLIAM SOMERVILE, Efq.
whofe youngeft Son, Mr. BENJAMIN,
was a very beautiful Perfon
and an excellent Scholar,
for which he was moft entirely
beloved of his Mother.
She bred him up at Eaton School,
and from thence removed him to
Oxford, where he died in the
nineteenth Year of his Age,
and was buried here by his
Grandmother TRACEY,
December 3, 1686.
This Monument was erected
by the Hon. Mrs. SOMERVILE,
to the worthy Memory of her moft
dear Mother, Sifter, and Son.

Arms ; Gules on a Fefs Argent three
Lions paffant purpure for OLDISWORTH.

GULIELMUS OLDISWORTH,
Filius natu maximus
JACOBI OLDISWORTH,
Rectoris de Kencott,
in comitatu Oxon,
Obiit Decem. 22, An. Salutis 1714,
Ætatis 41.
Vixit puræ Religionis Omnigenæque
Virtuti ab ipfis incunabulis,
fincere elevatus, vultu Moribus,
& Famâ Candidus & Venuftus,
Carus apud fuos, apud alienos
bene meritus,
apud omnes comis & benignus,
Civis fobrius, Mercator honeftus,
Pius Laicus, caftus Cælebs.

Arms ; OLDISWORTH as before.

Underneath lie the Remains of
Mrs. MURIEL LOGGAN
(Daughter of JAMES OLDISWORTH,
Rector of Kencott in Oxfordfhire),
who died April 18, 1754,
aged 74 Years.
A Woman of fuperior Strength of
Underftanding without Affectation,
whofe extenfive Benevolence
of Heart to the Poor
and warmeft Affection to her Relations,
whofe truly zealous and uniform
Devotion, and moft earneft Defire
of doing Good to all,
made her greatly refpected when living,
and fincerely lamented when dead.
To whofe Memory this Monument
was erected by her very Affectionate
and grateful Relation
Mrs. MARY MANN of Tewkefbury.

Arms ; OLDISWORTH, Creft, a Lion
rampant, Gules, holding a Scroll, Or.

Sacrum Reliquiis
Venerabilis Viri ;
JACOBI OLDISWORTH,
Cujus,
In Deo colendo Pietatem,
In curandis animis Diligentiam,
In Parochiali Regimine Authoritatem,
In Elemofynis largiendis Fidem,
In Oeconomiâ ordinanda Prudentiam,
In Hofpitiis celebrandis Alacritatem,
In Ecclefiis ornandis Munificentiam,
In omni demum vitæ ftudio, & colore
Integras Virtutes, moreíque caftos &
verè Chriftianos,
Tota hæc Vicinia,
Et ora omnium quibus innotuit,
Palàm clamant, abundeque teftantur ;
Dum in Pofteros efferunt
(Quod Hiftoriam potius quam
Epitaphium defideret)
Rarum & memorabile Exemplar
Obiit tertio die
Septembris MDCCXXII°,
Ætat. LXXXII°.

Arms ; OLDISWORTH impaling Argent
on a Fefs between two Cheverons Sable
three Crofcroflets, Or, for AUSTIN.

M. S.
GULIELMI OLDISWORTH,
Armigeri, Deum obfervanter colentis,
Mariti per-amantis
Patris prudenter indulgentis,
Amici fidelis, Pauperibus Advocati,

Medici & Difpenfatoris ;
Uxorem duxit MARIAM,
GULIELMI AUSTIN, in Comitatu
Suthriienfi Armigeri Filiæ,
per quam multiplicem habuit prolem.
Obiit 3° Die Octobriis 1680,
Anno Ætatis fuæ 71°.

ON FLAT STONES.

WITHIN THE RAILS.

Depofitum AUSTINI OLDISWORTH,
Profapia veteri utroque Nomine,
oriundi viri,
Inter Ecclefiæ Anglicanæ Fautores
Inter Rei Antiquariæ Studiofos,
Inter Affines, Cives, Amicos,
Et Familiares fuos,
diu multumque defiderati.
Obiit 27° Die Augufti,
Anno Salutis 1717,
Ætatis Climacterico.

Here lyeth the Body of
WILLIAM OLDISWORTH,
the eldeft Son of
JAMES OLDISWORTH,
who depated this Life
the 22d of December 1714,
aged 42.

Here lieth
WILLIAM OLDISWORTH, Efq.
who was buried in 1680.

M. KEBLE, 1744.

A. KEBLE, 1754.

ON A FLAT STONE WITHOUT THE RAILS.

Here lieth interred the Body of
WILLIAM BUTCHER, Sadler,
who gave Forty Pounds for the Ufe
to be given Wickly in Bred
to the Pore of this Parifh for ever,
and hee departed this Life
the 17th Day of June,
in the Yeare of our Lord God 1715,
and the 66th Yeare of his Age.

---

* This Monument without Infcription was erected to the Memory of ROGER LYGON, Efq. and KATHERINE his Wife in 1560. She was the Daughter of WILLIAM DENNYS, Efq. of *Pucklechurch*, and Relict of Sir EDMUND TAME and Sir WALTER BUCKLER, Knights.

ON

ON ATCHIEVEMENTS IN THE
NORTH AISLE.

N° 1. Azure, five Efcallops in Crofs Or, for BARKER, on an Efcocheon of Pretence Ermine, on a Bend Sable three Crefcents Argent, for
N° 2. Quarterly 1ft and 4th BARKER. 2. Gules, a Fefs between three Saltires Argent, charged with three annulets Sable, for GOLDSTONE. 3. Argent, on a Fefs between fix Crofcroflets Sable, three Efcallops, Or, for TYTTELEY.
N° 3. Quarterly 1ft and 4th, Sable on a Fefs, Or, between three Cinquefoils Ermine, a Lion paffant Gules between two Mullets fable for LAMBE; 2d and 3d Argent, a Bull paffant fable, armed Or, within a Bordure of the fecond bezanteè. COLE.

BANNEROLS.

1. BARKER impaling Argent, a Pomegranate proper for . . . . .
2. BARKER impaling Argent a Cheveron Gules frettè Or, between three Billets fable.

ON MONUMENTS IN THE
SOUTH AISLE.

Arms; Argent frettè Sable on a Chief Gules, three Mullets, Or, for HUNTINGTON.

Infria Sepultum jacet Corpus FRAMPTON HUNTINGTON, A. M. Qui in hoc mortali Ævo Vixit Annos 55, et fuit hujus Ecclefiæ Vicarius 27, unde Ex hâc ærumnofâ Vitâ Ad Dominum migravit 8vo. Die Aug. Annoq. Domini 1738.

Arms; Argent three Crofcroflets fable, on a Chief Gules a Lion paffant Or, for READY.

Near this place lieth the Body of SARAH, who was the Wife of THOMAS TOWNSEND of Sudeley, in this County, Gentleman. And after of ALEXANDER READY, of this Place, Gentleman. She was an excellent Wife to both, and had defervedly the Character of a very good Woman. She died Oct. 5, 1731, ætat. 39.

Arms; Azure, an Anchor erect Or, between two Dolphins Argent, collared and chained of the fecond for COLSTON.

Sacred to the Memory of ALEXANDER COLSTON, late of Filkins in the County of Oxford, Efq. and one of his Majefty's Juftices of the Peace for this County. He died December 1, 1775, in the 89th Year of his Age. He was always refpected for the Solidity of his Underftanding and Judgment, efteemed for his unblemifhed Integrity, and beloved for the Virtues of his Heart.

ON A FLAT STONE.

Here lyeth the Body of ANN, the Wife of Mr. WILLIAM HAYNES, who died March 21, 1723.

Alfo the Body of MARY HAYNES, who died the 27th of March 1754.

Alfo the Body of WILLIAM HAYNES, who died the 5th of Auguft, 1758.

ON MONUMENTS AGAINST THE
EAST END OF THE CHURCH.

Arms; Or a Gryphon fegreant Sable, for MORGAN, impaling Gules three Cheverons Argent, within a Bordure of the fecond, for AVERY.

To the pious Memory of MARY, the Dearly beloved Wife of EDMUND MORGAN, Gent. of Fairford in Gloucefterfhire, and Daughter of AVERY TIRREL, Gent. and MARY his Wife, of Weft Hagbourn in Berkfhire. She was an ingenious and virtuous Woman, a moft excellent Wife, a kind Miftrefs, a good Neighbour, and charitable to the Poor. She died on 18th March, 1715, in the 33d Year of her Age, and in the 2nd of Wedlock, leaving Iffue one Son. This Monument was erected by her moft loving and forrowful Hufband.

Near this Place lieth the Body of JOHN, the Son of JOHN and ELIZABETH CAREY of Quenington, who departed this Life the 25th day of May 1754, in the 33d Year of his Age.

Arms; Or, a Gryphon fegreant Sable, for MORGAN; 2 and 3 Gules, a Fefs vairè between three Unicorns Heads couped Or, for SAVERY.

In Memory of CHARLES MORGAN, Gent. of this Parifh, who departed this Life the 18th day of Auguft 1754, in the Fortieth Year of his Age. He was the only furviving Defcendant of a very ancient Family, whofe Virtues, together with their Poffeffions, he inherited; by the uniform and unaffected Practice of the one as well as by a liberal ufe of the other, he truly merited and univerfally obtained the diftinguifhing Character of a faithful Friend, a good Neighbour, and a worthy honeft Man.

Alfo of ELIZABETH his Wife, who exchanged this Life for a better the 12th day of October 1772, aged 58 Years. She fucceeded her Confort in the Care and Education of a numerous Family of Children, a Charge which fhe moft affectionately undertook and happily lived to accomplifh, and at her departure fhe left them, as the beft Rule of their future Conduct, the amiable pattern of her own Life and Manners. In grateful Teftimony of fo much maternal excellence they here unite their Common Tribute of filial Regard and Veneration to the beft of Mothers.

IN THE CHURCH YARD, ON TOMBS.

THOMAS MORGAN, was buried Nov. 28, 1632, aged 30.

ELIZABETH Wife of ROBERT MORGAN, Gent. buried 11th of June 1688. She was Daughter and Heirefs of RICHARD HOLFORD, Gent. She had Iffue one Daughter named ELIZABETH, and four Sons, viz. RICHARD, ROBERT, EDWARD, and HENRY, which RICHARD was buried 15th of Sept. 1705, aged 19 Years.

WALTER MORGAN, died 28th of September 1705, aged 57 Years.

Mr. ROBERT MORGAN, Son of EDMUND and MARY MORGAN, died on the 6th of June 1728, in the 77th Year of his Age.

MARY, Wife of CHARLES MORGAN, fen. died the 8th of Jan 1731, in the 64th Year of her Age.

Mr. EDMUND MORGAN, Widdower, (Son of ROBERT and ELIZABETH MORGAN) died the 19th, and was buried the 20th of March 1731, in the 49th Year of his Age.

CHARLES

CHARLES MORGAN, fen. Gent.
died June 30, 1738,
in the 83d Year of his Age.

RICHARD COMLEY,
Son of LAWRENCE and SABINA COMLEY,
departed this Life Nov. 9, 1752,
in the 57th Year of his Age.

VALENTINE STRONG (Freemafon)
departed this Life Dec. 26, A.D. 1662.

MARY, Daughter of DENNIS POPE,
died . . . . 14, 1712, ...

JACOB TELLING,
Son of WILLIAM and MARY TELLING,
died July 10, 1784, aged 29 Years.

WILLIAM TELLING
died Sept. 3, 1778, aged 56 Years.

MARY his Wife
died Feb. 3, 1784, aged 62 Years.

ISAAC TELLING their Son
died Jan. 2, 1776, aged 12 Years.

WILLIAM COOPPER, jun.
Son of WILLIAM and ANN COOPPER,
died June 10, 1754, aged 25 Years.

ANN his Grandmother
died May 25, 1729, aged 61 Years.

CHARLES WEEKS, Gent.
died June 26, 1740,
in the thirty-third Year of his Age.

ANN his Daughter
died Oct. 1, 1739.

Arms; Per Saltire Ermine, and lozengy Or and Gules, for BEDWELL.

ELIZABETH, Wife of
THOMAS BEDWELL,
of Furzy Hill,
died Aug. 18, 1740, aged 29 Years.

Alfo ELIZABETH their Daughter.

SARAH PRIOR, Daughter of
THOMAS and JANE HITCHMAN,
of Blunfdon, in the County of Wilts,
and Wife of JOHN PRIOR,
Mafter of the adjacent Free School,
died March 22, 1787,
in the 48th Year of her Age.

Six of their Children died in their Infancy.

WILLIAM WILLIAMS, fenior,
died June 21, 1762, aged 54 Years.

ANN his Wife
died Oct. 11, 1766, aged 68 Years.

JOHN their Son
died April 21, 1777, aged 40 Years.

JOSEPH LEWIS,
Son of HENRY and MARY LEWIS,
of this Town,
died Jan. 11, 1780, aged 57 Years.

JOSEPH WHITFORD
died Aug 10, 1722, ætatis 57.

WILLIAM LAKE
died July 10, 1751, aged 80 Years.

ELIZABETH WHITFORD,
aged 76.

ON A MONUMENT AGAINST THE FREE SCHOOL:

Near this Place
lie interred the Remains
of Mr. RICHARD GREEN,
late Mafter of this Free School,
who departed this Life the 9th Day of
November, 1767, in the fifty-fourth
Year of his Age.
The Integrity of his Life and Manners
had gained him the fincere Refpect
of his Neighbours; and the
uncommon Affiduity and Abilities
with which he difcharged the
Duties of his Profeffion for more than
fourteen Years in this School,
have m de his Death a publick Lofs,
and he will be long lamented by
all thofe that knew the Value
of fo ufeful a Character.

ON FLAT AND HEAD STONES.

	Died	Aged
George Meffeter	27 Aug. 1755	33
John and Ann Peachy		
Ann, Wife of Edward Trinder	18 Nov. 1759	63
William Smith	17 Jan. 1763	48
Hannah, Wife of Solomon Clinch	24 Aug. 1786	56
Sarah their Daughter	1 Jan. 1771	17
William their Son	10 June, 1775	—
Charles Price	9 Jan. 1755	27
Thomas Longden	4 Jan. 1762	54
Edward Hicks	13 June, 1776	66
William Howes	16 Apr. 1764	64
Catharine Howes	8 Aug. 1728	58
William Howes, fenior	8 Oct. 1725	72
Richard, Son of Thomas and Mary Howes	6 July, 1727	—
Thomas Price	6 Apr. 1747	36
Mary, Wife of John Bailey, junior	16 June, —	—
Thomas White	1 Apr. 1748	71
Mary his Wife	29 Aug. 1779	96
William their Son	30 July, 1773	38
Sarah, Wife of Thomas White	27 Oct. 1731	29
John, Son of John and Sarah White	16 Mar. 1779	8
George Hiett, fenior	24 June, 1759	81
Mary his Wife	22 Apr. 1753	73
George and Edward their Sons, buried	2 July, 1730	24
	30 May, 1734	22
Mary, Wife of Robert Hiett	17 Feb. 1747	93
Jane, Daughter of George and Mary Hiett	22 Nov. 1754	46
Ann Higgins	18 Sept. 1773	32
Sufannah, Wife of Charles Clinch	9 Mar. 1754	59
Charles Clinch, fenior	22 June, 1776	83
Zechariah Hinton	13 Jan. 1733	82
Sarah his Wife	3 Nov. 1737	80
Elizabeth, Wife of Thomas Price	16 Jan. 1750	64
James, Son of John and Mary Hill, of Burfcott	28 Mar. 1777	18
Jofiah Hill, fenior	12 Nov. 1734	83
Paul Silvefter	4 Oct. 1779 in Infancy.	31
John his Son		
Jane his Wife	11 Nov. 1749	36
Richard Duckett	11 June, 1742	71

	Died	Aged
Martha his Wife	20 Mar. 1751	81
Elizabeth, Daughter of Charles and Sarah Herbert	23 Nov. 1763	36
Sarah, Wife of Charles Herbert	1 Jan. 1758	—
Efther his former Wife	17 Oct. 1732	—
Sarah, Daughter of James and Sarah Carter	21 Jan 1766	24
Sarah, Wife of James Carter	24 Oct. 1769	74
James Carter, fenior	10 Dec. 1752	59
John Carter	15 Oct. 1784	60
Elizabeth his Wife	1 Aug. 1765	40
Daniel, Son of James and Sarah Carter	15 Apr. 1734	3
Daniel, Son of James and Sarah Carter	28 Mar. 1754	19
Sarah, Daughter of John and Elizabeth Wheeler	23 Dec. 1749	19
Elizabeth, Wife of John Wheeler buried	19 Feb. 1733	40
Charles Wheeler	10 Oct. 1743	27
Sarah his Wife	23 June, 1752	36
Ann, Wife of Charles Betterton	7 Feb. 1742	30
John Betterton	16 Mar. 1761	40
Robert his Son	4 June, 1777	20
Robert Goddard	22 Aug. 1759	61
John, Son of John and Jane Barrow	6 May, 1733	6
George, Son of John and Jane Barrow	2 June, 1733	—
George Stacey, fenior	25 Sept. 1734	76
Richard Gale	24 Dec. 1690	—
Mary, Daughter of Henry and Alice Simpfon	1 Nov. 1726	19
Henry Simpfon, fenior	25 Mar. 1756	84
Alice his Wife	2 Jan. 1766	87
Sarah, Wife of Allen Simpfon	25 Apr. 1753	72
Jonathan Telling	5 July, 1775	28
John Telling	14 Jan. 1778	78
Elizabeth, Wife of William Hiorns	1 Oct. 1755	55
John their Son	27 July, 1740	—
Sarah their Daughrer	24 May, 1742	5
John Holyoak	25 Apr. 1783	46
Elizabeth, Wife of John Telling	22 May, 1741	—

O N

ON FLAT AND HEAD STONES.

Name	Died	Aged
William Early - -	5 Nov. 1755	57
Mary Early - - -	12 Dec. 1752	57
William, Son of Richard and Mary Collett - -	28 Dec. 1762	—
William Early Collett -	20 Apr. 1772	—
Mary, Wife of Thomas Eycott	13 Sept. 1733	93
Rebecka, Wife of William Early	30 Jan. 1769	73
Thomas Cooper - -	25 Oct. 1756	48
Elizabeth his Daughter -	1 Aug. 1752	—
Jane, Wife of Henry Delawell	27 Aug. 17—	—
Mary, Wife of Richard Blowing	24 Sept. 1755	51
Hannah, Wife of Charles Heo	5 Apr. 1757	48
Deborah, Wife of Thomas Bond	13 Dec. 1762	40
Elizabeth, Wife of John Price	13 Mar. 1777	71
Mary their Daughter -	29 Sept. 1761	27
Ann their Daughter -	—	—
Three more of their Children died in their Infancy.		
Joseph Turner, junior -	1 Mar. 1752	39
Mary Turner - -	27 June, 1750	65
William, Robert, Thomas, and Anne, Children of William and Anne Williams, all died in their Infancy.		
William, Son of William and Elizabeth Green - -	22 Dec. 1743	3
John Tovey - -	19 Jan. 1766	45
Ann his Wife - -	9 Jan. 1766	41
Richard Tovey - -	10 July, 1780	24
John, Son of John and Ann Tovey	16 Mar. 1766	19
Sarah, Wife of William Gillett	20 June, 1765	50
Edward Panting -	2 June, 1751	40
William, Son of William and Sarah Ody - -	2 Aug. 1753	72
Sarah, Wife of Richard Brewer	21 Jan. 1774	21
Harry Tanner, senior -	26 Nov. 1731	72
Alexander his Son -	21 Mar. 1709	9
Deborah, Wife of Giles Newman	— Feb. 1744	33
Alice, Wife of Hugh Huseter	1 Jan. 1749	66
Hugh Huseter - -	23 Dec. 1738	72
William, Son of Robert and Betty Bartlett - -	26 Apr. 1761	4
Ann, Daughter of Henry and Esther Tovey - -	4 July, 1742	2
Henry Tovey - -	2 Sept. 1749	40
Esther his Wife -	4 June, 1778	66
Richard their Son - -	1 Aug. 1770	26
William Ebsworth Lewis, Son of John and Ann Lewis -	2 Mar. 1716	23
Ann, Wife of John Lewis, and Daughter of Richard and Ann Ebsworth - -	14 Jan. 1753	33
Mary, Wife of Henry Lewis, senior	13 Jan. 1755	72
Henry Lewis, senior, -	5 Sept. 1748	63
John Lewis - -		45
Ann, Daughter of Henry and Mary Lewis - -	13 Mar. 1763 / 11 Dec. 1767	60

Name	Died	Aged
Henry Lewis, junior -	17 Oct. 1766	55
Sarah, Wife of William Scotford	17 Oct. 1761	77
William Cowley - -	7 June, 1666	84
Elizabeth his Wife -	—	—
Richard Cowley -	1 July, 1748	86
Mary, Wife of Ambrose Folker, of Oxford, and Daughter of John and Mary Cowley -	2 Mar. 1788	54
Mary, Wife of John Cowley	6 Apr. 1778	72
Ann Boyle their Daughter	12 Sept. 1760	22
William Cowley -	18 Sept. 1732	64
Alice his Wife - -	23 Jan. 1731	62
William Reeves, senior, -	27 Mar. 1763	70
Thomas King - -	5 Mar. 1775	88
Mary his Wife - -	3 May, 1757	62
Thomas Reeves, senior -	29 Jan. 1733	72
Samuel Castle - -	— Aug. 1719	55
Anne his Wife - -	5 Feb. 1747	83
Hannah Palling buried	11 Dec. 1724	82
Sabina, Daughter of John and Mary Turner - buried	22 Aug. 1697	—
John Herbert - -	1 Apr. 1766	48
John Tackley - -	26 Oct. 1721	72
John, Son of William and Elizabeth Neal - -	8 Sept. 1742	24
Elizabeth, Wife of William Neal	16 Apr. 1749	70
Samuel Neal - -	14 July, 1764	59
Charles Herbert -	5 Nov. 1778	45
Thomas, Son of George and Mary Phillips - -	1 Nov. 1769	20
James, another of their Sons	9 Feb. 1761	7
George Phillips -	21 Sept. 1760	41
John Peachy - -	25 Apr. 1730	85
Arabella his Wife -	27 Mar. 1722	70
Sarah, Wife of Harry Herbert	8 Apr. 1702	76
Harry their Son -	1 May, 1740	17
John Adams - -	27 June, 1782	60
John, Son of Thomas and Hannah Russell - -	10 May, 1779	35
Thomas, Son of Robert and Syble King - -	13 Sept. 1753	25
John Luckman - -	14 Nov. 1758	60
Richard Luckman, senior -	16 Mar. 1734	64
Elizabeth his Wife -	11 May, 1744	75
Richard Luckman, junior -	8 July, 1753	39
Mary, Wife of Richard Walklett	12 Sept. 1711	69
Robert Cambray -	23 June, 1780	83
Robert Bishop - -	4 Dec. 1799	39
Robert Humphris - -	10 Jan. 1731	62
Richard, Son of Richard and Mary Humphris - -	13 Jan. 1770	56
Richard Humphris -	25 Aug. 1759	88
Mary his Wife - -	19 Apr. 1739	60
Charles Betterton -	14 Nov. 1722	65
Sarah his Wife - -	8 Sept. 1714	56

7 L

CXVIII.

AND in the moſt ancient Records *Tormentone*, or *Tormertune*; Names, which from their Reſemblance of *Tormarton*, another Pariſh in this County, have occaſioned no inconſiderable Confuſion in the Hiſtory of Property.

This Pariſh is ſituate in the open *Coteſwold*, in the Hundred of *Bradley*, two Miles Northward from *Northleche*, eight Weſtward from *Burford*, in *Oxfordſhire*, and from GLOUCESTER twenty-one on the Eaſt. The Boundaries form an oval of about nine Miles in Circumference. The Soil is light, inclining to Gravel, moſtly incloſed, and in Tillage, with 60 Acres of Woodland. This Diſtrict is deſervedly famed for a very ſuperior Breed of Sheep.

The Benefice is rectorial, in the Deanery of *Cirenceſter*, and appears to have been originally connected with *Northlech*, where the Inhabitants had a Right of Sepulture, and a Penſion of 6s. 8d. is claimed annually by the Vicar.

In the Church, dedicated to *St. Peter*, are no ſtriking Remains of Antiquity. It is a plain Building, with a low embattled Tower.

Tormentune was originally Parcel of the great Manor of *Leche*. In 1298, 26 EDW. I. it was granted by the Service of one Knight's Fee to HENRY DE ST. PHILIBERT, a Pictovin. His Grandſon, Sir JOHN DE ST. PHILEBERT, in 1352, 25 EDW. III. transferred this Manor, with the Advowſon of the Chapel, by Deed of Sale, for the Sum of 200 Marks, to WILLIAM DE EDINGTON, Biſhop of *Winton*, with which he endowed the College he had founded at *Edington*, co. *Wilts*, for a Dean and twelve Prebendaries, afterwards a Priory of the Order of *Bonhommes*, of *St. Auguſtine* *. A Confirmation of which Grant to them, and their Succeſſors, paſſed the great Seal in 1362, 35th of the ſame Reign †.

At the Diſſolution this Manor was purchaſed from the Court of Augmentations by MICHAEL AYSFIELD, or ASHFIELD, whoſe Deſcendant ROBERT ASHFIELD, Eſquire, re-ſold it to Sir RICE JONES, Knight, about the Year 1610. Sir HENRY JONES diſtinguiſhed himſelf in ſeveral Victories obtained in *Flanders*, in one of which he was ſlain. Upon his Death, this Eſtate paſſed to the Right Honourable RICHARD LUMLEY, the firſt Earl of *Scarborough*, who had married FRANCES his only Daughter and Heir ‡. Early in the preſent Century it was transferred by Purchaſe to EDMUND WALLER, Eſq. of *Beaconsfield*, co. *Bucks*, the Father of the preſent Proprietor. About the ſame Time the Manor-houſe was re-built in a modern Style, and is handſome and commodious.

The great Road from *Glouceſter* to *Oxford* leads nearly two Miles through this Pariſh.

No Benefactions to the Poor.

INCUMBENTS.	PATRONS.	INCUMBENTS.	PATRONS.
1298 ——————,	Henry de St. Philebert.	1690 Jacob Finnimore,	——————
1352 ——————,	Priory of Edington.	1692 Chriſtopher Baynes,	Earl of Scarborough.
* * * * * *	* * * * * *	1718 John Eykyn, LL.B.	Hon. Thomas Lumley.
1607 William Aſhfield,	Robert Aſhfield.	1734 Charles Spendelowe,	Edm. Waller, Eſq.
1621 Thomas Hughes,	King James.	1773 Thomas Beynon,	The ſame.
1641 Humphry Smith, M.A.	Richard Jones, Eſq.	1788 Harry Waller, M. A.	Edm. Waller, Eſq.
1687 Michael Geddes,	Sir Henry Jones.		

---

* WILLIAM DE EDINTON, Biſhop of *Winton*, founded at his native Place a large Chauntry or College, dedicated to *St. Mary*, *St. Katherine*, and *All Saints*, about the Year 1347. Theſe were afterward, at the Requeſt of EDWARD the Black Prince, changed into a reformed Sort of Friars of the Order of *St. Auguſtine*, called *Bonhommes*, who were ſettled there under the Government of a Rector, 1358. Its yearly Revenues amounted to 442l. 9s. 7d. DUGDALE. 521l. 12s. 5d. SPEED.
TANNER's Not. Mon.

† Pat. Clauſ. 35 EDW. III. m. 3. vel 19. " Pro Manerio de *Thormertune*, in com. *Glouceſtrenſ.*"
‡ COLLINS, vol. IV. p. 119. Title *Scarborough*.

4

PRESENT

PRESENT LORD OF THE MANOR,
EDMUND WALLER, Efq.

The only Perfon fummoned from this Parifh by the Heralds in 1682 and 1683 was
Humphry Smith, Rector.

At the Election in 1776, Three Freeholders polled from this Parifh.

The Regifter cannot be precifely afcertained, as to its earlieft Date.

ANNUAL ACCOUNT OF MARRIAGES, BIRTHS, AND BURIALS, IN THIS PARISH.

A.D.	Mar.	Bir.	Bur.	A.D.	Mar.	Bir.	Bur.	A.D.	Mar.	Bir.	Bur.	A.D.	Mar.	Bir.	Bur.
1781	2	6	3	1786	6	7	5	1791				1796			
1782	2	8	4	1787	—	3	—	1792				1797			
1783	1	8	5	1788	2	8	6	1793				1798			
1784	2	9	2	1789	2	8	4	1794				1799			
1785	1	7	4	1790				1795				1800			

INSCRIPTIONS IN THE CHURCH.

IN THE CHANCEL.

ON AN ATCHIEVEMENT AGAINST THE
SOUTH WALL:

Sable, a Cheveron Or between three
Snaffles Argent, for MILLS ;—impaling,
Ermine, a Lion rampant gardant Gules,
on a Canton Argent, a Spread Eagle of
the third, for

ON FLAT STONES.

Arms ; Sable, an Eagle difplayed
Ermine, for SMITH.

Hic jacet, vir doctrinâ,
moribus, & pietate, infignis
HUMFREDUS SMITH, A.M.
et hujus ecclefiæ annis
plufquam quadraginta rector,
qui obiit Feb. 26, 1687-8,
anno ætatis fuæ 75.

MARIAM juxta Uxorem,
JOHANNES EYKYN, LL. B.
hujus ecclefiæ rector,
diem hic expectat
fupremum.
Tu vero, lector, vigila !
Ne dies tremendus ille
tibi fuperveniat
inopinanti.

I. E. } obiit { July 21, 1734 } æt { 63.
M. E. } obiit { Nov. 24, 1729 } æt { 68.

C. B. *
hujus ecclefiæ Rector,
obiit
die Septembris,
Anno Dom.
MDCCXVIII.
ætatis fuæ LIII.

Here lie the Remains of
ELIZABETH,
the Infant Daughter of
ROBERT and BARBARA DINELY.
She departed this Life
the 3d of September, 1789,
aged 4 Months.

ON BRASS PLATES.

Here lieth the Body of
WINIFRED SMITH,
late Wife of
HUMFREY SMITH, Clerk,
who departed this Life
Feb. 20, 1652.

Here lieth the Body of
DOROTHY SMITH,
the Wife of
WILLIAM SMITH,
of Alvefcot, in the County of Oxon,
Clarke,
who died Auguft 26, 1668.

Here lieth the Body of
HUMFREY SMITH,
the Son of
HUMFREY SMITH,
who departed this Life
July 23, 1659,
aged 12 Yeares and 6 Moneths.

Here lieth the Body of
THOMAS COX,
of Lincoln's Inn, Barrifter,
who departed this mortal Life
May 18, 1658.

ON AN ATCHIEVEMENT
AGAINST THE NORTH WALL
IN THE NAVE:

Sable, three Walnut Leaves Or between two Bendlets Argent, for WAL-
LER ;—impaling, Argent, a Lion rampant Sable, collared and chained Or,
for PHILLIPS. Creft, on a Mount
Vert, an Oak Tree acorned prop e,
charged on the finifter Side, with an
Efcocheon, bearing the Arms of France.

IN THE CHURCH YARD, ON A TOMB.

CHARLES MILLER, Gent.
died October 7, 1778.

* CHRISTOPHER BAYNES.

ON

ON HEAD AND FLAT STONES.

	Died	Aged
Elizabeth, Wife of William Joynes	27 July, 1767	33
Sarah their Daughter - -	6 Apr. 1776	12
John Joynes	2 Mar. 1748	72
William Joynes - buried	17 Aug. 1762	83
Anna Maria his Wife buried	4 Aug. 1741	45
Anna Maria, Daughter of William and Elizabeth Joynes -	18 Sept. 1763	1
Elizabeth, Wife of Thomas Joynes	3 Nov. 1763	41
James and Joseph their Children died Infants.		
Thomas Simmons - -	3 Nov. 1736	65
Anne his Wife - -	1 Feb. 1765	78
John Joynes, Son of Thomas and Elizabeth Humphris -	21 Dec. 1772	
Susannah, Wife of Gabriel Addams	3 Nov. 1752	50
Gabriel Addams - -	4 Dec. 1774	90
Betty, Wife of Charles Gillett	23 Mar. 1772	36
John their Son -	19 June, 1770	
John Pearce - -	29 Dec. 1757	90
Mary, Wife of John Curtis	2 Feb. 1788	65
Elizabeth, Wife of John Joynes, of Hazleton	25 July, 1789	72
Thomas, Son of Thomas and Elizabeth Humphris, of Windrush	12 Jan. 1783	
Richard, Son of Richard and Martha Duffell - -	6 May, 1742	24

	Died	Aged
Hannah, Wife of Edmund Addams	8 Aug. 1752	22
Edmund, Son of Gabriel and Susannah Adams -	15 July, 1753	26
Elizabeth, Wife of Gabriel Addams	28 Jan. 1786	57
Ann, Wife of Thomas Joynes	6 July, 1788	34
Thomas Joynes - -	5 July, 1780	54
James, Son of Charles and Mary Gillett - -	28 Sept. 1779	
Rebekah their Daughter -	27 Mar. 1781	
John Townsend - -	14 July, 1740	60
Mary their Daughter -	25 May, 1731	38
Mary his Wife - -	——— 1720	—
William their Son - -	——— 1728	—
Jof. Hall - -	23 Nov. 1781	54
Betty Hall, Daughter of Caleb and Betty Hall - -	12 Feb. 1786	28
Caleb their Son - -	27 May, 1770	11
John their Son - -	14 June, 1780	12
Petty Hall - -	30 Oct. 1782	54
Ann, Wife of Thomas Rose	20 Oct. 1779	19
John, Son of Tho. and Eliz. Wheeler	9 Sept. 1779	29
John their Son - -	7 Sept. 1744	
Alice their Daughter -	11 Sept. 1758	1
Alice their Daughter -	27 Sept. 1758	
Ann their Daughter -	17 June, 1759	11
William Jones - -	26 May, 1717	—

CXIX.

IS a Parifh of fmall Extent, in the lower Divifion of the Hundred of *Berkeley*; fituate on the great Road from GLOUCESTER to BRISTOL, from the former of which it is diftant thirty, and from the latter four Miles. The Boundaries are nearly two Miles each Way, forming a Square; and the Soil, which is of a ftiff Clay, is with fmall Exception applied to Pafture. From a Survey made in 1791, it appears, that in this Parifh are 17 Houfes and 113 Inhabitants.

The following Account is tranfcribed from Mr. SMYTH's Collections:

" *Filton*, alias *Filton* and *Hay*, written alfoe *Felton*, a Townfhip not mentioned in the Booke of *Domef-*
" *dei*, but went under the Name of *Horfield*. In this Village are fix Meffuages, Parcell at this Day of
" the Poffeffions of the Bifhopricke of *Briftol*, erected in 34 HEN. VIII. and were Parcell of the Lands
" of the Monafterie of *St. Auguftine*, founded by ROBERT, Son of HARDINGE, in the Time of Kinge
" STEPHEN. But in what Parifh thefe fix Meffuages doe lie, Queftion hath of late been moved by the
" Inhabitants, which I determine not. The Bifhop, being Lord alfoe of *Horfield* adjoininge, draweth
" thefe fix Houfeholds to his Leet at *Horfield*, who are reputed a little Manor of themfelves. The other
" Part of this Village is, at this Day, the Inheritance of WILLIAM BALDWYNE, of *London*, Draper, whofe
" Father WILLIAM BALDWYN, was by Inquif. 19 JAC. I. found to dye feized of the Manor of *Filton*, holden
" of the Kinge by Knight's Service, but not *in Capite*. This little Manor confifteth of eight Houfeholds
" who are all within the great Leet of the Hundred of *Berkeley*, whereat they appear twice in each Yeere, and
" wherto the Wafte Grounds doe belong. And theis eight rule and order the other 6 Houfeholds, who
" are bound by what thefe doe (as all the 45 Yeeres of my being Steward hath byn accuftomed), and ap-
" pear thereat, by the Name of the Tythinge of *Filton* and *Hay*. As for that Part, called *Hay*, only
" one Houfe is nowe ftandinge thereon, the Inheritance of JOHN MALLET, Efquier. The faid WILLIAM
" BALDWYN, Father of WILLIAM, purchafed the Manor of JOHN YOUNGE, and hee of RICHARD NE-
" VILLE.

" Take the reft that concerneth this Village, as I obferved in the Recordes mentioninge it.

" By Patent Roll, in the Tower of *London*, 27 Edw. I. ELIAS DE FILTON arraigned an Affize againft
" the Abbot of *St. Auguftine*, for common of Pafture there. By Inquif. in 4 RICH. II. after the Death
" of EDMOND BLUNT, it is found, that he held joyntlie with his Wife MARGARET, who furvived, the
" Moietie of the Manor of *Filton* by Gift of THOMAS FITZ NICHOL and MARGERY his Wife, holden of
" REGINALD DE COBHAM in Right of ALIENOUR his Wife, by Knight's Service; and that WILLIAM
" BLUNT is his Son and Heire.

" By Rot. Clauf. 7 RIC. II. mem. 22. upon a " non intromittendo" to the King's Efchaetor, it is re-
" cited, that whereas EDMÙND BLUNT, decefed, held joyntly the Manor of *Filton*, not holden of the King,
" that the faid Moitie fhould be delyvered to MARGARET his Wife.

" By Inquif. 7 RIC. II. upon a Writ of " Ad quod Damnum," it was found, that befide other Ma-
" nors entayled by the faid Sir THOMAS FITZ NICHOL, there remained to him the Moietie of the Ma-
" nors of *Filton* and *Harryftoke*, holden of REGINALD COBHAM, by Knight's Service, in Right of ELI-
" NOR his Wife. In *Berkeley* Câftell is a Court Roll, 11 HEN. IV. which fhews, that ELIAS DE FILTON,
" Sonne of RALF DE FILTON, was then Lord therof.

" Inquif. 6 HEN. V. after the Death of Sir THOMAS FITZ NICHOL, fhews that he held the Manors of
" *Filton* and *Stokebenry* of the Lord of BERKELIE, but by what Service the Jurie find not, and that
" KATHERINE, the Wife of JOHN POINTZ, and JOHN, Son of JOHN BROWNINGE and ELINOUR his Wife,
" are as well Heires of the faid Sir THOMAS, the faid KATHERINE and MARGERIE being both his Daugh-
" ters and Coheires.

" Inquif. 8 HEN. V. after the Death of JOHN, Sonne and Heire of JOHN BROWNINGE, findes that hee
" dyed feifed of the Manor of *Filton* and *Harryftoke*, holden of the Lord BERKELEI, and that WILLIAM
" his Brother and Heir was then 20 Yeeres olde.

" Inquif. 32 HEN. VI. finds that WILLELMA, fometime the Wife of JOHN BLUNT, held for her
" Life the Manour of *Filton* of the Heire of ELEANOUR SCRYVET, decefed, and that EDMUND BLUNT
" was her Sonne and Heire. See alfo the Record of Michaelmas Term, 20 HEN. VI. in Sccio cum
" Rem, Thefaur."

7 M

From

From the Family of MALLET, the Manor paſſed to JOHN POPE, Eſq. of *Briſtol*, about the Beginning of this Century, and now belongs to the Right Honourable FREDERIC AUGUSTUS Earl of BERKELEY. The chief Eſtate was transferred to JOHN BRICKDALE, Eſq. and with another, the Property of the Family of GAYNER, is held under the Manor.

The Church, dedicated to *St. Peter*, is a ſmall and low Fabric, conſiſting of a Nave and Semi-tranſept projecting on the South Side.

The Benefice is a Rectory in the Dioceſe and Deanery of *Briſtol*, originally appropriated to the Abbey of *St. Auguſtine*, charged in the King's Books at the clear yearly Value of 36*l*. 11*s*. 8*d*. * The Advowſon was formerly attached to the Manor.

In the Sale made of Epiſcopal Eſtates, Jan. 30, 1649, the Manors and Impropriations of *Horfield* and *Filton* were purchaſed by THOMAS ANDREWS for 1256*l*. 14*s*.; but it appears, that the ſix Meſſuages before mentioned were the whole Property of the Biſhop in this Pariſh †.

B E N E F A C T I O N.

JOHN SILCOCKS, Gent. by Will, dated July 22, 1741, bequeathed the Sum of 200*l*. to CHRISTOPHER GRYFFITH the elder, and CHRISTOPHER his Son, and their Aſſigns, and the Miniſter and Churchwardens of the ſeveral Pariſhes of *Filton*, *Stoke Giffard*, *Winterbourne*, and *Almondſbury*, in Truſt, to apply the Intereſt to teach poor Children to read, whoſe Parents do not receive Alms, in an equal Number from each Pariſh. The annual Proportion of Intereſt to *Filton* is 2*l*. 10*s*.

INCUMBENTS.	PATRONS.	INCUMBENTS.	PATRONS.
—— Richard Knevett,	————.	1683 Scudamore Godwyn, B.A.	————————.
1563 Richard Johnſon,	————.	1702 Samuel Godwyn,	————————.
1597 William King,	————.	1705 James Pidding §,	Eliza Pope.
1645 Will. Blackwell ‡, B. A.	John Mallet, Eſq.	1730 Francis Baker,	Charles Hawkins.
1662 Thomas Stephens,	————.	1735 John Bound, M. A.	The ſame.
1668 Thomas Godwyn,	————.	1766 John Davie, M. A.	Matt. Brickdale, Eſq.
1675 Thomas Godwyn,	————.	1779 Edw. Blakeway, M. A.	The ſame.

PRESENT LORD OF THE MANOR,

The Right Honourable FREDERIC AUGUSTUS Earl of BERKELEY.

No Perſon was ſummoned from this Place by the Heralds in 1682 and 1683.

At the Election in 1776 One Freeholder polled from this Pariſh.

The Regiſter has its firſt Date in 1654.

ANNUAL ACCOUNT OF MARRIAGES, BIRTHS, AND BURIALS, IN THIS PARISH.

A.D.	Mar.	Bir.	Bur.	A.D.	Mar.	Bir.	Bur.	A.D.	Mar.	Bir.	Bur.	A.D.	Mar.	Bir.	Bur.
1781	—	1	6	1786	1	6	—	1791				1796			
1782	—	5	1	1787	1	5	3	1792				1797			
1783	—	2	1	1788	—	4	7	1793				1798			
1784	1	4	3	1789	2	3	3	1794				1799			
1785	1	2	1	1790	—	3	1	1795				1800			

I N S C R I P T I O N S   I N   T H E   C H U R C H.

ON FLAT STONES IN THE CHANCEL.

Here lyeth the Body of JANE, Daughter of JAMES PIDDING, Rector of this Pariſh, who departed this Life Dec. .. 1714, aged 13 Years and .. Months.	Alſo here lieth THOMAS, Son of the ſaid JAMES PIDDING, who departed this Life April 9, 1721, aged 3 Years.	Here lieth the Body of JANE, Wife of JAMES PIDDING, Rector of this Pariſh, who departed this Life Sept. 21, 1723, ætatis ſuæ 50.

* BACON's Liber Regis, p. 108.
EDWARD COLSTON, Eſq. who died in 1721, gave 6,000*l*. to augment ſixty ſmall Livings, of which Benefaction *Filton* partook in 1727.
† BARRET's *Briſtol*, p. 316. ECTON's Theſaurus, ed. WILLIS.
‡ Ejected for Nonconformity 1662.
§ At his own Coſt re-built the Eaſt End of the Parſonage Houſe in 1716, and in 1714 paved the Chancel with Brick.

Here

Here lieth ABIGAIL HULL,
who lived 13 Months,
and died Feb. 17, 1637.

IN THE SOUTH TRANSEPT.

Here lieth the Body of
JOHN WADE, of this Parish, Gent.
who departed this Life May 7, 1716,
aged 49 Years.

Alfo here lieth the Body of
ELINOR WADE, the Wife of
the abovefaid JOHN WADE,
who departed this Life April 19, 1741,
aged 80 Years.

Here lyeth the Body of
JOHN BLAKE,
who died Dec. . . 1682, aged . .

Here lyeth the Body of
GRACE BLAKE,
the Wife of JOHN BLAKE,
of this Parifh, Yeoman,
who departed this Life the 2d of April,
1690, aged 70.

IN THE CHURCH YARD, ON TOMBS.

WILLIAM BYSSE,
died Nov. 1, 1636, ætatis 44.

ANNE his Wife
died April 5, 1689, ætatis fuæ 80.

GEORGE FRETWELL

and

MARY his Wife.

Here lyeth the Body of
THOMAS AUSTIN, Ship Carpenter,
who departed this Life
the 6th Day of May, 1672, aged 55.

ON HEAD STONES.

	Died	Aged
William Millett, Yeoman	10 May, 1750	48
Elizabeth his Daughter -	21 Nov. 1745	17
Thomas his Son -	17 Nov. 1745	—
Mary his Daughter •	2 Nov. 1745	19
William his Son - -	21 Nov. 1745	6
Thomas Harding, of Briftol, Car-penter - -	19 Dec. 1765	44
Richard Hancock, of Pen Park, in the Parifh of Weftbury on Trim	6 Dec. 1766	45
Sarah Lewis, of Horfield -	7 May, 1760	61
Stephen Humphrys, Blackfmith	7 Feb. 1741	30
Martha his Relict, and Wife of John Spear, of Baptift Mills, in the Parifh of St. Philip and Jacob	28 June, 1768	—
John Weft - -	9 Nov. 1748	—
William Lake, of Briftol, -	11 Oct. 1758	55
Thomas Wade -	11 Jan. 173$\frac{4}{5}$	63
John Wade, Gent. -	13 Apr. 1705	83

	Died	Aged
John Wade, Yeoman -	24 Oct. 1760	64
Mary his Wife -	11 Oct. 1737	46
Ann his Wife - -	7 Jan. 1764	68
Jofeph, Son of Jacob and Mary Mil-lett - -	— — 1716	—
Jofeph, Son of Jacob and Mary Mil-lett - -	— — 1732	—
Hannah, Daughter of Jacob and Mary Millett -	— — 1723	—
Mary, Daughter of Jacob and Mary Millett -	— — 1730	—
Hefter, Daughter of Jacob and Mary Millett - -	— — 1716	—
William Owen - -	27 Feb. 1725	49
Hannah his Wife -	25 June, 1711	30
Ann their Daughter -	3 July, 1743	40
William, Mary, and William their Children died in their Infancy.		

CXX.

CXX. F L A X L E Y.

THIS Parifh is a Part of the Hundred of *St. Briavel*, in the Purlieus of the Foreſt of *Dean*, eleven Miles diſtant from GLOUCESTER on the North-eaſt, and three from *Newnham*. The Boundaries include about 1400 Acres, of a Soil varying from red Marl to Lime Stone, and chiefly in Paſture and Woodland. In the earlieſt Records Iron Forges are faid to have been eſtabliſhed here, and the Iron of this Manufactory has long been eſteemed of an excellent Quality.

The Abbey of *Flexely* or *Dene* was founded for *Ciſtertian** Monks, in the Reign of King STEPHEN, about the Year 114., by ROGER FITZ-MILO, the fecond Earl of *Hereford*, after the Conqueſt, in a Valley called *Caſtiard*, which was, from its retired and beautiful Situation, peculiarly adapted to that order of conventual Hermits. Their Endowment, originally ample, was confirmed and extended by various Charters (which are ſubjoined), during the reigns prior to the Diſſolution†. It does not, however, appear that their Number was ever great; and, as the Abbots had no pontifical Privilege, no Documents have reached us, by which their Succeſſion might have been more regularly aſcertained, than by the Regiſter of the Dioceſe of *Hereford*.

A B B O T S.

1288.	Nicholas.	1509. John.
1314.	William de Rya.	1528. William Beawdley ‡.
1372.	Richard Peyto.	1532. Thomas Ware §.

By which laſt, the Abbey was ſurrendered to the Commiſſioners in 1541; at which Time there were Nine Monks, whoſe Revenues were valued at £.112 13s. 1d. according to DUGDALE. A Grant and Confirmation of theſe were made to Sir WILLIAM KINGSTONE ||, Knight, by King HENRY VIII. in 1545, from which we collect that the conventual Church, Tower, Chapter-houſe, &c. were then undemoliſhed. He made it his Reſidence, and was ſucceeded by his Son Sir ANTHONY ** and his Deſcendants.

---

* *Ciſtertian* Monks were a Branch of the *Benedictines*, ſo called from *Ciſtertium* or *Ciſteaux*, in the Biſhoprick of *Chalons* in *Burgundy*. This Order, called likewiſe *Bernardines*, was eſtabliſhed in 1098. Their Monaſteries, which became very numerous (for STEVENS, vol. II. p. 31. ſays that they had in all 6000 Houſes), were generally founded in ſolitary and romantic Places, and all dedicated to the Bleſſed Virgin. DUGDALE's Mon. vol. I. p. 891. STEVENS's Mon. vol. II. pp. 37. 50.

† See in DUGDALE's Mon. Angl. vol. I. p. 884, the Charter of HENRY Duke of NORMANDY; and another, when King HENRY II. confirms the Donation of Earl ROGER, Pat. 22 RICHARD II. p. 3. m. 16, granting them in this County the Manor and impropriate Church of *Flaxley*; the Manors of *Blaiſdon*, *Newnham*, and *Ruerdeane*; diſtinct Manors in the Pariſhes of *Dean-Parva*, *Dymock*, and *Arlingham*; a Houſe in *Aubenhall*; and an Iron Forge in the Foreſt of *Dean*; and for the Supply of it, two Oaks Weekly, which being found prejudicial, a Wood called *Abbots Wood* was given by Patent, 42 HENRY III, in Lieu of them. The Foundation Charter gave them the Tythe of all the Cheſnuts growing within the Foreſt *(Decimam omnium Ceſtanearum)* then producing a conſiderable Income. Certain Tenants, within the Purlieus of the Royal Foreſts, had the right of Paſnagium or Pannage, i. e. of turning in a certain Number of Hogs to feed on the Acorns and Maſts, from the Feaſt of St. MICHAEL to that of St. MARTIN. The frequent inſtances of the Roofs of ancient Buildings having been conſtructed with Cheſtnut proves that it was generally cultivated in England as a Timber Tree, and the Fruit being uſed by the lower rank of People was conſidered as of greater Value than Acorns, and conſequently, ſubject to Decimation. If it be admitted that the Timber was tytheable, the Revenue muſt have been very conſiderable. By the ſame Grant they had a Fiſhery, "apud *Ridleiam* quæ dicitur *Neweria*," and a Moiety of the Fiſhery in the *Severn*, called *Hunwere*. Rot. in Turr. *Lond.* N. N. 39. Pat. 54 HEN. III. n. 58. And in a Charter, dated 25 EDWARD III. 1352. an annual Rent Charge of 36l. 19s. 1d. from the King's Tenants in the Foreſt of *Dean*. In 2 RICHARD II. 1387, certain Tenements in *Leye*, *Boſteley*, and *Rodley*. Pat. p. 1. m. 28. For farther Particulars conſult TANNER's Not. Mon. ed. NASMITH, GLOUCESTERSHIRE, N° XI.

LELAND, in his Itinerary, Vol. IV. p. 83, ſays, "*Flaxley* Abbay of White Monks ſtode in *Dene* Foreſt, a 5 or 6 Miles from "*Gloceſtre*;" and vol. VIII. p. 36, "ROGERus Earl of HEREFORDE, Founder of *Flexeley* in the Foreſt of *Deene*. Ther was a "Brother of ROGERus Earl of HEREFORDE that was kylled wythe an Arowe in Huntinge, in the very Place where the Abbay "ſyns was made. There was a Table of the Matter hanggid up in the Abbay Church of *Flaxley*. Ther was a Byſhope of "HEREFORD that holpe moche to the buildinge of *Flexeley*."

"ROGER Earl of HEREFORD, having in the decline of Life taken the Habit of a Benedictine, died S. P. in the Abbey of "*St. Peter* in *Glouceſter* in the Year 1154, 1 HENRY II." DUGDALE's Baronage, vol. I. p. 538.

‡ "1528, June 18. Father WILLIAM BEAWDLEY, Abbat of *Flaxley* of the Ciſtertian Order, opponent in Divinity." WOOD's Faſti, vol. I. p. 677.

§ THOMAS WARE, a Monk of the Ciſtertian Order, and ſome time a Student in *St. Bernard's* College in *Oxon*. He afterward's became the laſt Abbat of *Flexley* in *Glouceſterſhire* (in the Place of W. BEAUWDLEY), and living to fee his Houſe diſſolved, and himſelf and his Brethren turned out thence, he retired to *Aſton Rowant* near *Thame* in *Oxon*, where, ſpending the remaining Part of his Days in Devotion and Retiredneſs, he gave at length to Fate in a good old Age, Anno 1546; whereupon his Body was buried in the Yard belonging to the Church there. WOOD's Faſti. vol. I. p. 672. WILLIS's Mitred Abbies, vol. II. p. 85.

|| Of Sir WILLIAM KINGSTONE, LLOYD obſerves (Worthies, p. 464), that "he was one one of the beſt Courtiers at Maſks "and Revels, one of the beſt Captains at Sea, and one of the moſt valiant and ſkilful Commanders by Land. He was knighted "for his Service at *Tournay*, and made Marſhal for his Succeſs at *Flodden*."—"He was Captain of the Guard to King HENRY VIII. "and Lieutenant of the Tower; and conducted Cardinal WOLSEY upon his Attainder. Upon the Diſperſion of monaſtic Pro-"perty he ſhared very largely, having received from the King ſeveral Manors in this County, belonging to the diſſolved Priories "of *Llantony* and *Flaxley*." FULLER's Worthies, p. 368.

** "HENRY VIII, by his Letters Patent in 1545, regranted to Sir ANTHONY KINGSTONE the Site of the late Abbey of *Flaxley*, and all the Church, Bell Houſe, and Church Yard of the ſame, and all the Houſes, Granges, &c. as well within as without the ſaid Site, and alſo all other the Manors and Granges of *Flaxley*, *Howle*, *Goderith*, *Climperwell*, *Wolmore*, *Blaiſdon*, *Arlingham*, *Le Ronken*, *Ruardene*, *Newland*, *Dene Parva*, *Newenham*, *Pulton*, and *Dymock*, with their Rights, &c. in the County of *Glouceſter*; and the Houſe and Manor of *Rochelburgh*, com. *Somerſet*, belonging to the ſame; and all Advocations, Preſentations, &c. of the ſaid Pariſhes, at any time appurtenant to the ſaid Monaſtery, at the yearly Payment of 1l. 8s. 2d. to the Crown." MSS. SNELL.

3

Early

Early in the prefent Century, that Part of this venerable Pile which had been inhabited by the Abbot and Monks, remained nearly perfect *. It was a low Structure of great Length, containing in Front the Refectory, fixty Feet long, twenty-five wide, but fourteen only in height; the whole arched with Stone, with plain and maffy Ribs, interfecting the Vault. The firft Floor confifted of a very long Gallery, with which the Dormitories or Cells were connected; and at the South End a very fpacious Apartment, which is conjectured to have been the Abbot's chief Room, or ufed for the affembling of the Convent. Thefe are certainly Parts of the original Structure, much of which was deftroyed by Fire in 1777, which has been fince reftored, and many Additions made by the prefent Poffeffor. In feveral of the Apartments are fome fine old Portraits of the Families of CLARKE and BOEVEY. In 1788, the Site and Floor of the Chapter-houfe were difcovered at a fmall Depth in the Garden, extending about forty-five Feet, and twenty-four wide; at the upper End a circular Stone Bench, and in the Centre the carved Bafe of a Pillar. Seven Coffin Lids of Stone were then found fculptured with ornamented Croffes; but upon one a right Hand and Arm holding a Crofier, which Circumftance imports it to have been the Memorial of one of the Abbots, as their Office had not the Privilege, as that of Bifhops, of conferring Benediction.

In the Park, on the North-eaft, is a natural Terrace of confiderable Extent, commanding a moft interefting View of the cultivated Vale of *Severn*, and the City of GLOUCESTER, flanked by the whole Chain of the *Cotefwold* Mountains from *Bredon* to *Sodbury Hill*, a Line of more than fifty Miles. The frequent Windings of the River in the Fore-ground appear like fo many Lakes in Succeffion, and give a highly picturefque Effect to this fingularly pleafing Landfcape. The Benefice is a Donative, which receives 8*l. per Annum* from the Impropriation, and is farther endowed with the Profits of an Eftate purchafed with 1200*l.* bequeathed by CATHERINE BOEVEY, Relict of WILLIAM BOEVEY, Efq. for that Purpofe. In Purfuance of her Requeft, the Church was re-built by her Executrix MARY POPE about the Year 1730, which is fmall, with a low Spire; but on the Infide peculiarly neat. The Archdeacon of *Hereford* vifits it, as a Member of his Archdeaconry in the Diocefe of GLOUCESTER.

Before the year 1650, ABRAHAM CLARKE, Efq. purchafed the manerial Eftate, including the greater Part of the Parifh, of ANTHONY KINGSTONE, Efq. the fifth in Defcent from the firft Proprietor, and who left no Iffue. He was fucceeded by his Son ABRAHAM; after whofe Death WILLIAM BOEVEY, Efq. enjoyed it. By his Will, dated 1697, it paffed, fubject to Jointure, to THOMAS CRAWLEY, Efq. of GLOUCESTER, who affumed the Surname of BOEVEY; from whom it has defcended to his Grandfon, who, in 1789, fucceeded to the Dignity of Baronet, in virtue of a Limitation in the Patent of Creation of Sir CHARLES BARROW, Baronet, of *Highgrove*, bearing Date Jan. 22, 24 GEO. III. 1784. An Eftate, called the *Grange*, now vefted in the Family of SKIPP, is held by Leafe under the Manor.

B E N E F A C T I O N S.

1620, May 8. GEORGE CUSTANS, Gent. gave, by Will, Money, now producing 1*l.* a Year, to be given to the Poor.

1692, 1 Aug. WILLIAM BOEVEY, Efq. by Will fo dated, bequeathed 400*l.* which Legacy was confirmed by his Relict CATHERINE BOEVEY, by Will, dated March 30, 1726, to be applied to the apprenticing poor Children of the Parifh of *Flaxley*; the annual Produce of which is 14*l.*

PERPETUAL CURATES.	PATRONS.	PERPETUAL CURATES.	PATRONS.
1727 Thos. Tyrer, M.A.	Thos. Crawley Boevey, Efq	1742 Wm. Crawley, M.A.	T. Crawley Boevey, Efq.
—— William Lloyd, M.A.	—————.	1780 John Longden, M.A.	T. Crawley Boevey, Efq.

PRESENT LORD OF THE MANOR,
Sir THOMAS CRAWLEY BOEVEY, Baronet.

The only Perfon fummoned by the Heralds, in 1682 and 1683, was
Abraham Clarke, Efq.

At the Election in 1776 Two Freeholders polled from this Parifh.

I N S C R I P T I O N S   I N   T H E   C H U R C H.

ON MONUMENTS IN THE CHANCEL.

Arms; Ermine, a Bend, Parti per Bend Gules and Sable, charged with two Guties d'Or, between three Cornifh Choughs of the third, for BOEVEY;— impaling, Argent, three Annulets Azure, for RICHES.

M. S.
GULIELMI BOEVEY, Armig.
Qui fide et famâ ornatiffimus,
non fui parcus, non appetens alieni,
nemini notus ex injuriâ,
E beneficentiâ innumeris,
Maximam vitæ partem feliciter tranfegit;
tandem verò,
Cum mole corporis obefiffimi anima
oppreffa fufpiraret graviter et gemeret,
ut liberiorem fui copiam haberet,
Deo miferente,
ad fuperos migravit lætiffima
Aug. XXVI. A. D. M,DC,XVII.
ætat. XXXV.

H. M.
Catharina
conjux fidiffima
M. P.

Arms; BOEVEY, as before.

Hic dormit
ABRAHAMUS CLARK, Armiger.
beatam refurrectionem expectans,
in omni vitâ modeftus ac fobrius,
juftitiæ et æquitatis cultor eximius,
fummâ in amicos fide,
verâque in Deum.
Egenorum fautor ac patronus,
orphanorum pater,
liberalitatem exercere maluit
quam oftentare aliis, munificentiæ
teftes præter Deum
ægrè admifit.
Satis ei magnum ad virtutem
invitamentum rectè factorum
confcientia. Obiit Decem.
4, anno Domini 1683,
ætatis fuæ 61.

* See KIP's View of *Flaxley Abbey* in ATKINS's *Gloucefterfhire*.

7 N

Arms;

Arms; Ermine, a Saltire Gules, for
Lloyd.
Hoc juxta marmor
depofiti conduntur cineres
Gulielmi Lloyd, A. M.
de Stow cum novem ecclefiis
in agro Northonienfi,
Per annos XXXIV rectoris.
Viri
eximiâ probitate, fide & eruditione
inftructiffimi;
& cuilibet vel in ecclefia vel in orbe
literato muneri,
five fuftinendo, five ornando,
nifi fua obfuiffet modeftia
non imparis.
In hac capella concionatoris munere
per annos complures
feliciter perfunctus eft.
Londini natus,
in Oxonienfi academia enutritus,
bene latuit & bene vixit,
donec ad vitam beatiorem hinc
tranflatus eft
Julii XI die,

anno ætatis fuæ LXIX,
& æræ Chriftianæ
MDCCLIV·

Arms; Or, on a Chevron Sable, three
Eftoiles Argent, for Clarke.

Here lyeth entombed the Body of
Joanna Clarke, Lady of Flaxley,
who deceafed this Life, in the Feare of
God, upon Palm Sunday,
the 3d of April, in the 59th Year of
her Age, and in the Year of
our Lord God 1664.

ON FLAT STONES.

James, the Son of
Abraham Clarke, Efq.
died Feb. 11, 1669, aged 6 Days.

Jane his Daughter,
born March 16, 1670,
and died Sept. 9, 1677.

Elizabeth his Daughter,
born April 23, 1677,
and buried in this Chapel
Dec. 6, 1677.

Anne Riches,
Daughter of John Riches, Efq.
and onely Sifter to Mrs. Bovey,
of Flaxley, departed this Life
Oct. 5, 1689,
which fhe had paffed
in a religious Obfervance of her Duty
towards God and her Parents;
in tender Affection to her Relations;
in Charity and Kindnefs to all;
endued with this early Habit of Vertue,
Death, however fuddain,
did not furprife her
unprepared.

On a large plain Tablet of white Marble:

In the Vault near this Chapel is repofited the Body of
Mrs Catharina Bovey, Daughter of John Riches, Efq. of London, Merchant.
She was married to William Bovey, Efq. Lord of this Mannor of Flaxley, at the Age of 15,
was left a Widow, without Children, at the Age of 22, and continued fo all the reft of her Life.
She entertained her Friends and Neighbours with a moft agreeable Hofpitality; but always took Care to
have a large Referve for Charity, which fhe beftowed, not only on fuch Occafions as offered,
but ftudied how to employ it fo as to make it ufeful and advantageous.
Her Difpofition to do good was fo well known in the Diftrict about her, that fhe eafily became acquainted with
the Circumftances of thofe that wanted; and, as fhe preferved many Families from Ruin, by feafonable Loans or Gifts,
fo fhe conveyed her Affiftance to fome of better Rank, in fuch a Manner as made it doubly acceptable.
How far her Bounty extended was known to herfelf alone; but much of it appeared, to her Honour and God's Glory,
in frequent Diftributions to the Poor, and efpecially to the Charity Schools round about the Country,
in relieving thofe in Prifon, and delivering many out of it, in contributing to Churches of the Englifh Eftablifhment
abroad, as well as aiding feveral at home, in cloathing and feeding her indigent Neighbours,
and teaching their Children, fome of whom every Sunday, by Turns, fhe entertained at her Houfe,
and condefcended to examine them herfelf; befides this continual, it might be faid this daily, Courfe of Liberality
during her Life. She bequeathed at her Death, towards founding a College in the Ifland of Bermudas 500 l.;
to the Grey Coat Hofpital, in St. Margaret's, Weftminfter, 500 l.;
to the Blue Coat Hofpital in Weftminfter, 500 l.;
to the Charity School of Chrift Church, Parifh of Southwark, 400 l.;
to augment the Living of this Place, 1200 l.;
to put out poor Children Apprentices, the Intereft of 400 l. for ever; of which Summe 160 l. had been
left by Mr. Clarke and Mr. Bovey;
to be diftributed, as her Executrix fhould think fit, among thofe whom fhe had put out Apprentices in her Life-time 400 l.;
laftly, fhe defigned the re-building of this Chapel, which pious Defign of hers
was fpeedily executed by Mrs. Mary Pope.

A Monument is erected to her Memory in Westminster Abbey, with the following Inscription:

To the Memory of Mrs. Catharina Bovey,
whofe Perfon and Underftanding would have become the higheft Rank in Female Life, and
whofe Vivacity would have recommended her in the beft Converfation; but by Judgment,
as well as Inclination, fhe chofe fuch a Retirement as gave her great Opportunities in Reading and Reflection,
which fhe made Ufe of to the wifeft Purpofes of Improvement in Knowledge and Religion.
Upon other Subjects fhe ventured far out of the common Way of thinking; but in Religious Matters
fhe made the Holy Scriptures, in which fhe was well fkilled, the Rule and Guide of her Faith and Actions,
efteeming it more fafe to rely upon the plain Word of God, than to run into any Freedoms of Thought
upon revealed Truths, the great Share of Time allowed to the Clofet was not perceived in her Œconomy;
for fhe had always a well ordered and well inftructed Family, from the happy Influence,
as well of her Temper and Conduct, as of her uniform and exemplary Chriftian Life.
It pleafed God to blefs her with a confiderable Eftate, which, with a liberal Hand,
guided by Wifdom and Piety, fhe employed to his Glory, and the Good of her Neighbours.
Her domeftick Expences were managed with a Decency and Dignity fuitable to her Fortune;
but with a Frugality that made her Income abound to all proper Objects of Charity,
to the Relief of the Neceffitous, and Encouragement of the Induftrious, and the Inftruction of the Ignorant.
She diftributed not only with Cheerfulnefs, but with Joy, which, upon fome Occafions of raifing and
refrefhing the Spirit of the Afflicted, fhe could not refrain from breaking forth into Tears,
flowing from a Heart thoroughly affected with Compaffion and Benevolence.
Thus did many of her good Works, while fhe lived, go up as a Memorial before God;
and fome fhe left to follow her.

She died Jan. 21, 1726, in the 57th Year of her Age
at Flaxley, her Seat in Gloucefterfhire,
and was buried there, where her Name will be
long remembered, and where feveral of her Benefactions
at that Place, as well as others, are particularly recorded.

This Monument was erected, with the utmoft Refpect
to her Memory, and Juftice to her Character, by her
Executrix Mrs. Mary Pope, who lived with her near
40 Years in perfect Friendfhip, never once interrupted
till her much lamented Death.

To the Memory of Mary Pope,
Daughter of John Pope, of Briftol, Merchant,
the Friend of Mrs. Bovey, and Partner of her Virtues, who, after a Life fpent in
exemplary Piety, and full of good Works, died March 24,
in the Year of our Lord 1746, aged 81 Years.

I N

IN THE CHURCH YARD.

On a Tablet against the Church:

In Memory of the
excellent Mrs. Elizabeth Cowling,
Daughter of John Cowling, Efq.
who left this Life for a bleffed Eternity,
Sept. 16, 1759, aged 42 Years.

ON TOMBS.

William Heyley,
died July 20, 1784, aged 76.

Elizabeth his Wife
died July 25, 1785, aged 83.

Edward Williams
died June 5, 1755, aged 31.

Cecil his Mother
died Jan. 25, 1773, aged 84.

Thomas Hull
died Oct. 27, 1764, aged 83.

Elizabeth his Wife
died March 26, 1722, aged 39.

Mary his fecond Wife
died Sept. 28, 1723.

Edmund Green
died Sept. 8, 1721, aged 73.

Ephraim his Son
died Sept. 5, 1705, aged 12.

Margaret Green
died Dec. 30, 1732, aged 72.

Edmund Green,
died April 23, 1748, aged 52.

Blanch, the Wife of
John Smith, of the Grove,
in the Parifh of Weftbury,
died Jan. 13, 1785, aged 74.

ON HEAD AND FLAT STONES.

	Died	Aged
Elizabeth, Wife of Charles Rofe, of the Parifh of Chapel Hill, in the County of Monmouth	2 Apr. 1775	42
Elizabeth, Wife of Charles Rofe	31 Mar. 1780	47
Mary Trafford	7 Mar. 1778	63
Arnel Wallington	1 Jan. 1763	64
John Evens	21 Nov. 1735	45
Sarah his Daughter	—— 1732	6
Thomas Burgum	25 Nov. 1748	69
William Nourfe	11 Aug. 1771	68
Mary his Wife	12 Oct. 1749	45

	Died	Aged
Mary, Wife of Thomas Lodge	28 Nov. 1708	—
Thomas Lodge	7 Apr. 1722	55
Richard Conftable	3 June, 1733	35
Ann, Wife of Roger Blewett	8 Mar. 1721	79
Robert Hillier	12 Feb. 1779	67
Mary, Wife of Edmund Green, late Wife of Thomas Hill	7 Oct. 1769	62
James Mann	1 Nov. 1697	49
Mary his Wife	18 Dec. 1676	—
Richard Hazell	8 May, 1701	59
Richard Hazell	12 May, 1722	—

CXXI.

CXXI. FORTHAMPTON.

FORTHELMINTON, or commonly *Forthington*, is a Parifh of about five Miles in Extent, in the lower Divifion of the Hundred of *Tewkefbury*, from whence it is three Miles diftant Weftward, and eight North from the City of GLOUCESTER. The Boundaries are clofed on the North by a part of *Worcefterfhire*, and the River *Severn* forms them on the Eaft. The Soil is chiefly of a deep Clay, and applied to Pafturage: it is likewife very productive of Oak and Elm Timber.

The Benefice is a Cure, ftipendiary from the Impropriation, and in the Appointment of the Impropriator, who is charged with a yearly Payment of 13*l.* 6*s.* 8*d.* as fettled upon the Suppreffion of the Abbey of *Tewkefbury*. It is a Peculiar of *Deerhurft*.

In the Year 1789, fuch Repairs were made to the Church that no difcriminating marks of Antiquity remain. It is a fpacious Building, dedicated to *St. Mary*, with a ftrong embattled Tower. The neat Pews were made at the Expence of the Lord of the Manor.

As a Member of the great Lordfhip of *Tewkefbury*, this Manor was retained by the Crown, at the Compilation of Domefday. King HENRY II. granted it the *Benedictines* of *Tewkefbury* by Royal Charter, in whom it was vefted till the Diffolution. The Abbot had here a Country Refidence and private Chapel, the Site and Parts of which are the prefent Manfion. JOHN WAKEMAN, the laft Abbot, after his Refignation and Confecration as firft Bifhop of GLOUCESTER, frequently retired here, and died in 1549. But he muft be confidered as a Tenant only, for the Demefne was granted to GILES HARPUR in 1542, 23 HEN. VIII.

The Manor reverting to the Crown, was given by K. JAMES, in 1607, the 5th of his Reign, to ROBERT CECIL, Earl of *Salifbury*, and was afterward transferred to ARTHUR CAPEL, Earl of *Effex*, in the Reign of CHARLES II. His Son fold it to CHARLES DOWDESWELL, Efq. Son of RICHARD DOWDESWELL, Efq. of *Pull Court*, who was fucceeded by his Sons CHARLES and RICHARD. CHARLES DOWDESWELL, Son of the laft mentioned RICHARD, conveyed it, by Deed of Sale, to SAMUEL CLARKE, Efq. from whom it paffed, in the fame Manner, to Dr. ISAAC MADOX, Bifhop of *Worcefter*, about 1750, whofe Daughter and fole Heir is the Wife of the Hon. Dr. JAMES YORKE, fucceffively Bifhop of St. David's, *Gloucefter*, and *Ely*, who, in her right, is the prefent Proprietor.

The Family of HAYWARD, otherwife Cox, in the beginning of the laft Century, became poffeffed of confiderable Property in this Parifh, a great Part of which was lately purchafed by the prefent Lord of the Manor. HOPEWELL HAYWARD, Gent. has the only exclufive Eftate of confequence.

HAMLETS.—*Swailley* and *Down End*, of which is nothing worthy remark.

BENEFACTIONS.

1617. JOHN RESTELL gave, by Deed, Land for the Ufe of the Poor, now producing yearly 15*s.*
1738. Dec. 20, ELIZABETH HAYWARD bequeathed 5*l.* for Bread to be given to the Poor.
1784. Dec. 3. ELIZABETH NEWMAN left Money, the Annual Produce of which is 5*l.*, to be given to the Poor, at the Difcretion of her Executor.

* " Ego autem ipfe Rex HENRICUS dedi eidem Ecclefiæ unam villam quæ fuit de honore ROBERTI, filii HAIMONIS; poft " mortem ejufdem ROBERTI, dedi eam et pro animâ ipfius. Villa ipfa vocatur *Ferthelmenton*." DUGDALE Mon. vol. I. p. 163. Pat. 38 EDW. III. m. 13. " Pro tenementis in *Fordehampton*."

+ " Maner Places longing to the Abbate of *Tewkefbyri*. *Fordehampton* a faire Place upon *Severne* in dextrâ ripâ, a Mile beneth *Theokefbyri*." LELAND's Itin. vol. VI. p. 94.

‡ JOHN WAKEMAN, alias WICH, or as WOOD (FASTI, vol. I. p. 479) calls him, ROBERT WAKEMAN, was the laft Abbot of *Tewkefbury*. He continued till the Diffolution 1539, when he furrendered the Abbey with thirty-five of his Monks, and had a Penfion affigned to him of 266*l.* 13*s.* 4*d.* per. ann. as may be feen in BURNET's Hiftory of the Reformation. In Sept. 1541, being then B. D. he was confecrated the firft Bifhop of GLOUCESTER. He died about the Beginning of Dec. 1549. In his Life-time he erected a Tomb for his Place of Burial in the Abbey Church of *Tewkefbury*, in the North Side of a little Chapel, ftanding South-eaft from the high Altar. Bifhop GODWYN (*de Præfulibus Angliæ*) fays, that he was buried at *Worthington* (evidently meaning *Forthington*) in the County of GLOUCESTER, where he had a Houfe and Chapel. WILLIS's Mit. Abb. p. 259.

It is faid in HEARNE's Preface to ROBERT of GLOUCESTER, p. xxi. that in 1540, at a Convocation, feveral Bifhops were appointed to perufe the Tranflation of the Bible; and that the Revelations of St. JOHN were affigned to JOHN WAKEMAN, Bifhop of GLOUCESTER, and JOHN CHAMBERS, Bifhop of *Peterborough*.

PERPETUAL

<table>
<tr><td>

PERPETUAL CURATES.
1781 William Parsons, LL. B.
1789 Charles Platt, M. A.

</td><td>

PATRONS.
Dr. James Yorke, Bishop of GLOUCESTER.
Dr. James Yorke, Bishop of Ely.

</td></tr>
</table>

PRESENT LORD OF THE MANOR,

The Honourable and Right Reverend JAMES Lord Bishop of ELY.

The Person summoned from this Place by the Heralds in 1682 and 1683, was

Charles Dowdeswell, Esq.

At the Election in 1776, Four Freeholders polled from this Parish.

The earliest Date in the Register occurs in 1678.

ANNUAL ACCOUNT OF MARRIAGES, BIRTHS, AND BURIALS, IN THIS PARISH.

A.D.	Mar.	Bir.	Bur.	A.D.	Mar.	Bir.	Bur.	A.D.	Mar.	Bir.	Bur.	A.D.	Mar.	Bir.	Bur.
1781	4	10	4	1786	5	10	10	1791				1796			
1782	1	14	9	1787	3	17	3	1792				1797			
1783	4	11	6	1788	5	11	11	1793				1798			
1784	4	16	9	1789	6	13	8	1794				1799			
1785	1	16	11	1790	1	18	6	1795				1800			

INSCRIPTIONS IN THE CHURCH.

IN THE CHANCEL.

ON A MARBLE MONUMENT.

Arms ; Or, a Fefs wavy, between fix Billets Sable, for DOWDESWELL, impaling Gules, a Chevron Argent pellettee, charged with two Barrs Gemelles of the Field, between three Lions Heads, erafed Or, for COLLES.

Hic infra Reconduntur
Cineres Notabilis viri CAROLI
DOWDESWELL, ex hac Parochia
Amigeri.
Filius erat RICHARDI DOWDESWELL,
nuper de Pool-Court,
in Comitatu Wigorn,
Armigeri natu maximus,
vir Probitate et Induftria infignia,
quippe qui paternas opes laudabili
modo ampliavit.
Duos filios, CAROLUM fcilicet
et RICHARDUM ; et tres filias,
MARGARETAM,
GEORGIO SMYTH,
Armigero, de North Nibley,
in hoc comitatu, nuptam ;
ELIZABETHAM, GUALTERO
YATE de Bromfborowe,
in com. prædict. defponfatam ;
et ANNAM, adhuc Virginem,
fuperftites reliquit,
ex ELIZABETHA filia TIM. COLES,
de Hatfield, in comitatu Hertford,
Armigeri fufceptos. Annos vixit
feptuaginta et duos,
et tandem divitiarum
et deliciarum hujus mundi
fatur, melioribus politus,
obiit 21 die Octobris,
Anno Chrifti 1706.

ON A SMALL TABLET.

In Memory of my much honoured
Hufband JOHN RASTELL,
who died in the Yeare 1631.
ELIZABETH RASTELL,
mourning, did this.

ON FLAT STONES.

Here lieth the Body of
THOMAS COCKES, alias HAYWARD,
who died the 15th of May 1620.

Here lieth the Body of
THOMAS HAYWARD,
of the Lower Houfe,
who died Dec. 18, Anno 1641.

Here lieth the Body of
WILLIAM UNDERHILL, the Sonne of
JOHN UNDERHILL of Forthampton,
in the County of Gloucefter,
who departed this Life
the 10th Day of April
Anno Dom. 1647.

ON A MARBLE STONE.

Arms ; DOWDESWELL as before, impaling, Or, an Efcallop Sable, between two Bendlets Gules, for TRACEY.

This Marble Stone was laid
by the Widow, 1716,
in Memory of her much honoured
Hufband CHARLES DOWDESWELL, Esq.
late of Forthampton Court.
He married ANN eldeft Daughter
of the Hon. Mr. JUSTICE TRACEY,
by whom he had two Children.
His Son CHARLES is interred with him.
his Daughter ANN furvived him,
He died very much lamented,
the 30th of May 1713,
in the 26th Year of his Age.

Here lyeth the Body of
MARGARET, the Wife of
JOSEPH GEORGE of this Parifh,
who departed this life the
18th of Oct. 1761, aged 33 Years.

ON FLAT STONES IN THE NAVE.

Arms ; On a Bend cotifed three Cinquefoils for BETTS impaling COLLES as before.

Here lieth the Body of
ALICE BETTS, Widdow,
Wife of RICHARD BETTS, Gent.
and Daughter of JOHN COLLES, Efq.
who died July 22, 1694.

Arms; Argent, on a Bend Sable, three Fleurs de Lis, Or on a Chief of the fecond, a Lion Paffant, of the third, for HAYWARD, impaling a Crofs patonce for WARD.

Motto, " Virtute non Sanguine."
H. S. E.
HOPEWELLUS HAYWARD, Gen.
probitate et induftria infignis
Obiit 20 Die Jan. Anno Dom. 1722,
Ætatis 76°.
Hic quoque jacet
ELIZABETH HAYWARD,
ejus Uxor, Septem Liberorum mater;
Qualis erat Supremus ille
Dies indicabit in quo omnes
a Deo laudem accipient. Ob. 26°
Feb. 1728, Ætatis 50.

H. S. E.
24° Decembris 1746,
MARIA Chariffima Uxor
HOPEWELL HAYWARD, Gen.
filia GULIELMI SURMAN de Tredington
in Com. GLOUC. Armigeri,
quinque filiorum & feptem filiarum
Mater ; e quibus tres filii, viz.
HOPEWELL, æt. 9, PACKER 5
menfium, et MICHAEL unius anni,
et una filia ELIZABETHA,
fex menfium, jacent fepulti,
juxta cum Avo et Avia HOPEWELL,
et ELIZABETHA HAYWARD.
In eodum tumulo fepultus eft quod
mortale fuit HOPEWELL HAYWARD,
Gen. qui poft vitam laudabiliter actam
fummo bonorum luctu animam
afflavit fuam 13mo Octobris 1766,
Ætatis 63.

7 O

IN

IN THE CHURCH YARD, ON TOMBS.

PHILLIP HAYWARD, Gent.
died June 5, 1714, aged 62 Years.

PHILLIPPA and ELIZABETH
twin Daughters of the said
PHILLIP HAYWARD
died the 25th May 1715,
ELIZABETH died the 9th Oct. 1738.

————

THOMAS HAYWARD, Gent.
died July 31, 1742, aged 66.

MARY his Wife,
died April 18, 1759,
in the 91st Year of her Age.

Job. C. 17 and 14.
MARY, Wife of
PHILLIP HAYWARD, Gent.
and Daughter of JOHN STURMY,
of Swindon in this County, Gent.
died August 22, 1683, aged 34.

Also Mrs. ELEANOR STURMY,
only Sister to Mrs. MARY HAYWARD,
died Sept. 3, 1693, aged 54.

————

SUSANNAH Wife of RICHARD HILL,
of Dymock, Gent.
died July 14, 1730, aged 52 Years.

————

JOHN IRELAND, sen.
died April 12, 1785, aged 77 Years.

MARY his Wife,
died April 30, 1729, aged 77 Years.

MARY Daughter of
EDWARD and SARAH IRELAND,
died Jan. 10, 1784, aged 2 Years.

EDWARD their Son
died Dec. 9, 1785, an Infant.

PRISCILLA their Daughter,
died Oct. 18, 1787, aged 11 Months,

SARAH his Wife,
died Jan. 6, 1789, aged 27 Years.

ON FLAT AND HEAD STONES.

	Died	Aged
John Neast	16 Apr. 1755	62
George Rider	13 June, 1761	58
Samuel his Son by Ann his Wife	13 Nov. 1769	26
Richard Newman	25 Dec. 1732	60
Benjamin his Son	11 Feb. 1729	19
Richard his Son	24 Oct. 1766	56
William Penson	10 Nov. 1766	66
Sarah his Wife	4 May, 1744	35
Mary Wife of John Brookes	2 Sept. 1691	60
Ann Wife of Jonathan Stephens	2 May, 1707	—
Richard White	17 Mar. 1721	70
Margaret his Wife	15 July, 1750	76
Nicholas Hatton, sen. Gent.	17 May, 1681	74
John Hatton	24 Aug. 1669	—
Elizabeth his Wife	1 Dec. 1692	—
Canaan Wife of John Hatton	6 June, 1700	55
John Parish	21 Sept. 1785	51
William Perkins	13 Sept. 1734	42
Sarah his Wife	19 Feb. 1774	76
John their Son	9 Mar. 1767	36
Two of his Children died Infants		
William Maysie of Longdon	23 Feb. 1767	26
John Man	4 May, 1687	—
Mary his Wife	22 Apr. 1700	—
John Man, sen.	12 Aug. 1714	58
Margaret his Wife	6 Feb. 1712	55
Mary Wife of William Man	24 Nov. 1768	78
Mary Wife of Charles Mason	27 Feb. 1730	—
Robert Newman	5 Aug. 1713	40
Margaret Wife of John Willis	17 Mar. $172\frac{5}{6}$	53
Elizabeth his Wife, Daughter of the Rev. Mr. Thompson, Vicar of Eldersfield,	14 Apr. 1738	63
Hannah their Daughter	8 June, 1717	19
John Willis	17 Jan. 1725	57
Richard Foaks	2 June, 1731	67
Thomas Smith	13 July, 1741	23
Mary Wife of John George	30 Apr. 1746	46
Mary Daughter of Thomas and Mary Pensam	29 May, 1770	—
Margaret Tomb	2 Feb. 1746	40
Elizabeth Hartland	22 Oct. 1749	37
Samuel Jefferies, sen.	15 Aug. 1761	64
Samuel Jefferies, jun.	29 Oct. 1757	24
Sarah Wife of John Jefferies	10 Dec. 1701	—
John Son of Peter and M. Whithorne	25 Aug. 1759	23
Mary his Mother	13 Feb. 1777	68
Thomas Howbrook	21 Dec. 1784	39
John his Son	14 Dec. 1784	15
Thomas Weston	23 Apr. 1789	62
Elizabeth his Wife	10 Aug. 1788	38
James Evans	11 Sept. 1774	62
Elizabeth his Wife	18 Mar. 1770	56
Two of their Children died Infants		
John Stubbes	2 Jan, 1753	52
William Son of John and Hannah Bennett	5 Jan. 1763	7
William their sixth Son	26 Dec. 1768	
John Crees	24 Dec. 1785	41
Susannah his Daughter died an Infant		

CXXII.

CXXII. FRAMPTON COTTEREL,

OR *COTEL*, the Name of its ancient Proprietors, is a Parifh in the Hundred of *Langley* and *Swinef-head*, five Miles diftant from *Sodbury* on the South-weft, feven South from *Thornbury*, and thirty in the fame Direction from the City of GLOUCESTER. The Soil is of a red Grit, mixed with fer-ruginous Particles, and the greater Portion in Pafture, including more than 2000 Acres.

The Benefice is a Rectory, in the Deanery of *Hawkefbury*, endowed with an extenfive Glebe, the Advowfon of which was formerly annexed to the Manor. In 1744 WILLIAM SOUTHWELL, Efq. who had purchafed the Eftate of the Family of SYMES in this Parifh, prefented on that Claim; but in the Year 1765, it appearing that the Right had defcended in certain Parts to the Co-heirs of HENRY SYMES, Efq. and their Reprefentatives, the following Arrangement of Prefentation was confirmed. 1. His Grace HENRY Duke of *Beaufort*, by Defcent from ELIZABETH, the eldeft Daughter of the faid HENRY SYMES, the Wife of RICHARD BERKELEY, Efq. of *Stoke Gifford*. 2. and 3. WILLIAM SOUTH-WELL, Efq. by Purchafe from EDWARD BISSE HALE, Efq. whofe Grandmother was JANE, the fecond Daughter, and Wife of EDWARD BISSE, Efq. of *Inglefcombe*, co. *Somerfet*. 4. ROBERT BUXTON, Efq. Nephew of the late JOHN JACOB, Efq. of *Norton*, co. *Wilts*, whofe Mother was SUSANNAH, the youngeft Daughter and Co-heir. 5. Duke of BEAUFORT. 6. and 7. W. SOUTHWELL, Efq. 8. ROBERT BUXTON, Efq. 9. W. SOUTHWELL, Efq.

The Church, dedicated to *St. Peter*, is a Building in the neat Gothic Style of the middle Centuries, with a South Aile, and a Tower embattled and pinnacled, with Niches, in which are Effigies of Saints. The high Altar was dedicated in July 1315, by WALTER DE MAYDENSTONE, Bifhop of *Worcefter*. A MS. of Mr. SMYTH, dated 1607, mentions the following Arms as then remaining in the Windows; 1. Ermine, a Fefs chequè, Or, and Azure, ARDEN impaling Quarterly per Fefs, indented Argent and Azure ACTON. 2. ACTON impaling Argent, a Cheveron between three Falcons rifing, Gules. 3. Gules, three Lozenges in Fefs, Ermine; D'AUBENY impaling 1. Sable fix Swallows in Pile, Argent, ARUNDEL. 2. Azure a Bend and Label of three Points, Or; CARMINOWE. 3. Gules an Orle, within an Ina-luron, Argent, CHEDIOCKE, 4th as 1ft. 4. Barry of 8, Or, and Sable, POYNTZ. In 1315, 7 EDW. II. the Family of ACTON were feifed of a Mill and eighty Acres in this Parifh, and were probably Con-tributors to this Edifice.

In *Domefday*, the Manor taxed at five Hides was given by the CONQUEROR to WALTER, *Baliftarius Regis* *, or the Crofsbowman of the King's Perfon. His Defcendants took the Surname of COTEL, which Family became extinct in 1255, 39 HEN. III. To them fucceeded ROBERT WALERAN, who in 1285, 15 EDW. I. proved upon a *quo warranto* his Right to Markets and Fairs. In the next Reign 1319, JOHN DE WILLINGTON held it as of the Honour of WALLINGFORD, whofe Defcendants poffeffed it till it paffed by Marriage of JOAN WILLINGTON to JOHN WRATH or WRIOTHESLEY in 1397, 20 RICH. II. JOHN their Son dying S. P. in 1412, this Manor was divided between his two Sifters, ELIZABETH the Wife of Sir WILLIAM PULTON, and ISABEL the Wife of WILIAM BEAUMONT, who inherited her Sifters Moiety. Sir THOMAS BEAUMONT her Heir died 1451, 29 HEN. VI., and in 1505, 20th HENRY VII. the Manor was conveyed to the Crown. In 1515 GILES Baron D'AUBENEY, was appointed Conftable of the Caftle of *Briftol*, and had this Manor in Fee †, in both of which in the next Reign he was fuc-ceeded by EDWARD SEYMOUR Duke of *Somerfet*. After his Attainder, the Manor was demifed from the Crown in 1557 to the Family of BASSET. About 1730 it was transferred to WILLIAM PLAYER, Efq. of *Mangotsfield* and *Acton Iron*, whofe Defcendant of that Name fold it to CHARLES BRAGGE, Efq. in 175... In 1788 ROBERT TUCKER, Gent. became poffeffed of it by Purchafe from EDWARD HOSKINS, Efq. But the chief Eftate, upon which is a very large ancient Manfion, was detached from the Manor by K. HENRY VIII. and given to Sir JOHN SEYMOUR, the Father EDWARD Duke of *Somerfet*, and Sir HENRY SEYMOUR, to the latter of whom he bequeathed it. His Son and Succeffor was Sir JOHN SEYMOUR of *Bitton* and *Frampton Cottrel*, Knight of the Shire for this County. ANNE his eldeft Co heir was the Wife of HENRY SYMES, Efq. who purchafed the remaining Intereft in their Eftate. EDWARD BISSE, Efq. re-ceived it in Dower with JANE fecond Daughter and Co-heir of the faid HENRY SYMES. AMY Daughter of EDWARD BISSE married GABRIEL HALE of *Alderley*, Grandfon of Chief Juftice HALE, and was

---

* KING WILLIAM the Conqueror conftituted an Officer ftyled, " Arbaliftarius Rejes", who was continued by his Succeffors. His Lands were held in Capite of the King by the Service of prefenting annually a Crofsbow, and of finding thread to make a Crofsbow ftring as often as the King paffed through a certain Diftrict. KELHAM on *Domefday*, p. 157. BLOUNT's ancient Tenures, pp. 57. 70. 81. Pref. to *Grofe's* Antiq. p. 31.

† BARRET's *Briftol*, p. 221.

4

fucceeded

fucceeded by Edward Bisse Hale, Efq. who died in 1735, and the Eftate was foon after fold to William Southwell, Efq. who is the prefent Proprietor.

Wickwick is the only Tything, and is confidered as a feparate Manor: it was originally a Part of the Eftate of the Seymours in this Parifh. In the Reign of Q. Eliz. it paffed to Roger Kemys, Efq. and continued in his Defcendants till it was conveyed by marriage fettlement to Robert Brown, Gent. with Anne the eldeft Co-heir of William Kemys; by whom fhe left a Daughter Mary afterward the Wife of Clayton Milborne, who died in 1712.

Francis Brown, Efq. was the fubfequent Poffeffor, whofe eldeft Daughter married John Daubeney, Efq. of *Briftol*, who inherits in her Right.

No Benefactions to the Poor.

Incumbents.	Patrons.	Incumbents.	Patrons.
1553 Thomas Dylke,	Q. Mary.	1667 Miles Muggleworth, M.A.	The fame.
David Jones,	————	1671 Samuel Alway,	Henry Wafborough and
1571 John Albert,	John Seymour, Efq.		John Clements, *pro hâc vice.*
1573 Daniel Lane,	Arthur Baffet, Efq.	1704 George Bryant,	John Berkeley, Efq.
1574 Robert Colmore*,	Arthur Baffet, Efq.	1745 Thomas Moore, D.D.	Will. Southwell, Efq.
1622 Henry Baynham,	John Gilbert.	1765 John Wickes,	The fame.
1639 Thomas Davyes, A.B.	Anne Baynham.	1770 Phillip Blifs, M.A.	John Jacob, Efq.
1667 Edward Batten, M.A.	Humph. Hooke, Efq.		

Present Proprietors of the Manors,

Of Frampton Cotterel.

Robert Tucker, Gent.

Of Wickwick.

John Daubeney, Efq.

The only Perfons fummoned from this Parifh by the Heralds in 1682 and 1683, were

Henry Symes, Efq. and Clayton Milbourne, Efq.

At the Election in 1776 Twenty-eight Freeholders polled from this Parifh and its Hamlets.

The prefent Regifter commences in 1561, and is perfect to 1639 from which Period to 1653 no Entries were made; from 1653 to the prefent Time it is accurate and entire.

Annual Account of Marriages, Births, and Burials, in this Parish.

A.D.	Mar.	Bir.	Bur.	A.D.	Mar.	Bir.	Bur.	A.D.	Mar.	Bir.	Bur.	A.D.	Mar.	Bir.	Bur.
1781	4	30	12	1786	3	28	14	1791				1796			
1782	3	30	19	1787	13	42	18	1792				1797			
1783	5	28	14	1788	7	30	12	1793				1798			
1784	5	17	22	1789	5	41	20	1794				1799			
1785	11	35	24	1790				1795				1800			

INSCRIPTIONS IN THE CHURCH.
IN MILBORN'S AISLE.

On Atchievements.

1. Sable, a Cheveron between three Mullets Argent, for Browne; impaling, Vert, on a Cheveron Argent, three Pheons Sable, for Kemys.

2. Browne, quartering Kemys.

3. Argent, a Crofs moline Sable, in the dexter Chief Point a Mullet Gules, for Milborne; on an Efcocheon, Browne, quartering Kemys.

On Flat Stones.

Here lyeth the Body of Mary, the Wife of Clayton Milborn, Gent. only Daughter and Heir of Robert Brown, Gent. by his Wife Ann, Daughter and Co-heir of William Kemys, of Wickwick, Efq. who died January 13, 1707.

Alfo here lyeth the Body of the faid Clayton Milborn, Efq. who died January the 25th, 1712, aged 63 Years.

Alfo Here lieth the Body of Henry Milborne, Gent. only Son of the faid Clayton Milborn by the faid Mary his Wife, who died the 19th March 1715-6, aged 34 Years.

Here lyeth the Body of Ann Milborne, Daughter of Clayton Milborne, Efq. and Mary his Wife, who departed this Life the 4th Day of January 1755.

* " It appears from the Books of the Regiftrar of this Diocefe, that this Prefentation was difputed by John Seymour, Efq.
" who nominated Walter Roch, Clerk. A Writ " De Jure Patronatûs," to enquire into the Right of Prefentation, was iffued
" from the Chancellor's Court, Dec. 4, 1574, and on Feb. 3, 1574-5, Arthur Basset's Claim as Lord of the Manor was
" confirmed, and Robert Colemore received Inftitution."

5

Here

Here lyeth the Body of
ROBERT BROWN, Gent.
who died in September 1679.

Here lieth the Body of
ANN, Daughter and
Coheir of WILLIAM KEMYS,
of Wickwick, in this Parifh, Efq.
and Wife of ROBERT BROWN, Gent.
who died in September 1692.

Within this Ile are likewife
interred the Bodyes of the
faid WILLIAM KEMYS
her Father, ARTHUR KEMYS her
Grandfather, and ROGER KEMYS her
Great-grandfather, Efquires.

Arms; on a Lozenge, a Fefs cottifed, and in Chief two Mullets for
PLAYER.

Here lyeth the Body of
Mrs. ISABELLA PLAYER,
Daughter of WILLIAM, and Sifter of
THOMAS PLAYER, Efq.
the prefent Lord of this Manor,
who departed this Life
the 16th Day of June, 1736.

Here lyeth the Body of
JOHN SYMES, of Poundisford,
in the Parifh of Pitmifter,
in the County of Somerfet, Efq.
He was born on the 4th Day of March,
1572.
He lived foberly, righteoufly, and godlily,
and dyed on the 21ft Day of
October, 1661.

Arms; Azure, three Efcallops in
Pale Or, for SYMES.

Here lyeth the Body of
HARRY SYMES, Efq.
Son of JOHN SYMES, Efq.
under the adjacent Marble,
who marryed the Daughter of
Sir JOHN SEYMOUR, Knight,
formerly of this Parifh.
He departed this Life
the 1ft Day of November,
Anno Domini 1682, ætatis fuæ 73.
He was a loving Hufband, a good
Father, and ever a cordial Friend,
where he profeffed Friendfhip.

Here lyeth the Body of
ANN SYMES, Widow,
and Relict of HARRY SYMES, Efq.
who departed this Life
on the 25th Day of May A. D. 1686.
She was the Daughter of

Sir JOHN SEYMOUR, Knight,
formerly of this Parifh,
by Dame ANN his firft Wife,
the Daughter of WILLIAM POULETT,
of Cottles, in the County of Wilts, Efq.
Son of my Lord GILES POULETT,
fourth Son of WILLIAM POULETT,
Marquis of Winchefter, and
Lord High Treafurer of England.
Great was her Birth, greater her Virtues,
the beft of Wives, the beft of Mothers,
the beft of Women.

Reader! thou ftandeft on the facred
Duft of a virtuous handfome Maid,
AMY, the Daughter of
HARRY SYMES and ANNE his Wife,
Daughter of Sir JOHN SEYMOUR.
She was in her Deportment to her
Parents eximious, refpectful, dutiful,
obedient to a Proverb.
She never gave them Caufe to
afk her, why do you this?
She was fnatched from them by a
violent Sicknefs, which makes them
daily wafh their eyes with Salt Water.
She lies here in a ftill and quiet Sleep,
not to awake but by a loud Trump,
and then to rife in white, to fing
Hallelujahs to the Great GOD and Lamb
for ever. Amen.
She deceafed Jan. 9,
was buried Jan. 13, 1678.

ON A BRASS PLATE:

Arms; Azure, three Efcallops in Pale, Or, for SYMES;—impaling, Sable, two Hounds paffant Argent, for HORNER.

Reader, thou treadeft on the facred Afhes of JOHN SYMES, Efquire, who, in the late unhappy Times of Rebellion, was forc't (for his fignall Loyalty to his Prince) to leave his former Habitation at Poundisford, in the Parifh of Pitminfter, in the County of Somerfet, and
to feek a Repofe for his old Age in this Parifh. He was a Man greatly renowned for
Wifdom, Juftice, Integrity, and Sobriety; which Talents he did not hide in a Napkin, but
religioufly exercifed in the whole Conduct of his Life, efpecially in the Government of
that County, wherein he bore all the honourable Offices incident to a Country Gentleman, as
Knight of the Shire (elected, nemine contradicente) for the Parliament held at Weftminfter, in the 21ft Year of King JAMES, High Sheriff, Deputy Lieutenant for many Years,
and Juftice of the Peace for 40 Years and upwards. And as he was careful and folicitous
to difcharge his Duty to GOD, his Soveraigne, and his Country; fo GOD was pleafed to
beftow on him feverall Badges (alfo) of his fpeciall Favour, as Length of Days, accompanied with a moft healthy Conftitution of Body for above 80 Years, and of his Mind
to the laft; as alfo a numerous Pofterity, even of Children and Children's Children, to the
Number of 100 and upwards, defcended of his Loynes (by his only Wife AMY, the
Daughter of THOMAS HORNER, of Cloved, in the County of Somerfet, Efq.)
And when he was full of Dayes and Honour, having lived 88 Years, 7 Months, and 17 Days, and
feen the fafe Return of his Prince to his Crown and Kingdoms, after a long and horrible
exile, and thereby the flourifhing Condition, both of Church and State; having finifhed
his Work on Earth, he cheerfully refigned his Soul to GOD that gave it, the 21ft Day of
October, Anno Domini 1661, in full Affureance of a joyfull Refurrection.

ON FLAT STONES IN THE CHANCEL.

Here lyeth the Body
of JONATHAN TYLER,
who deceafed this
Life October the 28th,
aged 30 Years,
Anno Domini 1693.

M. S.
FRANCISÆ & ELIZABETHÆ
conjugum GEORGII BRYAN,
hujus Ecclefiæ Rectoris,
quæ fub hoc marmor
quiefcunt intumulatæ;
altera anno 1707,
altera 1732.
Cum filio impubere,
& filiâ feptemdecim annorum virgine.

M. S.
SIBYLEÆ uxoris MAURITII SMYTH,
Rectoris de Henton Bluet,
in comitat. Somerfet.

Et SUSANNÆ uxoris HENRICI DAVIS,
hujus parochiæ, generofi.
Altera hic compofita
anno exeunte 1737;
altera ineunte 1738.

Here lyeth the Body of
ELIZABETH, the Wife of
HENRY DAVIS,
of this Parifh,
who departed this Life
the 8th Day of February,
A. D. 1729, aged 32 Years.

HENRICI DAVIS,
hujus parochiæ, generofi.
Obiit Julii 18, A. D. 1754, æt. 74.

Alfo here lyeth the Body of
ELIZABETH, the Daughter of
HENRY and SUSANNA DAVIS,
who departed this Life
the 1ft Day of January,
A. D. 1732, aged 9 Weeks.

Here
lyeth the Body of
JANE, the Daughter of
GABRIEL HALE, Efq.
aad AMY his Wife,
who dyed the 30th Day of
November, 1699,
aged 7 Weeks.

---

7 P

Arms;

Arms; Sable, three Efcallops in Pale
Argent, for B I S S ;—impaling, Azure,
three Efcallops in Pale Or, for S Y M E S.

Here lyeth the Body of
J A N E, the Wife of
E D W A R D B I S S, Efq.
and Daughter of
H E N R Y S Y M E S, Efq.
both of this Parifh,
who died the 6th Day of Auguft, 1704.

Here lyeth the Body of
E D W A R D B I S S, Efq.
who departed this Life
the 20th Day April, 1696,
ætatis fuæ 48.

Here lyeth two Beauties,
two Vertues,
Daughters of H A R R Y S Y M E S, Efq.
and A N N E his Wife,
the Daughter of
Sir J O H N S E Y M O U R, of this Parifh.
E L I A N O R,   F R A N C E S,
deceafed
Sept. 26, 1672,   Dec. 17, 1671.
buryed
Oct. 1, 1672,   Dec. 21, 1671.

IN THE CHURCH YARD.   ON TOMBS.

Here lyeth the Body of
D A N I E L H O L D E R,
of this Parifh, Yeoman,
who departed this Life
the 27th Day of March, 1776,
in the 70th Year of his Age.

Alfo
S A M U E L, Son of
D A N I E L and M A R Y H O L D E R,
who died Sept. 18, 1773,
aged near 40 Years.

Alfo
J A M E S their Son
departed this Life Jan. 29, 1776,
aged 28 Years.

Underneath this Tomb
refteth the Body of
J O S E P H M I L L E T T,
of this Parifh, Yeoman,
who departed this Life
the 20th Day of Auguft,
Anno Domini 1690,
aged 57 Years.

Alfo
underneath refteth the Body of
F R A N C E S, the Wife of
J O S E P H M I L L E T T,
who departed this Life
the 17th Day of December,
Anno Domini 1702,
aged 65 Years.

In Memory of
J O S E P H M I L L E T T,
late of Stoke Gifford,
in this County,
who departed this Life
the 6th Day of January, 1768,
aged 85 Years.

In Memory of
J O H N, Son of
J O H N and H E S T E R H O R W O O D,
alias H A R W O O D,
of Grovenend, in the
Parifh of Alvefton,
who departed this Life
the 23d Day of January, 1748 9,
aged 22 Years.

Here lyeth the Body of
A N N W H I T E,
of this Parifh, Widow,
who departed this Life
the 14th Day of December, 1724,
ætat. fuæ 92.

Here lyeth the Body of
W I L L I A M S L O N D,
of this Parifh,
who died April 3, 1716,
aged 30 Years.

Here lyeth the Body of
G E O R G E, the fecond Son of
G E O R G E R O D M A N and
H A N N A H his Wife,
of this Parifh,
who departed this Life
the 2d Day of December,
Anno Domini 1708,
aged 16 Years and 10 Months.

Alfo
here lieth the Body of
W I L L I A M G I N G E L L,
of this Parifh,
who departed this Life
the 10th Day of February, 1750,
aged 44 Years.

Here alfo lyeth the Body of
E L I Z A B E T H his Wife
who died January 16, 1780,
aged 78 Years.

In Memory of
A N N, the Wife of
E D W A R D F R E E M A N,
of the City of Briftol,
and Daughter of
J O H N M I L L E T T and M A R Y his Wife,
of this Parifh,
who died Auguft the 19th, 1733,
in the 48th Year of her Age.

Alfo in Memory of
the aforefaid
E D W A R D F R E E M A N,
of the City of Briftol,
Haberdafher,
Son of F R A N C I S F R E E M A N,
of Bifhop's Froom, in the
County of Hereford, Gent.
who departed this Life
the 7th Day of May, 1739,
aged 44 Years.

Here lyeth the Body of
J A N E, Wife of W I L L I A M M I L L E T T,
of this Parifh, Gent.
and Daughter of D A N I E L C U R T I S,
of the Ifland of Jamaica, Efq.
who died May 6, 1765,
aged 51 Years.

Alfo
here lyeth the Body of the
aforefaid W I L L I A M M I L L E T T, Gent.
who departed this Life
December 22, 1769,
aged 55 Years.

Here lyeth the Body of
J O H N W A T K I N S,
who departed this Life
January 6, 1702, ætatis fuæ 60.

Here lyeth the Body of
S A R A H, the Wife of
J O H N W A T K I N S,
who departed this Life
June the 11th, 1712,
ætatis fuæ 72.

Underneath
lie the Remains of
the Rev. J A M E S B U L L E R, M. A.
Vicar of Kilton,
in the County of Somerfet,
who departed this Life
April 11, 1777, aged 72.

H. H. T.
G E O R G I U S B R Y A N,
H. E. R.
Obiit Martii 27°,
A. D. 1744,
æt. 71.

In Memory of
M A R Y, the Wife of
A B R A H A M D A V I S,
of this Parifh, Yeoman,
who departed this Life
June the 25th, 1705,
aged 39 Years.

Alfo
M A R Y their Daughter,
who departed this Life
November 15, 1711,
in the 7th Year of her Age.

Alfo
in Memory of
the aforefaid A B R A H A M D A V I S,
who was buried the
27th Day of December, 1741,
in the 62d Year of his Age.

O N

ON HEAD STONES.

	Died	Aged
Mary, Hannah, and Elizabeth, Daughters of Thomas and Betty Pullin, feverally died as follows: Mary, June 2, A. D. 1770, aged 11 Years. Hannah, June 6, A. D. 1770, aged 8 Years. Elizabeth, July 26, A. D. 1770, aged 14 Years. Likewife Sarah their Daughter, who died Dec. 29, 1772, aged near 6 Months.		
Henry Hibbs -	25 Aug. 1763	53
Joanna, Wife of Daniel Holder	10 Oct. 1765	40
Martha, Wife of Francis King	2 Nov. 1730	31
William Harris -	28 Apr. 1755	65
John Embly - -	17 Nov. 1770	50
Elizabeth, Wife of Joshua Bennett	4 Oct. 1725	53
James Gifford - -	1 Apr. 1757	50
Ann, Wife of James Gifford	13 Mar. 1779	75
George Bryant -	23 Jan. 1768	86
Elizabeth, Wife of George Bryant	14 Dec. 1753	74
Sarah, Joseph, and Jane, Son and Daughters of John and Martha Cook. Sarah died in 1743, aged 7 Weeks; Joseph, in 1751, aged 15 Years; and Jane, in 1753, aged 9 Years.		
Ralph Wickham -	8 May, 1758	73
Charles Parker -	20 July, 1749	55
Sarah, Wife of Charles Parker	— Nov. 1728	—
Abraham Huggins -	1 Apr. 1779	75
Susanna, Wife of Abraham Huggins	16 Mar. 1760	57
Abraham, Son of Abraham and Sufanna Huggins -	3 May, 1756	19
Alfo Isaac their Son -	6 Jan. 1772	33
Jacob Huggins, Son of the above	1 Apr. 1789	47
Joseph Gingell, fenior -	9 Jan. 1727	51
Joseph Gidgell, junior -	3 Mar. 1757	45
Ann, Wife of Joseph Gingell, fenior	10 Jan. 172 6/7	52
Ann, Widow of Joseph Gingell, jun.	6 Nov. 1762	43
Ann, Wife of Edward Webb	13 Aug. 1750	33
John Webb, fenior -	21 Apr. 1754	66
Joseph, Son of John Webb	27 Feb. 1737	12

	Died	Aged
Luke Webb - -	8 June, 1753	30
Mary Webb, Spinfter -	26 July, 1773	58
Mary, Wife of Isaac Jarratt	28 Jan. 1737	42
Ann, Daughter of Isaac and Mary Jarratt - -	22 July, 1737	14
Sufannna, Wife of Stephen Stout	8 Dec. 1737	67
Stephen Stout - -	10 Sept. 1760	61
Elizabeth, Wife of Stephen Stout	9 Feb. 1740	28
Simeon Turner -	14 Sept. 1768	36
Simeon his Son -	20 Jan. 1767	6
Elizabeth their Daughter -	5 June, 1770	1
Thomas Blanchard -	7 June, 1782	84
Ann, Wife of John Webb -	8 June, 1786	47
Elizabeth, Daughter of Thomas and Betty Hawkins -	14 May, 1770	4
Joseph Rodman - -	8 Jan. 1740	44
John, Son of William Millett, fenior	13 Apr. 1726	46
George, Son of William and Jane Millett - -	14 Aug. 1737	28
William Millett, fenior -	26 Mar. 1726	84
George Buck - -	15 Dec. 1745	72
Mary his Wife -	10 Jan. 1726	47
Rachel and Martha, two of their Daughters. Rachel -	13 Aug. 1712	10
Martha - -	6 Jan. 1713	10
Hannah, Daughter of Thomas and Hefter Smith - -	16 June, 1749	8
Simeon Turner -	4 Sept. 1711	49
Harry Chefter - -	29 Sept. 1731	46
Thomas Chefter -	20 Sept. 1733	38
Hannah, Relict of Thomas Chefter	— Jan. 1754	55
Bethiah Turner -	23 Oct. 1773	49
Richard Price - -	22 Dec. 1737	26
Ann, Wife of Mofes Pocock	11 Feb. 1779	54
John, the Son of Mofes and Ann Pocock - -	14 Jan. 1766	4
James Offer - -	31 Dec. 1775	47
William Offer - -	8 Sept. 1756	68
Martha his Wife -	6 May, 1783	80
William Flower -	28 Sept. 1762	55
Dinah, Wife of John Davis	26 Jan. 1768	32
Betty, Wife of Thomas Davis	16 Dec. 1777	74
John, Son of Thomas Davis and Betty his Wife -	12 Apr. 1757	26

FRAMPTON UPON SEVERN.

CXXIII. FRAMPTON upon SEVERN.

IN Diftinction, with refpect to the preceding Parifh, is fituate in the Hundred of *Whitftone*, which exercifes manerial Rights as paramount over all Parifhes within its Diftrict. It is diftant from *Stroud* eight Miles weftward, feven North from *Durfley*, five South from *Newenham*, croffing the River, and from GLOUCESTER ten on the South-weft. The whole Parifh is about two Miles fquare, of a Soil chiefly of fine Gravel; nearly equal Portions in Pafture and Tillage, including common arable Fields of 300 Acres. The Inhabitants have a Right of Commonage in *Slimbridge Warth*. The *Severn* forms the South-weft Boundary, and is more than a Mile acrofs; from the Shifting of the Sands, the current of the River is diverted from one Shore to the other; and it is remarkable, that of late Years, all Endeavours to prevent its Encroachments, have been infufficient.

The Living is vicarial, in the Deanery of *Durfley*. It is endowed with one third of the Profits of the Impropriation, and the Privy Tythes. It is faid, that the Impropriation belonged to the Abbey of *Cirencefter*; but is fo fpecified neither by DUGDALE or TANNER *. The Advowfon is annexed to it, and both were obtained by the Family of CLIFFORD; from whom they were transferred about the Beginning of the prefent Century, and are now vefted in ELIZABETH WICKS, Widow.

The Church was confecrated, and dedicated to *St. Mary*, in July 1315, by WALTER DE MAYDEN-STONE, Bifhop of *Worcefter* †. It is conftructed with a Nave, two Aifles, and a Chapel on either Side the Chancel. The Tower is of neat Gothic Architecture, having a deep and open embattled Parapet, with Pinnacles. In the North Aifle and Chapel, under Arcades, are two recumbent Effigies in Free-ftone, of a Croifader and a Lady, certainly of the CLIFFORDS; and a Conjecture is allowable, from the Date of the Dedication of the Church, and other Circumftances, that they were intended for WILLIAM CLIFFORD, who died in 1321, and CATHERINE DE MALTON his Wife. In the Eaft Window are Arms and Portraits of Saints. 1. Chequy Or and Azure, on a Bend Gules, three Lions paffant Or; CLIFFORD.

---

* Dr. PARSONS fays, that the Advowfon belonged to the Abbey of GLOUCESTER, and it feems to have been originally diftinct from the Impropriation. There is more room to fuppofe, that the Great Tythes were vefted in the Family of CLIFFORD at the Diffolution, and fo continued, than that they were forfeited by Attainder fince that Period, as Sir R. ATKINS afferts. For ED-MUND CLIFFORD prefented fo lately as 1691, as Heir of the elder Branch of the Family, after the Difperfion of their other Property. An Eftate, purchafed with Queen ANNE's Bounty, in the Parifh of *Slimbridge*, producing a neat annual Income of 33*l.* has been added to the Vicarage.

† THOMAS's Survey of the Cathedral of *Worcefter*, p. 162.

3

2. Argent,

2. Argent, a Crofs voided Gules; DE MALTON. 3. Gules, on a Bend Argent, a Martlet Sable; HOARE anciently. 4. Sable, an Eagle with two Heads difplayed Argent, within a Bordure engrailed of the fecond; HOARE modern. In another Window, BERKELEY *.

The CONQUEROR gave this Manor, taxed at nine Carucates or Plough-tillages, with other extenfive Grants in the Counties of *Hereford* and *Worcefter*, to his Follower DROGO FILIUS PUNTII, or FITZ-PONS, who died without Iffue in 1089. He was fucceeded by his Brother RICHARD †, who fettled it on his fecond Son WALTER, Lord of *Clifford Caftle*, co. *Hereford*, the Father of "*Fair Rofamond.*" RICHARD CLIFFORD ‡, a younger Son of the preceding, obtained it, and to Sir HUGH CLIFFORD his Heir, a Grant of Markets and Fairs was made in 1254, 38 HEN. III. which was confirmed in 1311, 4 EDW. II. In that Reign, it paffed to Sir JOHN CHIDIOCKE, who had married ISABEL, fole Daughter and Heir of ROBERT CLIFFORD. CATHERINE CHIDIOCKE was the Wife of Sir JOHN ARUNDEL, of *Llanberne*, in *Cornwall*, who died feized of the Manor in 1479, 19 EDW. IV. and bequeathed it to his Son Sir JOHN ARUNDEL, JOHN ARUNDEL, Efq. occurs in 1608, who, about 1630, fold it to HUMPHRY HOOKE, Alderman of *Briftol.* Sir HUMPHRY HOOKE died about the Clofe of the laft Century, leaving three Coheirs, from one of whom, the Family of GROVE, of *Ferns*, co. *Wilts*, derive their Right.

Concerning other Property, it appears, that HENRY, Brother of Sir HUGH CLIFFORD, purchafed Lands in *Frampton* of confiderable Value in 1284, 12 EDW. I. which paffed by regular Defcent to JOHN CLIFFORD, Efq. who died in 1684. MARY, the eldeft of his three Co-heirs, married NATHANIEL CLUTTERBUCK, of *Eaftington*, whofe Grandfon RICHARD CLUTTERBUCK, Efq. dying in 1775 left a Life Intereft in this Eftate to EDMUND PHILLIPS, Gent. and ELIZABETH his Wife, Daughter of WILLIAM BELL, Efq. of *Sainthurft* and *Gloucefter*, by CATHERINE his only furviving Sifter; and after their Demife to NATHANIEL WINCHCOMBE, Efq. of *Stratford Houfe*, in the Parifh of *Stroud*, and his Heirs, he being the only Son of ANNE, fecond Daughtea of the faid WILLIAM BELL, a lineal Defcendant from Sir THOMAS BELL, Knight, the munificent Mayor of *Gloucefter* in the Reign of King HENRY the Eighth §.

Upon the ancient Site, in 1731, R. CLUTTERBUCK, Efq. began the prefent Manfion, which is a large and handfome Edifice. The Houfe occupies the Centre with fpacious Wings as Offices, it is ornamented with Ionic Pilafters, and upon the Pediment, in bas relief, is an Efcutcheon, bearing, Quarterly, 1ft and 4th, Azure, a Lion rampant, and in Chief three Efcallops Argent, for CLUTTERBUCK; 2d and 3d, CLIFFORD. The extenfive Pleafure Grounds are very regular and neat, in the old Style of Gardening.

An Area, called *Rofamond's Green* **, of 750 Yards in length and 150 broad, forms the Entrance to this pleafant and populous Village on the North-eaft from the Church, and gives it an Air of fuperior Neatnefs and Cultivation. Thefe Improvements were made when the Manfion Houfe was re-built, and at the Expence of the fame Perfon.

Of another confiderable Eftate the earlieft Proprietors we can trace are as follows: from HENRY CLIFFORD it paffed in Dower with ALICE his Daughter, and Heir to WILLIAM TEST, about 1470, who was

---

* "In 1491, upon the Difinherifon of MAURICE LORD BERKELEY, by the Will of WILLIAM Marquis of BERKELEY, he regained a yearly Rent of twenty-two Marks in *Frumpton*, which did not pafs in the Settlement." DUGDALE, Baron. Vol. I. p. 366.

† WALTER FITZ-PONS having the Caftle of *Clifford*, Co. *Hereford*, in Dower with MARGARET Daughter and Heir of RALPH BARON DE TOENI affumed that Name. WALTER, his eldeft Son, was the Progenitor of the noble Branch of this Family; created Barons of CLIFFORD with the inherited Baronies of DE VIPONT, WESTMORELAND, and VESCI, in 1298; Earls of CUMBERLAND in 1525; Barons CLIFFORD of *Chudleigh*, Co. *Devon.* in 1672. RICHARD, the younger Brother, was the immediate Anceftor of the CLIFFORDS of *Frumpton*.

‡ In 1200, 2 JOHN, a Fine was levied between RICHARD DE CLIFFORD Petent, and WALTER CLIFFORD the eldeft Brother, Tenant of the Manors of *Corfhum*, *Cleys*, *Culmerton*, and the *Hay* of *Ernefeir*, Co. *Salop*, which were releafed to WALTER, who granted to RICHARD and his Heirs, by LETITIA DE BERKELEI his Wife, the Manor of *Frampton*, to be held of WALTER, by the Service of one Knight's Fee to the Caftle Guard of *Clifford*, Co. *Hereford*, for 40 Days, and paying to RICHARD, for his Life, an Annuity of ten Pounds, by the hands of HUGH DE DENE, and JOHN DE SOLERS. "*Fines levat. in Com. Salop.* 2 R. *Joh'is in Cur. Recept. Scacar.*" Of this Family the following have been Sheriffs of this County. In 1367, JOHN DE CLIFFORD; 1446, HENRY CLIFFORD; 1450, JAMES CLIFFORD; and in 1434, JAMES CLIFFORD, Efq. was fummoned as one of the Confervators of the Peace. FULLER'S *Worthies*, p. 363.

§ MSS. Pedigree.

** In the Manfion-houfe is preferved a Portrait of ROSAMOND, which is fomewhat different from one defcribed by HEARNE. " An Ancient and fine Picture of the beautiful ROSAMOND is now in the Poffeffion of SAMUEL GALE, Efq. who purchafed it " accidentally, and it was from him that I received the following Account of it. ' 'Tis painted on a Pannel of Wainfcot and " reprefents her in a three-quarter Proportion, dreffed in the habit of the Times—a ftrait-bodied Gown of changeable red Velvet, " with large fquare Sleeves of black flowered damafk faceings, turned up above the Bend of her Arms, and clofe Sleeves of a " Pearl-coloured Sattin, puffed out, but buttoned at the Wrift, appearing from under the large ones. She has feveral Rings fet " with precious Stones on her Fingers. Her Breaft covered with a fine flowered Linen, gathered clofe at the Neck like a Ruff. " Her Face is charmingly fair, with a fine blufh on her Cheeks. Her Hair of a dark-brown, parted with a Seam from the " Middle of her Forehead upwards, under her Coiffure, which is very plain, but a Gold Lace appears above it, and that co- " vered with a fmall Cap of Silk. She is looking very intenfly on the fatal Cup which fhe is going to drink: fhe holds it in " one hand and the Cover in the other. Before her is a Table of black Damafk on which there lies a Prayer-book open, written " in the black Character.' Mr. GALE fuppofes this Piece to have been done about HARRY the Seventh's Time." LANGTOFT's *Chron.* p. 561, 8vo.

Although every Portrait of ROSAMOND muft be imaginary, it is thought that this minute Account would not be unentertaining to fome of our Readers. There is an Anachronifm with refpect to the Drefs, which is that of the Court in the Reigns of EDWARD IV. and HENRY VII. with little Variation. *Fretherne* claims the Honor of her Birth, nor does any Account in the Englifh Hiftory contradict that Tradition.

7 Q   fucceeded

fucceeded by Lawrence Test, whofe Son Giles was an Ecclefiaftic; and at his Death in 1545 bequeathed it to Mary his Sifter, the Wife of Ambrose Codrington. He was fucceeded by Francis Codrington, Sheriff of *Briftol*, who died feifed of it in 1558. From that Family it was transferred by Deed of Marriage Settlement of Margaret, Daughter of Francis Codrington, to Edward Bromwich, Efq. of *Bromefberrow*, about 1650. In 1670, it was fold to Colonel Rice Yate, and feveral Purchafes were fubfequently made by Walter Yate, Efq. his Son. Robert Gorges Dobyns Yate, Efq. in 1779, fold it to Samuel Peach, Efq. of *Briftol*, by whofe Will it paffed to Samuel Peach Crucer his Grandfon, who affumed the Name of Peach by royal Sign Manual in 1787. The ancient Houfe of Timber Frame is now occupied as a Farm; in the Windows of which, thefe Arms are emblazoned: 1ft, Argent, a Fefs counter-embattled Sable, between three Lions paffant Gules; Codrington. 2. Codrington, impaling, Sable, on a Chevron Or, between three Falcons rifing Argent as many Roundlets. 3. Clifford. A Cypher *F. C.* (*Francis Codrington*) is very curioufly flourifhed *.

There were other competent Eftates, now difperfed, held by the Families of Selwyn and Haines; but excepting thofe already fpecified, the principal Landholders are Nathaniel Winchcombe, Efq. and Richard King, Efq. of *Alkerton*.

Richard Fitz Pons gave two Yard Lands in *Frampton*, of the yearly Value of 20 Shillings to the Knights Templars †, which Rent is now paid to *Corpus Chrifti College, Oxford.*

Iron Armour, confifting chiefly of Weapons of a rude Form, has been ploughed up in a Field there, where was traditionally a Skirmifh between the *Saxons* and *Danes.*

No Benefactions to the Poor.

Incumbents.	Patrons.	Incumbents.	Patrons.
—— Richard Sheppard,	———————.	1648 John Barnfdale,	The Parliament.
1554 Thomas Mafon,	Henry Clyfford, Efq.	1662 Jonathan Hefkyns,	Chriftian Clifford.
1558 John Robyns,	The fame.	1667 Nich. Paul, M.A.	S. Leet & Chriftian his Wife.
—— Peter Ovett,	———————.	1691 William Done,	Edmund Clifford.
1573 John Savacre,	James Clyfford, Efq.	1698 William Smith,	———————.
—— Walter Wiat,	———————.	1721 Charles Wallington,	———————.
1578 —— Clutterbucke,	———————.	1765 John Wicks, M. A.	John Wicks.
* * * * * * *	* * * * * * *	1770 William James, B. A.	Elizabeth Wicks.
1621 Thomas Pill,	John and Mary Cage.	1773 William Ellis, M. A.	The fame.
1622 Alan Bifhop,	———————.	1777 Thomas Rudge, B. D.	The fame.
1624 Thomas Pill,	John Cage, Efq.	1784 William Jenkin, LL.B.	The fame.

Present Lord of the Manor,

Thomas Grove, Esq.

The Perfons fummoned from this Parifh by the Heralds in 1682 and 1683 were

John Clifford, Efq. and George Lloyde, Gent.

At the Election in 1776, Twenty-nine Freeholders polled from this Parifh.

The Regifter commences with a Date 1624 ‡.

Annual Account of Marriages, Births, and Burials, in this Parish.

A.D.	Mar.	Bir.	Bur.	A.D.	Mar.	Bir.	Bur.	A.D.	Mar.	Bir.	Bur.	A.D.	Mar.	Bir.	Bur.
1781	12	21	13	1786	4	20	17	1791				1796			
1782	3	30	28	1787	5	27	9	1792				1797			
1783	5	30	20	1788	12	31	13	1793				1798			
1784	7	21	21	1789	6	22	17	1794				1799			
1785	5	17	25	1790				1795				1800			

* For feveral Years paft the River has taken its Courfe near the Banks which are in this Parifh. Thefe have been lately broken down, and every endeavour to keep the Flood within its bounds has failed, fo that the high Spring-tides overflow the Grounds adjacent to the Church, undermine the Banks and encroach on the Land, whereby many Acres are loft and are ftill lofing from this Eftate, occupied by Mr. Watts, which fink into the bed of the River.

† " Apud *Framptonam* ex dono Ricardi Filii Puntii duas virgatas, quas tenet Rogerus de Cautelo pro xx fol." Dugd. *Mon.* Vol. II. p. 530. Thefe Rents were originally paid to the Preceptory at *Quenington*, and were, foon after the Diffolution, purchafed by *Corpus Chrifti College, Oxford.*

‡ In the Regifter is a long detail of Damage done by a Storm on the 18th of Feb. 1662, which, in the fpace of four Hours, deftroyed twelve Barns, one dwelling-houfe, and rooted up 357 Trees, chiefly in Orchards. The Account is fubfcribed ' John Barnsdale, Vicar."

7

INSCRIPTIONS

INSCRIPTIONS IN THE CHURCH.

ON FLAT STONES IN THE CHANCEL.

Here lieth the Body of
. . . . . CLUTTERBUCK, and Vicare of this Church, deceased
the 30 Day of September, Anno
Domini 1579, annoque Regni
Reginæ ELIZABETH vicesimo.

Here lieth the Body of
WALTER WIAT,
Preacher and Vecare of this Ch . .
he decesed the 30
Day of September,
Anno Domini 15
78 Annoqe regni
Reginæ ELISABETH
vicefimo.

MARY, the Wife
of THOMAS BOWSER,
departed this Life the 2d of Sept. 1612.

THOMAS BOWSER, Gent.
departed this Life . . July, 1641.

Here lieth the Body of
ELEANOR, the Wife of THOS. BOWSER,
who died Sept. 20, 1669.

Here lieth the Body of
ALICE, the Wife of
JOHN BOWSER, Gent.
who died the 19th Day of
October, 1669.

ON FLAT STONES IN THE NAVE.

BRASS PLATES INSCRIBED
To the facred Memory of
JOSEPH MORGAN,
of this Parish, Gardener,
and MARY his Wife.
He was buried Sept. 15, 1766, æt. 69.
She   Jan. 12, 1763, æt. 63.

Underneath are interred the
Remains of RICHARD CORK,
of this Parish, Surgeon,
who was buried the
5th Day of October, 1769, aged 62.

Also of MARY his Wife,
and Daughter of MILES OATRIDGE,
of the Parish of Coaley, Gent.
who was buried the
15th of October, 1759, aged 39 Years.

Also of MARY their Daughter,
who was buried the
4th of September, 1785, æt. 42.

ON MONUMENTS IN THE NORTH AISLE.

Arms; Checquy Or and Azure, on a
Bend Gules, three Lioncels paffant of
the firft, for CLIFFORD.

In Memoriam
JOH'IS CLIFFORD, Gen.
Mafculorum antiquiffimi
Nominis CLIFFORDIORUM,
Infra hanc Paroch. ultimi;
Qui obiit XXVII die
Octobr. Anno Domini 1684;
Hoc erigitur.

Arms; Azure, on a Saltire between
four Fleurs de Lis Or, five Efcallops Sable, for WADE;—impaling, Sable, a
Chevron Or, between three Towers triple
towered Argent, for DUNCH.

ANNA WADE,
filia natu tertia JOHANNIS DUNCH,
de Puify, in Comitatu Berks, Armigeri,

Annæque uxoris ex majorum
apud Hamptonienfes Domo Familiis
Ambabus Religione pariter ac
generis fplendore confpicuis digna
Propago, conjux merito chariffima
THOMÆ WADE, Armigeri,
hujus oppidique Generofi, cui
quatuor peperit Liberos
(uno eodemque fuavi filiolo fuperftite)
Rei domefticæ ftrenuè perita,
nec minus in rebus Dei affidua Filia, Soror,
Uxor, Mater, Domina, Vicina,
Amica, Fœminarum Lectiffimis
annumeranda, luce a partu fexta
Ardenti febri correpta,
Ardentiori adhuc amore in
Patentia chari Redemptoris
Brachia fanctam expiravit animam
menfis Julii Die XVII,
Anno Æræ Chriftianæ MDCLXXXVII,
ætatis XXX.
Chariffimæ Uxoris M. S.
M. P. THOMAS WADE.

Arms; Quarterly, 1ft and 4th, Azure,
a Lion rampant, and in Chief three Efcallops Argent, for CLUTTERBUCK;
2d and 3d, CLIFFORD, as before.

M. P. S.
GULIELMI CLUTTERBUCK,
hujus Parochiæ, Generofi,
qui 15 Feb Anno Æræ Chriftianæ
MDCCXXVII,
ex hac vita deceffit Annos 67 natus.
ALIS CLUTTERBUCK, de Naftend,
in Parochia Eaftingtoniæ,
in hoc Agro, Generofi,
Filius, ex MARIA,
Uxore JOANNIS CLIFFORD,
hujus Parochiæ, Generofi,
maxima natu filia, quam una cum aliis
Hæredem Pater reliquerat.

ON A SMALL FREESTONE TABLET:

Arms; CLIFFORD, as before.

In Memoriam ANTHONII CLIFFORD,
Defuncti RICHARD CLIFFORD,
pofuit.

ON A NEAT MARBLE TABLET:

Arms; Quarterly, 1ft and 4th, Azure,
on a Cheveron engrailed, between three
Lapwings Or, as many Cinquefoils of the
Field, on a Chief of the fecond a Fleur
de Lis between two Spears Heads of the
firft, for WINCHCOMBE; 3d and 4th,
Sable, a Cheveron Ermine between three
Griffins Heads erafed Or, for GARDINER.
Upon an Efcocheon of Pretence, quarterly of 12, 1. Argent, a Cheveron between three Bells Gules, charged with
two Bars gemelles of the Field, on a Chief
of the fecond a Hawk's Lure between
two Hawks of the Field; BELL. 2. Azure,
a Lion rampant, and in Chief three Efcallops Argent, for CTUTTERBUCK. 3.
CLIFFORD. 4. HOARE anciently. 5.
HOGELINTON. 6. HOARE modern. 7.
Ermine, three Bars Gules; HUSSEY. 8.
Argent, on a Fefs nebulè Sable, three
Hare's Heads couped Or; HAREWELL.
9. Argent, a Cheveron Sable, in chief
two Croffes pattée, in bafe a Saltire of
the fecond; BEAUPENY. 10. Argent,
three Moor Cocks proper; DE LA MORE.
11. Argent, a Cheveron between three
Eagles difplayed Azure; CLOPTON. 12.
Vert, a Cheveron between three Wolve's
Heads erafed Argent; MIDDLETON.

NATH. WINCHCOMBE, Gent.
died October 22, 1766.

ANN his Wife, Daughter and Coheir
of WILLIAM BELL, Efq.
of Gloucefter, and Sainthurft, in this

County, by CATHARINE his firft Wife,
Daughter of WILLIAM CLUTTERBUCK,
Gent. of this Parifh, died Aug. 7, 1757.

ON FLAT STONES.

ON A LARGE BLUE STONE, WITH LETTERS INLAID WITH ALABASTER:

Hic jacet humatum corpus Elizabethe Clifford, que obiit vicessimo quarto die mensis Septembris Anno D'ni Mil'timo CCCCLXXIII. Sub eodem vero lapide jacet corpus Johannis Clifford, qui obiit Maii, An. D'ni Mil'timo CCCCLXXVII, quorum animabus propitietur Deus. Amen.

Arms; CLIFFORD, as before.

ANTHONIUS CLIFFORD,
Lond. Obiit hic fepult.
24 die Julii, A. D. 1650.

Arms; CLIFFORD, as before.
JOHN CLIFFORD, Gent.
died October 27, 1684.

Hic jacet
JOANA, Ux. JOHANNIS
CLIFFORD, Gent. quæ
obiit Feb. 4, 167..

Arms; Quarterly, 1ft and 4th, CLUTTERBUCKE; 2d and 3d, CLIFFORD,
impaling, WADE, as before.

Quod mortale fuit SARÆ,
nuper Ux. WILL. CLUTTERBUCKE,
Gen. & filiæ JOH'IS WADE, Ar.
fub hâc Petrâ repofitum eft
quæ obiit 25 die Junii,
Anno { ætatis fuæ 28.
       { falutis 1685.

Hic reconduntur Cineres
CLIFFORDI CLUTTERBUCK,
Filii natu max.
WILL. CLUTTERBUGK, Gen.
Qui obiit Nov. 1709.

Arms; WADE, impaing DUNCH,
as before.

ANNA WADE, Uxor THOMÆ WADE,
Generofi, doloribus puerperii prius
fracta adorienti protinus febri
fuccubuit, anni menfe menfifque
die quos hic juxta ftatutum
exhibet monumentum; tenellus
autem infantulus in maternum
conclufus eft tumulum die XIV
a quo ex utero materno exclufus
fuerat.

Here lieth the Body of
ROBERT CLUTTERBUCK
one of the Sons of
NATHANIEL CLUTTERBUCK, Gent.
who died Oct. 12, 1685,
aged about 20 Years.

THOMAS CLUTTERBUCK,
one other Son of the faid
NATHANIEL, who died Feb. 17, 1693,
aged about 24 Years.

Here lieth ABIGAIL,
fecond Wife of WM. CLUTTERBUCK,
of this Parifh, Gent.
Daughter of WM. CLUTTERBUCK, of
Mill End, in the Parifh of Eftington, Gent.
who died Aug. 15, 1707.

Alfo here lieth the abovementioned
WILLIAM CLUTTERBUCK,
of this Parifh,
who died Feb. 15, 1727.

SARAH,

SARAH, Daughter of
WILLIAM CLUTTERBUCK, Gent.
died October 27, 1709.

MARY CLUTTERBUCK,
Daughter of WM. CLUTTERBUCK, Gent.
died Jan. 17, 1711.

Hic fitus NICHOLAUS PAUL, A. M.
hujus ecclefiæ vicarius, vir integer
vitæ, regis fubditus fidelis, ecclefiæ
Sancta Catholicæ filius verus,
qui cum feptem de octaginta annos
Domino exegit die Paffionis
Domini deceffit MDCLXXX.
Juxta hic etiam deponitur SAMUEL PAUL,
filius ejus natu minimus,
viginti annos natus, naturâ
exit Januar. 17, 1670.

Underneath is interred
the Body of ANN, the Daughter of
JOHN and ELIZABETH PURNELL,
who died Dec. 11 1763, aged 25 Days.

JOSIAH TIPPETTS
died April 24, 1783, aged 65.

MARY CLUTTERBUCK,
Daughter of W. CLUTTERBUCK, Gent.
died Jan. 11, 1711.

IN THE SOUTH AISLE.

ON A TOMB.

HERE LIETH THE BODI
OF THE RIGHT WORSHIP-
FUL HENRY CLIFFORD, ESQUIER,
WHO DECEASED THE 4
DAY OF JUNE, 1558; AND
THE BODY OF MABEL HIS
WIFE, ONE OF THE DAUGH-
TERS OF SER JHON WE
LCHE, KNIGHT, WHO DE-
CEASED IN SEPTEMBER
1592; AND THE BODI
OF ANNE WATSON, DAUGH-
TER OF THE SAYDE
HENRY AND MABELL,
AT THE PROPER CHARG
OF WELLIAM WATSONE,
GENTLEMANE, 1595.

ON FLAT STONES.

Here lieth the Bo-
di of JOHN SIDENHAM,
decefed the 16 Day
of March, anno
Domini 1585.

Here lieth the Bo-
di of MARI SIDENHAM,
deceffed the .. Day
of Jan. Anno
Domini 15 ..

Here lieth the Bo-
di of NICHOLAS SID-
ENHAM, decefed the
11 Day of December,
Anno Domini 1584.

Here lieth the Body of
RICHARD BROMWICH, the Son of
EDWARD BROMWICH, Efq.
who died the 1ft Day of . . . . . 1626.

ON A MARBLE STONE:

Inter CLIFFORDORUM cineres hic
jacet EDRUS HAYNES, un. Attornat.
Cur. de Com. Banco; in cujus memor.
ROSAMUNDA, filia JOH'IS CLIFFORD,
mœftiffima fua relicta, hoc pofuit;
ob. 11 Junii, 1668.

Here lieth the Body of
CHARLES, the Son of
ZECHARIAH WINTLE,
who died May 10, 1682, aged 12 Days.

Alfo ROSAMUND his Daughter,
who died March 6, A. D. 1685,
aged almoft 2 Years.

Here lieth the Body of
ROSAMUND, the Wife of
ZACHARIAH WINTLE,
and Daughter of JOHN CLIFFORD, Gent.
who died the 23d of November,
A. D. 1686.

In Memory of MARY,
Wife of THOMAS PEARSON, and
Daughter of EDWARD HAYNES, Gent.
who died April 7, 1741, ætatis fuæ 75.

Alfo of MARY, the Daughter of
THOMAS and MARY PEARSON,
who died June 8, 1757, aged 65.

In Memoriæ THOMÆ PEARSON,
qui obiit 27 Junii, A. D. 1717,
æt. fuæ 51.

In Memory of MARY,
Daughter of WM. CLUTTERBUCK,
of Mill End, in the Parifh of Eaftington,
in this County, Gent.
who died Feb. 17, A. D. 1720-1.

Alfo of SARAH, Daughter of
WM. CLUTTERBUCK aforefaid,
who died Jan. 17, A. D. 1723.

In Memory of
JOHN WICKS, of this Parifh, Gent.
who died Oct. 29, 1746, aged 60 Years.

Alfo MARY his Wife
died Dec. 25, 1745, aged 60 Years.

Sacred to the Memory of
JOHN WICKS, Son of
JOHN and MARY WICKS,
of this Parifh, Clerk,
Rector of Frampton Cotterel,
in this County, and Impropriator of the
Great Tythes of this Parifh,
who departed this Life the 21ft of May,
1770, aged 50 Years.

Here lie the Remains of
JOSEPH WICKS, Gent.
Son of JOHN and MARY WICKS,
of this Parifh,
who refigned this Life the 3d Day of
November, 1771, aged 45 Years.

In Memory of
the Rev. STEPHEN MIDWINTER,
Curate of this Parifh,
who died the 13th of October, 1757,
aged 42 Years.

Alfo of HESTER his Wife,
who died March 31, 1776, aged 82.

Infcribed
to the facred Memory of
ROBERT VERREY, of this
Parifh, Yeoman, and
ELIZABETH his Wife.
She died May 25, 1778, aged 59.

IN THE CHURCH YARD.

ON A FREESTONE MONUMENT AGAINST
THE SOUTH CHANCEL:

In Memory of
JOHN BOND, of this Parifh, Yeoman.
He died Jan. 29, 1753, ætat. 75.

SARAH, the Wife of JOHN BOND,
died March 10, 1728-9, aged 38.

JOHN, the Son of JOHN BOND,
died May 18, 1724.

Alfo of MARY his Daughter,
died May 8, 1724.

ON TOMBS.
HENRY WINCHCOMBE,
died Dec. 20, A. D. 1723,
aged 74 Years.

ALICE his Wife
died June 19, A. D. 1715,
aged 60 Years.

ANNE their Daughter
died September 17, 1710,
in the 16th Year of her Age.

ALICE their Daughter
died April 20, 1723, aged 27 Years.

JOHN, Son of HENRY WINCHCOMBE,
died July 22, 1734, in his 47th Year.

ELIZABETH his Wife
died Dec. 8, 1728, aged 39 Years.

THOMAS their Son
died Aug. 26, 1719, aged 11 Months.

JOHN their Son
died March 27, 1747, aged 35 Years.

ANNE their Daughter
died June 4, 1735, aged 13.

ALICE their Daughter
died Jan. 18, 1725, an Infant.

MARY,

MARY, Daughter of
JOHN and ELIZABETH WINCHCOMBE,
died Jan. 10, 1755, aged 38 Years.

ELIZABETH their Daughter
died April 23, 1770.

———

THOMAS ROGERS
died June 19, 1703, in the
43d Year of his Age.

ABIGAIL his Wife
died June 8, 1741, aged 74 Years.

ELIZABETH their Daughter
died in 1693.

ABIGAIL their Daughter
died in 1699.

THOMAS ROGERS, Cler. A. M.
Cujus ne plures quære, lector, titulos
quos fi non tulerit, meruiffe conftat
(nec qui tulit magnus, fed qui meruit)
fumat ille tamen fine invidia honores
quæfitos meritis, quos incorrupta fides
fimplicitas, pudor, nudaque veritas,
morumque integritas, quam edocto
ingenio quo felicius alios doceret,
adjunxit abunde ei tribuerunt.
Vitâ his artibus culta atque honeftata
vacuaque pigri cruciatu morbi
(ipfâ profecto morte gravioris)
Telo libitinæ improvifo, in via
excuffus equo difceffit.
Difce hoc exemplo, mortem viro bono
quæ fubita venit, venire optimam.
Ob. die 17° Martii, A. D. 1736, æt. 38.

———

RICHARD DAVIS
died March 30, 1725, aged near 37.

ELIZABETH KING,
Relict of RICHARD DAVIS,
died Oct. 3, 1752, aged 59.

THOMAS their Son
died Jan. 5, 1761, aged 40.

HESTER his Wife,
Daughter of WM. MAYO, of Slimbridge,
died Sept. 16, 1763, aged 43.

They left four Children.

———

THOMAS BRADFORD
was buried June 11, 1748,
aged 80 Years.

ESTHER his Wife
died April 11, 1731, aged 57 Years.

ELIZABETH their Daughter
died April 23, 1712, aged 15 Years.

MARGARET the firft, and
MARGARET the fecond,
their Daughters, died Infants.

CORNELIUS BRADFORD,
buried April 6, 1757,
aged near 57 Years.

MARY, Wife of
THOMAS EVANS, and Daughter of
THOMAS and ESTHER BRADFORD,
buried Dec. 26, 1739,
aged near 41 Years.

JOHN BRADFORD
died Sept. 15, 1784, aged 76 Years.

MARY his Wife
buried June 22, 1777, aged 64 Years.

———

THOMAS WARNER
died Feb. 12, Anno Dom. 1684.

WILLIAM HINTON
died Nov. 7, Anno Dom. 1684.

WILLIAM his Son
died Feb. 13, 1682.

LYDIA HINTON
died July 23, 1721, aged 77.

LYDIA their Daughter,
Wife of the Rev. Mr. BROADHURST,
buried July 14, 1722, aged 51,
leaving two Daughters,
LYDIA and ELIZABETH.

ANN, Daughter of WILLIAM HINTON,
died May 25, 1682.

———

RICHARD LONGSTRETH
was buried Jan. 15, 1737.

JOHN his Son,
buried April 23, 1755, aged 55.

RICHARD, Son of
JOHN LONGSTRETH,
buried Jan. 1, 1756, aged 20.

ELIZABETH his Daughter,
buried April 14, 1753, aged 21.

ANN, eldeft Daughter of
RICHARD LONGSTRETH, Wife of
BRICE SEEDE, of Briftol,
died Oct. 14, 1766, aged 60.

JUDITH his youngeft Daughter,
Wife of THOMAS DAVIS,
Millwright, of Stroud,
buried Nov. 1, 1771, æt. 55,
leaving one Son.

———

JOHN GARDINER,
buried May 19, 1691.

EDWARD his Son
died Sept. 19, aged 42 Years.

EDWARD GARDINER,
buried May 6, 1761, aged 70 Years.

EDWARD his Son
died June 24, 1715, aged one Month.

JOHN his Son
died in 1744, aged 23.

ROSAMUND his Daughter
was buried Oct. 19, 1742,
aged 23 Years.

———

THOMAS ADY, of Frethorn,
buried June 20, 1756, aged 80 Years.

ELIZABETH his Wife,
buried May 19, 1746, aged 64,
with feveral of their Children.

THOMAS their Son,
buried June 26, 1761, aged 45 Years.

MARY his Wife
died May 9, 1789, aged 85 Years.

———

JOHN HAWKINS
died April 24, 1713, aged 45 Years.

MARY his Wife
died April 10, 1722, aged 53 Years.

JEREMIAH their Son
died March 21, 1714, aged 18.

JOHN their Son
died Aug. 11, 1725, aged 24.

DEBORAH their Daughter
died June 16, 1726, aged 31.

SARAH their Daughter
died Jan. 13, 1700, aged 5 Weeks.

ELIZABETH their Daughter
died July 24, 1726, aged 14.

ELEANOR their Daughter
died Feb. 2, 1726, aged 20.

SAMUEL HAWKINS,
buried July 2, 1758, aged 49 Years.

———

THOMAS WINTLE, Clothier,
died Aug. 26, 1728, aged 37 Years.

ANNA his Wife
died March 25, 1725, aged 32 Years.

———

ANN, Wife of
CHARLES KNIPE, Daughter of
RICH. and ELIZ. BOND, of Pitchcomb,
died Feb. 25, 1769, aged 51 Years.

———

JOHN WILLIAMS, Gent.
late of Goodrick, Herefordfhire,
who died by a Fall from his Horfe
June 8, 1774, aged 73 Years.

———

SEYMORE BUCKINGHAM,
died Aug. 9, 1709, aged 56 Years.

HANNAH his Wife
died Dec. 17, 1728, aged 63 Years.

THOMAS their Son
died Sept. 20, 1761, aged 57 Years.

MARY his Wife
died July 19, 1757, aged 49 Years.

SEYMORE his Son
by SARAH his Wife
died an Infant.

———

GILES HIERON
died June 11, 1727.

MARY his Wife
died Auguft 5, 1744.

ELIZABETH, Wife of
JOHN HIERON, jun.
his Grandfon, Daughter of
ROBERT and ELIZABETH HALL,
of Slimbridge,
died July 31, 1787, aged 26 Years.

———

SARAH, Wife of SAMUEL COLLINS,
died Aug. 5, 1782, aged 55 Years.

THOMAS, Son of
THOS. HUGHES and SARAH his Wife
(their Daughter)
buried Feb. 16, 1779.

Alfo two more Children died Infants.

———

THOMAS BARNARD
died June 17, 1749, aged 57 Years.

ELIZABETH his Wife
died March 6, 1764, aged 65.

WILLIAM, Son of
WM. and ELIZ. BARNARD,
died Nov. 3, 1783, aged 10 Years.

———

JOHN BARNARD
died April 21, 1695, aged 48.

ELIZABETH his . . . . .
. . . December . . 1733.

JOHN, Son of
JOHN and ELIZABETH BARNARD,
died May 23, 1695, aged 8.

ELIZABETH their Daughter
. . . September . . 1729, aged 4 Days.

———

7 R

In

In Memoriam
JOHANNIS SEYMORE,
qui obiit 27 die Julii, A. D. 1673.

THOMAS SAUNDERS
died May 31, 1719, aged 50 Years.

MARY his Wife
died June 6, 1733,
in the 63d Year of her Age.

SARAH their Daughter,
buried June 9, 1751, aged 51 Years.

MARY, another of their Daughters,
Wife of THOMAS FOWLER,
of Ouldings, in the Parish of Stonehouse,
buried April 20, 1770, aged 60 Years.

MARY, Wife of
PHILLIP GUY,
died Jan. 29, 1767, aged 27.

ON HEAD AND FLAT STONES.

Name		Died	Aged
Richard Blanch	-	11 Mar. 1745	58
Elizabeth his Wife	·	8 Feb. 1744	51
Joannah Pearson	-	20 Jan. 1729	70
Joseph Packer, Butcher	-	2 Jan. 1788	67
Esther, Wife of John Verney		14 Apr. 1742	52
John Verney	- -	28 Oct. 1746	51
Elizabeth, Wife of Joseph Merrett		6 Jan. 1730	44
Joseph Ayland	-	—— 1725	—
Judith, Daughter of William and Elizabeth Fryer	-	17 Oct. 1761	63
Thomas Ayland	buried	26 Dec. 1757	62
Mary his Wife	·	16 Oct. 1760	68
Thomas his Son	·	— Jan. 1721	2
George Day	- -	—— 1711	—
Daniel Hewlett	-	2 June, 1765	47
Mary, Wife of John Hyett	·	11 Nov. 1747	74
John Hyett	- ·	14 Nov. 1747	67
Elizabeth their Daughter	·	21 June, 1744	33
Thomas George	-	24 Mar. 1744⅝	60
William Burley,	buried	26 June, 1744	48
Ann his Wife	buried	29 Aug. 1747	51
Ruth, Wife of William Burley		9 Jan. 171⅞	61
William Burley, junior	·	13 Jan. 1729	—
Daniel Burley	- ·	16 July, 1739	41
Sarah his Wife	buried	12 Nov. 1771	72
Edward Evans	-	24 Dec. 1758	39
John, Son of Edward and Mary Evans	- -	24 Apr. 1771	45
William their Son	-	26 Aug. 1783	29
James Evans	· ·	12 Mar. 1777	53
Sarah his Wife	·	7 Feb. 1784	65
Thomas their Son	·	22 Dec. 1762	3
Sarah their Daughter	-	26 July, 1763	—
John Vaughan	·	17 Sept. ——	20
John his Son	- ·	26 Oct. 1762	32
John Spencer	- ·	5 Nov. 1747	40
John his Son	- ·	26 Oct. 1747	10
Mary, Daughter of Richard Avad		18 Feb. 1718	2
Richard Avad	-	12 Jan. 1729	52
Susannah his Wife	-	3 Nov. 1728	—
Samuel Guy	- ·	6 June, 1779	41
Thomas Guy	-	12 Nov. 1742	83
Ann, Wife of William Guy		6 Nov. 1762	59
John Parslow	- ·	25 Mar. 1744	49
Mary his Wife	-	3 June, 1734	28
Deborah their Daughter	-	11 Mar. 1739	11
Samuel Verrey	-	—— 1730	41
John his Son	- ·	—— 1740	21
Margaret Bradford	-	24 May, 1738	69
William Waring	-	9 June, 1740	40
Richard Roe	buried	25 May, 1766	52
Anne his Wife	-	——	—
Richard their Son		17 June, 1744	3
Betty and Ann their Daughters, buried at Durfley	-		
David Fletcher	-	8 May, 1770	52
William Fletcher	-	9 Aug. 1742	28
Elizabeth his Wife	-	5 Dec. 1736	29
John Fletcher	-	2 Dec. 1754	52
Betty his Wife	-	17 Mar. 1744	46
John their Son	·	31 May, 1743	7
Paul Edwards	- ·	20 May, 1729	81
John his Son	-	16 Sept. 1724	37
Esther, Wife of Paul Edwards		12 Aug. 1714	63
Joseph Coley, of Froombridge		4 Mar. 1788	83
Sarah his Wife	- -	1 Dec. 1707	68
William Webley Coley, Son of William and Elizabeth Fream Coley	- ·	21 Dec. 1783	—
George Coley	· -	10 June, 1771	35

Name		Died	Aged
John Johnson, of Froombridge		8 Apr. 1778	45
Ann his Wife	-	24 Aug. 1781	47
Thomas, Son of James and Elizabeth Barnard	-	17 Dec. ——	—
Sarah, Daughter of James Barnard		5 Feb. 1720	8
Samuel his Son	buried	11 Dec. 1743	4
James Barnard, Butcher	-	8 Dec. 1757	63
Elizabeth his Wife	buried	3 Oct. 1741	41
John their Son	- -	9 Oct. 1741	9
Sarah their Daughter	-	20 May, 1765	—
Abraham Lane	-	18 Feb. 1755	42
Anna, Wife of John Frape		29 Mar. 1756	56
Sarah their Daughter	-	26 Sept. 1740	14
Ann, Wife of Ephraim Smith		11 Jan. 1693	13
Margaret, Wife of Charles Ricketts		25 May, 1761	38
Sarah their Daughter	-	7 Sept. 1761	2
Lydia, Wife of William Browning		19 Mar. 1736	30
Samuel their Son	-	7 Oct. 1747	18
William Browning and Mary his Wife	-	——	—
Mary, Daughter of Thomas Evans, and Wife of William James		19 May, 1734	24
William their Son	-	19 Nov. 1732	—
Mary Evans	- ·	18 Apr. 1721	50
William, Son of Thomas Evans		19 Jan. 1743	49
Elizabeth, Daughter of Thomas and Mary Evans	-	20 Jan. 173⅞	29
John, Son of Thomas Evans		21 Oct. 1788	1
Samuel, Son of Thomas Evans		— June, 1764	—
Mary, Wife of John Wakefield, of Newnham, Mariner		5 May, 1761	25
Edward Evans	·	18 May, 1746	43
William his Son	- -	5 Dec. 1744	10
Thomas his Son	·	25 Oct. 1748	9
Martha his Wife	- ·	9 Mar. 1750	48
John, Son of Richard and Katharine Rowles	- ·	22 Sept. 1734	3
Daniel King	- ·	23 Mar. 1775	57
Mary his Wife	- ·	15 July, 1770	60
Susannah, Daughter of John and Hannah King	-	27 Oct. 1778	—
Susannah the second, their Daughter	- -	14 July, 1785	2
William Grindon	- ·	25 Feb. 1752	39
Elizabeth his Wife	-	29 June, 1785	76
Mary their Daughter	-	6 Aug. 1752	15
Sarah Ricketts, their Daughter		12 Nov. 1776	27
Richard Sanigear	-	15 Dec. 1765	57
Dinah, Daughter of Richard Blaynch		23 Feb. 1701	—
Thomas Haynes	-	7 Apr. 1734	—
Josephi Haynes, Gener.	-	6 Nov. 1712	—
Susannah, Daughter of Thomas and Elizabeth Holder	-	24 May, 1727	1
Elizabeth, Wife of Joseph Canter		19 Dec. 1788	65
Elizabeth their Daughter		3 Aug. 1765	5
Samuel, Son of Samuel and Sarah Daw	- -	31 May, 1772	21
Hester their Daughter, buried at King Stanley	-	— June, 1770	24
Thomas Bevan, Butcher	buried	1 May, 1739	—
Sarah his Wife	- buried	6 Feb. 1725	—
William Rogers	-	20 Mar. 1695	60
Dorothy his Wife	-	21 Oct. 1723	91
Mary their Daughter, Wife of John Hill	- -	15 May, 1748	74
William Knight	-	4 Jan. 1765	61
Susannah his Wife	-	15 Aug. 1760	55
John, William, and Joseph, their Sons.			
James Knight	- buried	15 Dec. 1719	67

ON HEAD AND FLAT STONES.

	Died	Aged
James his Son - -	27 May, 1711	12
John his Son - -	3 Apr. 1730	36
John Carefield -	18 May, 1738	43
Mary his Wife -	2 Mar. 1765	63
Elizabeth their Daughter -	7 July, 1732	—
John Carefield, sen. -	23 Feb. 1732	65
Anne his Daughter -	13 May, 1733	6
Jane, Wife of John Carefield	13 July, 1761	68
William Carefield -	8 Feb. 1774	38
Mary, Wife of John Carefield	—— —— 1727	—
Nathaniel, Son of John and Sarah Haynes, Clerk of this Parish	23 Apr. 1729	39
Sarah his Wife -	3 Oct. 1755	—
Thomas and Edith their Children.		
Joseph, Son of Joseph and Hester Brossar - -	2 Apr. 1730	—
Elizabeth, Wife of William Wintle	7 Aug. 1666	—
Elizabeth, Wife of Zechariah Wintle	4 Mar. 1710	—
William Wintle -	5 Oct. 1690	—
William his Son -	10 Dec. 1692	—
Zechariah Wintle -	11 Sept. 1689	—
Ann, Wife of Jacob Osborn, of Gloster, and Daughter of Thomas and Mary Haynes -	21 Dec. 1776	60
Edward Cage - -	13 June, 1695	—
Judith his Wife - -	26 Feb. 1740	—

	Died	Aged
John their Son, Surgeon -	8 June, 1727	41
John Mills, Bricklayer buried	15 Mar. 1761	52
Mary his Wife - -	20 Dec. 1780	63
John Mills - buried	4 Mar. 1721	53
Rosamund his Wife - buried	23 May, 1712	41
William Fords - -	11 Sept. 1741	61
Ann his Wife - -	11 Jan. 1730	54
William Tykell - buried	6 May, 1758	80
Judith his Wife - buried	12 Aug. 1728	45
John their Son - buried	11 July, 1729	25
Joseph their Son - buried	6 Jan. 1743	25
Sarah their Daughter, Wife of John Spencer - buried	1 Dec. 1732	27
Susannah another Daughter buried	28 Nov. 1781	72
James Keylock -	1 Apr. 1751	29
John Keylock -	29 May, 1760	56
Thomas Keylock - -	14 Oct. 1781	67
Richard Davis - -	30 Mar. 1725	36
Elizabeth King, Relict of the said Richard Davis -	23 Oct. 1752	53
Thomas their Son - -	9 Jan. 1761	40
Hester his Wife, Daughter of William Mayo, of Slimbridge	16 Sept. 1763	43
Johanna, Daughter of Robert Tippetts, by Sarah his Wife, Daughter of John and Mary Hawkins	9 Aug. 1774	43

In Memory of JOHN GRIFFIN, his six Wives, and four Children.

He was Lay Clerk of this Parish upwards of 59 Years,

and died Feb. 15, 1788, aged 84.

CXXIV. FRETHERNE.

CXXIV. F R E T H E R N E.

THIS ſmall Pariſh lies in the Hundred of *Whitſtone,* three Miles South-eaſtward from *Newnham,* eight Northward from *Durſley,* and nine from GLOUCESTER on the South-weſt. The Weſtern Boundary is made by the *Severn* ; the whole not exceeding ſix Miles in Circumference. The Soil is univerſally a very ſtiff, moiſt, Clay, nearly in equal Portions, Paſture and Tilled. In parochial Payments it is jointly rated with *Saul,* and *Putloe,* a Hamlet of *Standiſh,* with the former of which it is inter-mixed.

The Living is a Rectory, in the Deanery of GLOUCESTER, anciently endowed with forty-four Ridges of Land ; the Advowſon is veſted in the Family of YATE, of *Bromeſberrow *.* The Church, dedicated to *St. Mary,* is plain and ſmall †.

Domeſday ſtates this Manor to have been valued at three Hides only. In 1316, 9 EDW. II. it was the Property of NICHOLAS LE VELE, and a Family ſtyled DE FRETHERNE held it for ſeveral ſucceſſive Cen-turies. HENRY CLIFFORD obtained it by Deed, dated Oct. 25, 1425, 3 HEN. VI. from JOHN and LAWRENCE PRIDE, and LAWRENCE BAKER. JAMES CLIFFORD, Eſq. is recorded in 1608. He was an Officer of the Houſehold to Queen ELIZABETH, and is ſaid to have built a very ſumptuous Houſe in the Style of that Day for her Reception in her Progreſs to *Briſtol* in 1574. It had an eligible Situation, above the Church, commanding a very advantageous View of the *Severn* ‡.

After remaining long in a State of Dilapidation, it was entirely taken down about 1750, and ſeveral of the architectural Ornaments were removed to *Arlingham Court.*

About the Year 1623, the Manor paſſed to the Family of CAGE, or GAGE, Citizens of *London,* but whether by Connection or Purchaſe is not known. JOHN CAGE married MARY, only Daughter and Heir of JAMES CLIFFORD, who ſold it to WILLIAM BAYLY, Barriſter at Law, ſoon afterward, and it remained with the Deſcendants of the laſt mentioned for ſeveral Generations. In 1744 and 1745 the Manor was bought by the Truſtees of Colonel WALTER YATE, in purſuance of his Will ; one undivided fourth Part of JOHN PRITCHARD, and three fourths of WILLIAM HAYWARD, Serjeant at Law. In 1777 ROBERT GORGES DOBYNS YATE, Eſq. re-ſold it to RICHARD STEPHENS, Eſq. of *Eaſling-ton.* Other Eſtates belong to JOHN SKINNER STOCK, Eſq. Barriſter at Law, THOMAS MORSE, Eſq. of *Durſley,* and the Family of SAUNDERS. The Pariſhioners anciently claimed an Exemption from all Tolls of Fairs, and a free Paſſage over the *Severn* ; but by what Authority is not now to be collected.

Fretherne Cliff is a Hill riſing gradually to the Height of ſixty Feet above the Surface of the River. The Soil, of blue Clay, is hard and unfertile, in which theſe ſeveral Sorts of Foſſils are found : beauti-ful Maſſes of Mundic and Ammonites mundiciſed ; Gryphites, Aſteriæ, Oſtracites, and large Bivalves. In ſome Places Layers of Coal, very thin, but of a fine Quality, are inſerted in the Beds of Shells : likewiſe ſome Fragments of the pearly-ſhelled Nautili, of the largeſt Species.

In the Road leading to this Place is a Houſe, which, according to the moſt ancient and generally re-ceived Tradition, was the Site of the Reſidence of WALTER Lord CLIFFORD, where his Daughter, " Fair ROSAMOND," was born.

<hr>

* DOROTHY BAYLY, Spinſter, who died in 1727, left the Eſtate called *Jackſon's* Farm, in the Pariſh of *Wheatenhurſt,* to the Biſhop and Dean of GLOUCESTER in Truſt, who ſhall appoint a Curate at *Wheatenhurſt* under certain Reſtrictions ; and the other Moiety to the Rector of *Fretherne* for the Time being.

† Dedicated in 1315. THOMAS's Survey of *Worceſter* Cath. p. 216.

‡ " *Fretherne* Lodge, which is a ſtately Houſe, with a moſt noble Staircaſe and Turrets of Freeſtone, belonged to the CLIF-
" FORDS, who had here a Park. It was built by JAMES CLIFFORD, with a Deſign to entertain Queen Elizabeth. Arms ;
" in the little Parlour Window, 1. Chequy Or and Azure, on a Bend Gules, three Lions paſſant Or ; CLIFFORD. 2. Argent, a
" Chevron Azure, in chief three Birds ; FOLLIOT ; 3. Barry ſix Gules & Ermine ; HUSSEY ; 4. Sable, an Eagle diſplayed within
" a Bordure engrailed Argent ; HOARE ; 2. Quarterly, 1. Gules, a Chevron between three Bulls Heads affrontée Argent ;
" BAYNHAM ; 2. Gules, on a Bend Ermine, a Greyhound current Sable ; 3. Parti per Pale, Gules and Vert, guttée d'Or ;
" GREYNDOUR ; 4. Or, a Feſs between ſix Croſlets florctè Gules ; DE ABBENHALL.—3. Quarterly : CLIFFORD ; 2. 3. Ar-
" gent, Or, a Feſs nebulè Sable, three Hares' Heads couped Or ; HAREWELL.—4. Quarterly, 1. CLIFFORD ; 2. Argent,
" three Creſcents Sable ; HOGELINTON ; 3. HOARE : 4. Gules, on a Bend Argent, a Martlet Sable, HOARE anciently.—5.
" CLIFFORD, impaling HAREWELL ; and Or, on a Chief Sable, three Birds of the Field ; WOGAN. In the great Parlour,
" over the Chimney, 1. Per Pale Azure and Gules, over all a Saltire Or ; CAGE, or GAGE.— 2. CLIFFORD, with ſeven quar-
" terings. 3. Gyronnée of four Azure and Argent, over all a Saltire Gules ; DE GAGE." MSS. PARSONS, Muſ. Tih *Oxon.*

2

NO

No Benefactions to the Poor.

Incumbents.	Patrons.	Incumbents.	Patrons.
—— William Luffingham,	John Rolles, by Grant from James Clifford and Dorothy his Wife.	1690 Henry Higford,	William Bayly, Efq.
		1695 John Talbot,	The fame.
		1705 William Smith,	The fame.
		1720 Vincent Rice,	The fame.
1582 James Luffingham,	The fame.	17— William Deane,	The fame.
—— Richard Luffingham,	The fame.	1754 Yate Bromwich, M. A.	The fame.
1663 Thos. Wootton, B. A.	William Bayly, Efq.	1786 Henry Gorges Dobyns Yate, LL. B.	} R. G. D. Yate, Efq.
1673 George Perkins, M. A.	The fame.		

PRESENT LORD OF THE MANOR,

HENRY STEPHENS, Efq.

The only Perfon fummoned by the Heralds, in 1682 and 1683, was

William Bayly, Efq.

At the Election in 1776 Eleven Freeholders polled from this Parifh.

The firft Date of the Regifter is in 1631.

ANNUAL ACCOUNT OF MARRIAGES, BIRTHS, AND BURIALS, IN THIS PARISH.

A.D.	Mar.	Bir.	Bur.	A.D.	Mar.	Bir.	Bur.	A.D.	Mar.	Bir.	Bur.	A.D.	Mar.	Bir.	Bur.
1781	2	7	3	1786	—	6	5	1791				1796			
1782	1	6	—	1787	5	5	8	1792				1797			
1783	—	2	2	1788	2	7	4	1793				1798			
1784	1	7	3	1789	2	9	1	1794				1799			
1785	5	4	8	1790	3	6	3	1795				1800			

INSCRIPTIONS IN THE CHURCH.

IN THE CHANCEL, ON FLAT STONES.

HIC THOMÆ

WOTTÕ PROLES

TUMULO JACET ANĀ

DUM VENIET CHRIST

SUFFICIT ISTA DOMUS

Vº ID. FEBR.

1664.

HEARE RESTETH
THE BODY OF ANN
BAYLY, DAFTER OF
WILLIAM BAYLY, ESQ
VIER, WHO DEPARTED
THIS LIFE THE 27 OF
AVGVST, IN THE
YEAR OF OVR LORD
GOD
1666.

ON A TOMB:

Arms; In a Lozenge, an Efcocheon of Pretence, Parti per Pale for BAYLY;—impaling, Gules, three Stirrups leathered and buckled Or, for SCUDAMORE.

Here lies the Body of
RADEGUND, eldeft Daughter of
JOHN SCUDAMORE,
of Kentchurch, in the
County of Hereford, Efq.
and Relict of WILLIAM BAYLY,
of Frethorn, in the
County of Gloucefter, Efq.
who finifhed a virtuous Life June 15,
in the Year of her Age LXXX,
and of her Redemption 1702.

In Memory of
Mrs. DOROTHY BAYLY,
fecond Daughter of WM. BAYLY,
of Frethorn, Efq.
She departed this Life
the 25th Day of June,
Anno Domini 1727,
and lies here buried
in the 76th Yeare
of her Age.

Here refteth
the Body of JOYCE
BAYLY, deceffed the 9 Day
of December,
1663.

7 S　　　　　*I N*

F R E T H E R N E.

IN THE CHURCH YARD, ON TOMBS.

Near this Place lieth the Body of
Mrs. JANE DEANE,
Relict of the Rev. Mr. DEANE,
Rector of Columoe, in the
County of Nottingham,
the Gift of his Grace the
Duke of KINGSTONE.
She was the excellent Mother of
twelve Children, and worthy of all
Honour,
Grandmother to the Rev. Mr. W. DEANE,
late Rector of this Parish,
Minor Canon and Sacrist of the
Cathedral Church of Gloucester.
He departed this life the
9th of November, 1753, aged 42,
and lies buried on the Right Hand
of that Choir.

Mrs. DEANE died June 11, 1738;
and this Stone was directed to be

placed here by her Daughter
Mrs. ELIZABETH BAYLY,
third Wife of WM. BAYLY, Esq.
the last of that Name that possessed
Frethorn Lodge,
in his Time a good old Seat,
remarkable for a fine Staircase,
built by the noble Family of the
CLIFFORDS.

WILLIAM BAILY, Esq.
died at Worcester Aug. 20, 1726,
and was buried in the Chancel of
St. Swithin in that City.

———

WILLIAM ROWLES, Yeoman,
died Feb. 28, 1720, aged 38 Years.

ELIZABETH his Daughter
died Nov. 20, 1719, aged 2 Years.

———

ELIZABETH, Wife of
JOSEPH SINDERBY,
died April 19, 1754,
aged near 67 Years.

———

TOBIAS COULES,
1630.

———

MARGARET, Wife of
THOMAS KING,
died Jan. 2, 1731,
in the 64th Year of her Age.

RICHARD their Son
died Dec. 1, 1738, aged near 30 Years.

THOMAS KING
died Sept. 15, 1746, aged near 79 Years.

———

JANE, Wife of
WILLIAM MIDDLETON,
of the City of Gloucester, Gent.
died Jan. 8, 1777, aged 52 Years.

ON HEAD AND FLAT STONES.

	Died	Aged
Pearce Smith - -	8 —— 1655	—
Joseph his Son -	5 Mar. 1676	16
—— Wife of P. Smith -	— Oct. 1668	—
Edward Bendal - buried	— —— 1684	—
Thomas Evans -	12 Mar. 1773	38
Mary his Wife - -	3 Jan. 1770	35
Mary, Betty, John, Mary, and Thomas, their Children, died Infants.		
Ann, Wife of William Evans	12 Nov. 1746	27
Ann their Daughter -	in Infancy	
John Cowmeadow -	4 July, 1745	54
Elizabeth his Wife -	11 Jan. 1743	59
Elianor Warren } both drowned {	17 June, 1757	6
William Warren }	17 June, 1757	27
John Warren - -	19 June, 1778	63
Elizabeth, Wife of William Vaile	7 Jan. 1786	58
Hester, Wife of Joseph Hale	7 Aug. 1787	65

CCXXV. FROCESTER

LIES in the Hundred of *Whitſtone*, four Miles North-eaſt from *Durſley*, five Weſt from *Stroud*, and eleven South-weſt from *Glouceſter*. The Soil is very fertile, chiefly Paſture; in ſome Parts a fine binding Gravel or rich Braſh, and in a ſmall Proportion Clay. The common Arable Land is divided into ſix Fields, containing collectively 270 Acres. Upon a late Survey, the Terrier was found to include 1174 Acres belonging to the Right Honourable GEORGE Earl of WARWICK, and 600 of Paſture to the Right Honourable FRANCIS Lord DUCIE, beſide Woodland, called the *Buckholt* *, of uncertified Extent. In this Wood ariſe ſeveral Springs which form a Rivulet interſecting the Pariſh in its Courſe to the *Severn*, about two Miles below.

The ancient Village is ſaid to have been contiguous to the Church; but having been deſtroyed by Fire, was re-eſtabliſhed at the Diſtance of a Mile from it, upon the great Road from *Glouceſter* to *Bath*, from the former of which this Place is the firſt commodious Stage.

The Living is a Vicarage in the Deanery of *Stonehouſe*, and not in Charge in the King's Books, originally, with the Manor, belonging to the *Benedictine* Abbey of *St. Peter* in *Glouceſter*, to whom the Church is dedicated. It has a Nave and South Aiſle of equal Length with the Chancel, and a low obtuſe Spire. The only Reliques of Antiquity are ſeveral Stone Coffins, having Lids inlaid with the Croſſes of Alabaſter. In the laſt Century it was thought expedient to build the Chapel now frequented; for which purpoſe the Site was given by ANNE Baroneſs Dowager BROOKE; where all parochial Offices are now performed, excepting Sepulture.

Eccleſiaſtics are ſaid to have been ſettled at *Froceſter* † in the very remote *Saxon* Æra, which were made dependant upon the Abbey of *Glouceſter* by Grant of RAVENSWART, Brother of BEORNULF King of *Mercia*, in 822 ‡.

The Manor, ſtated in Domeſday to contain five Hides of Land, having been alienated, and annexed to the See of *York* by WOLSTAN the Archbiſhop, was regained by Abbot SERLO in 1072, from which time to the Reformation, it continued their Property §. In 1547, 1 EDW. VI. it was given to the Protector EDWARD Duke of SOMERSET, upon whoſe Attainder it was confirmed, in lieu of Dower, to ANNE his Relict. It lapſed to the Crown on her Deceaſe, and in 1574, 17 ELIZ. was regranted to Sir CHRISTOPHER HATTON, Knight. Sir WILLIAM DODINGTON, Knight, of *Bremer* co. *Hants*, is recited in 1608 as Poſſeſſor of this Manor, whoſe Son, JOHN DODINGTON, bequeathed it to his Daughter, and, at length, ſole Heir, ANNE the Wife of ROBERT GREVILLE the fourth Baron BROOKE, in which noble Family it is now veſted.

When the Eſtate of the Abbey at *Glouceſter* was diſpoſed of, the ancient Grange, Mill, &c. with the Demeſne Lands (now conſequently exempted from Tythes) and the Impropriation, were purchaſed from the Court of Augmentions by JOHN HUNTLEY in 1554; which were held by Sir GEORGE HUNTLEY, Knight, and his Deſcendants; who ſold them to Sir ROBERT DUCIE, Bart. about 1612. The Right Honourable FRANCIS Lord DUCIE derives his Right to them from the laſt mentioned Family.

The Court Houſe appears to have been rebuilt by the HUNTLEYS in the Reign of Q. ELIZABETH, and was perhaps repaired for her Reception here in 1574 ‖. It formerly made three Sides of a ſpacious Quadrangle, with Bay Windows, and other Ornaments in the Style of that Day. But a greater Curioſity

---

* Large Tracts of Woodland, which were exempted from the Foreſt Laws; and held by written Evidence, were called " Boc " holt " of which were ſeveral in this County. They were uſually Parcel of the Poſſeſſions of the Church.

† " *Froceſter*, wher ſometim was a Colledge of Prebendaries, ſuppreſſed: and given to *Gleuceſter* Abbey, diſtant from *Gloucſter* 8 Miles, and ſtandith a Mile beyond *Stanley* Priory. The King hath it nowe. It is an 100 Markes by the Yeare."
LELAND, Itin. vol. IV. part. II. p. 172. vol. VII. p. 76.

‡ " RAVENSWAART, frater regis BEORNULFI dedit manerium de *Frouceſter* Eccleſiæ *Sancti Petri Glouc.* tempore Clericorum " ibidem degentium." DUGDALE, Mon. vol. I. p 110.

§ Ibid. vol. I. p. 114. Cart. Edw. III. n. 4. " Pro liberâ Warennâ in *Frouceſtre*." TANNER, Not. Mon. *Gloucesterſhire*, No XII.

‖ From the Regiſter of the Pariſh. " Hoc Anno, die Feſti LAURENCII Martyris (Aug. 10, 1574) Sereniſſima Regina noſtra " ELIZABETHA hoc noſtrum Oppidatum acceſſit & inviſit; in eoque, in Ædibus GEORGII HUNTLEY, Armigeri, comiter be- " nigueeque & ſummâ cum humanitate tractantis pernoctavit; indeque *Barkel-yum Caſtellum* conceſſit."
See BIGLAND, on Pariſh Regiſters, 4to, 1764, p. 13.

3

FROCESTER.

CHAPEL at FROCESTER.

is the old Conventual Barn, which is 70 Yards in Length, and still entire. No Date of its building, which is usual in others in this County, has ever been discovered.

Southward from the Village is a very lofty Hill, the Summit of which seems evidently to have been one of the Faftneffes formerly occupied by the *Danes*; a Conjecture formed from the Appearance of Intrenchments and the Discovery of Skeletons. The Road leads down a winding Terrace, the Acclivities of which are made very picturefque by beautiful Beech Woods. Following this fingularly magnificent Profpect, as it prefents itself, flanked on the left Side by *Cam* Down, of a volcanic Shape, and the bold Promontory of *Stinchcombe*, two wide Reaches of the *Severn* are feen in the Foreground—an expanfive and cultivated Vale, interfperfed with Village Churches, which pleafingly mark the Diftances. Beyond, are the Foreft Hills, and, as we defcend, the Landfcape is clofed by the blue Mountains of *Malvern* and the Turrets of *Gloucefter* *.

Confiderable Property is held by renewable Life Leafes under the Manor; the chief of which are the Eftates of the Rev. George Hayward, M. A. Vicar, Richard Bigland, Efq. and the Families of Miles, Wetmore, Brooke, Webb, Heaven, Smith, Driver, Barnes, Garlick, and Sandford.

B E N E F A C T I O N S.

Ralph Bigland, Efq. Garter Principal King of Arms, by Will, dated 1784, gave 100*l.* to purchafe Land, vefted in Truftees, the Produce, Intereft, or Rent, arifing from the faid Donation, to be difpofed of as follows: 20*s.* for a Dinner, annually; 2*s.* 6*d.* to the Parifh Clerk; and the Remainder to the worthy Poor of the Parifh of *Frocefter* for ever. A Ground, called *Wet Mead*, in the Parifh of *Coaley*, formerly belonging to ——— Browning, Efq. containing 2 Acres, 1 Rood, and 16 Perches, is appropriated for the Purpofe directed by the faid Will.

A Tenement and Three Acres of Land, lying in the Parifh of *Coaley*, were given for the Repairs of the Church; the Donor, and the Time of Donation, unknown.

Incumbents.	Patrons.	Incumbents.	Patrons.
—— Kenelm Dene,	Abbey of Gloucefter.	* * * * * * * * * * * *	
1552 John Dyfton,	Edw. Walfh, by Grant from the Abbey of Gloucefter.	1663 Philip Lawrance,	Sir William Ducie.
		1664 Eliezer Marfhall, M.A.	The fame.
		1668 John Marfhall,	The fame.
1554 Edward Rutter,	George Huntley.	1686 Thomas Burton,	Frances Vifc. Downe.
1567 William Johns,	The fame.	1692 Edw. Smith, M. A.	The fame, and Philip Sheppard, Efq.
1570 William Tully,	George Huntley, Efq.		
1609 Nath. Baxter, B. D.	Sir George Huntley.	1729 John Hayward, M. A.	Matt. Lord Ducie.
1610 Richard Hathaway,	The fame.	1776 Geo. Hayward, M. A.	Thos. Lord Ducie.

Present Lord of the Manor,

The Right Honourable George Earl of Brook and Warwick.

The only Perfon fummoned from this Place by the Heralds in 1682 and 1683 was John Marfhall, Vicar.

At the Election in 1776 Six Freeholders polled from this Parifh.

The Regifter has its firft Date in 1559.

Annual Account of Marriages, Births, and Burials, in this Parish.

A.D.	Mar.	Bir.	Bur.	A.D.	Mar.	Bir.	Bur.	A.D.	Mar.	Bir.	Bur.	A.D.	Mar.	Bir.	Bur.
1781	3	6	7	1786	4	7	7	1791				1796			
1782	2	9	9	1787	6	15	9	1792				1797			
1783	2	2	4	1788	2	10	6	1793				1798			
1784	2	11	4	1789	5	14	10	1794				1799			
1785	6	9	20	1790	3	17	8	1795				1800			

* The Road defcending from the Hill, which was formerly very narrow and fteep, has been diverted, and brought by a more regular and eafy Courfe from *Nympsfield* acrofs *Coaley Pike*. This Improvement was fuggefted by the prefent Vicar of *Frocefter*, and completed in 1783, under his Infpection, to the great Accommodation of the Publick.

INSCRIPTIONS

INSCRIPTIONS IN THE CHURCH.

ON A FLAT STONE IN THE CHANCEL.

ANNO DOMINI 1570,
THE 14 OF AUGUST,
WAS BURIED THE BO-
DY OF JHON HVNTLEY,
THE SONNE AND HEYRE
OF GEORGE HVNTLEY,
ESQVIER, AND IN
THE 12 YEARE OF
THE RAIGNE OF OUR
SOVERAGNE LADY
ELIZABETH QUEENE.

ON FLAT STONES IN THE NAVE.

Under this Stone are depofited
the Remains of ELIZABETH,
the Wife of EDW. SMITH,
Vicar of this Parifh,
who was buried Feb. 8, 1712-13.

In Memory of the
Rev. Mr. EDW. SMITH, M. A.
late Vicar of this Parifh,
who died March 25, 1729,
aged 70 Years.

In Memory of
MARY, Relict of the
Rev. Mr. EDWARD TURNER,
late Vicar of Cam,
who deceafed May 3,
Anno Domini 1738.

ON A BRASS PLATE.

In Memory of
SAMUEL HALLIDAY and of
ELEANOR his Wife.
He died the 24th Day of Auguft, 1684,
aged 50 Years.
She died the 24th Day of June,
in the 80th Year of her Age, 1720.

**IN THE NORTH CHANCEL,
ON AN ALTAR TOMB.**

Hic jacet fub hoc tumulo
Corpus JOHANNIS HUNTLEY, Armigeri,
qui hanc vitam difceffit
decimo quarto die Augufti,
Anno Dom. 1570,
et etiam Corpus
GEORGII HUNTLEY, Militis,
& eidem JOHANNI
prædicto Hæredis, qui
hanc vitam difceffit
decimo tertio die Septembris,
Anno Domini 1622.

**ON FLAT STONES,
WITH A WALL BEFORE THEM.**

Here lyeth the Body of
ELIZABETH, Daughter of
the Rev. JOHN HAYWARD.
She died Jan. 2, 1768, aged 34.

Here lyeth the Body of
MARY, the Wife of
the Rev. JOHN HAYWARD,
Vicar of this Parifh.
She died May the 12th, 1768,
aged 58.

Here lyeth the Body of
the Rev. JOHN HAYWARD, M. A.
Vicar of this Parifh 47 Years,
and 18 Years Rector of Nymphsfield.
He died July 1776, aged 71.

Here lieth the Body of
MARY, Wife of
WILLIAM HOPTON,
and Daughter of
the Rev. JOHN HAYWARD.
She died June 21, 1769, aged 38.

IN THE CHURCH YARD.

ON TOMBS.

Arms ; Erminois, on a Bend Azure,
cottiled Sable, three Martlets Argent,
a Canton Or, charged with a Rofe Gules,
for WILKINS; on an Efcocheon of Pretence, Argent, on a Cheveron engrailed
Sable, between three Fleurs de lis Gules,
as many Bezants, for WOOD.

In Memory of
JOHN WILKINS, of this Parifh,
who died the 29th of April, 1736,
aged 69 Years.

Alfo of
ANNE, the Wife of the faid
JOHN WILKINS,
who died the 20th of July, 1730,
aged near 58 Years.

In Memory of
ELIZABETH, the Daughter of
JOHN WILKINS
and ANNE his Wife,
who died June the 17, 1729,
in the 28th Year of her Age.

Alfo of
EDITH, the Daughter of
JOHN WILKINS,
by ANNE his Wife,
who died the 14th of May, 1730,
in the 23d Year of her Age.

Near this Place lie the Bodies of
JOHN WILKINS,
late of this Parifh,
and ELIZABETH his Wife,
the Daughter of CHARLES WOOD,

of Stanley St. Leonard, in this County.
He departed this Life the
9th Day of March 1758, aged 64 Years ;
and fhe on the 8th Day of Auguft 1739,
aged 49 Years.

SARAH
their only furviving Daughter
(Wife of MILES OATRIDGE, jun.
of Coaley, in this County),
as a Pledge of her filial Affection,
caufed this Monument to be erected
to their Memories, anno 1760.

Alfo to the Memories of
JOHN (eldeft Son of the faid
JOHN and ELIZABETH WILKINS),
who died March 7, 1747,
aged 29 Years, and was buried here ;

CHARLES, fecond Son,
who died in London
Sept. 18, 1740, aged 19 Years,
was buried at Stepney in Middlefex.

ANNE, eldeft Daughter,
Wife of RALPH BIGLAND,
Citizen of London
(now Somerfet Herald),
who died there Dec. 1, 1738,
aged 25 Years,
and was buried at Stepney,
in the County aforefaid ;

ELIZABETH, fecond Daughter,
Wife of ARTHUR JEPSON,
Citizen of Briftol,
who died there Sept. 12, 1753,
aged 31 Years,
and was buried in St. Werburgh's
Church.

MARY, Daughter of
RICHARD and MARY BIGLAND,
died Nov. 25, 1766,
aged 16 Months.

JOHN WEBB
died Aug. 1, 1686, aged 70.

JOHN his Son
died Jan. 22, 1676,
aged 1 Year and 9 Months.

EDWARD BROWNING,
Son of EDWARD BROWNING,
defefed the 2d Day of April, 1687.

THOMAS BROWNING,
died in October, 1737, aged 76.

JUDETH his Daughter
Wife of SAMUEL FLETCHER,
died April 28, 1775, aged 74.

SAMUEL FLETCHER
died March 25, 1752, aged 40.

THOMAS EVANS
died July 30, 1779, aged 27.

ELIZABETH, Wife of
NICHOLAS BARON,
was here buried April 25,
Anno { Domini 1743,
{ ætatis 80.

THOMAS BARON
died Sept. 11, 1766, aged 64.

MARY his Wife
died Nov. 24, 1781, aged . . .

7 T　　　　　　　　　　　　　　THOMAS

THOMAS WETMORE, Yeoman, died August 24, 1758, aged 47.

ELIZABETH his Wife died April 25, 1748, aged 30.

MARY his second Wife died March 6, 1779, aged 60.

ELIZABETH, Daughter of WILLIAM and SARAH WETMORE, died May 31, 1787, aged 8 Years.

———

ELIZABETH, Wife of WILLIAM TROTMAN, died Sept. 20, 1771, aged 40.

Three of their Children died Infants.

———

ON A BRASS PLATE:

JOHN HEAVEN, late Servant to the Rev. PHILLIP SHEPPARD 33 Years. He departed this Life Oct. 7, 1779, aged 66 Years.

———

ON A FLAT STONE:

In Memory of SAMUEL, the Son of NATHANIEL WILKINS, of this Parish, and of ELIZABETH his Wife, the Daughter of JOHN PEGLER, of Nymphsfield, who died at Leghorn, anno 1758, aged near 40 Years.

Also of NATHANIEL WILKINS aforesaid, who died February 2, 1764, aged 65 Years.

ELIZABETH his Wife died in 1782, aged 84.

ELIZA their Daughter, Wife of JAMES BAYLIS, died March 3, 1753, aged 37 Years.

JOHN, 4th Son of the said NATHANIEL and ELIZABETH, died in London, Jan. 15, 1766, aged 22.

NATHANIEL, 2d Son, died in London, 1782, aged 60.

WILLIAM, 3d Son, died 1782, aged 49.

———

ON FLAT AND HEAD STONES.

	Died	Aged
William Chapman	16 Nov. 1692	61
Mary his Wife	21 Nov. 1726	84
Rebekah, Wife of Joseph Wilkins	25 Dec. 1675	—
William Wilkins	4 Sept. 1711	35
George Chapman Wilkins, Son of John and Ann Wilkins buried	27 Dec. 1712	—
Joseph, Son of John Wilkins	1 Mar. 1717	—
Mary, Daughter of Nathaniel Wilkins	4 Sept. 1734	3
Hannah, Daughter of Miles and Mary Oatridge	28 July, 1714	1
John, Son of John Heaven	12 July, 1707	8
Edith, Relict of William Heaven, senior	30 Jan. 1708	79
Ann, Daughter of William Heaven	4 Mar. 1728	1
Ursula, Daughter of William Heaven	4 May, 1736	19
Edward, Son of William Heaven	11 June, 1743	37
Elizabeth, Relict of William Heaven, junior	19 Feb. 1744/5	75
John Heaven	8 Feb. 1739	33
Martha his Daughter	31 May, 1745	8
Thomas Heaven	20 Oct. 1754	44
Alice, Wife of Richard Ronalds, and Relict of Thomas Heaven	30 Oct. 1770	64
Sarah, Wife of John Wettmore	6 July, 1711	—
Thomas Wettmore, senior	5 Apr. 1727	82
Henry Wettmore	14 Apr. 1729	97
Mary, Wife of John Wettmore	27 Aug. 1742	46
John Wettmore	14 Sept. 1745	62
Thomas their Son	2 Nov. 1753	26
William Daw	6 June, 1723	63
William, Son of William Daw, jun.	26 Apr. 1727	—
James, Son of William Daw, jun.	12 Oct. 1734	—
James, Son of Wm. Daw	22 Nov. 1727	—
Hannah, Relict of William Daw	19 July, 1733	—
Margaret, Daughter of Will. Daw	4 Jan. 1744	9
William, Son of George Smith, of Chester	21 May, 1758	4
William Daw	23 July, 1760	57
Sarah his Wife	28 Oct. 1777	71
George, Son of William and Sarah Daw	20 Jan. 1788	58
William and William, Sons of Geo. and Sarah Daw, died Infants.		
John Phelps	22 Dec. 1736	51
Margaret Phelps	2 Dec. 1757	67
Ann, Daughter of John Phelps	3 May, 17—	12
George Pegler	16 Dec. 1679	63
Thomas Pegler	26 Feb. 1692	—
Sarah, Wife of George Pegler	27 Oct. 1719	36
George Pegler	22 Aug. 1722	65
John, Son of George Pegler	3 May, 1721	—
James, Son of George Pegler	3 Mar. 1727	11
George Pegler	16 Oct. 1738	27
Thomas Pegler	26 Feb. 1764	48
Mary, Wife of Thomas Pegler	9 May, 1778	63
John Smith.		
Sarah, Wife of John Smith, senior.		
Richard Smith	20 Nov. 1686	—
John Smith	25 Oct. 1701	—
Michael Smith	30 July, 1702	—

	Died	Aged
George, Son of John Smith	14 Sept. 1720	—
Margaret, Wife of John Smith	27 Aug. 1721	—
William Smith	28 Dec. 1728	—
William Smith	26 Apr. 1729	30
Margaret Smith buried	15 Jan. 1768	70
Thomas, Son of William and Margaret Smith buried	4 Apr. 1781	53
Sarah his Wife buried	29 Dec. 1779	50
William Wood	11 Apr. 1729	73
Elizabeth his Wife	14 Oct. 1724	—
James their Son	14 May, 1704	—
Sarah their Daughter	6 Jan. 1724	—
John their Son	10 Mar. 1769	72
Elizabeth his Wife	29 Mar. 1748	46
William, Son of John and Margaret Wood	31 July, 1789	36
Mary, Daughter of John and Margaret Wood	11 May, 1790	41
Margaret, Wife of George Baron	3 Oct. 1685	—
Nicholas Baron	— May. 1708	—
Charles his Son	— —— 1733	33
Mary, Wife of George Baron	6 Aug. 1776	26
George Baron buried	8 Nov. 1785	42
Sarah their Daughter died in Infancy.		
Richard Barnes	13 Nov. 1748	50
Hannah his Wife	29 Sept. 1736	39
Hannah, Wife of Samuel Barnes	1 July, 1778	66
Daniel Bennett	26 Nov. 1728	66
Hannah his Wife	15 Sept. 1735	66
Daniel Bennett	4 Feb. 1788	88
Sarah his Wife	5 Feb. 1785	75
Richard Ronalds	18 Oct. 1731	42
Richard Ronalds	11 May, 1771	54
Mary Ronalds	23 June, 1777	93
William Andrews	13 June, 1777	69
Richard, Son of Giles Heaven	18 June, 1747	13
Richard Heaven	24 Mar. 1753	39
Anne, Wife of Samuel Heaven	6 Apr. 1748	36
Anne their Daughter	15 Dec. 1758	11
Samuel Heaven	25 Apr. 1767	48
Richard Heaven	14 Mar. 1758	82
Mary his Wife	25 Apr. 1748	85
Mary, Daughter of William and Sarah Heaven	24 Jan. 1787	18
James Wilkins	18 Mar. 1712	44
Sarah his Wife		
Ann, Wife of William Wilkins	1 Mar. 1730	—
Susannah, Wife of John Wilkins	24 Nov. 1750	29
Abigail, Wife of William Vaisey	25 Apr. 1748	—
Mary, Wife of Samuel Wilkins	2 Nov. 1762	70
Samuel Wilkins	17 July, 1765	67
Thomas Wilkins	— Mar. 1781	60
Sarah, Daughter of Sam. and Mary Wilkins.		
Mary, Wife of Samuel Wilkins	16 May, 1784	45
Samuel Wilkins	4 Dec. 1786	60
William, Son of Thomas Willis	1 June, 1726	4
Thomas Willis	19 Dec. 1760	66
Sarah his Wife	24 Mar. 1757	62
Thomas Willis, Schoolmaster	23 Nov. 1757	
John Willis	8 Jan. 1783	58

O N

ON FLAT AND HEAD STONES.

	Died	Aged
William, Son of William Nurfe	27 June, 1662	—
Samuel Nurfe -	11 Dec. 1711	36
Sarah, Wife of George Nurfe	8 Dec. 1755	—
Mary, Daughter of George Nurfe	— Sept. 1768	4
John Webb, fenior.		
John Webb - -	17 Oct. 1742	53
Charles, Son of William and Ann Webb - -	19 Feb. 1787	—
Ann, Wife of Simon Neall, of Cowley - - -	26 Jan. 1740	—
Sarah, Daughter of Daniel Neall, fenior - -	16 Mar. 1744	—
Sarah, Daughter of Daniel Neall, junior - - -	28 Nov. 1752	3
Mary, Wife of Richard Horftone		
Lucy Llan - -	14 Sept. 1747	—
John Davis - -	12 Jan. 1731	26
Edith his Wife -	5 May, 1736	29
Thomas Davis, Butcher -	20 May, 1787	81
William King, a Native of North Britain - - -	28 Oct. 1748	34
Elizabeth, Wife of Nathaniel Stephens - -	21 June, 1735	65
Mary their Daughter -	11 Aug. 1762	60
Samuel Wilkins - -	— — 1784	—
Judith, Wife of John Parflow.		
Elizabeth, Wife of Roger Parflow	31 Dec. 1732	64
Robert their Son -	28 Dec. 1732	44
Bartholemew Wicks -	30 Apr. 1684	—
N. Adams -	1 Oct. 1728	68
Judith his Wife -	1 Oct. 1725	63
Andrew Fletcher -	1 Jan. 1754	41
James, Son of John Fletcher	28 May, 1758	32
Robert Collins -	— — 1742	—
Betty his Wife -	— — 1748	—

	Died	Aged
Betty, Sarah, } Daughters of W. Collins {	— — 1750 / — — 1759	— / —
Stephen Hofkins -	24 June, 1733	70
William Cowley, Clerk of this Parifh	30 Mar. 1753	77
Hannah his Wife -	30 July, 1731	43
Samuel his Son - -	28 May, 1731	—
Samuel Woodman -	28 Aug. 1753	64
Alfo five of his Children.		
Mary, Wife of Thomas Woodman	19 Apr. 1755	33
Sarah, Wife of John French	29 Oct. 1789	69
Mary, Wife of John Turner, and Daughter of John and Sarah French - -	21 Aug. 1786	42
Jofeph Churches -	9 May, 1767	76
Martha his Wife -	28 Apr. 1743	63
Arthur Watts, Son of Arthur Watts	17 Feb. 1721	43
William Clark - -	— May, 1753	—
Sarah his Wife -	28 Apr. 1778	69
Hannah Clark -	28 June, 1754	23
William Clutterbuck -	17 Dec. 1785	36
Sarah his Daughter -	26 Feb. 1780	1
Thomas, Son of Thomas and Sarah Buckingham -	16 Mar. 1769	5
Thomas, George, Thomas, James, and Jofeph, their Sons, died Infants.		
Anthony Rowles -	4 Feb. 1789	77
John Crofs - -	19 Apr. 1731	50
Mary his Wife -	1 Apr. 1752	53
John Trotman - -	7 May, 1747	52
Samuel Browning -	17 Oct. 1731	39
George Perkeins - buried	22 Apr. 1712	—
Alfo three of his Children.		
Sarah, Wife of John Bond, of Stroud	4 Sept. 1783	58

CXXVI. GUITING

CXXVI. GUITING POHER*,

MORE commonly called *NETHER GUITING*, is a Parish of confiderable Extent, in the lower Divifion of the Hundred of *Kiftesgate*, fix Miles diftant Weftward from *Stowe*, fix Eaftward from *Winchcomb*, and nineteen North-eaft from the City of GLOUCESTER. The Soil is of light ftone Brafh, including about 4000 Acres; arable in a far greater Proportion; with fpacious Downs and Woodlands. The Downs are commonable, and are remarkable for the natural Produce of a great Number of Hawthorns.

The Living is a Vicarage, the Impropriation of which was given to the *Ciftertian* Abbey of *Bruerne*, in *Oxfordfhire*, foon after its Foundation in the Reign of King JOHN. The greater Part of the impropriate Tythes now belong to *Chrift Church* College, *Oxford*; and the Remainder to the Truftees of certain Charities, bequeathed by GEORGE TOWNESEND, of *Rowell*, in this County, Efq. anno 1683.

The Church, dedicated to *St. Michael*, retains the Architecture of the early *Norman* Centuries. The two oppofite Door-cafes confift of indented Mouldings, and what is remarkable, the Arch dividing the Nave from the Chancel, which is very pointed, has the fame Ornament. There is an embattled Tower at the Weft End.

The Manor was given by the CONQUEROR to WILLIAM GOIZENBODED, from whom it defcended to the DE QUINCEYS, Earls of *Winton*, under whom it appears to have been held by Leafe by the Mafter of the Knights Templars. ROGER DE WATTEVILLE had previoufly granted to them two Yard Lands, and certain Immunities, in this Parifh. In 1314, 14 EDW. II. it was found by an Inquifition, *poft mortem*, that ROGER CORBET had died feized of this Manor, with thofe of *Ebrington*, *Catteflade*, and *Fermecott*, from which Circumftance it feems that it was about that Time included in the Manor of *Ebrington*, which ftill exercifes manerial Jurifdiction as Paramount. ADAM DE HERMINGTON, and Sir JOHN BOTELER, of *Sudley*, are next mentioned as Proprietors. In the Reign of HENRY the Eighth, it was transferred from the Crown, where it had lapfed by Attainder of the BOTELERS, to WILLIAM WHORWOOD, Efq. Attorney General, who left two Daughters and Coheirs, ANNE, the Wife of AMBROSE DUDLEY, Earl of *Warwick*, and MARGARET, of THOMAS THROCKMORTON, of *Coughton*, co. *Warwick*, Anceftor of the prefent Sir ROBERT THROCKMORTON, Baronet; the former of whom dying without Iffue, one Moiety was inherited by her Nephew THOMAS WHORWOOD in 1573, 15 ELIZ.

The ancient Family of STRATFORD, already poffeffing large Property in the Parifh, purchafed the Manor about 1600; and retained it till 1715, when it was transferred to Sir JAMES HOWE, Bart. of *Berwick St. Leonard's*, co. *Wilts*, by Marriage with ELIZABETH, Daughter and Coheir of HENRY STRATFORD, Efq. In 1720 DAVID HUGHES, Efq. held the Manor of *Guiting Poher*, and was fucceeded by his Son, who, dying without Iffue in 1757, it paffed in equal Parts to his three Sifters and Coheirs, the eldeft of whom was the Wife of JOHN VERNON, Efq. Barrifter at Law, the fecond of WILLIAM SMART, Gent. and the youngeft of THOMAS HOLLAND, Gent. of *Mickleton*.

H A M L E T S.

Fermecotte, or *Farmcote,* diftant from the Church about three Miles, is a diftinct Manor, and is faid to have had anciently parochial Rights. It is a Chapelry annexed to *Guiting Poher*, to which it pays, in Lieu of Tythes, 6*l.* 8*s.* 4*d.* by an old Compofition. It is recited in *Domefday*; and in the fubfequent Centuries paffed to the Families of CORBET and GREVILLE. JOHN STRATFORD, who was fummoned to Parliament 12 EDW. II. 1320, then held this Manor. JOHN STRATFORD, the eighth in defcent from the abovementioned, was the Progenitor of three opulent Families fettled at *Farmcote, Temple Guiting*, and *Halling*. For this Eftate WILLIAM STRATFORD, Efq. paid to the Parliament 763*l.* 14*s.* on account of his Loyalty. About the beginning of the prefent Century it became by Purchafe the Property of ROBERT TRACY, Efq. of *Corfcombe*, who, dying without Iffue, left it to ROBERT PRATT, Efq. whofe Relict, re-married to STEYNOR HOLFORD, Efq. (fince deceafed) is the prefent Poffeffor.

In the Chapel, which is apparently ancient, is a Tomb for HENRY STRATFORD, Efq. in the Style of Queen ELIZABETH's Time, without Infcription. The Preceptory at *Quenington*, and the Abbey of *Hayles*, both held Lands in this Hamlet.

* The neighbouring Village of *Shipton* became the Property of HUGH POHER, in 20 HEN. III. which defcended to his younger Daughter, the Wife of SIMON SOLERS, from whom it obtained the additional Name of *Shipton Solers*. The POHERS are faid to have held large Poffeffions in the County of *Warwick*. DUGDALE's *Warwickfhire*, pp. 167, 276, &c. Sir HUGH POER accompanied STRONGBOW Earl of PEMBROKE in his Expedition into *Ireland*, and, fettling in that Kingdom, became the Anceftor of the Marquis of TYRONE.

2

Farmcote

Farmcote Wood, of 200 Acres, as appendant on the Lordſhip of *Sudley,* belongs to the Right Honourable George Lord Rivers.

2. *Guiting Grange* included the manerial Lands originally granted to the Abbey of *Bruerne,* and was the Grange in which their Corn-rents were received *. Upon the Diſſolution, theſe Lands were ſold, ſubjeʼct to a reſerved Rent to the Crown, to Anthony Stringer and John Williams in 1545. They were bought in 1620 by William Gardyner, Eſq. of *Bermondſey* in the County of *Surrey;* and by his Grandſon re-ſold, about 1720, to John Snell, Eſq. of *Glouceſter.* The Manſion-houſe is compaʼct and elegant, ſituate in a ſmall Park, which abounds in very beautiful Scenery. The *Coteſwold* Vallies, ſuch as theſe are, ſhew a ſuperior Cultivation.

3. *Catteſlade,* or *Caſtellet,* for it is ſaid, that a Caſtle built here was held by Edmund Earl of Stafford, in the Reign of Henry the Fourth †. This Hamlet is likewiſe mentioned in *Domeſday.* It became the Property of David Hughes, Eſq. by Marriage with the Heir of the Family of Colles, and is now that of the Repreſentatives of his Coheirs, Thomas Vernon and Thomas Holland, Gents.

A Stream which is the Source of the River *Windruſh* has its firſt Riſe in this Pariſh.

B E N E F A C T I O N S.

1615. Thomas Compeer, Gent. bequeathed 100*l.* the Intereſt of which to be expended in buying Materials for ſetting the Poor to work, or to be given them in Bread.

1635. Thomas Dean gave 30*l.* to the Poor.

1682. George Townesend, Eſq. of *Rowell,* left Lands, the Income of which is 2*l.* 12*s.* to be laid out in Bread, and other Lands, which produce 5*l.* a Year, for apprenticing a poor Boy, either from this Pariſh, or *Blockley* in *Worceſterſhire.*

Incumbents.	Patrons.	Incumbents.	Patrons.
1560 Baldwin Johnſon,	——————.	1737 John Parſons, M. A.	Coheirs of D. Hughes, Eſq.
—— Thomas Wood,	——————.		
1588 Henry Scriven,	Henry Stratford, Eſq.	1760 Thomas Darke,	Thos. Vernon, Eſq. and David Hughes Holland, Gent.
1621 William Gorton ‡,	Henry Stratford, Eſq.		
1658 Miles Huatſon,	Wm. Stratford, Eſq.		
* * * * * * *,	* * * * * *	1769 Eraſmus King,	The ſame.
1712 Thomas Humphreys,	David Hughes, Eſq.	1777 Charles Biſhop, M. A.	Elinor Vernon and John Holland.
1727 Henry Savage, B. A.	The ſame.		
		1780 Thomas Symondes,	The ſame.

Present Proprietors of the Manors,

Lord Paramount of *Guiting, Catteſlade,* and *Farmcote.*

The Right Honourable Hugh Earl Fortescue.

Claimants;

Of *Guiting* and *Catteſlade,*
Eleanor Vernon, Widow,

Of *Farmcote,*
Mary Holford, Widow.

Lord of the Manor of *Guiting Grange,*

Powel Snell, Eſq.

The only Perſons ſummoned from this Pariſh by the Heralds in 1682 and 1683, were William Gardyner, Eſq. and John Colles, Gent. of *Catteſlade.*

At the Election in 1776 Twelve Freeholders polled from this Pariſh.

The firſt Date of the Regiſter is in 1560.

Annual Account of Marriages, Births, and Burials, in this Parish.

A.D.	Mar.	Bir.	Bur.	A.D.	Mar.	Bir.	Bur.	A.D.	Mar.	Bir.	Bur.	A.D.	Mar.	Bir.	Bur.
1781	4	16	10	1786	3	21	7	1791				1796			
1782	2	15	10	1787	6	11	15	1792				1797			
1783	1	12	12	1788	5	14	7	1793				1798			
1784	3	13	20	1789	3	12	7	1794				1799			
1785	7	11	12	1790	1	14	7	1795				1800			

* Dugdale's Mon. vol. I. p. 835. Chart. 39 Edw. III. ni " pro liberâ warennâ in *Guyting Poer,* &c."

† MSS. Snell.

‡ William Gorton, B. D. of the Univerſity of *St. Andrew,* was incorporated July 9, 1639. He was now Vicar of *Lower Guiting,* com. *Glouc.* Wood's Faſti *Oxon.* vol. I. p. 898.

7 U

INSCRIPTIONS

INSCRIPTIONS IN THE CHURCH.

ON FLAT STONES IN THE CHANCEL.

Arms; Gules, a Cheveron vairè between three Crefcents Gules. Creft, a Buck's Head affronté Gules, attired Or.

HIC JACET CORPUS
EDMONDI GODDARD, DE SWINDON
IN COMITATU WILTONIENSI,
GENEROSI.
OBIIT 18 OCTOBRIS,
ANAQUE DOM. 1676,
ÆTATIS SUÆ 61.

Here lieth the Body of
WILLIAM COUES, Gent.
who departed this Life

December the 5, 1699,
and in the 76 Year of
his Age.

ON A BRASS PLATE AGAINST THE NORTH PILLAR BETWEEN THE NAVE AND CHANCEL:

Memoriæ Sacrum
Prope hunc locum in his cancellis
jacet Corpus MILETII HUATSONII,
Clerici,
PETRI HUATSONII Filii,
de Docker, Baroniæ,
Candalienfi comitatu Weftmorlandiæ,
hujus Ecclefiæ plurimis annis paftoris.
Obiit die menfis Julii 3,
anno æt. 79, & anno Salutis 1712.
Qui requiefcit in Domino.

IN THE NAVE.

ON A FLAT STONE:

In Memory of THOMAS CHARLES,
Mercer;

And of MARY his Wife.

THOMAS died Nov. 2, 1727, aged 42.

MARY died Aug. 10, 1731, aged 41.

Their Son RICHARD SMITH CHARLES died greatly lamented, and was buried here March 23, 1755, aged 38 Years.

IN THE CHURCH YARD, ON TOMBS.

WELTHIN, Wife of
HENRY HUMPHRIS,
died Jan. 27, 1758, aged 74.

HENRY HUMPHRIS
died Dec. 9, 1781, aged 87.

HENRY FREEMAN
died July 8, 16.7.

JOHN FREEMAN
Sept. 3, 1731, aged 48.

WILLIAM FREEMAN, Free Mafon,
died Jan. 31, 1730, aged 46.

THOMAS FREEMAN
died Feb. 26, 1775, aged 86.

Here lieth
a truly honeft Man,
JOHN HOWES,
Dyer, who
departed this Life the 26th Day of May,
1787, aged 77 Years,
by whofe unremitting Induftry
the Poor of this and the adjacent Parifhes
were many Years greatly relieved, by
the Employment of them
in the various Parts
of his Trade.
By an uniform Refpect for his Superiors,
he gained their good Will;
by a Generofity and Hofpitality to his
Equals,
he was bleffed with their Friendfhip;
and,
by a Hand ever open to the diftreffed,

he procured their unfeigned
Benedictions.
This fmall Tribute to his Memory
is placed by a near Neighbour.

Ye, to whom once this mortal Clay was
known,
Whofe focial Tongue oft chear'd the
Winter's Day,
Drop one foft Tear of Pity on this Stone,
Then move in facred Thoughtfulnefs
away.
'Twas mine, 'tis yours (perchance with
Grief) to fee
The Trifles of more fleeting Years re-
turn:
Then lift! redeem what 's loft with
Piety,
Left ye too late your Negligence
fhould mourn.

ON HEAD AND FLAT STONES.

	Died	Aged		Died	Aged
Charles Blackwell -	16 Mar. 1716	—	Elizabeth, Wife of John Williams	28 Apr. 1742	64
William Hanks -	5 Aug. 1757	36	Jofeph Thorndell -	1 Nov. 1785	65
Mary, Wife of Thomas Hyett buried	19 June, 1747	—	Sarah his Daughter, Wife of John Harris - -	28 Sept. 1776	29
Mary, Wife of Edward Wood	24 Aug. 1762	58	Sarah, Wife of Jofeph Thorndell	5 Apr. 1784	60
Efther, Wife of William Hayward	15 Aug. 1762	56	William Thorndell -	27 July, 1782	63
Thomas Jones -	9 Aug. 1713	15	James Taylor -	22 Nov. 1755	53
Margaret his Wife -	10 Oct. 1734	73	Hannah, Wife of Adam Mifflin	10 Nov. 1789	28
Deborah, Daughter of William and Deborah Wotton, of Ilminfter, and Wife of John Hayward	11 Aug. 1776	36	Harry Hayward -	25 Dec. 1776	42
			Thomas Freeman -	10 Mar. 1729	—
Ann, Daughter of John and Deborah Hayward -	18 Aug. 1778	2	John Freeman -	4 Feb. 1761	48
			Elizabeth Ruck -	8 June, 1689	85
William Phipps, late Bayliff to Powell Snell, Efq. -	8 Aug. 1773	60	Elizabeth, Wife of William Hunt	12 Apr. 1767	25
John Taylor - -	23 Oct. 1780	66	John, Son of Thomas and Mary Buttler - -	21 Feb. 1736	1
			John Wood -	5 Oct. 1749	71
Ann, Wife of William Arkell, of Caftelett - -	12 Feb. 1771	31	Mary his Wife	10 Nov. 1761	69
			John Wood, of Barton -	28 Dec. 1751	35
Sarah, Wife of William Luckett, late of Broadwell -	3 Oct. 1782	78	Edward Wood - -	—— 1673	—
Elizabeth, Wife of Robert Boulton	11 Apr. 1784	29	Hannah, Daughter of John and Mary Wood, and Wife of Edward Matthews - -	15 Aug. 1743	25
Ann, Wife of Nathaniel Mafon	19 Aug. 1784	50			
Elizabeth, Wife of William Hunt	12 Apr. 1767	25			
Efther, Wife of Robert Huton	6 Dec. 1782	73	Hannah, Wife of John Wood, of Barton - -	—— 1713	—
Ann, Wife of James Tayler	15 Jan. 1783	82			

ON

O N   H E A D   A N D   F L A T   S T O N E S.

	Died	Aged
Auguftine, Son of Auguftine and Mary Greening -	9 Apr. 1745	4
Thomas, Son of Auguftine and Mary Greening -	17 Jan. 1745	1
Auguftine Greening -	23 Dec. 1782	70
Mary King - -	20 May, 1743	—
Benjamin Charlwood -	3 Aug. 1747	40
Mary his Daughter -	15 Apr. 1745	4
Elizabeth, Wife of Edward Smith, junior - -	24 May, 1757	76
Hannah, Wife of John Turner	20 Apr. 1762	61
John Turner . -	28 Nov. 1778	78
Thomas Greening -	21 May, 1730	—
Grace his Wife -	15 Mar. 1728	66
William, Son of William Prefton, of Yanworth -	9 June, 1722	26
Elner, Daughter of John Skinner	20 Sept. 1701	24
John Stephens, fenior -	12 Oct. 1729	73
John Stephens, junior -	19 Mar. 1770	67
Hannah, Wife of John Stephens	6 Mar. 1747	45
Hefter, Wife of James Humphris, of Kyneton - -	11 June, 1755	49
Alice, Wife of John Humphris	10 Mar. 1782	59
Henry Humphris, of Kyneton	16 Nov. 1765	35
Elizabeth, Wife of John Turner	13 Dec. 1770	71
Thomas Wood -	28 Jan. 1729	43
Sarah his Wife -	24 Aug. 1731	45
John their Son - -	27 May, 1783	70
Mary, Daughter of Richard and Mary Belcher -	18 Apr. 1762	16
Eleanor, Wife of Juftinian Hatheway	23 Sept. 1744	68
Sarah, Wife of Jofeph Mufco buried	21 Dec. 1760	53
Anne, Wife of Thomas Hatheway	15 Dec 1751	88
Abiathan Hatheway -	—	—
Anne, Daughter of Jofeph	— Nov. 1720	—
Robert Etheridge -	6 Aug. 1746	17
John Etheridge -	17 Jan. 1748	48
John, Son of John and Elizabeth Etheridge - -	30 Nov. 1749	24
Elizabeth, Wife of John Etheridge	13 Aug. 1773	81
Elizabeth, Wife of John Humphris	4 Nov. 1739	78
John Humphris -	6 Mar. 1686	—
John Humphris -	7 May, 1740	57
Ann, Wife of Rich. Williams, fenior	14 Nov. 1724	67
John Williams - -	7 July, 1776	86
Mary his Wife -	20 Oct. 1744	46
Michael their Son -	12 Nov. 1772	29
Mary, Wife of Timothy Sadler	2 May, 1781	63
Ann, Daughter of Anthony and Ann Sadler -	24 June, 1752	26
John Blackwell -	8 Dec. 1714	—

I N   T H E   C H A P E L   A T   F A R M C O T E.

On a Tomb on the North Side of the Chancel are the Effigies of a Man in Armour, with a Woman, in the Drefs of the Times, fupplicating, and the following Arms, but no Infcription:—Barry of 10, over all a Lion rampant, for STRATFORD;—impaling a Bend engrailed, a Crefcent for difference.

ON FLAT STONES IN THE NAVE.

Here lieth the Body of
ARABELLA, the Daughter of

THOMAS and BETTY BAKER,
who departed this Life the
2d Day of June, in the Year 1765,
aged 17 Weeks.

Alfo here lieth the Body of
BETTY, the Daughter of
THOMAS and BETTY,
who departed this Life
the 11th Day of November,
in the Year 1767, aged 16 Years.

Heare

refteth, in hopes of a joyfull

Refurrection, the Body of

THOMAS BAKER,

who departed this Life

the 30th Day of September 1785,

aged 64 Years.

O N   H E A D   S T O N E S   I N   T H E   C H A P E L   Y A R D.

	Died	Aged
Hannah, Wife of Robert Baylis	26 June, 1750	53
Three of their Children died in their Infancy, buried within the Entrance of the Chapel.		
Robert Baylis -	21 Apr. 1767	64
Mofes, Son of Robert and Ann Baylis	15 June, 1762	26
Caleb, Son of Robert and Hannah Baylis - -	22 Oct. 1772	42
William, Son of Richard Baker, of Didbrooke - -	30 Aug. 1761	26
Anne, Wife of Thomas Wilfon, of Camden, and Daughter of Robert and Hannah Baylis -	24 Dec. 1774	49
Jane, Daughter of John and Ann Chadbourn - -	19 Nov. 1748	73

CXXVII.   GUITING

CXXVII. GUITING MILITUM TEMPLI,
OR
TEMPLE GUITING.

ADJOINS the preceding Parifh, and is fituate in the lower Divifion of the Hundred of *Kiftef-gate*, feven Miles North-weftward from *Stow*, five Eaftward from *Winchcombe*, and twenty from GLOUCESTER on the North-eaft. More than 4000 Acres are included within the Boundaries, of a light ftony Soil tilled ; with 400 Acres in Woodland, and very extenfive commonable Downs, upon which large Flocks are fed.

The Living is a ftipendiary Curacy, of the certified Value of 20*l.* 5*s.* paid from the Impropriation, which, upon the Diffolution of the Knights Hofpitallers of *St. John* of *Jerufalem*, was granted to *Chrift Church* College, *Oxford*.

The Church, dedicated to *St. Mary*, is conftructed with a Nave and a ftrong embattled Tower at the Weft End ; but the Chancel is evidently more ancient, fo that it appears, that the original Edifice was re-built, and moft probably by the Knights Hofpitallers. Dr. TALBOT, the late Incumbent, in 1745, at the Expence of 1,000*l.* entirely re-modelled the Infide in a high Style of modern Decoration, with a flat Roof, and furrounding Cornices.

Amongft the hundred and fixteen Manors given by the CONQUEROR to ROGER DE LACI (fixteen of which were in this County) was " *Getinge*." His Defcendant GILBERT DE LACI gave in 1120 twelve Hides and one Virgate of Land, with the Demefnes in *Guiting* to the Knights Templars, and afterward profeffed himfelf of that Order. But the Manor was referved to his Heirs, and held by Leafe in 1324, 17 EDW. II. from ALICE Countefs of LINCOLN by the Templars, who were about that Time fucceeded by the Knights Hofpitallers *. It was inherited by the Family of CLINTON DE SAY ; and in the Reign of HENRY VIII. was purchafed of Sir JOHN HUDDLESTONE, Knight, by Dr. RICHARD FOX, Bifhop of *Winchefter*, who fettled it on the Prefident and Fellows of *Corpus Chrifti* College, *Oxford*, by Charter of Foundation in 1517.

The only Freehold Eftate in *Temple Guiting* became in 1590 the Property of THOMAS BEALE, Gent. JOHN BEALE, Gent. dying in 1774, bequeathed it to his Daughter and fole Heir MARY, the Wife of JOHN BROWNE, Gent. of *Cold Salperton*, whofe fecond Son THOMAS BEALE BROWNE, a Minor, is the prefent Poffeffor. The principal Leffee under *Corpus Chrifti* College is GEORGE TALBOT, Efq. of an Eftate, long held by the Family of ALLEN. For more than a Century, the impropriate Tythes have been leafed by *Chrift Church* College to the Family of HAYWARD.

H A M L E T S.

1. *Ford* is a Conftablewick annexed to *Pynnock*, and had formerly a Chapel, now applied to fecular Ufes. It claims diftinct manerial Rights, and forms a Part of the Eftate of the Right Honourable THOMAS CHARLES LEIGH, Lord Vifcount TRACY. The Abbey of *St. Peter* in *Gloucefter* held a Mill here, the Donation of ROBERT CONSUL in 1120, during the Abbacy of WILLIAM GODEMON.

2. *Barton* was Parcel of the Templar's Eftate in *Guiting*, where they had two Mills, one of them a Fulling Mill, erected by the Hofpitallers, probably in the Reign of EDW. III. and amongft the firft in this County †. The chief Leffees under *Corpus Chrifti* College are WILLIAM RAIKES, Efq. of *London*, and

---

* At *Quenington*, in this County, was a Preceptory of Knights Templars, appendant on their chief Houfe in *London*. A few of them refided there, for the Purpofe of receiving the Rents of Lands contiguous, and belonging to them. Upon their Diffo-lution in 1320 the fame Eftablifhments were kept up, and called Commanderies by the Knights Hofpitallers.

" Summa redditûs pertinenentiarum ad *Guiting* XI*l.* X*s.* VI*d.* ob." DUGDALE, Mon. vol. II. p. 529.

† " Fratres fecerunt unum Molendinum fulerez apud *Beretone*, quod tenet *Wireht* pro XXXII*s.* Item ipfi fratres fecerunt aliud " Molendinum apud *Beretone* quod tenet idem *Wireht* pro XII*s.*" DUGDALE. ut fupra. This, it is prefumed, is the firft No-tice of any fulling Mill erected in this County ; and it is certain that the Manufacture was eftablifhed in the Towns of *Camp-den, Northleche, Fairford, Cirencefter*, and the adjacent Villages, before it was extended to the Diftrict called *Stroud Water*. For the greater Encouragement of it, an Act of Parliament was made in 1376, " that no woollen Cloth fhall be carried into any Part, " out of the Realm to be fulled," which was confirmed by fubfequent Statutes in 1 RIC. II. ch. 7. 7 EDW. IV. ch. 3. 3 HEN. VII. ch. 11. 19 HEN. VII. ch. 11. 8. ELIZ. ch. 15. Prior to this Period, the Wool grown on the *Cotefwold* was exported to *Flanders*, from whence this Kingdom was fupplied with Woollen Cloth.

JOHN

John Inglett Fortescue, Efq. of *Dawlifh*, co. *Devon*. Maurice Rodney held this Manor by Grant from Queen Elizabeth in the firft Year of her Reign.

3. *Kyngton* in 1350 belonged to the Families of Cook and Collett, but is now divided into feveral fmall Freeholds. One of the large Common Fields is appropriated to this Hamlet.

In a Survey made in 1770, the whole Parifh was found to contain 75 Houfes, and 428 Inhabitants.

Incumbents.	Patrons.	Incumbents.	Patrons.
1711 William Winde,	Chrift Church Coll. Oxf.	1777 Charles Bifhop,	Chrift Church Coll. Oxf.
——— ——— Parfons,	The fame.	1780 Thomas Symonds,	The fame.
1769 Erafmus King,	The fame.		

PRESENT PROPRIETORS OF THE MANOR,

The Prefident, Fellows, and Scholars of *Corpus Chrifti* College, *Oxford*.

The Perfons fummoned from this Place by the Heralds in 1682 and 1683, were

William Stratford, Efq. and John Beale, Gent.

At the Election in 1776, Three Freeholders polled from this Parifh.

The earlieft Date in the Regifter occurs in 1679.

ANNUAL ACCOUNT OF MARRIAGES, BIRTHS, AND BURIALS, IN THIS PARISH.

A.D.	Mar.	Bir.	Bur.	A.D.	Mar.	Bir.	Bur.	A.D.	Mar.	Bir.	Bur.	A.D.	Mar.	Bir.	Bur.
1781	7	9	11	1786	3	10	14	1791				1796			
1782	4	7	6	1787	2	9	11	1792				1797			
1783	2	16	6	1788	5	12	12	1793				1798			
1784	5	9	11	1789	2	14	4	1794				1799			
1785	4	11	15	1790	3	9	8	1795				1800			

INSCRIPTIONS IN THE CHURCH.

ON FLAT STONES IN THE CHANCEL.

To the Memory of
RICHARD HAYWARD, of Barton, Gent.
Impropriator of this Parifh,
and ANNE his Wife.
He died the 21ft of January, 1703,
aged 60.
She died the 24th of June, 1724,
aged 80.

ROGER and SUSANNAH,
two of their Children, died Infants.

Here lieth the Body of
AGNES HAYWARD,
Daughter of the above
RICHARD and ANNE HAYWARD.
She died April 8, 1760, in her 81ft Year.

To the Memory of
CHARLES HAYWARD, Gent.
Impropriator of this Parifh,
who departed this Life
the 15th Day of January,
in the Year of our Lord 1787,
aged 63 Years.

To the Memory of
CHARLES HAYWARD, Gent.
Impropriator of this Parifh,
who died July 25, 1764, aged 76.

Alfo of ANNE HAYWARD,
Wife of THOMAS HAYWARD, Gent.
who died the 8th Day of October, 1771,
aged 33 Years.

To the Memory of
THOMAS HAYWARD, Gent.
who departed this Life
the 16th Day of Auguft,
1785, aged 59 Years.

Here lyeth the Body of
JOHN ALLISON,
Citizen and Apothecary of London,
who had Iffue, by RUTH,
his dear and loving Wife,
three Sons, JOHN, RALPH, and ARTHUR,
and two Daughters,
PENELOPE and MILLICENT.

He died June 28, 1659,
aged above 40 Years,
to whofe Memory fhe erected this
Monument.

ON FLAT STONES IN THE NAVE.

Here lieth the Body of
MARY, the Wife of THOMAS DEANE,
of the Woodhoufe, Gent.
who departed this Life
the 3d Day of October, AnnoDom. 1708,
aged 55 Yeares.

In Memory of
MARGARET, the Wife of
LEWIS A'DEANE, of the Woodhoufe,
Gent.
She was Daughter of JAMES ROSS,
of the City of Edinburgh, Gent.
who defcended from the ancient Family
of the Houfe of Killarig and
Balling a Gowing, in the Shire of Rofs,
in the North of Scotland.
Her Father went Secretary to his Uncle
ARTHUR ROSS,
laft Archbifhop of Scotland, in the
Reign of King JAMES the Second.
She has left Iffue, by the faid
LEWIS A'DEANE, three Sons and four
Daughters. She departed this Life
Jan. 6, 1740, aged 42 Years.

Here

Here lieth the Body of Mrs. KATHERINE BRAYNE, of Barton, Relict of Mr. WILLIAM BRAYNE,
of Little Dean, in this County.   She died Nov. 22, 1727, aged 78 Years.

Alfo the Remains of ELIZBETH CURTIS, of Stow, in the County of Gloucefter,
who died the 22d Day of Feb. 1758, aged 72 Years.

ON MARBLE MONUMENTS IN THE NORTH WING.

Arms ; on a Chevron, between three Griffins, Heads erazed, as many Mullets,

In a Vault near this Marble
lie the Remains
of JOHN BEALE, Gent.
defcended from an ancient Family of this Place.
He died the IX Day of Auguft, MDCCLXXIV, aged LXXIV Years.

Alfo
in the fame Vault are depofited the Remains of
JOHN BEALE, of the City of London, Merchant,
a Gentleman juftly efteemed for his Integrity and Friendfhip.
He died the XXVII Day of October, MDCCLXXIV, aged XXVIII Years,
juftly lamented by all who knew him.
He was only Son and Heir of the firft—named
JOHN BEALE and MARY his Wife,
Daughter, and fole furviving Heir
of THOMAS ROBBINS, of Maugerfbury, in this County.

Arms ; Gules, a Lion rampant within a Border engrailed Or, a Mullet for difference, for TALBOT ;—impaling, Per Fefs Or
and Argent, an Eagle difplayed, with two Heads Sable, on the Breaft an Efcocheon Gules, charged with a Bend Vairè, for
BOUVERIE.

Sacred to the Memory
of that truly great and pious Divine the Honourable and Reverend GEORGE TALBOT, D. D.
(youngeft Son of CHARLES Lord TALBOT, Lord High Chancellor of Great Britain)
who finifhed his glorious Courfe of Life on the 19th of November, 1785, in the 71ft Year of his Age.
Stedfaft from his Infancy in the Profeffion of the true Faith, and conftant in the Practice of every Virtue,
he became in early Life, and continued to his laft Hour,
a fhining Pattern of Chriftian Excellence, and an Ornament to Human Nature.
Though bleft with every Endowment to difcharge with Dignity and Luftre the Duties of the higheft Office,
his Humility conftrained him to the loweft in the Miniftry.
Confcious of the Good he did in this Curacy, and dreading the Refponfibility of a more extenfive Truft,
he refufed a Bifhoprick ;
and for near thirty Years, until difabled by Infirmities, taught in this Church,
with the pureft Zeal, and moft perfuafive Eloquence,
the faving Truths of the Gofpel ; and converted many to Righteoufnefs.
His Charities were diffufive, but directed by Wifdom ; his Benevolence was unbounded ;
and his Labours to promote Peace, and the Temporal, as well as the Spiritual Intereft of all his Fellow Creatures,
ceafed only with his laft Breath.
He paffed through Life without an Enemy, and with the Affection and Veneration of all who knew him.
This Fabrick, fubftantially repaired and beautified at his fole Expence,
and the Hofpital of this County, which his Liberality and Exertions greatly contributed to found and eftablifh,
will be lafting Monuments of his Piety and Humility ;
but his good Name will furvive both.
This was erected by the Honourable CHARLOTTE BOUVERIE, at her exprefs Defire.

IN THE CHURCH YARD, ON TOMBS.

MARY WINDE, Relict of
JOHN WINDE, of Bruckthrop,
and Daughter of WILLIAM RANDAL,
of Cowley, who was buried
Feb. 28, 1684.

JOHN WILLIAMS,
Sept. 26, 1680.

JOHN WILLIAMS,
1696.

JOHN WILLIAMS,
Sept. 2, 1745.

THOMAS WILLIAMS, of Kyneton,
May 26, 1755, aged 70.

RICHARD TOWNSEND, Gent.
departed this Life MDCCLXXXIV.

SARAH KECK, Daughter of
ANTHONY and MARY KECK,
of Swindon, in this County,
died June 5, 1753, aged 16 Years.

4

ELIZABETH, Daughter of
JOHN and JOAN CLARK,
died May 21, 1760, aged 22 Years.

JOAN, Wife of JOHN CLARK,
died Jan. 27, 1783, aged 84 Years.

RICHARD their Son
died in his Infancy.

ERASMUS KING, Clerk,
a few Years Vicar of
Upper and Lower Guiting,
died March 1, 1777, aged 31 Years.

Clear was his Voice, and as his Reafon
ftrong,
With pious Care his well taught Flocks
among
He ftrew'd of Holy Writ the choiceft
Store;
Well fkill'd he was in Theologic Lore.
On his perfuafive Lips Attention hung,
For Truths divine flow'd fweetly from
his Tongue.

Rev. CHARLES BISHOP, M. A.
Minifter of this Parifh,
Vicar of Lower Guiting
and of Badgeworth, in this County,
died May 14, 1780, aged 28 Years.

If flow Confumption (fure Ally of Death)
Prey on thy wafting Limbs and lab'ring
Breath,
Reader ! be taught, without Complaint
or Tear,
Like him with patient Chearfulnefs to
bear ;
And when the long impending Stroke is
given,
Calmly refign, like him, this World for
Heaven.

ON

ON FLAT AND HEAD STONES.

Name	Died	Aged
Betty Crips - -	13 Sept. 1778	60
Richard Crips -	9 Apr. 1769	48
Betty their Daughter -	25 June, 1772	9
Giles Crips - -	28 May, 1737	30
Elizabeth his Wife -	31 Mar. 1754	44
Mary their Daughter -	1 Aug. 1745	10
William Crips	— —— 1747	—
Elizabeth, Daughter of Richard and Elizabeth Crips -	21 June, 1757	—
John Crips - -	14 Feb. 1758	83
Thomas, Son of John and Mary Crips - -	17 July, 1788	72
Mary, Daughter of Richard and Elizabeth Smith, of Cobberley, and Wife of Thomas Turner	16 Aug. 1777	33
Joseph Keck - -	23 Dec. 1729	75
Sarah Keck, Relict of Joseph Keck	12 Aug. 1762	100
Hester, Wife of Robert Keck	11 Feb. 1754	55
Robert Keck - -	24 July, 1777	76
Mary Keck, Wife of Anthony Keck - -	2 Nov. 1759	56
William, Son of Joseph and Sarah Keck - -	29 Jan. 1757	70
Elizabeth, Daughter of Joseph and Ann Keck - -	31 May, 1767	39
John Jones, Son of George Gilbert, and Margaret Jones, of Ford	18 Apr. 1771	21
Ann their Daughter -	11 Apr. 1773	21
Margaret, Wife of George Gilbert Jones - -	7 Oct. 1773	54
George Gilbert Jones -	17 July, 1778	59
George Gilbert Jones, junior	12 Dec. 1777	32
Mary, Wife of William Freebury, of Ford, junior -	27 May, 1777	29
Thomas Weale	24 May, 1706	65
Mary, Daughter of William and Frances Dowty -	— Mar. 1736	—
Mary, Wife of Richard Gillett	21 Apr. 1753	65
William Gillett - -	30 May, 1722	—
Sarah, Wife of Thomas Dunce, of Condicot - -	15 Oct. 1746	27
John Wiggett -	2 Feb. 1753	—
Alice, Wife of John Snow, of Ford	19 Oct. 1789	31
William their Son died in his Infancy.		
Thomas Morris -	3 Jan. 1766	82
Anne his Wife -	11 Aug. 1731	51
Anne his second Wife -	13 May, 1742	42
Anne, Wife of James Fardon, of Ford - -	9 Oct. 1758	53
Anne their Daughter -	3 Jan. 1770	21
Anne, Daughter of James and Anne Fardon, of Ford -	21 Aug. 1734	—
Benjamin Crips, Son of John and Mary Crips - -	— Oct. 1728	9
John their Son -	24 Aug. 1728	16
Mary, Wife of John Crips, senior	25 Feb. 1771	84
Jane, Wife of William Baylis, Daughter of William and Mary Attwood - -	— —— 1768	35
Robert, Son of William and Mary Chandler, died in his Infancy.		
Letty their Daughter -	13 Sept. 1768	73
Elizabeth, Wife of Simon Herretts	17 Feb. 1730	81
Joseph Chandler -	28 Mar. 1729	—
Giles Withorne -	6 Aug. 1704	56
Ann, Wife of Joseph Chandler		
Robert Chandler, of Kynton	11 Feb. 1734	39
Mary his Wife -	12 Aug. 1745	66
Elizabeth, Wife of Richard Smith, of Coberley, and Daughter of Robert and Dinah Flatcher, of Postlip - -	28 Jan. 1761	39

Name	Died	Aged
Robert, Son of Richard and Elizabeth Smith	22 Mar. 1761	—
William their Son -	17 Apr. 1764	19
Robert Baylis, of Sudeley -	24 Mar. 172½	59
Johannah his Wife buried	10 Jan. 17¾₀	72
Ann, Wife of John Lyes buried	21 June, 1776	—
Elizabeth, Daughter of William and Elizabeth Baylis -	4 May, 1728	22
Ann, Daughter of William and Elizabeth Baylis -	— June, 1713	—
William Baylis, senior -	2 May, 1723	63
Elizabeth his Wife -	14 Mar. 1758	77
John Smith, of Ford -	29 Sept. 1769	69
Elizabeth his Wife -	4 Apr. 1763	50
Richard Smith -	17 May, 1762	66
Mary his Wife -	25 Feb. 1745	38
Mary their Daughter -	20 July, 1746	—
Mary, Wife of Richard Perratt, senior -	30 May, 1754	70
John, Son of Richard and Mary Perratt - -	16 Mar. 1784	68
Sarah, Wife of Richard Perratt, junior - -	3 Apr. 1776	63
Mary, Wife of William Dowdeswell - -	8 Feb. 1787	35
Mary their Daughter died in her Infancy.		
John Perratt - -	28 June, 1688	41
Richard Surman -	10 Dec. 1719	—
Lucy, Wife of James Griffin	28 Feb. 1768	76
James Griffin -	25 July, 1764	80
John Dowdeswell -	17 Mar. 1784	65
Elizabeth his Wife -	6 Jan. 1781	59
Elizabeth, Wife of Thomas Dowdeswell - -	18 Feb. 1745	61
John, Son of John and Elizabeth Dowdeswell -	10 Mar. 1774	27
Elizabeth their Daughter died in her Infancy.		
Mary, Daughter of John and Elizabeth Smith	30 Jan. 1773	19
Mary, Daughter of Richard and Sarah Smith - -	25 Sept. 1715	24
John Clarck - -	14 Sept. 1767	66
Samuel Dowdeswell -	3 Apr. 1728	41
Anthony Dobbins -	23 June, 1768	70
Anthony Dobbins -	23 Sept. 1779	77
Eleanor, Wife of William Winchester - -	14 Feb. 1712	30
Adam their Son -	7 Feb. 1782	—
William Timmins - -	2 Mar. 1729	60
Sarah his Wife - -	9 July, 1764	86
Sarah Timmins - -	21 July, 1765	61
Jane Timmins - -	16 Mar. 1766	58
Mary, Wife of William Proctor	3 Feb. 1783	69
Katharine Luker - -	5 Mar. 1735	77
Adam Winchester - -	30 Sept. 1754	55
Elizabeth, Wife of Richard Langson -	26 Oct. 1788	60
Thomas Yardington, of Sudeley, in the Parish of Winchcomb	8 Mar. 1781	82
Edward Humphris -	25 July, 1766	57
Sarah, Wife of William Gillett	29 Jan. 1784	29
Naomi, Wife of John White, and Daughter of Thomas Deane, Gent. - -	14 Apr. 1749	79
Anne Williams - -	21 Jan. 1759	—
Anne, Wife of William Williams	14 Feb. 1781	70
William Williams - -	23 June, 1757	50
John Williams - -	17 Mar. 1762	—
Ann his Wife - -	17 Aug. 1762	68
Thomas Compere -	6 Mar. 1689	—
William Baylis -	14 Feb. 1786	54

O N

ON FLAT AND HEAD STONES.

	Died	Aged		Died	Aged
Charles, Son of Charles and Lucy Williams	29 Feb. 1772	7	Ann Deane	25 Dec. 1730	—
Thomas Williams	6 Mar. 1758	61	William Hatfield	14 Dec. 1787	41
Charles Williams	12 Mar. 1786	55	Ann, Daughter of William and Sarah Hatfield, died in her Infancy.		
Ann, Wife of Thomas Williams	20 Dec. 1775	77	Sarah, Daughter of William and Sarah Hatfield	19 Feb. 1787	5
William Compere	16 June, 1690	81			
Dorothy his Wife	3 Sept. ——	—	William Johnson	— May, 1721	22
Thomas Smith	25 May, 1745	61			

The Honourable and Reverend
GEORGE TALBOTT,
D. D.
died November 19, 1785,
aged 70.

H A M P N E T T,

OR *H A M P T O N E T*, is a Parish of the middle Dimensions, within the Hundred of *Bradley* and the Perambulation of *Cotefwold.* The Soil is light; which, fince the Inclofure, has been generally applied to Tillage. The Rivulet *Leche* has its Source here; and, in a flight Degree, a petrifying Quality near the original Spring. From *Northlech* this Village is diftant one Mile on the North-weft, and eighteen Eaftward from GLOUCESTER.

The Benefice is rectorial, having the contiguous Rectory of *Stowell* confolidated with it by Confent of the Diocefan and Patron in 1660 *. They are both in the Deanery of *Cirencefter.*

No curious Remains are obfervable in the Architecture of the Church, which is dedicated to *St. George,* conftructed with a Nave only, and an embattled Tower at the Weft End.

In *Domefday* the Manor was taxed at ten Hides; the Property of ROGER DE LUREI. Soon afterward it became appendant on the great Manor of *Bifley,* and was held by ROGER and EDWARD DE MORTIMER, Earls of *March.* In 1507, 23 HEN. VIII. it belonged to RICHARD HERCOURT and AGNES his Wife. EDMUND HORNE was feized of *Hamptonet* and *Stowell* in 1547, 1 EDW. VI.; and, in the next Reign, ANTHONY BOURNE, having married his Daughter and fole Heir, fucceeded to thefe Eftates. The next Poffeffor was RICHARD ATKINSON, Citizen of *Oxford,* who was Mayor in 1548, and received the Honour of Knighthood at the Coronation of Queen ELIZABETH 1559. ROBERT ATKINSON, Recorder of *Oxford,* fucceeded, and left one Son, Sir HENRY ATKINSON, Knt. who died without furviving Iffue; and one Daughter, ANNE, the Wife of Sir WILLIAM WENTWORTH, of *Wentworth Woodhoufe,* co. *York,* by which Connection they paffed to the Earls of STRAFFORD. About 1700, they were purchafed by JOHN HOWE, Efq. (the Father of the firft Baron CHEDWORTH), whofe noble Defcendant is the prefent Proprietor.

S T O W E L

Has had the fame Poffeffors as *Hamptnett* fince EDMUND HORNE abovementioned. Prior to him were the Family of MARTELL for feveral Generations, and the elder Branch of the TAMES, of *Fairford* †.

The Church is very ancient, but fmall; in which, fince the Confolidation with *Hampnett,* no divine Service has been performed.

The manerial Manfion-houfe is the only one within the Limits of the Parifh which was re-built with an embattled Front, &c. in the Reign of Queen ELIZABETH by ROBERT ATKINSON, whofe Arms (Azure, a Crofs moline Argent, between four Lioncels rampant Or) are carved over the Porch. It was the Refidence of the Lords CHEDWORTH till the Deceafe of the laft in 1780.

No Benefactions to the Poor.

INCUMBENTS.	PATRONS.	INCUMBENTS.	PATRONS.
		Hampnett.	
—— Hugh Bennet,	—— ——.	1602 Brian Atkinfon,	Q. Elizabeth.
1558 Edward Apdavid,	Anth. Buftard.	1621 Robert Knowles,	Charles Holte.
1577 John Bignell,	The fame.	1629 Tho. Hughes, M.A.	The fame.
		Stowel.	
—— ——————,	Agnes Hercourt.	1581 George Hayward, B.A.	Rob. Atkinfon, Efq.
—— Richard Conway,	—— ——.	1590 Edmund Bracegirdle,	The fame.
1551 John Edwards,	Walt. and Jane Bafkerville.	1602 Brian Atkinfon, B.A.	The fame.
1559 Walter Thurbet,	The fame.	1606 Francis Webb, B.A.	The fame.
1574 Meredith Evans,	Q. Elizabeth.	1613 Francis Webb, M.A.	Sir Hen. Atkinfon, Kt.
1578 Henry Fifher,	Rob. Atkinfon, Efq.	—— Thomas Hughes,	The fame.

* Lib. Reg. 10*l* " 64 acras terr' arab', & 4 acras prati." Terrier.
† " The elder Houfe of the TAMES is at *Stowel* by *Northleche.* Mr. HORNE, of *Oxfordfhire,* dwellinge by *Langeley,* hath " married this TAME, Daughter and Heir, and fhaul have by her 80*li.* of Land by the Yere." LELAND, Itin. vol. VI. p. 18.

VOL. II.   B   INCUM-

Incumbents.	Patrons.	Incumbent.	Patron.

Hamptnett cum Stowel.

1675 Tho. Hughes, M. A.	Wm. Earl of Strafford.	1771 Peter Hawker, M. A.	Henry Frederick Lord
1733 Simon Hughes,	Fridefwide Hughes.		Chedworth.

PRESENT LORD OF THE MANORS

Of *Hampnett* and *Stowel,*

The Right Honourable JOHN Lord CHEDWORTH.

From *Stowel,* at the Heralds Vifitation, in 1682 and 1683, was fummoned

James Stephens, Efq.

At the Election in 1776, only One Freeholder polled from this Parifh.

The earlieft Date in the Regifter occurs in 1591.

ANNUAL ACCOUNT OF MARRIAGES, BIRTHS, AND BURIALS, IN THIS PARISH.

A.D.	Mar.	Bir.	Bur.	A.D.	Mar.	Bir.	Bur.	A.D.	Mar.	Bir.	Bur.	A.D.	Mar.	Bir.	Bur.
1781	2	2	—	1786	1	4	—	1791				1796			
1782	1	5	1	1787	2	1	1	1792				1797			
1783	1	3	1	1788	1	5	1	1793				1798			
1784	—	7	2	1789	2	4	1	1794				1799			
1785	2	4	2	1790	—	4	2	1795				1800			

INSCRIPTIONS IN THE CHURCH.

ON FLAT STONES IN THE CHANCEL.

JANE, the Wife of
THO. HUGHES, Rect.
was buried
March 24,
1641.

JOHN yr Sone
was buried
Jan. 8, 1644.

ON FLAT STONES IN THE NAVE.

Here lyeth the Body of
JOHN LOVESEY,
who departed this Life Novem.
the 10, 1729, aged 70 Years.

Alfo here lieth the Body of
MARY his Wife.
She died September 2, 1741,
aged 77 Years.

In Memory of
WILLIAM LOVESEY, fenior,
who died October the
4, 1762, aged 72.

ANN his Wife
died October 11, 1775,
aged 65.

In Memory of
MARGARET, Wife of
LAWRENCE GLOVER,
who died January 5, 1757,
aged 55 Years.

Alfo of the faid
LAWRENCE GLOVER,
who died March 25, 1790,
aged 82.

IN THE CHURCH YARD.

ON A TOMB.

ELIZABETH, Wife of

STEPHEN TAYLER,

died October 20, 1789, aged 57.

SARAH, RICHARD, and REBECCA,

their Children,

died in their Infancy.

ON HEAD AND FLAT STONES.

	Died	Aged
John Wakefield	4 May, 1710	34
Anne his Wife	6 June, 1760	86
William Day	— Sept. 1717	57
William Mallings	8 Aug. 1710	76
Eliner, Wife of John Millard	27 Aug. 1707	62
Charles Lovefey	22 Feb. 172..	17
John Miller	17 June, 1673	—
Elizabeth, Wife of Richard Ballinge	13 Jan. 1734	—
William Radway	5 Nov. 1777	26
Hefter, Daughter of Robert and Mary Radway	27 Oct. 1784	33

I N

IN THE CHAPEL AT STOWEL.

ON MARBLE MONUMENTS.

Arms; On a Lozenge, Or, a Griffin fegreant Sable, for MORGAN.

In Memory
of the
truely excellent
Mrs. ANNE MORGAN, Daughter
and Coheirefs of Sir EDWARD MORGAN,
late of Lanternham, in the County of
Monmouth, Bart. who died the 24th of Auguft,
1712, in the 35th Year of her Age.
Her Perfon was beautifully agreeable.
She had Wit, without Levity; Knowledge,
without Affectation; a penetrating
Underftanding, with a found Judgement.
She was pleafant in Converfation;
modeftly referved, without Severity;
Juft, Beneficent, Charitable, and
Generous; endued with a fweetnefs
and firmnefs of Temper above the
Power of common Accidents; civill and
well-bred towards all; but where fhe
profeffed Friendfhip, in every Part of
that Duty without equall; for ever to
be honoured, loved, and lamented.

The LORD giveth, and the LORD
taketh away; bleffed be the Name of
the LORD!

Arms; On a Lozenge Or, a Fefs between three Wolves Heads couped Sable, for HOWE;—impaling, Azure, a Bend Or, for SCROPE.

In Memory of the truly pious,
the Lady ANNABELLA HOWE, one of the
Daughters of EMANUEL Lord SCROPE,
Earl of SUNDERLAND, the Widow of
JOHN GRUBHAM HOWE, of Compton,
and the moft indulgent Mother of
JOHN GRUBHAM HOWE, of Stowell,
in the County of Gloucefter.
She died the 20th Day of March, 1703-4.

Quem femper Acerbum,
Semper Honoratum,———Habebo.———

CXXIX. HAMPTON

CXXIX. HAMPTON MONIALIUM,
MINCHIN, or MOCHEL,

SO denominated from Monecchun, an old Word, fignifying a Nun *, is an an extenfive and very populous Parifh, in the Hundred of *Longtree*, four Miles diftant from *Stroud* on the South, fix from *Tetbury* in the oppofite Direction, ten eaft from *Cirencefter*, and fourteen South-weftward from the City of GLOUCESTER.

More than 4000 Acres are faid to be within the Boundaries, which, on the North and South Sides, are formed by the *Avening* Brook, and the Rivulet *Stroudwater*. The Soil is light, excepting in the Vallies; and chiefly in Tillage and Beech-woodland, exclufive of the great Common of 600 Acres, with very excellent Herbage.

The Benefice is a valuable Rectory †, with the Chapel of *Rodborough* annexed, in the Deanery of *Stonehoufe*. About the Year 1720, the Parfonage-houfe being dilapidated, PHILIP SHEPPARD, M. A. Rector, began the prefent upon a new Site. It is peculiarly commodious, and the Environs are laid out on a very neat and eligible Plan.

When *Domefday* was compiled, the Nuns of *Caen*, in *Normandy*, poffeffed, with the Manor, the Impropriation ‡; and about the Reign of King HENRY III. founded the Church, which was then dedicated to the *Holy Trinity*, and contains a Nave, Tranfept, and two fmall Aifles §. The dividing Arches are, on one Side, round and heavy; and, on the other, plain Gothic. In the Reign of RICHARD II. 1382, Sir JOHN DE LA MERE and MAUD his Wife re-built the South Tranfept; which is more lofty than its Oppofite, having a very large Window of beautiful Ramifications, and feveral others, with narrow lancet Arches, inferted between the Buttreffes. Under the great Window are two Arcades, with the recumbent Effigies of the Founders, as a Croifader and a Lady in the Drefs of that Age. Upon the Shield, almoft effaced, is an Eagle difplayed, Part of the Arms of DE LA MERE. At this Period, they held a Manfe, and 60 Acres of Land, in this Parifh. A Chantry was fubfequently eftablifhed by a Perfon named AINSLOW, of whom we can collect nothing farther; and RICHARD GRAVENOR, the laft Prieft, received an annual Penfion of 5*l.* ‖. In the North Tranfept is another Arcade, which contains a Sarcophagus, upon the Lid of which is carved a Crofs florettè; certainly intended for an Ecclefiaftick; and in various Parts of the Church are large blue Slabs, fome mutilated, and others entirely robbed of their Braffes. The Tower, which is placed in the Centre, had originally a Spire, the upper Part of which was blown down in 1602, when it was finifhed with an embattled Parapet **.

Minchin Hampton became a Town in 1213, 53 HEN. III. of whom the Abbefs of *Caen* purchafed the Privilege of a weekly Market on Tuefday, and two Fairs, which are held, according to the modern Calendar, on Trinity Monday, and the 29th of October. There are three Market-houfes; two of which were built by PHILIP SHEPPARD, Efq. in 1700, with a Defign of eftablifhing a Wool Market, but without Succefs ††. The Town is fituate upon a gradual Declivity, open to the South-eaft, from whence the Approach is very picturefque. It confifts of four Streets, lying at right Angles, but irregularly built. A beautiful Skreen of Wood furrounds it on the North-weft, in the higher Ground of the Park, which gives every diftant View of the fingularly fhaped Tower a very pleafing Effect, as it appears " bofomed high in tufted Trees."

---

* See HEARNE's Gloffary to ROBERT OF GLOUCESTER's Chronicle, vol. II. p. 685.

† Lib. Reg. 41*l.* 13*s.* 4*d.* Yearly Tenths 4*l.* 3*s.* 4*d.*

‡ " Here were Nunnes alfoe," faith LELAND, Itin. vol. VI. p. 74. " And from him CAMDEN, SPEED, and others, fay " that there was a Nunnery here, but I can not find any, and believe that this Place was called *Minchin Hampton*, only becaufe " the Manor was given to the Minchins, or Nuns of the Holy Trinity at *Caen*, in *Normandy*, by K. WILLIAM CONQ." TANNER's Not. Mon. *Glouc.* XIV. See farther, Cart. 53 HEN. III. m. 8. " de Mercatû & Feria conceff. Abbatiffæ de *Cadomo* apud " *Hampton Monialium*." Cart. 33 EDW. III. n. 9.

§ The great Altar was dedicated by WALTER DE MAYDENSTONE, Bifhop of *Worcefter*, in July 1315.

THOMAS's Survey of *Worcefter*, p. 220.

‖ WILLIS.

** MSS. PARSONS and WANTNER, in the Bodleian Library, *Oxford.*

†† The Grant of Market and Fairs was renewed to ANDREWS Lord WINDSOR in 1545.

I

Domefday

HAMPTON

Sir John De la Mere Kn.t 1382

647

Domesday specifies eight Hides belonging to the Manor in the Tenure of GODA, a Saxon Countefs, before it was given to the Nunnery of the *Holy Trinity*, founded at *Caen*, by MAUD, Wife of WILLIAM the CONQUEROR, in 1064 *. King HENRY V. when he diffolved the Alien Priories, gave it to the Nunnery of *Sion*, in *Middlefex*, founded by him in 1414, appendant on which it continued till the final Diffolution of monaftic Bodies. But this Grant was reverfionary, for Sir JOHN PHELIP had obtained it *in feodo*, by Patent, 2 HEN. V.; and, in the 22d Year of the next Reign, the Nuns of *Sion* were confirmed in it after the Deceafe of ALICE, the Relict of WILLIAM DE LA POLE, Duke of *Suffolk*†. Upon the final Diffolution of monaftic Corporations, the King referved this Manor to his own Ufe, which, in 1545, he gave, together with the Priory of *Bordefley*, in *Worcefterfhire*, in Exchange for Lands at *Stanwell* and *Hampton Court*, co. *Middlefex*, to Sir ANDREWS WYNDSORE, the firft Baron WINDSOR, fo created Nov. 3, 1529, 21 HEN. VIII. The Manors of *Minchin Hampton, Avening, and Pennebury*, were vefted in his immediate Defcendants, to THOMAS Lord WINDSOR, who died in 1642 without Iffue; when his Nephew, THOMAS HICKMAN, fucceeded to thefe Eftates, which were in the Court of Wards during his Minority ‡. About the Year 1664 they were purchafed by PHILIP SHEPPARD, Efq. and were inherited by the prefent Poffeffor, upon the Death of his elder Brother, SAMUEL SHEPPARD, Efq. in 1770, without Iffue Male.

The ancient Manerial-Houfe, formerly inhabited by the WYNDESORS, is faid to have been fituate in the Centre of the Town, to have been very fpacious, and to have had hanging Gardens open to the South. The large Manfion near the Church, called the Farm, was once occupied by the Firmarius, or Receiver of the Abbey Rents. P. SHEPPARD, Efq. when he purchafed it, made it his Refidence, and feveral of the Apartments have been fince added.

T Y T H I N G S and H A M L E T S.

1. *Hampton* Tything contains the following Hamlets: The *Box, Forwood*, and *Hawcombe*, or *Holcombe.* The *Box* and *Longford* were held in 1376, 49 EDW. III. of the BOHUNS Earls of HEREFORD; and *Forwood* belonged at the Commencement of this Century to a younger Branch of the Family of DRIVER, of *Afton*. In 1547, 1 EDW. VI. a Fine in Lands in *Hawcombe* was paffed by JOHN HYETT to WILLIAM WEBB, whofe Defcendants have been fince fettled there, and have formed feveral diftinct Houfes.

2. *Rodborough* Tything, in which are *Littleworth, Theefcombe*, and *St. Cloe*, or more properly *Saintlieu*, which laft was the Grange of certain Lands belonging to the Abbey of *Malmfbury*, and where a few Monks occafionally refided §. It was bought by the Truftees of NATHANIEL CAMBRIDGE, *Hamborough* Merchant, who, at his Deceafe in 1697, bequeathed 1000*l.* for the Eftablifhment of a Free School, confined to the Natives of this Tything, and the adjoining Parifh of *Woodchefter*. At *Theefcombe* the Family of CAMBRIDGE were originally fettled.

3. *Chalford* Tything, in which are included *Chalford, Hyde, Burley, Brimfcombe*, and *Cowcombe*. The beautiful Valley, called *Chalford Bottom*, is divided between this Parifh and *Bifley* by the Rivulet *Stroud Water*. The Springs which rife in the Hill on the North Side have, in a very peculiar Degree, the Quality of depofing a calcarious Sediment upon every Subftance with which they come in Contact; forming Incruftations, or Petrifactions, fome of which are highly efteemed by the Naturalifts ‖.

St. Mary Mills, in this Diftrict, and Lands adjoining, were the Corps of the Chauntry of *St. Mary*, in the Church of *Minchin Hampton* before mentioned, and probably the Refidence of the Prieft. The Houfe is partly ancient; and the Hall, before the modern Front was added, is faid to have been the Chapel for this Tything, and to have retained many Veftiges of *Romifh* Worfhip. There is a fmall Room, with a flat Stone Roof, called " Friar BACON's Study ;" but it is well known that he was not a

---

* Terra Ecclefiæ *Monialium* S'cæ *Trinit'* de *Cadoma*.

Ipfa Eccl'a ten' *Hantone*. Goda Comitiffa tenuit T. R. E. Ibi VIII Hidæ. In d'nio funt v Car', & XXXII Vill'i, & x Bord', " cum XXIII Car'. Ibi P'br & x Servi, & VIII Molini de XLV Sol', & xx Ac' P'ti, Silva II Levv' l'g, & dimid' Levv' lat'. Va- " let XXVIII Lib'."

" The Church of the Nuns of the *Holy Trinity* at *Caen* holds *Hantone*, in *Langetren* Hundred. GODA, the Countefs, held it in " the Time of K. EDWARD the Confeffor. There are eight Hides. Annexed to the Manor are five Plough Tillages (300 Acres), " thirty-two Villeins, or fuperior Hufbandmen; ten Bordars, who held fmall Portions of Land on Condition of fupplying the " Table of their Lord; and employed thirty-five Ploughs. There is a Prieft, and ten Servi, or menial Servants; eight Corn- " mills of forty-five Shillings Rent; twenty Acres of Meadow; a Wood, two Miles long, and half a Mile broad. The annual " Value of the whole is 28*l*." Domefday, p. lxxii.

† Pat. 2 HENRICI V. p. 2. m. 6. vel 7. Licentia JOANNI PHELIP, Arm. perquirendi in feodo Manerium de *Minchin Hampton* Parcell. poffeffionum Abbatiæ de *Cadomo*.

Pat. 22 HEN. VI. p. 2. m. 11. pro Manerio de *M. Hampton* concedendo Abbatiffæ & Conventui de *Syon* poft mortem ALICIÆ uxoris WILL. DE LA POLE, com. *Suff*.

Rec. in Scacc. 1 HEN. VII. Mich. Rot. 15.

‡ " WILLIAM Lord WINDSOR ob. 1558 feized of the Manor of *M. Hampton, Avening*, and *Pinburie*. Upon an Inquifition, " *poft mortem*, taken at *Cirencefter*, Sept. 9, 1576, EDWARD Lord WINDSOR was found to have died feized of the Manors of " *Minchel Hampton, Aveninge, Pinbury*, and *Loefmore*." COLLINS, Title *Plymouth*, vol. IV. p. 80.

§ Abb. de *Malmfbury* " de Terris in *Munchene Hampton*." DUGDALE, Mon. vol. I. p. 54.

‖ They are difcriminated by our ingenious Countryman Mr. KIRWAN, in his " Elements of Mineralogy," under the Name of *Tophi and Stalactites*, 8vo, p. 25. DA COSTA (Nat. Hift. of Foffils, 4to, 1757, p. 135.) fpeaks of the *Saxum Arenarium Tophus dictum*, which he confiders as differing in many refpects from thefe Incruftations.

VOL. II.   C   Native

Native of this County, as the Tradition reports. It appears, that this Eftate belonged, after the Suppreffion, to the Family of HALYDAY ; and, a few Years paft, to SAMUEL PEACH, Efq. by whom it was fold.

Hyde ; the prefent Poffeffors of which are the Families of WALBANK, CLUTTERBUCK, and BEALE.

Cowcombe. Lands in this Place were held by WILLIAM MULL, or MYLLE, of *Harefcombe*, and were efchaeted to the Crown, with others at *Duntefborne Militis*, during the Wars between the Houfes of *York* and *Lancafter.*

The greater Part of *Brimfcombe* lies in the Parifh of *Stroud.*

Amberley muft be noticed upon two Accounts ; being that large Tract given to poor Houfekeepers refident in the Parifh, and the Site of a very remarkable Entrenchment. The Family of HAMPTON were very anciently fettled here. ALICE, Daughter of JOHN HAMPTON, who died in 1556, is faid to have been " right beneficial to the Church and Parifh *." It is reafonably conjectured, that upon her becoming a Nun of *Sion*, fhe either purchafed *Amberley* for the Purpofes fpecified, or procured a Grant of it from the Convent *.

The great Vallum is irregular, with fmaller Trenches branching from it. It varies much in Height, at moft about eight Feet, compofed of the Rubble Stone of the Country, cemented and coated with Turf. Commencing at *Littleworth*, it extends for nearly three Miles to *Woeful Dane* Bottom; a fmaller fkirting the Brow of *Nailfworth* Hill, meets it at the Eaftern Extremity. By a tranverfe Vallation near the South-weft Point, an Area of about 10 Acres fquare, is inclofed ; a Circumftance obfervable in moft *Saxon* Camps. From the Eaft End of the Common it is continued through the Park ; where much of it is levelled. It then paffes through a large Field belonging to the Rectory ; in which, making an Angle, it ftretches fome Furlongs in a right Line to *Woeful Dane* Bottom. The Brow of the Hill from *Littleworth* to the laft mentioned Place was fufficiently fortified by its Abruptnefs.

It is left to more able Antiquaries to determine upon which of the following Occafions thefe Entrenchments were thrown up ; fhould they not confider them as originally *Britifh*. A very furious Battle was fought in 628, between PENDA King of *Mercia* and his rebellious Sons CYNEGILS and CWICHELM, near *Cirencefter*; nor are there Veftiges of *Saxon* Entrenchments nearer than thefe. In the fucceeding Centuries, the *Danes*, or *Pagans*, as they were ufually called in Monkifh Annals, when landing on this Side the *Severn*, proceeded to the higher Grounds, marking their Progrefs by the moft cruel Devaftation. In one of thefe predatory Incurfions in 918, during the Reign of King EDWARD the Elder, it is recorded in the *Saxon* Chronicle, " that the Inhabitants of *Herefordfhire* rofe in Arms, and being joined " by thofe of *Gloucefterfhire*, they fell on the *Danes*, and after a bloody Battle put them to Flight, with " the Lofs of HROALD, one of their Leaders †." EDWARD is faid to have been encamped at that Time near the Mouth of the *Avon*, on this Side *Severn* ; by which Means, every Communication was intercepted. Although the Name of *Woeful Dane* Bottom be allufive to fome fatal Overthrow of thefe Robbers, the other Bulwarks muft have been neceffary to protect the Inhabitants from their frequent Attacks, of which they lived in conftant Dread ; and are thus accounted for, without afcertaining any military Tranfaction in particular.

Two Common Fields, containing together 800 Acres, are fituate on the Eaft Side of the Town, which were originally Sheep Paftures ; the Number of them was regulated by the Proportion of Lands to which this Privilege was annexed. Soon after the Commencement of the prefent Century, the firft Inclofure was made, and called *Peach's Farm* ; upon a Plan which has fince been univerfally adopted ; that the Number of Acres inclofed in Severalty fhould be exchanged for Sheep Paftures, according to the Equivalent then ftipulated, and confirmed by general Agreement. In the farther of thefe Fields is a rude Fragment of Rock, fet upright, called " The Long Stone." At this Time, it is feven Feet above the Ground, and five Feet in Breadth, perforated by long Expofure to the Weather. It is undoubtedly a funeral Monument, but of whom we cannot venture to afcertain.

The Names of Families formerly of Property in this Parifh, as they are found in ancient Documents, are chiefly, HAMPTON, HALIDAY, A'DEANE, BUCKE, PINFOLD, ILES, SMALL, CLUTTERBUCK, and PEACH. At prefent, exclufive of the Manor, WALBANK and PINFOLD.

---

* The Brafs Effigies, which are placed as a Memorial for JOHN HAMPTON and his Children, have this Peculiarity. Of the nine Children feven are reprefented as Infants ; and two, as a Monk and a Nun, of larger Size. From whence it may be probable, that ALICE became the Heir of the Family, and was enabled to make fuch a Benefaction. Her Will, or Deed of Gift, is faid to be preferved amongft the *Tower* Records. Sir WILLIAM HAMPTON was Sheriff of *London* in 1462, and Mayor in 1472. See STOW's Survey of *London*, p. 570. FULLER's Worthies, *Glouc.* p. 363. Arms ; " Quarterly, 1. and 4. Gules, a Fefs " chequy Or and Azure, within a Bordure Argent ; 2. and 3. Lozengy, Argent and Gules." In 1314, 7 EDW. II. JOHN DE HAMPTON was Sheriff of this County, and was continued for four Years.

FULLER, ut fupra.

† LELAND's Collectanea, vol. III. p. 278.

3

The

The Lovers of Natural Hiftory will find here a Field for very ample Inveftigation *.

At the *Iron* Mills, *Scoria,* or Iron Cinders, have been dug up; but no fuch Manufacture has been carried on within the Memory of Man. The very numerous Inhabitants of this Parifh have been employed fince the Reign of Queen Elizabeth in the Manufacture of Woollen Cloth.

* Of thefe Curiofities the following Detail has been politely communicated to us, by Gentlemen, in whofe Collections they are preferved.

FOSSILS.

Patellæ—in great Abundance, though rare, in other Parts of the Kingdom.
Buccinæ.
Cylindri—rare.
Trochi.
Cochleæ—very fharp, and fome in their original Colours.
Anomiæ.
Cunæi—of the fmaller Kind.
Pectenoides—many of them in their original Colours.
Mytili—a Variety of fmaller *Bivalves* very fharp.
Spines of *Echini*—and beautiful Fragments of the *Echinus Mamillaris,* with, here and there, fmall Specimens of *Madripore.*

BOTANY.

RARE PLANTS.

Ophrys Apifera—Bee Orchis.
Ophrys Myodes—Fly Orchis.
Ophrys Nidus Avis—Bird's Neft.
Ophioglossum vulgatum—Adder's Tongue.
Linum Catharticum—Purging Flax.
Chlora perfoliata—Yellow Centaury. See GERARD, p. 547, the *Blaxtonia perfoliata* of HUDSON, and the *Gentia perfoliata* of LINNÆUS.
Chryfofplenium alternifolium—Alternate-leaved Saxifrage.
Aquilegia vulgaris five rubra—Common, or Red Columbine. GERARD, p. 1093.
Eadem oppofitifolium—Common Columbine.
Cardamine impatiens—Lady's Mantle.
Thymus Acinos—Sweet Bafil.
Paris Quadrifolia—True Love, or One-berry.
Polypodium Fragile—Brittle Polypody.
Ceraftium tormentofum—Woolly Moufe-ear Chickweed.
Afplenium Adriantum nigrum—Black Maiden Hair.
Geum Rivale—Water Avens.
Serapias Grandiflora—White-flowered Hellebore.
Eadem longiflora—Long-leaved Hellebore.
Convallaria multiflora—Solomon's Seal.
Monotropa Hypopithis—bird's Neft *Monotropa.* See HUDSON, p. 153. WITHERING, vol. I. p. 245.

MORE COMMON PLANTS.

Viccia Sativa—Common Vetch.
Viccia Lathyroides—Strangle Tare, or Wild Vetch.
Aftragulus Glycyphillos—Wild Liquorice, or Liquorice Vetch.
Adoxa Mufchattalina—Mufk Crowfoot.
Valeriana Officinalis—Great wild Valerian.
Lyfimachia nummularia—Money Wort.
Lyfimachia Nemorum—Yellow Pimpernel of the Woods.
Atropa Bella Donna—Deadly Nightfhade, or Dwale.
Agrimony Eupatoria—Common Agrimony.
Vinca Major—Great Periwinkle.
Campanula Trachelium—Great Throat Wort, or *Canterbury Bells.*
Caltha Paluftris—Marfh Marygold.
Potentilla reptans—Common Cinquefoil.
Galeopfis Galeobdolon—Yellow Nettle Hemp.
Circæa Lutetiana—Enchanter's Nightfhade.
Tormentilla reptans—Creeping Tormentil.
Polemonium Cæruleum—Greek Valerian, or Jacob's Ladder.
Tragopogon Pratenfe—Yellow Goat's Beard.
Polygonum Biftorta—Biftort, or Snakeweed.
Ribes Rubrum—Wild Currant.
Rubus Idæus—Rafpberry Bufh.
Alchemilla vulgaris—Lady's Mantle.
Viburnum opulus—Water Alder, or Guelder Rofe.
Ciftus Helianthemum—Dwarf Ciftus, or Little Sun-flower.
Melampyrum Arvenfe—Purple Cow-wheat.
Convallaria Majalis—Lilly of the Valley.
Enophorum polyftachium—Cotton Grafs.
Ervum tetrafpermum—Smooth Tare.
Polypodium dryopteris—Branched Polypody.
Ranunculus Lingua—Spear Wort.
Hypericum Androfæmum—Tutfan, or Park Leaves.

BENE-

B E N E F A C T I O N S.

URSULA TOOKE, Widow, devifed by Will, dated 1698, Lands, by Eftimation twenty Acres, and 80*l*, for improving the fame, for the following Ufes for ever, 2*l*. a Year to be paid to the Truftees, their Heirs, and Affigns, for their Care in the faid Truft; 8*l*. a Year for keeping fix Boys at School, and finding them Books; and 5*l*. a Year to be given to four poor People. If the Rents of the faid Lands fhould exceed, or fall fhort of 15*l*. a Year, a proportionable Addition or Abatement is to be made in the Schoolmafter's Salary, and in the Annuities to the poor People.

NATHANIEL CAMBRIDGE, of *Hamborough*, Merchant, in 1669, fettled by Deed, invefted in certain Truftees, the Sum of 1000*l*. with which, an Eftate called *Saintlieu*, alias *Sinckley*, in this Parifh, for teaching Boys (born in the Parifh of *Woodchefter*, and Tything of *Rodborough*, in this Parifh, being between the Ages of fix and fixteen) Reading, Writing, and Arithmetic, and fuch other ufeful Learning, having firft learned to read Englifh.

RICHARD CAMBRIDGE, of *London*, Merchant, gave by Will in 1702, Money, the Intereft of which is 2*l*. 10*s*. for the fame Purpofe as the former Benefaction.

BENJAMIN CAMBRIDGE, Gent. of *Theefcombe*, gave 100*l*. to be laid out in Lands, the yearly Amount of which is to be applied to bind and place out one or more Apprentices.

JOHN YEATES, Gent. left 100*l*. for apprenticing Boys educated at *Saintlieu* School.

HENRY KING, Gent. left by Will, in 1699, one Moiety of his Eftate, being 250*l*. (which Sum, the Truftees appointed by the Court of Chancery have fince laid out in purchafing Lands in the Parifh of *Randwick*, and one Acre at *Hyde*, in this Parifh) for teaching eight Boys Reading, Writing, and Accompts, nd providing them with Pens, Ink, and Paper.

WILLIAM WEBB, of *Howcombe*, in 1742, gave, by Will, a Rent Charge of 15*s*. yearly, to be diftributed between five poor Widows.

THOMAS YEATES, Gent. gave, by Will, 20*l*. the Intereft thereof to be annually diftributed amongft the Poor of *Rodborough* Tything.

MARY CHURCHES, Widow, in 1758, left 10*l*. for the fame Purpofe.

WILLIAM VICK, Gent. of *Briftol*, bequeathed, in 1754, 300*l*.; the Intereft to be difpofed of annually, by the Minifter and Churchwardens, on the 15th of November, for ever, as follows: for Prayers and a Sermon 1*l*. 1*s*.; to the Clerk 5*s*.; to the Sexton 2*s*. 6*d*.; to the Ringers 10*s*.; 1*l*. 1*s*. to be fpent by the Veftry at the *Talbot*, whilft a publick Houfe; and 5*s*. more to the Clerk for diftributing the Remainder in Bread at the Houfes of fuch Perfons as fhall be deemed proper Objects of Charity, preference being always glven to the aged and fober.

SARAH WEBB, Widow, left, by Will, 300*l*. vefted in the Rector and Churchwardens; the Intereft of which to buy twelve Brown Cloth, or Serge Gowns, and twelve Shifts, to be given to twelve Widows, or ancient poor Maidens, on the 3d of January annually, for ever.

REBECCA VICK, Spinfter, gave, by Deed, a Rent Charge of 5*l*. 4*s*. for teaching poor Children to read. She likewife, in 1768, bequeathed 200*l*. vefted in the Rector and Churchwardens; the Intereft whereof to be diftributed annually amongft the Poor of the Town of *Hampton*.

DANIEL WEBB, Gent. left, by Will, Land, the Produce of which is 10*l*. to be given to the Poor of the Parifh at large.

INCUMBENTS.	PATRONS.	INCUMBENTS.	PATRONS.
1538 Thomas Powel,	Agnes Abbefs of Sion.	1618 Hen. Fowler §, M. A.	Michael Halyday.
1551 Gilbert Bourne *,	Sir Edmond Peckham, by Affignment of a Grant from Agnes Abbefs of Sion, 1539.	1660 Tho. Warmftree ‖, D.D.	————.
		1665 John Farrer,	Philip Sheppard, Efq.
		1717 Ralph Willet, M. A.	————.
1558 Thomas Taylor,	Wm. Lord Wyndfore.	1720 Phil. Sheppard, M.A.	Samuel Sheppard, Efq.
1575 Thos. Freeman, M.A.	Sir Henry Carey.	1768 Rob. Salufbury Heaton, M.A.	S. Sheppard, Efq.
1584 George Byrch,	John A'Deane †.	1774 John White, D.D.	Edward Sheppard, Efq.
1612 Ant. Lapthorne‡, D.D.	King James.	1778 Honᵇˡᵉ Harbottle Grimftone, M.A.	The fame.
		1786 Hen. Cha. Jeffreys, M.A.	The fame.

* GILBERT BOURNE, Son of PHILIP BOURNE, of *Worcefterfhire*, elected Fellow of *All Souls* College 1531. In 1541 he "was made one of the firft Prebendaries of *Worcefter* by K. HENRY VIII.; Archdeacon of *Bedford* in 1549; confecrated Bifhop "of *Bath* and *Wells* in 1554, and appointed Lord Prefident of *Wales*. When Q. ELIZABETH fucceeded he was deprived of his "Bifhoprick for denying her Supremacy, and died at *Silverton*, in *Devonfhire*, Sept. 10, 1569, where he was buried."

WOOD, Ath. Oxon. vol. I. p. 598.

† "JOHN A'DEANE, hujus Rectoriæ Firmarius, fepult. 1602." Par. Reg.

‡ He was Chaplain to King JAMES the Firft.

§ "March 13, 1678. HENRY FOWLER (Son of the above mentioned), of *Oriel* College, who, after he had been a Graduate, "ferved very faithfully in his Majefty's Army during the grand Rebellion, begun by the godly Party, and afterward betook "himfelf to the Study of Phyfick, which he did with good Succefs in his own Country." WOOD's Fafti, vol. I. p. 881.

HENRY FOWLER, Rector of *Minchin Hampton*, is faid by WALKER (Sufferings of the Clergy, p. 242.) to have been treated with the moft cruel Indignities by —— BUCKE, a Captain in the Parliament Army in 1643, of which he gives a very minute Detail.

‖ "THOMAS WARMSTREY, Student of *Chrift Church* 1624, created D. D. 1642. At the Reftoration, 1660, he was inftalled "Prebendary of *Gloucefter*, and the Year following Dean of *Worcefter*. He was a frequent Writer."

WOOD's Ath. Oxon. vol. II. p. 250.

5

PRESENT

PRESENT LORD OF THE MANOR,

EDWARD SHEPPARD, Efq.

The Perfons fummoned from this Parifh by the Heralds in 1682 and 1683, were

Philip Sheppard, Efq.
John Bucke, M. D.
John Farrer, Rector,
Thomas Pinfold, Gent.
Edward Pinfold, Gent.

Giles Pinfold, Gent.
John Iles, Gent.
John Smith, Gent.
Richard Merret, Gent.

At the Election in 1776 One Hundred and Nineteen Freeholders polled from this Parifh.

The firft Date of the Regifter is in 1558 *.

ANNUAL ACCOUNT OF MARRIAGES, BIRTHS, AND BURIALS, IN THIS PARISH.

A.D.	Mar.	Bir.	Bur.	A.D.	Mar.	Bir.	Bur.	A.D.	Mar.	Bir.	Bur.	A.D.	Mar.	Bir.	Bur.
1781	26	88	65	1786	19	64	68	1791				1796			
1782	21	74	69	1787	31	55	70	1792				1797			
1783	24	70	71	1788	22	53	74	1793				1798			
1784	16	59	134	1789	32	57	53	1794				1799			
1785	31	77	111	1790	26	66	67	1795				1800			

INSCRIPTIONS IN THE CHURCH.
IN THE CHANCEL.

ON FREESTONE MONUMENTS.

Arms; Gules, a Chevron between three Bulls Heads caboffed Argent, armed Or, for BAYNHAM ;—impaling, Argent, a Chevron Gules, and in Chief a Bar engrailed Sable, for FREME.

Here lyeth the Body of
ANNE, Daughter to
JOSEPH BAYNHAM,
who was fecond Sonne to
JOSEPH BAYNHAM, of Weftbury,
Efquire.
Her Mother was ALICE,
fourth Daughter to
ROBERT FREAME, of Lypeat, Efquire.
She died the 16 Day of Auguft
Anno Domini 1632.

Arms ; Per Fefs nebulè Or and Sable three Bucks Attires fixed to the Scalp, all counterchanged, for BUCKE ; —impaling, Argent, on a Bend cotifed Sable, three Annulets Or, for SELWYN.

Piæ Memoriæ JEREMIÆ BUCKE,
Arm. qui, cum 35 foles
enumeraverat, fato correptus præpropero
die Dominico ante Nativitatem CHRISTI
Vitam cum morte commutavit.
Mœtiriffima conjux URSULA BUCKE
hoc marmor erigi curavit.

Arms; BUCKE, as before.

To the happy Memorie of
JEREMIAH BUCK, Batchelor,
the eldeft Son of
JEREMIAH BUCK, Efq.
and of URSULA his Wife,
who died May the 2d, Anno 1668.

Alfo ELIZABETH,
eldeft Daughter of the faid
JEREMIAH BUCK and URSULA,
who died May the 19, Anno 1663.

Near this Place
lyeth SARAH, the Daughter of
THOMAS DAVIS, of the Bourne,
by SARAH his Wife,
Daughter of the above
JEREMIAH and URSULA his Wife,
who died March 15, 1673.

Alfo three Children of
T. TOOKE, of Elmftree, Efq.
and URSULA his Wife,
Relict to the above
JEREMIAH BUCK, viz.

CHARLES, April 4, 1694;

ANNE, May 29, ...

ELIZABETH, died Septem. . . . . . .

NEAR THIS PLACE LYETH THE BODY OF JEFFERY BATHE, GENTLEMAN, WHO DEPARTED THIS LIFE THE 2nd DAY OF NOVEMBER, ANNO DOM. 1659.

ON MARBLE MONUMENTS.

Arms ; Azure, a Lion rampant, and in Chief three Efcallops Argent, for CLUTTERBUCK ;——impaling, SHEPPARD.

In this Church Yard
are depofited the Remains of
EDMUND CLUTTERBUCK,
of Hyde, Gent.
who died October 5, 1778,
aged 71 Years.

Arms ; a Chevron engrailed between three Wolve's Heads erafed, for RIDPATH.

Hic juxta fitus eft
PHILIPPUS,
filius unicus
GEORGII DE RIDPATH,
Cognomen ducens a Baronia de
Ridpath in Scotia,
Patrimonium avitum.   Juvenis
erat fummæ fpei,
Supra ætatem doctus, acri ingenio,
indole optima,
Aliifque eximiis animi dotibus
præditus.   Sanitatis
ergo, Parentum confenfu, ac
Medicorum confilio e Londino,
rus fe contulit ; at in itinere
Gloceftriam verfus, 3 idus Julii, 1705,
repentino dolore in tergo correptus,
Poftridie fummo mane, hac in urbe,
remediis fruftra tentatis, animam
piam ac puram placidè Deo reddidit,
ineunte vigefimo fecundo
ætatis anno.   Omnibus
cum quibus confuetudinem
habuit defiderium fui
non mediocre
Reliquit.

Arms ; on a Bend, three Horfefhoes, for FERRARS.

Near this Place lieth the
Body of the Reverend
Mr. JOHN FERRARS,
52 Years Rector of this
Parifh, who departed this
Life the 22d Day of
May, in the Year of our
Lord 1717, and in the
81ft Year of his Age,
an eminent Example
of Piety and Charity.

* In 1558 there were 28 Burials ; no Baptifms were entered till 1562; in 1563, 28 Baptifms. In 1711, Sir R. ATKYNS ftates the Births to be 33, and the Burials 31, annually ; the Houfes 377, and the Inhabitants about 1800.

VOL. II. D Arms ;

Arms; Ermine, on a Chief Sable, three Battle Axes Argent, for Sheppard;—impaling, per Fefs Gules, a Lion rampant between three Crofs Croflets fitchée Or, for Capel; 2. Gules, two Wings conjoined in Lure, for Seymour.

Haud procul hinc tumulo jacet
Philippus Sheppard, Armiger,
hujus Ecclefiæ & Manerii,
æque ac illius de Avening,
Patronus idem & Dominus.
Fideli erga Regem animo
ac in Vicinos perquam benevolo
(per annos quinquaginta & amplius)
Irenarchæ munus arduum
Rogatus fufcepit;
Adminiftrando ornavit;
Patriæ Salutis ergo & Confcientiæ caufa
in biennio tantum Jacobi II.
Conftanti animo detrectavit.
Parentis, Mariti, Magiftratûs, Heri,
fingulis ipfe perfunctus officiis
cum cura ftudioque maximo.
Exemplum Pofteris optimum reliquit;
Regi, Reipublicæ, & Ecclefiæ Anglicanæ
obfequentiffimus;
plus æquè penè fobrius,
Pacificus, pius.
Uxores duxit binas,
amantes viciffim ac amatas;
primam, Elizabetham Gamalielis
Capel, Militis, Filiam,
ex quâ tres liberos adhuc fuperftites
fufcepit,
Samuelem, Philippum, Saram;
præter Mariam & Elizabetham,
Olim in cœlos hinc receptas.
Secundam, Franciscam, viduam,
prænobili Domino Gulielmo
Domino Vicecomiti Downs,
Olim nuptam.
Rerum & dierum plenus,
Nullius morbi, nullius ægritudinis,
extremæ fenectutis tantum pondere
laborans,
lubens tandem hic requiem affecutus eft,
Anno { Domini 1713,
      { ætatis 82.

Hic juxta quoque fita eft
Elizabetha Sheppard,
prædictis { Philippo neptis,
          { Samueli filia,
virgo modefta, humilis, pudica
nec minus facili comitate morum
verè amabilis;
heu tamen immaturâ morte
quatriduum ante avum
abrepta,
anno ætatis 3omo.
Patri ac Filiæ clariffimis,
majora meritis,
Hoc qualecunque amoris & obfervantiæ
Monumentum
Samuel Sheppard,
Philippi fortunæ et virtutis
Heres,
μνημοσυνης ergô
poni curavit.

Arms; Sheppard, as before;—impaling, a Crofs quarterly; in the firft Quarter an Eagle difplayed, for Webb.

M. S.
Samuelis Sheppard, Armigeri,
(cujus quicquid mortale fuit
in propinquo Monumento reconditur)
viri per omnia vitæ ftadia;
fine fuco, pii, fobrii, jufti;
qui poft omnia Officia, quæ
vel Maritum, vel Parentem, vel
Hominem, denique Chriftianum
fpectant, religiosè præftita,

Uxore & numerosâ prole
Superftiti relictâ, Divinæ
Voluntati feipfum refignans,
Placidè in Domino obdormivit.
Obiit { die 29 Aug.
      { anno Dom. 1724,
      { ætatis fuæ 63.

Necnon Annæ Sheppard,
Samuelis fupradicti uxoris perdilectæ,
Ex affiduâ & alacri pietate in Deum
Tum palam tum fecreto largitate
in egenos,
merito femper admirandæ,
hinc in cœlum migravit
Anno { Christi MDCCXXXIV.
      { ætatis fuæ LXXVI.
In eodem etiam Tumulo jacet
Gamalielis
prædictorum Samuelis & Annæ
Sheppard,
filius quartus,
Anno { Dom. 1732,
      { ætatis fuæ 40.

Arms; Sheppard, as before.

Near this Place
lie the mortal Remains
of Frances, Rebecca, and
Thomas Sheppard;

And alfo of Sarah Day,
Widow, Son and Daughters of
Samuel Sheppard, Efq.
and Anna his Wife,

Frances died April 17, 1741,
aged 52.

Rebecca died July 24, 1741,
aged 47.

Thomas died Jan. 17, 1757,
aged 66.

Sarah died May 30, 1764,
aged 72.

Arms; Sheppard, as before;—impaling Sheppard.

I. H. S.
Eliza Sheppard,
Uxor Samu. Sheppard,
de Muffilhill, de hac Parochia.
Ob. Jun. 27, 1752, æt. 27.
Beati qui moriuntur in Domino.
In Memoriam
Conjugis fuæ
pofuit hoc maritus.

In the Vault behind this Chancel lie
the mortal Remains of
Mary, the Wife of
Phillip Sheppard,
Rector of this Parifh,
who ended this tranfitory Life
the 11th of May 1753, aged 49.
Honourable Age is not that which
ftandeth in Length of Time,
nor that is meafured by Number
of Years; but Wifdom is the
grey Hair unto Men, and an
unfpotted Life is old Age.
The World paffeth away, and the
Luft thereof; but he that doeth the
Will of God abideth for ever.

In the fame Vault are
depofited the mortal Remains
of the Rev. Phillip Sheppard,
Mafter of Arts,
Rector of this Parifh forty-nine Years,
who departed this Life
the 15th Day of December,
1768, in the twenty-third
Year of his Age,
in Hopes of a bleffed Refurrection.

Arms; Sheppard, as before;—impaling, Argent, on a Chevron Sable, between three Stags Heads, as many Branches Vert, for Whorwood.

Samuel Sheppard, Armiger.
Obiit XXIX die Octobris,
A. D. MDCCLXX, ætatis . . . .

In Cœmeterio haud procul hinc
quatuor liberi fupradicti
Samuelis Sheppard,
jacent fepulti.

On the South Side of this Chancel
lye depofited the Remains of
Robert Salusbury Heaton,
Clerk, M. A. Rector of
Minchin Hampton and Avening,
who died June 30, A. D. 1774,
aged 33 Years.

ON FREESTONE MONUMENTS.

Arms; a Bend between fix Mullets.

Near this Place refteth the
Body of Daniel Holbrow,
Baker, of this Town,
who died Oct. 9, 1727,
in the 72d Year of his Age.

Likewife the Body of
Daniel Holbrow, Surgeon,
who died Sept. 5, 1766,
in the 52d Year of his Age.

Alfo the Body of
Mary, the Wife of
Daniel Holbrow, Surgeon,
who died June the 4th, 1756,
in the 48th Year of her Age.

Near this Place lyeth the Body of
Clutterbuck Dean, Gent.
of this Parifh,
who departed this Life
the 8th Day of April,
Anno Dom. 1701.

And alfo the Body of
Ann his Wife,
who departed this Life
the 25th Day of March, 1690,
in hope of a glorious Refurrection.

Alfo Sarah their Daughter,
and Wife of John Shurmer, Clothier,
who died the 18th of June,
in the 56th Year of her Age, 1717.

ON FLAT STONES.

In Memory of
Elizabeth, the Wife of
Thomas Davis,
of this Town, Maltfter,
Daughter of James Wild,
of Yatton Keynell, in the
County of Wilts, Gent.
who died June 7, 1747, aged 50.

Hear lieth the Body of
Elizabeth Wild, Relict of
James Wild, of Yatton
Keynell, in the County of
Wilts, Gent. and Mother of
Elizabeth Davis abovementioned, who departed this
Life the 17 Day of May,
in the Year of our Lord 1748,
in the 75th Year of her Age.

Here

Here lieth the Body of
Ann Norris,
who departed this Life
Feb. 1, 1748-9, aged 69.

IN THE NAVE.

ON MARBLE MONUMENTS.

Arms ; a Fefs engrailed, and in Chief
three Fleurs, for Iles.

In Memory of
John Iles, of Chalford, Efq.
many Years a Juftice of Peace
for this County ;
religious, loyal, and beneficent ;
a Hufband moft affectionate,
Father moft tender ;
to all benevolent ;
in every Station, publick and private,
exercifing fuitable Virtues ;
and in the whole tenour of Life
a truly good Man.
He died March 27, 1727, aged 70.

Alfo of Mary his Wife,
whofe Life, from Youth, was a
continued Example of true Piety.
She died July 8, 1737, aged 78.

Alfo of Ann, the Wife of
John Iles, junior, Efq.
and Daughter of
Mr. John Hickes, of London,
Merchant ;
one of the moft agreeable, virtuous,
and beft of Wives,
who died Aug. 4, 1736, æt. 37.

Alfo in Memory of
John Iles, late of Chalford, Efq.
who died April 20, 1767, aged 66.

In Memory of
Thomas Iles, fecond Son of
John Iles, Efq.
a Perfon of fingular Probity,
Humanity, the kindeft Relation,
and fincereft Friend.
He died March 1, 1731, aged 29 ;

And of Mary his Wife,
eminent for her conjugal Virtues,
kind and amiable in her Deportment
to all.
She died Dec. 26, 1728, aged 27.

Alfo of Catharine and Mary,
their Daughters,
who died in their Infancy.

Arms ; Iles, as before.

Near this Place
lie interred the Remains of
Joseph Iles, Efq.
of the City of Briftol,
who died March 14, 1749,
aged 45.
He was youngeft Son of John Iles,
of Chalford, in this Parifh, Efq.

Arms ; Gules, a Crofs lozengy Or, between four Rofes.

Sacred be this Marble to the Memory of
Walter Butt,
late of Chalford, in this County,
Clothier.
He departed this Life Feb. 20, 1780,
aged 67 Years.

ON FLAT STONES.

HERE LIETH THE BODY OF
THOMAS, THE
SON OF JOHN ILES THE ELDER, OF
THIS PARISH, CLOTHIER, WHO
DEPARTED THIS LIFE THE 8TH
DAY OF . . . . DOM. 1686.

A Brass Plate on the same Stone:

IN MEMORY OF
MRS. MARTHA HICKES,
RELICT OF MR. JOHN
HICKES, OF LONDON,
MERCH^t, WHO DEPART-
ED THIS LIFE THE 14th
OF JANUARY, ANNO DOM.
1745, ÆT. 74.

ON BRASS PLATES.

Here refteth the Body
of Susannah, the Daughter
of Thomas Iles, who departed
this Life the 8th Day of
Auguft, Anno Dom. 1697.

Here lieth the Bodies of John
Phillips, of Brimfcomb,
Clothier, who departed this
Life the 11 Day of April,
Anno Dom. 1690,
ætatis fuæ 70 ;

And Sarah his Wife,
who died Auguft the 18th,
Anno { Dom. 1701,
{ ætatis 76.

Here lyeth the Body
of John Keyse, who
departed this Life
the 19th Day of January,
Anno Dom. 1696.

Here refteth the
Body of John Keyse,
junior, of the Parifh of
Hampton, Clothier, who
departed this Life the 21ft
Day of July, Anno Dom.
1718.

Here refteth the Body of
John Deane, Clothier,
of this Parifh,
who departed this Life
the 2d Day of September,
in the 68th Year of his Age,
Anno Dom. 1712.

Alfo Sarah his Wife,
who departed this Life
the 21ft Day of April,
in the 91ft Year of her Age,
Anno Dom. 1726.

Samuel Taylor
died Dec. 6, 1729, aged 63 Years.

Thomas Taylor
died March 5, 1730, aged 23 Years.

Elizabeth Gurney
died Aug. 1, 1757, aged 70 Years.

In Memory of
Mary Pierce, Daughter of
Elizabeth Gough, of Brimpfcomb,
by her firft Hufband
Edward Pierce, late of Devizes.
She died Jan. 21, 1727-8,
in the 16th Year of her Age.

In Memory of
Edward Pierce, of Brimf-
comb, in this Parifh, Clothier,
who departed this Life Dec. 2,
1746, in the 35th Yeare of his Age.

In Memory of
Thomas Gough, Son of Daniel
Gough, of Brimfcomb, Clothier,
who departed this Life Sept. 2,
1760, in the 36th Year of his Age.

IN THE NORTH CROSS AISLE.

On a Brass Plate :

Of yonr Charite pray for the Soules of
John Hampton, Gentleman Elyn his
Wife, and all their Children fpetiallie
for the Soule of Dame Alice Hampton
his Daughter, whiche was right beneficiall
to this Church and Parifh. Which John
deceffed in the Yere of o'r Lord
MCCCCLXII, on whofe Soules J'hu
have M'cy. Amen.

On a Marble Monument :

Arms ; on a Bend three Rofes in
the finifter Chief Point a Cheffrook,
for Small ; on an Efcocheon of Pretence, three Delves.

In Memory of
John Small, Efq. 4th Son of
George Small, Efq.
He married Elizabeth, one of the
Daughters and Coheirs of
John Ovey, of Greenville,
in the County of Oxon, Gent.
and died July 3, 1725, aged 61.
Reader !
let his Character be thine ;
juft and temperate,
loyal as by Law,
religious without Superftition.

Mary Small,
the 2d Daughter of
John Small, Efq.
died June the 23d, 1729.

Joseph, his youngeft Son,
died March the 8th, 1743, ætatis 34.

Elizabeth, his eldeft Daughter,
Wife of John Adye,
of Cirencefter, Gent.
who died Nov. 25, 1748, ætatis 61.

ON

ON FLAT STONES.

John Small, Efq.
died July . . . .

Sarah, youngeft Daughter of
George Small, Efq.
died . . July, 168 . .
. . . .

Here refteth the Body of
Henry Elshew,
of Burley, in this Parifh,
who departed this Life
the 3d Day of March, 1690,
ætatis fuæ 82.

Elizabeth, Wife of
John Small, Clothier,
of Pudhill, and Daughter of
Mr. John Ovy, of Greenfield,
died May 29, 1713, aged 42.

Subtus jacet Georgius Small,
Armiger,
Optimus Pacis Curator,
ditiffimufque hujus fæculi
Pannarius.
Obiit tertio die Octobris,
Anno { Domini 1704,
      { ætatis 77.

Mary Small,
Widow and Relict of
George Small, Efq.
departed this Life
Sept. 3, Anno Dom. 1719, aged 89.

IN THE NORTH AISLE.

On a Flat Stone:

Near this Place
lie the Remains of Frances,
late Wife of Richard Plummer,
of Burley, Attorney at Law.
She died the 17th of September 1746,
aged 72 Years.

Likewife the Remains of
Richard Plummer, late of Burley,
in this Parifh, Gent.
who departed this Life
the 1ft of January, 1769,
aged 91 Years.

Alfo the Remains of
Frances Plummer, Spinfter,
eldeft Daughter of the aforefaid
Richard and Frances Plummer.
She departed this Life
the 31ft of May, 1785, aged 76 Years.

IN THE SOUTH AISLE.

ON FREESTONE MONUMENTS.

Arms; three Doves between two
Chevronells, for Pinfold.

Near to this Place
lieth the Body
of Richard Pinfold,
Gent. of Hied Court,
who departed
this Life the tenth
Day of July, Anno
Dom. 1668.

Alfo Elizabeth his
Wife departed the 4th
Day of September, 1694.

To the Memory of
William Wallington,
of this Town, Mafon,
and of Rebeckah his Wife.
She died the 20th Day of
January, in the 47th Year of her
Age, 1699. He died 27 July, in the
67th Year of his Age, 1712. Alfo near
this Place lie fix of their Children.

To the happy Memory of
Mary, Wife of John Vick,
who departed this Life the 19th
Day of July, in the 34th Year
of her Age 1710.

Here under lieth the Body of
Jeremiah Buck, Mercer,
in this Parifh, who deceafed
the 5th Day of December,
Anno Dom. 1638.

ON FLAT STONES.

Here lieth the Body
of Nathaniel, Son of Samuel
Cambridge, of Theefcombe,
who departed the 23d of Feb.
1726, in the 67th Year of his Age.

Eusebius, the Son of Nathaniel
Cambridge, Clothier, departed
this Life the 25th Day of May, 1707,
in the 1ft Year of his Age.

In Memory of Sarah, the Daughter
of Nathaniel Cambridge, of
Woodchefter, who died the 25th Day of
January, in the 64th Year of her Age,
1702.

Alfo in Memory of Samuel,
the Son of Samuel Cambridge, of
Theefcomb, Clothier, who died the
24th Day of June, in the 30th Year of
his Age 1706.

Here refteth the Body of
Richard, the Son of Samuel
Cambridge, of Theefcomb,
who departed this Life the 17th Day of
October, in the 47th Year of his Age,
1726.

In Memory of Grace, the Wife of
Samuel Yeats, of the Dye-houfe,
Daughter of Edward Stephens, of
Eaftington, Gent. who departed
this Life April 19, 1714, aged 68.

In Memory alfo of
Samuel Yeats, Hufband to
the abovefaid Grace, who
departed this Life
May the 21ft, 1722,
in the 83d Year of
his Age.

In Memory of
Sarah, the Daughter of
Samuel Yeats, of the Dye-houfe,
who departed this Life
November the 24th, 1719.

Alfo Esther, the Daughter
of Samuel and Elizabeth Yeats,
who died Dec. 3, 1726, aged 3 Days.

In Memory alfo of the
faid Samuel, who departed
this Life the 19th of Auguft, 1729.

Here lieth the Body of
Elizabeth, the Daughter of
Nathaniel Cambridge, of
Theefcomb, who died the 10th Day of
February, 1727, in the 24th Year of
her Age.

IN THE SOUTH CROSS AISLE.

ON MONUMENTS.

Arms; Paly of fix, on a Chief a
Lion paffant guardant, for Blackwell;—impaling Webb, as before.

In hope of a joyful Refurrection
here reft the Bodies
of Mr. Archar Blackwell,
late of the Parifh of Bifley,
and of Katharine his Wife.
He died Jan. 13, 1749-50,
ætatis 75.
She died Oct. 12, 1749,
ætatis 68.

Near this Place lies alfo
the Body of Martha, their only
Daughter, who departed this Life
November 21, 1736,
ætatis 29.

Arms; Webb, as before.

This Monument is erected to the
Memory of Daniel Webb, Son of
John Webb, late of Giddinap, in
this Parifh, Gentleman, who departed
this Life the 2d of December, 1770,
aged 66.

On a Brass Plate fixed on a Freestone Monument:

Arms; a Chevron between three Swans,
for Lyte.

Near this Place lyeth
interred the Body of Nicholas
Lyte, Gent. who departed this
Life the 30th of October, Anno
Domini 1645, in certain hope
of a joyfull Refurrection
at the coming of Christ.

ON FLAT STONES.

A Brass Plate:

Of your Charitie pray for the Soule of
Edward Hollday and Margery his Wyfe
which Edward deceffed the 6th Day of
April, A. D. M·CCCCXIX.

Arms; Pinfold, as before.

In Memory of
Mary, the Wife of Edw. Pinfold,
Clothier, of this Parifh, who died
October the 10th, A. D. 1729, ætat. 23.

Alfo in Memory of the
aforefaid Edward Pinfold,
Son of Giles Pinfold,
of this Parifh, Clothier, who
departed this Life the
8th Day of September, 1740,
in the 38th Year of his Age.

Heare refteth the Body of
Thomas Holiday, Clother,
of Chalford, who departed
this Life the 21ft Day of January,
Anno Domini 1700.

Here

Here lyeth the Body of MARY, Wife of
JOHN VICK, junior,
and Daughter of
CHARLES SMITH, of Horfley, Gent.
She died July 22, 1742,
in the 64th Year of her Age.
Alfo of MARY, the Wife of
JOHN VICK, fenior,
who died October 7, 1709, in the 82d
Year of her Age.
Likewife of MARY their Daughter,
who departed this Life July 11, 1715,
in the 37th Year of her Age.

Here lieth the Body of JOHN
VICK, of Minchin Hampton, who departed this Life the 20th Day of
June 1692, ætatis 52.
Alfo here lyeth the Body of JOHN,
the Son of JOHN VICK, who departed
this Life the 2d Day of Auguft, 1747,
æt. 66 Years.

Here lyeth the Body of
WILLIAM VICK, junior,
who died Jan. 3, 1754.

———

REBECCA VICK
died July the 19th, 1768.

———

Her lies interred ANNE,
Wife of SAMUEL REMINGTON,
of Woodchefter,
and Daughter of JOHN and MARY VICK,
of this Town. She died June 6, 1763.

———

FRANCES VICK, Sifter of the
aforefaid ANN REMINGTON,
departed this Life Nov.
the 20th, 1781.

Arms; BLACKWELL, as before.

MARTHA BLACKWELL,
1736.

———

Here lyeth
the Body of SARAH WEBB,
Daughter of WILLIAM WEBB,
of Howcombe, in this
Parifh, who died May 3,
1748, aged 68 Years.

———

MARY DAY
died June 30, 1776.

———

In the fame Aifle, on two Flat Stones,
are two Figures, with Legends, but no
Infcription.

IN THE CHURCH YARD.

ON A FREESTONE MONUMENT, SOUTH
SIDE THE CHANCEL:

Near this Place
lyeth interred the mortal
Remains of ELIZABETH, the Wife
of JAMES CHAMBERS; but her
immortal and better Part
returned to GOD, and feparated from
fad furviving Friends,
is now, we hope, through JESUS CHRIST,
poffeffed with pure and endlefs Joy.
She departed this Life the 12th Day of
Auguft, in the . . Year of her Age,
Anno Dom. 1725.

———

ON A STONE FIXED IN THE SOUTH
WALL:

HERE UNDER LYETH INTERRED
THE BODY OF ELIZABETH DEANE,
LATE WIFE OF JOHN DEANE,
PHYSICIAN, WHO DIED THE 14TH
DAY OF JUNE AN° DOM. 1640.

———

ON A STONE AGAINST THE SOUTH
WALL, WEST END:

Arms; WEBB, as before.

Here lyeth interred
the Body of MARTHA,
Wife of WILLIAM WEBB, Gent.
of Howcombe, in this Parifh,
who died March 16,
1684.

Alfo of WILLIAM WEBB,
Gent. their Son, who
died May 15, 1742,
aged 72 Years.

Alfo of NATHANIEL WEBB, Gent.
of the Parifh of Avening.
He died March 19, 1742, aged 33 Years.

ON TWO MARBLE TOMBS:

Under this Marble Tomb
lie the Bodies of FRANCES
and REBECCA SHEPPARD
Daughters of SAMUEL
SHEPPARD, Efq. and ANNE
his Wife, whofe Remains
lie in the Chancel.

FRANCES died April 17, 1741, aged 52.

REBECCA died July 24, 1741, aged 47.

Arms; SHEPPARD, as before;—impaling, a Lion rampant crowned.

In Memory of
SAMUEL SHEPPARD, Efq.
A Gentleman of unblemifhed Integrity,
unaffected Piety,
and truly primitive Simplicity of Manners;
affable and courteous in his Behaviour,
eafy and inftructive in his Converfation,
juft and upright in all his Dealings,
without Partiality, without Hypocrify.
His Charity was as free from Oftentation
as his Nature from Difguife.
In all Social Offices he remarkably ex-
celled;
an eminent Example of Conjugal Affection;
a tender Parent, a kind Mafter, a fincere
Friend.
Thus adorned with an uncommon Sanctity
of Morals,
he fuftained the Miferies of human Life
with Chriftian Fortitude;
his Confcience not reproaching him
with the Omiffion of any Duty to GOD
or Man.
He was patient and refigned in his
death,
and his Hope was full of Immortality.
He died December the 20th, 1749,
in the 63d Year of his Age.

Here alfo are depofited the Remains of
ANNE SHEPPARD his Wife,
chearful and hofpitable in her Temper,
religious and devout in her Heart,
difcreet and prudent in the Management
of her Family,
freely diftributing to the Neceffities of
others,
and folicitous for the Welfare of all.
She died Auguft the 29th, 1749,
in the 59th Year of her Age.

———

Arms; BLACKWELL, as before. [duplicate placeholder]

ON A BRASS PLATE:
H. S. I.
JACOBUS BRADLEY, S. T. P.
Regalium Societatum
Londini, Lutetiæ Parifiorum,
Berolini, & Petropoli Sodalis; Aftro-
nomus Regius, Aftronomiæ apud
Oxonienfis Profeffor Savilianus.
Vir in rerum Phyficarum fcientiâ exco-
lendus,
præcipuè vero in penitiffimis arcanis
indagandis; tam felici diligentiâ & fagaci
ingenio, ut quotquot ubique gentium
iifdem honeftiffimis ftudiis navabant
operam, illi omnes libenter affurgerent;
tam fingulari interim modeftiæ, ut
quâ effet apud graviffimos judices
exiftimatione ipfe folus ignorâffe
videtur. Difceffit III id. Jul.
A. D. MDCCLXII, ætatis
LXX.

———

ELIZABETH, Daughter of
SAMUEL PEACH,
died April 17, 1717.
ELIZABETH his Wife
died May 25, 1737.

———

ON RAISED FLAT STONES.

Near this Place lies the Body of JANE,
Relict of WILLIAM BRADLEY,
late of Combend in the
Parifh of Elkftone, in this County, and
Mother to the Rev. Doctor BRADLEY,
of Greenwich, in the County
of Kent. She died Sept. 29, 1747,
aged 94 Years.

Arms; On a Bend between fix Martlets a broken Spear, for DALLAWAY;—
impaling, Or, a Fefs Azure, between
three round Buckles Gules, for BRAD-
LEY.

JOHN DALLAWAY, Gent.
of Brimfcombe,
in the Parifh of Stroud,
only Son of ROBERT DALLAWAY, of
Alton, com. Warwick, died March 9,
1764, æt. 65.
REBECCA his Relict,
youngeft Daughter of
WILLIAM BRADLEY,
and JANE his Wife,
died Oct. 25, 1765, æt 65.

———

Arms;

Arms ; DALLAWAY, as before ;—impaling, quarterly, 1. Gules, a Lion rampant, between eight Crofs Croflets fitchee Or, HOPTON ; 2. Azure, a Bend Argent, cottiled Or, between fix Crofs Croflets Or, the fecond within a Bordure Gules bezantee, HOPTON ancient ; 3. Paly bendy fix Or and Gules, KENSINGFORD ; 4. Azure, crufuly Or, three Boars' Heads couped of the fecond, HEVYN ; 5. Argent, crufuly Gules, two Pipes of the fecond, DOWNTON ; 6. Azure, a Lion rampant Argent, within a Bordure engrailed Or, TYREIL ; 3. Or, three Barrs Gules, ST. OWEN ; 8. Argent, a Lion rampant Sable, charged with a Trefoil Vert, EYTON ; 9. Paly fix, Sable and Or, on a Chief of the fecond two Pellets of the firft, over all an Inefcocheon Gules, charged with three Barrs Ermine, BURLEY ; 10. Brry fix Or and Azure, PEMBRUGE ; 11. Argent, three broad Arrows, Azure, HAYLES ; 12. Vert, a Chevron Or and Gules, between three Soles nayant Or, SOLLEY.

H. S. I.

GULIELMUS DALLAWAY, Armiger,
Obiit 7 Martii, 1776,
ætatis 55.

ELIZA Conjux, ex antiquiffimâ profapiâ de Hopton Caftello, in Agro Salopienfi, longo ftemmate oriunda,
Obiit Martii 3, 1775, æt. 38.

JACOBUS DALLAWAY, Generofus.
Ob. Maii die 12, 1787,
æt. 57.

Cujus Uxor MARTHA, ELIZÆ prædictæ foror unica, ob. Feb. 19, 1783,
æt. 44.

VALETE ! QUEIS JAM SUPERSTITIBUS DOMUS NOSTRÆ HEU ! CITIUS LAPSURÆ
QUALESCUNQUE NOBIS RESTABANT IPES !
QUEIS AUTEM DECEDENTIBUS, OMNES EXCIDERE.

Arms ; Barry of fix Argent and Azure, on a Chief Gules two Pellets Or ; over all a Spear in Bend proper, for DALLAWAY. Creft, a Demi-lion Sable, collared checquy Or and Azure, holding between his Paws a Shield Gules, charged with a Crofs Croflet fitchée Or.

Suorum Tumulum refectum voluit
I. D. A. M. S. A. S. 1790.

JOHN PEACH
died Dec. 28, 1738, in the 36th Year of his Age.

SARAH his Wife
died Dec. 20, 1738, in the 57th Year of her Age.

JOHN their youngeft Son, an Infant.

SARAH PEACH their Daughter
died March 22, 1761, ætat. 31.

CATHERINE PEACH their Daughter
died July 13, 1763, æt. 28.

JANE, the Wife of JOSEPH BEDDOME, of the City of Briftol, Merchant,
who died Jan. 21, 1778,
aged 55 Years.

RACHAEL BROKENBROW, Wife of WALTER BROKENBROW, Maltfter, departed this Life the 19th Day of May, 1785, aged 50 Years.

JAMES MOODY
died March 16, 1735, in the 67th Year of his Age.

JOAN his Wife
died June 13, 1733, in the 67th Year of her Age.

ELIZABETH their Daughter
died Dec. 11, 1721, in the 22d Year of her Age.

RICHARD FARMER,
late of Rodborough, Clothier,
Son of JOHN FARMER, of Nuneaton, in the County of Warwick, Woolftapler,
died at Culver Houfe, Nov. 29, 1782,
in the 54th Year of his Age.

DANIEL DAVIS,
late Schoolmafter at Burley, in this Parifh,
died May 8, 1756, aged 49 Years ;
of whom, to make no mention
would be the greateft Ingratitude to Merit, and Injuftice to Pofterity ;
for, without the leaft falfe Panegyrick
too common to Infcriptions of this Nature,
his Country has loft in him
a truly ufeful and valuable Member of Society ;
his Intimates a fincere, conftant, and unchangeable Friend ;
his Pupils a kind, inftructive, and excellent Mafter ;
the diftreffed Poor a continual Affifter and Benefactor ;
Mankind in general a living Example of the ftricteft Virtue ;
and Religion one of her firmeft Supporters and faithful Votaries.
His moft mournful and afflicted Widw,
deeply fenfible of the great Lofs fhe has fuftained
by the death of the tendereft and kindeft of Hufbands,
has caufed this Monument to be erected to his Memory.

MARY his Wife
departed this Life Dec. 8, 1773,
in the 70th Year of her Age.

DANIEL, Son of
THOMAS BUCKINGHAM,
died Sept. 29, 1772, in the 24th Year of his Age.

JOAN, late Wife of
THOMAS BUCKINGHAM,
of the Parifh of Rodborough,
died Oct. 29, 1768, ætatis fuæ 57.

PENELOPE his fecond Wife
died Sept. 27, 1789, aged 56.

ESTHER, Wife of
DANIEL BUCKINGHAM, fenior,
died June 12, 1769, ætatis fuæ 65.

DANIEL BUCKINGHAM, fenior,
died May 28, 1780, aged 82 Years.

JOHN BUCKINGHAM, Cutler,
died Oct. 1, 1770, ætatis fuæ 38.

MARY, Wife of
DANIEL BUCKINGHAM,
died Jan. 27, 1776, in the 51ft Year of her Age.

GEORGE, Son of
RICHARD and ANN COCKLE,
died Feb. 6, 1779, in the 17th Year of his Age.

THOMAS THATCHER,
late of Kidderminfter, in the County of Worcefter, Gent.
an Officer in the firft Royal Dragoons,
who departed this Life Feb. 28, 1784,
aged 46.
In him fhone the Man,
firm and valiant in his Profeffion,
the indulgent, kind and affectionate Hufband,
the conftant, fteady, and fincere Friend.

A VERY LARGE VAULT, RAILED ROUND :

In this Vault
are depofited the Remains of
SAMUEL WHITMORE, Efq.
late of Hyde Court,
who died March 4, 1783, aged 75 Years.

JOHN HOLLIDAY, Surgeon,
Son of JOHN and ANN HOLLIDAY,
died July 14, 1754, ætatis fuæ 26.

JOHN HOLLIDAY
died April 10, 1761, aged 78 Years.

ANNE his Wife
died June 1, 1764, æt. 74.

JOHN PRICE, of Avening,
who lived with SAMUEL SHEPPARD, Efq.
a faithful Servant 28 Years,
died July 28, 1763, aged 67 Years.

PRISCILLA, Daughter of
CHRISTOPHER and ELIZAB. GARDINER
died May 4, 1664, aged 13 Years.

ROBERT POOL, Ironmonger,
died Sept. 27, 1757, aged 65 Years.

ANN his Wife
died Aug. 23, 1739, aged 42 Years.

JOHN, SAMUEL, ELIZABETH,
PENELOPE, WILLIAM, and ANN,
their Children,
all died in their Infancy.

ANN, another of their Daughters,
died Aug. 6, 1736, aged 6 Years.

JONATHAN ESSEX
died in September 1722.

HESTER his Wife
died Feb. 19, 1750, aged 84.

CHARLES BELCHER
died Sept. 12, 1714.

THOMAS POOL
buried May 2, 1744, aged 60.

MARY his Wife
buried June 2, 1748, aged 73.

ROBERT POOL, of Avening,
died January 23, 1766, aged 48.

JANE POOL
died Nov. 23, 1767, aged 50.

ELIZABETH, Wife of
THOMAS SAUNDERS,
died March 21, 1782, aged 69 Years.

JOHN their Son
died June 23, 1782, aged 30 Years.

JANE their Daughter
buried Oct. 13, 1750, aged 3 Years.

WILLIAM their Son
buried May 15, 1752, in the 3d Year of his Age.

THOMAS SAUNDERS aforefaid
died April 18, 1783, aged 59 Years.

WILLIAM

WILLIAM HIERON
buried March 9, 1742, aged 60 Years.

SARAH his Wife
buried March 15, 1748, aged 54 Years.

SAMUEL HIERON
died Nov. 14, 1760, aged 44 Years.

MARY, Wife of THOMAS DEVERELL,
Clothier, died June 3, 1753, æt. 47.

THOMAS DEVERELL
died Jan. 13, 1767, ætat. 69.

MARTHA, Wife of
RICHARD BROWN, Surgeon,
and Daughter of
BENJAMIN and ANN HAYWARD,
died in 1777, aged 39 Years.

Likewife four of their Children,
who died in their Infancy.

THOMAS SEALE, Surgeon,
died in 1751, aged 40 Years.

ANN his Sifter,
Wife of BENJAMIN HAYWARD,
Apothecary,
died in 1774, aged 60 Years.

BENJAMIN, Son of
BENJAMIN and ANN HAYWARD,
died in 1740, aged 14 Days.

ANN their Daughter
died in 1763, aged 14 Years.

BENJAMIN HAYWARD,
died Oct. 13, 1787, aged 77 Years.

NATHANIEL WEBB, Clothier,
died March 10, 1753, ætatis 58.

ELIZABETH his Wife
died May 25, 1764, aged 79 Years.

EDWARD WEBB,
Son of RICHARD WEBB,
of Nailfworth, Clothier,
died Jan. 2, 1762, aged 44 Years.

JOHN WEBB,
Son of JOHN WEBB, of London,
and Grandfon of
NATHANIEL and ELIZABETH WEBB,
died Auguft 29, 1765, aged 2 Years and
10 Months.

DANIEL his Son
died Dec. 7, 1715.

RICHARD his Son
died Jan. 8, 1743, aged 21 Years.

JUDITH BOWYER,
died Aug. 6, 1778, aged 73 Years.

MARY his Daughter
died March 19, 1759, aged 21 Years.

JOHN WEBB, Clothier,
died May 26, 1754, aged 77 Years.

ANN his Wife
died April 12, 1749, aged 75 Years.

MARY WEBB, Spinfter,
Daughter of JOHN WEBB, Clothier,
of Giddiknap,
died March 3, 1761, aged 46 Years.

SARAH WEBB, Spinfter,
Daughter of JOHN WEBB aforefaid,
died Dec. 2, 1761, aged 52 Years.

ELIZABETH, Daughter of
MARY BROWN,
died Oct. 16, 1770, aged 15 Years.

JOHN WEBB
late of London, Factor,
died Aug. 23, 1773, aged 46 Years.

THOMAS HIATT, Clothier,
died March 25, 1779, aged 29 Years.

JOHN RICKARDS.
He was an Officer of Excife at Worfted,
County of Norfolk, 24 Years,
and died at Hawkefbury's Upton,
in this County,
Oct. 29, 1782, aged 59 Years.

SARAH, Relict of JAMES COOK,
and Daughter of THOMAS RICKARDS,
died Jan. 27, 1782, aged 74 Years.

GEORGE MAYNARD, Clothier,
was buried April 22, 1701, aged 29
Years.

GEORGE his Son
was buried near the fame Time, aged
2 Years.

SARAH his Wife
died April 3, 1763, aged 92 Years.

WILLIAM RIDLER,
of the Bourn, in the Parifh of Stroud,
Clothier, Grandfon of WILL. GRIME,
of the fame Place,
died Dec. 2, 1739, in the 68th Year of
his Age.

THOMAS DURINGFORD WINN
died July 5, 1781, aged 9 Years.

THOMAS FOWLER, fenior,
of Stroud, Clothier,
died Nov. 6, 1687, ætatis fuæ 51.

JOHN FOWLER,
Clothier, of this Parifh,
died Feb. . . 17 . .

JANE, Relict of the abovementioned
THOMAS FOWLER,
died Oct. 7, 1708, in the 79th Year of
her Age.

MARY, Wife of THOMAS FOWLER, jun.
of Stroud, Clothier,
died Aug. 2, 1722, ætatis fuæ 38.

JOHN their Son
died Sept. 16, 1728, in the 9th Year of
his Age.

THOMAS FOWLER, of Stroud, Clothier,
died Feb. 28, 1745, aged 64 Years.

SARAH his Daughter
died Oct. 27, 1734, aged 18 Years.

DANIEL his Son
died Feb. 14, 1753, æt. 40.

ELIZABETH, Daughter of
THOMAS and MARY FOWLER,
died March 15, 1784, in the 70th
Year of her Age.

JEREMIAH NICHOLLS
died May 25, 16 . 9.

DOROTHY, Wife of THOMAS POPE,
died Nov. 8, 1698.

ANNA, Wife of SAMUEL CAMBRIDGE,
1682.

ROBERT HARMAN, Staymaker,
died Dec. 24, 1778, aged 62 Years.

SARAH his Wife
died Nov. 18, 1779, aged 70 Years.

SARAH WHEELER their Niece
died Jan. 15, 1786, aged 44 Years.

BETTY, Daughter of
WILLIAM and MARTHA KIRBY,
died July 20, 1781, aged 2 Years and
a Half.

SAMUEL CLUTTERBUCK,
late of Howcombe, Clothier,
died March 28, 1766, aged 52 Years.

SARAH, MARTHA, and THOMAS,
three of his Children.

JOHN WEBB,
late of the Iron Mills, in this Parifh,
Clothier,
died Nov. 28, 1756, aged 41 Years.

ELIZABETH his Wife
died Aug. 6, 1767, aged 52 Years.

JAMES their Son
died Oct. 31. 1787, aged 18 Years.

PENELOPE COOK,
Daughter of SOLOMON and MARY COOK,
died April 9, 1756,
in the 28th Year of her Age.

Near this Place
lyeth the Bodies of three Sons of
HENRY SPERRY, viz.

JOHN died March 20, 1695.

DANIEL died Nov. 12, 1711.

HENRY died Nov. 14, 1711.

RICHARD PERRY
died Auguft 24, 1728.

HANNAH his Wife
died April 3, 1713.

JOSEPH PERRY, Clothier,
died Dec. 20, 1740, aged 45 Years.

REBECCA, Wife of SAMUEL COSBURN,
died Nov. 22, 1751, aged 19 Years.

DANIEL KEENE, Baker,
died Jan. 12, 1758, aged 48 Years.

DANIEL his Son
died Aug. 31, 1770, aged 31 Years.

CHARLOTTE, Daughter to
the firft mentioned DANIEL,
died Aug. 3, 1755, aged 12 Years.

CHARLES, Son of
SAMUEL and ELIZABETH KEENE,
died in his Infancy.

SARAH, Wife of
DANIEL KEENE, Baker,
died July 7, 1787, aged 77 Years.

MARY, Wife of JOHN CLIFT,
and Sifter to the aforefaid
SARAH KEENE,
died Nov. 2, 1790, in the 72d Year
of her Age.

ALICE LAMBURN, Spinfter,
died Feb. 26, 1755, aged 60 Years.

THOMAS LAMBURN
died Sept. 20, 1759, aged 67 Years.

THEOPHILUS FOWLE, Shear Maker,
died Oct. 24, 1729, ætatis fuæ 59.

JUDITH his Wife
died Feb. 7, 1720, æt. 55.

RICHARD PIMBURY,
of Upper Hyde, Waggoner,
died June 19, 1742, aged 81 Years.

CATHARINE, Wife of PETER MORRIS,
died Jan. 13, 1748-9, aged 60 Years.

ELIZABETH,

ELIZABETH, Daughter of
JEREMIAH and MARY ALDER,
died Feb. 11, 1731-2
in the 12th Year of her Age.

ELIZABETH, Wife of
HOPEFUL JACK,
died June 4, 1788, aged 70 Years.

SAMUEL RIDLER
died April 17, 1746, aged 36 Years.

NATHANIEL his Son
died Jan. 23, 1743.

Arms ; on a Chevron engrailed between fix Croffes patée fitchy, three Fleurs de lis, each charged with an Annulet.

JAMES SMITH
and MARY his Wife.

WILLIAM their Son
died May 16, 1758, aged 43.

JAMES FREEMAN
died May 18, 1774, aged 41.

JAMES SMITH,
Son of WALTER and ELIZAB. SMITH,
of Woodchefter,
died Jan. 5, 1766, in the 22d Year of his
Age.

MARY, Daughter of the faid
WALTER SMITH, and Wife of
the aforefaid JAMES FREEMAN,
died May 2, 1784, aged 50 Years.

ELIZABETH, Wife of
JOSEPH DANGERFIELD,
and Daughter of the aforefaid
WALTER SMITH,
died April 19, 1782, aged 36 Years.

MATTHEW SMITH
died Feb. 2, 1748-9, ætatis fuæ 28.

ZEPHANIAH his Son
died Nov. 28, 1747, an Infant.

ELEANOR, Wife of THOMAS BARBER,
died May 20, 1762, æt. 50.

THOMAS BARBER
died Nov. 4, 1773, aged 57.

Alfo three of their Children.

HESTER, Wife of RICHARD TAULEY,
died 8 of . . . . 1716, ætatis 57.

EDWARD PINFOLD, Clothier,
. . . . Auguft . . 1636.

EDWARD PINFOLD, Clothier,
died Feb. 16, 17 . . in the 63d Year of
his Age.

JOHN PINFOLD, Clothier,
died Oct. 12, 1713.

EDWARD, Son of EDWARD PINFOLD,
died Feb. 15, 1716-7.

JOSEPH PINFOLD, Clothier,
died May 1, 1728, in the 42d Year of
his Age.

EDWARD PINFOLD, Clothier,
died Nov. 9, 1728, in the 45th Year of
his Age.

EDWARD, Son of
JOSEPH and ANN PINFOLD,
died Nov. 20, 1746, in the 23d Year of
his Age.

JOANNA, Daughter of
JOSEPH and ANN PINFOLD,
died Jan. 19, 1729-30, in the 2d Year of
her Age.

ANN, Relict of JOSEPH PINFOLD,
and Daughter of JAMES WILD, Gent.
died Jan. 6, 1736-7, in the 37th Year
of her Age.

JUDITH STACKMORE,
died Jan. 4, 1778, in the 91ft Year of
her Age.
She was married firft to EDW. PINFOLD,
of this Town, Clothier,
afterwards to the
Rev. NATHANIEL HACKMAN,
Rector of Cherrington.

Alfo of WILLIAM WESTLEY,
who married the only Daughter of
JUDITH HACKMAN,
died March 14, 1779, aged 71 Years.

MARTHA his Wife
died Aug. 8, 1782, aged 68 Years.

JOHN HAINES, late of Stroud,
died Nov. 18, 1788, aged 35 Years.

WALTER WOODROOF
died Aug. 20, 1719, aged 36.

ELIZABETH his Wife
died March 10, 1748, aged 75.

MARY, Wife of
THOMAS EARLE, Maltfter,
died Jan. 17, 1764, in the 34th Year
of her Age.

THOMAS, WILLIAM, and ELIZABETH,
Children of
THOMAS and ELIZABETH EARLE,
all died in their Infancy.

HESTER, Daughter of
JAMES and HESTER CHAMBERS,
of Forwood, in this Parifh,
died March 13, 1765, aged 23.

THOMAS, FRANCIS, GEORGE, and
SARAH, their Children,
died Infants.

SARAH, Wife of
JOHN CAMBRIDGE, fenior,
died March 10, 1755, ætatis fuæ 67.

HENRY POULTON
died Nov. 23, 1684.

ALICE his Wife
died Oct. 24, 1692.

RY, Wife of JOHN SPARROW,
of Painfwick,
died May 1757, aged 38 Years.

AMBROSE COSBURN, fenior,
died Jan. 24, 1741, aged 53 Years.

MARY his Wife
died Feb. 11, 1779, aged 86 Years.

MARY and SUSANNAH, Daughters of
AMBROSE and ROSSANNA COSBURN.

MARY died July 21, 1770, in the
16th Year of her Age.

SUSANNAH died July 30, 1770,
in the 4th Year of her Age.

GILES GOUGH, of Brimfcomb,
died Oct. 30, 1665.

DANIEL GOUGH, of Brimfcomb,
died Feb. 10, 1766, aged 83.

ANN, Daughter of
JOHN and ANN CLIFT,
died Dec. 7, 1751, aged near 21 Years.

Three more of their Children
died Infants.

JOHN CLIFT, fenior,
died Sept. 16, 1750, aged 79.

MARY his Wife
died Jan. 21, 1758, aged 92.

ANN, Wife of JOHN CLIFT,
died Sept. 23, 1757, aged 70 Years.

JOHN CLIFT
died Feb. 19, 1769, aged 69 Years.

JEREMIAH DAY, fenior, Clothier,
died Jan. 31, 1733, in the 84th Year
of his Age.

BRIDGET his Wife
died Aug. 31, 1730, in the 73d Year
of her Age.

JEREMIAH DAY, junior, Clothier,
died July 10, 1730, in the 37th Year
of his Age.

RICHARD FOWLER, of Brimpfcomb,
Clothier, died July 7, 1627.

GEORGE, Son of
THOMAS HILL, Clothier,
died Sept. 28, 1700, aged 1 Year.

MARY, Wife of THOMAS HILL,
Clothier,
died Sept. 6, 1711.

THOMAS HILL, of Rodborough,
Clothier,
died June 16, 1735, aged 56 Years.

JOHN HILL, of Stroud, Butcher,
died Dec. 5, 1777, aged 75.

THOMAS HILL, Butcher,
died Aug. 10, 1718.

SARAH his Wife
died July 9, 1697.

SARAH, Wife of WM. DUTTON,
Butcher,
died Oct. 22, 1764, ætatis 73.

MARY their Daughter
died Jan. 15, 1763, ætatis 35.

WILLIAM DUTTON
died April 24, 1774, aged 79.

THOMAS his Son, late of the Bourne,
in the Parifh of Stroud,
died April 10, 1787, aged 64.

ROBERT PERKES, Surgeon,
died May 29, 1734, in the 57th Year
of his Age.

MARTHA his Wife
died Dec. 16, 1735, in the 47th Year
of her Age.

ROBERT and EDWARD their Sons.

FRANCIS PERKES
(Uncle of ROBERT PERKES, Surgeon),
died Anno Dom. 1685.

MARY, Daughter of
ROBERT and MARTHA PERKES,
and Wife of JOHN BACON, A. M.
Rector of Afton Ingham, in the
County of Hereford.
She departed this Life
July 31, 1744, aged 30.

MARY and ELIZABETH,
their Daughters died in their Infancy.

NATHANIEL PERKES, Efq. Son of
ROBERT and MARTHA PERKES,
died Feb. 9, 1782, in the 63d Year
of his Age.

WILLIAM

WILLIAM STEPHENS
died Sept. 30, 1663.

SARAH, Wife of
JOHN CAMBRIDGE, jun. Clothier,
at Brimpſcomb,
died Jan. 10, 1769, aged 59.

CATHARINE their Daughter
died March 23, 1748, an Infant.

JOHN CAMBRIDGE
died July 20, 1789, aged 74.

JOHN CAMBRIDGE
died Feb. 15, 1775, in the 99th Year
of his Age.

ANNAH, late Wife of
TOBY CAMBRIDGE,
died Oct. . . 1703.

JOHN THOMAS,
of the Lodge,
died Nov. 22, 1767, in the 79th Year
of his Age.

WILLIAM, Son of
JOSHUA and HESTER THOMAS,
died July 1, 1765, an Infant.

JOSHUA THOMAS, of the Box, Maltſter,
died Jan. 23, 1791, aged 65 Years.

HESTER his Wife
died June 27, 1785, aged 53 Years.

EDWARD RIMER, Clothier,
died Oct. 3, 1681.

EDWARD his Son
died Oct. 2, 1740.

EDWARD, Son of
EDWARD RIMER, Clothier,
died June 1721, aged 5 Years.

ON HEAD AND FLAT STONES.

Name	Died	Aged
Mary, Daughter of Daniel and Mary Wilts, of Burley	17 May, 1779	20
William Davis	15 July, 1750	45
Mary Teal	13 Feb. 1756	—
Samuel Teal, Clothier	27 Apr. 1729	60
William Bliſs	7 Sept. 1768	67
Timothy Rotten, late of the Bourn, in the Pariſh of Stroud	29 Nov. 1772	49
Suſannah his Wife	23 Mar. 1766	33
George Winn, of Strd	—— 1740	—
Ann his Daughter	—— 1721	—
Jane, Widow of John Bradley, of Elkſtone	19 Apr. 1752	63
William Bradley, late of Rodborough, Son of William Bradley, late of Toddington, and Grandſon of William Bradley, late of Combend	3 Oct. 1760	40
John Wilton, Collarmaker	12 May, 1751	29
Deborah, Wife of Samuel Manning	— May, 1762	36
Robert Milton, Shoemaker	25 Dec. 1763	38
Jonathan Smith	19 Feb. 1736	68
Ann his Relict	— July, 1743	82
Sarah, Wife of James Churches	15 Nov. 1781	57
Chriſtian his ſecond Wife	15 Dec. 1785	55
Elizabeth, Wife of Thomas Stratford, of the Bourn	4 Dec. 1765	45
S. Peach	17 Sept. 1769	65
M. Peach	12 Dec. 1769	69
Elizabeth their Daughter	30 Apr. 1737	—
Sarah, Daughter of Samuel and Mary Peach	15 Sept. 1773	30
Joſeph Harris	15 Sept. 1770	39
Daniel Day, of Littleworth	8 June, 1769	63
Daniel Day	28 Apr. 1744	66
Margery his Wife	29 Sept. 1756	76
John their Son	—— 1717	—
William Smith	5 Oct. 1757	43
Thomas, Son of Richard and Mary Pinbury, of Upper Hyde	17 Dec. 1713	—
Mary their Daughter	24 Jan. 1754	13
Joſeph Freeman	23 May, 1749	40
William Harris		
Sarah his Wife	13 Nov. 1736	95
Elizabeth, Daughter of John and Mary Baxter, of Derbyſhire	28 Aug. 1746	—
William Manning	—— 1765	26
Sarah, Wife of Abraham Bird	22 May, 1785	55
Urſula Merrett	28 July, 1753	72
Samuel, Son of Samuel Barnfield	20 Nov. 1724	61
John Barnfield, of Rodborough, Son of Samuel Barnfield	15 Nov. 1728	55
Hannah, Wife of Jonathan Pyrke	4 Mar. 1748	61
Elizabeth, Wife of John Weeb.		
Matthew Saunders	21 Apr. 1760	37
Mary his Daughter	14 Aug. 1759	4
Joſias Cloſe	10 May, 1675	—
Suſan his Wife	6 July, 1691	—
Stephen Warren, of Shriveham, co. Berks, late Butler to Samuel Sheppard, Eſq.	14 Jan. 1764	4

Name	Died	Aged
Abigail, Wife of John Robertſon	24 June, 1755	82
Elizabeth, Daughter of William and Sarah Moody	22 July, 1786	4
Thomas their Son	in his Infancy.	
Martha, Wife of Thomas Bingham	15 Nov. 1750	54
Thomas Bingham	9 Dec. 1749	58
Edmund Bingham	26 Feb. 1752	24
George Maſon	29 Apr. 1756	85
Sarah his Wife	8 Apr. 1771	88
Mary, Daughter of William and Mary Latham	16 Jan. 1729	—
Edward their Son	24 Feb. 1730	—
John their Son	27 Oct. 1757	18
John Eddels	21 May, 1770	84
Judith his Wife	3 Apr. 1749	58
Seven of their Children.		
John Keery	28 June, 1758	81
Sarah, Wife of John Marmon, of Brimpſcomb	— Oct. 1750	39
Elizabeth, Wife of William Newman.		
Elizabeth, Wife of James Canter	9 July, 1744	40
Suſannah and Martha their Daughters died Infants.		
Elizabeth their Daughter, Wife of Francis Soul	17 Sept. 1772	27
Richard Faux	26 Jan. 1765	79
Sarah his Wife	31 July, 1743	50
Elizabeth their Daughter	21 Mar. 1768	23
Samuel Gough, of Brimpſcomb	6 July, 1751	59
Judith his Daughter	30 Jan. 1752	32
Thomas Stockham	12 July, 1725	31
Mary, Wife of John Hiatt	3 Feb. 1758	32
John their Son	an Infant.	
Mary, Wife of Joſ. Hiatt	19 Jan. 1785	32
John their Son	an Infant.	
Thomas Yeaſt	13 Aug. 1751	28
Sarah, Wife of Thomas Barrett	—— 1738	—
James Fowler	8 July, 1781	51
Nathaniel Halliday, late of the Golden Valley	7 Jan. 1764	83
Mary his Wife	7 June, 1763	77
Five of their Children.		
Anna, Wife of Robert Snook	— Feb. 1750	—
William and Thomas their Sons.		
John Fletcher, Taylor	— Feb. 1736	—
Mary, Wife of John Fletcher	— Feb. 1738	33
John their Son	in Infancy.	
John Fletcher	7 Feb. 1756	56
Suſannah his ſecond Wife	— Nov. 1771	56
Thomas King	14 Feb. 1724	33
Obadiah Ball	— Dec. 1715	86
Thomas Daniells, Carrier	19 Sept. 1753	64
Richard Broad	6 Sept. 1745	—
John Broad his Brother	15 Sept. 1719	—
N. Hieron, Clothier	31 Mar. 1749	63
Edith his Wife	3 Oct. 1749	49
Katharine their Daughter		
Samuel, Son of Nathaniel Hieron	3 Apr. 1709	27
George Newman		
Daniel Newman	12 May, 1727	48
Thomas, Son of Samuel and Deborah Morton	26 Dec. 1760	1

ON HEAD AND FLAT STONES.

	Died	Aged
Samuel Morton -	11 Apr. 1782	51
Mary, Wife of Philip Farr	— Jan. 1759	76
Francis their Son -	— —— 1720	—
Mary, Wife of William Cloudsley, Clothier -	25 Dec. 1766	31
Sarah, Wife of Nathaniel Butt	27 Feb. 1770	55
Elizabeth, Wife of Jonathan Alden	19 Sept. 1757	49
Jonathan Alden -	9 Aug. 1784	76
Six Children of John and Mary Webb died Infants.		
John Newman -	10 Oct. 1704	—
Samuel King - -	— June, 175.	—
John King, Shoemaker -	— —— 172.	—
Elizabeth, Wife of James Parker	8 Aug. 1694	—
William Lyddiatt -	— July, 1687	—
Eleanor, Daughter of James Thomas - - -	2 Dec. 1732	10
Martha, Wife of Thomas Bingle	12 Apr. 1758	40
Thomas Bingle -	24 June, 1778	50
J. Rimer - buried	— —— 1674	—
Patience Clayfield, Relict of William Clayfield - -	15 Dec. 1775	66
Thomas their Son -	7 Apr. 1773	34
Jane their Daughter -	25 Jan. 1763	25
Mary, Daughter of James and Ann Newman - -	23 Dec. 1786	33
Thomas Holliday -	26 Oct. 1774	82
Deborah his Wife -	21 Mar. 1764	80
Richard, John, and Deborah, their Children.		
James Norton, sen. -	20 Aug. 1720	42
Mary his Wife - -	19 Jan. 1743	—
James Norton, jun. -	24 May, 1750	47
Martha, Wife of John Coxe	4 Oct. 1774	39
Abraham, Father of John Coxe	21 Mar. 1771	65
Elizabeth, Mother of John Coxe	10 Aug. 1772	63
Mary, Daughter of Stephen Cambridge - -	1 May, 1729	—
Martha his Daughter -	— Oct. 1730	—
Charles his Son -	— —— 1739	—
Judith, Daughter of Richard Norton, of Burley -	1 July, 1732	29
Susannah his Wife -	13 July, 1748	72
John their Son - -	28 June, 1711	—
Richard their Son -	12 Aug. 1729	—
Mary, Wife of Richard Essex	16 Dec. 1759	73
Mary, Daughter of William Hooleday - -	12 June, 1685	—
William Jacobs, Sadler -	— —— —	—
Thomas Wathen -	17 Sept. 1757	66
T. Pitt - -	— —— 1784	—
Thomas Hathen (41 Years Clerk of this Parish) - -	28 Jan. 1770	75
Susannah his Wife -	5 Oct. 1780	71
Giles their Son (succeeded his Father as Clerk 13 Years) -	16 July, 1783	41
John their Son - buried	24 June, 1784	48
John Cambridge -	— —— 1721	31
Joan, Daughter of John and Ann Cambridge -	— Dec. 1740/1	28
Elizabeth, Wife of Thomas Reynolds	6 Sept. 1742	37
Ann their Daughter -	27 Oct. 1733	—
Frances their Daughter -	15 Sept. 1734	1
Elizabeth Chester -	9 Mar. 1757	67
John Hooper -	— —— —	—
Arthur Hickes -	— May, 1728	40
Christian his Wife -	12 July, ——	—
Martha, Wife of Timothy Butt, sen.	27 Dec. 1718	75
John Waake - -	19 Jan. 1677	—
Margaret his Daughter -	— —— —	—
William Smith -	4 May, 1758	80
Richard Smith -	6 Dec. 1784	72
Martha his Wife -	27 Dec. 1784	77
Esther, Wife of John Simpkins, of Beverstone, and Daughter of Richard and Martha Smith	8 Dec. 1785	44
Four Children of John and Esther Simpkins died in their Infancy.		
Esther their Daughter -	18 Jan. 1770	6
John their Son -	11 June, 1770	1
Esther, Daughter of John Harmer	7 Feb. 1742/3	26

	Died	Aged
Walter Butt, Clothier -	6 Dec. 1720	—
Lydia his Wife -	19 Sept. 1751	—
Walter, Son of Walter Butt, of Chalford - -	3 Nov. 1754	1
Nathaniel Blifs, of Chalford	— Dec. 1724	—
John Blifs, of Chalford -	25 June, 1752	49
James Blifs, of Chalford -	12 Oct. 1751	—
Samuel, Son of Nathaniel Blifs, of Chalford -	25 Sept. 1758	47
Mary Smith, Daughter of Nathaniel Blifs -	27 Nov. 1758	53
Thomas, only Son of Thomas and Deborah Daniells -	13 Jan. 1749/50	15
Deborah, Wife of Thomas Daniells	25 May, 1736	33
Sarah their Daughter, Wife of Samuel Damford -	26 Dec. 1757	25
Sarah, Wife of Thomas Farmiloe	12 Mar. 1772	49
Jane, Daughter of William and Mary Bingle -	21 Mar. 1729	—
William, Son of Samuel and Mary Clift -	3 Nov. 1784	—
Hannah, Wife of John Roberts	30 Apr. 1784	66
Ann, Wife of John Cofburn	20 Jan. 1758	54
John their Son died in his Infancy.		
John Keeble - buried	— Feb. 1756	17
John Weaving -	— —— 1722	—
Anthony Stoner -	6 Jan. 1685	—
Nathaniel, Son of Giles and Susannah Pinfold -	29 Oct. 1734	28
Thomas their Son, Saddle-tree-maker -	30 May, 1740	29
Susannah, Relict of Giles Pinfold	27 Nov. 1754	73
Jane, Wife of William Gardner	20 Apr. 1722	27
Two Children of Samuel and Hannah Hill.		
Thomas Pinfold, of Burley, Clothier	— Mar. 172.	84
Robert Smith -	— June, 1725	43
James Stoner -	31 Jan. 1663	—
Deborah, Daughter of Savmercal Bridges -	31 May, 1680	—
Thomas Holder -	20 Dec. 1652	—
Thomas, Son of William and Martha Westley -	3 June, 1785	39
Daniel Corbett -	— Feb. 1720	31
Mary his Wife -	— Mar. 1750	66
Sarah, Wife of James Warthen, sen.	— —— 1677	—
Joseph Dangerfield -	28 Oct. 1755	49
Joannah his Wife -	25 July, 1766	49
Margery, Wife of Richard Dowdy	15 Jan. 1741/2	34
Elizabeth Hall -	9 Feb. 1745/6	62
Lydia Hall -	5 Jan. 1750/1	54
Richard Dowdy -	16 Feb. 1752/3	83
Sarah, Wife of Robert Dowdy	21 Feb. 1759	23
William Dowdy -	3 Mar. 1763	57
Stephen Averis -	22 Jan. 172.	—
Thomas Webb, Clothier -	10 Nov. 1731	38
Robert his Son -	2 July, 1750	21
Samuel Webb - -	20 Aug. 175.	—
Thomas his Son died an Infant.		
Richard Harmer, of Chalford	23 June, 1764	55
Mary his Wife -	25 June, 1764	54
Daniel Jones -	11 Feb. 1737	32
Thomas } Sons of Thomas and {	25 Oct. 1773	1
and John } Mary Aland {	25 June, 1786	2
William Bishop -	23 Dec. 1742	42
Edward and } Sons of Jeremiah and {	18 Oct. 1768	5
Jeremiah } Hester Vizard {	29 Sept. 1771	5
William Pierce -	31 July, 1741	45
Sarah his Wife -	7 Jan. 1779	73
Four Children of James Newman died Infants.		
Edward Sparrow -	10 Dec. 1781	58
Jeremiah Fowler, of Hyde	15 Oct. 1756	72
Elizabeth his Wife	26 Mar. 1772	85
Thomas Jordan, Baker -	2 Jan. 1763	59
Abraham Harrison -	— Dec. 1727	31
Mary, Wife of Thomas Fewster, sen.	— Nov. 1743	60
Mary, Wife of Leonard Smith, sen.	8 Jan. 1660	60
Leonard Smith -	17 Mar. 1782	83
Stephen Skinner -		
Isaac Scott, Gardner -	— Apr. 1733	—

O N

ON HEAD AND FLAT STONES.

	Died	Aged
John Pockeridge	24 June, 1746	38
Richard Child	28 Aug. 1678	—
Elizabeth his Wife	— Dec. 1697	—
John Child	27 Mar. 1763	63
Sarah his Wife	16 Mar. 1781	84
Mary their Daughter	27 Oct. 1783	52
Ann their Daughter	3 Sept. 1783	58
Thomas their Son	27 Sept. 1783	60
Three of his Children, by Mary his Wife, died in their Infancy.		
Thomas, Son of Thomas Cornwall	23 Dec. 1682	—
Richard Webb, sen.	19 May, 1761	69
Rachael his Wife	27 Dec. 1763	67
Jeremiah Mason.		
Deborah, Wife of Jeremiah Mason	12 June, 1712	—
Samuel, Son of Richard Webb	— —— 1755	34
Daniel, Son of Samuel and Elizabeth Walkley	1 May, 1791	34
Eunice Punter, Daughter of Isaac and Jane Punter	3 Sept. 1736	—
Sarah their Daughter	2 Apr. 1735	—
Isaac Punter	5 Apr. 1734	72
Jane his Wife	25 Sept. 1743	80
Edward Hill	8 Oct. 1729	—
Sarah his Wife	21 May, 1699	—
Edward Hill, jun.	5 Mar. 1723	33
Susannah, eldest Daughter of John Deverell	21 Oct. 1753	60
John Deverell, Clothier	15 Feb. 173⅔	68
Hannah his Wife	15 Nov. 1748	83
John and John } their Sons {	10 Oct. 1702	4
	— Sept. 1744	43
Hannah and Anne } their Daughters {	27 Apr. 1703	—
	19 Aug. 1715	19
Daniel, eldest Son of Daniel Webb	3 Dec. 1713	40
Samuel and Edward } Sons of Daniel Webb {	6 Dec. 1687	13
	8 May, 1729	50
Elizabeth, Wife of Edward Webb	19 Dec. 1737	66
Daniel Webb	18 Dec. 1698	66
Susannah his Wife	21 Aug 1713	66
Samuel, Son of John Webb	18 Aug. 1715	9
John his Son	30 Mar. 1725	24
Anne his Daughter	17 Mar. 1751	48
Hester, Daughter of John and Margaret Millard	28 Oct. 1737	6
S. Walkley	3 Sept. 1783	64
Charles Easey	11 May, 1754	—
Richard, Son of Robert Hill	— —— 1758	4
Mary, Daughter of Daniel King	2 Mar. 1637	—
Mary and Jane } Daughters of John and Katharine Wheeler {	— —— 1747	—
	18 Jan. 1749	4

	Died	Aged
John, Son of Thomas Gale	8 Dec. 1692	14
Thomas Gale	— Dec. 1681	40
Betty, Daughter of William and Martha Kirby	20 July, 1781	2
Samuel, Son of Richard Bowyer	25 Oct. 1755	—
Judith, Wife of Thomas Latham	— Oct. 1745	—
Elizabeth, Daughter of Mary Brown	16 Oct. 1770	15
Jane, Wife of Richard Smith	28 Apr. 1774	20
Richard Smith	7 May, 1786	46
Jonathan Danford, Cooper	20 Apr. 1742	57
Dinah, Wife of Giles Heaven, and Daughter of George Barrett	30 May, 1759	41
Mary, Wife of William Griffin	6 Mar. 1771	39
Thomas their Son died an Infant.		
Sarah his second Wife	30 Dec. 1776	32
Betty their Daughter died an Infant.		
Susannah his third Wife	6 Apr. 1789	59
James Cook	18 Nov. 1766	55
Thomas, Son of Thomas Cook	18 Aug. 1750	—
James Cook	2 May, 1722	39
Sarah his Relict	22 Aug. 1746	69
George Cook	— Mar. 1739	64
John his Son	24 Mar. 1751	24
Allis, Wife of Henry Mallard	19 July, 1752	29
Thomas Richards, sen.	2 July, 1738	59
Hannah his Wife	21 Dec. 1747	66
John his Son	— Dec. 1716	11
Elizabeth, Daughter of Joseph and Mary Perry	24 Aug. 1760	23
James Bailey, of Malmsbury	7 May, 1758	23
John, Son of John Johnstoun	— —— ——	—
Elizabeth, Daughter of John and Charlotte Chapman	31 May, 1744	—
Alice their Daughter	7 Oct. 1746	1
John Chapman	3 Nov. 1749	32
Mary and Samuel } Children of Daniel and Sarah Keene {	11 Apr. 1739	1
	4 Oct. 1742	—
Charles Cornwall	4 July, 1742	62
Charles his Son	15 May, 1717	—
Elizabeth his Daughter	16 Apr. 1722	—
Brice his Daughter	26 Oct. 1723	—
William, Son of William Wathen	4 July, 1742	—
Elizabeth, Relict of Charles Cornwall, Clothier	8 May, 1760	78
Thomas Chapman, Gent.	30 Nov. 1736	—
Sarah his Wife	2 Nov. 1769	—
Mary, Daughter of Nath. Young	— July, 1727	—
Thomas Sansum	28 Dec. 1757	72
Mary his Wife	14 Feb. 1728	43
Mary their Daughter	1 May. 1751	28

CXXX.

CXXX. H A R D W I C K E

LIES in the great Vale of *Severn*, and at a fmall Diftance from its Banks. It is Part of the Hundred of *Whitftone*, feven Miles diftant from *Stroud* on the North, and four weftward from the City of GLOUCESTER. The Soil is of a very ftrong Clay, of excellent Pafturage, with a fmall Proportion of arable Lands, and many Orchards.

The Benefice is vicarial, annexed to the Vicarage of *Standifh* as a Chapelry. In 1112, the Impropriation, with Lands in *Rudge* and *Farleigh*, were given to the Abbey of *St. Peter* in *Gloucefter* *; which have been fince annexed to the See, and held in Leafe by the Family of TRYE, from whom they paffed by Purchafe to the Earl of HARDWICK.

The Church, dedicated to *St. Nicholas*, has a Nave, an Aifle on the South fide, which is continued parallel with the Chancel, and a low embattled Tower. It is divided by very low pointed Arches. In the Reign of King HENRY VII. in purfuance of the Will of WILLIAM TRYE, Efq. the Nave was decorated with a new Roof of timber Frame, and Floor of painted Bricks; upon which, and the Joints of the Roof, are feveral Coats of Arms †.

The Manor was originally included in that of *Standifh*, and was held of the DE CLARES Earls of GLOUCESTER. Amongft the firft Tenants upon Record are the Family of KENN in 1400. But this Manor appears to have been diftinct from that called *Hardwick Park Court*, which had been long before held by the BOTELERS. Upon the Death of Sir ALMERIC BOTELER A PARK, in 1449, 27 HEN. VI. this Eftate was inherited, in Right of Marriage Dower, by JOHN TRYE, Efq. ‡. He had married ELIZABETH, the elder Co-heir; ISABEL the other, the Wife of JOHN KENN, received the Hamlet of *Park End*, in the adjoining Parifh of *Haresfield*, as her Portion. In the Family of TRYE the manerial Eftate remained vefted for the Space of more than three Hundred Years. THOMAS TRYE, Efq. about 1730, having been empowered by an Act of Parliament granted for that Purpofe §, fold it to the Right Hon. Sir PHILIP YORKE, Attorney General, who, being appointed Lord High Chancellor of *Great Britain*, was created Baron HARDWICK Nov. 3, 1733, 7 GEO. II. and Earl of HARDWICK April 2, 1754, 27th of the fame Reign. His Grandfon is the prefent Proprietor.

The Court, or Manfion Houfe, formerly encircled by a Park, is now inhabited as a Farm. It was built about the Beginning of the Reign of CHARLES the Firft, and has a very fpacious Hall, with many large Apartments. The external Cornice is that which was firft introduced by INIGO JONES. Upon the fame Site was the ancient Houfe of the BOTELERS, with a Moat, and other caftellated Appendages.

---

* " A. D. 1112, THOMAS ST. JOHN dedit Ecclef. *S. Petri Glouc.* terram de la *Rugge*, quæ jacet in *Standifh* in puram & per- " petuam Elymofunam liberam & quietam de Geldo, &c. quæ ad regem pertinebant, Rege HENRICO feniore confirmante *Petri* " Abbatis." DUGDALE, Mon. I. p. 118.

Cart. 28 E. III. n. 4. pro libera Warenn. in *Rugge* & *Farleigh*.

† Many of thefe Efcocheons are deftroyed by the late Repairs. What remain are, 1. BERKELEY, quartering DE BROTHERTON, WARREN, and MOWBRAY; WILLIAM Marquis of BERKELEY. 2. On a Chevron three Martlets, between as many Crofs Crofslets fitchè, and an Annulet in Chief, enfigned with a Mitre; FARLEIGH Abbot of *Gloucefter*. 3. DENNYS of *Dyrham*. 4. DENNYS, impaling BERKELEY. 5. A Chevron between three Leopards' Faces jeffant. 6. Or, a Bend Azure, impaling DENNYS; W. TRYE, Efq. And upon fome, Knots, and other Devices. The Bricks bear the Arms of the Abbey of *Gloucefter*, and Scrolls, " Ave MARIA Gra' plen'."

‡ Efchaet. 20 EDW. IV. 1480. The Family of TRYE are of *Norman* Extraction, as appears by a Roll of Arms compiled in the Time of the Crufade. " Monfieur BILEBATUD DE TRIE, d'Or a une Bende gobonnè d'Argent and Azure. Monfieur REY- " NALDE DE TRIE, d'Or a une Bende d'Azure." LELAND, Coll. vol. II. p. 612. The firft upon Record in *England* is RAWLIN TRYE, who, marrying the Daughter of THOMAS BERKELEY, received with her in Dower the Manor of *Alkington* in *Berkeley* about 1380. In 1434, JOHN TRYE was fummoned as one of the Gentry of this County; and in 1427 was High Sheriff. JOHN TRYE, Efq. his fecond Son, was Burgefs in Parliament, and the firft Mayor of the City of *Gloucefter*, when the Charter was granted by RICHARD III. in 1483. WILLIAM TRYE, Efq. reprefented it in the Parliaments of the 2d of WILLIAM and MARY, in the 7th of the fame Reign, and in the 1ft Year of Queen ANNE.

§ In 3 GEO. II. an Act paffed, intituled, " An Act for vefting in Truftees the Manors of *Hardwick* and *Haresfield*, with " the impropriate Tythes of *Haresfield, Coldrop*, &c. and other Lands in the County of *Gloucefter*, the Eftate of THOMAS TRYE, " Efq. to be fold for certain Purpofes expreffed in the faid Act."

4   *H A M L E T S.*

H A M L E T S.

1. *Rudge* and *Farleigh* were given, as before mentioned, to the Abbey of *Gloucefter* in 1107, and confirmed to them by King EDWARD III. in 1344. A Leafe is extant from EDWARD FOWLER, Bifhop of *Gloucefter*, to WILLIAM TRYE, Efq. dated 1708; which was afterward transferred with the other Eftates.

2. *Field Court*, or *La Felde*, had been more anciently held of WILLIAM CLINTON, Earl of *Huntingdon*, previous to its becoming the Property of EDMUND BEREWE, or BARROW, who died feifed of it in 1570, 12 ELIZ. THOMAS BARROW, Efq. fifth in lineal Defcent from EDMUND, upon his Demife in 1736, bequeathed this Eftate to ELEANOR his Daughter and fole Heir, the Wife of the Rev. THOMAS SAVAGE, whofe Son GEORGE SAVAGE, Efq. is the prefent Poffeffor *.

In parochial Payments this Parifh is jointly rated with the Hamlet of *Coldthrop*.

No Benefaction to the Poor.

The Lift of INCUMBENTS will be given in the Account of the Parifh of *Standifh*.

PRESENT LORD OF THE MANOR, AND LESSEE OF THE MANOR OF RUDGE AND FARLEIGH,

The Right Honourable PHILIP Earl of HARDWICK.

The Perfons fummoned from this Parifh by the Heralds in 1682 and 1683 were
William Trye, Efq. Thomas Barrow, Efq. and William Yate, Gent.

At the Election in 1776, Eight Freeholders polled from this Parifh and its Hamlets.

The Regifter commences with a Date 1566.

ANNUAL ACCOUNT OF MARRIAGES, BIRTHS, AND BURIALS, IN THIS PARISH.

A.D.	Mar.	Bir.	Bur.	A.D.	Mar.	Bir.	Bur.	A.D.	Mar.	Bir.	Bur.	A.D.	Mar.	Bir.	Bur.
1781	3	9	1	1786	3	11	7	1791				1796			
1782	1	6	2	1787	2	9	3	1792				1797			
1783	2	8	8	1788	3	17	6	1793				1798			
1784	5	7	8	1789	2	11	4	1794				1799			
1785	2	10	6	1790	1	17	5	1795				1800			

INSCRIPTIONS IN THE CHURCH.

IN TRYE'S SEPULCHRAL CHAPEL AT THE END OF THE AISLE.

A Monument of Freeftone, with an arched Canopy over a recumbent Figure in Armour; on one Side a fmaller Figure of a Child likewife in Armour.

Arms; Quarterly, 1. and 4. Or a Bend Azure, for TRYE; 2. and 3. quarterly, 1. and 4. Gules, three covered Cups Or, 2. and 3. Argent, a Buck's Head caboffed Gules, for BOTELER A PARK;—impaling, quarterly, 1. and 4. Argent, a Saltire between four Mullets Gules, for GORNEY; 2. and 3. Barry of eight Argent and Gules, over all a Lion rampant Or, for BRANDON. On the other Side, Argent, three Bars and a Greyhound current in chief Azure, for SKIPWITH, with many quarterings. Erected for JOHN TRYE, Efq. and MARGARET his Wife, Daughter of Sir WILLIAM SKIPWITH, Knight, in the Reign of Queen ELIZABETH.

Near this Place
lyeth interred the Body
of JOHN TRYE, Efquire, Lord of the
Mannour of Hardwicke, Father
of WILLIAM TRYE, Efquire, who
lived in the Time of King HENRY
the Sixth, and was then High
Sheriffe of the County of Gloucefter.

Near this Place
lyeth interred the Body of
WILLIAM TRYE, Efquire, Lord of the
Mannor of Hardwick, Sonn of
JOHN TRYE, Efquire. He lived in
the Time of King EDWARD the
Fourth, and married ISABELLA,
eldeft Daughter of JAMES Lord
BERKELEY, of Berkeley Caftle,
and Sifter to WILLIAM Lord
Marquis BERKELEY. He was at

the Charge of making and beautifying the Roof of the Body
of the Church of Hardwick,
as by his Will appears.

Arms; TRYE, with quarterings as before.

Here lyeth interred the Body
of JOHN TRYE the elder, Efq.
Lord of the Mannor of Hardwicke.
He married ELIZABETH, one of the Coheirs of Sir CHARLES BRANDON, Kt.
Duke of Suffolk, and Knight of the
moft noble Order of the Garter.
He died the 21 Day of April, 1579.

* This Eftate belonged to the Family of DE DEORHYRSTE. WALTER BEREWE, of *Awre*, married ELIZABETH, Daughter and Heir of THOMAS DE DEORHYRSTE, who was Burgefs in Parliament for *Gloucefter* early in the Reign of HENRY VI. 1431, 1445. MS Pedigree. Arms; Vert, a Bend between fix Crofs Crofslets Or.

Arms; as before.

HERE LIETH THE BODY OF
WILLIAM TRYE THE ELDER,
ESQUIRE, LORD OF THE
MANNOR OF HARDWICKE,
WHO MARRIED
MARY, SECOND DAUGHTER TO
SIR EDWARD
TYRRELL, OF THORNTON, IN
THE COUNTY OF
BUCKINGHAM, KNIGHT, AND DIED
THE 13TH DAY OF MARCH, A. D.
1609.

HERE RESTETH THE MEMORIAL
OF
CAPTAYNE HENRY TRYE, SECOND
SONNE OF THIS WILLIAM TRYE,
WHO DIED THE 20 OF OCTOBER,
1629,
AND LIETH BURIED IN ST. CLE-
MENT'S
CHURCH, LONDON.

Arms; as before.

Huic propinque loco jacet quod reliquum est spectatissimi adolescentis,
pietate, literis, nec non corporea claritu-
dine eximius, summæ spei & splendoris
sui nominis JOHANNIS TRYE, Gen.
filii & heredis GULIELMI TRYE,
Armigeri. Hujus soli Harwikensis
domini, qui postquam Collegio Lyn-
colnensi, Oxon. nec non honorabilissimo
divertiorio Lincolnensi, Londoni, summo
cum profectu constitutos transsisset
dies, in Domino placide obdormivit 21
die Augusti, anno Dom. 1651, ætatis
suæ 25.

Arms; TRYE as before;—impaling,
Azure, three Cinquefoils Argent, for
VINCENT.

Here lyeth the Body of
WILLIAM TRYE, Esq. Lord of this
Manor
of Hardwicke and Harsfield, nobly
descended by his Auncestors, and by
their matching in sundry noble
Families, the last was with one
of the Coheireses of Sir CHARLES
BRANDON,
Duke of Suffolk, Knight of the Most
Noble Order of the Garter.
He had, by his most virtuous
and charitable Wife Mrs. ANNE TRYE,
Fourteen Children,
descended of the Family of Sir FRANCIS
VINCENT, Baronet, of Stoke, in the

County of Surrey. He died on Tues-
day at
Night, the 20 Day of December, 1681,
aged above 84 Years.
His original Descent and Name is
from a Town beyond the Seas, called
Trye, from whence his Ancestors came
into England above Five Hundred Years
since.

Arms; TRYE as before;—impaling,
Azure, three Cinquefoils Argent, for
VINCENT.

Here lyeth interred the Body
of that virtuous and charitable
Mrs. ANNE TRYE, Wife of WILLIAM
TRYE, Esq. Lord of this Mannor of
Hardwicke and Harsfield, descended of
the Family of Sir FRANCIS VINCENT,
of Stoke, in the County of Surrey, Kt.
who died . . . . Day of April. . . . .
having been the Wife of the said
WILLIAM TRYE, Esq. 58 Years.
. . . .
and had by him 6 Sonnes and
8 Daughters.

Arms; TRYE;—impaling, Gules, a
Lion rampant Or, for JONES.

Dux Militarius THOMAS TRYE,
Filius GUL. TRYE, de Hardwicke,
Armig.
suis comitatuique Glevensi charus, Regi
& Ecclesiæ fidelis, utriusque
inimicis formidabilis; post quadraginta
annorum militiam hic tandem arma &
exuvias deposuit corona triumphali
emeritorum ultra omnia secula,
apud cælicolos decorandus.
Obiit 16 Feb. 1670.

In cujus memoriam dilectissima ejus
conjux trium filiarum ac cohæredum
RICARDI JONES, de Hanham, in agro
Glevensi, Armigeri, natu maxima
monumenta hoc mœrens extruxit.

Here also lyeth the Body of ANNE
TRYE, Relict of Capt. THOMAS TRYE,
and one of the Daughters of RICHARD
JONES. Esq. of Hanham, who departed
this Life April the 25th Day, 1703.

Arms; TRYE;—impaling, Azure,
a Chevron between three Bugle Horns
Or, for HORNE.

In Memory of WILLIAM TRYE, Esq.
Lord of the Mannour of Hardwicke
and Haresfield, who departed this Life
on the 29 Day of June, Anno Dom. 1717,
ætatis suæ 57.

Also in Memory of MARY TRYE,
Wife of WILLIAM TRYE, Esq. Lord of
the Mannours of Hardwick

and Haresfield, who departed this Life
on the 20 Day of April, 1724,
ætatis suæ 53.

WILLIAM, second Son of WILLIAM
TRYE abovementioned, died August
the 4th, 1739, aged 47 Years.

ON FLAT STONES
IN THE CHANCEL.

HERE LIETH THE BODY OF
HARRI DAVIS, WHO DECESSED
THE 6 DAY OF NOVEM. 1601.

HERE RESTETH THE BODY OF
SAMUEL HAWKINS, LATE
OF HARDWICKE, YEOMAN,
WHO DEPARTED THIS LIFE
THE 29 DAY OF NOV. 1675.

Arms; on a Cross five Roundlets.

In Memory of JOHN STRATTON,
of this Parish, Gent. who died
October 19, anno 1719, æt. 78.

In Memory of MARY STRATTON,
the Wife of JOHN STRATTON, of
this Parish, Gent. who departed
this Life the 21st Day of June, 1707,
aged 65 Years.

In Memory of REBEKAH, the
Wife of THOMAS STRATTON, of
this Parish, Gent. who died April
14, 1709, aged 28 Years.

In Hopes of a glorious
Resurrection here lyeth the Remains
of RICHARD MARTIN,
of this Parish, Yeoman, who (after
a Life well spent in Honesty, Care,
and Industry, performing the
Offices of a loving Husband, a
tender Father, a kind Neighbour,
and a good Christian) died greatly
regretted the 21 Day of Aug. 1765,
aged 50 Years.
Also of SARAH their Daughter,
who died an Infant.

Here lieth
the Remains of WILLIAM, the Son of
RICHARD MARTIN (by HANNAH his
Wife), who departed this Life the
13th Day of September, 1776,
aged 23 Years.

IN THE CHURCH YARD,   ON TOMBS.

Here resteth the Body of
HANNAH, the Wife of THOMAS SMITH,
who departed this Life the 5th Day
of January, 1702, ætatis suæ 67.

Here resteth the Body of
THOMAS SMITH.
who died the 11th Day of May, 1675.

Also HANNAH, the Wife
of WILLIAM BUCKLE, and Daughter
of THOMAS and HANNAH SMITH,
who died the 6th Day of June, 1695.

Under this Tomb lie the
Remains of JOHN PRIDE, Yeoman,
Native of this Parish, late resident
in the Parish of Charlton King's,
who departed this Life the 14th Day
of September, 1766,
aged 59 Years.

Also of SARAH his Wife,
who departed this Life the 12th Day
of Oct. 1777, aged 67 Years.

In Memory of
JOHN BISHOP, late of the
Parish of Hullavington,
in the County of Wilts,
who departed this Life April 2,
1782, aged 25 Years.

ON

ON FLAT STONES.

In Memory of
SAMUEL WHITE, of this Parish, Yeoman,
who died January the 2d, 1754,
aged 84 Years.

Also ELIZABETH GARDNER died 1747,
aged 74 Years.

In Memory of
ROBERT CAREFIELD, of this Parish, Yeoman,
who died July the 7th, 1769,
aged 39 Years.

Also of ANNE, the
beloved Wife of ROBERT CAREFIELD.
She died June the 3d, 1765,
aged 35 Years.

ON HEAD STONES.

	Died	Aged
Nathaniel Hawkins -	23 Mar. 170½	42
Mary, Wife of Nathaniel Hawkins	7 Feb. 1704	24
Thomas Hawkins, sen.	20 Sept. 1718	63
Sarah his Wife -	19 June, 1706	52
Thomas their Son -	3 Aug. ——	—
Ann, Wife of Nathaniel Hawkins	10 Oct. 1729	42
Samuel, Son of Thomas and Sarah Hawkins -	26 Oct. 1729	48
John Hawkins -	10 Nov. 1739	55
Thomas Hawkins -	28 May, 1767	80
Elizabeth his Wife -	24 Aug. 1759	65
Anne, Wife of Thomas Hawkins	1 Aug. 1770	65
Thomas, Son of Thomas Hawkins	14 Nov. 1755	—
Elizabeth, Wife of John Birt, of Epney, Daughter of Thomas and Eleanor Hawkins -	26 Apr. 1727	28
Thomas, Son of Nathaniel Hawkins	4 Dec. 1760	57
Anne, Daughter of George and Hester Matton -	12 Aug. 1769	18
William Carefield, senior -	15 Feb. 1756	60
Mary his Wife -	20 July, 1761	65
William their Son -	9 Feb. 1747	21
William Rowles, of Elmore	26 May, 1746	32
Elizabeth, Wife of John Rowles	15 Aug. 1750	63
Mary Fleming, Daughter of Elizabeth Rowles -	— July, 1722	—
Elizabeth, Wife of John Moore	26 Oct. 1766	55
Thomas their Son -	14 Mar. 1769	27
Thomas Pride -	5 Apr. 1712	—
Sarah his Wife -	28 Feb. 1714	—
Margaret, Wife of William Chamberlin - -	19 Oct. 1720	28
John Rowles -	7 Nov. 1737	50
Thomas Adey -	7 May, 1689	66
Oliver Holtham -	17 June, 1726	69
Sarah his Wife -	19 Mar. 1752	77
Samuel Holder -	17 Jan. 1757	40
Sarah, Relict of Samuel Holder, and late Wife of George Mans	15 Mar. 1770	54

	Died	Aged
Susannah Wife of William Holder	15 Dec. 1756	55
William Holder -	1 July, 1766	63
Elizabeth, Wife of William Roberts, of Haresfield, Daughter of William Holder - -	28 Sept. 1758	—
Thomas Merrett -	2 June, 1724	43
Thomas Dowdyn, of Elmore	31 Aug. ——	—
John Cooke -	23 Mar. 1705	32
John Wells -	31 Oct. 1735	68
William his Son -	30 May, 1729	36
Alice, Wife of John Wells	14 Feb. 175½	88
John their Son -	9 Apr. 1740	40
James their Son -	4 July, 1709	11
Hannah their Daughter -	27 May, 1699	2
Samuel Merret -	23 Apr. 1690	49
John Merret -	—— 1786	78
Prudence his Wife -	9 Mar. 1759	46
Mary their Daughter -	20 May, 1772	22
John Waife -	20 Feb. 1682	55
Thomas Baldwin -	30 July, 1679	—
Jane, Wife of Anthony Shaftford	30 Sept. 1681	—
Thomas Bailey -	6 Mar. 1763	70
Joan his Wife -	22 July, 1778	86
John, the Son of John and Mary Bailey - -	9 Feb. 1783	47
Anna, Wife of William Bailey	7 Aug. 1790	68
Daniel Mills, Schoolmaster	4 July, 1775	57
Philip Jenkins -	23 Nov. 1760	72
Sarah his Wife -	21 Oct. 1761	60
Samuel Organ -	6 Apr. 1729	65
Joan his Wife -	20 Apr. 1727	62
John Beach - -	9 Oct. 1773	62
Mary his Wife -	6 Jan. 1778	57
Anne, the Wife of Joseph Curtis	25 Dec. 1732	70
Eleanor, the Wife of Daniel Fryer	23 Mar. 1783	64
George Matton -	31 Mar. 1787	73
Hester his Wife -	7 Apr. 1788	78

CXXXI. HARESCOMBE,

CXXXI. HARESCOMBE, or HARSCOMBE,

IS a Parifh of fmall Extent, in the united Hundreds of *Dudftone* and *King's Barton*, fituate under the Eaftern Extremity of *Broadridge Hill*, two Miles diftant from *Painfwick*, and five South from GLOUCESTER. As the Soil is of Clay, the Pafture Lands greatly exceed the Arable; the whole is computed to contain about 700 Acres.

The Living is a Rectory, partly appropriated, and annexed to *Pitchcombe*. There are fourteen Acres of Glebe.

Amongft the ancient Endowments of the Abbey of *Gloucefter* was a Portion of Tythes in *Harfcombe*, which was confirmed to the Bifhops, upon the Eftablifhment of the See in 1541; and is now leafed to the Right Hon. JAMES Lord SHERBORNE.

The Church, dedicated to *St. John Baptift*, and in the Deanery of *Gloucefter*, is a fmall plain Structure, with a Nave only, and a low conic-formed Turret, which is not inelegantly finifhed by a Crofs. Such are not unfrequent in this County, and are fuppofed to have been moft in Ufe in the fourteenth Century. And Bifhop THOMAS has remarked from the Regifter of WALTER DE MAYDENSTONE, Bifhop of *Worcefter*, that this Church, with feveral others, were dedicated by him in 1315 [*].

In *Domefday*, the Accounts of this Manor are confufed; one Manor, however, probably including that of *Brockthrop*, is ftated to have been let by Earl LUREI for 46*l.* 13*s.* 4*d.* for the Ufe of the King [†]. The Abbey of *Gloucefter* held a Manor, in very early Times, by Donation of ADELISA DE IBREIO, which was connected with *Brockthrop*, and recited in the Charter of the Eftablifhment of the See. Of this the Family of WOOD were fometime Leffees; they were fucceeded by Sir ROBERT COCKS, of *Dumbleton*, from whom it paffed by Will to the prefent Tenant.

But, the original Manor is faid to have belonged to the RUFI, or LE ROUS, of *Duntefborne Militis*, the firft of whom died feifed of it in 1273, 2 EDW. I.; and it defcended, after five Generations, to JULIANA LE ROUS, firft the Wife of Sir ANDREW HERLE, Knight [‡], and afterward of THOMAS MILL, Efq. of *Tremill*, co. *Devon*.

THOMAS MULL, or MILL, his Heir, fettled at *Harfcombe* in 1360, and was the Progenitor of a Family, which remained there till the middle of the laft Century; when their Eftate, much diminifhed, paffed to SANDFORD and ROBERTS; after whom, to the MICHELLS, of *Randwick*; and fome Years fince, to MILES HUNTLEY, Gent. to whofe Reprefentatives it now belongs. Other Property is nearly equally divided. The Site of their ancient Refidence is now faintly traced, at the Foot of the Hill, above the Church; but no Buildings are preferved.

BENEFACTION.

GILES COX, Gent. 1620, devifed, by Will, for the Ufe of Poor Houfeholders not receiving Alms, of feveral Parifhes, of which *Harefcombe* is one, an Eftate, which when it produces 50*l.* a Year, this Parifh is to receive 12*s.* fubject to Taxes ond Repairs; the annual Produce is now 12*s.* The Feoffees are Sir RICHARD SUTTON, and Sir JOHN GUISE, Barts.; SAMUEL HAYWARD, HOWE HICKS, BENJAMIN HYETT, ROBERT CAMPBELL, and THOMAS MEE, Efqrs.; DANIEL LYSONS, M. D. RICHARD ROGERS, and MARTIN BARRY, Clerks.

---

[*] THOMAS's Survey of *Worcefter* Cathedral, p. 162.

[†] " In *Herfecombe* tenebat *Wiflet* III virg' terræ liberas ficut & *Ealmer*. Ibi habebat II car' & II bordar' & v fervos & prata " carucis. Has eafdem ROGERUS DE LUREI pofuit ad firmam pro XLVI lib' & XIII fol' & VI den'." Domefday.

[‡] Efchaet. anno 15 RIC. II. " Terras & tenementa ANDREÆ DE HERLE, Militis, qui obiit anno 15 Regis RIC. II. *Herfecome* " & *Duntefborne Rous*, co. *Glouc.*"

I

INCUMBENTS.	PATRONS.	INCUMBENTS.	PATRONS.
	Of *Harefcombe* and *Pitchcombe.*		
1569 Richard Rawlins,	Thomas Mill, Efq.	1696 Charles Stock,	Charles Stock, fen.
—— Peter Hogg,	————.	1709 Jonathan Blague, B. A.	————.
1596 John Rowles,	Thomas Mill, Efq.	1726 Thomas Rawlins,	Mary Blague.
1606 Peter Hogg,	The fame.	17— Charles Neale,	————.
1612 Thomas Lloyd,	Thomas Mill and William his Son.	1769 Rice Jones,	John Purnell, Efq. and Eliz. Purnell, Spinfter.
—— Richard Horeton,	————.	1791 Chas. Wallington, M.A.	Thomas Purnell Purnell, Efq.
1684 Thomas Stock,	William Mill, Efq.		

PRESENT LESSEE OF THE MANOR,

ANNE BUSBY, Spinfter.

No Perfon was fummoned from this Place by the Heralds in 1682 and 1683.

At the Election in 1776 Fourteen Freeholders polled from this Parifh.

The Regifter has its firft Date in 1618.

ANNUAL ACCOUNT OF MARRIAGES, BIRTHS, AND BURIALS, IN THIS PARISH.

A.D.	Mar.	Bir.	Bur.	A.D.	Mar.	Bir.	Bur.	A.D.	Mar.	Bir.	Bur.	A.D.	Mar.	Bir.	Bur.
1781	1	11	2	1786	3	8	3	1791				1796			
1782	1	11	2	1787	2	10	1	1792				1797			
1783	1	4	2	1788	1	6	2	1793				1798			
1784	1	5	3	1789	—	12	4	1794				1799			
1785	—	12	5	1790	1	8	4	1795				1800			

INSCRIPTIONS IN THE CHURCH.

ON MONUMENTS IN THE CHANCEL.

In Memory
of the Rev. Mr. Jonathan Blague, B.A.
Rector of Harefcombe and
Pitchcombe eighteen Years,
who departed this Life
Auguft 31, 1726,
ætatis fuæ 62.

In
Memory of
CHARLES STOCK,
jun. Rector de Harefcombe.
He departed this Life the 2d Day
of Feb. in the Year 1707-8,
aged near 53 Years.

In Memory of MARY,
the Wife of CHARLES STOCK, jun.
who departed this Life July 6,
Anno Dom. 1709, aged 48.

ON FLAT STONES IN THE CHANCEL.

Here refteth the Body
of JOHN MICHELL, Gent.
who departed this Life January
the 9, 1700.

Here lieth the Body
of JOHN MICHELL, Gent.
who was buried Sept. 13, 1727.

HERE RESTETH THE BODY
OF MARGARET, THE WIFE
OF JAMES MICHELL,
GENT. WHO DIED 5 DAY OF JUNE,
IN THE YEARE OF OUR LORD
GOD MDCLIII.

Here lyeth the Body
of MARY, the Wife of THOMAS
HUMPHRIES, of Stonehoufe, who
died July 10, 17 . . in the 22
Year of her Age.

HERE LYETH THE BODY
OF THOMAS ROBERTS, GENT.
WAITING
FOR A RESURRECTION
TO GLORY. HE
DECESSED JAN. 20,
ANNO 1632.

ON FLAT STONES IN THE CHURCH.

Here
refteth the
Body of THOMAS,
the Son of JAMES
MICHELL, Gent. who died
the 27 November 1676,
his Age 8 Years and
near 7 Monthes.

CHARLES, the Son
of JAMES MICHELL, Gent.
died 25 Oct. 1657.

Alfo
CHARLES his Brother
died 14 Nov. 1658.

And
MARY their Sifter
died . . . . . 1678.

In Memory of
THOMAS ROBERTS, of
this Parifh, Gent. who died
March 13, 1751,
aged 84.

In Memory of
ABIGAIL his Wife, who
died Oct. the 28,
Anno Dom. 1739,
aged near 85.

IN THE CHURCH YARD.

ON MONUMENTS AGAINST
THE CHURCH.

Arms; three Bugle Horns.

To the Memory of
MILES HUNTLEY, of this Parish, Gent.
who, after a long and painful Illnefs,
which he bore with great Firmnefs
and Refignation, departed this Life
Oct. 25, Anno Dom. 1765,
in the 80th Year of his Age.

Alfo
of ABIGAIL his Wife, who departed
this Life Feb. 6, A. D. 1743,
aged near 50 Years.

BRIDGET their Daughter, and
three Sons, viz. JAMES, JAMES, and
CHARLES,
were likewife interred near this Place.

Arms; HUNTLEY, as before.

In Memory of
MILES HUNTLEY, of this Parish, Gent.
who departed this Life the 12th Day of
September, Anno Dom. 1790,
aged 70 Years.

MARTHA, the Wife of
MILES HUNTLEY, of this Parish, Gent.
She departed this Life July 10, 1789,
aged 54 Years.

Near this Place lie the Remains
of SAMUEL LAMBRICK, fen.
(late of this Parish, Yeoman) who
departed this Life Jan. 13, 1778,
aged 62 Years.

Alfo WILLIAM and BETTY, Children
of the abovefaid, who died in their
Infancy.

ON TOMBS.

Here refteth the Body of MARY,
the Wife of JOHN HUNTLEY, Gent.
who deceafed the 9th of May, 1698.

Here refteth the Body of JOHN HUNTLEY,
of this Parish, Gent.
who deceafed Feb. 15, 1670.

ELIZABETH, the Wife of
MILES HUNTLEY, Gent.
who died Oct. 20, 1710,
aged 29 Years and 9 Months.

Arms; Azure, three Leopards' Faces
Or, a Chief embattled Ermine, for
MICHELL.

Hic jacet corpus CAROLI MICHELL, Gen.
Qui fuit unus ex coronatoribus ad Regiam
Majeftatem pro hac comitatû
finceri Regi ac patriæ hac vita difceffit
Aprilis die 27, 1694, ætatis fuæ 56.

Arms; MICHELL; as before;—impaling, per Pale, Argent and Gules, a
Lion rampant Sable, for ROBERTS.

Here refteth the Body of
JAMES MICHELL, junior, Gent.
who departed this Life
the 20th Day of Nov. A. D. 1689,
ætatis fuæ 31.

5

Here
lieth the Body of JAMES
MICHELL, Gent.
who departed
this Life Sept. the 9th, 1698,
in the 76th Year of his Age.

Here refteth the Body of BRIDGET,
the Wife of JAMES MICHELL,
Gent. who was deferving
in her Life, and lamented in
her Death. She deceafed
the 25th Day of June,
Anno Dom. 1685,
aged 56 Years.

Arms; a Fefs wavy between three
Lions' jambs erafed.

In Memory of thefe worthy
Brothers THOMAS CLENT and
WILLIAM CLENT, Gentlemen. The
which THOMAS died October 26,
aged 24 Years; and
WILLIAM died 30 of the fame
Month, 1671, aged near 21 Years.

In Memory of
MARY COPNER, of the Parish of
Haresfield, Wife of WILLIAM COPNER,
who died October the 2d, 1718,
aged 71 Years.

In Memory of
JOHN COPNER, Son of
WILLIAM and MARY COPNER,
of the Parish of Haresfield, Yeoman,
who died March 19, An. Dom. 1719,
aged 39 Years.

In Memory of
ELIZABETH COPNER, Daughter of
WILLIAM and MARY COPNER,
of the Parish of
Haresfield, Yeoman, who died April
10, An. Dom. 1720,
aged 37 Years.

In Memory of BENJAMIN
COLLINS, of this Parish, Yeoman,
who departed this Life
the 25th Day of Dec. 1724, in the
64th Year of his Age.

In Memory of ALICE,
the Wife of BENJAMIN COLLINS,
who departed this Life
the 16th of July, 1728,
in the 77th Year of her Age.

In Memory of
JOHN SMALLDRIDGE, of this
Parish, who departed this Life
Oct. the 18th, 1736, aged 40.

In Memory of
ELIZABETH, the Wife of JOHN
SMALLDRIDGE, of this Parish, Yeoman,
who departed this Life Jan. 17, 1750,
aged 66 Years.

In Memory of RICHARD
LEWIS, of this Parish, Yeoman,
who departed this Life June 6, 1723,
aged 89 Years.

Here refteth the Body of
RICHARD HARBERT,
aged about 69 Years, who departed
this Life Feb. 7, 1682.

Here
refteth the Body of STEPHEN
TOWNCELL, of Colthrop, in the
Parish of Standifh, Yeoman,
who departed
this Life Aug. 19, An. Dom. 1768,
aged 62 Years.

Alfo MAGDALEN his Wife
departed this Life
June 26, 1784,
aged 83 Years.

Underneath
lies interred the Body of MARY,
the Wife of RICHARD BIDDELL, jun.
only Daughter of STEPHEN and
MAGDALEN TOWNCELL, of the
Parish of Standifh, Yeoman.
She departed this Life Sept. 19, 1768,
aged 25 Years.

Here refteth the Body
of THOMAS COLE, of the Parish of
Haresfield, who died Sept. 16,
An. Dom. 1760, aged 72 Years.

Alfo of SARAH, Wife of the
abovenamed THOMAS COLE. She died
June 4, 1767, aged 67 Years.

In Memory of
THOMAS COLE, of Coldthrop,
in the Parish of Standifh, Yeoman.
He departed this Life Oct. 11,
1789, aged 73 Years.

To the Memory of MARY,
the Wife of GEORGE COPNER,
of the Parish of Haresfield.
She died Dec. 8, 1785,
aged 55 Years.

In Memory of ROBERT ARCH,
of the Parish of Haresfield, fenior,
Yeoman, who departed this Life
Dec. 28, 1762, aged 62 Years.

Alfo ELIZABETH his Wife
died Jan. 19, 1779.
aged 80 Years.

Near this Place lieth
the Body of ROBERT ARCH, jun.
of the Parish of Haresfield,
who died Dec. 12, 1775,
aged 42 Years.

In Memory of JOHN,
Son of ROBERT ARCH,
of the Parish of Haresfield, fen.
who died April 26,
Anno Dom. 1779,
aged 41 Years.

In Memory of
WILLIAM MILL, of this Parish,
who departed this Life July 5, 1739,
aged 60 Years.

Alfo of ANN his Wife.
She died Nov. 21, 1776,
aged 72 Years.

In Memory of
MARY, the Wife of THOMAS MILL,
of the Parish of Haresfield,
who departed this Life
Nov. the 5th, 1785, aged 55 Years.

GEORGE

GEORGE NEALE
died Aug. 16, 1763,
aged 81 Years.

Hic juxta cineres paternos
corpus fuum fepiliri voluit
CAROLUS NEALE, A. B.
hujufce parochæ rector fidelis.
Vir
literis facris & humanis
a prima ætate innutritus,
in munere concianotorio
operofus & felix,
ad omnia officii paftoralis munia
promptus femper & alacris
Filius, frater, amicus,
inter præftantiffimos
erga omnes hominum ordines
egregie benevolus,
quas eximias dotes invicta
celavit modeftia
Obiit 14 ⎰ Salutis humanæ 1769,
Jun. anno ⎱ ætat. fuæ 50.

Multum dilectus, multum defideratus.

———

ELIZABETH, the Wife of GEO. NEALE,
died Jan. 2, 1748,
aged 58 Years.

———

ON FLAT STONES.

In Memory of
RICHARD DOWDSWELL, of this Parifh,
Yeoman, and JANE his Wife.
He died the 4th of May, 1773, aged 71.
She died Nov. 21, 1771, aged 59.

In Memory of RICHARD,
eldeft Sond of RICHARD DOWDSWELL,
of this Parifh, Yeoman, who died
May 3, 1760, aged 18 Years.

———

In Memory of LEWIS,
the eldeft Son of THOMAS ROBERTS,
of this Parifh, Gent. who departed
this Life Aug. 23, Anno Dom.
1733.

———

In Memory of ELIZABETH,
Wife of JOHN PARTRIDGE, of Colthrop,
in the Parifh of Standifh, who
died Feb. 19, 1766,
aged 28 Years.

In Memory of JOHN JORDAN,
of the Parifh of Haresfield,
who died Nov. 30, 1755, aged 84 Years.

In Memory of
KATHARINE, Wife of JOHN JORDAN,
of the Parifh of Haresfield, who died
December . . 1745, aged near 67.

———

In Memory of
HUMPHRY LAND, fenior, of this Parifh,
Yeoman ; and alfo of ELIZABETH
his Wife.
He died April 16, 1757, aged 81 Years.
She died Oct. 18, 1759, aged 83 Years.

HUMPHREY their Son
died Sept. 14, 1772, aged 64.

THOMAS their Son
died Sept. 14, 1742, aged 22.

JOHN their Son
died July 8, 1755, aged 40.

———

In Memory of GEORGE COPNER,
of Haresfield,
Yeoman ; and alfo ANNE his Wife.
He died Feb. 24, 1741, aged 59 Years.
She died April 17, 1747, aged 47.

———

ON HEAD STONES.

	Died	Aged
Edward Mill, of Haresfield	6 May, 1752	78
Jane his Wife, Daughter of Giles Gardner, Gent. -	27 Jan. 1735	63
John Harris - -	19 Nov. 1768	62
Elizabeth his Wife -	19 Apr. 1769	55
William Lane -	4 Feb. 1727	40
Thomas Mills, of Stroud -	17 Oct. 1738	41
William his Son -	6 Sept. 1760	27
John Mills, fenior -	13 May, 1786	56
William Steel -	14 Nov. 1711	56

	Died	Aged
Mary, Daughter of Rich. Hayward, of Ampney St. Peter -	26 July, 1751	22
Thomas Michell, of Haresfield	8 Mar. 1758	—
James Clifford, of Gloucefter	20 Mar. 1761	—
Richard Andrews -	13 Sept. 1769	—
Sarah his Wife - -	26 Feb. 1770	—
John Browning, of Haresfield	24 Nov. 1700	27
Elizabeth his Wife -	6 Nov. 1753	80
Ann, Wife of Jeremiah Greening	30 Apr. 1725	56

CXXXII.

IS a Parifh of the middle Dimenfions, lying in the Vale of *Severn*, and Hundred of *Whitftone*; five Miles North-weft from *Stroud*, and fix South from the City of GLOUCESTER. By a Ridge of very lofty Hills, it is furrounded on the Eaft. The Soil, of a deep Clay, is applied in a Proportion of two thirds to Pafturage, and is very fertile. About 2500 Acres are included within the Limits of the Parifh, with large Meadows near the *Severn*, which are ftinted to certain Days and Number of Cattle.

The Living is vicarial, not in Charge in the King's Books, and in the Deanery of *Gloucefter*. There are twenty Acres of Glebe. It is not certainly known at what Time the Church Revenues were appropriated to the Abbey of *Llanthony*; but the Donation was originally made by HENRY CONSUL, between the Years 1154 and 1199 *. In 1605, 3 JAMES I. the impropriate Tythes were granted to LAWRENCE BASKERVILLE and WILLIAM BLAKE, fubject to an annual Payment of 9*l.* 18*s.* 8*d.* to the Crown, and were afterward held by the Family of TRYE. Of the WEBBS, of *Slimbridge*, they were purchafed by the late Earl of HARDWICK.

The Structure of the Church confifts of a Nave, two Chancels one beyond the other; and at the Weft End a neat embattled Tower and Spire, which appears more modern than the other Parts. It is dedicated to *St. Peter*. The only Antiquities worth Notice are three recumbent Effigies under Arcades, a Croifader, and two Females. There are good Reafons to prefume that they are Memorials of that Branch of the Family of DE BOHUN who were refident at *Haresfield*. The late Repairs on the Infide are faid to have interfered with many other Veftiges, which are concealed or deftroyed.

The Manor, connected with thofe of *Newnham* and *Wheatenhurft*, was anciently a local Dignity. Soon after the Conqueft it paffed to MILO Earl of *Hereford*, and Lord High Conftable of *England*, by grand Sergeanty. Upon the Demife of all his Sons without Iffue, this Office defcended to MARGARET, his only Daughter; who conveyed it to HUMPHRY DE BOHUN her Hufband, with the Earldom of *Hereford* †. HUMPHRY DE BOHUN, the firft Earl of that Name, had by his fecond Wife, MAUD DE AVENBURY, JOHN DE BOHUN; upon whom he fettled in Fee Farm the Manor of *Haresfield*, referving the Dignity ‡. He died in 1236, 20 HEN. III. and left EDMUND BOHUN, the Progenitor of a Family eftablifhed here. But it appears, that the STAFFORDS were confidered as Lords of this Manor, being Heirs general of the elder Branch of the abovementioned Proprietors, till the Attainder and Death of EDWARD Duke of BUCKINGHAM in 1520, when the Crown reclaimed the Manor, and abolifhed the Office, as an hereditary and local Tenure. In 1553, King EDWARD VI. granted it to Sir ANTHONY KINGSTONE, from whom it was transferred to Sir HENRY JERNINGHAM, the Son of Sir EDWARD JERNINGHAM by MARY, fecond Wife of his Father Sir WILLIAM KINGSTONE. Soon after the Commencement of the laft Century it belonged to the Family of WARNER §, from whom, to GEORGE MYNETT, Efq. before the Year 1643. WILLIAM TRYE, Efq. of *Hardwick Court*, died feifed of it in 1681; and by his Defcendant it was re-fold, with other Eftates, to the firft Earl of HARDWICK in 1726.

The Priory of *Llanthony* held confiderable Eftates, which, according to the Practice of Ecclefiaftics, were termed a Manor; not as poffeffing any Jurifdiction, but Exemption only from the Suit and Service at the Court Baron.

T Y T H I N G S and H A M L E T S.

1. *Haresfield* Townfhip. The chief Eftate is attached to the *Moat Place*, which was re-built in its prefent Form by JOHN ROGERS, Efq. in 1670, who was defcended from the Family fettled at *Dowdefwell*. RICHARD PULTON, Gent. inherited from his Uncle JOHN ROGERS in 1683, and of his Heirs it

---

* DUGDALE, Mon. vol. II. p. 72.

† See COKE's Inftitutes, Part I. ch. viii. p. 106. edit. HARGRAVE; or BLOUNT's Ancient Tenures, edit. BECKWITH, pp. 10. 12.

‡ " HUMPHREDUS DE BOHUN, Comes quintus de *Hereford*, defponfaverat etiam alteram mulierem dictam MATILDAM de " *Avenbury*, de qua procreavit Dominum JOHANNEM DE BOHUN Dominum de *Haresfield*, fratrem Domini EDMUNDI DE " BOHUN. Ob. 1275." Stemma com *Hereford*. DUGDALE Mon. vol. II. p. 68.

§ " JOHN WARNER, Son of WILLIAM WARNER, of *Haresfield*, in *Gloucefterfhire*, was born there, entered into *Magdalen* " *Hall* in 1628, being aged 17 Years, took his Degrees in Arts; and at length became Vicar of *Chrift Church*, in *Hampfhire*, " where he was much reforted to by thofe of the Prefbyterian Perfuafion. He wrote feveral Tracts in Divinity."
WOOD, Ath. *Oxon.* vol. II. p. 142.

3

was

was purchafed in 1760 by SAMUEL NIBLETT, and is now the Property of his Son JOHN NIBLETT. Efq. The *Mount* and Eftate were held in the laft Century by the Family of ROBERTS. With a female De-fcendant of LEWIS ROBERTS, Gent. they paffed in Marriage Dower to EDWARD SMYTH, of *Nibley*, Efq. who was a Juftice of *Wales*; and afterwards were transferred by Purchafe to the Earl of HARD-WICKE. Other Property in this Tything belonged to the Family of WARNER, from whom to the TRYES, having been bequeathed by WILLIAM TRYE, Gent. younger Son of WILLIAM TRYE, Efq. of *Hard-wick Court*, to JOHN LONGFORD, Clerk, M. A. who re-built the Manfion-houfe. The prefent Proprietor is the Grandfon of the laft mentioned, CHARLES BRANDON TRYE, Gent. of *Gloucefter*. GEORGE SA-VAGE, has likewife an Eftate here.

2. *Harfecomb* Tything includes that Divifion which adjoins the Parifh of *Harfcombe*, and is faid to have formerly been the Demefnes of a Caftle built by the DE BOHUNS, which they inhabited *. The Family of ROBERTS had a confiderable Eftate, which defcended by Marriage to the WOODS of *Brock-throp*, and is now jointly vefted in the Families of CLUTTERBUCK and PEACH.

3. *Park End* Tything. Several Eftates in this Diftrict are exempted from Tythes, having belonged to the Priory of *Llanthony*. In 1397, 20 RIC. II. Sir ALMERIC BOTELER died feifed of the Manor of *Park End*, which he gave to his younger Coheir the Wife of JOHN KENN, whofe Defcendants enjoyed this, with Land, called *Beaurepeire*, till the Reign of HENRY VI. †. Another Branch of the Family of ROGERS were poffeffed of an Eftate called *Okeys*, which is now divided in Moiety between EDWARD BEARCROFT, Efq. Chief Juftice of *Chefter*, and —— JONES, Efq. in right of their Wives. Befide thefe, the principal Proprietors are the Right Hon. the Earl of HARDWICKE, DANIEL LYSONS, M. D. and JOHN NIBLETT, Efqrs.

4. *Broad Ridge*, or *Broad Barrow Green*, lies on the Summit of the Hill, and is a commonable Field unftinted, of about 200 Acres. It is the Site of a very fingular Camp; the firft Divifion of which is made by a fingle Vallum fifteen Feet high, and 600 Yards in Length, from one Side of the Hill to the other. It is thought to have been a *Britifh* Station after the *Roman* Invafion. The very bold Promon-tory, called the *Beacon Hill*, inclofed by a tranfverfe Vallation fifty Feet deep, and containing fifteen Acres, is connected with the former, but in the Parifh of *Standifh*. A Spot refembling a Prætorium is ftill apparent; upon which probably the Beacon was afterward placed; but the whole is now in too rude a State to afcertain Conjectures refpecting its Origin and Application. But the Profpect deferves fuperior Powers of Defcription. The South eaft Side fhews the Chain of wooded Hills from *Selfley* to *Stinchcombe*, with the whole of the beautiful Amphitheatre which they enclofe. On the South-weft are the high Cliff at *Auft Ferry*, with the Mouth of the *Briftol* Channel, and the two broad Reaches of the *Severn* at *Beach-ley* and *Frampton*. We are then led to the Foreft of *Dean*, *May's Hill*, and the whole Range of the *Malvern* Mountains, encircling the great Vale of *Severn*; more particularly marked by *Robinhood* and *Churchdown* Hills in the Centre. The Abbey Towers of *Gloucefter* and *Tewkefbury* are diftinguifhed from thofe of many Villages, which are fo frequently difperfed in this luxuriant Tract of Country. The North eaft View exhibits *Cleeve*, *Leckhampton*, *Crickley*, *Birdlip*, and *Painfwick*, Cliffs, in Succeffion; each, with bold and rocky Headlands, is the Boundary of many fpacious Dells, either cultivated, or of the moft beautiful Woodland; which afterward fpread into the great Vale, and in Contraft with thofe bare Summits have a truly picturefque Effect.

B E N E F A C T I O N S.

THOMAS TEEKLE, Gent. by his laft Will, bearing Date Dec. 1675, gave the yearly Sum of 5*l*. for ever, for the Relief of fetting to Work the Poor.

JOHN ROGERS, Gent. in his Life-time, gave the Church Clock; and by his laft Will, dated Jan. 22, 1695, gave *Stars Mead Houfe* for a Dwelling for the Parifh Clerk, if fufficient (or other Perfon able), to ring the great Bell every Morn and Even, from All Saints to the Purification of the bleffed Virgin MARY.

ANN PULTON, fen. gave a Silver Plate for the Ufe of the Communion Table.

ANN PULTON, late Widow of SAMUEL PULTON, gave 40*l*.; the Intereft of which is to be annually employed towards the Relief of the Poor.

SAMUEL PULTON, Gent. gave 40*l*. for ever; the Intereft thereof to be yearly difpofed of to the Poor.

ELIZABETH PULTON his Relict, in her Life-time gave a Silver Flaggon, for the Ufe of the Communion Table; and at her Death 20*l*. for ever; the Intereft thereof to be yearly difpofed of to the Poor.

The Rev. JOHN LONGFORD, by his laft Will, gave 50*l*. to this Parifh for ever; the Intereft thereof to be applied in apprenticing out poor Children.

MARY CAPEL by her laft Will gave 20*l*. to this Parifh for ever; the Intereft thereof to be applied in teaching poor Children to read.

---

* " Caftellum de *Havyfcombe* prope *Paynynfwicke*, in *Glouc.* com." Itin. W. WYRCESTER, p. 280.
" *Elmore* Court Houfe was built with Part of the Stone that came from the Caftle of the DE BOHUNS at *Harefcombe*."
MSS. PARSONS. Bodl. Lib.

† See Efchaet. 20 EDW. IV. 1480.
Inquifit. poft mort. ALMERICI BOTELER A PARK, Militis.

VOL. II. I DANIEL

HARESFIELD.

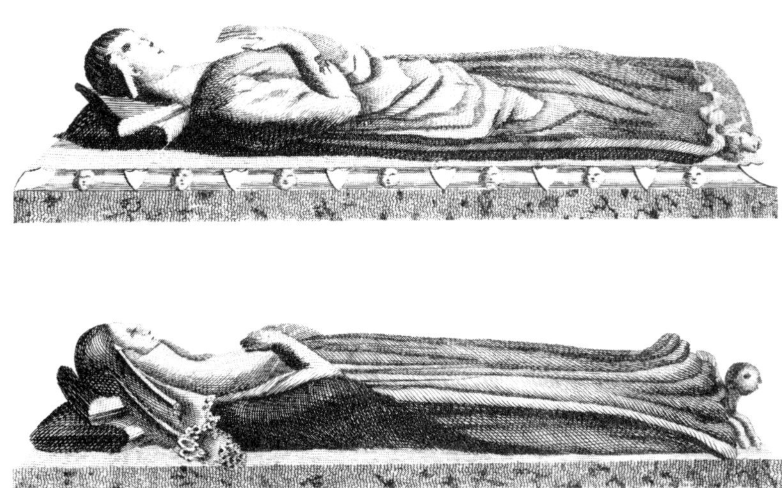

FIGURES IN HARESFIELD CHURCH.

DANIEL NIBLETT, of this Parish, Gent. by his Will, gave to the Ministers and Churchwardens of this Parish 100*l.* upon Trust, to apply and dispose of; the Interest thereof for the teaching and instructing poor Children of this Parish to read and write.

ELIZABETH NIBLETT, Relict of the said DANIEL NIBLETT, April 29, 1783, left 20*l.*; the Interests and Profits to be applied yearly at Christmas, for the Use of the Poor for ever.

INCUMBENTS.	PATRONS.	INCUMBENTS.	PATRONS.
—— William Houghton,	Priory of Llanthony.	—— Anthony Andrews, Clerk,	——————.
1546 Henry Kyrke,	Sir Anth. Kingstone.	1679 Richard Capel, M. A.	William Trye, Esq.
1554 Richard Hudson,	The same.	1712 Henry Abbot,	The same.
—— John Jennings,	——————.	1737 James Commelyne, M.A.	——————.
1571 Thomas Lewis,	Sir Henry Jernegan.	1780 Will. Steele, LL.B.	Philip Earl of Hardwicke.
1577 Thomas Woodcock,	Dame Franc. Jernegan.	1780 Thomas Rudge, B.D.	The same.
1624 Thos. Woodcock, jun.	John Stubbs.		

PRESENT LORD OF THE MANOR,

The Right Honourable PHILIP Earl of HARDWICKE.

The Persons summoned from this Parish and its Hamlets by the Heralds, in 1682 and 1683, were

Edward Warner, Esq. Lewis Roberts, and Rowland Wood, Gents.

At the Election in 1776 Twenty Freeholders polled from this Parish.

The Register, which commences in 1654, has this Entry respecting the Population in 1668:

" Ther were numbred in this P'rish, People of all Ages and Sexes, 591." And in 1783, 110 Families were found within this Parish.

ANNUAL ACCOUNT OF MARRIAGES, BIRTHS, AND BURIALS, IN THIS PARISH.

A.D.	Mar.	Bir.	Bur.	A.D.	Mar.	Bir.	Bur.	A.D.	Mar.	Bir.	Bur.	A.D.	Mar.	Bir.	Bur.
1781	2	8	—	1786	3	16	3	1791				1796			
1782	7	10	6	1787	5	4	11	1792				1797			
1783	3	11	8	1788	3	16	8	1793				1798			
1784	4	13	9	1789	4	10	5	1794				1799			
1785	2	8	10	1790	6	8	5	1795				1800			

INSCRIPTIONS IN THE CHURCH.

ON MONUMENTS IN THE CHANCEL.

Arms; Argent, a Mullet Sable, on a Chief Gules a Fleur de lis Or, for ROGERS;—impaling, Gules, three Lions rampant Argent, for PAUNCEFOOTE.

M. S.
Cum de mortuis
nec omnia tacere fas sit
nec omnia effundere,
sciant posteri
JOHANNEM ROGERS, Generosum,
non solum multis ingenii
dotibus iisque eximiis
verum etiam & animæ
virtutibus quamplurimis
exornatum claruisse;
qui ergo omnium amorem
dum adhuc in vivis esset
facillime attraxit
idem luctum omnium funebrem
cum fato cederet jure merito
excitavit.
Vixit ille annos 58.
Obiit anno 1698.

M. S.
Dominæ MARIÆ ROGERS,
hic juxta sepultæ;
fœminæ, si qua alia
merito celebrandæ,
non tamen ob paucas virtutes
quod facile est infirmioribus
si modo velint,
sed ob plurimas fere omnes
easque præclarissimas,
quas ut a majoribus receperat
sancte observandas,
ita posteris omnibus exemplo suo
Reliquit observandas.
illustriores factas
Vixit illa annos 56.
Obiit anno 1697.

In vita & moribus
ita morte & sepultura
conjunctissimi.

———

The Mirrour of
JOHN ROGERS, of this Parish, Gent.
who died Jan. the 7th, 1670, aged 53.

ANNE ROGERS his Wife,
second Daughter of THOMAS SURMAN,
of Tredington, Gent.
who died Oct. 16, 1668, aged 49;
both Persons of great Piety, Providence,
and Goodness.
They had two Sons, JOHN and WILLIAM
(He died Aug. 18, 1673, aged 29),
and three Daughters, viz. ELIZABETH,
(who died March 20, 1669, aged 26),
ANNE and ELEANOR.

Arms; ROGERS, as before.

In Memory of
JOHN ROGERS, eldest Son of
JOHN ROGERS, Gent. and MARY his Wife,
Daughter of POOLE PAUNCEFOOTE,
of Newent, Esq.
who was born the 9th of August, 1672,
and died August the 19, 1683.
A Lad of rare Piety, Beauty, Docibility,
Wit, and good Nature.

Of gentle Blood his Parents only Trea-
sure,
Theyr lasting Sorrow, and theyr vanish'd
Pleasure,
Adorn'd with Features, Vertues, Wit,
and Grace,
A large Provision for so short a Race.
More mod'rate Gifts might have pro-
long'd his Date;
Too early fitted for a better State.
But knowing Heav'n, his Home to shun
delay,
He leap'd o'er Age, and took the short-
est Way *.

———

* This Epitaph, written by DRYDEN, is published in the first Volume of his Miscellanies.

4

UPON

Arms; 1. a Lion rampant; 2. upon a Cheveron three Efcallops between three Cinquefoils, and in Chief a Garb.
Creft, a dexter Arm vambraced holding a Sword.

LO HERE THE END OF FLESHE AND BLOODE, BLAVNCHE OVIATT DOTH DESCRIE,
WITH PETERE EKE HER YOUNGEST SONNE, BOTHE WHICH IN TOUME HERE LIE,
THE AIEGHT OF MAYE DEPARTID HE, THE LORD DID SO PROVID,
THE THRE AND TWENTITHE OF APRILL, HERSELF THEN LIKEWISE DIED.
MATRIS DECESSUS 1592.
FILII DECESSUS 1588.

ON A BRASS PLATE:

HERE RESTETH THE BODY OF
RICHARD ROBYNS,
OF HARSFIELD, GENT. WHO
CHANGED THIS LIFE THE 28 DAY
OF OCT. ANNO DOM. 1638.

OF FLAT STONES IN THE
CHANCEL.

Arms; Parti per Pale Argent and
Gules, a Lion rampant Sable, impaling,
Gules, feven Lozenges, 3, 3, and 1,
conjoined vairè, on a Canton Or, a Mullet Sable, for GUISE.

DEPOSITUM
LUDOVICI ROBERTS, GEN.
QUI OBIIT IX DIE JUNII,
MDCLXXIX.

Depofitum
Rev. RICARDI CAPELL,
tres annos fupra trigeffimum
hujus Ecclefiæ Parochialis
Vicarii.
Obiit anno XII. MDCCXII.
ætatis 63.

JAMES his Son, born Dec. 9, 1686,
died July 23, 1688.

ELIZABETH his Daughter
died Sept. 20, 1697, aged 2 Years 11
Months.

ANNE his Daughter died Sept. 1, 1697,
aged 13 Years.

Hic jacet
RICHARDUS ROGERS, Gen.
Qui obiit VII die Maii,
A. D. MDCLXXII.

M. S.
JACOBI COMMELINE, A. M.
hujus ecclefiæ
per annos quadraginta Vicarii fidelis,
qui officio affidue functus eft.
Ob vitæ integritatem
morumque fuavitatem non minus infignis,
five conjux, five parens, five amicus,
fuit nemini fecundus.
Obiit Julii 29, 1780, ætatis fuæ 75.

Hic jacet ROBERTUS HUMPHREYS,
Gener. qui obiit 23 die Novembris,
anno 1695, ætatis fuæ 70.

In Memory of Mrs. FRANCES CAPELL,
Relict of Mr. RICHARD CAPELL,
late Vicar, and Daughter of
ROBERT HUMPHREYS, Gent.
who departed this Life the 17th Day of
Auguft 1732, aged 79 Years.

In Memory of the Reverend
Mr. HENRY ABBOTT, late Vicar
of this Parifh,
who died the 25th of March, 1737,
in the 78th Year of his Age.

Alfo in Memory of MARY,
the firft Wife of Mr. HENRY ABBOTT.
She died Sept. 10, 1714, aged 57.

Arms; Gules, a Saltire voided Or;—
impaling, Ermine, on a Chief Sable,
three Battle Axes Argent, for SHEP-
PARD.

Hic jacet
ANTONIUS ANDREWS, Cler.
Qui obiit
IIII die Septembris, MDCLXXVIII.

Arms; on a Fefs between three Mullets three Roundlets, for PULTON;—
impaling, ROGERS, as before.

Here lyeth the Body
of RICHARD PULTON, Gent.
who died 17 July,
An. Dom. 1701,
aged 55 Years.

ANN ROWLES, Relict of
Mr. JOHN ROWLES,
and Daughter of RICHARD and
ANN PULTON, Gent.
died Feb. 6, 1762, aged 82 Years.

Arms, as before.

Here refteth the Body
of ANN PULTON, the
Wife of RICHARD PULTON, Gent.
who died the 5th Day
of May, A. D. 1724,
aged 72 Years.

MARY PULTON, Daughter of
RICHARD and ANNE PULTON, Gent.
died Aug. 14, 1763, aged 73.

Arms; PULTON, as before;—impaling, a Lion rampant between three
Fleurs de lis.

Here lieth the Body
of SAMUEL PULTON, Gent.
who died the 4th of
Jan. Anno Dom. 1744,
aged 61 Years.

Alfo ELIZABETH, Relict of
SAMUEL PULTON,
died Jan. 18, 1752,
aged 58 Years.

Arms; PULTON, as before;—impaling
PULTON.

Here lieth the Body
of ANN PULTON, the Wife
of SAMUEL PULTON, Gent.
who died the 2d Day

---

of Oct. A. D. 1726,
aged 30 Years.

ELIZABETH, eldeft Daughter of
RICHARD and ANN PULTON,
died 9 May, 1731, aged 33.

Arms; PULTON, as before.

Here lieth the Body of
JOHN PULTON, Gent. Son of
RICHARD and ANN PULTON, of
this Parifh, who departed this
Life May 17, 1729, in the 53d
Year of his Age.

Arms; PULTON, as before.

RICHARD PULTON,
of this Parifh, Gent. departed
this Life Nov. 8, 1758,
aged 47 Years.

Alfo MARY, Relict of
RICHARD PULTON, Gent.
died Feb. 27, 1760, aged 40 Years.

Alfo SARAH died an Infant.

ON FLAT STONES IN THE
SOUTH PORCH.

Arms; Paly of fix; over all a Bend;
for LONGFORD;—impaling, Or, a Bend
Azure, for TRYE.

Vir Reverendus
JOHANNES LONGFORD, A. M.
Clericus, morum candore & vitæ
fanctitate
vere Infignis.
Obiit 24 Feb. Anno { Salutis 1759.
{ Ætatis 69.

GULIELMUS LONGFORD,
Filius JOHANNIS & ELIZABETHÆ
LONGFORD
bonæ indolis & fpei juvenis.
Ob. 27 Aug. Anno { Salutis 1750.
{ Ætatis 19.

Arms; On a Lozenge, Paly of fix;
over all a Bend, for LONGFORD.

M. S.
ELIZABETHÆ LONGFORD,
Filiæ natu fecundæ
Reverendi JOHANNIS LONGFORD.
Obiit idæ Martii 1770.

I N

I N   T H E   C H U R C H   Y A R D.

ON A MONUMENT AGAINST THE
CHURCH:

Beneath this Place lies the Body
of FRANCES, Relict of
WILLIAM VAISEY,
and Daughter of the Rev. Mr.
RICHARD CAPEL, late Vicar of this
Parish.
She died March 13, 1764, aged 74.

Alfo MARY CAPEL, Spinfter,
Daughter of the faid RICHARD CAPEL,
who died Feb. 20, 1762, aged 64.

CAPEL, Son of the
abovefaid WILLIAM VAISEY,
died Jan. 19, 1771, aged 50 Years.

ON   TOMBS.

In Memory of WILLIAM
BUCKLE, who died 22d Day of
April, in the 62d Year of
his Age, anno Dom. 1704.

Here refteth the Body of
ROGER BUCKLE, de Colthrope,
who departed this Life the
16th Day of October, 1703,
ætatis fuæ 68.

Here refteth the Body of
KATHERINE, the Wife of
EDMUND FLETCHER, of Painfwick,
Gent. She departed this Life
April 7, anno Dom. 1689,
aged 52 Years.

In Memory of
ABIGAIL, Daughter of
NATHANIEL SYMES
and ELIZABETH his Wife.
She departed this Life
April 5, anno Dom. 1711,
aged 16 Years.

In Memory of
NATHANIEL SYMES, of Colthroop,
Yeoman,
who departed this Life Aug. the 7,
1741, aged 85.

Alfo ELIZABETH his Wife, who died
May 5, 1743, aged 72.

MARY their Daughter died Aug. 19,
1725, aged 28 Years.

Here
refteth the Body of JOHN SYMES,
fen. late of Colthroop, Yeoman,
who departed this Life Aug. 22,
1768, in the 64th Year of his Age.

Alfo ELIZABETH, Relict of the abovefaid,
died Sept. 10, 1778, aged near 69.

RICHARD, Son of
THOMAS and JANE SYMES,
died Oct. 21, 1778, aged 28 Years.

HERE RESTETH THE BODY OF
ROGER LONGE, YEMAN,
WHO DECEASSED THE
7 DAY OF SEPTEMBER, ANNO DOM.
1639, WAITING FOR A JOYFUL
RESURRECTION.

HERE RESTETH THE BODY OF
JHONE LONGE, THE WIFE OF
ROGER LONGE,
DECESSID THE EIGHTEENTH DAIE
OF DECEMBER, AN. DOM. 168 . .

HERE RESTETH THE BODY OF
MARGARET WARNER, DAUGHTER
OF WILLIAM WARNER,
WHO DECEASED THE 1 DAY OF
NOVEMBER, AN. DOM. 1619.

HEARE RESTETH THE BODY OF
WILLIAM WARNER, CLOTHIER,
WHO DECEASED
THE 20 DAY OF SEPTEMBER,
AN° DOM. 1632,
WAITING FOR A JOYFUL
RESURRECTION.

HEARE RESTETH THE BODY
OF ANN WARNAR, THE WIFE
OF WALTER WARNER, WHO
DECEASED THE FIFTH DAY
OF APRILL, ANNO DOM. 1645.

HERE RESTETH THE BODY OF
THOMAS DORNEY, CORDINER,
WHO DECEASED MARCH
THE 7, ANNO D'NI 1643. AND OF
ROBERT DORNEY,
WHO DECEASED MAY THE FIRST,
AN° DOM^i 1647.

HEARE RESTETH THE BODY
OF RICHARD DORNEY, GENTEL-
MAN,
WHO DECEASED THE 10 DAY OF
NOVEMBER, AN° D'NI 1646.

Here lieth the Body of ELIZABETH,
the Wife of ROBERT PIKE,
of the City of Gloucefter, Gent.
the eldeft Daughter
of PHILIP WATKINS,
of this Parifh, Clothier,
who died the 24th Day
of Feb. 1701, aged 57.

To the Memory of
ALICE, the Wife of
DANIEL NIBLETT, of this Parifh,
Yeoman,
who departed this Life the 18th Day of
April, anno Dom. 1699.

Alfo WILLIAM, the Son of
DANIEL NIBLETT and ALICE his Wife,
who departed this Life
the 9th Day of June, 1699,
aged 8 Years.

In Memory of DEBORAH,
the Wife of DANIEL NIBLETT, of
this Parifh, Yeoman, who died
July 7, Anno Dom. 1743,
aged 68 Years.

In Memory
of JUDITH, the Wife
of DANIEL NIBLETT,
Yeoman, who departed
this Life the 16th Day of
Jan. Anno Dom. 1694,
ætatis fuæ 32.

In Memory of
DANIEL NIBLETT, fenior,
of this Parifh, Yeoman,
who departed this Life March 22,
Anno Dom. 1749,
aged near 83.

In Memory of JOHN HARRIS,
of this Parifh, Yeoman,
who departed this Life the 29th
Day of Nov. 1695,
ætatis fuæ 63.

In Memory of
DANIEL NIBLETT, of this Parifh,
Gent. who departed this Life
Nov. 8, 1772, aged 63 Years.

In Memory
of ELIZABETH, the Wife of
DANIEL NIBLETT, of this
Parifh, Gent. who departed
this Life April 29 1783,
aged 65 Years.

In Memory of JOHN
NIBLETT, Son of JOHN and
DEBORAH NIBLETT, of this
Parifh, who departed
this Life Dec. 1,
1721, aged 26 Years.

Alfo SUSANNAH, Daughter of
JOHN and DEBORAH NIBLETT,
died Aug. . . Anno Dom. 1731, aged 33.

In Memory of JOHN NIBLETT,
of this Parifh, Yeoman,
who died Jan. 1, A. D. 1737,
aged 70 Years.

In Memory
of MIRIAM, Daughter of
JOHN and DEBORAH
NIBLETT, of this Parifh,
who died Jan. 22, 1728,
aged 20 Years.

In Memory of
SAMUEL NIBLETT, Son of JOHN
NIBLETT, of this Parifh, Yeoman,
who died Feb. 16, 1736,
aged 35 Years.

To the Pious Memory of
SAMUEL, Son of SAMUEL and
ELIZABETH NIBLETT, of this Parifh,
Yeoman,
who died Dec. 15, 1763,
aged 32 Years.

In Memory of
WILLIAM, Son of SAMUEL
and ELIZABETH NIBLETT, who
died Dec. 18, 1788,
aged 54 Years.

HERE RESTETH THE BODY OF
ALICE HARRIS, THE WIFE OF
WILLIAM HARRIS
THE YOUNGER, WHO DECEASED
THE FOWER AND TWENTIETH DAY
OF NOVEMBER, ANNO DOM. 1638.

In

In Memory of John Harris,
who deceafed June 2, 1706,
aged 21 Years.

John Harris died 1696.

Anne, the Wife
of John Harris, who
died May 1, Anno Dom. 1734,
aged 75 Years.

In Memory of
Samuel Birt, of this Parifh,
Yeoman, who departed this Life
the 25th of Feb. 1712, aged 58 Years.

Alfo Eleanor his Wife
departed this Life Aug. 24, 1718,
aged 65 Years.

HERE RESTETH THE BODIE OF
GEORGE MINIET, LORD OF THIS
MANNVR
OF HARSFIELDE, ESQVIER, WHO
DECEASED THE 1O DAY OF OCTO-
BER, ANNO DOMINI 1643.

Here refteth in Hope
the Body of John Rowles,
fen. of this Parifh, Yeoman,
who departed this Life 3
Nov. An. Dom. 1711,
aged 70 Years.

In Memory of
John Rowles, of this Parifh,
Gent. who departed this Life
the 27th of Feb. Anno Dom. 1750-1,
aged 73 Years.

In Memory of
Sarah, the Wife of John Rowles,
of this Parifh, who departed
this Life the 16th Day of
Nov. Anno Domini 1710,
aged 70 Years.

In Memory of
William Rowles, Son of John
Rowles, of this Parifh, who departed
this Life Oct. 15, Anno Domini 1709,
aged 28 Years.

ON FLAT STONES.

In Memory of Ann,
Daughter of John White, of Colthrop,
Yeoman, who died June 19, Anno
Dom. 1779, aged 38 Years.

Here refteth the Body of
John White, of Colthrop, fenior,
who died Feb. 4, Anno Dom. 1780,
aged 81 Years.

Here refteth the Body of
Mary White, Daughter of George
and Elizabeth White, of this Parifh,
who died Aug. 13, 1769, aged 55
Years.

Charles White,
of Colthrop, departed this Life
June 10, 1788, aged 77 Years.

In Memory of
Richard Denn, of the Parifh of
Standifh, who died Jan. 11, 1699.
aged 70.

Jane his Wife died in June 1715,
aged 80.

Alfo Ann Atkins, Widow,
Daughter of the above,
died March 7, 1737, aged 75.

In Memory of
Henry Westbury, of this Parifh,
Farrier, who departed this Life
Aug. 17, 1757, aged 53.

In Memory of Anselm Bayley,
of this Parifh, Yeoman,
who died Aug. 31, A. D. 1743,
aged 70 Years.

Ann his Wife died in October, 1729,
aged 56 Years.

ON HEAD STONES.

Name	Died	Aged
William Randle	4 Nov. 1724	75
Alice his Wife	26 Sept 1727	81
Richard Buckle	12 Apr. 1711	68
Hefter, Daughter of Thomas and Jane Symes, of Moreton Valence	19 Apr. 1788	30
Mary Webb	9 Feb. 1736	30
Thomas Gregory	19 Sept. 1726	42
Sarah, Wife of George Watkins	26 Feb. 1780	50
Thomas Rowle	7 Mar. 1684	—
Elizabeth his Wife	25 Mar. 1728	93
Elizabeth Abbot, Daughter of the Rev. Henry Abbot	26 Aug. 1754	72
Thomas Stephens	23 Nov. 1763	45
Abigail his Wife	29 Oct. 1766	70
John Andrews, Gent.	24 Oct. 1700	—
Elizabeth his Wife	27 July, 1690	57
Nathaniel Cobb	2 May. 1730	54
Mary his Wife	5 Sept. 1735	60
George Vail	7 Feb. 1760	82
Hefter his Wife	2 May, 1738	62
Saran their Daughter, Wife of Thomas Chandler	12 Feb. 1734	28
Ann, Daughter of Daniel Vail	22 Aug. 1735	30
Sarah, Wife of J. Willis, of Weftbury	1 Sept. 1712	67
Samuel Niblett, fen.	3 Dec. 1760	64
Sarah his Wife	28 Nov. 1765	78
Samuel Niblett	—— 1711	39
Daniel Niblett	22 June, 1742	17
William Niblett	15 Aug. 1762	58
Anthony Mill	31 Aug. 1726	28
Robert Mill	19 July, 1740	82
Mary his Wife	3 Dec. 1734	74
John Window	4 Oct. 1769	63
Deborah his Wife	27 Oct. 1769	75
Richard Heaven	12 Nov. 1759	54
Hefter his Wife	3 Mar. 1763	43
Giles Merret	11 June, 1762	86
Hefter his Wife	20 Nov. 1755	78
John Bayley	6 Mar. 1762	55
Mary his Wife	26 Apr. 1744	32
Richard Peer	17 Sept. 1771	80
Ann his Wife	10 Apr. 1767	84
Robert Stratford	2 Mar. 173$\frac{2}{3}$	83
Jane his Wife	27 Oct. 1749	75
John their Son	33 Jan. 1741	33
John Gabb	21 Mar. 1699	42
Ann, Wife of Eleazer Flower	1 Feb. 1783	29
Thomas Newman	7 Dec. 1755	78
John Lee	14 Aug. 1768	63
Dorcas his Wife	30 Apr. 1778	69
Hefter, Wife of Eleazer Flower	13 July, 1777	30

Name	Died	Aged
John White	9 Dec. 1725	57
Hannah his Wife	9 Aug. 1751	68
Margaret, Wife of John White, of Colthrop	10 Dec. 1716	55
Elizabeth, Wife of John White, of Colthrop	27 Apr. 1754	55
George White, of Colthrop	8 Dec. 1775	35
Thomas Birt	2 Dec. 1713	60
John Smith	6 Apr. 1784	20
Richard Browne	14 Sept. 1710	16
Elizabeth Browne	15 Mar. 1730	73
Giles Ham	— Nov. 1721	40
Elizabeth his Wife	—— 1723	36
Sarah their Daughter	18 May, 1769	52
William Lee	14 Oct. 1777	72
Anne, Wife of John Gainer	1 Oct. 1724	—
Robert Rowles	29 Aug. 1679	35
Sarah, Wife of Griffith Williams	17 July, 1719	70
Sarah, Wife of William Wells	16 Aug. 1709	36
Walter Wells	8 May, 1773	71
Elizabeth his Wife	11 May, 1743	51
Charles Rowles	22 June, 1759	51
Efther his Wife	7 Mar. 1755	45
William Rowles	30 Jan. 1766	46
Robert Rowles	3 July, 1754	74
Mary his Wife	24 July, 1747	70
Sarah their Daughter	7 May, 1742	38
William Parker	18 Nov. 1700	22
James Harris	10 May, 1763	60
Elizabeth his Wife	26 June, 1747	59
Daniel Munden	9 Jan. 1753	70
Mary his Wife	25 May, 1761	82
John Buckingham	2 Dec. 1770	79
Elizabeth his Wife	26 Aug. 1742	57
Ann, Daughter of Thomas and Mary Buckingham	19 Dec. 1775	20
Mary Ludlow	27 Apr. 1771	46
William Bright	29 Jan. 1776	89
Ann his Wife	—— 1746	50
Mary their Daughter	27 Aug. 1773	35
Daniel Teaft	18 Sept. 1764	66
Thomas Eagles	27 June, 1770	40
Elizabeth, Relict of Thomas Eagles, and Wife of George Mans	— June, 1772	29
William Merrett	30 May, 1788	26
Charles Bright	18 May, 1790	55
James Wilkins	18 Jan. 1762	67
Sarah his Wife	10 Jan. 1767	73
William Wilkins	30 Nov. 1787	37
John Wilkins	12 Feb. 1774	51
Sarah, Wife of Thomas Maning	23 Mar. 1785	58

CXXXIII. HARNHILL, OR HARNHULL.

O F this fmall Parifh very few Materials of Topography are found, as it contains nothing interefting either to the Naturalift or Antiquary. It is Part of the Hundred of *Crowthorne* and *Minety*; three Miles diftant from *Cirencefter* on the Eaft, and twenty South-eaftward from GLOUCESTER. Being fituate upon a Declivity, the Soil is chiefly of a fertile Clay, almoft equally Arable, and upland Pafture, with Quickfet Inclofures, comprifing about 700 Acres.

The Benefice is a Rectory, which includes the Tythes of the whole Parifh, in the Deanery of *Cirencefter*.

Nothing is worthy Remark in the Church, which is dedicated to *St. Michael,* and has a fmall Spire at the Weft End.

Domefday fpecifies " *Harehill*" to contain five Hides, the Property of RALPH TODENI. The Manor defcended to HUMPHRY DE BOHUN, Earl of *Hereford,* and was held of the Honour of *Hereford* by WILLIAM DE HARNHULL, in the Reigns of EDWARD the Second and Third. In 1383, 6 RICH. II. EDWARD STONOR occurs as Lord of this Manor, and it continued in that Family till the Reign of HENRY the Eighth. Sir EDMUND TAME, of *Fairford,* died feifed of it in 1545; when it paffed with his other large Property in this County to his three Coheirs. THOMAS AWBREY, Efq. occurs in 1608. About 1660 it was purchafed by HUMPHRY SMITH, M. A. Rector of *Farmington*; and in 1787 was re-fold by the Executors of the late THOMAS SMITH, Efq. of *London,* to RICHARD WATTS, Efq. of *Wotton Baffet,* co. *Wilts,* the prefent Proprietor.

Another Eftate of equal Extent was the Property of the late SAMUEL BLACKWELL, Efq. of *William-ftrip.*

B E N E F A C T I O N S.

Two Perfons unknown gave 15*l.* the Intereft whereof is 12*s.* to be annually diftributed among poor Houfe-keepers.

1719. ROBERT PLEYDELL, Efq. bequeathed by Will an Eftate, then valued at 80*l.* a Year, for the Eftablifhment of a School, for the joint Benefit of the Parifhes of *Ampney St. Mary, Ampney Crucis, Ampney St. Peter,* and *Harnhill.*

INCUMBENTS.	PATRONS.	INCUMBENTS.	PATRONS.
1577 John Adams,	Q. Elizabeth.	1715 James Thorne,	The fame.
1585 Robert Harding,	William Harding.	1723 Tho. Ball, B. D. (refigned)	Thos. Smith, Efq.
1608 William Awbrey,	Thomas Awbrey, Efq.	1731 Thomas Finch, M. A.	The fame.
16— —— Ham,	——————	1735 Thomas Ball, D. D.	The fame.
16— John Ham,	——————	1748 Thomas Bray, D. D.	The fame.
1666 Richard Jackfon,	Humphry Smith, Efq.	1777 Richard Dennifon Cum-	
1700 Sam. Adams, B. D.	Thomas Smith, Efq.	berland, LL. B.	Thos. Smith, Efq.

PRESENT LORD OF THE MANOR,

RICHARD WATTS, Efq.

At the Heralds Vifitation, in 1682 and 1683, the only Perfon fummoned from this Place, was

Thomas Smith, Efq.

It does not appear that any Perfon polled from this Parifh at the Election in 1776.

The earlieft Date in the Regifter occurs in 1730.

ANNUAL

ANNUAL ACCOUNT OF MARRIAGES, BIRTHS, AND BURIALS, IN THIS PARISH.

A.D.	Mar.	Bir.	Bur.	A.D.	Mar.	Bir.	Bur.	A.D.	Mar.	Bir.	Bur.	A.D.	Mar.	Bir.	Bur.
1781	3	2	2	1786	—	3	3	1791				1796			
1782	1	3	—	1787	1	1	1	1792				1797			
1783	1	4	2	1788	—	1	—	1793				1798			
1784	—	3	1	1789	—	1	3	1794				1799			
1785	—	2	1	1790	1	3	1	1795				1800			

INSCRIPTIONS IN THE CHURCH.

ON FLAT STONES IN THE CHANCEL.

Here resteth the Body of
Mr. JOHN HAM,
who was a faithful and diligent Preacher
of the Gospel of CHRIST.
He departed this Life the 2d Day of
July, Anno Domini 1666.
His Father and he were Ministers
here 70 Years.

Here lyeth the Body of
RICHARD JACKSON, Clerk,
Rector of this Church,
who departed this Life
April . . Anno Dom. 1700.
He was buried April 8, 1700.

Here lyeth the Body of
GEORGE SUMMERTON, Esq.
who departed this Life the
. . . . 1730.

GEORGE, the Son of
GEORGE and MARY SUMMERTON,
buried Nov. 10, 1730,
aged 16.

SARAH, Daughter of
GEORGE and MARY SUMMERTON,
buried Nov. 18, 1730,
aged 25.

In
Memory of
ELIZABETH STOTHER,
who departed
this Life
Sept. 13, 1775,
aged 71.

IN THE CHURCH YARD.   ON TOMBS.

ANTHONY PETERS, alias MIFLIN,
died Dec. 7, 1736, aged 72.

FRANCES his Wife
died Dec. 18, 1701.

ISABELLA his Wife
died May 19, 1706.

THOMAS BEDWELL
died Nov. 29, 1776, aged 39.

JACOB HEWLINGS, sen.
died Jan. 18, 1766, aged 59 Years.

SARAH his Wife, Daughter of
EDWARD WHITE, of Ampney Crucis,
died Nov. 19, 1777, aged 62 Years.

SARAH their Daughter
died March 28, 1769, aged 14.

ON FLAT AND HEAD STONES.

	Died	Aged
Sarah, Daughter of Jacob and Sarah Hewlings	27 Dec. 1752	18
Hannah their Daughter	16 Mar. 1735	—
Thomas Matthews. jun.	— Oct. 1728	—
John Pasley	20 Dec. 1733	42
Sarah his Wife, Daughter of Thomas and Elizabeth Matthews	16 Feb. 1760	68
Thomas Embury	21 Nov. 1757	83
William Eldridge, sen.	13 Apr. 1747	45
Mercy his Wife, Daughter of Thomas Embury, of Arlington, in the Parish of Bibury	8 Mar. 1772	62

	Died	Aged
William, Mercy, and Elizabeth, their Children.		
Mrs. Jane Jackson, Widow of Mr. Richard Jackson	22 Feb. 1722	—
Thomas Hall, Gent.	2 Apr. 1710	—
John, Son of George and Mary Summerton buried	10 Dec. 1730	16
Sarah their Daughter	18 Nov. 1730	25
Mary, Wife of George Summerton	5 Feb. 1754	80

CXXXIV.

CXXXIV. H A R T P U R Y.

THIS Parish is a Part of the united Hundreds of *Dudstone* and *King's Barton*, six Miles eastward from *Newent*, nine South from *Tewkesbury*, and five North-west from GLOUCESTER.   It is bounded on the North-east by the Parish of *Stanton* in *Worcestershire*.   But its more ancient Name was *Merewent*, a Member of the great Manor of *Barton Regis*; it was first called "*Hardepcry*" in the Reign of HENRY the First.

Of the Soil, which is deep and fertile, including 3000 Acres, the greater Portion is Arable, with very rich and extensive Meadow and Pasture Land.   By the Rivulet *Leden* the lower Parts of the Parish are subject to frequent Inundations.

The Living is a Vicarage, endowed with certain of the Impropriate Tythes at the Suppression, when the Advowson was confirmed to the See of *Gloucester* *.   The Impropriation is now in Lease to CATHE-RINE and JANE BERKELEY.

Nothing interesting now remains in the Church, which is in the Deanery of *Gloucester*, and dedicated to *St. Mary*.   It has a spacious Nave only, with a low Tower at the West End; against which is affixed an Escocheon with the Arms of COMPTON, a Lion passant between three Helmets.

Merewent, the ancient Manor, was the Donation of OFFA King of *Mercia* to the Nunnery established at *Gloucester* in *Saxon* Times †; and continued Parcel of the Possessions of the *Benedictine* Abbey of *St. Peter* till the final Dissolution of monastic Bodies.   In the Reign of EDWARD VI. it was granted to Sir WILLIAM HERBERT, Knight of the Garter, the first Earl of *Pembroke*, of that Name.   WALTER COMP-TON, Esq. obtained it from the last-mentioned by Deed, bearing Date Feb. 20, 1551, 4 EDW. VI. ‡; and it passed to his Descendant WILLIAM COMPTON, who was created a Baronet May 6, 1686, 2 JAC. II. Sir WALTER COMPTON, Bart. the fifth and last who bore the Title, died in 1777 without Issue, when this Manor and Estate devolved in Moiety to his surviving Sisters CATHERINE and JANE, HELEN the younger being then deceased.   The eldest married EDWARD BEARCROFT, Esq. of *Droitwich*, co. *Worcester*, and died in 1775 without Issue.   JANE the younger was the Wife of JOHN BERKELEY, M. D. of *Hereford*, and of that Branch of the Family which is settled at *Spetchley*, co. *Worcester*, by whom she left two Daughters, CATHERINE and JANE BERKELEY, Minors, who are the present joint Proprietors of this Estate.   The Manor-house, now much dilapidated, was anciently called *Abbot's Place*, which was one of the Country Residences of the Abbots of *St. Peter's* §, and, during many Years, of the Family of COMPTON.

A competent Estate has been for many Generations vested in the Family of PULTON, very anciently established here; and another now belongs to CHARLES HAYWARD, Esq. of *Woolstrop*, which, with the Manor, comprises the principal Property of the Parish.

H A M L E T S.

1. *Morewent End.* Twenty Acres of Woodland were given to the Poor by WILLIAM DE MEREWENT which was laid Waste during the Siege of *Gloucester*. 2. *Moor End* is a commonable Meadow on the Banks of the *Leden*. 3. *Corse End*; so called from being contiguous to that Parish. 4. *Blackwell's End.* 5. *Lamper's End.* 6. *Butter's End.*

The Boundaries of the Parish toward *Woolridge Common* are very indistinct; a considerable Tract is claimed by the Lord of the Manor, which is said to have been immemorially considered as Part of the Parish of *St. Mary de Lode*, within the City of *Gloucester*.

Governor MASSIE placed a Garrison at *Hartpury* during the Siege; and a decisive Skirmish was fought between this Village and *Stanton*; when Colonel MYN, of the Royal Party, suffered great Loss ‖.

* " In the Taxation of Ecclesiastical Preferments 19 EDW. I. Ecclesia de *Hartpury* valet 10 Marc.   Portio Vicarii 7 Marc. " & dimid."   MSS. SNELL.
† DUGDALE, Mon. Ang. vol. I. p. 93.
‡ Eschaet. Inquisition. 1565, 7 ELIZ.
§ LELAND, Itin. vol. IV. part II. p. 172.   WILLIS, Mitred Abbies, &c.
‖ CORBET's Military Hist. of *Glouc.* pp. 69. 102.

I   B E N E-

B E N E F A C T I O N S.

For the Relief of Widows, or other poor Perfons, that do not receive Alms from the Parifh, Land in the Parifh of *Hartpury*, originally vefted in Truftees, who are now dead, nor is it known in whom the Right of choofing others now lies ; the annual Produce is 8*l.* 10*s.*

Giles Cox, Gent. gave, by Will, for poor Perfons that do not receive Affiftance from the Parifh, Land, vefted in Sir John Guise, and other Gentlemen of the City and County of *Gloucefter* ; the annual Produce about 3*l.*

Some Land in the Parifh of *Langley* was given for the fame Purpofe as the above, fuppofed to be vefted in the Churchwardens and Overfeers ; the annual Produce is 3*l.* 7*s.* 3*d.*

Incumbents.	Patrons.		Incumbents.	Patrons.
—— Philip Oxenforde,	Abbot of Gloucefter.	1663	William Grove, M. A.	——————.
1551 Richard Wheelar,	John Bp. of Gloucefter.	1687	Henry Jennings,	——————.
* * * * * * * * * * * * * *		1728	Will. Alexander, M.A.	——— ——.
1611 Thos. Ridgewall, M.A.	Bifhop of Gloucefter.	1742	Edward Sparkes, B. A.	————— —.
1634 Edm. Attwood, M. A.	——————.	1785	George Rollo, B. A.	Caroline Cornewallis,
1653 W. Chamberlaine, Clk.	——————.			Widow.

Present Proprietors of the Manor,

Catherine and Jane Berkeley *(Minors)*.

The Perfons fummoned from this Parifh by the Heralds in 1682 and 1683 were

William Compton, Efq. John Pulton, and John Madocke, Gents.

At the Election in 1776, Ten Freeholders polled from this Parifh.

The Regifter commences with a Date 1571.

Annual Account of Marriages, Births, and Burials, in this Parish.

A.D.	Mar.	Bir.	Bur.	A.D.	Mar.	Bir.	Bur.	A.D.	Mar.	Bir.	Bur.	A.D.	Mar.	Bir.	Bur.
1781	4	21	4	1786	—	22	9	1791				1796			
1782	2	14	9	1787	7	12	8	1792				1797			
1783	5	15	12	1788	4	18	11	1793				1798			
1784	1	10	10	1789	3	14	11	1794				1799			
1785	3	21	18	1790	3			1795				1800			

I N S C R I P T I O N S   I N   T H E   C H U R C H.

ON MONUMENTS.

In Memory
of Anne, the Wife of
William Webb, Daughter of
Richard Pulton, who was buried
Aug. 30, 1701,
aged 85 Years.

Alfo Anne, Daughter of William and
Anne Webb, was buried Feb.
15, 1709, aged 64 Years.

Erected by Joan Hadnock,
de Brocktherup.

In
the Church Yard lie buried
the Body of Thomas Biddle, jun.
of this Parifh, who was interred
Oct. 7, 1728, aged 31 Years and
upwards.

IN THE CHANCEL.

On a Brass Plate :

HERE LYETH THE BODY OF
WALTER COMPTON, ESQ.

LATE LORD OF THE
MANNOR OF HARTPURY, WHO DE-
PARTED THIS LIFE JUNE 12, AN°
DOMINI 1627.

Here lyeth buried the
Body of Dorothie Comp-
ton, late Wife of Walter
Compton, Efquire, the
Daughter of Sir John
Higforde, who departed
this Life . . Day
of June, ...

On a Brass Plate :

Arms ; Argent, a Bar nebulè Gules, on a Chief of the fecond a Helmet between two Falcons Heads erafed Or, for Compton ;—impaling, Paly of fix, Argent and Azure, on a Chief Gules, three Croffes païée Or, for Meux.

HERE LYE THE BODYS OF WILL.
COMPTON, ESQ.
LORD OF THE MANNOR OF HART-
PURY, AND ELINOR
HIS WIFE, DAUGHTER OF Sᵣ JOHN

MEUX, Kᵗ. SHE
DIED ANNO 1631 ; HE DIED
ANNO 1641 ;
TO WHOSE MEMORY THEIR DEAR
DAUGHTER
DAME ELINOR BUTTON, WIFE OF
Sᵣ ROBERT
BUTTON, BARᵗ, HERE PUT THIS
MONUMENT.

ON FLAT STONES.

Arms ; as before, differenced with a Crefcent.

Round the Verge :

HERE LYETH THE BODY OF
WILLIAM COMPTON, SONNE OF
WILLIAM
COMPTON, ESQ. BURIED THE 13
DAY OF
NOVEMBER, 1614.

John Compton, Gent. fecond Son of Walter Compton, died the 7 Day of May, 1660.

Here lieth buried the
Body of SARAH, the Wife
of RICHARD PULTON, Gent.
who departed this Life
the 14 Feb. 1652.

RICHARD PULTON, of this
Parifh, Gent. being by
Death divorced from
his Wife for 19 Years,
returned to her Bed
in Peace the 19 Day
of January, 1671.

Here lyeth the Body
of JOHN PULTON, of this
Parifh, Gent. who departed
this Life the 6th of June, 1682,
aged 44 Years.

Here lyeth alfo the Body
of THOMAS PULTON,
Sonne of the faid JOHN PULTON,
who departed this Life the
2d Day of Oct. Anno Dom. 1708,
aged 40 Years.

Here lyeth
the Body of ELIZABETH, the
Relict of JOHN PULTON,
of this Parifh, Gent. who
died Aug. 11, 1689.

Here lyeth the Body of
SARAH, the Wife of JOHN
PARKER, of Hasfield, Gent.
eldeft Daughter of RICHARD PULTON,
of this Parifh, Gent.
who was born in 1637,
married 1672, and died 6 Sept.
1708, in the 72d Year of her Age.

RICHARD, the Son of JOHN
PULTON, Gent. was buried
the 30 June, 168..

In Memory of ANNE, the Wife of
PAUNCEFOTE PULTON, of this
Parifh, Gent. who departed this
Life the 14th Day of November,
Anno Dom. 1716,
aged 28 Years.

In Memory of SARAH, the Daughter
of THOMAS PULTON, of this Parifh,
Gent. who departed this Life the 16th
Day of Feb. anno Dom. 1716,
aged 19 Years.

SARAH PULTON, Daughter of
THOMAS PULTON, of the City

of Gloucefter, Gent. and MARY
his Wife, died Feb. 15, 1776,
aged 49 Years.

EXUVIÆ HIC REPONUNTUR
THOMÆ RIDGEWELL, ARTIUM
Mr, HUJUSQUE PAROCHIÆ OLIM
VICARIJ, QUI OB. 4 DIE
MAIJ, A. D. 1634.
POSTQUAM ANNOS 53 NATUS
EGERATQ. HIC 23.

HERE LYETH THE BODY
OF JOHN TERRETT,
WHO DEPARTED
THIS LIFE THE 20
DAY OF APRIL,
AN. DOM. 1651.

EDMUNDUS ATTWOOD,
Artium Magifter,
Stantoniæ Rector,
necnon hujus Parochiæ
Vicarius, hic requiefcit ;
cujus anima ad Cœium
evolavit 1mo 8bris, annoq.
D'ni 1653.

Here refts
the Body of JOHN BELLAMY, who
died Oct. 3, 1705, aged 79 Years
and 11 Months.

Here lieth the Body of
JUDITH, the Daughter of
WILLIAM and ELIZABETH BELLAMY,
who departed this Life
June 30, 1712, aged
1 Year and 4 Months.

MR. GUIL. GROVE,
SPECTATISS. DOCTRINA PIETATIS
ET EXIMIJ CANDORIS VIRI
MEMORIÆ
HEU WILHELME TACES. DIA LO-
QUETA.

. . . .

. . . .

ROUND THE VERGE :

MOLE SUBTRAC. DORMIT GULIEL-
MUS NOMINE GROVUS.

Arms ; Azure, a Bend Or, between
three Boys Heads with Snakes round
their Necks in chief, 2. and 1. proper,
and three Griffins Heads erafed in bafe
Argent.

Here lyeth the Body
of JOHN MADOCKE, Gent.
of this Parifh, Alderman of
the City of Gloucefter,
and once Mayor, who departed
this Life the 19th Day of
Decem. 1657.

ROUND THE VERGE :

HERE LYETH THE BODY OF AN-
THONY GELFE, MASTER GUNNER
OF THE KING'S MAJESTIE.

HERE LYETH THE
BODY OF JOOIN MASON,
THE WIFE OF
JOHN MASON, WHO
DEPARTED THIS LIFE
THE 26 DAY OF FEB.
ANNO DOM. 1669.

HERE LIETH BURIED
THE BODY OF RICHARD
PULTON, WHO DECEASED
THE XXIII DAY OF
JULY, IN THE YEARE OF
OUR LORD GOD . . . .

Here lyeth
the Body of DOROTHY,
Wife of RICHARD PULTON, Gent.
who departed this Life May
6, 1654, aged 74 Years.

Alfo ANN, the Wife
of WILLIAM WEBB, and Daughter
of RICHARD and DOROTHY
PULTON, who departed
this Life Aug. 28, 1701,
aged near 85 Years.

Here lyeth the Body of
ANN, the Daughter of WIL-
LIAM and ANN WEBB, who
departed this Life the 14
Day of Feb. Anno Dom.
1709, aged 65 Years.

IN THE CHURCH YARD, ON TOMBS.

Arms ; on a Fefs between three Mullets
three Roundlets.

In Memory of
THOMAS PULTON, late of the City of
Gloucefter, Gent. who departed
this Life in May, 1742.

Near the Remains of her Hufband,
here lies buried the Body of MARY
PULTON, Wife of THOMAS PULTON
aforefaid, Gent. who died Aug. 29,
1770, aged 68 Years.

In Memory of
THOMAS SLOPER, of this
Parifh, Gent. whofe furviving Children,
by JOANE his only Wife, are the
Rev. Mr. CHARLES SLOPER,
Chancellor of Briftol ;
WILLIAM SLOPER, one of the Attorneys
of the Common Pleas at Weftminfter ;
JANE, the Wife of GEORGE GITHENS ;
and CATHERINE SLOPER.

Near to this Side lies the Body of
the faid JOANE SLOPER.
He departed this Life 13 April, 1703.
She departed this Life 2 Sept. 1676.

Near to this Side lyes the
Body of MARY SLOPER,
Daughter of the fayd
THOMAS SLOPER and JOANE
his Wife.

Near this Place lyeth the Body of
WILLIAM CARTER, of this Parifh, who
died Dec. 9, 1724.

Alfo the Body of MARK (Son of HENRY)
NOBLE, of the Parifh of Afhlerworth,
who died Jan. 19, 1730, aged 59 Years.

Alfo ELIZABETH, the Wife of
MARK NOBLE,
of the Parifh of Afhlerworth, in this
County, who was here interred
April 6, 1729, aged 48 Years.

Here lyeth the Body of
HENRY NOBLE, of this Parifh,
Yeoman, who was buried March
the 29, Anno Dom. 1674,
aged 66 Years.

Alfo MARY his Wife, who
was here buried Feb. 18,
Anno Dom. 1692, aged
62 Years.

ON A FLAT STONE :

To the Memory of SARAH HOOPER,
Wife of JOHN HOOPER,
late of this Parifh.
She died Aug. 29, 1768,
aged 86.

ON

O N   H E A D   S T O N E S.

	Died	Aged		Died	Aged
Elizabeth, Wife of Ralph Houly	25 Jan. 1727	39	James their Son -	—— 1738	21
Grace Peace - -	16 Mar. 1745	21	Ann, Daughter of John Matthews	—— 1742	19
John Matthews, fen. -	2 Oct. 1737	55	Thomas Drew -	3 Nov. 1719	60
George Tayler -	28 Aug. 172.	84	Elizabeth his Daughter -	15 Jan. 1750	45
William Garter -	29 Aug. 1691	37	Mary, Relict of John Viner	3 Sept. 1689	40
Mary his Wife -	22 Jan. 1706	42	John Phillips, fen. -	4 May, 1723	66
Mary, Daughter of John and Mary Jenkins - -	6 Aug. 1740	23	William Cooke -	13 May, 1737	61
Sarah her Sifter -	6 Feb. 1745	20	Samuel Overthrow -	15 Jan. 1747	44
John Ockley - -	29 June, 1720	29	Mary, Wife of Thomas Broadftock	7 Feb. 1759	29
Mary, Wife of Thomas Humppidg	20 Jan. 1763	57	John Drew -	24 Feb. 1686	58
John Partridge -	25 Nov. 1745	80	Elizabeth, Wife of William Keake	15 Oct. 1693	33
William Sheppard -	1 Oct. 1745	49	Thomas, Son of Thomas Smith, of Tiberton -	24 Feb. 1759	12
Thomas Bevan -	7 Apr. 1762	29	John Hale -	13 Apr. 1757	66
Richard Atkins - -	21 June, 1755	40	Sarah his Wife -	25 Mar. 1770	72
Elizabeth, Wife of Thomas Atkins	10 Nov. 1712	—	William Hunt -	2 Feb. 1755	54
John Birt - -	12 Dec. 1772	47	Jane his Wife -	6 Aug. 1736	32
William Coulfey, of Gloucefter, Gent. -	25 Mar. 1714	33	Mary, Wife of John Moody	2 Mar. 1772	40
Ralph Turner -	23 Nov. 1671	—	John Lane -	8 Nov. 1764	42
William Dobbins -	— Apr. 1700	61	Richard Coopey -	17 Feb. 1713	74
John Howell - -	12 Oct. 1699	50	William Dobbins -	22 July, 1729	73
John his Son -	— Jan. 1706	18	Francis Fifher -	3 May, 1731	43
William White, of Maifemore	27 Mar. 1712	44	Bazel Wagftaff -	2 Dec. 1728	56
Joane, Wife of John Fletcher	24 Dec. 1710	74	Mary Butt, Widow -	11 June, 1714	64
Sarah, Wife of William White, and Daughter of Richard Stock	30 Oct. 1706	23	Richard Butt -	9 Aug. 1694	45
Mary, Daughter of Richard Stock	9 Oct. 1706	17	Thomas Jones -	3 May, 1728	40
Richard Stock -	21 Nov. 1696	61	Mary, Wife of Jonathan Gof	21 May, 1735	47
Thomas Laughton -	2 May, 1711	59	Jofeph Hooper -	9 Mar. 1747	65
Joan, Wife of John Holland	11 Sept. 1665	—	John Hooper -	12 Oct. 1785	60
John Lane, Gent. -	8 Mar. 1748	78	Richard Smith, of Highleadon	18 Apr. 1721	50
Thomas Price - -	5 Jan. 1713	66	Elizabeth his Wife -	19 Mar. 1721	20
Elizabeth his Wife -	2 Nov. 1697	—	Elinor Taylor -	26 May, 1747	60
Sarah, Wife of Abraham James	—— 1714	—	John her Son -	24 Dec. 1745	28
Thomas Farmer -	9 Mar. 1727	30	Richard Tayler -	2 Aug. 1769	63
Mary, Wife of Richard Matthews	20 Apr. 1749	25	Betty, Daughter of William Danford	20 Oct. 1710	16
Chriftian their Daughter	27 Oct. 1753	6	Ruth, Wife of James Oakey	9 Jan. 1735	36
Richard Matthews -	7 Mar. 1789	77	James their Son -	10 Apr. 1751	16
John Afton - -	7 Feb. 1723	50	Thomas Farmer -	28 July, 1760	43
Sarah his Wife -	10 Dec. 1747	88	Ann his Wife -	14 Aug. 1762	54
William Bick - -	5 Nov. 1748	58	Thomas Humpidge -	27 Oct. 1775	54
Richard Forty -	9 Feb. 1685	—	Michael Wells -	14 Aug. 1734	70
Elizabeth Gribble -	2 Mar. 1697	77	Thomas Biddle -	27 Mar. 1702	—
John Hale - -	9 Sept. 1692	25	Thomas Randell -	5 June, 1708	—
Mofes Ferris -	5 Jan. 1768	71	William Oakey -	2 June, 1716	50
Sarah Ferris - -	14 Nov. 1777	19	Elizabeth Eldridge -	20 May, 1706	75
Charles Ferris -	15 Aug. 1774	15	Thomas Bullock -	19 Sept. 1711	49
Abraham Eagles -	2 Aug. 1727	35	Elizabeth his Wife -	24 Mar. 1724	02
Sarah his Wife -	7 May, 1727	38	Sarah Tayler, Widow -	7 Dec. 1711	81
John Matthews -	6 Oct. 1730	50	Alydea, Wife of William Gough	18 Sept 1720	42
Hannah his Wife -	22 Nov. 1749	62	Sarah, Wife of Robert Williams	29 Apr. 1767	53
			Jonathan Brooks -	25 Feb. 1766	58
			Hannah his Wife -	1 Nov. 1755	44

CXXXI. HASFIELD,

CXXXV.   H A S F I E L D,

WHICH is fituate in the lower Divifion of the Hundred of *Weftminfter*, is diftant fix Miles Eaft from *Newent*, five South from *Tewkefbury*, and eight from GLOUCESTER on the North. The Soil is of fine Clay, within a Terrier of 1400 Acres, of which 125 only are Arable, and 40 Woodland. There are feveral Lot Meadows on the Banks of the *Severn*, in the Privilege of which, certain Eftates in the adjoining Parifh of *Afhleworth* have an equal Claim *.

The Benefice is a Rectory, but not endowed with Tythes of the whole Parifh †. For the Priory of *Deerhurft* were poffeffed of Tythes of Lands near the *Severn*, which at the Diffolution were in the Court of Augmentations, from whence they were fold in 1558 to FRANCIS PHILIPS and RICHARD MOORE. Another Portion in 1571 was bought by RICHARD HILL and WILLIAM JAMES. As the fame Property they were long vefted in the Family of BROWNE, from whom they were transferred, by Purchafe, to the Family of HYETT, of *Gloucefter*.

The Church, dedicated to *St. Mary*, is a Peculiar of *Deerhurft*. It has a Nave only, and a Tower at the Weft End. In the Chancel Window were anciently thefe Arms: 1. Gules, fix Plates; 2. Gules, three Lioncels rampant Argent; PAUNCEFOTE. 3. Or, a Lion rampant, and femée of Crofslets Gules. 4. BRYDGES. By the prefent Incumbent the Parfonage Houfe has been re-built.

In *Domefday* Book one Hide and a Half is faid to be held under the Church of *Weftminfter*, who claimed " *Hasfelde*" as a Member of their great Manor of *Deorhyrfte*. But it appears that the Manor was granted in 1245, 33 HEN. III. to RICHARD DE PLANCO PEDE, or PAUNCEFOOT, from whom it paffed to his Son GRIMBALD PAUNCEFOOT ‡, and remained with his Defcendants till the Reign of Queen ELIZABETH. In 1608, PAUL TRACY, of *Stanway*, was Proprietor, and by his Heir Sir HUMPHRY TRACY it was fold to JOHN PARKER, Efq. of *Northlech*, in 1655. He was a lineal Defcendant from the Father of WILLIAM PARKER, alias MALVERNE, the laft Abbot of *St. Peter* in *Gloucefter*.

Hasfield Court, the manerial Houfe, is eligibly fituate above the Meadows and River; it is fpacious, and in the Style of the laft Century. Near it ftands a large Portal or Gateway, with feveral blank Efcocheons, and apparently of much higher Antiquity.

Another Eftate belonged, in 1437, 15 HEN. VI. to EDWARD BRUGES, of *Lone*, the Brother of Sir GILES BRYDGES, of *Coberley*, and is called a Manor in the Inquifition taken after his Death. EDMUMD Lord CHANDOS, of *Sudley*, died in 1573, 15 ELIZ. feifed of this Manor in *Hasfield* §.

Lands given in *Saxon* Times to the Abbey of *Weftminfter* were ftyled a Manor. In 1681, 33 CAR. II. a Suit was tried refpecting its Jurifdiction, when it appeared from the Court Rolls, that in 1335, 8 EDW. II. it was held of the Heirs of WILLIAM RUSSELL, by the Service of prefenting a Ger. Falcon yearly.

The Family of BROWNE became poffeffed of confiderable Property in this Parifh about the Year 1600, which was purchafed by the Anceftor of the prefent Proprietor BENJAMIN HYETT, Efq. of *Painfwick*.

---

* From a Survey of thefe Meadows, taken about the Year 1770, it appears, that they contained, feparately, as follows: *Mowing Lot* Meadow 386 Acres; *Wynhales*, or *Wynholte*, 123 Acres; *Widenham*, 356 Acres. This laft mentioned is commonable to certain Eftates in *Afhelworth*, which were Parcel of the Poffeffions of the Priory of *St. Ofwald* in *Gloucefter*. The Lord of the Manor of *Hasfield* could formerly command the Ufe of Men, Waggons, and Horfes, during Harveft, in compenfation for this Privilege. About the Reign of King HENRY VI. this Service was commuted for a Payment of 50*s.* yearly, as it has fince remained. In *Hasfield* Meadow are 403 Acres.

† " Gleb' 5 Acr' Terr' Arab' 3 Acr' Prati in *Wydnam*, & 4 Acr' in *Winholter*." BACON's Liber Regis.

‡ In a Roll of the Names and Arms of Knights and Efquires in the Camp of HENRY the Third, in 1220, amongft thofe of the County of *Gloucefter*, is, " GRYMBALD PAUNCEVOD, Chivaler; Goulis, 111 Lionceles Argent."

§ COLLINS's Peerage, Title *Chandos*, vol. II. p. 245.

Efchaet. fub ann. 15 HEN. VI. n. 36.

Efchaet. fub ann. 12 ELIZ. MSS. Bibl. Harl.

4   BENE-

B E N E F A C T I O N S.

A Meſſuage and Paſture Ground, containing three Acres, ſituate at *Wickeridge*, a Hamlet in this Pariſh, with four Acres and a Quarter of Meadow, lying in the common Meadows of *Wyddenham* and *Wynnals*. The Donors not known. But the Uſes ſpecified in the Feoffments, which bear Date in the 5th Year of the Reign of Queen ELIZABETH, aıe, the Arming of Soldiers within the ſaid Pariſh in Time of War for the Defence of the Kingdom; for the Repairs of common Highways; or for the Mending of the *Severn* Banks within the Pariſh; the Cloathing and Maintenance of the Poor for the Time being; and the Repairs of the Pariſh Church.

There is a Rent Charge of 5*s.* on a Ground, called *Branmayne's Croft*, belonging to THOMAS PULTON, Eſq. given by LAWRENCE GILBERT, for the Repairs of the Church, in the Reign of HENRY VIII.

In 1726, ELEANOR PARKER gave, by Will, the Sum of 100*l.*; the Intereſt of which is to be appropriated towards the apprenticing of Poor Children.

MARGARET PARKER, 1724, left, by her laſt Will, 40*l.* and which, according to particular Direction, was laid out in Land at *Redmarley*, in the County of *Worceſter*; the Rent of which is ſet apart towards the Education of Poor Children.

INCUMBENTS.	PATRONS.	INCUMBENTS.	PATRONS.
1547 Hugh Wall,	Richard Pauncefote, Eſq.	1664 James Alderſon,	——————.
1570 William Baldwyn,	John Pauncefote, Eſq.	1684 John Price, B. A.	John Parker, Eſq.
1614 John Rhodes, B. A.	Sir Richard Tracy, Kt.	1727 Will. Moſeley, M.A.	Edward Parker, Gent.
1626 Thomas Alanſon,	——————.	1753 Charles Parker, M.A.	John Parker, Eſq.
⁕ ⁕ ⁕ ⁕ ⁕ ⁕ ⁕ ⁕ ⁕ ⁕ ⁕ ⁕ ⁕ ⁕		1787 Saunders Will. Miller, B.A.	Will. Miller, Gent.

PRESENT LORD OF THE MANOR,

JOHN PARKER, Eſq.

The Perſons ſummoned from this-Place by the Heralds, in 1682 and 1683, were

John Parker, Eſq. William Browne, Eſq. and James Alderſon, Rector.

At the Election in 1776 Twenty-five Freeholders polled from this Pariſh.

The firſt Date of the Regiſter is in 1653.

ANNUAL ACCOUNT OF MARRIAGES, BIRTHS, AND BURIALS, IN THIS PARISH.

A.D.	Mar.	Bir.	Bur.	A.D.	Mar.	Bir.	Bur.	A.D.	Mar.	Bir.	Bur.	A.D.	Mar.	Bir.	Bur.
1781	1	8	4	1786	1	9	4	1791				1796			
1782	1	3	3	1787	1	3	5	1792				1797			
1783	2	4	2	1788	—	13	6	1793				1798			
1784	1	7	3	1789	3	7	6	1794				1799			
1785	1	6	5	1790	1	8	2	1795				1800			

INSCRIPTIONS IN THE CHURCH.

ON MONUMENTS IN THE

CHANCEL.

Arms; Argent, on a Feſs Gules, three Cheſſrooks Or, in chief as many Martlets Sable, for BROWNE.

Eximii Viri HENRICI BROWNE, Gen. Qui obiit April 18, anno Dom. 1620, Et Lectiſſimæ Matronæ ALOISIÆ, uxoris illius, Quæ obiit 9 Sept. 1626.

In Memory of JAMES ALDERSON, late Rector of this Church, who departed this Life June 25, Anno Domini 1684.

ANNE, the Wife of JOHN PRICE, Clerke, Daughter of EDWARD MORTIMER, of Preſtbury, Gent.

departed this Life March the 9, Anno Dom. 1703.

ON AN OLD TOMB:

Arms; Gules, three Lioncels rampant Argent.

ROUND THE VERGE,

HERE LYETH DOROTHY PAUNCE-FOTE, LATE THE WYDOWE OF . . . . . PAUNCEFOTE . . . .

ON FLAT STONES.

HERE LIETH THE BODY OF ALICE BROWNE, WIFE OF HENRY BROWNE, ESQ. WHO DEPARTED THIS LIFE THE 9 SEPT. 1626.

HERE LIETH ALSO THE BODY OF MARY BROWNE, WIFE OF WILLIAM BROWNE, ESQUIRE, WHO DEPARTED THIS LIEE THE 16 DAY OF JULY, ANNO DOM. 1665.

ALSO HERE LIETH THE BODY OF MARGARET BROWNE, DAUGHTER OF HENRY BROWNE, ESQ. AND ELEANOR HIS WIFE, WHO DEPARTED THIS LIFE THE 18 DAY OF FEB. ANNO DOMINI 1685.

ALSO ELEANOR, THE WIFE OF HENRY BROWNE, ESQ. WHO DIED FEB. 28, 1715.

VOL. II.

M

Here

Here lyeth the Body of
HENRY BROWNE, of Hasfield, Esq.
who departed this Life the 18th Day
of April, Anno Dom. 1620.

Here also lyeth the Body of
WILLIAM BROWNE, Esq. Sonne
of the abovesayde HENRY BROWNE,
who departed this Life the 3d Day
of Novem. Anno 1658.

Here also lyeth the Body of
HENRY BROWNE, Esquire, Sonne
of the sayd WILLIAM BROWNE,
who departed this Life the 5th
Day of July, Anno Domini 1678.

ROUND THE VERGE,

HERE LIETH THE BODY OF
RICHARD GILBERT, WHO DE-
CEASED
THE 12 DAY OF FEB. AN. DOM.
161..

ON THE MIDDLE,

HERE LYETH THE BODY OF CYCELY
WILLIS, WIFE OF THOMAS WILLIS,
WHO DIED 19 SEPT. 1644, OF
HER AGE 79.

Arms; Azure, three Lozenges in Fefs
Or, for FREEMAN;—impaling, Per
Pale Argent and Gules, a Lion rampant
Sable, for ROBERTS.

ROUND THE VERGE,

HERE LYETH INTERRED THE
BODY OF

MARY FREEMAN, WIDOW, LATE
WIFE OF
JOHN FREEMAN, OF BUSHLEY,
AND DAUGHTER
OF JOHN ROBERTS, OF FIDDING-
TON, GENT.
WHO DIED 29 MAY, ANNO DOM.
1658.

Beneath this Stone
lyeth the Body of
EDWARD PARKER, Gent.
Son of JOHN PARKER, Esq.
late of Hasfield Court,
who departed this Life
the 29th Day of March,
1728, ætatis 56.

Also MARTHA, Relict of the
said EDWARD PARKER,
Ob. 2 May, 1749,
ætat. 77.

MARIA Uxor CAROLI
PARKER, hujus Ecclesiæ
Rectoris. Ob. 12 Mart. 1753.

EDV. \
JOH. / Infantes. Ob. { Aug. 8, 1747.
       { Oct. 22, 1748.

Infra
ANN, Filia CAROLI & MARIÆ PARKER.
Ob. Sept. 29, 1765, ætat. 13.

Juxta
SARAH, second Uxor CAROLI PARKER,
Ob. Dec. 24, 1777.

Here lyes the Body of HANNAH,
Daughter of JOSEPH and HANNAH
BROCK, who died May 12, 1680.

HERE LYETH THE BODY OF
LAWRENCE BLINCKCOE,
WHO DIED THE XV OF MAY,
ANNO DOM. 1640.

Arms; on a Fess between three
Pheons, a Stag's Head affrontée between
two Roundlets, for PARKER.

MICHAEL and JOHN, Twin Brothers,
the Sons of JOHN PARKER, Gent.
and MARY his Wife, born
and baptized Sept. 23, 1655,
and interred here the Day
following in one Coffin.

CHARLES,
the Son of THOMAS HALSY,
was buried here
Dec. 3, Anno Dom. 1654.

JOHN PRICE, Rector
of this Church, departed
this Life on the 6th Day of
Sept. Anno Dom. 1727,
in the 75th Year of his
Age.

Here lie the Bodies of ANNE
and ISABELLA, the Wives of
JOHN PRICE, Clerk, who
departed this Life,
ANNE June 5, 1687,
ISABELLA May 15, 1723.

ELIZABETH, the Daughter
of WILLIAM MOSELEY, Rector
of this Church, and Grand-
daughter of the aforesaid
JOHN PRICE, departed this
Life May 7, Anno Dom. 1729,
in the 13th Year of her Age.

IN THE CHURCH YARD, ON TOMBS.

In Memory of HENRY GOODCHEP, who
departed this Life Aug. 19, 1728,
aged near 92 Years.

Also of DOROTHY his Wife,
who departed this Life
the 9th September, 1696.

And also of
ETHERINGTON and BENJAMIN
their Sons.

RALPH TOVEY deceased the
26th of August, 1663.

ELIZABETH, the Wife of
RALPH TOVEY,
ended this Life the 5th Day of April,
1662.

Here lies also
the Body of CHARLES,
Sonne of RALPH
and ELIZABETH TOVEY,
who died
February the 2,
Anno Dom. 1682.

CAROLUS PARKER,
Rector & hujus Ecclesiæ
fidelis pius Pastor.
Obiit 7 Februarii,
Anno Dom. 1787,
ætatis suæ 72.

Here lieth the Body of MARY, the
Wife of WILLIAM CUMBERSUM,

of the Parish of Tirley. She died
the 6th Day of Nov. 1759,
aged 36 Years.

ON FLAT STONES.

In Memory of
HENRY WHITEMORE,
late of this Parish,
who died June 14, 1760,
aged near 55 Years.

In Memory of ANN, the Daughter
of JOHN and SARAH SIZMORE, of
this Parish, who departed this Life
Nov. the 1st, 1767,
aged 1 Year.

Here
lyeth the Body
of WILLIAM TERRETT, late
of Redmarley, who departed
this Life the 12th Day of May,
Anno Dom. 1754, aged 62.

Also
here lyeth the Body of
ANN, the Wife of WILLIAM
TERRETT, who departed this
Life March 19, Anno
Dom. 1745, aged 52 Years.

Here
lieth the Body of Mrs.
ANN, Daughter of WILLIAM

TERRETT, Gent. by ANN his
Wife. She died the 20th Day of
Sept. 1774, aged 43 Years.

In Memory of
MARTHA, the Wife of
WILLIAM FLETCHER,
of the Parish of Rutford,
Yeoman, who departed this Life
April 21, 1760, aged 40 Years.

Also in Memory of
JOHN, the Son of CHARLES and JEAN
ROAN, of this Parish, Yeoman,
who departed this Life Nov. 6,
1760, aged 37 Years.

Also here lyeth the Body of SARAH, the
Daughter af WILLIAM and
MARTHA FLETCHER,
late of Highleadon Court, in the Parish
of Rutford, who departed this Life
Oct. 15, 1778, aged 28 Years.

Here
lieth the Body of WILLIAM FLETCHER,
late of Highleadon Court, in the
Parish of Rutford, who departed
this Life May 26, 1776,
aged 63 Years.

Here resteth the Body
of CHARLES, Son of CHARLES and
JANE ROAN, of this Parish, Yeoman,
who departed this Life March 31,
1751, aged 23 Years.

In

In Memory
of SARAH, the Wife of CHARLES ROAN,
of this Parish Yeoman, who departed
this Life Aug. 2, 1763,
aged 70 Years.

Also CHARLES ROAN,
of this Parish, Yeoman,
departed Oct. 7, 1770, aged 75 Years.

Here
lieth the Body of CHARLES ROAN,
late of this Parish,
who departed this Life Oct. 18, 1775,
aged 23 Years.

ON HEAD STONES.

	Died	Aged
William Lane, of Maisemore	24 Feb. 1781	62
John Willis	1 Feb. 1705	70
Thomas Jones	9 Dec. 1693	54
Margaret his Wife	22 Dec. 1697	67
James Butt	1 May, 1771	71
Thomas Goodchep	31 Apr. 1726	42
Thomas Stroud	20 Jan. 1721	29
Margaret, late Wife of Edmund Collins, of the County of Devon, Gent.	22 Aug. 1727	—
James Woodcock	15 May, 1710	40
Henry Stephens, of Ashlerworth	2 Dec. 1768	51
Eugena his Wife	15 June, 1770	53
Jonathan Daw	—— 1719	—
Richard Daw, jun.	12 Jan. 1726	37
Anne, Daughter of Thomas and Mary Roberts	30 Sept. 1721	12
Thomas Roberts	30 July, 1720	48
John Ricketts	17 Aug. 1724	50
William Bayley	31 Dec. 1727	65
Ann his Wife	5 Dec. 1726	67
Robert Middleton	13 June, 1693	—

	Died	Aged
Richard Wall	16 Sept. 1704	73
Anne, Wife of Richard Bick	10 Oct. 1708	54
Mary Wall	25 Feb. 1726	55
William Whitemore	10 June, 1728	70
William Moreden, of Pendock	21 Apr. 1714	61
Mary his Wife	14 Oct. 1715	68
John Turner	23 Aug. 1753	42
James Turner	13 June, 1761	38
Benjamin Harris	30 June, 1777	67
Rebekah his Wife	9 May, 1784	84
Benjamin Eatly	31 Mar. 1770	13
Mary, Wife of James Clark, of the City of Gloucester	2 Feb. 1778	42
William Barnes	15 Dec. 1788	44
Timothy Barnes, senior, of Corfe Court	28 May, 1782	63
Mary his Wife	31 Dec. 1779	61
James their Son	31 May, 1772	18
Mary, Wife of Timothy Barnes, jun. and Daughter of Nathaniel Hawkins, of Tirley.	24 July, 1781	32

CXXXVI. HASLETON;

CXXXVI. H A S L E T O N;

IN the high *Cotefwold*, and Hundred of *Bradley*, is a fmall Parifh of an oval Shape, about two Miles long, and one Mile and a Half acrofs in the wideft Part. The Soil is of Stone-brafh, and nearly in equal Portions tilled and upland Pafture. The Diftance from *Northleche* is three Miles North-weftward, and from GLOUCESTER feventeen on the Eaft.

The Benefice is rectorial, with the Chapelry of *Yanworth*, or *Endeworth*, annexed, in the Deanery of *Stowe*. At the late general Inclofure, Lands were given in Lieu of Tythes; the Glebe is now fixty Acres. The Advowfon belonged fucceffively to the Abbies of *Winchcombe* and *Hayles*; and fince the Suppreffion, it has been vefted in the Crown.

The Church, dedicated to *St. Andrew*, is a fmall Building, confifting of a Nave only, with a low embattled Tower *.

Ten Hides are defcribed in *Domefday* as held by SIGAR DE CIOCHES; the Parifh had then gained parochial Rights, as a Prieft is exprefsly mentioned. In 1251, 35 HEN. III. this Manor was given to the Abbey of *Winchcombe* by ROBERT GYVES; although a prior Donation of it is recited by TANNER †. At the Diffolution, it was granted to THOMAS COLEPEPER the younger, referving a Rent Charge to the Crown of 16*l.* 8*s.* 4*d.* a Year. Livery of the Manor was confirmed to ALEXANDER COLEPEPER in 1558, who was fucceeded by his Son.

From this Family it paffed to the WYATTS of *Kent*, and in the laft Century was transferred to WILLIAM BANASTER, of *Turkdean*, who had been before poffeffed of a confiderable Eftate in this Parifh, which Records fhew was in the Reign of EDWARD IV. the Property of THOMAS BYSELEY, of the City of *Gloucefter* ‡. By WILLIAM BANISTER, Serjeant at Law, or his Heirs, it was fold, together with the Manor of *Turkdean*, to EDMUND WALLER, Efq. of *Farmington*, whofe Defcendant is the prefent Proprietor.

H A M L E T.

Yanworth, or *Enworth*, which is divided from *Hafleton* by the Parifh of *Hampnett*, is by one third Part of fmaller Extent. The Chapel is an inconfiderable Building, with an Aifle on the North Side, and a fmall Tower. It had anciently no Right of Sepulture; and in 1366 WILLIAM WITLESEY, Bifhop of *Worcefter*, made a Decree between the Abbot of *Winchcombe* and the Rector of *Hafleton*, by which a Chaplain was eftablifhed here.

RADULPH LE ZOUCH gave " *Janeworth*" to the Abbey of *St. Peter* in *Gloucefter*, and REGINALD THOKYS made a farther Donation; both which were confirmed by STEPHEN and HENRY II. §

The Manor, at the Suppreffion, was granted with *Hafleton* to RICHARD COLEPEPER. From Sir RICHARD HOWE, of *Compton*, it has defcended to the noble Family of CHEDWORTH. But other Property, which is ftyled a Manor, belonged to the Abbey of *Winchcombe*; and being fold out of the Court of Augmentations, was fucceffively vefted, during the Reign of JAMES I. in the Earls of ARUNDEL and BEDFORD.

No Benefaction to the Poor.

---

* It appears in the Books of the Regiftrar of this Diocefe, that a Faculty was obtained for re-building the Tower about 1670.

‡ DUGDALE, Mon. Ang. vol. I. p. 95.

" Carta Antiq. E. n. 8. fcilicet regis JOHANNIS confirm' Donat' GULIELMI ATREBATENSIS, de *Hafylton, Hawling*, &c."
TANNER, Not. Angl. *Glouc.* No. XXXIII.

‡ " JOHAN' BYSELEY, Filius & Hæres, & THOMAS BYSELEY, nuper de Civitat. *Glouc.* concefsêre W. DE NOTTINGHAM &
" WALTERO DE BROCKHAMPTON omnes terras & tenementa fua in *Hafleton*." Clauf. Rot. 4 EDW. IV. n. 29.

" WILLIAE BANASTER died feifed of a capital Meffuage and ten Yard Lands, with Meadow and Pafture; and of another
" Meffuage, called *Nether-houfe*, in the Parifh of *Hafleton*, in 1601, 43 ELIZ." Efchaet. Inquif. poft mortem.

§ DUGDALE, Mon. Angl. vol. I. p. 93.

3

INCUMBENTS.

INCUMBENTS.	PATRONS.	INCUMBENTS.	PATRONS.
1182 ——————,	Abbey of Winchcombe.	* * * * * * * * * * * * * *	
—— Reginald Taylor,	Anthony Aylworth and Thomas Warne, by Grant from the Abbey of Winchcombe, 1534.	—— Bartholomew Dobſon,	——————.
		1669 Daniel Mewe, M. A.	K. Charles II.
		1675 Charles Seward,	——————.
1546 Walter Turbot,	——————.	1715 John Sedgewick,	K. George I.
1573 Gervaſe Carrington,	Q. Elizabeth.	1726 Thos. Lodge, Clerk,	——————.
1586 Sam. Jennings, M.A.	——————.	1749 Jonath. Rawlins, Clerk,	K. George II.
		1785 James Preedy, Clerk,	K. George III.

PRESENT PROPRIETORS OF THE MANORS,

Of *Haſleton*,   Of *Yanworth*,

EDMUND WALLER, Eſq.   Right Hon. JOHN Lord CHEDWORTH.

No Perſon was ſummoned from this Place by the Heralds in 1682 and 1683.

At the Election in 1776 only One Freeholder polled from this Pariſh.

The Regiſter has its firſt Date in 1590.

ANNUAL ACCOUNT OF MARRIAGES, BIRTHS, AND BURIALS, IN THIS PARISH.

A.D.	Mar.	Bir.	Bur.	A.D.	Mar.	Bir.	Bur.	A.D.	Mar.	Bir.	Bur.	A.D.	Mar.	Bir.	Bur.
1781	2	2	3	1786	—	5	2	1791				1796			
1782	3	4	1	1787	—	2	—	1792				1797			
1783	1	1	1	1788	1	1	1	1793				1798			
1784	—	4	1	1789	1	1	1	1794				1799			
1785	—	—	—	1790				1795				1800			

INSCRIPTIONS IN THE CHURCH.

IN THE CHANCEL.

AGAINST A PEW:

Depoſitum
BARTHOLOMÆI DOBSON, Rectoris
Hujus Eccleſiæ, qui obiit
Januarii die 19, 1669.

Depoſitum
CATHERINÆ DEWY,
GULIELMUS Uxoris.

Obiit Aprilis 26, Anno { Salutis . . . / Ætatis 33.

IN THE CHURCH YARD, ON A TOMB,

Here lyeth the Body of JOHN LORDE the younger,
who departed this Life May 12, Anno Domini 1644.

ON HEAD AND FLAT STONES.

	Died	Aged
Thomas Dowdeſwell, Gent - - - - - -	26 Oct. 1767	86
Thomas Bateman, of Withington - - - - - -	27 Oct. 1757	88
Elizabeth his Wife - - - - - - -	—	—
Elizabeth, Wife of John Buttler - - - - -	1 July, 1770	65
John Bubb - - - - - - - -	6 July, 1773	72
Elizabeth his Wife - - - - - - -	5 May, 1782	82
Ann, Daughter of John and Mary Goodall - - - -	2 Nov. 1759	5
Elizabeth, Wife of John Wakefield - - - - -	25 Feb. 1786	32

CXXXVII.   H A T H E R O P,

W H I C H is fituate in the Hundred of *Brightwell's Barrow*, is diftant feven Miles South-eaft from *Northleche*, ten Eaftward from *Cirencefter*, and twenty-feven in the former Direction from the City of GLOUCESTER. The Soil varies from Clay to a very ftiff Loam, and is chiefly Arable, including, by Computation, more than two Thoufand Acres, and bounded on the South-eaft by the River *Colne*.

Of the Benefice, which is a Rectory, in the Deanery of *Fairford*, the Right of Advowfon was given, in 1232, to the *Auguftine* Nuns eftablifhed at *Lacock* in *Wiltfhire*, by ELA Countefs of SALISBURY; and, at the Diffolution, was granted, with the Manerial Eftate, to Sir WILLIAM SHERRINGTON in 1548, 2 EDW. VI. * It appears that the Church, which is dedicated to *St. Nicholas*, and confifts of a Nave only and a low, flated Tower, was re-built at the Expence of the Convent, and the Architecture leads us to conjecture about the Middle of the fifteenth Century. Very decent Pews have been lately erected.

In 1222, WILLIAM DE LONG ESPE †, Earl of *Salifbury*, affigned this Manor for the Maintenance of a *Carthufian* Priory, which he founded here; but the Monks, diffatisfied with this Situation, obtained the Confent of ELA his Relict to remove to *Henton*, co. *Somerfet*, where, in 1227, fhe founded a Monaftery for their Reception ‡.

There were, when *Domefday* was compiled, two Manors within the Boundaries of this Parifh; the greater, containing feven Hides, then belonged to ERNULPH DE HESDING, from whom it foon paffed to the Barons DE CADURCIS, or CHAWORTH. WALTER DE EWE received it in Dower with SYBELLA CHAWORTH. He founded the Priory of *Bradenftoke* in *Wiltfhire*, and endowed it with certain Lands appendant on this Manor §. ELA || before mentioned, Daughter and fole Heir of WILLIAM DE EWE, Earl of *Salifbury*, was the Wife of WILLIAM LONG ESPE, natural Son of King HENRY the Second by FAIR ROSAMOND, who, in her Right, fucceeded to that Honour. She beftowed this Manor upon her Foundation at *Lacock* **. When the monaftic Lands were difperfed, it was granted to Sir WILLIAM SHERRINGTON, who fold it foon afterward to JOHN BLOMER, Efq. of a very ancient Family fettled in *Weftmoreland*, and about this Time at *Cowley* in this County. By the Demife of JOHN and WILLIAM BLOMER, Efqrs. MARY, their only furviving Sifter, became, in 1686, poffeffed of this manerial Property. By her firft Hufband, RICHARD DRAYCOTT, Efq. of *Painfley*, co. *Stafford*, fhe left no Iffue; but, re-marrying with Sir JOHN WEBB, Bart. of *Canford*, co. *Dorfet*, her Defcendants have fucceeded to this Eftate. Sir JOHN WEBB, the prefent Proprietor, is the fifth in Defcent from Sir JOHN WEBB, created a Baronet, by Patent, dated April 2, 1644, 10 CAR. I. in reward of his eminent Services to the royal Caufe.

Of the leffer Manor, it is defcribed in *Domefday* to have contained two Hides only, and to have been given by the CONQUEROR to ROGER DE LACI, from whom it paffed to the DE SPENCERS. In 1299, 27 EDW. I. JOHN DE HANDELO, Governor of the Caftle of *St. Briavel*, levied a Fine. ISABEL DE ST. AMAND, Relict of RICHARD DE HANDELO, held it in Jointure, connected with the Manors of *Wyke* and *Williamfthrop*. She died in 1355. In 1363, 37 EDW. III. a Partition was made between her Coheirs, MARGARET, the Wife of JOHN APULBY, and ELIZABETH of EDMUND DE LA POLE, when this Eftate was confirmed to the elder ††. About the fame Period Sir WILLIAM SHERRINGTON purchafed both Manors, and no Diftinction between them has been fince preferved.

The Manor-houfe is very fpacious, fituate above the River *Colne*, and was built by JOHN BLOMER, Efq. early in the Reign of ELIZABETH. As it has long ceafed to be the Refidence of the WEBB Family,

---

* " 80 acr' terr' arab' in gleb'." BACON's Liber Regis.
When the late Inclofure was completed, Lands were allotted to the Rectory in Lieu of Tythes.
† " Vide in Afpilogia cl. JOHANNIS ANSTIS, (MS. n. 94.) conventionem inter ELAM com' WARWIC', de maner' de *Hetherop* " conceffo comitiffæ durante vita (Ib. n. 95) confirmationem donationum matris fuæ ELÆ per WILL. DE LONGESPE."
‡ DUGDALE's Mon. Ang. vol. I. p. 960. vol. II. pp. 341. 931.
§ TANNER's Not. Ang. *Wilts*, No. V.
|| See Lives of LELAND, HEARNE, and WOOD, vol. I. Append. p. 139.
** STEVENS's Supplement, Append. p. 354. See Charter of ELA Countefs of SARUM granting the Manor of *Hatherop*.
Pat. Fin. 33 HEN. III. " pro Manerio de *Heytherop*."
Pat. Rot. 13 HEN. IV. " de Manerio de *Heytherop*."
†† This Partition is proved by Clauf. Rot. 36 EDW. III. m. 28.

2   it

it is much dilapidated, and wears an Appearance of Decay. It was formerly very fuperbly furnifhed, in the old Style, with a large Collection of Portraits *.

There are no Eftates of Confequence independent of the confolidated Manors.

B E N E F A C T I O N S.

Sir HENRY BLOMER gave a Rent Charge of 4*l.* a Year (Time unknown); one Moiety for poor Families, to be given in Bread; the other for beautifying the Church.

Lady WEBB gave a Rent Charge of 18*l.* 13*s.* 4*d.* (Time not known) iffuing out of *Dean Farm* in the faid Parifh, for the Ufe of the Poor, according to the Direction of the Romifh Prieft officiating in the Manfion-houfe of the Parifh for the Time being; the Hon. SOMES TALBOT, and others, Truftees.

Some others of the Family of the WEBBS gave Monies, the Intereft whereof, amounting to 12*l.* is alfo difpofed of by the Romifh Prieft for the Time being, as follows, viz. one Half of a Bull to the Poor of the Parifh cf *Eaftleach*, and the other Half, with Bread, and the remaining Part of the Money, to the Poor of the Parifh of *Hatherop*.

INCUMBENTS.	PATRONS.	INCUMBENTS.	PATRONS.
—— James Watfon,	Nunnery of Lacock.	1673 William Wyatt, M.A.	The fame.
1560 Thomas Anne,	William Blomer, Efq.	1679 John Wyatt,	William Dowdefwell.
1562 Nathaniel Harford,	The fame.	1686 Wm. Bourchier, B.A.	Sir John Webb, Bart.
1563 William Selyter,	William Matthews.	1709 Wm. Boftock, M. A.	Univerfity of Oxford.
1572 George Bath, B. A.	Queen Elizabeth.	1710 John Bradley, M. A.	Sir John Webb.
1589 Rob. Hartland, B. A.	William Blomer, Efq.	1742 Rich. Hutchins, M.A.	Univerfity of Oxford.
1591 Richard Pullen,	Queen Elizabeth.	1749 Wm. Sanford, B. D.	The fame.
1601 Thomas Pullen, M.A.	William Blomer, Efq.	1782 J.Weekes Bedwell, B.A.	Mary Smith, Spinft.
—— John Jones,	John Blomer, Efq.		

PRESENT LORD OF THE MANOR,

Sir JOHN WEBB, Bart.

The only Perfon fummoned from this Parifh by the Heralds, in 1682 and 1683, was

John Blomer, Efq.

At the Election in 1776 no Freeholder polled from this Parifh.

The Regifter commences in 1657; and it is faid that the preceding Notices were deftroyed.

ANNUAL ACCOUNT OF MARRIAGES, BIRTHS, AND BURIALS, IN THIS PARISH.

A.D.	Mar.	Bir.	Bur.	A.D.	Mar.	Bir.	Bur.	A.D.	Mar.	Bir.	Bur.	A.D.	Mar.	Bir.	Bur.
1781	1	5	4	1786	—	11	5	1791				1796			
1782	—	6	5	1787	1	6	2	1792				1797			
1783	—	4	3	1788	3	2	5	1793				1798			
1784	3	8	5	1789	1	4	4	1794				1799			
1785	—	5	3	1790	1	13	6	1795				1800			

INSCRIPTIONS IN THE CHURCH.
ON MARBLE MONUMENTS IN THE CHANCEL.

LADY MARY WEBB was the Daughter of JOHN and the Hon. FRANCES BLOMER. She was twice a Wife, and twice a Widow, and confpicuous for her Prudence and Virtue in each State of Life.

She married RICHARD DRAYCOTT, of Painfley, in the County of Stafford, Efq. by whom fhe had one Son and one Daughter; and afterwards Sir JOHN WEBB, of Great Cranford, in the County of Dorfet, Bart. by whom alfo fhe had one Son

and one Daughter: Her life was fo exemplary that we have reafon to hope fhe is in Expectation of a bleffed Refurrection.

---

* Befide many Portraits of the Families of BLOMER and WEBB, was a Series of whole Lengths of the STUARTS from JAMES I. to JAMES II. Likewife of the three Daughters of Sir JOHN WEBB and their Hufbands: ANNA MARIA, who married JAMES RADCLIFFE, the unfortunate Earl of *Derwentwater*; MARY, the Wife of JAMES Earl of WALDEGRAVE; and BARBARA, the Wife of ANTHONY Lord Vifcount MONTACUTE. From this Houfe the firft mentioned Nobleman went on his ill-fated Expedition to join the Scotch Army in 1715. MSS. SNELL.

Arms;

Arms ; Gules, on an Inefcocheon Argent, a Lion rampant of the firft, within a Bordure of the fecond, for Blomer ;—impaling, Sable, three Lions paffant between two Cottifes Argent, for Browne.

To the pious Memory
of John Blomer, Efq. fixth Son to
William Blomer, of Hathrope,
in the County of Gloucefter, Efq.
of Frances his Wife, Daughter to
Anthony Vifcount Montacute,
by whom he had Iffue three Sons,
John, William, and Anthony,
which laft died in the 19th Year of his
Age;
and three Daughters,
Catharine, Frances, who died
Infants, and Mary,
who firft married Richard Draycott,
of Painfley, in the County of Stafford,
Efq.
and afterwards
Sir John Webb, of Cranford,
in the County of Dorfet, Baronet.
Thefe were all Branches of
John and Frances Blomer,
who were both Inftances of fingular
Piety and Goodneffe,
The one continually promoting
the Peace of the Neighbourhood;
the other ftill feconding of him
in all Chriftian Virtues;
which fhining moft confpicuoufly in her
through the three feveral Conditions
of her Life, when
Maid, Wife, Widow,
gave a true Glory and Luftre to her
high Birth.
He died the 26th of December,
in the Year of our Lord 1640,
in the 64th Year of his Age.
She died the 1ft of October,
in the Year of our Lord 1657,
in the 57th Year of her Age.

Arms; Blomer, as before.

Near this Place are likewife interred
John and William Blomer, Efqrs.
Sons of John and Frances Blomer,
of Hathrope, who died
Batchelours,
were exemplary in their Lives,
eminent for their Charity,
and their Love to each other
made them in a Manner one
whilft Living;
and, in their Deaths,
they were not long divided.
The former dying the 19th of September,
in the 56th Year of his Age,
the Year of our Lord 1685.
The latter dying the 27th of March,
in the 53d Year of his Age,
in the Year of our Lord 1686.

Arms; Azure, three Barrs wavy Argent, for Sanford ;—impaling, Or, fix Annuletts Sable, for Lowther.

Sacred
to the Memory of
William Sanford, D. D.
and Rector of this Parifh,
by Prefentation of the Univerf.ty of
Oxford.
In him
Society diftinguifhed the agreeable
Companion;
the County an able and upright
Magiftrate;
the Church a zealous and faithful Paftor;
religious without Oftentation;
complaifant without Meannefs, and
liberal without Profufion.
He lived univerfally efteemed
to the Age of Seventy-two;

and
died as univerfally regretted
on the xviii Day of February,
MDCCLXXXIII.

ON FLAT STONES OF MARBLE.

Arms ; Blomer ;—impaling,
as before.

Hic jacent corpora
Johannis Blomer, Armigeri,
& Franciscæ uxoris ejus,
Octobris trigefimo primo defunctæ,
& incarnationis Domini
Millefimo fexcentifimo quinquagefimo
feptimo,
Die quem fpero felicem
ut tandem poft aliquot annos disjuncti
placide in Domino
per omnem æternitatem requiefcant.

Arms ; a Fefs between three round
Buckles, for Bradley.

In Memory of
the Rev. Mr. John Bradley,
Vicar of Great Barrington,
and Rector of Hatherop,
who died the 2d of April, 1741,
aged 82 Years.

On a Brass Plate :

S. I. R.
Henrici Tourville,
Generofi,
qui obiit 20 die Octobris,
anno falutis 1754.

Requiefcat in pace.

ON FLAT STONES.

Arms; Blomer, as before.

Hic jacent corpora
Johannis Blomer, Armigeri,
defuncti decimo nono die Septembris,
anno falutis millefimo fexcentefimo
octagefimo quinto,
& Gulielmi Blomer, Armigeri,
defuncti vigeffimo feptimo Marcii,
anno falutis milleffimo fexcentiffimo fexto
Filiæ Johannis & Franciscæ Blomer,
de Hatherope, & focii ut fpero æternæ
beatitudinis.

Arms ; on a Lozenge, a Crofs between
four Falcons clofe, on an Efcocheon of
Pretence, Blomer, as before, for
Webb ;—impaling, a Bordure Ermine,
an Efcocheon of Pretence, Blomer.

In Remembrance
of
Mary Lady Webb,
whofe Body was here interred, and who
departed this Life the 29th of March,
in the Year 1709, and of her Age 74.
This Marble Stone was laid by her moft
affectionate Son Sir John Webb, Bart.
She was a moft loving Wife,
a tender Parent,
a kind Miftrefs,
a fincere Friend,
a Lady of meek and condefcending
Temper,
of an extenfive Charity and Beneficence,
and ripe in Virtue.
She died lamented by all who knew her,
efpecially by the Poor.

The Reverend
Mr. Richard Hutchins, B. D.
late Fellow of Corpus Chrifti College,
in Oxford,
and Rector of this Church,
departed this Life
March 5, 1749.

HERE LYETH THE BODY
OF JOHN JONES, RECTOR,
AND CATHARINE JONES,
THE WIFE OF THE
FORESAID JOHN JONES,
DECESSED THE 29TH DAY
MARCH, IN THE YEARE OF
OUR LORD 1673, AND
KATHARINE HIS WIFE,
DECESSED THE 22ND DAY
OF NOVEMBER, IN THE
YEARE OF OUR LORD 167V.

ON FLAT STONES IN THE NAVE.

Here lieth the Body of
Mrs. Mary St. Leger,
who died the 7th Day of January,
1704-5,
in the 21ft Year of her Age.

Here lieth the Body of
Mrs. Elizabeth Bloore,
Widow of Mr. Richard Bloore,
Mother of Mrs. St. Leger,
by a former Hufband,
and Mother alfo of
Richard Bloore, the
younger. She departed
this Life the 6th Day
of April, 1739, in the 79th
Year of her Age.

Here lieth the Body of
Richard, the Son of
Richard and Elizabeth Bloore,
who died May the 22d, 1705,
in the 4th Year of his Age.

Alfo
here lieth the Body of
Mr. Richard Bloore, the Father,
who departed this Life on
the 9th Day of Auguft, in the
Year of our Lord 1728,
and in the 55th Year of his Age.
He was a truly affectionate Hufband,
a juft and fkilful Steward,
a kind and charitable Neighbour,
an humble and pious Chriftian,
and his Death lamented by all
who knew him.

Here lieth, in hopes of a glorious
Refurrection to eternal Life, the
Body of Mr. Thomas Reynolds, who
departed this Life the 27th Day of
January, in the Year of our Lord
God 1714, aged 59 Years.

Alfo
near this Place lieth the Body of
Mary Reynolds, Wife of
Thomas Reynolds,
who departed this Life
the 12th of December, anno 1727,
aged 58 Years.
She was an affectionate Wife,
a tender Mother and kind Neighbour,
and in each Station of Life,
of a Maid, a Wife, and a Widow,
a zealous and pious Chtiftian.

Under

Under this Stone lieth interred
the Body of Mr. THOMAS JOLLEY,
Gentleman to Sir JOHN WEBB, Bart.
He died on the 20th of October,
in the Year 1721,
and about the 54th Year of his Age.

In Memory of
BRYAN REYNOLDS,
who departed this Life
April 27, 1738, aged 38.

Alfo of SARAH his Wife,
who departed this Life
July 15, 1771, aged 68.

Alfo of
JOHN KNAPP their Son,
who died an Infant.

In Memory of
MARY, the Wife of
THOMAS REYNOLDS,
who departed this Life
March 24, 1777, aged 34.

Alfo JOHN their Son
departed this Life
June 25, 1771, aged 2 Years
and 8 Months.

Alfo BRYAN their Son
departed this Life
November 2, 1770.

Alfo JOHN BRYAN
their Son departed this Life
June 26, 1773.

Alfo JOHN their Son
departed this Life July 19, 1775.

In Memory of
CATHARINE, the Wife
of BRYAN REYNOLDS,
junior. She died
November the 4th, 1768,
aged 28 Years.

And SARAH their
Daughter died May
the 4th, 1769, aged fix
Months.

IN THE CHURCH YARD, ON TOMBS.

MARY, Wife of THOMAS BALDWIN,
and Daughter of
RICHARD and ALICE EBSWORTH,
died Dec. 14, 1763, aged 55 Years.

THOMAS BALDWIN
died March 29, 1772, aged 61.

JAMES BOULTAR.
Ob. non. Julii, Anno { falutis 1762.
{ ætatis 67.

JOHN HUMPHRIS
died April 22, 1763, aged 63 Years.

ELIZABETH his Wife
died January 19, 1780, aged 80.

JOHN FREEMAN
DIED MAY 22, 1738, AGED 43.

ANN HIS WIFE
DIED SEPTEMBER 2, 1770,
AGED 73.

ON HEAD AND FLAT STONES.

	Died	Aged		Died	Age
John Ebfworth, of Bibury	29 Sept. 1747	86	Anne, Wife of William Latham	1 Feb. 1764	44
Elizabeth, Wife of John Ebfworth	6 Apr. 1705	—	John Latham	11 Dec. 1773	60
Richard Ebfworth	14 Feb. 1752	75	Dorothy his Wife	22 May, 1773	59
Elizabeth his Daughter	10 Jan. 1761	44	William, Son of William and Winifrede Browne	14 May, 1735	2
Robert Ponting	5 Apr. 1705	—	John Weavihg	23 July, 1758	83
Elizabeth his Daughter	18 July, 1699	4	Mary his Wife	21 June, 1747	61
Alexander Midwinter buried	6 Jan. 1681	—	Robert Weaving	15 Apr. 1748	66
Edward Midwinter	—	—	Catharine, Wife of Thos. Lapworth	27 June, 1747	63
John Midwinter	11 Jan. 1701	—	Anne, Wife of Thomas Ebfworth, junior, of Netherton	12 Aug. 1710	—
John Midwinter	5 Oct. 1733	65	Alice, Wife of Richard Ebfworth	23 Feb. 1726	50
Margaret Midwinter	20 Jan. 1712	—	Richard Holloway, jun. of Netherton	1 Jan. 1722	35
John, Son of Giles Midwinter	29 May, 1696	—	Winifrede, Wife of Edward Tombes, of Hayle, in Oxfordfhire	8 Mar. 1741	57
Margaret, Daughter of John and Margaret White, of Brailes, in Warwickfhire	8 June, 1742	42	Frances, Wife of William Turner	30 Mar. 1754	72
Sufannah, Daughter of William and Mary Hands, of Henlyarden, in Warwickfhire	20 July, 1741	27	Frances, Wife of Walter Green	13 June, 1758	36
Ann, Wife of John Howes, and Sifter of Sufannah Hands aforefaid	2 Dec. 1743	36	Mary, Daughter of John and Jane Hawkins	4 Jan. 1776	26
John Howes	8 May, 1774	80	Elizabeth, Daughter of John and Elizabeth Humphris, and Wife of Thomas Niblett	11 Apr. 1788	65
William, Son of John Latham	— 1716	—	Thomas Ebfworth	23 Nov. 1730	73
Mary Latham	2 May, 1721	—	William Ebfworth	11 Sept. 1722	57
Amy, Daughter of John and Hefter Latham	11 May, 1729	—	William Turner	10 Aug. 1729	72
John Latham	20 Jan. 1738	60			

O

CXXXVIII.

HAWKESBURY.

The Right Hon.ble Sir Charles Jenkinson Bar.t
BARON of HAWKESBURY
contributes this Plate.

CXXXVIII. HAWKESBURY.

TH E Extent of this large Parifh is faid never to have been afcertained by Perambulation ; but is calculated, with its feveral Hamlets, to exceed thirty Miles in Circumference. It lies in the upper Part of the Hundred of *Grumbald's Afh*, four Miles North-eaft from *Sodoury*, four Eaft from *Wickwar*, and twenty-five on the South from the City of GLOUCESTER. A confiderable Divifi n of this Parifh extends over the great Ridge of the lower *Cotfwold* Hills, which is confequently of a dry, light Soil ; but fertile in Corn ; the Vale abounds in rich Pafture. There are two very large Commons, *Ingleham* and *Hawkefbury*. The Proportion of Arable to the Pafture Lands is about four Parts in five ; and the Woodlands are fome Hundred Acres. The Village is built upon the Hill, and generally called *Hawkefbury Upton* ; but the Church, Manor, and Vicarage Houfes, are fituated in a clofe Valley, at the Foot of a very picturefque Knowl.

Of the Benefice *, which was formerly impropriate, and annexed to the *Benedictine* Abbey of *Perfhore*, co. *Worcefter*, the Right of Advowfon is now connected with the Manor. The great Tythes were granted with it at the Suppreffion, 1546, to JOHN BOTELER, which have been fince divided into feveral Parcels, and attached to particular Eftates ; the total annual Amount of which is 294*l.* 6*s.* 6*d.* at a moderate Valuation.

The Church is the Chief of a Deanery, and is dedicated to *St. Mary.* It is capacious and handfome, with a Nave, two Aifles, and a heavy embattled Tower at the Weft End. By the Abbey of *Perfhore* the original Structure was probably built ; but it is conjectured, from the Arms of BOTELER (three covered Cups), now remaining in carved Stone, and from the Shape of the Windows, that it was nearly re-erected by that Family in the fixteenth Century. In the upper Part of the South Aifle was STINCHCOMB's Chantry eftablifhed in 1452, 30 HEN. VI. to which belonged a Gild or Fraternity, with Lands for its Endowment at *Chalkeley* in this Parifh, which are ftill fubject to the Repairs †. To *Hawkefbury* are annexed the Chapels of *Badminton Parva*, *Trefham*, and *Hilfley* ; the latter of which is now totally dilapidated ; its laft Incumbent was THOMAS SWETHEMAN, who was difcharged at the Suppreffion with a Penfion of 5*l.* per Annum ‡.

Domefday § recites the Manor as belonging to the Church of *St. Mary* of *Perfhore*, containing feventeen Hides, of the yearly Value of 10*l.* The Convent obtained a Licence for a Fair, Markets, and free Warren, in the early Centuries, which were confirmed to them upon a *Quo Warranto* ; and many Tenants in Demefne were appointed by them.

By King HENRY VIII. in 1546, it was granted to Sir JOHN BOTELER, of *Badminton*, upon whofe Death in 1552 this Manor was left in Settlement upon SYLVESTER his Relict (Daughter of JOHN GUISE, Efq. of *Elmore*), who was fucceeded by JOHN BOTELER in 1565. In 1608, the Manor, including the Hamlets of *Hilfley*, *Kilcott*, *Trefham*, *Seddlewood*, *Upton*, and *Gufton*, were held by NICHOLAS BOTELER, Efq. It was transferred in 1612 to ARTHUR CREWE, Efq. of *Alderley*, by whofe Executors it was fold to the Anceftors of the prefent Proprietor.

Sir ROBERT JENKINSON, Knight, of *Walcot*, co. *Oxford*, became poffeffed of it about the Year 1620. His Patent of Creation, as Baronet, bears Date May 18, 1661. Upon the Deceafe of Sir BANKS JENKINSON, the fixth who bore the Title, it devolved to the next Heir Male, the Right Honourable CHARLES JENKINSON, Chancellor of the Dutchy of *Lancafter*, one of his Majefty's moft Honourable Privy Council, and Prefident of the Committee of Council for Trade and Plantations, who was created Baron of *Hawkefbury*, by Patent, dated Aug. 8, 1786, 26 GEO. III. The manerial Houfe, never well conftructed or fituated, is now a Ruin. It was for fome Years the Refidence of the Family of JENKINSON.

The Convent of *Bonhommes* of *Edington*, co. *Wilts*, are faid to have held Lands in this Parifh, which were transferred to the Knights Templars and Hofpitallers, and fold by the Court of Augmentations.

---

* BACON's Thefaur. p. 341.

† The Chantry was founded by one of the Family of STINCHCOMBE, whofe Arms, Quarterly, 1. and 4. a Fefs engrailed between three Annulets braced with another ; 2. and 3. a Chevron between three Garbs are ftill extant. Sir ABRAHAM ELTON, Bart. of *Briftol*, was poffeffed of *Chalkley* at the Time of his Deceafe in 1780, which has defcended to his Heirs.

‡ WILLIS's Mitred Abbies, vol. II. p. 86.

§ In *Grimboldeftov* Hund'. Ipfa eccl'a ten' *Havochefberie*. Ibi xvii hide. In d'nio v car', & xviii vill'i, & xxv bord', cum xv car'. Ibi ii fervi & vii colib'ti. Ibi iii molini de xix fol' & ii den', & i ac p'ti. Silva de ii leuc' l'g & una lat'. Valuit xvi lib' modo x lib'. Domefday.

Cart. 37 HEN. III. m. 6. pro Mercatâ & Feriâ apud *Hawkefbury*.

Efchaet. *Glouceft.* 14 RICH. II. n. 137. de Manerio de *Hawkefbury*.

2 *H A M L E T S.*

H A M L E T S.

1. *Hilderſley*, or *Hiliſley*; ſo ſpecified in *Domeſday*. In 1316, 9 EDW. II. ROBERT LYNETT proved his right to certain Lands, and was admitted Tenant of others under the Abbey of *Perſhore*. Other Tenants are likewiſe enumerated. Here was a Chapel dedicated to *St. Giles*, now uſed for ſecular Purpoſes; the Advowſon of which, in the Reign of HENRY V. was veſted in Sir THOMAS BERKELEY and MARGARET his Wife. FRANCIS THYNNE, Eſq. Son of FRANCIS THYNNE, of *Kempsford*, held this Manor in 1623. Of the Family of SYMONDS, of *Dorſetſhire*, it was purchaſed in the laſt Century by EDWARD COSYN, Eſq. of *Great Stoughton*, co. *Huntingdon*, and was conveyed in Marriage Dower by ELIZA his Daughter and ſole Heir to GEORGE TIPPING, Eſq. third Son of Sir THOMAS TIPPING, of *Oxfordſhire*. It has ſince paſſed from the Families of HALE and SPRINGETT, of *Alderley*, to MATTHEW A'DEANE, Eſq. the preſent Proprietor. This Hamlet is divided into ſeveral ſmall Eſtates, the chief of which belongs to —— THOMAS, Gent. of the County of *Somerſet*. The Village is ſmall, but pleaſantly ſituated.

2. *Treſham*. The earlieſt Record of this Hamlet is in 1348, 21 EDW. III. when THOMAS KENNETT and MARGARET his Wife levied a Fine of Lands. The Manor now belongs to JOHN BLAGDEN HALE, Eſq. and the principal Eſtate to TIMOTHY THOMAS, Gent. of *Uley*. The Chapel is ſmall, and contains no Monument or Antiquities worthy Notice.

3. *Killcott*. The Manor, with free Warren in *Kilcott*, was confirmed to MATILDA DE EVERS 1287, 15 EDW. I. It afterwards paſſed to the Families of BODISANT and STANSHAWE. Of ROBERT POYNTZ, Eſq. of *Alderley*, it was bought by SAMUEL BARKER, Eſq. of *Fairford*, and re-ſold to WILLIAM SPRINGETT, Gent. MATTHEW A'DEANE, Eſq. is the preſent Proprietor.

4. *Seddlewood* belonged for many Generations to the Family of WORKMAN. Some Years ſince it was ſold by TIMOTHY THOMAS, Gent. to DANIEL ADEY, Eſq. who is ſucceded by his Nephew. *Treſham, Kilcott*, and *Seddlewood*, compoſe one Tything.

5. *Upton* is a very extenſive Tything, ſituate on the Hill. JOHN CODRINGTON and ALICE his Wife levied a Fine of Lands in *Hawkeſbury Upton* in 1459, 39 HEN. VI. By their Deſcendant it was ſold to Sir ROBERT JENKINSON, and is now annexed to the manerial Eſtate. An Eſtate belonging formerly to ROBERT WICKSEY, Gent. and by him purchaſed of —— BENCE, of *Sherſtone*, co. *Wilts*, is now veſted in JAMES WOOD, Eſq. of *Glouceſter*. Another was the Property of the late JAMES CLEARE, Eſq. of *Briſtol*.

6. *Waſte*, or *Le Waſte* *. This Manor was transferred from the Abbey of *Perſhore* to that of *Glouceſter*. It was ſold by the CODRINGTONS to his Grace the Duke of BEAUFORT.

7. *Badminton Parva*, already deſcribed.

B E N E F A C T I O N S.

MATTHEW POYNTZ, Eſq. in 1600 gave by Deed, for the Relief of Poor Perſons, one Houſe and Garden, value 4*l.* a Year.

RICHARD THYNNE, Gent. gave by Will, dated Sept. 23, 1704, Land, the yearly Produce of which is 8*l.* to be diſpoſed of on the 26th of December, yearly, for ever, to Poor Children and old indigent People of the Pariſh not receiving Alms, veſted in Truſtees.

DANIEL BELSIRE, Gent. gave by Deed, March 25, 1733, 1*l.* 10*s.* payable out of one fourth Part of Lands in the Pariſh called *Hawkeſbury Barns*, to be diſtributed annually, on the 25th of December, to ſuch Poor Perſons in the Pariſh as ſhould moſt want it, at the Diſcretion of the Churchwardens.

DANIEL WALKER, Gent. gave by Will, dated Dec. 24, 1734, 100*l.* veſted in the Miniſter and Churchwardens; the Intereſt for ever to be applied for educating poor Boys, of this Pariſh.

INCUMBENTS.	PATRONS.	INCUMBENTS.	PATRONS.
1548 Chriſtopher Wootton,	John Boteler,	1612 John Cooper, B. A.	Arthur Crewe, Eſq.
1549 Roger Lawrence,	Sylveſter Boteler.	1644 John Pell,	Sir Robert Jenkinſon.
1556 Thomas Broadhead,	The ſame.	1679 Henry Stephens,	Sir Robert Jenkinſon.
1559 Hugh Kyrke, M. A.	The ſame.	1707 William Ballard, B.A.	The ſame.
1561 Michael Jones,	The ſame.	1712 John Ryland,	The ſame.
1569 Chriſtopher Seaborn,	W. Boteler, Eſq.	1726 John Warneford, M.A.	Sir Robert Jenkinſon.
1570 Thomas Thackham,	The ſame.	1731 Potter Cole, M. A.	The ſame.
1584 Thomas Hooke,	Queen Elizabeth.		

* " *Waſt*. The Abbat and Convent of *Perſhore* granted a Licence, 47 EDW. III. to THOMAS BEVERSTON, Clerk, and JOHN
" GODWELL, to give their Manor and Lands of *Waaſt*, in the Manor of *Hawkeſbury*, to the Abbey of *Glouceſter*, on Condition
" that the latter do grant to the Abbat of *Perſhore*, and his Succeſſors, 6*s.* 8*d.* out of thoſe Lands, on the Death of every Abbat
" of *Glouceſter*. And accordingly BEVERSTON and GODWELL gave the ſame Manor, with the Advowſon of the Chapel, to
" the Abbey of *Glouceſter*, by their Deed executed at *Standiſh*, 49 E. III." MSS. SNELL.

PRESENT

H A W K E S B U R Y.

Present Proprietors of the Manors,

Of *Hawkesbury* and *Hawkesbury Upton*,
The Right Hon. Charles Lord Hawkesbury.

Of *Kilcott*,
Matthew A'Deane, Esq.

Of *Tresham* and *Hillsley*,
John Blagden Hale, Esq.

Of *Seddlewood*,
Daniel Adey, Esq.

Of *Le Waste* and *Badminton Parva*,
His Grace the Duke of Beaufort.

The Persons summoned from this Parish by the Heralds, in 1682 and 1683, were

Sir Robert Jenkinson, Bart.
Edward Cosyn, Esq.

Edward Workman, Gent.
———— Aylway, Gent.

At the Election in 1776 Forty-four Freeholders polled from this Parish.

The earliest Date in the Register is 1602.

Annual Account of Marriages, Births, and Burials, in this Parish.

A.D.	Mar.	Bir.	Bur.	A.D.	Mar.	Bir.	Bur.	A.D.	Mar.	Bir.	Bur.	A.D.	Mar.	Bir.	Bur.
1781	21	30	24	1786	13	29	29	1791				1796			
1782	6	27	29	1787	7	33	19	1792				1797			
1783	5	24	25	1788	9	37	23	1793				1798			
1784	5	34	17	1789	12	38	32	1794				1799			
1785	9	29	37	1790	11	46	23	1795				1800			

INSCRIPTIONS IN THE CHURCH.

IN THE CHANCEL.

On a very handsome Marble Monument:

Arms; Azure, on a Fess wavy Or, a Cross pattée Gules, in Chief two Estoiles of the first. Crest, a Sea Horse assurgent Or, maned Azure, supporting a Cross pattée Gules.

In Memory of Sir Robert Jenkinson, Bart.
who departed this Life August 8, in the Year of our Lord 1766, in the 46th Year of his Age.
He was the eldest Son of Sir Robert Banks Jenkinson, Bart. by Catharine his Wife,
third Daughter of Sir Robert Dashwood, of Northbrook, in the County of Oxford, Bart.
He married Mary, the Daughter of Sir Jonathan Cope, Bart.
but left no Issue ;
yet let his Name be preserved to Posterity
for his filial Piety, his conjugal Love, and fraternal Affection ;
and all those Virtues which best adorn the honest English Gentleman and sincere Christian.
Fortified with these, he bore with Patience a long and painful Illness,
till he resigned his Soul, with Faith and Confidence, into the Hands of his Creator.
Disdain not, Reader!
what, from too high a Veneration for more glaring and ostentatious Characters,
thou mayest be taught to think a very humble Encomium ;
for, remember that purity of Heart, and integrity of Manners,
will receive the truest Praise at the last Day
from Him who is the Supreme Judge of all Virtue and Merit,
and who alone can assign them their due Reward.

The following Inscription is intended for a Monument to be erected:

Near this Place
reposeth the Body
of
Amelia Jenkinson,
first Wife of the Right Honourable Charles Jenkinson,
now Lord Hawkesbury.
She was the eldest Daughter of William Watts, Esq.
President of the Council of Fort William in Bengal
at that memorable Period
when the Arms of Great Britain
first acquired an Ascendancy in India.
She was born in 1750 ;
She was married in 1769 ;
She died, alas ! on the 7th Day of June, 1770,
after having given Birth to her only Child
the Honourable Robert Banks Jenkinson, M. P.

Hence, Adulation ! to proud Sculpture fly,
Nor wound this honest Marble with a Lie ;
The Truth she lov'd inscribe her gentle dust,
Which almost blushes yet at Praise, though just.
Of Symmetry, the coldest breast to charm,
Of Modesty, to check a Wish too warm ;
Of Manners soft, by Elegance refin'd,
Nature's pure Gift, with not an Art combin'd ;
O'er ev'ry Gesture, all she look'd, or said,
Propriety its happy Polish shed ;
In her soft Converse chearfully sedate,
Joy affum'd Wings, and Grief forgot its Weight.
Superior to the World, on Life's gay Stage,
She liv'd, a Heav'n-born Pattern to the Age!

O N

MONUMENT OF

Sr Robt Jenkinson Bart

ON FLAT STONES.

HERE LYETH BRIDGET, THE WIFE OF THOMAS WORKMAN, OF THIS PARISH, GENT. WHO WAS BVRYED THE 28 DAY OF MARCH, A° D'NI 1674.

HERE LYETH RICHARD, LATE SON OF THOMAS WORKMAN, OF THIS PARISH, WHO WAS BVRIED THE 21 DAY OF AUGUST, 1690.

VNDER THIS STONE WAS INTERRED THE BODY OF THOMAS WORKMAN, LATE OF TRESHAM, GENT. WHO DEPARTED THIS LIFE THE 12 DAY OF NOVEMBER, AND WAS BURIED THE 15 DAY OF THE SAME MONTH, ANNO DOM. 1694, ÆTATIS SUÆ 61.

HERE RESTETH THE BODY OF JOHN WORKMAN, LATE OF SEDDLEWOOD, GENT. WHO DEPARTED THIS LIFE THE 23 DAY OF JANUARY, ANNO DOMINI 1717, ÆTATIS SUÆ 50.
HERE ALSO LYETH THE BODY OF ANNE, THE WIFE OF THIS JOHN WORKMAN, GENT. WHO DYED DECEM. THE FIRST, 1734, AGED 66.

HERE RESTETH THE BODY OF THOMAS WORKMAN, GENT. SON OF THIS JOHN WORKMAN, OF SEDDLEWOOD, GENT. WHO DEPARTED THIS LIFE THE 12 DAY OF OCTOBER, ANNO DOMINI 1717, ÆTATIS SUÆ 25.

HERE ALSO RESTETH THE BODY OF ANNE SYMONS, WIFE OF WILLIAM SYMONS, DAUGHTER OF JOHN WORKMAN, GENT. SHE DEPARTED THIS LIFE JVLY THE FIRST, ANNO DOM. . . . . . AGED 26 YEARS.

HERE LYETH THE BODY OF ELIANOR POYNTZ, WIDD. LATE WIFE OF JOSEPH POYNTZ, GENT. WHO ENDED THIS LIFE THE 5 DAY OF SEPTEMBER, AN. DOM. 1699.

HERE LYETH THE BODY OF FRANCIS THYNNE, GENT. OF THIS PARISH, WHOE DEPARTED THIS LIFE ON THE 20 DAY OF JANVARY, ANNO DOM. 1670.

VOL. II.

HERE LYETH THE BODY OF ELIZABETH, THE WIFE OF RICHARD THYNNE, OF THIS PARISH, GENT. WHO ENDED THIS LIFE THE 8 DAY OF APRIL, ANNO DOM. 1680.

HERE LIES INTERRED THE BODY OF RICHARD THYNNE, OF THIS PARISH, GENT. WHO DEPARTED THIS LIFE THE XXI DAY OF NOVEMBER, AN° DOM. 1704, ÆTATIS SUÆ 81.

HERE LYETH THE BODY OF PENELOPE THYNNE, OF THIS PARISH, SPINSTER, WHO DEPARTED THIS LIFE THE 3 DAY OF JANUARY, IN THE LXXVI YEARE OF HER AGE, ANNOQ. DOM. 1709.

HERE LYETH THE BODY OF JOHN FRANKCOM, WHO DEPARTED THIS LIFE THE 2 DAY OF JANUARY, 1728, AGED 51 YEARS.

HERE ALSO LYETH THE BODY OF MARGARET HIS WIFE, THE DAUGHTER OF THOMAS WORKMAN, OF TRESHAM, GENT. SHE DEPARTED THIS LIFE THE 19 FEBRUARY, 1757, AGED 74 YEARS.

HERE LYETH THE BODY OF JOHN FRANKCOM, OF TRESHAM, WHO DIED THE 16 OF JANUARY, 1764, AGED 25 YEARS.

IN THE NAVE.

On a marble Monument:
Arms; Per Pale, three Suns. Creft, a demi Lion rampant, holding a Mullet, for CLEARE.
Near this Place lie the Remains of JAMES CLEARE, Efq. who died April 2, 1790, aged 62 Years.

Arms; Argent, a Bend engrailed Azure, between two Fire Balls proper, for SYMONDS.
Erected to the Memory of MATTHEW SYMONDS, of this Parifh, Gent. and ELIZABETH his Wife. He left Ifiue only one Daughter, BARBARA, married to WILLIAM MOUNTJOY, jun. of Biddefton, in the County of Wilts, Gent. He died June 3, 1719, æt. 65. She died Nov. 2, 1719, æt. 63.

P

Arms; on a Fefs between fix Billets three Rofes, for WASTFIELD.
Before this Place lie interred the Body of Mrs. BARBARAH WASTFIELD, who was buried Nov. 3, 1666.
Mrs. ANN WASTFIELD, who was buried May 30, 1709.
Mr. RICHARD WASTFIELD, who was buried June 5, 1716, aged 85 Years.
Mr. RICHARD WASTFIELD, who was buried Nov. 3, 1738, aged 77 Years.
Mr. JOHN WOOLVIN, who was buried Nov. 30, 1739, aged 41 Years.

ON A FLAT STONE:
Under this Stone lieth the Body of MARY, the Wife of WILLIAM RICE, who died Jan. 29, 1763, aged 62 Years.

Alfo here lieth the Body of ROBERT, the Son of WILLIAM and MARY RICE, who died June 8, 1762, aged 32 Years.

Likewife under this Stone lieth the Body of the faid WILLIAM RICE abovementioned, who died April 24, 1778, aged 73 Years.

IN THE SOUTH AISLE.
ON VERY HANDSOME MONUMENTS.
DANIEL ESBURY, Gent. died Sept. 4, 1780.
MARY ESBURY his Daughter, Dec. 14, 1782.
This Monument is erected in Memory of THOMAS ESBURY, Son of DANIEL ESBURY, of this Parifh, Gent. He was a dutiful Son, a fincere Friend, and a good Chriftian. He died Auguft the 28th, 1766.

Alfo of SARAH ESBURY, Wife of the faid DANIEL ESBURY. She died December the 8th, 1766.

Alfo of GRACE FORDER, Sifter of the faid SARAH ESBURY, who died January the 19th, 1766.

Arms; a Bull within a Bordure, charged with eight Roundles, for COLE; —impaling, Gules, a Chevron Ermine, between three Pheons Argent, for ARNOLD. Creft, a demi Dragon.
Sacred to the Memory of HARRY COLE, Son of the Rev. Mr. POTTER COLE and SARAH his Wife, who departed this Life June 12, 1756, aged 15 Years.
Alfo of ELIZABETH COLE their Daughter, who died March 16, 1762, aged 23 Years.
Alfo of FRANCES COLE their Daughter, who died May 15, 1768, aged 16 Years.
Alfo of WILLIRM COLE their Son, who died Sept. 10, 1773, aged 30 Years.
And alfo of SARAH COLE their Daughter, who died Aug. 20, 1786, aged 48 Years.

Arms;

Arms; on a Crofs engrailed, between four Pheons, a Rofe of the Field,
for JOBBINS.

Sacred to the Memory
of
MARY, Wife of
Mr. JOHN JOBBINS,
who was buried May 24, 1754,
aged 52.

Alfo of
JOHN JOBBINS their Son,
who was buried June the 2d, 1743,
aged 19.

Alfo of
MARY JOBBINS their Daughter,
who was buried April 13, 1752,
aged 24.

ON FLAT STONES.

H. S. E.
SARAH MARIA COLE.
Ob. 26 Dec. 1729,
ætatis 23.

HERE RESTETH THE BODY OF
THOMAS WESTON, OF
HILLSLEY, SURGEON, WHO
DEPARTED THIS LIFE THE 12TH
DAY OF NOVEM. A. D. 1716.

FRANCIS JOBBINS, Efq. Obiit
Jan. 22, 1784.

THOMAS CURTIS, Efq. Obiit
April 4, 1784.

Alfo here lieth the Remains
of JANE JOBBINS, the Wife of
FRANCIS JOBBINS, who died June 27,
179', aged 60.

ON A TOMB:

Arms, Argent, a Chevron Ermines,
between three Wolves Heads erafed Sable, for COSYN;—impaling, Or, a Bend
Azure, for TRYE.

Dedicated to the Memory
of EDWRRD COSYN, Efq. of Hillfley,
in this Parifh, Lord of the Mannor of
Charley, in the County of Leicefter,
who departed this Life the 20th Day of
February, Anno Dom. 1689,
ætatis fuæ 88,
who marryed FRANCES, eldeft Daughter
of WILLIAM TRYE, Efq. of Hardwick,
in this County.

ON GRAVE STONES.

HERE LIETH THE
BODY OF SARAH, THE
WIFE OF NICHOLAS
HORWOOD, WHO DEPAR-

TED THIS LIFE THE 8
DAY OF . . . . 1675.

Here lieth the Body of JOHN
PELL, who was above 33 Yeares
Minifter of this Parifh,
who deceafed the 18th Day of
March, Anno Domini 1678.

And neare him lieth MARY
his Wife, and two
of his Sons, and one
Daughter.

IN CHALKLEY CHANCEL.

ON FLAT STONES.

HERE LYETH THE BODY OF
NICHOLAS STINCHCOMB, OF
THIS PARISH, YEOMAN, WHO
DEPARTED THIS LIFE THE 5
DAY OF JULY, ANNO DOM.
1693.

HERE LYETH THE BODY OF
THOMAS STINCHCOMB, WHO
DEPARTED THIS LIFE THE 22
DAY OF FEBRUARY, ANNO DOM.
1689.

IN THE CHURCH YARD.

ON TOMBS.

Here lieth the Body of SARAH
MACHIN, Widd. late Wife of WILLIAM
MACHIN, fenior, who departed this
Life the 17th of January, Anno
Domini 1702.

Here lyeth the Body of WILLIAM
MACHIN, fen. who departed this
Life the 29th of February, An. Domini
1687, ætatis fuæ 67.

Here lyeth the Body of JOHN
MACHIN, who departed this
Life the 18th of July, An. Dom.
1717, ætatis fuæ 31.

In Memory of MARY, the
Wife of WILLIAM GILES,
of Wickwar, Gent. but
formerly the Wife of
Mr. WILLIAM MACHIN,
of this Parifh, Clothier.
She departed this Life the 21ft Day
of July, Anno Dom. 1729,
aged 69 Years.

Here lyeth the Body of
WILLIAM MACHIN, who
departed this Life the 30th
of June, 1703, ætatis 50.

Here lieth the Body of WILLIAM
LARTON, the Son of Mr.
WILLIAM LARTON, late of Hillfley,
Clothyer, who departed
this Life the 11th of May,
Anno Domini 1724,
ætatis fuæ 21.

To the Memory of
MARY, the Wife of EDMUND ROUCH,
of Hillfley, here interred,
who died the 23d of December,
1763, ætatis 50 Years.

Likewife five Children died Infants.

HERE LYETH THE BODY
OF JOHN COOPER, ONCE
MINNISTER OF THIS PLACE,
WHO DEPARTED THIS
LIEE THE 20 DAY OF
NOVEMBER, 1644,
AGED 85.

Here lyeth the Body of
ELNER COOPER, Wife of
JOHN COOPER, Minnifter
of this Place, who left
this Life the 6th Day of
May, 1645, aged 88.

Here lyeth the Body of
ROBERT ROBERTS, of this Parifh,
who deceafed the 9th of
March, 1683;
buryed by CORNELIUS GINGELL.

Here lyeth the Body of ANNE,
Wife of THOMAS TUCKER, of this
Parifh, who departed this Life
the 12th Day of July, 1727,
aged 49 Years.

And alfo THOMAS, the Son of the
faid THOMAS and ANNE TUCKER,
who departed this Life the 31ft
Day of May, 1723, aged 14.

Here lyeth the Body of ANNE,
Daughter of THOMAS and

ANNE TUCKER, who departed
this Life the 20th of December,
1732, aged 18.

In Memory
of ANN, the Wife of
WILLIAM WILLIAMS, who
died the 30th of May, 1757,
aged 54 Years.

Alfo WILLIAM HARRIS died
the 11th of July, 1757,
aged 4 Years and 4 Months.

Here alfo lieth MARTHA,
the Wife of MORGAN DAVIS,
of Petty France,
who died the 7th of April, 1763,
aged 40 Years.

Near this Stone lieth the Body of
WILLIAM WILLIAMS, of Petty France,
who died the 13th of January, 1767,
aged 67 Years.

Here lyeth the Body of ESTHER,
late Wife of MATTHEW SYMONDS,
of this Parifh, who departed
this Life the xvith Day of September,
in the xxviith Year of her Age,
Anno Dom. 1697.

HERE LYETH THE BODY OF
ELIZABETH, SECOND DAUGH-
TER OF MATTHEW SYMONDS,
OF THIS PARISH, GENT.
BEING A TWINN, WHO DE-
PARTED THIS LIFE THE 13TH
DAY OF MAY, ANNO
1696,
ÆTATIS SUÆ 3.

Here

Here lyeth the Body of ARTHUR
VENN, fen. who departed this
Life the 20th Day of April, Anno
Dom. 1715, ætatis 53.

Alfo MARY his Wife, who departed this Life the 5th Day of
. . . . 1726, ætatis 70.

In this Place was interred WILLIAM
VENN, Father to the faid ARTHUR
VENN, who departed this Life the
16th Day of May, An. Dom. 1682.

Beneath this Stone lyeth repofed
the Bodys of WILLIAM and ANN
VENN, Son and Daughter of ARTHUR
and MARTHA VENN. ANNE died the
17th of Jan. 1754, aged near 2 Years.

In Memory of . . . . Son of
Mr. ARTHUR and MARTHA VENN,
of Hillfley,
who departed this Life April 3, 1779,
in the 21ft Year of his Age.

In Memory
of EDWARD WEEKES,
jun. who departed this
Life the 5th Day of July, 1706,
aged 37 Years.

In Memory of MARTHA, the Daughter
of DANIEL BIDDLE, of Hillfley,
and MARY his Wife,
who was the Widow of the faid
EDWARD WEEKES,
who departed this Life July 17, 1729,
aged 7 Years.

In Memory of MARY, the Wife of
WILLIAM SYMONDS, formerly the
Wife of EDWARD WEEKES.
She died the 25th of December, 1761,
æt. 83 Years.

In Memory of EDWARD WEEKES,
of this Parifh, who died Aug. 24, 1768,
aged 66 Years.

Alfo of EDWARD his Son,
who died May the 26th, 1769,
aged 20 Years.

And likewife of
ELIZABETH, Wife of
Capt. JOHN PURNELL,
of the City of Briftol, and Daughter of
EDWARD and ELIZABETH WEEKES,
who died Dec. 26, 1768, aged 32 Years.

WILLIAM PURNELL their Son died in
his Infancy.

Alfo in Memory of the abovefaid
Capt. JOHN PURNELL,
who died the 31ft Day of March, 1791,
aged 60 Years.

HESTER, the Daughter of EDWARD
and ELIZABETH WEEKES before mentioned, died Dec. 27, 1771, in the
33d Year of her
Age.

Beneath
this Stone lies interred
the Body of MARY
BENCE, Spinfter, of this
Parifh, who departed
this Life the 12th Day of
June 1746, in the 80th
Year of her Age.

In Memory of
JOAN, the Wife of
SAMUEL HOLBOROW,
Daughter of
JOHN and ANN
BENCE, of this

Parifh, who de-
parted this Life
May the 18th, 1726,
in the 58th Year
of her Age.

Near this Place lies the Body of
JOHN BENCE, fen. of Upton,
who departed this Life the
20th Day of Feb. 1675, in the
61ft Year of his Age.

And alfo the Body of ANNE his Wife,
who departed this Life the 24th of
Auguft, 1715, aged 77 Years.

Alfo JOHN, the Son of JOHN BENCE,
who died the 5th of April, 1725,
aged 62 Years.

This Tomb is erected to preferve the
Memory of WILLIAM RODWAY,
of this Parifh,
who was buried December the 31ft, 1772,
aged 84 Years.

Alfo of MARTHA his Wife,
who died June 17, 1721, aged 33.

Alfo of WILLIAM their Son,
who died May 24, 1768, aged 47.

Alfo of ELIZABETH, Daughter of
WILLIAM RODWAY, by
DEBORAH his fecond Wife,
who died June 11, 1763, aged 26 Years.

In Memory of
WILLIAM, the Son of
EDWARD and HESTER RODWAY,
who died June 19, 1774,
aged 10 Months and 3 Weeks.

In Memory of DEBORAH,
the fecond Wife of
WILLIAM RODWAY,
who died October the 27th, 1779,
aged 75 Years.

In Memory of
WILLIAM WITCHELL, of Trefham,
who departed this Life the 2d of Dec.
1767, aged 82 Years.

In Memory of WILLIAM WITTS,
who departed this Life the 26th of Aug.
1763, aged 73 Years.

In Memory
of JOHN ALWAY,
of this Parifh, Yeoman,
who died the 5th Day of Auguft,
1681.

Likewife in Memory of
DANIEL ALWAY,
who died the 18th of April, 1772,
aged 74.

In Memory of WILLIAM ALWAY,
of this Parifh, Gent. who
departed this Life the 15th of
April, 1718, ætatis fuæ 60.

Alfo MARY, Wife of
WILLIAM ALWAY, of this Parifh, Gent.
who departed this Life the 22d Day
of Jan. 1740, ætatis fuæ 72.

Alfo near this Tomb
was interred the Body of
THOMAS ALWAY,
Son of DANIEL and HESTER
ALWAY,
of this Parifh, who died
the 4th Day of Jan. 1790,
aged 49 Years.

HESTER, Wife of DANIEL ALWAY,
died the 9th Day of March, 1791,
aged 89 Years.

In Memory of SAMUEL WALKER,
of this Parifh, Yeoman, who died
the 15th of April, 1755, aged 78.

Alfo JANE his Wife died
Nov. 6, 1757, aged 78.

Alfo two Sons of JOHN and SILVESTER
WALKER, both JOHNS, died Infants.

Beneath this Tomb lieth the
Body of JOHN WALKER, of this Place,
who died Sept. 3, 1768, aged 58.

In Memory of
DANIEL SHAKESPEAR, of Trefham,
Mafon, who died Auguft the 28th,
1770, aged 53 Years.

Alfo SARAH his Wife died the
6th of June, 1770, aged 58 Years.

Here
lieth the Body of MARY,
Wife of RICHARD WICKS,
of Kilcott.
She died Dec. 5, 1774,
aged 67 Years.

Alfo here lieth the Body of
RICHARD WICKS.
He died Dec. 26, 1783,
aged 68 Years.

Here lyeth the Body of Mr. JOHN
WAITE, late Citizen and Dyer of
London, who departed this Life
the 27th Day of January, Anno
1701-2, ætatis fuæ 49.

Here lyeth alfo the Body of
SARAH, the Daughter of
MATTHEW and ELIZABETH TAUNTON,
who departed this Life Jan. 31, 1701-2,
ætatis fuæ 17.

Here lyeth the Body of MARY,
the Wife of OWEN LARTON, late
of London, Silk Dyer, who
departed this Life the 12th Day
of Auguft, 1698,
ætatis fuæ 51.

Under this Tomb lieth alfo the
Body of WILLIAM LARTON,
of this Parifh, Clothier,
who was the third Son
of OWEN LARTON and MARY his Wife,
who departed this Life the XIV Day
of March, in the XXXIV Year of
his Age, Annoque Dom. 1709.

Here alfo lieth the
Body of JOHN LARTON,
eldeft Son of OWEN and
MARY LARTON, who departed
this Life the 20th of December, 1722,
aged 51.

Near this Stone
lieth the Body of
THOMAS HORWOOD, fen.
of this Parifh, Yeoman ;
and alfo ELIZABETH his Wife.
She died April 15, 1750, aged 72.
He died Nov. 21, 1752, aged 74.

In Memory of ANNE, the Wife
of THOMAS PARSONS, who died the
15th of July, 1763, aged 53.

In Memory of JOHN HORWOOD ;
and alfo of MARY his Wife.
He died Nov. 26, 1770, aged 57.
She died March 25, 1771, aged 59.

Here

Here lyeth the Body of
MARY FAIRFAX, Relict of
GEORGE FAIRFAX, late of
London, Gent. who departed this Life
the 10th of April, Anno Dom. 1712,
ætatis suæ 64.

Alfo the Body of GEORGE FAIRFAX,
of this Parifh, Gent.
who departed this Life the
21ft Day of Auguft, Anno Dom. 1735,
aged 42.

In Memory of MARY, the Wife of
THOMAS ESBURY, of Hillfley, Gent.
formerly the Wife of GEORGE FAIRFAX,
Gent. who died Jan. 30, 1755,
ætat. 52.

Here lyeth the Body of JOHN ROD-
MAN, who died the 12th Day
of July, 1678.

Alfo the Body of SARAH,
the Wife of this JOHN RODMAN, who
departed this Life the 29th Day of
July, Anno Dom. 1701.

Here lyeth alfo the Body of
JOHN RODMAN, Son of this
JOHN and SARAH RODMAN,
of Hillfley, Yeoman,
who departed this Life
Jan. 31, 1723,
ætatis fuæ 72.

Here lyeth the Body of JOHN STINCH-
COMBE, of this Parifh, Yeoman, who
departed this Life the laft Day of
December, Anno Dom. 1723,
ætat. fuæ 71.

Alfo in Memory of
MARTHA STINCHCOMBE, Widdow,
who was buried May the 22d,
in 1696.

Here lyeth the Body of
THOMAS STINCHCOMBE,
who departed this Life Dec. 14, 1737,
aged 64 Years.

HERE LYETH THE BODY OF
WILLIAM HANCOCKE,
LATE OF THIS PARISH,
FARMER, WHO WAS BURYED
THE 25 DAY OF MAY,
ANNO D'NI 1674.

HERE LYETH THE BODY OF
ANNE, THE WIFE OF
RICHARD HANCOCKE,
OF THIS PARISH, WHO
DIED THE 6 DAY OF
MARCH, 1755, AGED 83.

ALSO WILLIAM, SON OF
RICHARD AND ANNE HANCOCKE,
DIED 15 SEPT. 1737, AGED 50.

In Memory of
SHADRACH WEERRIT,
who departed this Life the 12th of
September 1767, aged 67 Years.

Alfo of HESTER his Wife,
who departed this Life 22 Sept.
1765, aged 72 Years.

And 4 of their Children which died
in their Infancy.

In Memory of
SHADRACH WEERRITT, Son of
SHADRACH and HESTER WEERITT,
who died May the 28th. 1781,
aged 45 Years.

Alfo of JOHN his Brother,
who died Oct. 7. 1781,
aged 54 Years.

In Memory of THOMAS ESBURY,
who died the 19th Day of Nov. 1703,
aged 49 Years.

Alfo of JOANE his Wife, who died
the 30th Day of Dec. 1744,
aged 84 Years.

In Memory of THOMAS ESBURY,
of Hilfley, in this Parifh, Gent.
who departed this Life the 25th of Dec.
1771, aged 79 Years.

In Memory
of MARY, Daughter of
THOMAS and HANNAH DAVIS,
of this Parifh, who died Jan. 11,
1777, aged 2 Years and 9 Months.

Near this Tomb
lieth the Body of
THOMAS HORWOOD,
who died Jan. 25, 1764,
aged 82 Years.

Alfo THOMAS, Son of
SAMUEL TROTMAN,
who died May 22, 1757, aged 32 Years.

In Memory of
BETTY, the Daughter of
FRANCIS and MARTHA HOWELL,
of the Parifh of Little Sodbury,
who died May the 8, 1763,
in the 17th Year of her Age.

Alfo in Memory of MARTHA,
Wife of the faid FRANCIS HOWELL,
who died Dec. 14, 1778,
aged 55 Years.

In Memory of
FRANCIS HOWELL,
late of Little Sodbury,
who was interred beneath
this Tomb,
the 26th Day of March, 1788,
in the 66th Year of his Age.

Here lyeth the Body of GEORGE
HEWES, of Kingfwood, fen.
who departed this Life
April 26, 1712, aged 77 Years.

Near this Tomb, at the
lower End, lyeth the Body of
DAVID HEWES, Son of this
GEORGE HEWES, fenior, who departed this Life the 25th Day
of February, 1720,
aged 29 Years.

Near this Tomb lyeth the
Body of MARTHA, Daughter
of this GEORGE HEWES, fen.
who departed this Life
the 15th of May, 1717,
aged 14 Years.

Here lyeth the Body of
SAMUEL HEWES, Son of the faid
GEORGE HEWES, of Kingfwood,
who departed this Life the 2d Day of
March, Anno Dom. 1711, aged 22 Years.

Here lyeth the Body of GEORGE,
the Son of GEORGE HEWES, of Kingfwood, who departed this Life the 8th
Day of April, 1707, aged 26.

Near
this Place lyeth

the Body of
MARY, the Wife of GEORGE HEWES,
of Kingfwood, fen. who departed this Life the 1ft Day
of June, Anno Dom. 1736,
in the 80th Year of her Age.

Here lyeth the Body of
MARY, Wife of WILLIAM COMPEER,
of the Parifh of Kingfwood, Yeoman,
who departed this Life
the 6th of Auguft, 1724,
aged 60 Years.

Here lyeth the Body of STEPHEN
COMPEER, fen. late of Trefham,
in this Parifh ; and of SARAH his Wife.
STEPHEN died April 6, A. D. 1689;
SARAH, Nov. 10, A. D. 1696;
had Iffue JOAN, MARY, ROBERT,
THOMAS, STEPHEN, and WILLIAM.

Near this Tomb lyeth the Body
of MARY, the Daughter of
WILLIAM and CHRISTIAN GOWEN,
of this Parifh, who departed
this Life the 4th Day of June,
Anno Dom. 1734, in the
2d Year of her Age.

Here lyeth the Body of PATIENCE,
the Wife of WILLIAM THOMPSON,
who died Nov. 5, 1780,
aged 36 Years.

Alfo ISAAC their Son, who died
March . . . . aged 19 Years.

Erected
in Memory of JAMES COMELEY,
late of this Parifh,
who died the 29th Day of March, 1779,
in the 49th Year of his Age.

Alfo of ELIZABETH, Wife of the
faid JAMES COMELEY abovementioned,
who died the 18th Day of Dec. 1790,
in the 67th Year of her Age.

Likewife of 4 Children by ELIZABETH
his Wife, who were ftill-born.

In
Memory of ANN,
the Wife of JOHN WHEELER,
who died Sept. 17, 1783,
aged 60 Years.

Here
lieth the Remains
of THOMAS HOLLIDAY,
who died Feb. 17, 1787,
aged 55 Years.

To the Memory of SUSANNA,
the Wife of HENRY ANDREWS,
who departed this Life
Dec. 24, 1776,
in the 27th Year of her Age.

Alfo two of their Children ;
HENRY died in his Infancy ;
THOMAS Jan. 7, 1783, aged
11 Years and 10 Months.

Underneath this Tomb lies
interred the Body of WILLIAM TURNER,
who departed this Life
May the 25th, 1790, aged 58 Years.

Alfo MARY his Daughter. She died
Aug. 25, 1783, aged 6 Months.

ON

O N   H E A D   S T O N E S.

Name	Died	Aged
William, Son of John and Ann Webb	19 Feb. 1777	15
Sarah, Wife of James Chappell	21 Feb. 1782	46
John, Son of John Robinfon	26 Feb. 1767	12
Samuel Chappell -	4 Dec. 1782	70
John Chappell -	16 Apr. 1768	32
Sarah Chappell -	3 Oct. 1773	66
Sarah, Wife of James Rodway	19 Sept. 1782	35
Ann their Daughter -	29 May, 1782	9
Mary Latham -	9 June, 1764	80
James Buck - -	3 Sept. 1777	67
Thomas Buck - -	5 Feb. 1780	44
Betty his Daughter -	3 Jan. 1780	6
Gerteres, Wife of Daniel Niblett	2 July, 1782	48
Ann their Daughter -		10
James Tomfon - -	15 July, 1769	50
James his Son -	22 Nov. 1785	26
Margaret, Relict of William Clark	27 Nov. 1769	76
Edward Clark - -	9 Sept. 1774	78
Jane his Wife, Daughter of Giles Jenkins - -	8 Oct. 1768	74
Sarah, Wife of Robert Pritchard, of Thornbury, Daughter of Edward Clark - -	11 Oct. 1790	55
Giles Jenkins - -	21 June, 1740	81
Giles Bick - -	21 Feb. 1743	45
Mary, Wife of Nathaniel Tandy	3 Aug. 1717	45
William Reeve - -	10 Feb. 1710	—
Richard Longden •	16 Sept. 1784	74
Hefter his Wife - -	19 Dec. 1785	75
Robert Collins - -	13 Feb. 1737	43
Sarah his Wife - -	22 Dec. 1755	54
Aaron Worluck - -	9 Aug. 1748	40
Sarah, Wife of Thomas Arthurs	— — 1736	52
Elizabeth, Wife of Robert Witts, Daughter of the above Thomas Arthurs - -	22 June. 1732	34
Thomas Ford - -	7 Feb. 1776	31
William Ford - -	12 Feb. 1776	76
Ann his Wife - -	30 Sept. 1784	74
William Sanfum -	1 Apr. 1743	—
Ann his Wife - -	8 Feb. 1747	37
William Rodway -	13 June, 1709	81
Giles Rodway - -	13 Aug. 1722	70
Martha Rodway -	17 June, 1727	33
Charles Rodway -	8 Jan. 1741	74
Giles Rodway - -	27 July, 1760	67
James Rodway -	8 Aug. 1761	57
Mary his Wife -	5 Jan. 1744	47
Ruth Davis - •	15 Apr. 1743	—
Sarah, Wife of John Davis	21 June, 1714	—
John Davis - -	2 Oct. 1748	70
Ann his Wife - -	18 Apr. 1754	70
Sarah, Daughter of William and Rofe Davis - -	17 Feb. 1791	15
John Witts - -	— Sept. 1740	80
John Witts - -	19 Mar. 1744	55
Ifabella, Wife of William Witts	1 Aug. 1752	51
Samuel Witts -	7 Oct. 1784	63
John Witts - -	29 Oct. 1789	72
Sufannah his Wife -	11 Apr. 1785	71
Nathanael Woodrough -	8 Dec. 1737	52
William Frape - -	1 Dec. 1785	64
William Afhbee -	14 Dec. 1726	33
Robert, Son of George and Mary Afhbee - -	29 Mar. 1773	13
Mary, Wife of Henry Afhbee	19 Jan. 1745	87
Robert Afhbee - -	19 Feb. 1765	78
Ann his Wife -	17 June, 1764	79

Name	Died	Aged
William Rouch -	8 Mar. 1698	70
Martha his Wife -	— Feb. 1722	89
William Rouch -	25 Mar. 1732	60
Robert Rouch - -	11 Oct. 1733	59
Martha his Daughter -	9 Jan. 1781	81
Ann Rouch - -	19 Jan. 1742	74
Edward Hall - -	10 July, 1705	37
Mary Stinchcomb, late Wife of E. Hall	10 Dec. 1758	86
Ifaac, Son of Thomas and Ann Afhbee - -	6 May, 1775	21
Martha, Wife of William Witchell	14 Oct. 1721	39
Mary, Wife of Jones Witchell	14 Nov. 1785	73
Thomas Andrews -	8 Feb. ——	—
Sarah his Wife -	24 Nov. 1763	68
William Savage -	23 Mar. 1782	62
William, Son of Daniel and Sarah Stinchcomb -	11 Apr. 1770	16
Samuel Cook -	2 Apr. 1756	74
Margaret his Wife -	20 Aug. 1757	86
Henry Box -	1 May, 1697	—
Rebekah, Wife of Daniel Frankcom	24 Feb. 1746	40
Nicholas Trotman -	11 Nov. 1765	79
Sarah his Wife -	1 July, 1774	67
Nicholas their Son -	17 Dec. 1780	45
Humphry Pinkcot -	7 July, 1745	80
Mary, Wife of Weekes Pincot	6 Apr. 1774	50
John Compeer -	8 Aug. 1743	43
Francis Camm, Gent. -	9 Oct. 1690	75
Daniel his Son -	3 Mar. 1723	75
Either, Wife of Samuel Stiff	17 Apr. 1710	75
Thomas Stiff - -	19 Dec. 1740	—
Matthew Stiff -	22 Aug 1763	85
Martha his Wife -	18 Apr. 1710	35
James Rouch •	26 Apr. 1748	74
Mary his Wife -	14 Oct. 1755	70
Daniel their Son -	2 Nov. 1781	51
Ann their Daughter -	11 Aug. 1740	23
Chriftian, Wife of William Gowen	11 Mar. 1751	48
Stephen Eftmat -	10 July, 1748	74
Robert, Son of Robert Bruton	5 Feb. 1735	15
Betty, Daughter of Nicholas and Betty Stinchcomb, of Badminton	28 Oct. 1786	36
Richard Whittern -	3 Nov. 1767	56
Sufannah his Wife •	2 July, 1790	83
Thomas Jobbins -	12 Nov. 1679	72
Joan his Wife -	24 Aug. 1701	—
Nathanael, Son of Henry Horwood	27 June, 1708	18
Martha, Wife of William Coles	8 Feb. 1743	80
John May -	1 Jan. 1731	83
Either his Wife -	25 Dec. 1747	80
Giles Allen -	1 Mar. 1741	67
Giles, Son of Giles and Sarah Allen	20 Apr. 1779	28
Mary, Daughter of John and Elizabeth Wicks -	8 July, 1751	26
Sarah their Daughter -	19 July, 1750	24
Mary, Wife of Jofeph Cooper	1 Mar. 1753	64
Sarah, Daughter of William and Hefter Cooper -	20 Aug. 1770	11
Mary, Daughter of Jofeph and Elizabeth Cooper -	22 Feb. 1775	21
Sarah, Wife of Arthur Pritchett	23 Mar. 1744	42
William Baily -	4 Nov. 1731	75
John Baily - -	15 May, 1748	55
Samuel, Son of Samuel and Elizabeth Mills -	15 Apr. 1736	—
Ann, Wife of Giles Trotman	6 July, 1753	81

CXXXIX.   H A W L I N G

IS a Parifh in the *Cotefwold*, fituate in the Lower Divifion of the Hundred of *Kiftefgate*, fix Miles North-weft from *Northleach*, five in the oppofite Direction from *Winchcombe*, and feventeen North-eaft from the City of GLOUCESTER. The Terrier includes about 3,000 Acres, of a Soil varying from Stone Brafh to Loam or Clay, one Third only of which are Pafture, with 100 Acres of Woodland. The Common Fields, containing 977 Acres, were inclofed by Act of Parliament in 1756.

The Living is a Rectory, in the Deanery of *Winchcombe*; the Advowfon of which is annexed to the Manor. Nothing worthy the Attention of an Antiquary remains in the Church, which is dedicated to *St. Edward the Martyr*. It has a Nave only, with a low embattled Tower in the Middle, and has undergone frequent Repairs.

Domefday ftates the Manor (which appears to have at all Times included the whole Property of the Parifh) as belonging to SIGAR DE CIOCHES, a *Norman* Knight. The *Benedictine* Abbey of *Winchcombe* obtained it, with the Manor of *Hafelton* as the Donation of ROBERT GYVES, in the Reign of King JOHN. It was confirmed to them in the fubfequent Centuries by various Charters *. At the Suppreffion it was granted to WILLIAM WHORWOOD, Efq. Attorney General, and defcended to the fame Proprietors as the Manor of *Guiting Poher*, already defcribed +, till the Demife of RICHARD STRATFORD, Efq. in 1692. It then paffed to his Sifter and Coheir the Wife of WILLIAM WYNDHAM, Efq. a younger Son of Sir WADHAM WYNDHAM, Knight, Juftice of the King's Bench, who was the feventh Son of JOHN WYNDHAM, Efq. of *Orchard*, co. *Somerfet*, and has continued in that Family. The ancient Manor Houfe was long the Refidence of the STRATFORDS, and appears to have been erected in the Reign of Queen ELIZABETH.

R O W E L L

Has been confidered as extra-parochial, maintaining its own Poor, but is ufually connected with this Parifh. It is recited in *Domefday* as containing ten Hides; and that the King took it from WOLNARD, the *Saxon* Poffeffor, and beftowed it upon the Church of *St. Ebrulph*, at *Utica* in *Normandy*, and that it paid a yearly Rent of 20*l.* ‡ It was purchafed by RICHARD YDEBURY, Abbot of *Winchcombe*, in 1319, 12 EDW. II. of the Abbot of *St. Ebrulph*, for the Sum of 550*l.* and annexed to his Convent §. Sir RALPH SADLIER obtained it at the Diffolution, and the Manor and Impropriation confirmed to him, who appears foon to have difpofed of it, for Livery was granted to BRYAN CARTER and MARY his Wife in the 1ft Year of Queen ELIZABETH's Reign. It was purchafed by the Barons CHANDOS of *Sudley* by GEORGE TOWNSEND, Efq. who died in 1693, and of his Executors by CHRISTOPHER MONTAGUE, Efq. Brother of the firft Earl of HALIFAX, and now belongs to that Family ||. The Chapel has long been demolifhed, and 1*l.* 10*s.* yearly are paid to the Rector of *Hawling* in Lieu of Tythes.

No Benefactions to the Poor.

INCUMBENTS.	PATRONS.	INCUMBENTS.	PATRONS.
—— Thomas Stock,	William Bafkerville, by Grant from the Abbey of Winchcombe, dated 1538.	1676 Charlton Barkfdale,	King Charles II.
		1702 GerardClements,B.A.	Wm. Wyndham, Efq.
		1722 William Barford,	Wm. Wyndham, Efq.
		—— John Fry,	The fame.
1544 William Cobley,	————.	1730 John Baynes, M. A.	The fame.
1581 Philip Scriven,	William Hobbs, Efq.	1752 John Hughes, M. A.	Wm. Wyndham, Efq.
1584 Charles Hurft,	————.	1765 John Lawrence, Clerk,	The fame.
1606 Nath. Hurft,	Henry Stratford, Efq.	1768 John Wyndham, Clerk,	The fame.
* * * * * * *	* * * * * * *	1772 John Lawrence, Clerk,	The fame.

* Cart. Antiqua, fcil' JOANNIS Regis, confirmans Donationes GULIELMI ATREBATENSIS, de *Halynge*, *Hafylton*, &c. Ex Vitâ ROBERTI quarti *Winchelcumbenfis* cænobii Abbatis. "Quod Dominia de *Yanworthe*, *Hafylton*, & *Halynge*, cum advocatione Ec-" clefiarum amplius quam quingentis quinquaginta & octo libris nobis primo adquifivit."
DUGDALE, Mon. Addit. in primum vol. p. 856.

+ See vol. I. of this Work, No. CXXVII.

‡ "In *Holeford* Hund'. Eccl'a *S. Ebrulfi* ten' de Rege RAWELLE WLUUARD tenuit T. R. E. Ibi x Hide. In d'nio funt " IIII car', & XVI vill'i, & II bord', cum VI car'. Ibi III fervi. Val' & valuit x lib' hoc M, nunq' geldavit." Domefday. " De dominio meo dono in *Gloucefterfcirâ* villam quæ *Ravella*, id eft capreæ fons dicitur." Cart. GULIELM. Conqueft. pro Abb. S'eti *Ebrulphi* apud *Uticam*. DUGDALE, Mon. vol II. p. 966.

§ "Idem RICARDUS, cum manerium de *Rowell*, quod eft contiguum maneriis fuis de *Hawling Cotyfdene*, & bofco fuo de " *Winchelcumba* immediatè, venale fuiffet; idem Abbas cepit dictum manerium ad feodi firmam, pro quo folvit, cum fuis perti-" nentiis quingentas & quinquaginta libras." DUGDALE, Mon. Addit. in primum vol. p. 857.

‡ COLLINS's Peerage, vol. V. p. 3.

PRESENT

6

PRESENT PROPRIETORS OF THE MANORS,

Of *Hawling,*
WILLIAM WYNDHAM (*a Minor*).

Of *Rowell,*
———— MONTAGUE, Efq.

The Perfons fummoned from this Parifh by the Heralds in 1682 and 1683 were Henry Stratford, Efq. and George Townfend, Efq. of *Rowell.*

At the Election in 1776, Three Freeholders polled from this Parifh.

The Regifter commences with the Date 1677.

ANNUAL ACCOUNT OF MARRIAGES, BIRTHS, AND BURIALS, IN THIS PARISH.

A.D.	Mar.	Bir.	Bur.	A.D.	Mar.	Bir.	Bur.	A.D.	Mar.	Bir.	Bur.	A.D.	Mar.	Bir.	Bur.
1781	1	4	7	1786	2	6	3	1791	5	6	5	1796			
1782	—	5	2	1787	—	5	5	1792				1797			
1783	2	3	1	1788	4	7	2	1793				1798			
1784	1	8	3	1789	1	12	3	1794				1799			
1785	2	2	3	1790	1	10	5	1795				1800			

INSCRIPTIONS IN THE CHURCH.

IN THE CHANCEL.

ON FLAT STONES.

THE FIVE FOLLOWING ARE ON BRASS PLATES:

HERE LYETH THE BODY OF HENRY STRATFORD, ESQUIRE, LORD OF THE MANOUR OF HAWLINGE AND GUYTING, WHO DEPARTED THIS LIFE SEPT. .. 1649.

Arms; in a Lozenge, barry of 10 Argent and Azure, over all a Lion rampant Gules for STRATFORD.

HERE LYETH THE BODY OF MARGARET, THE WIFE OF HENRY STRATFORD, OF HAW-LINGE, GENT. WHO DECEASSED 7 JUNE, 1665.

Arms; STRATFORD, as before.

HERE LIETH THE BODY OF HENRY STRATFORD, ELDEST SON OF HENRY STRATFORD, OF HAW-LINGE, GENT. WHO DIED 20 OCT. 1671.

HERE LYETH THE BODY OF ANN STRATFORD, DAUGHTER OF GEORGE STRATFORD, OF FARMCOATE, ESQUIRE, AND WIFE TO HENRY STRATFORD, OF HAWLING AND GUYTINGE, WHO DEPARTED THIS LIFE NOV. 23, 1671.

HERE LIETH THE BODY OF ANNE STRATFORD, DAUGHTER OF HENRY STRATFORD, OF HAWLINGE, ESQUIRE, WHO DEPARTED THIS LIFE 30 NOV. 1667.

HERE LYES THE BODY OF HENRY STRATFORD, ESQ. LORD OF THE MANNOVRS OF HAWLING AND GUYTING, WHO DEPARTED THIS LIFE

ANNO { ÆTATIS 30. DOM. 1672.

HERE LIETH THE BODY OF ALICE STRATFORD, SECOND DAUGHTER OF HENRY STRATFORD, GENT. AND ANN HIS WIFE, WHO DEPARTED THIS LIFE ON THE ELEVENTH DAY OF DECEMBER, ANNO DOM. 1699.

Arms; STRATFORD, as before.

M. S.
RICHARDI STRATFORD, ARMIGERI, DE HAWLING ET GUYTING, TOPARCHÆ JUVENIS MORIBUS SUAVISSIMIS OMNIBUSQ. DOTIBUS ET ANIMI ET CORPORIS SUPRA COÆVOS SUOS, ILLUSTRIS. QUI 4 ANNIS IN ACADEMIA OXON. FELICTER POSITUS

SPEM VIRI EGREGII OMNIBUS FECIT NEC FEFELLISET NISI ILLUM FEBRIS VOTA DEO, ECCLESIÆ, PATRICE NONCUPATA REDDITURUM PRÆRIPUISSET

ANNO { ÆTATIS 22. DOM. 1692.

Arms; Or, a Fefs between three Wolves' Heads couped Sable, for HOWE; on an Efcocheon of pretence, STRATFORD, as before, and in Chief the Arms of Ulfter; impaling, STRATFORD, as before.

Here lieth the Body of Dame ELIZABETH HOWE, Wife of Sir JAMES Howe, of Berwick St. Leonard's, Bart. in the County of Wilts, Daughter and Coheir of HENRY STRATFORD, of Hawling, Efq. by ELIZABETH his Wife, Daughter of WILLIAM BANNASTER, of Turkdean, Efq. in the County of Gloucefter, who, after a fhort Race well run, pioufly refigned up her Soul to GOD, January 21,

In the Year of { her Age 35. our Lord 1702.

IN MEMORY OF THE REVEREND JOHN BAYNES, RECTOR OF THIS CHURCH, WHO DIED DEC. THE 3, 1751, AGED 45.

I N

IN THE CHURCH YARD, ON TOMBS.

GEORGE TOWNSEND, of Rowell, Gent.
was buried July 24, 1693, aged 57 Years.

RICHARD and MARY his beloved Son
and Daughter are buried here by him.
MARY, Feb. 21, 1687, aged 21 Dayes.
RICHARD, Sept. 7, 1689, æt. 9 Years.

GEORGE, Son of GEORGE TOWNSEND,
buried Sept. 4, 1701, aged 17 Years.

———

THOMAS TOWNSEND, Gent.
of the Wadfield, in the Mannor of
Sudeley,
departed this Life the 31ft of May, 1719,·
aged 33 Years.

———

ANN, Wife of ISAAC BAYLIS, of Pinnock,
and Daughter of WILLIAM and
MARY COOK,
of this Parifh, died Aug. 21, 1765,
aged 42 Years.

ISAAC BAYLIS (of Pinnock)
died June 25, 1777, aged 55 Years.

MARY, HANNAH, ROBERT, and REBECCA,
4 of their Children, died in their Infancy.

ON HEAD AND FLAT STONES.

	Died	Aged
Margaret, Reliĉt of Leonard Price, and after Wife to Richard Falconer	23 Apr. 1764	82
Benjamin, Son of Benjamin and Mary Prefton - -	9 Feb. 1771	30
Mary, Wife of Benjamin Prefton, of Sevenhampton -	5 June, 1780	66
Richard Parrett, of Charlton King's	4 Apr. 1718	39
Jane, Daughter of Thomas and Mary Woollam - -	20 Oĉt. 1778	21
Thomas Woollam, of Comney in Wilfhire, but late of Hawling	24 Dec. 1785	69
Jane his Daughter -	29 Nov. 1781	—
Edward his Son -	10 Sept. 1783	—
Jane his Daughter -	8 Sept. 1785	—
Margaret, Daughter of Nathaniel and Ann Cook -	1 Apr. 1758	2
Edward Ruck -	25 May, 1760	72
Edward his Son -	29 Sept 1725	2
John his Son - -	14 July, 1726	—
Ann his Wife -	20 Mar 1762	74
Emmit their Daughter -	24 Apr. 1726	6
Edward their Son -	22 Feb. 1712	—
Thomas their Son -	14 Mar. 1713	—
Richard their Son -	28 Apr. 1714	—
Richard Ruck -	24 Dec. 1768	46
Thomas Ruck, of the Weftfield	22 Mar. 1782	66
Nathaniel Cook, Cordwainer	4 Jan. 1775	54
Nathaniel Cook Skinner, Son of William and Margaret Skinner	26 July, 1786	1
John Harris - -	—— —— 1683	—
Ann, Daughter of Harry and Ann Baylis - -	14 Feb. 1772	5
Emmit, Wife of Thomas Collett	13 July, 1729	71
Thomas Collett, Collar-maker	27 Aug. 1732	75
John Cook - -	12 May, 1780	50
Catharine, Reliĉt of James Akerman, after Wife of John Collett, of Naunton - -	21 May, 1755	88
Betty, Wife of Richard Cook	23 Mar. 1765	36
Jane, Wife of Thomas Maflen	22 July, 1770	64
William Cook -	4 Mar. 1714	68
Sarah his Daughter -	17 May, ——	—
Thomas Humphris, of Rowell	3 May, 1727	77
Mary, Wife of Thomas Newman	14 Feb. 1763	74
Ann, Wife of William Newman	16 Oĉt. 1784	58
Mary, Wife of John Ruck, late of Aylworth, and Daughter of William and Mary Cook -	3 July, 1787	38
William Cook -	6 Feb. 1780	60
Mary, Wife of William Cook	6 Oĉt. 1753 O.S	65
Thomas, Son of Thos. and Ann Crofs	28 July, 1720	—
Sarah their Daughter -	2 Aug. 1722	—
Mary their Daughter -	8 Aug. 1725	—
Ann their Daughter -	28 June, 1726	—
William their Son -	24 Nov. 1725	—
Thomas, Son of William and Mary Cook - -	1 May, 1750	—
John their Son -	26 Oĉt. 1722	1
William Cook -	12 Sep. 1753 O.s	66
John Clapon - -	8 Apr. 1753	68
Mary his Wife -	24 Dec. 1748	57
Thomas Green -	28 July, 1771	65
Mary, Daughter of John and Elizabeth Green - -	23 Oĉt. 1775	—
Richard, Son of John Clapon and Mary his Wife -	10 Sept. 1726	—
Hannah their Daughter -	10 Dec. 17.9	—
John, Son of John and Mary Maflen	11 Aug. 1771	—
John Perry, of Dinton, Wilts, but late of Hawling Lodge -	5 Mar. 1780	73
Elizabeth his Wife -	29 Nov. 1781	76
John Maflen - -	23 Feb. 1774	38
Mary, Wife of John Maflen, Baker	1 Oĉt. 1777	58
Guy Hamblett -	11 Jan. 1785	74
Mary, Daughter of John and Betty Fletcher - -	26 Sept. 1778	25
Mary, Daughter of Aaron and Elizabeth Marchant -	10 Aug. 1778	2
Martha, Wife of Robert Mifflin	15 Nov. 1776	41
John, Son of John and Hannah Gardiner - -	20 Nov. 1762	—
William Prim - -	21 Feb. 1717	28
Jof. Marchant - -	26 Jan. 1734	40
Thomas Keeble -	18 July, 1762	60
Robert Keeble - -	28 June, 1758	66
Jofeph Halford -	10 Feb. 1773	30
Mary his Wife -	27 Oĉt. 1779	47
William Carpenter -	6 July, 1754	75
Dorothy his Wife -	25 Jan. 1771	80
Mary their Daughter -	20 Sept. 1724	1

CXL. HAYLES

IS a Parifh fitutate in the lower Divifion of the Hundred of *Kiftefgate*, beneath the *Cotefwold* Hills, more than two Miles diftant from *Winchcombe* on the North-eaft, ten Eaftward from *Tewkefbury*, and feventeen North-eaft from GLOUCESTER. It is interfected by a Rivulet which joins the *Avon* at *Evefham*. The Soil is chiefly of ftrong fertile Clay, and applied to Pafture, with a large Tract of Woodland; the whole containing 1364 Acres.

The Living is a Curacy, ftipendiary from the Impropriation, annexed in 1738, by Confent of the Patron and Diocefan, to the Vicarage of *Didbroke*, and in the Deanery of *Campden*. GODFREY GIFFARD, Bifhop of *Worcefter*, by Deed, dated at *Henbury*, Oct. 10, 1270, compelled the newly-erected Convent of *Hayles* to allow ten Marks yearly to the Chaplain *. The rectorial Tythes were granted in 1576, 18 ELIZ. to JOHN DUDLEY and JOHN AYSCOUGH, and are now held with the Manor.

The Church was conftructed from the Ruins of the conventual Chapel before the Year 1603 by WILLIAM HOBBY, Efq. It is very fmall, and retains nothing worthy Notice.

WILLIAM LUERIE, a *Norman* Knight, received this Manor from the CONQUEROR, and is ftated in *Domefday* to hold Eleven Hides, &c. at " *Heile* †." Parts of it are faid to have been given to the Abbey of *St. Ebrulph*, at *Utica* in *Normandy* ‡. After various Poffeffors, it came in 1226 to tne Crown, and was given by King HENRY the Third to his Brother RICHARD PLANTAGENET, Earl of *Cornwall*, King of *Almaine* and the *Romans*, for the Purpofe of founding a Convent for Monks of the *Ciftertian* Order. This Inftitution was completed in 1246, in purfuance of a Vow which he had made when endangered by a Tempeft in the *Englifh* Channel returning from *Gafcony* §. He removed twenty Monks from the *Ciftertian* Abbey of *Beaulieu*, in the *New Foreft* in *Hampfhire*, which had been eftablifhed by his Father, and conftituted one of them their Abbot. He is faid to have informed MATTHEW PARIS, the Hiftorian, that he had expended 10,000 Marks in various Edifices for their Reception §. On the 9th of November, 1251, the Dedication of the Abbey of *Hayles* to *St. Mary* and *All Saints*, was folemnized with unufual Magnificence and Splendour. At this memorable Solemnity were prefent King HENRY the Third and his Queen, thirteen Bifhops and Abbots, many of the Nobility, and a Retinue of 300 Knights, who were moft fumptuoufly entertained. The Church, Cloifters, and Refectory, were then finifhed, and formed a very beautiful Structure, in the beft Style of Architecture of that Age ‖. In 1271, the greater Part of the Monaftery was deftroyed by Fire, but repaired by the Founder at the Expence of 8,000

---

* Regift. *Vigorn*. De ordinatione Vicariæ de *Hayles* 1270.

† In *Greteftan* Hund. Itd' W' ten' *Heile*, *Ofgot* tenuit T. R. E. Ibi xi hide. In d'nio funt iii car' & viiii vill'i & xi bord' cum viii car'. Ibi erant xii fervi quos Will'us liberos fecit. Ibi molin de x folid'. Silva una leuua l'g & dimid' lat'. Valuit xii lib' modo viii lib'.

‡ DUGDALE, Mon. vol. II. Cænobia Gall. p. 966.

§ " Prout in mari voverat, quando a *Gafconiá* rediens, in mari fuborta tempeftate, periclitabatur, vix portum attingens in " Cornubiâ." MATT. PARIS, 1251. Ex ore fundatoris.

HOLINSHED's Chron. pp. 627.—" The faid Earle of *Cornewall*, togyther wyth the Earles of *Pembrooke* and *Hereforde*, and " dyvers other Noblemen tooke the Sea; and after manye Daungers efcaped in theyr Courfe; at lengthe, on Sainéte *Lucie's* " Daye, they arrived in *Cornewall* , though fome of the Veffels that were in the Companye were dryven, by force of the tem- " peftuous Weather, uppon other contrarye Coaftes." Idem, p. 704. KENNET's Paroch. Antiq. p. 239.

‖ " The Abbey of *Hailes* was dedicated, which was founded by RICHARD Earl of CORNEWALL; the Building whereof had " coft him 10,000 Marks. At this Dedication was kept a folemn Feaft, at the which was prefent, the King, the Queene, and " almoft all the Nobility of *England* fpirituall and Temporall." STOWE's Chron. p. 189.

WHARTON's Anglia Sacra, p. 492.

" Anno millefimo ducentifimo quinquagefimo primo, nono Novembris, vigiliâ Sancti LEONARDI Comes RICARDUS folemniter " & magnificè nimis fecit dedicari ecclefiam de *Hales*, quam magnis fundaverat fumptibus & ædificia conftruxerat, prout in mari " voverat quando à *Gafconia* rediens in mari fuborta tempeftate pereclitabatur, vix portum attingens in Cornubiâ. Erant autem " immemoratâ dedicatione præfentes, dominus Rex & Regina & ferè omnes *Angliæ* magnates & prælati. Epifcopi vero tredecim, " qui omnes miffam die dedicationis celebrarunt, quilibet vero ad fuum altare *Lincolnienfifque* ad majus altare miffam folem- " niter valde decantavit. Erat autem dies dominica in qua fplendidè & ordinatè cum epifcopis & aliis carne vefcentibus coëpu- " labantur. Religiofi vero pifcium multitudine & varietate reficiebantur feorfum collocati. Erantque ibidem milites plufquàm " trecenti. Iftius nempè fefti folemnis & convivii magnitudinem ad plenum fidefcriberem, limites tranfgredi dicerer veritatis : mihi " autem MATHEO PARIENSI fuper hoc edoceri, cupienti, ne falfa huic libro infererem fub indubitata certitudine. Comes fignifi- " cavit quod omnibus fumptibus computatis in ipfius ecclefiæ conftructione decem millia marcarum expofuerat, addens quoddam " verbum memorabile immo & commendabile unitam Deo complaceret ut omniaque in caftro de *Walingoford* expenditam fa- " pienter & tam falubriter expendiffem." MAT. PARIS, Hift. Angl. p. 827. n. 40. DUGDALE, Mon. vol. I. p. 928.

" Anno Domini millefimo ducentefimo quinquagefimo primo, confummata eft ecclefia de *Hales*, cum dormitorio, clauftro & " refectorio, expenfis in operationibus octo marcarum millibus." LELAND, Itin. vol. V. p. 5.

VOL. II.   R   Marks,

Marks, who, dying in the next Year, was buried near the high Altar *. Senchia his Queen had been interred there in 1261, as was Edmund Earl of *Cornwall* their Son in 1300 †. The firſt Abbot that appears to have been ſummoned to Parliament was Walter de Flagge in 1307, 1 Edw. I. at the great Council of the Nation held at *Carliſle* ‡. At what Period the Mitre and Pontificals were conceded to them we have not been able to aſcertain.

SUCCESSION OF ABBOTS.

1298	John.	1420	William Henley.
1305	John de Glouceſter.	——	—— Landrake.
1306	Walter de Flagge.	1464	William Whitchurch ‖.
1314	Bartholomew.	1479	Richard Wootton.
1332	John.	1483	John Combecke.
1380	Robert §.	1503	Thomas Stafford.
1402	John.	1526	—— Whally.
——	Robert.	1530	Stephen Sagar **.

The Poſſeſſions of this Abbey were valued at the Surrender at 357*l.* 7*s.* 8*d.* †† annual Rent, and their Jewels and Furniture were extremely valuable, ariſing chiefly from the Oblations and Altarages, which were made when they exhibited a Veſſel which was ſuppoſed to contain the Blood of Christ. This Relique was to them, in thoſe Days of Credulity, an exhauſtleſs Source of Wealth ‡‡.

The

** " Such the Deide the olde Quene biȝonde the Se withoute faile
    That our Kinge's moder Henri was and the Earl of Cornewaile
    Hir Sone bi gan to aere the Abbeie of Hailis
    As in ȝer of Grace tuelf hundred & ſix & fourti ubis."

" The Quene Sſenche deide ſuth the of Alemalne purs
    At Berchamſtede in Novembre ; & ibured was & is
    In the quer of Hailes on hey in a vair Place
    Twelf hundred and on & ſexti as in ȝer of Grace."

Rob. of *Glouc.* f. 1496.

Idem, p. 534.

Wharton's Anglia Sac. p. 498.
† Stowe' Chronicle, p. 208.
‡ Idem, p. 211.
§ Buried at *Dowdeſwell.* See vol. I. p. 484, No. XCVIII.
‖ Buried at *Didbroke.* See vol. I. p. 475, No. XCIV.
** " To Stephen Sagar, laſt Abbot ther, a Penſion of 100*l.* a Yeare, and alſo to have of the Kyng's Majeſtie the ca-
" pital Meſſuage or Manſion Houſe callyd *Coſtcombe*, alias *Coſton*, within the Pariſh of *Didbroke*, with the Stable ther, and oon
" Cloſe nere onto adjoining ; and the firſte Veſture of oon lityl Mede adjoyning to a Grove callyd *Coſton Grove*, with the lytyl
" Garden ; and the Courte there duringe the natural Lyffe of the ſaid Stephen, until the ſaid Stephen be promoted by the
" Kynge's Majeſtie to ſome Benefice of the Summ aboveſeid ; and further to have forty Lodes of Fyre Wode and Houſebote
" owt of the Woodes callyd *Hayles Wode*, &c." Penſions.
" To John Dawson, B. D. Prior, and Philip Brode, 8*l.* each. Richard Eddon, B. D. and Roger Rede, B. D. 7*l.*
" each. John Sylvester, Kitchener, Thomas Farr, Celerar, 6*l.* 6*s.* 8*d.* each. William Choo, ſenior, and John Gryf-
" fyth, 6*l.* each. Thomas Hopkyns, J. Richard Dawnser, ſub Prior, 5*l.* 6*s.* 8*d.* Reginald Lane, Adam Tyler,
" William Netherton, Richard Woodward, William Halyday, and Thomas Rede, 100 Shillings each. Elias
" Dugdel, John Hatt, and Christopher Hodgeson, 53 Shillings and 4 Pence each. John Holme 40 Shillings.
" Richard Dene, 26*s.* and 8*d.*" Willis's Hiſtory of Abbies.
* Vide in Bibl. Bodl. *Oxon.* MS. Dodsworth, vol. XXIV. f. 8. cartam 10 Edw. II. pro abbate & conventu de *Hailes*, f.
35. cartam 2 Ed. III. pro eiſdem. Cartas rentalia rotulos curiarum & alia munimenta ad hanc abbatiam ſpectantia penes præ-
honorabilem Gulielm. dom. Tracy. Cart. antiq. Hen. III. H. n. 13. Clauſ. 6 Hen. III. m. 17. Cart. 17 Hen. III. m.
3. Plac. apud *Weſtm.* 27 Hen. III. n. 12. 13. Cart. 29 Hen. III. m. 2. Cart. 33 Hen. III. m. 2. Cart. 35 Hen. III. m. 6.
Pat. 37 Hen. III. m. 15. de terris in *Pynoke.* Cart. 6 Edw. I. n. 7. pro ecclef. de *Hemelhempſted*, com. *Hert.* Pat. 22 Edw. II.
pro licentia kernellandi. Cart. 29 Edw. I. n. 42. pro manerio de *Lechlade*, in feod. firm. pro c marcis. Pat. b. 2 Edw. II. m. 6
& 8. de terris in *Netherſwelle.* Id. m. 22. pro advocatione hoſpitalis & vicariæ de *Lechlade.* Pat. 12 Edw. II. de manerio de
Sodyntune. Pat. 39 Edw. III. m. 26. pro ecclef. de *Todynton* appropriandâ. Pat. 11 Ric. II. m. 26. pro ecclef. de *Todington*,
cum capellâ de *Stanley Pont Larch.* Clauſ. 11 Hen. IV. m. 17. Pat. 1 Hen. V. p. 4. m. 13. pro terris in *Pynokeſhire.* Pat.
6 Edw. IV. p. 2. m. 23. Recept. in ſcacc. 9 Hen. VIII. pro manerio de *Redborne*, com. *Wilts*, &c.
†† Ad cænobium de *Hayles* ſpectat fragmentum quoddam antiquum in Collectaneis meis adſervatum è quibus hic loci ſubjicere
operæ pretium duxi. " The Yere of our Lorde MCCLXX, Edmond the nobyll Earle of Cornuale brought a Porcyon of
" precyous Blode of Cryste Jhesu that he ſhedde for Mankynde upon the Croſſe, un to the Abbey of *Haylis* upon Holyrode
" Day in Hervifte, where God daylie ſhewithe Miracles throwe the virtue of that precyous Blode. And therefore Pope John
" XXIIIIth hath grauntede for evermore to the Abbat of that Monaſterii of *Haylys* power to ſyne 2 Confeſſors, the whiche
" may here Confeſſion of all Pylgrymes, and aſoyle them of all Synnes, excepte the Poyntes that bethe reſervede to the Pope's
" own Perſon. Alſo the ſeyde Pope John hath grauntede to all Bretherne and Syſterne of the Chapter Houſe of the ſeyd
" Monaſterii, power to chele hem a Confeſſor, the whiche may confeſſe and aſoyle them in the Poynt of Dethe of all Synnes,
" none excepte. Alſo Pope Eugeni IVth hathe grauntede to the Abbot of the ſeyde Monaſterii power to ſyne 7 Confeſſors at
" the Feſte of Corpus Chriſti, the whiche may aſoyle all Pylgrems of all here Synnes. Moreover, the ſeyde Pope Eugeni
" hathe graunted 7 Yere and 3 Lentes to all thoo that gevythe any Thinge to the Worſhip of God, and that precyous Blode
" and other Relykis that bethe in that Place. Alſo Pope Calixt the IIIde hath grauntede full Remiſſion at the Feſte of Corpus
" Chriſti, and at the principall Feites in the Yere, that ys to ſey, at Holyroday in May, and Holyroday in Hervefte, at yche
" of thes Feſtys, with 4 Days followynge ; and alſo the 3d Weke in Lent, and iche of thes 4 full Remiſſion of all Synnes.
" Alſo 15 Cardynals hathe grauntede yche be hemſelfe 100 Dayes of Pardon to all hem that honoure that precious Blode, and
" other Reliquies whiche be in that forſayde Place, and put to ther helpynge Hondes to the Welfare of that forſayde Monaſ-
" terii of *Haylis*." Leland's Collectanea, vol. VI. p. 291.
" The fourthe Nones of Aprill, as ſome have, or in the Moneth of Februarie, as others write, in the 56 Yere of King
" Henrie's Reign, at *Berkhampſted*, died Richard King of *Almayne* and Erle of *Cornwal*, and was buried in the Abbey of
" *Hailes*, which he himſelf had founded. He was a worthye Prince, and ſtood his Brother King Henry in great Stead in
" handling Matters both in Peace and Warre. He left behind him Iſſue begot of his Wife Sanctia two Sons Edmunde and
" Henry. This Edmunde was he that brought the Blood of *Hayles* out of *Germanie*, for as he was there uppon a Time
" with his Father, it chaunced that as he was beholding the Reliques, and other precious Monuments of the auncient Empe-
" rors,

The Convent appears to have been, when originally founded, of quadrangular Conſtruction, with a Cloiſter, incloſing an Area about 40 Yards ſquare. The ruined Arches are ſtill to be traced, chiefly Lancet, with Trefoils in the Heads. The Abbot's Lodgings at the South-weſt Angle, now nearly deſtroyed, were re-built but a few Years prior to the Diſſolution. An embattled ſquare Building, more lofty than the other Parts, contained the chief Room, with large Bay Windows. In theſe were Arms in ſtained Glaſs, which are now removed to *Toddington*, the Seat of Lord Viſcount TRACY : 1. Or, an Eagle diſplayed Sable ; Legend, " 𝔯icardus 𝔭lantagenet ſemper 𝔞guſtus 𝔣undator noſter." 2. *England*, the Eſcocheon upon a Croſier. 3. Gules, fretty Argent, impaling, Argent, a Lion rampant Sable ; Sir JOHN HUDDLESTONE. 4. Quarterly, *France* and *England*, enſigned with the Crown ; on each Side 𝔥. 𝔨. HENRY VIII. and KATHERINE PARRE ; Motto, " 𝔥oni ſoit," &c. 5. *France* and *England* ; with a Label Argent ; on either Side 𝔢. 𝔭. * Likewiſe a Chimney Piece of carved Stone with Arms, quarterly, 1ſt, a Feſs between three Hawks ; HOBBEY ; 2d, three Battle Axes ; 3d, three Lozenges conjoined in Feſs ; 4th, HOBBEY, impaling, 1. an Eagle diſplayed ; 2. a Lion rampant ; 3. a Pomegranate ; 4. a Lion regardant ; 5. a Chevron between three Boars' Heads couped ; 6. as the firſt.

In the Chancel at *Todington* are preſerved nine Figures of the Apoſtles, about 18 Inches in Height ; over which are Labels, upon which are inſcribed Sentences of the Apoſtolic Creed. They are delicately finiſhed, and were probably a Part of the ſplendid Embelliſhments of the Chapel. Arms, Argent, a Lion rampant Gules, within a Bordure Sable bezantee, which, from the rude Delineation, muſt be contemporary with the Founder.

The Site of the Monaſtery perfectly accorded with the *Ciſtertian* Inſtitution, being ſurrounded on all Sides, except the Weſt, with very lofty Hills covered with Wood. Some of the Offices are now inhabited as Cottages, and are diſtinguiſhable only by Arches, and other Members of Gothic Architecture, which are frequently diſcerned by the Eye of an Antiquary. The Conventual Barn is ſtill intire ; but the greater Part of the Buildings which are deſcribed by KIP and BUCKE became totally a Ruin in 1760 †.

After the Suppreſſion it was granted, with the greater Part of the Manor (probably *Hayles Wood*, *Pinnock's Wood*, and *Hayles Park*, containing 500 Acres, value 65*l*. 14*s*. 8*d*.) to Sir THOMAS SEYMOUR, in Fee, Aug. 19, 1 EDW. VI. He being attainted of High Treaſon, and afterwards beheaded, the Site of the Monaſtery, and the reſt of the Lands, were granted to WILLIAM Marquis of NORTHAMPTON, June 12, 4 EDW. VI. the Marquis, on the 16th of June, in the ſame Year, leaſed it to JOHN HODGKINS for twenty-one Years, at 159*l*. 16*s*. It ſeems afterwards to have been in the Crown, for Queen ELIZABETH July 18, in the 7th Year of her Reign, leaſed it again to HODGKINS for twenty-one Years for the ſame Conſideration. HODGKINS had three Sons ; but he bequeathed this Eſtate to his Daughter ALICE, who married WILLIAM HOBBY, Eſq. of *Hurſley*, co. *Berks*, of whoſe Family this Manor and Eſtate was purchaſed by JOHN Lord Viſcount TRACY, in the Reign of CHARLES the Firſt, whoſe Deſcendant, THOMAS CHARLES LEIGH, Lord Viſcount TRACY, of *Rathcoole*, in the Kingdom of *Ireland*, is the preſent Proprietor.

Many ancient Evidences confound this Monaſtery with that of *Hales Owen*, in the County of *Salop* ; particularly as the Abbots of both Places were indiſcriminately ſummoned to Parliament. ALEXANDER DE HALES, the celebrated Doctor, was certainly of the latter ; and that unfortunate Abbot, who was executed in the Reign of HENRY IV. for ſiding with the Earl of NORTHUMBERLAND againſt the King, and was taken in Armour in the Field at *Braham Moor* in *Yorkſhire*, belonged to that Monaſtery ‡. The Conventual Seal bore an Eſcocheon charged with a Chain and a Shackbolt at each End, between three Mitres.

" rors, he eſpyed a Boxe of Golde, by the Inſcription whereof he perceyved (as the Opinion of Men then gave) that therein
" was conteined a Portion of the Blood of our SAVIOUR. He, therfore, being deſirous to have ſome Part thereof, ſo intreated
" hym that had the Keping of it, that he obteined his Deſire and brought it over wyth hym into *Englande*, beſtowyng a third
" Part therof after his Father's Deceaſe in the Abbeye of *Hayles*, as it were to adorne and enryche the ſame, bycauſe that
" therein both hys Father and his Mother were buryed ; and the other 2 Partes hee dydde reſerve in his owne Cuſtodie, tyll
" at lengthe moved uppon ſuche Devotion as was then uſed, he founded an Abbey a little from his Manor of *Berkhamſted*,
" which Abbey was named *Aſhrugge*, in the which he placed Monks of the Order of *Bonnehommes*, being the firſt that ever had
" bin ſeene of that Order here in *England*. And herewith he alſo aſſigned the two other Partes of that Bloud to the ſame
" Abbey. Whereupon followed great Reſort of People to thoſe two Places, induced thereunto by a certaine blynde Devotion."
HOLINSHED, p. 781.

" A little Treatiſe of divers Miracles ſhewed for the Portion CHRIST's Blood at *Hayles* Abbey, in Metre, how it was brought
" thither ; the Pardons graunted by the Popes and Reliques there," 4to, *ſans* Date, printed by RICH. PYNSON.
AMES's Typog. Antiq. edit. HERBERT, vol. I. p. 285.

It was reported by the Viſitors at the Reformation, that this was the Blood of ſome Animal frequently renewed and put into a Cryſtal Bottle, one Side of which was more opaque than the other. At Confeſſions, the bright Side was ſhewn only to thoſe who offered conſiderable Sums of Money or Jewels.

* At *Guiting Temple*, in the Houſe belonging formerly to the Family of BEALE, are Arms brought from hence : 1. HEN. VIII. imp. JANE SEYMOUR, with ſix Quarterings, 1ſt, on a Pile Gules, between ſix Fleurs de Lys Azure, three Lions of *England* ; 2d, Gules, two Wings conjoined in Lure Or, for SEYMOUR ; 3d, Vairè Argent and Azure, for BEAUCHAMPE of *Hache* ; 4th, Argent, three Demi Lions rampant and couped Gules, for STURMY ; 5th, Parti per Bend Argent and Gules, three Roſes in Bend counterchanged, for MAC WILLIAMS ; 6th, Argent, on a Bend Gules, three Leopards' Faces Or.—2. EDW. VI.

𝔢. 𝔭. Coronet and Label both encircled with Bordures charged with the Roſes of *York* and *Lancaſter* alternately. Beſide theſe *France* and *England*, more ancient, repeated.
When the Abbey was diſſolved, the Ornaments, ſuch as painted Glaſs and Bricks, were collected by many of the neighbouring Gentry, and applied as Embelliſhments of their own Houſes, particularly at *Southam*, &c. See vol. I. p. 377, of this Work.

† ATKINS's Hiſt. *Glouc.* p 470 ; and BUCK's Antiq. of *England*, edit. 1730.
‡ HOLINSHED, Chron. p. 1154.

4

Hayles

Hayles Wood, containing 102 Acres, is reported to have belonged to the Abbey of *Tewkesbury,* and was granted to Robert Cecil, Earl of *Salisbury,* in 1607, 5 James I. It is now held in Leafe by Lord Vifcount Tracy, fubject to an annual Payment to the Moft Noble the Marquis of Salisbury. Other Lands in this Parifh, which were held by Theophilus and Richard Adams in 1583, 25 Eliz. now belong to —— Stratford, Efq.

The Series of Incumbents is given under *DIDBROKE.*

No Benefaction to the Poor.

Present Lord of the Manor,
Thomas Charles Leigh Lord Vifcount Tracy.

No Perfon was fummoned from this Place by the Heralds in 1682 and 1683.

At the Election in 1776 Three Freeholders polled from this Parifh.

The firft Date of the Regifter is in 1603.

Annual Account of Marriages, Births, and Burials, in this Parish.

A.D.	Mar.	Bir.	Bur.	A.D.	Mar.	Bir.	Bur.	A.D.	Mar.	Bir.	Bur.	A.D.	Mar.	Bir.	Bur.
1781	1	4	2	1786	3	5	2	1791				1796			
1782	2	5	1	1787	—	3	1	1792				1797			
1783	3	2	—	1788	1	2	2	1793				1798			
1784	—	3	3	1789	1	3	3	1794				1799			
1785	1	3	—	1790	—	4	2	1795				1800			

INSCRIPTIONS IN THE CHURCH.

ON FLAT STONES IN THE CHANCEL.

Here lieth the Body of John Langley, Efq. Son of Philip Langley, of Mangersfield, Efq. and Frances his Wife, Daughter to the Right Hon. John Lord Vifcount Tracey, of Toddington, who died the 14th Day of July, Anno Domini 1699, in the 61ft Year of his Age.

Alfo here lieth the Body of the Rev. Mr. John Holbrooke, who died the 4th Day of Oct. Anno Dom. 1764, ætatis 68.

Here lyeth the Body of John Peak, of Hailes, who departed this Life the 20th Day of May, Anno Dom. 1683.

ANN, THE WIFE OF JOHN PEAK, OF HAILES, WAS BURIED SEPTEMBER 27, 1685.

Here lieth the Body of John Hull, who departed this Life Sept. 9, 1734, aged 64 Years.

Alfo Judith, the Wife of John Hull, who died Auguft 30, 1752, aged 72 Years.

In Memory of Stephen Gregory, who departed this Life April 2, 1731, aged 27 Years.

Here lyeth the Body of John Stiles, fen. who departed this Life the 6 Dec. Anno Dom. 1715, aged 92 Years.

Alfo here lieth the Body of William Stiles, who departed this Life the 6th Day of May, in the Year 1772, aged 61 Years.

Here lieth the Body of Ann, the Wife of John Stiles, fen. who departed this Life March the 9, Anno Dom. 17 .. aged 73.

Alfo in Memory of Elizabeth, the Daughter of John and Elizabeth Stiles, and the Wife of James Mason, of Winchcombe, who departed this Life Feb. 4, 1735-6, aged 28 Years.

Here lyeth the Body of Elizabeth. the Wife of John Stiles, who departed this Life the 12th Day of Feb. in the Year 1728.

Alfo here lyeth the Body of James Dobbins, who departed this Life the 30th Day of Sept. in the Year 1762, aged 52 Years.

Here lieth the Body of John, the Son of John and Ann Stiles, who departed this Life the 10th Day of November, Anno Domini 1723, aged 53 Years.

Alfo here refteth, in Hope of a joyful Refurrection, the Body of Sarah, the Daughter of James and Mary Dobbins, of Grove Lays, in this Parifh, who departed this Life the 13th Day of May, Anno Dom. 1787, aged 33 Years.

Here lieth the Body of Elizabeth, the Wife of Isaac Baylis, fen. who departed this Life September the 30th, Anno Dom. 1724, aged 59.

Here lieth the Body of Isaac Baylis, fen. who departed this Life June 8, Anno Dom. 1716, aged 50 Years.

IN THE CHURCH YARD.

ON A TOMB.

Here lyeth the Body of Sarah, the Wife of Jorden, of Bourton on the Water, in this County, Gent. who departed this Life the 11th Day of Jan. A. D. 1769, in the 60th Year of her Age.

ON HEAD STONES.

	Died	Aged
Alice, Wife of John Eaft	3 Mar. 1769	40
Elizabeth, Wife of Thomas Eaft	19 Mar. 1783	19
Richard, Son of Sam. and Ann Deckins	19 May, 1747	22
Robert Mafon	31 July, 1737	53
Hannah his Wife	11 Oct. 1715	38
Sarah his fecond Wife	7 June, 1751	65
Mary, Daughter of J. and Ann Fardon	— May, 1737	27
John Fardon, fenior	9 Mar. 1742	69

2

CXLI.

CXLI. HEMPSTED, or HEMSTEED;

AND more anciently *HEY-HEMPSTED*, is a Parish of small Extent, in the united Hundreds of *Dudstone* and *Barton Regis*, distant one Mile on the South-west from the City of GLOUCESTER, upon an easy Eminence above the great Road to *Bristol*, declining from every Side. The Soil is of fertile Clay, and applied in the greater Portion to Pasturage.

The Benefice was made rectorial in 1662, 14 CHARLES II. by an Act of Parliament enabling JOHN Lord Viscount SCUDAMORE to endow certain Vicarages with their impropriate Tythes. With the Consent of WALTER DE CANTILUPO, Bishop of *Worcester*, the Portion allotted to the Vicar was ascertained, and the great Tythes given in 1137 by Earl MILO were confirmed to the *Augustine* Canons of *Llanthony* about the Year 1240 *. At the Dissolution these Tythes were held by Sir CHRISTOPHER HATTON, from whom they passed to HENRY POWLE, Esq. who, in 1662, sold them to Lord SCUDAMORE previous to this Benefaction, to which he added the whole Tythes of the adjacent extra parochial Demesne of *Llanthony*; of all which the present Rectory of *Hempsted* consists †. It is likewise subject to farther Augmentation from the Estate, settled by the Will of SYLVANUS LYSONS, Esq. for charitable Purposes, after the precise Claims are answered ‡.

Of the Church, dedicated to *St. Swithin*, and included in the Deanery of *Gloucester*, the Architecture is of the early Part of the fourteenth Century. It has a Nave only, with a Tower dividing the Chancel from it, neatly finished, but low; it may be more modern than the other Parts. The Inside of the Church was formerly very handsomely decorated; paved with painted Bricks, and furnished with open carved Benches; in the Windows are rich Remains of painted Glass. Under Canopies two female Figures representing the Meeting of MARY and ELIZABETH, with their Names superscribed. The Font is of very curious Form §. In 1315, WALTER DE MAYDENSTONE, Bishop of *Worcester*, consecrated the high Altar here; the Church was then annexed to that of *St. Owen* in *Gloucester*, now totally destroyed ‖.

* " View of the ancient and present State of the Churches of *Door*, *Home Lacey*, and *Hempsted*, endowed by the Right Hon.
" JOHN Lord Viscount SCUDAMORE, by MATT. GIBSON, M. A." 4to. Appendix, No. VIII. A Chirography of the Estimation of the Altarage, Small Tythes, and Obventions of *Hempsted* Chapel, " Ad perpetuam existentiam vicariæ memoratæ Ro-
" BERTO DE FROMA, Clerico, suo & successoribus suis pro rationabili sustentatione, portiones subscriptas assignarunt, videlicet,
" minutas decimas altelagii ecclesiæ Sancti *Audoeni*, &c.—Item, minutas decimas & obventiones altelagii capelle de *Heyhampstede*,
" que estimantur, communibus annis, sexaginta sol' & eo amplius, cum manso & curtilag', & gardino, ad ipsam capellam per-
" tinentibus: Quod gardinum est amplum & bene fructuosum. Item, adjiciunt eisdem omnes decimas provenientes de tribus
" virgatis terre in eadem villa, tam in feno quam in garbis, quas tenent in *Heyhamstede* ADAM KINEMON, ROGERUS KEYS,
" ALICIA DRAKE, &c. Quarum quidem uniuscujusque virgate per se sumpte valet decima, communibus annis, septem solid'
" & eo amplius, quarum vero portion' assignationem, &c." E. Registro *Lanthon*' Signum I. Num. CXII.
 † By a Conveyance, bearing Date 17 Jan. 13 CAR. II. anno 1661, HENRY POWLE, Esq. of *Williamstrop*, in the County of *Gloucester*, for the Sum of 576*l*. " sold, granted, and confirmed to JOHN Lord Viscount SCUDAMORE the Vicarage-house and
" Garden, and Orchard, the Parsonage Close and Barn, and a Parcell of Meadow Ground in *Hempsted Moor*, the Church-house,
" and Church, and Chancel, and Church Yard of *Hempsted*; together with the perpetual Advowson, or perfect and absolute
" Patronage of the said Church; and all the said HENRY POWLE's Portion of Tythes, Oblations, and Obventions whatsoever,
" renewing and growing within the tytheable Places of the said Parish of *Hempsted*: to have and to hold in as large and ample
" Manor as the said HENRY POWLE, or his Ancestors, or his or their Tenants, held and enjoyed the same. Charged never-
" theless with, and subject and liable to, the Payment of the yearly Rent of 40*s*. unto the King's Majesty, his Heirs and Suc-
" cessors, for and out of the said Impropriate Tythes."
 Certain Lands and Tythes in *Hempsted*, with a Fishery in the *Severn*, which lately belonged to the Priory of *Llanthony*, were granted to ARTHUR PORTER, 32 H. VIII. and descended to Lord SCUDAMORE, to which he added the Church Yard of the late dissolved Priory of *Llanthony*; and all Manner of Tythes whatsoever, arising from his Demesne Lands of the said Priory: which had, by the Laws and Statutes of this Realm, been freed and discharged from all Manner of Tythes before.
 GIBSON, ut sup. pp. 169, 170, 171.

 ‡ Extract from the Will of SYLVANUS LYSONS, Esq. dated Nov. 13, 1731:
 He devises all his Manors, Lands, &c. in *Hempsted*, *Haresfield*, *Whaddon*, *Standish*, and *Harscombe*, and elsewhere, in the City and County of *Gloucester*, vested in PHILIP SHEPPARD, BENJAMIN NEWTON, and JOHN GREGORY, Clerks, CHARLES HYETT, and JOHN RADCLIFFE, Esqrs. and their Successors, in Trust, after the Death of MARY LYSONS his Wife (which happened July 17, 1750), that 20*l*. per Ann. should be severally paid to nine Widows of Clergymen who have been educated at one of the Universities of *Oxford* or *Cambridge* as a Clergyman of the Church of *England* ought to be, and have been ordained Ministers as the Law directs, and have severally died Incumbents of some Church or Chapel, within such Part of the Diocese of *Gloucester* as is not in the *Forest* Deanery, as Rector, Vicar, or Perpetual Curate thereof. The Salary to be paid so long as they shall continue unmarried. The Trustees are required to elect within one Month after each Vacancy; 1*l*. 1*s*. to the Rector of *Hempsted*, for a Sermon on Ascension Day; and 4*l*. for a Dinner at his Mansion at *Hempsted* on the same Day; the Residue of the Rents and Profits, if any, to be applied as an Augmentation to the Rectory for ever.
 § Archæologia, vol. X. p. 188. plate XXV.
 ‖ THOMAS's Survey of *Worcester*, p. 162.

Daniel Lysons M.D. LORD OF THIS MANOR contributes this Plate.

Our Lady's Well at Newark.

When the new Rectory was founded, the ancient Houfe affigned for the Officiating Minifter, and for building which the Convent of *Llanthony* had expended three Marks and a Half, was dilapidated. The prefent Houfe was erected by Lord Scudamore at the Expence of 700*l*. *

The Manor, at the Compilation of *Domefday*, was held by Edric Lang, a Thane of Earl Harold, and entitled " *Heckanftede* †." In the next Century it became Parcel of the immenfe Territory of Milo the great Earl of Hereford, by whom, in 1136, 2 Stephen, it was given to his newly eftablifhed Priory of *Llanthony*, who, in the fubfequent Reigns, received frequent Confirmation of their Rights ‡. In 1546, 37 Hen. VIII. Thomas Atkins, Efq. of *Tuffley*, and Margaret his Wife purchafed it, together with a Fifhery on the River *Severn*, from the Court of Augmentations, and it vefted in their immediate Defcendants to Sir Robert Atkins, Knt. Lord Chief Baron of the Exchequer, who, about 1708, fold it, with other Eftates in this County, to Allen Bathurst, Efq. of *Cirencefter* (afterward Baron, and now Earl Bathurst), of whom it was purchafed by Daniel Lysons, Efq. whofe Grandfon Daniel Lysons, Efq. M. D. is the prefent Proprietor.

Under the Priory of *Llanthony* many Leafes determinable by Lives were granted of Lands within this Parifh, which Mode was continued by the fucceeding Lords of the Manor for many Years ; but the chief Part is now Freehold. About the Year 1630, the Family of Lysons, of *Gloucefter* and *Hempfteed*, Defcendants from that of *Nether Lay*, in the Parifh of *Weftbury upon Severn*, became principal Leffees. The prefent Manor Houfe, which has a moft eligible Situation, commanding a delightful View of the City and Vale of *Gloucefter*, was began to be built about the Clofe of the laft Century by Daniel Lysons, Efq. in the Infancy of his Son (who afterwards purchafed the Manor), and was finifhed by the Son's Truftees.

H A M L E T S.

1. The *Rhee*, or *Rea*, now belongs to T. W. Payne, Efq. It is bounded on the North by the River *Severn*, and on the Weft by the Parifh of *Quedgeley*, and South by the Road leading from *Gloucefter* to *Briftol*.

2. *Podgemead* is a Farm of confiderable Value and Extent in this Parifh, Parcel of the Endowment of the Priory of *Llanthony*. The Scite of the Manor of *Poddefmead*, with Lands in the Parifhes of *Brockworth*, *Bentham* in *Badgworth* and *Elmore*, were fold to Joan Cooke §, Relict of John Cooke, Alderman of the City of *Gloucefter*, to be held by the tenth Part of a Knight's Fee, paying yearly 30*s*. to the Crown, in Confideration of the Sum of 266*l*. 6*s*. 8*d*. This Eftate was afterwards held by Henry Hoskins, Gent. who, in 1653, granted it by Will to the Corporation of the City of *Gloucefter*, on Condition that they fhould renew to the Heir Male of his Defcendants a Leafe for thirty-one Years at a certain referved Rent, fubject to a Fine. The prefent hereditary Leffees are George Phelps, Gent. and the Family of Hope.

B E N E F A C T I O N S.

Mary Harris gave by Will, in 1720, 1000*l*. vefted in Daniel Lysons, M. D. Samuel Lysons, Clerk, Benjamin Hyett, and George Savage, Efqrs. to purchafe Lands ; the annual Income of which is 42*l*. to be applied in the following Manner : viz. for a Sermon and Sacrament on the 27th Day of June ; for Gowns of Grey Cloth to four Widows of *Hempftead*, and two Widows of the Parifh of *Whaddon* ; for Boys to be apprenticed, two of *Hempftead* to one of *Whaddon* ; the Overplus, if any, for Cloth Gowns to poor Men, two of *Hempftead* to one of *Whaddon* ; alfo a Sermon and Sacrament at *Whaddon*, upon the fame Day, being that of her Death.

Giles Cox, in 1620, gave by Will 1044*l*. with which Lands were purchafed, and are now vefted in Sir Richard Sutton, Bart. Sir John Guise, Bart. Sir How Hicks, Bart. Samuel Hayward, and Robert Campbell, Efqrs. Daniel Lysons, M. D. and others, for the Relief of Poor Houfeholders in feveral Parifhes not receiving Parifh Relief, fo that, when the Eftate neats 50*l*. a Year, the Parifh of *Hempftead* fhall have 20*s*.

Incumbents.	Patrons.	Incumbents.	Patrons.
1662 Geo. Wall, M. A.	John Ld. Vif. Scudamore.	1715 Digby Cotes, M. A.	James Lord Scudamore.
1669 John Gregory, M. A.	The fame.	1726 Thos. Wilkes, D. D.	Henry Duke of Beaufort.
1678 John Gregory ‖, M. A.	The fame.	1737 John Webb, M. A.	The fame,
1690 John Gregory, D. D.	The fame.	1753 John Tayler, Clerk,	Frances Fitz Roy Scu-
1708 Bernard Gardiner **, LL. D.	——————.		damore.

* Gibson's View, p. 174 ; and the Entry in the Parifh Regifter, copied in the Appendix.
† Domefday, p. 69.
‡ Cart. Fund. Priorat. *Lanthonienf. Milonis*, com. *Hereford*, p. 69. " Capella de *Heccamftudâ* cum decimis villanorum in " omnibus." Dugdale's Monaft. vol. II. p. 70. Tanner's Not. Mon. No. XXI. Cart. 21 Edw. I. m. 17, pro liberâ Warennâ in *Heyhamftede*, *Podefmede*, &c.
§ By Indenture tripartite, made the 11th Jan. 31 Hen. VIII. between Dame Joan Cook, Widow, the Mayor and Burgeffes of the Town of *Gloucefter*, and the Bailiff and Citizens of the City of *Worcefter*, thefe Eftates were given for the Foundation and Eftablifhment of a Free Grammar School in the Parifh of *St. Mary de Crypt*, and the repairing the Weft Bridge and Caufeways.
Corporation MSS.
‖ Wood, Fafti *Oxon*. vol. II. p. 823, gives an Account of this Family, feveral of whom were eminent for their Works in Divinity.
** Elected Warden of *All Souls College*, *Oxford*, 1702, ob. 1726.

7   Present

PRESENT LORD OF THE MANOR,
DANIEL LYSONS, M. D.

The Perfons fummoned from this Place by the Heralds, in 1682 and 1683, were

Daniel Lyfons, Efq. Thomas Lyfons, Gent. and John Gregory, M. A.

At the Election in 1776 Two Freeholders polled from this Parifh.

The Regifter has its firft Date in 1558, and has been kept with great Regularity.

ANNUAL ACCOUNT OF MARRIAGES, BIRTHS, AND BURIALS, IN THIS PARISH.

A.D.	Mar.	Bir.	Bur.	A.D.	Mar.	Bir.	Bur.	A.D.	Mar.	Bir.	Bur.	A.D.	Mar.	Bir.	Bur.
1781	3	6	8	1786	4	4	1	1791				1796			
1782	3	6	2	1787	—	4	2	1792				1797			
1783	2	8	4	1788	8	3	4	1793				1798			
1784	4	6	9	1789	11	5	4	1794				1799			
1785	3	3	7	1790	12	3	3	1795				1800			

INSCRIPTIONS IN THE CHURCH.

ON A MARBLE MONUMENT:

Arms; Gules, a Chief Azure, on the latter Part thereof a Cloud, the Sun's Rays iffuant proper, for LYSONS;—impaling, a Chevron between three Fleurs de Lys, for HARRIS.

Here reft the Bodies of Mr. THOMAS LYSONS, of Hempftead, who died Feb. 21, 1713, aged 77 Years.

THOMAS, Son of Mr. THOMAS LYSONS, who dyed June 7, 1683, aged 8 Years.

SILVANUS LYSONS, Efq. died 9 Dec. 1731, aged 66 Years.

MARY, Wife of SILVANUS LYSONS, died July 19, 1750, aged 76 Years.

ANNA MARIA, Daughter of Mr. SILVANUS LYSONS, of Hempftead, who dyed Nov. 27, 1704, aged 17 Weeks.

MARY, Daughter of Mr. SILVANUS LYSONS, who died April 17, 1720, aged 19 Years.

ELIZ. Daughter of SILVANUS LYSONS, died Feb. 11, 1728, aged 27 Years.

Here alfo reft the Bodies of MARY, Daughter of Mr. THOMAS LYSONS, and Wife of Mr. JAMES HARRIS, of Abergavenny, who died June 27, 1721, aged 48 Years.

LOVISA, Daughter of Mr. JAMES HARRIS and MARY his Wife, who died Oct. 29, 1701, aged 10 Years.

Here lyeth the Body of MARGERY BARNES, Widdow, and formerly Wife of JOHN HILL, of Ridford, Yeoman, who died February the 18th, 1688.

Alfo here lyeth the Body of JOHN HILL her Son, who died May the 15th, 1671.

Here lyeth the Body of FRANCES GREGORY, Spinfter, who lived a faithful Servant in the Family of DANIEL LYSONS Efq. 35 Years, without ever giving or receiving Warning to quit her Place, for which fhe was much refpected, and died greatly regretted by her Friends and Acquaintance the 24th of October, 1766.

IN THE CHANCEL.

ON A BRASS PLATE FIXED IN THE NORTH WALL:

Arms; Baron and Femme; Quarterly, 1ft and 4th, Gules, five Mer Lion's Wings in Saltire Argent, for PORTER; 2d, Argent, three Helmets clofe Sable, garnifhed Or; 3d, Argent, three Bars Sable, over all as many Ropes coiled Or. 2. Quarterly, 1ft and 4th, Gules, a Chevron Ermine between three Pheons Or, for ARNOLD; 2d and 3d, Sable, a Chevron Or between three Hawk's Lures Argent.

𝔥ere this 𝔭lace lyeth the 𝔅odyes of
𝔑icholas 𝔭orter
𝔥enry 𝔯oger and 𝔑icholas, jun.
eully and 𝔅rigid
𝔰onnes and 𝔇aughters to 𝔄rthur 𝔭orter,
𝔈fquyor, and 𝔄lys his 𝔚yfe 𝔄nno 𝔇ni
𝔐DLLIII, on whofe 𝔰ouls 𝔍hu have
𝔐ercy

A RAISED TABLE TOMB, UPON WHICH IS THE EFFIGY OF A MAN EXTENDED AND SUPPLICATING, DRESSED IN A JUDGE'S ROBES AND COIF, CARVED IN FREESTONE, AND PAINTED.

Arms; Argent, a Crofs cotifed florettée between four Mullets pierced Sable, for ATKINS;—impaling, Gules, a Horfe's Head couped Argent, between three Croffes Croflets fitchée Or, for MARSHE.

Here lyeth ELINOR, the Wife of RICHARD ATKINS, Efqvior, and Daughter of THOMAS MARSHE, of Warefleie, in the Countie of Huntington, Efqvior, who died the 3 of April, An° D'ni 1594. Her godly Life, her bleffed Death, her Hope and Confolation, were Signes to us, and Seales to her of Joyful Refurrection.

ON FLAT STONES.

HERE LYETH BURIED THE BODY OF RICHARD ATKINS, OF TUFFLEY, ESQVIOR, WAIGHTING FOR THE RESURRECTION TO GLORY, AND WAS BURIED THE 8 DAY OF NOVEMBER, ANNO 1610.

Arms: Ermine, on a Chief embattled Sable, three Battle Axes Argent, for SHEPPARD.

WILLIAM SHEPPARD, Ar. Obiit 26 die Martii, An. Dom. 1674.

Et ALICIA Uxor ejus 29 Julii, 1693.

Arms; Argent, two Bars Sable, in Chief a Lion paffant of the laft;—impaling, Sable, a Lion rampant Argent.

JOHN GREGORY, 2d Rector of this Church, and Archdeacon of Glofter, died Decemb. 10, 1678, in the 50th Year of his Age.

SARAH, the Wife of JOHN GREGORY, 3d Rector of this Church, and Daughter of ARTHUR LYSONS, of this Parifh, Gent. died Sept. 20, and buried Sept. 21, 1682.

HERE LYETH THE BODY OF THOMAS, THE SON OF HENRY HOLMAN, GENT. who WAS BURIED JUNE 26, 1635.

HERE

HERE LYETH THE BODY OF
SUSANNA, THE WIFE OF
JEIFFRY FLETCHER,
DAUGHTER OF HENRY HOSKINS,
OF PODGMEAD, WHO
DEPARTED THIS LIFE
JUNE THE 9TH,
1653.

Arms ; Per Pale three Lioncels rampant
Argent.

Here lyeth the Body of HOLMAN
HOSKINS, of Podgmead, in this Parish,
Gent. who departed this Life July 25,
in the Year { of our Lord 1717,
{ of his Age 44.

Here also lyeth the Body of HOLMAN
his Son, who died Oct. 3, 1714,
aged 6 Years.

Also here lyeth the Body of
ELIZABETH, Wife of the said HOLMAN
HOSKINS, who died Sept. 17, 1719.

Likewise MARY their Daughter
died the 21st of March, 1723,
aged 9 Years.

Also ELIZABETH their Daughter
died the 11th of July, in the 15th Year
of her Age, An. Dom. 1724.

Here lyeth the Body
of ELIZABETH, the Relict
of THOMAS HOSKINS, of
Podgmead, Gent. who
deceased the 13th of October,
Anno Dom. 1712,
aged 70 Years.

HERE LYETH THE BODY OF
JOHN GREVESTOCK,
CLARKE OF THIS CHURCH,
WHO WAS CLARKE HERE
39 YEARS AND A HALF,
AND DIED THE 26 DAY OF
DEC. AN. DOM. 1620.

Here lyeth the Body of
JOHN HOPE, Gent.
who departed this Life May 12, 1770,
aged 62 Years.

Also
one Son and two Daughters
of the said JOHN HOPE,
of Podgmead, Gent.

Here rests the Remains of
MARY FISHER,
who died Aug. 2, 1786, aged 71.

ON A HANDSOME MARBLE MONUMENT :

Upon two Efcocheons : Arms ; 1. LYSONS, impaling, Vert, three Scythes Argent, on a Chief of the fecond a Bull paffan
Gules, for RIDLER ; 2. LYSONS, impaling, a Chevron between three Goats' Heads erafed, for MEE.

M. S.
DANIELIS LYSONS,
Ejufque filii natu maximi,
Necnon eorum Conjugum & Liberorum.

	Nat.	Ob.		Nat.	Ob.
DANIEL LYSONS, Pater	2 Dec. 1672	6 Sept. 1736	DANIEL LYSONS, Filius	1 Dec. 1697	8 Jul. 1773
ELIZ. RIDLER, Conjux	25 Dec. 1670	15 Jan. 1708	ELIZ. MEE, Conjux	2 Oct. 1702	22 Dec. 1785
ANNA LYSONS	22 Jan. 1693	10 Apr. 1697	SAMUEL LYSONS	24 Jul. 1728	26 Jul. 1720
ELIZ. LYSONS	2 Dec. 1695	28 Sept. 1752	ELIZ. REEVE	3 Jan. 1729	1 Jul. 1772
SARA LYSONS	2 Jul. 1714	8 Sept. 1726	ANNA LYSONS	25 Feb. 1732	11 Nov. 1784
ANNA LYSONS	1 Maii, 1699	2 Dec. 1703	THOMAS LYSONS	10 Dec. 1725	26 Maii, 1737
MARIA LYSONS	25 Oct. 1700	8 Jun. 1780	JOHANNES LYSONS	28 Dec. 1736	6 Oct. 1743
THOMAS LYSONS	7 Mar. 1701	22 Jul. 1702	ESTHERA LYSONS	26 Nov. 1739	19 Feb. 1764
THOMAS LYSONS	19 Feb. 1704	2 Aug. 1728	PRISCILLA LYSONS	10 Oct. 1743	3 Maii, 1764
JOHANNES LYSONS, LL. D.	28 Dec. 1706	12 Sept. 1760			

Hoc Marmor
In Avi, Patris, & Gentis memoriam,
DANIEL LYSONS, M. D.
Piè pofuit 1789.

IN THE CHURCH YARD,   ON TOMBS.

HERE LIETH BURIED THE
BODY OF JOHN BRIDGES,
YEOMAN, WHO DIED
JAN. 7, A. DOM. 1613.
AND ALSO OF JOANE
HIS WIFE, WHO DIED
JAN. 20, A. DOM. 1613.

Here resteth the Body of
THOMAS COOK, who was buried Feb. 10,
An. Dom. 1728, aged 62 Years.

Also here resteth the Body of
MARTHA, the Wife of THOMAS COOK,
who was buried Oct. 12, An. Dom. 1723,
aged 45 Years.

Near this Tomb rests the Bodies of
four Children of THOMAS COOK
by MARTHA his Wife,
three Sons and one Daughter.

THOMAS COOK, who was buried
Aug. 28, 1720, aged 22 Years.

HESTER COOK was buried
Dec. 29, 1721, aged 2 Years.

SAMUEL COOK was buried
July 30, 1732, aged 28 Years.

WILLIAM COOK was buried
Dec. 6, 1732, aged 25 Years.

Near this Place lieth the Body
of RICHARD, the Son of RICHARD

and SARAH FRANKS, who died
June 11, 1750, aged 2 Years
and 5 Months.

Arms ; Azure, three Lozenges in Fefs
Or.

Hic jacet JOHANNES FREEMAN, Centurio
Equeftris, Filius JOHANNIS FREEMAN,
de Bufhleij, comitatu Wigorn, Armigeri,
Caftris Regiis obfidione Gleuenti
Sclopetariæ Glandis Ictu Trajectus
Die Augufti 14,
Salutis 1 1643.
Ætatis J 23.

In Memory
of JOHN BUBB, of
this Parifh, who was buried
the 20th of April, 1722.

Also of ANNE his Wife, who was
buried the 6th of March, 1741-2.

Likewise JOHN BUBB
their Son, who was buried the
31st of Jan. 1760.

In Memory
of JOHN, the Son
of THOMAS and MARY JENNINGS,
of the Parifh of Elmore,
who died the 9th of Feb. 1764,
aged 39 Years.

In Memory of WILLIAM,
the Son of THOS. and MARY JENNINGS,
who died Aug. 28, 1770, aged 33 Years.

In Memory of
THOMAS JENNINGS, of the Parifh
of Elmore, who departed this Life
the 21st of Feb. 1767, aged 71.

Also MARY, Relict of the above
THOMAS JENNINGS, who died the
22d of Feb. 1774, aged 77.

In Memory
of JOHN SMITH,
of this Parifh, Yeoman,
who departed this Life the 21st
of July, 1752, aged 62.

Also of ELIZABETH his Wife,
who died Sept. 12, 1719,
aged near 29.

In Memory of
JOHN SMITH, jun. of this
Parifh, Yeoman, who died
the 10th of April, 1769, in the
50th Year of his Age.

In Memory of
ANN, the Wife of JOHN SMITH,
of this Parifh, Yeoman, who died
Oct. 14, 1780, aged 69.

In

In Memory of
JOHN HEARD, of this Parish, Yeoman,
who departed this Life July 25, 1779,
aged 52 Years.

In Memory of
ROBERT HEARD, of this Parish,
Yeoman,
who departed this Life Feb. 9, 1780,
aged 48 Years.

Alfo MARGARET, Wife of
JOHN MANN, of Norton, Yeoman,
who died Mar. 22, 1785, aged 53 Years.

ON A FLAT STONE:

In Memory of . . . . .
Wife of JOHN SMITH, of this
Parish, Yeoman, who departed
this Life Dec. 5, 1731,
aged 32.

Alfo MARY, the Wife of
JOHN SMITH,
died May the 6th, 1752, aged 70.

ON HEAD STONES.

	Died	Aged
John Shill, of Withington -	20 Sept. 1726	21
Robert Heard - -	28 Aug. 1728	74
Joan his Wife -	16 Nov. 1729	76
Samuel Heard, of Churcham	24 Dec. 1765	64
Elizabeth his Wife -	17 May, 1756	55
Charles their Son -	23 May, 1765	24
Robert Heard -	25 July, 1753	64
Margaret his Wife -	20 Jan. 1742	51
William Halling - -	12 May, 1775	60
Sarah his Wife -	21 Oct. 1783	78
William their Son -	11 Oct. 1783	38
Ifabel, Wife of John Witcomb	26 Dec. 1696	90
John, Son of John and Mary Wit-comb, of Tuffley -	15 Oct. 1784	36
Rebecca, Wife of George Ellis	2 Mar. 1782	34
Mary Belcher - -	14 Oct. 1755	40
Mary, Wife of James Johnfon	5 Apr. 1781	35
John Miles, fen. -	2 Oct. 1770	62
Sarah his ft Wife -	23 Dec. 1730	30
Sarah his 2d Wife -	9 Mar. 1771	62
John their Son -	18 Jan. 1775	25
Hannah, Wife of William Bullock, Daughter of John and Sarah Miles - -	17 Apr. 1782	31
Jane, Wife of George Stevens	15 Apr. 1791	56
Mary, Wife of Charles Driver, Daughter of Thomas and Eliza-beth Priddy -	8 June, 1789	60
Edmund, Son of Edmund and Mary Barnwood - -	— Mar. 1707	—
John Keys - -	— May, 1756	70
Ann his Wife - -	30 Jan. 1776	81
John their Son - -	— Feb. 1771	32
Sufannah Smith - -	18 July, 1708	32
John Smith - -	26 Aug. 1723	72
William his Son -	22 Apr. 1724	—
William Jennings -	9 June, 1685	—
Margaret his Wife -	20 Jan. 1683	—
Elizabeth, Wife of Richard Child	27 Mar. 1716	—
John Prieft - -	2 Aug. 1727	59
Elizabeth his Wife -	10 May, 1735	59
Robert Bubb, who was murdered in his Return from Gloucefter	17 Nov 1697	63
Ann his Wife - -	6 Dec. 1679	—
John Bubb - -	8 Apr. 1722	58
Henry Jennings -	20 Sept. 1682	—
John Nourfe - -	13 July, 1679	—
John Nurfe - -	16 Oct. 1697	60
John his Son - -	27 Mar. 1699	17
Mary his Daughter -	2 Aug. 1700	16

CXLII.   H E N B U R Y,

WHICH is of great Extent, and by which, and the contiguous Parifh of *Weftbury*, the Hundred, anciently called *Bernintreu*, is formed, is fituate near the *Briftol* Channel and the River *Avon*, from which Circumftance it is ftyled, in moft ancient Records, " *Henbury in falfo Marifco.*" It is diftant four Miles from *Briftol* Northward, and thirty-five Weftward from GLOUCESTER. The Extent is faid to be fix Miles from North to South, and four acrofs in the wideft Part, and the Soil chiefly of fertile Clay or Sand, and applied, with fmall Exception, to Pafturage. The Village of *Henbury* has much beautiful Scenery refulting from the greateft Cultivation, with many elegant Houfes, of which its Vicinity to *Briftol* was the primary Caufe ; and it has long been the Refidence of fome of the more opulent Citizens.

The Benefice is vicarial, appropriated to the See of *Worcefter* by Bifhop WOLSTAN, who died in 1095 ; to which the Tythes of Hay were added by SIMON his Succeffor in 1140. In 1549 the Impropriation was alienated by NICHOLAS HEATH, then Bifhop, to JOHN DUDLEY, Duke of *Northumberland*, and has been fince held with the Right of Advowfon and the Manor *.

The Church is dedicated to *St. Mary*, and has a very fpacious Nave with two Aifles, one of which is continued parallel with the Chancel ; from the Windows of which it appears to have been built early in the fourteenth Century, when the *Norman* lancet Arches fucceeded to the heavy *Saxon*. Many Repairs have fubfequently taken Place, by which the external Form is much altered, probably about the Reigns of HENRY the Seventh or Eighth. It is decorated in the Infide with much Judgement, and in a fingularly decent Style.

Thirty Caffats of Land at Ɖeanbupẏ anɖ Ȝuꞃꞇın (*Henbury and Auft*), with the Fifheries of the River *Severn*, were given to the See of *Worcefter*, in 691, by OSFTOR, the fecond Bifhop. In 795 King OFFA added twenty Manfes †. *Domefday* recognized *Huefberie*, in *Bernintreu* Hundred, as belonging in *Saxon* Times to the Church of *St. Mary* in *Worcefter*, with its Members, *Henbury*, *Redwicke*, *Stowicke*, and *Yate* ‡. In 1196 King RICHARD I. confirmed by Charter to JOHN DE CONSTANTIIS, Bifhop of *Worcefter*, the fame Privileges and Liberties in *Henbury*, &c. as in his other Manors, which, in 1200, were ratified by his Brother King JOHN §. Free Warren in *Henbury*, and other Lordfhips, was granted by King HENRY III. in 1255, to WALTER DE CANTELUPO, then Bifhop. In 1275 Pope GREGORY X. took under his Protection the Temporalities of the See of *Worcefter*, confirming to it the Manor of *Henbury*, and other Poffeffions ||. Soon after the Conqueft, the Bifhops of *Worcefter* founded a Palace here, and imparked many Acres. THOMAS PEVERELL, the fixtieth Bifhop, died here in 1418, and HENRY WAKEFIELD, his Predeceffor, iffued a Mandate thence againft WICKLIFFE in 1387 **. Some ruinous Buildings near the Church feem to mark the Site of the Palace, which was their occafional Refidence.

In the 1ft Year of EDWARD VI. this Manor, and its Dependences, were alienated by NICHOLAS HEATH, and granted to JOHN Duke of NORTHUMBERLAND, upon whofe Attainder they reverted to the See. But, by virtue of an Act, paffed in the 1ft of ELIZABETH, 1559, impowering the Queen, upon the Avoidance of any Bifhoprick, to refume the Temporalities, recompenfing the Value of them with Parfonages impropriate, this and other Manors were feized by the Crown ††. This Tranfaction was, however, merely formal ; for, Sir RALPH SADLIER was then in Poffeffion, and had gained twenty one other Manors from the Spoils of the Church. GERTRUDE was the Daughter, and at length Heir of Sir THOMAS SADLIER, and the Wife of Sir WALTER ASTON, of *Tixal*, co. *Stafford*. WALTER Lord ASTON, their Son, fold the Manerial Eftate, with the Advowfon of the Vicarage, to THOMAS YATE, Efq. of *Gray's Inn*, *London*, and GREGORY GEARING, of *Denworth*, co. *Berks*, Efq. in

---

* THOMAS's Surv. *Worc.* pp. 92, 109, 213. TANNER, Not. Mon. *Worc.* No. XXI.

† Idem, pp. 7, 22.

‡ " Terra Eccl'e de *Wireceftre*. In *Bernintreu* Hund', *S'c'a Maria de Wireceftre* tenuit & ten' *Huefberie*. Ibi fuer' & funt ι
" Hide. In d'nio funt II Car' & VIII Vill'i & VI Bord', cum VIII Car'. Ibi IIII Servi & una Ancilla. Ad hoc M p'tı᷉ ' h'
" Membra: *Henberie, Redeuuiche, Stoche, Giete*. In his funt VIIII Car' in d'nio & XXVII Vill'i & XXII Bord', cum XXVI Car'.
" Ibi XX Servi & II Ancille & XX Colib'ti cum X Car' & Molin' de XX Den'." Domefday, No. IIII.

§ THOMAS, Surv. *Worc.* pp. 120, 121. Cart. I JOHAN. p. I, n. 151.

|| Idem, pp. 132, 139. A D. MCCLXXV. VII Idus Julii fuit duellum pro ballivâ de *Hembury* ; & pugil Epifcopi vicit pugilem PHILIPPI DE STOK WHARTON, Anglia Sacra, vol. II. p. 501.

** THOMAS, ut fupra, pp. 186, 191.

†† Idem, p. 213.

1675,

1675, who re-fold them in 1680 to Sir SAMUEL ASTRY*, Knight, Clerk of the Crown, who was a lineal Defcendant of Sir RALPH ASTRY, Lord Mayor of *London* in 1594, and of *Woodend*, in the County of *Bedford*. They afterwards defcended in equal Parts to his three Daughters and Coheirs, ELIZABETH, Wife of Sir JOHN SMYTH, Bart.; DIANA, Wife to RICHARD ORLEBAR, Efq. and ARABELLA, Lady of CHARLES WILLIAM, the feventh Earl of SUFFOLK, whom fhe furvived, and bequeathed her Share to her elder Sifter. Sir JOHN SMYTH, her Nephew, fold a Moiety of that Share to the Heirs of EDWARD COLSTON, Efq. who had before purchafed ORLEBAR's Partition. A Moiety was then in Sir JOHN SMYTH, whofe three Sifters and Coheirs fold it to Sir JARRIT SMYTH, Bart. who married FLORENCE, one of the faid Coheirs; and the other Moiety defcended to the two Daughters and Coheirs of THOMAS EDWARDS, Efq. of *Filkins*, co. *Oxon*, one of whom married FRANCIS Lord MIDDLETON, the other ALEXANDER READY, Efq. who hath fince taken the Name of COLSTON, and died in December 1775. THOMAS SMYTH, Efq. is the prefent Owner of one Moiety, and the other belongs to the Right Hon. HENRY Lord Vifcount MIDDLETON and ALEXANDER COLSTON, Efq. Grandfon of the former.

The Tything of *Henbury* contains about 1000 Acres; the principal Proprietors of which are EDWARD SAMPSON, Efq. (of a Family long eftablifhed in the Parifh), JOHN SCANDRETT HARFORD, Gent. and the Heirs of MICHAEL MILLER, Efq. *Blaife Hill* rifes above the Village on the South-weft Side, and was probably the Site of a Chapel dedicated to *St. Werburgh* (*Capella St. Warburgæ fuper montem Hembirie fita*), though more generally thought to have been to *St. Blazius*, from whom it received its prefent Name †. Many *Roman* Veftiges lately difcovered evince that it was a *Specula*, or Out-poft; and in the latter Ages there is faid to have been a Beacon for the Ufe of the Ships in the *Briftol* Channel ‡. Upon the

* " REBECCA, Relict of Sir SAM. ASTRY, was his fecond Wife, and Daughter of THOMAS CLARKE, Efq. of *Henbury*. " She re-married with Sir SIMON HARCOURT, afterward Lord High Chancellor of *England*, and enjoyed this Eftate in Jointure " till her Death." COLLINS, vol. VI. p. 73.

† THOMAS, ut fup. p. 121.

‡ The following Coins were found at *Henbury*, in the Year 1708, by Sir SIMON HARCOURT:

Face, or Obverfe.	*Reverfe.*
CONSTANTIUS MAGNUS.	ROMULUS and REMUS.
TRAJAN; a very fair Medal in Copper, of a large Size.	A female Figure fitting, in her Left Hand a Cornucopia, in the Right the Rudder of a Ship, fubfcribed, " S. C."
MARCUS AURELIUS ANTONINUS.	A female Figure, facrificing on an Altar, " Salut. AUG. " S. C."
VESPASIAN; feveral middle fized Copper.	A large Altar, fubfcribed, " Reverentia."
CONSTANTIUS; very fair, in fmall Copper.	A Mars marching, circumfcribed, " Confervatio."
Ditto; fmall Copper.	" Felix Temporum reparatio."
Ditto.	A Caftle, and circumfcribed, " Provident. AUG."
LICINIUS.	" Genio Populi Romani."
GETA; fmall Silver.	" Invictus."
MARCUS AURELIUS ANTONINUS.	A funeral Pile, " S C."
ADRIAN; large Copper.	A Ship, with feveral Figures.
TRAJANI FAUSTINA.	
ANTONINUS PIUS.	A female Figure captive, " BRITANNIA."
A *Britifh* Gold Coin, coined at *Malden*, or *Colchefter*, in *Effex*; an Ear of Corn on one Side.	A Horfe, " C. A. M. O."
CALIGULA; large Copper.	
NERO; ditto.	
JULIAN, the Apoftate.	" Votis X. Mulctis XX."
DOMITIAN; middle-fize Copper.	
NERVA.	Two Hands joined. " Exercituûm Concordia."
Ditto.	" Fortuna Redux."
GALIENUS; a radiated Crown.	A Deer, " Cof. AUG."
PROBUS.	" LÆTITIA AUG."
D. N CONSTANS P. F. AUG.	Drawing a Captive out of his Den.

The following Coins were dug up at *Sea Mills*, 1712:

" Imp. CÆS. VESPASIANUS P. F. AUG."	" Concordia Militum."
Ditto.	A Temple in the Exergue, " Providentia."
" Imp. DIOCLESIANUS P. F. AUG."	A fitting Figure.
" Imp. CÆS. DOMITIANUS AUG."	A Figure holding a Flower in her Hand.
" Imp. CÆS. ANTONINUS P. F. AUG."	A Figure holding a Cornucopia.
" D. N. CONSTANTINUS P. F. AUG. P. P."	A Man transfixing a fuppliant Captive with a Dart.

The following were difcovered at *St. Blaze Hill, Henbury*, 1768:

" Imp. CÆSAR DOMITI AUG. GERM. Cos. XIII. CENS. " PERP. P. P." within a Laurel Crown.	" Virtuti AUGUSTI S. C." a Soldier, holding in his Right Hand a Dart, in his Left a Parazonium.
" Imp CÆS. DOMIT. AUG. GERM. Cos. XI. CENS. PERP. " P. P."	A winged female Figure, or Victory, holding in her Right Hand a Shield, " S. C."
" Imp. CÆS. NERVA TRAJAN AUG. GERM. P. M." a radiated Head.	" T. R. POT. Cos. III. P. P. S. C." a Figure fitting with a Staff between two Cornucopias.
" D. N. GRATIANUS P. F. AUG." bright Silver.	" Virtus Romanorum."
" Imp. CÆS. CARAUSIUS P. M."	" Pax AUG." a female Figure with an Olive-Branch.
" CRISPINA AUGUSTA."	A fitting Figure; in her Right Hand fhe holds a Patera to a Serpent afcending from an Altar.
" Imp. CÆS. ALECTUS P. F. AUG." a radiated Head.	" Virtus Auguft. Q. C. Navis."
" D. N. MAGNENTIUS P. F. AUG." a naked Head.	" Salus D. N. AUG. & CÆS." a Monagram of the Name of CHRIST, " I. M. B." in a Crofs with Alpha and Omega.
" Imp. C. M. POSTHUMUS P. F. AUG."	" Victor. AUG."
" Imp. CÆS POSTHUMUS P. F. AUG."	A Figure of ÆSCULAPIUS, with a Serpent.

Face,

the Summit of this very picturefque Knowl ftands a caftellated Building of confiderable Height and Dimenfions. It refembles the Citadel or Keep of an ancient Caftle ; fuch as are frequent on the Fron- tiers of *Wales.* confifting of a large circular Tower flanked by three embattled Turrets. It is moft ad- vantageoufly feen from the North, as the Turrets are from that Point of View diftinct, and the whole beautifully embofomed in Wood. From this Eminence the fame grand Scenery is difplayed as at *Kings- wefton.* This Structure was begun in 1769 by T. Farr, Efq. and completed with much Tafte, and at a great Expence.

By fome Antiquaries this Spot has been called the *Abone* of the *Romans,* who allege, in Confirmation of that Conjecture, that certain Lands near it were ftyled in a Rental of Sir Ralph Sadlier, dated 36 Hen. VIII. one Acre in *Campo de Abone-town.*

TYTHINGS and HAMLETS.

1. *Kingswefton.* Few Defcriptions would do Juftice to this Situation. In the Park are many beautiful Inequalities of Ground, which are interfperfed with the moft luxuriant Plantations, particularly of Elm- Trees. The Manfion-Houfe was re-built by Sir R. Southwell, from a Defign of Sir J. Vanbrugh, and may be faid to be rather handfome than fumptuous, yet it is certainly lefs heavy than many Works of that Architect. The Portal, finifhed with *Corinthian* Pilafters, leads to the great Hall, which is very lofty, and decorated, as are moft of the other Apartments, with a Series of Portraits of the Southwell Family and their Connections, by the moft eminent Artifts *. The View which this Spot commands is

truly

Face, or Obverfe.	*Reverfe.*
" Imp. Cæs. Vespasian. Aug. Cos. VIII. P. P."	" S. C." an Eagle, with his Wings expanded, fitting on a Globe.
" Imp. Antonin. Aug. Pius, P. P. Tr. P. P. Cos. IIII." Head crowned with Laurel.	A ftanding Figure holds out a Patera to a Serpent rifing from an Altar.
" Magnentius Nob. Cæs." a naked Head.	" Victor. D. D. N. N. Aug. & Cæs." two Victories fuftain- ing a Globe, on which is " Vot. V. Mult. X."
Constantius Carausius—feveral of them with their In- fcriptions worn out.	
Valentinianus—feveral of them.	" Securitas Reipublicæ."
" Imp. Nerva Cæs. Aug. P. M. T. R. P. Cos. III. P. P.	" Fortuna Augusti."
" Imp. Claud. August."	
" Urbs Roma," a Head with a Helmet—feveral of them.	A Wolf fuckling two Infants.
" Marcus Aurel. Antonin. Aug."	
" Antoninus Aug. Pius, P. P."	
" T. R. Pot. Cos. III. S. C."	A Mars marching.
Constantinus, Gratianus, Constantius ; and many other Coins of various Sizes.	

* Portraits in the Great Hall.

Full Lengths.
Thomas Cromwell, Earl of *Ardglafs,* in his Robes of State, nat. 1594, ob. 1653, by Vandyke.
Wingfield Cromwell, Earl of *Ardglafs,* in his Robes of State, nat. 1622, ob. 1668, by Ditto.
Lady Elizabeth Cromwell, Wife of Edw. Southwell, Efq. by Kneller.
Edw. Southwell, Efq. and Katherine Watson his Wife, by Dahl.
Half Lengths.
Sir Richard Southwell, of *Wood Rifing,* æt. 33.
Rob. Southwell, Efq. nat. 1607, ob. 1677 ; and Helena Gore his Wife, nat. 1613, ob. 1679.
Sir Rob. Southwell, Knt. nat. 1636, ob. 1702 ; Eliz. Dering his Wife, nat. 1648, ob. 1681.
The laft four by Vandyke.
Lord Chancellor Finch, fitting, in his Robes of Office.

In the Green Room.

Thomas Cromwell, Earl of *Effex,* by Hans Holbein, fitting at a Table.
Rich. Cromwell, æt. 95.
Sir Rich. Cromwell, 1554, by Sir Antonio More.
Mrs. Southwell, Maid of Honour to Q. Elizabeth, fmall Half Length, by Corn. Jansen.
Sir John Percivall, Half Length, by Vandyke.
Will. Ashburnham, Efq. æt. 70, 1679, by Lely.

In the Breakfaft-Room.

Full Lengths.
Mrs. Ashburnham, Wife of Sir Edw. Dering, Knt. 1623, æt. 18, by Corn. Jansen.
The Dutchefs of Mazarine, by Lely.
Countefs of Marlborough, by Ditto.
Half Lengths.
Lady Eliz. Cromwell, by Kneller.
Katherine Watson, Wife of Edw. Southwell, Efq. in the Character of *St. Katherine,* with the Symbols of Martyrdom, by Ditto.

In the Eating-Parlour.

Thomas Cromwell, Earl of *Effex,* fitting and holding his Wand of Office, by Kneller, full Length. The Head copied from the Original.
Lady Eliz. Cromwell ftanding, in a Fancy Drefs, by Ditto.

In

4

truly magnificent.   In the Fore Ground is a very flat Tract of Country called *Salt Marsh*, which appears beautifully verdant and cultivated ; the Channel and great Æstuary of the River *Severn*, with the bold Shores and Mountains of *Glamorgan*, and the Entrance of the Port of *Bristol*, frequently crowded with Shipping.

" *Kingesweston*; in the Booke of *Domesdei*, written *Westone*, wherein WILL'M the CONQUEROR had
" (as that Booke faith) 7 Hides and one Yard Land holden of the Crowne by Knight Service *in Capite*,
" and nowe the Inheritance of Sir JOHN WINTOUR, of *Lidney*, Knight, Sonne of Sir EDW. WINTOUR,
" Sonne of Sir WILL. WINTOUR, Vice Admirall of *England*, who, in the 12th Yeare of Queene ELIZ.
" purchafed the fame of Sir RICHARD BERKELEY, of *Stoke Gifford*, Knt. and lyeth within the Parish
" of *Henbury*.

" This Manor of *Westone*, nowe altogether called *Kingesweston*, was by Kinge H. II. in the first Yeare
" of his Raigne, granted (amongst others) to ROBERT, the Sonne of HARDING, and his Heires then,
" Parcell of the great Manor of *Berkeley*, and passed under the Wordes, in that Kinge's Grant, of *Berke-*
" *lei Hernesle*, as being one of the Nookes or Corners thereof, neere to the utter Bounds of this County
" of *Glouc.* not far from the Paffage over the River of *Hungrode*, called *Crock* and *Pill*, leading into
" *Somerfetshire*.   Shortly after which Grant of Kinge H. II. to the faid ROBERT, the Sonne of HARDING,
" he conveyed the fame, with the Manor of *Beverston*, to ROBERT his third Sonne, and his Heires, who
" was comonly written ROBERTUS Filius ROBERTI, Filii HARDINGI, and fometimes ROBERT Lord of
" WERE, neare *Axbridge*, in the County of *Somerfet*, which ROBERT DE WERE had Iffue MAURICE and
" EVE, and died in temp. JOH'IS.   The faid MAURICE was comonly called MAURICE DE GANT, and
" died without Iffue, in 14 H. III. leaving this Manor, with many others, to difcend to the Sonne of
" the faid EVE his Sifter, who was married to ——— GURNAY, who died in 53 H. III. leavinge Iffue
" ANSELM DE GURNAY, who died in 14 E. I. leavinge Iffue JOHN DE GURNAY, who died in 19 E. I.
" leavinge Iffue ELIZABETH, his only Dau'r and Heire, married to Sir JOHN AP ADAM; in what Yeare
" the faid ELIZ. died I have not obferved ; but the faid Sir JOHN her Hufband died in 5 E. II. to both
" whom the faid Sir THOMAS AP ADAM was Sonne and Heire, who, in 4 E. III. fold this Manor of
" *Kingesweston*, with that other of *Elberton*, to Sir MAURICE BERKELEY, Knt. who left Iffue Sir THO-
" MAS BERKELEY, called of *Ewley*, who had Iffue Sir MAURICE, Father of Sir MAURICE, Father of
" Sir WILL', Father of RICHARD, Father of Sir JOHN, Father of Sir RICHARD BERKELEY, who, in
" 12 ELIZ. fold this Manor to Sir WILL' WINTOUR.

" Rot. Paten. 4 H. III. pars 1. membr. 7. fhewes that Kinge's Licence granted to Sir MAURICE
" BERKELEY to demife his Landes in *Kingesweston* and *Ailberton*, to his Tenants, for Yeares or Lives.

" Placita in banco Hill. Term. 10 H. III. rot. 7. JOH'ES CORDWAINER & WILL'US filius ADAMI,
" appo' : fe verfus JOH'EM, de *Lantemersh*, filium SIMONIS, pro Manerio de *Westun* : which I take to
" be this.

" By Inq. after the Death of KATHERINE Lady BERKELEY, in 9 R. II. it is found, that fhe died
" feized for Life of a Meffuage and Carucate of Land in *Kingesweston*, holden of Sir JOHN THORPE,
" Knight, as of her Manor of *Kingesweston*, by Knight Service ; which Sir JOHN THORPE was fecond
" Hufband to KATHERINE BERKELEY, of *Stoke Gifford*, Widowe of Sir THOMAS BERKELEY, who held
" in Jointure the Manor of *Kingesweston*, which KATHARINE died in 11 R. II. and JOHN BERKELEY, Knt.
" was her Sonne and Heire, which is fo likewife found to be holden after the Death of the faid Sir
" JOHN BERKLEY by Inq. in 6 H. VI. but in 38 H. VI. after the Death of Sir MAURICE BERKELEY,
" Sonne of the faid Sir JOHN, and in 14 E. IV. after the Death of Sir MAURICE his Sonne and Heire,
" and in 2 H. VII. after the Death of Sir WILL. BERKELEY his Sonne and Heire, the faid Meffuage
" and Carucate of Land is found to be holden in Soccage, which now is the Freehold of ——— HORT,
" and others, lyinge in *Lawrence Weston*."

Mr. SMYTHE is very accurate in this Account, as far as his own Period.—Sir EDWARD WINTOUR was feized of it in 1614; by him it was conveyed to HUMPHRY HOOK, Alderman of *Briftol*, whofe Son, Sir HUMPHRY HOOK, re-fold it to Sir ROBERT SOUTHWELL, Knt. in 1679, who was lineally defcended from RICHARD SOUTHWELL, Efq. of *Wood Rifing*, co. *Norfolk*, conftituted one of the Truftees to the Will of King HENRY VIII. in 1546.   In that Family it has been fince vefted, and is now the Property of the Right Hon. EDWARD Baron DE CLIFFORD, *Weftmoreland*, *Vefci*, and *Appleby*, in Fee, firft fummoned in 1298 *.

The

In the Dreffing-Room.

Miniatures.

GEORGE CLIFFORD, Earl of *Cumberland*, in gilt and burnifhed Armour.

ANNE CLIFFORD, the celebrated Countefs of *Dorfet*, *Pembroke*, and *Montgomery*, in full Court Drefs, with her Coronet on her Head.

ANNE of *Denmark*, Queen of JAMES I. when young.

A very fatisfactory Mode has been adopted with thefe Portraits, that of annexing the Armorial Bearings to each ; by which the precife Connection is elucidated.   This Catalogue does not include the whole Collection ; but fuch Pictures only as appeared to be of greater Merit or Curiofity.

* ROGER DE CLIFFORD, Lord *Clifford* of *Clifford Caftle*, in the County of *Hereford*, was fummoned to Parliament in 1298. He married ISABEL, eldeft Daughter and Coheir of ROBERT DE VIPONT, Lord and Baron of *Weftmoreland*.   One of his

<table>
<tr><td>VOL. II.</td><td align="center">U</td><td align="right">Defcendants</td></tr>
</table>

The impropriate Tythes of the Hamlet of *Kingefwefton*, Parcel of the original Donation of ROBERT FITZHARDING to his Monaftery of *St. Auguftine* at *Briftol*, were granted to that See, and are now held by Leafe by Lord DE CLIFFORD. This Tything contains about 1400 Acres.

2. *Lawrencewefton.* The Manor of *Lawrencewefton* is likewife held by Lord DE CLIFFORD, with the Impropriation. This Tything contains about 1100 Acres; it had formerly a Chapel.

3. *Stowick* Tything, containing about 2500 Acres, the greater Part of which is the *Salt Marfh*, upon the Banks of the *Severn*. The Manor and Tythes, excepting thofe of *Crookmarfh*, which are in Difpute, belong to Lord DE CLIFFORD. Other Proprietors of Lands are, EDWARD SAMPSON, THOMAS SMYTH, SAMUEL EDWARDS, SAMUEL PEACH-PEACH, and SAMUEL THOMAS, Efqrs. the Families of EASTON and FRAMPTON.

4. *Charlton* Hamlet and Tything, containing about 1000 Acres, are faid to be annexed to the Manor of *Weftbury*; the principal Proprietors of which are, FIENNES TROTMAN, Efq. the Families of TEAST, HARFORD, and POWELL. Confiderable Eftates were held by the Family of STOKES till the Beginning of the prefent Century.

5. The Tything of *Northwick* and *Redwick*, including, jointly, about 1400 Acres, ftretches along the Banks of the *Severn*. The Chapel is fmall; of the Architecture of the later Centuries. Lands in this Tything are held by THOMAS LEWIS, Efq. of *St. Pierre*, JOSEPH TOMPKINS, ANDREW DAUBENEY, Efqrs. and JOHN MARSH, Gent.

B E N E F A C T I O N S.

ROBERT STOAKES gave by Deed of Feoffment, 1583, Lands, vefted in Feoffees, the yearly Produce of which is 80*l.* 16*s.* 2½*d.* to and for the needful Reparations of the Parifh-Church of *Henbury*, from Time to Time, when and fo often as Need fhall require; and to and for the Suftentation and relieving the pooreft and needieft People of the Parifh of *Henbury* aforefaid, being born within the faid Parifh, of good Name and honeft Converfation; and alfo to and for the Repairing and Amending the High-ways, and of the Sea Walls of *Severn*, from Time to Time, needful to be amended within the faid Parifh; and to and for Relieving, Helping, and Advancement of poor young Men and Maidens, born and abiding within the faid Parifh, being of honeft and chafte Converfation; and to and for fuch other charitable, good, and godly Ufes, Deeds, and Purpofes, as to the faid Feoffees, their Heirs and Affigns, fhall be thought good and meet. From this Fund a Saving has been accumulating fince the Year 1771, which produces an additional annual Income of 12*l.*

ANTHONY EDMUNDS gave by Deed of Feoffment, dated Nov. 15, 1628, Lands, the annual Income of which is 128*l.* for erecting and eftablifhing a Free Grammar School for all Children born within the Parifhes of *Henbury*, *Weftbury*, and *Horfield*, and for founding an Hofpital for the Lodging, Cloathing, and Maintenance of a certain Number of Poor Boys, as the Feoffees from Time to Time, fhall think meet.

Mrs. GRACE JAYNE gave by Will, dated Dec. 3, 1728, a Rent Charge of 20*s.* a Year for ever, to the Poor of the Tything of *Lawrencewefton*, to be paid out of Lands there, now in the Poffeffion of SUSANNAH WITHERLY, of *Briftol.*

CHRISTOPHER COLE gave by Will, dated Dec. 6, 1736, Moneys, vefted in EDWARD HARFORD, the Intereft of which is 27*l.* for the better Increafe and Maintenance of the Poor Boys of the aforefaid Free School in this Parifh.

WILLIAM COTTERILL, in 1754, gave by Will 10*s.* yearly, for ever, for a Sermon on Good Friday, charged on an Eftate called *Baker's Leaze.*

WILLIAM BURROUGHS gave (Time unknown) 20*s.* yearly, for ever, for a Sermon on Trinity Sunday, charged on an Eftate in *Kingswefton.*

ROBERT SANDFORD gave by Will, dated Oct. 6, 1755, Money, vefted in Truftees, the Intereft of which is 105*l.* to be applied to the Increafe and better eftablifhing of the aforefaid Free School. He likewife gave 100*l.* vefted in the Vicar of *Henbury* for the Time being, the Intereft whereof to be applied as follows, viz. 20*s.* yearly in Bread to twenty poor People, and the Remainder to the Minifter, for two Sermons on Good Friday and St. Thomas's Day.

Defcendants married the Heirefs of Lord VESCY. ANNE, fole Daughter and Heir of GEORGE, 17th Lord CLIFFORD, and third Earl of *Cumberland*, fucceeded to the Baronies of *Vefcy*, *Vipont* and *Clifford*, on the Death of HENRY fifth Earl of *Cumberland*. She married, 1ft, RICHARD third Earl of *Dorfet*; 2dly, PHILIP fourth Earl of *Pembroke:* By this laft fhe had no Iffue; by the firft fhe had Iffue two Daughters; Lady MARGARET SACKVILLE, the eldeft, was married to JOHN fecond Earl of *Thanet*, and had Iffue; Lady ISABELLA SACKVILLE, the fecond, was married to JAMES COMPTON, third Earl of *Northampton*, and had no Iffue remaining. THOMAS Earl of THANET, the Son of Lady MARGARET, in 1691, laid claim to the above-mentioned Baronies, which Claim was allowed him; but, he dying in 1729, they fell into Abeyance amongft his Daughters and Coheirs; when his late Majefty was pleafed, in 1734, to revive the fame in the Perfon of Lady MARGARET TUFTON, the third Daughter. She married THOMAS Lord LOVELL, afterwards Earl of *Leicefter*; and, leaving no furviving Iffue at her Death in 1776, his prefent Majefty was pleafed, in that Year, to confirm the faid Baronies to EDWARD SOUTHWELL, Efq. he being Son of KATHARINE Vifcountefs SONDES, eldeft Daughter of the above THOMAS Earl THANET.

EDW. SOUTHWELL, Efq. after his Marriage with the Lady ELIZABETH CROMWELL, who was Heir General to THOMAS Earl of *Effex*, created Baron CROMWELL of *Oakham* in 1540, claimed that Dignity upon the Death of ANNE Baronefs CROMWELL, in the Reign of Queen ANNE; but his Claim was not allowed by the Houfe of Lords.

Mrs.

Mrs. MARY WHITE gave (Time unknown) the Intereſt of 2o*l.* for ever to poor Houſekeepers not receiving Alms, veſted in Lord DE CLIFFORD.

Mrs. ANN SMYTH, in 1760, gave by Will, an Annuity of 1o*l.* for ever, iſſuing out of an Eſtate called *Redcliff Meads*, for teaching poor Girls to read, knit, and few, to be appointed by the Miniſter and Churchwardens, veſted in EDWARD GORE, Eſq.

INCUMBENTS.	PATRONS.	INCUMBENTS.	PATRONS.
1627 Henry Brereton,	Ralph Sadlier, Eſq.	1726 William Holmes,	Sir John Smyth.
1668 John Saunders,	Walter Lord Aſton.	1729 John Gardiner,	Thomas Edwards, Eſq.
1672 John Chetwynd,	John Stump.	1780 John Davie, D. D.	Robert Yatcombe.
1690 Thomas Stump,	Elizabeth Goldenham.	1786 Alex. Colſton, LL. B.	Lord Middleton.
1712 Arthur Derby,	—————.	1792 (Vacant.)	

PRESENT PROPRIETORS OF THE MANORS.

Of *Henbury*,
THOMAS SMYTH, Eſq. The Right Honourable HENRY Lord Viſcount MIDDLETON,
and ALEXANDER COLSTON, Eſq.

Of *Kingweſton, Lawrenceweſton*, and *Stowick*,
The Right Hon. EDWARD Baron DE CLIFFORD.

The Perſons ſummoned from this Pariſh and its Hamlets by the Heralds, in 1682 and 1683, were

Sir Samuel Aſtry, Knt. Dame Katharine Hooke, Francis Fane, Gent.
Sir Robert Southwell, Knt. Henry Stokes, Gent. Thomas Waſhbourn, Gent.
Edward Sampſon, Eſq. Edward Parker, Gent. Richard Kingſtone, Gent.

At the Election in 1776 Fifty Freeholders polled from this Pariſh.

The earlieſt Date in *Henbury* Regiſter is 1538.

ANNUAL ACCOUNT OF MARRIAGES, BIRTHS, AND BURIALS, IN THIS PARISH.

A.D.	Mar.	Bir.	Bur.	A.D.	Mar.	Bir.	Bur.	A.D.	Mar.	Bir.	Bur.	A.D.	Mar.	Bir.	Bur.
1781	9	47	39	1786	10	29	50	1791				1796			
1782	11	29	37	1787	10	36	38	1792				1797			
1783	13	50	41	1788	11	51	55	1793				1798			
1784	7	40	35	1789	11	44	36	1794				1799			
1785	7	55	41	1790	3	31	34	1795				1800			

The Regiſter of the Chapelry of *Northwick*, not including the Marriages, has its firſt Date in 1667.

ANNUAL ACCOUNT OF BIRTHS, AND BURIALS, IN NORTHWICK CHAPELRY.

A.D.	Bir.	Bur.	A.D.	Bir.	Bur.	A.D.	Bir.	Bur.	A.D.	Bir.	Bur.
1781	1	5	1786	4	4	1791			1796		
1782	2	3	1787	1	2	1792			1797		
1783	3	1	1788	3	3	1793			1798		
1784	2	1	1789	6	4	1794			1799		
1785	1	4	1790	3		1795			1800		

I N   T H E   C H A P E L   A T   N O R T H W I C K.

ON FLAT STONES.

Here lyeth the Body
of THOMAS HOLLISTER, of this
Tything, Yeoman who departed
the 14th Day of April, 1729, aged 43.

Alſo two Sons of the above named
THOMAS HOLLISTER, both named
EDWARD, were buried here.

Alſo here lyeth the Body
of MARTHA, the Wife of
the aboveſaid THOMAS
HOLLISTER, who died Decemb.
the 29th; 1747, aged 63 Years.

Alſo here lyeth the Body of
RICHARD HOLLISTER, of this Tything,
Son of the aboveſaid THOMAS,
who departed this Life
the 30th Day of April, 1753.

———

In Memory of
JOHN BRIGHT, obit 7th July,
1759, aged 2 Years.

Alſo of JOHN, Son of RICHARD
HOLLISTER, obit 5 May, 1760,
aged 18 Years.

Alſo of JOHN HOLLISTER,
obit 4 January, 1767.

Alſo of GEORGE HEWETT,
obit 9 February, 1771,
aged 52 Years.

Alſo of ANN BRIGHT, obit
30 April, 1775, aged 60 Years.

Alſo of JOHN BRIGHT, obit
27th November, 1775,
aged 64 Years.

———

ON GRAVE-STONES IN THE CHAPEL-YARD.

William Orchard, of Olveſton,	died 27 July, 1694, aged	—	John his Son	-	died 11 Oct. 1763, aged	9
Grace his Widow, and late Wife of			Roger Hicks	-	15 Oct. 1729	50
William Boulton	29 Sept. 1727	—	Elizabeth his Wife, and Relict of			
John Brewer	-	21 Oct. 1766	38	Thomas Hitchings	-	22 Dec. 1752	57

2

INSCRIPTIONS

INSCRIPTIONS IN THE CHURCH OF HENBURY.

IN THE CHANCEL ON MARBLE MONUMENTS.

Arms; Argent, three Cinquefoils Gules, each charged with five Annulets Or, for SOUTHWELL;—impaling, Or, a Saltire Sable, for DERING. Creft, a demi Goat Argent, eared and gorged with a ducal Coronet, and charged with three Annulets in Bend Gules.

Here lyeth
the Body of Sir ROBERT SOUTHWELL,
of King's Wefton, in the County of Gloucefter, Knt.
He was eldeft Son of ROBERT SOUTHWELL, of Kinfale
in Ireland, Efq. and of HELENA, the Daughter
of Major ROBERT GORE.
He was born at Ballyn Varwick, on the River of Bandon,
near Kinfale, the 31ft of Decem. 1635;
he came for his Education into England, in 1650;
and fpent his younger Years at Queen's College
in Oxford, in Lincoln's Inne, and in Travel abroad.
He was, by King CHARLES the Second, made one of the Clerks
of his Moft Honourable Privy Council in Septem. 1664.
He married ELIZABETH, eldeft Daughter of Sir EDWARD DERING,
of Surronden-Dering, in Kent, Bart.
by whom he had Iffue 6 Children.
He was employed in feveral Foreign Negotiations;
firft, in quality of Envoy, with Powers to mediate a Peace
between Spain and Portugal, proving happily
inftrumental in giving a Period to that War
which had continued 28 Years without Intermiffion.
He was fent a fecond Time to the Court of Portugal
in quality of Envoy Extraordinary;
afterwards with the like Character to the Governor of Flanders,
the Conde de Montery in 1672;
and with the fame Commiffion to the Elector
of Brandenburg at Berlin, in 1680, attending in his Way
the Prince of Orange at the Hague, by whofe Councels
that Negotiation was to be directed.
After his Return he retired from publick Bufinefs,
living at King's Wefton till King WILLIAM
was advanced to the Throne.
He was then by his Majefty made Principal Secretary
of State for Ireland, and attended him in his Expedition
in 1690, for the Reduction of that Kingdom,
holding the faid Office till his Death.
He had ferved in three Parliaments, and was 5 Times
chofen Prefident of the Royal Society.
He dyed at King's Wefton the 11th Day of Sept. 1702,
aged 66 Years.

Arms; on two Efcocheons, 1ft, SOUTHWELL as before; on an Efcocheon of Pretence, quarterly, Or and Azure, four Lions paffant counterchanged, for CROMWELL; 2d, SOUTHWELL, impaling, Or, two Bendlets engrailed Sable, for BLATHWAIT.

To the Memory of
EDWARD SOUTHWELL, Efq.
who, after leaving the Univerfity of Oxford,
was early entered into Bufinefs,
under the Conduct of his Father Sir ROBERT,
who then attended King WILLIAM into Ireland
as Principal Secretary of State of that Kingdom,
in which Employment he fucceeded his Father,
and continued in it till his Death.
His Skill and Experience in Bufinefs
recommended him to four Princes fucceffively,
whom he attended as Clerk of the Councill.
He was thrice joint Commiffioner of the Privy Seal,
twice Chief Secretary to the Lord Lieutenant of Ireland,
Clerk of the Crown in Ireland, and Vice Admiral of Munfter.
In thefe feveral Stations
he improved his Family Eftate with Integrity and Induftry;
he was helpful to all Mankind, and affectionate to his Family;
he enjoyed Life with Chearfulnefs and Innocence;
and bore a moft long and painful Sicknefs
with Patience, Firmnefs, and Refignation.
He was born the 4 Septem. 1671, and died 4 Dec. 1730.

Here lyeth the Right Hon. the Lady ELIZABETH, fole Daughter and Heirefs of VERE ESSEX CROMWELL, Baron of Oakham, Vifcount Lekale, and Earl of Ardglafs, by CATHARINE HAMILTON. She was tenth Defcendant from THO. CROMWELL, firft Baron of Oakham, and Earl of Effex, Vicar General, and chief Promoter of the Reformation in the Reign of HENRY VIII. She was born 3d of December, 1674, married to EDWARD SOUTHWELL, Efq. 29 October, 1704, and died 31 of March, 1709, leaving Iffue EDWARD, ROBERT, THOMAS, and ELIZABETH; the three laft died in their Infancy.
She was a Lady diftinguifhed by a fuperior Genius and Underftanding, and her Affection to her Hufband and Family. Her Charity, and the Refolution with which fhe bore her laft Illnefs, and forefaw her Death, are ever to be remembered to her Honour, and to be recommended to the Imitation of Pofterity.

Here alfo lyeth ANN, the Daughter of WILLIAM BLAITHWAIT, Efq. by ANN WYNTER, of Dyrham, in the County of Gloucefter, a Lady of fingular Virtue and Merit, who died much lamented 1 July, 1717, aged 27, a Year after her Marriage with EDWARD SOUTHWELL, Efq. leaving one Son WILLIAM SOUTHWELL.

Arms;

Arms; SOUTHWELL, as before;—impaling, Or, a Saltire
Sable, for DERING

ELIZABETH,
eldeft Daughter of Sir EDWARD DERING, of Surren-
den Dering in Kent, Baronet (one of the Lords Commiffioners
of his Majefty's Treafury), and of Dame MARY his Wife,
lies here interred.
She die! in London on the 13th of Jan. 1681, in the 33d Year
of her Age, and was here depofited (in Hopes of a bleffed
Refurrection) on the 26th Day of the fame Month.
She was married on the 26 Day of January 1644, to Sir
ROBERT SOUTHWELL. Knt. then one of the Clerks attending his Majefty King CHARLES the Second, in his moft
Honourable Privy Councel.
They had iffue
RUPERT, EDWARD, HELENA, ELIZABETH, MARY
(who died an Infant), and KATHARINE.
RUPERT,
who was born in London the 21 of May, 1660,
and dyed there on the eighth of May, 1678, lyes here now alfo
interred.
Such a Sonne, and fuch a Wife, deferve fomething
more durable than Marble to the Memory of their Virtues.
She had all the Perfections of Beauty, Behaviour, and Underftanding, that could adorn this Life; and all the inward Blef-
fings of Virtue and Piety which might intitle her to a better.
The Boy was in his Years only a Child, fo that none had fo
much Hope of what he might be, as of Defpair that he was not
intended for this World.
To the Memory of both (who lived too fhort for thofe they left
behind the affli&ted Hufband and Father Sir ROBERT
SOUTHWELL, of King's Weiton, in the County of Gloucefter,
Knt. erects this Stone.

Arms; SOUTHWELL as before.

To the Memory of
the Right Hon. EDWARD SOUTHWELL,
Son of EDWARD SOUTHWELL and Lady ELIZAB. CROMWELL,
born 17 June, 1705;
he married, 21 Aug. 1729,
KATHARINE WATSON, Daughter of EDWARD Lord SONDES,
Son of LEWIS Earl of ROCKINGHAM;
their Children were,
EDWARD, born 6 June, 1738,
KATHARINE, born 10 Dec. 1739; fhe died 17 March, 1748,
and is buried near her Father,
who exchanged this Life for a better 16 March, 1755.
He was chofen Member of Parliament for the City of
Briftol in the Year 1739; and re-chofen for the fame Place
the two following Parliaments in the Difcharge of
which Truft, his Conduct was uninfluenced by the
Temptations of Ambition, Avarice, or Popularity;
equally true to his King and his Country, and ever fteady
to what he thought right. In private Life he was Juft,
Charitable, Benevolent, Friendly; a tender affectionate
Hufband and Father; a kind Landlord and Mafter; and,
what comprehends all civil and moral Virtues, a fincere
pious Chriftian.

IN THE SOUTH AISLE.

Arms; Quarterly, 1ft and 4th, SOUTHWELL as before; 2d
and 3d, Or and Azure, a Fefs Gules, for CLIFFORD;—impaling, gyrony of eight, Gules and Ermine, for CAMPBELL.

To the Memory
of EDWARD SOUTHWELL, Baron CLIFFORD,
only Son of the Right Honourable EDWARD SOUTHWELL,
of King's Weiton, in the County of Gloucefter,
by CATHARINE, only Daughter, and fole Heir of EDW. WAT-
SON, Vifcount Sondes,
firft Son of LEWIS Earl of ROCKINGHAM, by
CATHARINE, eldeft Daughter, and Coheir of
THOMAS TUFTON, Earl of Thanet and Baron Clifford.
On the Deceafe of the faid Earl of THANET in 1729,
the Barony of Clifford fell into Abeyance,
and was conferred upon MARGARET Countefs
of LEICESTER, his third Daughter, and
Coheir; on whofe Demife in 1775,
the Barony again falling into Abeyance,
was conferred, in April 1776, on
the faid EDWARD SOUTHWELL, who,
journeying to a milder Climate for the
Benefit of his Health, died at Avignon,
the firft of Nov. 1777,
in the fortieth Year of his Age.

IN THE NAVE.

TO THE MEMORY
OF THE HONOURABLE
CATHARINE SOUTHWELL,
WIDOW OF EDWARD SOUTHWELL,
ESQUIRE,
OF KING'S WESTON,
ONLY SURVIVING ISSUE
OF EDWARD
LORD VISCOUNT SONDES,
SON OF LEWIS WATSON,
EARL OF ROCKINGHAM,
BORN
SEPTEMBER MDCCXI,
DIED
APRIL . . MDCCLXV.

ON A MARBLE MONUMENT IN THE CHANCEL:

Arms; Quarterly, 1ft and 4th, Barry, wavy of fix Argent
and Azure, on a Chief Gules, three Bezants, for ASTRY; 2d
and 3d, three Croflets, on a Chief, three Efcallops.

H. S. E.
Juvenis, tum genere tum virtutibus fpectabilis,
SANCTUS JOHANNES ASTRY, Armiger,
Utroq. à nomine ornatus,
Utriufq. fimul ornamentum.
Quippe
Familiæ de ASTRY, apud Woodend, in agro Bedfordienfi, fera
foboles,
Stemmate gaudens ob antiquitatem haud ignoto.
Uxore ductâ de STIRPE ST. JOHN, de Fletfho nobili,
Filius alter, unicus fuperftes
SAMUELIS ASTRY ex ELIZABETHA, filiâ & herede GEORGII
MORSE, de Henbury, Arm.
Qui quidem SAMUEL titulo Equeftri donatus,
fi merita fpectes, omni titulo major,
Per XL circiter annos continuos
Clerici Coronæ munus arduum nec inhoneftum
Summâ fide pariter ac folertiâ obivit.
Juvenis hic patre dignus,
Gentilitios quotquot funt, honores proprios fecit;
Ob paternas virtutes clarus, etiam fine ijs clariffimus;
Animo benigno moribus ingenuis pollebat fine æmulo fuis,
Egregiæ Vir humanitatis. Jufticiæ alias inauditæ:
Erga pauperes liberalem, erga omnes benevolum,
Profequebantur omnes amore vivum, morientem defiderio.
Obiit die XXI Novemb. Anno { Salutis noftræ MDCCXII.
{ Ætatis fuæ XXVII.
Cujus memoriæ facrum effe voluit hoc marmor,
foror natu minima,
ARABELLA ASTRY,
fororum amantiffima heredum mœftiffima.

ON HANDSOME MONUMENTS IN THE SOUTH AISLE.

Arms; a Crofs fleury between four Efcallops for SAMPSON;—
impaling, a Lion rampant, between fix Croflets, for LONG.

To the Memory
of EDWARD SAMPSON, of Henbury, Gent.
who departed this Life the 1ft Day of Feb. 1695,
aged 45 Years.
He was fecond Son of JOHN SAMPSON, of
Charleton, in this Parifh, Gent.
He fpent his younger Years at Nevis,
and other the Weftern Iflands, where he
refided as a Factor until the Death of
his elder Brother JOHN SAMPSON, of the
Inner Temple, London, Efq. and then
returned to England, and married MARY,
fole Daughter and Heirefs of EDWARD LONG,
of Olvefton, in this County, Gent.
She died the 14 of April, 1716, aged 66 Years,
and lieth here interred.
They had Iffue three Children;
MARTHA, JOHN, and MARY.
MARY died an Infant.
MARTHA fubmitted to inexorable Fate
the 24 of June, in the Year of our Lord
1710, and of her Age the 25th.

Arms ; three Swords in Pale, Points in Chief hilted ;—impaling, quarterly, 1ft and 4th. a Crofs flory, between four Efcallops ; 2d and 3d, a Crofs.

In Memory of
JOHN SAMPSON, of Charlton, in this
Parifh, Gent. who departed this Life the 24th
of Auguft, 1732, aged 55 Years. His Corpfe was
firft interred in a Vault in the Church Yard,
and removed to the Vault beneath,
7 Nov. 1766.

Alfo of JAMES TEAST, of the City of Briftol,
Stationer, who died 12 March, 1767, aged 39 Years.

Alfo of MARY, Wife of the abovefaid
JOHN SAMPSON, who departed this Life 22 Sept.
1769, aged 86 Years.

Alfo of SIDENHAM TEAST, of the City
of Briftol, Gent. who departed this Life
22 January, 1773, aged 72 Years.

____

To the Memory of
CHRISTOPHER COLE, Gent.
Son of JAMES COLE, of
Briftol, Merchant,
who gave the Refidue of his
Eftate, amounting to near
one Thoufand Pounds,
for the better Maintenance
and Increafe of the poor Boys
belonging to the Free School
of this Parifh.
He deceafed the 21 March, 1736,
aged about feventy,
and lies interred near
this Monument.

____

To the Memory of
WILLIAM COTTERELL,
of this Parifh, Gent.
who departed this Life
Feb. 18th, 1754, aged 40 Years.

Alfo
of MARY, the Wife of
WILLIAM JONES,
of this Parifh, Yeoman,
who died 12 Nov. 1770,
aged 44 Years.

____

Arms ; Per Chevron Sable and Ermine, in Chief two Boars'
Heads couped Or, for SANDFORD ;—impaling, Azure, a Bend
between three Leopards' Faces Or.   Creft, a Boar's Head
couped Or.

Ex adverfo hujufce loci
(Profpiciens ipfe fibi fepulchrum)
Exuvias fuas deponi voluit
ROBERTUS SANDFORD, Armiger,
Patre quidem Cive Briftolienfi,
Proavis de Sandford Hall, in agro Salopienfi, oriundus,
Improles obiens
Quas accepit a fuis opes
(Auctiores ipfius induftria redditas)
Teftamentum condens ita difpertivit,
Ut dum liberalem fe in fuos præftavit,
Utilitatis publicæ non immemor extaret
Beneficentiæ Monumenta rogas ?
En qui teftentur paræciæ iftius incolæ,
Quippe quibus mille & fexcentas libras legavit,
Quum fuiffet jamdiu in negotiis verfatus,
Otio tandem aliquantifper ut frueretur
(Suadentibus item annis, & uberiori reditu)
Bathoniæ feceffum quæfivit,
Ubi annum agens fexagefimum tertium,
Arthritide correptus, deceffit 29° Jan. 1756.

____

To the Memory of
WILLIAM DAVIE, Efq. Son of
Sir JOHN DAVIE, Baronet, of Creedy,
in the County of Devon,
who died the 14 of Nov. 1757, aged 51.

____

Arms ; Argent, a Chevron Sable, between three Mullets
pierced Gules ;—impaling, Per Pale dancette Or and Azure two
Fleurs de Lys counterchanged.

H. S. E.
Reverendus JOHANNES DAVIE, S. T. P.
hujus Ecclefiæ aliquandiu Paftor,
Cui muneri utcunque arduo
Strenue & feliciter invigilavit,
Multis & eximiis Animi dotibus,
Dignitatem contulit & Gratiam peculiarem,
Mira Corporis venuftas
ut in illo
Comitas, Benevolentia, Fides,
non Pectoris tantum incolæ,
at Fronti palam afpectabiles infediffe
viderentur.
Optimo Marito ac dilectiffimo
Hoc noftri defiderii Monumentum
Conjux nuper felix
Vidua heu ! nunc derelicta
cum Lachrymis pono.

S. D.

____

Near this Place
are depofited the Remains
of THOMAS SHEWELL,
late Citizen of London,
who died at the Hotwell
16 Ap. 1770, aged 70.

____

IN THE NORTH AISLE.

Arms ; Quarterly, 1ft and 4th, a Crofs flory, between four
Efcallops, for SAMPSON ; 2d and 3d, a Fefs wavy, between
three Fleurs de Lys, for HICKES.

Near this Tablet
are intombed the Remains
of JOHN SAMPSON, Efq.
Son of EDWARD SAMPSON, of this Parifh, Gent.
who departed this Life
on the twenty-firft of December,
one Thoufand feven Hundred and fifty-three,
in the fixty-fixth Year of his Age.
After the ufual Time dedicated to his Studies
at the College of St. John in Oxford,
He was affianced in Marriage to MARY,
Daughter and Coheirefs of NICHOLAS HICKES, Efq.
Alderman of the City of Briftol,
by whom he had Iffue
four Sons and two Daughters,
none of whom furvived the Period of Minority
except JOHN, who deceafed at the Age of twenty-eight,
and EDWARD, who, in Remembrance of an indulgent Father,
erected this Monument.

____

Near this Place
are interred the Remains
of MICHAEL MILLER, Efq.
Born at St. Gall, in Switzerland,
22 September, 1703.
Died at Henbury
23 May, 1785.

____

IN THE NAVE.

Arms ; in a Lozenge, Gules, on a Chevron between three
Cinquefoils Argent, each charged with an Annulet of the firft,
as many Leopards' Heads Sable, for SMYTH.

Sacred to the Memory
of ANNE SMYTH,
eldeft Daughter of Sir JOHN SMYTH, Baronet,
of Long Afhton, in the County of Somerfet.
She lived a confpicuous Example
of all Chriftian Virtues ;
her Piety was without Hypocrify ;
her Charity without Oftentation,
and her Hofpitality without Extravagance.
Such was her amiable Difpofition ;
and fuch her unbounded Beneficence,
that fhe was alike refpected and beloved
by the Rich and Poor.
Her Liberality ftill remains

in

in her pious Bequefts :
to the Parifh of Long Afhton,
and to the Parifh of Henbury,
She left refpectively the Sum of ten Pounds for ever.
Obiit Decemb. 21, 1760, æt. 68.
This Monument was erected
by her Nephew EDWARD GORE, Efquire,
of Kiddington, Oxfordfhire.

Arms ; Chequy Or and Azure, on a Fefs Gules, three Lozenges Argent.

Prope jacet
Corpus EDVARDI
CAPELL, nuper Civis
& Mercatoris Civitatis
Briftoll, qui exceffit e
vita fecundo die Junii,
Anno ætatis fuæ,
fexageffimo quinto,
Annoque Domini Mill'imo
Sexcenteffimo
Octagefimo
Primo.

ON FLAT STONES IN THE CHANCEL.

Arms ; Ermine, a Bull within a Bordure engrailed Sable, charged with twelve Bezants, for COLE ;—impaling, within a Bordure, a Pomegranate, for WHITSON.

HERE LYETH THE BODY OF CHRISTOPHER COLE,
OF CHARLTON, ESQ. WHO DECEASED THE 11TH
DAY OF MAY, ANNO DOMINI MDCLXXXXIX,
AGED LXXVI YEARS. HE HAD 6 CHILDREN ; CHRISTO-
PHER, AND CHARLES, MARY, BRIDGET, ANN,
AND ELIZABETH, OF WHOM ANN IS THE ALONE
SURVIVOR, MARRIED TO RICHARD HAYNES,
OF ABSTON, IN THIS COUNTY, ESQ.
HE WAS EXQUISITELY VERSED IN OUR LAWS AND CONSTI-
TUTION, EXERTING HIS KNOWLEGE TO THE HONOUR OF HIS
PRINCE, AND BENEFIT OF HIS COUNTRY, NO LESS
STUDIOUS OF RIGHT AND EQUITY, THAN SKILFUL IN
DISTRIBUTING JUSTICE, NOT REGARDING HIS PRIVATE SO
MUCH AS THE PUBLICK GOOD, WHEREBY HE DISCHARGED
THE OFFICE OF A TRUE JUSTICIAR.
HE WAS DEVOUT TOWARDS GOD, AND REMARKABLE
AMONG MEN, FOR AN ANCIENT FREEDOM AND INTEGRITY
OF MIND, PROTECTING THE INNOCENT, PUNISHING AND
REPRESSING THE INJURIOUS, ACTING BY PERSUASION AND
MILDNESS, RATHER THAN BY EXTREMITY AND FORCE,
COMPOSING DIFFERENCES, AND PROMOTING PEACE,
WHEREBY HE DISCHARGED THE DUTY OF A TRUE CHRISTIAN.

ALSO HERE LYETH THE BODY OF MRS. ANN JEFFERIS,
OF CHARLTON, WHO DIED 28 DEC. 1780,
AGED 69 YEARS.

HERE LYETH THE BODY OF
BRIDGET COLE, THE
DAUGHTER OF CHRIS-
TOPHER COLE, ESQ.
WHO DEPARTED THIS
LIFE THE 31 OF OCT.
ANNO DOM. 1683,
AGED 21 YEARS.

ALSO ELIZABETH HIS DAUGHTER
DIED THE 11 SEP. 1674,
AGED 1 YEAR.

HERE LYETH THE BODY OF
CHRISTOPHER COLE, GENT.
SON OF CHRISTOPHER COLE,
OF THIS PARISH, ESQ. WHO
DEPARTED THIS LIFE THE
2D DAY OF APRIL, 1683,
AGED 24 YEARS.

ALSO BRIDGET, THE DAUGHTER
OF CHRISTOPHER COLE, JUN.
DIED THE 14 AUG. 1683.

ALSO CHARLES COLE, GENT.
THE 2D SON OF CHRISTOPHER
COLE, ESQ. WHO DEPARTED 31
OF MAY, ANNO DOMINI
1685,
AGED 25 YEARS.

HERE LYETH THE BODY OF
BLANCH, THE WIFE OF
CHRISTOPHER COLE, OF THIS
PARISH, ESQ. WHO DIED
JULY 9, 1690, AGED
61 YEARS.

Arms ; on a Bend, a Fifh, a Crefcent for Difference.

In a Vault beneath this Marble
the Remains of three Daughters of the Rev. JOHN DOLMAN
and REBECCA his Wife are depofited ; viz. SARAH,
REBECCA, and ANN, neither of whom furvived the Period
of Infancy except REBECCA, on whom Nature had beftowed
every Embellifhment that could excite the pleafing Hopes
of her fond Parents. But, alas ! this lovely Innocent,
unable to refift the Violence of a fevere Ilinefs,
to the ineffable Lofs of her afflicted Relatives,
funk into the cold icy Arms of Death,
Dec. 15, 1779, aged 5 Years.
To the Memory of whom
may this laft Tribute of Parental Affection
be held facred.

The Rev. JOHN DOLMAN, B. A. Rector of Broome,
in the County of Worcefter,
exchanged the Sorrows of this World
for the joyful Society
of his happy Progeny in a better,
April 4, 1783, aged 45.

IN THE SOUTH AISLE, ON FLAT STONES.

Here lyeth the
Body of THOMAS WASBOROW, of
Penpark,
in the Parifh of Weftbury,
Gent. who departed this Life
the 27th Day of Auguft, 1721,
aged 58 Years.

Alfo here lyeth the Body of
CICELIA, Daughter of
HENRY WASBOROW, Gent. and
CICELIA his Wife, of Penpark,
in the Parifh of Weftbury,
both deceafed. She departed this Life the 11 Day of
September, Anno Dom. 1701,
ætatis fuæ 31.

In Memory
of MARTHA, Wife of THOMAS WAS-
BOROW,
who died the 9 of Feb. 1739,
aged 43.

Alfo of the faid
THOMAS WASBOROW,
who died 2 Jan. 1746,
aged 48.

Likewife
JOHN WASBOROW,
of the City of Briftol,
Merchant, who died
thd 7 of April, 1767,
aged 36.

HERE LYETH THE BODY OF
THOMAS WASBOROW, OF
THIS PARISH, YEOMAN, WHO
DEPARTED THIS LIFE THE
12 DAY OF OCTOBER, ANNO
DOMINI 1679,
AGED 63 YEARS.

HERE LYETH THE BODY OF
SARAH, THE WIFE
OF THOMAS WASBOROW,
YEOMAN. SHE DEPARTED
THIS LIFE THE 26
OF DECEM. 1669,
AGED 46 YEARES.

MARY,

MARY, DAUGHTER OF
THOMAS AND SARAH
WASBOROW, DIED THE
LAST OF AUG 1681,
AGED 18 YEARS.

HERE LYETH INTERRED THE
BODY OF HENRY WASBO-
ROW, LATE OF PEN PARKE,
IN THE PARISH OF WESTBURY
UPON TRIM, YEOMAN, WHO
DEPARTED THIS LIFE
THE 22 DAY OF JULY, ANNO
DOMINI 1674,
AGED 57 YEARES.

HERE LYETH ALSO THE BODY
OF THOMAS,
SON OF THE SAIDE HENRY WAS-
BOROW,
WAS BURIED DEC. 29, AN. DOM.
1724,
IN THE 2CTH YEAR OF HIS AGE.

HERE LIES THE BODY OF
CICELY ELBRIDGE,
WIFE OF THE ABOVESAID HENRY
WASBOROW, AND LATE WIFE TO
JOHN LAMBE, ESQ.
WHO DEPARTED THIS LIFE
JUNE 13, 1693, AGED 52.

Here lyeth the Body of SARAH
WASBOROW, of Henbury, Widow,
who departed this Life
May 24, 1726, aged 56 Years.

Alfo here lyeth the Body of
HENRY WASBOROW, Son of HENRY
WASBOROW and EDITH his Wife,
of Penpark, in the Parifh of
Weftbury upon Trym. He
was buried the 26 Jan. 1743,
aged 20 Years and 4 Months.

Alfo here lyeth the Body of
HENRY, the Son of JOHN
and ELIZABETH WASBOROW, of this
Parifh, who departed this
Life the 24 of September,
Anno Dom. 1711,
aged 23 Years.

Alfo the Body of HANNAH,
the Daughter of THOMAS
WASBOROW and SARAH his
Wife, of this Parifh, who died
June the 5th, 1732,
aged 67 Years.

H. S. E.
SARAH STANDFAST, Daughter of
THOMAS and SARAH WASBOROUGH,
ob. January the 23, 1732.

Here lyeth the Body of
JOSIAS NORTON, of this Parifh,
who departed this Life
the 14 of January, 1680,
aged 34 Years.

IN THE NAVE.

Sacred
to the Memory of
the Rev. Mr. THOMAS STUMPE,
late Vicar of Henbury,
who, exchanging this
mortal State
for Immortality,
departed this Life
the 23 of April, 1712.

FRANCES his Wife
was buried Jan. 12, 1729.

MARY their Daughter
died Novem. 5, 1697,
aged 6 Years.

THOMAS their Son, buried
June 26, 1718,
aged 19 Years.

Arms; Per Chevron crenelle three
Eagles difplayed.

Here lyeth the Body of
ARTHUR DERBY, Vicar of Henbury,
who departed this Life the 21 Day
November . . . . . in the 40 Year of
his Age. Alfo two of his Children,
JOHN and ARAB . . . . . .

Here lyeth the Body of CATHERINE,
the Wife of THOMAS GEERING,
Yeoman, who departed this Life
the 7th of March, 1686-7.

Here lyeth the Body of CORNELIUS
JAYNE, of this Parifh, Yeoman,
who departed this Life 2 Ap. 1713,
aged 73.

GRACE his Wife died the 31ft of . . . .
1731, aged . .

Here lieth interred
the Remains of JOHN AUST,
of this Parifh, Yeoman,
who died 17 Oct. 1767,
aged 73 Years.

SARAH his Wife died the 16th
of Oct. 1746, aged 55 Years.

JOHN their Son died 22 Novem.
1746, aged 25 Years.

Here lyeth the Body of MORRIS
OWELAND, of this Parifh, ...
who departed this Life the
30 Day of . . . . ber, 1651, aged 73.

MARY HOLLISTER died 1734.

In Memory of WILKINS WADE,
of Briftol, Gent. who died
July the 8th, 1748 aged 23 Years.

Alfo of MARY WADE, Widow,
Mother of the faid WILKINS
WADE, who died the 19 Feb. 1755,
aged 67 Years.

Here lyeth the Body of JOSEPH CHOCK,
of this Parifh, Schoolmafter,
who departed this Life the 30 of Nov.
1725, aged 55 Years.

H. S. E.
RICHARD GAY,
who died 28 March,
1761, aged 68.

The Rev. JOHN PRICE, M. A.
late Minifter of St. James, in the
City and Diocefe of Briftol, 1772.

IN THE NORTH AISLE.

To the Memory of JANE, the
Wife of THOMAS BAKER, of
this Parifh, Yeoman, who departed
this Life March 28, 1758, aged 63.

ALICE CREED, aged 59 Years,
Wife to EDWARD CREED 45 Years,
deceafed the 6th Septemb. 1626.

Under this Stone are depofited the
Remains
of JOHN RUSSELL, Gent. late of
Shirehampton.
Faithful to his GOD,
a Friend to Mankind,
a Relation to Relations,
ferved his King and Country
53 Years.
His Liberality and Charity to the Poor
were without Bounds.
We therefore hope, that, at the laft Day,
his Body will be received in Glory,
being fnatched away by Death,
which he had long expected with
conftancy.
He went to a better Life Dec. 2, 1789,
having lived 72 Years, 8 Months, and
28 Days.

Here
lies, in Hopes of a joyful Refurrection,
the Remains of MARGARET, the
Wife of ROGER PROSSER,
of the City of Briftol, Victualler.
She departed this Life the 16 Day of
May, 1780,
aged 77 Years.

IN THE CHURCH-YARD, ON TOMBS.

HERE LYETH THE BODY OF
DANIEL SAMPSON,
OF WOODLAND, IN THE PARISH
OF ALMONDSBURY, SON OF JOHN
SAMPSON, WHO DEPARTED THIS
LIFE JANUARY 24, 1678.

HERE LYETH THE BODIES OF
TWO SAMUELS, THE SONS OF
RALPH SAMPSON, GENT.
WHO DIED IN THEIR INFANCY.

Here lyeth the Body of
JOHN SAMPSON,
late of this Parifh, Gent.
who departed this Life
20 April, 1727, aged 32.

Here

Here lyeth the Body of
MARTHA, Daughter of JOHN
SAMPSON, of Charlton,
Gent. who departed this
Life the 8 Day of July, 1663,
aged 14 Years.

. . . . of this Parifh, Gent.
Son of DANIEL SAMPSON. of Wood-
land, Gent. who departed this
Life Aug. 24, 1732, aged 55.

Here lyeth the Body of EDWARD
SAMPSON, Gent. Son of RALPH
SAMPSON and MARTHA his Wife, who
departed this Life, for a Life of
Immortality, the 6 Day of May,
Anno Domini 1722, ætatis fuæ 31.

Here lyeth the Body
of the Rev. JOHN PRIEST, A. B.
Mafter of the Grammar School
of this Parifh, and Rector of Langfton,
in the County of Monmouth,
who died 22 Feb. 1779, aged 90.

In Memory of JOHN HOLLY,
of this Parifh, Yeoman, who
died Sept. 30, 1701, aged 43.

Alfo of JOHN HOLLY, Yeoman,
who died Dec. 30, 1729, aged 34.

Alfo of JOHN HOLLISTER HOLLY,
Son of JOHN HOLLY, by ANN his Wife,
who died Dec. 11, 1753,
aged 27 Years.

And of SARAH, the Wife of the
above JOHN HOLLISTER HOLLY, who
died May 21, 1755, aged 41 Years.

Here
lyeth the Body of
THOMAS ADLAM,
of this Parifh, Yeoman,
who departed this Life
the 8 Day of May, in the
Yeare of our Lord 1724,
aged 54 Years.

Alfo here lyeth the Body of
SUSANNAH, the Wife of THOMAS
ADLAM, fen. who departed this Life
the 11 of March, 1725, aged 46 Years.

Alfo here lyeth the Body of
THOMAS ADLAM, jun. Son of
THOMAS and SUSANNAH ADLAM,
who died March 29, 1726,
aged 25 Years.

Here lies the Body of CHARLES ADLAM,
of this Parifh, Gent.
who departed this Life the 8 Day of
April, 1743, aged 39 Years.

Here lyeth the Body of
ESTHER, the Wife of
CHARLES ADLAM, of this Parifh,
Gent. who died 21 Jan.
1737, aged 29 Years.

Alfo of MARY, Wife of the
above CHARLES ADLAM, who
died Feb. 13, 1773, aged 64.

Here lyeth the Body of
PHILIP BAKER, of this Parifh,
Yeoman, who departed this Life
the 6 of March, 1727-8, aged 63 Years.

Alfo PHILIP BAKER, jun. who died
the 11 of June, 1743, aged 41.

And ESTHER his Wife, who
died 20 Feb. 1742, aged 42.

HANNAH, Wife of PHILIP BAKER,
departed this Life 26 Mar. 1728.

VOL. II.

Here lieth the Body of MARY, the Wife
of RALPH BAKER, of this Parifh, who
died 23 Aug. 1788, aged 53 Years.

Alfo
in Memory of PHILIP BAKER, of this
Parifh, who died the 31 Jan. 1783,
aged 49 Years.

Arms; on a Chevron between three
Griffins' Heads erafed four Fleurs de
Lys.

In Memory of ANNE, the Wife of
RICHARD POPE,
of this Parifh, Yeoman, who died
July 8, 1752, aged near 60 Years.

In Memory of KATHARINE POPE, the
Wife of
RICHARD POPE, of this Parifh,
Yeoman, who died
16 Jan. 1776, aged 55 Years.

Alfo of GEORGE EDWARDS, the Son of
WILLIAM and HANNAH EDWARDS,
Grandfon of RICHARD and ANNE POPE,
who died 22 Oct. 1776, aged 20 Years.

In Memory of THOMAS POPE,
of this Parifh, Yeoman, Son of
JOHN and ELIZABETH POPE,
who departed this Life Dec. 10, 1751,
aged 29 Years.

In
Memory of
ELIZABETH, the Daughter of
JOHN and ELIZABETH POPE,
of this Parifh, who died
Nov. 8, 1743, aged
33 Years.

In Memory of
CORNELIUS GROVE HORT,
Gent. who died 26 Novemb. 1762,
aged 38.

Alfo of AMELIA his Daughter, who
died 21 Dec. 1762, an infant.

In Memory of JENKIN LEWIS,
of this Parifh, Yeoman, who departed
this Life Feb. 19, 1745-6, aged 72.

Alfo of MARGARET his Wife, who died
March 17, 1734, aged 66 Years.

Here lyeth the Body of HESTER,
the Wife of WILLIAM CHAMBERS,
of this Parifh, who departed this Life
the 10th of Jan. 1762, aged 36 Years.

HERE LIETH THE BODY
OF JOSEPH WILLS, OF LONG ASH-
TON,
IN THE COUNTY OF SOMERSET,
GARDINER,
WHO DEPARTED THIS LIFE THE
29 DAY OF AUGUST, 1720,
AGED 45 YEARS.

Arms; two Garbs, in bafe a Lamb,
a chief chequy;—impaling, Gules, on
a Bend Or, between two Efcallops Argent, a Cornifh Chough proper between
as many Cinquefoils Azure, on a Chief
of the fecond, a Rofe between two Fleurs
de Lys of the firft, for PETRE.

Memoriæ Viri fui chariffimi
GEORGII PETRE, quondam de
Charlton, Generofi. ELEONORA
Uxor ejus mœftiffima condidit
hunc tumulum. Vixit ad annos
72. Mortem obiit Febr. 23, 1630,

Y

Extitit enim Pater 22 liberorum,
quorum duo inter vivos
numerantur; reliqui unâ cum
Patre placide dormiunt, denuo
Expectantes futuram corporis
Refurrectionem vitam æternam.

Here lyeth the Body of GEORGE PETRE,
of Charlton, Gent. who departed this
Life the 20 Day of May, 1698,
aged 81 Years.

Alfo the Body of ELIZABETH his Wife,
who died the 10 July, 1705, aged 86.

Here alfo lyeth the Body of ELIZABETH,
Wife of SAMUEL ROACH, of the Parifh
of Weftbury upon Trim, Merchant,
who departed this Life 6 Nov. 1710,
aged 32 Years.

H. S. E.
GEORGIUS PETRE, de Charlton, obiit
27° Aug. 1728, ætatis fuæ 83.

Arms;   a Chevron   between
three Childrens' Heads couped

HERE LYETH THE BODY
OF WILLIAM GWIN VAUGHAN, SON
OF WILLIAM GWIN VAUGHAN, OF
TREBARRIED, IN THE COUNTY OF
BRECON, ESQ. AND OF MARTHA
HIS WIFE, SOLE DAUGHTER AND
HEIR OF SAMUEL ROACH,
OF SHIREHAMPTON, IN THE
COUNTY OF GLOUCESTER, ESQ.
HE DIED THE 21 DAY OF AUGUST,
1737, AGED 5 MONTHS AND 20
DAYS.

Alfo here lyeth the Body of
MARTHA VAUGHAN, who departed
this Life the 3 Feb. 1750, aged
39 Years.

Here lyeth the Body of
THOMAS WITHERLY, of Charlton,
in this Parifh, Yeoman, who departed this Life the 26 Feb.
Anno Dom. 1725, aged 69 Years.

Alfo here lyeth the Body of
MARTHA, the Wife of THOMAS WI-
THERLY,
Daughter of GEORGE PETRE, Gent.
who changed this mortal Life
for a Life of Immortality . . .
Day of March, 1722,
aged 73 Years.

In Memory of
ROBERT WITHERLY, Shipwright, late
Refident of the City of Briftol, who
departed this Life the 18 Jan. 1782,
aged 47 Years.

GEORGE CHARLTON, Gent, died 27
Aug. 1728,
aged 83 Years.

HERE LYETH THE
BODY OF EDWARD
STOKES, OF CHARLTON,
IN THIS PARISH, YE-
OMAN, WHO DEPARTED
THIS LIFE THE 31 OF
JULY, 1645.

HERE LYETH THE BODY OF ALCE,
THE FIRST WIFE OF EDWARD
STOKES, WHO DECEASED THE 4
OF JUNE, 1625.

ALSO

ALSO HERE LYETH MARGARET, THE SECOND WIFE OF EDWARD STOKES, WHO DECEASED THE 24 DAY OF DECEM. 1631.

HERE LYETH THE BODY OF KATHARINE, THE THIRD WIFE OF EDWARD STOKES, WHO DEPARTED THIS LIFE 23 NOV. 1667.

ALSO HERE LYETH THE BODY OF HENRY STOKES, YEOMAN, SON OF EDWARD STOKES, WHO DEPARTED THIS MORTAL LIFE 29 JANUARY, 1684, AGED 54 YEARS.

ALSO THE BODY OF CHRISTIAN EDMONDS, WIDOW, THE SISTER OF EDWARD STOKES, WHO DECEASED THE 17 JAN. 1667.

Here lyeth the Body of GRACE, the Wife of HENRY STOKES, who died the 21 of June, An. Dom. 1712, aged 79 Years.

Alfo here lyeth the Body of EDWARD STOKES, Gent. Son of HENRY STOKES and GRACE his Wife, who died the 16 Oct. 1726, aged 63 Years.

Alfo feveral Children of EDWARD STOKES, of Charlton, Gent. and ELIZABETH his Wife.

Here lyeth the Body of BETTY, the Wife of EDWARD WALL STOKES, of Charlton, in this Parifh, Gent. who departed this Life 7 Jan. 1735, aged 28 Years.

Alfo the aforefaid EDWARD WALL STOKES, of Charlton, in this Parifh, died the 28 June, 1782, aged 81 Years.

ANNA, Daughter of EDWARD WALL STOKES and BETTY his Wife, died the 14 Nov. 1747, aged 12 Years.

Alfo HENRY their Son died Dec. 31, aged 37 Years.

Beneath this Stone lie the Remains of ALICE STOKES, of the Parifh of St. Michael, Briftol, Relict of HENRY STOKES, of the Ifland of Jamaica, Mariner, who departed this Life 20 April, 1780, aged 73 Years.

To the Memory of WILLIAM, the Son of THOMAS and ANN CAMBOURNE, who died Jan. the 17th, 1728, aged 9 Years.

Alfo of MARY, Daughter of THOMAS and ANN CAMBOURNE, who died April the 4, 1732, aged 12 Years.

In Memory of THOMAS CAMBOURNE, of Lawrence Wefton, in the Parifh of Weftbury upon Trim, Yeoman, who died June 26, 1747, aged 56 Years.

Alfo of ANN, the Wife of THOMAS CAMBOURNE, who died May the 15, 1730, aged 39 Years.

In Memory of SARAH, the Wife of THOS. BROWNING, of this Parifh, Yeoman, who died the 16 of Auguft, 1770, aged 43 Years.

Alfo in Memory of the above THOMAS BROWNING, who departed this Life Nov. 7, 1771, aged 40 Years.

Beneath this Tomb lies interred the Body of WILLIAM VIMPANY, of this Parifh, Gent. who departed this Life the 4 of May, 1751, aged 61 Years.

HERE LYETH THE BODY OF KATHARINE, WIFE OF RICHARD SPRATLEY, WHO DEPARTED THIS LIFE THE 23 OF FEB. 1670.

ALSO RICHARD THEIR SON WAS BURIED THE 12 DAY OF MARCH, 1659.

HERE LYETH THE BODY OF ANNE WILLIAMS, WIDOW, SISTER TO RICHARD SPRATLEY, WHO DEPARTED THIS LIFE THE 15 DAY OF MAY, 1692, AGED 63 YEARS.

To the Memory of MOLLY CHURCH, Wife of RICHARD CHURCH, of the New Paffage, who departed this Life the 18th of May, 1788, aged 48 Years.

To the Memory of ABRAHAM JONES, of Charlton, in this Parifh, Yeoman, who departed this Life Sept. 7, 1782, aged 61 Years.

Alfo here lyeth the Body of ELIZABETH his Wife, who died Sept. 8, 1789, aged 65 Years.

HERE LYETH THE BODY OF JOHN SQUIRE, OF SHIREHAMPTON, MARINER, WHO DEPARTED THIS LIFE ..... 1676.

ALSO HERE LYETH THE BODY OF WILLIAM KEINTON, SHIPWRIGHT, THE SON OF GEORGE KEINTON, OF ...... IN THE COUNTY OF MONMOUTH. HE DIED OCT. 29, 1709, AGED .. YEARS.

Here lyeth the Body of WILLIAM CROOKER, of this Parifh, Yeoman, who departed this Life the 29 of April, 1731, aged 35 Years.

Alfo three of his Children.

In Memory of WILLIAM CROOKER, Son of WILLIAM CROOKER, of this Parifh, who departed this Life Jan. 23, 1767.

In Memory of ELIZABETH, the Wife of JOHN LAWRENCE, of this Parifh, who departed this Life the 7 Day of Aug. 1742, aged 42 Years.

Alfo the above named JOHN LAWRENCE, who died 8 Feb. 1777, aged 70 Years.

In Memory of ELIZABETH, the Daughter of EDWARD RUSSELL, of Kingfwefton, who died the 31ft of Jan. 1770, in the 6th Year of her Age.

Alfo of EDWARD their Son, who died the 23d of April, 1776, aged 17 Years.

WILLIAM SPICER, late of Kingfwefton, died 18 Mar. 1779, aged 41 Years.

ABRAHAM COLLINS, of Shirehampton, in the Parifh of Weftbury upon Trim, Yeoman, died 4 April, 1780, aged 65 Years.

Alfo ANNE, the Wife of ABRAHAM COLLINS, died 11 Aug. 1790, aged 79 Years.

WILLIAM COLLINS, Yeoman, the Son of ABRAHAM and ANN COLLINS, of Shirehampton, in the Parifh of Weftbury upon Trim, died 15 June, 1771, in the 27th Year of his Age.

To the Memory of ROBERT POYNTER, of the County of Norfolk, Gent. who departed this Life 26 Feb. 1786, aged 73 Years.

Alfo to the Memory of MARTHA, Widow of the faid ROBERT POYNTER, Gent. who departed this Life April 8, 1786, aged 73 Years.

ON A FLAT STONE AT THE ENTRANCE OF THE SOUTH PORCH:

Hic jacet J. G. hujus Parœciæ per Annos XLIX Vicarius, qui obiit Jan. XXVII. MDCCLXXIX. ætatis Anno LXXXIV.

O N

ON HEAD AND FLAT STONES.

Name	Died	Aged
Benjamin Tanner -	1 May, 1743	39
William, Son of John and Ann Thomas - -	25 Aug. 1745	1
Thomas Pearce -	— Oct. 1763	56
William, Son of Thomas and Mary Pearce -	1 Sept. 1775	40
Sarah, Wife of Thomas Pearce, of St. Stephen's, in the City of Bristol	25 Feb. 1773	50
Anna Maria Pinkney, of London	28 Oct. 1788	23
Richard Collins, of Shirehampton	30 Oct. 1770	65
Edward, Son of Abraham Collins, of Shirehampton	16 Oct. 1728	24
Abraham Collins, senior, of Shirehampton	10 Aug. 1741	77
Thomas Cox, of Stoke Gifford	20 Nov. 1743	52
Edward Wall, of Westbury upon Trim -	20 Feb. 1764	76
Mary, Relict of Thomas Cox and Edward Wall -	1 July, 1765	58
Robert Cullimore -	26 June, 1764	53
Grace his Wife -	28 Mar. 1780	64
Sarah their Daughter -	11 Oct. 1754	2
William, Son of Richard and Elizabeth Wait -	20 July, 1767	19
Elizabeth, Daughter of John and Elizabeth Turnpenny, of Bristol	19 Apr. 1786	9
Hannah, Wife of John Jaques	12 Sept. 1783	28
Hannah his second Wife -	24 Oct. 1785	30
Ann, Wife of John Bayley, of Bristol	21 Feb. 1783	28
Rebekah, Wife of Thomas Stratton, of Compton, in the Parish of Almondbury, Daughter of Stephen Hollister -	11 Dec. 1753	26
Stephen Hollister, of Northwick	7 Aug. 1728	78
Rachel his Wife -	16 Dec. 1708	—
Mark, Son of Stephen Hollister, of Northwick - -	28 Dec. 1752	27
Stephen his Son -	25 Apr. 1760	25
Richard Wedlock -	24 Mar. 1713	40
Betty his Wife -	18 Nov. 1760	83
William Wedlock -	7 Sept. 1772	65
Rebekah his Wife -	19 Nov. 1709	46
Sarah their Daughter -	3 Nov. 1770	13
Thomas Joyner, of Westbury	3 Mar. 1699	—
John Crocker - -	7 Oct. 1761	47
Edward Long -	14 Mar. 1760	68
Mary his Daughter -	27 Apr. 1764	37
John Plomley - -	26 May, 1701	—
Mary his Wife -	4 Mar. 1686	—
William Newport -	25 Oct. 1762	87
Dorothy his Wife -	10 Nov. 1708	65
Ann his Wife - -	7 July, 1760	71
John Parker - -	18 Mar. 1739	63
Mary his Wife -	22 Sept. 1739	66
Edward their Son -	1 Jan. 1729	16
Elizabeth, Wife of Henry Edgworth, of Bristol -	9 Aug. 1770	29
William Creed -	—— 1689	38
Elizabeth his Wife -	7 Oct. 1724	71
Thomas Creed - -	14 Feb. 1784	40
Mary, Wife of John Proffer	31 Mar. 1789	37
Francis Binning -	24 Nov. 1742	43
John Watkins - -	— Dec. 1710	49
Jane his Wife -	—— 1710	42
John Watkins - -	10 May, 1784	48
Thomas Watkins, of Almondsbury	8 Dec. 1756	39
Daniel Lovering •	12 Dec. 1726	60
John Lovering -	2 May, 1729	66
Henry Sage, of Almondsbury	1 Sept. 1742	55
Martha his Wife -	1 Aug. 1758	63
Elizabeth their Daughter -	7 May, 1753	18
Thomas Joyner -	13 July, 1737	29
William Joyner -	15 June, 1782	37
Thomas Wallis -	14 June, 1728	38
Susannah, Wife of William Tippeler	18 Aug. 1742	49
William, Son of Daniel and Anne Webb - -	9 Jan. 1779	21
James Davis - -	6 Feb. 1774	63
William Perks - -	10 Oct. 1778	26
Christopher Reynolds -	12 Sept. 1778	45
Richard Wheeler -	8 Sept. 1751	51

Name	Died	Aged
Thomas Banson, of Shirehampton	29 June, 1737	36
Richard Jones -	2 July, 1749	53
William Powell -	5 Feb. 1729	93
Mary, Wife of Nathaniel Simmons	13 Jan. 1764	57
Nathaniel Simmons -	29 Mar. 1759	57
Thomas Bickerton -	2 July, 1786	39
John Oliff - -	9 Sept. 1760	71
Elizabeth his Wife -	31 Mar. 1746	50
Bridget their Daughter -	11 Apr. 1748	26
John Sumerell -	— Feb. 1736	30
Edward Sumerell -	20 Feb. 1712	91
Daniel Esbury, of Bristol -	10 Jan. 1736	41
Thomas Hopkins - -	19 Jan. 1734	71
Ann his Wife - -	23 Nov. 1741	77
Jacob Hayman -	9 Nov. 1779	65
Rachel his Wife - -	25 Apr. 1733	57
Thomas Jenkins -	7 Mar. 1720	29
William Jenkins -	— Oct. 1737	—
John Bevin, sen. -	22 Apr. 1741	64
Esther his Wife - -	7 Sept. 1740	56
Ann their Daughter -	3 June, 1734	8
Ann, Wife of Abraham Bevin	29 Apr. 1743	28
Francis Burroughs -	2 Mar. 1785	90
Jane his Wife - -	17 Feb. 1758	59
Lucy Pearce - -	18 Mar. 1771	39
William Martin - -	1 May, 1699	55
John Franckom -	2 July, 1791	72
Mary his Wife -	18 Jan. 1779	95
Betty his second Wife -	18 Sept. 1791	57
Jane, Wife of John Small -	23 Mar. 1778	40
Thomas Edwards -	6 Nov. 1733	46
Mary, Wife of William Young, of Westbury - -	8 Mar. 1743	31
Hannah Worgan her Daughter	23 Mar. 1762	27
James Joyner, of Hungroad	6 June, 1738	51
Margaret his Wife -	8 Nov. 1749	56
Sarah, Wife of William Joyner, of Clifton - -	19 Aug. 1763	42
Margaret, Daughter of James Joyner	7 Oct. 1745	49
Katharine, Wife of Thomas Maylor	14 Feb. 1747	33
Richard Pope -	11 Apr. 1720	68
Elizabeth his Wife -	7 Dec. 1696	—
James Sims - -	26 Jan. 1767	45
Lucy, Wife of William Horrill, of Westbury - -	14 Feb. 1782	91
Mary Averis - -	14 Aug. 1784	89
Sarah, Wife of Francis Wilding	27 Sept. 1735	26
Jane, Wife of Jonathan Neat	9 Mar. 1736	41
Sarah his second Wife -	22 Jan. 1738	32
Mary his third Wife -	30 Mar. 1747	33
Sarah his sixth Wife -	2 Oct. 1781	69
John his Son - -	19 Sept. 1742	13
Emy his Daughter -	29 —— ——	14
Thomas his Son -	1 July, 1784	41
Sarah, Wife of Thomas Neat	12 May, 1783	42
John Legg - -	1 Apr. 1718	—
Mary his Daughter -	11 June, 1720	—
Sarah, Daughter of George Legg, Wife of Peter Williams	— July, 172.	31
Mary, Wife of William Morgan	1 June, 1681	21
Patience, Wife of Thomas Parsley	1 Dec. 1772	34
Jonathan Marshall -	29 Mar. 1778	33
Mary, Wife of John Miller -	25 Sept. 1781	24
Mary, Daughter of William and Cecilia Dawes - -	1 Feb. 1777	14
Elizabeth, Wife of Moses Hunt	31 Aug. 1738	29
Edward Fill - -	17 Oct. 1733	64
Hester, Wife of John Dawes	3 Feb. 1788	33
Elizabeth, Wife of Edward Boulton - -	9 Dec. 1763	44
Richard their Son -	20 Sept. 1770	17
John Farr - -	1 May, 1730	50
Mary his Wife -	15 Nov. 1743	64
Thomas their Son -	4 June, 1735	28
Susannah, Daughter of Stephen and Hannah Farr -	11 Aug. 1740	9
William Humphris -	31 May, 1749	60
Nicholas Edye - -	11 Aug. 1737	47
William Beale - -	1 Mar. 1768	52
Elizabeth, Daughter of Peter and Elizabeth Cullimore -	6 Apr. 1771	31
James their Son -	24 May, 1775	40

O N

ON HEAD AND FLAT STONES.

	Died	Aged
Mary, Wife of John James, of St. Stephen's, in Briſtol -	19 Sept. 1761	27
John Webb - -	— Mar. 172⅚	32
Thomas Webb - -	6 Mar. 173⅚	39
Edward Fiſhpool -	3 Jan. 1731	65
Sarah his Wife -	21 Oct. 1730	65
John their Son - -	12 May, 1731	38
Sarah, Wife of Samuel Lewis	9 Dec. 1760	24
Samuel Child - -	27 Feb. 1719	67
Daniel, Son of William and Joan Child - -	4 June, 1734	—
Mary, Wife of Thomas Pentry	14 Jan. 1782	65
Eſther his ſecond Wife, Daughter of Joſeph Turton - -	15 Dec. 1786	57
William Savage -	10 Dec. 1777	35
Philip Thomas, of Weſtbury	27 Jan. 1728	58
Henry Brown - -	4 Jan. 1722	50
William Brown -	— — 1730	56
Stephen Keel - -	28 Jan. 1769	35
John England -	4 Mar. 1729	36
Sarah Clark his Daughter -	22 July, 1757	39
Sarah England - -	15 — 1752	—
John Cook - -	20 Nov. 1706	52
Heſter his Wife -	6 Apr. 1710	44
Heſter Cook - -	23 Mar. 1752	55
Chriſtopher Rudder -	1 Nov. 1740	45
Sarah his Wife -	18 Oct. 1753	63
Thomas Philips -	1 Dec. 1788	43
Elizabeth Willis - -	20 Aug. 1785	76
Cecilia Jayne - -	27 Jan. 1766	64
Cecilia her Daughter -	29 June, 1744	19
John Yeels - -	17 July, 1768	22
Jane, Wife of John Hewett	17 June, 1774	28
Ann Webb - -	28 Nov. 1783	73
Ann, Daughter of George and Sarah Ralph - -	1 Dec. 1768	16
Mary their Daughter -	31 Dec. 1768	19
Thomas, Son of Edward Kemp	23 Jan. 1740	21
Henry Williams -	19 May, 1782	62
Hannah his Wife - -	5 Jan. 1783	44
Mary, Wife of Samuel Child	15 Dec. 1748	52
Sarah, Daughter of John and Elizabeth Wade - -	9 Jan. 1772	17
Henry Jones - -	23 Sept. 1776	52
Sarah his Wife -	24 Nov. 1779	58
Sarah Jones -	21 Nov. 1754	32
John Jones - -	2 Sept. 1770	14
William Watkins -	18 Mar. 1739	27
Elizabeth Watkins -	26 Jan. 1736	58
Edward Long - -	3 Jan. 1727	—
Mary Vimpeny -	20 Feb. 1723	92
Mary, Wife of Anthony Leach	29 Sept. 1725	26
Henry Jayne - -	31 Sept. 1713	40
Elizabeth, Wife of Cornelius Jayne	14 Apr. 1729	55
William Jayne - -	4 Nov. 1737	36
Abel Jayne - -	13 Jan. 1766	52
Sarah his Wife -	6 Jan. 1745	36

	Died	Aged
Elizabeth his ſecond Wife -	4 Feb. 1789	66
William Jane - -	12 May, 1777	42
James Keniſon, of Horfield	26 Mar. 1790	40
Thomas Richards, of the New Paſſage - -	20 Oct. 1761	65
Jane his Wife - -	10 Mar. 1731	39
Ann his ſecond Wife -	28 Jan. 1746	50
William Tuck, of Shirehampton	28 May, 1758	38
John Blake, of Weſtbury -	8 July, 1744	35
Joſeph Baker - -	— May, 1721	35
Elizabeth, Wife of William Roſſer	2 Feb. 1746	30
Iſaac Pearce - -	1 Apr. 1790	43
Robert, Son of Luke and Mary Tovey	5 Jan. 1770	8
John James - -	2 Apr. 1730	26
Robert Player -	20 May, 1760	49
Mary his Wife -	13 Dec. 1780	77
Robert Player - -	11 Aug. 1763	25
Robert Baker - -	6 Mar. 1728	49
Ann Smith - -	6 May, 1756	34
George Andrews -	27 Nov. 1742	35
Mary, Wife of William Symes	28 Feb. 1749	50
Samuel Leach - -	— — 1704	43
Anthony Leach -	5 Apr. 1745	45
Joan his Wife - -	20 Mar. 1745	32
Iſaac Leach, of Shirehampton	8 Oct. 1749	29
Sarah his Wife -	19 July, 1764	41
Iſaac their Son - -	25 Nov. 1789	43
Sarah, Wife of John Webb	7 Dec. 1727	30
Chriſtiana Suſannah, Wife of Philip Jones, of Briſtol -	22 Dec. 1789	25
Thomas Crooker -	18 Sept. 1741	37
Elizabeth his Wife -	20 Nov. 1770	72
Thomas their Son -	3 Mar. 1777	48
Hannah, Wife of Thomas Croſſman, of Almondſbury -	23 Apr. 1789	22
Dorothy, Wife of Thomas Hooper	21 Feb. 1760	60
William, Son of Thomas and Joyce Scriven - -	28 June, 1748	26
John Thomas, of Olveſtone	23 Oct. 1743	57
Elizabeth his Wife -	27 Feb. 1743	52
Francis Thomas -	21 Oct. 1766	31
John Matthews - -	17 Dec. 1764	65
Mary his Wife -	17 Dec. 1755	54
Suſannah Webb -	16 Aug. 1788	—
Henry Calder - -	22 Mar. 1740	35
James his Son -	15 Aug. 1749	9
Ann, Wife of George Thomas, of Weſtbury -	2 Sept. 1765	60
Joſeph Wheeler -	30 Apr. 1746	31
John his Son - -	9 Apr. 1746	10
James Pains - -	28 Apr. 1789	29
William, Son of Samuel and Suſannah Pains - -	5 Nov. 1764	27
Jane Pains - -	— — 1732	21
John Willis - -	— — 1754	37

CXLIII.

CXLIII. H E W E L S F I E L D,
O R
H U A L D E S F I E L D,

IS a Parish of the middle Extent, in the Hundred of *St. Briavel's,* divided from *Tyntern,* in the County of *Monmouth,* by the River *Wye,* fix Miles diftant North from *Chepftow,* feven South from *Coleford,* and twenty-four from GLOUCESTER on the South-weft.

The Site of the Village is on the high Lands of the Foreft of *Dean,* and the Soil partakes of the great Variety for which that Tract is remarkable; the Declivities to the River are abrupt, but cloathed with Timber and low Wood of the greateft Luxuriance, and forming many delightful Landfcapes, which are fo juftly celebrated by thofe who have inveftigated the Shores of the River *Wye.*

By the Sheriff, in the Return made of all the Hundreds and Vills in this County in 1281, 9 EDW. I. this Parifh was included in that of *Lidney,* and its Inhabitants claim the Privileges of the Duchy of *Lancafter,* to which Court they are amenable. With other Liberties in the Foreft of *Dean* and the Purlieus, they are allowed a Right of Common and Wood in *Hart Hill.*

The Living is annexed as a Chapelry to the Vicarage of *Lidney,* and endowed with the whole Tythes.

There is nothing remarkable in the Architecture of the Church, which is a plain Building, with a low embattled Tower, and fepulchral Chapel belonging to the Family of GOUGH.

In *Domefday* this Manor is taxed at three Hides only, and included in the Foreft by the efpecial Command of the King. JOHN DE MONEMOUTH, Conftable of *St. Briavel's Caftle,* gave it to the Hofpital which he had founded in that Town; but, being efcheated, with his other Property to the Crown, King EDWARD the Firft re-granted it in free Alms to the Abbot of the *Ciftertians* at *Tynterne.* When that Houfe was diffolved it was given to HENRY Earl of WORCESTER, who, by an Inquifition taken after his Death in 1550, was found to be feifed of it, with other adjoining Eftates. From that Time it has been vefted in his noble Defcendants the Dukes of BEAUFORT. Another confiderable Eftate in this Parifh was transferred to JOHN MADOX in 1500, 21 HEN. VII. GEORGE GOUGH, in 1558, obtained it in Marriage Dower with MARY, Daughter and Coheir of WILLIAM WARREN. RICHARD GOUGH, his Grandfon, left it in Moiety between his Daughters, ALICE, the Wife of Sir NICHOLAS THROCKMORTON, and ELEA-NOR, the Wife of Sir WILLIAM CATCHMAYE, Knights. Of the Coheirs of Sir NICHOLAS THROCKMOR-TON their Partition was purchafed by ROBERT SYMONDS, Efq. and is now the Property of THOMAS POWELL SYMONDS, Efq. of *Pengethly,* co. *Hereford.* The other Share defcended to TRACY CATCH-MAYE, Efq. whofe Daughter was the Wife of Major JAMES ROOKE, who died in 1771. WARREN JANE, Efq. of a Family long eftablifhed in this Parifh, is the prefent Proprietor.

H A M L E T.

Brockwere, or *Brockwear* on the *Wye,* is a Village fituate in a wooded Recefs or Cove, at the Foot of the lofty Foreft Hills, and has a fmall Port, from which Iron and Timber are conveyed to *Briftol.*

B E N E F A C T I O N S.

ELIZABETH WILLIAMS, in 1724, gave Land, vefted in ALEXANDER THORN; the annual Produce of which is 1*l.* to be divided between eight poor Widows.

Other Land, the yearly Produce of which is 5*s.* was given for the Ufe of the Poor; but by whom, or when, is not known.

The Series of Incumbents will be given in the Account of *LIDNEY*.

PRESENT LORD OF THE MANOR,

His Grace HENRY Duke of BEAUFORT.

The Perfons fummoned from this Parifh by the Heralds in 1682 and 1683 were

George Gough, Efq. Edward Madox, Gent. and Edward White, Gent.

At the Election in 1776, Fourteen Freeholders polled from this Parifh.

The Regifter commences with the Date 1664.

ANNUAL ACCOUNT OF MARRIAGES, BIRTHS, AND BURIALS, IN THIS PARISH.

A.D.	Mar.	Bir.	Bur.	A.D.	Mar.	Bir.	Bur.	A.D.	Mar.	Bir.	Bur.	A.D.	Mar.	Bir.	Bur.
1781	2	9	8	1786	3	9	8	1791				1796			
1782	3	6	7	1787	4	10	7	1792				1797			
1783	3	8	6	1788	2	11	9	1793				1798			
1784	4	9	9	1789	2	12	8	1794				1799			
1785	4	12	10	1790	3	10	8	1795				1800			

INSCRIPTIONS IN THE CHURCH.

ON A MONUMENT IN THE CHANCEL:

Arms : Argent, on a Chevron Sable, three Bugle Horns of the firft, between three demi-Lions rampant Gules, for BOND.

Near this Place lieth the Body of EDMUND BOND, of Aylfmore, Gent. who died October the 22d, 1743, aged 70.

Near this Place lies the Body of RICHARD BOND, of Aylfmore, Gent. Nephew to the faid EDMUND BOND, who departed this Life the 25 Day of March, 1754, aged 41.

ON A MONUMENT IN THE NAVE:

Near this Place lies interred the Body of ANNE, only Daughter of JOHN EDDY, of Lidney, by MARY his Wife, Daughter of WILLIAM CARPENTER, of St. Briavell's in this County, Gent. She died the 29 of November, 1768, aged 60 Years.

Sir NICHOLAS THROCKMORTON, Knt. was buried the 2d June, 1664.

ON FLAT STONES IN THE CHANCEL.

HERE LYETH THE BODY OF THOMAS JONES, ESQ. SONN OF CHARLES JONES, OF NASS, ESQ. OF THE PARISH OF LIDNEY, WHO

DEPARTED THIS LIFE THE 16 DAY OF APRIL, ANNO DOM. 1720.

Here lyeth the Body of MARY, Relict of THOMAS JONES, Efq. who departed this Life the 26 of October, 1757, aged 82.

Here lyes the Body of EDWARD PERKINS, of Huelsfield, Gent. the Son of EDWARD PERKINS, of Pillfton, Efq. who departed this Life the 24 of April, 1726.

Here lyeth the Body of MARY, the Wife of EDMOND BOND, of Aylfmore, Gent. who departed this Life the 8 Aug. 1711.

Alfo the Body of MARY APPLEBE, the Daughter of EDMUND BOND, of Aylfmore, Gent. who died 5 July, 1737.

To the pious Memory of MARY, Relict of RICHARD BOND, Gent. Ob. 2 July, 1760, æt. 50.

JOHN, THE SON OF EDMUND HADDOCKES, GENT. WHO DEPARTED THE 9 DAY OF FEBRUARY, 1683.

TO THE PIOUS MEMORY OF THE MOST VIRTUOUS LADY DAME ELINOR CATCHMAY OF MOST EXEMPLARY LIFE AND CONVERSATION, WHO DIED THE 10 DAY OF MARCH, ANNO DOMINI 1661.

HERE LIETH THE BODY OF MARY, WIFE OI WILLIAM GOUGH, OF PARSLEY-HILL, AND DAUGHTER OF SIR NICHOLAS THROCKMORTON, WHO DEPARTED THIS LINE THE 28 DAY OF JULY, 1718.

HERE LYETH THE BODY OF ELIZABETH, THE DAUGHTER OF THOMAS JONES, GENT. AND MARY HIS WIFE, WHO DIED 7 JANUARY, 1711.

ALSO HERE LYETH THE BODY OF TERESA, THE DAUGHTER OF THOMAS JONES, GENT. AND MARY HIS WIFE, WHO DEPARTED THIS LIFE THE 28 NOVEMBER, 1712, BOTH GRAND-DAUGHTERS OF CHARLES JONES, OF NASS, ESQ.

Here lyeth the Body of MARY, the Wife of JOHN HARDWICKE, late a Minifter of God's Word, of Michaelftroy, in the County of Monmouth, Daughter to WILLIAM GOUGH, of this Parifh, who departed this Life the 11 Day of Dec. 1685.

In

In Memory
of John Prosser,
Surgeon, of the Town of
Monmouth, who departed
this Life June the 23d, 1771,
aged 40 years.

ON FLAT STONES IN GOUGH'S BURIAL CHAPEL.

HERE LYETH THE BODY OF ISRAEL GOUGH, WHO DECEASED THE 4 DAY OF FEBRUARY, A. D. 1672.

ALSO HERE LYETH THE BODY OF GEORGE GOUGH, GENT. WHO DIED THE 24 SEPT. A. D. 1689.

ALSO HERE LYETH ELIZABETH, WIFE TO GEORGE GOUGH, GENT. WHO DIED 7 AUGUST, 1726.

ALSO THE BODY OF GEORGE GOUGH, GENT. WHO DEPARTED THIS LIFE THE 22D DAY OF MAY, 1711, AGED 60 YEARS.

Here
lyeth the Body
of Mary, the Daughter of
Richard Gough, who died
the 8 Day of April, An. Dom.
1673.

Hic etiam jacet corpus
Elizabethæ, uxoris Johannis
Roberts, de St. Briavel's,
& Filiæ Jacobi Gough, Gent.
de urbe Briftol. quæ ob.
22 Novembris, Anno Dom. 1726,
æt. 29.

ON FLAT STONES IN THE NAVE.

Here lies the Body of Matthew Driver, of Brockware, who died the 18 Feb. 1707.

Mary, Daughter of Matthew and Jane Driver, died 24 Feb. 1707.

HERE LIETH THE BODY OF JOHN JANE, WHO DECEASED THE 4 OF MAY, 1646.

HERE LIETH THE BODY OF WILLIAM JANE, OF BROCKWARE, GENT. WHO DEPARTED THIS LIFE THE 15 DAY OF APRIL, 1655.

Nicholas, Son of Warren Jane, died 15 January, 1693-4.

Magdalen, Wife of Warren Jane, departed this Life January 1699.

Eleanor, Relict of William Jane, Gent. departed this Life the 30 Day of May, 1786, aged 82.

IN THE CHURCH YARD,

Here lieth the Body of John Sinor, of Brockwear, who departed this Life the 11 Day of June, 1728, aged 57 Years.

Alfo here lieth the Body of Richard Synor, who departed this Life the 27 Day of April, 1777, aged 63 Years.

Here lyeth the Body of Mary, the Daughter of William and Mary Thomas, of the Parifh of Woollafton, who died April 5, 1721.

In Memory of Elizabeth, the Wife of Henry Brown, of Brockwear, who died Sep. 12, 1685, aged 55 Years.

Here lyeth the Body of Ann, the Wife of George Man, of Brockweare, who departed this Life the 10 Day of Aug. An. Domini 1706.

Here lieth the Body of Tacey, the Wife of George Man, of Brockwear, who departed this Life 22 Day of February, Anno Domini 1715, aged 32 Years.

Alfo in Memory of Ann, the Daughter of George and Tacey Man, of Brockwear, who departed this Life the 12 Day of April, 1716.

Here
lieth, in Hopes of a joyful Refurrection, the Body of George Man, of Brockwear, Mariner, who departed this Life the 2d Day of November, 1753, aged 77 Years.

Here lyeth the Body of Ann, the Daughter of George Man, of Brockwear, who departed this Life the 7 Day of July, 1692.

And alfo here lyeth the Body of Mary, the Daughter of George Man, of Brockwear, who departed this Life the 22d Day of December, 1693.

Alfo here lyeth the Body of George, the Son of George and Tacey Man, who departed this Life the 11 Day of Jan. 1713.

In Memory of Dinah, the Wife of George Man, of Brockwear, Mariner, who died the 17 of Oct. 1777, aged 84.

Alfo in Memory of Ann, Daughter of the above George and Dinah Man, who died the 5 March, 1788, aged 60 Years.

Here lieth the
Body of Frances, the
Wife of Charles Lewis,
of Brockwear. She
departed this Life April
20, 1747, aged 74 Years.

In Memory of
Thomas Harris, of
the Parifh of Wollafton,
who departed November
the 22, 1705.

Alfo here lyeth the Body
of Elizabeth, Wife of
Thomas Harris, who died
Dec. the 24 Day,
1729.

Alfo in Memory of
John, the Son of George
and Martha Cole, of
Brockwear, who died
the 31 of Jan. 1787,
aged 7 Years.

ON TOMBS.

Alfo in Memory of
Martha their Daughter,
who died the 8 Day of
June 1787, aged 6 Years.

In Memory of Alexander Moxley, who departed this Life the 26 of Aug. 1773, aged 38 Years.

Here lieth the Body of Francis Raulings, who departed this Life the 24 Day of June, 1702.

Alfo Esther, the Wife of Francis Raulings, died July the 7th, 1717.

Alfo in Memory of John Raulings, deceafed June 8, 1729, aged 36 Years.

Here lieth the Body of George, the Son of George and Elizabeth Rawlings, of Brockwear, who departed this Life the 21 Day of September, 1742, aged 22 Years.

Alfo here lieth the Body of Walter, the Son of Benjamin and Elizabeth King, of Brockwear, who died June 6, 1758, aged 5 Years.

In Memory of Benjamin, the Son of Benjamin and Elizabeth King, of Brockwear, who died the 5 Day of November, 1751, aged 1 Year and 8 Months.

Alfo in Memory of Martha, the Daughter of Benjamin and Elizabeth King, who died the 25 Day of January, 1751, aged 5 Years.

In Memory of Mary, the Daughter of Benjamin and Elizabeth King. She died the 1 Day of June, 1767, aged 13 Years.

Here

Here lyeth the Body of
ELIZABETH, the Wife of
GEORGE RAULINGS, who
departed this Life the
12 Day of September, 1720,
aged 28 Years.

In Memory of MARTHA,
Daughter of GEORGE and MARTHA
RALLINGS, deceafed July 19,
1728.

Alfo in Memory of MARTHA, the
Wife of GEORGE RALLINGS,
deceafed December 18,
1731, aged 36 Years.

In Memory of GEORGE RAWLINGS, of
Brockwear, Mariner, who departed
this Life
the 26 Day of March, 1770, aged 84
Years.

Here
lieth the Body of
ANN, the Daughter of WILLIAM
and ANN PAGE, of Brockwear,
who died June 27, 1755,
aged 18 Years.

Alfo in Memory of WILLIAM PAGE,
who died Oct. 20, 1783,
aged 77 Years.

Alfo ANN his Wife died the 14
of May, 1787, aged 87 Years.

HERE LYETH THE BODY OF
DORITY, THE WIFE OF
WALLTER PARY, WHO
DEPARTED THIS LIFE THE
6 OF NOVEMBER, 1709.

Here lyeth the Body of HENERY
ROGERS, of Brockwore, who departed
this Life the 11 Day of December,
Anno Dom. 1694.

HERE LYETH THE BODY OF
JANE, THE WIFE OF HENRY
BEVEN, OF BROCKWEAR,
WHO DEPARTED THIS LIFE
THE 21 DAY OF
DECEMBER, 1702.

In Memory of JANE, the Wife
of JOHN PHILIPS, of Brockwear,
who departed this Life the 2
Day of March, 1714.

In Memory of MARY, the Wife
of WILLIAM LEWIS, of Brockwear.
She died June 10, 1745,
aged 70.

In Memory of JANE, the Wife
of GEORGE GETHING, of Tinton.
She died Nov. 17, 1761, aged 22.

Here lyeth the Body of
JANE, the Wife of BENJAMIN LEWIS,
of Brockwear,
who departed this Life Oct. 9, Anno
Dom. 1735, aged
32 Years.

Alfo here lyeth the Body
of MARY LEWIS, the Daughter of
BENJAMIN and HANNAH LEWIS,
of Brockwear, who departed this Life
the 10 Day of May, in the Year of our
Lord, 1749, aged 5 Years.

JANE their Daughter died Jan. 7, 1772,
aged 6 Years.

Under this Tomb lie the Remains
of ARTHUR PITCHER, of this Place,
who died March 24, 1770,
aged 74.

MARTHA, the Wife of WILLIAM
PITCHER, who died 8 March, 1780,
aged 27.

WILLIAM, the Son of WILLIAM
and MARTHA PITCHER, died 7 Sep.,
1780,
aged 4 Years and 6 Months.

WILLIAM, Son of ARTHUR and JANE
PITCHER, died 11 May, 1787,
aged 41.

In
Memory of JANE, the Wife of
CHARLES WADE,
late of Magget,
who died the 28 Feb. 1780,
aged 74 Years.

Alfo in Memory of CHARLES,
the Son of WILLIAM and SARAH WADE,
who died March 18, 1782,
in his Infancy.

Alfo in Memory of CHARLES WADE,
who died the 19 Day of
Feb. 1788, aged 74 Years.

Alfo WILLIAM, Son of the above
WILLIAM and SARAH WADE, who
died the 8 Day of July, 1788,
in his Infancy.

Here refteth
the Body of
JOHN PARRY,
who departed
this Life Ap-
ril 11, 1680.

Alfo here ly-
eth the Body
of JOHN PRICE,
who died
January the 14,
1702.

Alfo here lyeth
the Body of JOHN
PARROTT, of this Place,
who died the 1 Day
of February, 1776,
aged 63 Years.

Here lyeth the
Body of ANN
PRICE, who died
July 23, 1717.

HERE LIETH THE BODY
OF BLANCH, THE WIFE OF
THOMAS HOPKIN, OF
HUELSFIELD, WHO DECEAS-
ED NOVEMBER THE 4,
AN° DOM. 1627.

ALSO BARBARA, THE WIFE OF
WILLIAM CATCHMAY, DEPARTED
THIS LIFE THE 4 DAY OF JAN-
VARY, 1712, AGED 72.

ALSO HERE LYETH THE BODY OF
WILLIAM CATCHMAY, OF
HVELSFIELD,
WHO LIVED PEACABLY, AND
DEPARTED THIS LIFE THE 10 DAY
OF NOVEMBER,
1691.

IN MEMORY OF WILLIAM, THE SON
OF JOHN AND MARY JANE, OF

CHEPSTOW,
WHO DIED THE 11 SEPTEMBER,
1777, AGED 6 YEARS.

IN MEMORY OF JOHN JANE, OF
CHEPSTOW,
SON OF JOHN JANE, LATE OF
HUELSFIELD,
WHO DIED THE 20 MAY, 1778,
AGED 53.

In Memory
of JOHN JANE, of this Place.
He died May 10, 1770,
aged 70.

In Memory of EDMUND, the Son
of JOHN and ELIZABETH JANE,
who died the 21 March, 1775,
aged 50 Years.

Here lieth the Body
of WILLIAM HARRIS, of
Howelsfield, who was
interred the 30 Day of
March, 1684, aged 106 Years.

Alfo here lieth the Body
of MARY his Wife, who was
interred the fame Day.

Alfo here lyeth the Body of
MATTHIAS HARRIS, of Brockwear,
who departed this Life
the 29 Day of May,
1749, aged 84 Years.

Alfo in Memory of
BRIDGET, the Wife of
JAMES HOPKIN, of this
Parifh. She died the 3 Day
of April, 1771, aged 63
Years.

Here lyeth the Body of
JAMES HOPKIN, who departed
this Life the 1 Day of Decem.
1786, aged 79 Years.

Here lyeth the Body of ELIZABETH
CUTTER, late Wife of AMBROSE CUTTER,
of Briftol, who died the 30 Day of
Sept. 1741, aged 51 Years.

Alfo here lyeth the Body of
ELIZABETH BOND, Daughter of
RICHARD BOND, of Aylimore,
by ELIZABETH his Wife, who died
Dec. 24, 1742, aged 7 Years.

WILL'US CATCHMAY, de
Huelsfield, Gen. obiit
octavo die Februar.
annoque D'ni 1713,
ætatis fuæ 49.

ON FLAT STONES.

Here lyeth the Body of ELIZABETH,
the Daughter of JAMES and ELIZABETH
HOPKINS, of Brockwear, who
departed this Life the 26 Day
of November, 1734,
aged 22 Years.

Here lyeth the Body of ANN, the
Wife of THOMAS HOPKINS, of
Brockwear, who departed this
Life March 29, 1763, aged 49.

Here
lyeth the Body of
ELIZABETH, the Wife of JAMES
HOPKINS, of Brockwear, who
departed this Life the 29 Day
of Jan. 1753, aged 73 Years.

Here

Here lyeth the Body of
ELIZABETH WILLIAMS, who
departed this Life the 8 Day
of Oct. 1724, aged 33 Years.

Here lyeth the Body of
ANN WHITE, Daughter of
JOHN and ANN WHITE, of the
Parish of St. Stephen, in the
City of Briftol, who departed
this Life the 17 Nov. . . . . .
aged 22 Years.

Here lyeth the Body of WILLIAM
WILLIAMS, who departed this Life
the 14 Day of Dec. An. Dom.
1695.

Alfo here lyeth the Body of
WILLIAM WILLIAMS, junior, who
departed this Life the 9 Day of
Feb. Anno Dom. 1717.

Alfo ANN, Wife of RICHARD WILLIAMS,
who departed this Life 14 July,
1727.

Here refteth the Body of MARGARET,
Wife of WILLIAM WILLIAMS, who
departed this Life Jan. 9, 1701.

Alfo ELIZABETH, the Wife of WILLIAM
WILLIAMS, departed Nov. 18, 1707.

Alfo here refts the Body of RICHARD
WILLIAMS, who departed this Life the
16 Day of Dec. 1711, aged 61 Years.

BETTY, Daughter of BENJAMIN and
MARY GAY, departed this Life
Aug. 18, 1751, aged 15 Years.

Here refteth the Body of
JOHN HARRIS, of Brockwear, who
departed this Life the 1 Day of July,
An. Dom. 1702.

HERE LYETH INTERRED THE BODY
OF GEORGE KEACHMENT, OF
BROOKWER, WHO DEPARTED
THIS LIFE THE 30 DAY OF AUG.
IN THE YEAR OF OUR LORD
GOD 1658.

AND ALSO HERE LYETH
INTERRED THE BODY OF
FRANCES, THE WIFE
OF GEORGE KEACHMENT, OF
BROCKWER ABOVESAID, WHO
DEPARTED THIS LIFE THE
20 DAY OF JVNE, IN THE
YEAR 1680.

HERE LYETH THE BODY OF
THOMAS GEORGE, OF BROCKWERE,
WHO DEPARTED THIS LIFE THE 8
DAY OF MAY, 1708.

HERE LYETH THE BODY OF
HENRY ROGERS, OF THIS PARISH,
MARINER, WHO DEPARTED
THIS LIFE THE .. DAY OF OCT.
1680.

HERE LYETH THE BODY
OF MARY, DAUGHTER OF
HENRY ROGERS, OF THIS
PARISH, THE YOUNGER, WHO
DEPARTED THIS LIFE THE 28 DAY
OF FEB. 1680.

Here lyeth the Body
of HENRY SCUDAMORE,
who departed this Life
the 27 Day of April, 1719,
in the Parifh of Ragland,
in the County of Monmouth.

Alfo here lyeth the Body
of SARAH, the Wife of
THOMAS RICHARDS, of
Brockwear, who died
the 16 Feb. 1751.

Here lyeth the Body of
BRIDGET, the Daughter of
JOHN MORGAN, who died
June 1697.

Alfo here lyeth the Body
of EDWARD MORGAN, of

Brockwear, who died
the 10 July, 1719.

Here lyeth the Body of
WILLIAM BADDAM, Shipwrite,
of the Citty of Briftol, who
died the 4 of Jan. 1709,
aged 49 Years.

Here lyeth the Body of
MARGARET, the Wife of
FRANCES RAWLINS, of
Brockwear, deceafed
the 30 Day of Dec.
1684.

Here lyeth the Body of
RICHARD RALLINGS, who
departed this Life the 23d
of Dec. 1715, aged 44.

Alfo here lyeth the Body of
JOAN, Wife of JOHN TYLER,
of Brockwear, who died
the 2 Day of April, 1713,
aged 66 Years.

Here lyeth the Body of
THOMAS HARRIS, who departed
this Life 1684.

MARY his Wife, Nov. . . 170 . .

HERE LYETH THE BODY OF
ELINOR, DAUGHTER OF
THOMAS WHITE, WHO
DEPARTED THIS LIFE THE
1 DAY OF DEC. 1696.

Here lyeth the Body of
THOMAS WHITE, of this
Parifh, who died 4 Nov.
1695.

MARY WHITE died 11 June, 1694.

MARY, Wife of THOMAS WHITE,
died 26 Oct. 1708.

THOMAS, Son of JAMES CUTT,
deceafed Feb. 3, 1727.

JAMES his Son died 2 Ap. 1743.

O N   H E A D   S T O N E S.

	Died	Aged		Died	Aged
Mary, Daughter of Edward Evans	16 Mar 1706	—	Ann, Wife of Job Marfhall	5 Jan. 1764	43
Edward Evans	27 Mar. 1706	—	James Williams	10 Dec. 1708	—
Thomas, Son of Jno. and Alice Hughes	12 Mar. 1769	17	Richard Thorn	31 Oct. 1719	—
Eleanor their Daughter	30 Aug. 1770	22	Ifaac Williams	20 June, 1728	70
Diana, Daughter of George Man	25 Sept. 1742	20	Elizabeth Williams	15 Aug. 1736	60
Thomas Thorn. of St. Briavell's	10 Apr. 1783	50	Jane, Wife of Francis Williams	18 Dec. 1765	29
Hannah, Daughter of John Ravenhill	11 Nov. 1781	9	William Moxley	12 Mar. 1776	72
Elizabeth, Daughter of William and			Jane his Wife	7 Apr. 1762	59
Alice Ball	27 Apr. 1777	20	James their Son	4 May, 1762	23
James Hall	28 Feb. 1769	46	Mary, Daughter of Philip Moxley	7 Jan. 1777	20
Richard Lewelling	21 Dec. 1756	60	William, Son of Morgan and Hannah		
Elizabeth his Wife	9 Jan. 1773	85	Dibdon	6 Jan. 1781	22
Thomas Marfhal, of Tiddenham	25 July, 1778	76			

CXLIV. H I L L, or H U L L,

S O called from its elevated Situation, is a fmall Parifh within the Hundred of *Berkeley*, from which
Town it is diftant three Miles, four North from *Thornbury*, and twenty-two South-weftward from
GLOUCESTER.

The Lands fhelving from the Hill extend in a level Direction for about two Miles to the River *Severn*,
divided into fpacious Meadows, of a deep Soil, very fertile, and fubject to frequent Inundations.
About 2,000 Acres are included in the Terrier.

The Living is a Donative. Being, with the whole Tythes, Parcel of the Endowment of the Abbey
of *St. Auguftine's* in *Briftol*, it was granted, upon their Eftablifhment, to the Dean and Chapter of that
See; and is now held under Leafe.

The Church is dedicated to *St. Michael*, and belongs to the Deanery of *Durfley*. It appears to have
been new-modelled by Sir EDWARD FUST, when he re-built the Manor-houfe to which it adjoins. Open
carved Benches are the only Remains of an early Date. It has a Nave, and low obtufe Spire.

In the *Domefday* Survey, *Hill* is fpecified as a Member of the great Lordfhip of *Berkeley*. Mr SMYTHE
proceeds with the Hiftory of its Proprietors: " *Hill*, in *Domefdei* Booke foe written; but fince, and of
" late Years, *Hill*, als *Hull*, an ancient Manor within the Parifh of *Berkeley*, holden of the Kinge by
" Knight Service *in capite*, wherein WILLIAM the CONQUEROR, and before him Kinge EDWARD, called
" the CONFESSOR, had foure Hides of Land, as the faide *Domefdei* Booke fhews.

" And in this Manor, in the Time of Kinge E. II. JOHN FITZ NICHOLL, then Lorde thereof, had
" two Parkes, as by Deeds with Sir ROBERT POYNTZ, whofe Father's this late was, which I have feen
" appears.

" This Manor was amongft many others given by Kinge H. II. in the firft Yeare of his Raigne, to
" ROBERT, the Son of HADINGE, and his Heires, to hold of him by Knight Service, by which Grant
" alfo he was created a Peere and Baron of the Realme. This Manor the faid Lord ROBERT not long
" after, in the faid Kinge's Time, gave to NICHOLAS his fecond Sonne, and his Heires, by his Deed in
" theis Words: " Sciato me dediffe & conceffiffe NICHº filio meo *Hullam* & *Nimdesfield*, cum oñbus
" ptinentiis fuis, quas dni Rex mihi dedit fervicio meo in feodo & hereditate fibi & heredibus fuis, fa-
" ciendo illi oñi fervicium dimidii militis liberas & quietas ab omni alio fervicio. Tefte Riĉo Abbate
" Sĉi *Auguftino*," &c. as by the Deed remaining with Sir EDWARD COKE, late Chief Juftice of the
" King's Bench, which I copied out, appeareth; and after the faid Lord ROBERT dyed in 17 H. II. as
" by the great Pipe Roll of that Yeare appears.

" This NICHOLAS was a Baron and Peere of the Realme, and paid feveral Efcuages to the faid K. H. II.
" in the 7th, 8th, 32d, and 33d, Yeares of that Kinge, and alfo Aid for Maryage of MAUD his Daugh-
" ter to the Duke of *Saxony*, and dyed in the 6 Yeare of Kinge R. I. leaving Iffue ROGER, who was
" written ROGERIUS filius NICHOLAI, filii ROBERTI filii HARDINGE, and dyed in 15 H. III. leaving Iffue
" NICHOLAS; betweene which NICHOLAS and MAURICE Lord BERKELEY, the fecond of that Name,
" arofe Suites in Lawe for Services which that Lord required of him for this Manor of *Hill*, and for that
" of *Nimdesfield*, to his Lawe Dayes at *Berkeley*; and after thofe Suites ended by Compofition, the faid
" NICHOLAS, Sonne of ROGER, died in 46 H. III. leaving Iffue RAPH, ufually written RAPH, Sonne of
" NICHOLAS, Sonne of ROGER, which RAPH died in 19 E. I. leaving Iffue NICHOLAS, Sonne of RAPH,
" and THOMAS Lord BERKELEY, the fecond of that Name, arofe Suites alfo about the fame Services
" for their Manors of *Hill* and *Nimdesfield*; and after the faid NICHOLAS dyed in 6 E. III. leaving Iffue
" JOHN, between which JOHN and the faid THOMAS Lord BERKELEY were alfo Suites in Law about the
" fame Services for the faid Manors, as by feveral Compofitions thereupon made, which I have read in
" *Berkeley Caftle*, and elfewhere, appeareth; and afterwards the faid JOHN dyed in 49 E. III. leaving
" THOMAS, Sonne of REGINALD, Sonne of him the faid JOHN his Grandchild and Heire.

" The faid THOMAS, ufually written THOMAS FITZ NICHOLL, had only two Daughters, viz. KATHA-
" RINE, who, in the Time of Kinge RICHARD the Second, was maryed to ROBERT POYNTZ; and
" ALIENOR, maryed to JOHN BROWNINGE.

" The

" The faid Thomas Fitz Nicholl, by a Fine in the Court of Comon Pleas, levied in 12 H. IV.
" entayled this Manor of *Hill* to himfelfe and to Agnes his fecond Wife, and to the Heires Male of
" his Body, the Remainder to the faid Robert Poyniz * and Katharine his Wife, Daughter of him
" the faid Sir Thomas, for the Term of their Lives, the Remainder to Nicholas Poyntz, Sonne of
" them the faid Robert and Katharine, and to the Heires Male of his Body, with fix other Remain-
" ders over, which Agnes, fecond Wife of the faid Sir Thomas Fitz Nicholl, died without Iffue in
" the Life time of her Hufband; and after the faid Sir Thomas died in 5 H. V. without Iffue Male of
" his Body, whereby this Manor of *Hill* remained, and came to the faid Robert Poyntz and Katha-
" rine; and after their Deaths (after fome Deviations by Conveyances amongft their Children and
" Nephews), as their Records will fhewe, viz. Paten. 10 H. VI. p. 2. 15 rot. pardon 15 H. VI. in 27 clauf.
" 34 H. VI. m. 10. in dorfo Clauf. 35 H. VI. m. 1. dorfo finis 37 H. VI. m. 1. finis 39 H. VI. m. 1.
" & 4. finis 49 H. VI. m. 4. which was 10 E. IV. this Manor fettled in Sir Robert Poyntz, Heire at
" Comon Lawe to the faid Robert and Katharine, who was a learned and remarkable Gent. bredd
" an vtter Barrifter in *Graie's Inne*. Knight for the Body to Kinge Henry, a Councellor, and Chan-
" cellor to Queene Katharine, firft Wife to Kinge H. VIII. and High Steward of the Lordfhip and
" Hundred of *Berkeley*, and dyed in 12 H. VIII. and left Iffue Anthony Poyntz, Knight, who was by
" Kinge H. VIII. oft employed in very honorable Services at Home and Abroade, in Times of Warre
" and Peace, by Sea and Land in important Services, and died in . . H. VIII. leavinge Iffue Sir Nicho-
" las, who died 3 & 4 Ph. and Mary, who left Iffue Sir Nicholas, who dyed 28 Eliz. who leaft
" Iffue Sir John Poyntz, who, in . . Eliz. aliened this Manor of *Hill* to Nicholas Dimery, and his
" Heires, who fhortly after fold the fame to Henry Fleetwood, and hee foon after to Richard Fuist,
" by whofe Death, in 12 Jacobi K's, it defcended to Edward his Sonne, an underftandinge Gent. who
" nowe holdeth the fame, anno 1639.

" Of this Village, through the lowe Scituation and bad Water, it is faid to be " Hieme mala, æf-
" tate molefta, nunquam bona;" evil in Winter, grievous in Summer, and never good for Habitation;
" wherein are the moft remarkable Places, *Brighampton, Bibury, Woodend, Wickftowe, Shepwarden*, als *She-
" perdine*; in which *Sheperdine*, where a Paffage is over *Severne*, was a Chapel built, whereof Thomas
" Lord Berkeley was Founder, whereunto his Heires prefented as to a Chantry, till the Diffolution
" thereof by Act of Parliament, and whereto, in 25 E. III. he gave competent Lands to maintaine a
" Prieft to finge there.

" Inter Plta coram rege apud *Glouc.* 37 E. III. rot. 27. thus, Joh'es Fitz Nicholl, dus de *Hull*, non
" proteft dedicere quin tenetur folus mundare quendam gurgitem apud *Hull*, per quam aqua folebat
" currere ad *Severne* qui obftructus fuit tempore prefentationis, fed nunc mundatur.

" The Copyhold Rents of this Manor of *Hill* were, in anno 40 Eliz. about 51*l. per Ann.* nowe lef-
" fened, accuftomed to be granted for one Man's Life, and for foe long as his Wife furviving him fhall
" continue fole and chafte, and foe the Poffeffion, by the Death of every Copyhold Tenant, revertinge
" to the Lord to bee again granted to whom it pleafeth him; alfo the Copyholder's Eftate is forfeited
" by committinge of Wafte, as fellinge of Timber without Licence, &c. and by beinge not refident upon
" his Copyhold Tenement and Lands, by not performance of his Service at Courts, by demifing for
" more than one Yeare, and other the like, as by an old Survey which I have feen appeareth.

" Freeholds within this Townfhip of *Hill* which I thought fitteft to Remembrance, viz. an ancient
" Meffuage, with 20 Acres of Land thereto belonginge, called *Scotlands*, the Inheritance of Thomas
" Mallett, of *Rockhampton*, and by him purchafed of Thomas Veel, Efq. late before the Lands of
" Richard Bridges, and fome Time the Land of William Holfrfd, and before Clarkes, and be-
" fore the Land of Richard Moore, of *Hill*, and are holden of George Lord Berkeley, as of his
" Manor of *Hame*, by the yearly Rent of 12*d.* fute to his Hundred Court of *Berkeley*, from three Weeks
" to three Weeks, and by . . . .

" In this Townfhip, in a Place *Woodends* leis, are about 7 Acres of Land, late the Lands of James Par-
" lyn, Sonne of Thomas, the Inheritance whereof is in the three Sifters and Coheires of the faid James,
" viz. Alice, marryed to Richard Adams, of *Oldbury*, who had a third Part; Thomas Rich, of
" *Cleverton*, in *Wiltfhire*, Sonne of another Sifter, another third Part; and the third third Part is parted
" betweene the two Daughters and Coheireffes of ——— Dimery, Sonne of a third Sifter of the faid
" James Purlyn, and are holden of George Lord Berkeley, as of his Manor of *Hame*, by the yearly
" Rent of 2*s.* and Sute of Court to the faid Manor.

" And, by Inq. in 44 Eliz. after the Death of Maurice Tovy, of *Thornbury*, it is found that he
" dyed feized of a Meffuage, Orchard, Garden, one Curtilage, one Clofe of Arrable, and Pafture
" Land, called *Hifefield*, als *Hewifhfield*, containing 12 Acres in *Pedington, Hame, Hill*, and within the
" Parifh of *Berkeley*, holden of Henry Lord Berkeley, as of his Manor of *Canonbury*; but by what

---

* " Pontz of *Gloceftre* cam owte of a Houfe of a youngger Brother of Sutton Pontz: and they had by Heire General
" of one Fitz Nicol or Nicholas, a youngger Sunne of one the Barkeleys, a goodly Lordfhip caullid *Hulle*, and com-
" munely *Hille*; ftanding on the hither Ripe of *Severne*. This Lordefhip was gyven owte of the Berkeleys' Landes. And
" they had after, by Heyres Generales of Acton, the Lordfhip of *Afton*." Leland's Itin. vol. VI. p. 54.

" Service

" Service the Jury knew not; and that MARY, the Wife of JOHN BABOR, JONE, the Wife of NICHOLAS
" BAKER, and FRANCES, the Wife of THOMAS TAYLOR, are his Daughters, and Heires of full Age.

" This Land MAURICE TOVY aforefaid, by Deed, dated in Jan. anno 27 ELIZ. purchafed of ROBERT
" TILLADAM, and are Part of the Lands called *Purlyns*."

From Sir EDWARD FUST laft mentioned, who was created a Baronet, by Patent, dated Auguft 21,
1662, 14 CHARLES II. it has paffed to Sir JOHN FUST, the fifth Baronet, who died in 1779, without
Iffue Male, and bequeathed his manerial Eftate to Dame PHILIPPA his Relict. The Family of FUST
originated in *Switzerland*; and about 1420 obtained confiderable Eftates in the County of *Suffex*. JOHN
FUST, of *Mentz* in *Germany*, allied to this Branch, was the Inventor of the Art of Printing in 1430.
THOMAS FUST, of *Ware*, co. *Herts*, fuffered Death for the Proteftant Perfuafion in 1555; and EDWARD
FUST was an eminent Loyalift during the Civil War.

The prefent Manor-houfe was erected by Sir EDWARD FUST, the fourth Baronet, the more ancient
Refidence, probably built by the Families of FLEETWODE or POYNTZ (of which KIP has given a View),
and is faid to have held out againft the Parliamentary Forces. It confifts of one Side of an intended Square,
and is very extenfive; the Centre is occupied by the Hall, a Room 80 Feet long, and excellently pro-
portioned; it is furnifhed with many Portraits of the Family of FUST and their Connections, with their
Arms, and thofe of their Alliances. Each Portrait is marked with the armorial Bearing, impaled or
quartered, of the Perfons reprefented, with Memoirs of them, printed in gold Letters *.

From the Site of this Houfe the Profpect to the Weft opens to a very fine Reach of the *Severn*;
and beyond it the Cliffs of *Monmouthfhire*, and the *Welfh* Hills, with thofe of the Foreft of *Dene*, are feen
at the Extremity.

The only Property diftinct from the Manor is an Eftate purchafed with the Benefaction of Sir JONA-
THAN DAWES, of *London*, Knight, (who died April 18, 1672) to the Parifh of *Wotton-under-edge*.

BENEFACTION.

MABEL MALLET, Widow, gave, by Deed, dated in 1653, a Clofe of Ground in this Parifh, of the
annual Value of 1*l*. 2*s*. a Moiety of which to be applied towards the Relief of poor, aged, and impotent Perfons, in each of the Parifhes of *Hill* and *Rockhampton*, at the Difcretion of the major Part of
the Truftees for the Time being.

INCUMBENTS.	PATRONS.	INCUMBENTS.	PATRONS.
—— Lancelot Law,	——————.	1745 Robert Lowle, Clerk,	Sir Francis Fuft.
—— William Pritchard, M.A.	——————.	1757 Thomas Robins, Clerk,	The fame.
1744 Richard Jones, B. A.	Sir Francis Fuft.		

PRESENT LADY OF THE MANOR,

Dame PHILIPPA FUST, Widow.

At the Heralds Vifitation, in 1682 and 1683, the only Perfon fummoned from this Place was

Sir John Fuft, Bart.

At the Election in 1776, Ten Freeholders polled from this Parifh.

The earlieft Date in the Regifter occurs in 1766; the preceding is not to be found.

ANNUAL ACCOUNT OF MARRIAGES, BIRTHS, AND BURIALS, IN THIS PARISH.

A.D.	Mar.	Bir.	Bur.	A.D.	Mar.	Bir.	Bur.	A.D.	Mar.	Bir.	Bur.	A.D.	Mar.	Bir.	Bur.
1781	4	8	4	1786	1	3	2	1791				1796			
1782	3	8	3	1787	3	9	4	1792				1797			
1783	—	4	2	1788	2	9	5	1793				1798			
1784	1	3	6	1789	2	7	2	1794				1799			
1785	5	4	4	1790	3	8	1	1795				1800			

* Amongft this very large Collection of Family-Portraits, thofe that are moft ancient are moft valuable. Two three-quarter
Portraits, one of CHARLES BERKELEY, Earl of *Falmouth*, and the other of JAMES Duke of ORMOND, are original, and
worthy Notice.

4. *INSCRIPTIONS*

INSCRIPTIONS IN THE CHURCH.

ON A HANDSOME MARBLE MONUMENT:

Arms; Quarterly, 1. Argent, on a Chevron between three Bills Sable, as many Mullets pierced of the Field, for Fust; 2. Argent, three Chevronels Gules, between as many Martlets Sable, for Singleton; 3. Azure, a Chevron between three Lozenges Or, for Hyde; 4. Argent, two Bars Gules, in Chief three Cinquefoils Sable, for Denton; 5. Sable, a Chevron between three Stags' Attires Argent, for Cocks; 6. 1ft and 4th, Gules, a dexter Arm embowed, covered with a Maunch Ermine, holding a Fleur de Lys Or, for Mohun; 2d and 3d, Or, a Chevron between three Lozenges Azure, on a Chief Gules, an Eagle difplayed Or, for Hyde;—impaling, 1ft and 4th, Gules three Cinquefoils Argent, Hamilton modern; 2d and 3d, Argent, a Ship Sable, Hamilton antient.

Within this Vault is interred,
with his illuftrious Anceftors,
the Body of Sir John Fust,
Son of Sir Francis Fust, Bart. of the adjacent venerable Manfion Hill-Court, Gloucefterfhire.
He died,
the laft Male of his ancient Family,
April 16th, 1779, aged 53.

He was of the middle Stature, of
a benign and comely Countenance
expreffive of his Mind,
which was active, amiable, and generous.
In Youth he was difpofed to feek for Honour,
in the only true Field of Glory,
his Country's Defence,
but his Defires were limited
by Paternal Tendernefs.
However, in the Year 1745, he accepted
a Captain's Commiffion, under Earl Berkeley,
to aid in repreffing an
unprovoked Rebellion,
and prove his Duty to his Sovereign and Country.
In this he followed thofe Paths
his magnanimous Progenitors
had trod.
When Rebellion was fuppreffed, he retired,
and made all around him happy, in the Character
of a liberal, benevolent, country Gentleman.
He was poffeffed of true Chriftian Virtue
and Refignation, joined with manly Fortitude,
exemplified in Life and Death.

Through all the Sufferings of a long
and painful Illnefs, he well fupported
a Dignity of Character
and Rectitude of Heart.
That Heart was Integrity itfelf;
his Judgement was ftrong,
his Manners were gentle,
the tendereft Hufband,
the trueft Friend,
the kindeft Mafter.
Reader, this Character is drawn
by her who knew him beft;
not by the Pen of Flattery,
but the Pencil of Truth.
Infpired by Gratitude, and emulative
of the Virtues he poffeffed, his
afflicted Relict
confecrates thefe unadorned Lines
to a Memory fo precious
to conjugal Affection;
who hopes, when her Soul is
permitted to join the deceafed, her
Body may reft with his
in this awful Manfion.

Sir John Fust married Philippa, third Daughter of John Hamilton, Efq.
late of Chilfon in Kent, Nephew to the Right Honourable James Earl of Abercorn.

Sacred to the Memory of
Thomas Hobby,
only Son of Thomas and Mary Hobby,
of Ham, in the Parifh of Berkeley,
who died the 6 Dec. 1781,
aged 33 Years.
This Monument was erected by his
Parents
as a Teftimony of his Worth,
and their Affection.

Alfo of Thomas Hobby, fen. who died
the 9 Aug 1783, aged 67 Years.

Alfo of Mary Hobby, Relict of the above
Thomas Hobby, who died 18 June, 1788,
aged 75 Years.

ON A FREESTONE MONUMENT:

PIÆ MEMORIÆ
VENERAB. VIRI LANCELOTTI LAW,
S. S. T. B. PIETATIS, PATIENTIÆ
ET TEM-
PERANTIÆ EGREGII EXEMPLARIS;
QUI EODEM SCLOPPO QUO AVIVM
PETEBAT VITAM INCAVTE AMISIT
SVAM DEC. 7,
1650.

ON FLAT STONES.

Round the Verge:

HERE LYETH THE BODY OF MARY,
THE DAUGHTER OF WILLIAM
QUINTON, WHO
DIED THE 6 OF JUNE, 1631, AND
THE FIRST THAT WAS BURIED IN
THIS CHANCEL.

Round the Verge:

VNDER THIS STONE DOTH LYE
THE BODY OF
RALPH DARBIE, WAYTING FOR A
BLESSED RESVRRECTION, WHO
DECEASED
THE 30 OF JANUARY, 1643, AND
IN THE
66 YEARE OF HIS AGE.

Under
this Stone lieth the
Body of John Wade, of
this Parifh, Yeoman, who
died March the 10, 1770,
aged 44 Years.

Round the Verge:

HERE RESTETH THE BODY OF
MARGARET
TROTMAN, WIFE OF WILLIAM
TROTMAN,
WHO DECEASED THE 9 DAY OF
OCT. 1648.

HERE LYETH THE
BODY OF KATHRIN
SMYTH, THE WIFE
OF ROBERT SMYTH,
WHO DEPARTED THIS LIFE
THE 16 DAY OF SEPTEMBER,
IN THE YEARE OF OVRE
LORD 1655.

IN THE CHURCH-YARD, ON TOMBS.

Here lyeth
under this Tomb
the Body of RALPH PEARCE,
of Hill, Yeoman, who was
buried the 1st Day of
March 1719, aged 75.

Also here lyeth the Body
of MARY his Wife, who was
buried the 2d Day of
Nov. 1707,
aged 60 Years.

In Memory of EDWARD PEARCE, late
of Greenstreet, in the Parish
of Berkeley, Gent. who
departed this Life the 27
Day of Feb. 1756,
aged 37 Years.

In Memory of
EDWARD PEARCE, of Hill, Yeoman,
who was buried the 2d Day of March,
1728, aged 41 Years.

Also in Memory of ELIZABETH his Wife,
who was buried the 25 Day of Feb. 1728,
aged 40 Years.

Also in Memory of THOMAS his Son, who
was buried the 5 Day of March, 1728,
aged 6 Years.

In Memory of ANN, Wife
of JOHN Cox, of Nubdown,
in the Parish of Rockhampton,
Yeoman, who departed this
Life Feb. 18, 1743, aged 22 Years.

Also in Memory of WILLIAM
their Son, who died
Dec. 26, 1743, aged 11 Years.

In Memory of ELIZABETH,
Daughter of the said JOHN and
ANN Cox, who was buried
March 7, 1744, aged 1 Year.

In Memory of ELIZABETH, the Daughter
of WILLIAM Cox, of this Parish,
who died March 14, 1744, aged 14 Years.

Also ANN, the Daughter of
THOMAS KING, of this Parish,
who died March 14, 1744,
aged 2 Years.

In Memory of THOMAS KING,
of this Parish, who died Jan.
the 24, 1758, aged 60 Years.

Also of ELIZABETH his Wife,
who died Dec. 14. 1753,
aged 61 Years.

In Memory of ELIZABETH, the
Daughter of THOMAS KING,
of this Parish, and Wife of
THOMAS NELMES, of Claptor,
in the Parish of Berkeley,
who died Jan. 19, 1758,
aged 22 Years.

In Memory of JOAN,
the Wife of WILLIAM SPILLMAN, of
Berkeley, in this County, who died the
7 Feb. 1722, aged 39 Years.

In Memory of JOHN SPILLMAN,
of Nupdown, in the Parish of
Rockhampton, who was buried
July 12, 1736.

Also of ELIZABETH his Wife,
and late Wife of JOHN APPERLEY,
of this Parish, jun. who
died Oct. the 2d, 1766,
aged 68 Years.

ON FLAT AND HEAD STONES.

	Died	Aged
Joseph Deacon -	12 Mar. 1721	60
Mary his Wife - -	15 Apr. 1712	46
John Perrett - -	23 Apr. 1767	69
Elizabeth his Wife -	31 Mar. 1760	65
William Perrett - -	25 Aug. 1756	24
Thomas Allin - -	4 June, 1765	44
William Smith, Butler to Sir Francis and Sir John Fust -	28 May, 1784	74
John, Son of John Tayler -	7 June, 1724	12
John Tayler - -	27 Jan. 1729	63
Mary, Widow of Joseph Everett, of Berkeley - -	3 Mar. 1774	58
Samuel Thomas -	20 Apr. 1751	—
Ann his Wife - -	1 July, 1742	—
Ann, Wife of William Davis	16 Jan. 17—	—
Elizabeth, Wife of William Thomas	25 Dec. 1748	39
Mary, Wife of Philip Osborne	16 Dec. 1764	56
Sarah, Daughter of Thomas Price	28 Apr. 1764	26
Thomas Price - -	7 May, 1705	39
John Champnies -	10 Nov. 1751	30
William Hobby - -	1 May, 1769	74
Thomas Pride - -	8 May, 1705	—
John Summers, of Thornbury	6 Mar. 1728	—
Ann, Daughter of William and Sarah Signett - -	18 Oct. 1761	31
Judith, Relict of Thomas Davis, of St. Oulard, in the County of Monmouth - -	21 Sept. 1766	63
James Phipps -	9 Jan. 1784	33
Betty his Wife - -	24 May, 1781	30
James King - -	7 Oct. 1762	43
Jane his Wife -	14 May, 1778	73
William Pritchard, of Berkeley	11 Dec. 1787	81
Mary his Wife - -	19 Dec. 1787	61
Moses Summers - -	9 Feb. 1790	72
Sarah, Wife of Thomas Eyles	11 July, 1784	78
Ann, Wife of Samuel Merrett	29 Jan. 1762	53
John Spillman - -	10 Jan. 1723	—
William Cox - -	23 Feb. 1728	33
Sarah, Wife of Thomas Nelmes, Daughter of Thomas Pearce	7 May, 1763	49
Elizabeth, Relict of Thomas Hobby	10 May, 1785	67
Edward Fowler -	25 Apr. 1744	42
William Atwood - -	22 Dec. 1728	—
William Atwood -	6 July, 1729	48
Sarah his Wife - -	18 June, 1746	58
Elizabeth his Daughter -	28 June, 1729	18
Edward Knight -	15 Apr. 1764	67
Sarah his Wife - -	22 Sept. 1766	71
Jane their Daughter, Wife of Thomas Werrett - -	16 Feb. 1763	32
Elizabeth their Daughter -	26 Oct. 1766	42
Aaron Summers -	3 Feb. 1728	42
Esther his Wife - -	9 Jan. 1755	79
Anthony Hollway -	19 Oct. 1742	65
Jeane, the Wife of Nathaniel Garland - - -	27 May, 1689	—
Samuel Liddiatt - -	8 Sept. 1736	29
Mary, Wife of Richard Andrews	2 Aug. 1722	44

CXLV.

William
(Baker Esq.
LORD OF
THIS MANOR.
contributes
this Plate.

KEMERTON.

CXLV.   H I N T O N,
O R
HYNNYNGTON SUPER VIRIDEM,

MORE commonly called *HINTON ON THE GREEN*, lies in the Hundred of *Tibbold-ftone*, in the Vale of *Evefham*, whence it is diftant three Miles on the South, eight Weft from *Campden*, and twenty-one North-eaftward from GLOUCESTER. The Terrier includes 2214 Acres, in nearly equal Parts, of rich Pafture and Arable, which, from its fuperior Verdure, gives a Name to the Place. The Soil is of a deep Clay, interfected by a Rivulet, called the *Ifbourn*, which falls into the *Avon*.

The Living is a Rectory, endowed with thirty-two Acres of Glebe, one third Part of the great, and all the fmall Tythes. As the others were Parcel of the Endowment of the Abbey of *St. Peter in Gloucefter*, they were confirmed to the Bifhops, under whom they are now held by Leafe for twenty-one renewable every feven Years.

About the Year 1315, the Church was re-built, at the Charge of the Abbey of *Gloucefter*, and dedicated to *St. Peter **. It is conftructed with a Nave and embattled Tower of the neat Architecture of that Age, and is a Member of the Deanery of *Campden*. Some Years fince, a large Slab was taken up, with this Infcription : " Hic fepelitur corpus D'ni WILL'MI HALFORDIÆ, quondam Abbatis de *Bordefleya*, " qui feliciter obijt XII die Septbris, Anno D'ni Millefimo CCCXVII." TANNER notices WILLIAM HAYFORD as Abbot of *Bordefley* in *Worcefterfhire* from 1293 to 1317.

In the Year 981, ELFLEDA, Sifter of King ETHELRED, at that Time wealthy, and advanced in Years, gave the Manor of *Hynetun*, and it is fpecified in *Domefday* under " Terra S. Petri de Glowcefl'," as containing fifteen Hides. She obtained peculiar Exemptions from all Charges, which Liberty was allowed in 1166 †. In 1287, 15 EDW. I. Free Warren, Market, and Fairs, were confirmed to the Abbey in their Manor of *Hynetun* upon a *Quo Warranto* ; and, in the fame Year, a Fine was levied upon a View of Francplege in the Hundred Court of *Tibboldftone* before the Juftices in Eyre ‡. Under the Abbey, the Family of DASTON, of *Wormington*, were Leffees in the Reign of HENRY the Eighth.

At the Suppreffion, the Manor and Advowfon were fold, from the Court of Augmentations in 1545, 36 H. VIII. to Sir EDWARD WORTH, Knight, to whom fucceeded THOMAS BERNERS, or BARNES, whofe Daughter and fole Heir was the Wife of THOMAS BAKER, and their Son Sir THOMAS BAKER was Proprietor in 1608. It afterwards paffed to Sir JOHN HANMER, and from him to Sir ROBERT JASON, of *Broad Somerford*, co. *Wilts*, who was created a Baronet by Patent, dated Sept. 5, 1661. The Relict of the laft mentioned re-married with Sir CHRISTOPHER AYRES, and, furviving him, with DAVID WARREN, Efq. She enjoyed this Eftate in Jointure till her Death in 1713. In 1738, JOSEPH SWAYNE, Efq. of *Briftol*, married the Widow of a fucceeding Sir R. JASON, and, having gained entire Poffeffion of this Manor, he fold it to JAMES STEPHENS, LL. D. of *Comerton*, co. *Somerfet*, who bequeathed it to his Brother PHILIP STEPHENS, Efq. In 1792 it was purchafed by WILLIAM BAKER, Efq. of *London*. The Manor-houfe is large and commodious, built about the Commencement of the laft Century, and repaired by the firft-mentioned Sir ROBERT JASON, Bart.

Although the general Face of the Country be fo level, from a Hill called the *Downs*, of no great Eminence, a moft extenfive Profpect may be feen of the great Vales of *Gloucefter* and *Evefham*, and upwards of thirty Parifh Churches diftinctly pointed out.

---

* THOMAS's Survey of *Worcefter*, p. 168.

† " De *Hynetone*. Anno Domini MCCCCLXXXI. ELFLEDA, foror Regis ETHELREDI, dedit ecclefiæ *Sancti Petri, Glouc.* " *Hynetone* pro anima fua, erat tunc ipfa vetula fterilis & minus egena cumque de eadem poffeffiuncula exigerentur quinque ho- " mines in expeditione Regis, & invenire non poffent, venerunt clerici qui tunc præerant ecclefiæ *S. Petri, Glouc.* & requifierunt " dominam illam porro illa, in die Nativitatis Domini cum effet Rex in convivio fuo, proftravit fe ad pedes ejus & obtinuit, tunc " & deinceps, ut liberæ fit poffeffio illa & quieta."
     DUGDALE's Monaft. vol. I. p. 115. MS Regift. Abb. *S. Petri, Glouc.* inter Cod. MSS. *Coll. Regin. Oxon.* affervatum.

‡ Arbitration made in 15 EDW. I. 1287, before the Juftices in Eyre at *Gloucefter*, preferved, with many others, amongft the Archives of the Dean and Chapter. The Seals of the twelve Jurors are appendant to it.

In the Excheq. Taxation, temp. EDWARD I. of the Abbey of *Gloucefter*, " Apud *Hynton* tres carucatas terræ & valet carucata " per ann' 25s. Et de redd' affif' 13s. & 4d. Et de relaxatione 50s. & de duobus molendinis 30s. Sum' 8l. 8s. 4d."
          Regift. Abb. *Glouc.* MS. p. 34.

    View of Franc-plege of the Manor of *Hynton*. Ibid. p 36,

    Leafe of the Manor of *Hynton* to GEORGE DASTON and WILLIAM his Son for eighty Years, at an annual Rent of 30l. 6s. 8d. dated 1530. Ibid. p. 42.

4   No

No Benefaction to the Poor.

Incumbents.	Patrons.	Incumbents.	Patrons.
—— William Lynfcombe,	——————.	1671 Jonathan Clerke,	Bifhop of Gloucefter.
1572 William Willis,	Anthony Dafton, Efq.	1700 Anthony Johnfon,	David Warren, Efq.
1575 William Willis,	The fame.	1726 Thos. Savage, M.A.	Bifhop of Gloucefter.
1596 Wm. Bufted, } double prefentation.	{ Thomas Baker } confirmed to the former.	1727 John Chefter, M.A	Sir Warren Jafon, Bart.
John Morell, }	{ John Savage }	1753 Hen. Stephens, LL.D.	Philip Stephens, Efq.
1644 Paul Knell,	King Charles I.	—— John Raynolds, M.A.	The fame.
—— William Payton, B.D.	——————.	1774 Edm. Goodenough, M.A.	The fame.
1667 Timothy Wharton,	Sir John Hanmer.	1783 Francis Mills, B.A.	James Stephens, Efq.

PRESENT LORD OF THE MANOR,
WILLIAM BAKER, Efq.

No Perfon was fummoned from this Place by the Heralds in 1682 and 1683.

It does not appear that any Perfon polled from this Parifh at the Election in 1776.

The Date of the oldeft Regifter now preferved is in 1735.

ANNUAL ACCOUNT OF MARRIAGES, BIRTHS, AND BURIALS, IN THIS PARISH.

A.D.	Mar.	Bir.	Bur.	A.D.	Mar.	Bir.	Bur.	A.D.	Mar.	Bir.	Bur.	A.D.	Mar.	Bir.	Bur.
1781	2	6	8	1786	1	8	6	1791				1796			
1782	2	4	7	1787	2	5	5	1792				1797			
1783	—	10	5	1788	1	4	8	1793				1798			
1784	2	3	1	1789	1	7	1	1794				1799			
1785	1	8	4	1790	3	7	1	1795				1800			

INSCRIPTIONS IN THE CHURCH.

Arms, on an Atchievement, Quarterly, 1. and 4. Azure, a Toiffon d'Or, within a double Treffure counterflory of the fecond, on a Canton, the Arms of Ulfter, for JASON; 2. and 3. Gules, a Lion paffant guardant Argent, on a Canton of the laft, a Crofs of the firft, for LYON. On an Efcocheon of Pretence, Ermine, a Fefs chequy, between three Lions paffant Sable.

ON FLAT STONES.

ROUND THE VERGE:

𝕳ic jacet 𝕿homas 𝖂𝖞𝖐𝖐𝖞𝖘, quondam firmarius cujus anime, qui obiit XXIIII die Octobris, A° D'ni M°CCCCLXXX°, et Joanna uroris, quon . . . .

ROUND THE VERGE:

𝕳ic jacet 𝕵annetta 𝖂oolmer, quondam uror 𝕿homæ 𝖂oolmer. Cujus anime . . . . . propitietur 𝕯eus. Amen.

HERE LYETH
THE CORPSE OF
MR. WILLIAM PEY-
TON, B.D. WHO
ENDED THIS LIFE
THE 8 OF JAN.
ANNO 1666.

H. S. E.
JONATHAN CLARKE,
Vir pius, probus, &
Verbi præco affiduus;
Qui cum per ann' 29
Hujus ecclefiæ curam
Cum laude fuftinuit,
Ex hac vita ad feliciorem migravit
Octavo kalend' Decembris,
Anno reparatæ falutis 1700,
Ætatis fuæ LV.

Here lieth the Body of ANNE, Wife of Sir ROBERT JASON, of Broad Sumerford in Wiltfhire, Baronet, Relict of DAVID WARREN, Efq. of Greet, in the County of Gloucefter, who was born July 1644, and departed this Life January the 29th, 1713.

Here refts the Body of DAVID WARREN, Efq. the Son of JOHN WARREN, of Greet, in the County of Gloucefter. His Charity and Knowledge rendered him very ufeful to the Poor; his Learning and Converfation, beloved by all his Acquaintance. He died the 28 of September, in the Year of our Lord 1708, aged 56.

Here lieth the Body of CATHARINE, Relict of JOHN WARREN, of Greet, in the County of Gloucefter, Dr. of Laws. She was the Daughter of THOMAS, the fecond Son of Sir DAVID WILLIAMS, Baronet, of Guernevet, in the County of Brecon, and one of the Barons of the Exchequer. She died May the 30th, 1709, aged 84.

Here lyeth the Body of JOHN CHESTER, late Rector of this Church. He departed this Life May the 16th, 1740, aged 40 Years.

IN THE CHURCH YARD.
ON HEAD STONES.

	Died	Aged
Richard New	11 May, 1776	67
Hannah his Wife	17 Aug. 1788	88
Ann their Daughter	14 Oct. 1754	20
Richard Lloyd	18 Jan. 1783	68
William Woollams	22 Feb. 1706	58
Mary Mufgrove	21 Dec. 1694	—
Rebekah, Wife of Jofeph Smith	25 Apr. 1737	36
Jane his fecond Wife	20 June, 1745	38
Thomas Hill	27 Apr. 1753	67
Thomas, Son of Thomas and Alice Hill	14 Dec. 1781	52
John Bevin	11 Oct. 1781	57

	Died	Aged
John Ryland	2 May, 1747	42
Margaret his Daughter	18 Jan. 1728	15
Mary his Wife, late Wife of John Bevin	18 Mar. 1782	69
John Ryland	23 Dec. 1727	61
Samuel Ryland	10 Jan. 1728	58
John Ryland	3 Aug. 1713	79
Mary his Daughter, Wife of Thomas Baylis	12 Dec. 1719	55
Thomas Baylis	12 June, 1720	66
William Tandy	13 Apr. 1729	29

2

CXLVI. HORFIELD.

CXLVI. H O R F I E L D.

THIS fmall Parifh is contained in the Extremity of the lower Divifion of the Hundred of *Berkeley*, two Miles North from the City of *Briftol*, nine South from *Thornbury*, and thirty-two from Gloucester, in the fame Direction. The River *Trim* has its Source in this Parifh; the greater Divifion of which is rich Pafture Ground, of a ftrong Soil, principally Clay.

The Impropriation belonged to the Abbot of *St. Augufine in Briftol*, and was confirmed to the See in 1545; the certified Value of the Curacy being only 3*l.* In 1718 it was augmented by Queen Anne's Bounty, and the Benefactions of Edward Colston and Thomas Edwards, Efq.

Nothing curious remains in the Church, which is very fmall, with a Nave only, and low Tower. It is in the Deanery of *Briftol.*

The Manor is thus defcribed by Mr. Smythe: " *Horefeild*; in *Domefdei-booke*, *Horefelle*; a Townfhip
" within two Miles of the Citie of *Briftoll*, wherein Will'm the Conqueror, which alfo Edward the
" Confessor had, as that Book telleth us, eight Hides of Land in Demefne, now Parcell of the Pof
" feffions of the Bifhoppricke of *Briftoll*, and hath for its Neighbour Borderers the fower *Stokes*, of
" *Great Stoke, Little Stoke, Stoke Gifford*, and *Harry Stoke*.

" This Manor and Townfhip was Part of the ancient Poffeffions of the Abbot and Convent of *St. Au
" gufine's* by *Briftoll*, and one of the Manors given by Robert, Sonne of Hardinge, when in the Time
" of Kinge Stephen hee firft founded the fame, whereof fee before, in *Almondfbury*, &c. and continued
" in the Hands of thofe Abbots till the Diffolution of that Monaftery in 31 H. VIII.; and, upon that
" Kinge's erecting of the Bifhoppricke of *Briftoll*, in the 34 Yeare of his Reigne, became by his Grant
" parcell of the Poffeffions of the Bifhoppricke.

" For Freewarren, and other Liberties granted by Kinge E. I. and after recited and confirmed by
" Kinge E. IV. fee before, in *Almondfbury.*

" A Booke of Knight's Fees in the Exchequer, with the Remembrancer to the Lord Treafurer, faith,
" John Gifford holds half a Knight's Fee in *Horefield* of Thomas de Berkeley, which is now the
" Land of . . . .

" In the Yeare 1472, A° 12 E. IV. a Compofition was made between Walter Newberry, then
" Abbot of the Monaftery of *St. Augufine's* by *Briftoll*, and Will'm Meredith, then Rector of the
" Parifh Church of *Filton*, in the Dioces of *Worcefter*, concerning certain Tythes, real, mixt, and per
" fonal, out of Lands in the Limitts and Borders of the Chaple of *Horefeild*, called *Brewefhold*, whereby
" the Abbot was to have the Tythes, and to pay the Rector of the Church of *Filton* 6*s.* 8*d. per Ann.*
" at Michmas, which was confirmed by John then Bifhopp of *Worc.* and is to this Day paid by the
" Bifhopp of *Briftoll*, within which Deanery of *Briftol* this Chaple or Church is."

The Leafe of the Manor was long held by the Anceftors of Thomas Mitchel, Efq. Barrifter at Law, whofe fole Daughter and Heir was Isabella, the Wife of John Shadwell, Efq. of *Cork*, in *Ireland.* Three Defcents of the Family of Walter, of *Stapleton*, prior to 1656, are faid to have held Eftates at *Horfield*, now divided between the Families of Cave, Wetherell, Harding, and Davies.

Nothing worthy Remark, relating either to Antiquities or Natural Hiftory, is found within this Parifh.

B E N E F A C T I O N.

A Rent Charge of Land, in the Tything of *Stowick* and Parifh of *Henbury*, the Property of Lord Clifford, 16*s.* annually, whereof one Half is given to the Minifter for a Sermon on every Firft of January, and the other Half to the Poor on that Day.

PRESENT LESSEE OF THE MANOR,
John Shadwell, Clerk.

The only Perfon fummoned from this Parifh by the Heralds, in 1682 and 1683, was Edward Hancock, Clerk.

At the Election in 1776, only One Freeholder polled from this Parifh.

INSCRIPTIONS IN THE CHURCH.
IN THE CHANCEL.

ON MARBLE MONUMENTS.

In Memory
of John Shadwell, Efq.
Barrifter at Law, and late Lord of this Manor,
who,
poffeffing a confiderable Share of Know-ledge,
applied it to the wifeft of all human Purpofes,
that of being an affectionate Hufband,
an exemplary Father,
and honeft Man.
Ob. 18 April, 1777, æt. fuæ 42.

In Memory
of Isabella, Daughter of
John Shadwell, of the City of Cork, Efq.
Lord of this Manor.
She died the 3d of July, 1763,
aged 3 Years and 2 Months.
Her Mother, Isabella, was Daughter of
Thomas Mitchell, Efq.
late Lord of the faid Manor,
to whofe Anceftors it had belonged
for a long Series of Years.

From an experienced Senfe
of the many amiable Qualities
which, in every Relation, formed the Character
of
Richard Jennings, Efq.
late of this Parifh
(whofe Remains lie here interred),
his grateful Widow,
Rachael Jennings,
caufed this Stone to be erected.
He died the 9th of March, 1776,
in the 54th Year of his Age.

In a Vault near this Place
lie interred the Remains of Hester Pye,
the loving, and beloved Wife of
Samuel Pye,
of Briftol, Surgeon.
This Monument was erected by her afflicted
Hufband, as the laft Teftimony of his unfeigned
Affection for a truly virtuous Wife, a fond Parent,
and fincere Friend.
She departed this Life January 15, 1780,
aged 50.

Alfo of three of their Children,
Samuel, Frances, and Sophia,
who died in their Infancy.

Alfo of Margaret Pye,
Mother of Samuel Pye, who died
21 April, 1771,
aged 80.

ON FLAT STONES.

Round the Verge:

Here lieth the Body of John Walter, late of Horfield, in the Countie of
Gloucefter, who departed this Life in the Faith of Christ Jesus the eaight Day of
September, in the Year of our Lord
1624,
ætatis fuæ 65.

Mors fit mihi vita.

Round the Verge:

Here lieth the Body of Thomas Walter, of this Parifh, Efq. who departed this Life

the 27 Day of November, Anno Dom. 1656.

Here lieth the Body of Elizabeth, the Wife of John Reave, of this Parifh, Yeoman, who died 8 Oct. 1723, aged 84 Years.

Here lyeth the Body of John Reeve, who died the 16th of October, 1725, aged 90 Years.

Here lyeth the Body of Grace, the Wife of John Organ, of Horfield Farm,
Yeoman, who died 21 Sept. 1728, aged 41 Years.

Alfo the Body of John Organ, of faid Farm, who died Nov. 22, 1744, aged 76 Years.

Alfo Hannah their Daughter, who died Jan. 7, 1752, aged 30 Years.

Here lieth the Body of William Thomas, of this Parifh, who departed this Life the 28th Day of February, in the Year of our Lord 17 .. aged 78 Years.

Here lyeth the Body of Elisabeth, the Wife of William Thomas, late of this Parifh, who died 27 Jan. 1729, aged 30 Years.

Here lyeth the Body of Joseph, Son of William and Elizabeth Thomas, of this Parifh, who departed this Life the 14 of Oct. 1729, in the 18 Year of his Age.

IN THE CHURCH YARD. ON TOMBS.

Mary, the Wife of John Lambe, Gent. died April 30, 1743, aged 77 Years.

Elizabeth, Relict of John Jones, of the City of Briftol, died Jan. 27, 1775, aged 74 Years.

ON HEAD AND FLAT STONES.

	Died	Aged
Grace, Wife of John Thomas	26 Feb. 1779	29
John Hughes, Yeoman	6 Apr. 1787	59
Betty, Wife of Job Hughes	1 May, 1782	—
Mary, Sifter to Job Hughes	24 May, 1774	20
Elizabeth, Wife of William Bennett	12 May, 1754	45
Sarah, Wife of John Bennett	13 Apr. 1753	41
Mary, Wife of John Taylor, of Clouerwall	5 June, 1716	—
Elizabeth, Relict of Thomas Latcham, of Filton	19 Sept. 1757	82
Thomas Latcham	1 Aug. 1749	83
James Alway	8 Jan. 1716	46
Sarah Alley, Wife of James Alley	4 —— 1707	—
Ann, Daughter of James and Ann Hill	9 Apr. 1782	—
Elizabeth, Wife of George Alway	20 Apr. 1788	42
Mary, Wife of Jofeph Wheeler	16 Jan. 1781	61
Mary, Daughter of John and Grace Organ	19 Aug 1716	—
Hannah, Daughter of John and Grace Organ	18 Jan. 1719	—
Thomas Stone, Soapmaker, of Briftol	4 Feb. 1760	58
Sarah his Wife	10 Feb. 1786	71
Thomas their Son	22 Mar. 1760	6
Eight of their Children.		
John Organ, Butcher	5 May, 1786	35

CXLVII. HORSLEY,

CXLVII. HORSLEY, HORKESLEIGH,
OR
HURSTLEGH,

IS Part of the Hundred of *Longtree*; three Miles diftant from *Minchin Hampton* on the South-weft, four North from *Tetbury*, and feventeen South from the City of GLOUCESTER.

The Terrier is computed to contain 4000 Acres, one Half of which are Arable, and the other Woodland and Pafture. The Face of the Country is here very irregular, and broken into many very fteep Acclivities, with narrow Valleys, watered by fmall Rivulets, upon which Mills are erected for the Manufacture of Cloth, which in its various Branches gives Employment to the numerous Inhabitants.

Ecclefiaftics feem to have taken an early Poffeffion of *Horfley*. Before the Compilation of *Domefday*, a Cell, confifting of a Prior and a few Monks, was eftablifhed here, and annexed to the Abbey of *St. Martin*, founded at *Troarne* in *Normandy* by ROGER DE MONTGOMERI Earl of SHREWSBURY [*]. In 1372, 45 E. III. an Exchange was made between the Prior of the *Auguftine* Abbey of *Bruton*, co. *Somerfet*, and the abovementioned, in Lieu of Lands in *France*; and it continued as a Cell to that Body till the Diffolution of monaftic Eftablifhments [†]. Still to be difcovered are the Foundations of a confiderable Building, and the old Gateway remains entire, ftanding very near the Church.

The Tythes of this Parifh were appropriated by HENRY WAKEFIELD, Bifhop of *Worcefter*, in 1376, to the Abbey of *Bruton*; and, in 1280, he appointed twelve Marks to be paid annually to the officiating Prieft, which Stipend has not been increafed [‡]. In 1733, the Vicarage was farther augmented by Queen ANNE's Bounty, and a Benefaction of PAUL CASTLEMAN, Efq. The Impropriation was granted in 1564, 6 ELIZ. to Sir WALTER HUNGERFORD, Knight, of *Farley Caftle*, co. *Wilts*, and has paffed from the Families of WILLETT and HILLIER to JOHN SELFE, Efq. and JOHN LEVERSAGE, Gent.

The Church is in the Deanery of *Stonehoufe*, and dedicated to *St. Martin*, and was probably re-built by the Abbey of *Bruton* in the middle Centuries. It is fpacious, with a heavy embattled Tower, a Nave, Aile, and a Chapel appendant to the Chancel. In painted Glafs are Efcocheons: 1. Gules, a Chevron Ermine, between ten Croffes pattee Argent, for BERKELEY of *Uley*. 2. Argent, a Chief chequy Or and Azure, . 3. Quarterly, Gules and Or, a Bend Argent, for FITZ NICHOLL.

After the Diffolution, this Manor, with its Appendages, was confirmed, in 1542, to Sir THOMAS SEYMOUR (afterward Lord Protector); and, upon his Attainder and Death, in 1553, it was re-granted to Sir WALTER DENNYS, of *Dyrbam*, by whofe Son RICHARD DENNYS, Efq. of *Sifton*, it was fold to the Family of STEPHENS, of *Eaftington*. RICHARD STEPHENS, Efq. in the Reign of Q. ELIZ. built the prefent Manfion-houfe at *Chavenage* in this Parifh, and fettled this Eftate in Jointure upon ANNE his Wife, Daughter of JOHN STONE, of *London*, in 1589 §. It has fince continued in that Family, as their principal Refidence.

---

[*] " *Horkefleigh*, or *Horfley*, Alien Priory. ROGER OF MONTGOMERY, Earl of SHREWSBURY, temp. WILL. CONQ. endowed
" the Abbey of *St. Martin*, which he had founded at *Troarn* in *Normandy*, with this Manor; and here were fettled a Prior and
" Monks dependant on that foreign Monaftery, till the Prior and Convent of *Bruton* in *Somerfetfhire* gave fome Lands they had
" in *France* to the Abbat and Convent of *Troarn*, in Exchange for this and other Eftates in *England*, and then *Horfley* became
" a Cell to *Bruton*, but afterward was quite diffolved, having neither Prior nor Canon; however, it continued Parcel of the
" Eftate of *Bruton* Monaftery, and as fuch was granted, 7 EDW. VI. to Sir WALTER DENNYS."
TANNER, Not. Mon. edit. NASMITH. *Glouc.* XVII.

† DU MONSTRIER, Neuftria Pria, p. 563.—DUGDALE, Mon. Ang. vol. I. pp. 604, 605. II. p. 1002.—Pat. 1 RIC. II. p.
5 m. 37.—NEWCOURT's Repertorium, vol. II. pp. 335, 336.—STEVENS's Supplement, vol. II. p. 16.—Cart. 4 EDW. III. n.
81. confirm. excambium Abb. & Convent. de *Troarn* de Ecclef. de *Whitenhurft* & *Horkefley*, com. *Glouc.* & maneriis conceffis Priori & Convent. de *Bruton* pro Ecclef. & Maner. de *Lyon* in *Normannia*.

‡ THOMAS's Survey of *Worcefter*, p. 185.—BACON's Thefaurus.
A. D. 1380. Ordinatio Vicariæ de *Horfley*, e Regifterio Diocef. *Vigorn*. Extract. " HENRICUS, &c. Epifcopus *Vigornienfis* de
" affenfu & fpontaneâ voluntate Prioris & Conventûs de *Bruton*, &c. ftatuimus & ordinamus vicariam perpetuam confiftere in
" ecclefiâ de *Horfley* & vicarium qui pro tempore fuerit, duodecim marcas fterlingorum de dictis priore & conventu percipiendas
" & quatuor charactelas bofci five focalium per liberationem cuftodis dictorum prioris & conventûs ad quatuor anni terminos
" ufuales liberandas. Habebitque dictus vicarius & fucceffores fui unum manfum competentem non longe diftantem ab ecclefiâ
" de *Horfley*, quem prior & conv. primâ vice erigere tenentur, & ex tunc vicarii fuftentare, propriis fumptibus."
§ Efcheator's Return, fub anno.

2   Other

Other Estates were held by the Families of Smythe of *Nibley*, Webb, and Butler, which now belong to Edward Wilbraham, Paul Castleman, Esq. and others. Very extensive Beech Woodlands, formerly called the Prior's, are the Property of Sir John Hugh Smythe, Bart. This was the last Property in the Parish of *Horsley* which was sold by the Family of Dennys.

T Y T H I N G S.

1. *Down End.*

2. *Nupp End,* or the *Upper End.*

3. *Barton End,* where was the Barton for storing the Corn Rents belonging to the Abbey of *Bruton.* By the Family of Webb it was bequeathed to Paul Castleman, Esq. and has been since purchased by John Remmington, Gent. Certain manerial Privileges are claimed by this Tything.

4. *Nailsworth*; the greater Part of which very populous Village is included in the Parish of *Avening,* and already described *.

Pursuant to an Act of Parliament, passed in 1783, a Penitentiary and House of Correction have been lately completed at *Horsley,* upon Land given by Henry Stephens, Esq. for the adjoining Hundreds. The Plan is particularly judicious, and calculated to answer every Purpose of a reformed Police.

B   E   N   E   F   A   C   T   I   O   N   S.

Walter Chambers gave, in 1714, 10*l.* vested in Mrs. Castleman; the Interest of which to be laid out in Bread for the Poor.

The Rev. Henry Stubbs gave (Time unknown) 20*l.* vested as above; the Interest to be laid out in purchasing Testaments for the Poor.

Edward Webb, in 1744, gave by Will 200*l.* vested as before; the Interest to be disposed of to the Poor, at the Discretion of Trustees.

Mrs. Castleman gave by Deed, in 1752, 200*l.* vested in Trustees, to support a Free School.

Joseph Browning, in 1770, gave by Will Moneys vested in William Smith; the Interest of which is 1*l.* to buy Testaments for the Poor.

Mrs. Castleman, in 1775, gave 30*l.* to support a Free School, vested in Trustees.

Incumbents.	Patrons.	Incumbents.	Patrons.
1554 Henry Wodehouse,	Thomas Bennet, by Grant from the Abbey of Bruton, dated 1536.	1640 Richard Horston,	King Charles I.
		1690 ——— Collins,	King William III.
		1733 Rich. Wallington, M.A.	King George II.
1558 Richard Devys,	Queen Elizabeth.	1764 George Gwinnet, M.A.	King George III.
1608 Samuel Cradock, M.A.	King James I.	1779 Richard Davies, Clerk,	The same.

Present Lord of the Manor,

Henry Stephens, Esq.

The Persons summoned from this Place by the Heralds, in 1682 and 1683, were

Thomas Davis, Gent. and John Hillier, Gent.

At the Election in 1776 Thirty-seven Freeholders polled from this Parish.

The first Date of the Register occurs in 1590.

Annual Account of Marriages, Births, and Burials, in this Parish.

A.D.	Mar.	Bir.	Bur.	A.D.	Mar.	Bir.	Bur.	A.D.	Mar.	Bir.	Bur.	A.D.	Mar.	Bir.	Bur.
1781	16	44	48	1786	24	31	57	1791				1796			
1782	16	31	33	1787	25	29	25	1792				1797			
1783	15	25	36	1788	31	40	24	1793				1798			
1784	15	27	52	1789	21	46	25	1794				1799			
1785	17	23	46	1790	14	53	30	1795				1800			

* See vol. I. p. 92, of this Work.

INSCRIPTIONS

INSCRIPTIONS IN THE CHURCH.

IN THE CHANCEL.

ON MARBLE MONUMENTS.

Arms, a Lion rampant, for WAL-
LINGTON;—impaling, Azure, a Caſtle
triple-towered Or, for CASTLEMAN.

M. S. ALICIÆ,
RICHARDI WALLINGTON,
hujus ecclefiæ vicarii, uxoris, quæ
gemellos enixa, &, non multo poſt
febre correpta, diem obiit
ſupremum 12° Mar. A. D. 1738,
æt. 3. Gemelli quoque,
JOHANNES & PAULUS, ſub eodem
fere tempore vitâ ceſſerunt.

Arms, three Fleurs de Lys, in Chief a
Crofs Crofslet, for HILLIER.

Near this Place lie the Remains
of JOHN HILLIER, formerly of this
Parifh, Gent. who died January
the 26th, 1743, in the 90th Year
of his Age.

Alſo the Remains of JOHN HILLIER,
late of this Parifh, Gent. Nephew
of the abovementioned JOHN HILLIER,
who died June 30, 1768,
aged 60.

Alſo of ELIZABETH, Wife of the
late JOHN HILLIER, who died
September the 22, 1750, aged 32.

And alſo of ELIZABETH their
Daughter, who died Feb. 20,
1764, aged 21.

In Memory of
THOMAS STRATFORD,
Miniſter of this Parifh,
who died Feb. the 19th, 1732,
ætatis ſuæ 45.

And alſo of ELIZABETH
his Wife, who died
March 10, 1739,
aged 69 Years.

Arms, a Crofs quarterly, quartered
in the firſt Quarter, an Eagle difplayed,
for WEBB.
In Memory of
RICHARD WEBB,
Clothier, and MARY his Wife.
She died May 1, 1749,
ætatis 30; and he April
2, 1750, ætatis 37.

Alſo of MARY their Daughter,
who died July 24, 1746,
ætatis 2.

Arms, Or, a Chevron Sable, between
three Mullets pierced of the Field, for
DAVIS.
In Memory of
THOMAS DAVIS, fen. Gent. of this Parifh,
who died Oct. 6, 1749, aged 78 Years.

ANNE DAVIS his Wife,
who died Aug. 31, 1730,
aged 59 Years.

ANNE SMITH, Widow,
their elder Daughter,
who died June 15, 1782, aged 83 Years.

THOMAS DAVIS, jun. Gent.
their eldeſt Son,
who died Nov. 2, 1743, aged 64 Years.

SAMUEL DAVIS, Gent. their fourth Son,
who died May 15, 1741, aged 32 Years.

And of NATHANIEL and DANIEL
DAVIS, Twins,
their fifth and ſixth Sons.
NATHANIEL died an Infant, May 17,
1712, aged 6 Months.
DANIEL DAVIS, Gent. died Sept. 1,
1783, aged 72 Years.

ON FLAT STONES.

HERE LYETH BURIED
THE BODY OF MARY,
THE WIFE OF JOHN WATTS,
THE DAUGHTER OF TOBYE
CLUTTERBUCKE, WHOE
DEPARTED THE 18 OF
APRIL, 1646.

Here lyeth the Body
of MARY KYRLE, Widow,
late Wife of ROBERT
KYRLE, of Walford,
Efq. youngeſt Daugh-
ter of WILLIAM SEL-
WYN, of Matfon, Efq.
who departed this
Life the 30 Day of March,
Anno Dom. 1677,
æt. ſuæ 63.

ELIZABETHA, nata
RICHARDI HORSTON,
hujus ecclefiæ
vic. mortalitati
vale dixit die Julij, Anno
D'ni 1690.

Hic jacet
Reverendus
GEORGIUS GWINNETT, M. A.
hujus ecclefiæ
nuper vicarius.
Diem obiit fupremum
Anno { ætatis ſuæ 62.
{ Domini 1779.

Here lyeth the Body
of JOHN WOOD, of this
Parifh, Clothier, who
died Nov. 6, 1751,
aged 63 Years.

ON MONUMENTS IN THE NAVE.

Arms, WEBB, as before.

In Memory of
Mr. EDWARD WEBB,
Clothier, who departed
this Life on the 15 Day
of April, in the Year
of our Lord 1751,
aged 52 Years.
He gave 200l.
to the Charity School
of this Parifh.

In Memory of
WILLIAM LOKIER, who
departed this Life
July 24, 1711.

Alſo of MARY, Wife of JOHN
HARRIS, who died May 12,
1728, aged 59 Years.

Alſo in Memory of WILLIAM
DEVERELL, who died March 15,
1779, aged 71.

Alſo of JOAN his Wife, who
ended this tranfitory
Life April 5, 1787,
ætat. 67.

In Memory of
PAUL CASTLEMAN, Efq. and
ELIZABETH his Wife.

Likewife of
EDWARD their Son, and ELIZABETH
their Daughter,
1790.

ON A FLAT STONE:

In Memory of
CHARLES SMITH, Gent.
who died April 5, 1729,
aged 87 Years.

Alſo FRANCES his Wife,
who died January
the 13, 1677,
aged 23 Years.

Alſo MARY, Wife of CHARLES
SMITH, who departed this
Life Anno 1719.

IN THE BURIAL CHAPEL,
ON MONUMENTS.

Near this Place lies the Body
of THOMAS DAVIS, Clothier, who
died March 1, 1715, ætat. ſuæ 87.
Likewife his Daughters, SARAH,
who died Sept. 12, 1713; and
MARY, who died Sept. 21, 1713,
æt. 34.

Near this Place reſteth, in
Hope of a joyful Refurrection, the
Body of SARAH, Wife of THOMAS
DAVIS, Clothier. She died Jan. 14,
and was interred the 18, A. D. 1694.

In Memory of
MARY CASTLEMAN,
who died
Anno { ætatis 36.
{ Domini 1735.

Alſo of
ELIZABETH, Daughter of
PAUL and ELIZABETH CASTLEMAN,
who died Anno { ætatis 3.
{ Domini 1740.

Likewife of THOMAS, Son of
PAUL and MARY CASTLEMAN,
who died Anno { ætatis 17.
{ Domini 1741.

SOUTH AISLE.

In Memory
of JOSEPH CHAMBERS, of
this Parifh, Clothier, who died
Auguſt 21, 1722, æt. 57.

Alſo of KATHARINE his Wife,
who died May 1, 1739,
ætatis 75.

IN THE CHURCH PORCH.

On a Monument :

In Memory of
MARY, Daughter of
Mr. NATHANIEL WEBB,
who died August 1, 1731,
aged 25 Years.

AGAINST THE PORCH, ON THE OUTSIDE.

In Memory of
Mr. NATHANIEL WEBB,
Clothier, who died 31 Jan. 1723,
ætatis suæ 83. Likewife of
SARAH his Wife, who died Sept. 29,
1710,
ætatis suæ 45. And three of their Sons;
SAMUEL died June 20, 1712 ;
DANIEL, April 26, 1716; and
THOMAS, Sept. 29, 1727.

Near this Place lie the Bodies
of EDWARD WEBB, Clothier, and
ALICE his Wife. He departed this
Life Jan. 29, 1691. She departed
this Life June 10, 1687.

In Memory of
NATHANIEL WEBB,
of the Parifh of
Hampton, Clothier,
who died 19th
March, 1736,
æt. fuæ 99.

HENRY HOWELL died
June the 1, 1714.

. . . .
. . . .

Near this Place lieth the Body
of GYLES BISHOP, of
this Parifh, Clothier, who
departed this Life 23 June, 1703,
aged 69.

Alfo SARAH his Wife departed
this Life 4 Nov. 1741, aged
80 Years.

In Memory of
ELIZABETH, Wife of ABRAHAM SHIPTON,
of this Parifh, who died 12 Jan. 1721,
aged 56 Years.

THOMAS STEELE died May 4, 1728.

JANE his Wife died April 14, 1740.

In Memory of THOMAS HALLIN
who departed this Life . . . . .

In Memory of
MARY, the Wife of THOMAS HALLING,
who departed this Life Oct. 22,
Anno Dom. 1716.

FRANCIS WHITE,
from Malmfbury,
died, unmarried, April
16, 1762, aged 49.

In Memory of
JOHN BISHOP, late of this
Parifh, Yeoman ; and alfo MARY
his Wife. He died Feb. 21, 1771,
aged 74.
She died June 10, 1765, aged 77.

Alfo in Memory of three Children ;
MARY died Jan. 30, 1752, aged 27 ;
DEBORAH, Nov. 25, 1754, aged 31 ;
SARAH, Sept. 16, 1765, aged 38.

IN THE CHURCH YARD.

AGAINST THE SOUTH SIDE OF THE CHURCH.

Near
this Place lie the Remains
of WILLIAM WILKINS, late of
Nailfworth, in this Parifh,
Carpenter, who departed this
Life February 26, 1761,
aged 72.

Alfo of ELIZABETH his Wife,
who departed this Life
Sept. 26, 1750, aged 75.

Alfo WILLIAM their Son,
who departed this Life March 25,
1768, aged 46.

To the Memory of
ROBERT WILKINS, of this
Place, Yeoman, who departed
this Life May the 4th, 1767,
aged 76.

Alfo of DEBORAH his Wife,
who departed this Life
Jan. 31, 1766, aged 75.

Alfo five Children of
THOMAS and SARAH WILKINS,
who died in their Infancy.

In Memory of
FRANCIS WHITE, who died
April 16, 1762, aged 49 Years.

Alfo near this Monument lieth
the Remains of DANIEL WHITE,
of this Parifh, Miller and Baker,
who departed this Life
the 20 Day of Auguft,
1710, aged 64 Years.

ON TOMBS.

In Memory of
ARTHUR EMLY, of Brimfcomb,
in the Parifh of Stroud, Clothier,
who deceafed November 12, 1683.

In Memory of
Alice, the Wife of GILES CHAMBERS,
who died February 23, 1716,
in the 84 Year of her Age.

In Memory of
SAMUEL HOLLIDAY,
of this Parifh, who
died Dec. 22, 1663,
ætatis suæ 87.

In Memory of
FRANCIS CLAYFIELD, Clothier,
and ELIZABETH his Wife.
He died December 2, 1709, aged 66.
She died February 28, 1739,
ætatis suæ 86.

Alfo RICHARD their Son died
January 14, æt. 21 ; and ELIZABETH
their Daughter, Wife of THOMAS
SMITH, died Jan. 6, 1769, aged 84.

In Memory of
THOMAS, Son of
FRANCIS CLAYFIELD,
who died March 17, 1740,
aged 47 Years.

SAMUEL LOCKIER died the
27 May, 1700, aged 35.

Under this Tomb lie the
Remains of BETTY, Wife
of WILLIAM WALLIS, of
this Parifh, Yeoman. She
departed this Life
April 18, 1762, in
the 49 Year of her Age.

5

Under this Tomb lie the
Remains of JOHN WALLIS,
who died April the 1, 1791,
aged 52 Years.

Alfo near this Tomb lie the
Remains of ROBERT WALLIS,
who died April 3, 1789,
aged 41 Years.

In Memory of
JOHN ATWOOD PEGLER, late of
Hampton, Surgeon, who died
Sept. the 22, 1772, aged 40.

To the Memory of
JEREMIAH PEGLER, late of this
Parifh, Surgeon, who died July
17th, 1768, aged 80.

Alfo of
JUDITH his Wife, who
died July the 26, 1762, aged 62.

Alfo of
AMELIA their Daughter,
who died Dec. the 10, 1761,
aged 32.

In Memory
of HANNAH, the
Wife of WILLIAM
ENGLISH, who died
May the 1ft, 1761,
aged 81 Years.

In Memory of SARAH, the Wife of
RICHARD WOODLANDS, who died the
15 of Novem. 1769, aged 48 Years.

Alfo of
WILLIAM and RICHARD, Sons of the
faid RICHARD and SARAH WOODLANDS,
who died young.

Alfo of
RICHARD WOODLANDS, who died
the 28 of Feb. 1777, aged 60 Years.

Underneath

Underneath
this Monument
lies interred the Remains
of WILLIAM, Son of WILLIAM
and MARY FROST, of this
Parifh, Yeoman, who died the
14 Day of Auguft, 1782, aged 25.

In Memory of DANIEL BOWN, of
this Parifh, who died
the 1ft Day of March, 1780, aged 72.

Alfo of ANN his Wife, who
died Feb. the 17, 1781, aged 73.

Alfo of eight of their Children,
who died in their Infancy.

Underneath
this Stone lie the Remains
of ELIZABETH, Wife of WILLIAM
JONES, of this Parifh, Yeoman,
who departed this Life the
22d Day of April, 1770, aged 62.

Alfo near this Stone lie the
Remains of the aforefaid
WILLIAM JONES, who departed
this Life the 11 Day of December,
1783, aged 75 Years.

Alfo near this Stone lieth the
Remains of three Daughters of
RICHARD and BETSY HILL, of
this Parifh, who died in Infancy.

In Memory of
JAMES EVANS, who died
Dec 22, 1740, aged 52.

Alfo of ANN his Wife,
who died March the 29,
1776, aged 90.

Near this Tomb lie the Remains
of WILLIAM FARMILO, late of
Nailfworth ; alfo MARGARET
his Wife. He died Dec. 14, 1765,
aged 62.
She died Dec. 30, 1763,
aged 63.

Alfo five of their Children, viz.
JOHN, JOHN, WILLIAM, HESTER, and
ANN.

Under this Tomb lie the Remains
of RICHARD HEAVEN, late
of Nailfworth, who died
May 19, 1775, aged 36.

Near adjoining to this
Monument of Mortality
lies interred MARGARET,
Wife of NATHANIEL DYER,
of Nailworth, who departed
this Life the 25 Day of July,
1781, in the 39 Year of her Age.

Near this Tomb lie the
Remains of JOHN, Son of
PHILIP and HESTER LOCK,
of Nailfworth in this Parifh,
who departed this Life the
24 Day of Auguft, 1766,
in the 18 Year of his Age.

Alfo of the aforefaid
PHILIP LOCK, who departed
this Life the 24 of Auguft,
1781, aged 60 Years.

Alfo the Remains of HESTER,
WILLIAM, HESTER, ROBERT, and
SARAH, Sons and Daughters of
the faid PHILIP and HESTER
LOCK, who all died Infants.

This is to keep the Memory of
SUSANNAH, late Wife of JOSEPH LOCK,
of Nailfworth, in this Parifh, Malfter.
She departed this Life the 10th of
Jan. 1787, in the 31ft Year of her Age.

Alfo of two of their Children, viz.
JOSEPH and HANNAH, who died in Infancy.

In Memory of LYDIA,
Wife of OBADIAH BURGHESS,
who died Feb. the 29, 1743,
in the 49th Year of her Age.

Alfo in Memory of HESTER,
Daughter of JOHN and
SARAH BURGHESS. She
died Nov. 19, 1775, in
the 8th Year of her Age.

Arms, a Chevron between three Fleurs
de Lys, for CROOME.

In Memory of
JOHN CROOME, fen. who died
Dec. 26, 1726, aged 55 Years.

ELIZABETH his Wife, who died
Feb. 4, 1733, aged 62 Years.

JOHN CROOME, jun. who died
May 18, 1738, aged 45 Years.

SARAH his Wife, who died
March 5, 1767, aged 72 Years.

JOHN their Son, who died
March 5, 1739, aged 16 Years.

In Memory
of JAMES, Son of
JOHN CROOME, jun.
and SARAH his Wife,
who died April 28,
1749, ætatis 20.

In Memory of
ELIZABETH HALLING, Daughter of
JOHN CROOME, jun. died
June 2d, 1757, aged 39.

ELIZABETH HALLING her
Daughter died Jan. 17,
1754, aged 16.

In Memory of SAMUEL
WEBB, of this Parifh. Clothier,
who died Jan. 19, in the
67 Year of his Age, 1701.

. . . .
. . . .

In Memory of
MARY, Wife of
JOHN WOOD, of
this Parifh, Clothier.
She died March 19,
1772.

O N   F L A T   S T O N E S.
In Memory of
THOMAS, Son of THOMAS and REBECCA
LOCKIER, who died Sept. 25, 1747,
aged 25.

Alfo of ELIZABETH, Daughter of
THOMAS and DEBORAH LOCKIER,
Wife to WILLIAM WALLIS,
who died March 1773, aged 26.

In Memory of
ELIZABETH, Wife of THOMAS
OATRIDGE. She died June
23, 1777, aged 58 Years.

And of ELIZABETH their
Daughter, who died an Infant.

In Memory of
MARY, Wife of PHILIP HOWELL,
of this Parifh, who departed
this Life Jan. 16, 1744.

Near this Stone
lieth the Remains of
ANNA MARIA, Daughter
of DANIEL WALKLEY,
who departed this Life the
12 of November, 1782.

ON A BRASS PLATE :

Here lie the Remains
of THOMAS PEGLER,
and ELIZABETH his Wife.
He died May the 12,
1750, aged 55.
She died May the 26,
1766, aged 78.

IN HOPES OF A BLES-
SED RESURRECTION,
HERE RESTETH THE
BODY OF JAMES
TERET, WHO DE-
PARTED THIS LIFE
THE 17 DAY OF JUNE,
ANNO DOM. 1697.

ON A BRASS PLATE :

Near this Place lie
the Remains of MARY
BUMPASS, of this Parifh,
who died December 12,
1781, aged 56.

In Memory of PHILIP HOWELL,
of this Parifh, who departed
this Life April 3, 1761,
aged 74 Years.

Alfo of HESTER his late
Wife, who departed
this Life Sept. 20, 1781,
aged 74 Years.

In Memory of
ELIZABETH, the Daughter
of JAMES and JANE
ASHMAN, who died
Dec. 3, 1726.

In Memory of
JANE ASHMAN, who
died June 29, 1748, æt. 84.

In Memory of
JAMES EVANS, who died
Dec. 22, 1740, aged 52,

Alfo ANN his Wife, who
died March 29, 1776,
aged 90.

In Memory of
JOHN COOK, who died
Feb. 21ft, 1752,
aged 66 Years.

Here lieth the Body
of LIDDY, the Wife of
GILES KNIGHT, who
departed this Life
the 20 Day of May,
1695.

In Memory of
GILES KNIGHT, who dep-
arted this Life Dec. 1712.

In

In Memory of
THOMAS ENGLISH, who
departed this Life the
19 Day of Auguſt, 1732,
aged 43 Years.

Alſo of MARY his Wife,
who departed this Life
the 28 Day of April, 1788,
aged 66 Years.

Alſo of JANE, Daughter of
EDWARD and BETTY ENGLISH,
of Stroud, who departed
this Life the 23 Day of
Feb. 1785, aged 3 Years.

In Memory of
MARY BRINCKETT, who died
July the 7, 1765,
aged 61 Years.

In Memory of
HANNAH, Wife of EDWARD
DYER, who died Sept. 4,
1738, aged 50 Years.

MARY their Daughter
died Jan... 1750.

In Memory of
EDWARD DYER, who
died Mar. 9, 17 .. in
the 57 Year of his Age.

In Memory of
WILLIAM BARNFIELD, who
departed this Life June 19,
1712.

Alſo of WILLIAM TEAKLE
and ELIZABETH his Wife. He

died Oct. 13, ætatis 80; and ſhe
Nov. 25, 1761, ætatis 8..

In Memory of MARY,
the Wife of JOSEPH
BARNFIELD, who died the
17th Day of April, 1786,
aged 46 Years.

In Memory of
GEORGE, Son of STEPHEN
and HANNAH TEAKLE,
who departed this Life
May the 29, 1767, aged 18.

Alſo of HANNAH, Wife of
STEPHEN TEAKLE, who died
Feb. 3, 1781, aged 64.

O N H E A D S T O N E S.

	Died	Aged
Elizabeth, Wife of Thomas Black-well, jun.	23 Nov. 1753	55
Heſter their Daughter	27 Mar. 1745	12
Samuel Bird	11 Dec. 1756	61
Ann his Wife	13 Dec. 1756	60
Jane, Wife of Thomas Ricketts	19 Apr. 1778	45
Ann their Daughter	16 Dec. 1773	12
David Ricketts	—— 1777	—
Dinah, Wife of Jeremiah Niblett	28 Feb. 1754	53
Mary, Wife of Thomas Harvey	8 May, 1766	59
Lydia, Wife of Obadiah Burgeſs	29 Feb. 1743	49
Thomas Kench	17 Sept. 1779	84
Thomas Hillier	10 May, 1766	34
Heſter Chambers	26 May, 1752	27
Richard, Son of Richard and Eliza-beth Turk	25 Feb. 1745	18
Richard Turk	12 June, 1756	70
Elizabeth his Wife	3 Feb. 1761	81
John Smith	7 Apr. 1707	29
Matthew Orcher	13 Dec. 1784	82
Sabina his Wife	26 Mar. 1751	58
John their Son	3 May, 1756	27
James Manning	21 May, 1774	67
Elizabeth his Wife	15 July, 1777	67
Rebekah, Wife of Daniel Manning	30 Apr. 1789	71
Martha, Wife of Francis Corbett	25 Mar. 1750	46
John Smith	17 Nov. 1735	34
Mary his Wife	13 Feb. 1752	—
Thomas Lockier	20 July, 1758	73
Rebecca Lockier	27 July, 1760	77

	Died	Aged
Elizabeth, Wife of Nicholas Gazard	22 Nov. 1762	52
Thomas Webb	12 Nov. 1785	66
Emma, Daughter of Richard Clark	11 June, 1707	35
Richard Clark	21 Dec. 1725	85
Emma his Wife	12 Feb. 1732	95
Thomas Clark	18 May, 1717	46
Thomas his Son	17 Aug. 1733	—
William Creed	16 —— 1740	61
Mary his Wife	23 Mar. 1745	64
Richard Creed	22 May, 1741	37
Elizabeth, Wife of Thomas Hewer	25 July, 1762	40
Elizabeth, Wife of Joſeph Sparrow	10 Apr. 1731	77
Joſeph, Son of Richard Sparrow	17 July, 1751	28
William his Son	2 Oct. 1738	—
Thomas Hill	8 Aug. 1723	40
Sarah his Wife	19 Jan. 1710	—
Mary, Daughter of Richard Soule	— Feb. 1729	—
Mary, Daughter of John and Sarah Croom, and Wife of John Wall	1 Jan. 1754	35
Ann, Wife of Joſeph Evans	6 Dec. 1762	46
Deborah, Wife of Thomas Barnard	11 Dec. 1752	34
Abigail his ſecond Wife	2 July, 1780	58
Elizabeth, Wife of John Bateman	9 Aug. 1752	38
Grace, Wife of James Creed	8 June, 1751	56
Edith, Reliĉt of Giles Creed	8 Sept. 1723	71
Richard Bicknell	24 June, 1760	78
Elizabeth his Wife	30 Mar. 1736	—
Sarah, Wife of James Morgan	24 June, 1742	47
John Hopkins	29 Sept. 1743	53
Iſaac Punter	10 Mar. 1759	58

CXLVIII. HORTON,

IN the Hundred of *Grumbald's Aſh*, is a Pariſh of middle Extent, two Miles diſtant North-eaſt from *Chipping Sodbury*, four South-eaſt from *Wickwar*, and twenty-eight South from GLOUCESTER.   Nearly equal Portions of Land are ſituate upon the lofty Ridge of Hills and in the Vale; and the Soil varies accordingly, from Clay to Stone Braſh.

The Benefice is rectorial, and endowed with the whole Tythes, and thirty Acres of Glebe; the Advowſon of which is annexed to the Manor.   It is exonerated from a Penſion of 1*l.* 2*s.* to the Prebendary of *Horton*, in the Cathedral Church of *Sarum* *.

The Church is dedicated to *St. James*, and a Member of the Deanery of *Hawkeſbury*.   It is conſtructed with a Nave, North Aiſle, Chancel, Porch, and embattled Tower, all of contemporary Erection, and of the neateſt Maſonry, in the Style which prevailed about the Cloſe of the fourteenth Century.

In painted Glaſs are Figures of Eccleſiaſtics and Cherubs holding Eſcocheons, upon which are, 1. Or, a Feſs Gules, over all a Bend Azure; 2. Or, on a Bend Gules, three Mullets pierced Argent.   PASTON's Sepulchral Chapel is divided by an Arch, and has a beautifully carved Timber Roof.

In *Domeſday* the Manor is ſtyled " *Horedon*," and taxed at ten Hides, the Property of ROBERT DE TODENI †.   From the Families of DE ABBINGTON and KAYLEWAY it was transferred to the BRADSTONES in the Reign of EDWARD the Third, who held it for ſeveral Generations.

WILLIAM KNIGHT, Eſq. Prothonotary of the Common Pleas, in the Reign of King HENRY VIII. is ſaid to have built the Manor-houſe; and from him it paſſed afterwards to EDWARD PASTON, Eſq. of *Appleton* in *Norfolk*, who died ſeized of it in 1640.   WILLIAM PASTON, Eſq. was ſucceeded by his Brother CLEMENT PASTON, upon whoſe Death, in 1789, without Iſſue, this manerial Property, including the far greater Part of the Pariſh, was bequeathed to his third Wife MARY-ISABELLA, Daughter of JOHN KEMPSON, Eſq. of *Sandon*, in the County of *Stafford*.

The Church and Manſion-houſe are ſituate upon a ſmall Eminence, at the Baſe of wooded Hills ſurrounding them, except on the North Side, which opens to a fine View of the Vale of *Severn*.   The whole Scene, from the beautiful Inequality of Ground, is extremely ſtriking and picturefque.

The Court-houſe, though ſaid to have been built by W. KNIGHT abovementioned, exhibits many Veſtiges of higher Antiquity.   The Chapel (now uſed for the *Romiſh* Service) has Door-caſes with *Saxon* Mouldings, over which is an Eſcocheon, bearing a Saltire, charged in the Centre with two Annulets braced.   Another Door-caſe of the principal Entrance is ornamented with Sculpture, ſuch as firſt appeared in *England* in the Reign of HENRY VIII. under the Auſpices of HOLBEIN; has an Eſcocheon with a Spread Eagle, enſigned with a Cardinal's Hat, which Device is repeated upon the Chimney-pieces.

Another reputed Manor, called *Horewood*, in this Pariſh, was the Corps of a Prebend founded in the Cathedral Church of *Saliſbury* by AGNES DE RYA and HENRY her Son during the Prelacy of RICHARD POER.   In 1287, 15 Edw. I. a *Quo Warranto* was brought againſt RALPH DE YORK, then Prebendary, whoſe Claim to this Manor was allowed †.   This Prebend, valued at 64*l.* 15*s.* 9*d. per Annum*, was exonerated and diſſolved by King HENRY VIII. ‡   In the next Reign, the Protector SOMERSET obtained it, after whom it was re-granted, in 1554, to CLEMENT PASTON, Eſq. Father of EDWARD PASTON, by whoſe Deſcendants it has been ſince enjoyed and conſolidated with the other manerial Eſtate.

Lands, which in old Deeds are called " *Frayers Hay*," belonged to the Preceptory of Knights Hoſpitallers at *Quenington*.

The only Eſtate independent on the Manor is held by GEORGE HARDWICK, M. D. of *Chipping Sodbury*, which Borough has the Privilege of an extenſive Common in this Pariſh.

---

* BACON's Theſaurus, p. 340.
† MSS. SNELL.
‡ BACON's Theſaurus, p. 867.

Leland, in his Defcription of the Camps which are continued along the Brow of the lower *Cotefwold* Hills, notices a fmall Outpoft at *Horton* *. It is of a fquare Form, but no Difcovery, either of Armour or Coins, has been hitherto made.

No Benefactions to the Poor.

Incumbents.	Patrons.	Incumbents.	Patrons.
1401 John Cooper,	Prebendary of Horton.	—— Tho. Gwynne, Clerk,	——————.
—— Richard Walker,	The fame.	1703 James Harris, Clerk,	Richard Whitehall.
1562 Guy Eaton, B. D.	Clement Pafton, Efq.	1730 Edward Draper, M.A.	William Nourfe, Efq.
1577 Roger Cooper, LL.B.	The fame.	1777 Rich. Budworth, M.A.	John Unwin, Efq.
—— Andrew Thomas,	——————.	1778 Paul Hitch, Clerk,	Charles Hitch, Efq.
1618 Roger Fielding,	Edward Pafton, Efq.		

Present Lady of the Manor,

Mary Isabella Paston, Widow.

The Perfons fummoned from this Parifh by the Heralds in 1682 and 1683 were

John Pafton, Efq. and —— Stokes, Gent.

At the Election in 1776, Three Freeholders polled from this Parifh.

The Regifter commences with the Date 1567.

Annual Account of Marriages, Births, and Burials, in this Parish.

A.D.	Mar.	Bir.	Bur.	A.D.	Mar.	Bir.	Bur.	A.D.	Mar.	Bir.	Bur.	A.D.	Mar.	Bir.	Bur.
1781	1	13	5	1786	2	9	8	1791				1796			
1782	3	5	10	1787	1	7	9	1792				1797			
1783	—	11	9	1788	2	8	5	1793				1798			
1784	1	5	7	1789	2	10	4	1794				1799			
1785	3	8	7	1790	5	11	6	1795				1800			

INSCRIPTIONS IN THE CHURCH.

IN PASTON'S SEPULCHRAL AISLE.

ON MARBLE MONUMENTS.

Arms ; Argent, fix Fleurs de Lys Azure, a Chief indented Or, for Paston ;—impaling, Argent, a Chevron between three Martlets Sable, for Lawson. Supporters, for the finifter, a Bear muzzled Sable, collared and chained Or, for the dexter, an Oftrich Argent, holding a Horfefhoe Or. Creft, a Griffin Or.—Motto, " De mieux je penfe en mieux."

☩
DOM. B. M. V.
Cineres
Gulielmi Paston & Mariæ uxoris
Hâc ædicula commifcentur,
Hic in agro Norfolcienfi, ex antiquo & præclaro genere,
Ob. 24 Martii, 1673.

Illa Jacobi Lawson, Armigeri, filia, in Eboracenfi
Comitatu, ftirpe non minus celebri, obiit 23 Sept. 1679.

In quibus vera in Deum pietas, in proximum Charitas,
In alterutrum fidiffimus Amor, refulfit.
Nec non
Trium conjugalis amoris pignorum,
Quorum Gulielmus, 14 annum agens,
Maximæ fpei juvenis, mortem eheu fubiit, Junii 5, 1677.

Sub hoc marmore
Deponuntur exuviæ Franciscæ Paston,
Johannis Paston, Armigeri, uxoris,
Henrici Tichborn, Baronetti, et Mariæ Arundell,
Uxoris, filiæ natalibus ab utroque latere nobiliffimis,
Quæ pietate, ingenio, prudentia, forma, in adverfis
Fortitudine et animi conftantia, fexum fuperavit ;
Et poftquam 18 annos conjugis amantiffimæ, et matris
Chariffimæ, omnibus exemplum præbuiffet, infelici
Puerperio, 10 Aprilis, 1712, obiit ;—non obiit, vivit !

Eternùm in progenie illuftriffima,
Præfens gaudium, abfens amicorum et mariti gemitus ;
Qui, pietatis et amoris ergo,
Hoc monumentum mœtiffimus pofuit.

O Deus ! quot bona
Parvula æde conduntur—
Ut requiefcant,
Tu, lector, de profundis !

Arms ; Paston ;—impaling, Paly of fix, Or and Sable, over all a Bend counterchanged, for Calvert.

☩
Beneath this Stone refteth the
Body of the Honourable Ann Paston,
Daughter of the Right Honourable
Charles Calvert, Baron Baltimore
of the Kingdom of Ireland. She
was Wife to Edward Somerset,
of Pauntley Court, in the County
of Gloucefter, Efq. ; and after his Deceafe
married John Paston, of Horton
Court, in the faid County, Efq.
She having punctually performed
all the Duties of a moft loving
Wife, a tender Mother, and faithful
Friend, in the Care fhe took of her
laft Wife's Children by his
firft Wife, her dear Friend, who here
lyes interred by her, ended her Life by
a moft tedious and painful Sicknefs,
fuffered with the greateft Courage
and Patience,
on the 10th of February,
MDCCXXXI.

Cujus animæ propitietur Deus.

* Leland's Itin. vol. VII. p. 96.

Arms ;

Arms ; PASTON ;—impaling, Sable, a Fefs couped, and a Canton Argent, for BOSTOCK.

☩

D. O. M.
Hoc Tumulo
conduntur exuviæ
JOHANNIS PASTON,
olim de Appleton, in agro
Norfolk, nuper de Horton,
in com. Glouc. Armigeri.
De numerosâ prole,
quam ex primâ conjuge
FRANCISCA, HENRICI TICHBOURNE,
de Tichborne in com. Hants,
Baronetti, filiâ, fufcepit, tres
duntaxat natos, GULIELMUM,
CLEMENTEM, & JACOBUM, duaſque
filias, MARIAM fcilicet & FRANCISCAM,
Superſtites reliquit.
Alteris nuptiis,
ANNÆ CALVERT, CAROLI Baronis de BALTIMORE,
& demum CATHARINÆ, NATHANIELIS BOSTOCK,
de Wixhall, in agro Salop. Armigeri,
filiæ (quam mœſtam reliquit viduam)
conjunctus fuit.
Po t vitam DEO verè piam,
ſponſis fidelem amicis fuavem et
benignam, proli autem maximè defideratam.
Diem obiit fupremum poftridiè nonas
Octob. anno falutis 1737, ætatis 68.

Cujus animæ propitietur Deus.

ON A MARBLE MONUMENT OF VARIOUS COLOURS:

Arms: PASTON ;—impaling, Checquy Or and Gules, a Chief variè, for CHICHESTER; on an Efcocheon of Pretence Or, three Torteauxes, a File of as many Points Gules, for COURTENAY.

☩

Sacred to the Memory of WILLIAM PASTON, late of Horton, Efq.

A Man, enrich'd by Nature and by Art,
With what could pleafe, and intereft every Heart :
In upper Life, by all who faw, approv'd,
In lower Life, by all who knew him, lov'd :
No Epitaph his Virtues need proclaim,
His Actions ever will endear his Name ;
An upright, generous, open-hearted Friend !
Horton, deplore thy Lofs! lament his End !

He was twice married ; his firſt Wife was MARY, Daughter of JOHN COURTENAY, of Molland, in the County of Devon, Efq. one of the Coheireffes of her Brother JOHN COURTENAY, of the fame Place, Efq.
She died Oct. the 29, A. D. 1747.
His fecond Wife was MARY, Daughter of GILES CHICHESTER, of Arlington, in this County, Efq. who, as a grateful Teftimony of her fincere Love and Affection, caufed this Monument to be erected to the deceafed.
By his firſt Wife he had Iffue one Daughter, ANNA MARIA, married to GEORGE, the only Son of Sir ROBERT THROCKMORTON, of Wefton Underwood, in the County of Bucks, Bart.
By his fecond and furviving Wife he had no Iffue.

He died January the 11th, anno { Dom. 1769. { ætatis fuæ 69.

Requiefcat in pace.

ON A FLAT STONE:

☩

JOHN BISHOP,
Son of
RICHARD BISHOP,
of Brayls, Efq.
and of FRANCES
his Wife, the
Daughter of
JOHN PASTON, Efq.
aged 14 Days,
Anno D'ni 1720.

IN   THE   CHANCEL.
ON A BRASS PLATE:

In Memory of
FRANCIS, the Son of FRANCIS and BETTY FRANCKCOM, of this Parifh, who died the 2 May, 1767, aged 21 Years.

ON ANOTHER:

Here lyeth the Body of GEORGE, the Son of GEORGE and MARY SHEPHEARD, who departed this Life the 20 Day of December, 1711, aged 10 Years.

ON FLAT STONES:

In Memoriam
ANDREÆ THOMAS, hujus ecclefiæ rectoris, qui obiit 25° die Martii, A. D. 1618.

In Memory alfo of
ELIZABETH, the Wife of RICHARD BARNARD, of this Parifh, Gent. who departed this Life the 23d Day of February, Anno Dom. 1712, aged 69 Years.

ROUND THE VERGE:

HEARE LIETH THE
BODY OF EDMUND CONOLDI,
LATE OF HORTON, GENT. WHO
MARRIED ELIZABETH, THE DAUGHTER
OF CHRISTOPHER KINGSCOTE, AND HAD
BY HER TWO SONNES AND ONE DAUGHTER,
HE DYED ON THE LAST DAY MAY, IN THE
YEARE 1665.

Hic ad terram reverfum eft
Quicquid terreftre fuit
THOMÆ GWYNN,
Qui hanc eccleſiam pie 47 annos
Rector digniffimus,
Et eruditione fumma, moribus
Incontaminatis . . . .
Obiit Junii, anno { D'ni 1703. { ætatis fuæ 81.

Corpus ELIZABETHÆ, uxoris THOMÆ GWYNN, hujus Ecclefiæ Rectoris. Obijt
. . . .
Sexto die Decembris, anno D'ni 1697, Ætatis fuæ 74.

D. O. M.
☩
Hic jacet CHRISTOPHERUS CORBETT, Qui obiit 12° Novembris, 1732.

Animæ cujus propitietur Deus.

ON A BRASS PLATE:

In Memory
of RACHEL, late Widow
of WILLIAM WALKER,
of this Parifh,
who died Nov. 14, 1767,
aged 84 Years.

I N

IN THE NAVE.

HERE LYETH THE BODY OF
MORDECAY RICHARDS,
SONNE OF . . . .
RICHARDS, ...
THE 11 DAY OF DECEMBER,
ANNO DOM. . . . . . .

HERE LYETH THE BODY OF WILLI-
AM STOKES, OF THIS PARISH, GENT.
WHO DEPARTED THIS LIFE THE
18 DAY OF SEPTEMBER, ANNO
DOM. 1694,
ÆTATIS SUÆ 49.

Here lyeth the Body of RICHARD
AMARSON, who departed this Life
the 25 Day of March,
Anno Dom. 1724,
ætatis fuæ 79.

HERE LYETH THE BODY OF JOHN
STOKES, OF THIS PARISH, GENT.
WHO DEPARTED THIS LIFE THE 29
DAY OF NOVEMBER, ANNO DOM.
1694,
ÆTATIS SUÆ 84.

Here lyeth the
Body of MARTHA, the
Wife of JOHN STOKES,
of this Parish, Gent.
who departed this
Life the 7 Day of June,
1696.

HERE LYETH THE BODY OF
WILLIAM WALKER, OF THIS
PARISH, YEOMAN, WHO DE-
PARTED THIS LIFE THE
. . DAY OF APRIL,
ANNO D'NI 1694,
ÆTATIS SUÆ 75.

ON BRASS PLATES.

Here lyeth the Body
of WILLIAM WALKER,
Gent. who departed
this Life the 26 Day
of June, 1736,
aged 28 Years.

Alfo MARY WALKER, Widow,
who died 12 Day of May,
1757, aged 65 Years.

In Memory of ANNE, the Wife of
EDWARD BARNES,
of the City of Chefter, Mercer, and
Daughter
of WILLIAM and JOYCE WALKER,
of this Parifh, who
departed this Life Aug. the 4, 1730,
aged 30 Years.

Alfo in Memory of ANNE, Daughter of
the faid EDWARD and ANNE BARNES,
who
departed this Life Feb. 26, 1730,
aged 3 Weeks.

Here lyeth the Body of
THOMAS WALKER, Son of WILLIAM
and JOYCE WALKER, who departed
this Life the 25 Day of Oct.
Anno Dom. 1717, ætatis fuæ 23°.

Here lyeth
the Body of JOYCE WALKER,
the Wife of WILLIAM
WALKER. Gent. who de-
parted this Life the 3
Day of October, 1744,
aged 74 Years.

IN THE NORTH AISLE.

In Memory of DANIEL, the Son of
EDWARD and MARTHA RICE, of
Little Sodbury,
who was loft at Petty France
7 Nov. 1761, and found the 15th at the
fame Place, aged 35 Years.

In Memory of HESTER, the Daughter
of
EDWARD and MARTHA RICE, of
Little Sodbury,
who died April 13, 1769,
aged 32 Years.

In Memory of
EDWARD RICE, late of Little Sodbury,
who died July 24, 1774,
aged 79 Years.

Alfo
in Memory of MARTHA,
Wife of EDWARD RICE
abovementioned, who died
June 9, 1777,
aged 80 Years.

In Memory of
MARY BAYLIS, Wife of JOHN BAYLIS,
of this
Parifh, and Daughter of EDWARD and
MARTHA RICE,

---

of the Parifh of Little Sodbury, who
departed this Life the 13 April, 1756,
aged 33 Years.

Alfo
to the Memory of JANE BAYLIS,
Mother of JOHN BAYLIS, of this
Parifh, who departed this Life the
24 Day of Feb. 1775,
aged 84 Years.

HERE RESTETH THE BODY
OF THOMAS EMERSON, OF
THIS PARISH, YEOMAN, WHO
DEPARTED THIS LIFE THE
23D DAY OF MAY, ANNO
DOM. 1692,
AGED 40 YEARS.

Here lyeth the Body of
MARGARET, the Wife of
THOMAS BUTLER, and
Daughter of RICHARD EMERSON,
of this Parifh, fen.
who died Dec. 25, A. D. 1696,
aged 56.

Alfo an Infant of SAMUEL and
MARY PARDOS, of the City of
Briftol, was here interred,
Feb. 25, 1731-2.

HERE LYETH THE BODY OF MAR-
GARETT CAM, OF THIS PARISH,
WIDD.
WHO DEPARTED THIS LIFE THE 3
DAY OF DECEM. ANNO DOM.
1694,
ÆTATIS SUÆ 67.

HERE LYETH THE
BODY OF JAMES
CAM, OF THIS PARISH,
GENT. WHO DEPARTED
THIS LIFE SEPTEMBER
THE 25, ANNO DOM.
1708,
AGED 68 YEARS.

ON A BRASS PLATE:

In Memory of
THOMAS HALL, Yeoman,
who died 4 Jan. 1784,
aged 78 Years.

Alfo of MARGARET, Widow of the
above, who died the 7 Day of
July 1789, aged 83 Years.

IN THE CHURCH YARD, ON TOMBS.

In Memory
of THOMAS ISAAC, of this Parifh,
who died
March 27, 1774, aged 82 Years.

Alfo of JANE his Wife, wdo died
Aug. 19, 1772, aged 83 Years.

In Memory
of HANNAH, Wife of JOSEPH ISAAC,
of this Parifh, Yeoman, who died
25 April, 1779,
aged 48 Years.

Alfo of SAMUEL their Son, who died
the 4 July, 1779, aged 2 Years.

Likewife
in Memory of the faid
JOSEPH ISAAC,
of this Parifh, who departed this Life
the 4 Day of April, 1785,
in the 47 Year of his Age.

2

In

In Memory of CHRISTOPHER SLADE,
of this Parish, Yeoman,
who died April the 11, 1759,
aged 79 Years.

In Memory of
ELIZABETH, the Wife of
CHRISTOPHER SLADE, who
died September the 26,
1760, aged near 86 Years.

Here lieth the Body of
ANNE, Wife of
ROBERT SLADE.
She died June the 7,
1772,
aged 44 Years.

In Memory of
RICHARD HALL, of Little Sodbury,
who died May the 16, 1763,
aged 59 Years.

Also of two of his Sons, by ANNE his Wife,
JOHN and JAMES, both died Infants.

In Memory
of
ANN, late Widow
of the said
RICHARD HALL,
who was interred
near this Tomb
on the 9 Day of Feb.
1778,
in the 74 Year
of her age.

Here lyeth the Body of
CATHARINE, the Wife of
RICHARD BENNETT, of this
Parish, who departed this
Life the 29 Day of April,
1698, aged 54 Years.

Here
lieth the Body
of RICHARD BENNETT,
of this Parish,
who departed this Life
the 30 Day of Oct.
1736,
aged 85 Years.

Also
under this Tomb
lieth the Body of
WILLIAM BENNETT,
Son of RICHARD BENNETT
before mentioned,
who died May 30,
1778,
aged 72 Years.

Here lieth the Body of
ELIZABETH BENNETT,
of this Parish, who departed this
Life the 14 of Aug. 1770,
aged 66 Years.

Near this Place
lieth interred the Body
of JOHN CLARK;
and also JOANE CLARK his Wife.

She } died { 18 Aug. } 1711, æt. { 61.
He }   { 25 Dec. }   { 66.

Near this Place
lieth interred the Body
of RICHARD CLARK;
and also SILVESTER CLARK
his Wife.

She } died { 18 Feb. 1732, } æt. { 71.
He }   { 25 Jan. 1753, }   { 75.

Here lyeth the Body of HANNAH,
the Daughter of JOHN and HANNAH
CLARK, who departed this Life
the 31 May, 1728, in the
23 Year of her Age.

In Memory of JOHN RITCHENS,
of this Parish, who died
Oct. 3, 1777, aged 80 Years.

Also of ANN his Wife,
who died Oct. 1, 1774,
aged 79 Years.

In Memory of
ELIZABETH,
Daughter of JOHN and
ELIZABETH ALWAY,
of this Parish, who
died Dec. 2, 1775,
aged 2 Years and 5 Months.

In Memory of
ROBERT SMITH, who
died Dec. 6, 1751,
aged 56 Years.

Also of HANNAH, Wife of
ROBERT SMITH,
who died October 23,
1755, aged 59 Years.

Also in Memory of
MARY, Daughter of
ROBERT and HANNAH SMITH,
who died 6 April,
1753, aged 21 Years.

Here lyeth the Body of
LEWIS HIGGS, jun. who departed
this Life Oct. . . 1729, æt. 48.

Here lyeth the Body of RUTH HIGGS,
Widow, who departed this Life
June 24, 1729, aged 85 Years.

In Memory of LAZARUS HIGGS,
of this Parish, who departed this
Life 7 Feb. 1739, aged 65 Years.

To the Memory of MOSES HIGGS,
of this Parish, who departed
this Life June the 21, 1728,
ætatis suæ 69.

In Memory of
THOMAS HIGGS,
of this Parish, who
died Dec. 17, 1771,
aged 52 Years.

In Memory of ANNE Wife
of WILLIAM HIGGS. She died
Jan. 29, 1740,
aged 55 Years.

Also in Memory of NATHANIEL
HIGGS. He died Sept. 28, 1721,
aged 70 Years.

Also in Memory of JANE,
Wife of NATHANIEL HIGGS.
She died Aug. 18, 1709,
aged 58 Years.

In Memory
of WILLIAM HIGGS, jun.
who departed this Life
the 23 Dec. Anno D'ni 1748,
aged 33 Years.

Also in Memory of
WILLIAM HIGGS, sen.
who departed this Life
the 18 July, 1758,
aged 74 Years.

Also in Memory of ANNE,
Wife of PHILIP BURGES, and Daughter
of WILLIAM and ANNE HIGGS,
who died April 25, 1741,
aged 23.

Here lyeth the Body of
JAMES THRESSELL, of this
Parish, Yeoman, who
departed this Life March
9, 1743-4, aged 71 Years.

In Memory of MIRIAM, the
Wife of JAMES TRESSELL, of this
Parish,
who departed this Life 11 Day of Nov.
1741,
ætatis suæ 77.

In Memory of
MARY, Wife of THOMAS LUDLOW,
of Westonburt, and Daughter of JAMES
TRESSELL, of this Parish, who departed
this Life the 13 April, 1720,
aged 25 Years.

Beneath
this Tomb lies interred
JOHN MANING,
late of this Parish,
who died Feb. 11, 1761,
aged 86 Years.

Likewise
near this Tomb lie
interred JEREMIAH RUSSELL
and MARTHA his Wife.
He died Oct. 1, 1763,
aged 79 Years.
She Sept. 16, 1774,
aged 94 Years.

In Memory
of GILES RUSSELL, of
this Parish,
who departed this
Life the 21 Day of
March, 1787,
in the 79 Year of his Age,
and was interred near this
Tomb.

O N   H E A D   S T O N E S.

	Died	Aged		Died	Aged
Frances, Wife of John Walker, of Yate	21 Feb. 1777	36	Hester, Daughter of Robert and Anne Slade	20 Mar. 1764	7
Sarah their Daughter	2 —— 1768	2	John, Son of Caleb Monin	30 Nov. 1776	21
John their Son	6 Jan. 1775	6	Sarah, Wife of Samuel Pullin	23 Feb. 1780	56
William Walker	—— —— 1752	34	William Alway	12 Aug. 1779	58
Elizabeth his Wife	—— —— 1757	34	Mary his Wife	30 Dec. 1786	60
Christopher May	31 Dec. 1731	43	Hester their Daughter	23 Apr. 1779	17
Thomas his Son	12 Sept. 1768	37	Thomas Horwood	28 Sept. 1758	69
William May, sen.	4 July, 1786	80	Mary his Wife	15 Apr. 1774	90
Daniel his Son	17 Aug. 1748	17	William Pain	— July, 1750	62
Philip, Son of William and Jane May	1 Mar. 1777	38	William Paine	5 Sept. 1764	35
Charles Bryant	26 June, 1777	77	Edward his Son	22 Mar. 1772	7
John Cooper	4 Apr. 1749	44	William Weston	21 Nov. 1790	74
Sarah Cooper	15 May, 1759	59	Robert his Son	26 Nov. 1782	32
Jane, Daughter of Richard and Sarah Brown	5 Sept. 1732	4	Richard Curtis	1 Sept. 1773	66
George Perrott	14 June, 1772	91	David St. George	9 July, 1761	33
Samuel Perrott	1 Aug. 1782	88	Sarah, Wife of John Pullen	18 Mar. 1783	46
Miriam, Wife of George Perrott	26 Aug. 1761	76	Joseph Lewis	28 Oct. 1743	85
Robert Sarjent	10 Oct. 1727	48	Eleanor his Wife	4 Sept. 1733	75
Sarah, Wife of Moses Tiler, of Tormarton	10 Aug. 1745	76	Daniel Reed	4 Apr. 1784	81
Sarah, Wife of Morris Tilor	6 June, 1761	64	Ann, Wife of John Blunson	25 Nov. 1763	28
Mary, Wife of Daniel Holbrow, of Kingswood, co. Wilts, Daughter of Christopher Sleed	21 Aug. 1740	70	John Washbourn	12 June, 1767	64
			Ann his Wife	15 Jan. 1779	73
			William Clark, sen.	29 Mar. 1755	76
			Martha his Wife	2 Mar. 1714	27
			William Clark	1 Apr. 1771	58

CXLIX. HUNTLEY

CXLIX. H U N T L E Y

IS a Parifh fituate upon the Confines of *Herefordfhire*, included within the Foreft of *Deane*, and the Dutchy of *Lancafter*, five Miles North-eaft from *Michel Dean*, eleven Eaftward from *Rofs* in *Herefordfhire*, and feven from GLOUCESTER on the Weft. Of the Soil, certain Parts are Stonebrafh, Sand, and Loam : the Arable is exceeded by the Pafture ; but the Woodlands were by much the more extenfive : the whole within a Circumference of eight Miles. About one Third Part of the Parifh was formerly confidered as Wafte Land, but much has been lately inclofed and appropriated as a Nurfery for Timber. *Yarcledene*, or *Yartleton*, but more commonly called *May Hill*, is on one Side, within the Limits of this Parifh, and is faid to abound in Iron Ore. It is a very confiderable mountainous Tract, of a regular Form, and, being the higheft Ground in the Foreft Divifion, commands a very extenfive Profpect.

The Village lies on the great Road between the Cities of *Gloucefter* and *Hereford*.

Of the Benefice, which is a Rectory, in the Foreft Deanery, the Advowfon, detached from the Manor, is now vefted in the prefent Incumbent.

It was granted in the early Centuries by WIHENOC DE MONMOUTH to the *Benedictine* Priory, which he founded within the Caftle of *Monmouth*, as a Cell to the Abbey of *St. Florence de Salurmo* *.

In the Church, dedicated to *St. John Baptift*, are no remaining Veftiges, either of peculiar Architecture or of Antiquities. Its Dimenfions are very fmall, a Nave and Chancel, with a low flated Tower at the Weft End. The Rectorial-houfe, having been burnt, was re-built by JACKMAN MORSE, M. A. in 1720. A Yew-Tree of Twenty Feet in Girth ftill flourifhes in the Church-yard †.

Domefday recites this Manor as belonging to WILLIAM the Son of BADERON, and to contain Two Hides of cultivated Land, and a Wood two Miles broad and one in Length. In 1271, 53 HEN. III. REGINALD DE GREY purchafed Free-warren in *Huntley*; and ROBERT DE SAPYE died in 1327, 20 EDW. II. poffeffed of the fame Privilege. In the next Reign, it paffed to RICHARD Baron TALBOT of *Goderick Caftle*, co. *Hereford* ; from whom it defcended in a Right Line to Sir JOHN TALBOT, Earl of *Shrewfbury*, fo celebrated for his Victories in *France*, who was flain at the Siege of *Chaftillon* in 1456 ; and from him to GILBERT the Sixth Earl, who, dying in 1616, 14 JAMES I. bequeathed this, and other Eftates in this County, to ELIZABETH his fecond Daughter; fhe was the Wife of HENRY GREY, Earl of *Kent*, who died without Iffue. This Property, however, did not revert to the TALBOT Family, but lapfed to ANTHONY GREY, the next Male Heir, with whofe Defcendants it continued till the Demife of HENRY Duke of *Kent* in 1740. His large Eftates in the Counties of *Hereford* and *Gloucefter* being then fold, this Manor was purchafed by Sir EDMUND PROBYN, Knight, one of the Juftices of the King's Bench, whofe Heir, EDMUND HOPKINS PROBYN, is the prefent Proprietor. Independent of the Manor, there are few Eftates of confiderable Value.

The Parliament eftablifhed a Garrifon at *Huntley*, during the grand Rebellion, which was betrayed into the Hands of the Royalifts ‡.

---

* " Ecclefia de *Eililde-hopa*, cum capella de *Huntley*."

Cart. Fund. DUGD. Mon. vol. I. p. 600. TANNER's Not. Mon. *Monmouth*, N° XI.

† The laft Statute, made in the Reign of EDW. I. 1307, was entitled, " Ne Rector arbores in cœmeterio profternat," in the Preamble of which it is ftated, that Yew-Trees in a Church-yard were generally planted to fkreen the Church from the Wind : low as the Village Churches were then ufually built, the thick Foliage of the Yew anfwered that Purpofe better than any other Tree. See BARRINGTON's Obfervations on the Statutes, p. 169.—This Tree is here noticed for its extraordinary Bulk.

‡ " The Enemy were amazed at the fudden and unexpected Encounter, forced back with Fear, and retreated to *Huntley*, " where Sir JOHN WINTER had fecured his own Perfon ; but, diftracted by the ftrange Repulfe, marched off in great Confu- " fion at the Approach of fifteen Horfe that fell in among the whole Brigade, flew feven or eight, and took ten Prifoners."

CORBET, Mil. Gov. *Glouc.* p. 62.

" Suddenly after this Repulfe we loft two fmall Garrifons at *Weftbury* and *Huntley* by the Treachery of Captaine THOMAS " DAVIS, who fold them at a Rate to Sir JOHN WINTER. This DAVIS commanded the Guard at *Huntley*, where himfelf, by " Night—fome Diftance from the Houfe, attended the Enemies' comming, went in before them as Friends from *Gloucefter*, gave " them Poffeffion ; and, having accomplifhed that Peece of Treafon, immediately marched to *Weftbury*, where he was received " for a Friend, and led in his Traine of Cavaleers, that both Places were furprized in two Houres, and above eighty Men " and Armes loft in that great Exigence. This Villaine was pofted on the Gallowes in *Gloucefter*, and the Lord Generall (ESSEX) " was defired that his Name might ftand upon the Gibbet in all the Parliament Garrifons." Ibid. p. 71.

4

His

His Grace ALEXANDER GORDON, Duke of GORDON, was created Baron GORDON, of *Huntley,* in the County of *Gloucefter,* and Earl of NORWICH, &c. by Patent, bearing Date July 2, 1784.

B E N E F A C T I O N S.

Tenements and Land, vefted in Feoffees, the yearly Produce of which is 7*l.* have been given, by whom or when is not known, to be diftributed among the Poor at Chriftmas.

HENRY WOODWARD gave, by Will, 20*l.* and other Parifhioners, in 1663, gave 12*l.* with which Land was purchafed, and vefted in Feoffees, which produces annually 2*l.* 9*s.* given to the Poor at Chriftmas.

WILLIAM ELLIS and Lord KENNEDY gave 7*l.* vefted in the Minifter and Churchwardens; the Intereft of which to be given in Bread to the Poor.

JOHN WYMAN gave, by Will, 5*l.* vefted in the Minifter and Churchwardens; the Interest to be given in Bread to the Poor on the Feaft of St. JOHN the Evangelift.

ELIZABETH HARTLAND, in her Life-time, gave 20*l.* vefted as above, 5*s.* of the Interest of which to be given to the Poor in Bread on the Feaft of St. JOHN the Evangelift; the Remainder for teaching two poor Children to read.

INCUMBENTS.	PATRONS.	INCUMBENTS.	PATRONS.
1548 Richard Taylor,	Francis E. of Shrewfbury.	* * * * * * * * * * * * *	
—— John Hoddy,	——————.	—— Ifaac Hague,	——————.
1558 Lawrence Fowle,	Thomas Hooper and John Fowle.	1688 Abraham Morfe,	Henry Earl of Kent.
		1726 Jackman Morfe, M.A.	Edward Morfe.
1613 Thomas Vychan,	Francis E. of Shrewfbury.	1765 John Morfe,	Ann Morfe, Widow.

PRESENT LORD OF THE MANOR,

EDMUND PROBYN, Efq.

The Perfons fummoned from this Place by the Heralds, in 1682 and 1683, were

William Jones, Gent. George Kingftone, Gent. and Ifaac Hauge, Rector.

At the Election in 1776 Sixteen Freeholders polled from this Parifh.

The firft Date of the Regifter occurs in 1680.

ANNUAL ACCOUNT OF MARRIAGES, BIRTHS, AND BURIALS, IN THIS PARISH.

A.D.	Mar.	Bir.	Bur.	A.D.	Mar.	Bir.	Bur.	A.D.	Mar.	Bir.	Bur.	A.D.	Mar.	Bir.	Bur.
1781	2	17	5	1786	1	11	3	1791				1796			
1782	1	11	5	1787	—	15	4	1792				1797			
1783	1	8	6	1788	3	9	4	1793				1798			
1784	2	6	12	1789	2	18	5	1794				1799			
1785	2	25	11	1790	1	17	4	1795				1800			

I N S C R I P T I O N S   I N   T H E   C H U R C H.

ON A FLAT STONE:

Here refteth, in Expectation
of a glorious Refurrection, the
Body of MARGARET, the Wife
of WILLIAM ELLIS, and Daughter of
WILLIAM ATWOOD, of Pauntley
Court, Gent. who deceafed
the XXIX of December,
Anno Dom. 1686,
ætatis fuæ XXIIII.

ON A MONUMENT AGAINST THE CHURCH:

S. H. M.
Depofitæ funt Exuviæ
Reverendi Viri ABRAHAMI MORSI,
Hujus Ecclefiæ
Triginta & octo annos
Eximii Rectoris;
Vir vere dignus,
Si quid valeant
Pietas, Jufticia, Charitas;
In munere paftorali vigilans &
laboriofus;
In negotiis affiduus & fidelis,

In pace promovenda maxime ftudiofus,
Omnibus amicus promptus & fincerus.
Eheu pofteri negabitis!
Plus in aliorum, quam fui ipfius,
Aut fuorum, commodum,
Seipfum exercuit.
Hunc
Maxime defideratum, et variis ærumnis,
Et infirmitatibus pergravatum,
Mors vità fpoliavit
XXV die Octobris,
Anno Domini
MDCCXXVI,
ætatis fuæ
LXXVIII.

I N

IN THE CHURCH-YARD, ON TOMBS.

FEBRUARY THE 15, 1666.
THEN DEPARTED THIS LIFE
WILLIAM HOPTON, THE SON OF
WILLIAM HOPTON,
OF HUNTLEY, BEING OF THE
FAMILY
OF SIR WALTER HOPTON, AT
HOPTON CASTLE
IN THE COUNTIE OF SALOP.

Here refteth the Body of
PETER CHARLES, who departed
this Life the 25 Day of January,
1708, aged 48 Years.

Alfo here lyeth the Body of ABIGAIL,
the Wife of PETER CHARLES. She
died January 26, 1729, aged 67 Years.

Here refteth the Body of JAMES
CHARLES, who departed this Life
the 19 June, 1728, aged 61 Years.

Here lyeth the
Body of THOMAS MORGAN,
of the Parifh of Newland,
who died Feb. 14, 1737,
aged 51 Years.

Alfo here refteth the Body of
THOMAS MORGAN, of this Parifh,
Nephew to the abovementioned
THOMAS MORGAN, who departed
this Life Oct. 5, A. D. 1762,
aged 45 Years.

Here lyeth the Body of
ANTHONY ASHLEY, Yeoman, of
this Parifh, who departed this
Life May 10, An. Dom. 1701,
aged 92 Years.

Here lyeth the Body of JOHN, the
Son of ANTHONY ASHLEY,
Yeoman, who
died Sept. 7, An. Dom. 1747, aged 75
Years.

To
the Memory
of
JAMES DRINKWATER,
of this Parifh, fen.
who died Oct. 12, 1751,
aged 78 Years.

And alfo
in Memory of ANN,
the Wife of the faid JAMES
DRINKWATER, who died
Oct. 24, 1758, aged
71 Years.

Alfo THOMAS, the Son of
JAMES DRINKWATER, jun. by SARAH
his Wife. He died April 15,
1760, in the 7 Year of his Age.

ON A BRASS PLATE:

M. S.
of RICHARD CLARK,
a zealous Afferter of the Proteftant
Religion and his Country's
Liberties, a Guardian to the
Fatherlefs and Widow, and a
provident and induftrious
Manager of his own Concerns.
He was born at Barntley, lived
at Painfwick, and died here
June 24, 1717,
aged 55 Years.

Alfo JANE, the Wife of
RICHARD CLARK. She died
January the 22d in 1741,
aged 67 Years.

To the pious Memory alfo of
ELIZABETH, the Wife of THOMAS
DRINKWATER, and Daughter of
RICHARD and JANE CLARK aforefaid.
She departed this Life the 30 Day
of July, Anno Domini 1750,
and in the 41ft Year of her Age.

Alfo BETTY their Daughter, buried
here.

In Memory of
THOMAS DRINKWATER,
who died Auguft 3, 1757,
aged 42 Years.

In Memory
of the
Rev. Mr. ABRAHAM MORSE,
who was thirty-eight Years
Rector of this Church;
and, after an active Life of 70 Years,
anfwered to the Call of GOD,
and to the Law of Mortality,
October the 28,
in the Yeare of our Lord
1726.

In
Memory of
ROBERT FOWLE,
who was one of the
Feoffees of this Parifh,
and, after a careful Life ended,
was here interred November
29, 1757, aged 67 Years.

Alfo in Memory of
DEBORAH, the Wife of the
faid ROBERT FOWLE, who was the
Daughter of the Reverend
Mr. ABRAHAM MORSE, Rector of
this Church, and was laid with
her Hufband in this Grave Feb.
11th, in the Year 1758, aged 71.

Here lieth the Body of HESTER,
the Wife of THOMAS ELLIOTT. She
died December 19, 1777,
aged 33 Years.

ON A FLAT STONE.

Underneath
lies the Body of JOHN WYMAN,
late of the City of Gloucefter,
Cordwainer, who departed this
Life March the 19, 1720,
aged 69 Years.

Here refteth, in
hopes of a glorious
Refurrection, the Body
of ELIZABETH HARTLAND,
Daughter of the above
JOHN WYMAN. She died
Jan. 17, 1763, aged 80.

ON HEAD-STONES.

	Died	Aged
Thomas Aftman	30 Jan. 1712	40
William Conftans	26 Feb. 1692	74
Richard Conftans	2 June, 1691	63
Ifabell his Wife	17 Nov. 1686	—
John, Son of William Jones	2 Aug. 1695	26
Sufannah, Daughter of John Fowle	19 June, 1684	—
James Hampton	18 Apr. 1744	67
James, Son of Even Price	3 May, 1750	8
Richard Worme	19 Sept. 1723	60
Frances Harding	—— —— 1741	41

761

O N   H E A D - S T O N E S.

	Died	Aged
Hannah, Wife of Thomas Reece	10 Feb. 1776	60
Thomas their Son	16 Nov. 1768	21
John Billingham	6 Apr. 1773	67
Thomas Jones	31 Aug. 1783	34
Sarah his Wife	16 Nov. 1787	39
Joſeph, Son of Stephen and Ann Baylis	22 Apr. 1776	25
William Haile	23 June, 1717	60
James Haile	24 June, 1750	56
Elizabeth his Wife	30 May, 1762	69
John Haile	7 Nov. 1779	52
Robert Haile	7 Sept. 1780	42
Mary his Wife	11 Sept. 1784	41
John Smith, ſenior	23 July, 1769	60
Ann his Wife	22 June, 1742	33
Eſther, Wife of John Smith, junior	23 Oct. 1779	29
Eſther, Wife of John Williams	4 May, 1781	30
James Sanford	2 Jan. 1780	64
Mary his Wife	4 June, 1780	66
Elizabeth, Wife of Joſeph Braban	6 Mar. 1720	24
Samuel Rudge	30 Dec. 1687	—
Elizabeth, Wife of Richard Crockett	29 Nov. 1724	29
Martha their Daughter	14 Nov. 1738	19
John Uzett	5 Apr. 1772	63
Mary his Wife	20 Jan. 1777	64
Mary Charles	15 July, 1694	—
Mary, Wife of John Weale	9 July, 1756	28
Thomas Hawkins	14 June, 1761	51
Mary his Wife	22 Nov. 1750	49
Thomas Hill	6 Dec. 1773	30
John Hyett	12 Nov. 1772	32
Thomas Hyett	4 Feb. 1764	32
Thomas Fowle	24 Feb. 1732	34
Ann, Daughter of James Dobbs	29 Aug. 1779	5
John Viner	16 May, 1721	51
Sarah, Wife of Samuel Fowle	13 Dec. 1745	27
Ann, Wife of Thomas Bond, and Daughter of Richard Clarke, Gent.	27 Apr. 1758	55
Mary, Daughter of Thomas Bond	1 Mar. 1759	25
Ann, Relict of John Middleton, Daughter of Thomas Bond, of the City of Gloucester	24 Apr. 1763	31
Jane, Wife of George Lodge	11 July, 1780	35
Robert Hooper	9 June, 1765	27
Thomas Turner	28 Feb. 1732	51
Oſwell Bryan	6 Sept. 1729	45
Ann, Wife of Paul Gardener	11 Aug. 1773	71
William, Son of Richard and Mary Hill	27 Sept. 1715	15
John Fifield	26 July, 1699	—
Elizabeth, Wife of George Parſons	17 Sept. 1734	54

L. KEMERTON.

L.   K E M E R T O N.

THIS Parifh is a Part of the lower Divifion of the Hundred of *Tewkefbury*, bounded on the Weft by *Bredon*, on the North-eaft by *Overbury*, and on the South by *Tredington*, in *Worcefterfhire*; the Rivulet *Carrant* dividing the Counties.

The Diftance from *Tewkefbury* is four Miles on the North-eaft, feven North-weftward from *Winchcombe*, and fourteen on the North from the City of GLOUCESTER. It lies in the great Vale of *Evefham*, at the Bafe of *Bredon-Hill*, Part of which is included in it. DRAYTON, in his " Poly-Olbion," celebrates *Bredon Hill*, in which many extraneous Foffils are found; and a few Years fince, within the Vallations of the Summit, feveral *Roman* Coins of bafe Metal and the later Empire have been difcovered.

The Terrier ftates the Parifh to contain 1400 Acres, one Half of which, being commonable Land, was inclofed by Act of Parliament in 1772. Of the Soil the chief Part is of fandy Loam or Clay; and the Pafture is exceeded by the Arable.

The Living is rectorial, in the Deanery of *Campden*, the Advowfon of which having been obtained by GODFREY GOODMAN, Bifhop of *Gloucefter*, who had been prefented to the Rectory in 1631, by Indenture made between him and the Mayor and Burgeffes of the City of *Gloucefter*, he fettled it upon them fubject to the fubjoined Conditions *.

Neither WILLIS or ECTON mention the tutelar Saint of the Church, which is a capacious Building, and confifts of a Nave and two Aifles, with a plain embattled Tower at the Weft End. The oppofite dividing Arches are *Saxon* and Lancet; but the whole appears ancient, and has been frequently repaired.

In the Particulars of the great Manor of *Tewkefbury*, recited in *Domefday*, " *Chenemertone*," as a Member of it, is faid to be eight Hides, having diftinct manerial Rights. In the early *Norman* Reigns it was granted to the CLARES, Earls of GLOUCESTER, and is ftill within the Jurifdiction of the Court of that Honour. A Grant of Markets was obtained in 1218, 2 HEN. III. By various Defcents, this Manor paffed to THOMAS Earl of ARUNDEL, whofe Sifter and Coheir was JOAN, the Wife of WILLIAM BEAUCHAMP, Baron *Bergavenny*, the Parents of RICHARD Earl of WARWICK, who died in 1470, feized of this Manor, which he bequeathed to his Son HENRY Duke of WARWICK; upon whofe Demife it came to his Sifter and Heir ANNE, the Wife of RICHARD NEVILLE, Earl of *Salifbury*, and (in her right) of *Warwick*. By an Act of Parliament, the Countefs was deprived of this Manor, and it was fettled on ISABEL her elder Daughter, Dutchefs of CLARENCE; but in 1488, 3 HEN. VII. was reftored to her by that Prince, who obtained the final Poffeffion of her vaft Property by a fraudulent Deed. ROBERT Lord WILLOUGHBY DE BROKE having married ...., Daughter and Coheir of Sir RICHARD BEAUCHAMP; fhe died feized of this Manor in Jointure in 1515, 6 HEN. 8. Their Son EDWARD WILLOUGHBY left three Daughters and Coheirs, ELIZABETH, Wife of Sir FULKE GREVILLE, Father of the firft Lord BROKE; ANNE, who died unmarried; and BLANCH, who married Sir FRANCIS DAUTRY, Knight. Upon the Death of ANNE, the laft-mentioned inherited her Partition of the Manor. In the Reign of Q. ELIZABETH the Families of HEWES and LYGON became Proprietors. It was held, in 1608, by THOMAS HEWES, Efq. and Sir ARNOLD LYGON, Knt. of whom it was purchafed by JOHN PARSONS, Efq. a few Years afterward, and has paffed to JOHN PARSONS, Efq. the feventh in lineal Defcent, to whom it now belongs.

---

* Extract from the Indenture of Prefentation, dated July 24, 1637, between G. GOODMAN, Bifhop of *Gloucefter*, and the Mayor and Burgeffes, " that his Meaning and Intention is, that, whenfoever the faid Living fhould become void the fecond Time after " his Death, the Avoidance fhall be made known to the Wardens to the Hofpital of *Ruthyn* and the Aldermen of the faid Bo- " rough, to the Intent that fome of the Blood of GOODMAN fhould be prefented. One of the Defcendants of EDWARD GOOD- " MAN, Grandfather of the faid GODFREY—thofe of Name and Blood before Blood only—and the Son of the eldeft Sifter before " the Son of the younger—and, if none fo qualified offer, then the Son of the Mayor of *Gloucefter*—the Alderman and Common " Council in Rotation according to Seniority, or a Minifter ferving within the faid City. And further, it is the Will and Defire " of the faid Reverend Father, that, whereas the Parfonage of *Kemmerton* is a fufficient Maintenance for an able Scholar, being " worth £. 200 per Annum at the leaft, that whofoever fhall happen to be prefented by the Mayor and Burgeffes, having a Be- " nefice with Cure of Souls, fhall, upon his Admiffion and Induction into the faid Church, refign his former Benefice to the " Ufe of the Son of a Burgefs or Freeman, to be prefented by the Mayor and Burgeffes. Ten Pounds are directed to be paid, " to be beftowed upon a Dinner for the Poor of *St. Bartholomew's Hofpital* upon the Enfealing of the Prefentation, and one Quar- " ter of Wheat yearly to be delivered to the Treafurer of the faid Hofpital in the Week before Eafter."

2   In

In the Village are two commodious Manfion-houfes, called the Upper and Lower Courts, upon the manerial Eftate; but it is not to be collected from any record that there were two diftinct Manors.

The Property, unconnected with the manerial Eftate, is not confiderable; the Lands which were held by KENELM WRIGHT at the beginning of the laft Century, are now vefted in the Families of MUMFORD and TIDMARSH.

B E N E F A C T I O N S.

CHARLES PARSONS, Efq. gave, by Will, dated in 1735, a rent Charge of £. 1. *per Annum*, to be diftributed to the Poor in Bread on Chriftmas-day.

Alfo Land, the annual produce of which is 10 *s.* was given for the Relief of the Poor of *Kemerton*; but by whom is not known.

INCUMBENTS.	PATRONS.	INCUMBENTS.	PATRONS.
1340 ————	Alice Beauchamp.	1596 John Fownes,	Thomas Hewes, Efq.
1541 Thomas Raynold,	K. Henry VIII.	1631 GodfreyGoodman,D.D.	K. Charles I.
—— Michael Raynold,	————	1655 John Hinman,	————.
1560 William Clynton,	William Lygon, Efq.	1657 Nat.Lye,D.D.	W.Scudamore,Efq. and others.
1568 Geo. Swatt,	————	1738 John Lloyd, M. A.	Corporation of Gloucefter.
1572 Ralph Ecton,	Chriftopher Moody.	1762 Godfrey Goodman, M. A.	The fame.
1588 William Stephens,	————	1786 Roger Parry, M. A.	The fame.

PRESENT LORD OF THE MANOR,

JOHN PARSONS, Efq.

The Heralds, in 1682 and 1683, fummoned from this Parifh

John Parfons, Efq. and Thomas Surman, Gent.

At the Election in 1776, Eight Freeholders polled from this Parifh.

The Regifter has been kept with laudable Accuracy. It commences with the Year 1572.

ANNUAL ACCOUNT OF MARRIAGES, BIRTHS, AND BURIALS, IN THIS PARISH.

A.D.	Mar.	Bir.	Bur.	A.D.	Mar.	Bir.	Bur.	A.D.	Mar.	Bir.	Bur.	A.D.	Mar.	Bir.	Bur.
1781	3	9	7	1786	2	9	11	1791				1796			
1782	4	13	4	1787	3	6	3	1792				1797			
1783	—	7	9	1788	4	8	6	1793				1798			
1784	4	7	8	1789	3	8	3	1794				1799			
1785	3	9	11	1790	2	5	7	1795				1800			

INSCRIPTIONS IN THE CHURCH.

IN THE CHANCEL.

ON FLAT STONES.

In hopes of a joyful
Refurrection here lyeth
the Body of JOHN LLOYD,
Rector of this Parifh,
He died 6 May, 1762,
ætat. 49.

Here lyeth the Body of JOSEPH
HATCH, Clerk. He died Oct.
the 25th, 1727, aged 71.

Here lyeth the Body
of ELNER STEPHENS, Gent.
She died Oct. 31, 1727,
aged 77.

ANNA, Uxor JOSEPHI HATCH,
Clerici, obiit Nov. 28, 1713,
Anno ætat. 54.

ON A BRASS PLATE:

COLIBERY, uxor JOSEPHI HATCH,
obiit Jan. 31, 1687,
ætat. fuæ 24.

IN THE NAVE.

ON FLAT STONES.

Here lyeth the Body of
DANIEL NEWMAN.
He died May the 27th, 1681,
aged about 30 Years.

Here alfo lieth the Body
of THOMAS, the Son of
THOMAS and HANNAH
NEWMAN, of the Blue
Boar Inn, Holborn, London. He
died Aug. 8, 1734,
aged 20 Years.

SAMUEL NEWMAN
died Dec. 4, 1766, æt. 75.

In Memory of
WILLIAM COLE, who
departed this Life
September the 27,
Anno Dom. 1722,
aged 74.

Here lieth the Body of
ANNE, the Wife of
WILLIAM COLE, who died
September the 23,
Anno Dom. 1728,
aged 77.

Here
lyeth the Body of
JOHN, Son of JOHN COLE
and MARY his Wife, who
died 24 Nov. 1769, aged 33.

Here

Here
refteth, in hopes of
a joyful Refurrection,
the Body of JOHN COLE,
who departed this Life the 6
Day of March, A. D. 1786,
in the 96 Year of his Age.

Alfo here lyeth the Body of
MARY, Wife of the above,
who departed this Life the
28 Day of April, A. D. 1788,
aged 78 Years.

Here lyeth interred the
Body of BETTY COLE, the
Wife of THOMAS COLE, who
departed this Life the 21
February, 1774, aged
26 Years.

Alfo JOHN COLE, Son of the above
named, who died in his Infancy.

Beneath this Stone
lie the Remains of
Mrs. MARY HARTGILL,
who died the 21 Dec. 1789,
aged 63 Years.

N O R T H   A I S L E.

SUSANNAH PARSONS,
the Wife of JOHN PARSONS, fen.
Gent. She died Novem. 3, 1697,
aged 73.

Here lyeth the Body of
MARY PARSONS, the Wife of
CHARLES PARSONS,
Gent. She died Decem. the 28, 1720,
aged 23.

JOHN PARSONS,
Gent. died the firft Day of June,
Anno Dom. 1704, in the 75th
Year of his Age.

Here lyeth the Body of
JOHN PARSONS,
jun. Efq. who died March the
10th, 1721, aged 72.

SUSANAH, the fecond
Daughter of JOHN PARSONS, Efq.
and DEBORAH his Wife, died
the 16th of December, 1738,
in the 5th Year of her Age.

CHARLES PARSONS,
Gent. Son of JOHN PARSONS, jun.
Efq. and ELIZABETH his Wife. He
died Novem. the 21, 1721,
aged 28.

JOHN PARSONS, Efq.
He died June the 23d, 1757,
aged 59 Years.

DEBORAH PARSONS,
Widow, died 25 Feb. 1788,
aged 79 Years.

Here lyeth the Body of Mrs.
ELIZABETH PARSONS,
the Wife of JOHN PARSONS, Efq.
She died December the 3d. 1736,
aged 78.

Here lyeth the Body of
WILLIAM, the Son of WALTER
and JUDITH JONES. He died
April the 20, 1725, aged
5 Months.

EDWARD PARSONS,
fourth Son of JOHN PARSONS, Efq.
and DEBORAH his Wife
(Lieutenant in his Grace the Duke
of RICHMOND's Regiment),
died April 4, 1764,
aged 21.

ON A MARBLE MONUMENT:

Arms; Azure, a Cheveron Ermine between three Trefoils Argent, for *Parfons*;
—impaling, Azure, a Chevron between
three Lions' Heads erafed Or, for *Wyndham.*

ANNE, the lamented Wife of
JOHN PARSONS, Efq.
fecond Daughter of THOMAS WYNDHAM,
of Clearwell, in this County, Efq.
Obiit 17 April, 1785, ætatis 53.

O N   F L A T   S T O N E S.

ELIZABETH, the Wife of
JOHN CUFF, who died
May 11, 1770, aged 72.

JOHN CUFF died 22 March,
1766. æt. 66.

JOHN CUFF, jun. died 1 Sept.
1769, aged 32.

SARAH,
fecond Daughter of JOHN
CUFF and ELIZABETH his Wife,
died the 7th of May,
1767, æt. 32.

IN THE SOUTH AISLE.

ON FLAT STONES.
Here refts the
Body of MARGARET,
the Daughter of
NICHOLAS STAIGHT and
HANNAH his Wife,
was buried Oct. 15,
1685.

Here lyeth the Body of FLORENCIA,
the Wife of CONAN DAWBNEY, who,
having difcharged the Duty of
a faithful Wife,
a tender Mother,
a good Neighbour, and
a pious Chriftian,
departed this Life November the 4th,
Anno Dom. 1695, ætat. 74.

JOHN PEART, Mafon,
and Clerk of this Parifh,
died Feb. 8, 1765, æt. 67.

Here
lieth the Body
of BETTY, Wife of JOHN BARNES,
of this Parifh, who died the
20th of July, 1773, æt. 41.
Alfo here lieth the Body of
MARY BARNES, the Wife of
JOSEPH BARNES, who died April
the 15, 1780, æt. 27 Years.
Alfo WILL. BARNES, Son of the
above, who died in his Infancy.

IN THE CHURCH-YARD, ON HEAD STONES.

	Died	Aged
Thomas Dudfield, fen.	29 May, 1729	54
Barbara his Wife -	26 Aug. 1727	53
Samuel Dudfield -	12 May, 1733	60
Mary his Wife -	27 May, 1767	85
John Dudfield -	29 Jan. 1769	52
Betty his Wife -	31 Mar. 1781	57
Elizabeth, Wife of Samuel Dudfield	20 Oct. 1727	40
John, Son of William Dudfield	19 July, 1729	62
Samuel his Son -	14 Dec. 1728	53
Thomas Bird -	5 Jan. 1760	68
Elizabeth his Wife -	1 Oct. 1768	83
Richard Stephens -	12 June, 1763	52
Timothy Barnes -	9 Jan. 1761	72
Mary his Wife -	16 Dec. 1765	82
Ann, Wife of Jofeph Barnes	23 Feb. 1778	65
John Pace - -	3 Nov. 1753	78
Sarah his Wife -	10 Feb. 1743	60
John Pace - -	29 Sept. 1770	47
Eleanor, Wife of William Pace	28 Dec. 1715	63
Eleanor Pace -	26 Mar. 1773	73
Thomas Pace -	14 June, 1772	24
Betty, Wife of William Pace	13 June, 1778	39
Thomas Stephens -	30 Oct. 1711	44
Hannah his Wife -	2 Sept. 1711	32
Richard Stephens -	3 Mar. 1741	71
Sarah his Wife -	29 Jan. 1736	64
Richard Stephens -	12 June, 1763	52
Sarah, Wife of Ifaac Peart	30 Jan. 1714	54
William Cole -	17 Apr. 1732	67
Mary his Wife -	9 Nov. 1727	—
Richard Cole -	16 Dec. 1700	47
Eleanor his Wife -	25 Aug. 1694	32
Mary, Daughter of T. and Kat. Cole	18 Nov. 1719	68
Anne their Daughter -	13 Mar. 1729	71
John their Son -	18 May, 1720	75
Sarah their Daughter -	1 Nov. 1723	69
William Cole. -	17 Apr. 1732	67
Mary his Wife -	9 Dec. 1727	42
Samuel Rickards -	15 Apr. 1726	42
Mary his Wife -	17 Aug. 1760	75
Samuel Rickards -	20 Nov. 1770	53
William Rickards -	27 Mar. 1786	83
John Ricketts - -	2 Dec. 1783	73
John Tinker -	11 June, 1696	27
Mary Tinker -	26 Apr. 1776	73
William, Son of John Thornhill	28 Mar. 1750	17
William, Son of W. and E. Bincher	25 Mar. 1742	26
Robert Bradford -	6 Jan. 1702	68
Ann, Wife of John Overbury	28 Nov. 1775	38
Job Smith - -	9 Apr. 1775	77
Charles, Son of Ben. and Mary Stanly	11 May, 1785	22
Alice, Wife of Edward Morgan	17 Apr. 1711	59
Thomas Tavener -	8 Mar. 1675	27
William Stew -	11 Apr. 1783	57
John his Son -	10 Sept. 1786	27
Mary his Daughter -	23 Nov. 1769	13
Thomas Johns, fen. -	3 Jan. 1759	87
Joyce his Wife -	31 July, 1746	60
Mary, Wife of Thomas Johns, jun.	9 Mar. 1766	46
Mary his fecond Wife -	5 Aug. 1775	50
Thomas their Son -	19 May, 1781	24
Jofeph Farley -	10 Oct. 1769	52
Robert Dennis -	2 Feb. 1760	71
Mary his Wife -	13 Feb. 1757	82
Mary, Wife of William Cormell	21 Nov. 1735	29
William Sheen -	14 Oct. 1737	84
Ann his Wife -	22 May, 1750	73
Elizabeth Cormell -	19 May, 1729	13

CLI.   K E M P L E Y,

WRITTEN in antient Evidences *KENEPELEGH*, is a Parish fix Miles in Circumference, in the Hundred of *Botloe*; bounded on the Weft by *Much Marcle* in the County of *Hereford*, five Miles Northweft from *Newent*, and fifteen in the fame Direction from GLOUCESTER.

The Soil is of a ftiff red Clay or Loam, and peculiarly fertile, the Pafture Lands are more than the Arable, but in no great Proportion. It has been a Practice in this Diftrict to plant univerfally wide Rows of Fruit Trees both in Arable and Pafture Fields, which produce Cider and Perry of a good Quality *. The Oak and Elm flourish here with great Luxuriance.

The Living is a Vicarage in the *Foreft* Deanery, endowed with the impropriate Tythes of the whole Parish, excepting of *Prior's Court*, which is therefore charged with the Repairs of the Chancel. The great Tythes were given by GEOFRY DE LONGCAMP to the Prior and Brethren of the Hofpital of *St. Katharine* in *Leabury*, founded by HUGH FOLLIOTT, Bifhop of Hereford, in 1232, and re-eftablifhed by Act of Parliament, paffed in the Reign of Q. ELIZABETH, by which the Dean and Chapter of *Hereford* were conftituted Guardians and Patrons.

Of the Church, dedicated to *St.* ———, the Dimenfions are fmall; having a Nave only divided from the Chancel by a heavy Arch, with *Saxon* Mouldings and a Door-Cafe of the fame Style of Architecture. The low Spire is covered with Shingles.

ROGER DE LACI held " *Chenepelei*," containing three Hides, as *Domefday* Book recites; and, in the Reign of RICHARD the Firft, the Manor was held by HENRY DE GREY, in whofe Defcendants it was vefted 'till the Year 1460, 1ft of EDW. IV. JOHN ABRAHALL, Efq. fucceeded them, and it paffed, in 1539, to WILLIAM PIGOT, Efq. HENRY PIGOT, his Grandfon, left ANNE, his fole Daughter and Heir, who married HENRY FINCH, Efq. of the Family of the Earls of WINCHELSEA, who died in 1631, feized in her Right of the Manor of *Kempley*. FRANCIS FINCH, Efq. only Son and Heir, was the Father of JOHN FINCH, by whom this Eftate was fold in the laft Century to Sir THOMAS HOWE, Knt. third Son of JOHN HOWE, Efq. of *Compton Abdale*, who died without Iffue.

Soon after, a Purchafe was made of it by REGINALD PYNDAR, Efq. who was Lord of this Manor in 1711, and was fucceeded by his Son THOMAS PYNDAR, who died in 1722.—REGINALD PYNDAR LYGON, Efq. of *Madresfield*, in *Worcefterfhire* (which latter Name he has affumed), is the prefent Proprietor, and is one of the Reprefentatives in Parliament for that County.

The Manerial-Houfe is fpacious, having been built by HENRY FINCH, Efq. in 1610, as appears from that Date, and his armorial Bearings carved in fome of the Apartments. It has fharp Pediments and bay Windows in the Style of that Age. It is now being refitted as a Farm.

By the Prior and Brethren of *St. Bartholomew* in *Gloucefter*, Lands were anciently granted in Leafe, fubject to a Rent of three Cranocs (half Quarters) of Wheat, and two Quarters of Oats.

The only Eftate of Confequence, independent on the Manor, is held by DANIEL HULLETT, Gent.

B E N E F A C T I O N S.

JOANE WOTON gave, by Will, dated 31 Jan. 1706, a Rent Charge of 10*s. per Annum*, to be diftributed among the Poor.

ELIZABETH PYNDAR gave, by Deed, dated 5 June, 1755, four Acres of Land, vefted in REGINALD LYGON, Efq. and others, the annual Produce of which to pay for teaching two poor Children to read, and the Remainder to be diftributed among the Poor.

MARY WORRELL, about the Year 1752, gave, by Will, two Acres of Land, vefted in the Parish Officers, the annual Produce of which to pay for teaching poor Children to read.

* See MARSHAL's Rural Œconomy of *Glouc.* vol. II. p. 152.

INCUMBENTS.	PATRONS.	INCUMBENTS.	PATRONS.
1548 John Came,	Hofpital of St. Katharine in Ledbury.	1660 Rich. Wilkinfon, M.A.	King Charles II.
1572 William Scott,	The fame.	1666 John Lewys,	D. and Chap. of Hereford,
1575 Hum. Taylor, alias Cradock,	The fame.	1694 Peter Senhoufe, M. A.	The fame.
1606 Tho. Nicholas, } double prefen-	{ Margery Pigot.	* * * * * * * * * * * *	
R. Atkyns, M.A. } tation.	{ Abp. of Canterbury.	1760 John Stephens, L.L. D.	The fame.
1607 John Cradock,	Dean and Chap. of Hereford.	1762 ——— Bourne, Clk.	The fame.
		1787 Robert Squire, M. A.	The fame.

PRESENT LORD OF THE MANOR,

REGINALD PYNDAR LYGON, Efq.

The Heralds, in 1682 and 1683, fummoned from this Parifh

Reginald Pyndar, Efq.

At the Election in 1776, Six Freeholders polled from this Parifh.

The firft Date of the Regifter occurs in 1663.

ANNUAL ACCOUNT OF MARRIAGES, BIRTHS, AND BURIALS, IN THIS PARISH.

A.D.	Mar.	Bir.	Bur.	A.D.	Mar.	Bir.	Bur.	A.D.	Mar.	Bir.	Bur.	A.D.	Mar.	Bir.	Bur.
1781	2	6	4	1786	1	16	5	1791				1796			
1782	—	—	—	1787	3	12	1	1792				1797			
1783	4	10	2	1788	—	14	4	1793				1798			
1784	3	8	3	1789	3	6	2	1794				1799			
1785	1	16	5	1790	3	12	3	1795				1800			

INSCRIPTIONS IN THE CHURCH.

IN THE CHANCEL.
ON A MONUMENT.

Arms ; Quarterly, 1ft, Argent, a Cheveron engrailed between three Griffins paffant, Sable, for FINCH ; 2d, Sable, three Pick-axes Argent, for PIGOT : 3d, Gules, three Lions Argent, for ..... ; 4th, Argent, within a Bordure engrailed, three Pikes hauriant Sable ; 5th, Parti per Feſs indented Argent and Sable, four hunting Horns counterchanged ; 6th, FINCH.

P. M. S.
Macte Marmor.
Eloquere !
nec taceas Cineres HENRICI FINCH,
Armigeri hic effe
Reconditos,
fitq; tibi non ingratum Munus Fidelitatis
fuæ Symbolum ;
In { Principem, Patriam, Amicos } exftare.
Efferto Vivis, Pofteris Annuncia, Temporibufq; propalato
Futuris.
Quam

Sincerus	Numinis	Cultor,
Sedulus	Veritatis	Indagator,
Candidus	Æquitatis	Difpenfator,
Acerbus	Fraudis	Exoior,
Beneficus	Paupertatis	Suftentator,
Studiofus	Hofpitii	Propugnator.

Vixit Occiditq;
Deo, Ecclefiæ, Amicis, Optimis, Proximis, Omnibus } Fuiffe { Supplicem, Morigerum, Charum, Jucundum, Familiarem, Comem.
Bis octo Annorum Luftra in vivis peregiffe,
Et
Supremam non metuiffe fed exoptaffe Horam.

Illumq;
Votum fuum Precibus et Sufpiriis ufq; adeo expetitum
22° Auguft e Cœlorum Gremio accipuiffe
An°. fui Jefu, MDCXXXI.
Porro non fine Piaculo conticefcas
ANNAM, ex non obfcura PIGOTORUM prolapia fideliffima,
Confortem, hic Lateri ejus dormientem adjacere ;
Quorum
Socialis Amor Morte non finitur, fed unitur.
Hanc
Unicum Marito peperiffe Filium quem amabant unice,
Qui { Amoris, Obfequii, Pietatis } ergo
In P. Parentum M.
Hæc
non fine Lachrymis
Dicavit
Æ. C.
MDCXXXIII.

Arms, Azure three Urchins Or.

Beneath this Marble lyeth the Body of DORCAS LEWES, the Wife of JOHN LEWES,
Paftor of this Church, who changed this Life for a better
Nov. 3, 1672, aged 32.

ESTHER LEWES here lyeth interred with her Mother, Auguft 2, 1673.

ON FLAT STONES.

Hic jacet
Corpus HENRICI POOLE,
Generoſi, de Parochia de Kempley, qui fepultus eft Die Jun. 10mo 6to,
Anno Dom. 1688.

Hic etiam
jacet Corpus ELIZABETHÆ
olim ejus Uxoris, quæ fepulta eft Die Feb. 10mo 8vo,
Anno Dom. 1717.

Here lyeth the Body of HENRY POOLE, of Great Malvern, in the County of Worcefter, Gent. who departed this Life the 29th Day of Oct. in the Year of our Lord 1735, aged 65.

IN THE NAVE.

On a handfome MARBLE MONUMENT.

Arms ; on two Efcocheons ; 1ft, Azure, a Cheveron between three Lions Heads erafed Or, ducally crown'd, for PYNDAR ;—impaling, Azure, three Piles Or. on a Chief of the fecond, a Lion paffant of the Field, for LOGGIN ; 2d, PYNDAR as before, impaling, Argent, two Lions paffant Gules, for LYGON.

Near this Place
lyeth interred,
THOMAS PYNDAR, REGINALD PYNDAR,
Efq. only Son of
who died   THO. PYNDAR and
May the 18,   ELIZ. his Wife, who
Ann. { Dom. 1722, Ætat. 60. }   died July 10,
Anno { Dom. 1721, Ætat. 33. }

ELIZABETH PYNDAR
died Jan. 10, 1759,
Ætat. 92.

WILLIAM PYNDAR,
Son of
REGINALD PYNDAR,
died Oct. 16, 1787,
aged 70 Years.

ON

ON FLAT STONES.

In Memory of
WILLIAM, the Son of
WILLIAM JAMES,
of this Parish, by
JOANE his Wife,
who was buried
June 27, 1731,
aged 18.

Here lyeth the Body of
RALPH WOOTTON, alias CULTON, late of
the City of London, who died
in this Parish, Jan. 22, An. Dom.
1706, aged 54 Years.

Here lyeth
the Body of MARY, the
Wife of ANTHONY SENHOUSE,
late of Thornhaugh, in the
County of Northampton,
who died Dec. Anno { Dom. 1709.
{ Æt. —.

Here also lyeth
the Body of ELIZABETH,
the Daughter of PETER SEN-
HOUSE, Clerk, Vicar of this
Church, and MARY his Wife,
who died Aug. the 1st,
Anno { Dom. 1712,
{ Ætat. 6.

IN THE CHURCH YARD.

Successus selectus JOHANNIS LEWYS,
Olim hujus Parochiæ de Kempley,
Clerici officiosissimi.
Qui fidem in Deum
Religiose coluit,
Hospitem exhibuit,
Pauperes benigne hillaravit,
Literas multifarias coluit,
Literatos ample evexit,
Pietatæ cæterifque virtutibus
Emicuit,
Moribus his & artibus
Has acquisivit Virtutes
Obiit 11 Sept.
Anno { Salutis 1695,
{ ætatis 58.

To the Memory of
JAMES EDWARDS, of this Parish,
who died Feb. 11, 1764,
aged 64 Years.

In Memory of
THOMAS NOTT, sen.
late of Sayfells, in this
Parish, who departed this Life
July the 19, 1761, aged 80 Years.

In Memory of
HENRY EVANS, who was
here buried December
the 10th, 1719, aged 79.

In Memory of
JAMES GURNEY, who was
here buried May the 5,
1743, aged 87 Years.

In Memory of JANE,
the Wife of JAMES GURNEY,
who was buried May the 1st,
1735.

In Memory
of
LETTICE, the Wife of JAMES
GURNEY, who departed this Life,
February the 22d, 1753,
aged 52 Years.
Also in Memory of
the abovesaid JAMES GURNEY, of
this Parish, who departed
this Life March 29, 1766,
aged 67 Years.

Here lies interred the Body
of HENRY MATTHEWS,
who departed this Life the
Nov. 13, 1776, aged 90 Years.
In Memory of ANNE, the Wife
of HENRY MATTHEWS, she died
May the 30th, 1764, aged 69.

To the
Memory of ANNE, the Daughter of
HENRY MATTHEWS, by ANNE his Wife,
and grand-daughter of JAMES GURNEY,
by JANE his Wife, who died May 25,
1757, she was in the 19th Year of her age.

In Memory of
HENRY, the Son of
HENRY MATTHEWS, by
ANNE his Wife, who died
May the 2d, 1725,
aged four Months.

ON TOMBS.

To the
Memory of WILLIAM MATTHEWS
Son of HENRY and ANNE MATTHEWS,
who died June 30, 1770, aged 41.

In Memory of
DANIEL WORRELL, who died August,
the 28th, 1732, aged 95 Years.

Also MARY his Wife, died Feb.
the 26th, 1750, aged 87 Years.

In Memory of ANTHONY,
the Son of DANIEL
WARRELL, by MARY his Wife,
who died Sept. 12, 1730,
aged 30 Years.

In Memory of
ISAAC THOMAS,
late of this Parish,
who died Nov. the 24th, 1787,
aged 69 Years.

Also of ELIZABETH his Wife,
who died Aug. the 21st, 1788,
aged 65 Years.

Here
lyeth the Body of THOMAS
Cocks, who departed this
Life April the 4th, 1702,
Ætatis 67.

Also ANNE, the Wife of
the abovenamed THOMAS
Cocks, who died May 28,
1718, aged 74.

ON HEAD STONES.

	Died	Aged
Thomas Coxe, junior	22 May, 1735	60
Sarah his Wife	10 Aug. 1742	78
Joan, Wife of Joseph Hooper	15 Jan. 1741	82
Joseph Hooper	3 Dec. 1730	70
Elizabeth their Daughter	22 June, 1727	27
Alice, Wife of John Davis, Daughter of Henry Mayl	19 Jan. 1682	—
Henry Mayl	12 Nov. 1691	54
Mary Davis	3 Oct. 1720	50
Elizabeth, Wife of Thomas Symonds	18 Feb. 1771	45
Joan, Wife of Ralph Wootton	1 Feb. 1706	—
Margaret, Daughter of William and Mary Lane	4 Jan. 1770	23
John Brooke	18 Dec. 1712	62
Mary his Wife	21 Nov. 1727	69
John Brooke	16 May, 1729	38
John Brooke	17 July, 1780	65
Esther his Wife	10 July, 1765	46
Jane, Wife of Joseph Griffiths, and Daughter of John Brooke	7 July, 1773	53
William Baker	10 Sept. 1727	68
Hester his Wife	15 May, 1725	72
Daniel Lodge	1 Mar. 1745	75
Margaret his Wife	30 June, 1742	73
Daniel Lodge	19 Jan. 1757	54
Richard Holmes	9 Feb. 1712	—
Sarah his Wife	14 Sept. 1729	63
Thomas Phelps	22 Sept. 1719	78
Stephen Sergeant	21 Dec. 1737	60
Stephen, Son of Stephen and Hester Sergeant	6 Aug. 1765	21
Richard How	28 Jan. 1709	63
Mary, Daughter of William and Joan James	11 Apr. 1727	40
Joyce Elsemere	1 July, 1761	72
John Hill	30 July, 1725	—
John Hill	7 Nov. 1726	—
Thomas Edwards	1 May, 1734	56
Margaret his Wife	30 May, 1753	72
John Edwards	5 Nov. 1701	—
Elizabeth his Wife	8 Nov. 1718	—
Elizabeth, Wife of Joseph Bonnor, of Weston	29 Apr. 1741	60
Mary, Wife of Richard Proffor	18 July, 1761	67
John Probit	— May, 1690	—
Thomas Drew	20 Dec. 1688	—
John Wingod	14 Feb. 1694	62
Alice his Wife	6 Oct. 1709	80
William Wingod	11 Apr. 1712	50

5

CLII. KEMPSFORD.

LII. K E M P S F O R D.

THE Dimenfions of this Parifh, upon a general Comparifon with others, are of the middle Degree, not exceeding 2,0co Acres, divided in no unequal Proportion between Arable and Pafture, the latter of which confifts of Meadows upon the Banks of the Rivers *Colne* and *Ifis*, which laft named feparates this County from the the Parifh of *Hannington*, in *Wiltfhire*. The Soil varies but little from a fertile Clay.

Kempsford is included in the Hundred of *Brightwel's Barrow*, four Miles South-weftward from *Lechlade*, nine Eaftward from *Cirencefter*, and thirty-five from GLOUCESTER, in a fimilar Direction, inclining to the South.

The Benefice is vicarial, endowed with a certain Portion of the impropriate Tythes, which, with the Advowfon, were given to the *Benedictine* Abbey of *St. Peter in Gloucefter* by ERNULF DE HESDING, a *Norman* Knight, who accompanied WILLIAM the CONQUEROR, which Grant was afterward confirmed by HENRY I. Thefe, with the Impropriation of the Tything of *Welford*, were conveyed to the See of *Gloucefter* in 1544, and more fully in 1552.

The Church is dedicated to *St. Mary*, and is a Member of the Deanery of *Fairford*. Many concurring Circumftances prove this Edifice to have been built in the fourteenth Century, and at the Expence of HENRY Duke of LANCASTER. There is a Nave only, with a lofty Tower in the middle; againft the fupporting Pillars of which are thefe Efcocheons: 1. EDWARD CONFESSOR; 2. LANCASTER; 3. CLARE; 4. CORNWALL, or, as fome have thought, the Stool of a Tree eradicated within a Bordure bezanted, being the Cognizance of the Houfe of PLANTAGENET. The Architecture of the whole is contemporary, and very neat; the Windows of the Chancel were once embellifhed with richly ftained Glafs, now mutilated.

Domefday records the Manor as belonging to King HAROLD, and ftyled *Kynemeresford*, as fuch it was beftowed on ERNULPH DE HESDING abovementioned. It was fo confiderable as to contain Twenty-one Hides, in which were Twenty-four Plough Tillages, and four Corn Mills, the Meadows paying yearly nine Pounds, befide finding Hay for the Oxen and Sheep, the whole Produce being fixty-fix Pounds, in the Reign of WILLIAM CONQUEROR *. The great Family of DE CADURCIS, or CHAWORTH, immediately fucceeded him, and held it to the Reign of EDWARD the Second; when it was conveyed to HUGH LE DESPENSER, who had married ISABEL, Relict of PATRICK DE CHAWORTH. Her Daughter MAUD inherited upon her Death, and was the Wife of HENRY Earl of LANCASTER, Nephew of King EDWARD I. In 1355, 28 EDW. III. HENRY Duke of LANCASTER granted this Manor to the College of *St. Mary the Great in Leicefter*, which, in 1330, had been founded by his Father for the Maintenance of a Dean and twelve Prebendaries †. Free-warren was confirmed to them, by Patent, in 1357, and it continued their Property till the Diffolution. King EDWARD the Sixth, in the Third Year of his Reign (1549), gave thefe Eftates to Sir JOHN BOTTEVYLE, otherwife THYNNE, the Favourite of the Protector SOMERSET, who had been much enriched by the Spoils of the Church. In his Defcendants they were vefted to THOMAS, the prefent Marquis of BATH (fo created by Patent, dated 1789), by whom they were fold to the late GABRIEL Lord COLERAINE, and are now held in Dower by his Relict. There is a wellfounded Tradition that *Kempsford* was the Site of a royal Palace in the *Saxon* Times, and that the CHAWORTHS and PLANTAGENETS refided in their Caftle there, which was re-built by Sir THOMAS THYNNE, in the Reign of King JAMES I. This manerial Manfion, within a few Years levelled with the Ground, was a quadrangular Structure of very large Dimenfions, ornamented in the Style of that Day. KIP has engraven a Plate of it, more happily than fome which appear in Sir ROBERT ATKYNS's Hiftory of this County ‡.

---

* " In *Brictuoldefbury* Hund. ERNULPHUS DE HESDING ten. *Chenemeresford*. Ibi xxi hid' geldat'. In dcminio funt vi car',
" & xxxviii vill'i, & viii bord'i, & i rad'chenift, cum xviii car'. Ibi xiii fervi & iiii molini de xl fol' & xl den. Ei de
" p'tis viii lib' pr't pafturum boum & de ovili cxx penfas cafeorum. Tot. T. R. E. val'b't xxx lib' modo lxvi lib' & vi fol'
" & vi den." Domefday, N° IX.

† TANNER's Notitia Mon. *Leicefterfhire*, N° XVI.

‡ P. 490.

In the Year 800, a Battle is faid to have been fought in a Plain near *Kymneresford*, between ÆTHEL-MOND and WEARITAN, Chiefs of the *Wiccii* and *Walfati*, two *Saxon* Provinces, now the Counties of *Wilts* and *Gloucefter*, in which the latter were victorious. Several Remains of Military Furniture, fuch as Spear-heads and Iron Bits for Horfes, were dug up in 1670, which Circumftance fixes the Site of this Tranfaction.

H A M L E T S.

1. *Horcote*, which once belonged to the Family of FORSTER. A Corn Mill in this Hamlet was given to the Monks of *Gloucefter*, in the Time of WILLIAM the Abbot, by PATRICK DE CHAWORTH.

2. *Dunville*.

3. *Welford*, which is the moft confiderable, was granted to the faid Abbey by PAYAN DE CHAWORTH, with all Tythes belonging to it *.

Moft of the Lands within the Limits of this Parifh are held by Copyhold renewable Leafes under the Manor.

B E N E F A C T I O N.

THOMAS Lord Vifcount WEYMOUTH gave, by Deed of Settlement, dated November 2, 1709, the Sum of 10*l*. annually, to teach poor Children to read and write.

INCUMBENTS.	PATRONS.	INCUMBENTS.	PATRONS.
1557 Thomas Allen,	Bp. of Gloucefter.	1686 Dennis Huntington, M.A.	Bp. of Gloucefter.
1565 Humphry Halimote,	The fame.	1711 Thomas Dreffer,	The fame.
1576 Anthony Higgins,	The fame.	1714 Jofeph Cookfon,	The fame.
1578 John Brooke,	George Lloyd.	1715 George Gerrard, M. A.	The fame.
1597 Henry Blackburne,	Q. Elizabeth.	1735 Samuel Clarke, M. A.	The fame.
1638 Godfrey Goodman, D.D.	*(In Commendam.)*	1757 John Warren, M. A.	The fame.
1642 Edw. Hitchman, LL. B.	Bp. of Gloucefter.	1761 William Price, M. A.	The fame.
1672 John Scott,	The fame.		

PRESENT LADY OF THE MANOR,

ELIZABETH Baronefs Dowager COLERAINE.

The only Perfon fummoned from this Parifh by the Heralds, in 1682 and 1683, was

Sir Henry Frederick Thynne, Bart.

At the Election in 1776, Eleven Freeholders polled from this Parifh and its Hamlets.

The firft Date of the Regifter is in 1573.

ANNUAL ACCOUNT OF MARRIAGES, BIRTHS, AND BURIALS, IN THIS PARISH.

A.D.	Mar.	Bir.	Bur.	A.D.	Mar.	Bir.	Bur.	A.D.	Mar.	Bir.	Bur.	A.D.	Mar.	Bir.	Bur.
				1786	3	13	7	1791	6	19	14	1796			
1782	5	17	9	1787	7	18	14	1792	3	20	16	1797			
1783	3	19	17	1788	6	15	12	1793				1798			
1784	5	22	16	1789	13	25	12	1794				1799			
1785	4	20	9	1790	4	18	12	1795				1800			

* MSS. Regift. Abb. *Glouc.*

INSCRIPTIONS

INSCRIPTIONS IN THE CHURCH.

IN THE CHANCEL.

ON A MARBLE MONUMENT:

Arms; a Saltire, for SCOTT;—impaling, quarterly, 1ft and 4th, on a Fefs three Lions paffant, for OLDYSWORTH; 2d and 3d, four Lozenges in Bend, each charged with a Rofe.

Infra fepultus jacet JOHANNES
SCOTT, Scotus, plurimæ
Eruditionis & integritat's
Vir, 14 Annos hujus Ecclef.
Vicarius; uxorem duxit MARIAM,
EGIDII OLDISWORTH (de Burton fuper
Monte, in hoc Comitatu, Rectoris
Filiam) quam cum triplici Prole
deplorantem reliquit, & in
Cœlos migravit 18 die Julii,
1686.

ON FLAT STONES.

ON A VERY LARGE STONE ARE THE FIGURES, INLAID IN BRASS, OF A MAN, A WOMAN, AND FOUR CHILDREN, WITH THE FOLLOWING INSCRIPTION ROUND THE VERGE:

Oſt your Charitie pray for the Soule of
Walter Hichman here buryed, which
deceſſed the XXVIII Day of September, in
the IIII Yere of the Reign of kinge Henry
the VIII, Anno D'ni Millimo CCCCC
III°, and for the Soule of Chriſtyan his
Wyffe, which had togedder IIII Sonnes
viz. Thomas, John, Robert, and John, on
whoſe Soules, and all Xpen Soule, J'h'u dave
Mercy. Amen.

ON THREE COARSE STONES, INSCRIPTION ROUND THE VERGE:

EDWARDUS HITCHMAN, LL. BAC. PRÆB.
Wellenfis, hujus Ecclefiæ Anno XXIX
Vicarius, Vir probus ac vere Chriftianus.
Obiit in Domino XXI Aug. MDCLXXII,
ætat. LXII.

Arms; Barry of ten, on a Canton, the Arms of Ulfter, for THYNNE;—impaling, Sable, a Fefs Ermine between three Crefcents Or, for COVENTRY.

Here lyeth, expecting a happy Refurrection, the Body of Sir HENRY FREDERICKE THYNNE, Kt. and Bart. defcended in a right Line from GEOFFREY BOTEVILE, who came into England General of an Army of Poicteuins, to affift King JOHN againft his Barons. He was Son of Sir THOMAS THYNNE and Mrs. KATHARINE HOWARD, Grand-daughter of THOMAS Vifcount BINDON, and MARY, one of the Daughters of THOMAS Lord COVENTRY, Keeper of the Great Seale

of England, and by her had Iffue three Sonnes and two Daughters, all now living; viz. THOMAS, now Vifcount WEYMOUTH, JAMES, and HENRY-FREDERICKE; MARY, married to RICHARD HOWE, Efq. and KATHARINE to Sir JOHN LOWTHER, of Lowther, Bart. He was a Man of excellent Parts, great Loyalty to his Prince, a conftant Affertor of the Church of England in the worft of Times, kinde and obliging to his Family and Friends, and dyed March the 6, 1680, aged 66 Years and 5 Days.

The Memory of the Juft is bleffed!

Arms; Gules, a Chevron between three Heads erafed Or, for GODDARD.

JOHN PARKER, Gent.
died Sept. 27, 1697.

Arms; Gules, a Chevron vairè between three Crefcents Or, for GODDARD.

Here lyeth the mortal Part of
ROBERT GODDARD, Gent. only Son of
RICHARD GODDARD, Clerk, late Rector
of Caftle Eafton (who was Son of
EDWARD GODDARD, of Eaftwoodhay, Efq.)
He was a peaceable and hofpitable Neighbour,
charitable to the Poor, and an excellent Mafter.
He died Aug. 22, 1706 (without Iffue),
aged 63, much lamented by all that knew him.
This (as a grateful Acknowledgement to his
worthy Benefactor) is here placed by his
loving Nephew ALEXANDER READY, Gent.

Hic jacet
beatam Refurrectionem expectans
GEORGIUS GERRARD, Collegii Wadham,
olim Socius maxime fenior, & hujus
Ecclefiæ octodecim annos Vicarius
Vir (fiquis alius) probus, verecundus,
humilis, beneficus, pacis amans
in omnibus vere Chriftianus
qui febre intermittente
diu & animofe conflictatus eft;
aft viribus fenfim labantibus,
& ehu tandem abfumptis,
pie & placide (uti vixit) obiit
triceffimo die menfis Julii,
Anno Domini Milleffimo
feptingentefimo tricefimo quinto.

Here lyeth the Body of
THOMAS DRESSER, Vicar of
this Parifh, who deceafed
April 25, Anno Dom. 1714;
by him ANNA-MARIA
his Daughter.

In Memory of MARY,
the Wife of ROBERT
KING, who died
January the 15th, 1772,
aged 65 Years.

IN THE CHURCH YARD,   ON TOMBS.

HENRY PACKER,
of Horcutt, in this Parifh,
died May the 4th, 1748, aged 84 Years.

THOMAS PACKER, fenior,
died May 4, 1756, aged 79.

RICHARD PACKER
died December 22, 1746, aged 51.

THOMAS PACKER
died June 19, 1783, aged 73.

JANE his Wife
died Dec. 26, 1784, aged 76.

FRANCIS WILKES
died XXII March, 1634.

5

HENRY

HENRY PACKER and CATHARINE his Wife.
She was buried Jan. 16, 1719;
and he Aug. 27, 1727, in the 78th Year of
his Age.

JOHN their Son
died April 1, 1743, aged 55.

HENRY their Son
died March 16, 1743, aged 53.

SARAH his Wife
died March 24, 1767, aged 73.

			Aged
HENRY, THOMAS, JOHN, and ISAAC,	their Sons, died	March 23, 1724,	1.
		March 4, 1730,	3.
		June 26, 1732,	13.
		Jan. 14, 1734,	1.

ANNE, Wife of JAMES JENNER,
died October 13, 1743, aged 64.

MARY, Wife of JOSEPH DAGE,
died December 18, 1760, aged 49.

DOROTHY, Wife of JOHN ARKELL,
died December 25, 1780, aged 50.

THOMAS POPE, fenior,
died Oct. 24, 1759, aged 84.

ANN his Wife
died Jan. 11, 1767, aged 88.

HUMPHRY their Son
died Jan. 11, 1782, aged 76.

JOAN, Wife of THOMAS POPE, junior,
died Feb. 11, 1776, aged 56.

ON HEAD AND FLAT STONES.

	Died	Aged
Thomas Smith - -	22 Sept. 1745	59
Vincent Davis, fenior -	8 Apr. 1750	70
Elizabeth his Wife -	22 Oct. 1740	63
William Jacobs - -	30 Mar. 1764	74
Margaret his Wife -	3 Dec. 1745	57
Jeremiah Hewer, fenior -	4 Feb. 1729	63
Alice his Wife - -	30 July, 1735	72
Catharine their Daughter -	9 Oct. 1755	61
Jeremiah Hewer -	21 Oct. 1741	45
Robert Lack -	13 Nov. 1740	83
Rachael his Wife -	6 May, 1736	68
Leonard Cowling -	27 Sept. 1728	58
Elizabeth his Wife -	25 Dec. 1731	59
Leonard Cowling, fenior -	13 May, 1708	76
Catharine his Wife -	23 June, 1708	79
Eleanor their Daughter -	23 Sept. 1748	83
Anne, Daughter of Thomas and Anne Pope -	3 Jan. 1740	30
Edith Pope, Widow -	27 Oct. 1734	80
Elizabeth Humphris, Widow bur.	14 Feb. 1724	85
Walter Edwards -	17 Mar. 1697	—
Richard Kirby -	18 Apr. 1722	24
Elizabeth, Wife of Rowland Kirby	23 Mar. 1776	—
Thomas Smith -	22 Sept. 1745	59
William Smith -	11 Oct. 1774	53
Robert, Son of Thomas and Bridget Smith - -	11 Feb. 1737	25

	Died	Aged
Samuel Green -	3 May, 1784	83
Jane his Wife -	21 Oct. 1783	71
Sarah, Wife of William Brown, and Daghter of Samuel and Jane Green	8 Sept. 1768	24
Jane Brown their Daughter	15 July, 1767	3
Robert Godwin -	8 Aug. 1770	46
Elizabeth his Wife -	27 Apr. 1787	67
Margaret, Wife of William Jacobs	3 Dec. 1745	57
William Jacobs -	30 Mar. 1764	74
Sufannah, Wife of Cornelius Eyres	14 Nov. 1779	70
Robert King - -	10 Mar. 1767	52
John, Son of Robert and Rachael Lock - -	7 Oct. 1748	45
Walter Cowling -	24 Mar. 1693	25
Elizabeth, Daughter of Thomas and Margaret Cowling	20 Apr. 1696	—
Elizabeth, Wife of John Edwards	20 Oct. 1744	73
Elizabeth, Daughter of Robert Jenner	17 Jan. 1780	64
Robert Jenner - -	22 June, 1773	73
John Jenner - -	6 Mar. 1762	61
Joan, Wife of Francis Packer	3 May, 1719-20	39
Thomas Pope -	7 Feb. 1722	87
Francis Hewer -	23 Mar. 1789	82
George, Son of Rich. and Jane Penn	17 Oct. 1745	25
John, Son of W. and Martha Herbert	16 Dec. 1709	—
Heary, Son of John and Dorothy Arkell - -	20 Apr. 1777	4

CLIII. KINGSCOTE

CLIII.   K I N G S C O T E

IS a Parifh of the middle Extent, fituate in the Upper Divifion of the Hundred of *Berkeley*, five Miles diftant North-weft from *Tetbury*, five Eaft from *Wotton Underedge*, and fixteen South from Gloucester. In the Terrier 1300 Acres are defcribed of a light Stonebrafh Soil, chiefly in Tillage and Woodland; the Site of the Village is faid to be fome of the higheft Ground in that Divifion of the Country. There are feveral very deep Valleys, the Acclivities of which are covered with Groves of Beech.

The Living is a Portion of the Rectory of *Beverftone* annexed to it as a Chapelry, and the Chapel, dedicated to *St. John Baptift*, is not a very antient Structure, having a Nave only, and a low embattled Tower.

Mr. Smyth's Account of the Manor is fo accurate and minute, that we cannot hefitate to fubjoin it, as more authentic than that given by Sir R. Atkyns.

" *Kingefcote*, in *Domefdei* Booke written *Chingefcote*, wherein Will'm the Conqueror had, as that
" Booke fpeaketh, fower Hides of Land in Demefne, holden of George Lord Berkeley, as of his
" Manor of *Berkeley*, by Half a Knight's Fee, and Sute to his Hundred Court of *Berkeley*. A Manor
" whereof Anthony Kingscote, Efq. is Lord, confiftinge of 30 Families; in Reputation a Parifh, but
" *re vera*, a Chaple within the Parifh, and belonginge to the Mother Church of *Beverftone*, yet ufeth all
" ecclefiaftical Rights there which belonge to a Parifh.

" This Manor and Tithinge of *Kingefcote*, was, by Kinge H. II. in the firft Yeare of his Raigne, given
" to Robert, the Sonne of Hardinge, and his Heires, with many others, then Parcell of his Barony
" of *Berkeley*, whereof the faid Robert, was then, by that Grant, created a Baron of Parliament, and
" Peere of the Realme, according to the Manner of thofe Times.

" Shortly after which Grant the faid Lord Robert gave this *Kingefcote* to Nigell, the Sonne of
" Arthur, in Marryage with Aldena his Daughter, to hold of him by Halfe a Knight's Fee; which
" Guift, the faid Kinge Henry the Second, by his Deed confirmed; both which I have feene under
" Seale, with Mr. Anthony Kingescote, which Nigell made *Combe* the Jointure of the faid Aldena,
" as witnefleth another Deed with him.

" The faid Nigell and Aldena had Iffue betweene them, Adam and Robert; Adam had Iffue
" Richard, who, after his Father's Death, and his own full Age, died withoute Iffue, leavinge the faid
" Robert his Uncle to be his Heire, which Robert had Iffue Nigell and Richard, to which Ni-
" gell, and his Heires, Robert Lord Berkeley, the fecond of that Name, in the Time of Kinge
" R. I. by the Name of Robert de Berkeley, Sonne of Maurice, Sonne of Robert, Sonne of
" Hardinge, confirmed this Manor of *Kingefcote*, which (faith the Deede which I have feene) Robert
" his Grandfather gave to Nigell his Grandfather in Marryage with Aldena his Daughter, which
" Nigell afterwards died without Iffue, leavinge the faid Richard his Brother and Heire, which
" Richard had Iffue Nigell, who died in 12 E. II. and was Father of Will'm, Father of Nicholas,
" Father of Will'm, Father of John, who died in the Life-time of his Father, leavinge Iffue Will'm,
" who was Ward to Will'm Lord Berkeley, Father of Will'm, who died in 16 H. VIII. and was
" Father of Will'm, who died in 32 H. VIII. and was Father of Will'm, who died in 25 Eliz. Fa-
" ther of Christopher, who died in 5 Jac. and was Father of the faid Anthony, that nowe holdeth
" the A° 1639.

" I have alfo feene a Deed, whereby Maurice de Berkeley, the firft of that Name, in the latter
" End of the Reign of Kinge H. II. confirmed to Adam his Nephew, Sonne of Nigell, Sonne of
" Arthur, the Manor of *Kingefcote*, which Robert, the Sonne of Hardinge, his Father gave to the
" Father of the faid Adam, and to Aldena, Sifter of the him the faid Maurice, to hold of him by
" Half a Knight's Fee for all Services.

" Upon Exchanges of late Time made, by Christopher Kingescote, fome fmall Parts of this
" Manor are nowe the feverall Inheritances of Will'm Workeman, Richard Heaven, and others.
" It may be faid of this ancient Gentleman, and of his Family, as, doubtlefs, of noe other in this
" County, nor, I think, of many others in this Kingdome, that hee and his lineal Anceftors have con-
" tinued in this little Manor nowe aboute 500 Yeares, never attainted, nor dwellinge out of it elfewhere,
Vol. II.   K k   " nor

Robert Kingscote Esq?
LORD OF THIS MANOR
contributes this Plate.

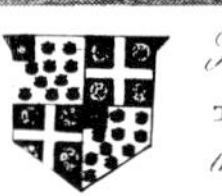

Cenotaph for the Family of
KINGSCOTE.

774

" nor hath the Tide of his Eftate higher or lower flowed or ebbed, in better or worfe Condition ; but,
" like a fixed Star in his Firmament, to have remained withoute Motion in this his little Orbe, withoute
" any remarkable Change ; and as to the Name of the firft Anceftor that is not perished, Ansgerus,
" it importeth that it is hereditary *Saxon.*

" By Patent Roll, 37 H. III. Barthol' de Owlepen, arr^d affifam vēfus Nigellum de Kingescote
" de communia pafture in *Kingefcote.*

" An ancient Booke of Knight's Fees, with the Lord Treafurer's Remembrancer, in the Exchequer,
" fol. 237, hath this : ' Ricardus de Kingescote tenet dimidium feodum in *Kingefcote,* de Thoma
" de Berkeley.''

" By Inquifition, in 14 E. I. after the Death of Anselm de Gurney, Lord of *Beverfton,* it is found
" that he died feized of a Yardland and of one Wood, pertaining to *Kingefcote,* holden of Richard
" de Kingescote, by the Yearely Rent of 12*d.*

" Freeholds in this Tything—Here is one Meffuage, called *Bares-court,* with 12 Acres of Land
" thereto belonginge, holden of the Kinge by Knight's Service *in capite* ; which Henry Lord Berke-
" ley, by Deed, d..ted 10 Junii, a° 9 r. Jacobi, granted to Will' Shipton, and his Heires, and was
" till that Time reputed Parcell of the faid Lord's Manor of *Wotten-forren,* and is nowe, 1639, the
" Inheritance of . . . . . . Here alfo certaine Lands, called *Redecrofts,* lying betweene the olde Leis
" and the Larder, containing . . . . Acres, nowe the Inheritance of . . . . purchafed of . . . .
" Thorpe, by Deed, which had continued in his Anceftors' Poffeffion from the Time of E. I. if not
" longer before, and then were the Lands of Thomas de Stone, and by Alice his Daughter and Co-
" heir, came to John Swonhunger, and foe to the Name of Thorpe, as there appears, and by other
" Deeds which I have feene without Date.

" Nigell of Kingescote gave " totam illam dimidiam virgatam terræ in territorio de *Hafilcote,*" to
" Alice his Daughter, and her Heires, rendringe a Rofe for all Services, " falvo regali fervicio," &c.
" which is Knight's Service ; one of which Deeds is to her in Taile, and are now in *Berkely* Caftle.

" By an Inquifition, 5° Jacobi, Leonard Lockier is found to die feized in a Fee, of a Meffuage
" and 15 Acres of Land, and 7 Acres of Pafture, in *Kingefcote,* holden of Christopher Kingescote,
" of *Kingefcote,* Efq. by the 40th Part of a Knight's Fee, and that John Lockier was his Sonne and
" Heire, 4 Yeares old, whofe Wardfhip the faid Christopher had ; and, after full Age, fold his faid
" Lands to Anthony Kingscote aforefaid, Sonne and Heire of the faid Christopher, whereby the
" Menalty being deftroyed, the faid Meffuage and Lands, came to be holden immediately of the faid
" George Lord Berkeley, as the reft of that Manor is.

" Will'us D'us de Kingscote, by Deed, 5 E. III. releafed for that Yeare to the Abbot of *Kingef-*
" *wood,* unam faldam ducentas ovium quas tenebatur invenire fuper terras per D'um Will'm de campo
" de *Kingefcote.*''

Anthony Kingscote, Efq. the laft mentioned, died in 1665, leaving Abraham Kingscote, Efq.
his Son and Heir, and who, upon his Deceafe in 1670, was fucceeded by William Kingscote, Efq.
the Great-grandfather of the prefent Proprietor, who is the twenty-third in lineal Defcent from the original Grantee of this Manor. Nigel Kingscote, Efq. died in 1773, without Iffue, and bequeathed
this, and other Eftates, to Robert, the eldeft Son of Robert-Fitzharding Kingscote, his only
Brother.

To the antient Manor-houfe and Refidence of this Family confiderable Additions have been lately
made, with much Judgement ; the adjacent Scenery is picturefque, and improved by Art, commanding
a very interefting Profpect.

Of *Roman* Antiquities, feveral Specimens have been difcovered by Ploughmen in a large Field, called
the *Cheftles,* probably a corrupted Word, which may prove it to be the Site of Military Tranfactions. Befides Coins of the Lower Empire, the *Tefferæ* of the Pavement of a Pretorian Tent, a large Statue of
Stone, with many *Fibulæ* and Beads of Glafs, have been formerly found ; but this is a Tradition only,
for it is not known whether they were preferved in any Collection. The Outpofts are fo frequent upon
the lower Range of the *Cotefwold* Hills, and have fo little Variety, as to Form or Veftiges difcovered, that
they fall under one general Defcription.

Three Hamlets, or Places, are fpecified within the Limits of this Parifh ; *Binley, Hazlecote,* and
Hunter's Hall ; the latter of which is a commodious Inn, upon the great Road from *Gloucefter* to *Bath.*

B E N E F A C T I O N.

Given for the Ufe of the Poor of *Kingscote,* Land, the yearly Produce of which is 2*l.* but by whom,
or when, is unknown.

4   The

The Lift of INCUMBENTS are given in *B E V E R S T O N E.*

PRESENT LORD OF THE MANOR,
ROBERT KINGSCOTE, Efq.

The only Perfon fummoned from this Parifh by the Heralds in 1682 and 1683 was
William Kingfcote, Efq.

At the Election in 1776, Two Freeholders polled from this Parifh.

The Regifter commences with the Date 1651.

ANNUAL ACCOUNT OF MARRIAGES, BIRTHS, AND BURIALS, IN THIS PARISH.

A.D.	Mar.	Bir.	Bur.	A.D.	Mar.	Bir.	Bur.	A.D.	Mar.	Bir.	Bur.	A.D.	Mar.	Bir.	Bur.
1781	—	8	4	1786	2	14	2	1791				1796			
1782	1	9	3	1787	1	7	4	1792				1797			
1783	1	11	2	1788	1	15	3	1793				1798			
1784	—	13	—	1789	2	9	7	1794				1799			
1785	2	7	6	1790	2	17	2	1795				1800			

IN THE CHURCH-YARD, ON TOMBS.

Arms ; Argent, ten Efcallops Sable, on a Canton Gules, a Mullet pierced Or, for KINGSCOTE.

HERE LYETH THE BODY OF ANTHONY KINGSCOTE, OF KINGSCOTE, ESQ. WHO FELL ASLEEP IN THE LORD ON THE 29TH OF AUGUST, IN THE YEARE OF CHRIST 1654, WHO LIVED AND DIED IN A LIVING HOPE OF A BLESSED RESURRECTION TO ETERNAL LIFE THROUGH JESUS CHRIST.

HERE LYETH THE BODY OF TROYLUS KINGSCOTE, GENT. WHO DID SERVICE AS A COMMANDER FOR THE PRINCE OF ORANGE, 40 YEARS, AND BEING 80 YEARS OLD, ENDED THIS LIFE UPON THE 10 DAY OF SEPTEMBER, A. D. 1656.

ON FLAT STONES.

HERE RESTETH THE BONES OF ALLIDAY, THE WIFE OF TROYLUS KINGSCOTE, GENT. WHO DEPARTED THIS LIFE THE 17 DAY OF AUGUST, ANNO DOMINI 1662.

KATHERINE, THE WIFE OF ANTHONY KINGSCOTE, ESQ. DECEASED THE 2 DAY OF DECEMBER, 1665.

ON A BRASS PLATE :
HERE LYETH THE BODY OF ANNE KINGSCOTE, THE 4TH DAUGHTER OF ANTHONY AND KATHERINE KINGSCOTE, WHO ENDED THIS LIFE UPON THE 9TH

DAY OF NOVEMBER, IN THE YEAR OF CHRIST 1657.

ON A TRIANGULAR PYRAMIDAL MONUMENT :

Arms ; Argent, ten Efcallops Sable, on a Canton Gules a Mullet pierced Or, for KINGSCOTE.

NIGELLUS DE KINGSCOTE, ARTHURI ab antiquis Britannis orti filius, ALDEVAM ROBERTI FITZHARDING Natam duxit uxorem.
Hujus ROBERTI Danorum Rex, avus erat Évaque GULIELMI illius Normanni Neptis, uxor.
Sedem Kingfcotienfem cum manerio Hic NIGELLUS cum ALDEVA illâ Dotem
Terram de Comba
(Meritorum in MATILDAM Imperatricem gratià)
Donatam accepit :
Hanc fedem tum ipfe tum pofteri Ornarunt vivi ;
Mortuos autem (maximâ ex parte) Ecclefia hæc cum cœmeterio fervat.
ANTONIUS KINGSCOTE (Ar.) primus (Ne majorum cineres violaret)
Hoc cœmeterium defignavit locum, Quo fe et fuos
ABR'UM fcil. filium & WILL'UM nepotem Sepeliendos fore voluit.
Domus hujus non pauci
Arma geftarunt nec inglorii,
Hoc Pictonum & Agincortii arva,
Hic idem MAURITIUS AURASINIS Princeps teftati funt ;
Omnes ad unum
Contra quamcunque Tyrannidis fpeciem, Tam in facris, quam in civilibus, Strenue & femper certaverunt.

GULIELMUS KINGSCOTE (Ar.) (Ab ARTHURO vicefimus primus Muneribus magiftratus, amici, patris fumma cum laude functus)
Obiit
Omnibus nifi fibi immature Menfe Octobris,
Anno { D'ni MDCCVI. / ætatis XL.

Huic genitus
Vir cariffimus, quibus notus fuit, GULIELMUS deceffit
Anno Domini 1731,
Ætatis 41.

Poft patrem
Ad hanc proerabaut fedem
ANTONIUS
Annum agens viceffimum,
Et HENRICUS
Qui undeviceffimum nondum compleret
Anno Dom.
1740.
1746.
De quibus merito tradendum,
Quod illorum fpes maxima fuit omnibus,
Adeo profecerunt,
Hic prudentiâ juris civilis,
Ille quippe fatellitum præfectus
Rebus militaribus.

Here lieth the Body of MARY, the Wife of NATHANIEL CAMBRIDGE, and eldeft Daughter of ANTHONY KINGSCOTE, of Kingfcote, Efq. who, on the 10 Day of . . . . 1692, ended this mortal Life.

ON A TOMB :
ABRAHAM KINGSCOTE, OF KINGSCOTE, WHOSE BODY LYES HERE DIED JUNE THE 28, A. D. 1670.

ON FLAT STONES.

In Memory of Mrs. JOAN KINGSCOTE, Relict of ABRAHAM KINGSCOTE, of Kingfcote, Efq. who died the 2d Day of Auguft, 1717.

And alfo of WILLIAM KINGSCOTE, their Great-grandchild, who was born and died in October following.

ABRAHAM an Infant, and next Brother to WILLIAM, lyes buried in London.

Here lieth the Body of NIGEL KINGSCOTE, of Kingfcote, who departed this Life on the 28th of June, A. D. 1773, aged 53 Years.
In Memory of MARY, Daughter of ROBERT and MARY KINGSCOTE, who died Jan. 29, 1786, aged 29 Years.

On

ON A MARBLE MONUMENT IN THE CHURCH:

In Memory
of THOMAS CREED,
of this Parish,
who died March 14, 1789,
aged 73 Years.
This Monument was erected
by his two youngest Sons,
JOHN WORLOCK CREED
and WILLIAM CREED,
in grateful Remembrance of
their affectionate Father.

ON TOMBS.

HEARE LYETH THE BODY OF JOHN WIGHT, WHO DEPARTED THIS LIFE THE 22 DAY OF SEPTEMB. 1651.

Here lyeth the Body
of WILLIAM WIGHT, senior, of this
Parish, Yeoman, who departed
this Life the 1st Day of February,
1706.

In Memory of
BETTY PAIN, Daughter
of JOHN and ELIZABETH WIGHT.
She departed this Life November
the 1st, 1775, aged 29 Years.

In Memory of
JOHN WIGHT, Yeoman,
who died March 17, 1732, aged
76 Years.

In Memory of
WILLIAM WIGHT, Yeoman,
[who died February 18, 1742,
aged 85 Years.

HEARE LYETH THE BODY OF EDMOND BALL, WHO DEPARTED THE .. DAY OF APRIL, IN THE YEARE 1662.

In Memory of RICHARD BALL, of
this Parish, Yeoman, who died the 6
of February, 1728, ætatis suæ 88.

Also of MARY his Wife
who died the .. Day of August, 1726,
ætatis 71.

In Memory of
RICHARD, the Son of
RICHARD BALL, who died
May the 25th, 1710.

In Memory of
EDMUND BALL,
who died August the 2d,
1761, aged 74.

In Memory of ROBERT HOPKINS,
who died April 10, 1767,
aged 69 Years.

In Memory of
JEREMIAH HOPKINS,
of this Parish, Yeoman,
who died July 6, 1775,
aged 73.

SUSANNAH, the Wife of
JEREMIAH HOPKINS,
died Mar. 12, 1766,
aged 72 Years.

Here lyeth the Body of WILLIAM
HOLBROW, senior, who departed this
Life the 2d Day of April,
in 1688, aged 83.

In Memory of
JOHN HOLBROW, of this Parish, Yeoman,
and MARY his Wife.
She died the 25th of March,
in the 75th Year of her Age;
and he the 20th of August,
in the 85th Year of his Age,
1729.

Near this Place lyeth the Body
of JOHN CLARK, Yeoman, of the
Parish of Newington Bagpath,
who died July the 30th, 1735.

Here lyeth the Body of DANIEL
WELLSTEED, of this Parish, who departed this Life the 11th Day of Sept.
1709, in the 75th Year of his Age.

Under this Tomb lie the
Remains of WILLIAM HATHAWAY,
late of this Parish, Blacksmith,
who died Dec. 30, 1775, aged 75.

Also of BEATE his Wife,
who died Sept. 1, 1737, aged 33.

In Memory of
ROBERT BROOKS,
Yeoman, who died Dec.
the 2, 1749, aged 60 Years.

Also of HESTER his Wife,
who died Nov. 2, 1766,
aged 77 Years.

In Memory of MARY,
Daughter of THOMAS
and MARY BROOKS, of
this Parish, who died July 26,
1760, aged 18 Years.

In Memory of THOMAS,
the Son of ROBERT and
HESTER BROOKS, who departed
this Life April 26, 1762,
aged 52 Years.

Also of MARY his Wife,
who departed this Life
April 7, 1771,
aged 67 Years.

In Memory of
WALLIS BROOKS, who
died May the 6, 1768,
aged 35 Years.

ON FLAT STONES.

In Memory of
SARAH, the Wife of THOMAS
NEWMAN, of this Parish, who
died Jan. 14, 1780, in the
26th Year of her Age.

In Memory of
THOMAS HATHAWAY, of
this Parish, who departed this Life
April the 21st, 1716. Also of THOMAS
his Son, who died Oct. 31, 1777,
in the 72d Year of his Age.

ON HEAD STONES.

	Died	Aged		Died	Aged
Elizabeth, Wife of John Wight	7 Mar. 1764	47	Sarah, Wife of Thomas Ball	5 June, 1757	45
Ann, Wife of John White	20 Mar. 1750	49	Joan, Wife of John Shrieve	10 Apr. 1738	39
John Wight	30 Apr. 1756	89	Thomas Faux	9 Nov. 1762	79
Mary his Wife	20 Mar. 1770	95	John Faux	7 Jan. 1760	80
Robert, Son of Robert and Mary Hopkins	12 Aug. 1760	27	Hannah his Wife	4 Apr. 1745	71
Hester their Daughter	30 Apr. 1766	25	Daniel, Son of Richard Browne	13 June, 1729	24
Ann their Daughter, Wife of Daniel Dangerfield	28 Nov. 1766	28	Richard Browne	28 Nov. 1706	72
			Jane his Wife	7 Oct. 1739	81
Martha, Wife of Thomas Hopkins, Daughter of James Habgood	16 Oct. 1780	28	Thomas, Son of William and Mary Morse	30 Apr. 1773	19
John Creed	10 May, 1749	43	Susannah, Wife of William Shipway	1 Apr. 1781	24
Katharine, Wife of Thomas Creed	25 June, 1748	24	William Putly	25 Sept. 1728	53
William Ball	4 Dec. 1752	82	Robert Hopkins	8 Mar. 1713	—
Hannah his Wife	15 Jan. 1739	63	Joseph Sparks	18 Mar. 1767	82
			Ann his Wife	15 Nov. 1759	61

CLIV.

CLIV. K I N G S W O O D.

THERE are few Counties in *England* from which certain Parishes or Hamlets are not detached and insulated by others. *Kingswood*, although in the Hundred of *Chippenham* and County of *Wilts*, was included in the See of *Gloucester* at the Time of its Establishment by HENRY VIII. and we therefore follow Sir R. ATKYNS, in giving a Description of it.

The Parish contains about 3000 Acres, of a deep rich Soil, of which not fifty are tilled ; and is distant five Miles from *Wickwar*, two from *Wotton Underedge*, and twenty from GLOUCESTER.

Domesday does not recite this Place under the Title of " Terra Regis," nor amongst the Lands of ROGER DE BERKELEY in *Wiltshire*, neither was it surveyed with the adjacent Parishes in this County *.

The Abbey of *Kingswood* was founded by WILLIAM DE BERKELEY, Lord of *Dursley*, in 1139, and made dependent upon the *Cistertian* Monastery at *Tinterne*, co. *Monmouth*. Their Establishment was in early Times much interrupted by vexatious Law Suits ; for, having purchased *Haseldene*, in the Parish of *Rodmarton*, of JOHN DE ST. JOHN, which, though granted to him by King STEPHEN during the Civil Wars, was the real Property of REGINALD DE ST. WALERICK, he refused to allow their Claim, unless they would consent to remove their Convent from *Kingswood* to *Hasyldene* †.

On account of many Inconveniences which they found there, they were again removed to *Tetbury* ; and lastly, upon the Remonstrance of ROGER DE BERKELEY, the Heir of the Founder, firmly established at *Kingswood*, and the Patronage taken from the Abbey of *Tinterne*, after 28 Years quiet Possession.

A B B O T S   O F   *K I N G S W O O D.*

1318 Richard.	1415 Walter Dering.	1503 John Sodbury.
1351 Nicholas Hayle.	1446 John Woodland.	1511 Robert Woolaston.
1369 Richard Hampton.	1468 Thomas Reade.	1532 William Bendlowe.

It does not appear that they had pontifical Privileges, or were ever summoned to Parliament.

At the Dissolution, the Abbey was surrendered by WILLIAM BENDLOWE, Abbot, and thirteen Monks, and, it is presumed, that their Number was seldom greater ‡. Various Accounts are given of the Value of their Endowment §. In 1560, the Site and Demesnes were granted from the Court of Augmentations to Sir JOHN THYNNE, Knight, from whom it passed to the Family of SMYTH, of *Nibley*, and from them to the MITCHELLS' early in this Century. Of the Family of KNOWLES, it has been purchased by JOHN BLAGDEN HALE, Esq.

There are considerable Remains of the Conventual Building now divided into several Tenements. The Abbots' Lodgings appear to be the most perfect, which are accurately given in a very elegant

* WYNDHAM's *Wiltshire Domesday* Book. *Gloucestershire Domesday* Book.

† TANNER, Not. Mon. *Wilts*, N° XX. DUGDALE's Mon. Ang. vol. I. p. 811. LELAND's Collectanea, vol. I. pp. 31, 65, 104.
Ex Libro Donationum Monaster. de *Kingeswood :*
GUL. DE BARKELEY dedit Abbatiæ de *Tinterne Kinggeswood* ad fundandam ibi Abbatiam. Illi de *Kingeswood* emerunt *Haseldene* à Domino de S. JOANNE, cui rex hanc terram tempore hostilitatis. Nam erat REGINALDI DE S. WALERICO. REGINALDUS DE S. WALERICO suis restitutus terris abegit monachos de *Haseldene*. Postea autem recepit eos & pars major conventus de *Kinggeswood* translata est ad *Haselden*. Postea propter aquæ penuriam REG. DE S. WALERICO transtulit eos ab *Haselden* ad *Tettebyri*. ROGERUS BARKELEY, filius GUL. BARKELEY, conabatur aut reducere monachos de *Tettebyri* ad *Kingeswood*, aut *Kingeswood* eis auferre tanquam suum fundum. BARNARDUS DE S. WALERICO fundator ecclesiæ de *Tettebyri* emit *Mireford* prope *Kingeswood* à ROGERO BERKELEY, & eo quia *Tettebyri* ligni copia carebat, monachos transtulit. REG. BARKELEY dedit manerium suum de ACHOLTE monaster. S. *Mariæ* de *Kingeswood*. HENRICUS LOVEL testis. ROBERTUS DE BERKELEY filius ROBERTI DE BERKELEY. PHILLIPPUS & OLIVARIUS, fratres ROBERTI Junioris. Testis ROGERUS comes HEREFORD.
HAWISIA, uxor D'ni de VEEL. NICOLAUS KINGESTON, Miles.
Charta MATILDIS DE VEEL, uxoris GAUFRIDI DE VEEL. ROBERTUS DE VEEL, filius GAUFRIDI.
GAUFRIDE DE WROKESHAL, Miles. JOANNES CHANSY, Miles. PETRUS DE VEEL, Miles. JOANNES DE WELLINGTON, Miles. THOMAS DE VEEL, Miles, filius PETRI. GUL. DE BRADELEGA, *Duddelegh* pratum. Manerium de *Hakesbyri*. Manerium de *Acholte*, alias *Kingeswood*. THOMAS DE S. WALERICO, BERNARDI filius. ROBERTUS DE LA MARE.
LELAND, Itin. vol. VI. p. 44.

‡ WILL. BOWDELEY, alias BENDELEY, last Abbot, surrendered his Abbey with thirteen Monks, Feb. 1, 1539, and had a Pension of 50l. a Year assigned him. WILLIS, Hist. Mitred Abbeys, vol. II. p. 86.
Pensions assigned to the Religious at the Surrender—WILL. BENDLOWE, Abbat, 50l. REDING, Prior, 6l. 13s. 4d. JOHN WESTBURY, JOHN SETHAM, WILL. WOTTON, 4l. 6s. 8d. each. WILL. HUGHES, JOHN SODBURY, NIC. HAMPTON, WILL. PARKER, EDW. ERMINGHAM, THO. ORCHARD, 4l. each. JOHN STANLEY, Novice, NIC. ACTON, Cellerer. 4l. 13s. 4d. each.
Ib. App. p. 10.

§ In Libro Nigro Scaccarii, p. 166 de *Kingeswoda* tent. DE ROGERO DE BERKELEY.
In Bishop KENNET's Parochial Antiquities, &c. pp. 113, 126, of the Monks removing to *Haselden*, and returning to *Kingswood*. Registrum Abbatiæ de *Kingswood* penes JOANNEM SMITH, de *Nibley*, in com. *Glocestr.* arm. 1651. Cart. 11 H. III. p. 1. n. 109. pro maner. de *Acholt*, ex donatione ROGERI DE BERKLE, Plac. in com. *Glocestr.* 53 H. III. rot. 9. d. pro 2 partibus maner. de *Chelesworth*.
Pat. 3 E. I. m. 34. d. pro comun. pastur. in *Tettebury*. Pat. 3 E. II. m. 19. de mess. & terris in *Hull, Berkele, Rochampton*, &c. Pat. 5 E. II. p. 1. m. 13. pro terris in *Culkerton*.
It was rated. 26 HEN. VIII. at 244l. 11s. 2d. per ann. DUGD. 254l. 11s. 2d. SPEED. 239l. 19s. 7d. ob. q. clare. 2 l. 5s. 1cd. summa totalis, MS. valor. TANNER, Not. Mon.

Work *. From the Diftance of fome of the Ruins, the Site of the Abbey muft have been extenfive, though the Materials of the greater Part were difperfed and fold.

The Faculty for re-building the prefent Church, dedicated to *St. Mary*, was granted in 1719, in which it is ftated, that it fhould be erected upon the Site of the conventual Church, then much decayed. It was completed in 1723, and confifts of a Nave only without a Tower. In the Chancel Window are the Arms of the Founders, preferved from the Abbey.

The Benefice is a perpetual Curacy in the Deanery of *Durfley*, endowed with a yearly Payment of 26*l.* 16*s.* from the Eftates in the Parifh in due Proportion, by virtue of a Decree in the Court of Exchequer; and the Right of nominating the Curate is vefted in the Inhabitants.

The Clothing Manufacture has been long eftablifhed at *Kingswood*, which is a large and populous Village; but the Houfes are very irregularly placed. Principal Eftates are now held by the Families of TYLER (by Inheritance from the WEBBS), PARTRIDGE, POPE, TROTMAN, OSBORNE, and JONES.

The Foreft of *Kingswood* is a very large Tract extending to the Gates of the City of *Briftol*. The Office of Keeper was antiently annexed to the Conftablefhip of *Briftol Caftle*; but the whole is now difafforefted, and belongs to various Proprietors †.

B E N E F A C T I O N S.

Mr. JOSIAH SHEPPARD, of *London*, gave 800*l.* for the Purchafe of Lands, the neat yearly Income thereof to be equally divided on New Year's Day yearly, between ten poor Houfekeepers of this Parifh, not receiving Alms, to buy them Coats or Firing. He likewife gave 500*l.* for the Purchafe of Lands, the neat Produce of which to be diftributed weekly amongft the Poor of this Parifh, in Six-penny Bread.

JOHN MAYO, of *Bayford*, in the County of *Hertford*, Efq. gave the Free-fchool to this Parifh (being the Place of of his Birth) to educate the Poor Children of this Parifh in the Proteftant Religion, and to teach them to read and write.

ROBERT WEBB, of *Wotton Underedge*, Gent. gave to this Parifh, out of Land, called *The Grange*, 13*l.* a Year for ever, fome Part of it to be given to the Poor in Bread every Sunday to twenty-four Houfekeepers; and 2*l.* to forty poor Houfekeepers upon *St. Thomas's* Day; the Remainder for a Dinner for the Officers at giving up their Accompts.

Mr. BEN. BIDDLE, of *London*, gave to this Parifh 400*l.* for purchafing of Land, and the Income of it to be given in Bread on Sundays to poor Houfekeepers of the Communion of the Church of *England* having no Collection, at the Difcretion of the Minifter and Churchwardens.

Mr. ROBERT DRIVER, of *Woodford*, gave certain Lands in the Parifh of *Berkeley* to this Parifh, the Income of which is to be difpofed of as follows: 1*l.* a Year to the Truftee over it, 6*s.* every firft Thurfday in the Month for a Sermon. The reft to be given in Bread to poor Houfekeepers not having Collection.

Mrs. MARY BLAGDEN gave a Velvet Pulpit Cloth and Cufhion, for the Ufe of the Church, 1723. At her Death fhe gave 50*l.* for the purchafing Land, the Income of which is to be given in Bread to poor People at Chriftmas. Likewife 20*l.* for the purchafing Land, out of which 10*s.* is to be given to the Minifter yearly for a Sermon on Good Friday, and the Reft to be given in Bread to poor Widows not having Collection, at the Direction of JOHN BLAGDEN during his Life, and afterwards by the Minifter and Churchwardens.

RICHARD BLINCO, of *Briftol*, gave the Branch; SARAH his Wife the Sockets, for the Ufe of the Church.

THOMAS BLAGDEN, late of *Wotton Underedge*, Clothier, bequeathed 60*l.* to this Parifh, to be laid out for a Cloth and Plate for the Communion Table of this Church; and alfo 30*l.* to be immediately diftributed amongft the poor Houfekeepers of this Parifh; and 100*l.* more to the Poor of this Parifh, at the Deceafe of his Widow, to be diftributed at the Difcretion of his Executor RICHARD OSBORN, of *Wortley*, or his Heirs.

The prefent Curate is THOMAS THOMAS, Clerk, elected in 1777.

PRESENT LORD OF THE MANOR, JOHN BLAGDEN HALE, Efq.

The firft Date of the Regifter occurs in 1709.

ANNUAL ACCOUNT OF MARRIAGES, BIRTHS, AND BURIALS, IN THIS PARISH.

A.D.	Mar.	Bir.	Bur.	A.D.	Mar.	Bir.	Bur.	A.D.	Mar.	Bir.	Bur.	A.D.	Mar.	Bir.	Bur.
1781	7	19	24	1786	14	18	12	1791	7	22	19	1796			
1782	4	19	15	1787	6	28	15	1792				1797			
1783	3	17	13	1788	6	18	14	1793				1798			
1784	6	15	7	1789	5	22	22	1794				1799			
1785	2	9	11	1790	7	22	13	1795				1800			

* Etchings of Views and Antiquities in the County of *Gloucefter*, Plate XII. the Gateway of *Kingswood* Abbey. Sir ROBERT ATKYNS, in his Hiftory of *Gloucefterfhire*, p. 493, fpeaking of this Abbey, fays, " The Gatehoufe is ftill to be feen, and a confiderable Part of the Abbey is yet ftanding, but divided into feveral Tenements. There is carved, and ftill remaining over the Kitchen Chimney of the Abbey, a Tyger, an Hart, an Oftridge, a Mermaid, an Afs, and a Swan; the firft Letters of which Creatures fpell THOMAS, the Name of the Lord BERKELEY, who was a confiderable Benefactor, and Patron to that Foundation." This was probably THOMAS Lord BERKELEY, who died 35 E. III. and was a great Benefactor to many religious Houfes; as the Building, from the Style of its Architecture, appears to have been built about that Time. Over the Gateway is a very elegant Window, the Jamb of which is formed by a Lily in a Flower pot carved in Stone, and the Gable End over it is terminated by a Figure of the Crucifixion. Over the Gateway is a Room, the Cieling of which is elegantly ornamented. The Walls have been painted with Figures, a few Fragments of which ftill remain. This Room is now employed by a Clothier in fome Part of his Manufactory.

† Perambulation of the Foreft of *Kingswood*, temp. ELIZ. MSS SMYTH. Writ of Infpeximus, dat 1572.

INSCRIPTIONS

INSCRIPTIONS IN THE CHURCH.

ON A MONUMENT:

Arms; Or, on a Bend Sable, three
Efcallops Argent, for WEBB.

In Memory of his dear Father
THOMAS WEBB,
late of Kingfwood,
Son of RICHARD WEBB, of Wotton
Underedge, Gent.
who died May 24, 1674,
aged 84.
His obfequious Son RICHARD WEBB fet
up this Monument;
and
in Memory of
his vertuous Mother

PERSIS, the Daughter of
ANTHONY WEBB,
who died 15 Years before,
viz. April 17, 1659.

ON FLAT STONES.

To the Memory of
WILLIAM TANNER, jun.
of this Parifh, Clothier;
and of ANNE his Wife.
He died Oct. 30, 1725, aged 43 Years.
She Aug. 28, 1718, aged 27 Years.

Alfo of MARY their Daughter,
who died July 2, 1719, aged 11 Months.

And alfo of MARY, the Wife
of THOMAS TANNER,
of this Parifh, Clothier,
who died June 16, 1750, aged 42 Years.

Alfo two of their Children,
who died, WILLIAM June 7, 1739,
aged 3 Weeks and 3 Days;
MARY Jan. 31, 1747, aged
2 Years and 9 Months.

ELIZABETH WHITE
died March 7, 1768,
aged 77 Years.

IN THE CHURCH YARD.

AGAINST THE CHURCH.

SOUTH SIDE.

To the Memory of HESTER,
Daughter of ROBERT GAINER,
who died March 9, 1760,
aged 50 Years.

Alfo of BETTY, Daughter of ROBERT
and HESTER GAINER, who died April
27, 1760, aged near 25 Years.

In Memory of WILLIAM ELSLEY,
who died April 17, 1764,
aged 51 Years.

EAST END.

In Memory of AMBROSE LEWIS,
who died June 4, 1754, aged 76 Years.

And of ANNE his Wife,
who died June 23, 1755, aged 81 Years.

Alfo of WILLIAM their Son,
who was buried near this Place.

And alfo of ELIZABETH and REBECCA,
their Daughters, who was buried here.

Near
this Place lieth
the Body of MARTHA,
Wife of THOMAS ENGLAND,
who was buried Nov. 22,
1741, aged 58 Years.

Likewife the faid THOMAS ENGLAND,
Clark of this Parifh. He was buried
May 3, 1748, aged 75 Years.

Alfo WILLIAM and HANNAH,
Children of the faid THOMAS ENGLAND,
were buried,
WILLIAM, Dec. 30, 1729, aged 23;
HANNAH, Aug. 14, 1730, aged 5.

Alfo of SARAH, Wife of JOEL ENGLAND,
who died Feb. 23, 1761, aged 48.

Likewife the faid JOEL ENGLAND,
Clerk of this Parifh, died April 6,
1764, in the 43 Year
of his Age.

Near
this Place was
interred the Body of
SARAH, Wife of THOMAS ENGLAND, jun.
who was buried Dec. 30, 1741, aged 42.

And JOHN his Son was buried
Oct. 27, 1736, in the 2d Year of his Age.

And alfo SARAH, Daughter of
THOMAS and SARAH ENGLAND, died
July 11, 1754, aged 22 Years.

In Memory
of THOMAS CHARD,
of this Parifh, Clothier,
who departed this Life Feb. 1,
1738, aged 51 Years.

Alfo of JOHN his Son, of this Place,
Baker, who departed this Life
the 28 April, 1747,
aged 25.

Alfo MARY, Daughter of the faid
THOMAS CHARD, and Wife of
WILLIAM BAMFORD,
of Tetbury, Woolftapler,
died June the 12, 1762, aged 37.

Alfo HESTER, Wife of the abovefaid
THOMAS CHARD,
who died Auguft 9,
1770, aged 77 Years.

ON TOMBS.

Here lieth the Body of
THOMAS LEWIS, of this Parifh, Gent.
who departed this Life this 5 Day
of April, 1745,
in the 59 Year of his Age.

In hopes of a joyful
Refurrection, here
refteth the Body of
ELIZABETH, the Wife of
THOMAS LEWIS, of this
Parifh, who departed this
Life June 23, 1736,
in the 44 Year of her Age.
And of REBECCA, Widow of
JOHN RUSSELL,
Daughter of RICHARD LEWIS
the elder, who departed this Life
Aug. . . . 1757, aged 75.

Here lyeth the Body of ELIZABETH,
the Wife of RICHARD LEWIS, who
was buried May 26, 1704.

Alfo here lyeth the Body of
ELIZABETH NAPP their Grand-daughter,
who was buried March 20,
1700.

In Memory of
CHARLES GALE, of this Parifh,
Clothier, who was buried April 12,
1736, in the 61 Year of his Age.

Alfo of SARAH, PRUDENCE, and
MARY, his Wives,
who were buried,
SARAH, Sept. 16, 1714, aged 29;
PRUDENCE, July 23, 1719, aged 33;
MARY, May 7, 1737, aged 43.

Here refteth the Body of ROBERT
ITHELL, fenior, of the Parifh of
Charfield, who died the 13 of April,
1727, aged 58 Years.

To the Memory of
JOHN COUNSELL,
of this Parifh, Clothier,
who died Oct. 10, 1699, aged 45 Years.

Alfo of THOMAS COUNSELL, Clothier,
who died Aug. 20, 1739, aged 57.

Alfo of HESTER his Wife,
who died Sept. 7, 1749, aged 59.

This Tomb was
erected to the Memory
of JAMES COUNSELL,
of this Parifh, Clothier,
Son of THOMAS and HESTER COUNSELL,
who died Feb. 16, 1768,
aged 54 Years.

Alfo of REBEKAH his Wife,
who died Feb. 6, 1768,
aged 47 Years.

This Tomb was
erected to the Memory
of SAMUEL COUNSELL,
of this Parifh, Clothier,
who died Nov. 17, 1766,
aged 42 Years.

In Memory of
DANIEL MORTON,
of this Parifh, and of HESTER
his Wife.
He died Oct. 3, 1726, aged 48 Years.
She died Jan. 6, 1730, aged 48 Years.

WILLIAM their Son died, 1726,
an Infant.

MARGARET, the Wife of
DANIEL MORTON, fen.
died Jan. 3, 1767, aged 63 Years.

Here

Here lieth the Body
of ROBERT BLISSON,
of this Parish, Clothier,
who departed this Life
March 20, 1747,
aged 77.

Also of MARY his Wife,
who died May 20, 1731,
aged 79 Years.

In Memory of
RICHARD GODSELL, Clothier,
who was buried May 10, 1720, aged 56.

MARGARET his Wife was buried
Oct. 24, 1737, aged 69.

Also JOHN COLE was buried here
Oct. 20, 1742, aged 22 Years.

In Memory of
RICHARD GODSELL, jun.
of this Parish, Clothier,
who died June 5, 1770, aged 72 Years.

ELIZABETH, Wife of
RICHARD GODSELL, jun.
died Jan. 29, 1768,
aged 66 Years.

Here resteth the Body of WILLIAM
TANNER, sen. Clothier, who departed
this Life Nov. 27, 1729, in the
85 Year of his Age.

And MARY his Wife, who departed
this Life Nov. 5, 1728, aged 74.

Also under this Tomb lie the Remains
of JOHN, the Son of WILLIAM and
MARY TANNER, who departed this Life
Oct. 30, 1759, aged 58 Years.

Under, and near this Tomb was
interred the Bodies of MARY,
the Wife of NATHANIEL TANNER,
of this Parish, the 15th Day of
September, 1711, aged 57,
and several of their Children.

Under this Tomb is interred the Body
of NATHANIEL COPE, senior,
Clothier and Craper,
who departed this Life the 2d Day of
November, 1735, aged 83 Years.

Near this Tomb lieth the Body
of ELIZABETH, the Wife of JONATHAN
COPE, Daughter of M. STEPHEN
COLLIER, Rector of Rodmarton,
She died Dec. the 27th, 1747,
aged 60 Years.

In Memory of
JOHN FOWLES, of this Parish, Shearmaker,
who died Aug. 11, 1751, in the
52 Year of his Age.

Here resteth the Body of
ROBERT PERRY, senior, Esq.
who departed this Life the
14th Day of January, 1722,
in the 88th Year of his Age.

Here resteth the Body of
MARGARET, the Wife of
ROBERT PERRY, Esq.
who departed this Life the 6th
Day of March, 1706,
aged 60 Years.

Here lyeth the Body of
REBECCA, Wife of Mr. ROBERT
PERRY, jun. and Daughter of
AMBROSE AWDREY, of Melksham,
in the County of Wilts, Gent.
She departed this Life in
August 1706.

Here resteth the Body of ROBERT PICK,
senior, who departed this Life
Jan. 6, 1722, aged 85 Years.

Also ELIZABETH his Wife, who
departed Jan. 6, 1710, aged 68.

In Memory of JOHN PICK, sen.
who departed this Life February
the 21st, 1751, aged 58 Years.

Also of ELIZABETH his Wife,
who departed Nov. 10, 1770,
aged 69 Years.

Also four of their Children.

ON A BRASS PLATE:

Juxta requiescit Reverendus
RICHARDUS NELMES, A. M. C. C. C.
apud Oxoniensis quondam socius,
Theologus acutus, medicus sagacissimus,
omnibus in artibus quæ vitam &
ornant, & utilissimam reddunt, excelluit.
Mors tua, vir præstantissime,
ecclesiæ semper luctuosa,
patriæ funesta, bonis omnibus acerba,
divinâ qua inituit scientia,
quæ Deo juvante jam sæpe
Et feliciter aliorum morbis
& languoribus sanitatem
Restituit, sua solum fata retardare heu!
Frustra tentavit ; medio enim cursu morte
Triumphante Natura lugente correptus.
Nov. die X,

Anno { CHRISTI MDCCXXIII.
{ Ætat. XLI.

Hic etiam jacent exuviæ RICHARDI &
CATHARINÆ NELMES,
Filii & Filiæ RICHARDI NELMES
supradicti.

In Memory of
PAUL PARK, senior,
of this Parish, who departed Sept. 21,
1746, aged 58 Years.

MARY his Wife dept. 15, 1756,
aged 89 Years.

In
Memory of
JOSIAH FERNLEY, Clothier,
who departed this Life
Oct. 23, 1759,
aged 63 Years.

Also of ANN his Wife,
who died April 16, 1782,
aged 74 Years.

And of JOSIAH their Son,
who died April 18, 1756,
aged 15 Years.

In
Memory of
ANNE POYER,
Relict of JOHN POYER,
late of Grove, Pembrokeshire,
South Wales, Esq.
who died Nov. 16, 1783,
aged 82 Years.

Here
rests the Body of THOMAS
WILTSHIER, who departed this
Life July 5, 1776,
aged 74 Years.

In Memory of
SAMUEL EYLES,
and of ELIZABETH his Wife.
He died Jan. 25, 1731,
aged 68 Years.
She May 26, 17 . .
aged 89 Years.

In
Memory of
THOMAS PHILLIPS,
of Nind, in this Parish,
who departed this Life the
15 Day of Feb. 1789,
in the 36 Year of his Age.

Likewise
SARAH his Daughter,
departed this Life the
28 Nov. 1786,
aged 11 Months.

In Memory of
WILLIAM DOWNS,
of Watson, in this Parish,
who departed this Life the
26 Dec. 1786,
in the 50th Year of his Age.

CHARLES HOPKINS,
of the Grange,
died May the 31st, 1749,
aged 60 Years.

MARY his Wife
died Sept. 5, 1738, aged 56 Years.

MIRIAM, the Daughter of
CHARLES and MARY HOPKINS,
died Jan. 23, 1748, aged 25 Years.

Under
this Tomb lieth the Body
of AMBROSE LEWIS, of this Parish,
Dyer, who departed this Life April 1,
A. D. 1697, aged 70 Years. And of his
Wife MARTHA, who departed this
Life Sept. 29, A. D. 1706, aged 53 Years.

And also the Body of their Son
WILLIAM LEWIS, who departed this
Life Mar. 23, A. D. 1705-6,
aged 22 Years.

In Memory of
THOMAS, Son
of THOMAS and MARY
WEBB, whose
Remains were here
deposited the 24th Day
of December, anno
Domini 1699, aged
22 Years.

Dedicated to
the Memory of
MARTHA, Daughter
of JOHN and ELIZABETH
BAKER, of this Parish,
whose Remains were
here deposited the
26 Nov. 1711, ætatis suæ 16 Years.

In Memory of
THOMAS, Son of
EDWARD WEBB, of this
Parish, Clothier, who
departed this Life the
14 October,
1702,
in the 69 Yeare
of his Age.

In Memory of
MARY, the Wife of
THOMAS WEBB, who
departed this Life the
20th Day of Dec. 1713,
in the 67 Yeare
of her Age.

In

In Memory
of THOMAS TYNNDALE,
fen. of this Parifh,
and of ANNE his Wife.
He died July 15, 1757,
in the 74th Year of his Age.
She Jan. 5, 1755, in
the 69 Year of her Age.

In Memory of ANNE, the Wife
of THOMAS TYNDALE,
who died Feb. 29, 1768,
in the 65th Year of her Age.

In Memory of REBECCA,

Wife of WILLIAM HOLLIDAY,

and Daughter of

THOMAS and ANNE TYNDALE,

who died Oct. 9, 1761,

in the 35th Year of her Age.

ON A FLAT STONE:

In Memory
of JOHN SUMMERS, and of REBECCA
his Wife.
He died Aug. 10, 1765, aged 72.
She died July 20, 1760, aged 65.

Alfo of MARY their Daughter,
and Wife of WILLIAM RODWAY,
who departed Sept. 21, 1758, aged 33.

Alfo three of their Children
died in their Infancy.

ON HEAD STONES.

	Died	Aged
John Lewis	20 Apr. 1744	44
Betty his Wife	8 Mar. 1773	73
John Tanner, fenior, Cloth-dreffer	28 June, 1789	85
Prifcilla, Wife of James Mafey	8 Sept. 1772	29
Mary, Wife of Arthur Bifs, fenior	6 Apr. 1769	33
Sarah, Wife of Edward Tanner, Daughter of John Exell	8 Sept. 1741	30
Abraham, Son of Daniel and Hannah Workman	25 May, 1736	28
Elizabeth Smith	17 Feb. 1737	—
George Parker, Officer of Excife	11 Apr. 1780	87
Betty, Wife of Nathaniel Summers	1 Nov. 1747	55
James Summers	28 Mar. 1751	54
Peter Harris, of Ludlow, in Shropfhire, Officer of Excife	8 Sept. 1765	42
Mary, Wife of Daniel Horwood Park	— Dec. 1750	29
Thomas Andrews	10 Sept. 175.	66

IN THE OLD CHURCH-YARD.

ON BRASS PLATES:

HENRY SMYTH, Gent. SARAH his
Relict, and feven of their Children,
are here interred.

HENRY died April 23, 1713,
aged 53 Years.

SARAH June 26, 1734,
aged 66 Years.

To the Memory of SARAH,
Wife of THOMAS TANNER,
of this Parifh, Clothier,

and Daughter of HENRY SMYTH, Gent.
and of SARAH his Wife.
She died Feb. 6, 1761,
aged 53 Years.

THOMAS SMYTH, Efq.
departed this Life May 2, 1752,
aged 54 Years.

ON A RAISED FLAT STONE:

In Memory
of Mr. ROBERT FERNLY, Clothier,
who departed this Life Oct. 23,
1772, aged 66 Years.

Alfo of MARY his Wife,
who died Sept. 23, 1772, aged 68.

Alfo of ROBERT their Son,
who died Nov. 25, 1765, aged 31.

Alfo of SARAH their Daughter,
who died July 18, 1771, aged 30.

Alfo of OBADIAH their Son,
who died Aug. 7, 1772, aged 39.

CLV. L A S S B O R O U G H

IS a Parifh of very fmall Extent, in the Hundred of *Longtree* and Lower *Cotefwold*, five Miles Eaft from *Wotton Underedge*, five Weft from *Tetbury*, and nineteen from Gloucester on the South. The Soil is light Stonebrafh, chiefly in Tillage, and producing confiderable Quantities of Grain.

The Benefice is a Rectory, in the Deanery of *Durfley*, not in Charge in the King's Books. It has claimed to be a free Chapel, but is inftitutive by the Diocefan.

The Church is a fmall Building, and apparently not very ancient.

The Bifhop of *Lifeaux* in *Normandy* held this Manor when *Domefday* was compiled, and Hugo Mami-not was his Tenant. It was then taxed at five Hides. William de Lasseburgh died feized of it in 1259, 43 Hen. III. and after his Defcendants it paffed to the Bassets of *Uley*, the laft of whom died in 1398, leaving Margaret his fole Daughter and Heir, the Wife of Walter Browne.

Of the Family of Hunter, otherwife Perry, this manerial Property was purchafed by Sir Thomas Estcourt in the Reign of King James the Firft. He built the large Manfion-houfe in the Style of that Age, and inclofed the Park. There is a Tradition, that he entertained King James the Firft there, when upon one of his Progreffes; and a rude emblazoning of the Royal Efcocheon is ftill fhewn as a Memorial of that Event.

Edmund Estcourt, Efq. the laft in lineal Defcent, bequeathed this Eftate, with many others, to Thomas, Son of Matthew Estcourt, of *Cam*, who is the prefent Poffeffor.

Some Years fince, a *Roman* fepulchral Stone was ploughed up in *Bowldown* Field in this Parifh. The Infcription was fo much obliterated, that nothing more than a conjectural Account could be given of it.

Lands in this Parifh belonged to the free Chantry of *St. Catharine*, in the Church of *Chipping Campden*, now incorporated with the other Eftate.

No Benefactions to the Poor.

Incumbents.	Patrons.	Incumbents.	Patrons.
1548 John Serche,	Thos. and Anne Perry.	1664 Edward Fido,	John Eftcourt.
1561 William Alye,	Anne Perry.	1667 Thomas Bryan,	Thomas Eftcourt.
1563 Philip ap Gryffith,	The fame.	1678 Thomas James,	King Charles II.
1538 John Jones,	Dame Anne Perry.	1684 Stephen Banning,	Walter Eftcourt.
1589 Tho. Wythers, A.B.	Robert Webb.	1719 Ifaac Gale, B. A.	The fame.
1591 Robert Cheeke,	The fame.	1750 Edm. Eftcourt Gale,	Edmund Eftcourt.
1593 John Chantrel,	The fame.	1771 Thomas Clare, B. D.	—————.
—— Edward Williams,	————.	1778 Cha. Wallington, B.A.	Thomas Eftcourt.
1609 Thomas Iles, M. A.	Sir Thos. Eftcourt, Knt.	—— W. Goodenough, M.A.	The fame.
1663 William Hodges,	John Eftcourt.		

Present Lord of the Manor,

Thomas Estcourt, Efq.

The only Perfon fummoned from this Parifh by the Heralds in 1682 and 1683 was

Richard Horfield, Efq.

At the Election in 1776, only One Freeholder polled from this Parifh.

As there are but three Houfes in the Parifh, Entries in the Regifter are very few.

INSCRIPTIONS

INSCRIPTIONS IN THE CHURCH.

IN THE CHANCEL.

On an elegant Monument of Black and White Marble, under a Canopy, with Effigies supplicating, supported by Corinthian Pillars:

Arms; Quarterly, 1ſt and 4th, Ermine, on a Chief indented Gules, three Eſtoiles Or, for Estcourt; 2d and 3d, Sable, a Feſs between three Eagle's Heads eraſed Or. On two Eſcocheons; 1ſt, Estcourt as before; 2d, Argent, ſix Lions rampant Sable, for Savage.

VITA INTROITUS MORTIS   MORS ÆTERNITATIS.

DEATH FOLLOWETH LIFE, LIFE DEATH!
WHEN GOOD MEN DIE,
THEIR BURIAL IS A NEW NATIVITIE!

THEN, GENTLE READER, CALL
NOT THIS A TOMBE;
BUT OF A SECOND LIFE THE
HAPPY WOMBE!

HERE REST THE BODIES OF Sᴿ THOMAS ESTCOURT, OF THE
EST COURT IN SHIPTON MOYNE IN THIS COUNTY, KNIGHT,
AND OF DAME MARY HIS WIFE, THE DAUGHTER OF WILLIAM
SAVAGE, OF ELMLY CASTLE IN THE COUNTY OF WORCEŠ, ESQ.
HE WAS A PILLAR OF THIS COUNTY, AND MUCH HONOURED
AND BELOVED FOR HIS WISDOME AND HOSPITALITY. HE LIVED
RELIGIOUSLY, AND (IN HIS RETURN FROM THE PARLIAMENT,
BEING THEN ONE OF THE KNIGHTS FOR THIS COUNTY)
DIED AT CIRENCESTER THE 4TH OF JULY, Aᵒ D'NI
1624.
IN WHOSE MEMORY HIS AFORESAID WIFE CAUSED THIS MONUMENT
TO BE ERECTED.
THIS MONUMENT WAS REPAIRED
AND BEAUTIFIED BY THOMAS ESTCOURT, ESQ.
1744.

Here lyes the Body of John Geale,
who died the 26 of March,
1686.

William,
Son of Henry and Sarah Dutton,
of Letchlade, in this County,
died at Bowldown, 22 June, 1752,
aged 16.

CLVI. LASSINGTON,

CLVI. LASSINGTON,
OR
LASSINGDON.

THIS fmall Parifh lies in the Hundred of *Dudftone* and *Barton Regis*, eight Miles South from *Tewkefbury*, and two North-weftward from GLOUCESTER. Upon the North Side it is bounded by the Rivulet *Leden*, of a rich Soil, containing not more than 500 Acres, one Third of which only is arable, and the others fertile Pafture, with fmall Exception.

The Benefice is a Rectory, with eight Acres of Glebe, in the Deanery of *Gloucefter*, charged with an annual Payment of Eight Shillings to the Dean and Chapter of *Briftol*, a Penfion formerly due to the Prior of *St. Ofwald's* in *Gloucefter*. The Heirs of DENNIS COOKE, Efq. and the Bifhop of *Gloucefter*, are the prefent Patrons ; but the firft named have two Turns.

The Church, dedicated to *St. Ofwald*, is a low Edifice, of fmall Dimenfions, and has nothing in it worthy Obfervation.

When *Domefday* was compiled, *Leffedune* was held in Demefne of the Archbifhop of *York*, and valued at thirty Shillings. The Family of *Mufgros* were poffeffed of two Thirds of it for feveral Generations, which, from the Heirs of JOHN COOFFE, were transferred to THOMAS RALEGH, Efq. of *Farnborough* in *Warwickfhire*, in 1390, 13 RIC. II. WILLIAM RALEGH was feized of them in the Reign of HENRY VI. who fold them to Sir JOHN SCUDAMORE, with whofe other Eftates they were efcheated to the Crown by King EDWARD the Fourth, whence they were granted to WILLIAM WHORWOOD, Efq. Attorney Gene-ral to King HENRY the Eighth, and paffed to his Coheirs, with other Manors in this County. The other third Part, lying in the Parifh of *St. Mary de Lode*, was given by JOHN PYRIE to the Abbey of *St. Peter* in *Gloucefter*, and confirmed to them by Patent, bearing Date 1272, 1 EDW. I. and included in the Endowment of the See.

JOHN ARNOLD, Efq. obtained a Leafe of it in 1536, 27 HEN. VIII. * and purchafed the other two Parts; and it has defcended, with the Manor of *Highnam*, to Sir JOHN GUISE, Bart. the prefent Proprietor.

Amongft the Foffil Productions in this Parifh are the Aftroites, or Star Stone. They are ftriated and pentangular, about three Inches in Length, and of the Shape of a Star at the Ends : with much eafe they are broken into thin *lamina* in a tranfverfe Direction.

No Benefaction to the Poor.

INCUMBENTS.	PATRONS.	INCUMBENTS.	PATRONS.
1538 Richard Morgan,	Abbey of Gloucefter.	1660 Thomas Grayle,	Jane Cooke, Widow, and W. Cooke, Efq.
—— Will. Barker,	——————.	1709 Sam. Lawrence,	John Nicholfon, Efq.
1572 William Mawfon,	William Huntley.	1723 Henry Church,	Edward Cooke, Efq.
—— Owen Lewis,	——————.	1733 John Whinfield, M.A.	Dennis Cooke.
1583 Richard Rogers,	George Burrell, Efq.	1735 Stephen Phillips, B.A.	Bifhop of Gloucefter.
1606 Elias Wrench, M.A.	John Rogers.	1782 J. Harris, B. A.	Sir John Guife, Bart.
1663 Ezra Grayle,	Robert Cooke, Efq.		
1648 Thomas Tyrer,	——————.		

PRESENT LORD OF THE MANOR,

Sir JOHN GUISE, Bart.

No Perfon was fummoned from this Place by the Heralds in 1682 and 1683.

At the Election in 1776 only One Freeholder polled from this Parifh.

* MS. Regift. Abb. *Glouc.*

The

The Date of the oldeſt Regiſter is in 1655.

ANNUAL ACCOUNT OF MARRIAGES, BIRTHS, AND BURIALS, IN THIS PARISH.

A.D.	Mar.	Bir.	Bur.	A.D.	Mar.	Bir.	Bur.	A.D.	Mar.	Bir.	Bur.	A.D.	Mar.	Bir.	Bur.
1781	—	2	3	1786	3	4	2	1791				1796			
1782	—	2	6	1787	—	3	2	1792				1797			
1783	1	2	4	1788	1	3	3	1793				1798			
1784	—	5	7	1789	1	3	—	1794				1799			
1785	1	1	3	1790	—	—	—	1795				1800			

INSCRIPTIONS IN THE CHURCH.

IN THE CHANCEL.

ON FLAT STONES.

Here lyeth the
Body of JAMES
HYETT, Yeoman,
who departed this Life
the 15 of Feb.
Anno Dom. 1672.

Here lyeth the Body of
DOROTHY, the Wife
of JAMES HYETT, Yeo-
man, who departed
this Life March
the 14, Anno 1666.

Here lieth the Body of
ELIZABETH, the Relict
of JAMES HYETT, Yeoman,
who departed this Life
16 . 1.

Here reſts the Body of
JOHN STREET, of Stoke,
next Guildford, in Surrey,
Gent. who departed this
Life Aug. 17, An° 1702,
aged 34.

Hic jacet Corpus ESRÆ
GRAILE, filii EDMUNDI
GRAILE, Medici, qui
pûre & orthodoxe Evangelium
CHRISTI per Annos 14 diſpen-
ſavit Laffingtoniæ, & Mortem ob. 23 February, Anno
1648,
ætatis ſuæ 41.

Etiam THO. GRAILE, fil.
Supradic. ES. GRAILE,
Obiit 25 Junii,
A. D. 1709,
ætat. 73,
Et hujus Eccleſiæ Rectoris
Annos 48.

Here reſts the Bodyes of
ESTHER, the Wife of
THOMAS GRAILE,
Rector of this Church,
who departed this Life
the 21ſt of April Anno Dom. 1682,
aged 52 Years.

And of SARAH their Daughter,
who departed this Life
the 16th Day of Aprill, An° Dom. 1682,
aged 13 Years.

In Memory of
ESTHER, the Wife of JAMES
BEARD, and Daughter of the
Rev. THOMAS GRAILE,
formerly Rector of this
Church. She departed
this Life the 8 Decemb.
Anno Dom. 1734,
aged 70 Years.

In Memory of
JAMES BEARD, of Staunton, in the
County of . . . . . .
the Huſband of ESTHER,
Daughter of the Rev.
Mr. THO. GRAILE, Rector

of this Church, who departed
this Life the 4th Day
of May, 1713, aged 72.

HERE LYETH THE BODY OF
JOHN WATTS, OF LASSINGTON,
YEOMAN, WHO DEPARTED
THIS LIFE THE 20TH DAY OF
APRILL, ANNO DOM. 1647.

Here reſt
the Remains of HENRY PEARCE,
of this Pariſh,
who departed this Life Aug. 20,
1786,
aged 56 Years.

IN THE NAVE.

ON A MONUMENT:

In Memory of
THOMAS GOSLING,
of Highmam, Yeoman, who died
the 28 of March, 1736,
aged 24 Years.

Alſo in Memory of MARY
his Wife, Daughter of PEREGRINE
PURROCK, of Highnam Lodge.
She died May 15, 1736,
aged 26 Years.

IN THE CHURCH-YARD, ON TOMBS.

HENRY PEARCE,
born at Haydon Farm, in the
Pariſh of Boddington, in the Year 1702,
was buried here in 1781.

ELIZABETH his Wife
died Nov. 27, 1782, aged 74 Years.

Here reſts
the Remains of SARAH, the Wife
of JOHN BOYCE, of Down Hatherly,
in this County, and Daughter of
HENRY and SARAH PEARCE, late
of this Pariſh, who departed
this Life July the 4th, 1788,
aged 35 Years.

Here lyeth the Body of
JOHN PURROCKE, of Highnam Lodge,
who, for his Readineſs and Abilities
in doing good, was deſervedly eſteemed
while he lived, as the loſs of him was
univerſally lamented by his
Friends, Neighbours, and Acquaintance.
He died the 4th of Auguſt, 1724,
aged 48 Years.

In Memory
of MARY, Relict of
JOHN PURROCKE aforeſaid, who
departed this Life . . . .
1734.

Here reſteth the Body of
ELIZABETH, the Wife of RICHARD
PETERS, of Highnam, who departed
this Life the 9th Day of Sept 1762,
aged 64 Years.

Alſo SARAH his ſecond Wife,
who departed this Life the
27 Day of March, 1779,
aged 54 Years.

Alſo in Memory of
RICHARD PETERS, Huſband of the
aboveſaid ELIZABETH and
SARAH PETERS,
who died September 9, 1779,
aged 76 Years.

Underneath this Stone lieth the Body of Mr. WILLIAM HEATH, late Citizen of London, Coachmaker. He departed	this Life the 7 Nov. 1777, aged 39. He died single, leaving his Fortune to his Niece JANE HEATH,	of Chigwell in Essex. In gratitude thereof she erected this Stone.

O N   H E A D   S T O N E S.

	Died	Aged
William Russell	11 Sept. 1769	42
Susanna, Wife of Thomas Cannon	2 Oct. 1738	69
James, Son of James and Susanna Halford	26 Sept. 1669	—
Jane, Daughter of John Watts	23 Oct. 1708	—
John Hannis	28 Apr. 1720	57
Richard Engly	24 Jan. 1729	41
Joanna his Wife	25 Mar. 1738	61
Stephen Pitthorn	9 July, 1761	78
Elizabeth his Wife	— May, 1751	55
Betty their Daughter	25 Dec. 1760	30
Anthony Pitthorn	23 May, 1774	45
Mary his Wife	9 Jan. 1776	53
Matthew Pumfrey	18 Mar. 1723	—
Mary, Daughter of John Morris	19 July, 1720	38
Ann Morris	11 May, 1720	34
William Jones	— Aug. 1712	70
Anne his Wife	— June, 1712	60
Thomas Wicksteed	24 Mar. 1714	73
Ann, Daughter of John Little	16 Nov. 1698	—
John Little	14 May, 1718	60
Eleanor his Wife	17 Oct. 1696	36
Betty, Wife of John Merrick	14 Aug. 1784	32
Thomas Bayce	14 Dec. 1777	73
William his Son	14 Mar. 1768	18
Edward Overthrow	8 July, 1771	72
Sarah Sanford	20 Feb. 1782	20
Henry Marchant	17 Dec. 1776	59
Peregrine, Son of Peregrine Purrocke, of Highnam	— May, 1737	24
William Purrocke	9 Sept. 1712	34
Salathiel Coldrick	10 Feb. 1781	71
Mary his Wife	17 Mar. 1782	61
Thomas May		
Hester his Wife	7 Aug. 1693	—
Sarah, Wife of John Ferret	23 Oct. 1697	—
Richard Salcombe, of Highnam	29 Oct. 1737	65
Elizabeth his Wife	27 Oct. 1737	57
James Salcombe	21 Jan. 1731	63
Mary his Wife	16 Feb. 1754	78
William their Son	28 Dec. 1738	19
James Salcombe	30 July, 1741	35
Elizabeth, Wife of William Taylor	9 Feb. 1757	34
William Morrell	2 Dec. 1694	—
Hester his Wife	27 Sept. 1703	—
Ann Gaze	11 July, 1782	34
Sarah, Wife of James Dyer	22 Sept. 1729	42
Thomas Brooke	— 1698	—
Francis Carter	9 Dec. 1712	—
Joseph Wood	22 Aug. 1748	51
Joan his Wife	22 Feb. 1727	43

CLVII. L E A,

THE fmaller Divifion of this Parifh, including the Village, lies in the Hundred of *St. Briavel's*, in the Foreft of *Dean*, and the other in the County of *Hereford*, diftant two Miles North from *Michel Dean*, fix South from *Newent*, and twelve Weft from GLOUCESTER, upon the great Road to *Rofs*. The Soil is univerfally of Sand, and applied in a Portion of about three Fourths to Tillage.

The Living is a perpetual Curacy, annexed as a Chapelry to the Vicarage of *Linton* in *Herefordfhire*, but is a Member of the Foreft Deanery. When augmented by Queen ANNE's Bounty the certified Value was 4*l. per Annum*. The impropriate Tythes were held by the late WILLIAM LANE, Efq. of *Gloucefter*, who received it from the Family of COCKS.

The Church, dedicated to *St. John Baptift*, is of the Architecture of the middle Centuries after the Conqueft, and confifts of a Nave, divided from the North Aifle by light Pillars, and a fepulchral Chapel, with a low Spire at the Weft End. In one of the Windows are feveral Efcocheons remaining in ftained Glafs; 1. Barry of fix Argent and Azure, in Chief a Label of five Points Gules, for GREY DE WILTON; 2. the fame, with a Canton Gules, charged with three Mullets Or.

Concerning the Manor, we find in *Domefday* Book that it belonged to the Bifhop of *Conftance*, and contained only one Hide and two Plough Tillages in demefne, of the Value of 20*s*. From the MARSHALS it defcended to the TALBOTS, and belonged to JOHN TALBOT, the great Earl of *Shrewfbury*, and to his Son and Succeffor, who was flain at the Battle of *Northampton* in 1450, 38 HEN. VI. Having then been confifcated, it was then obtained by the Family of THROCKMORTON, in whom it was vefted for feveral Centuries. RICHARD HAMMELINE held in 1608. In the laft Century it was transferred to Sir DUNCOMBE COLCHESTER, Knt. and remains with his Defcendant.

B E N E F A C T I O N.

THOMAS NOURSE, in 1675, gave, by Will, Lands, the yearly Produce of which is 2*l*. to be diftributed amongft the Poor in Wheaten Bread on the Sunday before Chriftmas Day, and the Sunday before Candlemas Day, annually, vefted in the Churchwardens, Overfeers, and three of the moft fubftantial Inhabitants.

The prefent Curate is THEOPHILUS PROSSER.

PRESENT LORD OF THE MANOR,
JOHN COLCHESTER, Efq.

The only Perfon fummoned from this Parifh by the Heralds, in 1682 and 1683, was
Giles Wynter, Efq.

At the Election in 1776, Four Freeholders polled from this Parifh.

The firft Date of the Regifter is in 1581.

ANNUAL ACCOUNT OF MARRIAGES, BIRTHS, AND BURIALS, IN THIS PARISH.

A.D.	Mar.	Bir.	Bur.	A.D.	Mar.	Bir.	Bur.	A.D.	Mar.	Bir.	Bur.	A.D.	Mar.	Bir.	Bur.
1781	3	9	5	1786	—	7	3	1791				1796			
1782	—	4	3	1787	—	7	4	1792				1797			
1783	—	6	3	1788	—	3	3	1793				1798			
1784	1	5	7	1789	1	8	3	1794				1799			
1785	—	5	3	1790	—	5	5	1795				1800			

INSCRIPTIONS IN THE CHURCH.

IN THE NAVE.

ON FLAT STONES.

HERE
RESTETH IN
THE LORD THE
BODY OF MARGERY,
THE WIFE OF THO-
MAS BACHE, WHO

DEPARTED THIS
LIFE THE 3 DAY OF
JANUARY, ANNO
DOMINI 1668.

HERE LYETH THE BODY OF
THOMAS BACHE, OF
THIS PARISH, BLACK-

SMITH, WHO DEPARTED
THIS LIFE OCTOBER
Y* 22, ANNO DOM.
1679.

Here lyeth the Body of
ANN, the Wife of
RICHARD MILLER, who
died October the 24th, 1698.

IN

2

IN THE NORTH AISLE.
ON FLAT STONES.

Here lyeth the
Body of BRIDGET,
the Wife of
WILLIAM PHELPOTS,
of Aſſen, who
departed this Life
24 of December,
Anno Domini 16.0.

In Memory of
JOHN RUDGE, of Caſtlend,
who departed this Life
Dec. 20, Anno Dom. 1710,
ætatis ſuæ 81.

Alſo BRIDGET, the Wife of WILLIAM
PHILLPOTTS, of the Warren, in the
Pariſh of Aſton Ingham, was
here buried Dec. 25, Anno 1680,
ætaːis ſuæ 29.

Alſo BRIDGET, the Daughter of
WILLIAM PHILLPOTTS and BRIDGET
his Wife, was here buried April
the 8, Anno 1681, ætat. 3 Months.

IN THE BURIAL CHAPEL.
ON FLAT STONES.

Arms ; two Bars, in Chief a Lion paſſant, for GREGORY ;—impaling, a Feſs
between two Cheverons, for NOURSE.

Here lyeth the Body of . . . . . the
Wife of ROBERT GREGORY . . . . .
Daughter of JOHN NOURSE, Eſq. by
ANN his Wife, of Weſton under Penyard,
in the County of Hereford, who died
December the 4, Anno { Dom. 172 . / ætatis 50.

Arms ; a Feſs between two Cheverons ;
—impaling two Lions paſſant.

In Memory of
ROBERT GREGORY, of Caſtlend, Eſq.
He was buried Nov. 11, 1731, aged 45.

Alſo of PHILIP NOURSE, Eſq.
who was buried Nov. 5, 1742,
aged 36.

Likewiſe of MARY NOURSE,
Widow and Reliſt of

PHILIP NOURSE, and Daughter of
WILLIAM GARNONS, of Trelough,
Eſq. She was buried Oct. 26, 1769,
aged 64.

Here lyeth the Body of JANE,
the Wife of THOMAS WELLINGTON,
of Caſtlend, who was buried
the 27th Day of March, 1716.

Here lyeth the Body of
THOMAS WELLINGTON, of
Caſtlend, who departed
this Life March 13, 1750,
in the 67th Year of his Age.

Alſo in Memory of ANN,
the ſecond Wife of the above
THOMAS WELLINGTON,
who was here interred May 25,
1764, aged 67 Years.

In Memory of SAMUEL,
the Son of WILLIAM GARDNER,
by MARY his Wife, who was here
buried November the 11th, 1731,
aged 20 Years.

IN THE CHURCH YARD,

Here lies interred the Body of
STEPHEN YEARSLEY, late
of this Pariſh. He died Aug. the
23, 1742, aged 78 Years.
In Memory of JOSEPH, the Son
of STEPHEN YEARSLEY, by MARY
his Wiſe.
He died June 29, 1693, aged 13 Weeks.
As alſo of
MARY their Daughter. She died
Aug. 31, 1711, ætat. ſuæ 18.

In Memory of JOHN YEARSLEY, who
died June 26, 1782, aged 60 Years.
Alſo JOYCE, the Wife of the above
JOHN YEARSLEY,
died Nov. 20. 1783, aged 60 Years.

In Memory of JONE, the Wife of MOSES
PHILLIPS, who was here buried
Aug. 15, 1718.

In Memory of
BRIDGET, the Wife of
ROBERT PHILLIPS, who
departed this Life Oct. 11,
1725, aged 32 Years.

Here lies interred
the Body of KATHERINE, the Wife of
WILLIAM PHILLIPS, of this Pariſh, who
departed this Life the 25th of Oct.
1769, aged 65 Years.

In Memory of MARY, the Wife of
EDWARD LEWIS, of Caſtlend,
who daparted March 27, 1756,
aged 34 Years.

Alſo SARAH, the Daughter of
EDWARD LEWIS, by MARY his Wife,
who died May 7, 1756.
In Memory of ANN, the Daughter of
THOMAS WELLINGTON, by ANN his
Wife, late of Caſtlend, in this Pariſh.
She died Auguſt 25, 1750, aged 26.

In Memory of MARTHA, the Wife of
THOMAS BUTCHER, of this Pariſh.
She departed the 27 Day of March, 1772,
aged 70 Years.

ON FLAT STONES.

Under
this Stone lies interred the Body of
EDWARD LEWIS, late of Caſtlend,
in this Pariſh, who departed this Life
Sept. 22, 1775, aged 60 Years.

In Memory of ABRAHAM ASTILE,
who died May 26, 1762,
aged 82 Years.

In
Memory of WILLIAM KEYES, who
died Nov. 25, 1749, aged 69 Years.
Alſo MARY, the Wife of WILL. KEYES,
who died Nov. 22, 1762,
aged 98 Years.

JOHN SYMONDS died
May 13. 1763, aged 41 Years.

In Memory of
ELIZABETH, the Daughter

ON TOMBS.

of WILLIAM LODGE, by
ELIZABETH his Wife,
who died Sept. 15, 1776,
in the 20 Year of her Age.

Here lieth the Remains of
ROBERT TURNER,
who died Dec. 6, 1785,
aged 63 Years.

Here
lyeth the Body
of WILLIAM GARDNER. He
died Feb. 21, 1745,
aged 51 Years.
Alſo
of ELIZABETH his Wife,
Dec. 1, 1784, aged
75 Years.

Here
lyeth the Body of ANN, the Wife of
ABRAHAM ASTILL, who
died Dec. 2, 1747, in her 67th Year.

In Memory of
MARTHA, the Wife of
ROBERT PHILLIPS, who
was here buried Feb. 16, 1728, aged 42.

Alſo JAMES, the Son of
ROB. PHILLIPS, by MARTHA his Wife,
was here buried Feb. 9, 1728.

To the Memory of JAMES PRICHARD,
who died May 12, 1752, aged 34.

Alſo MARY, the Wife of
JAMES PRICHARD, who
died January .. 1755, aged 53.

ON HEAD STONES.

	Died	Aged
Moſes Phillips - -	8 Nov. 1750	107
John Surman - -	6 May, 1729	68
Samuel James - -	7 Apr. 1786	65
Elizabeth, Wife of William Sindry	6 Oct. 1719	—
William Sindry -	12 June, 1731	85
John Drinkwater -	26 Apr. 1762	57
Thomas Barnett - -	9 Feb. 1777	75
Betty, Wife of Jonathan Bennett	1 Feb. 1780	31
Thomas Bennett -	26 Oct. 1783	66
Benedicta his Wife -	8 Feb. 1781	67
Benedicta, Wife of Charles Lewis	15 Apr. 1790	37
Elizab Dau. of Rob. and Betty Hook	5 Mar. 1788	15
Jacob Phillips -	31 July, 1743	61
William Phillips - -	2 May, 1773	89
William Maduks -	23 Jan. 1676	—
John Palmore - -	11 Nov. 1749	71
Samuel his Son - -	30 May, 1741	22
Ann, Wife of Thomas Norton	18 June, 1716	—
Richard Boner -	29 May, 1729	67
Mary his Wife -	19 Feb. 1741	59
Boner -	12 Feb. 1743	22
James Read - -	19 Aug. 1770	42
Betty his Daughter by Mary his Wife	14 July, 1784	26
John their Son -	31 July, 1785	23
Elizabeth, Wife of Stephen Yearſley	23 May, 1738	40
Joſ. Son of Steph. and Mary Yearſley	29 June, 1693	—
Jane, Wife of Joſeph Lodge	8 Feb. 1731	22
Alexander Dobbs -	23 Feb. 1784	84
Joan, Wife of James Phelps	— — 1694	—
Robert Furney - -	28 Apr. 1740	44
Hannah his Dau. by Mary his Wife	7 June, 1763	29
Robert his Son, by Hannah his Wife	15 Feb. 1769	17
Jane, Wife of Richard Boner	15 Dec. 1717	—
Richard, Son of Edward Jones	16 May, 1745	—
Francis Wellington -	3 May, 1733	43
William Brown and Blanch his Wife	23 Oct. 1709	—
John Brown - -	12 Aug. 1681	—
Philip, Son of Thomas Sutton	31 July, 1700	—
Richard Millard -	11 June, 1724	—
Ann Daughter of Richard Millard	2 Mar. 1728	68
Job Jones - -	30 Mar. 1750	63

CLVIII. LECHELADE,

John Twinyhow.

Figures in Lechlade Church.

CLVIII. LECHELADE, OR LEACHLADE.

WHAT the ancient Topographers relate concerning the Origin of this Name, with Reference to an Univerſity for teaching the Latin Language, is totally unworthy of Credit. It owes the Appellation more probably to the Circumſtance of the Rivulet *Leche* diſcharging itſelf here into the *Iſis*.

This Pariſh lies in the Hundred of *Brightwell's Barrow*, upon the Confines of the County of *Berks*, twelve Miles Weſtward from *Cirenceſter*, and twenty-nine in a ſimilar Direction from GLOUCESTER. The Arable Lands are greatly exceeded in Quantity by rich Meadow and Paſture upon the Banks of the Rivers, of a Soil varying from Stonebraſh to Gravel and Clay. The Terrier includes more than 4,000 Acres, and the Boundaries form a narrow and very irregular Figure.

Lechelade has long enjoyed the Privileges of a Market-town, with two Fairs, for Cattle, Cheeſe, and other Commodities, which are much frequented, eſpecially that which was held in a Meadow near *St. John's Bridge* on the 9th of September, now transferred to the Town. The other Fair is held on the Feaſt of *St. Lawrence*, and the Market Day is Friday. RICHARD Earl of CORNWALL firſt obtained the Grant from King HENRY III. One of the great Roads to the Weſtern Counties leads through it, and to this Place. The chief Part of the Cheeſe made in the County of *Glouceſter* and Part of *Wiltſhire*, amounting to above 3,000 Tons annually, is brought in Waggons, where it is put on-board Veſſels which convey it down the *Thames* to *London* *.

The Benefice is a Vicarage, the Patronage and Impropriation of which formerly belonged to the Priory of *St. John*, founded in this Place, and ſince the Diſſolution had paſſed with the Manor, till bequeathed by LAWRENCE BATHURST, Eſq. by his Will, dated Sept. 16, 1670, as an Endowment of the Vicarage. It is a Member of the Deanery of *Fairford*.

The Church, dedicated to *St. Lawrence*, is a very handſome Edifice, and of contemporary Erection. It was built in the Reign of EDWARD IV. by CONRAD NEY, then Vicar, and the Benefactions of the Priory and Inhabitants. The Plan is ſyſtematic and complete, and the Ornaments in the beſt Style of *Gothic* Architecture. The Dimenſions are ſpacious, containing a Nave, divided from the Aiſles by light Pillars, Chantries at each End, and a Spire of very elegant Proportions. No Arms or ſtained Glaſs are now to be diſcovered. The Pulpit and Font are of ſculptured Stone.

Of the Priory or Hoſpital at *Lechelade*, RICHARD Earl of CORNWALL and SENCHIA his Wife are recorded to have been the Founders, as well as of *Hayles* Abbey, who endowed it with the Hermitage of *Lovebury*, in the Foreſt of *Whichwood*, and dedicated to *St. John Baptiſt*. King EDWARD IV. in 1472, granted the Patronage to CICELEY Ducheſs of YORK, with Licence to convert it into a Chantry, to be ſerved by three Chaplains, to celebrate daily at the Altar of our Lady at *Lechelade*. To theſe JOHN TWINIHOW, of *Cirenceſter*, added another, dedicated to *St. Blaiſe*, which was included in the former Incorporation †. Soon afterward UNDERWODE, Dean of *Wallingford*, procured the Removal of two of them to his College. JOHN LECHE, the laſt Incumbent of TWINYHOW's Chantry, which was endowed with ten Marks yearly, received a Penſion of 5*l.* in 1553. The Site of the Priory is not now known with certainty ‡.

In

* "As I rode over *Iſis* I lernid that ulter ripa was in *Gloceſtreſhir*, and citerior and *Barkſhir*, and *Oxfordſhir* not far of. At
" the End of *St. John's Bridge* in ripa ulteriori on the right Hond I ſaw a Chapelle in a Medow, and great Encloſures of Stone
" Waules. Heere was in Hominum Memoria a Priory of Blake Chanons of the Patronage of the Duke of CLARANCE of YORK.
" When this Priory was ſuppreſſid there were 3 Cantuaries erectid in the Church of *Lechelade :* and ther remaynid ontylle of
" late Dayes one UNDREWOODE, Decane of *Wallingforde*, founde Meanes that 2 of theſe Cantuaries ſhould be at *Wallingford*
" *College,* and the third to remaine at *Lechelade*. From S. *John's Bridge* to *Lechelade*, about half a Mile. It is a praty olde
" Village, and hath a pratie Pyramis of Stone at the Weſt Ende of the Chirch. From *Lechelade* to *Fairford* about a 4 Miles
" al by low Ground, in a Maner in a Levelle moſt apt for Graſſe, but very barein of Woodde." LELAND, Itin. vol. II. p. 47.
† Theſe Chantries were confirmed by JOHN CARPENTER, Biſhop of *Worceſter*, May 24, 1476.
Regiſt. Vigorn. CARPENTER, vol. II. p. 78. THOMAS's Survey of Worc. p. 198.
‡ A Priory of Black Canons, or rather an Hoſpital of a Maſter or Prior and certain poor and infirm Brethren, dedicated
to *St. John Baptiſt*, was founded here upon a Piece of Ground called *Lade,* near the great Bridge over the *Thames* (hence called
St. John's Bridge), given to that good Uſe by the Lady ISABEL FERRERS, ſometime Wife of HUGH MORTIMER, before 30
H. III. But this Houſe being run into great Decay, K. EDW. IV. a. r. 12, gave his Mother CICELY Ducheſs of YORK Leave
to get it diſſolved, and then to apply the Revenues of it to the endowing of a perpetual Chantry of three Prieſts at the Altar
of *St. Mary* in the Pariſh-Church here, which continued till Dean UNDERWOOD, temp. H. VII. found Means to place two of
theſe Chantry Prieſts at *Walingford College*, and let the third remain at *Lechelade*, and ſo the Site of this Priory, as Parcel of
the Poſſeſſions of *Walingford College*, was granted to DENNIS TAPPES, 14 ELIZ. Vide in Mon. Ang. tom. II. p. 218 & 222.
paucula de fundatione. Ib. p. 451. Cart. 39 HEN. III. m. 8. confirm. fundationem. Cart. 54 HEN. III. m. 9. pro Heremitagio de *Lovebyri,* cum pertinentiis in Foreſta de *Wichewode* huic hoſpitali concedendo. Pat. 12 E. IV. p. 2. m. 28 pro mutatione hujus hoſpitalis in cantarium trium capellanorum. Inter Collect. FRANCISCI PECK in Muſeo Britannico, vol. V. ordinationem

In *Domefday* Book the Manor of *Lechelade* is defcribed as being extenfive *, and the Property of HENRY DE FERRERS, from whom it was inherited by the MORTIMERS. King HENRY III. gave it to his Brother RICHARD Earl of CORNWALL, upon the Death of whofe Son EDMUND it reverted to the Crown. It then paffed in Succeffion through the TALBOTS, DESPENCERS, HOLLANDS, and GREYS, till confirmed by EDWARD IV. to his Mother CICELEY Duchefs of YORK, who died in 1495.

The Manor and Town, with Tolls of Markets and Fairs, were Parcel of the Jointure of CATHARINE of ARAGON, which fhe enjoyed after her Divorce, after whofe Deceafe they were granted to DENNIS TOMPES and DOROTHY his Wife, in Exchange for *Ruckholts*, co. *Effex*, referving a Rent of 27*l.* 4*s.* 3*d.* to the Crown. Early in the Reign of JAMES I. the manerial Eftate was transferred to ROBERT BATHURST, Efq who appears to have been then newly fettled at *Lechelade*, defcended from the BATHURSTS of *Horfemunden* in *Kent*. His Right to it is faid to have been derived from EDWARD DODGE, Efq. Sir EDWARD BATHURST, was knighted in 1643; and, on December 15, in the fame Year, he was created a Baronet. Sir EDWARD his Grandfon died during his Minority in 1677, and was fucceeded in this Property in Moiety by his Sifters and Coheirs, ANNE, the Wife of JOHN GREENING, Gent. and MARY, the Wife of GEORGE COXETER, Efq. of *Kennington*, co. *Berks*. JOHN GREENING bequeathed his Partition to ELIZABETH his Heir and Niece, who married NICHOLAS HARDINGE, Efq. of the *Inner Temple*, by whom a Partition was obtained by a Decree in Chancery, dated 1698. His Share was afterward fold, Jan. 11, 1718, to Sir FRANCIS PAGE, Knt. one of the Juftices of the King's Bench, by whom, after his Relict Dame FRANCES PAGE, it was devifed to her fecond Brother, afterward Sir GEORGE WHEATE, Bart. in 1730. After many Suits at Law refpecting the Claims of GREENING's Defcendants, the fole Right was confirmed to the late Sir JACOB WHEATE, Bart. in 1774, upon whofe Demife, in 1783, the Title defcended to his Brother the Rev. Sir JOHN THOMAS WHEATE, Bart.

Two very fpacious Houfes belonging to the Manor were taken down by Sir JACOB WHEATE. One of them, called the Lantern-houfe, from a large Cupola of Glafs upon the Top of it, was built by Sir EDWARD BATHURST, and upon its Site the prefent Manfion was erected.

Other Eftates in this Parifh, as we collect from ancient Evidences, were held of the Families of TWINIHOO, MORTON, and COLLET, and fince them by LODER, OATRIDGE, and AINGE. The prefent Proprietors, exclufive of the Manor, are JOHN WEBB, Efq. of *Henbury*, Sir JOHN WEBB, Bart. of *Hatherop*, Dr. LOVEDAY, the Families of LODER, MARSHAM, OATRIDGE, and the Rev. JOHN CHAUNLER.

Near *St. John's Bridge* was a Chapel noticed by LELAND; the Ruins of which have been lately difcovered, and it is faid to have been appendant to the Hofpital abovementioned.

The long projected Junction of the Rivers *Thames* and *Severn* has been completed near this Place; of which a more ample Account is fubjoined †.

B E N E-

CECILIÆ Duciffæ EBOR. de cantaria MARIÆ de tribus capellanis, nec non de Cantaria S. *Blafii* de uno capellano, in ecclefia parochiali de *Lechelade*. 13 E. IV. Cart. 30 H. III. m. 6. de *Lodenmill* paftura v vace. Pat. 4 E. II. p. 2. m. 14. de terris in *Uplambourn* perquirend. de JOANNE SWINE, temp. E. I. Cart. 6 E. II. n. 22. de advocatione hofpitalis conceffa per EDM Comitem CORNUBIÆ Abbatiæ de *Havles*. Pat. 43 E. III. p. 1. m. 23. pro ten. in eadem villa. Rec. in fcac. 17 RIC. II. Mich. rot. 19. de terris de *Borowneflon (Berks)*. TANNER, Not. Mon.

* Terra HENRICI de FERRERS. In *Brictuoldeberg* Hund', HENRICUS DE FERRERES ten' *Lecelade* ^{BAR.} SIUUARD tenuit ibi XV hide, T. R. E. geldantes fed ipfe rex c'ceffit VI hid' quietas a geldo. Hoc teftat' om'nis comitatus & ipfe qui figillum regis detulit. In d'nio funt IIII car', & XXVIII vill'i, & X bord', & unus francig' ten' t'ram unius vill'i. Int' om's h'nt XVI car'. Ibi XIII fervi, & III molini, de XXX folid', & pifcaria de CC anguill' XXV minus. De pratis VII lib', & VII fol', p'ter fenum boum. In *Wicelcumbe* II burgenfes rede' XVI den', & unus in *Glouuc'*, fine cenfu. Tot' M. T. R. E. val'b' XX lib' & modo fimiliter.

Domefday Book.

† The Execution of this Work, agitated as it had been in Parliament in the Time of CHARLES II. and depicted in the Fancy of a Poet in the Time of GEORGE I. was referved for our own Day, and was undertaken, upon the Survey and Report of that able Engineer, Mr. ROB WHITWORTH, in 1782, at the Inftance and Rifk of feveral private Perfons; particularly of the refpectable Baronet in *Staffordfhire*, and of the very well-informed and opulent Merchants in *London*, hinted at by your former Correfpondent, who had no local Intereft in either of the Counties of *Gloucefter* or *Wilts*, through which the Canal paffes. Thefe Gentlemen agreed fome Time in the Month of November, 1782, to proceed to the Execution of their Defign, and accordingly introduced a Bill into Parliament for that Purpofe in the Month of February following. In the Courfe of that Seffion the Bill paffed into a Law (23 Geo. III. c. xxxviii.), and is entituled, " An Act for making and maintaining a Navigable Canal from the " River *Thames* or *Ifis*, at or near *Leachlade*, to join and communicate with the *Stroudwater* Canal at *Wallbridge*, near the " Town of *Stroud*; and alfo a Collateral Cut from the faid Canal, at or near *Siddington*, to or near the Town of *Cirencefter*, " in the Counties of *Gloucefter* and *Wilts*." Agreeably to the Eftimate of the Expence of this projected Undertaking, 130,000*l.* were ftated in the Act to be raifed by the Proprietary, who was incorporated, and had a Power of borrowing the farther Sum of 60,000*l.* upon Mortgage, under their Common Seal.

It fhould not be omitted to be obferved, that, previous to the Commencement of this Undertaking, a Canal had been made from the *Severn* to *Wallbridge* near *Stroud*, by virtue of an Act of Parliament which paffed for that Purpofe in 1730, and afterwards amended by another in 1776. The Length of this Canal from the *Severn* at *Framiload* to *Wallbridge*, is 7 Miles, 6 Furlongs, and 8 Chains and a Half, and the Rife above the Level of *Severn* is 102 Feet, 5 Inches. The Defign and Works therefore, of the Undertakers of this New Extenfion of Navigation commence at *Wallbridge* near *Stroud*, and reach to near *Leachlade* on the *Thames*, a Diftance of 30 Miles, 7 Chains and a Half.

The

B E N E F A C T I O N S.

Edward Dodge, Efq. by his laft Will, dated in 1599, gave 5l. yearly to the Poor of this Parifh, payable out of Land, vefted in the Executors of the late Sir Jacob Wheate.

In 1602, William Blomer, Efq. and his Heirs, were commanded by a Writ of Execution to deliver five Bufhels of Wheat, and five of Barley, to the Vicar and Churchwardens on St. Mark's Day, to be diftributed among the Poor, out of the Profits of Dolemead, vefted as above.

Richard Welman gave, by Will, in 1703, 10s. yearly, to be diftributed in Bread to ten fuch Poor Widows as receive the Sacrament on Chriftmas-Day, out of Land, vefted in Richard Hughes.

Francis Loder, by Will, dated in 1720, gave the Intereft of 100l. for ever to the pooreft Orphans, or pooreft Widowers or Widows, born in the Parifh, or towards erecting a School, vefted in Robert Loder.

Robert Loder gave, by Will, in 1721, 1l. yearly, payable out of Land, vefted as above, to be diftributed in Bread on New-Year's Day.

Richard Ainge, in 1725, gave, by Will, 1l. a Year, to be diftributed in Bread on St. Mark's Day, payable out of Land vefted in Catharine Hughes.

Rev John Loder, by Will, dated in 1748, gave to the Poor of the Parifh not receiving Alms, Houfes, vefted in the Parifh, the yearly Produce of which is 4l. 10s.

Anne Simmonds, in 1769, gave, by Will, 200l. in the Funds, the annual Produce of which to be diftributed among fuch of the Poor as do not receive Alms, vefted in the Minifter and Churchwardens.

Incumbents.	Patrons.	Incumbents.	Patrons.
1470 Conrad Ney,	Hofpital of St. John.	1618 William Phipps,	Robert Bathurft, Efq.
1554 John Gyley,	Queen Mary.	1645 Thomas Davis,	Sir Edw. Bathurft, Bart.
1561 John Gowfyth,	—————.	1688 Richard Caftle, M. A.	J. and Anne Greening.
—— John Snowfhil,	—————.	1737 John Whitmore,	Ann Pearfall, Widow.
1572 John Dormer,	Queen Elizabeth.	1761 Rich. Bowles, M. A.	Sir Geo. Wheate, Bart.
—— Henry Herbert,	—————.	1774 Sir J. T. Wheate, Bart.	John Moreton, Efq.

Present Lady of the Manor,

Dame Avice Wheate.

The Perfons fummoned from this Place by the Heralds, in 1682 and 1683, were

Sir Edward Bathurft, Bart.	Robert Keble, Gent.	Robert Oatridge, Gent.
Robert Bathurft, Efq.	John Loder, Gent.	William Jordan, Gent.
Sir Thomas Cutler, Knt.		

The feparate and united Admeafurements of this Diftance I will tranfcribe from Mr. Whitworth's Plan, laid down from actual Surveys, and dated 1783, and immediately connected with the Act of Parliament.

	Length.			Rife.		Fall.	
	M.	F.	Ch.	F.	In.	F.	In.
From the Head of the Stroud Canal at Wallbridge to Danaway Bridge	7	0	5	241	3	0	0
From Danaway Bridge to the Entrance of the Tunnel near Sapperton	0	2	5	0	0	0	0
The Length of the Tunnel	2	3	0	0	0	0	0
From the End of the Tunnel in Coates Common Field to Upper Siddington	5	3	3½	0	0	0	0
The Branch to Cirencefter	1	2	5	0	0	0	0
From Upper Siddington to (near) Cricklade	5	4	4	0	0	102	2
From Cricklade to (near) Leachlade	8	0	5	0	0	28	4
	30	0	7½	241	3	130	6

The general Width of the Canal is 40 Feet at the Top, and 30 feet at the Bottom. In many Parts, where the Ground is on a dead Flat or Level, it is confiderably wider, having the Banks entirely made with the Soil from the Bed of the Canal. The Tunnel is (as before ftated) two Miles three Furlongs in Length; it is 14 Feet 3 Inches wide, and 16 Feet in Height, including fix Feet of Water. It is lined with Mafonry, arched at the Top, and having an inverted Arch at the Bottom, excepting fome few Places where Rock has made it unneceffary. On April 20, 1789, Mr. Josiah Clowes, the operative Engineer, paffed this Tunnel, for the firft Time, in a Veffel of 30 Tons. The Boats are 12 Feet wide, and 80 Feet long, drawing 4 Feet of Water when loaded, and carrying 70 Tons. The Tonnage is regulated by the Commodity, and charged not by the Mile, but by certain Stations mentioned in the Act of Parliament.

The Junction with the Thames was actually made near Leachlade Nov. 14, 1789, as is chronicled on the Key-ftone of the Bridge adjoining the Lock there; and, on the 19th of the fame Month, the firft Veffel paffed laden into the Thames in the Prefence of great Numbers of People, who were affembled on the Occafion. In order to form any adequate Judgement of the commercial Importance of this Undertaking, it will be neceffary to take a larger View of the Intercourfe between the Ports of Wales, Briftol, Gloucefter, Worcefter, and Shrewfbury, of the inland Navigation connected with the Staffordfhire and Worcefterfhire Canal, and of the intermediate Courfe of the Thames from Leachlade, by Oxford, Wallingford, and Reading, to London, than can be fully expreffed in this Place. The Extent of the Exports from Briftol up the Severn, and which will be conveyed by this Canal into the Thames, includes many Articles, as Metals, &c. &c. of Indian and American Produce. The Returns down the Severn are ftill more important; Coal, Cider, Perry, Grain, Wool, Cheefe, Salt, and Manufactures of almoft every Kind. If we confult the Courfe of the Thames, and the inland Country through which this Canal paffes, it is not eafy to exprefs the Advantages which the Inhabitants living on the Banks of this extenfive Communication will derive from it; which, connected as it is in its Effects with the Oxford Canal Navigation, leading to Birmingham, Staffordfhire, Yorkfhire, Chefhire, &c. form a Line of Intercourfe between the interior Parts of the Kingdom and London, by the Way of the River Thames. The Returns from the Capital by thefe two great Canals (the Oxford and the Thames and Severn Canals) will probably be of the greateft Importance to the City of London, and will proportionably awaken its Traders to fome additional Attention to thefe great Works now they are completed.

5

The

The firſt Date of the Regiſter occurs in 1586.

ANNUAL ACCOUNT OF MARRIAGES, BIRTHS, AND BURIALS, IN THIS PARISH.

A.D.	Mar.	Bir.	Bur.	A.D.	Mar.	Bir.	Bur.	A.D.	Mar.	Bir.	Bur.	A.D.	Mar.	Bir.	Bur.
1781	8	15	19	1786	4	25	17	1791				1796			
1782	4	28	18	1787	4	29	18	1792				1797			
1783	0	24	29	1788	4	26	22	1793				1798			
1784	12	24	31	1789	4	24	15	1794				1799			
1785	4	26	33	1790	8	35	24	1795				1800			

INSCRIPTIONS IN THE CHURCH.

IN THE CHANCEL.
ON FLAT STONES.

Arms ; Azure, two Bars, in chief three Croſſes patée Or, on an Ineſcocheon, the Arms of Ulſter, for BATHURST ; — impaling, a Chevron between three Talbots, for MORRICE.

Here lyeth, in hopes of a bleſſed Reſurrection, the Body of Sir EDWARD BATHURST, Knt. and Baronett, who departed this Life the ſixth Day of Auguſt, Anno Dom. 1674, ætatis ſuæ 61.

Arms ; BATHURST as before ;—impaling a Croſs. Creſt, a Horſe paſſant.

Here lyeth the Body of ROBERT BATHURST, eldeſt Son of Sir EDWARD BATHURST, Bart. by his ſecond Lady, and MARGARET his Wife, eldeſt Daughter of Mr. ROBERT OATRIDGE, of Butler's Court in this Pariſh. He died May 30, 1692, aged 48. She died March 20, 1718, aged 69. They had 16 Children, 8 died in their Infancy, and lie near this Place.

Arms ; BATHURST as before ;—impaling, on a Bend, three Roſes, and in the dexter Canton a Cheſſrook, for SMALL.

HERE LIETH THE BODY OF ROBERT BATHURST, ELDEST SON OF ROBERT AND MARGARET BATHURST, WHO DIED OCT. 6, 1726, AGED 59.

ALSO ELIZABETH HIS WIFE, DAUGHTER OF GEORGE SMALL, OF MINCHIN HAMPTON, IN THIS COUNTY, ESQUIRE, WHO DIED FEB. THE 5TH, 1748, AGED 81.

ALSO JAMES SMALL, BROTHER OF ELIZABETH BATHURST, WHO DIED FEB. 13TH, 1749, AGED 86.

Arms ; BATHURST as before ;—impaling a Chevron between three Cocks Heads eraſed, for COXETER.

Here lieth interred the Body of ROBERT BATHURST, of Clay-hill, Gent. who departed this Life February 28, 1765, aged 67.

Alſo Mrs. ELIZABETH BATHURST, died May the 7, 1788, aged 77.

Arms ; ſix Annulets, for LODER ; the ſame on an Ineſcocheon.

HERE LIETH THE BODY OF JANE LODER, WIFE OF JOHN LODER, GENTLEMAN, ONE OF THE DAUGHTERS AND COHEIRESSES OF CHARLES LODER, OF HINTON, IN THE COUNTY OF BERKS, ESQUIRE, WHO DIED MARCH 31, 1736, AGED 36.

ALSO NEAR TO THIS PLACE LIETH THE BODY OF FRANCIS, SON OF JOHN AND JANE LODER.

HERE LIETH THE BODY OF JOHN LODER, GENTLEMAN, SON OF ROBERT LODER, LATE OF LECHELADE, GENTLEMAN, AND PENELOPE HIS WIFE, WHO DIED THE 29TH OF OCTOBER, 1746, AGED 59.

Arms as before.

Heie lieth the Body of FRANCIS LODER, Gentleman, Son of ROBERT LODER, late of Lechelade, Gentleman, and PENELOPE his Wife, who died the 19 Day of Novem. 1741, aged 56.

Arms ; a Bend engrailed between two Fireballs, for SIMONS ;—impaling, a Bend guttée, between two Corniſh Choughs, a Chief checquy, for PLEYDELL.

HERE LIES INTERRED THE BODY OF ROBERT SIMONS, ESQ. WHO DEPARTED THIS LIFE THE THIRD DAY OF APRIL, MDDXXII, ÆT. LXIX.

ALSO HIS NEPHEW JOHN SHERMER, ESQUIRE, OF HANNINGTON,

IN THE COUNTY OF WILTS. HE DIED JULY 13, 1786, AGED 81 YEARS.

Arms as before, on a Lozenge.

Here lies interred the Body of ANN SIMONS, late Wife of ROBERT SIMONS, Eſq. and one of the Daughters of EDWARD PLEYDELL, of Cricklade, in the County of Wilts, Gent. who departed this Life the ſixth Day of April, MDCCXXIX, æt. LXXV.

Alſo MARY, the Wife of JOHN SHERMER, Eſquire, of Hannington, in the County of Wilts. She died Feb. 4, 1774, aged 48 Years.

Arms ; two Bars, on a Canton, a Caſtle ; —impaling, LODER.

In Memory of the Rev. RICHARD CASTLE, Vicar of this Place 43 Years, who departed this Life Oct. 3, 1737, aged 70.

Here lieth, in hopes of a joyful Reſurrection. the Body of LETTICE, the Wife of RICHARD CASTLE, who departed this Life Sept. 4. 1723, aged 33 Years.

Arms ; billettée, on a Chief three Garbs.

HENRY, the Son of HENRY and SUSANNAH BAMPTON, ob. March 31, 1765, æt. 35.

ANN, the Daughter of HENRY and SUSANNAH BAMPTON, ob. April 5, 1753, æt. 13.

Alſo HENRY BAMPTON their Father lies here, who died Dec. 3, 1769, aged 67.

SUSANNAH BAMPTON, Wife of HENRY BAMPTON, and Daughter of ROBERT and ELIZABETH BATHURST, of Clay Hill, died June 8, 1777, aged 77.

Arms ;

Arms, as before ;—impaling a lion with two heads.

Here lieth the Body of
Mr. SAMUEL BAMPTON,
late Oilman, of
Grace Church Street,
London, Son of HENRY and
SUSANNA BAMPTON,
of this Place.
He died y͏ᵉ 21 of
November, 1773,
aged 40 Years.

ON A HANDSOME MARBLE MONUMENT:

Arms; on a Lozenge Or, a Bend engrailed Vert, between
two Fire Balls Gules.

Near this Place
lie the Remains
of Mrs. ANN SIMMONS,
whofe Life compleated the true Character
of the Gentlewoman, the Friend, and the Chriftian.
She was fincere in her Friendfhip,
affable and candid in her Converfation,
pious in her Devotion,
liberal and fecret in her Charity.
Her Acquaintance have loft a real Friend ;
the Poor a daily and conftant Benefactrefs.
She lived to a good old Age ;
and though fhe declined gradually,
through the Weaknefs and Infirmity of Body,
yet fhe retained a chearful Temper
and Vivacity of Spirits to the laft.
She is gone to receive the Reward of her Virtue ;
and has left her Friends to imitate her Example.
She died the 24th of September, 1769,
aged 76.

S O U T H   A I S L E.
ON A MARBLE MONUMENT :

Arms ; on three Efcocheons ; 1. Argent, a chevron between
three Cocks' Heads erafed Gules, for COXETER ;—impaling,
Gules, three Daggers, between feven Mullets Argent, on a
Canton Sable, a Lion paffant guardant Or. 2. Quarterly, 1ft
and 4th, COXETER ; 2d and 3d, Azure, two Bars Or, in chief
three Croffes pattée of the laft, for BATHURST. 3. BATHURST;
—impaling, Argent, a Fefs between two Lions paffant Gules.

To the pious Memory
of the hopeful Youth GEORGE COXETER,
eldeft Son of GEORGE COXETER, Efq.
and MARY his Wife, the only furviving
Offspring of that noble Benefactor
to the Church LAWRENCE BATHURST, Efq.
and SUSANNAH his Wife, who both
lye interred in the Chancel.
LAWRENCE died in the Year 1671 ;
SUSANNA, in the Year 1687 ; GEORGE,
the 28th September, 1699,
in the 13 Year of his Age.

Alfo
to the pious Memory of GEORGE COXETER,
Efq, who died Jan. the 18th, 1701,
in the 42d Year of his Age,

ON A MONUMENT :

Arms ; a Chevron between three Hickwalls.

Near this Place lyes interred
the Body of Mrs. ELIZABETH PINFOLD,
Wife of EDWARD PINFOLD, fen. of this
Parifh, who departed this Life
June the 2d, in the 25 Year of
her Age.

ON A FLAT STONE.

Here lieth interred
ELIZABETH, the Wife of
WALTER PARKER, who
departed this Life October
the 5th, 1729, aged 24 Years.

IN THE NORTH AISLE.

ON   MONUMENTS.
Arms ; Azure, a Chevron Ermine between three Croffes
pattée Argent ;—impaling LODER.

Near this Place
lieth interred, in the Grave of his Anceftors,
RICHARD AINGE, Gentleman, who died April 9, 1778,
in the 57 Year of his Age.
His Acquaintance have loft a Friend, the Poor a Benefactor,
and the World an honeft Man.
He married LETTICE, the Daughter of ROBERT LODER,
of this Parifh, Gentleman.
She died Nov. 11, 1775, in the 53d Year of her Age,
univerfally lamented.

Near this Place lieth the Body of Mr. EDWARD HUGHES,
who died Sept. 3, 1786, aged 57 Years.
He married CATHARINE, the fole furviving
Sifter of RICHARD AINGE.

Near this Place
lye the Remains of
EDWARD BATHURST, Gent.
born the 9th of Feb. 1705,
obiit the 29 of Auguft, 1762.

Alfo in the fame Place
BARBARA his Wife,
born the 3d of Auguft, 1701,
obiit the 12 Feb. 1785.
She was the only Daughter of
RICHARD COXETER, Efq.
of Bampton, in the County
of Oxford.

IN THE CHURCH YARD.

ON MONUMENTS AGAINST
THE CHURCH.

To the Memory of
EDWARD WALKLETT, who
died the 7 of July, 1757, in
the 73d Year of his Age.

Near
this Place
lieth interred the
Body of THOMAS BLAGROVE,
fen. who departed this Life
April 28, 1746, aged 57,
who left a Widow and ten
Children to lament the Lofs

of the beft of Hufbands,
and a tender Parent.

MARY, the Wife of
THOMAS BLAGROVE, died Aug. 17, 1762,
aged 69 Years.

MARGARET, the Daughter of
THOMAS and MARY BLAGROVE,
died July 21, 1757,
aged 23 Years.

ON   TOMBS.

In Memory of ROBERT NEWMAN,
of Downington, who died
the 21 Day of November, in 1708.

Alfo MARY his Wife
died 10 Dec. in the Year 1743,
aged 84 Years.

Under this Tomb lyeth the Body of
JOHN NEWMAN, their only Son,
who departed this Life Feb. the 20th,
in the Year of our Lord 1760,
aged 77 Years.

In Memory of
MARTHA, Wife of
JOHN NEWMAN,
who departed this Life
October 16, 1770,
aged 71 Years.

Here lies the Body of
Mr. Robert Anderson,
Citizen and Grocer
of London, late of
Leachlade, Agent and
Wharfinger, who died
Oct. the 9, 1769, in the
56 Year of his Age.

In Memory of
Isaac Wells,
who died 31 of Jan. 1763,
aged 66 Years.

Here lyeth the Body of the Wife of
Robert Gearin, who was
buryed anno 1689.

Here lyeth the Body of Richard
Gerin, the Son of Robert, who
was buried May the 24, 1699.

Here lyeth the Body of
Robert Gerin, who was
buried 28 June, 1706.

Here alfo was buried Simon, the Son
of Simon Gerin, July 30, 1702.

Here lyeth the Body of Simon,
the Son of Robert Gerin, who was
buried Dec. the 11, 1710.

Alfo here was buried the Wife
of Simon Gerin, Mar. 14, 1705,
and Ann, the Daughter of Robert
Gerin, was buried Anno Dom. 1691.

In Memory of
Thomas Baldwin,
who died at Thornhill Farm,
in this Parifh, 15 June, 1740,
aged 60 Years.

To the pious Memory of
Eleanor, the Wife of Thomas
Baldwin, who departed this Life
15 Jan. 1764, aged 91 Years.

In Memory of Eleanor,
Daughter of George and
Elizabeth Grinnuf. She
died March the 30, 1757,
aged 28 Years.

Mary, Daughter of Thomas and
Martha Perrin, of Aylberton,
in this County, ob. 5 May, 1746,
aged 28.

Sarah, Wife of William Day,
and 2d Daughter of Thomas and
Eleanor Baldwin, died 11 Oct.
1738.

In Memory of
Justinian Stocker, Gent.
who died Aug. 16, Anno D'ni 1742,
ætatis 27.

Elizabeth, Wife of William Stiles,
ob. 24 June, 1728, aged 70 Years.

William Stiles died 14 March,
1729, aged 68 Years.

Jane, Wife of William Stiles,
died 8 July, 1732, aged 29.

Here lies the Body of
Anne, the Wife of John Strange,
Gent. who died Nov. 28, 1763,
aged 68 Years.

Here lyeth the Body of
John Niblett, fen.
who departed this Life
May .. 1713, aged . . . . .

Near this Place lyeth Elizabeth,
the Mother of John Niblett,
aged 70 Years.

Here lyeth the Body of
Sarah, the Wife of Robert Raikes,
of Gloucefter.

Near this Tomb
lyeth the Body of
John Boarding.
He died January 1738.

Alfo of Rebecca Boarding
his Wife. She died
March 9th, 1774, in the 71ft Year of
her Age.

In Memory of
Elizabeth, Daughter of
James and Elizabeth Ayling.
She died March 11, 1774, aged 7 Years.

In Memory of
Miriam, the Wife of
John Harding,
of Leachlade, in the
County of Gloucefter,
Gentleman, deceafed.
She died Auguft
the 14, 1775,
aged 85 Years.

In Memory of
John Green, Son of
Thomas and Sarah Green,
who died Sept. 6, 1783,
aged 40 Years.

Here
lie the Remains of
Thomas Oatridge, Gent.
who departed this Life
November 12, A. D. 1789,
aged 60 Years.

To the Memory of
Ann Lambert,
who departed this Life
Novemb. 28, in 1771,
and in the 71ft Year of her Age.

To the Memory of
Elizabeth Lewis,
of Leachlade, Spinfter,
who departed this Life the
8 of May, Anno Domini 1776,
in the 66 Year of her Age.

Mr. William White,
and Mrs. Sarah White his Wife,
departed this Life,
in Hopes of a bleffed Immortality;
the former on the 4 Day of April, 1767,
aged 59;

---

the latter on the 4 Day of Auguft, 1769,
aged 72.

Mary Robins
departed this Life
November 30, 1770.

Mrs. Elizabeth Spencer
departed this Life
January the 31, 1766.

Here lieth interred
the Body of
Frances Phillips,
Wife of John Phillips,
and Daughter of George
Radburn, of Leachlade,
who departed this Life
the 1ft of May, 1781,
aged 60 Years.

In Memory of
Martha Luckett, the Wife of
James Luckett. She died Nov. 8,
1774, aged 56 Years.

In Memory of
Thomas Luckett, who died Jan.
the 24, 1773, aged 55 Years.

Alfo
Thomas Luckett,
the Son of Thomas and
Martha Luckett,
who died October the 27, 1765,
aged 8.

In
Memory of
Thomas Walker,
who died March the 6th,
1758,
aged 68 Years.

In Memory of
William Hughes. He was
buried Nov. 1, 1765,
aged 70 Years.

Alfo of Elizabeth
his Wife. She was buried
January the 9th, 1767,
aged 78 Years.

ON FLAT STONES.

In Memory of
William Jackson,
Son of James and Sarah Jackson,
who died July 23, 1789.

In Memory of
William Gearing
and Ann his Wife.
He died Auguft the 20th, 1767,
aged 67 Years.
She died Feb. 20, 1784,
aged 79.

O N

ON HEAD-STONES.

	Died	Aged
Robert Hobbs	14 June, 1736	49
Robert Hobbs	14 Apr. 1776	61
Elizabeth his Wife	4 June, 1785	69
Elizabeth, Daughter of William and Catharine Hobbs	13 Feb. 1789	—
Richard Grain	15 Apr. 1729	26
Elizabeth Luckett	17 Nov. 1746	63
James Hancock	18 Apr. 1729	57
John Barker	7 May, 1755	55
William Hooper	29 Mar. 1779	63
William Day	11 Feb. 1783	76
Sarah his firft Wife, Daughter of Thomas and Elizabeth Baldwin	11 Oct. 1738	34
Mary, Wife of Thomas Bailey	26 Oct. 1781	68
Mary Tuckey	3 May, 1690	—
John Tuckey, fen.	3 Nov. 1718	55
John Tuckey, jun.	24 June, 1718	20
Alexander Gearing	8 Feb. 1736	84
Mary Gearing	— Nov. 1737	—
Richard, Son of Robert and Catharine Gearing	19 Sept. 1758	26
John Gearing	9 Nov. 1747	39
Robert Gearing	14 Aug. 1728	—
Robert Gearing	8 July, 1757	74
Mary his Wife	4 Sept. 1762	66
Henry Gearing	11 Jan. 1756	61
Sarah, Wife of Richard Gearing	6 Sept. 1734	76
William Gearing	30 Aug. 1767	67
Robert Gearing	2 July, 1768	70
Catharine his Wife	12 Aug. 1757	68
Simon Gearing	10 May, 1749	19
Catharine, Daughter of Robert and Elizabeth Gearing	23 Apr. 1780	16
Thomas Luckett	6 July, 1731	42
Elizabeth his Wife	16 July, 1731	42
William Edmondes	14 Mar. 1686	—
Phillis, Wife of Edward Davis	12 Feb. 1733	52
Thomas Day	— May, 174.	41
Elizabeth Day	9 Oct. 1732	—
Simon Temple	19 Aug. 1719	—
Sarah his Wife	26 July, 1683	—
Ann his fecond Wife	13 Nov. 1700	—
Simon his Son, Parifh Clerk 60 Years	5 Jan. 1768	—
Ann, Wife of John Temple	28 Dec. 1722	34
Jane, Wife of Simon Temple, Daughter of William Edwards	2 June, 1741	63
Thomas Berry	6 Feb. 1700	—
Sibble his Wife	— May, 1717	—
Ann Cullam	23 Oct. 1697	—
Margaret, Wife of Robert Borton	14 Feb. 1700	—
James Pearce	8 Mar. 1672	—
Mary, Daughter of William and Elizabeth Bailey	12 July, 1702	—
Richard Bailey	11 July, 1723	61
Mary, Wife of Charles Godwin	7 Aug. 1706	33
John Davis	15 Feb. 1710	—
William Davis	10 Feb. 1710	81
Mary, Wife of David Smith	— —— 1700	—
Mary, Wife of John Turnor	25 Feb. 1680	—
Damaris, Wife of —— Smith	19 Sept. 1727	63
William, Son of Wm. and Mary Pullin	1 July, 1725	19
Robert Wormer	7 May, 1753	36
William Adams	— May, 1729	28
Richard Hinton	23 July, 1711	—
Richard his Son	12 Mar. 1724	—
John Hinton	24 July, 1738	55
William Stiles	— Mar. 1724	63
Elizabeth, Wife of Francis Harber	— July, 1728	62
William Garnbury	11 Jan. 1744	—
Katharine Sweatman	10 Nov. 1746	62
Mary Sweatman	24 June, 1755	—
James Knight	19 Feb. 1751	61
Jane his Wife	18 Oct. 1744	57
Jane their Daughter	5 Mar. 1748	24
James their Son	29 May, 1749	24
John Knight	9 Apr. 1770	51
Thomas Morris	13 Apr. 1737	48
Jane, the Wife of Stephen Chadwell	3 Nov. 1731	67
Catharine, Wife of Daniel Gibbins	10 Nov. 1758	50
Efther, Wife of William Yells	16 Sept. 1755	74
John Gilford	22 Sept. 1748	30
James Knipe	4 Dec. 1735	68
Francis Whiting	17 Mar. 1735	38
Ann, Wife of William Hughes	24 July, 1786	66
John Hughes	23 Apr. 1770	39
Eleanor, Wife of William Watkins	— Apr. 1730	43
Thomas Richman	— Aug. 1728	62
Hannah, Wife of Arthur Brown	10 Oct. 1745	33
Mary, Wife of Robert Keble	15 Sept. 1750	27
Joan, Wife of Anthony Morfe	— 1730	70
Anthony Morfe	13 July, 1728	—
Mary, Daugh. of T. and Ann Rodway	27 Oct. 1747	19
James Rodway	6 Dec. 1789	31
Edmund Strange	16 Oct. 1777	51
Stephen Smith	24 July, 1728	35
Ann his Wife	22 June, 1755	63
Thomas Smith	12 Apr. 1777	51
Richard Walker	12 Oct. 1720	—
Richard Walker	17 Nov. 1737	28
Joanna, Daughter of Charles and Elizabeth Pinfold	25 Aug. 1745	23
Mary, Wife of Samuel Stanly	26 Mar. 1751	60
Samuel Stanly	6 July, 1752	62
Nathaniel Crew	19 June, 1785	73
Mary his Wife	21 Apr. 1743	25
Matthew, Son of John Pain	24 —— 1725	25
Ifaac Pain	— 1729	57
Catharine his Wife	7 Feb. 1748	75
Ann, Wife of John Day	17 Apr. 1732	22
John Francis	21 May, 1730	73
Mary his Wife	24 July, 1738	72
John Francis	3 Oct. 1773	27
Margaret, Daughter of John and Mary Francis	12 Aug. 1775	23
Ann, Wife of William Smith	17 July, 1751	91
Anne, Wife of William Cook	4 Mar. 1752	57
Ann, Wife of John Everton	4 July, 1733	29
Francis Galloway	29 June, 1765	75
Anabell his Wife	2 Feb. 1741	47
Ann their Daughter	5 May, 1746	26
Thomas Elliott	18 May, 1712	69
David Smith	19 Dec. 1709	—
Bartholomew Day	13 July, 1721	82
Robert Hall	23 Apr. 1710	45
Urfula Apworth	10 Oct. 1745	49
Lawrence Wyett	3 Jan. 1734	40
—— Luckett	6 July, 1731	42
Thomas, Son of Jofeph and Frances Manfield	16 Mar. 1753	22
Mary, Wife of Robert Hobbs	12 May, 1737	49
John Parker	7 May, 1755	55
Mary Lewis	17 Mar. 1749	65
Elizabeth Wentworth	6 Mar. 1742	59
Mary, Wife of Thomas Ebfworth	1 Feb. 1764	28
William Houfe	23 Oct. 1729	55
John Hooper	10 Dec. 1755	57
Richard Hooper	8 Mar. 1730	57
Mary, Wife of William Hooper	10 Mar. 1730	37

CLIX. LECKHAMPTON

IS a Part of the Hundred of *Cheltenham*, from which Town it is diftant about three Miles, twelve from *Cirencefter* on the North-weft, and eight Eaftward from the City of Gloucester. The Terrier includes 1200 Acres, and is divided between rich Pafture of a mixed Soil of Sand and Loam, and a mountainous Tract, the Acclivities and Summit of which are extenfive Sheep Walks, partly converted, the Inclofure, to Arable Land.

The Ridge of *Leckhampton* Hills are fome of the boldeft and moft lofty of the *Cotefwold*; they are broken more precipitately, and exhibit a greater Extent of bare Rock of granulated Stone than any other. Near the Precipice, upon a very grand Terrace, are Veftiges of a Vallation or deep Trench acrofs the Point, which, as the Sides were defended by Nature, muft, in the rude State of War, have been an impregnable Faftnefs.

The Benefice is a Rectory, in the Deanery of *Winchcombe*, but not endowed with the Tythes of the whole Parifh. Certain Portions of them appear to have been divided between the Abbey of *Fifchamp* in *Normandy* and the *Benedictine* Nunnery of *Ufk* in *Monmouthfhire*. To the former belonged the Advowfon and certain Lands, which, after the Cuftom of the Ecclefiaftics, were ftyled a Manor. At the general Inclofure, Lands were allotted in Lieu of Tythes.

About the middle of the fourteenth Century, the Church was re-built, with the ufual Architecture of that Æra. It has a Nave and South Aifle, with a very neat Spire in the Middle, of confiderable Height and exact Dimenfions.

The Manor in *Domefday* is faid to have been held in two Parts, one by William Leuric, containing three Hides, and the other by Britric, taxed at four Hides, and valued at 1*l.* 10*s.* a Year. Adam le Despencer, fo named from his Office of Steward of the King's Houfehold at the great Feftivals, obtained the whole of this, with other Manors, which he held by grand Serjeanty. A Grant of a Fair, Markets, and free Warren, was made to him in 1249, 57 Hen. III. the Right of which was allowed in 1287, 15 Edw. I. and finally confirmed in 1618, 16 James. In the Reign of Edward III. it paffed to the Family of Giffard, a younger Branch of the Barons of *Brimpsfield*, and thofe of *Stoke Giffard*, in which it remained till 1486, when it was held in Marriage Dower by John Norwood, who married Eleanor, Daughter and Coheir of John Giffard, Efq. from whom, in a right Line, it has defcended to Henry Norwood, Efq. the prefent Proprietor *.

Of the Manor-houfe there are fome ancient Remains. The Form of the Windows of the Hall, and the brick Chimneys, which are twifted Columns, prove the Date of Erection in the Reign of Henry the Seventh; and make a Conjecture allowable, that the firft mentioned John Norwood was the Founder of this Structure. In the Beginning of this Century, a fpacious Addition was made by the Rev. Thomas Norwood in the modern Style. Although fituate at the Bafe of the lofty Hills before mentioned, it commands a very extenfive and interefting Profpect over the Vale of *Gloucefter*.

Eftates, independent on the Manor, are now held by the Families of Critchet and Pride, which were formerly vefted in thofe of Selwyn of *Mattefden* and Isles of *Minchin Hampton*.

No Benefactions to the Poor.

Incumbents.	Patrons.	Incumbents.	Patrons.
—— Robert Ffynch,	————.	* * * * * * * * * * * * *	
1549 Rhees Jones,	Ralph Norwood.	1707 Tho. Norwood, M. A.	Arthur Charlet, D. D.
1570 Ralph Gynes,	William Norwood.	1734 Richard Arthur,	————.
1571 Anthony Higgins,	William Rogers.	1738 Clement Headington, B. A.	Will. Norwood.
* * * * * * * * *		1743 John Trye, B. A.	William Trye.
—— Robert Jones,	————.	1766 William Draper, M. A.	Charles Norwood.

* The Family of Norwood is of high Antiquity and Confequence, and is regularly traced from John de Northwode, of *Northwood Chafteners*, in the Ifle of *Shepey*, co. *Kent*. John de Norwode was fummoned as a Baron of Parliament in 1294, 22 Edw. I. which Barony became extinct in 1375. The Defcendant of a Brother of the firft Baron migrated into this Country, and, in Confequence of his Marriage with Eleanor Giffard, became poffeffed of the manerial Eftate at *Leckhampton*.

Present

Present Lord of the Manor,
Henry Norwood, Efq.

The Heralds, in 1682 and 1683, fummoned from this Parifh
Henry Norwood, Efq. Oliver Partridge, Gent. and Richard Banafter, Gent.

At the Election in 1776, Five Freeholders polled from this Parifh.

The firft Date of the Regifter occurs in 1679.

Annual Account of Marriages, Births, and Burials, in this Parish.

A.D.	Mar.	Bir.	Bur.	A.D.	Mar.	Bir.	Bur.	A.D.	Mar.	Bir.	Bur.	A.D.	Mar.	Bir.	Bur.
1781	2	5	2	1786	1	8	2	1791				1796			
1782	—	3	—	1787	1	3	3	1792				1797			
1783	2	6	5	1788	1	6	4	1793				1798			
1784	1	5	2	1789	1	5	1	1794				1799			
1785	1	8	3	1790	2	3	1	1795				1800			

INSCRIPTIONS IN THE CHURCH.

IN THE CHANCEL.

ON A MONUMENT.

Chara Fidem non verba dedi, jam Fata
vocârunt ;
Ecce Virum cineres mifceat urna facros.

Juxta reliquias conjugis
Fidelis conditur in quod
Mori potuit Roberti Jones,
Art. M. non ita pridem
Reverendi hujus ecclefiæ
Rectoris, fummâ morum
Pietate, litterarumq; fcientiâ,
Inter fuos fpectabilis, qui
Viduitatis languens in
Mœrore multæq; fenectutis
Pondere depreffus, placidus
Sanctam efflavit animam
Die Septembris 29,
An. D'ni 1707, ætat. 84, viduit. 13.

In fpem futuræ Refurrectionis
fubtus depofitum eft corpus
Elizabethæ Roberti Jones,
Conjugis dilectæ, que expiravit Maij 8te,
Anno { D'ni 1694.
{ Ætatis 72.
{ Conjugij 40.

IN THE SOUTH AISLE.

On a Brass Plate in the South
Wall, with the Effigies of a
Man, Woman, nine Sons, and
two Daughters, kneeling.

Arms ; Ermine, a Crofs engrailed
Gules, for Norwood ;—impaling, Ar-
gent, two Lions paffant Gules, for
Lygon.

ELIZABETHA NORWOOD, VXOR
GULIELMI NORWOOD,
ARMIGERI, CVI PEPERIT NOVEM
FILIOS, FILIAS DUAS,
ANNOS NATA 5C, APRILIS 16 AN'O
D'NI 1598, PIE
ET FELICITER EXPIRAVIT IN
CHRISTO.

ON FLAT STONES.

Arms ; Norwood as before.

Here was buryed the Body
of William Norwood, Efq. who
died September the 23, 1632.

As alfo the Body of Henry
Norwood, the youngeft Son
of Henry Norwood, Efq.
who departed this Life the 14
Day of Sept. An° D'ni 1689.

HERE LYETH THE BODY
OF RICHARD NORWOOD,
THE ELDEST SON OF
WILLIAM NORWOOD,
ESQVYER, WHO DECI-
ASED THE XII DAY OF
JANUARY, ANNO DOM'
1630.

Jane, the endeared
Wife of Richard, eldeft
Son of Francis Norwood,
Efq. deceafed in Child
bed the 15th Auguft, 1682,
aged . . Indued with
Piety, Patience, and Charity,
beloved by all, and
her Death much lamented.

Here lyeth the Body
of Richard Norwood, Efq.
the eldeft Son of
Francis Norwood, Efq.
who died March 14,
1689, in the 57 Yeare
of his Age.

Mary Norwood was buried Aug.
the 31, 1727.

Thomas Trye, Efq. was
buried February 16,
1730, aged 46.

The Rev. Thomas Norwood,
Jun. died September the 12
1724.

Francis, fixth Son of
Francis Norwood,
Efquire, here buried
Nov. 6, 1700.

The Rev. Thomas
Norwood, fen. died
the 11th Aug. 1734,
aged 83.

Mary, Wife of the
Rev. Thomas Norwood, died
Auguft the 25, 1723.

On a Marble Slab :

Arms ; Norwood as before, on an
Inefcocheon of Pretence, three Trefoils,
in chief a Greyhound current, for
Palmer.

William Norwood, Efq.
died the 24th of June, 1764,
aged 65 Years.
This Stone was engraved to his Memory
by the Order of Anne his Relict.

HERE LYETH INTERRED THE
BODY OF ROBERT HIDE
BORNE FROM WILLIAM HIDE,
OF DENCHWORTH IN BARK-
SHIRE, WHO DEPARTED THE . .
DAY OF DECEMBER, 163 . .

Thomas Sadler, A. B.
of Univerfity Coll. Oxon. Son
of Thomas Sadler, of
Leckhampton, Yeoman,
died the 27 of July, 1710,
ætatis fuæ 22.

In Memory of
William Hazleham and
Elizabeth his Wife,
Daughter of Thomas
and Mary Sadler, who
died June the 8th, 1776.

ELIZABETH, Wife of
WILLIAM TRYE, Efq.
of Sudgrove,
in this County,
died November 8th,
1742, aged 22.

IN THE NAVE.

ON FLAT STONES.

SAMUEL ROGERS, Clerke,
was buried May 17, 1728.

Arms ; Or, a Bend Azure, for
TRYE ;—impaling, Paly of fix, over all
a Bend, for LONGFORD.

In Memoriam diuternam
JOHANNIS TRYE,
Ecclefiæ hujus Parochialis Rectoris.
Obiit hic die Novemb. 22,
Anno falutis 1766,
ætatis 49.

Necnon & JOHANNIS filii fui,
Qui vita defunctus eft Jan. 15,
Anno Dom. 1757.

Necnon MARIÆ JOH. TRYE, uxoris,
& JOH. LONGFORD, Cler. filiæ. Obiit die
Aprilis 30, anno falutis 1768, ætatis 46.

I N T H E C H U R C H - Y A R D, O N T O M B S.

HERE LYETH THE BODYE OF
RICHARD HOWSE AND
LETTICE HIS WIFE. HEE
DECEASED MARCH THE 12,
1621 ; AND SHE DECEASED
THE 10 OF MARCH, ANNO
1636.

This Tomb is erected to the
Memory of RALPH PUMFRET
and BARBARA his Wife, who were
here buried, by each other. He
died on the 9 Day of May, 1699,
aged 90 Years : and fhe was
buried on the 11 Day of June, 1687,
in the 78 Year of her Age.

ROBERT, Son of RALPH
PUMFRET, was buried
neere this Place on
the 22 Day of April, 1699,
aged 65.

ELIZABETH BROWN,
Daughter of RALPH
PUMFRET, is neere
this Place interred
Aug. the 26, 1680,
aged 45.

In Memory of
RICHARD CAFFORD, of this Parifh,
Yeoman,

who died Dec. 19, 1726, aged near
80 Years.

Alfo of MARY his Wife, who died
Oct. 18, 1732, aged 76 Years.

Near this Tomb is buried
RICHARD CAFFORD, Yeoman,
the Son of RICHARD and MARY
CAFFORD. He died March 13, 1755,
aged 70 Years.

Near this Place lieth
MARY, the Wife of RICHARD CAFFORD.
Ob. 11th of Oct. 1759, æt. 76.

MARY, Wife of WILLIAM TAYLER,
died the 16 of March, 1761,
aged 44.

In Memory of
JAMES, the Son of
JAMES and ELIZABETH SADLER, of
the Parifh of Uphatherly, who died
October the 10, 1741.

In Memory of
EDMUND BELLENGER, fen. Yeoman.
He died Nov. 27, 1749, aged 88 Years.

Here lyeth the Body of
JOHN BELLENGER, fen. of the Parifh of
Cuberley, Yeoman, who departed
this Life June the 5, 1766,
aged 63 Years.

In Memory of JOHN ROSE,
who died July the 19, 1762,
aged 74 Years.

Alfo in Memory of ANNE, Wife
of JOHN ROSE, who died Aug. 12, 1766,
aged 75 Years.

In Memory of WILLIAM ROSE, who
died March 7, 1792, aged 76 Years.

In Memory of WILLIAM HESLEHAM,
who departed this Life
Sept. 10, 1720, aged 58.

Alfo of JANE his Wife. She died
Feb. 1, 1745, aged 78 Years.

Alfo in Memory of JAMES HESLEHAM,
Son of WILLIAM and JAMES HESLEHAM,
who died the 1ft of March, 1783,
aged 75 Years.

ELIZABETH, the Daughter of
WILLIAM HESLEHAM, jun., died
Nov. the 4, 1726, aged 21 Years

In Memory of WILLIAM HESLEHAM,
who died May 1692, aged near 70 Years.

Alfo MARY SPARROW, Daughter of
WILLIAM and JANE HESLEHAM,
She died Sept. 22, 1769, aged 68.

O N H E A D - S T O N E S.

	Died	Aged		Died	Aged
John True	— July, 1717	70	Jane his Wife	26 Nov. 1759	78
Thomas, Son of —— Gybfon	5 June, 1708	19	Samuel Cherington	21 Nov. 1779	59
William Wheeler, fen.	2 May, 1709	67	Dorcas his Wife	10 Jan. 1769	50
Elizabeth, Daughter of George Balldwin, of Swyndown	3 Mar. 1711	38	William Cherington	14 Feb. 1761	85
Richard Webb	18 May, 1747	40	Elizabeth his Wife	—— 1746	80
John Lawrence	17 Jan. 1788	50	Samuel, Son of W. and Mary Arkell	22 May, 1717	25
William, Son of Ralph and Fr. Randoll	— Nov. 1672	—	Elizabeth, Wife of Lewis Nothen	18 Sept. 1746	68
Alice, Wife of John Clerk	11 Aug. 1725	71	Jane Clark	2 Jan. 1699	68
William Ballinger	25 Sept. 1742	86	Thomas Williams	—— 1719	—
Thomas his Son	25 Apr. ——	20	Eleanor his Wife	9 Feb. 1755	80
William his Son	10 Jan. 1715	26	Ann their Daughter	6 June, 1756	50
Mary, Wife of Will. Ballinger, fen.	22 Feb. 1710	82	Mary, Wife of Walter King, fecond Wife to Daniel Frame	—— 1681	66
Mary their Daughter	23 Dec. 1694	—	Mary, Daughter of Ralph Crump, Wife of Richard Blifs	2 Dec. 1716	31
John Davis	—— 1741	21	Richard Blifs	7 Apr. 1741	59
Thomas Sadler	26 Apr. 1732	72	John Allen	16 June, 1776	70
Mary his Wife	3 July, 1751	88	Mary, Wife of Richard Clapton	29 Mar. 1783	55
Timothy their Son	7 May, 1744	46	Giles Bridges	2 Nov. 1675	27
Jane, Dau. of John and Jane Sadler	27 Nov. 1742	15	Ann his Wife, late Wife of Edmund Carpent	13 Nov. 1727	84
Mary, Wife of Jofeph Sadler	8 Jan. 1780	69			
Samuel Cherington	28 Mar. 1746	70			

CLX. LEYGH,

clx. LEYGH, LYE, or THE LEIGH;

SO denominated, according to the *Saxon* Etymology, from its extreme flatnefs of Situation, is a Parifh in the Vale of *Gloucefter*, containing 950 Acres, and divided between the Hundreds of *Deerhurft* and *Weftminfter*. It is fix Miles diftant from *Cheltenham*, four South from *Tewkefbury*, and fix from GLOU-CESTER in the oppofite Direction. The Soil is a rich Clay, and chiefly applied to Pafture, particularly a Common of fome Hundred Acres, the Right of which is jointly poffeffed by this and the Parifh of *Deerhurft*, who, fome Years fince, refifted the Divifion of it by a Trench, and obtained uninterrupted Communication by a Suit at Law.

The Living is a Vicarage in the Peculiar of *Deorhurft*, which, with the Impropriation, were given to the Abbey of *St. Dennis* at *Paris*, and afterward annexed to *Deorhurft*; but, when the Alien Priories were fuppreffed, it was confirmed to the *Benedictine* Monks at *Tewkefbury*. Out of the Court of Augmentations the impropriate Tythes were purchafed, in 1574, 16 ELIZ. by RICHARD PATE, Efq. who conveyed them in Truft to the Prefident of *Corpus Chrifti College, Oxford*, for the Maintenance of the Free-fchool at *Cheltenham*, fubject to an annual Rent Charge of 10*l*. 10*s*. to the Crown.

The Church is dedicated to *St. James*. It retains no Peculiarity of Architecture, and was probably built, at the Charge of the Priory, in the fourteenth Century.

Domefday confirms the Property of one Hide to *St. Dennis* of *Paris* in *La Legh*; but the Manor was either never held by them, or afterward alienated; for, in 1334, 7 EDW. III. GILBERT DE KYNARDS-LEY grants it, with other Eftates, to JOAN DE RODBOROUGH, of *Notgrove*, who was fucceeded by her Son. JOHN BROWNING, or FITZ NICHOL, of *Coaley*, having married the Heir of that Family, it paffed (1415), in Default of male Iffue, to CICELY BROWNING, the Wife of Sir GUY WHITTINGTON. THO-MAS WHITTINGTON, Efq. dying in 1547, left fix Coheirs, upon which it was fold to RICHARD BROWNE, Efq. and by his Defcendants to Lord Vifcount TRACY, about 1686. At the Clofe of the laft Century it belonged to STEPHEN COOKE, Efq. whofe Son, RICHARD COOKE, bequeathed it to his Sifter and Heir, the Wife of RICHARD DALTON, Efq. of *Sunning-hill*, co. *Berks*, whofe Daughter and fole Heir is SOPHIA, married to EDMUND PROBYN, Efq. of *Newland*, who is the prefent Proprietor in her Right.

The only Property of confequence, befide the Manor, are the Eftates of ANN HILL, Widow, WIL-LIAM MEEKINGS, Gent. and that held for the Purpofes abovementioned by *Corpus Chrifti College, Oxford*.

Evington is the only Hamlet.

B E N E F A C T I O N S.

ROBERT BUTT gave, by Will, a Rent-Charge of 6*s*. on Land in this Parifh, vefted in the Church-wardens and Overfeers, to be diftributed among the Poor of *Leigh End* on Good Friday annually.

Mrs. LEECH gave Land, the annual Produce of which is 1*l*. 4*s*. to be given to the Poor on *St. Tho-mas's* Day, vefted as above.

JOHN FLUCK, Efq. by Will, gave a Rent-Charge of 2*l. per Annum*, vefted in the Parifh-Officers, to be diftributed among the Poor of this Parifh on the 22d of July.

ELIZABETH FLUCK gave, by Will, vefted as the foregoing, an annual Rent-Charge of 1*l*. to be divided amongft the Poor, on Chriftmas Day.

Dr. ROBERT HUNTINGDON, Bifhop of *Raphoe*, gave, by Will, in 1701, a Rent-Charge of 2*l. per Annum*, vefted in the Minifter and Churchwardens, for apprenticing poor Children alternately, with the Parifh of *Deorhurft*.

BENJAMIN HUNTINGDON gave 5*l*. vefted as above, the Intereft to be given to the Poor annually.

INCUMBENTS.

Incumbents.	Patrons.	Incumbents.	Patrons.
—— Edward Ap Jenkins,	——————.	1625 Jerome Yonge,	King Charles I.
1559 James Williams,	——————.	—— Robert Huntingdon,	——————.
1561 John Davis,	Q. Elizabeth.	1664 Samuel Kendrick, M.A.	King Charles II.
1564 Morgan Ap Howel,	Hugh Evans, by a Grant from the Abbey of Tewkesbury, dated 1539.	1675 John Beard,	——————.
		1683 John Mower, M. A.	——————.
		1728 John Mower, B. A.	King George II.
		1729 Daniel Bond, B. A.	——————.
1577 John Davis,	Q. Elizabeth.	1757 Samuel Jones, Clerk,	——————.
1588 Richard Taylor,	——————.	1759 Richard Neale,	——————.
1618 Joshua Elliott, M. A.	King James I.	1775 John Chester, M. A.	King George III.

Present Lord of the Manor,

Edmund Probyn, Esq.

The only Person summoned from this Parish by the Heralds, in 1682 and 1683, was

Richard Browne, Esq.

It does not appear that any Person polled from this Parish at the Election in 1776.

The first Date of the Register is in 1634.

Annual Account of Marriages, Births, and Burials, in this Parish.

A.D.	Mar.	Bir.	Bur.	A.D.	Mar.	Bir.	Bur.	A.D.	Mar.	Bir.	Bur.	A.D.	Mar.	Bir.	Bur.
1781	2	4	3	1786	2	7	5	1791				1796			
1782	3	5	7	1787	3	5	2	1792				1797			
1783	1	2	4	1788	—	6	7	1793				1798			
1784	—	6	6	1789	2	3	4	1794				1799			
1785	4	5	3	1790				1795				1800			

INSCRIPTIONS IN THE CHURCH.

ON FLAT STONES.

Arms; on a Fess, three Chessrooks, in chief three Martlets, for Browne; —impaling, Gules, a Lion rampant guardant Or, holding a Rose, for Master.

Mary, eldest Daughter of Sir William Master, Kt.

and Wife of Richard Browne, Gent. who departed this Life Novem. the 29, 1683.

———

Arms; Browne as before.

Thomas, the Sonne of Richard Browne, Gent. died November 1667.

———

Hic subtus reconduntur cineres
Johannis Mower, A. M. hujus ecclesiæ per annos XLIIII vicarii
Necnon
Johannis filii A. B.
Unici anni successoris.
Pater ob. 1° Aprilis, 1728, æt. 71.
Filii ob. 4° Aprilis, 1720, æt. 29.

———

IN THE CHURCH-YARD.

ON MONUMENTS AGAINST
THE CHURCH.

Near
this Place
lyeth the Body of
Mary, the Wife of William Lane,
of this Parish, Yeoman,
who died the 17 of Novem.
1726, aged 55 Years.

———

In Memory of John Butt,
an honest substantial Man of
this Neighborhood. He departed
this Life the 20 of May, in the
78 Yeare of his Age, and Yeare of our
Lord 1708.

Also of Anne, Relict of the said
John Butt, who departed this Life
the 12 Sept. 1712, aged 54 Years.

Also of Giles their Son, who departed
this Life the 27 Jan. 1711, aged 26.

Robert Huntingdon, Vicar
of this Church above 16
Yeares, died April 1st, 1664,
and Elizabeth his Wife
Dec. 24, 1649.

———

ON TOMBS.

Here lyeth the Body of
Richard Wells, late of
this Parish, Gent. who departed
this Life 11 Nov. 1686.

———

In
Memory of John Wells, Gent.
late of this Parish, who departed
this Life the 7 of Octob. 1731,
ætat. 31.

In Memory of Mrs. Elizabeth Pope,
late of this Parish, who
for her first Husband married John
Wells, Gent. late of this Parish.

She departed this Life the 15 of
Feb. 1755, ætat. 55.

———

Regretted
by her Friends and Acquaintance
lie here interred the Remains of Esther,
the beloved Wife of William Lane,
who (after a Life worn out with
Care and Industry, performing the
Office of a loving Wife, a tender
Mother, a kind Neighbour, and a
good Christian) willingly resigned
her Soul to God, in Hopes of a blessed
Immortality, the 21 of Sept. 1764,
in the 56 Year of her Age.

———

ON A BRASS PLATE:

HERE LYETH THE BODY
OF IOHN WELLS, GENT.
WHO DEPARTED THIS LIFE
THE IOTH DAY OF APRIL,
IN THE YEAR OF OUR
LORD GOD 1663.

———

ON

S

ON HEAD STONES.

	Died	Aged
William Lane	27 June, 1745	76
John Lane	6 July, 1719	—
Lydia Lane	30 May, 1704	—
Mary, Daughter of William Lane, and Wife of Richard Gooding	10 Sept. 1722	—
Edmund Merryman, fenior	25 Feb. 1742	65
Joan his Wife	12 Nov. 1760	73
Edmund Merryman	1 Feb. 1763	53
Sarah his Daughter	23 Mar. 1767	22
Martha his Daughter	1 May, 1775	16
Thomas, Son of Richard and Elizabeth Merryman	24 Mar. 1769	—
Hefter, Wife of Edmund Merryman, and Daughter of Samuel Healing	24 Feb. 1770	22
Elizabeth, Wife of Jofeph Barnard, and Daughter of Edmund and Sarah Merryman	28 Feb. 1770	29
John Bigling	24 June, 1729	52
William Bifhop	24 Mar. 1789	73
Edward Green	9 July, 1772	—
Anne, Wife of Thomas Drinkwater	14 May, 1681	—
Jofeph Drinkwater	7 Apr. 1727	68
Richard Hawker	25 Sept. 1734	30
Chriftopher Dorrell	12 Mar. 1692	59
Chriftopher his Son	12 Mar. 1694	—
Thomas Longford	4 Apr. 1707	50
Thomas Wood	18 June, 1705	51
Lydia, Wife of William Watts	5 Aug. 1714	75
Jane Butt	22 Mar. 1696	96
Samuel Smith	15 Sept. 1715	62
Bartholomew Cleve	16 Apr. 1713	37
William, Son of John and Anne White, of Norton	25 Oct. 1786	22
Elizabeth, Daughter of Jofeph and Mary White	15 June, 1750	19
Frances, Wife of John Afhly	12 Apr. 1719	67
Edmund Etheridge	17 Dec. 1682	—
William Hill	10 June, 1744	70
Rebecca his Wife	20 Apr. 1739	62
William Hill	31 Jan. 1766	26
Anne, Wife of John Hill	6 July, 1770	30
William Hill	9 Dec. 1775	70
Hannah his Wife	5 June, 1745	40
Thomas Roberts	11 June, 1725	33
Elizabeth his Wife	10 Jan. 1721	35
George Greenway	7 June, 1781	82
Hefter his Wife	2 Mar. 1784	70
Richard Barnes	20 Jan. 1777	30
William Oakey	14 Mar. 1756	72
Anne his Wife	5 May, 1742	55
William James, of Ewyas Harold	26 Dec. 1765	20
Thomas Merry	13 Dec. 1753	52
Hannah his Wife	4 Nov. 1790	87
John Cox	18 Oct. 1770	72
John Cook	3 Nov. 1774	68
Mary his Wife	18 Jan. 1766	58
Anna, Wife of Matthew Clent	12 Sept. 1733	27
Joanna, Wife of Giles Ham	22 Oct. 1740	57
James Hancock	18 Apr. 1731	60
Henry Hancock	31 Oct. 1741	35
Judith Oakey his Daughter	28 Apr. 1757	25
Elizabeth, Wife of William Hancock	26 Apr. 1767	33
Sarah, Daughter of John and Hefter Tyler	5 May, 1735	—
John Tyler	12 Aug. 1739	70
William Lane	16 May, 1702	60
Thomas Lea	3 June, 1762	59
Mary his Wife	16 Dec. 1784	78
John their Son	6 Jan. 1760	25
Elizabeth their Daughter	20 July, 1775	23
Daniel their Son	19 Apr. 1766	28
Mary their Daughter, Wife of Philip Holloands	15 Jan. 1758	25
Thomas White, of Apperley	27 Sept. 1737	63
Eleanor his Wife	19 Mar. 1728	52
Ann, Wife of Samuel Vernon	22 Feb. 1789	57
Edward Fauks	13 Mar. 1733	62
Richard Smith	— Dec. 1727	38
Tacey his Wife	7 Nov. 1728	—

THIS fmall Parifh is fituate in the upper Divifion of the Hundred of *Tewkefbury*, upon the Confines of *Warwickfhire*, five Miles diftant South-eaft from *Campden*, five South weft from *Skipton upon Stour*, and thirty in the oppofite Direction from the City of GLOUCESTER. The Soil, which varies from Gravel to Sand, is nearly equally applied to Tillage and Pafture, and is included in a Terrier of about 700 Acres.

The Living is a perpetual Curacy in the Deanery of *Campden*, originally ftipendiary from the Abbey of *Tewkefbury*, who held the Impropriation, which is ftill charged with 10l. annually, to which is added Queen ANNE's Bounty, obtained in 1737. The Impropriation, now annexed to the Manor, was formerly held by the Family of GREVILLE of *Seifincote*. Of the Church, which is fmall, the Architecture is of the middle Centuries, and very plain.

The manerial Eftate, including the whole Parifh, was amongft the original Grants to the Abbey of *Tewkefbury*, and is recited in *Domefday* amongft the Poffeffions, as containing Twenty-four Hides. For many Generations the Family of PALMER * enjoyed the Leafe under the Abbey. After the Diffolution it was purchafed, in 1576, 18 ELIZ. out of the Court of Augmentations, by AMBROSE SMITH, Efq. by whofe Heirs it was transferred to Dr. W. JUXON, afterward Archbifhop of *Canterbury*, who bequeathed it to his Nephew Sir WILLIAM JUXON, Bart.

Upon the Deceafe of SUSANNA Lady Vifcountefs FANE, in 1792, this Eftate devolved by Heirfhip to Sir ROBERT HESKETH, Bart. of *Rufford*, in the County Palatine of *Lancafter*, who has affumed the Name of JUXON by Royal Sign Manual, who has re-fold to MICHAEL CORGAN, THEOPHILUS and WILLIAM WALFORD, and WILLIAM MEYRICKE, Efqrs.

B E N E F A C T I O N S.

Dr. WILLIAM JUXON, Archbifhop of *Canterbury*, gave by Will, dated in 1662, 100l. for the Ufe of the Poor, vefted in HUMPHRY MARRIOTT, Efq. GEORGE HALFORD, and JOHN ROACH, Yeoman ; the annual Produce of which is 4l. 6s. 2d.

The JUXON Family are feized in Fee, as Truftees for the Poor of *Lemmington*, of the Freehold Inheritance of two Clofes of Ground, formerly called *Walker's Clofes*, in the Parifh of *Battesford*, in the County of *Gloucefter* ; the annual Rent of which is 6l.

The prefent INCUMBENT is the Rev. WILLIAM BAKER, Clerk.

CLAIMANTS OF THE MANOR,
MICHAEL CORGAN, THEOPHILUS and WILLIAM WALFORD, and WILLIAM MEYRICKE, Efqrs.

There does not appear to have been any Perfon fummoned from this Parifh by the Heralds in 1682 and 1683; nor any Freeholder polled at the Election in 1776, from this Parifh.

The firft Date of the Regifter is in 1685.—Marriages, in 1790, 2 ; Births, 3 ; Burials, 1.

IN THE CHURCH.

ON A BRASS PLATE :
Arms ; Sable, on a Crofs engrailed Or, five Pellets,
for GREVILL.

HERE LYE THE BODIES OF CHARLES GREVILL

AND PETER GREVILL, ESQUIORS, WHOE WERE

NATURAL BRETHREN, AND LATE PATRONES OF

THIS CHAPPELL ; THEY WERE BROUGHT UP, AND

LIVED TOGETHER IN A VERTVOVS AND PIOVS COVRSE

AND TAKING TRUE CONTENT AND COMFORT ONE

IN THE OTHER, LEDD SINGLE LIVES, AND DIED

BATCHELLORS, ANNO DOMINI 1636.

IN THE CHURCH-YARD.

ON A FLAT STONE :

Here lyeth interred the
Body of FOUCKE WOOLLOSTON ;
and alfo the Body of
SUSANNA WOOLLOSTON his
Wife. He departed this
Life December the 11,
in the Year 1711 ;
She departed this Life
May the 13, in the
Year 1710.

ON HEAD STONES.

	Died		Aged
Anne, Wife of Thomas Halford	14 Jan.	1748	33
Mary, Wife of George Halford, fenior	10 Apr.	1782	58
Hannah, Wife of George Halford, jun.	24 May,	1781	37
Francis Andrews	12 Feb.	1744	54
John Andrews	11 July,	1768	70
Hannah Roach	18 Dec.	1763	64

---

* " The eldeft Houfe of the PALMERS of *Warwickfhire* is at *Ilmington*, and the Landes of it at this Tyme is about a Hun-
" derith Pound by the Yere. The Heire of this at this Tyme dwelhth in *Herefordfhire*, by reafon of a Wife that he married.
" PALMER of *Calays*, one of the Officers there, is Son to the aforefaid PALMER : and there is a nother Brother of them a very
" riche Man that dwellith at *Kentifchtoun* without *London*.
" PALMER of *Lemington*, in the very Egge of *Glocefire*, a 3 Miles from *Rolleriche* Stones, cummith oute of the aforefaid Houfe
" of the PALMERS of *Warwickfhire*. He began firft with a very fmaul Portion of Lande : and being a galant Felow, and
" clothid yn migtie Colowrs, got a riche Widow in *Lemington* Ton to Wife, a 80 Yeres or more hens : and fins there hath
" plantid themfelves, and buildid a faire Houfe, and bought faire Landes to it. He that now hath it maried one of the GRA-
" VILLES Daughters of *Milcot*." LELAND, Itin. vol. VI. p. 18.
2

CLXII. L I D N E Y.

CLXII. L I D N E Y.

THIS Parifh is fituate upon the Shore of the River *Severn* in its broadeft Part, and extends about eight Miles. It is included in the Hundred of *Blediflowe*, in the Foreft Divifion, ten Miles South-eaft from *Monmouth*, eight North-eaft from *Chepftow*, and twenty in a nearly oppofite Direction from GLOUCESTER ; the great Road from which City to *South Wales* leads through *Lidney*. The Soil in fo confiderable a Tract of Land necefferily varies, the greater Proportion confifts of Meadow and Pafture, with Arable and large Woodlands. Coal and Paving-ftone are the Foffil Productions, with Iron, which pervades the whole Diftrict of the Foreft of *Dean*. Several Hundred Acres of rich Pafture, called *The New Grounds*, have been recovered from the Channel of the *Severn*; the Courfe of which, during the Lapfe of many Years, has been diverted. The Boundaries of the Parifh, both on the Eaft and Weft, are formed by fmall Rivulets.

The Benefice is vicarial in the Foreft Deanery; the Impropriation of which belongs to the Cathedral Church of *Hereford*, having been obtained by them upon the Diffolution of Alien Priories from the Abbey of *Lyra* in *Normandy*; to it are annexed the Chapelries of *Aylberton*, *Huelsfield*, and *St. Briavel's*, and it is further endowed with Glebe at *Aylberton*.

The Church, dedicated to *St. Mary*, is a capacious Building, the Style of which has been frequently varied by Alterations and Repairs. It has a Nave, two Ailes, with a very lofty Spire. The Chantry at the end of the North Aifle was built and endowed by JOHN CHARDBOROUGH and JULIAN his Wife, in 1376, 49 EDW. V. whereof JOHN COOK, the laft Incumbent, retired with a Penfion of 5*l.*

We collect from the earlieft Records that there were two Manors in *Lidney*, for, fuch are recited in *Domefday*, one as the Property of WILLIAM FITZ BADERON, taxed at fix Hides; and the other of Earl WILLIAM, which, being more extenfive, produced a Rent of 7*l.* befide the Demefne.

The chief Manor was vefted in the Earls of *Warwick* for many Centuries, having belonged to WALEROND Earl of WARWICK in the Reign of HENRY III. ANNE DE BEAUCHAMP, Sifter and Heir of HENRY Duke of WARWICK, the Wife of RICHARD NEVILLE, Earl of *Warwick*, fucceeded to this Manor after the Death of CICELEY Dutchefs of WARWICK, who held it in Jointure. Her Daughters and Coheirs were ISABEL, married to GEORGE Duke of CLARENCE, and ANNE, the Queen of RICHARD the Third. King HENRY the Seventh, pretending the Injuftice done to ANNE Countefs Dowager of WARWICK, procured from Parliament the Difinherifon of her Daughters; and afterward fraudulently perfuaded her to convey the whole of her vaft Property to him in Truft, and *Lidney*, amongft other Manors, was then vefted in the Crown. Under the Defcription of WARWICK and NEVILLE's Lands it was given to Sir THOMAS SEYMOUR, Lord High Admiral in 1547, 1 EDW. VI. and upon his Attainder reverted to the Crown. Queen ELIZABETH granted in Fee to Sir WILLIAM WYNTOUR, Vice Admiral of *England*, for his valiant Services againft the *Spanifh* Armada in 1588 *. He built the ftately Manor-houfe called the *White Crofs*, which, during the Civil War, was garrifoned by his Grandfon Sir JOHN WYNTOUR, one of the moft ftrenuous Supporters of the Royal Caufe. CORBET fpeaks of him with unufual Virulence, which affords Proof of his unremitted Exertions †.

Upon

---

* FULLER's Worthies, *Glouc.* p. 357.

† " Another Guard was fet at *Weftbury* on the Edge of the Forreft to Sir JOHN WYNTOUR, a moft active Enemy, and one " chief Agent of the Popifh Faction." Military Government of *Gloucefter*, pp. 60, 61.

" About this Time Sir JOHN WINTER entred upon the Government of *Newnham*; whereupon he took the Courage to plun-" der the Villages neare *Gloucefter:* his Horfe came within three Miles of the City, and drove away ftore of the Country Cattle. " The Governour receiving Intelligence, drew forth his fmall Number of Horfe, not exceeding feventy, made after them and " purfued them to the Entrance of their new Garrifon, where they had already fecured their Plunder: in the Retreat five " Troops of the Lord HERBERT's Regiment fell on the Reare: our Men drew up in a narrow Lane ready to receive the Charge, " fired upon them, and put them to a running Retreat; an Officer, with twelve Troopers, made the Purfuit, took one Horfe, " Colours, and fome Prifoners, and killed a Cornet and Quarter Mafter, which Event made Sir JOHN WINTER, for prefent, " quit that Government with much Diftraction.

" At that Time there was no lofty Stage of Action, becaufe the prefent Enemy did yeeld no gallant Opportunity. Sir JOHN " WINTER was wife for himfelf, nimble in inferior Bufinefes, delighted rather in petty and cunning Contrivance than open " gallantry, referred all his Induftry to his own Houfe, or the Limits of the Forreft, vexed his Neighbours more than weak-" ened his Enemy, and advanced the Catholicke Caufe no other Way then by the Plague and Ruine of the Countrey." P. 62.

" The next Day, by an over-ruling Hand of Providence, our Party was led back to *Gloucefter*, contrary to the Hope of Sir " JOHN WINTER and his Complices. Thefe having Intelligence of the Governor's Abfence, with a ftronge Party, and fuppofing " the Garrifon thereby weakened, fent to all the Quarters of the Forreft, *Monmouth*, and *Herefordfhire*, to draw together and " advance for the Surprifall of *Gloucefter*. It was afterwards fufpected a Complotment, to be managed by the Affiftance of Ma-" lignants

Upon the Death of Sir CHARLES WYNTOUR, the manerial Eſtate was bequeathed to his Relict, of whom, or his Heirs, it was purchaſed by BENJAMIN BATHURST, Eſq. younger Brother of the late Earl BATHURST, about the Beginning of this Century. He was ſucceeded by THOMAS BATHURST, Eſq. who died in 1790, and bequeathed it to his Brother POOLE BATHURST, Eſq. who died in 1792, and upon the Demiſe of his Relict it will devolve to CHARLES BRAGGE *, Eſq. the Son of ANNE his eldeſt Siſter, SUSANNA the younger and Relict of POWEL SNELL, Eſq. having no Iſſue. The Manſion-houſe, which is large and commodious, was built by BENJAMIN BATHURST, Eſq. and is ſurrounded by a Park which has many ſingular Beauties, both with reſpect to the picturesque Variety of Ground, and the very extenſive and intereſting Views which it commands.

Of the other Manor, now conſolidated by unity of Poſſeſſion, the early Records mention the Families of HATHEWAY and BUTLER, from whom it paſſed by Marriage with a female Heir to GILBERT Lord TALBOT, in the Reign of EDW. III. In 1474 it belonged to HUMPHREY STAFFORD, Duke of *Bucking-bam*, as appears by the Eſcheator's Roll, ſince which Period no diſtinct Account is preſerved.

Lidney is a Spot very fertile in *Roman* Antiquities †. Many Arguments of much Plauſibility are adduced to ſupport an Opinion that the *Abone* of ANTONINUS was this Place, and neither *Alvington* nor *Hanham*, which

" lignants in the City. Late at Night the Governor had Notice of the Enemy in the Forreſt. Thereupon he commanded Cap-
" taine CRISPE to draw fifty Muſketiers from the Guards, and march three Miles that Way, making good a Houſe that ſtood
" on the Paſſage. As yet there was no Suſpition of a Plot; but, before our Party had paſſed a Mile and a Halfe, they encoun-
" tered the Enemy, who were drawn up, Horſe and Foot, in a broad Lane near *Highnam Houſe*, inſtantly fired upon them,
" ſlew a Captaine, and ſome foure common Souldiers. The Enemy were amazed at the ſudden and unexpected Encounter,
" forced back with Feare, and retreated to *Huntly*, where Sir JOHN WINTER had ſecured his own Perſon, but, diſtracted by
" the ſtrange Repulſe, marched off in great Confuſion at the Approach of fifteen Horſe that fell in among the whole Brigade,
" ſlew ſeven or eight, and took ten Priſoners.
" After this Diſpatch the Governor marched to *Lidney Houſe*, with Purpoſe to attempt according to what he ſhould find meet,
" and in the firſt Place ſummoned the ſame to ſurrender, which being refiſted, and he finding the Houſe exceedingly well forti-
" fied, and no leſſe provided with Victual and Force, engaged not upon it; and underſtanding that Col. MYN, with a conſider-
" able Strength of Horſe and Foot, aſſiſted by the Lord HERBERT's Forces, and Sir JOHN WINTER, was come as far as Co-
" *ford,* he was enforced with more Expedition to draw off, for the gaining of the Hill towards them, there expecting the
" Enemies Advance till towards Evening, when he marched off his wearied Men to *Glouceſter*, firſt having fired Sir JOHN WIN-
" TER's Iron Mills and Furnaces, the maine Strength of his Eſtate and Garriſon." P. 89.
" The Earl of *Worceſter*, the Lord HERBERT, and their Agent Sir JOHN WINTER, beſtirre themſelves to patch up the lin-
" gring Life of the Garriſon at *Lidney*, and have procured from Prince MAURICE at *Worceſter* a Regement of Horſe and Dra-
" goones, by whoſe Aſſiſtance he was confident to have beaten up our ſmall Guards in the Forreſt, and enlarge his owne Quar-
" ters; to bring the Forreſt once more under his Power to the Deſtruction of the People, and the great Advantage of the
" King's Army, and *Briſtoll* in ſpeciall, furniſhing them with Iron, Wood, and Coales. The reminding of ſo greate a Miſchiefe
" to the Parliament's Service made the Governor careful to prevent him, and with an anſwerable Number of Horſe and Foote
" advanced into the Forreſt towards *Lidney*, where Sir JOHN and his Party got in before him; but, after a few Skirmiſhes to no
" valuable Loſſe on either Side; the Governor ſet Guards upon all the Paſſages, and impriſoned the Enemy in their own ſtrong
" Hold, and againe drew off the maine Body in the View of the Garriſon. The Enemy obſerving his March, and ſuppoſing
" the Expedition for *Gloucеſter*, ſallied out upon *Sully Houſe* at a Mile's Diſtance, and a temporary Garriſon for the blocking up
" of *Lidney*.
" In the Inſtant of Time the Governor returnes to this Guard, and, underſtanding by the Scouts their neere Approach,
" drew out a forlorne Hope, faced and charged them, retreated a little, and faced them againe with the Exchange of few
" Shot, till the Enemy were brought up ſo high that they diſcovered our Body. Hereupon they make a ſudden Retreate, our
" forlorne Hope fall on and the Body followes, turned their Horſe to Flight, who forſooke the Foote, and left moſt of them to
" our Mercy. Here wee tooke one Captaine, with five-and-twenty common Souldiers, having ſlaine a Captaine, two Lieute-
" nants, and twenty-five Souldiers.
" The whole Action upon thoſe Forces from *Worceſter* was performed onely with the Loſſe of twenty Horſes, and a few
" Men ſurprized in their Quarters; which, neverthleſs, coſt the Enemy the Life of a Major." The Paſſages from *Lidney* are
" all guarded by our Horſe to ſtarve thoſe within, and preſerve the Forreſt from their Plunder." P. 124.
" Meane while Sir JOHN WINTER's Reliefe lyes under the Arreſt, yet ſo as we would gladly ridde our Hands: for the
" Guards ſet round his Houſe to the Safety of the Forreſt did always diſtract our Deſignes. Theſe Horſe are impatient of a
" longer Impriſoment, and after a ſore Diſtreſſe breake their Way through our Quarters into the utmoſt Parts of the Forreſt
" towards *Chepſtow*, and joyne with a Partie of Foote from *Chepſtow* landed at *Lancaught*, where they intended to fortify and to
" make good the Paſſe over *Wye*; by which Meanes they might iſſue out of *Wales* at their Pleaſure. The Place containes foure
" Hundred Acres, having a very ſtraight Entrance. Hereupon our ſeverall Guards drew together, and ſummoned the Country
" to aide, and came up to the Enemy, who were divided in Opinion; one Part held it meete to make good the Paſſage, the
" reſt perſuaded to draw out into the Field and fight. Theſe latter prevailed, and for a while both Parties faced each other.
" Our Men drew out a forlorne Hope of Foote, the Place ſo requiring, next unto theſe a forlorne Hope of Horſe, and the reſt
" were appointed for a Reſerve. Their Horſe violently charged our forlorne Hope of Foote, who were ready to give backe
" when our Horſe came in very opportunely and played their Parts, whereat the Foote tooke Courage, and fell on altogether,
" and with one Charge turned the Enemy to Flight, that they killed few on the Place, but drove them up to the River Side, and
" fell upon the Hacke in the Purſuite, and ſo cooped them up that few eſcaped their Hands. About fourſcore were ſlaine, of
" whom were Colonell GAMME and Colonell VANGERRIS; of the Reſidue ſome adventured the River to recover the Frigate;
" many were drowned, of whom Colonel POORE, Governour of *Berkeley Caſtle*; but Sir JOHN WINTER and his Brother, with
" ſome few beſides, eſcaped onely of an Hundred Men from *Chepſtow*, and an Hundred and fourſcore Horſe and Dragoones
" from *Lidney Houſe*. The Remainder fell into our Hands, an Hundred and twenty taken Priſoners, of whom two Lieutenant
" Colonells, foure Captaines, and divers inferiour Officers. This was the laſt Blow of three which Sir JOHN WINTER received
" one in the Neck of another." P. 128.
" Sir JOHN WINTER, the Plague of the Forreſt, once more importuned the Reliefe of *Lidney Houſe*, and obtaines from the
" Prince about two Thouſand Horſe, and fifteene Hundred Foote, who break in to deſtroy the Country and diſarme the Inha-
" bitants. The Governor, with what Strength he could make, marched to *Weſtbury*, and quartered within a Mile and a Half
" of the Enemy, and gave Orders to the Guards that beſet *Lidney*, that the Foote be drawn off to the Garriſon of *Naſt* and
" *Highmeadow*, and the Horſe repaire to the Rendezvouze, which was done without Loſſe, when the Forreſt was full of the
" Enemy." P. 133.
" Sir JOHN WINTER, deſpairing of longer Subſiſtance and Livelyhoode, deſerted and fired his Houſe at *Lidney*, having firſt
" ſpoiled the Forreſt, and ſo beforehand with Revenge." P. 136.
* Amongſt the Portraits at *Lidney Houſe* are thoſe of ALLEN Lord BATHURST, a full Length, in his Robes; the late Duke and Dutcheſs of BEAUFORT, BENJAMIN BATHURST, and THOMAS MASTER, Eſqrs. and others.
† CAMDEN's Brit. edit. GIBSON, vol. I. p. 270.
" *Lidney* Park, &c. Here, on two Hills of conſiderable Eminence, ſtand two Camps or Forts overlooking the *Severn*, and
5 " which

which is the Conjecture of Camden and Dr. Gale, the learned Comentator upon the Itinerary of Antoninus. There are too many Vestiges to ascertain it to have been a *Roman* Station to admit of any Doubt. Amongst other Remains are two large Statues of Stone, Coins of the latter Empire, Fragments of Pottery, and *Tesseræ* which once composed a Pavement. The Outworks of a *Speculum* upon an Eminence are easily traced; and at some Distance from it the Ruins of an Hypocaust, of an oval Form, the longest Diameter of which is about seventeen Feet, and the other seven; the Walls below the Surface being still entire. It is uncertain whether it was first intended for a Kiln or Bath. The whole Site of these Remains occupies about eight Acres, within the Park-pale.

H A M L E T S.

1. *Aylberton* lies a Mile Westward from the Church. From the Family of *Harptre* it passed through the Gournays, De Gaunts, and Ap Adams of *Beverstone*, as appendant to that Lordship, to the Berkeleys of *Kingsweston*. Sir William Berkeley having been a Partizan with King Richard the Third, his Successor estreated this Estate and granted it to Jasper Duke of Bedford for his Life. By the Woodroffes it was transferred by Purchase to the Wyntours, and joined the manerial Estate. The greater Part of this Tything is Pasture, with very large Commons and Woodlands. The principal Proprietor is George Morgan, Esq.

There is a small Chapel for the Service of this District. When the Priory of *Lantoney* was dissolved, their Lands in this Tything were granted to William Wyntour in 1541, 52 Hen. VIII.

2. *Pyrton*, or *Purton*, is three Miles Southward from the Church. It appears to have had the same Proprietors as the last mentioned. The Estates of the Family of Doning, who were antiently and long established here, are now vested in the Right Hon. Lord Elliott, Johanna Jones, and ——— Townley, Esq.

At *Purton* is one of the Passages across the *Severn*, the Shores of which afford an ample Field of Investigation for the Collectors of Fossils *.

3. *Nass*, about two Miles South-eastward from the Church. It is noticed in *Domesday* as taxed at nine Hides, and held by Earl Harold. In the early Centuries it belonged to the Greyndours, of *Michel Dene*, and descended, with their other Property, to the Baynhams. The Ancestor of the present Proprietor, Roynon Jones, Esq. obtained it early in the Reign of Queen Elizabeth, and built the Mansion-house, to which a considerable Estate is annexed.

4. *Alliston* lies at the same distance. *Domesday* mentions two Hides only without Demesne held by William de Owe. The Similarity of this Name to *Alveston* has occasioned much Confusion in the History of Property in both Places. It includes *Rodleys* and *Hurst*, held in the last Century by the Morgans. The principal Proprietors of Lands are Edward Jones, Esq. of *Monmouth*, and the Mayor and Burgesses of the City of *Gloucester*.

5. *Soilwell*, or *Sulley*, is likewise a Part of *Alliston*, and belonged as a distinct Manor to Edward Duke of York, in the Reign of Henry V. About the Commencement of the last Century it was vested in the Family of James; and it has since passed, by Purchase, to John Townshend, Esq. of *Chiswick*, co. *Middlesex*.

The Iron Foundries at *Lydney* are of very ancient Establishment, and some of the most considerable in the Forest of *Dean*.

" which, with some Works on the opposite Side, on a Spot now called *Oldbury*, mentioned by Camden, entirely command the
" Passage of that River, supposed formerly to have been not more than one Fourth of its present Breadth, which Supposition is
" not only corroborated by a Tradition, but also by the Remains of a Number of Oak trees visible at low Water, all laying one
" Way, that is, with their Roots to the North-east, the Soil on which they grew having been washed away by the Incroachment
" of the Tide. The largest of these Camps, which is of an oblong Form, in Length 830 Feet, and 370 in Breadth, stands on
" the Northernmost or highest Hill, and is surrounded with a single Ditch, excepting towards the East, where the Descent
" being less steep it has a double one. South of this is another Hill, separated by a Valley 28 Yards over; on this there is a
" small round Camp or Fort, encompassed likewise by a single Ditch. As the Command of such a River as the *Severn* made these
" Parts of considerable Consequence, they were undoubtedly entrusted to Officers of some Rank, and accordingly they appear to
" have had all necessary Accommodations for the *Roman* Style of Living. Near the Western Edge of the largest Work a very
" elegant Bath is still pretty entire (of which a Plate is given in the Antiquarian Repertory), and in other Parts the Foundations
" of divers Buildings, some of which had tessellated Pavements. Various *Roman* Coins are found here, particularly a Silver one
" of Galba, with many of Adrian and Antoninus.
   " As there are no Traces of any Encampment in *Alvington* Parish, we may conclude, that these were the first Stations occu-
" pied by the second Legion after they crossed the *Severn*." Archæologia, vol. V. p. 208.
   * Extraneous Fossils in the Rocks at *Pyrton Passage* to be found at low Water; and particularly at the Vernal Equinox, when the Wind happens to be Easterly, by which the Mud being washed away, a greater Space of them is laid bare:
Coralloids. Asteriæ. Trochi. Bivalves of several Kinds, such as Gryphites, Pectenoides, &c. Ammonites in great Abundance, many of them two Feet in Diameter.
   See Woodwards Catalogue, Part II. p. 81, 8vo, 1729; and Lludij Lythophylacii Britannici, 8vo, 1760. Millepora, p. 2—8. Nautilites Rhombellatus, p. 16. Pectenites Flabelliformis, p. 31. Musculites Myofus Littoralis, p. 38. Mytelopectunculus, p. 43. Aculeius minor, coloris lividi eburnei nitoris, p. 51. Astacopodium asperum Anthracinum, p. 62. Dorsale asperum, id.

Vol. II.   S s   B E N E-

BENEFACTIONS.

There are no Donations belonging to the Poor of the Parifh of *Lidney*, except *5l.* left by Mrs. ELEANOR LEWIS, whofe Will is now under Litigation.

CHRISTOHHER WILLOUGHBY, Efq. in 1680, gave by Deed a Portion of Tythes, in the Parifh of *Milton*, alias *Milton Abbotts*, in the County of *Wilts*, for the Ufe of the Poor of the Tything of *Aylberton*; *viz.* to two old Women, *3l. 4s.* each; to the Minifter for a Sermon 16*s.*; for keeping a Regifter 16*s.*; to four poor Perfons 18*s.* each; to the Chapel Warden 16*s.*; to the Clerk of the Chapel 8*s.*

A Perfon unknown gave three fmall Pieces of Land and Pafture in the *Warf* for repairing the Chapel of *Aylberton.*

INCUMBENTS.	PATRONS.	INCUMBENTS.	PATRONS.
—— Thomas Hopkyns,	——— ———.	1660 Help-on-high Foxe,	D. and C. of Heref.
1549 Henry Haye,	Dean and Ch. of Hereford	1662 Edward Jones, M. A.	K. Charles II.
—— Robert Greenfield,	The fame.	1681 Daniel Pilfworth, M. A.	D. and C. of Heref.
1570 Thomas Turner,	Sir William Wyntour.	1694 Thos. Matthews, M. A.	The fame.
1594 Antony Stirrey,	Sir Edward Wyntour.	1712 Thomas Gwillim, M. A.	The fame.
1623 John Lake, B. A. / T. Philipotts, M. A. (double prefentation.)	Edward James, Efq. / D. and Ch. of Heref.	1726 Robert Breton, M. A.	The fame.
1638 Bennet Richardfon, M. A.	Herbert Richardfon.	1769 John Evans, M. A.	The fame.
1641 Morgan Goodwyn, LL.D.	D. and C. of Heref.	1783 Charles Morgan, M. A.	The fame.

PRESENT PROPRIETORS OF THE MANORS,

Of *Lidney,*

ANNE BATHURST, Widow.

Of *Nafs.*

ROYNON JONES, Efq.

The Perfons was fummoned from this Place by the Heralds, in 1682 and 1683, were

Charles Wyntour, Efq.

Charles Jones, Efq.

William Morgan, Efq.

Thomas Cromp, Gent.

Thomas Doning, Gent.

John Hyckes, Gent.

At the Election in 1776 Twenty-fix Freeholders polled from this Parifh.

The earlieft Date in the Regifter occurs in 1678.

ANNUAL ACCOUNT OF MARRIAGES, BIRTHS, AND BURIALS, IN THIS PARISH.

A.D.	Mar.	Bir.	Bur.	A.D.	Mar.	Bir.	Bur.	A.D.	Mar.	Bir.	Bur.	A.D.	Mar.	Bir.	Bur.
1781	3	33	17	1786	7	37	23	1791				1796			
1782	8	37	16	1787	6	38	33	1792				1797			
1783	3	25	21	1788	10	44	19	1793				1798			
1784	2	41	14	1789	4	29	18	1794				1799			
1785	7	39	31	1790	2	27	19	1795				1800			

INSCRIPTIONS IN THE CHURCH.

IN THE CHANCEL.

ON A MARBLE MONUMENT:

To the Memory
of ELEANOR LEWIS, Widow,
eldeft Daughter of
RICHARD MORGAN, of Hurft, Efq.
by ELEANOR his Wife,
who died Jan. 2, 1785,
aged 74 Years.

ON FLAT STONES.

HERE LYETH THE
BODY OF THOMAS
MORGAN, OF HURST,
ESQ. WHO DIED THE
2 OF MAY, 1664.

HERE LYETH INTERRED
THE BODY OF MARY,
LATE THE WIFE OF
THOMAS MORGAN,
OF HURST, ESQ. THE
DAUGHTER OF THOMAS
MORGAN, LATE OF ST.
GEORGIS, IN THE COUNTY
OF SOMERSET, ESQ. SHE
HAVING COMPLEATED IN
THIS PARISH 35 YEARS
A RELIGIOUS LIFE TOW-
ARDS GOD, A VIRTUOUS
AND LOVING WIFE TO HER
HUSBAND, A FRIENDLY
NEIGHBOUR, CHARITABLY
DISPOSED TOWARDS THE
POOR, DIED THE 28TH OF

NOVEMBER, 1657, IN THE
57 YEAR OF HER AGE.

HERE RESTETH THE BODY OF
DOROTHY MORGAN, LATE THE
WIFE OF THOMAS MORGAN,
OF HURST, ESQ. DECEASED
THE DAUGHTER OF GEORGE PRO-
BERT OF PANCLASE, IN THE COUN-
TY OF MONMOUTH, ESQ. DE-
CEASED. SHE DEPARTED THIS
LIFE THE 28
DAY OF NOVEMBER, 1658, AGED
ABOVE 90 YEARS, LEAVING
BEHIND HER
TWO SONS AND TWO DAUGHTERS,
THOMAS AND WILLIAM, ANNE
AND JANE.

HERE

I

HERE LYETH THE BODY OF
THOMAS MORGAN, OF HURST,
ESQ. WHO DIED APRIL 20, 1704,
AGED 37 YEARS.

HERE LYETH THE
BODY OF RICHARD
MORGAN, OF HURST,
ESQ. WHO DEPARTED
THE 5 DAY OF FEBR'Y,
ANNO DOM. 1716.

HERE LYETH THE BODY OF
RICHARD MORGAN, THE SON OF
RICHARD MORGAN, OF HURST,
ESQ. AND ELEANOR HIS WIFE,
WHO DEPARTED THIS LIFE THE
. . DAY OF FEBRUARY, 1706.

GEORGE, THE SON OF RICHARD
MORGAN, OF HURST, ESQ. AND
ELEANOR HIS WIFE, DEPARTED
THIS LIFE THE 28 DAY OF SEP-
TEMBER 1719.

HERE
LYETH THE BODY OF
ELEANOR MORGAN, DAUGH-
TER AND COHEIR OF HENRY
PROBERT, OF PENALT,
IN THE COUNTY OF
MONMOUTH, ESQ. AND
WIDOW OF THE LATE RI-
CHARD MORGAN, OF HURST,
ESQ. SHE DEPARTED THIS
LIFE MARCH THE 28,
ANNO DOMINI 1754,
AGED 71.

Arms; three Fleurs de lis.

Under this Stone
lies buried the Body of
ABIGAIL, the Wife
of RICHARD MORGAN, of
the Argoed, in the
County of Monmouth,
Efq. Daughter of THO-
MAS PHELPS, late of Durfley,
in this County, Efq. She
died the 16 of November,
1748, aged 38.

Alfo
the Remains of RICHARD MORGAN,
of the Argoed, in the County of
Monmouth, Efq. fecond Son of
RICHARD MORGAN, late of Hurft,
in this Parifh, Efq. by ELEANOR
his Wife, Daughter and Coheirefs
of HENRY PROBERT, late of the
Argoed, in the County of Monmouth, Efq. who departed this
Life the 21ft Day of June, 1782,
aged 71 Years.

MAGDALEN, one of the Daughters
of RICHARD MORGAN, late of Hurft,
Efq. deceafed. She died the 10th of
January, 1743, aged 28.

Here lyeth the Body of
Captain THOMAS MORGAN,
youngeft Son of RICHARD,
and ELEANOR MORGAN, of
Hurft, who departed this
Life the 11 Day of September, 1772,
aged 57 Years.

In Memory of PROBERT MORGAN,
Efq. of Hurft, in this Parifh,
who died May 31, 1759,
aged 50.

HERE LYETH THE BODY
OF IOHN DONING, THE
ELDEST SON OF WILLIAM
DONING, OF PURTON, WHO
DEPARTED THIS LIFE
APRIL 2, 1637.

HERE LYETH THE BODY
OF WILLIAM DONING, OF
PURTON, WHO DIED
THE 28 OF NOVEMBER,
IN THE YEAR 1642.

HERE LYETH THE BODY OF JOANE
DONING, THE DAUGHTER OF
WILLIAM DONING, OF PURTON,
WHO DECEASED OCTOBER 10, IN
THE YEAR OF OUR LORD GOD
1656.

HERE LYETH THE BODY OF
THOMAS, THE SON OF THO-
MAS DONING, OF PURTON,
WHO DEPARTED THIS LIFE
THE 1 OF AUG. AN. DOM.
1681.

HERE LYETH THE BODY
OF IOANE, THE WIFE OF
IOHN DONING, WHO DECEASED
THE 1 DAY OF OCTOBER,
ANNO DOMINI 1684.

HERE LYETH THE BODY
OF IOHN, THE SON OF
THOMAS DONING, WHO
DEPARTED FEBRUARY
THE 27, 1670.

THOMAS, THE SON OF
THOMAS DONING DE-
PARTED THE 9 DAY OF
SEPTEMBER, 1677.

HERE LYETH THE
BODY OF THOMAS
DONING, OF LIDNEY,
GENT. WHO DEPARTED
THIS LIFE THE 22
DAY OF MARCH,
1693.

AND ALSO DORCAS,
THE WIFE OF THOMAS
DONING, HIS BELOVED
CONSORT AND RELICT,
WAS HERE INTERRED
OCTOBER THE 25,
ANNO DOMINI 1704,
ÆTATIS 89.

HERE LIETH THE BODY OF
WILLIAM DONING,
GENT. OF NURSEHILL, IN
THIS PARISH, ÆT. 25.
OB. 28 SEPT. 1743.

HERE LYETH THE
BODY OF MARGARET,
THE WIFE OF THOMAS
DONING, OF PYRTON,
GENT. WHO DEPARTED
THIS LIFE THE 3 DAY
OF FEBRUARY, 1712,
IN THE 64 YEAR OF HER
AGE.

HERE LYETH THE BODY
OF THOMAS DONING,
OF PYRTON, GENT.
WHO DEPARTED THIS
LIFE THE 13 DAY OF
FEBRUARY, ANNO
DOMINI 1713, IN
THE 65 YEAR OF HIS
AGE.

HERE LYETH
THE BODY OF JOHN
DONING, OF NURSE-
HILL, GENT. WHO DEP-
ARTED THIS LIFE THE
17 DAY OF MARCH,
ANNO DOMINI 1742,
AGED 60 YEARS.

HERE LYETH THE
BODY OF JOANE
SCHINTELL, LATE
WIFE OF THOMAS
MANSELL, DECEASED
THE 23 OF MARCH,
1662.

HERE ALSO LYETH THE BODY
OF THOMAS MANSELL, WHO
DEPARTED THIS LIFE THE
. . DAY OF SEPTEMBER,
ANNO DOMINI 1683.

HERE LYETH THE BODY
OF THOMAS PHILPOTTS,
OF TIBERTON, VICAR OF
LIDNEY, PREBENT OF WELLE,
AND CHAPLAINE UNTO
THE RIGHT HONOURABLE
HENRY THE LORD OF
HVLLAND, WHO DEPARTED
THIS LIFE THE 4 OF
SEPTEMBER 1638.

HERE LYETH THE BODY OF
DANIEL PILSWORTH, A. M.
PREBENDARY OF HEREFORD,
AND VICAR OF LIDNEY,
WHO DEPARTED THIS LIFE THE
3D DAY OF JANVARY, ANNO DOM.
1693.

HERE LYETH THE BODY
OF THOMAS GWILLIM,
VICAR OF LIDNEY, WHO
DEPARTED THIS LIEE THE
2 OF JUNE, 1726.

HERE

HERE LYETH THE BODY
OF MARGARET, DAUGHTER
OF THOMAS CORKE, OF
NASS, WHO DECESSED THE
26 OF MAY, 1629.

IN THE NAVE.

ON FLAT STONES.

Requiefcit hic
pars mortalis
ELIZABETHÆ,
Reverendi
HOELIJ POWELL, &
ANNÆ Uxoris ejus,
filiæ que 19° die
Octobris nata vi°
Martii fepulta
fuit 1712.

HERE LYETH THE BODY OF
WILLIAM PRINC, GENT.
WHO DECEASED THE 28 DAY
OF OCTOBER, 1630.

HERE LYETH THE BODY OF
ANN, THE WIFE OF WILLIAM
PRINC, WHO DECEASED THE
28 SEPTEMBER, 1647.

HERE LYETH THE BODY OF
HENRY PRINC, DECEASED
APRIL THE 11, 1636,
THE SON OF EDWARD PRINCE.

JANE, THE DAUGHTER OF
CHARLES ELLIS, DEPARTED
THIS L. THE 7 DAY OF
APRIL 1639.

HERE LYETH THE BODY OF
IOAN, THE WIFE OF CHARLES
ELLIS, WHO DEPARTED THE
9 OF . . . . . IN THE YEAR
OF OUR LORD GOD 1663.

HERE RESTETH
THE BODY OF JAMES
ELLIS, THE SONNE
OF CHARLES ELLIS.

ALLSO THE SONNE OF JOANE
ELLIS, WHOE DEPARTED
THIS LIFE THE 16
DAY OF APRIL, IN
THE YEAR OF OUR LORD
GOD 1658.

HERE LYETH THE
BODY OF WILLIAM
STRINGER, WHO
DECEASED THE 29
OF AUGUST, IN
THE YEAR OF OUR
LORD GOD 1663.

JOANE, the
Daughter of WILLIAM
STRINGAR, died the 10
Day of September, 1680.

Here
lyeth the Body of
THOMAS JAMES, of
Rodleys, in this Parifh,
Gent. who departed this Life
the 24 of March, 1761,
aged 62.

HERE LYETH THE BODY OF
ANNE, THE WIFE
OF RICHARD MORGAN, DAUGHTER
OF JOHN
BELLINGHAM, ESQUIRE, THIRD
BROTHER TO
SIR EDWARD BELLINGHAM, OF
POYNEINGS
PLACE, NEAR LEWES, IN THE
COUNTY OF
SUSSEX, KNIGHT, WHO DEPARTED
THIS LIFE THE 29 DAY OF
SEPTEMBER, ANNO DOM.
1669.

HERE LYETH ELIZABETH BEL-
LINGHAM, WHO DIED IN THE
MONTH OF DECEMBER,
1669.

HERE LYETH THE BODY OF
WILLIAM DVNNINGE, OF
WOOLLOSON, WHO DIED
THE 30 OF JUNE, 1668.

HERE LYETH THE BODY OF
ELIZABETH, THE WIFE OF
WILLIAM DONING, OF
NURSHILL, GENT. WHO WAS
THE DAUGHTER OF THOMAS
DONING, OF THE WILLHOVSE,
GENT. WHO DEPARTED THIS
LIFE THE 4TH DAY OF DECEMB.
ANNO DOM. 1692.

HERE RESTETH THE BODY OF
THOMAS DONING,
OF PYRTON, GENT. WHO
DEPARTED THIS LIFE FEB. 13,
1713, IN THE
65 YEAR OF HIS AGE.

HERE LYETH THE BODY OF MARY,
THE WIFE OF THOMAS DONING, OF
PYRTON, GENT. WHO DEPARTED
THIS LIFE THE 3 FEB. 1712,
AGED 64.

HERE LYETH THE BODY OF
ELIZABETHE, THE WIFE OF
JOHN DONING, OF NVRSHILL,
GENT. WHO DIED THE 16 OF
JUNE, 1739, AGED 63 YEARS.

HERE LIES THE BODY OF
JOHN DONING, OF NURSHILL,
GENT. WHO DEPARTED THIS LIFE
THE 17TH OF MARCH, 1742,
AGED 60 YEARS.

IN THE SOUTH AISLE.

ON FLAT STONES.

Arms ; a Lion rampant ;—impaling,
a Chevron lozengy between three
Cinquefoils.

Underneath this Stone lies
buried the Body of ROYNON JONES,
of Nafs, Efq. who died July the
26, A. D. 1732, aged 69,
in a Vault made by ANNE JONES
his Wife, Daughter of EDWARD COOK,
of Highnam, Efq. in that Part of
this Ifle which was the ancient bu-
rying Place of his Anceftors, Lords of
the Manor of Nafs, in this Parifh.

Here lyeth the Body of HENRY
STEPHENS, who departed this Life
the 10 of March, Anno Dom. 1716.

In Memory of MARY, the Wife
of WILLIAM STEPHENS, who died
April the 8th, 1752,
aged 70 Years.

In Memory of DAMARIS, the Wife
of WILLIAM STEPHENS, of Blakeney
Lodge, who died May the 14th, 1754,
aged 28 Years.

Alfo of JOHN their
Son, who died 2 May, 1754.

Alfo WILLIAM, Son of WILLIAM and
SARAH STEPHENS, of Blakeney Lodge,
died April 20, 1790,
aged 34 Years.

Hic in CRISTO quiefcit HOPWEL
FOXE, in Artibus Magifter, hujus
Ecclefiæ Vicarius vigilantiffimus,
qui obijt 2° die Aprilis, 1662.

Hic fpe Refurrectionis beatæ
mifericordia Divina per
CHRISTUM redemtiorem fepelitur
WILL'US POWLET, ferviens ad legem,
qui natu XIX Aug. MDCXXXI.
ob. III die Octob. MDCCIII.

Here lyeth the Body of
HANNAH, the Wife of JOHN
EDWARDS, and Daughter of
JOSEPH SHILLAM, of Tortworth,
who departed this Life the
17 of February, A. D. 1662.

HERE LIETH THE
BODY OF RICHARD GREENE,
WHO DEPARTED THIS LIFE
. . . . IN THE YEAR OF
OUR LORD GOD 1673.

HERE UNDER LYETH THE
BODY OF ADAM GREENE,
OF NASS, WHO DEPARTED
THIS LIFE THE 4 OF AUG. 1640.

MARGARET CRUMPE, THE
WIFE OF THOMAS CRUMPE,
DECEASED THE 12 OF OCTOBER,
1607.

HERE LYETH THE BODY OF
ISABEL, THE DAUGHTER OF
JOHN AND MARY BUCK,
WHO DEPARTED THE 3 DAY
OF MARCH, A° 1705.

Here

Here lyeth the Body of
MARY, the Wife of JOHN
BUCK, who departed
this Life the 10 of
January, 1716,
aged 58 Years.

Here lyeth the Body
of WILLIAM, the Son
of JOHN and MARY
BUCK, who departed
this Life the 5 of
Auguſt, 1725.

IN THE NORTH AISLE.

ON MONUMENTS.

In Memory of JOHN CAPLE, of this
Town, who was buried the 28 Dec.
1722.

And alſo ANNE, the Wife
of JOSHUA BRACE, and Reliĉt of the

above JOHN CAPLE, who was buried
Dec. 2, 1750, aged 65 Years.

Alſo in a Vault underneath
this Monument lie interred the
Body of DANIEL CAPLE SMITH,
Son of GEORGE and ELIZABETH SMITH,
of the City of Briſtol,
who departed this Life Feb, 24, 1787,
aged 4 Years.

And alſo ANNE, the Wife of
DANIEL CAPLE,
of the Town of Chepſtow, who
departed this Life the 29 Day of March,
1788, aged 65 Years.

Underneath this Place
lies interred the Body of MARY,
the Wife of WILLIAM ANDREWS, Gent.
Purveyor of his Majeſty's Foreſt
of Dean, who departed the 10
of April, 1777, aged 64.

Alſo WILLIAM ANDREWS. He died
the 10 June, 1787, aged 74.

Underneath this Place
lies the Body
of ANNE, the Wife of MARK LEE, of
Plymouth, Mariner,
who departed this Life the 9th of
Auguſt, 1775, aged 37.

Here lyeth the Body
of MARY, the Daughter
of ARTHUR BOON,
who departed this
Life the 19 of Feb.
1682.

Here lies interred
JAMES BELL,
of Edinburgh,
Steward of this
Manour. He died
Auguſt the 14th,
An. Dom. 1731.

IN THE CHURCH-YARD.

ON TOMBS.

MEMORIÆ SACRUM RHEBECCÆ
COSTER,
FILIÆ UNICÆ IOHANNIS ET
ANNÆ COSTER,
QUÆ NATA ERAT XXVII DIE
DECEMBER,
ANNO DOMINI MDCLI, OBIJT
OCTAVO
DIE JANUARII, ANNO DOM.
MDCLXVI,
CUM VIXISSET XVI ANNOS ET XIII
DIES.

HERE LYETH THE BODY OF ANNE,
THE WIFE OF JOHN COSTER,
GENT. LATE OF WHITE CLEEVE,
WHO DEPARTED THIS LIFE
THE 21 DAY OF
DECEMBER, 1688.

HERE LYETH THE BODY OF
RICHARD GILL, OF NAWAN,
MERCER, WHO DEPARTED
THIS LIFE THE 29 DAY OF MAY,
1676.

HERE LYETH THE BODY OF
MARY, THE WIFE OF
RICHARD GILL, WHO
DEPARTED THIS LIFE THE
13 DAY OF
SEPTEMBER, 1689.

Here lieth the Body of ANNE,
the Wife of HENRY KING, of
this Pariſh, who died July 21,
1761, aged 73.

Here lies interred the
Body of HENRY KING, of this
Pariſh, who departed this Life
the 14 of May, 1772, aged 59.

Here lyeth the Body of
RICHARD BENFIELD, of this Pariſh.
He died July 16, 1760, aged 33.

Here lyeth the Body of EDMUND
BERROW, of Gerſhill, in this Pariſh,
Gent. and ALES his Wife. She
died the 4 March, 1630; and he the
15 July, 1647.

Here lyeth the Body
of WILLIAM LONGDON,
of this Pariſh, who departed
the 7 Dec. 1744, aged 47.

Alſo here lyeth the Body
of ELIZABETH, the Wife of
WILLIAM LONGDON, of this
Pariſh. She departed this
Life the 31 Day of May,
1756, aged 68.

Here
lyeth the Body of
ANN, the Wife of JOHN
HOPKINS, of this Pariſh.
She died May 16, 1750.

Alſo JOHN HOPKINS died
January 12, 1757.

In
Memory of ELIZABETH, the Wife
of CHARLES INMAN, of Purton Paſſage.
She died Oĉt. 8, 1760, aged 45.

Here lyeth the Body of CHARLES
INMAN, of Purton Paſſage, who
departed this Life the 8 Decemb.
1779 aged 69.

Here lies interred
the Body of MARTIN INMAN, of
Purton Paſſage.
He was born at Totenham Court, in
St. Pankridge, in the County of
Middleſex.
He died Jan. the 29th, 1733,
aged 55 Years.

Alſo REBEKAH INMAN.
She died the 29 Sept. 1754.

Here
lies interred the Body of JOHN,
the Son of THOMAS and MARY WADE,
of this Pariſh. He died the 24 July,
1765, aged 34 Years.

In Memory
of MARY, the Wife of THOMAS WADE.
She died Jan. 11, 1732,
aged 25 Years.

Sacred to the
Memory of JAMES WADE,
who departed this Life April 13, 1778,
aged 67 Years.

Alſo SARAH, Wife of JAMES WADE,
who departed this Life May the
23, 1773, aged 57 Years.

In Memory of
THOMAS WADE, of this Pariſh, who
died the 12 November, 1776,
aged 78 Years.

Sacred to the Memory of
HENRY HEWLET, of this
Pariſh, who departed this Life
the 9 of March, 1786,
aged 36 Years.

HERE LIETH THE BODY OF
ELINOR, THE WIFE OF
JOHN EDDY, OF LIDNEY,
WHO DECEASED THE 1 OF MAY,
IN THE YEAR OF OUR LORD GOD
1624.

Here lyeth the Body of ELIZABETH,
the Wife of ROBERT EDDY,
of the Chantry, who died
15 March, 1671, the Mother of ſeven
Sons and five Daughters.

Alſo the Body of
JOHN EDDY, of the Chantry,
who died 28 July, 1682.

Here lyeth the Body of ELIZABETH,
the Wife of WILLIAM EDDY, and
Daughter of ROBERT EDDY
and ELIZABETH his Wife, who deceaſed
Auguſt the 20, 1668.

Alſo the Body of
ANN DUFFUL, the Daughter of
THOMAS EDDY, of Upper Street.

Alſo the Body of
THOMAS EDDY,
who died 26 Feb. 1682.

Here

Here lyeth the Body of ROBERT
EDDY, who departed this Life the
22 of May, Anno Domini 1703.

Alfo here lyeth the Body of
JOHN EDDY, of this Parifh, who
departed this Life the 23 Day of
January, Anno Dom. 1744,
aged 69 Years.

MARY, the Wife of JOHN EDBY,
died the 26 of Decemb. 1746,
aged 75 Years.

HERE LYETH BURIED THE BODY
OF JOHN BERRINGTON,
OF COW . . . .
IN THE COUNTY OF HEREFORD,
GENTLEMAN, WHO DIED THE
8 DAY OF NOVEMBER, IN THE
YEARE OF OUR LORD 1666.

Here lies interred the Body of
ANNE, the Wife of GEORGE TAYLOR,
of Aylberton,
who died 12 Nov. 1758,
aged 63 Years.

In Memory of
CHARLES COWLS,
of this Parifh. He died May 11,
1769,
ætatis fuæ 72 Years.

In Memory of
JOHN COWLS,
of this Parifh. He died the 30 July,
1778,
ætat. fuæ 42 Years.

Here lyeth the Body of
SARAH, the Wife of THOMAS
DAVIS, of this Parifh, who
departed this Life the 30 of
March, 1745, aged 39 Years.

Here lyeth
the Body of
MARTHA, the Daughter
of GEORGE and MARY
WINTER, of this Parifh, who
died the 27th Decem. 1776.

Alfo JOHN their Son died
June the 19, 1780.

Here lyeth the Body of
WILLIAM WINTER, who
departed this Life July 2, 1754,
aged 58 Years.

Alfo here lyeth the Body
of MARTHA his Wife, who
departed this Life the 12
Mar. 1785, aged 84.

Here lyeth the Body
of MARY, the Wife of WILLIAM
TRAFFORD, who departed
this Life the 9th Day of
April, A. Dom. 1725.

Here alfo lieth the Body of
WILLIAM TRAFFORD, who
departed this Life the 2
Day of September, Anno
Dom. 1727, aged 67 Years.

Alfo JOHN TRAFFORD. He died
the 18 Nov. 1743, aged 40.

Alfo MARTHA, the Wife of
JOHN MADDOX, of Churcham,
in this County, and Relict of
JOHN TRAFFORD. She departed
this Life 29 Day of Sept. 1780,
aged 70 Years.

I

HERE UNDER LYETH THE BODY
OF MARGARET, THE WIFE OF
THOMAS CRUMPE, WHO
DEPARTED THIS LIFE THE
20 DAY OF APRIL, ANNO DOMINI
1640.

HERE UNDER LYETH INTERRED
THE CORPS OF THOMAS CRUMPE,
OF NASS,
YEOMAN, WHO DECEASED THE
XXVII DAY OF NOVEMBER,
ANNO DOMINI 16 . .
ÆTATIS SUÆ LVIII.

This Tomb is erected
in Memory of MARY and ANNE, the
Daughters of THOMAS CRUMPE,
of Nafe, Gent.
MARY departed this Life the 11 Day of
January, 1680 ; and ANN the 14 of
September, 1684.

RICHARD, THE SON OF THOMAS
CRUMPE, OF NASE, GENT. DYED
THE 10 OF SEPTEMBER, 1661.

HENARY, SON OF HENARY
BROWNJOHN, GENT. DIED THE
8 DAY OF MARCH, 1670.

Here refteth the Body of
JOHN CRUMPE, of Nafs,
who departed this Life Nov. 15, 1686.

Here lyeth the Body of
ELEANOR SHERLE, who departed
the 28 Day of July, Anno Dom.
1714.

Dominæ ELIZABETHÆ DAVIDSON,
optimæ puellæ 1687.

HERE LYETH THE BODY
OF ROBERT FARRINGTON,
WHO DEPARTED THIS LIFE
THE 10 DAY OF MARCH,
ANNO DOM. 1719.

HERE LYETH THE
BODY OF ELIZABETH, THE
WIFE OF THOMAS WADE,
WHO DEPARTED THIS LIFE
MARCH 24, 1727, AGED 40.

HERE LYETH THE BODY OF
ELIZABETH FARRINGTON, WHO
DIED THE 22 JAN. 1769,
AGED 52.

Here lyeth the Body of
ROBERT JENKINS. He died
the 6 May, 1707.

MARY his Wife died
the 10 of May, 1711.

ROBERT JENKINS died
the 24 January, 1724.

WILLIAM JENKINS died
the 5 September, 1752,
aged 32 Years.

BLANCH, Wife of JEREMIAH
HARRIS, Relict of the above,
died the 15 of September, 1776,
aged 84 Years.

In Memory of ANNE
FREEMAN, of this Parifh,
who died June the 6th,
1754, aged 69.

Here lyeth the Body of
MARGARET, the Wife of
FRANCIS SEABORN, of
Nafe, who departed this
Life the 21 December,
Anno Dom. 1727, aged 80.

Here lyeth the Body of
MARGARET HAMMAN,
the Wife of JOHN HAM-
MAN, who departed the
20 June, 1658.

HERE LYETH THE BODY OF
ANTHONY HAMMOND, OF
NEWARN, IN THE
PARISH OF LIDNEY, TANNER,
WHO DECEASED THE 6 DAY OF
AUGUST, ANNO DOM. 16 . 6.

HERE LYETH THE BODY OF
MARGARET HAMMOND, THE
WIFE OF ANTHONY HAMMOND,
WHO DEPARTED THIS LIFE
DECEMBER . . 1675.

In
Memory of ANNE, the Wife
of JOSEPH TAMPLIN,
of this Parifh. She died the 9th
of May, 1778, ætatis 67.

Here lyeth the Body of
JOSEPH TAMPLIN, who died
April the 7, 1778, aged 66.

In
Memory of
MARGARET, the Daughter
of JOSEPH and
ANNE TAMPLIN,
of this Parifh, who
died the 12 of January,
1783, aged 47 Years.

Here lyeth the Body of
ELIZABETH, the Wife of
EDWARD TAMPLIN,
of this Parifh, who departed
this Life the 16 of June,
1745, aged 45.

Alfo
EDWARD TAMPLIN.
He died the 14 of April,
1770.

Here
lyeth the Body of ANNE,
the Daughter of JOHN
and ANNE PEAD, of this
Parifh, who departed this
Life Aug. 1, 1781, aged 26.

HERE LYETH THE BODY OF
THOMAS, THE SON OF THOMAS
KNAGGS, WHO DIED THE 11
MARCH, 1631.

HERE LYETH THE BODY OF
JAMES AYRES, KEEPER
TO THE LADY WINTOUR,
OF LIDNEY, WHO DIED
MARCH 1, 1717.

HERE

HERE LYETH THE BODY OF
MARGERYE NORTH, WHO DIED
THE 28 OF MAY, IN THE YEAR
OF OUR LORD 1633.

MARGARET, THE WIFE OF
JOHN THAWER, DEPARTED
THIS LIFE THE 19 DEC-
EMBER 1654.

HERE LYETH INTERRED THE
BODY OF EDMUND BERROW,
OF THIS PARISH, GENT.
AND ALSO HIS WIFE.
SHEE DECEASED THE 4 DAY OF
MARCH, ANNO DOMINI 1632;
AND HE DEPARTED THE
15 DAY JULY, ANNO
DOMINI 1647.

HERE LYETH THE BODY OF
ELIZABETH, WIFE OF JOHN
LONGDON, DAUGHTER OF
RICHARD AND SARAH
WILLIAMS. SHE DIED
MARCH 8, 1757, AGED 35.

Here
lyeth the Body of DAVID
TRAFFORD. He died Jan. 28,
1759, aged 60 Years.

Alfo here lyeth the Body
of SILVESTER his Wife,
who died the 27 Dec. 1765,
aged 81 Years.

Alfo DAVID their Son,
who died the 18 of April, 1770,
aged 58 Years.

Here lyeth the Body of
JOHN, the Son of THOMAS
and MARY STEPHENS, who
died the 30 March, 1728.

Alfo here lyeth the Body
of SARAH, Daughter of
THOMAS and SARAH STEPHENS,
who was buried Jan. 3,
1743.

Alfo here lyeth the Body of
THOMAS STEPHENS, of this Parifh,
who died the 7 March, 1760,
aged 72 Years.

Alfo SARAH his Wife
died Dec. 8, 1769.

Here lyeth the Body
of ELIZABETH,
the Wife of JOHN TAYLOR,
who departed this Life the
16 of May, 1722.

Here alfo lyeth the Body
of MARTHA, Wife of JOHN
TAYLOR, who died the 6 of
May, 1729.

In Memory of
MOSES, the Son of RICHARD
and SARAH MORSE, of
this Parifh, who died the
21 July, 1785.

MARGARET, Wife of RICHARD
MORSE, died 7 January, 1763,
aged 57 Years.

Alfo RICHARD MORSE died
the 25 Nov. 1777, aged 82.

Here lyeth the Body of MATTHEW
MORGAN, who departed this Life
the 24 Day of January, Anno 1646.

Alfo here lyeth the Body of THOMAS
MORGAN, who died the 24 . . . . . 1668.

ON FLAT STONES.

HERE RESTETH THE BODY
OF HENRY HUNTER,
WHO DEPARTED THIS
LIFE THE 2 DAY OF
DECEMBER, 1681.

In Memory of GEORGE
DUNING, who departed
this Life . . May, 1689.

Alfo JOAN his Wife
departed 4 Aug. 16 . 5.

To
the Memory of
the Rev. Mr. EVANS, who
died the 17 June, 1789,
aged 40 Years.

In Memory of
ANNE WILLIAMS, who died the
9th of October, 1788,
aged 21 Years.

Here lyeth the Body of CHARLES
JAMES, of Aylberton,
who departed this Life
December the 8th, 1730,
aged 70 Years.

Alfo ALICE, the Wife
of CHARLES JAMES. She
died 16 February, 1747,
aged 58 Years.

HERE LYETH THE
BODY OF ELIZABETH,
THE DAUGHTER OF
FRANCIS AND MAR-
GARET SEABORN,
WHO DEPARTED THIS
LIFE THE 25 DAY OF
JANUARY, 1704.

HERE LYETH THE
BODY OF FRANCIS
SEABORN, WHO
DEPARTED THIS
LIFE THE 27 DAY
OF MARCH, ANNO
DOM. 1723.

HERE LYETH THE
BODY OF JOHN
CHEWETT, OF ALISTON,
WHO DEPARTED THE
15 OF APRIL, 1695.

HERE LYETH THE
BODY OF JOHN
CHEWETT, OF AILBERTON,
WHO DEPARTED
THIS LIFE THE
3 DAY OF AUG. 1723,
AGED 64.

HERE LYETH
THE BODY OF
JOHN, THE SON

OF JOHN AND
MARY CHEWETT,
OF AILBERTON, WHO
DEPARTED THIS LIFE
JAN. THE 15 ANNO DOM.
1723, AGED 23.

HERE LYETH THE
BODY OF ELIZABETH,
THE DAUGHTER OF
ANTHONY KING,
WHO DEPARTED THE
3 DAY OF FEBRUARY,
ANNO DOMINI 1713.

HERE LYETH THE
BODY OF SARAH,
THE DAUGHTER
OF ANTHONY AND
MARY KING, WHO
DEPARTED THE 10
DAY OF APRIL, ANNO
DOMINI 1714.

ALSO HERE LYETH
THE BODY OF
ANTHONY KING, WHO
DEPARTED THIS LIFE
THE 5 DAY OF MARCH,
1725.

ALSO MARY HIS WIFE
WAS INTERRED DEC. 8,
1742, AGED 71 YEARS.

JOHN TRAFFORD THE
YOUNGER WAS BORN
THE 13 DAY OF MARCH,
ANNO DOMINI 1653,
AND DEPARTED THIS LIFE
THE 8 DAY OF APRIL,
ANNO DOMINI 1664.

HERE LYETH THE BODY OF
JAMES, THE SON OF JAMES
TRAFFORD, WHO DEPARTED
THIS LIFE THE 22 DAY OF
NOVEMBER, AN. DOM. 169 . .

HERE LYETH THE BODY OF
MARY, THE WIFE OF
JAMES TRAFFORD, WHO DE-
PARTED THIS LIFE THE 12
OF AUGUST, AN. DOM. 1703.

HERE LYETH THE
BODY OF JOHN
TRAFFORD, WHO
DEPARTED THE 25
DAY OF JANUARY,
ANNO DOM. 1690.

ALSO
HERE LYETHE THE BODY
OF JAMES TRAFFORD,
WHO DEPARTED THIS
LIFE THE 9 OF MAY,
ANNO DOMINI 1729,
AGED 71 YEARS.

IN MEMORY OF
MARY, THE WIFE OF
JAMES TRAFFORD.

SHE

SHE DIED JUNE THE 15, 1750, AGED NEAR 71 YEARS.

HERE LYETH THE BODY OF BLANCH TRAFFORD, THE WIFE OF JOHN TRAFFORD, WHO DEPARTED THE 26 DAY OF MAY, ANNO DOMINI 1687.

HERE LYETH THE BODY OF JAMES, THE SON OF JAMES AND MARY TRAFFORD, WHO DEPARTED THIS LIFE THE 29 OF SEPTEMBER, ANNO DOM. 1706.

HERE LYETH THE BODY OF THOMAS BUCK, OF AILBERTON, WHO DEPARTED THIS LIFE THE 02 DAY OF DECEMBER, ANNO DOM. 1677.

AND ALSO THE WIFE OF THOMAS BUCK, WHO DE-

PARTED THIS LIFE THE 18 DAY OF JUNE, AN° DOM. 1683.

HERE LYETH THE BODY OF SUSAN STEPHENS, WHO DEPARTED THIS LIFE THE 7 DAY OF DECEMBER, ANNO DOM. 1708.

AND ALSO HERE LYETH THE BODY OF JAMES, THE SON OF JOHN AND SARAH STEPHENS, WHO DEPARTED THIS LIFE THE 11 DAY OF AUGUST, AN° DOM. 1712.

HERE LYETH THE BODY OF JOHN, THE SON OF JAMES STEPHENS, AND SARAH HIS WIFE, WHO DEPARTED THIS LIFE THE 19 DAY OF FEB. ANNO DOMINI 1708.

ALSO HERE LYETH THE BODY OF JAMES STEPHENS, OF AILBERTON, WHO WAS INTERRED THE 9 OF NOVEMBER, ANNO DOM. 1727.

Here lyeth the Body of JEREMIAH COWLS, who departed the 21 Day of December, Anno Domini 1707.

Here lyeth the Body of JANE, the Wife of JOHN TAINTON, of Ailberton. She died February the 7, 1745, aged 63 Years.

In Memory of JOHN GILL, who departed this Life the 16 Day of October, in the Year of our Lord GOD 1703.

Also here lyeth the Body of MARY, the Daughter of JOHN and MARY GILL, who departed the 2 Day of July, Anno Domini 1689.

In Memory of FRANCIS, the Wife of RICHARD GILL, who died August the 7, 1726.

In Memory of SARAH, the Daughter of GEORGE WYRHALE and SARAH his Wife, who died 13 October, 1756.

And of JOHN their Son, who died 6 July, 1758.

ON HEAD-STONES.

	Died	Aged
Suſannah, Wife of Robert Tampler	5 Dec. 1681	—
Mary, Wife of Stephen Howell	8 Dec. 1741	41
Thomas Marſhman	18 Jan. 1681	—
Samuel, Son of William Smith	6 Sept. 1703	—
Richard Kays	— Oct. 1739	66
Margaret his Wife	8 Dec. 1740	76
Ann, Wife of John Hewlet	18 Oct. 1779	33
Richard Hewlet	7 Dec. 1786	84
Heſter his Wife	26 Mar. 1786	76
Edward Hored	24 Jan. 1615	—
John Hawker	22 Mar. 1762	66
Jone, Wife of John Reynold	4 May, 1731	—
Joan Morgan	22 Feb. 1765	—
Arthur Hicks	2 Oct. 1695	—
Mary his Wife	22 Feb. 1719	—
William Hurtnol	19 Mar. 1749	70
Mary his Wife	22 Feb. 1719	—
William Hurtnol	31 Dec. 1765	55
Elinor his Wife	15 July, 1748	37
William Davis	21 May, 1717	—
John Caplew	23 Feb. 1722	—
William Davis	22 Dec. 1729	—
Thomas Freeman	14 Oct. 1749	73
Suſannah, Wife of Richard James	8 May, 1723	—
Jane, Wife of William James	— Jan. 1668	—
William Page	6 Oct. 1725	—
Elizabeth, Wife of Richard Morgan	6 May, 1755	38
William Jones	7 Mar. 1781	45
Sarah his Wife	10 Apr. 1747	33
Thomas Matthews	16 Apr. 1740	41
John Manning	11 Jan. 1722	—
George Teebay	29 July, 1734	61
Heſter his Wife	15 Nov. 1740	67
James Day	23 Dec. 1733	64
David Trafford	17 Dec. 1720	—
Elizabeth his Wife	7 Dec. 1720	—
John Trafford	1 Aug. 1726	—
Elizabeth his Wife	27 Oct. 1719	—
William Proſſer, of Etlac	27 Apr. 1729	42
Joan, Wife of Robert Walding	23 Nov. 1729	55
John Worgan	27 Aug. 1747	64
William Tregany, Gent.	18 Sept. 1718	—
Jane his Wife	16 May, 1710	—
Margaret, Wife of Thomas Perkins	2 May, 1722	—
Ann, Wife of John Linch	11 Dec. 1715	—
James Linch	24 June, 1733	40
John Linch	5 June, 1729	40
Mary Hayward	1 Jan. 1785	76

	Died	Aged
Daniel Imm	3 Apr. 1785	90
Sarah his Wife	25 Aug. 1769	72
Sarah their Daughter	23 Nov. 1752	24
Robert Freeman	15 Aug. 1716	—
James Freeman, of Stroud	8 Dec. 1730	42
Ann Freeman	6 June, 1754	79
Alice, Wife of James Hawkins	14 Oct. 1786	26
Elizabeth, Wife of James Hawkins	21 Sept. 1788	50
William Hawkins	13 Sept. 1788	25
Mary, Wife of William Davis	3 Jan. 1758	49
Giles Davis	16 June, 1787	33
Ann, Daughter of Richard and Sarah Wilſon	15 Nov. 1728	—
Richard Williams	27 Jan. 1738	82
Sarah Williams	25 July, 1755	70
Richard Matthews	5 Mar. 1743	68
Mary his Wife	20 Mar. 1737	55
Mary, Wife of William Lane	2 Nov. 1728	27
John, Son of Peter Griffiths	6 Feb. 1739	32
George James	— Aug. 1744	78
Mary, Wife of Thomas James	5 Sept. 1764	46
Ann, Wife of Samuel Tipins	13 Dec. 1734	—
George Tipins	10 Aug. 1770	63
Richard Baldwin	16 Sept. 1742	60
John Walker	10 Oct. 1751	—
Mary his Wife	15 Dec. 1753	—
Charles Walker	19 Aug. 1779	61
William Walker	15 Dec. 1769	63
Elizabeth his Wife	27 July, 1741	—
William Morgan, Gent.	14 June, 1719	—
Joſeph Bilbie, of Briſtol	15 Oct. 1744	70
Thomas Howell	14 June, 1730	60
Ann his Wife	23 May, 1781	95
Thomas Day Meredith	10 Apr. 1787	21
Ann, Wife of John Pead	15 Sept. 1778	50
Prudence Allen	26 Sept. 1727	—
Samuel Hains	10 Dec. 1727	—
Robert Hicks	21 Jan. 1789	88
Ann Cawdron	15 Sept. 1758	41
Rachel Evans	12 May, 1728	79
Thomas Evans	12 Jan. 1741	61
Morgan Corſlet	30 May, 1736	48
Margaret his Wife	3 Apr. 1730	—
George Greene	5 Oct. 1724	—
Jane his Daughter	3 Jan. 1720	—
John Lewis	18 Mar. 1746	54
Elizabeth his Wife	6 Dec. 1736	—
Eaſter Lewis	24 May, 1764	56

O N

ON HEAD-STONES.

Name	Died	Aged
Mary Buckle	27 July, 1713	—
William, Son of Richard Scoot	30 Mar. 1727	—
Sarah, Wife of William Boughton	8 Dec. 1788	50
George Wintour	11 Apr. 1709	—
Richard Etherton	17 Apr. 1766	74
John Philpot	13 July, 1741	23
Frances, Wife of Thomas Philpot	27 May, 1729	67
Ann, Wife of William Philpot	23 Nov. 1733	48
Isabel, Wife of William Dibdon	25 May, 1720	71
John Hughes	4 Oct. 1760	62
Margaret his Wife	17 Nov. 1758	56
John Bedford	28 Mar. 1720	—
Elizabeth, Wife of George Byford	8 Aug. 1755	44
Solomon Dibdon	27 Mar. 1753	48
Joseph Martin	4 Nov. 1743	80
William Peters	22 Mar. 1769	66
Thomas Thomas	11 Feb. 1768	33
Richard Mason	6 Apr. 1789	58
Benjamin Mason	15 Aug. 1788	—
Walter Pritchard	27 May, 1719	—
Susannah, Wife of Lewis Watkins	10 Mar. 1782	80
George Perefte	6 July, 1680	—
William Hart	20 Dec. 1684	—
Thomas Evans	17 Apr. 1747	44
Abraham Evans	8 Feb. 1729	—
Elizabeth his Wife	1 Sept. 1734	47
Sarah Evans	17 Feb. 1729	30
William Peters	9 Dec. 1727	—
James Jones	8 Aug. 1769	68
Mary his Wife	4 Sept. 1779	68
Hannah, Wife of Richard Jones	24 Sept. 1786	42
Henry King	20 Nov. 1757	16
Matthew Pritchard	10 Mar. 1711	—
Robert White	10 Sept. 1730	70
Matthew his Son	11 Feb. 1732	—
James Parrey	10 June, 1758	52
Dorothy, Wife of John Scuff	24 Dec. 1706	—
Nathaniel Greenning	15 May, 1752	70
James, Son of Richard and Elizabeth Heath	17 Feb. 1778	26
Thomas Etell	16 Apr. 1729	52
David Hughes	25 Dec. 1762	63
Griffith Facey	18 Aug. 1754	22
James Pugh, of Monmouth	11 Dec. 1729	39
George Lewis	26 Nov. 1781	36
John Morgan	13 Sept. 1781	50
Elizabeth, Daughter of James and Jane Hunt	18 Aug. 1754	20
Robert Shepard	1 Feb. 1719	—
Ann his Wife	25 Oct. 1740	74
Thomas Tombes	25 Jan. 1728	—
Ann, Daughter of Thomas and Ann Hughes	9 June, 1774	28
Mary Jones	26 Dec. 1714	—
Efther, Wife of William Williams	24 May, 1769	30
John, Son of William Chewett	21 Sept. 1683	—
John Davis	4 Aug. 1738	66
James Davis	23 Nov. 1745	31
John Davis	17 June, 1761	53
Jane Davis	23 Feb. 1779	76
Martha, Wife of John King	7 Mar. 1727	—
Sarah, Wife of Edward Maddocks	7 July, 1706	—
John, Son of John Watts	19 Apr. 1704	—
Mary, Wife of Edward Hughes	23 Dec. 1743	41
George Baldwin	14 Aug. 1746	35
John Baldwin	8 Dec. 1754	39
Elizabeth, Wife of William Thomas	5 Nov. 1736	52
Betty, Wife of Charles Dowle	23 Feb. 1788	34
William, Son of James and Mary Pitcher	30 May, 1738	—
Stephen, Son of Mills and Mary Gwin	4 Feb. 1749	—
James Pitcher	14 May, 1746	56
John Pritchard	20 Jan. 1773	66
Mary Bartlem	21 Feb. 1758	29
John Jones	29 May, 1723	—
Andrew Parfons, of London, Gent.	19 June, 1735	—
Jane, Wife of Thomas Davis	24 Mar. 1782	53
Thomas their Son	21 June, 1780	19
Sufannah, Wife of Thomas Davis	20 Aug. 1727	42
Mary Eaton	26 Oct. 1780	90
Ann, Wife of David Jones	14 Oct. 1714	—
Ann Jones	8 June, 1719	—
David Jones	5 Jan. 1749	—
Joseph Williams	15 June, 1765	46
Mary his Wife	10 Oct. 1763	66
William Taylor	22 Aug. 1740	33
William Nation	2 Sept. 1731	33
Elizabeth, Wife of Thomas Sims, Daughter of John and Betty Read	21 Apr. 1783	19
Sarah, Wife of John Stephens	16 Jan. 1766	42
James their Son	28 Aug. 1769	24
Richard, Son of Abel and Hefter Lee	11 June, 1756	37
Hefter, Wife of Abel Lee	17 Jan. 1750	73
Thomas Perrin	15 Nov. 1740	35
Jane his Wife	12 Mar. 1740	34
William Evans	24 June, 1735	34
Martha, Daughter of William and Elizabeth Perrin	18 Apr. 1758	23
William, Son of Richard and Sarah Crofs	11 July, 1787	15
Sarah, Wife of Thomas Dyer	18 Aug. 1775	26
Mary, Wife of Thomas Wade	11 Jan. 1732	25
Philip Jarrett	4 May, 1751	33
Frances, Wife of Thomas Jarrett	16 Sept. 1748	63
Jane, Wife of Charles Inman	9 Sept. 1780	59
Martin, Son of Charles and Elizabeth Inman	23 Nov. 1776	39
Elizabeth, Wife of John Simmons	13 Feb. 1784	67
John their Son	30 Jan. 1770	22
George Simmons	8 Feb. 1752	37
John Williams	22 Jan. 1752	56
Mary his Wife	25 Dec. 1725	—
John Williams	1 June, 1752	34
Charles Williams	6 Nov. 1726	—
Benjamin Hopkin	22 Jan. 1748	28
James Duffell	30 July, 17—	—
Margaret his Wife	9 Nov. 1720	—
Charles Duffell	22 —— 1663	—
John, Son of John Long	20 Mar. 1698	—
John Davis	9 Aug. 1694	—
William his Son	22 Apr. 1725	—
Giles Woodruff	9 Sept. 1742	—
Alice his Wife	11 Oct. 1743	—

CLXIII. L O N G B O R O U G H

I S fituate in the upper Part of the Hundred of *Kiftefgate*, three Miles North from *Stow*, feven South from *Camden*, and twenty-five Eaft from Gloucester.

The Village lies upon an eafy Declivity, open to the Eaft, and commanding an interefting View over contiguous Parts of the Counties of *Warwick* and *Oxford*. The Soil is light, but fertile of Corn, and the greater Part of the Parifh uninclofed, with very extenfive Common Fields, containing in the whole about 1000 Acres.

The Benefice is a Vicarage in the Deanery of *Stow*, appropriated to the Abbey of *Hayles* by Thomas Cobham, Bifhop of *Worcefter*, in 1235, who, in the next Year, endowed the Vicarage with the Tythes of fixteen Yard Lands, and all privy Tythes, excepting of Lamb and Wool. He ordained, likewife, that, if they fhould not amount to 10*l.* a Year, the Abbot fhould be bound to make good the Deficiency *. Since the Diffolution the Impropriation has been attached to the Manor. Francis Earl of Guildford has the third Turn in the Prefentation.

The Church is dedicated to *St. James*, and confifts of a Nave, handfome embattled Tower, with Pinnacles, and a fepulchral Chapel, belonging to the Family of Leigh. It probably owes its Erection to the Abbey of *Hayles*. The Floor was made of painted Bricks, with the Arms of Boteler of *Sudeley*, and other Devices, frequently repeated, and the Windows were once filled with ftained Glafs.

Domefday records two Boroughs under the Title of *Langeberge*, one held by the Crown, and the other by Earl Moriton †. Thefe were afterwards either confufed or confolidated when they were granted by King Henry III. to his Brother Richard Earl of Cornwall and King of the *Romans* previoufly to his Foundation of the Abbey of *Hayles* in 1246 ‡. The Abbot's Right to this Manor, with Free Warren, Market, and Fairs, was confirmed upon a *Quo Warranto* in 1287, 15 Ed. I. and proved to be holden as of the Honour of *Wallingford*, which Claim continued till the Difperfion of their Property. It was not granted from the Court of Augmentations before 1554 to Sir Rowland Hill and Thomas Leigh, Efq. Livery was confirmed to Rowland Leigh, Efq. in 1573, 15 Eliz. whofe Heirs have enjoyed this manerial Eftate, including the greater Part of the Parifh, to the prefent Time.

H A M L E T.

Blank's-fee, Bank's-fee, or *South-field*, by which feveral Names it is recognized in antient Evidences. It is divided between this Parifh and *Condicote*, and was probably one of the Manors recited in *Domefday*. Richard le Blanc was poffeffed of one Meffuage and three Plough Tillages, called *Blank's-fee*, in the Reign of Edw. I. The College of *Weftbury upon Trim* held *South-field* in *Thornbury*, and not this Manor. William Freeman died feized of it in 1578, 20 Eliz. during whofe Reign it paffed to John Talbott. In 1636 it was purchafed by Sir Charles Shuckborough, Bart. and of his Defcendants, in 1753, by John Scott, Efq. who has re-built the antient Manfion in a commodious Style, which has many Advantages of Situation.

Veftiges of a *Roman* Out-work are to be traced upon the old *Fofs* Road, which leads near the Village.

---

* The fame Year he appropriated the Church of *Langberg,* or *Longbarrow*, in the Deanery of *Stow*, to the Abbot and Convent of *Hayles*; and, on the 4th of April, 1326, he ordained the Vicarage to the Value of 10*l.* per Annum.
 Cobham, f. 112. al. cxix. Thomas, Survey of *Worcefter*, p. 167.

† In *Cheftefiat* hund' tenuit E. rex *Langeberge* cum uno membro no'e *Mene*, in utroq' erant viii hide & in d'nio i car' & xii vill'i & viii bord', cum xiv car'. Ibi unus fervus & molin' de v fol' & vi fervi pratum de x fol'. T. R. E. reddeb' vicecom' de hoc m' q'd exibat ad firmam modo redd' xv lib' cum ii hund' quos ibi vicece' appofuit.
 Terra Comitis Moriton.
 In *Witelai* hund', Comes Moriton ten *Langeberge*. Toni tenuit T. R. E. Ibi ii hide in d'nio s't ii car' & iii vill'i & unus bord' cum i car' & iiii fervi, valuit iiii lib' m'o xl fol' & geld'. *Domefday*.
 Cart. 18 Ed. I. n. 64. pro manerio de *Langberg*. Pat. 17 Ed. II. p. 2. m. 6. de advoc' eccl' de *Longberwe* & *Rodburn (Wilt)*, ex dono Hugonis le Despenser, Cart. 19 Ed. II. n. 2.

‡ Pat. 39 Ed. II. p. 2. m. 14. pro ten' in *Longberwe*. Ibid. m. 25.
Pat. 11 Ric. II. p. 2. m. 18. Pat. 16 Ric. II. p. 1. m. 17. pro ten' in *Rodborn, Netherfwell*, & *Longberew*
 Tanner's Notitia Monaftica.

B E N E-

B E N E F A C T I O N.

THOMAS BARKER, in 1707, gave, by Will, 10s. a Year, to be given to the Poor at *Chriftmas*, charged on a Ground, called *Cafwell's*, in this Parifh, now in the Poffeffion of ANTHONY GISBORN.

INCUMBENTS.	PATRONS.	INCUMBENTS.	PATRONS.
1545 Richard Goodwyn	King Henry VIII.	1660 Edward Smallbone,	Dame Eliz. Leigh.
1546 William Fifher,	The fame.	1663 Auguftine Martyn,	The fame.
1554 John Webfter,	Sir Rowland Hill.	1672 Robert Hill,	Theophilus Leigh.
1606 John Riddel	—————.	1726 Thomas Dodwell, B. A.	William Leigh.
1641 William Lowle,	Dame Eliz. Leigh.	1751 Thomas Leigh, M. A.	Thomas Leigh.

PRESENT LORDS OF THE MANORS,

Of *Longborough*,

JAMES HENRY LEIGH, Efq.

Of *Blank's-fee*,

JOHN SCOTT, Efq.

The Perfons fummoned from this Place by the Heralds, in 1682 and 1683, were Jofeph Witham, and ———— Witham, Efqrs.

At the Election in 1776 Six Freeholders polled from this Parifh.

The earlieft Date in the Regifter occurs in 1676.

ANNUAL ACCOUNT OF MARRIAGES, BIRTHS, AND BURIALS, IN THIS PARISH.

A.D.	Mar.	Bir.	Bur.	A.D.	Mar.	Bir.	Bur.	A.D.	Mar.	Bir.	Bur.	A.D.	Mar.	Bir.	Bur.
1781	4	15	16	1786	4	12	5	1791				1796			
1782	1	13	12	1787	4	9	12	1792				1797			
1783	2	10	9	1788	4	10	15	1793				1798			
1784	3	11	12	1789	4	8	7	1794				1799			
1785	6	13	17	1790	2	8	4	1795				1800			

INSCRIPTIONS IN THE CHURCH.

IN THE TRANSEPT, OR BURIAL CHAPEL.

Arms, Gules, a Crofs engrailed, and in the firft Quarter a Lozenge Argent, for LEIGH;—impaling, on a Chevron, between three Bucks' Heads affrontée a Crefcent, for WHORWOOD.

MEMORIÆ SACRUM
GULIELMI LEIGH MILITIS
NEC NON
ELIZABETHÆ CONJUGIS.
HIC
EX UTROQ; STEMMATE, LEIGH &
BERKELEY, NOBILI SANGUINE
DITATUS,
UTRAMQUE FAMILIAM SUIS VIR-
TUTIBUS
ORNAVIT, OXONIÆ JUVENIS PER
BIENNIUM
BONIS LITERIS NON INFELICI-
TER OPERAM
DEDIT; ÆTATE INTEGRA, SUS-
CEPTO MATRI-
MONIO, RES PRIVATAS MAJORUM
MORE
PIE AC LIBERALITER, NEC SINE
DISPENDIO
EROGAVIT, EIRENARCHÆ OFFI-
CIO, PER

PLURES ANNOS, SUMMA CUM
ÆQUITATE
NON SUMMO JURE, FUNCTUS;
PHTHISI
TANDEM CORREPTUS, VITAM
HANC
MELIORI COMMUTAVIT, MENSE
NOVEMB.
ANNO SALUTIS 1631, ÆTATIS 46°.

E QUATUOR FILIJS TOTIDEMQ;
FILIABUS HUJUSCE CONNUBIJ
FRUCTU, HARUM
TRES, VIZ^t. ISABELLA, ELIZA-
BETHA, ET
ANNA, UTRIQ; PARENTI SUPER-
VIXERE.
BINOS ILLORUM, NEMPE GULI-
ELMUM
AC GEORGIUM, PATER RELIQUIT
SUPERSTITES; MATER TANTUM
NATU
MAJOREM.

ILLA
GULIELMI WHORWOOD MILITIS
STAFFORDIENSIS FILIÆ
ORBATA VIRO, PER ANNOS 34^or
VIDUITATE PERPETUA VITAM
PROTRAXIT
VERE RELIGIOSAM, ÆDES SUAS

PROXIMIS HOSPITIUM EGENIS
XENO-
DOCTRIUM, SUBDITISQ; REGIS
FIDELIBUS
(ARDUISSIMIS TEMPORIBUS) A-
SYLUM
SEMPER PRÆBUIT. H. M. NON IN-
DECORUM OPTIMO MARITO SI-
BIQUE IPSI
VIVENS POSUIT FILII NATU MI-
NORIS
LIBERIS LIBERA MANU DOTATIS;
MATURA DEMUM MORTE IMMOR-
TALITATEM ACQUISIVIT 23°
MARTIJ ANNO
x^ti 1664-5, SUIQ; 83°.

ON A FLAT STONE:

M. S.
ELIZABETHÆ
filiæ GULIELMI LEIGH, Armig. ex
MARGARETTA
Conjux GULIELMI GUISE, de Elmore,
Militis, nata
GIDEONI HARVEY, M. D. Connubio
junctæ,
Quæ obijt
XIII° die Maij, anno falutis MDCXCIV,
ætatis 58°.

GIDEON HARVEY, jun. proles unicè
fuperftes
H. M. P.

6

IN THE CHANCEL.

On a Flat Stone:

Here lyeth interred the Body of Joseph Alcock, who departed this Life the 9th of October, Anno Domini 1694, ætatis suæ 64.

IN THE NAVE.

ON FLAT STONES.

Here lyeth the Body of James Dodwell, second Son of Thomas Dodwell, Vicar, who died June 12, 1732, aged 4 Months.

Also the Body of James Tredwell Dodwell, third Son of Thomas Dodwell, who departed this Life May the 12th, 1742, aged 2 Years, 9 Months, 3 Weeks, and 4 Days.

Here lieth the Body of Thomas Dodwell, Rector of Seisincot, and Vicar of Longborough, who departed this Life July the 7, 1751, aged 50.

Here lyeth the Body of Charles Shuckburgh, eldest Son of Charles Shuckburgh, Esq. who died December the 28, 1719, aged one Month.

And also the Body of Charles Shuckburgh, second Son of Charles Shuckburgh, Esq. who died March 18, 1720-1, aged 3 Months, 2 Weeks, and 3 Days.

Arabella, second Daughter of Charles Shuckburgh and Sarah his Wife, died July the 22, 1730, aged 7 Months and 1 Day.

IN THE CHURCH YARD, ON TOMBS.

In Memory of Samuel Rowsham, who departed this Life November 14, 1776, in the 93 Year of his Age.

In Memory of Jane, Wife of Anthony Gisborn, Daughter of Thomas Roberts, of Lower Slaughter, who departed this Life the 16 Day of February, 1783, aged 50 Years.

HERE LYETH THE BODIE OF THOMAS MATHEW THE YOUNGER, IN TYME WITH HIS FATHER, BURIED THE 4 OCTOBER, IN THE YEAR 1622.

ON HEAD-STONES.

	Died	Aged		Died	Aged
Jane, Wife of John Whitehead	20 Jan. 1736	—	James Hall	19 Feb. 1786	42
William Whitehead	8 Feb. 1741	74	Benjamin Hudson	13 Feb. 1779	60
Philippe, Wife of J. Sutton	16 Mar. 1763	—	Richard Baker	24 Jan, 1750	81
Anthony Fletcher	18 Dec. 1780	72	Mary his Wife	11 July, 1747	67
William Paxford	22 Aug. 1703	61	Thomas Baker	10 Aug. 1692	65
Richard Clarke	31 May, 1714	70	Thomas Baker	27 Apr. 1717	83
Joan his Wife	29 Apr. 1727	75	Thomas Walford	3 Feb. 1766	50
John Collins	24 Jan. 1722	67	Charles Vickaridge	22 Mar. 1687	—
Mary his Wife	6 Oct. 1718	56	Katharine, Wife of Will. Rowsham	24 Sept. 1755	28
Edward Cudd	13 Oct. 1779	71	Richard Wells	2 June, 1763	67
Elizabeth Clarke	10 May, 1739	81	Thomas Grayhurst	10 May, 1703	73
Stephen Clarke	10 Mar. 1755	65	Ann his Wife	14 Feb. 1720	73
John Clarke	29 July, 1759	65	Thomas Grayhurst	24 Sept. 1717	49
Thomas Collet	8 Oct. 1720	66	Isaac, Son of Samuel Snow	25 Nov. 1715	36
Hannah Collet	3 Jan. 1725	72	Isaac Snow	18 Apr. 1762	49
Esther Collet	28 Mar. 1726	36	Alexander Williamson	17 June, 1781	39
Mary Collet	16 Aug. 1741	26	Thomas Perkins	28 Oct. 1759	83
Richard Collet	6 Dec. 1768	55	Mary his Wife	14 Sept. 1751	75
Ruth, Wife of John Collet	18 Sept. 1761	64	Henry Meadows	29 Sept. 1777	72
Joseph Collet	22 May, 1779	70	Sarah his Wife	15 Jan. 1788	73
Sarah his Wife	1 Nov. 1761	51	Hannah, Wife of Nicholas Hine	9 Nov. 1745	81
Henry Green	6 Jan. 1719	59	Nicholas their Son	23 Nov. 1758	61
William Hall	22 Jan. 1778	58			

CLXIV LONG HOPE,

CLXIV.   L O N G   H O P E,

DISTINGUISHED from *MANSEL HOPE*, not far diftant from it in *Herefordfhire. Hope* is a *Saxon* Word, fignifying a Valley, and applies to the Situation of this Village, which lies in the Hundred of the Dutchy of *Lancafter*, is about ten Miles in Circumference, diftant three North-eaft from *Mitchel Dean*, and nine Weft from GLOUCESTER.

The Turnpike Road from *Gloucefter* to *Rofs* leads through this Parifh.   The Soil is Stonebrafh, Sand, and Clay ; the Arable and Pafture Lands nearly equal, and the Woodlands of confiderable Extent *.

The Benefice is a Vicarage in the Foreft Deanery.   The Advowfon was originally given to the Abbey of *Lyra* in *Normandy* by ROBERT DE CHANDOS foon after the Conqueft ; and, upon the Suppreffion of the Alien Priories, the Impropriation was re-granted to the Priory of *St. Mary* and *St. Florence* in *Monmouth*.   In the Year 1675, the Impropriation belonged to THOMAS NOURSE †, Efq.   In 1701, his Defcendant, NOURSE YATE, Efq. very confiderably increafed the Value of the Living by reftoring the impropriate Tythes to the Vicarage, to which the Advowfon is now annexed.

The Church, which is dedicated to *All Saints*, confifts of a Nave with a Tranfept of large Dimenfions, and a Steeple at the Weft End, of the Architecture of the fourteenth Century.

With refpect to the Manor of *Long Hope, Domefday* fpecifies it to have been held by FERNE and ULFEG, two *Saxons*, in the Reign of King EDWARD the CONFESSOR, and afterwards attached to the Conftablefhip of the Caftle of *Monmouth* by King WILLIAM the CONQUEROR, who beftowed it on WILLIAM FITZ-BADERON, one of his Followers.   It was then taxed at five Hides.   In 1256, 40 HEN. III. upon the Demife of JOHN FITZ-BADERON, it was granted to EDWARD Prince of WALES, afterwards EDWARD I. and foon after to GILBERT TALBOT, who married GUENTHLIEN, Daughter of RHESE AP GRIFFETH, Prince of *Wales*.   It afterwards devolved to the noble Family of GREY DE WILTON, with whom it remained for feveral Centuries, and was fold, in 1740, with other Eftates of HENRY Duke of KENT, to Sir EDMUND PROBYN, Lord Chief Baron of the Exchequer, whofe Nephew and Heir EDMUND PROBYN, Efq. is the prefent Proprietor.

Confiderable Property, exclufive of the Manor, was vefted in the laft Century in the Families of BROMWICH, NOURSE, and YATE, and at this Time of SERGEAUNT and BAYLY.

In this Parifh are found no Matters of curious Refearch, either of Antiquities or Natural Hiftory.

B E N E F A C T I O N S.

THOMAS NOURSE.   See Note † below.
There is alfo a Piece of Land, value 20*s. per Annum*, given, by Will of THOMAS HODGES, formerly to buy Garments for the Poor at Chriftmas, now vefted in WILLIAM EDWARDS.   Likewife fundry Rents

---

* EDMUND PROBYN, Efq. has a Right to cut a Coppice called *Long Hope Wood*, which is then preferved for feven Years, and afterwards becomes commonable to the Inhabitants at large.

† The Donation of THOMAS NOURSE, of *Long Hope*, Gent. by his laft Will :

" I give and bequeath unto ten old antient People (Men and Women), of the Parifh of *Long Hope* aforefaid, that have Relief
" and Alms out of the faid Parifh, the Sum of 10s. a-piece to buy them Coates, or other Garments, every Year for ever ; and
" the fame to be paid by my Executors of this my laft Will out of the Rents, Iffues, and Profits, of my aforefaid Parfonage
" of *Long Hope*, yearly for ever, upon *St. Andrew's* Day, unto the Churchwardens, for the Time being, of the faid Parifh, to
" be by them layd out upon the faid Cloathes for the faid ten Perfons ; and the faid ten Perfons are to be chofen and appointed
" out by the faid Churchwardens, with the Confent and Approbation of four fubftantial Inhabitants of the faid Parifh of
" *Long Hope*.
" Item, I give and bequeath to the Parifh of *Long Hope*, for ever, the yearly Sum of 5*l.* to be yearly paid unto the Church-
" wardens of the faid Parifh for the placing out of one or two poor Children of the faid Parifh, whofe Parents, or themfelves,
" are upon the Almes of the Parifh, to be appointed in *London, Briftol, Gloucefter*, or fome Market-town, to a Trade there, and
" the Sum of five Pounds *per Annum*, to be yearly paid unto the faid Churchwardens for the Ufe aforefaid ; out of the Rents,
" Iffues, and Profits, of my Parfonage of *Long Hope* aforefaid ; and the faid Monies to be laid out by the faid Churchwardens,
" by the Confent and Approbation of four fubftantial Men of the faid Parifh, and not otherwife," &c.

<table>
<tr><td>VOL. II.</td><td align="center">X x</td><td align="right">iffuing</td></tr>
</table>

iſſuing from three Tenements, and divers Lands, amounting to 47*l.* 7*s.* given for the Reparation of the Pariſh Church of *Long Hope* aforeſaid, and for the Relief of the Poor and impotent People, and Orphans, belonging to the Pariſh, veſted in the following Perſons : EDMUND PROBYN, Eſq. 3*l.* 10*s.*; THOMAS PARRY 10*s.*; WILLIAM EDWARDS 2*l.* 5*s.*; CORNELIUS BLEWETT 18*s.*; THOMAS DOBBS 5*l.*; ELIZABETH HODGES 2*l.* 10*s.*; WILLIAM WATKINS 19*s.*; JOHN PHELPS 4*l.* 10*s.*; JOSEPH ACTON 9*l.*; THOMAS CONSTANCE 2*l.* 10*s.*; WILLIAM REECE 15*s.*; MARY BLEWETT 1*l.*; THOMAS RUDGE 2*l.*; NATHANIEL VAUGHAN 12*l.* Total 47*l.* 7*s.*

INCUMBENTS.	PATRONS.	INCUMBENTS.	PATRONS.
—— Thomas Brumſton,	———— .	1742 Yate Bromwich, M.A.	Mary Yate, Lancelot Bromwich and Priſcilla his Wife, Henrietta-Arabella Yate, and Frances Yate, Spinſters.
1561 Henry Deyce,	Richard Turner.		
1577 James Mutloe,	John Baker.		
—— Thomas Rudge,	The ſame.		
1618 John Adamſon,	John Cadle.		
1663 George Dutton,	Biſhop of Glouceſter.	1774 David Jones,	William Matthews and Priſcilla Bromwich.
1700 Charles Hoſkins,	Nourſe Yate.		
1703 George Venn,	Joſeph Venn.	1786 William Probyn,	Edmund Probyn.
1717 Thomas Mantle, B.A.	Francis Yate, Walter Yate, and W. Hodges.		

PRESENT LORD OF THE MANOR,

EDMUND PROBYN, Eſq.

The Perſons ſummoned from this Pariſh by the Heralds, in 1682 and 1683, were

Nourſe Yate and Edward Serjeaunt, Eſqrs.

At the Election in 1776, Forty Freeholders polled from this Pariſh.

The firſt Date of the Regiſter is in 1742.

ANNUAL ACCOUNT OF MARRIAGES, BIRTHS, AND BURIALS, IN THIS PARISH.

A.D.	Mar.	Bir.	Bur.	A.D.	Mar.	Bir.	Bur.	A.D.	Mar.	Bir.	Bur.	A.D.	Mar.	Bir.	Bur.
1781	2	20	14	1786	3	16	5	1791				1796			
1782	4	13	10	1787	2	18	9	1792				1797			
1783	4	18	7	1788	1	9	10	1793				1798			
1784	5	11	17	1789	2	23	11	1794				1799			
1785	3	14	23	1790	7	13	14	1795				1800			

INSCRIPTIONS IN THE CHURCH.

IN THE CHANCEL.

ON FLAT STONES.

Arms, a Lion rampant, holding a Roſe, for MASTER.

Here reſts
the Body of THOMAS
MASTER, Gent. who
died July the 13,
Anno Domini 1682.

Here reſteth alſo the
Body of BRIDGET, the
Wife of the aforeſaid
THOMAS MASTER, Gent.
who died the 24 Feb.
An. Domini 1697.

Arms, in a Lozenge, a Feſs, in chief two Mullets, for YATE ;—impaling, a Feſs embattled Ermine, between three Creſcents, for GLOVER.

PRISCILLA, the Wife and Relict of
NOURSE YATE, Eſq
and Daughter of HENRY GLOVER, Gent.
of Oldſwinford, in the County
of Worceſter, who died Jan. 4,
Anno Domini 1719-20, aged 61 Years.

Alſo FRANCES, youngeſt Daughter
of NOURSE YATE, Eſq. by PRISCILLA
his Wife, died the 28th of June, 1747,
ætatis 45.

Arms, YATE as before.

Here lyeth the Body of
CHARLES YATE, Eſq.
Son of NOURSE YATE, Eſq. late of
this Pariſh, deceaſed, who died the 14
Day of Feb. in the 33d Year of his Age,
Annoq; Domini 1729.

Alſo
HENRIETTA, fourth Daughter to
NOURSE YATE, Eſq. by PRISCILLA his
Wife, who died March the 9, 1725,
aged 60 Years.

Arms, in a Lozenge, YATE as before.

Here reſteth the Body of
MARY YATE, eldeſt Daughter of
NOURSE YATE, Eſq. Obijt 26 of
June, 1761, ætatis 78.

In Memory of ARETHUSA YATE,
5th Daughter to NOURSE YATE, Eſq.
by PRISCILLA his Wife.
Obijt the 10 of April, 1752, ætatis 60.

Arms, a Lion rampant;—impaling YATE, guttée du ſang, for BROMWICH.

Here reſts, in hopes of a glorious
Reſurrection, the Body of
LANCELOT BROMWICH, Gent.
Obiit 17 of March, 1752, ætatis 72.

Alſo
PRISCILLA, ſecond Daughter to
NOURSE YATE, Eſq. and Relict
of the above LANCELOT
BROMWICH, Gent. who died
December 20, 1763, aged 79.

Arms as above.

Sacred to the Memory of
YATE BROMWICH, Clerk, M.A.
Vicar of this Pariſh, Proprietor
of the Rectorial Rights of the ſame
by his Grandfather NOURSE YATE, Eſq.
and Patron of the ſaid Vicarage. He
died April 28, 1774, aged 60 Years.

Arms, a Chevron between three Unicorns' Heads couped, for LEIGH ;—impaling, barry of ten; over all, ſix Eſcocheons, for CECILL.

M. S.
ANNÆ Uxoris THOMÆ
LEIGH, de Medio Templo
Londin. Gen. ex patre
filiæ Honorabili GULIELMO
CECILL, Arm. filio GULIELMI
nuper Comitis
Sariſburienſis. Obijt
Anno { ætatis 27.
{ ſalutis 1677.

Arms,

Arms, in a Lozenge, a Mullet within a Bordure engrailed;—impaling, a Cross between four Leopards' Faces, for KINGSTONE.

Here lyeth the Body of BRIDGET, the Relict of ROGER ANDREWES, Gent. who died January the 6th, 1683.

WILLIAM READ DEPARTED THIS LIFE THE 3 DAY OF JUNE, 1671.

Here lyeth the Body of HUMPHRY BASKERVILLE, Gent. who deceased this Life Jan. the 3d, Anno Dom. 1689, ætatis suæ 72.

Infra reconduntur exuviæ THOMÆ MANTLE, Clerici Denati Julij 29, Anno Salutis 1742, ætatis suæ 58.

In Memoriam ANNÆ, dilectissimæ Uxoris THOMÆ MANTLE, A. M. hujus Ecclesiæ Vicarii, que mortem ob. 15 Feb. Anno Dom. 1735, ætatis suæ 33.

In Memory of THOMAS HARTLAND, who died July the 9, 1753, aged 90 Years.

JOAN BULLOCK died . . . . . . 1689.

Also in Memory of WILLIAM DOBBS, who died November the 11t, 1689.

To the Memory of JANE, the Wife of WILLIAM DOBBS, who deceased May the 26th, 1715.

Here lieth the Body of JOAN, the Wife of the above THOMAS HARTLAND, who died Jan. 17, 1727, aged 57 Years.

In Memory of JOANNA, Wife of THOMAS SANSOM, and Daughter of THOMAS HARTLAND, by JOAN his Wife, who died March 8, 1744, aged 43 Years.

IN THE NAVE.

ON FLAT STONES.

Here lyeth waiting for a glorious Resurrection the Body of THOMAS BRIGHT, of this Parish, who died August the 31, 1753, aged 73 Years.

Also here lyeth, in Hopes of a glorious Resurrection, the Body of JONE, the Wife of THOMAS BRIGHT, who died August 26, 1752, aged 67.

Also near to this Place lieth the Body of JONATHAN BRIGHT, of this Parish, who departed this Life April 3, 1758, aged 29 Years.

Here lieth the Body of SARAH, the Wife of JOSIAH BRIGHT, of the Parish of Taynton, and Daughter of JAMES and MARY MOTTLEY, of the Parish of Ruardeane, who died Feb. 16, 1773, aged 37.

Also in Memory of JOSIAH BRIGHT, Husband of the aforesaid, who died March the 16, 1777, aged 52 Years.

Here was buried . . . . . . WEALCH, who deceased August the 31, Anno 1662.

Here also lyeth the Body of MARY, the Wife of JOHN WELCH, sen. who deceased Life the 14 of September, Anno Dom. 16 ætatis suæ 58.

Here lyeth the Body of JOHN WELCH, sen. who departed this Life Nov. the 10, Anno Dom. 16 . . aged 75 Years.

Here lyeth the Body of THOMAS HODGES, Gent. who died May the 20th, 1736, aged 90.

Here lyeth the Body of ROBERT DAWES, sen.

Also here lyeth the Body of JOAN MORWENT, who died Sept. 5, 1744, aged 74 Years.

IN THE SOUTH TRANSEPT.

ON FLAT STONES.

Arms, a Fess between two Chevrons, for NOURSE.

Sepulchrum THOMÆ NOURSE, Gen. qui obiit XVI die Julij, MDCLXXV.

Here lyeth the Body of WILLIAM BRIGHT, of this Parish, Yeoman, who departed this Life the 9 Day of November, 1729.

Here lyeth the Body of HENRY BATSON, who deceased Jan. 31, 1668.

And also the Body of AVIS, the Wife of WILLIAM WINGOOD, who dyed September the 16, 1686.

IN THE NORTH TRANSEPT.

ON FLAT STONES.

What was mortal of SAMUEL WINTLE, of Blaysdon, and MARY his Mother, lies here. She was the Wife of Mr. ROBERT WINTLE, of Blaysdon, and afterwards of Mr. JOHN WELCH, of this Parish. Those in higher Rank might worthily imitate him. He acquired nothing by Fraud or Oppression. She died 21 January, 1699; He 12 August, 1749, aged 57.

Here lyeth the Body of EPHRAIM SANSOM, who died May the 16, 1741, aged 39 Years.

MARK, the Wife of the above EPHRAIM SANSOM, was here buried March 31, 1774, aged 70 Years.

IN THE CHURCH-YARD.

ON A MONUMENT AGAINST THE CHANCEL:

In Memory of JUDITH, seventh Daughter of JOHN ARROWSMITH, D. D. by MARY PERCIVAL his second Wife, who lived the truly Pious, and died March the 13, 1710, the much lamented Wife of GEORGE VEN, M. A. Vicar, aged 52.

ON TOMBS.
In Memory of EDMUND FOWLE, sen. who departed this Life Sept. 1685, ætatis suæ 80.

In Memory of MARY, Wife of JOHN FOWLE, who died July the 4, 1778, aged 56 Years.

In Memory of JOSIAH FOWLE, who died July 21, 1759, aged 53 Years.

In Memory of ELIZABETH, Wife of JOHN POWELL, who departed this Life Jan. 3, 1746, aged 53.

Here lyeth the Body of JOHN POWELL, who departed this Life Dec. 6, 1769, aged 70 Years.

In Memory of SUSANNAH, the Wife of JONATHAN WINTLE, and Daughter of JOHN BULLOCK by JANE his Wife, who died March 2, 1766, aged 43 Years.

In Memory of ANN, the Wife of THOMAS DOBBS, who died July 2, 1737, aged 80 Years.

Also JONE, the Wife of WILLIAM CHARLES, and Daughter of the above THOMAS and ANN DOBBS, who died March 6, 1772, aged 78 Years.

In Memory of WILLIAM CHARLES, who died December the 22, 1777, aged 82 Years.

To

To the Memory of
ROBERT HOOPER, of this Parish,
who departed this Life
the 2d of Feb. 17.6, aged 88 Years.

And also in Memory of MARY,
the Wife of the above ROBERT HOOPER.
She died March 27, 1718, aged 33 Years.

———

Under this Tomb lie the Remains
of ROBERT HOOPER, late of this Parish,
who departed this Life January the 21st,
1785, in the 69th Year of his Age.

Also in Memory of THOMAS, the Son of
ROBERT HOOPER, by MARY his Wife,
who died March 1, 1715, aged 2 Years.

———

In Memory of SUSANNAH FOWLE,
who died November the 22d, 1705,
aged 59 Years.

In the Memory of ELIZABETH, the
Daughter of JOHN FOWLE by MARY his
Wife, who died May the 12th, 1700,
aged 5 Years.

———

In Memory of WILLIAM BROWNE,
who died December the 3d, 1757,
aged 84 Years.

Also in Memory of SARAH his Wife,
who died January the 7th, 1747, aged 80.

———

Arms ; Argent, on a Pale Rayonée Or, a
Lion rampant of the first, for COLMAN.

To the Memory of
JOSIAH COLMAN, jun. who
departed this Life the 19th of
November, 1776, aged 59 Years.

In Memory of JOHN COLMAN,
who died July 1, 1753, aged 70 Years.

Also in Memory of JOAN his Wife,
who died October the 9th, 1728,
aged 48 Years.

———

In Memory of JOHN
COLMAN, who departed this

Life December 3, 1732, aged
78 Years.

Here lyeth the Body of
ELIZABETH, the beloved Wife
of JOHN COLMAN, who died
May the 9, 1726, aged 72 Years.

———

In Memory of JOSEPH COLMAN,
who died June 29, 1768, aged 75.

JOHN COLMAN, a Son of the
abovesaid, died December 31, 1770,
aged 35 Years.

GRACE, the Wife of JOHN COLMAN,
died January 30, 1770.

———

In Memory of GARDNER,
Son of ZACHARIAH and
ELIZABETH PITTMAN, who
died April 11, 1758, aged 20.

———

O N   H E A D   S T O N E S.

	Died	Aged
Martha, Wife of Richard Pittman	31 Aug. 1745	46
Priscilla, Daughter of William and Elizabeth Pittman	17 Aug. 1723	22
William their Son	12 Jan. 1726	21
Hannah, Wife of Thomas Pitman	27 Sept. 1764	38
Elizabeth, Wife of Richard Price	26 Apr. 1721	43
Mary, Wife of George Lodge	7 July, 1757	58
Jane their Daughter	18 Apr. 1763	29
James, Son of James and Sarah Baylis	18 June, 1758	18
Rowland Wintle	18 July, 1751	67
Joyce his Wife	19 Nov. 1758	76
John their Son	5 Feb. 1732	23
Thomas their Son	8 May, 1754	35
Thomas Bright, of this Parish	—— 1708	124

CLXV. LITTLETON,

 # L I T T L E T O N,

CALLED, from its Situation, *WEST LITTLETON*, originally a Tything in the adjacent Parifh of *Tormarton*, lies in the Hundred of *Grumbald's Afh*, two Miles North-weftward from *Marfhfield*, fix South-eaft from *Sodbury*, and thirty-one South from GLOUCESTER. It now claims diftinct parochial Rights. In the Soil there is little Variety, chiefly of light Stonebrafh, and the Terrier does not exceed 1000 Acres.

The Benefice is annexed as a Chapelry to *Tormarton*, in the Deanery of *Hawkefbury*. The Church is a fmall Structure, in the Style of the middle Centuries, confifting of a Nave only, with a low octangular Turret.

This Manor, in the CONQUEROR's Survey, is not diftinguifhed from *Tormarton*, and appears to have been firft feparately held by RICHARD DE CLARE, Earl of *Gloucefter*, in 1263, 47 HEN. III. afterward by the Families of WILLINGTON of *Sandhurft*, DE LA RIVIERE, and ST. LOE. In 1600, GEORGE TALBOT, Earl of *Shrewfbury*, was feifed of it, and Sir R. ATKYNS afferts, in Right of Marriage with ELIZABETH, Widow of Sir WILLIAM ST. LOE, Knight, which Circumftance COLLINS, in his Account of the Peerage, difproves; it is, however, certain, that he left no Iffue. It was next conveyed to WILLIAM CAVENDISH, Duke of *Devonfhire*, and has been fince fold, with the manerial Property, in detached Parts, to the Families of FRANCOMBE, FISHER, and OSBORNE. His Grace the Duke of BEAUFORT claims to be Lord Paramount.

No Benefactions to the Poor.

The INCUMBENTS will be inferted in the Defcription of *TORMARTON*.

No Perfon was fummoned from this Place by the Heralds, in 1682 and 1683.

At the Election in 1776, Six Freeholders polled from this Parifh.

The firft Date of the Regifter occurs in 1679.

ANNUAL ACCOUNT OF MARRIAGES, BIRTHS, AND BURIALS, IN THIS PARISH.

A.D.	Mar.	Bir.	Bur.	A.D.	Mar.	Bir.	Bur.	A.D.	Mar.	Bir.	Bur.	A.D.	Mar.	Bir.	Bur.
1781	—	4	1	1786	—	2	3	1791				1796			
1782	1	1	2	1787	—	2	4	1792				1797			
1783	2	1	3	1788	1	4	3	1793				1798			
1784	—	3	2	1789	—	3	1	1794				1799			
1785	1	2	—	1790	1	2	2	1795				1800			

I N S C R I P T I O N S   I N   T H E   C H U R C H.

ON MARBLE MONUMENTS.

In Memory of the
Rev. Mr. WILLIAM ALSOP,
Rector of Langridge,
and Vicar of Stanton Drew,
in the County of Somerfet,
who died September 17, 1750,
aged 38 Years.

Alfo of MARY, Relict
of the above
WILLIAM ALSOP, who
departed this Life
February the 7th, 1780,
aged 70 Years.

In Memory
of FRANCIS
FRANKCOM, Gent.
who died the 14th of 1748,
aged 48 Years.

Alfo BETTY his Wife,
who died Sept. 1, 1789,
aged 72 Years.

In Memory of EDITH, Wife of
JAMES OSBORNE, of Warminfter,
in the County of Wilts, who died
March 30, 1782, aged 41 Years.

Alfo of RICHARD FRANKCOM, Gent.
who died June 11, 1787,
aged 48 Years.

ON FLAT STONES.

Arms, a Fefs, in chief three Cinquefoils.

Here lyeth the Body of
ROBERT HALE, of this Parifh,
who died the 28 Auguft, 1723, in
the 97th Year of his Age.

Alfo here lyeth the Body of ELIZABETH,
Wife of JOHN FISHER, of this Parifh,
Gent. and Daughter of the abovefaid
ROBERT HALE and ELIZABETH
his Wife, who died January 5,
1736, in the 49th Year of her Age.

Here alfo lyeth the Body of
SARAH, the Wife of EDWARD THOMAS,
late of the Parifh of Durham, Gent.
She died October 17, 1752,
aged 75 Years.

Here lyeth the Body of
ELIZABETH, the Wife of ROBERT
HALE, of this Parifh, who died the
8th Day of November, 1722,
in the 67th Year of her Age.

Alfo here lyeth the Body of MARY,
the Daughter of the abovefaid
ROBERT and ELIZABETH HALE,
who died the 27th of June, 1732,
in the 49th Year of her Age.

IN THE CHURCH-YARD.

ON TOMBS.

In Memory of
WILLIAM ALSOP,
who died the 22 Day of September,
1663.

Alfo of
WILLIAM ALSOP,
a great Grandfon
of the abovementioned, who died
the 31ft Day of December,
1770,
aged 85 Years.

Likewife in Memory
of SARAH, late Wife of
WILLIAM ALSOP, great Grandfon
beforementioned,
who died March 31, 1778,
aged 90.

And of AMY WALLINGTON ALSOP
their Daughter, who died the 16
of April, 1728.

In Memory
of MARGARET
ALSOP, who died
October the 2d, 1620.

Alfo JOAN ALSOP,
who died Auguft 4,
1644.

Alfo in Memory
of ROBERT ALSOP.

Here lyeth the Body of
ROBERT ALSOP, who died
. . . . 1663, aged 36 Years.

And here lyeth the Body of
. . . . ALSOP, who was the Wife
of WILLIAM ALSOP, and Mother of
the faid ROBERT ALSOP, who
died the 26th of February, 1670,
aged 74.

Here alfo lyeth the Body of
ROBERT ALSOP,
who was Grandfon of
the beforementioned ROBERT
ALSOP. He died the 22d of July,
1757, aged 73 Years.

In Memory of
HUGH ALSOP, Apothecary,
Son of WILLIAM and SARAH
ALSOP, who died October the 4th,
1786, aged 62 Years.

Here
lyeth the
Body of GILES
LONGDEN, of this Parifh,
Yeoman, who departed this Life
the 27th of June, 1724,
aged 52 Years.

Alfo
here lyeth the Body of
SARAH, the Wife of GILES LONGDEN,
who departed this Life the 2d of March,
1755, aged 85 Years.

Beneath this Stone
lies interred the Body of
NATHANIEL OSBORN,
of this Parifh, Yeoman,
who departed this Life the 23d
of March, 1752, aged 87 Years.

Alfo beneath this Stone
lies interred the Body of
SARAH his Wife, who departed
this Life the 21ft of October, 1769,
aged 97 Years.

Here lyeth the Body of
NATHANIEL OSBORN, of this Parifh,
fen. who departed this Life the 5th
of May, 1691, aged 80 Years.

Alfo here lyeth the Body
of SARAH, the Wife of
NATHANIEL OSBORN, fen.
who departed this Life the
14th of April, 1723,
aged 84 Years.

Beneath this
Stone lies the
Body of MARY,
Wife of CHARLES
PALMER, late of
Rodbourn, in the
County of Wilts.
She died the 7th of
July, 1756,
aged 85 Years.

In Memory
NATHANIEL OSBORN,
who died the 6th Day of
February 1771,
aged 73 Years.

In Memory of ROBERT,
Son of WILLIAM and BETTY SNELL.
He died June the 4th, 1765,
aged 34 Years.

In Memory of WILLIAM SNELL.
He died December the 30th, 1766,
aged 69.

In Memory of
PHILIP WEST,
who died March the 4th, 1770,
aged 56 Years.

ON HEAD-STONES.

	Died	Aged
Mary, Wife of Michael Hulf	8 Aug. 1741	31
John Smart	15 Jan. 1723	76
John Smart, jun.	5 Nov. 1773	90
Iffaac, Son of Thomas Millard	31 Mar. 1708	—

CLXVI. LITTLETON

CLXVI. LITTLETON upon SEVERN.

THIS Parifh lies in the Hundred of *Langley* and *Swincfhead*, three Miles Weftward from *Thornbury*, ten North-weftward from *Chipping Sodbury*, and twenty-fix Weftward from GLOUCESTER. The Terrier includes about 800 Acres, extending to the Banks of the *Severn*, in which a Right of Fifhery is attached feverally to each Eftate. The Soil is chiefly in Pafture, of Sand and Marle in fome Parts, but moftly Clay.

The Living is a Rectory, the Emolument of which arifes from an Eftate of 30*l*. a Year in Lieu of all Tythes. *Domefday* recites a Church and Thirty Acres of Meadow Land for the Maintenance of a Prieft, when it belonged to the Abbey of *Malmfbury* in *Wiltfhire*. The Patronage has defcended from the Family of HAWKSWORTH, of *Thornbury*, to CHRISTOPHER WILLOUGHBY, Efq.

The Church is in the Deanery of *Briftol*. It is a fmall low Building, with a South Aile and flated Tower, and retains nothing worthy of farther Remark.

Before the Compilation of *Domefday* Book, *Littleton* was the Donation of fome *Saxon* Prince to the Abbey of *Malmfbury*, and continued to be a Part of their Revenues till the Diffolution in 1542. In that Year it was granted, fubject to a referved Rent to the Crown of 18*l*. 4*s*. 4*d*. to Sir RICHARD LONG, Knight, from whom it foon paffed, by Purchafe, to RICHARD HAMPDEN and his Defcendant. Early in the laft Century it belonged to WILLIAM HOPTON, Efq. of *Cam* and *Berkeley*, a collateral of the Family of HOPTON, of *Stanton Lacey*, co. *Salop*. Sir ROBERT CANN, Bart. afterward poffeffed it; and it has fince paffed as Parcel of his Eftates to Dame CATHERINE, Relict of Sir HENRY LIPPINCOTT, Bart. of *Stoke Bifhop*. Other Eftates belong to THOMAS PRITCHARD and WILLIAM TAYLOR, Gents.

No Benefaction to the Poor.

The prefent Rector is WILLIAM TRUMAN, Clerk.

No Perfon was fummoned from this Place by the Heralds, in 1682 and 1683.

At the Election in 1776 Seven Freeholders polled from this Parifh.

The firft Date of the Regifter is in 1699.

ANNUAL ACCOUNT OF MARRIAGES, BIRTHS, AND BURIALS, IN THIS PARISH.

A.D.	Mar.	Bir.	Bur.	A.D.	Mar.	Bir.	Bur.	A.D.	Mar.	Bir.	Bur.	A.D.	Mar.	Bir.	Bur.
1781	1	3	6	1786	1	3	3	1791				1796			
1782	1	5	4	1787	1	5	3	1792				1797			
1783	3	5	2	1788	—	3	2	1793				1798			
1784	—	6	1	1789	—	6	6	1794				1799			
1785	—	6	2	1790	2	2	—	1795				1800			

INSCRIPTIONS IN THE CHURCH.

IN THE CHANCEL.

ON A FLAT STONE:

HERE LIETH THE BODY
OF MR. JOHN HVMFRID,
RECTOR OF THIS PARISH
OF LITTLETON, WHO
DIED JAN. 15, 1704,
AGED 65 YEARS.

IN THE NAVE.

ON A MONUMENT:

In Memory
of JOHN ALLIN, of
this Parifh, Yeoman, who
died January the 25th, 1768,
aged 51 Years.

Alfo of HANNAH his Wife,
who died December the 6th, 1764,
aged 62 Years.

ON FLAT STONES.

HERE LIETH
THOMAS
ARCHARD
. . . . . .
ANO DOM'I
1580.

HERE LYETH THE BODY
OF RICHARD ARCHARD,
YEOM. HE DECEASED
THE 27 OF JULY, 1619.

HERE

HERE LYETH THE BODY
OF EDMUND CHAMPNIES.
HE DECEASED THE 18
OF MARCH IN THE
YEARE OF OUR LORD
GOD 1622.

Here lyeth the
Body of ELEANOR, the Wife
of ROBERT ANDREWS, of Kirton,
in the Parish of Thornbury,
Yeoman, who departed this Life
January the 1st, 1731,
aged 57 Years.

Under this Stone lieth interred
the Body of ANNE COX,
Daughter of the aforefaid
ELEANOR ANDREWS,
and Relict of THOMAS COX, of Kington,
Yeoman,
who deceafed November the 2d, 1767,
aged 67 Years.

IN THE AISLE.

ON A BLACK MARBLE TOMB:

Here lyeth the Body of
ANNE, the Wife of
WILLIAM STEPHENS,
of this Parifh, Yeoman.
She died the 24th Day of April, 1680,
ætatis fuæ 51.

Alfo here lieth the Body of
JOHN STEPHENS, Son of the
abovefaid WILLIAM STEPHENS.
He died the 15 Day
of September, Anno Domini 1708,
ætatis fuæ 51.

Neare unto this Place lieth the Body
of WILLIAM STEPHENS,
Son as aforefaid.
He died the 3d Day of December,
Anno Dom. 1682, ætatis fuæ 18.

This Tomb was erected by
KATHERINE, Wife of the
abovefaid JOHN STEPHENS, in
Memory of her dear Hufband.

ON FLAT STONES.

HERE LIETH THE BODIE
OF PHILIP WITHER,
DECEASED AN⁰ DOMINI
1600.

Here lieth the Body
of SARAH BEVEN, the
Daughter of THOMAS
BEVEN, of Berkeley,
Alderman, who de-
parted this Life the
1st Day of Nov. 1716.

IN THE CHURCH-YARD.

ON HEAD-STONES.

	Died	Aged
William Allen	29 Mar. 1771	56
Mary his Wife	22 July, 1760	32
Ralph Nicholas	14 Mar. 1782	57
Thomas Nicholas	1 Nov. 1768	48
Edward Parker	11 June, 1711	33
Martha Woofly	23 Apr. 1750	45
Nicholas Stephens	25 Dec. 1705	46
Thomas his Son	4 Dec. 1705	19
John Gingell	— Sept. 1715	35
Jonathan Ruffell	29 July, 1749	41
Thomas Ruffell	26 June, 1767	65
Benjamin, Son of Benjamin and Hannah Dobbins, died an Infant.		
Allen Hill	30 Aug. 1706	77
William Morgan	20 June, 1770	43
Ann, Wife of William Bendall	10 Mar. 1760	55
Thomas Thomas	2 Oct. 1788	59

CLXVII.

L O N G N E Y,

A PARISH in the Hundred of *Whitſtone,* ſeven Miles North-weſt from *Stroud,* four Eaſt from *Newnham,* and ſeven South-weſt from GLOUCESTER. It forms the Banks of the *Severn* for the Space of four Miles. The Terrier includes 1500 Acres of a ſtrong Clay Soil, chiefly Paſture, and producing a great Quantity of Cider; one Sort of which, called *Longney Ruſſet,* originates here, and is eſteemed excellent.

The Benefice is a Vicarage, in the Deanery of *Glouceſter,* and in the Preſentation of the Crown, of which the Impropriation was veſted in the Abbey of *Malvern* in *Worceſterſhire.* About eighty Acres, called *Sten Meadow,* having been Parcel of their Property in this Pariſh are Tythe free. As an Appendage to the Manor it was purchaſed by the Truſtees of the Charities founded by the Will of HENRY SMITH *, Alderman of *London,* who have allowed 10*l.* a Year in Augmentation.

The

---

* HENRY SMITH, Eſq. whoſe Name is well known on Account of his various Benefactions to the Poor, died at his Houſe in *Silver Street,* on the 30th of January, and his Funeral " was worſhipfully ſolemnized at *Wandſworth* it being his Deſire to be there buried, becauſe it was the Place of his Nativity." He was once married, but his Wife dying many Years before him without Iſſue, he made over his Eſtate, real and perſonal, in the Year 1620, to Truſtees for charitable Purpoſes, referving out of the Profits thereof 500*l.* a Year for his own Maintenance. By his laſt Will, bearing Date April 24, 1627, he bequeathed legacies to various Perſons to the Amount of nearly 1000*l.* among which was 200*l.* to the Counteſs of DORSET; and 100*l.* to Lady DELAWARE; 1000*l.* to his Nephew, HENRY JACKSON; 1000*l.* to his poor Relations; 10,000*l.* to buy impropriations for godly Preachers; 150*l.* to found a Fellowſhip in *Cambridge* for his own Kindred; 1000*l.* to redeem poor Captives taken by *Turkiſh* Pirates; 500*l.* to the Pariſh of *Wandſworth*: 1000*l.* to *Richmond*; and 1000*l.* to *Reigate* to buy Lands for the Uſe of the Poor; the Reſidue of his Eſtates, real and perſonal, he bequeathed to his Executors, to be allotted to the Poor of various Pariſhes, according to their Diſcretion. In this Diſtribution the County of *Surrey* has been principally regarded. It may be obſerved, that whenever it has been aſſerted that Mr. SMITH left a Sum of Money to any of the Pariſhes here mentioned (though they have recorded it as a ſpecific Bequeſt in their reſpective Tables of Benefactions), it is erroneous, and would have been more accurately ſtated if it had been ſaid that they received it as an Allotment out of Mr. SMITH's Charity.

It may be collected from his Will and Declaration of Uſes, that his Object was to ſet ſuch poor People to Work as were able; to relieve the Impotent with Cloaths and Proviſions; to educate Children, and to bind them Apprentices. A Schedule of the preſent Amount, as paid in the Year 1791 (obligingly communicated by WILLIAM BRAY, Eſq. of *Great Ruſſell Street,* the Treaſurer), with the Names of the Eſtates out of which they iſſue:

	£.	s.	d.			£.	s.	d.	
Addington	1	0	0—Bexhill, Suſſex.		Morden	1	0	0—Bexhill.	
Barnes	5	13	0—Kemſing, Kent; Reigate, Surrey.		Mortlake	5	13	0—Kemſing, &c.	
					Newington Butts	18	16	0—Ibid.	
Batterſea	7	10	0—Ibid.		Peterſham	5	14	0—Iwood, Suſſex.	
Beddington	2	0	0—Bexhill.		Putney	11	6	0—Kemſing, &c.	
Camberweil	7	10	0—Kemſing, &c.		Richmond	97	0	0—Kemſing, &c. and Telleſcomb, Suſſex.	
Carſhalton	2	0	0—Bexhill.						
Cheam	4	12	0—Worth, Suſſex.		Rotherhithe	18	16	0—Kemſing, &c.	
Clapham	2	0	0—Bexhill.		Streatham	5	13	0—Ibid.	
Lambeth	18	16	0—Kemſing.		Sutton	2	0	0—Bexhill.	
Malden	1	10	0—Warbleton, Suſſen.		Tooting	2	0	0—Ibid.	
Merton	1	0	0—Bexhill.		Wandſworth	27	0	0—Stoughton, Leiceſterſhire.	
Mitcham	4	0	0—Ibid.		Wimbledon	5	13	0—Kemſing, &c.	

The Allotments to *Richmond* and *Wandſworth* are excluſive of the Sums left to thoſe Places by Mr. SMITH's Will. The Eſtate at *Bexhill* being a Fee Farm Rent, is not improvable; a Part of the *Kent* Eſtate having been advantageouſly exchanged with the Duke of DORSET for Lands at *Reigate,* the Allotments paid out of it are much augmented, and are capable of further Improvement. The Pariſhes of *Kingston* and *Croydon* have their Eſtates in their own Hands, and receive, therefore, nothing from the Truſtees. The Pariſh of *Streatham,* in Addition to the Sum abovementioned, receives about 4*l.* a Year, out of an Eſtate at *Longney* in *Glouceſterſhire,* which, from eventual Circumſtances, produced nothing in the Year 1791.

The Story of SMITH's having been a Beggar reſts upon a very vague Tradition: Its Fallacy, ſo far as it relates to his excluding *Mitcham* from the Benefits of his Charity becauſe he was whipped out of that Pariſh, may be deduced from the foregoing Account. It appears, nevertheleſs, that he was a Perſon of very humble Extraction, from his leaving Money to his poor Kindred, viz. ſuch as were aged, impotent, and unable to keep themſelves. Upon being aſked, which of his poor Kindred he meant? he ſaid, the pooreſt of his Siſter's Children, and their Children.

Mr. SMITH was buried in the Chancel: on his Tomb is the following Inſcription;

" Depoſitum HENR. SMITH, Senatoris Londinenſis.
Mole ſub hac quæris quis cenditur optime lector,
Cujus & qualis, quantus in orbe fuit.
A dextris muri, ſtatuam tu cernere poſſis
Oranti ſimilem, marmore de Pario;
Subter quam ſtatuam cernatur tabula ſculpta
Auratis verbis quæ tibi cuncta notant."

MARSHFIELD.

The Church, dedicated to *St. Lawrence,* is a neat Gothic Structure, with embattled Nave and Tower, probably erected during the middle Centuries by the Abbey of *Malverne.*

It appears by *Domefday* Book, that the Manor, containing five Hides, was held by ELSI, a *Saxon,* and was granted foon after the Conqueft to OSBERN FITZ PONZ, who beftowed it upon the *Benedictine* Abbey of *Great Malvern,* which Right was afterwards confirmed to them by HENRY I. and remained with them till the Diffolution. No Proprietor is mentioned before Sir HENRY BOND, in 1608. Soon after the Year 1627, the Manor and Eftates, extending over the greater Part of the Parifh, were purchafed for the Purpofes of the Will of the abovenamed HENRY SMITH, which have been fince vefted in Truftees. This Place furnifhes no other Subject of Detail *.

B E N E F A C T I O N.

HENRY SMITH, Efq. by Deed enrolled in Chancery, in 1626, gave 100*l.* to purchafe Land; and, in 1641, his Truftees added what now produces 8*l.* 15*s.* 3*d.* for the Maintenance of the Poor.

INCUMBENTS.	PATRONS.	INCUMBENTS.	PATRONS.
—— Roger Matthew,	Priory of Great Malvern.	1662 Richard Littleton,	K. Charles II.
1543 John David,	K. Henry VIII.	1713 Henry Abbot,	Q. Anne.
1562 Robert Clayfield,	Q. Elizabeth,	1728 William James,	K. George II.
1609 Thomas Potter,	K. James I.	1744 William Moreland,	The fame.
—— William Halke,	The fame.	1772 Thomas Lewis,	K. George III.
1613 William Bennet,	The fame.	1774 Jofeph Chefter, D. D.	The fame.
—— John Trotman,	————.		

The prefent PROPRIETORS of the MANOR are the Truftees of the Charity of HENRY SMITH, Efq.

At the Heralds Vifitation, in 1682 and 1683, no Perfon was fummoned from this Place.

At the Election in 1776 Five Freeholders polled from this Parifh.

The firft Date of the Regifter occurs in 1660.

On the Eaft Wall a Monument has been erected to his Memory with his Effigies kneeling at a Defk in the Attitude of Devotion; underneath is a Tablet infcribed as follows:

" Here lyeth the Body of HENRY SMITH, Efq. fome Time Citizen and Alderman of *London,* who departed this Life the 30th Day of January, Anno Dom. 1627, being then neere the Age of 79 Yeares, whome while he lived gave unto thefe feveral Townes in *Surrey* following;—one thoufand Pounds apeece to buy Lands for Perpetuity for the Reliefe and fetting poor People on Worke in the faid Townes, viz. to the Towne of *Croydon* one Thoufand Pounds; to the Towne of *Kingfton* one Thoufand Pounds; to the Towne of *Guildford* one Thoufand Pounds; to the Towne of *Darking* one Thoufand Pounds; to the Towne of *Farnham* one Thoufand Pounds; and by his laft Will and Teftament did further give and devife, to buy Lands for Perpetuity and fetting the Poore aworke unto the Towne of *Reigate,* one Thoufand Pounds; to the Towne of *Richmond* one Efpecialty or Debt of a Thoufand Pounds; and unto this Towne of *Wandfworth,* wherein he was borne, the Sum of five Hundred Pounds, for the fame Ufe as before; and did further will and bequeath one Thoufand Pounds to buy Lands for perpetuity to redeem poor Captives and Prifoners from the *Turkifh* Tyranny; and not here ftinting his Charity and Bounty, did alfo give and bequeath the moft Part of his Eftate, being to a great Value, for the purchafing Lands of Inheritance for ever, for the Reliefe of the Poore and fetting them aworke; a Pattern worthy the Imitation of thofe whome GOD has bleffed with the Abundance of the Goods of this Life to follow him therein." LYSONS's Environs of *London,* vol. I. p. 512.

His Truftees, purfuant to the Directions of his Will, purchafed, amongft other Eftates, the Manor of *Longney,* with the Demefne Lands, and Rectory, and Parfonage; the Income of which to be difpofed of in Charities. And the Manor, &c. ftill continue vefted in fuch Truftees, who hold a Court Leet and Court Baron here.

The Demefne Lands and Parfonage of *Longney,* with the Quit-Rents of the Manor, are allotted to pay the following Sums annually, viz. to

	£.	s.	d.			£.	s.	d.
Bath Eafton, co. Somerfet	10	0	0	Northill, co. Bedford ——		4	0	0
Newton St. Loe, co. Somerfet	30	0	0	Odiham, co. Hants ——		10	0	0
Stanton Priors, co. Somerfet	10	0	0	Ormfkirk, co. Lancafter ——		9	0	0
Chippenham, co. Wilts	10	0	0	Perfhore, co. Worcefter ——		50	0	0
Calne, co. Wilts ——	10	0	0	St. Sepulchre, London ——		10	0	0
Chedefton, co. Suffolk ——	10	0	0	St. Giles's Cripplegate ——		10	0	0
Chipping Barnet, co. Herts ——	10	0	0	St. Olave Old Jewry ——		10	0	0
King's Langley, co. Herts ——	5	0	0	St. Vedaft Paternofter Lane ——		10	0	0
Chrift Church, co. Surrey ——	10	0	0	St. Martin in the Fields ——		12	0	0
Horne, co. Surrey ——	10	0	0	Radnor in Wales ——		5	0	0
Streatham, co. Surrey ——	4	0	0	Warbleton, co. Suffex ——		8	0	0
St. Thomas, Southwark ——	6	0	0					

Which Sums have been increafed as the Rent of the Farm has been improved.

* Plac. in com *Glocefir.* 32 H. III. rot. 18*d.* pro terris in *Langenei.* TANNER, Not. Mon. *Worc.* No. XV.

ANNUAL ACCOUNT OF MARRIAGES, BIRTHS, AND BURIALS, IN THIS PARISH.

A.D.	Mar.	Bir.	Bur.	A.D.	Mar.	Bir.	Bur.	A.D.	Mar.	Bir.	Bur.	A.D.	Mar.	Bir.	Bur.
1781	2	13	3	1786	2	8	5	1791				1796			
1782	2	7	9	1787	3	10	6	1792				1797			
1783	2	11	9	1788	1	8	7	1793				1798			
1784	3	8	6	1789	2	15	11	1794				1799			
1785	1	10	8	1790	1	7	7	1795				1800			

INSCRIPTIONS IN THE CHURCH.

IN THE CHANCEL.

ON A MONUMENT:

Arms; a Fefs between three Efcallops.

In Memory of
the Rev. Mr. RICHARD LITTLETON,
M. A. who was Minifter of this Place 58
Years. He was pious, painful, and
profitable,
in his Office. He finifhed his Courfe,
and was gathered among his People
October the 6th, Anno Domini 1713,
aged 79.

Here alfo lyeth MARY
his beloved Wife, who died
Auguft 24, in the 86th Year of her Age,
1714.

Alfo in Memory of WILLIAM
his Son, who was buried December
the 3d, Anno Domini 1695,
aged 22.

ON A FLAT STONE, ROUND THE
VERGE:

ELIZABETH, DAUGHTER OF
JOHN TROTMAN, VICAR,
DECEASED 17 MARCH, 1652.

IN THE NAVE.
ON FLAT STONES.

Here refteth the Body of
WILLIAM, the Son of
THOMAS ARUNDEL, Clothier
and of SARAH his Wife, who died
Auguft 28, Anno 1685,
aged 21 Weeks.

Here lyeth the Body
of JAMES HEARNE, Gent.
who deceafed the 23d of April,
1688, ætatis fuæ 32.

Alfo JAMES, JANE, and JANE, his Son
and Daughters, who died Infants.

IN THE CHURCH YARD.

In Memory of JOAN COPE, Widow,
the late Wife and Relict of
JOHN GOUGH, of Stonehoufe,
in this County, Clothier,
who died June 11, A. D. 1740,
in the 80th Year of her Age.

Alfo in Memory of THEOPHILUS,
the 4th Son of the
Rev. Mr. WILLIAM JAMES,
Vicar of this Parifh,
and Grandfon of the faid JOAN COPE,
who died the 28th Day of January,
1728, aged about 10 Months.

In Memory of
JOHN GOUGH, jun.
Son of JOHN GOUGH, late of the
Parifh of Stonehoufe,
He departed this Life the 6th Day of
April, Anno Dom. 1719,
in the 19th Year of his Age.

In Memory of
THOMAS COPE, of this Parifh,
Yeoman, who died April the 6th, 1719,
aged 61.

Alfo in Memory of MARY,
Relict of HENRY CLARKE,
of this Parifh, Yeoman,
and Daughter of the abovefaid
THOMAS COPE. She died
December 14, A. D. 1753,
aged 61 Years.

Here lieth the Body of
SARAH, the Wife of
THOMAS COPE, of this Parifh, Yeoman,
who departed this Life
the 9th Day of April, 1704, aged 48.

Here lyeth the Body of
JOHN COPE, who died the 17th of
December, 1745, aged 48 Years.

In Memory of
ANNE, the Wife of
JOHN COPE, who was buried
the 15th Day of December, 1725,
in the 30th Year of her Age.

Alfo JONATHAN their Son,
who died the 20 Day of July, 1726.

This Tomb is erected to the
Memory of WILLIAM ELLIS, of
this Parifh, Yeoman,
who died June 17, 1774,
aged 70 Years.

In Memory of WILLIAM ELLIS,
Son of JONATHAN and ANNE ELLIS,
of this Parifh, who died Dec. the 22,
1778, aged 20 Years.

In Memory of
JOHN BROWNING,
of this Parifh, who
died July 31, 1788,
aged 62 Years.

Here lyeth the Body of
ELIZABETH, the Wife of
WILLIAM ROWLES, who died
the 6th of June, 1740,
aged 40 Years.

Alfo JOHN ROWLES, late of
Minfterworth, who died
the 8th Day of December, 1746.

In Memory of
WILLIAM ROWLES, of this Parifh,
who died Dec. 22, 1775,
aged 77 Years.
In Memory of
ELIZABETH ANDREWS,
Daughter of the above
WILLIAM ROWLES.
She died Feb. 14, 1782, aged 56.

ON TOMBS.

In Memory of THOMAS JEFFERIS,
fenior, of this Parifh. Yeoman,
who was buried the 2nd Day of
September, 1726. aged 80.

Here lyeth the Body of
WILLIAM PACE, of this Parifh, Gent.
who departed this Life
the 1ft of June, 1720,
in the 72d Year of his Age.

Here lyeth the Body of MARGARET,
the Wife of WILLIAM PACE, Gent.
who died the firft Day of October,
A. D. 1692, ætatis fuæ 40.

In Memory of JOHN HOW, fen.
of this Parifh, Yeoman,
who died the 11th of June, 1706,
aged 78 Years.

In Memory of JOHN HOW, jun.
of this Parifh, Yeoman,
who died the 24th of September, 1724,
aged 70 Years.

In Memory of SARAH the Relict of
RICHARD YEALFE, of this Parifh, Sen.
who deceafed December 13, 1686.

Here refts the Body of
ESTHER YEALFE,
Daughter of RICHARD YEALFE,
of this Parifh, Sen.
who deceafed Jan. 19, 1695,
aged 37 Years.

Alfo of
SAMUEL and ELIZABETH GAINER.
SAMUEL died March 1770,
aged 65.
ELIZABETH died April 6, 1764,
aged 60.

She was eldeft Daughter of RICHARD
and ELIZABETH YEALFE, Jun.

Iu

In Memory of JOHN, the Son
of JOHN HOW. He deceafed
the 25 Day of September,
1727, aged 37 Years.

In Memory of
SARAH, the Wife of JOHN HOW, Sen.
who died the 25th Day of March, 1728,
aged 70 Years.

———

To the Memory of
Mrs. ELIZABETH RIDER,
Wife of Mr. JAMES RIDER,
of Painfwick Lodge in this County,
and Daughter of Mr. HENRY HODGES,
and ELIZABETH his Wife,
who departed this Life
the 27 Day of Auguft, 1747,
aged 40 Years.

———

In Memory of
HENRIETTA the Wife of
Mr. WILLIAM ROWLES,
of Gloucefter,
late of this Parifh.
She departed this Life
the 27th Day of May, 1771,
aged 67 Years.

———

Here lyeth the Body of
STEPHEN SIMONS,
of this Parifh, Yeoman,
who died in the Year 1626.

And alfo the Body of
JOAN his Wife,
who anciently lived in Longney,
and deceafed the 4 Day of Sept.
in the Year 1640.

Here lyeth the Body of
WILLIAM SIMONS, Son of
JEREMIAH SIMONS,
of this Parifh of Longney,
who deceafed the 20th Day of
January, 1675.

———

Here lyeth the Body of ELIZABETH,
the Wife of JEREMY SIMONS,
who departed this Life
the 9th Day of November, 1693,
ætatis fuæ 52.

Here lyeth the Body of ELIZABETH,
the Wife of THOMAS DYER,
and Daughter of
THOMAS and ABIGAIL ROBERTS,
of the Parifh of Harefcomb,
Gent. who died Oct. 15, 1756,
aged 76 Years.

———

Here refteth the Body of
JEREMY SIMONS,
of this Parifh, Yeoman,
who departed this Life the
12 Day of June, 1707,
ætatis fuæ 70.

Here refteth the Body of
SARAH, late Wife of
JEREMY SIMONS, of this Parifh,
Yeoman,
who departed this Life
the 25 Day of December, 1719,
ætatis fuæ 73.

———

Here refteth, in Expectation of a
joyous Refurrection,
the Body of JOHN HAYWOOD,
who departed this Life
the — of June, Anno Domini 1682,
aged 31 Years.

———

Here refteth the Body of
THOMAS HAYWOOD, of this
Parifh, Yeoman, who departed
this Life the 6th Day of Oct. 1706,
ætat. fuæ 62.

In Memory of MARY, the Wife
of THOMAS HAYWOOD, who
died the 2d of February, 1721-2,
aged 76 Years.

In Memory of WILLIAM HAY-
WOOD, of Downing in this Parifh,
Yeoman, who died the 8th of May,
1725, aged 45 Years.

———

Here refteth the Body of
THOMAS HAYWOOD,
of this Parifh, Yeoman,
who departed this Life
the 6th Day of June, 1714,
ætatis fuæ 33.

Here lyeth the Body of
ELIZABETH, the Wife of
THOMAS HAYWOOD,
of this Parifh,
who departed this Life
February the 1ft, Anno Domini 1732-3,
aged 47.

———

In Memory of
JOHN HAYWOOD, of this Parifh,
Yeoman, who died in 1736,
aged 45 Years.

In Memory of THOMAS ASTMAN,
of this Parifh, Yeoman,
who died Auguft the 17th, 1775,
aged 75 Years.

———

Here refteth the Body of
SARAH, the Wife of WILLIAM PACE,
of this Parifh, Gent.
who departed this Life the
1ft Day of February, 1714,
ætatis fuæ 43.

Here refteth the Body of
JOAN, the Wife of CHRISTOPHER
BELLOMEY, of this Parifh, Yeoman,
who departed this Life
the 12 of April, 1716, ætatis fuæ 70.

In Memory of MARY, the Wife of
WILLIAM FRYER, of this Parifh,
and Daughter of
JOHN and SARAH PRIDE,
of Charlton King's, in this County,
who departed this Life
Jan. 20, 1770, aged 36 Years.

Alfo of SARAH their Daughter,
who died March 15, 1772,
aged 14 Years.

To the Memory of
WILLIAM FRYER,
of this Parifh, Yeoman,
who departed this Life
October the 30, 1774, in the
61ft Year of his Age.

———

Underneath are depofited
the Remains of JOHN FRYER,
of the Parifh of Wheatenhurft,
Yeoman, who died Dec. 23, 1783,
aged 65 Years.

Alfo of HANNAH his Wife,
who died April the 10th, 1766,
aged 42 Years.

Alfo of MARY their Daughter
who died . . . . . the 15th, 1772,
aged 22.

———

In Memory of
WILLIAM PALMER,
of this Parifh, who died
November 26, 1782,
aged 56 Years.

Alfo of SARAH his Wife,
who departed this Life
June the 28th, 1791,
aged 59.

In Memory of
ANN, Wife of GILES PALMER,
of the Parifh of Tibberton,
who died February the 18th, 1778,
aged 42 Years.

———

ON A FLAT STONE:

Here lyeth the Body of
MARY the Wife of
THOMAS WEYMAN, Sen.
of this Parifh,
Daughter of CHARLES JONES,
of Maufick, in the Parifh of Newent
in this County,
who was buried Auguft 28, 1754,
aged 78.

Near this Place lieth the Body of
THOMAS WEYMAN, of this Parifh,
who departed this Life
November the 26th, 1780,
aged 80 Years.

———

O N

O N   H E A D   S T O N E S.

	Died	Aged		Died	Aged
Ann, the Wife of Thomas Weyman	20 Oct. 1697	27	Richard Sims	18 Jan. 1786	—
Thomas Weyman	10 June, 1731	60	Sarah his Wife	23 Mar. 1790	77
Elizabeth, Wife of Joseph Ellis, Daughter of Thomas Cope	17 Jan. 1728	—	Giles their Son	7 Feb. 1786	34
Jonathan Ellis	29 Mar. 1767	61	Thomas Stratford	11 Oct. 1717	49
William Ellis	21 Dec. 1720	78	Ann his Wife	27 May, 1728	46
Matthew Fryer	10 Jan. 1730	55	William Jackson	25 Oct. 1738	64
Sarah his Wife	27 Mar. 1744	60	Mary his Wife	30 Apr. 1746	76
Walter Rowles	16 Oct. 1768	37	Elizab. their Dau. Wife of Ri. Mayo	20 Jan. 1746	—
Hannah his Wife	29 July, 1758	50	Sarah, Wife of E. Stradling Westbury	26 Mar. 1755	33
William Bullock, sen.	2 Jan. 1701	68	Robert Bullock	15 Apr. 1679	—
William Bullock	26 Apr. 1721	52	Elizabeth his Wife	13 Sept. 1682	—
Anne his Wife	25 Dec. 1723	45	Anselme Bailey	27 Dec. 1769	63
Sarah their Daughter, Wife of John Baldwin	29 July, 1726	—	William, Son of Tho. and Anne Fryer	24 Sept. 1768	20
Robert Bullock	6 Sept. 1777	62	Sarah, Wife of Joseph Hale	12 May, 1764	61
Betty his Wife	23 May, 1770	41	Giles Lewis	2 Oct. 1757	40
John Bullock, of Bristol	20 June, 1782	73	Thomas Jefferis, jun.	13 Apr. 1724	45
Richard Cowmeadow	3 Nov. 1762	60	Josiah Howe	22 Aug. 1735	58
Anna his Wife	20 Sept. 1772	67	William Howe	9 Sept. 1736	46
Anna their Daughter	19 Dec. 1765	16	Anselme Browning	29 May, 1762	76
Thomas Cowmeadow	23 Feb. 1754	45	Joan his Wife	18 Sept. 1759	65
Grace his Daughter	18 Feb. 1784	37	William their Son	25 Feb. 1749	19
Sarah, Wife of William Jones	30 Jan. 1774	43	Thomas Browning, of Westbury	19 Apr. 1767	39
Thomas their Son	15 Aug. 1787	19	Thomas Rowle	6 Feb. 1731	43
Rachel, Wife of Joseph Hale	10 Mar. 1777	55	Temperance his Wife	16 Mar. 1739	56
William Stephens	10 Feb. 1778	73	Thomas Palmer	15 Apr. 1733	39
Thomas Fryer	10 Oct. 1787	67	Sarah his Wife	2 Mar. 1753	62
Ann his Wife	13 Mar. 1780	61	William How	25 July, 1700	42
Sarah, Wife of James Birt	20 Oct. 1778	31	Sarah his Daughter	6 May, 1716	18
John their Son	29 May, 1780	27	William How	6 Aug. 1730	45
John Eagles, senior, of Standish	21 Oct. 1771	72	Mary, Wife of William How, sen.	4 Mar. 1740	80
Elizabeth, Wife of Thomas Long	29 Aug. 1788	62	Richard Closs	27 June, 1716	48
Joseph Young, of Westbury	17 Mar. 1719	22	James his Son	5 Mar. 1737	31
Thomas Browning	5 Nov. 1720	65	Thomas Hannis	8 Mar. 1685	—
Sarah his Wife	18 Mar. 1711	49	Dorothy, Daughter of Rev. G. Venn	15 Mar. 1714	60
Sarah, Daughter of James Byrkin	5 June, 1752	20	Mary, Daughter of John Haywood	12 July, 1676	—
Ann, Daughter of Richard Bishop	29 Sept. 1682	—	Daniel Barrow	—— —— 1740	42
Mary, Wife of John Walter, of Westbury upon Trim	6 Nov. 1692	78	Sarah his Wife, Daughter of Richard and Elizabeth Yealfe	9 Jan. 1739	35
John Clarke	10 Mar. 1721	70	Anthony Fryer	16 Aug. 1771	60
Sarah his Wife	3 Dec. 1725	74	Susannah his Wife	2 July, 1771	60
Hester their Daughter	9 Mar. 1722	32	Edward Land	10 Aug. 1762	56
John their Son	18 Mar. 1714	33	Anne his Wife	4 Sept. 1777	59
William their Son	7 Nov. 1725	22	William Sly	26 July, 1775	46
Joan, Wife of John Clarke	6 Apr. 1765	94	Martha, Wife of Thomas Bright	19 Mar. 1785	53
Sarah, Wife of John Harnons, Gent.	3 Dec. 1728	65	Elizabeth, Wife of William Merrett	15 June, 1760	47
Joseph Sims	17 May, 1721	47	Thomas Cope	20 July, 1753	63
			Mary his Wife	15 Sept. 1714	19
			Mary, Wife of Thomas Guisden	7 Dec. 1734	37

CLXVIII. MANGOTSFIELD.

VARIOUS Etymologies have been offered concerning this Name, but they do not seem sufficiently applicable to deserve Repetition. The Parish of *Mangotsfield* is situate in that Part of the Hundred of *Barton Regis* which is contiguous to the City of *Bristol*, whence it is distant four Miles on the North-east, seven in the opposite Direction from *Chipping Sodbury*, and thirty-two South-west from GLOUCESTER. It contains about 3000 Acres, of a fertile Soil, with extensive Commons * ; and the Fossil Productions are Coal and Paving Stone, of a superior Quality.

The Benefice is only a stipendiary Curacy, arising from an annual Charge upon the Impropriation and Queen ANNE's Bounty, which was procured by the Benefactions of JOHN DOWEL and EDWARD COLSTON, Esqrs. It was originally a Chapel of Ease to the Church of *St. Peter in Bristol*, and belonged, with the Tythes, to the Cell of *St. James* in that City, under the Patronage of the Abbey of *Tewkesbury*. At the Dissolution they were purchased by JOHN BRAYNE, and afterwards belonged to the Family of DOWEL of *Almondsbury*, by whom they were again sold in severalty to the Proprietors of the Estates in this Parish, which have since been exempted.

The Church is a neat Gothic Structure, dedicated to *St. James*, consisting of a Nave and North Aisle, embattled with a Tower and Spire on the South Side. Some Conjectures have arisen with respect to the Founder, as there were formerly two Figures in the North Aisle (only one of which remains), with these Arms, Argent, two Bars Azure, over all, an Escarbuncle of eight Rays Gules, pomettée and floretté Or, for BLOUNT of *Bitton*, with other quartered Escocheons, which are repeated on the Outside of the Porch.

Under the Title of the great Manor of *King's Barton*, *Mangotsfield* was included as a Member, and so recited in *Domesday* Book. It appears to have been afterward divided into three distinct Parts. Of the Principal the earliest Proprietors for many Generations, were the BLOUNTS of *Bitton* abovenamed. WILLIAM PLAYER, Esq. purchased *Cleeve Hill*, with this manerial Estate, in the Reign of JAMES the First; and it remained with his Descendants till the Beginning of the present Century, when it was transferred to CHARLES BRAGGE, Esq. whose Son has resold it to JOHN GORDON *, Esq. retaining the Manor.

Another Manor belonged, in the early Reigns, to the Family of DE PUTOT. WILLIAM DE PUTOT built a Chapel in his Manor-house, and obtained a Grant of a free Chantry. It afterwards passed to the Families of LANGLEY and MEREDETH, and was purchased by the late EDWARD COLSTON, Esq. in whose Heirs the Right Hon. HENRY Lord MIDDLETON and ALEXANDER COLSTON, Esq. it is now vested.

A third Manor, consisting of Part of the Manor of *Sturdon*, which extends into other Parishes, has passed from EDWARD SEYMOUR, Earl of *Hertford*, to the Family of SMYTH, of *Long Ashton*, co. *Somerset*, and is now held by the Descendant THOMAS SMYTH, Esq.

H A M L E T S.

1. *Downend* is a considerable Village, and, having a very eligible Situation, is very populous.

2. *Morend* is likewise mentioned as a distinct Hamlet.

The principal Proprietors of Lands in this Parish, beside those already enumerated, are EDWARD ANDREWS, and WILLIAM HAYWARD WINSTONE, Esqrs. with several others.

B E N E F A C T I O N.

ISABELLA PLAYER bequeathed 100*l.* Date unknown, the Interest to be divided between the Parishes of *Mangotsfield* and *Frampton Cotterel*.

---

* By an Agreement with the Parishioners, JOHN GORDON, Esq. has inclosed 300 Acres of Waste Land in this Parish, for which he is to pay, in Aid of the Poor Rate, 80*l.* a Year.

6

The

The prefent Incumbent is Christopher Haines, Clerk.

Present Proprietors of the Manors,

Charles Bragg, Efq.   Right Hon. Henry Lord Middleton,
Thomas Smyth, Efq.   and Alexander Colston, Efq.

The Perfons fummoned from this Place by the Heralds, in 1682 and 1683, were
John Meredeth, Efq. William Player, Efq. Jonathan Tucker, Gent. and Robert Gueft, Gent.

At the Election in 1776 Sixty-three Freeholders polled from this Parifh.

The earlieft Date in the Regifter occurs in 1620.

Annual Account of Marriages, Births, and Burials, in this Parish.

A.D.	Mar.	Bir.	Bur.	A.D.	Mar.	Bir.	Bur.	A.D.	Mar.	Bir.	Bur.	A.D.	Mar.	Bir.	Bur.
1781	19	51	29	1786	11	87	49	1791				1796			
1782	13	84	42	1787	10	69	41	1792				1797			
1783	17	67	46	1788	12	74	20	1793				1798			
1784	18	77	38	1789	17	80	34	1794				1799			
1785	16	67	32	1790	16	83	34	1795				1800			

INSCRIPTIONS IN THE CHURCH.

IN THE NAVE.

ON MONUMENTS.

Arms; a Fefs Gules, between three
Mullets.

M. S.
Thomæ Player, de Cleeve Hill,
In agro Glouceftrienfi, Armigeri;
Cujus exuviæ jacent Collegio Briftolienfi.
Ingenio acri, judicio fagaci, memoria felici,
Fuit præditus.
Erga æquales fuavem, erga fuperiores
gratum,
Erga pauperes benevolum
fe præbuit;
Meliora meruiffe contentus.
Officium irenarchæ prudenter exercere,
Pacem & juftitiam inter vicinos ftabilire,
Maluit.
Variis diu laffus fatigatufque morbis
Podagra præcipuè cruciatus
Naturæ conceffit,
Primo die Novembris
1739.

Arms; on a Bend cottifed three Mullets;—impaling, on a Crofs four Mill-
rinds pierced.

To
the Memory
of an humble but fincere Member
of the Eftablifhed Church
Edward Andrews, Efq.
of Hillhoufe, in this County,
who died the 18th of July, 1758,
aged 49.
This Monument
is erected
by Elizabeth his Relict,
the fecond Daughter
of Edward Turnor, Efq. of
Stoke Rochford,
in the County of Lincoln,
by whom
he had Iffue
four Sons, now furviving,
and
one Daughter, Elizabeth,
who died July the 8, 1749,
and

lies buried with him
in a Vault
near adjoining to this Place.

Elizabeth his Relict
died March 10, 1772,
aged 54 Years.
Her Remains are depofited
in the fame Vault.

IN THE CHANCEL.

ON FLAT STONES.

Here lyeth the Body of
Dionisia, the Daughter of John
Meredeth, Efq. Lord of this
Mannour by Elizabeth his Wife,
Daughter of William Bassett, of
Claverton, in the County of Somer-
fet, Efq. who died the 3d of
March, Anno Domini 1702,
ætatis fuæ 36.

Here lyeth the Body of
Elizabeth, the Relict of
John Meredeth, Efq.
of this Parifh,
who departed this Life
the 22 July, 1705, aged 75 Years.

H. S. E.
Hanna uxor Roberti Guest,
hujus parochiæ, Gen. Adami Baynham, de Yate, Gen. & Sylvestriæ
Uxoris ejus Filiique; obijt tertio
. . . . die Decembris, anno Domini
Milleffimo feptingentefimo feptuagefimo
quinto. Etiam Robertus primo-
genitus
Roberti Guest & S . . . . uxoris, qui
obijt octavo die Augufti.
Etiam Maria foror fua . . . .
. . . . . deceffit
Etiam Theophilus filius fecundus
Roberti Guest & . . . . . uxoris ejus,
qui obijt quinto die Decembris,
Anno Domini milleffimo feptingentefimo
feptuagefimo tertio, viginti duos
annos natus.

Here lyeth the Body of
Edward Dobbins, Gent. of this
Parifh, who departed this Life
the 4th January, 1712,
aged near 73 Years.

Alfo here lyeth the Body of
Susannah, the Wife of Edward
Dobbins, Gent. of this Parifh,
who departed this Life the 3d
Day of Auguft, 1714,
aged 63 Years.

Alfo here lyeth the Body of
Elizabeth, the Wife of Thomas
Collins, and Daughter of the
abovefaid Edward Dobbins and
Susannah his Wife, who dep-
parted this Life the 22 of
June, 1718, aged 30 Years.

Here lyeth the Body of
Samuel Bampton, of this
Parifh, Gent. who departed
this Life the 23d of Sept.
1734, in the 63d Year of his Age.

Alfo here lyeth the Body of
Samuel Bampton, Son of the
abovefaid Samuel Bampton,
Gent. who departed this Life
the 12 of November, 174..
aged 30 Years and a Half.

Here lyeth the Body of
Mrs. Anne Bampton, Widow
of Samuel Bampton the elder,
of this Parifh, Gent. deceafed,
who departed this Life the
27 Day of Octob. 1758,
aged 82 Years.

IN THE NAVE.

ON FLAT STONES.

In Memory of
Robert, Son of Jonathan and Anne
Lennott. He died Sept. 23,
1762, aged 30 Years.

In

In Memory of MARY
PAGE, Daughter of JOHN
and ANNE MILATT, late
of this Parifh, who departed
this Life Dec. the 1ſt, 1762,
aged 75 Years.

Here lyeth the Body of
SUSANNA, the Wife of WILLIAM
SARTAIN, of this Parifh, Yeoman,
who departed this Life the
30 Day of Sept. Anno Dom.
1724, in the 51 Year of her Age.

HERE LYETH THE BODY OF
JOHN LANE, OF THIS PARISH,
YEOMAN, WHO DEPARTED THIS
LIFE THE 30 DAY OF DECEM-
BER, 1708, AGED 67 YEARS.

Here lieth the Body of
THOMAS STEWARD, of this
Parifh, who departed
this Life the 8 Day July,
Anno Dom. 1716, aged 55.

Alſo here lyeth the Body
of MARY, the Wife of THOMAS
STEWARD, of this Parifh, who
departed this Life the 19th
of March, 1729, in the 56
Year of her Age.

To
the Memory of JOHN BOOTH,
Glafs-mafter,
of the Parifh of Bedminfter,
who died April 18, 1770,
aged 34 Years.

Here lyeth the Body of
FARNAM, Son of CHARLES and
MARY LATHAM, who died the
19 Day of April, 1789.

Here under lieth the Body of JANE,
Daughter of STEPHEN and MARY
WATTS, of this Parifh,
who departed this Life
the 30 of April, Anno
Domini 1764, ætatis fuæ 34.

Alſo JOANNA SHIPLEY, Daughter
of the above, who departed
this Life the 23 of Nov. 1769,
aged 42 Years.

Here
under lieth the Body of
STEPHEN WATTS, ſen. Gent.
who departed this Life the
24th of March, A. D. 1768, ætat. 72.

Alſo Mrs. MARY WATTS, Wife
of the above, who departed this
Life the 23 of Sept. 1773,
aged 74 Years.

Here
under lieth the Body of STEPHEN
eldeſt Son of STEPHEN and MARY
WATTS, who departed this Life
the 27 of Sept. A. D. 1765, æt. 28.

Alſo BETTY, Wife of
HENRY WATTS, who
departed this Life the 23 of
May, 1778, aged 40 Years.

ON MONUMENTS IN THE
NORTH AISLE.

Arms ; Sable, a Croſs patonce Argent;—impaling, Or, a Chevron between
three Bulls Sable.

To the Memory of LUCY,
Wife of WILLIAM ALLEYN,
Merchant, of Briſtol,
Sifter of CHARLES BRAGGE, Efq.
of Cleeve Hill.
In her Perfon fhe was amiable;
in all her Actions virtuous;
for uncommon Sweetnefs of Temper,
unaffected Goodnefs, and univerfal
Benevolence,
fhe was admired, efteemed, and loved,
leaving few Equals, and fewer
Superiors.
She died in Child-bed, greatly lamented,
Dec. 14, 1741, and with her Infant Son
lies here interred in a Vault near this
Place.

Near this Place lieth the
Body of DANIEL LAWRENCE,
of this Parifh, Yeoman,
who departed this Life the 4 Day
of Sept. 1716, aged 44 Years.

ON A BRASS PLATE IN THE NORTH
WALL :

Here under lieth the Body of
OBADIAH TUCKER, of this
Parifh, Yeoman,
who deceafed Auguſt the 15,
Anno { Dom. 1680.
       { Ætatis 80.

HERE LYETH THE BODY OF
JOHN TUCKER, OF MOREND,
WITHIN THIS PARISH, YEOMAN,
WHO DECEASED THE 15 OF AUG.
ANNO DOM. 1657, BEING
AGED 59 YEARS.

ALSO HERE LYETH THE BODY OF
JONATHAN TUCKER, OF MOREND,
WITHIN THIS PARISH, YEOMAN,
SON OF THE ABOVESAID
JOHN TUCKER,
WHO DECEASED THE 20 OF
OCTOBER,
ANNO DOMINI 1712,
IN THE 75TH YEAR OF HIS AGE.

Here lieth the Body of
BENJAMIN, Son of
DANIEL and ELIZABETH NICHOLS,
of this Parifh, who died the 2 of
Decemb. 1765, aged 34 Years.

Alſo underneath this Stone
lies interred the Remains
of the abovefaid DANIEL NICHOLS,
who died 13 March, 1789,
aged 86 Years.

In Memory of WILLIAM TIPPETT,
of Winterborne, ob. 22 July, 1743,
ætat. 73.

Alſo BRIDGET, Wife of
WILLIAM TIPPETT,
ob. 5 Oct. 1758, ætat. 73.

IN THE PORCH :

MARY EMETT,
Wife of CHARLES EMETT, ſen.
died May the 19, 1779,
aged 81 Years.

IN THE CHURCH YARD.

ON TOMBS.

Under this Tomb lieth the
Body of ANNE, Wife of
JONATHAN LENNOTT, who
died the 21 of April, 1769,
aged 77 Years.

Here lyeth the Body of
CHRISTOPHER FOWLER,
of this Parifh, ſen.
who departed this
Life the 28 of Jan. Anno Dom. 1697,
aged 64 Years.

Alſo the Body of ELIZABETH,
the Wife of CHRISTOPHER FOWLER,
of this Parifh, ſen.
who departed this Life the 23 of Dec.
17 . . . . .

Here lieth the Body of THOMAS, the
Son of CHRISTOPHER and
ELIZABETH FOWLER,
of this Parifh, who departed this Life
the 7 of June, Anno Domini 1694,
aged 27 Years.

Alſo the Body of JANE FOWLER,
Spinfter,
who departed this Life. . January, 1733,
aged 63 Years.

Here alſo lies the Body
of CHRISTOPHER, the Son
of CHRISTOPHER and ELIZABETH
FOWLER, of this Parifh, who
departed this Life the 29
Day of Auguſt, 1726, aged
53 Years.

Near this Place lyeth
the Body of JOHN, the Son
of WILLIAM and ELIZABETH
CHURCHILL, of this Parifh,
who departed this Life the
30 Decemb. 1723, aged
20 Years.

Alſo here lyeth the Body
of SAMUEL, the Son of
WILLIAM and ELIZABETH
CHURCHILL, of this Parifh,
who departed this Life the
13 April, 1723, aged 21 Years.

MARY-ANNE COCKAYNE
died June the 25, 1791,

Here

Here lyeth the Body of
SAMUEL, the Son of SAMUEL
BISHOP and MARY his Wife,
of this Parish, who departed
this Life the 20 of October,
1693, aged 19 Years.

Also here lyeth the Body
of MARY, the Relict of
SAMUEL BISHOP, of this
Parish, who departed this
Life the 21 of August,
Anno Dom. 1712,
aged 77 Years.

Here
lieth the Body of
ELIZABETH, Wife of
THOMAS PULLEN, of this Parish,
who died the 23d of March, 1772,
aged 72 Years.

Also ELIZABETH their Daughter
died February 18, 1770, aged
44 Years.

Near this Tomb lieth the Body
of THOMAS HARDING, of this
Parish, who departed this Life
in the Year 1745, aged 57 Years.

Also near this Tomb lieth interred
the Body of JOHN BENDALL,
late of this Parish, Butcher,
who died Oct. 5, 1749, æt. 67.

Also the Body of
SOLOMON BENDALL, Son of
JOHN and ESTHER BENDALL,
who died 16 August 1738,
æt. 21.

Also ANNE, Wife of
WILLIAM BENDALL,
of this Parish, Butcher,
who died 16 August, 1751,
aged 36 Years.

Also the Body of
WILLIAM BENDALL,
sen. of this Parish,
who died 25 of January, 1760,
in the 36 Year of his Age.

Here lyeth the Body
of RICHARD SIMMONS,
late of this Parish, Yeoman,
who departed this Life
the 30 June, A. D. 1724, ætatis 72.

Also the Body of ANNE,
Wife of the abovesaid
RICHARD SIMMONS, who died
the 14 January, 1724, ætatis 57.

Here lyeth the Bodies
of JOHN and BENJAMIN, Sons
of RICHARD and .... PONTING.
JOHN died the 15 Day of August,
1721, aged 16 Years.
BENJAMIN died the 17 Day of
Dec. 1721, aged 15 Years.

Here lieth the Body
of JOHN BENNETT, of this
Parish, Yeoman, who
departed this Life the first
Day of Dec. Anno Dom. 1726.

Here lieth the Body of
SAMUEL BENNETT, who
departed this Life
the 4 Nov. 1777, aged 42 Years.

In Memory of
MARY, the Wife of DANIEL
BENNETT, of this Parish, who
died 16 April 1777, aged 64.

Also here lieth the Body of
DANIEL BENNETT, Husband
to the above, who died May
the 4, 1780, aged 62 Years.

Here lyeth the Body of
RICHARD POWELL, of this
Parish, Yeoman, who died April
the 25, 1730, aged 30 Years.

Sacred
to the Memory of
JACOB HICKS,
buried June 1, 1743;

MARY his Wife,
buried January 15, 1755;

WILLIAM their Son,
buried July 6, 1750.

This Tomb was erected in the Year
of our Lord 1784, by their Son
SAMUEL HICKS, Esquire,
in Testimony of filial Duty
and brotherly Affection.

In Memory of
JOANNA, Wife of WILLIAM BALL,
of the Parish of St. Philip and Jacob,
who died the 23d of February, 1781,
aged 53 Years.

ON FLAT STONES.

Here lyeth the Body of
JOHN PALMER,
of the Parish of St. James,
in the City of Bristol,
who departed this Life
May the 20, 1747, aged 48 Years.

Here lyeth the Body of
THOMAS SUTTON, of this Parish,
who departed this Life
Oct. 28, 1789, in the 17th Year of
his Age.

Here lyeth the Body of
SOPHIA TILY, Wife of
WILLIAM TILY, of the Parish of
Stapleton,
who died 17 March, 1791, in the
25 Year of her Age.

Here lyeth the Body of
SAMUEL FRANKUM, of this
Parish, senior, who departed this
Life the 5 Day of March, 1725,
aged 69 Years.

Here lyeth the Body of
JOHN ARTHUR, of this Parish,
who departed this Life the 9 of
Jan. 1708-9, aged 86 Years.

Also here lyeth the Body of
MARTHA, the Wife of the
abovesaid JOHN ARTHUR,
who departed this Life the
10 of May, 1708, aged 83 Years.

O N   H E A D - S T O N E S.

	Died	Aged
Mary, Wife of James Tanner	29 July, 1775	44
John Daws - -	20 Nov. 1752	75
Sarah his Wife -	10 Jan. 1723	38
Mary, Wife of Elias Bryan	24 Oct. 1759	86
Christopher Bryan -	13 Dec. 1773	70
Thomas Wilson, of the County of Hereford - -	14 July, 1768	39
William Witts, of Badminton	15 Sept. 1778	23
Thomas Bedford, of Ireland	22 May, 1779	50
Richard Noad - -	15 May, 1749	—
John Whitewood, jun. -	29 May, 1726	58
John Hedges - -	5 Apr. 1734	42
John Morton - -	20 Apr. 1773	84
Thomas Canter -	19 Nov. 1761	61
Hester his Wife -	14 July, 1768	75
Edward Humphreys -	25 Dec. 1741	49
Jane, Wife of Stephen Dando	28 Jan. 1698	38
Anne, Wife of Richard Simmons	30 Sept. 1749	68
Edward, Son of John and Hannah Emmett - -	3 Sept. 1756	—
William, Son of John and Mary Burchell - -	22 July, 1761	18
Thomas James -	3 Oct. 1762	42
Daniel Arnott - -	1 Apr. 1758	40
John Summers -	24 June, 1730	70
Hester, Wife of Thomas Summers	28 June, 1740	22
Ruth his second Wife -	3 June, 1748	30
Sarah, Wife of John Summers	17 Aug. 1745	62
Mary, Wife of Charles Perks	25 Oct. 1768	61
John Cook - -	8 Feb. 1758	24
Thomas Cook -	15 Sept. 1777	20
Anne, second Wife of John Sartain	4 Aug. 1731	28
Richard, Son of Andrew and Sarah Emerson - -	1 Mar. 1739	21
Jane, Wife of Nathaniel Hill	18 Feb. 1784	80
Thomas Lovell -	12 Mar. 1778	30

ON HEAD-STONES.

	Died	Aged
Sarah, Wife of Joseph Haſkins	8 July, 1768	56
Celia, Daughter of John and Heſter Fry	24 Dec. 1769	17
George their Son	3 Jan. 1783	25
William Puxton	14 Feb. 1783	63
Martha his Daughter	13 Feb. 1774	21
Elizabeth, Wife of George Puxton	2 Jan. 1776	21
George Puxton	18 Feb. 1777	27
Jonathan Haywarden	4 Dec. 1763	28
Thomas Harriſon	31 Mar. 1775	18
Ann, Wife of William Lewis	3 Apr. 1769	—
Arthur Sutton	21 Jan. 1760	45
Thomas Cambridge	12 Mar. 1751	21
Stephen Bennett	20 Mar. 1749	—
Anne Moreman his Widow	12 May, 1776	68
William Drew	25 Nov. 1783	75
Elizabeth his Wife	27 Aug. 1759	49
William Frame	— Dec. 1710	35
Judith his Wife	25 Jan. 1755	78
Stephen Frame	17 Mar. 1766	56
Mary, Wife of Poyntes Smith	14 Apr. 1769	41
Thomas Rouch	30 Jan. 1755	21
Eſther, Wife of Iſaac Rouch	16 Sept. 1755	26
Richard Phillips	30 Aug. 1764	37
Heſter, Daughter of Thomas and Mary Shepard	18 Oct. 1745	24
Samuel Shipley	6 July, 1741	84
Elizabeth his Wife	1 Apr. 1745	77
William Shipley	2 Feb. 1787	80
Mary his Wife	8 Nov. 1788	79
William their Son	27 Feb. 1787	35
Silas their Son	15 Mar. 1789	34
William Stenard, Officer of Exciſe	28 Dec. 1766	28
Jane, Daughter of John and Elizabeth Hall	9 Aug. 1782	19
Ann, Wife of William Lane	11 Dec. 1766	60
Robert Cambridge	12 Nov. 1783	65
Mary his Wife	10 Nov. 1783	65
John Knott	6 Dec. 1752	21
Charles Palmore	3 Oct. 1782	71
Heſter his Wife	25 Dec. 1738	24
Suſannah his ſecond Wife	14 Jan. 1769	55
Thomas, Son of Edward and Anne Watts	27 Apr. 1761	27
Thomas, Son of George and Hannah Powell	25 Feb. 1770	22
Daniel Pierce	7 Mar. 1775	68
Joſhua, Son of Caleb Edney	17 Dec. 1713	20
William Skuce	16 Dec. 1776	75
Sarah his Wife	5 Feb. 1757	44
Thomas their Son	25 July, 1773	33
Edward Nichols	13 May, 1761	62
Robert Nichols	25 May, 1766	59
Elizabeth, the Wife of James Wally	24 May, 1779	59
Robert Screen	7 Oct. 1741	64
Edward Smith	25 Oct. 1728	70
Mary his Wife	25 — 1741	—
Thomas Robins	23 Feb. 1764	39
William Bryant	3 Aug. 1764	74
Mary his Wife	14 June, 1756	70
Hannah, Daughter of Moſes and Sarah Lewellin	3 Mar. 1741	21
George their Son	19 July, 1743	26
William Lewellin	2 Dec. 1773	86
Hannah his Wife	17 Feb. 1773	74
John Parker	16 July, 1746	57
Heſter his Wife	16 Apr. 1749	56
John their Son	24 June, 1776	52
Thomas Moreman	2 May, 1776	78
Joan his Wife	17 July, 1735	50
Sarah his ſecond Wife	18 Nov. 1743	42
Mary his third Wife	22 Feb. 1748-9	49
John Hooper	11 Apr. 1763	60
Abigail his Wife	18 Nov. 1770	58

CLXIX. MARSHFIELD

CLXIX. MARSHFIELD

LIES in the upper Part of the Hundred of *Thornbury*, upon the Borders of the Counties of *Wilts* and *Somerfet*, feven Miles diftant from *Bath* on the North-eaft, as many South-eaft from *Chipping Sodbury*, thirteen Eaft from *Briftol*, and thirty five South from Gloucester. The Parifh extends about five Miles, and is three in the narroweft Part, of a Soil varying from Stonebrafh to the richer Kinds, equally applied to Tillage and Pafture, with a large Common, and confiderable Woodlands of Oak and Afh Timber.

The Town of *Marfhfield* ftands in the Centre of the Parifh, confifting of one Street of a Mile in Length, through which the great Road from *London* to *Briftol* is conducted. Its Situation is pleafant and healthful. Some Years fince, the principal Trade of the Inhabitants was the making of Malt, which ftill flourifhes in a confiderable Degree.

The reputed Borough is within the Jurifdiction of the Honour of *Gloucefter*, and has a Bailiff for its chief Officer, annually elected at the Court Baron, whofe Power is lefs extenfive at prefent than traditionally. He has a Serjeant at Mace to attend him in the Examination of Weights and Meafures, and other Jurifdiction. The Market on Thurfday, and two Fairs on the 24th of May and 24th of October, were firft granted to the Abbot of *Keynfham* in 1262, 50 Hen. III. 1287, 15 Edw. 1. and 1379, 2 Ric. II. and re-granted by Charter of Edw. IV. in 1462, which Privilege was finally confirmed by King James the Firft.

The Benefice is vicarial * in the Deanery of *Hawkefbury*, which has at various Periods received very confiderable Augmentations. The Impropriation and Advowfon belonged to the Abbey of *Keynfham*, by whom they were transferred to the Monks of *Tewkefbury*, and after the Diffolution given in Exchange by Queen Mary to the Warden and Scholars of *New College, Oxford*, for *Steepinglee*, and other Lands in the Counties of *Effex* and *Bedford*. The Leafe of the great Tythes has been long in Poffeffion of the Family of Mereweather.

The Church, dedicated to *St. Mary*, is fpacious and handfome. A very lofty Nave, two Ailes, and a well-finifhed Tower, complete this Structure, which owes its Erection to the Abbey of *Tewkefbury*, in the Reign of Edward the Fourth, affifted by the Contributions of the principal Inhabitants. The Architecture exhibits the neat Proportions of that Age. On the left Hand of the high Altar are three *Subfellia* or Stone Stalls, with light Canopies and Finials, intended for the Officiating Priefts. There were two Chantries in this Church : *Jefus* Chantry, of which Henry Neal was the laft Incumbent ; and *St. Clement's* Chantry, of which Robert Savage was the laft Incumbent, each of whom enjoyed a Penfion of : *l.* 10s. in the Year 1553.

In the Year 1529, Thomas Parker, who was Chancellor, and Vicar General to Jeronimus de Ghinucciis, or de Nugutiis, an *Italian*, Bifhop of *Worcefter*, at the Requeft of John Gosselat, the Bailiff, and Lord of the Vill of *Marysfield* as it is called in a certain antient Writing), and the greater Part of the Community of the fame Vill eftablifhed a Gild in this Church, with Rules or Statutes for the Government of all that fhould enter into that Fraternity. More of the Nature of thefe Gilds may be feen under *Dyrham*. The fame Thomas Parker new built the Vicarage-houfe, but that was taken down, and a very commodious one built on the Site of it by John Carey, M. A. the Vicar, about the Year 1734.

Soon after the Conqueft, the Manor, which confifts of fourteen Hides of cultivated Land, and was Parcel of the antient Demefnes of the Crown, was given to the See of *Wells*, to be holden as of the Honour of *Gloucefter*. William the fecond Earl of Gloucester endowed the Abbey of Black Canons which he founded at *Bath* with his Manor and Hundred of *Marfhfield* in 1217.

When the Manor was vefted in the Court of Augmentations, Sir Anthony Kingston obtained a Leafe of it for fix Years, at the yearly Rent of 80*l.* and Thomas Lord Willoughby and Sir Thomas Heneage, Knight, procured the Grant of Inheritance. Edward Duke of Somerset purchafed it, and by his Attainder it reverted to the Crown ; Sir Henry Sydney held it for his Life ; after which Queen

---

* The Vicarage was augmented in the Year 1725 with a Donation of 200*l.* by Sir William Perkins and Queen Anne's Bounty.

Elizabeth

Elizabeth gave it to Thomas Ratcliff, Earl of *Suffex*, for his military Services; by him it was fold to John Gorstlett, Efq. in the greater Share, jointly with John Chambers, Nicholas Richmond, alias Webb, and Thomas Crispe, which laft-named died in 1600, feized of many Eftates in this Parifh; William Gorstlett left a Daughter and fole Heir, who was the Wife of John Harrington, Efq. of *Kelwefton*, co. *Somerfet*, by whofe Defcendant it was transferred by Purchafe to Sir William Codrington, Bart. under whofe Will it is now held by Christopher Codrington, Efq.

T Y T H I N G S and H A M L E T S.

Befides the Borough are three Tythings, with their proper Officers.

Of the Hamlets are, 1. *Weft Town*, formerly called *Old Marfhfield*, or *Little Marfhfield*, which, according to antient Tradition, had diftinct parochial Rights under the Name of *St. Pancras*. The principal Proprietor is John Huddlestone, Gent.

By the other Hamlets another Parifh was formed, under the Denomination of *St. Nicholas*.

2. *Okeford*. For feveral Generations this Eftate was vefted in the Family of Jacobs, originally of *Norton*, in the County of *Wilts*, by whom a handfome Manfion-houfe, called *The Rocks*, was built, and was their Refidence. Upon the Demife of the laft Heir Female of that Family, it paffed to Isaac Webb Horlock, Efq.

3. *Eyeford* is annexed to the manerial Property.

4. *Afhwick*. About the Commencement of the laft Century, the Family of Webb, alias Richmond, obtained a competent Eftate in this Tything, which is inherited by Isaac Webb Horlock, Efq.

5. *Bicks* was the antient Settlement of the Family of Crispe, afterwards of Sir William Deanes, Knight, and now belongs to John Vickeris Dickenson, Efq.

Befide thefe was the Manor of *Meers*, attached to the Honour of *Thornbury*, which was forfeited by the Attainder of Edward Duke of Buckingham, but afterwards granted to Henry Lord Stafford. Henry Howard, Efq. now receives the chief Rents of this Demefne.

Upon the great Common, called *The Downs*, are Veftiges of Intrenchments ftill apparent, near which are five *Tumuli*, or Barrows, the largeft of which, being called Oswald's Tomb, feems to authorize a Conjecture of its having been the Grave of Oswald King of the *Northumbrians*, who was conquered and flain by Penda King of the *Mercians*, in his victorious March from *Cirencefter* to *Bath*, but well-authenticated Facts prove the contrary.

B E N E F A C T I O N S.

Ellis and Nicholas Crispe gave by Deed, in 1625, an Alms-houfe, with a Garden, for eight poor Perfons having no Children, vefted in Truftees.

The fame Ellis and Nicholas Crispe gave alfo, by Deed and Will, feveral Rent-Charges on Land and Houfes, to the Amount of 38*l.* 13*s.* 4*d.* a Year, to be divided amongft the Perfons in the faid Alms-houfe, vefted as above.

Rev. Robert Kening, by Will, dated in 1709, gave 120*l.* the Intereft of which to be applied yearly, viz. every fifth Year, to apprentice a poor Boy of *Kelwefton*, in *Somerfetfhire*, and in each of the other four Years a poor Boy of *Marfhfield*. He likewife gave 20*l.* the Intereft of which to be employed for the Benefit of the Charity-School in *Marfhfield*; both vefted in the Rector of *Kelwefton* for the Time being.

John Bearpacker gave by Will, dated in 1715, a Rent-Charge of 5*l.* a Year, vefted in the Churchwardens and Overfeers of *Marfhfield*, towards providing Coats for ten poor Men of *Marfhfield* on the 1ft of January yearly.

John Harrington, Efq. by Will, dated Jan. 20, 1724, gave certain Chief Rents amounting to 6*l.* annually, vefted in the Bifhop of *Gloucefter*, and others, to the Charity School at *Marfhfield*.

Dionysia Long, by Deeds, dated in February 1731, gave Lands, the Produce of which is 28*l.* a Year, to be applied as follows: viz. 20*l.* annually for teaching twenty poor Boys, and the Refidue for Cloaths, Books, and Firing for them.

Alfo other Lands, producing annually 27*l.* and upwards, to be equally divided amongft fix poor Widows, Parifhioners of *Marfhfield*; vefted in the Bifhop of *Gloucefter*, and others.

Likewife fhe gave, in Aid of the above laft-mentioned Charities, 800*l.* in South Sea Annuities, the annual Produce of which is 24*l.*; vefted as above.

Benjamin Viner gave by Will, 100*l.* in New South Sea Annuities, the Intereft of which to be given to the Poor Half-Yearly; vefted in the Vicar, Churchwardens, and Overfeers.

Sir Robert Gunning gave a Rent-Charge of 5*l.* a Year, to be diftributed in Bread amongft the Poor on New Year's Day; vefted as above.

3   Incumbents.

Incumbents.	Patrons.	Incumbents.	Patrons.
1559 John Moore, A. M.	New College, Oxford.	1704 Benj. Wooton, LL. B.	New College, Oxford.
1567 Rob. Harrifon, A. M.	The fame.	1711 Francis Edmonds, A. B.	The fame.
1576 John Meredeth, A.M.	The fame.	1714 Philip Smith, A. M.	The fame.
1642 John Oglander, A. M.	The fame.	1715 John Burton, A. B.	The fame.
1666 Robert Keining, A. M.	The fame.	1720 John Cary, A. B.	The fame.
1681 Will. Manning, LL. B.	The fame.	1756 Lancelot Mitchel, LL. B.	The fame.
1686 William Wallis, A. M.	The fame.	1779 John Herfent Thorpe, A.M.	The fame.
1687 Tho. Fecknaham, A.M.	The fame.	1781 John Burton Watkin, A. M.	The fame.

Present Proprietors of the Manors,

Of *Marfhfield*,	Of *Afhwick*,	Of *Beeks*,
Christopher Codrington, Efq.	Isaac Webb Horlock, Efq.	John Vickeris Dickenson, Efq.

The Perfons fummoned from this Parifh by the Heralds, in 1682 and 1683, were

William Webb and Thomas Crifpe, Gents.

At the Election in 1776, Forty Freeholders polled from this Parifh.

The firft Date of the Regifter is in 1653.

Annual Account of Marriages, Births, and Burials, in this Parish.

A.D.	Mar.	Bir.	Bur.	A.D.	Mar.	Bir.	Bur.	A.D.	Mar.	Bir.	Bur.	A.D.	Mar.	Bir.	Bur.
1781	5	32	29	1786	5	32	21	1791				1796			
1782	3	32	33	1787	6	32	9	1792				1797			
1783	8	27	32	1788	7	34	24	1793				1798			
1784	7	39	56	1789	9	38	30	1794				1799			
1785	12	37	32	1790	9	26	26	1795				1800			

INSCRIPTIONS IN THE CHURCH.

IN THE CHANCEL.

On a Monument:

Arms; a Bend.

Beneath this Place lyeth interred the Body of Elizabeth, late Wife of Robert Webb, of this Parifh, Gentleman, eldeft Daughter and Child of Thomas Codrington, late of Dodington, Clerk. She, having attained her Age of forty-feven Years, departed this Life in her Houfe in Bath on the 15 of April, 1705.

At the Feet of the fame Body lyeth alfo interred the Body of Elizabeth Webb, late Daughter of the faid Robert and Elizabeth. She, having entered into the thirtieth Yeare of her Age, left this Life, in the fame Houfe, on the 17 of April, 1711.

In the North Wall:

Neere this Place lyeth the Body of Mary, the Wife of Samuel Bertram, of this Towne, who died Auguft, Anno Dom. 1678.

ON FLAT STONES.

Under this Stone is the Body of Elizabeth Webb, who died the 15 of Sept. 1761, aged 43 Years.

She was Daughter of William Webb, Gent. and Elizabeth his Wife, one of the Daughters of William Webb, of Afhwick, Gent.

Alfo of the faid Elizabeth, the Mother, who died the 22 of March, 1776, in the 92d Year of her Age.

Here lieth interred the Body of Elizabeth Crisp, Wife of Samuel Crisp, who departed this Life the 23 Day of January, 1689, in the 23 Yeare of her Age.

Alfo here lyeth interred the Body of Sarah, Daughter of Samuel Crisp, who died the 14 June, 1690.

Alfo George, the Son of Samuel Crisp, who died Oct. 24, 1692.

Here lieth interred the Body of Thomas Crisp, fen. Gent. who departed this Life the 29 Day of April, Anno Domini 1691, in the 74th Yeare of his Age.

Here lyeth the Body of Mary, the late Wife of Thomas Crisp, fen. who departed this Life the 18 Day of January, Anno Domini, 1701, in the 68th Year of her Age

Here refteth the Body of Thomas Crisp, who departed this Life July the 22, 1752, aged 67 Years.

Alfo Mary his Wife. She departed this Life April the 24, 1766, aged 78 Years.

Here lyeth the Body of Elizabeth, the Wife of Thomas Crisp, who departed this Life, March 30, 1784, aged 63 Years.

Here lyeth interred the Body of Thomas, Son of Thomas Crisp, Gent. who departed this Life . . Oct. Anno Domini 1686, ætatis fuæ 37.

Here lyeth interred the Body of Mary Crisp, the Daughter of Thomas Crisp, of Beeks, Gent. who departed this Life July, Anno Domini 1654.

Here lyeth the Body
of Joseph Hook. He died
October 1665.

Here lyeth the Body
of Deborah, the Wife
of George Giles,
of this Town. She died
the 19 Day of March,
Anno Domini 1743,
aged 79 Years.

In Memory of
George Giles, who died June the 4,
1763,
aged 93 Years.

Sub hoc Lapide
sepultus jacet
Alworth Merewether, M. D.
Obiit 24 die Novembris,
Anno Domini 1791,
ætatis suæ 60.

Juxta jacet
Johannes Merewether, Chirurg.
qui obiit 2 die Decembris,
Anno Domini 1792,
ætatis suæ 58.

HERE LYETH THE BODY OF
JOHN DEARING, YEOMAN,
WHO DEPARTED THE 4 DAY
OF JULY, 1730, AGED 70.

Here lyeth the Body of
Joseph Holloway, who
died January the 7, A. D.
1726, aged 37 Years.

In Memory of
Elizabeth Waterford,
Widow, late Wife of
Andrew Waterford, jun.
of this Town. She died
7 April, 1742, aged 56.

Also William their Son,
who died the 1 of March,
1735, aged 10 Years.

And also Andrew
Waterford, who
died Nov. 11, 1786, aged 64.

Here
lyeth the
Body of Sarah
Waterford, who
died the 6 Day of
December, 1734,
aged 77 Years.

In Memory of Sarah,
Wife of Thomas Brown, Yeoman.
She died January the 22,
1769, aged 47.

Here lies, in the fame Grave
with his firft Wife,
Thomas Brown,
of this Parish, Yeoman, who
departed this Life the 12th,
Day of January, 1773,
in the 53d Year of his Age.

HERE LIETH
THE BODY OF
JOHN BATCHELOR, OF
THE CITY OF BRISTOL,
PEWTERER, WHO DIED
THE 31 DAY OF AUGUST,
ANNO DOM. 1708, AGED
57 YEARS.

ALSO HONNER,
DAUGHTER OF THE SAID
JOHN AND HONNER
BATCHELOR, DEPARTED
THIS LIFE THE 14TH OF
MARCH, 1737,
AGED 49 YEARS.

In Memory of
Elizabeth Hosy, Widow, who
died the 3d of April, 1701,
aged 88 Years.

Here also lyeth the Body of
of John Waterford, who
died the 30 July, 1762,
aged 67 Years.

IN THE NAVE.

ON HANDSOME MONUMENTS:

Arms; Sable, a Bend Or, on a Chief
Argent, two Cornish Choughs proper.

This Monument
is erected in Memory of
Mr. Benjamin Viner, of the
City of Briftol, Merchant,
deceafed, whofe Body lies interred
under a black Marble near this
Place; leaving, by Will, one
Hundred Pounds to the Poor of
this Parish, the Interest thereof
to be given them Half-Yearly, on
the 10th of March, and the 10th of
September, for ever; the faid Sum
was placed out on Government
Security in New South Sea
Annuities, in the Year 1748,
in the Name of the Rev.
Mr. John Cary, Vicar of
this Parish.

Near this Place refteth the Body of
Mr. Thomas Fecknaham,
late Vicar of this Parish, who
departed this Life the 2d Day
of April, Anno Domini 1704.

Mary, Wife of
John Fecknaham, Gent.
died June the 21ft, 1768,
aged 74.

Arms; Sable, a Chevron Or, between
three Efcallops Argent;—impaling, a
Fefs checky between ten Billets.

To the Memory
of the Rev. Lancelot Michell, LL.B.
who died on the 1ft of March, 1779.
Elizabeth Michell caufed this
Monument
to be erected as a Tribute of Affection
to her deceafed Hufband.
She died March the 16th,
1786.

ON FLAT STONES.

Here lyeth the Body of
Deborah, the Wife
of Thomas Wigmore,
who departed this Life
the 1ft Day of March,
1708, aged 70 Years.

S. W.
1722.

Here lyeth the Body of
Sarah, the Daughter of Edward
and Jane Tiley. She died the
12 of Feb. 1733.

Here lyeth the Body
of Thomas Osborne,
who departed this Life
the 17th Day of May, 1733,
aged 37 Years.

ON A BRASS PLATE:

Here refteth the Body
of Robert Powell, of
this Parifh, Yeoman,
who departed this Life
the 25 Day of April,
1733, in the 66
Year of his Age.

Alfo here lyeth the Body
of Mary, the Wife of
Robert Powell, who died
the 24 of Nov. 1756,
aged 85 Years.

HERE LYETH INTERRED
THE BODY OF JOHN,
SON OF JOSEPH ENGLAND,
WHO DIED AUGUST THE
18 ANNO DOM. 167..

Here lyeth the Body
of Bridget, the Wife of
John England, who
departed this Life the 2d
Day of July, 1720,
aged 65 Years.

Here lyeth the Body of
John England, of this
Parifh, Gent. who
departed this Life
March the 15, 1740,
aged 52 Years.

HERE LYETH THE BODY
OF MARY, WIFE OF
MARK MARFOLD,
WHO DECEASED SEPTEMB.
ANNO DOM. 1679.

Here lyeth the Body of
Nicholas Webb, Gent.
who departed this Life
the 21 Day of December,
Anno Domini 1695,
aged 51 Years.

Here lyeth the Body of Mary,
the Wife of Joseph Bushe, jun.
who departed this Life the 13
Day of March, 1721, in the
23d Year of her Age.

Here lyeth the Body of
Hannah, the Wife of Thomas
Hart, of this Town, who dep-
arted this Life the 31 Day of
Jan. 1736, aged 50 Years.

Here lyeth the Body of
Thomas Hart, of this Town,
who died Sept. 8, 1738, aged 69.

Alfo John, the Son of Thomas
Hart, by Hannah his Wife,
died March 6, 1740,
aged 32 Years.

IN

IN THE NORTH AISLE.

ON MARBLE MONUMENTS.

Arms ; in a Lozenge Sable, two Flaaches Ermine, a Lion rampant between fix Crofs Croflets Argent, for LONG ;—impaling, Sable, a Fret Argent, for HARRINGTON.

Interred near this Place lieth the Body of DIONYSIA LONG, Widow of CALTHROP LONG, of Whaddon, in the County of Wilts, Efq. and Daughter of JOHN HARRINGTON, of Kelfton, in the County of Somerfet, Efq. who departed this Life Dec. the 4, 1744, aged 86.

Arms ; Argent, three Battle Axes Sable :—impaling, HARRINGTON.

Here lyeth the Body of ELIZABETH GIBBES, Relict of Alderman HENRY GIBBES, of the City of Briftol, Merchant, and eldeft Daughter of JOHN HARRINGTON, Efq. of Kelfton, in the County of Somerfet, who departed this Life the 12 of October, Anno Domini 1723, aged 67 Years.

NEAR THIS PLACE RESTETH THE BODY OF JANE, THE WIFE OF JOHN HODGES, OF THIS TOWNE, WHO DEPARTED THIS LIFE FEBRUARY THE 2, AN. DOM. 1696.

Juxta hoc monumentum jacet MARIA Confors GEORGII BENNET Dilecta, ex hoc oppido; Mille virtutibus ornata, Integritate vitæ infignis, Dolifque procul omnibus, Omnigenæ Charitatis exemplar Cognatis benigna, amicifque fida ad omnia Pietatis munia Prompta femper & alacris, In Pace & Spe læta æternæ vitæ Per JESUM CHRISTUM Servatorem fuum Animam effluxit, Julii die 2°, Anno Domini MDCCLII, ætatis fuæ LVI.

Arms ; Gules, a Chevron engrailed Ermine, between three Pheons Or.

Near this Place lyeth interred the Body of JOHN GOSTLETT, Efq. who departed this Life January the 24, MDCXCII. in the LXVII Year of his Age.

Near this Place lieth interred the Body of MARY GOSTLET, Widow of JOHN GOSTLET, Efq. and Daughter of JOHN HARRINGTON, of Kelfton, in the County of Somerfet, Efq. by Lady DIONESSA LEGH, Daughter and Coheirefs of the Rt. Hon. JAMES Earl of MARLBOROUGH, who departed this Life Oct. the 27, 1693.

ON FLAT STONES.

PETER, Son of ROBERT and MARY POWELL, died the 24 Jan. 1775, aged 33 Years.

Alfo ROBERT POWELL, jun. died Oct. 13, 1783, aged 46.

Alfo MARY, Wife of ROBERT POWELL, fen. died May 30, 1784, aged 79.

Here lyeth the Body of ELIZABETH, the Wife of RICHARD TIELY, who departed this Life the 22 Day of Dec. 1712, aged 53 Years.

Here lyeth the Body of ANNE, Wife of JOHN TIELY, who departed this Life the 13 Day of May, 1763, aged 63 Years.

Alfo JOHN TIELY, who departed this Life April the 21, 1777, aged 78.

Here lyeth the Body of MARY, the Wife of JOHN TIELY, who departed this Life Jan. 10, 1778, aged 56.

In Memory of VERTUE, Wife of JOHN HIGGISSON, Gent. Daughter of JOHN HARRINGTON, Efq. of Kelfton, who was interred near this Place October 20, 1704.

Beneath this Stone lyeth the Body of MARY, Wife of GEORGE BENNETT, who departed this Life July the 2, 1752.

In Memory of VERTUE, Wfie of the late THOMAS OSBORNE, Daughter of JOSHUA HIGGISSON, Gent. who departed this Life Dec. the 15th, 1759.

In Memory of MARY, Daughter of THOMAS and VERTUE OSBORNE, who departed this Life the 10th Day of November, 1765.

Here lyeth the Body of GEORGE ADAMS, Gent. who departed this Life May 17, 1727, aged 64 Years.

Alfo here lyeth the Body of JANE, the Wife of GEORGE ADAMS, Gent. who departed this Life the 1ft Day of December, 1739, aged 75 Years.

Beneath this Stone lieth the Body of GEORGE BENNET, who departed this Life April the 25th, 1776.

Here lyeth the Body of Mr. SAMUEL WORKMAN, who departed this Life the 19 Day of January, in the Year of our Lord 1735-6.

Alfo here lyeth the Body of RUTH, the Wife of SAMUEL WORKMAN, who departed this Life the 5 Day of July, 1739, aged 66 Years.

Hoc fub lapide jacent JOHANNES FOX, Generofus, & Filia ejus ELIZABETHA, dilecta Conjux JOHANNIS VINER. Obiit ille 13 die Octobris, anno ætatis fuæ 40, & Redemptionis noftræ 1676; obiit illa 7 die Martii, anno ætatis 47, annoque Domini 1705.

Here alfo are interred BENJAMIN VINER, late of the City of Briftol, Merchant, who died 25 January, 1747, in the 58 Year of his Age.

And his Brother THOMAS VINER, of this Parifh, who died 22 June, 1749, aged 65 Years.

Under this Stone lies the Body of CHARLES YOUNG, Gent. who departed this Life July 9, 1766, aged 81 Years.

Alfo the Body of NASH ELIZABETH CLARK, Wife of THOMAS CLARK, and Daughter of the above CHARLES YOUNG, who died Nov. 23, 1767, aged 54 Years.

IN THE SOUTH AISLE.

ON MONUMENTS.

HERE LIETH BURIED WITH HER TWO CHILDREN ANNE, THE WIFE OF NICHOLAS WEBB, OF ASHWICK, GENT. WHO DECEASED FEB. 3, 1651.

Arms; on a Bend engraied three Crofs Croflets fitché, for WEBB ;—impaling, a Crofs Patonce between four Mullets, counterchanged.

Hic jacet NICHOLAUS WEBB, Generofus, & filius CHRISTOPHERI WEBB, qui mortem obijt 10 die Martii, anno Dom. 1670

Hic jacet CHRISTOPHERUS WEBB, Generofus, qui migravit ex hac vita 30 die Novembris, anno Domini 1676.

ON

On a very handsome Monument:

Arms; quarterly, 1ft and 4th, WEBB as before; 2d and 3d, a Crofs Patonce, between four Mullets as before.

WILLIAM WEBB,
of Afhwick, Gent. was buried near this
Place April 23, 1724;

And
ELIZABETH his Wife was buried in the
fame Tomb Dec. 5, 1719.
This was
erected to their Memory in the Year of
our Lord 1746,
by
LUCY WEBB, of Afhwick, their eldeft
Daughter, who died Auguft 3, 1746,
and was buried here.

MARY, their youngeft Daughter, and
Wife of JOHN MORRIS, A. M.
Vicar of Aldbourn,
in the County of Wilts, died Nov. 1,
1737,
and was buried in the fame Tomb.

GEORGE WEBB, youngeft Brother of
the abovenamed WILLIAM WEBB,
was buried here May 3, 1746.

WILLIAM and MARY, Son and
Daughter of the abovenamed
JOHN and MARY MORRIS,
were alfo buried here.

WILLIAM died the 24 February, 1736,
and MARY the 6 May, 1774.

The faid JOHN MORRIS was alfo buried
here, who died the 29 July, 1774,
aged 75.

On a handsome Monument:

Arms; on two Efcocheons, 1ft, a Lion
paffant between three Crofs Croflets
fitchée; 2d, a Chevron between three
Croflets fitchée.

Near this Place refteth the Body
of JOHN BEARPACKER, of
the City of Briftol, Merchant,
who departed this Life the 27
Day of November, Anno Dom. 1715,
aged 60 Years,
who gave one Hundred Pounds, the
Profit thereof to be laid out yearly
on ten Coats, to be given to ten Poor
Men of this Parifh, not receiving Alms,
on every New Year's Day for ever.

Near
this Place lyeth
the Body of ROBERT POWELL,
fen. of this Parifh, who
died May 21, 1774,
aged 67.

Near this Place
lyeth the Body of SAMUEL
BRISCOE, who departed this
Life the 14 Day of February,
1694.

Alfo the Body of HESTER, the Wife
of SAMUEL BRISCOE, who departed
this Life the 9 Day of April,
1696.

Arms; Argent, a Chevron Or.

Beneath this Place
lyeth interred the Body of
JOHN BRISCOE who departed
this Life the 14 Day of Feb.
Anno Dom. 1733,
aged 68 Years.

Near this Place
lies the Body of
WILLIAM BRISCOE, Mariner,
of the City of Briftol. He
died the 2 Auguft, 1736,
ætatis 82.

Near
this Place lies interred
the Body of EDWARD,
Son of EDWARD and
ELIZABETH TYLER. He
died July the 11, 1764.
aged 29.

Alfo
EDITH, Wife of ISAAC
GALE, and Daughter of
EDWARD and ELIZABETH
TYLER. She died April 24,
1761, aged 23.

In
Memory of
EDWARD TYLER,
of this Parifh, Yeoman,
who departed this Life
the 2 Day of July, 1749,
in the 34 Year of his Age.

Alfo ELIZABETH his Wife,
who departed this Life
the 15 Day of Auguft,
1779, aged 77 Years.

On an Atchievement:

Arms; Argent, within a Bordure bezanté, a Fefs between three Lions rampant Gules, for WILLIS.

Beneath, on a Flat Stone:

Underneath this Stone
are depofited the Remains
of THOMAS WILLIS, LL. B.
Rector of Blecheley,
in the County of Buckingham,
who died December 26, 1789,
aged 46.

ON FLAT STONES.

Arms; a Lion rampant.

Sub hoc lapide mi . . . .
Jo . . . . MEREDETH . . . .
. . . .
Gen. qui obiit 9 Feb. 1641.

JOHANNES filius, de Mangotsfield,
in hoc comitatu, Armiger,
qui obijt 11 July, 1697.

ROUND THE VERGE:

JOHN, SON OF CHARLES HARFORD
AND MARGARET HIS WIFE.
HE DEPARTED THIS LIFE THE
27 OF APRIL, ANNO DOMINI
1623.

To the Memory of MARK HARVARD,
who ended this Life March the
21, 1682, aged 70. Alfo MARY
his Daughter, who died Jan.
15, 1679, her Age 35.

And SARAH his . . . . who died
Jan. 26, 1687, aged 77.

Alfo the Body of SARAH his
Daughter, who died July 28,
1691.

Here lyeth the Body of
THOMAS HARFORD, who
departed this Life the
7th Day of May, Anno
Domini 1710, aged 83 Years.

Here lyeth the Body of
MARK HARVARD, fen.
who departed this Life
the 13 Day of January,
Anno Domini 1720,
aged 71 Years.

HERE LYETH THE
BODY OF MARK
HARVARD, OF THIS
PARISH, WHO DEPART-
ED THIS LIFE THE
21 DAY OF MARCH,
1729, AGED 35.

Here lyeth the Body of
MARY, Wife of MARK HARVARD,
who died July the 25, 1740,
aged 37 Years.

Here lyeth the Body of
ANDREW WATERFORD, fen.
who departed this Life the
5 Day of June, Anno Domini
1717, aged 53 Years.

Alfo here lyeth the Body of
ANDREW WATERFORD, jun. who
departed this Life the 24 Day
of March, 1729, aged 33 Years.

Alfo here lyeth the Body of
JOHN WATERFORD, who departed
this Life the 6 Day of Aug.
1778, aged 58 Years.

In Memory of
JOHN HELSAM. He died in March 1742.

In Memory of
RICHARD, Son of JOHN and ELIZABETH
HILMAN, who died Aug.
31, 1777, aged 23 Years.

Near this Place lyeth the Body
of MARY, the Wife of THOMAS
HELSOME, who departed this
Life the 3d Day of March,
1710.

Beneath this Stone lieth the
Remains of GEORGE MARTIN,
of the City of Briftol, Gent.
who died in October 1748,
aged 33 Years.

Likewife HESTER ARTHUR his Wife,
being twice married,
who died the 18 March, 1777,
aged 60 Years.

Here lyeth interred
the Body of HENRY
NICHOLS, of this Town,
Yeoman, who departed
this Life June 19, 1717.

Here lyeth the Body of
SUSANNA NICHOLS, who
died the 1ft Day of May,
1736, aged 76 Years.

Beneath

Beneath
this Stone lyeth the Body
of WILLIAM TYLER,
of this Parifh, Yeoman, who
departed this Life the 12
Day of October, 1744,
aged 69 Years.

Here lyeth the Body of
EDWARD TYLER, of this Parifh,
Yeoman, Batchelor,
who departed this Life the
27 Day of February, 1754,
aged 85 Years.

Alfo here lyeth the Body
of CHRISTOPHER TYLER, of this
Parifh, who died the 22 Day
of December, 1708,
aged 35 Years.

Here
lyeth the Body of ELIZABETH,
the Wife of WILLIAM TYLER.
She died Sept. 20, 1761,
aged 77 Years.

Beneath this Stone refteth
the Body of ELIZABETH, Wife
of JOHN PRIOR, who departed
this Life . . June, 1757.

Under this Stone lies
the Body of CHARLES
YOUNG, Gent. who departed
this Life July 9, 1766,
aged 81 Years.

Alfo the Body of
NASH ELIZABETH CLARK, Wife
of THOMAS CLARK, and Daughter
of the above CHARLES YOUNG,
who died November 23, 1767,
aged 54 Years.

Near this Place
lie the Bodies of
THOMAS HELSAM
and MARY his Wife.
He died March 19, 1749;
fhe died March 1, 1719.

Alfo near lies the Body of
CATHARINE, the Wife of
RICHARD HELSAM, who
died April 6, 1759,
aged 84.

Here lies interred alfo
the Body of RICHARD
HELSAM, who died
March 7, 1764,
aged 82.

Here lyeth the Body of
THOMAS TILEY, who departed
this Life April 6, 1758,
aged 80 Years.

In Memory of
SUSANNAH, Daughter
of ROBERT and MARTHA
TILEY, who died Auguft
the 20, 1763, aged 22.

IN THE CHURCH-YARD, ON TOMBS.

Beneath this Stone lyeth the Body of
MARTHA, the Wife of THOMAS MILLAR,
of this Parifh, who departed this
Life December 26, 1740, aged 25.

In Memory of
THOMAS MILLER,
of this Town, who died
May 3, 1776, aged 64.

Alfo MARY his Wife,
who died March the 20,
1769, aged 54.

Here
refteth the Body of
RICHARD MERRICK,
of this Town, who died
January 26, 1766,
aged 67 Years.

Alfo MARY, Wife of
RICHARD MERRICK.
She died May 22, 1746,
aged near 44 Years.

Near this Tomb lieth
interred MARY, the Wife
of SEAL EMERSON, who died
June 4, 1777, aged 47.

Beneath this Tomb
lyeth the Body of
ANGEL SHAPLAND, V. D. M.
He exchanged this Life for
a glorious Immortality the
19 Day of May, 1748,
aged 57.

Alfo MARY his Wife, who
died the 30th of May, 1753,
aged 51.

Alfo beneath
this Tomb is interred the
Body of JOHN, the Son of
JOSEPH DAVIS, fen. who
departed this Life the
30 Day of January, 1721,
in the 19 Year of his Age.

Beneath this Tomb
lyeth the Body of JOSEPH
DAVIS, who died October the 14th,
1721, aged 75 Years.

Alfo ELIZABETH, the Wife of
JOSEPH DAVIS, who died
October the 28th, 1711,
aged 37 Years.

To the Memory of ANNE,
Wife of JOSEPH SHAPLAND,
of the City of Briftol,
who departed this Life
the 26 Day of October, 1782,
aged 60 Years.

Alfo in Memory of
. . . . . SHAPLAND, Gent.
who died Nov, 16, 1781,
aged 52.

Near this Place
refteth the Body of MARY, Wife
of THOMAS GUNNING, and Daughter
of ANGEL and MARY SHAPLAND,
of this Town. She departed this
Life Dec. 6, 1765, aged 34.

Beneath this Stone lyeth
the Body of WILLIAM BLAND,
who departed this Life the 16th
of December, 1748, aged 70.

Beneath
this Stone refteth the Body
of MARY, the Wife of WILLIAM
OLAND, who departed this
Life the 1ft Day of January,
1740, ætatis fuæ 58.

Underneath
is inhumed the Body of
DANIEL OLAND, Gent.
who died Dec. 28, 1763,
aged 44.

In Memory of
JOHN OLAND, Gent.
who died the 31ft of March,
1759, aged 33.

This Tomb is erected
to perpetuate the Memory
of that amiable,
ufeful, and worthy Man
Mr. WILLIAM OLAND,

of this Place,
who died June the 28, 1785,
aged 62 Years.

In Memory of
Mr. WILLIAM OLAND,
who died April 2, 1788,
aged 30.

Beneath
this Stone refteth the
Body of WILLIAM EVE,
who departed this Life
the 26 Day of February,
1740, ætatis fuæ 25.

In Memory of
JOSEPH WOODWARD, fen.
who died the 3d Day of April,
1739, aged 36 Years.

Alfo ELIZABETH his
Wife, who died January
16, 1771, aged 60 Years.

Beneath this Tomb
lieth the Body of MARY
WOODWARD, Widow, who
died the 12 Day of July, 1752,
aged 82 Years.

ANN, the Wife of JOHN
WOODWARD, died July 7,
1722.

Here lyeth the Body of
JOSEPH WOODWARD. He died
the 27th Day of Sept. 1742.

Here lieth the Body
of JOHN WOODWARD, of
Oakford, in this Farifh, Yeoman,
who died July 10, 1740, in the
66 Year of his Age.

Alfo BETTY, Wife of
FERDINANDO WOODWARD.
She died October 9, 1763,
aged 39 Years.

In Memory of JOHN WOODWARD,
who died May 10, 1774, aged 23.

Alfo WALTER WOODWARD,
died Sept. 9, 1785, aged 27 Years.

In Memory of THOMAS
WOODWARD, who died April
13, 1780, aged 26 Years.

In Memory of MARY,
Wife of THOMAS RICKETTS,
of the Parifh of Batheafton,
and Daughter of FERDINANDO
and BETTY WOODWARD, who
departed this Life June the 7,
1785, aged 27 Years.

In Memory
of FERDINANDO WOODWARD,
who died Sept. 18, 1778,
aged 50 Years.

Alfo JAMES WOODWARD,
died Nov. the 25, 1792,
aged 27 Years.

In Memory of SAMUEL COX,
who died Nov. 28, 1771,
aged 64 Years.

Alfo of HESTER his Wife,
who died July the 15, 1757,
aged 59 Years.

HESTER, Wife of THOMAS JONES,
died April 13, 1771, in the
34 Year of her Age.

In Memory of
JOSEPH MUNDAY, who
died March 19, 1780,
aged 69 Years.

Alfo SARAH his Wife died Auguft
the 26, 1784, aged 74 Years.

In Memory of
MARTHA, Daughter of JOSEPH
and SARAH MUNDAY, who
died May the 15, 1779,
aged 27 Years.

Near this Tomb are interred
the Bodies of GEORGE SEAL
and EDMUND his Son.

Alfo the Bodies of ESTHER
his firft Wife, and SARAH
the fecond Wife of GEORGE SEAL.

Underneath this Tomb
lieth the Body of CHARLES
RUDDER, who departed this Life
the 30 Day of May, 1739,
aged 79 Years.

Alfo of HESTER, the Wife of CHARLES
RUDDER, who departed this Life the
11 Day of March, 1704, aged 40 Years.

Here refteth the Body of
HANNAH, the Wife of HAMOYS
EMERSON, who departed this
Life .. June, 1738, aged 41.

Alfo HAMOISE EMERSON, who
died the 24 of Jan. 1743, aged 54.

In Memory of
MARY, Daughter of SEAL
and MARY EMERSON, who
departed this Life Dec. 31,
1781, in the 18 Year of her Age.

Here
lyeth the Body
of HOTSON TIPPER,
who departed this Life
the 6 Day of December,
Anno Domini 1723,
aged 57 Years.

Alfo here lyeth the Body of
MARY, the Wife
of HOTSON TIPPER, who
departed this Life the
19 Day of Sept. 1731,
aged 57 Years.

In Memory of
WILLIAM TIPPER,
who died July the 14,
1780, aged 78 Years.

Here lyeth the Body of
THOMAS TILEY, who died
April 6, 1758, aged 80.

SUSANNA, Daughter of
THOMAS and SUSANNA TILEY,
died in Oct. 1737, aged 30.

In Memory of SUSANNA,
Daughter of ROBERT and
MARTHA TILEY, who died
Aug. 20, 1763, aged 22.

Beneath this Tomb
lyeth the Body of ELIZABETH,
Wife of JOSEPH BARKER, who died
Feb. 2, 1713, aged 47 Years.

Beneath
this Stone lyeth the
Body of JOSEPH BARKER,
who died the 4 Day of July,
1750, aged 60.

Near this Tomb is interred
JOYCE, the Wife of JOSEPH BARKER,
jun. who died
March 1, 1717.

Beneath this Tomb
lyeth the Body of JOSEPH
BARKER, fen. who died
April 1, 1727, aged 76 Years.

Alfo near this Stone
lyeth the Body of MARTHA
BARKER, who died the 13
July, 1754, aged 40.

In Memory of
NICHOLAS GOLDISBOROUGH,
of Auford ... He died the
2d of September, 1712, aged
near 40.

Here lyeth the Body of MARY,
formerly the Wife of
NICHOLAS GOLDISBOROUGH,
and late the Wife of JOSEPH
BARKER, of this Parifh, who
died 29 of May, 1745,
aged 68 Years.

Here lies the Body
Mrs. SARAH FISHER, Wife of
JOHN FISHER, of North Wrexall, Gent.
who departed this Life the 12 Day
of October, 1728, aged 34 Years.

I. H. 1651, buried.

Alfo here refteth the
Body of JOHN HARFORD.
He died the 21 Day of Jan.
1711, aged 70.

E. H. 1662, buried.

Here refteth the Body of
HANNAH, the Wife of
JOHN HARFORD, who died
29 Dec. 1715, aged 68.

Here refteth
the Body of Mr. JOHN HARFORD
the elder, who departed this Life
the 24 of Feb. 1734. in the 60th
Year of his Age.

Alfo near this Tomb refteth
the Body of SARAH the Wife
of JOHN HARFORD, fen. who
departed this Life May the
19, 1733, aged near 59.

Here refteth
the Body of HANNAH,
the Wife of JOHN HARFORD,
who departed this Life the
25 Day of October, 1743,
aged 32 Years.

Near this Place
refteth the Body of
JOHN HARFORD, Gent.
who died the 11 Day of
April, 1764, aged 56.

In Memory
of JOHN HARFORD, jun.
Gent. who died June 8,
1776, aged 39.

Beneath
this Tomb lies
interred the Body of
ELIZABETH BRYAN,
Relict of WILLIAM BRYAN,
of the City of Briftol,
Clothworker. She died the
3 Day of May, 1749, aged 85.

In Memory
of JOHN BRYAN, who
died December the 14th
1772, aged 70.

In Memory of JOHN, Son
of RICHARD and ELIZABETH
BAILY, who died Feb. 9, 1767.

Under this Tomb lyeth the Body
of NICHOLAS HOLLISTER, of the Parifh
of St. Philip, Briftol, Father of
JOHN and CECILIA HOLLISTER,
of this Parifh,
who died on July 27, 1727, æt. 35.

Under this Tomb
lyeth the Body of JACOB
SALMON, Son of JACOB and
JOYCE SALMON, of this Parifh,
who departed this Life 14 Feb.
1732, aged 47 Years.

EDWARD ISAAC
died February 28, 1761,
aged 45 Years.

SARAH his Relict
died January 27, 1786,
aged 71 Years.

In Memory of
ELIZABETH WARREN,
Wife of JOHN WARREN,
of the City of Bath, who
died July 4, 1791, ætat. 36.

AGAINST THE CHURCH:
Here lyeth the Body of
FELIX MOON. He died 8 of Dec.
1704, aged 94 Years. Alfo neare this
Place lyeth the Body of SARAH, the
Wife of FELIX MOON. She died 9 Day
of June, A. D. 1704, aged 82 Years.

On

ON A BRASS PLATE:

ANNE, the Wife of
JOHN WOODWARD, died
July 7, 1723.

ON FLAT STONES.

Here lyeth the Body of
JOSEPH WOODWARD. He died the
27 of September, 1742.

Underneath
lieth the Body of
WALTER WOODWARD, sen.
late of Cold Ashton, Yeoman,
who departed this Life April 5,
1765, aged 79 Years.

JANE his Wife died
September 17, 1773,
aged 68 Years.

In Memory
of EDWARD TIPPER,
who died Oct. 15, 1774, aged 70.

Also SARAH his Wife, who
died Nov. 25, 1762, aged 56.

And also WILLIAM their Son,
who died Feb. 24, 1762,
aged 24.

In Memory of JANE, Daughter
of EDWARD and SARAH TIPPER,
who died in August 1762, aged 22.

Also ELIZABETH their Daughter
died Dec. 30, 1758, aged 16.

THOMAS their Son died August 22,
1749.

ANN BLETCHLEY,
Wife of Mr. THOMAS BLETCHLEY,
of Bath Easton, died Octob. 15,
1781, aged 64.

WILLIAM BLETCHLEY
died July 20, 1791, aged 45.

THOMAS GUNNING,
Son of THOMAS and MARY
GUNNING, died Oct. 1788,
aged 34.

ON HEAD-STONES.

	Died	Aged
John, Son of William and Mary Yeeles	17 July, 1757	24
Robert their Son	9 Feb. 1771	50
Elizabeth, Wife of William Yeeles	— June, 1718	—
Joseph Robbins	31 Mar. 1772	81
Mary his Wife	24 Dec. 1765	66
Samuel their Son	7 Feb. 1754	28
William, Son of William and Margaret Robbins	7 Dec. 1769	23
Betty their Daughter	1 Oct. 1774	26
William Bush	9 Apr. 1761	66
Hester his Wife	31 May, 1787	86
George King	13 Dec. 1740	—
Hester his Wife	14 Jan. 1738	68
Thomas Griffin	29 Sept. 1756	72
Mary his Wife	31 Mar. 1720	40
Robert Milsom	8 May, 1746	53
William Milsom	1 July, 1771	34
Mary, Wife of George Milsom	19 Oct. 1774	59
William Robbins	13 Feb. 1725	72
Anne his Wife	— Nov. 1718	—
Sebbatin, Daughter of Edward and Sarah Fowles	2 Oct. 1740	—
Michael Huff	1 Nov. 1732	63
John Huff	13 May, 1757	—
Ann his Wife	31 May, 1766	64
James their Son	28 Feb. 1767	34
Benjamin Reacy	23 Sept. 1759	59
Mary his Wife	22 May, 1782	82
Mary, Wife of Joseph Cooke	30 Mar. 1766	52
Joyce Pope	26 Mar. 1760	61
William Tipper	13 June, 1772	67
Anne his Wife	15 Feb. 1752	43
Hutson Tipper	4 Feb. 1765	53
John Tipper	6 Dec. 1769	61
Moses Matthews	18 Nov. 1771	60
Anne his Wife	23 Nov. 1760	44
John Woodham	17 Mar. 1752	63
Elizabeth his Wife	28 Nov. 1763	68
Elizabeth, Wife of Joseph Woodham	8 May, 1772	60
Jeremiah Hopkins	8 Nov. 1761	92
Jeremiah Hopkins	7 Dec. 1779	57
Thomas Barnes	2 Apr. 1775	68
Susanna his Wife	28 Feb. 1773	54
William Barnes	29 Apr. 1779	39
Charles King	10 Dec. 1760	38
John Tayler	28 Dec. 1738	—
Elizabeth his Wife	26 Oct. 1729	—
William Taylor	17 Nov. 1787	63
George Payne	12 Dec. 1775	63
Elizabeth his Wife	27 June, 1764	66
Joseph Summers	17 Mar. 1751	58
Ann, Wife of William Pritchell	17 July, 1749	41
Henry Winchester	3 Nov. 1741	30
William Nichols	26 Mar. 175..	—
Mary his Wife	20 Apr. 1769	58
James Emerson	16 Feb. 1771	83
John Emerson	19 Dec. 1769	36
Anne his Wife	18 Nov. 1759	30
Edward Isaac	28 Feb. 1761	43
Richard Hulbard	9 Sept. 1751	74
George Britten	27 Oct. 1770	57
Ann his Daughter	8 Apr. 1772	36

	Died	Aged
Benjamin Perriman	7 Oct. 1773	51
William England	3 Nov. 1769	53
Sarah, Daughter of Joseph Shipton	27 Mar. 1788	—
James Fisher	13 Sept. 1790	82
Mary his Wife	15 Nov. 1758	72
Elizabeth, Wife of James Fisher	28 Nov. 1763	68
Elizabeth, Wife of John Coates	6 Aug. 1789	79
William Jefferis	11 Aug. 1785	74
Sarah his Wife	21 Sept. 1760	42
Hester, Wife of Thomas Jones	13 Apr. 1771	33
Samuel Cox	28 Nov. 1771	64
Hester his Wife	15 July, 1757	56
Daniel, Son of Robert and Betty Cook	11 Dec. 1774	22
Betty, Wife of Richard Aust	19 Feb. 1782	36
Mary, Wife of Joseph Tiley	26 July, 1767	52
Henry Burchell	25 Sept. 1746	49
William Gabbell	20 —— 1756	66
Hannah his Wife	8 Mar. 1767	78
Thomas Neemes	1 June, 1788	66
Mary his Wife	21 Aug. 1754	33
Hester his Wife	1 Jan. 1789	54
Elias Chambers	28 Jan. 1754	68
John, Son of Richard and Mary Chambers	23 Nov. 1778	21
Thomas their Son	27 Feb. 1788	25
Sarah, Daughter of John and Sarah Little	21 Sept. 1786	—
Robert Spicer	14 Aug. 1783	67
John Smith	14 Oct. 1781	75
Elizabeth, Wife of Richard Lovelock	8 May, 1759	62
Thomas Kingscote	2 Apr. 1777	82
William Kidd	21 July, 1785	32
William Humfrey	6 May, 1750	70
Anne his Wife	13 Feb. 1745	70
Benjamin Bullock	25 Oct. 1761	63
Mary his Wife	5 Dec. 1776	84
Samuel Shadwell	17 June, 1732	—
Anne his Wife	23 Feb. 1723	—
James, Son of Richard and Mary Beale	6 Nov. 1740	27
Richard Beale	26 Mar. 1734	59
Joseph Beale	20 Mar. 1754	—
John, Son of William and Mary Lewis	31 Dec. 1776	15
Ann, Daughter of Joseph and Jane Tayler	3 May, 1789	21
Robert Tayler	3 May, 1743	72
Anne his Wife	10 June, 1744	75
Nathan Tayler	31 Oct. 1753	—
George Tayler	18 Sept. 1754	—
William Tayler	14 Aug. 1778	76
Ann, Wife of Isaac Bence	14 Mar. 1779	69
Betty their Daughter	16 Feb. 1763	22
John Tuckey	15 Nov. 1777	58
Ann, Wife of Robert Tuckey	21 Feb. 1778	55
John Osborne	30 Nov. 1739	81
Richard Allingham	21 Sept. 1752	48
James Cannings	— Nov. 1721	40
Elizabeth his Wife	14 Apr. 1766	83
Martha, Wife of Benjamin Perriman	20 Oct. 1737	73
Isaac Bence	15 Mar. 1762	58
Sarah his Wife	9 Apr. 1761	57
Susannah, Wife of John Bence	11 Oct. 1776	70

4

ON

ON HEAD-STONES.

	Died	Aged		Died	Aged
John Bence	18 Sept. 1783	75	John Wait	21 Aug. 1773	75
Sarah, Wife of Ezza Davis, Daughter of Francis and Joan Webb	14 Oct. 1711	34	Eleanor his Wife	10 Jan. 1744	36
William King	10 Sept. 1735	38	Betty, Wife of William Wait	10 Dec. 1771	27
Elizabeth his Wife	18 July, 1760	66	Mary, Wife of Robert Penn	21 Dec. 1757	81
Jane, Wife of John Palmer	11 Sept. 1741	—	Edmund Roach, who was murdered	18 July, 1761	38
William Palmer	19 Jan. 1768	77	Hannah, Wife of James King	15 Nov. 1758	45
Joseph Palmer	14 Apr. 1770	78	Robert White	1 Mar. 1747	76
John Palmer	16 Oct. 1783	53	Mary his Wife	17 Mar. 1746	71
William Yeeles	16 Feb. 1778	60	Joseph White	26 Apr. 1784	80
Joseph Dier	12 June, 1760	62	John Nichols	9 Oct. 1758	75
Mary, Wife of John Bryan	20 Aug. 1744	45	Mary his Wife	12 Dec. 1763	74
William Bryan	17 Feb. 1768	67	Henry Garner	14 Oct. 1783	79
Ann, Daughter of John and Jane Kington	22 Dec. 1729	—	Sarah his Wife	4 May, 1790	76
Elizabeth Reynolds	2 Feb. 1766	67	Robert Keepin	3 May, 1775	59
Hannah, Wife of Edward Osborne	30 Dec. 1757	27	Elizabeth his Wife	6 Nov. 1771	55
William Gunning	17 June, 1766	82	Ann, Wife of Samuel Abbott	3 Oct. 1784	35
John Ladd	6 Nov. 1753	49	Hester White	24 Nov. 1759	69
Ann his Wife	9 Jan. 1774	79	Rachel, Wife of Thomas Noad	22 Mar. 1753	85
Edith, Wife of Samuel Abbott	22 Jan. 1779	26	Thomas Noad	1 Nov. 1760	37
George Kidd	20 June, 1745	64	Martha his Wife	12 Apr. 1782	55
Thomas Kidd	11 Jan. 1748	30	Nicholas Smith	24 Jan. 1776	80
Jane, Wife of George Kidd	1 Nov. 1745	75	Henry White	24 Nov. 1746	42
Elizabeth, Wife of James Bedford	16 Nov. 1789	42	William Helps	21 Mar. 1776	79
John Hulbert	23 Oct. 1754	47	Alice his Wife	14 Mar. 1776	79
Samuel Hulbert	8 Mar. 1751	50	Ann, Wife of John Howell	15 Apr. 1775	28
Mary his Wife	13 Feb. 1765	70	John Ranger	26 May, 1776	32
Edward Hulbert	11 Nov. 1761	27	John Phillips	7 Nov. 1778	63
Ann, Wife of Samuel Watts	28 May, 1726	30	Robert his Son	22 Jan. 1788	29
Calvin Elridge	11 Oct. 1761	75	Mary his Daughter	24 Aug. 1790	37
Ann his Wife	21 Jan. 1768	72	John, Son of John and Jane Greeneand	8 May, 1760	20
Ann, Wife of Thomas Burcombe	21 Aug. 1784	61	James Huff	31 July, 1777	42
Sarah their Daughter	9 Nov. 1778	18	Mary his Wife	16 July, 1783	50
Mary, Wife of William Greenland	9 June, 1774	23	Jane, Wife of Michael Huff	25 Sept. 1785	30
Eleanor, Wife of Samuel Edwards	29 Dec. 1742	33	William Sweatman	2 June, 1782	52
Margaret, Wife of Joseph White	19 Apr. 1779	79	Grace, Wife of Richard Fletcher	23 Dec. 1772	54
William Vernon	26 Jan. 1710	—	Mary Smalkomb	2 Feb. 1762	31
Hannah his Wife	17 Jan. 1746	77	Mary, Daughter of James and Ann Woodward	14 Apr. 1745	20
Ruth, Wife of William Smith	15 Jan. 1779	31	Robert Want	27 Mar. 1776	67
James Bond	13 Oct. 1747	75	Susannah his Wife	4 Mar. 1777	67
Elizabeth his Wife	11 Apr. 1762	63	Rebekah, Wife of William Woodham	3 Nov. 1764	66
Samuel Bond	25 Mar. 1759	70	Samuel Newth, Officer of Excise	20 Oct. 1761	77
Mary his Wife	29 Dec. 1779	71	Edith his Wife	20 —— 1778	85
John, Son of John Bond	25 Jan. 1755	23	Betty their Daughter, Wife of William Matthews	15 Jan. 1778	49
John Elridge	13 June, 1744	24			

CLXX. MARSTON,

CLXX. MARSTON, MARSTON SICCA, DRY OR LONG MARSTON;

IN Diftinction from *Broad Marfton* in *Pebworth*, by which Denominations this Parifh is known. It is fituated in the upper Divifion of the Hundred of *Kiftefgate*, in the extenfive and fertile Vale of *Eve-fham*, upon the Confines of the County of *Worcefter*, fix Miles South-weft from *Stratford upon Avon*, as many North from *Camden*, and thirty-four from the City of GLOUCESTER. The Terrier includes about 1500 Acres of inclofed and cultivated Land, of a ftiff Clay, which, although parched and dry in Summer, is in other Seafons fubject to frequent Inundations. There is no Subject of curious Inveftigation for either the Naturalift or Antiquary.

The Benefice is rectorial, in the Deanery of *Camden*; the Emolument of which, fince the general Inclofure in 1773, has been greatly increafed, arifing from the Allotment of Lands in lieu of Tythes, from which about 120 Acres of the ancient Demefne had been exempted from Time immemorial. The Advowfon was annexed to the Manor until the Purchafe of it from the Family of LOGGIN, of whom is the prefent Incumbent.

The Church is a fmall Structure, confifting of a Nave only, with a low Tower at the Weft End, covered with Lead, and contains no remarkable Architecture.

The Manor is recited in *Domefday* as Parcel of the Endowment of the *Benedictine* Priory of *Coventry*, whofe Right to Free-warren, Markets, and Fairs, appears to have been confirmed by fubfequent Grants in the Reigns of HENRY III. and EDWARD I. *. During the Reign of EDWARD III. the Manor, with all its Privileges was alienated by Purchafe, and attached to the Abbey of *Winchcombe*, who retained a full and free Poffeffion of them till their Diffolution †.

Out of the Court of Augmentations the manerial Eftates were granted to ROBERT DUDLEY, Earl of *Leicefter*, in 1566, 8 ELIZ. upon whofe Demife reverting to the Crown, they were fold in various Parcels; but the Royalty of the Manor, vefted in the Family of SHELDON of *Wefton* and *Beoley*, by whofe Defcendant, WILLIAM SHELDON, it was transferred by Purchafe to WILLIAM LOGGIN, M. A. the prefent Incumbent, who has lately built a commodious Manfion-houfe. The Records fhew that fome of the manerial Lands were purchafed by HENRY COOPER, Gent. and inherited by his Defcendants. The principal Proprietors at prefent are ROBERT BURTON, Efq. the Heirs of PETER CALMEL, Efq. the Heirs of —— HAINE, Gent. JOHN TOMES, WILLIAM MORRIS, and —— HARBRIDGE, Gents.

BENEFACTIONS.

Mrs. SARAH FLETCHER gave, by Will, 10*l.* at what Time not known, to be placed out at Intereft for the Benefit of poor Widows within the Parifh.

JOHN COOPER, Gent. gave, by Will, dated 14th March, 1743, 300*l.* for erecting and maintaining a Free School in *Long Marfton*, or *Marfton Sicca*, for ever, now invefted in Land, fituate in the Parifh of *Chipping Norton*, in the County of *Oxford*, the annual Produce of which is 32*l.*

INCUMBENTS.	PATRONS.	INCUMBENTS.	PATRONS.
1578 Richard Clark,	Queen Elizabeth.	1661 W. Hollington, D.D.	Ralph Sheldon, Efq.
1595 Thomas Pembruge ‡,	The fame.	1686 Richard Day, M. A.	John Newfham.
1595 Sam. Burton, M. A.	Ralph Sheldon, Efq.	1697 John Loggin,	William Dewes.
1634 —— Tolton, D. D.	William Sheldon, Efq.	1731 William Loggin,	Anne Loggin, Widow.
1645 William Cooper,	The Parliament.		

* Cart. 41 Hen. III. m. 4. pro lib' warren' in Man' *Merfton*, &c.
Plac' in com' *Glouc'* 15 EDW. I. quo warranto rot' 2. d. pro libert' in *Dry Marfton*. Not. Mon. *Warwickfhire*, No. IX.
† Pat. 13 EDW. III. p 2. m. 17. pro ten' in *Dry Merfhton*. Id. *Gloucefterfhire*, No. XXXIII.
‡ See WOOD's Fafti, *Oxon.* vol. I. p. 141.

VOL. II.   E e e   PRESENT

PRESENT LORD OF THE MANOR,
WILLIAM LOGGIN, M. A.

The Perfons fummoned from this Place by the Heralds, in 1682 and 1683, were Richard Cooper, Samuel Rawlins, and John Loggin, Gents.

At the Election in 1776 Seven Freeholders polled from this Parifh.

The earlieft Date in the Regifter occurs in 1528.

ANNUAL ACCOUNT OF MARRIAGES, BIRTHS, AND BURIALS, IN THIS PARISH.

A.D.	Mar.	Bir.	Bur.	A.D.	Mar.	Bir.	Bur.	A.D.	Mar.	Bir.	Bur.	A.D.	Mar.	Bir.	Bur.
1781	4	10	5	1786	3	5	7	1791				1796			
1782	3	8	4	1787	1	6	6	1792				1797			
1783	1	10	11	1788	4	9	5	1793				1798			
1784	1	7	7	1789	—	8	5	1794				1799			
1785	4	6	5	1790	—	8	13	1795				1800			

INSCRIPTIONS IN THE CHURCH.

IN THE CHANCEL.

ON BRASS PLATES:

CINERES R^{di} VIRI M^{ti} SAMVELIS
BVRTON
SVB HOC LAPIDE QVIESCVNT,
QVEM STAFFORDIENSIS AGER
EDUXIT, ÆDES
CHRISTI OXON. IN RE LITERARíA
EDUCAVIT, ET
ACADEMIA NOVIT THEOLOGṼ
ERVDITṼ; QVEM
INCOLÆ HVJVS LOCI PER 36 PLVS
MINVS ANNOS
HABUERVNT DOCTVM PERSPICVṼ
ET ASSIDVṼ PRÆ-
CONEM, PIVM ETIAM ET PACIFICṼ
RECTOREM,
QVEM QVINQVE GLOVCESTRENSES
EPISCOPI
PROBARVNT ACVTVM VIGILAN-
TEM, DIOCESIS
EXPERTA FVIT PRVDENTEM AR-
CHIDIACONVM,
COMITATVS PERITVM IVSTICIA-
RIVM.
HIC POST LABORES 66 ANNORṼ
IN ERGASTVLO
HVMANÆ CARNIS FORTITER
EXANTLATOS ET
EMENSOS TERRENA RELIQVIT, ET
IN DOMINO PLACIDE
OBDORMIVIT 14° JVNII, ANNO
POST CHRISTI NATṼ. 1634
LVGENS POSVIT
I. S.

HIC JACET DOROTHEA UXOR
RICHARDI COOPER FILIA VERO
REVERENDI THOMÆ DILLING-
HAM DE OVERDEAN BED-
FORDIENSIS. OBIJT 12° MAIJ,
1650.

HERE LYETH THE BODY
OF ELIZABETH, WIFE OF RICH-
ARD COOPER, WHO DECESSED
THE 14 FEB. 4°, 1657,
AGED 75.

IN THE NAVE.

ON FLAT STONES.

Here lyeth the Body of
RICHARD COOPER,
who departed this Life Auguft
the 17, Anno Dom. 1688,
aged 33 Years.

ON A BRASS PLATE:

HERE LYETH THE BODY OF
JOAN, THE WIFE OF WILLIAM
COOPER, RECTOR OF THIS CHURCH,
WHO DECEASED THE 4 OF
NOVEMBER 1658.

Here lyeth the Body of
ELIZABETH COOPER, Wife of RICHARD
COOPER, Gent. who departed
this Life the 12 of May, 1711.

Here lyeth the Body of
ROBERT COOPER, Gent.
the laft of this Family,
who departed this Life July 23,
1725, aged 39.

Arms; Party per Chevron, three
Mullets.

Sacrum Memoriæ RICHARDI DAY, A.M.
Ecclefiæ Anglicanæ filii obfervantiffimi,
pietate, literis, hofpitalitate celeberrimi,
in refurrectione ædis dilapidatæ
non minus munifici,
& morbo tandem repentino
non fenio & in rore confectus,
ager decubuit:
Et in hac Ecclefia,
quam per undecim annos religiofiffimè
miniftravit, mortalitatis exuvias,
in fpe beatæ refurrectionis,
anno Sal. 1697.
Pie depofuit, anno ætat. 38,
menfis Sexilis die 22.
Nullo non dignus elogio,
eo vero dignior qued nullo fe dignum
exiftimavit.
Epitaphiam uxor mœftiffima
ANNE DAY,
merito defideratiffima pofuit fuperftes.

Here lyeth the Body of
RALPH POOLE, who departed this Life
Auguft 7, 1707, in the 27
Year of his Age.

H. S. E.
Quod mortale fuit CICELIÆ BARTLETT,
RICARDI BARTLETT, Pharmacopolæ,
Stratfordienfis uxoris.
Requievit in Domino, Apr. 14,
Anno { Domini 1703.
{ ætatis 29.

Here lyeth the Body of
JOHN TOMES, who departed
this Life September the
26, 1736, aged 77 Years.

IN THE CHURCH YARD.

ON A MONUMENT AGAINST THE
CHURCH:
Near this Place lyeth the Body
of MARY TOMES, who died
Feb. 10, 1751,
aged 53 Years.

Alfo near the fame Place lyeth
the Body of ANNE, the Wife of
WILLIAM TOMES. She departed
this Life Feb. 16, 1756,
aged 48 Years.

ON TOMBS.

In Memory of JOHN HAYNES, Gent.
late of this Parifh, who
departed this Life Feb.
the 27, 1774, aged 83 Years.

H. S. E.

H. S. E.
EDMUNDUS COTTERELL, FRANCISCI
COTTERELL,
de Milcoat, & SARAH uxoris, filius
unigenitus.
Annis adolefcentibus,
Explorata morum gravitate fenibus,
Annumerandus.
FELIX EDMUNDUS,
Qui præpropera laborans maturitate
commutavit,
Vitæ exuvias cum immortalitate,
Anno { Salutis 1700,
       { ætatis fuæ 10,

Depofitum
SARÆ FLETCHER,
viduæ finceræ, religiofæ,
JOHANNIS LOGGIN, de Swalcliff,
in agro Oxon. Gen.
et SARÆ uxoris ejus
filiæ
primum FRANC. COTTERELL, Gen.
Uxoris,
CHRISTO obdormivit,
Anno { 5to die Jan.
      { Dom. 1726.
      { Ætatis fuæ 63.

Here lyeth the Body of
JOHN COOPER, Gent. deceafed the
14 of March, 1643, who was a
Lover of the Gofpel, a Benefactor
to the Poor, and, at his Death, gave
the Sum of Three Hundred Pounds
for the erecting and maintaining
of a Free School in Long Marfton
for ever.

ON HEAD STONES.

	Died	Aged
John Kecke	19 Nov. 1766	—
Maria his Wife	6 May, 1708	—
William Kecke	26 July, 1716	59
John Kecke	13 Apr. 1718	63
Sarah, Wife of John Tomes	9 Dec. 1787	53
William Tomes, Gent.	11 Mar. 1783	73
Simon Bifhop	2 Aug. 1684	56
Mary his Wife	7 Aug. 1686	48
Ann, Wife of Simon Bifhop	17 Apr. 1708	53
Robert Bifhop	14 Apr. 1721	—
William Cannin	24 Feb. 1761	61
John Haynes, Gent.	27 Feb. 1774	83
Eleanor his Wife	2 May, 1728	25
Anne his fecond Wife	24 Apr. 1739	39
Elizabeth Haynes	3 July, 1740	72
John Haynes, Gent.	3 Mar. 1790	58
William Morris	17 Sept. 1750	52
William Morris	18 June, 1758	32
Anthony Goodin	12 May, 1730	66
Elizabeth his Wife	24 Jan. 1730	58
John Goodin	9 May, 1758	66
Mary his Wife	7 Sept. 1783	79
Jofeph Knight	7 July, 1785	55
Richard Mumford	10 May, 1734	46
Jane his Wife	28 Nov. 1720	35
Ann, Wife of John Mumford	30 Jan. 1739	51
Richard Mumford	28 Feb. 1761	36
James Durham	7 Nov. 1720	68
William Durham	1 Feb. 1722	26
James Durham	13 Sept. 1721	—
Sarah, Wife of John Lee	— Oct. 17—	—
William Hood	— —— 1700	—
William Timbs	10 Mar. 1782	60
Joan, Wife of John Campden	15 Mar. 1672	69
Thomas Campden	29 —— 1700	—
Thomas Lamly	16 Aug. 1671	—
John Weffon	23 May, 1787	76
Sarah his Wife	18 Jan. 1767	49
Richard Webb	8 Mar. 1731	34
Mary his Wife	23 Dec. 1728	—
John Webb	29 Jan. 1736	76
William Sollis	13 Oct. 1783	56
Mary his Wife	13 Oct. 1762	31
Ann, Wife of John Weffon	17 July, 1709	75
William Johnfon	2 Aug. 1767	68
Thomas White	22 Oct. 1750	72
Mary his Daughter	22 June, 1747	21
William Widdowes	15 Oct. 1714	—
William his Son	27 July, 17—	42

CLXXI. MATSON,

CLXXI. MATSON, OR MATISDEN;

BUT in ancient Deeds denominated *MATISKNOLLE*, is a Parish of very fmall Dimenfions, containing nearly 300 Acres of Pafture, and 23 only of Arable Land, of a fertile Clay or Loam. It lies in the Hundred of *Dudftone* and *King's Barton*, ten Miles diftant from *Cheltenham* on the South-weft, eight North from *Stroud*, and two South-eaftward from the City of GLOUCESTER.

The Situation is peculiar, and extremely picturefque, fpreading round the North fide of a very beautiful Hill; which, rifing from the great Vale, is perfectly infulated and detached. As a ftriking Feature of the magnificent Landfcape, it correfponds with that of *Churchdown*; and, being in a parallel Direction, might probably fuggeft the legendary Idea of ROBIN HOOD's Butts, whofe Name it bears. Its Declivities are cloathed with the richeft Verdure, and Plantations grouped with much Tafte; the Summit is cleft into irregular Eminences, which produce a very pleafing Effect. In earlier Ages, the Manufacture of Iron eftablifhed at *Gloucefter* was fupplied with Ore from *Matifknolle*, before the more eafy Communication with the *Foreft of Deane*. Many broken Scars and the Appearance of exhaufted Mines evince this Fact, which is farther proved by feveral ferruginous Springs; and the Aqueducts, by which both the Monaftery and City of *Gloucefter* were fupplied, are mentioned in fome of the more ancient Evidences *.

The Living is a Rectory in the Deanery of GLOUCESTER, augmented by the Queen's Bounty and Legacies. In *Saxon* Times, it was given by ERNULPHUS to the Monks of *St. Peter*, and was confirmed at the Diffolution to the Dean and Chapter †. In 1739, ALBINIA, Relict of WILLIAM SELWYN, Efq. rebuilt the Church, upon a fmall and neat Plan, connected with the old Chancel.

Mattifden is not fpecified in *Domefday Book*. About the Reign of HENRY III. feveral Eftates, within its Limits, claimed manerial Privileges or Exemptions, but the chief Manor was held under HUMPHREY DE BOHUN in the fourteenth Century, whofe Tenant was ELIAS DAUBENEY, from whom feveral Leafes are ftill extant, during the Reign of EDWARD the Third ‡.

There is prefumptive Evidence that the whole Demefne was antiently attached to the Conftablefhip of *Gloucefter*, and that one of the Family of DE BOHUN beftowed Parcel of it upon the Priory of *Llanthony*, of their Foundation §. This Eftate, at the Suppreffion, was purchafed by the Mayor and Burgeffes of *Gloucefter*, by Deed, dated *September* 11, 1543. 34 HENRY VIII. who obtained the King's Licence to reconvey the fame to THOMAS LANE, Efq. their Recorder, from whom, in the fucceeding Reign, it was transferred to RICHARD PATE, Efq. He left three Daughters and Co-heirs, one married to RICHARD BROOKE, and another to RICHARD LYGON. SUSANNAH BROOKE inherited this Eftate, and conveyed it in Marriage Dower to Sir AMBROSE WILLOUGHBY, Knt. From Sir AMBROSE WILLOUGHBY this Eftate paffed by Purchafe in the latter part of Queen ELIZABETH's Reign to JASPER SELWYN, Efq. Counfellor at Law, of *Stonehoufe* in this County; which JASPER was the fourth in Defcent from JOHN SELWYN, who came into the faid County from *Suffex* about the Reign of RICHARD III. where that Family had been fettled for many preceding Generations.

On purchafing this Eftate he entailed it on the Male Heir, and it paffed fo entailed through four fucceeding Generations to Col. JOHN SELWYN, eldeft Son of Major General WILLIAM SELWYN, who was Governor of *Jamaica*, and died in that Ifland. But the above JOHN SELWYN joining with his eldeft Son of the fame Name, a few Months before the Deaths of both, in 1751, cut off the ancient Entail on the Male Heir, and re-entailed it on the Defcendants of his Daughter, who was married to the Hon. THOMAS TOWNSHEND, fecond Son of CHARLES, fecond Vifcount TOWNSHEND and one of the Tellers

---

* WILL.'US GERAND, de *Mattifden*, Abb' & Conv' *Glouc*', conceffit, " totam illam aquam quam in terra mea de *Mattifknolle*, " invenerunt aut invenire potuerunt, una cum quadam placea terræ ubi fitum eft receptorium aquæ & conftructum."

MSS. Arch. Cathed. Glouc'.

"PHILLIPPUS DE MATTISDEN conceffit, &c. Domum lapideam quam conftruxerunt dicti religiofi fubtus *Mattifknolle* ad " Aqueductum." Id. ut fup.

† In the Time of HAMMELINE, Abbot of *St. Peter's*, PHILIP DE MATTISDENE gave to that Church, " capellam de *Matif- " den* quæ eft juxta domum meam; quam pater meus eis prius donavit; et cum predicta capella vacaverit, liceat Abbati predicto " libere et fine reclamatione inftituere perfonam, &c." And THOMAS BREDON, a fucceeding Abbot, gave to WALTER HUNT " Capellam de *Mattifden*, fub annua penfione 10 folid'." Id. ut fup.

‡ Deed, dated April 3, 1365. Leafe of the Manor of *Mattefden* from ELIAS DAUBENY to Sir GILBERT GIFFARD, Knight, for Term of his Life, in virtue of a prior Leafe from the Abbey to the faid ELIAS DAUBENY, dated May 9, 1350. Id. ut fup.

§ Lib' taxat' ecclef' temp. EDW. I. " Prior *Llanthonienfis* tenet apud *Mattifden* unam car' terræ & valet 28 fol'."

MSS. Bodl. Lib.

2   of

of the Exchequer.   After which, being left by Will, during the Term of Life, to the second Son George Augustus Selwyn, it remained in his Poffeffion till his Demife in 1791, when it devolved, according to the new Entail, on Thomas Lord Vifcount Sydney, eldeft Son to the aforefaid Thomas Townshend and of Albinia his Wife, only Daughter of Col John Selwyn.   The defcendents in the original line of Entail are thofe of Henry Charles Selwyn, Efq. eldeft Son of Charles Jasper Selwyn, M. A. Rector of *Beverfton* in this County, eldeft Son of Henry, third Son of Major General William Selwyn before-named.

Another manerial Eftate was conferred on the Abbey of *St. Peter* for the Eftablifhment of two additional Monks and a Chantry, by William Nottingham, Efq. the King's Attorney Generel, by Deed, dated *Auguft* 10, 1470, 10 Edward IV. * of which the Family of Robyns, otherwife Bocher, were Tenants, and continued through feveral Defcents under the Dean and Chapter, by whom a Leafe was fome Years fince granted to the late G. A. Selwyn, Efq.

The Manor-Houfe, built by Sir Ambrose Willoughby, during the remarkable Siege of *Gloucefter*, afforded a Refidence for the Royal Perfon and Court, being in the Rear of the Army, which were ftationed in *Tredworth Field*.   Corbet relates, that the " King lay within a Mile of the Town ;" but without fpecifying the Place ; but, in the " Iter Carolinum," minute mention is made †.

When this Place came into the Poffeffion of George Augustus Selwyn, Efq. in 1751, he exerted that true Tafte by which he was diftinguifhed, in repairing and improving it in a Style fingularly appropriate to the Age in which it was built, placing in it fuch Appendages as correfponded with and ferved to elucidate its Anecdotes and former hiftory ; particularly thofe Parts which referred to the Refidence of King Charles the Firft, during his unfuccefsful attempt to reduce the City of *Gloucefter* ‡.

* William Nottingham, Efq. grants his Manor of *Mattefden* to the *Abbey* of *Gloucefter*: " ut invenerint duos capellanos
" regulares de feipfis ad oxorand. fingulis diebus pro animabus mei & Cæciliæ uxoris, & Elizæ nuper uxoris meæ, & Johan-
" nis de la Bere, nuper Epifcopi *Menevenfis*, &c."   MSS. Arch. Cathed. *Glouc.*

† Amongft feveral Public Acts done by King Charles the Firft, and dated from his Court at *Matfon*, is the following :

    " *CHARLES* R.

" Charles, by the Grace of God, King of *Great Britain*, *France*, and *Ireland*, Defender of the Faith, &c.   To our trufty
" and weil beloved Henry Tracie, Efq. greeting.—Wee doe hereby conftitute and appoint you to be Serjeant Major of the
" ——— Regiment of Foote, under the Command of our right trufty and wellbeloved George Lord Chandois.   And far-
" ther, that you be Captaine over one Company in the faid Regiment ; which, by Virtue of this our Commiffion, you are forth-
" with to imprefs and reteyne, of fuch as will willingly and voluntarily ferve us for our Pay, and for the Defence of our Royall
" Perfon, the two Houfes of Parliament, the Proteftant Religion, the Lawe of the Land, the Liberty and Property of the Sub-
" ject, and Priviledges of Parliament, to bring them to our Royall Standard, and caufe them to be duly exercifed in Arms,
" commanding all inferior Officers and Souldiers, as well of the faid Regiment as of your faid Company refpectively, you to obey
" as their Serjeant Major and Captaine of a Company of Foote, according to this our Commiffion, hereby given unto you.   And
" you yourfelf alfo to obferve and follow fuch Order and Direct on as from Time to Time you fhall receive either from us or
" from our Generall, Lieutenant Generall, Generall of our Horfe, your Colonell, or other fuperior Officer of our Armey, ei-
" ther already by us appointed, or hereafter to be appointed, according to occafion, and the difcipline of Warr.   And in all
" Things to governe yourfelfe as unto your Duty and Place of Serjeant Major of a Regiment, and Captaine of a Company of
" Foote. doth of Right appertayne and belong.   Given under our Signe Manuall, at our Court at *Matfdowne*, this Fourteenth
" of *Auguft*, 1643, in the Nineteenth Year of our Reigne."

‡ In a Window are ftill preferved the Arms of Peregrine Bertie, Lord Willoughby, of *Erefby*, in Right of his Mother
Katharine, fole Daughter and Heirefs of William Lord Willoughby, of *Erefby* ; which William died 17 Hen. VIII.
The faid Peregrine Lord Willoughby died 1601, and was buried at *Spilfby* in *Lincolnfhire*.   It is probable Sir Ambrose
Willoughby, being a collateral Relation to Peregrine Lord Willoughby, of *Erefby*, brought thofe Arms from fome
other Houfe, and put them up here as a Memorial of the Connection between the Lords Willoughby of *Erefby* and *Parham*,
quarterly, 1ft, Sable, a Crofs engrailed Or, Ufford ; 2d, Argent, three battering Rams barways proper for Bertie ; 3d,
fretty Azure, Willoughby ; 4th, Gules Crofs moline Argent, Beke ; 5th, quarterly, Azure, a Lion rampant Or and Argent, fretty Sable, Fitz Allan ; 6th, Or, a Lion rampant Sable, Malthravers ; 7th, Gules, a Fefs Dancette between fix
Crofles pattée Or, Enghain ; 8th, barry of fix Ermine and Gules, three Crefcents Sable, Welles.   Creft a Saracen's Head
proper between two Wings conjoined fretty Or and Sable.

This Place was for many Years after her Widowhood the Refidence of Albinia, Relict of his Excellency Major General William Selwyn.   She was fecond Sifter and Coheir of Sir Edward Bettenson, Baronet, of *Scadbury Park*, Co. *Kent*.   She had
three Sons ; firft, John, who was Colonel of a Regiment of Foot, Paymafter of the Marine, and Member in Parliament for the
City of *Gloucefter*.   Second, Charles, who was a Major in the Army, and Member in Parliament for the Borough of *Lugger-
fhall, com. Wilts*, and died S. P. ; and, third, Henry, who was Captain of a Troop in the Royal North Britifh Regiment of
Dragoons, and afterwards Receiver General of the Cuftoms, in which Office he died, and was buried at *Matfon* ; leaving Iffue
by his Wife Ruth, Daughter of Anthony Compton, of *Gainflow*, near *Berwick upon Tweed*, Efq. two Sons and feven Daughters.   Charles Jasper, the eldeft Son, is Vicar of *Blockley*, Co. *Wigorn*, Rector of *Beverfton*, Co. *Gloucefterfhire*, and Prebendary of *Sarum*, and has Iffue four Sons and three Daughters.   William, the fecond Son, of *Lincoln's-Inn*, Counfellor at Law,
and has Iffue two Sons and two Daughters.   Albinia, the eldeft Daughter of Henry Selwyn, married the 26th of *Auguft*,
1764, Sir William Irby, who was afterwards created Lord Boston, and by him Mother to Frederick the prefent Lord
Boston, to the Honourable William Henry Irby, to the Right Honourable Augusta Georgina, Elizabeth Lady
Walsingham ; the other Daughters were Mary, Charlotte, Frances, Catharine, Hannah, and Louisa.   Mrs.
Albinia Selwyn had alfo three Daughters ; firft, Albinia, fecond Wife of Major John Hanbury, of *Pontypool*, Co. *Monmouth*.   Second, Frances, married to Thomas Hayward, of *Quedgly*, Co. *Gloucefter*, Efq. Grandfather to the prefent Pof-
feffor of that Place.   Third, Margaret, who died unmarried ; and departing this Life in 1738, An. Æt. 80, fhe was buried
at *Matfon*, on the North Side of the Church-yard, under the Windows near the Chancel, where is alfo buried her youngeft Son
Henry aforefaid.

In the Collection of ancient Portraits made by the late G. Selwyn, Efq. were thofe of Ambrose Dudley, Earl of *Warwick*,
and his brother the more celebrated Earl of Leicester, Louis XI. of *France*, and his Wife Mary Queen of Scots, brought
from the *Louvre*, King Charles the First, and Henrietta his Queen, &c.   In the Gallery was placed a moft beautiful Buft
of that ill-fated Prince, in white Marble, by Roubiliac, upon a Pedeftal of Rofe-wood, enfigned with the royal Arms impaling
France, and infcribed round the Bafe, " King Charles came to *Mattefden* with his two Sons, *Aug.* 10, 1643."
Mattefden was honoured by the Notice of his prefent Majefty in 1788, accompanied by his auguft Family.

Vol. II.F f fBENEFACTION.

B E N E F A C T I O N.

A Portion of the Legacy of Giles Coxe, of *Ablond's Court*, in 1643, already mentioned,
is given to this Parish.

Incumbents.	Patrons.	Incumbents.	Patrons.
1536 Tho. Hale,	By Grant from the Abbey of of St. Peter in Gloucester.	1697 Mathew Yate,	Dean and Chap. of Glouc.
1556 Richard Brooke,		1747 Edward Nicholls,	Lord Chancellor.
Walter Cooper,		1763 Hugh Price,	Dean and Chap. of Glouc.
Roger Wheelar,		1767 Daniel Evans,	The same.
1570 Lewis Crones,	Richard Robins,	1769 Tho. Turner, M.A.	The same.
1626 Will. Anfell, M. A.	John Robins, by Grant from the D. and C. of Glouc.	—— Ja. Edwards, A.B.	The same.
1665 Edward Jackson,	King Charles.	1778 Tho. Parker, M.A.	The same.
1670 Edward Fidkin,	Dean and Chap. of Glouc.	1783 Wil. Gyllet, M.A.	The same.
1695 Edward Pain,	Bishop of Gloucester.	1785 Charles Palmer,	The same.
		1788 Edw. Jones, M. A.	The same.

Present Lord of the Manor,

The Right Honourable Thomas Lord Viscount Sydney.

At the Heralds Visitation, in 1682 and 1683, the only Person summoned from this Place was
Joseph Knight, Esq.

At the Election in 1776 One Freeholder polled from this Parish.

The first Date of the Register occurs in 1553.

Annual Account of Marriages, Births, and Burials, in this Parish.

A.D.	Mar.	Bir.	Bur.	A.D.	Mar.	Bir.	Bur.	A.D.	Mar.	Bir.	Bur.	A.D.	Mar.	Bir.	Bur.
1781	1	1	—	1786	—	—	—	1791				1796			
1782	1	—	1	1787	—	2	1	1792				1797			
1783	—	—	1	1788	—	—	2	1793				1798			
1784	1	—	1	1789	—	—	1	1794				1799			
1785	—	—	—	1790	1	—	1	1795				1800			

INSCRIPTIONS IN THE CHURCH.

ON MARBLE MONUMENTS.

Arms : Argent, on a Bend cottised Sable, three Annulets
Or, for Selwyn; impaling, Gules, a Fess between two Che-
veronells Argent, for Nourse.

MEMORIÆ SACRUM
GULIELMI, THEOPHILI, ET JASPERI, FILIORUM
GULIELMI
SELWYN, ARM', ET MARGARETTÆ, VXORIS EJUS, QVI
VNO EODEMQVE FATALI MORBO CORREPTI FATO
CESSERE IMMATVRO. GULIELMVS, PARENTUM PRI-
MOGENITVS, QVINQVENNIVM PENE EXPLETVS, 7mo
DIE
AUGVSTI, AN° 1649, OBJIT, THEOPHILVS TRIEN-
NIUM,
JASPERUS MENSEM ÆTATIS VNDECIMVM, PER-
AGENTES
PARVM IN MORTE SEPARATI OCCVBVERE, HIC 27mo,
ILLE
29 DIE SEPTEMBRIS, AN°. 1655.

Beneath this Tomb is interred
the Body of Margaret Selwyn, Widow
of William Selwyn, Esquire, and Daughter of
Edward Nourse, of Gloucester, Esq. She was married
at the Age of Seventeen; she was a dutiful Child to her
Parents, an Example of Piety to her Neighbours, a faithful

Wife to her Husband, and a tender Mother to her Children.
Her Virtues were rewarded by a mature Age, and
a fruitful Issue. She lived to see Sixty of her Posterity,
and died the 18th of January,
in the Year of our Lord 1715-6.
her Age 91.

Arms; on two Escocheons; 1st, Selwyn, as before; 2d,
Selwyn, impaling, Gules, a Fess within a Bordure Argent,
for Betenson.

In Memory of his Excellency William
Selwyn, Esquire, who died at Jamaica April
the 6th, 1702; was Governor and Commander
in Chief, both by Sea and Land, of that
Island, was Major General and Colonel
of a Regiment of Foot in the Wars of
King William the IIId, and Governor of
Tilbury Fort.
This Monument was erected many Years
before her Death, by his most affectionate
Widow, Albinia Selwyn, Sister and Coheir
to Sir Edward Betenson, Bart. of the
County of Kent. She died December the
29, Anno 1738, aged about 80 Years.

Here also lies buried
Henry Selwyn, their youngest Son,
who died Receiver General of
the Customs under King George II.

4

In

In Memory
of HENRY SELWYN, Efq.
who died September, 1734, aged 45.

His Widow,
one of the Daughters of
ANTHONY COMPTON, of Gainflow,
near Berwick upon Tweed, Efq.
who died 3 May, 1761, aged 63.

And alfo of two of their Daughters,
ALBINIA, Lady Bofton,
who died 2 April, 1769, aged 49.
And HANNAH SELWYN,
who died 15 Nov. 1756, aged 31.

In a Vault near this Place
lies the Body of the Hon. ALBINIA
TOWNSHEND, Wife of the
Hon. THOMAS TOWNSHEND,
2d. Son to the Right Hon. CHARLES
Lord Vifcount TOWNSHEND,
Principal Secretary of State to their
Majefties GEORGE the Firft and Second,
and Daughter to JOHN SELWYN, Efq.
She died September, 1739,
aged 25 Years,
and left five Children.

ON FLAT STONES.

Here lyeth the Body of JASPER SEL-
WYN, Efquire, Counfellor at Law, and
one of his Majefties Juftices of Peace
for the Coun ty of Glouc. who deceafed
the thirteenth Day of January, 1634,

and waiteth for a glorious
Refurrection.

Hic jacet GULIELMUS
SELWYN, Armigeri, filius
JASPERI SELWYN, armig',
qui obijt 28 die Octob.
Anno Domini 1643.

Quicquid mortale GULIELMI, filii
GULIELMI SELWYN, armigeri,
hic acquiefcit, fpes magna
parentum, familiæque decus, futurum
in luctum parentum, at perpetuam
fibi felicitatem
Augufti nondum quin . . . . .
Anno Domini 1649.

Arms; Per Pale, Argent and Sable,
two Flaunces and three Fleurs de Lis
counterchang'd, for ROBINS; impaling
Barry of ten, over all a Lion rampant,
for STRATFORD.

In Memory of ANNE, the Wife of
JOHN ROBINS, of the Manor of Matfon,
in the Parifh of Upton St. Leonard's, in
the County of Glouc. Efq. She was
the Daughter of WILLIAM STRATFORD,
of Farmcote, in the County of Glouc.
Efq. She was interred the 11 Day
of May, Anno Domini 1663.

Alfo
in Memory of DOROTHY, the
Wife of WILLIAM ROBINS, of Mat-

fon aforefaid, Gent. Grandfon of
the abovenamed JOHN and ANNE ROBINS.
DOROTHY was the Daughter of THOMAS
BACON, of Manfell, in the County
of Somerfet, Efq. a Gentleman
of an ancient good Family, and
in the Commiffion of the Peace for
that County to the Time of his Death.
She departed this Life the 26 Day
of May, 1732, aged 31 Years.

Here refteth the Body of
JANE WELLS, of the City of
London, and Daughter of
WILLIAM MADOCKS, of the
City of Gloucefter, Gent.
She departed this Life
the 19 Day of July, Anno
Domini 1725, her Age
52 Years.

HENRY Son of JAMES DOBBINS, and
GRACE his Wife, was buried the 25
of September, 1743.

In Memory of JOHN GREEN,
of the City of Gloucefter, who
was buried April the 3, 1747.

Here lyeth the Body
of JOHN HORNEDGE,
of Wootton, who was
buried the 16 Day of
April, 1749.

IN THE CHURCH-YARD.

ON FLAT STONES.

In Memory of
ISABELLA LONG, late
Wife to GEORGE LONG,
of Boddington Manor.

She departed this Life
May the 28, 1754.
Aged 62 Years.
ANNE, Wife of JOHN WITCOMB,
of this Parifh, Yeoman, was
buried 17 Oct. 1721, aged 63.

In Memory
of ANNE the Wife of GEORGE LONG,
of the Parifh of Sandhurft, Yeoman,
who departed this Life the 9 May,
1779, aged 48.

ON HEAD-STONES.

	Died	Aged
John Witcombe	9 Feb. 1726	81
Thomas Witcombe	29 Aug. 1739	37
Sarah his Wife	9 Jan. 1738	34
John Witcombe	19 Feb. 1761	65
Bridget his Wife	19 May 1759	60
Henry Hains, of Gloucefter	22 Oct. 1722	52
John Harris	6 July 1752	35
William Dower	15 Jan. 1773	72
Prifcilia his Wife	12 Jan. 1769	62
Thomas Canning	2 June 1739	38
William Canning	13 Nov. 1782	45
John, Son of Wil. and Prifc. Dower	31 Oct. 1770	21
Mary their Daughter	20 Feb. 1770	28
Jane Wells	19 July, 1725	—
Robert Curtis	4 Feb. 1725	—
Dorothy, Wife of William Robins	27 May 1732	—
Mary, Wife of William Print	28 Jan. 1766	88
John Print	21 Oct. 1769	46
Anne his Wife	3 May 1761	32

CLXXII. MAYSEMORE.

CLXXII. M A Y S E M O R E.

THE Name of this Place does not occur in *Domefday* Book, it being annexed to the Parifh of *St. Mary de Lode*, in *Gloucefter*, at the Period when that Record was compiled.

The Village is fituated on the Bank of the River *Severn*; over which is a Bridge, built in 1785, kept in Repair by a Toll granted by Parliament in 1777. It lies in the Hundred of *Dudftone* and *King's Barton*, eight Miles South-weftward from *Tewkefbury*, and one North-weftward from the City of GLOU-CESTER, bounded on the Weft Side by the River *Leaden*. It has one fmall Hamlet called *Overton*, of which there is nothing worthy of Remark.

The Boundary comprifes about 1900 Acres of Land. Of the Soil, the Nature varies from deep Clay to Gravel, and the greater Portion is applied to Pafture.

The Church, dedicated to *St. Giles*, is a fmall Fabric, confifting of a Nave and Chancel only, with a handfome embattled Tower at the Weft End.

The Living is a perpetual Curacy in the Patronage of the Bifhop of GLOUCESTER, which was augmented in 1719 and 1733 by Donations from the Bifhops of *Winchefter* and *Gloucefter*, by a Legacy left by Mr. HODGES, and Queen ANNE's Bounty. The Impropriation antiently belonged to the Abbey of *Gloucefter*; but, in 33 H. VIII. it was granted to the Bifhoprick, and confirmed 6 E. VI.

In confequence of a recent Act of Parliament obtained for inclofing the Common Fields, a certain Portion of Land is allotted to the Impropriator in Lieu of Tythes *.

The Manor remained in the Hands of the Monks of *Gloucefter* from the fecond of the Reign of King HENRY I. till their Suppreffion, when it was added to the Revenues of the Bifhoprick, and is now held by BENJAMIN HYETT and WILLIAM PITT, Efqrs. as Leffees under the Bifhop of *Gloucefter*.

CORBET †, in his Hiftory of the Military Government of the City of *Gloucefter*, relates, that " Co-" lonel NICHOLAS MIN, who commanded the *Irifh* Brigade, in the firft Entrance began to lafh out, and " made Affayes of Action, cut down the Bridge at *Mafemore*, allarmed the City from the Vineyard Hill, " and took divers of our Men that iffued out upon a Sally over the River in a Boate."

The whole of this Parifh confifts of Leafehold and Copyhold Lands.

B E N E F A C T I O N S.

—— Cox, prior to the Year 1683, gave, by Will, a Rent Charge of 1*l*. 6*s*. 8*d*.
GRACE WHEELER, 1675, gave, by Will, a Rent Charge of 1*l*. 4*s*.

INCUMBENTS.	PATRONS.	INCUMBENTS.	PATRONS.
* * * * * * * * * * * * * *		1745 James Pitt,	Bp. of Gloucefter.
* * * * * * * * * * * * * *		1784 Martin Stafford Smith,	The fame.
1735 Wm. Huddlefton, Clk.	Bp. of Gloucefter.	1793 Richard Raikes, M. A.	The fame.

LESSEES OF THE MANOR, UNDER THE BISHOP OF GLOUCESTER,

WILLIAM PITT and BENJAMIN HYETT, Efqrs.

No Perfon was fummoned from this Place by the Heralds, in 1682 and 1683.

At the Election in 1776, Three Freeholders polled from this Parifh.

---

* Contentions between the Citizens of *Gloucefter* and the Parifh of *Mayfemore*, concerning Right of Common in the Abbey of *Gloucefter*, Lands without and near the Weft Gate. Agreements dated 4 H. III. 9 H. III. and 25 H. VI. MSS. FURNEY. PONTZ de *Mayfemore*. MSS. FURNEY.
† P. 85.

6

AN-

ANNUAL ACCOUNT OF MARRIAGES, BIRTHS, AND BURIALS, IN THIS PARISH.

A.D.	Mar.	Bir.	Bur.	A.D.	Mar.	Bir.	Bur.	A.D.	Mar.	Bir.	Bur.	A.D.	Mar.	Bir.	Bur.
1781	2	3	4	1786	3	6	8	1791	1	11	7	1796			
1782	6	9	7	1787	1	16	7	1792	3	16	7	1797			
1783	2	2	8	1788	3	3	4	1793	2	9	7	1798			
1784	3	4	7	1789	1	12	8	1794				1799			
1785	5	4	3	1790	4	6	3	1795				1800			

INSCRIPTIONS IN THE CHURCH.

IN THE CHANCEL.

ON MONUMENTS.

Arms; a Fefs engrailed between fix Crofs Crofslets fitché.

Sacred to the Memory of
EDMUND REDISH, Gent.
A Man fteady and unfhaken in Friendfhip, a true Lover of Englifh Hofpitality and plain Dealing, a zealous Maintenance of the Rights and Privileges of this Parifh when living, and dying bequeathed fourty Pounds to the Inhabitants of the fame, the Intereft whereof to be given to the Poor in Bread monthly for ever.   He exchanged this Life for a better the 23d of November,
Anno { ætatis 81.
{ Domini 1708.

Arms; three Bars, in chief three Eftoiles, for PITT; on an Efcocheon of Pretence, quarterly of eight, 1ft, barry of fix Or and Azure, on a Bend Gules, three Martlets Argent, for PEMBRUGE; 2d, Argent, a Bend Lozengy Gules, a Chief Azure, for GAMAGE; 3d, Argent, a Chevron Gules, between three Hurts, for BASKERVILLE; 4th, Argent, on a Crofs Sable, a Leopard's Face in the Centre Or, for BRYDGES; 5th, Gules, a Fefs Or, between three Efcallops Argent, for PYTCHARD; 6th, Argent, on a Bend Gules, three round Buckles Or, for SAPYE; 7th, Lozengy, Argent and Gules, a Bordure Azure, for HALGOTT; 8th, Or, on a Pile in Point between fix Eftoiles Sable, three in Pale of the Field, for BAGYNDEN.

In a Vault near this Place is depofited the Remains of the Rev. JAMES PITT, Rector of Barrington, in this County, and Vicar of Taynton, in Oxon, who departed this Life the 25th Day of March, 1784, aged 59 Years.

Alfo of ELIZABETH his Relict, Grand daughter of WILLIAM PEMBRUGE, Efq. a Family long refident in this Parifh. She died the 14th Day of June, 1784, in the 66th Year of her Age.

ON FLAT STONES.

HERE LYETH ANNE,
THE DAUGHTER OF HENRY
WOODDESON, WHO DIED
NOVEMBER THE 20,
1633.

Arms; a Fefs engrailed between three Rooks.

Here lyeth the Body of
THOMAS ROOKE,
only Son of THOMAS ROOKE, of this Parifh, Gent. by JANE his Wife, Daughter of ANTHONY PEMBRUGE, who died Auguft 23, 1714, aged 33 Years.

Mr. HENRY WAGSTAFFE died the 27 of December, 1725, aged 51 Years.

And alfo, two Sons and one Daughter.

Here lieth the Body of
ALEXANDER READY, of Mayfmore, Gent. who died the 2d of May, 1639.

ANNE, the Daughter of EDMUND READY, Gent. was buried the 9 of Auguft, 1689.

EDMUND REDISH, Gent. 1708.

Here lyeth the Body of JAMES GREENE, of this Parifh, Gent. who died the 2d Day of January, 1679, aged about 31 Years.

In Memory of ELIZABETH, the Wife of WILLIAM COOKE, of the Parifh of Churchdown, Yeoman, who departed this Life Auguft the 20, 1700, aged 44.

Here lyeth the Body of ELIZABETH, Relict of Mr. ROBERT BIGGS, of Birdlip, and late Wife of the Rev. Mr. JOHN WALL, Minifter of this Parifh.   She departed this Life Jan. 31, 1727, in the 51ft Year of her Age.

Here lyeth the Body of the Reverend JOHN WALL, who was many Years Minifter of this Parifh, and Vicar of Brockworth.   He died Feb. the 19, 1746-7, aged 73 Years.

Here alfo lyeth the Body of the Rev. Mr. GEORGE WALL, M. A.

Son of the abovementioned Mr. JOHN WALL, Rector of Mungewell, in the County of Oxford, and Minifter of this Parifh, who died the 4 of June, 1776, in the 61 Year of his Age.

ON MONUMENTS IN THE NAVE.

Arms; Or, fretty Azure.

Hic jacet ROBERTUS WILLOUGHBIE, filius THOMÆ WILLOUGHBIE, de Bore Place, in comitatu Cant. Armig.
. . . .
Milit. Collegii Magdalenienfis olim focius in . . . . bus magift. necnon . . . . Baccalaureus, qui mortem obiit vicefimo quinto die Augufti anno falutis 1641.

Arms; PEMBRUGE as before;—impaling, Azure, a Fefs lozengy Or.

Sacred to the Memory of
WILLIAM PEMBRUGE, late of this Parifh,
a Gentleman of an ancient honourable Family, that lived in good Reputation, and whofe good Qualities procured him the Love and Efteem of his Friends and Acquaintance.
He truly defcended from Sir HENRY PEMBRUGE, Knight, who, in the 1ft Year of EDWARD the I. was feized of the Lordfhip and Caftle of Pembruge, in the County of Hereford.   He departed this Life the 13 April, in the Year 1738, aged 70 Years.

To the Memory of EDMUND PEMBRUGE, of this Parifh, Gentleman, Son and Heir of the abovementioned WILLIAM PEMBRUGE.
He departed this Life the 27 of October, 1766, aged 78.

Alfo in Memory of KATHARINE, Daughter of the faid WILLIAM PEMBRUGE, who departed this Life the 19th of September, 1722, aged 32 Years.

Arms;

Arms; Barry of fix, Or and Azure, on a Bend Gules three Mullets Argent, for PEMBRUGE.

M. S.
ANTONII PEMBRUGE, Generofi,
viri, natalibus clari,
morum probitate,
Erga regem fidelitate,
Erga liberos manfuetudine,
Erga proximum charitate,
Celeberrimi.
Obiit Oct. 7, A. D. 1696,
ætatis 79.

Necnon
ANTONII, prædicti ANTONII, filii
natu maximi,
filii vere pii,

qui, morte numis propera raptura vivis,
Obiit Martii 21, 1681, ætatis 21.
Parenti fuo & fratri chariffimis
Monumentum hoc GULIELMUS fuperftes.

———

Arms; a Chevron between three Leopards' Faces; — impaling, a Chevron between three Stags' Attires, for COCKS.

Infra repofiti fuerunt Cineres
FRANCISCI WHEELER, de Mayfemore,
Generofi,
& GILBERTI filii ejus primogenti,
anno ætat. XXXIX, dies XIX
Novembris;

Patrem vero in ætatis fuæ LXX, dies
XVII. Apritis XIX.
Quorum gratia relicta FRANCISCI
chariffima
Hoc marmor pofuit
In memoriam
Cujus etiam quod mortale fubtumulatum
fuit
die 18 Maii, anno 1680.

———

ON A FLAT STONE:

MARY, the Wife of
JOHN VALLENDER, died
May the 24, 1731,
aged 67 Years.

IN THE CHURCH-YARD.

ON A MONUMENT AGAINST THE
CHANCEL:

M. S.
In fpe beatæ refurrectionis,
Quod mortale fuit hic depofuit
ROB. CARPENTER, Gen.
Vir (fi quis alius)
Spectatiffima fide, morum integritate,
Quem liberi parentem vere benignum,
Ecclefiæ Anglicanæ genuinum filium,
Omnes defideratiffimum habuere.
Hunc inter vitæ tedia duobus annis
plus minus colluctantem inveterata
Phtyfis (vel invito Efculapio) corripuit
in cœlum, 16 Junii, anno ætatis 43,
Domini 1675.

Hoc quale ROBERTUS filius natu
maximus
in perpetuam obfervantiæ monumentum
L. M. Q. P.

———

ON TOMBS.

Here lyeth the Body of
GILES COOK, of this Parifh,
Yeoman, who died the 30 of
Sept. 1723, aged 60 Years.

In Memory of
MARY, the Wife of GILES COOK, of
this Parifh, Yeoman,
who departed this Life
January the 14th, 1740,
aged 49 Years.

WILLIAM their Son died Sept. 21,
1763, aged 48 Years.

In Memory of
GEORGE SILLY, of this Parifh,
Yeoman, who died Dec. 10, 1750,
aged 46 Years.

Alfo ELIZABETH his Wife died
Nov. the 15, 1766, aged 52.

Alfo five of their Children:

GEORGE died April 5, 1773,
aged 40.

RICHARD died October 28, 1766,
aged 31.

GILES died April 28, 1764,
aged 24.

EDWARD died Sept. 29, 1766,
aged 18.

ANNE died Sept. 15, 1747.

———

In Memory of
WILLIAM JELFE, of this Parifh,
Yeoman,
who departed this Life
Nov. 19, 1771, aged 93.

———

In Memory of
RICHARD SPILLMAN, of the City
of Gloucefter,
who departed this Life
January the 10th, 1768,
aged 63 Years.

Alfo
JOYCE, the beloved Wife of
RICHARD SPILLMAN,
who departed this Life
Sept. 25, 1779, aged 74.

In Memory of
JOHN MARTIN, of this Parifh,
Yeoman,
who departed this Life
January 2, 1738, aged 48 Years.

Alfo in Memory of MARY,
the Wife of JOHN MARTIN,
of this Place, Yeoman,
who departed this Life
November the 13th, 1766,
aged 77 Years.

———

In Memory of
ANNE, the Wife of
BENJAMIN VALLENDER,
of this Parifh, Yeoman,
who departed this Life
Oct. 24, 1757, aged 58.

Here lyeth the Body of
BEMJAMIN VALLENDER,
of this Parifh, Yeoman,
who departed this Life
May the 4th, 1775,
aged 77 Years.

———

Here lyeth the Body of
THOMAS ROOKE, fen.
of this Parifh, Gent.
who was buried the 13th of October,
the Year of our Lord 1684, aged 28.

And alfo the Body of JANE ROOKE
his Relict, who died April 6, 1729,
in the 76th Year of her Age.

ON HEAD STONES.

	Died	Aged
Sarah, Wife of Thomas White	22 May, 1787	38
Anne, Daughter of Samuel Haines, Wife of George Collings, of Stourbridge	9 June, 1789	22
Richard Howell	1 Nov. 1762	70
Betty his Wife	16 Aug. 1775	82
Sarah their Daughter	20 Apr. 1750	27
Anne, Wife of William Allard	24 Jan. 1702	26
Lawrence Allin	17 July, 1692	—
William Littel	17 May, 1702	—

	Died	Aged
John Little	21 Sept. 1666	—
Anne his Wife	— Feb. 1680	—
Richard Wintle	13 Nov. 1683	—
John Bubb	18 Dec. 1713	50
Jane, Wife of Thomas Gough	4 Mar. 1760	33
Richard Holland	17 Mar. 1715	60
Charles Holland	15 Sept. 1750	59
Mary, Daughter of Benjamin and Ann Vallender	26 Oct. 1775	45
Thomas Gardiner	21 June, 1752	69

7

ON

O N   H E A D - S T O N E S.

	Died	Aged
Jane, Wife of William Clark	31 Dec. 1754	74
Mary their Daughter	3 Apr. 1757	56
Hannah, Wife of Thomas Whitmore	22 Feb. 1754	80
Chriftian, Wife of Jófeph Whitmore	11 Mar. 1757	—
James Bifhop	24 June, 1753	57
Armel Miles Felfteed	1 July, 1759	21
Jofeph Randal	15 May, 1760	24
Joan, Wife of James Evans	4 Sept. 1701	79
John, Son of John Adderton	5 Feb. 1760	22
Deborah, Wife of George Finch	7 June, 1731	40
Nathaniel Hawkins	24 June, 1750	28
William Lea	8 July, 1756	64
Thomas Rogers	14 Dec. 1775	91
John Wingate	9 Apr. 1785	70
John Edwards	27 Nov. 1720	74
Richard Young	1 Aug. 1726	33
Edward Stock	7 Oct. 1738	59
John, Son of John Roan	23 Oct. 1728	30
Edward Roan	14 Apr 1765	52
Elizabeth his Wife	1 Nov. 1766	49
Giles Roan	20 Jan. 1770	63
Giles Roan	30 Mar. 1784	39
Ann, Wife of Giles Roan	16 Nov. 1777	68

	Died	Aged
Efther, Wife of Thomas Vallender	9 Sept. 1776	38
Elizabeth, Wife of William Holfey	26 Apr. 1765	54
Sarah, Wife of Thomas Longe	8 Aug. 1705	—
Thomas Wilkins	9 June, 1753	39
Mary his Wife	30 Dec. 1749	35
Elizabeth, Wife of John Wilkins	22 Jan. 1676	—
Anne, Wife of Thomas Wilkins	27 Feb. 1783	22
Mary, Wife of Thomas Woodcock	23 Dec. 1765	65
John Etheridge	29 Apr. 1758	54
Elizabeth his Daughter	27 June, 1755	23
William Fletcher	26 Jan. 1726	85
William Fletcher	10 Jan. 1753	65
Thomas, Son of Thomas and Mary Coucher	6 Apr. 1713	27
Charles, Son of John and Margaret Clarke	3 June, 1697	—
Ann, Wife of Thomas Gardiner	22 Mar. 1769	79
Richard Silley	28 May, 1762	62
Mary his Wife	1 Nov. 1774	69
Richard their Son	6 Nov. 1759	20
Gyles Silley	15 July, 1693	—
Alice Silley	19 Apr. 1695	—
Elizabeth, Wife of Edward Stock	28 Dec. 1737	49

CLXXIII. MEYSEY

CLXXIII. MEYSEY HAMPTON.

THIS is one of thofe Parifhes which, in the Courfe of Topographical Refearches, furnifhes but little Matter for curious Inveftigation.

It lies in the Hundred of *Crowthorne* and *Minety*; is diftant fix Miles Weft from *Lechelade*, fix in the oppofite Direction from *Cirencefter*, and twenty-three South-Eaft from GLOUGESTER.—The River *Thames* bounds it on the South, and the Road from *Cirencefter* to *London* paffes within a fhort Diftance of the Village.

About 1800 Acres are included in the Terrier, of a Soil varying from Stone-brafh to Clay ; and the Portion of Arable exceeds that of Pafture.

The Church is a fmall Fabric, dedicated to St. MARY, and confifts of a Nave and Tranfept, with a low embattled Tower. The Window in the Chancel is of curious Architecture, of the *Norman* Style, ornamented with the Nail-head Moulding ; and on painted glafs are the Arms of DE CLARE, Earl of *Gloucefter* and *Hertford*.

The Benefice is a Rectory in the Deanery of *Fairford*. In 1573 (15th of ELIZ.), Livery of the Advowfon was granted to GILES BRIDGES, Lord *Chandos*.

In the Reign of HEN. III. the Manor was held of the Honour of *Gloucefter*, and the Parifh is now within the Jurifdiction of that Court. In the fame Reign it paffed to the Family of MEYSEY, from whom the Prenomen of this Place was taken, the Manor being vefted in that Family till the Year 1329, when NICHOLAS DE ST. MAUR, who married ELIANOR, only Daughter and Heirefs of JOHN DE MEYSEY, died feifed of it. The SEYMOURS held it till 1409, the 10th of HEN. IV. when it paffed, by the Marriage of ALICE, only Daughter and Heirefs of Sir RICHARD SEYMOUR, to WILLIAM Lord ZOUCHE, whofe Daughter married WILLIAM SANDERS, who had Livery of this Manor, 26th of HEN. VIII. and levied a Fine thereof to EDMOND Lord CHANDOS. In 1608, Sir JOHN HUNGERFORD occurs as Lord of the Manor; and, at a fubfequent Period, Mr. BARKER, of *Fairford*, conveyed the Manor of *Alderley* to Sir MATTHEW HALE, in exchange for the Manor of *Meyfey Hampton* *.

The prefent Lord of the Manor is RAYMOND BARKER, Efq. Other principal Eftates in this Parifh are held by ESTCOURT CRESSWELL, Efq. and the Families of JENNER, BEDWELL, and FORSHEW.

This Parifh comprifes the extenfive Hamlet of *Marfton*, which lies in the County of *Wilts*, and is a feparate Manor. It has a fmall, neat Chapel, of which the Rector of *Meyfey Hampton* is Patron ; the Stipend has been augmented by Queen ANNE's Bounty. It was confecrated by MARTIN Lord Bifhop of *Gloucefter*, 25th of July, 1742.

1739	Clement Headington, A. B.	Licenfed	Bifhop of Gloucefter.
1782	Charles Coxwell, A. M.	Licenfed	Mr. Camplin, B. D. Rector of Meyfey Hampton.

BENEFACTIONS.

Three Tenements given to the Church.

RICHARD SAMWAIES, B. D. in 1650 gave ten Pounds, one Moiety to this Parifh for ever, and the other Moiety to the Village of *Marfton*. The Intereft to be divided amongft the Poor annually.

John Beale, D. D. gave, in 1712, the Intereft of five Pounds annually to the Poor of this Parifh for ever.

ANNE FORSHEW, Widow, gave to the Poor, in 1706, the Intereft of five Pounds for ever.

THOMAS GEGG, Gent. in 1715, gave five Pounds, the Intereft to be annually applied to the Relief of the Poor.

JOHN FORSHEW, Gent. gave to the Poor of *Meyfey Hampton*, in 1721, the Intereft of five Pounds annually for ever.

JOHN KIRCHEVALL, D. D. gave, in 1725, fixty Pounds to each Town, the Intereft of which to be applied to put poor Children Apprentice, or pay for their fchooling.

JOHN JENNER, Gent. in 1576, gave twenty Pounds, the Intereft thereof to be applied to the Relief of the Poor of this Place.

* MSS. Snell.

2

INCUMBENTS.

INCUMBENTS.	PATRONS.	INCUMBENTS.	PATRONS.
—— John Strange,	——————	1669 Henry Fowler,	——————
1570 Walter Turbat,	Edmund Lord Chandos.	—— Wil. Fulman‡,MA.	——————
1573 John Brooks,	Giles Lord Chandos.	1697 John Beale, D. D.	C. C. C. Oxon.
1584 John Aiftell,	Anthony Bridges, Efq.	1712 Jn.Kirchevall§, DD.	The fame.
1600 Walter Brickes,	William Lord Chandos.	1725 John Long, B. D.	The fame.
1605 Sebaftian Benefield*, M.A.	King James.	1749 Jn.Thompfon, B.D.	The fame.
1630 Hen. Jackfon, B.D.	——————	1773 Wil.Camplin, B.D.	The fame.
1662 R.Samwaies†, B.D.	——————	1793 George Clarke, B.D.	The fame.

PRESENT LORD OF THE MANOR.

JOHN RAYMOND BARKER, Efq.

The Perfons fummoned from this Place by the Heralds, in 1682 and 1683, were

—————— Trotman and William Fulman, Clerks.

At the Election in 1776 Seventeen Freeholders polled from this Parifh.

The firft Date of the Regifter is in 1570.

ANNUAL ACCOUNT OF MARRIAGES, BIRTHS, AND BURIALS, IN THIS PARISH.

A. D.	Mar.	Bir.	Bur.	A.D.	Mar.	Bir.	Bur.	A.D.	Mar.	Bir.	Bur.	A.D.	Mar.	Bir.	Bur.
1781	8	3	6	1786	3	8	5	1791				1796			
1782	1	14	6	1787	3	8	7	1792				1797			
1783	8	7	5	1788	5	9	3	1793				1798			
1784	3	7	11	1789	2	8	4	1794				1799			
1785	3	7	10	1790	2	13	5	1795				1800			

INSCRIPTIONS IN THE CHURCH.

IN THE CHANCEL.

ON A MONUMENT WITH THE EFFIGIES OF A MAN, TWO WIVES, NINE SONS, AND THREE DAUGHTERS.

Arms; on feveral Efcocheons ; 1. Quarterly, 1ft and 4th Argent, a Bend chequy Or and Gules, for VAULX; 2d and 3d, Sable, a Pelican Argent, vulned proper.

2. Quarterly, 1ft, Sable, 3 Bendlets engrail'd Argent, a Canton Or, for HORTON; 2d, Argent, a Bend Sable, with a File of three Points, ; 3d, a Fefs chequy Or and Sable, ; 4th, Argent, a Lion rampant Sable,

3. , three covered Cups, for JENNER.

4. VAULX; — impaling, chequy lozengy Argent and Vert, on a Bend Gules, Heads erafed.

5. VAULX ;—impaling, Sable, three Bendlets engrailed, Argent, a Canton Or.

Here refteth the Body of EDITHA JENNER, who, the 18 Day of Auguft, 1617, being called to the Joys of a better Worlde, lefte before her ix Sonnes and III Daughters, all of them the Pledges of that conjugall Love that was between herfelfe and her furviving hufband, who was

That famous Practitioner in Phyfick and Chirurgery JAMES VAULX, Efquer, who deceafed March 17, 1626, to the general Lofle of the whole Countrey, the private Griefe of all his Friends, more particularly of his forrowful then wife, who was

PHILIPE HORTON, Daughter to WILLIAM HORTON, of Staunton, in the County of Worcefter, Efq. who in Grief and Heavinefs, parting with her deareft Confort, is left behind to cherifh the Hopes of three Sonnes, now living, one Daughter being called to Heaven before her Father.

——————

ON A MARBLE MONUMENT.

Sacred to the Memory of JOHN JENNER, of Marfton Mefey, Wilts, whofe Remains reft underneath near thofe of his Father and Mother, of the fame Place. He died on the 2 Day of Oct. 1787, in the 67th Year of his age. MARY JENNER erected this humble Monument in honour of her departed Father, 1790.

ON FLAT STONES.

Here refteth the Body of JACOB, the Son of JOHN and MARY JENNER, who departed this Life September the 27, Anno Domini 1689.

Here lyeth the Body of WILLIAM, the Son of JOHN and MARY JENNER, of Marfton, who was buried Sept. the 1ft, 1692.

Here lyeth the Body of JOHN JENNER, of Marfton, who departed this Life Aug. 17, A. D. 1699. This is put in Memory likewife of ANNE, the Daughter of JOHN JENNER, of Marfton, and MARY his Wife, who was buried March 18, 1695-6.

ELIZABETH, the Daughter of JOHN JENNER, of Marfton, and MARY his Wife, who was buried June 28, 1696.

MARY, the Wife of JOHN JENNER, of Marfton, died March the 5th, 1752-3.

---

* He was born at *Preftbury*, in this County, was fourteen Years Margaret Profeffor in the Univerfity of *Oxford*, a Man of great learning, and publifhed feveral Things on religious Subjects, befides upwards of fixty Sermons. He was buried in the Chancel of this Church. Wood's Ath. Ox. p. 549.
† Wood's Ath. Ox. Vol. II. 310.
‡ Walker's Sufferings of the Clergy.
§ Wood's Ath. Oxon. Vol. II. p. 624.
‖ Ibid. Vol. II. p. 308.

VOL. II.   H h h   1 N

IN MEMORY OF
WILLIAM, SON OF
JOHN AND MARY
JENNER, OF MARSTON,
WHO DIED MAY THE
14, 1738, AGED 39.

ALSO OF
CATHERINE HIS WIFE,
WHO DIED JAN. 13,
1764, AGED 61 YEARS.

HERE LYETH THE BODY
OF THE REVEREND
DOCTOR JOHN
KERCHEVAL, RECTOR
OF MEYSEY HAMPTON,
WHO WAS BURIED
SEPT. 13, 1725.

IN THE NORTH TRANSEPT,

On a Monument:

Arms; a Griffin fegreant.

This Monument is erected in
Memory of HENRY MORGAN, of
South Hill, Gent. Son of HENRY
and ELIZABETH MORGAN, late of
Brewen Grange, in the County
of Oxford; a loving and beloved

Child, who died at London, Aug. 7,
Anno Domini 1754, in the
19 Year of his Age.

In Memory of ELIZABETH, the Wife
of the late HENRY MORGAN,
and Mother to the abovefaid
HENRY MORGAN. She died May
the 11, 1766, aged 72 Years.

Arms; per Saltire Chequy & Ermine.

Near this Place
are interred the
Bodies of JOHN BEDWELL, Gent.
and ANNE his Wife; he died
January the 8th, 1766, aged 78.
She died May 15, 1753, aged 48.

Alfo
ANNE, the Daughter of
FRANCIS and MARY BEDWELL,
who died April 19, 1766,
aged 11 Weeks.

IN THE SOUTH TRANSEPT
ON FLAT STONES.

HERE LYETH THE BODY OF
SARAH THE WIFE OF MR.
JOHN STRANGE, WHO DEPARTED
THIS LIFE THE 8 OF AUGUST,
IN THE YEARE OF OUR LORD
1690.

Here lyeth the Body
of WILLIAM BICK, of
Marfton, who was buried
May the 1ft, 1698.

On a Monument:

Arms; a Fefs between two Greyhounds collar'd, impaling a Bend in
chief, a Chevron in bafe.

THESE STONES ERECTED FOR
THE MEMORIE OF
MARGARET GUISWALD,
WHO DIED JUNE 23, 1625.

IN THE NAVE.

Flat Stone.

Here lyeth the Body of
EDWARD ARCHER,
of Marfton, who was buried
April the 17th 1696.

Alfo
JOANE, Wife of EDWARD
ARCHER, buried July 27,
1699.

I N   T H E   C H U R C H - Y A R D.

ON MONUMENTS AGAINST
THE CHURCH.

In Memory of
ANNE LARGE, who
died May the 22, 1759,
aged 74 Years.

Near
this Place lyeth the
Bodys of THOMAS JOULINS, and MARY
his Wife; THOMAS JOULINS,
aged 77,
and MARY his Wife,
aged 86.

In Memory of
JOHN, the Son of
WILLIAM and SUSANNAH JENNER,
who was buried October
22, 1718, aged 2 Years and
9 Months.

MARGARET, their Daughter,
was buried July 18, 1757,
aged 6 Years.

Near this Place
lieth interred the Body
of ROBERT JENNER,
who departed this Life
April 5, 1777, aged 77 Years.

In Memory of
ANN, the Wife of
WALTER PRICE, who died
September the 8th, 1764,
aged 52 Years.

ON TOMBS.

Here lyeth the Body of
THOMAS JENNER,
who departed this Life
Auguft 28, 1684.

In Memory of THOMAS
JENNER, of Marfton, Gent.
who died March 7, 1711,
aged 74 Years.

Alfo of ANNE,
his Wife, fhe died
A. D. 1716.

Alfo in Memory of
JOHN their Son, who departed
this Life May the 21, 1748,
aged 78 Years.

In Memory of ELEANOR, the Wife
of JOHN JENNER, of Marfh-Hill,
Sifter to the Rev. Mr. JAMES BRADLEY,
Aftronomy Profeffor in the Univerfity
of Oxford. F. R. S.
She was buried underneath this Tomb
March the 14th, 1715, aged 36 Years.

In Memory of MARTHA, fecond Wife of
JOHN JENNER, of Marfh-Hill, fen.
who died June the 29, 1736,
aged 3 Years.

In Memory of JOHN JENNER,
of Marfh-Hill, fen who
died March 20, 1750,
aged 72 Years.

In Memory of MARGARET, the
Wife of JOHN JENNER, fen.
who died Auguft the 23, 1729,
aged 65 Years.

In Memory of ELIZABETH,
the Wife of JOHN JENNER, who
died June 11, 1737, aged 58.

In Memory of
JOHN, Son of ROBERT and ANNE
JENNER, who died October, 25, 1773,
aged 29 Years.

In Memory of JOHN JENNER,
who died September the 19th, 1756,
aged 36 Years.

In Memory of JOHN, the Son
of JOHN and JANE JENNER: he
died September 16, 1784,
aged 15 Years.

This Tomb is erected in Memory of
WILLIAM JENNER,
of Marfton, in this Parifh,
who died May the 18, 1765, aged 70.

In Memory of SUSHNNAH JENNER, fen.
who died April 21, 1754, aged 84.

Alfo ELEANOR, the Daughter of
WILLIAM and ELEANOR JENNER,
died June 21, 1750, aged 53 Years.

In Memory of ELEANOR, the Wife of
WILLIAM JENNER, fen who died
June 11, 1726, aged 56 Years.

CATHARINE, Daughter of WILLIAM
and ELIZABETH JENNER,
lieth near this Place.

In Memory of JAMES, the Son of JOHN
and ELEANOR JENNER, who died Feb.
the 12, 1775, aged 65 Years.

In

In Memory of ELIZABETH, Wife of JOHN JENNER, and Daughter of HENRY and ELIZABETH HANCOX. She died March 11, 1780, aged 50 Years.

In Memory of the Daughter of CHRISTOPHER and JANE KING, of Marfton Mezey, fhe died Aug. 17, 1772, aged 69 Years.

In Memory of JANE, the Wife of CHRISTOPHER KING. She died May the 13, 1740, aged 77.

In Memory of MARY, the Wife of WILLIAM COULING, and Daughter of WILLIAM and ELEANOR JENNER, who died March the 27, 1778, aged 77.

In Memory of DOROTHY, the Wife of STEPHEN BARLY, who died November the 9th, 1752, aged 85 Years.

In Memory of ANNE, Daughter of WILLIAM and ELEANOR, and ELEANOR JENNER, who died Oct. the 3d, 1759, aged 53 Years.

In Memory of THOMAS, the Son of JOHN and BEATA JENNER, who died October 8, 1770, aged 55 Years.

In Memory of Beata, the Wife of JOHN JENNER, of Marfton, fen. who died Dec. 30, 1743, aged 64 Years.

In Memory of JOHN JENNER, of Water Eaton, Son of JOHN and BEATA JENNER, of Marfton, who died Nov. 24, 1763, aged 46.

Alfo ELIZABETH, the Wife of JOHN JENNER, Daughter of THOMAS and JANE MILLER, of this Place, who died Sept. 28, 1791, aged 76 Years.

In Memory of ELIZABETH and MARY, Daughters of JOHN and BEATA JENNER. ELIZABETH died March 7, 1781, aged 74. MARY died Auguft 6, 1786, aged 77.

HEARE LYETH THE BODY OF THOMAS JACOVETTS, DECEASED OCTOBER THE 18, ANNO DOMINI 1671.

In Memory of ELIZABETH, the Wife of HENRY HANCOX, and Daughter of CHRISTOPHER and JANE KING. She died June 23, 1777, aged 85.

In Memory of HENRY HANCOX, of Frampton Mancell, he died Dec. 10, 1759, aged 68.

In Memory of JOHN KING, of Marfton, who died June the 8, 1782, aged 75 Years.

In Memory of MARY, the Daughter of THOMAS and JANE MILLER, who died March 25, 1743, aged 30 Years.

In Memory of THOMAS MILLER, who died March 18, 1722, aged 33.

Alfo JANE, the Wife of THOMAS MILLER, who died January 31, 1765, aged 75 Years.

In Memory of JOHN MILLER, who died March 13, 1779, aged 60 Years.

Here lyeth the Body of MARTHA, the Wife of WILLIAM SEWELL. She died May 9, 1775, aged 38.

In Memory of ALBERT SAVARY, who died Nov. 5, 1729, aged 80.

In Memory of ELIZABETH, the Daughter of ALBERT and MARY SAVAGE, who died May the 4th, 1730, aged 25 Years.

In Memory of JOHN FORSHEW, fen. who died Jan. 14, 1768, aged 55 Years.

Alfo of JANE his Wife. She died Sept. 13, 1785, aged 83 Years.

In Memory of JANE, the Daughter of JOHN and JANE FORSHEW, who died Sept. 29, 1776, aged 42 Years.

In Memory of ANNE, Daughter of JOHN and JANE FORSHEW, who departed this Life December the 13th, 1781, aged 42 Years.

Here lies the Remains of JOHN HARRIS, he died Nov. 29, 1785, aged 86 Years.

Alfo of MARY his Wife. She died Sept 25, 1785, aged 75 Years.

ON HEAD-STONES.

	Died	Aged		Died	Aged
John Day	8 Aug. 1738	63	John Forfhew	24 May, 1775	74
Thomas Lewis	1 Feb. 1743	34	Elizabeth his Wife	24 Apr. 1780	83
Thomas Lewis	2 Aug. 1760	60	Edward Forfhew	24 July, 1770	60
Jane, Wife of John Tombs	28 Mar. 1766	47	William Booker	24 Oct. 1764	52
Edward Tombs	24 Jan. 1746	69	William, Son of John Davis	12 Aug. 1699	—
Mary his Wife	16 Nov. 1738	50	Henry Curtis	2 Apr. 1694	—
Edward their Son	27 Sept. 1750	36	Thomas Curtis	19 Oct. 1738	64
Thomas Tombs	31 Jan. 1757	42	Elizabeth his Wife	14 Mar. 1734	70
Hannah Sanders	12 Feb. 1771	16	John Jenner	5 Dec. 1769	65
John Betterton	7 Mar. 1764	87	Robert Jenner of Cirencefter	26 May, 1786	58
Sarah his Wife	4 Dec. 1766	75	Robert Rodborn	1 May, 1732	85
Ann, Wife of Edward Betterton	4 Oct. 1764	51	Katharine his Wife	3 June, 1684	29
John Betterton	26 May, 1780	72	Robert Rodborn	28 Jan. 1760	75
Thomas Bridges	24 Nov. 1756	51	Katharine his Wife	28 Dec. 1758	52
Richard Bridges	7 Nov. 1744	66	Robert their Son	10 Mar. 1759	23
Elizabeth his Wife	6 Feb. 1749	66	Elizabeth, Wife of John Rodbarn	23 May, 1777	32
Mary, Wife of Thomas Bridges	14 Sept. 1784	77	William Page	19 Nov. 1768	74
Walter Price	29 Oct. 1739	77	Mary his Wife	23 Jan. 1765	62
Catharine his Wife	25 Apr. 1717	59	Charles Arkell	16 Sept. 1732	—
William, Son of Wil. and Ann Price	4 June, 1733	—	Roger Fletcher	24 Mar. 1768	65
William Hatherill	10 Jan. 1728	74	Jane his Wife	30 Sept. 1774	70
Thomas Snowfell	17 Jan. 1730	62	Harry Fletcher	4 May, 1786	75
Anne his Wife	15 Jan. 1730	52	Anne his Wife	23 Apr. 1759	51
Chriftopher King	9 Jan. 1734	74	Robert Miller	25 Aug. 1721	70
Chriftopher King	10 June, 1755	59	Alice his Wife	17 Mar. 1749	87
Anthony King	8 June, 1759	68	Daniel their Son	4 Oct. 1730	45
Samuel Weake	10 Jan. 1766	74	Thomas Miller	8 Apr. 1763	75
Hannah his Wife	21 Feb. 1731	30	Sarah his Wife	3 Nov. 1759	61
Charles Heris	27 May, 1724	32	Daniel their Son	19 Feb. 1765	33
Elizabeth Harris	10 July, 1714	28	Mary their Daughter	10 Feb. 1778	52
Elizabeth, Wife of Richard Harris	11 July, 1720	62	John Soudby	22 Sept. 1733	73
Richard Harris	2 Mar. 1758	66	Elizabeth his Wife	13 Sept. 1729	67
Mary, Wife of Richard Harris	28 Mar. 1779	38	John Soudly	29 Nov. 1765	69
John Forfhew	4 Oct. 1720	—	Samuel Robins	2 Feb. 1722	31
Anne his Wife	30 Oct. 1720	—	Henry Miles	18 Dec. 17—	65
Edward Forfhew	15 May, 1748	75	Ann his Wife	19 Feb. 1745	77
Sarah his Wife	25 Sept. 1723	—	Dorothy, Wife of Stephen Barly	9 Nov. 1752	85
Alice, Wife of Robert Forfhew	28 Aug. 1742	78			

CLXXIV. MICKLETON;

 # M I C K L E T O N;

CALLED by the *Saxons MYCCLANTUNE*, as being at that Time more confiderable than thofe of the neighbouring Tuner or Villages in its Neighbourhood, and in *Domefday* Book ftyled *Muceltude*, lies in the upper Divifion of *Kiftefgate* Hundred, three Miles North from *Campden*, and thirty-one North from Gloucester.

The Village is fituate in a rich Vale, and comprifes, by Computation, nearly 4000 Acres of Pafture Land, with a very fmall Exception of Arable, and of a Soil chiefly Clay.

The Church, dedicated to *St. Lawrence*, is a handfome Structure, confifting of a fpacious Nave and two Aifles, with a Spire of elegant Proportions.

On painted Glafs in the Eaft Window of the North Aifle, are the following *Saxon* Characters, written in two Compartments :

EADLARUS REX
DEDIT
MYLLANTUNE
BRIÐNOTO DULI
ET ILLE
ÆÐELMARO DULI
ULTIMO
LOMMISIT DONO
QUI
POSTEA EAM
MONASTERIO DE
ELNESÞAM.

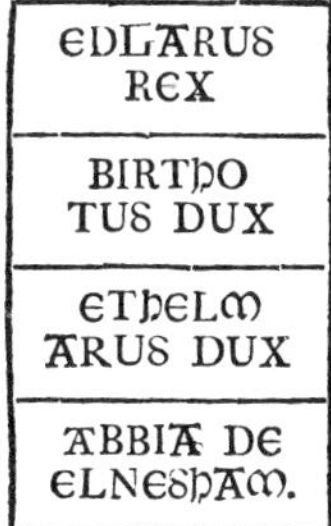

EDLARUS
REX

BIRTÞO
TUS DUX

ETÞELM
ARUS DUX

ABBIA DE
ELNESÞAM.

And in the fame Window are feveral Efcocheons with the Arms of Graves impaling thofe of Swan and Bates; alfo *France* and *England* quarterly.

In the Chancel is exhibited on painted Glafs, of beautiful Colours, an Efcocheon, with the Arms of Fisher varioufly quartered.

The Living is vicarial; the impropriate Tythes belonged to the Abbey of *Eynfham* till the Diffolution.

The Rectory was granted to Roger Mannors, Efq. 18 Eliz.   is the prefent Impropriator. Other Tythes in this Parifh, and in the Tything of *Hedecote*, belonged to the Abbey of *Winchcombe*, and were granted to Sir Thomas Seymour, 1 Edw. VI.

In the Reign of King Edgar the Manor was in the Crown. The Abbey of *Eynfham* held it for upwards of 500 Years; but, at the Diffolution, it was re-annexed to the Crown, where it continued till the 33d Year of Elizabeth's Reign, who granted it by Letters Patent under the Great Seal of *England* to Richard Lukenore, Richard Brown, Efqrs. and John Lampton, Gent. to them and their Heirs in Fee, to hold the fame *in capite* by Knight's Service; but referved to herfelf, her Heirs and Succeffors, the Right of Patronage to the Vicarage. In 36 Eliz. the Manor was fold to Edward Grevill, of *Milcote*, in the County of *Warwick*, Efq. from whom it paffed by Sale to the Family of Fisher, Defcendants from the antient Family of the Fishers, of *Fifherwicke upon Trent*, in the County of *Stafford*. In the Year 1612, the two Fields, called the Upper Field and Lower Field, were inclofed; before which Time many of the Tenants were Copyholders, but fince they are all Freeholders.

In 1656, the Rectory or Parfonage Impropriate was fold, together with Part of the Lands, to Mr. John Hervey, of *London*, Merchant; and fhortly afterwards the Manor or Lordfhip, and the Demefne

3   Lands

Lands and Manor-houfe were purchafed by RICHARD GRAVES *, of *Lincoln's Inn*, Efq. and conveyed to him and his Son JOHN GRAVES, and their Heirs, in Fee, by an Indenture, bearing Date the 22d of April, 1656; but JOHN dying before his Father, it defcended to SAMUEL the next Son and Heir, who fucceeded his Father in this Manor in the Year 1669; and at his Death it devolved to RICHARD GRAVES †, Efq. Son of the above SAMUEL, in whofe Defcendants it has been vefted to the prefent Poffeffor WALWYN GRAVES, Efq who occupies the Manor-houfe.

The Parifh comprifes two Hamlets, *Hidecote,* or *Hidcote,* and *Clopton,* which are diftinct Manors.

When *Domefday* was compiled, Lands in the Tything of *Hedecote* were held by the Abbey of *Winchcombe,* and at the Diffolution were granted to JOHN WYLEY and JOHN SCUDAMORE, Efqrs. The Manor afterwards paffed to the Family of KEYTE, and is now held by Mr. WILLIAM FREEMAN. WILLIAM GOIZENBODED, at the general Survey, held the Manor of the Hamlet of *Clopton,* from whom it paffed to the Priory of *Bonhommes,* at *Edington, Wilts,* and was granted to MICHAEL ASHFIELD, 32 HEN. VIII. It was afterwards vefted in the feveral Families of OVERBURY, ROWNEY, and NOEL, from whom it paffed to Lord FORTESCUE, who is the prefent Lord.

Other Eftates are held in this Parifh by Lord COVENTRY, Lord WENTWORTH, and the Families of HOLLAND, MILLER, ROBERTS, SMITH, CORBET, GROVES, and HIRON.

In this Parifh a Court Baron and a Court Leet is held; the latter by a fpecial Grant from the Crown. King JAMES the Firft, not long after he had knighted Sir EDWARD FISHER, granted him, by Letters Patent, the Perpetuity of holding a Leet within the Manor, Village, and Hamlets of *Mickleton* and Precincts of the fame.

The Arms of the PORTERS, formerly Inhabitants of this Place, and Benefactors to the Parifh, were, Sable, three Bells Argent; Creft, a Portcullis Or.

Meen Hill, the Beauties of which are defcribed by the Poet DRAYTON, and upon which are Veftiges of an Encampment, lies partly in this Parifh, and partly in *Queinton.*

B E N E F A C T I O N S.

RICHARD PORTER, Gent. gave by Will, in 1513, a Meffuage and a Yard Land in *Mickleton,* and a Clofe in *Overton,* for ever, for repairing of *Mickleton* Church, and other charitable Ufes; the annual Produce of which is 78*l.*

In 1612, the Landowners fet out a Part of the Inclofure, amounting to 33 Acres, for the Poor of this Parifh for ever; the yearly Income of which is 44*l.*

THOMAS PERKS gave, by Will, in 1623, a Rent Charge of 1*l.* a Year to the Poor of *Mickleton* for ever.

DOROTHY SWAN, by Will, dated in 1678, gave a Rent Charge on TYMS's Clofe in *Mickleton* of 2*l.* a Year for ever, to be applied in Manner following: 10*s.* for a Sermon on Chriftmas Day in the Afternoon; 10*s.* each Day in Bread to the Poor who fhall attend Divine Service on Chriftmas Day, Eafter Monday, and Whit Monday.

* The above RICHARD GRAVES was for many Years one of the Benchers of *Lincoln's Inn,* and at length Reader of that Society 1669. There is an Engraving of him by VERTUE, whereon he is faid to be Clerk of the Peace and Receiver General of the County of *Middlefex.* At firft, he was a great Friend of OLIVER CROMWELL, but afterwards they differed in Opinion, and had a perfonal Quarrel. Vide GRANGER's Biog. Hift. vol. III. p. 374.

He was feized in Fee of the Manors of *Mickleton, Afton,* and *Wefton Subedge,* in this County, *Powden,* in the County of *Worcefter, Portfwede,* in the County of *Southampton,* and the Royalty of the Hundred of *Kiftefgate,* in the County of *Gloucefter.*

SAMUEL GRAVES, fourth Son and Heir of RICHARD, fucceeded his Father in the above Manors and Eftates in the Year 1669, and was Father to

† RICHARD GRAVES, Efq. a Gentleman eminent for his literary Abilities; particularly for his Knowledge of Hiftory, Antiquities, and Heraldry. His Portrait is engraved by VERTUE. Vide GRANGER's Biog. Hift. vol. III. p. 374, 8vo edit. The following Account is given of him by BALLARD in one of his Manufcript Letters, preferved in the Bodleian Library at *Oxford:*

" He was a Gentleman endued with all thofe excellent Qualifications which might entitle him great and good. He was a com-
" plete Mafter of the *Greek, Latin,* and *Saxon* Tongues; was admirably well read and fkilled in the *Roman* and *Britifh* Antiqui-
" ties; and was a moft curious Hiftorian, Antiquary, and Medalift. He died (to the great Grief of all true Lovers of Anti-
" quity, as well as of thofe that knew him) upon *Wednefday,* about feven o'Clock in the Morning, being the 17th of *September,*
" an. 1729, in the 53d Year of his Age. He had made vaft Collections towards the Hiftory and Antiquities of thofe Places,
" where the feveral Parts of his Eftate lay; which he had collected with very great Pains and Expence from *Doomfday* Book, from
" Manufcripts and Records in the *Tower,* and divers other Places, which he defigned by way of Annals, in Imitation of KEN-
" NET's Parochial Antiquities; and juft before his Death had defigned to have methodized and compiled them in three Volumes,
" Folio. After his Death thofe Papers were purchafed by JAMES WEST, Efq. a Gentleman of very extraordinary Accomplifh-
" ments, and who, for his excellent Knowledge in the Hiftory and Antiquities of our Nation, may juftly be ftyled the Prince of
" our *Englifh* Antiquaries. His Collection of Medals (which were about 500, among which were many very valuable Pieces) con-
" fifted chiefly of *Greek* and *Roman* Coins; a great Part of which I collected for him from *Worcefter, Gloucefter, Cirencefter, Marl-*
" *borough, Devizes,* and feveral other Places; all which Coins were purchafed (after his Death) by ROGER GALE, Efq. (an intimate
" Acquaintance of Mr. GRAVES's) who is a great Mafter of thofe Studies, and many other ufeful Parts of Learning."

The above Papers, among other valuable Manufcripts, at the Deceafe of JAMES WEST, Efq. in 1773, were fold to WILLIAM PETTY Earl of SHELBURNE.

The Latin Infcription to RICHARD GRAVES was written by the above JAMES WEST, Efq. Prefident of the Royal Society.

The Portrait of MORGAN GRAVES, Efq. is done in Mezzotinto by VALENTINE GREEN; and an elegant Marble Monument is erected in the fame Aifle with his Father's, with an Englifh Infcription, written by his eldeft Son and Heir WALWYN GRAVES, Efq.

Incumbents.	Patrons.	Incumbents.	Patrons.
—— Thomas Perks,	————.	1593 Francis Wells,	Queen Elizabeth.
—— Thomas Rofe,	————.	1628 Henry Hurft *,	King Charles.
—— John Penn,	————.	1685 Henry Kirkham,	King James.
—— William Sweetman,	————.	1707 George Yardly,	Queen Anne.
1572 Thomas Rotton,	William Steward.	1746 Benjamin Field, B. A.	Lord Chancellor.
—— Chriftopher Perryn	————.	1781 Rich. Morgan Graves, D.D.	The fame.
1587 John Wells,	Queen Elizabeth.		

PRESENT LORDS OF THE MANORS,

Of *Mickleton*,	Of *Hidcote*,	Of *Clopton*,
WALWYN GRAVES, Efq.	WILLIAM FREEMAN, Efq.	Lord FORTESCUE.

The Perfons fummoned from this Parifh by the Heralds, in 1682 and 1683, were

Francis Keyte,
and
Samuel Graves, Efqrs.

Edward Perkes,
John Bonner,
William Rofe, Gents.

At the Election in 1776, Twenty-fix Freeholders polled from this Parifh †.

The firft Date of the Regifter is in 1641.

ANNUAL ACCOUNT OF MARRIAGES, BIRTHS, AND BURIALS, IN THIS PARISH.

A.D.	Mar.	Bir.	Bur.	A.D.	Mar.	Bir.	Bur.	A.D.	Mar.	Bir.	Bur.	A.D.	Mar.	Bir.	Bur.
1781	2	17	11	1786	1	15	11	1791				1796			
1782	1	14	6	1787	4	16	8	1792				1797			
1783	1	12	5	1788	1	10	9	1793				1798			
1784	3	11	4	1789	5	10	10	1794				1799			
1785	1	13	10	1790	3	14	10	1795				1800			

INSCRIPTIONS IN THE CHURCH.

IN THE CHANCEL.

OVER A BLACK MARBLE TOMB:

Arms; on feveral Efcocheons; 1. Quarterly, 1ft, Gules, three demi Lions rampant Or, a Chief of the laft, for FISHER; 2d, Argent, on a Fefs engrailed Azure, three Croffes pattée Or, ; 3d, Azure, three Eagles difplayed Or, ; 4th, Ermine, five Chevronels Gules, on a Canton of the laft, a Lion of England, ; 5th, Barry of ten, Argent and Gules, within a Bordure Azure, charged with ten Martlets Or, ; 6th, Vairé Azure and Argent, a Pale Sable, ; 7th, Gules, three Cufhions Argent, taffeled Or, ; 8th, Barry of ten, Argent and Gules, over all a Lion rampant Sable, ; 9th, Argent, three Horfefhoes Sable, ; 10th, quarterly, 1ft and 4th, Gules, 2d and 3d, Vairé, Vert and Or, over all a Lion rampant Argent, ; 11th, Argent, a Fefs vairé Or and Gules, between three Eagles difplayed of the laft, ; 12th, Paly of fix Argent and Gules, over all a Bend vairè, 2d, FISHER;—impaling, two Bars gemelles Argent, a Bend Sable, on a Chief of the firft, a Caftle triple towered Azure, for

2. FISHER;—impaling, a Chevron between three Cherubs, with 15 other quarterings.
3. FISHER;—impaling, quarterly, on a Bend Argent, three Trefoils proper, on a Canton Or, a Leopard's Face Gules, ; 2d, Or, on a Fefs Sable, three Bee-hives of the firft; 3d, Or, a Fefs between three Bulls' Heads erafed; 4th, Or, an Eagle difplayed Sable.

M. M. S.

Subter aut prope hunc lapidem
reconduntur Heroum vere nobilium
& colendiffimorum exuviæ

EDVARDI FISHER, Armigeri,
qui uxorem duxit Aviciam, filiam
digniffimam digniffimi illius RICHARDI
THORNHILL, de Bromley, in comitatu
Cantiano, Armigeri,
EDVARDI FISHER, militis, cui uxor erat Deo
& hominibus chara Domina MARIA,
filia primogenita eminentiffimi viri, armis
literifque clari,
THOMÆ CHALONERI, militis, auguftiffimo
Principi HENRICO GUBERNATORIS,
Dominorum hujus Manerii, ex prenobili
& antiquiffima ftirpe FISHERORUM,
de Fifherwick, fuper Trentam,
in Comitatu Staffordiæ,
oriundum.
E. F. Armig. H. M. M. T. P. Anno Dom. 1659.

On the Top of the Tomb are four Efcocheons:

1. FISHER, quartering as above. Underneath,
Qui obiit 16 Septemb. 1627.

2. Two Bars gemelles Argent, a Bend Sable, on a Chief of the firft, a Caftle triple towered Azure, for Underneath,
Quæ obiit 8 July, 1604.

3. As the firft. Underneath,
Qui obiit 29 Decemb. 1654.

4. Quarterly, 1ft, a Chevron between three Cherubs; 2d, a Chevron between three Stags Heads cabofhed; 3d, a Lion rampant Azure, with many others. Underneath,
Quæ obiit 8 Novemb. 1642.

---

* WOOD's Athen. vol. II. p. 639.
† Sir ANTHONY KECK, an eminent Lawyer, was born in this Parifh, and was conftituted one of the Lords Commiffioners of the Great Seal of *England* in the Year 1688.
THOMAS WIDDOWES was alfo a Native of this Place. WOOD's Athenæ, vol. II. p. 572.

I

ON

On a neat Marble Urn:

Utreciæ Smith,
Puellæ fimplici, innocuæ,
eleganti,
R. G.
Unâ ætæ memor pueritiæ
Lugens pofuit
MDCCXLIV.

Underneath, on a flat Stone, an Infcription for the fame Perfon, with Arms in a Lozenge, three Greyhounds curfant between ten Croffes patté fitché;—impaling a Fefs between three Fleurs de Lis.

ON FLAT STONES.

Arms; Quarterly, Argent and Gules, in the 2d and 3d Quarters a Fret Or, on a Bend Sable, three Efcallops of the firft, for Spencer;—impaling, Azure, on a Chevron between three Kites' Heads erafed Or, as many Trefoils Gules, for Keyt.

Here lyes the Body of Alice Keyt,
Daughter of Sir William Spencer, of
Yardington, in the County of Oxford,
Baronet, and of Constance his Wife, the
Daughter of Sir Thomas Lucy, of Charlecott,
in the County of Warwick, which faid Alice
was the late Wife of Francis Keyt, of Hithcoat,
Efq. and deceafed the 29 of May, in the Year 1687.

Arms; in a Lozenge, Keyt as before.

Here lyeth the Body of
Mifs Jane Keyt, Daughter of
Mr. Francis Keyt and
Alice his Wife, of Hitcoat,
who deceafed this Life the
30 Day of June, Anno Dom.
1674, ætatis fuæ 28.

Arms; a Chevron Ermine between three Swans,

Here
lyeth the Body of Captain
Richard Swann, who had
made fix Voyages to the Eaft Indies,
and departed this Life the 30
of June, 1676,
ætatis fuæ 59.
He was the Son and Heir of Capt. Rich. Swan,
fome time an Admiral in the Indian Seas
(by Damaris, Daughter and Coheir of Capt.
Andrew Shilling) who being Admiral
of the Englifh, obtained a fignal Victory
over the Portugueze in two Sea-fights
near Jafques in the Gulph of Perfia,
but, receiving a mortal Wound, dyed
fhortly after, and was buried there in 1620.

Arms; on a Bend three Martlets, for Danvers.

Here lyeth the Body of Mrs. Dorothy
Swann, Relict of Captain
Richard Swann, who
died the 15 Day of Jan.
1688,
ætatis fuæ 74.

In Memory of
the Rev. William Smith,
Clerk, late Vicar of Toddington,
and many Years Curate of this
Parifh, who died Feb. 22, A. D. 1768;

And of Utrecia his Wife, who died
November 7, A. D. 1760.

Alfo of Mary and Utrecia
their two Daughters.

Mary died Jan. 23, 1777.

Utrecia died March 5, 1743.

All of whom lie interred
in this Chancel.

Arms; a Crofs engrailed between four Roundlets, each charged with a Pheon.

M. S
Arthuri Fletcher, de Paxford,
in com. Wigorn. Gent.
Qui obiit 25 Feb. An. Dom. 1717,
ætatis fuæ 60.

ON MONUMENTS.

Looking for the bleffed Hope,
near this Place refteth the Body of
the Reverend Mr. Henry Hurst,
Minifter of this Parifh 58 Years.
He flept in the Lord Oct. 25, 1685,
aged 84.

Underneath this Place
lyes the Body of
Richard Richmond, Gent.
who departed this Life Dec.
the 20, Anno Dom. 1723,
aged 56 Years.

Heare lyeth intombed John Bonner,
Sonne of .... Bonner, of Pebworth,
who died the 17 October, 1618.

ON FLAT STONES.

Here lyeth the Body of
Mary Holland, the Wife of
David Hughes Holland, of
Norton, in the Parifh of Wefton
Subedge, Gent. who departed
this Life the vii of Nov. 1765.

This Stone
is facred to the Memory of
the Rev. Benjamin Field,
who was 35 Years Minifter of this
Parifh, and Rector of Afton Subedge,
a Gentleman, whofe excellent
Talents and great Abilities
rendered him very ufeful
in this Parifh and Neighbourhood.
He died the 10 of Auguft, 1781,
ætatis 70.

Alfo Caroline, Wife of the above
Benjamin Field.
She died April 17, 1789, aged 83.

In Memory of
Nathaniel Taylor, who departed
this Life September .. Anno
Domini 1728, aged 27 Years.

IN THE NORTH AISLE.

On a Monument:

Arms; on the Top, quarterly of fix, 1ft, Gules, an Eagle difplayed Or, crowned Argent, between eight Crofs Croflets of the 2d, for Graves; 2d, Vert, two Greyhounds currant Argent, on a Chief Or, three Fleurs de Lis Gules, for Menseir; 3d, Sable, a Fefs engrailed Argent between three dexter Hands couped Or, for Bates; 4th, Azure, a Chevron Ermine between three Swans proper, for Swan; 5th, Sable, on a Bend Argent three Martlets of the Field, for Shilling; 6th, Graves.

On the Sides are ten feparate Efcocheons, with thefe Arms: 1. Graves. 2. Argent, a Crofs engrailed and voided between four Eftoiles Gules, for Gurney. 3. Bates. 4. Swan. 5. Sable, a Chevron between three Pheons Argent, for Morgan. 6. Menseir. 7. Vert, on a Chevron between three Stags Or, as many Cinquefoils Gules, for Robinson. 8. on a Bend three Martlets, for Danvers. 9. Shilling. 10. Argent, on a Pale Gules, three Leopards Faces of the Field, in the dexter chief an Annulet, for Brayne.

At

At the Bottom, quarterly, GRAVES, MENSEIR, SWAN, and SHILLING; and on an Efcocheon of Pretence, quarterly, 1ft and 4th, MORGAN; 2d and 3d, BRAYNE.

To the Memory of
JOHN GRAVES, of Beamefley, in Yorkfhire, Gent.
of the Family of GRAVE, of Heyton, in that County,
who married the Dr and Hr of MENSIER. He died at Lond.
1616, aged near 103, and was buried at St. Martin's Ludgate.

RICH. GRAVES, S. of I. Citin of Lond. who, by FRANCES, Dr of WILL. GURNEY, Efq. had Iffue 4 Sons and 5 Drs. He died 1626, æt. 54, and was buried at St. Martin's Ludgate.

RICH. GRAVES, S. and Hr of R. Lord of the Royalty of the Hundred of Kiftefgate, and of the Manrs of Mickleton, Afton, and Wefton, in this County; for many Years one of the Benchers, and at length Reader of Lincoln's Inn, who by two Wives had 19 Child. viz. by ELNr, Dr and Hr of TH. BATES, Gent. 6 Sons and 9 Daughters; and by ELIZ. Dr of Jo. ROBINSON, Efq. 4 Drs. He died 1699, æt. 59; ELNr, 1056, æt. 39; and ELIZ. 1713, æt. 66; and he and ELIZ. were buried at Clarkenwell; and ELNr at Richmond.

SAM. GRAVES, S. and Hr of R. Ld of this Manr, who by SUS. Dr and Cohr of Capt. RI. SWANN, and DOR. DANVERS his Wife, S. of Capt. RI. SWANN, fen. by DAMARIS, Dr and Cohr of Capt. ANDREW SHILLING, had Iffue 6 Sons and 3 Drs. He died 1708, æt. 59; and fhe 1719; æt. 68: and were both buried here.

RICH. GRAVES, S. and Hr of S. who married ELIZ. Dr and Coheir of Capt. TH. MORGAN by ELIZ. Daughter and Coheir of JA. BRAYNE, Gt. caufed this Monument to be here erected in 1721, who alfo hath had 3 Sons bur. here, viz. RICHd, who died 1710; SAM. 1712; and SAM. a Twin, 1719; all in their Infancy.

ON AN ELEGANT MARBLE MONUMENT:

Arms; Quarterly, 1ft and 4th, GRAVES; 2d and 3d, MORGAN.

Subtus requiefcit
RICARDUS GRAVES, Armiger, hujufce Manerii Dominus:
Vir, fi quis alius, defideratiffimus,
Qui eximias animi dotes mirâ indolis fuavitate temperans,
Tam charus omnibus vixit, quam effufâ erat erga omnes bene-
volentiâ.
Liberos tenerrimo affectu,
Amicos inconcuflâ fide femper profecutus.
Inter hæc otii literarii ftudiis efflorefcens
Ruris feceffum Hiftoriarum varietate eleganter diftinxit:
Non vero, ut doctis fepe contingit nullibi nifi in Patria fuâ
peregrinis
Cum res Græcas Romanafque penitus perfpectas haberet
Noftras faftidiofe prætermifit.
His profecto unice deditus, inveftigandis
Acerrimam operam navavit
Dilucidandis omnem adhibuit diligentiam.
Antiquitates demum loci vicinitate commendatas,
Propriis illuftrare fcriptis occepærat,
Inchoati operis gloriam adeptus
Confummati famâ, Mortis interventu, privatus.
Uxorem duxit ELIZABETHAM filiam & coheredem
THOMÆ MORGAN, Armigeri.
Ex qua
Quatuor filios duafque filias fuperftites reliquit,
Qnarum una (pro dolor!) fubtus paterno lateri adhæret.
Obiit ille decimo feptimo Septembris, anno Domini 1729,
æt. 53.
Ne tantas patris virtutes nefcirent pofteri
Hoc Monumentum pofuit
MORGAN GRAVES, Arm.
Filius natu maximus.

ON A HANDSOME MARBLE URN:

To the Memory of DANVERS GRAVES, Efq.
Chief Agent to the Hon. E. India Company in Perfia,
where he greatly diftinguifhed himfelf
by his Refolution and Fidelity
during the Commotions in that Kingdom,
and died at Gambroon
MDCCLII.

6

Arms; GRAVES as before;—impaling, Gules, a Bend and Bordure Ermine, in chief a Talbot paffant Or.

In Memory
of MORGAN GRAVES, Efq.
Lord of this Manour,
and a Bencher of the Inner Temple.
He married ANNE,
Daughter of ——— WALWYN, of Longworth, Efq.
by whom he had three Sons and four Daughters,
and died 26 Dec. 1770, aged 63.
With every Quality to merit the efteem
he was particularly diftinguifhed
by thofe which gain the Love of Mankind.
He was generous, friendly, and humane;
and, by conftantly promoting the Happinefs of others,
He greatly augmented his own.
In fhort,
his Virtues rendered him truly amiable in this Life,
and will, we truft,
make him compleatly happy in a better.

Arms; on a Chevron between three Caftles,
a Pair of Compaffes.

In Memory
of THOMAS WOODWARD,
of Afton Subedge,
and ELIZABETH his Wife.
He died May 1, 1716, aged 71.
She died July 21, 1686,
aged 52 Years.

Near this Place lyeth
MARY HOLTHAM,
who died Auguft 18,
1753, aged 63.

Alfo
GILES HOLTHAM
died Oct. 22, 1767, aged 76.

ON FLAT STONES.

Near
this Place lie the Remains
of Mrs. MARY BARNES,
late Wife of
Mr. WILLIAM BARNES,
who departed this Life
Nov. 4, 1779, aged 54 Years.

Alfo Mr. WILLIAM BARNES, who departed this Life the 14 of Octo. 1788, aged 64 Years.

IN THE SOUTH AISLE.

Here lyeth the Body of ELIZABETH, the Wife of THOMAS BLOXAM, who departed this Life January the 28, Anº Dom. 1678, ætatis fuæ 27.

Beneath this Stone at their joint Requeft are depofited the Remains of JOHN IZOD, Gent. and MARY his Wife, 3 Sons, and a Daughter, of JOHN and MARY IZOD. JOHN, EDWARD, HENRY, and ESTHER.

Alfo ANN IZOD. She, the laft Survivor, died May the 7, 1772, aged 50 Years.

Alfo of MARY HARWARD, Wife of WILLIAM HARWARD, Gent. She departed this Life March 19, 1710, aged 66 Years.

To

To the Memory of ELIZABETH,
the Wife of
JOHN LEA, Schoolmaster
of this Parish, who departed this Life
the 13 Day of Oct. 1769, aged 36 Years.

ON A MONUMENT IN THE PORCH:

In Memory of
STEPHEN BRADLEY,
Vicar of Overbury,
in the County of Worcester,
who departed this Life
Nov. the 1st, anno Dom.
1627, aged 77 Years.

I N   T H E   C H U R C H - Y A R D.

ON A MONUMENT AGAINST THE CHANCEL:

Near this Place lieth interred all
that was mortal of ELIZABETH,
Wife of THOMAS TIDMAN,
of Quinton. She departed
this Life the 17 of Jan. 1783,
in the 32d Year of her Age.

ON A LOFTY PYRAMIDAL MONUMENT:

This Monument was erected
by HENRY ROBERTS
and ANNE his Wife, of Upper
Clapton, in this Parish, to the
Memory of their Daughter
MARGARET, as a Testimony of their
tender Love and paternal Affection.
She departed this Life April 19,
in the Year of our Lord CHRIST
1742, aged 6 Years and 6 Months.

To the Memory of
THOMAS ROBERTS,
buried 18 March, 1710, aged 54;

ELIZABETH his Wife,
buried 18 Aug. 1727, aged 75;

HENRY ROBERTS their Son,
buried 7 Aug. 1762, aged 75;

ANNE, Wife of HENRY ROBERTS,
departed this Life 14 May, 1774,
aged 79.

ON A TOMB:

In Memory of JOHN FREEMAN,
Gent. who departed this Life
Oct. 4, 1788, aged 85.

In Memory of MARY, the
Wife of JOHN FREEMAN, Gent.
who departed this Life
the 1st of May, 1752, aged 38.

O N   H E A D - S T O N E S.

	Died	Aged		Died	Aged
Charles Taunton	12 Feb. 1788	54	Esther, Wife of Thomas Kitchin	28 May, 1725	—
Ann his Wife	7 Aug. 1788	51	Anne Cotterell	14 July, 1785	56
William Summers	15 Apr. 1737	57	Susannah, Wife of Robert Tidman	5 July 1758	33
John Dutton	8 Apr. 1705	55	Robert their Son	12 Sept. 1780	27
William Dutton	13 Apr. 1760	83	Elizabeth, Wife of Edward Williams	16 Nov. 1772	54
Elizabeth his Wife	18 Nov. 1762	73	Mary Such	3 Apr. 1785	64
William Bishop	22 Aug. 1749	58	William Such	16 June, 1790	72
Sarah his Wife	5 Feb. 1761	74	Ann, Daughter of John and Anne		
Ann, Wife of John Stockford	19 Aug. 1710	—	Coleman	4 Sept. 1739	20
Esther, Wife of Barnabas Fletcher	5 May, 1699	—	Dee their Son	11 Oct. 1740	22
Piercy Grove	17 Oct. 1784	35	Robert Millaway	11 May, 1728	76
Thomas Rose	8 May, 1758	66	Thomas Jackson	21 Oct. 1756	42
Mary his Wife	11 May, 1734	47	Thomas Cresby	10 Dec. 1727	69
John their Son	3 Oct. 1745	23	Alice his Wife	14 Oct. 1736	73
John Meads	26 Oct. 1781	71	Thomas Wimblet	22 Feb. 1725	82
Thomas his Son	15 Dec. 1768	27	William Harris	21 Dec. 1715	52
Thomas Orsborn	18 Apr. 1742	—	Cornelius Harris	17 Apr. 1724	60
Sarah, Wife of John Price	1 Dec. 1770	25	Bridget Harris	6 Aug. 1728	—
John Tayler	6 Mar. 1713	36	Thomas Harris	11 Feb. 1687	69
Thomas Tayler	18 Mar. 1715	63	Bridget his Wife	11 Mar. 1699	74
Thomas Tayler	4 Apr. 1739	75	Thomas Harris	14 Apr. 1757	55
Sarah his Wife	18 July, 1758	84	Elizabeth Holtom	14 Aug. 1711	87
Hazlewood Clayton	18 Sept. 1788	32	Giles Holtam	17 Apr. 1722	65
Robert Robins	27 Nov. 1767	72	Millicent his Wife	17 Apr. 1740	82
Richard Robins	17 July, 1773	62	John Burnit	24 Mar. 1722	53
Mary his Wife	18 July, 1773	49	Henry Ward	29 July, 1723	68
William Robbins	25 Nov. 1769	65	Henry Greene	26 Feb. 1749	57
John Robbins	22 July, 1784	79	Nicholas Greene	16 Jan. 1772	76
Nicholas Canning	19 Jan. 1728	67	Joseph Nichols	4 Jan. 1734	29
Susannah, Wife of William Goldby	8 June, 1740	41	Elizabeth Braggins	11 Oct. 1708	55
Elizabeth his second Wife	21 Nov. 1743	79			

CLXXV. MINSTERWORTH,

DENOMINATED in *Domefday* Book *M O R T U N E*, as defcriptive of its Situation near the *Severn*; from *Mor*, which in *Britifh* fignifies the Sea, or fome large River.

Prior to the Reign of King JOHN, it was annexed to the Minfter or Abbey of *Gloucefter*, when the prefent Appellation was given it. This Parifh lies in the Hundred of the Dutchy of *Lancafter*, in the Foreft Divifion, and on the Turnpike Road leading from *Gloucefter* to *Newnham* *, whence it is diftant fix Miles North-eaft, feven Eaft from *Mitchel Dean*, and three South-weft from the City of GLOUCESTER.

The Soil is chiefly Clay, with fome Sand; and a greater Portion of Pafture Land than Arable. It is fingularly intermixed with *Elmore* Parifh on the oppofite Side of the River, at a Place called *Elmore's Back*. A Divifion fo extraordinary allows a probable Conjecture, that the Abbey of *Gloucefter*, having Land in *Elmore*, procured them to be annexed to the Parifh of *Minfterworth*, where their Property was more confiderable. About 1850 Acres are included in this Parifh; and an extenfive Common, bordered on the South Side of the River *Severn*.

The Benefice is a Vicarage, the Impropriation of which was appropriated to the Priory of *St. Ofwald* in *Gloucefter*, 22 RIC. II. It afterwards belonged to the Monaftery of *Boxleau* in *Hampfhire*; and the Rectory and Advowfon of the Vicarage were granted to the Bifhoprick of *Briflol*, 34 HENRY VIII. and then paffed in Leafe for three Lives.

The King's Auditor pays annually 10*l.* to the Vicarage, and the Impropriator four Loads of Hay; it has alfo been augmented by Queen ANNE's Bounty.

The Church, dedicated to *St. Mary*, confifts of a Nave and Aile of equal Length, with a Chancel, feparated by an Arch, ornamented with the zig-zag Moulding. In the Chancel Window are thefe Arms: Gules, three Lions of *England*. The Steeple and Bells were deftroyed by Lightning in the Beginning of the prefent Century. There is at prefent a low Tower at the Weft End; and in the Church a Stone Font, curioufly fculptured with Quaterfoils and other Ornaments that mark its Antiquity.

The Abbey of *Gloucefter* is recited in *Domefday* Book to have been poffeffed of this Manor when that Record was compiled. HENRY DE BOHUN releafed his Right in all his Lands in *Minfterworth* to King JOHN, in the firft Year of his Reign. SIMON DE MONTFORT, Earl of *Leicefter*, was feized of it 43 HENRY III. from whom it paffed to EDMOND Earl of LANCASTER, Brother to King EDWARD I. as appears by an Infpeximus, and Continuation in the . . . Year of the Reign of RICHARD II. who gave it to WILLIAM GRANDISON, a domeftic Servant of the Earl's, as a Reward for his Services. This WILLIAM GRANDISON was Brother and Heir to OTHO DE GRANDISON, who was fummoned as a Peer to Parliament 27 EDWARD I. By Failure of Male Iffue, the Manor reverted to the Houfe of *Lancafter*; and, in the third Year of HENRY V. it was granted to the Archbifhop of YORK, and others, in Truft, and afterwards held by feveral Leafes granted from the Crown. In 7 JAMES I. it was held in Fee, under an annual Rent of 20*l.* 6*s.* 11¾*d.*

About the middle of the laft Century, the Manor became vefted in the Family of PURY, from whom, after feveral fucceffive Purchafes, it came at length into the Poffeffion of the late Sir CHARLES BARROW, Bart. for many Years one of the Reprefentatives of the City of *Gloucefter*, and is now held by CHARLES EVANS, Efq.

Certain Copyhold Eftates of Inheritance in this Parifh are held by Tenures fimilar to thofe at *Cheltenham*, and fome other Places.

Three Hamlets are included in *Minfterworth*, *Morcote* or *Boyfield*, *Hampton*, and *Dunny*.

1. *Morcote*, fo called by the *Britons*, from *Coed*, a *Wood*, and by the *Normans*, *Boyfield*, from *Bois*, which are fynonymous Terms, is a reputed Manor, and at the general Survey is recited in *Domefday* Book

---

* This Line of Country is very hilly and picturefque, for the Road runs all the Way by the *Severn*, which has a bold Shore, finely wooded, and breaks upon the View in a very pleafing Manner.

YOUNG's Six Weeks Tour through the Southern Counties.

3

to

to have been in the Hundred of *Langebridge*, and held by WILLIAM, the Son of NORMAN. ULFEGH held it in the Time of King EDWARD. RICHARD VEEL was feized of *Morcote* 16 EDWARD III.; and, in the 36th of the fame Reign, it was held by JOHN BOTELER. It afterwards paffed to the Family of the KENNS, and was fold to THOMAS ELMBRIDGE, 27 HENRY VII. whofe Son and Heir JOHN ELMBRIDGE, dying without Iffue, it came into the Poffeffion of Sir JOHN DANET, 17 HENRY VIII. whofe Son fold it to the Family of ATKYNS, to whom a confiderable Eftate in this Parifh belonged, and whofe Reprefen-tatives EDMUND JOHN CHAMBERLAYNE and ANNE HORDE, the Heirs General of that Family, fold it to Mr. JOSEPH HAWKINS and Mr. JEREMIAH HAWKINS.

2. *Hampton* Hamlet is fituate in the Centre of the Parifh adjoining the Ham or great Common. ROGER DE BOYFIELD, who probably took his Name from his Place of Refidence in the Hamlet of *Boy-field*, was feized of one Meffuage and one Yard Land in *Hampton*, Parcel of the Manor of *Minfterworth*, 15 EDWARD II.

3. *Dunny*, of which there is nothing worthy of Remark. Tythes of the Fifheries in this Hamlet are allowed to the Parfon.

The principal Eftates of this Parifh are held by CHARLES EVANS, Efq. the Lord of the Manor of *Minfterworth*, Mr. JEREMIAH HAWKINS, Mr. JOSEPH HAWKINS, Mr. DANIEL ELLIS, Mr. JOHN OAKEY, and Mrs. MARTHA DRAYTON.

Sir ROBERT ATRYNS mentions that JOHN GUELLEM, eminent for his Book of Heraldry, was born at *Weftbury*, and refided moft of his Time in *Minfterworth*.

BENEFACTIONS.

JOHN HYETT, in 1719, gave by Will, for apprenticing fome poor Man's Son (born in this Parifh) every fecond Year, Land; the annual Produce of which is 10*l.*; now vefted in the Hands of the Over-feers and Churchwardens.

1722, JOSEPH WINTLE gave, Land, by will, in the Parifh of *Minfterworth*, the annual Produce of which is 1*l.* 10*s.* 1*d.*; vefted in the Overfeers and Churchwardens, to be diftributed in Bread to twenty poor Houfekeepers, at Chriftmas, for ever.

1764, SUSANNAH CRUMP gave, by Will, 2*l.*; vefted in Mr. SAUNDERS, of *Gloucefter*, for putting five poor Children to School.

1784, DANIEL ELLIS gave, by Will, 100*l.*; vefted in Mr. JOHN TURNER, Banker, in *Gloucefter*, to build a School.

INCUMBENTS.	PATRONS.	INCUMBENTS.	PATRONS.
—— John Whitmaye *,	——————.	1633 Thos. Ofbern, M. A.	King Charles I.
1555 William Bouge,	Robert Cole, by Grant of St. Ofwald's Priory.	1747 Edw. Draper, M. A.	Lord Chancellor.
1561 William Forte,	Queen Elizabeth.	1777 William Gyllet, A. B.	Bifhop of Briftol.
* * * * * * * * * * * * *		1783 William Gyllet, A.M.	The fame.

PRESENT LORD OF THE MANOR,

CHARLES EVANS, Efq.

At the Heralds Vifitation, in 1682 and 1683, the only Perfon fummoned from this Place was Daniel Griffith, Efq.

At the Election in 1776 Fourteen Freeholders polled from this Parifh.

ANNUAL ACCOUNT OF MARRIAGES, BIRTHS, AND BURIALS, IN THIS PARISH.

A.D.	Mar.	Bir.	Bur.	A.D.	Mar.	Bir.	Bur.	A.D.	Mar.	Bir.	Bur.	A.D.	Mar.	Bir.	Bur.
1781	3	16	3	1786	4	—	—	1791				1796			
1782	1	9	4	1787	7	8	5	1792				1797			
1783	2	7	5	1788	4	7	7	1793				1798			
1784	2	9	4	1789	10	10	7	1794				1799			
1785	4	8	4	1790	3	10	1	1795				1800			

* Athen. vol. I. p. 577.

INSCRIPTIONS

INSCRIPTIONS IN THE CHURCH.

IN THE CHANCEL.

On a Monument :

Arms ; Argent, a Fefs wavy between three Lions Paws erafed Sable ;—impaling, Azure, three Bars wavy, between three Rocks Argent.

To the Memory
of Mrs. Anne Clent, late Wife of
John Clent,
of this Parifh, Gent. She departed
this Life the 30 Day of May, 1668,
aged 38.

ON FLAT STONES.

Arms as above.

John Clent, Gent.
died May the 4th,
1672.

Here lyeth the
Body of William,
the Son of John
Clent, who departed
this Life the 19 of
April, 1657.

Here lyeth the Body
of Sibell, the Wife of
Robert Very, who
departed this Life
Auguft 11, Anno Dom.
1666.

Here lyeth Phillis,
the Daughter of Robert
Very, who died the 29
of March, 1676.

Here lyeth the Body of
Richard Bosley,
who departed this Life the
. . Day of March, 16 . .

Alfo the Body of Joane,
the Wife of Richard
Bosley, who departed
this Life the 7 of Dec.
An. D. 1625.

HERE RESTETH THE BODY OF
NEAST ARNOLD,
WHO DEPARTED THIS LIFE
THE LAST DAY OF OCTOB.
ANNO D'NI 1643.

HIC JACET CORPUS
E. W. VIDUÆ QUÆ
OCTAVO DIE NOVEM
FATIS CONCESSIT
1643.

IN THE NAVE.

ON FLAT STONES.

HERE LYETH THE BODY OF
WILLIAM SPARRY, WHO
DEPARTED THIS LIFE
THE II DAY OF MAY,
ANNO DOMINI 1663,
AGED 14 YEARS.

HERE LYETH BURIED
ISABEL, LATE WIFE OF
ANTHONY KEYLOCKE,
OF THIS PARISH, WHO
DEPARTED THIS LIFE THE
6 DAY OF SEPTEMBER,
AN. D'NI 1638.

HERE LYETH THE BODY OF
JOHN SPARRY, OF MINSTER-
WORTH, WHO DEPARTED THIS
LIFE THE 17 DAY OF SEPTEM.
1645.

HERE LYETH THE BODY
OF JOHN SPARRY, WHO
DEPARTED THIS LIFE THE
28 OF JUNE, ANNO DOM.
1650.

In Memory of Samuel, the Son
of Edward Wells, by Elizabeth
his Wife, Daughter of William
Cook. He departed this Life the
10 Day of July, Anno Dom. 1715,
aged near 30 Years.

In Memory of John
Brown, of the Parifh of Minfterworth, who died Nov. 5th,
1752, aged near 50 Years.

In Memory of
Joseph Brown, of this Parifh,
who died univerfally beloved
October the 24, 1781, aged near
71 Years.

Alfo within this Vault refteth the
Body of Elizabeth, the Wife of John
Oakey, of this Parifh, who departed
this Life June the 26, A. D. 1783,
aged 46.

Here lyeth the Body of
Elizabeth, the Wife of
Thomas Gybbe, of Stone-
houfe, who died 2 March,
1630.

Here lyeth Amy, the Daughter
of James Gittos, of Tirley, Clerk,
and of Elizabeth his Wife,
Daughter of Thomas Wintle,
of Minfterworth, and of Amy
his Wife, who died Sept. 11, 1666.

Amy, the Wife of
Thomas Wintle, was buried
the 8th Day of April, 1665.

Here refteth the Body
of Thomas Wintle, of this Parifh,
Gent. who deceafed Nov. 15,
1668, aged 49 Years.

Alfo the Body
of Jane his fecond Wife,
Daughter of James Pritchard,
of the Parifh of Grifmont,
in the County of Monmouth,
Efq. who deceafed Jan. the 12,
1700, aged 71 Years.

In Memory of
Joseph Wintle, Gent. who died
December the 22, 1722.

Alfo in Memory of Mrs. Anne
Weale, who died January the
23, 1722-3.

Alfo John Wintle, Gent. who
died June the 7, 1740, aged 35.

And William his Son died
1744.

In Memory of Anne, late
Wife of Thomas Hooper, of the
Parifh of Churcham, who dep-
arted this Life the 28th June,
Anno Dom. 1772, aged 70.

Here lyeth the Body of
Martha, the Wife of
Arthur Barrett, of this
Parifh, who departed this
Life the . . of April, 1663.

Here lyeth the Body of Matthew
Gough, late of this Parifh, Yeoman,
who departed this Life 19 Sept. 1687,
ætatis fuæ 61.

Here lyeth the Body of Susanna,
the Wife of John Callowe, who
deceafed the 8 of October, Anno
Domini 1668.

Here lyeth the Body alfo of
Margaret, the Wife of John
Frleman, late of the Parifh of
Weftbury, who departed this
Life the 21 of November,
Anno Domini 1689.

I N

IN THE AISLE.

ON A HANDSOME MARBLE MONUMENT:

Arms; Argent, three Bears Heads erafed Sable, muzzled Or, on a Chief Azure, the Arms of ULSTER.

Near this Place reft the Remains of
Sir CHARLES BARROW, of Hygrove, in this Parifh, Baronet, LL. D.
Recorder of Tewkefbury, and Reprefentative of the City of Gloucefter
in feven fucceffive Parliaments.
As a Senator, he was a zealous Affertor of the conftitutional Rights
and Interefts of his Country.—
As a Magiftrate, thoroughly verfed in the Municipal Laws;
and vigilant and active in the Execution of them.—
As a Friend, warm in his Attachments, both Public and Private.—
In focial Intercourfe, affable, engaging, courteous;
with a conciliating Addrefs, happily fuited to all Ranks and Conditions:
by which he acquired and retained a Popularity with his Conftituents,
equalled by few, and exceeded by none.
He died on the 10th Day of January, 1789,
in the 80th Year of his Age.

IN THE CHURCH YARD, ON TOMBS.

In Memory of MERIAM,
the Wife of JAMES CHURCH,
who died Jan. 9, 1759,
aged 55 Years.

Alfo of SAMUEL RIDER, and
ELIZABETH his Wife.
He died Nov. 16, 1736, aged 68.
She died Dec. 31, 1747, aged 78.

Near this Side refteth the
Body of MARY, the Wife of
JOHN CHURCH, of the Hamlet
of Over, who departed this
Life Nov. the 4, 1788, aged 50.

Here refteth the Body of
JAMES CHURCH, fen.
who departed this Life June 6,
Anno Domini 1771, aged near 70 Years.

In Memory
of WILLIAM WINTLE, who departed
this Life the 8th of December,
1692, aged 41.

In Memory of MARY, the Daughter
of WILLIAM WINTLE, who departed
this Life in November, 1751, aged
64 Years.

In Memory of SAMUEL, the Son
of EDWARD WELLS by ELIZABETH his
Wife, Daughter of EDWARD COOK,
who died 10 July, 1715, aged 30.

Here lyeth the Body
of NICHOLAS PHELPES,
of this Parifh, Yeoman,
who departed this Life
March the 20, Anno
Domini 1668.

In Memory of THOMAS
PURTON, of this Parifh,
who died November the 19,
1766, aged near 64 Years.

In Memory of ELIZABETH,
Wife of SAMUEL SMITH, of this
Parifh, and late Wife of RICHARD
PITT, of the City of Worcefter,
who departed this Life the 15th
of Sept. 1732, aged 64 Years.

In Memory of
SARAH, the Wife of WILLIAM
SMITH, of this Parifh, Yeoman, who
died May 14, 1729, aged 47 Years.

Here refteth the Body alfo of
WILLIAM SMITH, of this Parifh,
fen. who departed this Life
the 1 Day of May. 1753, aged 67.

JOHN NICHOLAS,
of the City of Gloucefter,
died the 3d of June, 1775,
aged 69 Years.

In Memory of
JOHN HAWKINS, of this
Parifh, who departed this Life
Sept. 11, 1764, aged 45 Years.

SARAH, the Daughter of
JOHN and ANNE HAWKINS, died
Oct. the 28, 1761, aged 5 Years.

In Memory of
JOSEPH HAWKINS, of this Parifh,
and ELIZABETH his Wife.
He died April 12, 1740, aged 46.
She died March 11, 1780, aged 73.

In Memory
of JOHN BURNETT. He died
the 10 of Sept. 1781, aged 77 Years.

Alfo ANNE, the 1ft Wife of the above
JOHN BURNETT, who died the 10 of
October, 1739,
ætat. 34 Years.

Alfo MARY his fecond Wife died the
25 Aug. 1765, ætatis 66 Years.

ON HEAD-STONES.

Name	Died	Aged	Name	Died	Aged
John Nicholas	—— 1729	51	Sarah, Wife of James Bodnum	27 Apr. 1775	28
Mary his Wife	—— 1744	67	Jofeph Young	14 Nov. 1745	51
William Hafkins	7 July, 1775	54	Mary, Wife of John Hill	2 June, 1707	55
Ann Broban	3 May, 1761	65	Jane, Wife of Samuel Allcock	7 Feb. 1729	69
Ralph Barret	18 May 1711	67	William Jones	18 Nov. 1760	54
Hannah, Wife of Abraham Pool	29 Dec. 1728	56	Richard Parfons	8 Apr. 1722	—
Anne, Wife of Abraham Pool	5 Nov. 1765	61	William Hawkes	12 Aug. 1768	68
Edward Pool	22 Nov. 1770	26	Ann his Wife	— June, 1762	53
Mary Goff	30 Sept. 1780	75	John their Son	9 Dec. 1787	44
Martha, Wife of Chriftopher Dugan	6 Mar. 1784	62	Thomas Hide	3 Dec. 1783	32
Ann, Wife of Jofeph Boughton	16 Nov. 1786	32	William Varnham	8 Oct. 1717	68
William Graceing	—— 1716	39	Ann his Wife	27 Oct. 1697	40
John Bagnel	5 Mar. 1741	49	Elizabeth, Daughter of Thomas Smith	4 Dec. 1681	—
Martha, Wife of John Hayward	18 Mar. 1720	34	Thomas Smith	27 July, 1682	76
Alice, Wife of John Bodnum	10 May 1741	49	Edward Surman	21 Oct. 1729	46
Mary, Wife of Robert Bodnum	10 Nov. 1765	64	William Watts	—— 1712	84
John Bodnum	28 Sept. 1768	73	Richard his Son	5 Apr. 1675	—
Mary his Wife	— Aug. 1767	53	Thomas Bradley	2 Oct. 1689	—
John their Son	22 Nov. 1770	29	Anfelm Littleton	1 June, 1712	50
Robert Bodnum, of Quedgley	30 Mar. 1777	57	Ruth his Wife	22 July, 1719	61
Hannah his Wife	23 May, 1782	62	John Littleton	11 Nov. 1719	—
Hannah their Daughter	12 Aug. 1782	29			

ON HEAD-STONES.

	Died	Aged
Mary, Wife of William Littleton	12 May, 1784	60
Margaret, Wife of John Hyett	12 May, 1687	76
John Hyett	31 Dec. 1711	61
Mary his Wife	—— 1713	52
Hefter, Wife of Anfelm Wooles	26 Feb. 1764	38
Sarah, Wife of Edward Overthrow	18 Nov. 1741	41
Margaret, Wife of William James	24 May, 1689	25
Ephraim Smith	10 Dec. 1775	48
Obadiah Allen	6 Oct. 1766	62
William, Son of John Trigg	11 Oct. 1728	—
Thomas Trigg	3 May, 1729	54
Robert Trigg	6 Oct. 1751	50
Thomas, Son of Stephen and Mary Brooke	25 Aug. 1760	18
Ann, Wife of John Lloyd	9 May, 1779	36
Thomas Church	28 Mar. 1721	65
John Church	9 Mar. 1739	43
John Church	26 Feb. 1748	56
James, Son of James and Miriam Church	5 May, 1750	22
William Grafing	10 May, 1777	46
Mary, Wife of Samuel Jackfons	17 Jan. 1771	72
Jofeph. Son of John Leighton	2 Nov. 1687	—
Edith, Wife of Edward Wells	26 Feb. 1783	—
William Phelps	3 Jan. 1786	6)
Elizabeth his Wife	20 June, 1779	57
Silvefter, Wife of Samuel Hyett and Daughter of Robert Daniel	19 June, 1716	63
Elizabeth, Wife of Edward Wells	8 July, 1690	—
Anne, Daughter of John and Frances Rowles	16 Apr. 1729	33
Anne, Wife of William Hayward	9 May, 1703	81
Mary Hayward	99 June, 1715	57
William Little	3 July, 1699	37
Alice his Wife	3 Nov. 1727	76
Jofeph Hawkins	13 Dec. 1776	40
Richard Barrett	12 Oct. 1712	86
Elizabeth his Wife	2 June, 1685	—
Richard Barrett	15 July, 1706	32
John Barrett	17 Dec. 1768	73
John Wathan	26 Feb. 1785	65
Mary his Wife	10 Nov. 1779	58
Hefter, Wife of John Craft	15 Mar. 1745	58
John Craft	1 May, 1752	62
Elizabeth, Daughter of Richard and Elizabeth Crump	16 Mar. 1729	19
Elinor, Wife of Matthew Aulen	23 June, 1677	—
Elizabeth, Wife of William Davis	22 May, 1727	—
Thomas Jones	27 Aug. 1784	50
William Hobbs	31 May, 1787	31
James Browne	4 Mar. 1745	45
Elizabeth his Wife	1 Oct. 1759	50
Robert Very	11 Mar. 1684	—
Samuel Very	5 Apr. 1699	—
Samuel his Son	16 Apr. 1699	—
Robert Colwell	12 Sept. 1685	—
Samuel Rider	16 Nov. 1736	63
Samuel Rider	2 Dec. 1778	77
Sarah his Wife	12 July, 1777	66
Thomas Drew	30 July, 1681	—
Jone his Wife	3 Apr. 1724	84
Thomas Bartlam	31 Dec. 1734	28
Thomas his Son	—— 1759	23
William Window	5 Oct. 1706	26
Elizabeth his Wife	13 Dec. 1751	75
William Goodwin	30 Oct. 1689	—
Jofeph Goodwin	15 Dec. 1697	45
John Cook	—— 1727	51
Joan his Wife	—— 1728	52
William Hooper	10 Feb. 1768	35

CLXXVI. MISERDEN,

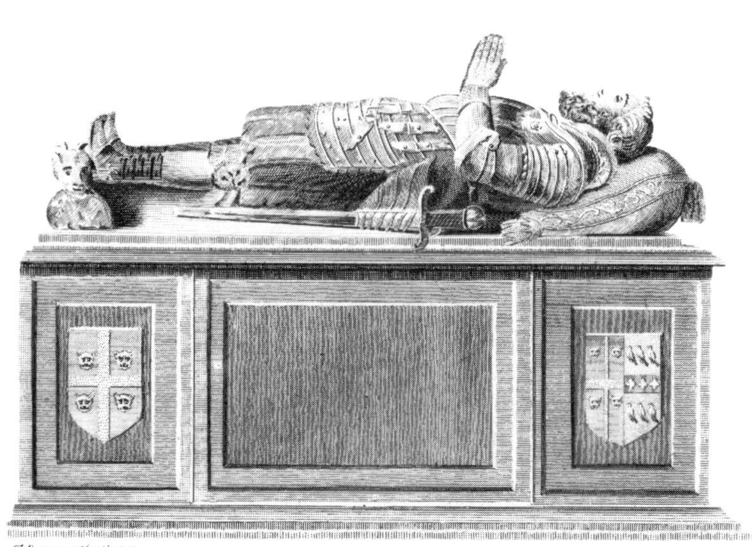

KINGSTON *Tomb* in MISERDEN.

CLXXVI. MISERDEN, OR MUSARDEN,

IN *Domefday* Book ftyled *GRENHAMSTEDE*, is fituated on the South-weft Side of the *Irmin* Street, or *Roman* confular Road, feven Miles North-weftward from *Cirencefter*, and nine South-eaftward from GLOUCESTER. The Family of the MUSARDS, who accompanied the CONQUEROR in his Expedition to this Kingdom, were Proprietors of this Parifh from that Period till the Reign of EDWARD I. and from them it took the Name of *Mufarden*, now corruptedly called *Miferden*. The Situation of the Caftle, in which fome of the Family refided, fuggefted the latter Part of the Name; *Den* fignifying a Dale, or deep woody Valley.

It includes a Circuit nearly of fifteen Miles, and about 1500 Acres of a Soil, chiefly Gravel, with fome Clay; which is applied to Tillage in a Proportion of two Parts to three. 300 Acres lie uninclofed in Downs and Common Fields.

Few Places can boaft of more natural Advantages than the Park, which is feven Miles in Circumference, uneven in Surface, clothed with fine Beech Wood, and exhibiting many picturefque, fequeftered, and romantic Scenes. In the middle of the Valley which the Park enclofes, now overgrown with Trees, and devoted to Solitude, is a circular Mound furrounded by a Moat, on which ftood the ancient Caftle, founded by RALPH MUSARD, who was Sheriff of this County from 17th JOHN to 9 HENRY III. and great Grandfon to the original Proprietor.

The Manerial-houfe, fituated on an Eminence in the Park, has the Appearance of Antiquity, and is reported to have been built with the Materials of the old Caftle; but the Period at which the one was deftroyed, and the other rofe from its Ruins, cannot now be accurately afcertained. The Rooms are capacious, but have fuffered greatly from Neglect and Decay. The Chimney-piece in the Dining-room is ornamented with the Arms of SANDYS, viz. Or, a Fefs dancetté between three crofs Croflets fitche Gules; a Crefcent, with an Annulet, for Difference; and in different Apartments are a Number of Family Portraits of Antiquity and Merit, a Defcription of which we have fubjoined *.

Miferden was garrifoned during the Civil Wars †, of which CORBET has given an Account, with his ufual Minutenefs and Accuracy; and, at the Siege of *Cirencefter*, a Detachment of Horfe and Foot advanced to *Cirencefter* ‡.

---

* Catalogue of the Portraits at the Manor-houfe at *Miferden* of the Family of SANDYS, with the Dates authenticated by the Pedigree:

N° 1. Sir WILLIAM SANDYS, Knight, who purchafed *Miferden* of HENRY JERNEGAN, Efq. of *Coffey*, co. *Norfolk*, about 1620, ob. 1640, æt. 77.

N° 2. Dame MARGARET his Wife, Daughter and Heirefs of WALTER COLEPEPPER, of *Hanborough*, co. *Oxford*, ob. 1644, æt. 64. Done late in Life.

Thefe Portraits are Full-length, and were fent to *Rome*, from which the Effigies in Alabafter are copied upon the Tomb in the Church.

N° 3. Full-length, Sir MILES SANDYS, of *Brimpsfield*, Member of Parliament for *Cirencefter*, 1605, 1 CHARLES I. in a Court Drefs, his Hand refting on a Greyhound, ob. vit. pat. 1626.

N° 4. Full-length, Dame MARY his Wife, Daughter of Sir JOHN HANBURY, of *Kelmarfh*, co. *Hants*, leading MARY her Daughter, an Infant, afterwards a Nun in *France*.

N° 5. Full-length, in Armour, laced Band, WILLIAM SANDYS, Efq. ob. 1649, æt. 25, in the Royal Army.

N° 6. Three-quarter Length, VANDYKE, Drefs Sattin, ELIZABETH his Wife, Daughter of STEPHEN SOAMES, of *Haydon*, co. *Effex*, died in *France*.

N° 7. Three-quarter Length. laced Cravat, holding a Hawk on his Thumb, MILES SANDYS, Efq.

N° 8. Half-length, flowing Wig, laced Cravat, WILLIAM SANDYS, of *London*, Brother of MYLES SANDYS.

N° 9. Oval Half-length, loofe drefs, flowing Wig, WILLIAM SANDYS, of *Miferden*, ob. 1712, æt. 35.

N° 10. Oval Half-length, fame Drefs, MYLES SANDYS, ob. 1706, æt. 24.

N° 11. Oval Half-length, loofe Drefs, BARBARA his Wife, Daughter and Coheir of Sir W. KERLE, Governor of *Carolina*, married 1701, ob. 1746, æt. 63.

N° 12. Her Sifter.

† " At which very Time we had longed three Hundred Foote within *Mufarden* Houfe fent thither the Day before, with Orders " to defend it as a Garrifon, who had no Knowledge of the Enemy's Approach till they came within Halfe a Mile. They re- " mained in the Houfe according to Command, but in no defenfible Pofture, neverthelefs expecting the Onfet every Moment. " The Surprizal of thefe Men was prevented by a mere Accident of the Governor's Arrivall, who faced the great Body with no " more than Sixty Horfe, till the Foote were drawne off the Hills." CORBET, Mil. Hift. p. 121.

‡ " Fifteen Colours of Horfe arrived at *Cirencefter*, and Five Hundred Horfe and Foot advanced to *Saperton* and *Mufarden*, " within ten Miles of the Garrifon. There were of the Enemie's Forces round about, near fix or feven Thoufand." Ib. p. 71.

3A Rivulet

A Rivulet which runs through the Park, and adds to its natural Beauties, is the Boundary of this Parish, and the adjacent ones of *Duntesborne* and *Winson*.

The Benefice is a Rectory, in the Deanery of *Stonehouse*, to which are annexed ninety Acres of Glebe Land, forty-four of which lie in Common Field.

The Church, dedicated to *St. Andrew*, consists of a Nave, and two cross Ailes of modern Structure, with a low embattled Tower at the West End. In the North Window are some Fragments of painted Glass, with the Cognizance of the Duke of YORK *; and over the Arch which separates the Nave from the Chancel are Escocheons for the Family of SANDYS. A Chapel on the South Side of the Chancel, appropriated to the Family of SANDYS, is decorated with various military Trophies and Infignia, and contains a costly and magnificent marble Tomb, with the recumbent Effigies of Sir WILLIAM SANDYS and his Lady in Alabaster, their Heads supported by a Cushion, and their Feet resting on their separate Crests. The former is in complete Armour; the latter in the most courtly and fashionable Dress of the Times. The Sculpture is very accurately copied from two Paintings of Sir WILLIAM SANDYS and his Lady by Sir CORNELIUS JOHNSON, which were sent to *Italy* for that Purpose, and even the nicest Parts of the female Dress are exquisitely finished. On the Sides of the Tomb, decorated with Escocheons of Arms, are the kneeling Figures of their ten Children. This superb Monument cost £.1000, and is still in the highest State of Preservation.

The Manor is specified in *Domesday* Book to have been held by ERNESI in the Reign of King EDWARD the Confessor, whose Successor HASCOIT MUSARD † was rewarded at the Conquest with several Manors in the Counties of *Buckingham, Warwick,* and *Derby,* and with six Lordships in *Gloucestershire,* of which *Miserden* was one. He was a Baron of the Realm, and this Estate was comprehended under the Title of the Barony of *Musarden* ‡. RICHARD MUSARD held it by Inheritance, to whom succeeded HASCOIT, who died 33 HENRY II. and to him RALPH MUSARD, who founded the Castle as before related. ROBERT his Son had Possession of the Castle §, 14 HENRY III. paying 60*l.* for Relief, who, dying without Issue, it devolved to his Brother RALPH MUSARD, a Minor, put under the Care of JEFFREY DESPENCER, who in Consideration thereof paid 500 Marks to the Crown. His Son JOHN MUSARD had Livery of the Manor 15 EDWARD I. and died two Years afterwards, leaving *Seyntbury* and the Castle of *Musarden,* then totally ruinous, to NICHOLAS his Uncle, who died without Issue, 29 EDW. I. His Heirs Sir RALPH FRESCHEVILLE, Son of AMICIA, eldest Sister of NICHOLAS MUSARD, and two younger Sisters, MARGARET MUSARD and JOAN, Wife of WILLIAM DE CHELARDISTON, had Livery of the Manor granted them, 29 EDW. I. HUGH LE DISPENCER soon afterwards possessed it, and after his Attainder the Manor was granted to JEOFFRY MORTIMER, Son of ROGER MORTIMER, Earl of *March.* He being also attainted and executed at *Smithfield,* it reverted to the Crown, and was granted to EDMOND of WOODSTOCK, Earl of *Kent,* second Son of King EDWARD I. and was then valued at 22*l.* yearly. He was afterwards attainted and executed at *Winchester,* 4 EDW. III. when JOHN his Brother, notwithstanding the Attainder, succeeded him in his Honours and Estate, and died seized of *Miserden,* 26 EDW. III. whose Widow ELIZABETH held it in Dower till her Death, 12 HEN. IV. JOAN, commonly called The Fair Maid of *Kent,* was Sister and Heir to JOHN, and was married to Sir THOMAS HOLLAND, created Earl of *Kent.* ROGER Earl of MARCH, who married ELIANOR, Sister and Coheiress of the Family of the HOLLANDS, held the Manor in the Reign of EDWARD III. whose Son EDMOND MORTIMER dying without Issue, it descended to ANN, Sister and Co-heiress of EDMOND, who was married to RICHARD Duke of YORK, Heir to the Crown of *England.* At his Death it was vested in the Crown, and remained till the latter End of King HENRY VIII. when the Manor and Park were granted to Sir ANTHONY KINGSTON; and the Letters Patent recite that it had been Part of the Dower Estate intended for Queen CATHARINE his (the King's) first Wife, had she survived him. His Son Sir WILLIAM KINGSTON was Provost Marshal in the Reign of King EDWARD VI. ‖ This Family enjoyed it for several successive Generations till the Year 1608, when WILLIAM KINGSTON, Esq. sold it to the JERNINGHAMS of *Norfolk,* of whom it was purchased by Sir WILLIAM SANDYS, who is descended from WILLIAM SANDYS, of *Rottenby* Castle, in the Parish of *St. Bees* in *Cumberland,* living in the Reign of HENRY VI. ** From 1608, the 5th of JAMES I. the Manor has descended through several Collateral Branches to the present Proprietor SAMUEL SANDYS, Esq.

---

* The Cognizances of the Brothers, of the House of *York,* EDWARD and RICHARD, are very frequently alluded to by SHAKSPEARE, in his historical Drama:
        " Made glorious Summer by this *Sun* of *York.*"

" But his favourite Cognizance was the Falcon and Fetterlock, with an unequivocal Motto, which, Mr. WALPOLE observes,
" ' had not even Delicacy to excuse the Witticism.' It is still to be discovered, either carved, or painted on Glass, in those
" Structures to which he contributed, or had himself built." DALLAWAY's Heraldic Enquiries, p. 385.

† " *Musard,* a Lingerer, or lazy Fellow, from *Musard,* French." HEARN's Glossary to PETER LANGTOFT's Chron. p. 623.
‡ ATKYNS, p. 293.
§ DUGDALE, Bar. vol. I. p. 512.
‖ This Sir WILLIAM KINGSTONE was famous in Chronicle for his sportive Cruelty. He ordered the Mayor of *Bodmin* to erect a strong and lofty Gallows in the Market-place; and, when he had well feasted with him, he trussed up Mr. Mayor upon his own well-built Gallows, to experiment the Strength and Firmness of it. He hanged up a Miller's Man, who pretended to be the Master, saying he could not do his Master better Service than to hang for him. ATKYNS, Hist. p. 294.
** For the Pedigree of the SANDYS, see ATKYNS, p. 294.

4   *H A M L E T S.*

SANDYS MONUMENT.

Published according to Act of Parliament by Rich.d Ragland July 1.st 1788.

H A M L E T S.

1. *Wifhanger* *, or *Rifeanger*, was given by Asculf Musard to the Fraternity of Knights Templars, and from whom it paffed to the Knights Hofpitallers of *Jerufalem.* After their Diffolution it was granted to Sir Thomas Palmer, 6 Edw. VI. and upon his Attainder to William Lord Howard, 1 Mary. Christopher Bumpsted levied a Fine of the Manor of *Whifhanger* to John Brown, 4 Mary, from which Time to the prefent Period it has been vefted in the Family of Partridge. *Hazelhoufe*, formerly belonging to the knightly Family of Kingstone †, is within this Hamlet, and is the Refidence of the Family of Mills. A Valley, called the City, containing a few Cottages, and on the oppofite Side a Spot which is commonly denominated the Camp, is alfo within this Hamlet.

2. *Sudgrove*, alias *Southgrove*, applying to its Situation on the South-weft Side of the Village, where is a modern Edifice, the Refidence of John Selfe, Efq. Milo, Conftable of *Gloucefter*, gave the Tithes of *Sutgrove-Reftald* to the Church of *Llanthony.*

3. The *Slad*, or *Slade*, from the *Saxon* Word Slaꝺe, a Slip of Ground, which lies three Miles North-weft of the Village of *Miferden.* Of this Hamlet there is nothing worthy remark.

The principal Eftates are vefted in the Lord of the Manor, John Selfe, and Theyer Townshend, Efqrs. and in the Families of Mills and Partridge.

B E N E F A C T I O N S.

1659, Thomas Muggleton gave, by Will, for the Benefit of the Poor of this Parifh, Land and Wood; the annual Produce of which is 15*s.* vefted in the Overfeer of the Poor of *Duntefbourne-Abbots* for the Time being. The Coppice Wood to be cut every fourteenth Year, and the Produce thereof (after paying the Expences) to be equally divided between the four Parifhes of *Duntfbourne-Abbots, Miferden, Side,* and *Winfon.*

1758, Mary Barnsdale gave, by Will, for the Benefit of the fecond Poor of this Parifh, 50*l.* in Money, now vefted in Mr. John Mills and Mr. John Coates; the annual Produce of which is 2*l.*

Incumbents.	Patrons.	Incumbents.	Patrons.
1590 Robert Madrin,	Queen Elizabeth.	1681 John Durfton,	The fame.
—— William Woulds,	——————.	1728 Giles Mills,	Barbara Sandys.
1673 William Wooley,	King Charles.	1785 Jofeph Green, M. A.	Samuel Sandys, Efq.
—— Samuel Rufh,	Miles Sandys, Efq.	1790 John Wafhbourn, D. D.	The fame.
—— William Hanfbey,	The fame.		

Present Lord of the Manor,

Samuel Sandys, Efq.

The Perfons fummoned from this Parifh by the Heralds, in 1682 and 1683, were

Miles Sandys, Efq. and Henry Partridge, Gent.

At the Election in 1776, Eight Freeholders polled from this Parifh.

The firft Date of the Regifter, March 12, 1574. At p. 18 of this Book, is the following curious and concife Memorandum : " The x o January was buried old Joan, out of Mr. Partridge Howfe."

ANNUAL ACCOUNT OF MARRIAGES, BIRTHS, AND BURIALS, IN THIS PARISH.

A.D.	Mar.	Bir.	Bur.	A.D.	Mar.	Bir.	Bur.	A.D.	Mar.	Bir.	Bur.	A.D.	Mar.	Bir.	Bur.
1781	3	18	6	1786	4	11	12	1791	3	11	17	1796			
1782	0	11	12	1787	4	19	9	1792	2	20	12	1797			
1783	4	16	5	1788	3	12	6	1793	2	8	7	1798			
1784	2	10	5	1789	2	14	11	1794				1799			
1785	4	6	7	1790	4	14	8	1795				1800			

* Ƿicinᵹaꝼ, in the *Saxon* Language, fignifies *Rovers* or *Privates.*
† Edmund Kingstone, of *Hazelhoufe*, ob. 1623, Heir of his Nephew William Kingstone. MSS.

INSCRIPTIONS IN THE CHURCH.
IN THE CHANCEL.

ON A MONUMENT:

Arms; Argent, on a Chevron Sable, an Eagle difplayed of the firft.

Sifte, Viator.
Neve fileret ætas infida, nimus loquatur faxum.
Juxta requiefcit fpe beatæ Refurrectionis
Quod mortale fuit tam patris quam filii,
In gremio matris
Delitefcentium,
Quorum nomina, ipfâ vel invitâ invidiâ,
Tanquam Αϲθότουον è radice fertili fatis
Memoriam fpirant immarcefcibilem.

Obijt ætatis 64. Anº falutis 70.

Patris fcilicet GULIELMI WOLLEY, A. M.
Hujus Ecclefiæ fpatio fere annorum quadraginta
Rectoris vigilantiffimi,
Qui quidem ufque & ufque meruit
Quicquid grata memoria in illum conferat;
Si fidelitas Regi CAROLO Regum optimo
Martyrum beatiffimo, fi charitas egenis,
Si omnibus extenfa benignitas exemplar,
Si denique labor indefeffus in Vineâ Domini
Laudem promeruiffe videatur.

Obijt { ætatis 50. Anº { falutis 59.

Conjugem habuit ELIZABETHAM,
Piam, caftam, fidelem;
Filium reliquit GULIELMUM WOLLEY,
Meritorum & ecclefiæ optimo jure
fucceflorem.

Obijt { ætatis 38. Anº { falutis 81.

Qui poft fluctus etiam vel decurrianos
(fed Σκαϲ⊙ τὸ ιϲχον Φορλιον βαιαϲιι)
Exuvias mortalitatis cœlebs depofuit;
Numerofâ tamen progenie clariffimus,
Abundans fcilicet opimis operibus:
Ab ærumnis avocavit mitiffimus pater

Nihil occultum quod non revelabitur.

ad αιωνον βάρ⊙ δόξης & ab ira τῶν ατοχων:
Dum moritur medium fedulus inter opus:
Abi, viator, & æternum præpone caducis.
Hoc quale quale pietatis monumentum pignus
Obfervantiæ in memoriam chariffimi parentis
Charique fratris, mœrens pofuit JANA WOLLEY, foboles
Unica fuperftes.

ON A MONUMENT, WITH THE EFFIGIES OF A MAN, WOMAN, AND FOUR CHILDREN, KNEELING BEFORE AN ALTAR:

Arms; Chequy, on a Bend three Efcallops, for PARTRIDGE;—impaling, Or, a Fefs embattled between three Catharine-wheels Sable, for CARTWRIGHT.

HERE LYETH THE BODY OF ANTHONY PARTRIGE, OF WISHANGER, GENT. SONNE OF ROBERT PARTRIGE, ESQUIER, WHO MARRIED ALICE, DAUGHTER OF TIMOTHY CARTWRIGHT, GENT. BY WHOM HE HAD ISSUE THREE SONNES AND ONE DAUGHTER, WHO DEPARTED THIS LIFE THE 25 DAY OF MARCH, ANNO DOMINI 1625, AGED 57.

ON AN ALTAR TOMB, A CUMBENT FIGURE IN ARMOUR, WITH A GOAT AT THE FEET:

Arms; Azure, a Crofs Or, between four Leopards Faces Argent, for KINGSTON.

HERE LYETH THE BODY OF WILLIAM KINGSTON, OF MISERDEN, ESQVIER, SONNE AND HEIRE TO ANTHONY KING-
6

STON, ESQVIER, WHO MARRIED MARY, DAUGHTER TO JOHN WASHBORNE, OF WICKENFORD IN THE COVNTY OF WORCESTER, ESQVIER, THE WHICH WILLIAM KINGSTON WAS FAITHFUL TO HIS PRINCE AND LOVING TO HIS COVNTREY, BEING HIGH SHERIFF OF THIS COVNTY, DEPARTED THIS LIFE THE 12 DAY OF DECEMBER, ANNO DOMINI 1614, ÆTATIS 39.

ON FLAT STONES.

ROBERT, THE SONNE OF HENRY PARTRIGE, LYETH HERE, WHO DIED THE 1 DAY OF JANUARY, 1645.

HERE LIETH THE BODY OF WILLIAM PARTRIGE, THE THIRD SON OF ANTHONY PARTRIGE, OF WISSINGER, GENT. WHO DEPARTED THIS LIFE THE 23 DAY OF APRILL, AN. DOMINI 1651.

Arms; PARTRIDGE as before.

Here lyeth the Body of HENRY, the Sonne of . . . . PARTRIGE, Gent. who departed this Life March . . Anno Dom. 1696, ætatis fuæ 25.

Arms as before.

In Memory of HENRY PARTRIGE, Gent. the only Son of THOMAS and HESTER PARTRIGE, of Wifhanger in this Parifh, Gent. who departed this Life the 17 Day of Auguft, Anº Dom. 1730, aged 36 Years.

Here lyeth the Body of ELIZABETH WOLLEY, the Daughter of WILLIAM WOLLEY, who departed this Life Jan. 16, 1619, aged 10 Years.

Mr. JOHN DURSTON, interred here, was born at Ripple, Worcefterfhire, educated at Winchefter, elected into New College, Oxford, prefented by that College to the Rectory of Alton, Wilts, Rector likewife of this Church above 40 Years, died the 29 of Feb. 1727, aged 82.

Arms; Per Fefs embattled Sable and Argent, fix Croffes pateé counterchanged, for WARNFORD.

In Memoriam
THO. WARNEFORD, Civis Londonenfis,
Filii natu maximi
THO. WARNEFORD, Generofi,
de Sutgrove,
Pofuit
HEN. WARNEFORD, confanguineus et
Hæres ex Teftamento.
Ob. 9 Jan.
Anno { Dom. 1717.
        { ætatis 63.

To the Memory of THOMAS MILLER, late of Wifhanger, in this Parifh, Yeoman. He died the 30 of January, 1749, aged 64.

Alfo of MARGARET, Relict of the aforefaid THOMAS MILLER. She died the 19 of May, 1766, aged 73.

And of WILLIAM MILLER their Son, who died the 26th of June, 1766, aged 36.

IN A CHAPEL ON THE SOUTH SIDE OF THE CHANCEL.

On a very handfome Marble Tomb are the Effigies of a Man and Woman at full Length, in the Drefs of the Times. The Man has a Griffin at his Feet, and the Woman a Falcon. Round the Sides are five Sons and five Daughters, kneeling; the whole is exquifitely finifhed.

Arms, on feveral Efcocheons; Or, a Fefs dancetté between three Crofs Croflets fitché Gules, for SANDYS. Argent, a Bend engrailed Gules, for CULPEPER.

On a Monument at the Head of the Tomb:

Arms; Quarterly, 1ft, SANDYS; 2d, CULPEPER; 3d, Argent, a Chevron Gules, between ten Martlets Sable, for HARDRESHULL; 4th, Or, a Crofs engrailed

grailed Gules, in the firft Quarter a Bird Sable, for HAWTE ; 5th, Argent, on a Bend Sable, three Martlets Or, for BEDGBERIE ; 6th, Azure, a Fefs between two Cheveronels Or ; 7th, Ermine, on a Chief Azure, three Lions rampant Or, for AUCHER ; 8th, Azure, fretty Argent, on a Chief Or, two Mullets Or ; 9th, Argent, femé Fleurs de Lys Azure ; 10th, Ermine, a Crofs Argent voided Gules ; 11th, Argent, three Bears Heads erafed Sable, muzzled Or.

HERE LYETH THE BODIE OF SIR WILLIAM SANDYS,

OF MUSÆRDEN, IN THE COUNTIE OF GLOUC. KNIGHT.

HE DEPARTED THIS LIFE MARCH THE 2, 1640, AGED 77.

AND DAME MARGARET HIS WIFE, DAUGHTER AND HEIRE

OF WALTER CULPEPPER, OF HANBURROGH, IN Yᵉ COUNTIE

OF OXON, ESQUIER, AND SHE DEPARTED THIS LIFE JUNE THE 13, 1644, AGED 64.

IN MR. MILLS'S BURIAL CHAPEL.

ON HANDSOME MARBLE MONUMENTS.

Arms ; barry of ten Argent and Vert ; over all, fix Efcocheons Gules, for MILLS ;—impaling, Azure, on a Chevron between three Fleurs de Lis Or, three Mullets Sable.

M. S.

GULIELMI MILLS, de Hafelhoufe, & SARÆ uxoris ejus. Ille vir probus et honeftus omnibus carus morte correptus fuit Anno 1724, ætatis 68. Ipfa vidua plorans Mater pia & benigna tandem efflavit animam Anno 1761, ætatis 91.	Item ELIZÆ uxoris GULIELMI MILLS, de Hafelhoufe, Armigeri, quæ ob caftitatem fanctitatem & pietatem eximia illuftris ex hac Vita in fpem melioris difceffit anno 1746, ætatis 48. Item GULIELMI MILLS, de Hafelhoufe, Armig. Obiit anno 1776, ætatis 82.

Arms, in a Lozenge, MILLS as before.

M. S.

ESTHERÆ MILLS, de vico vulgo dicto The Edge, GULIELMI MILLS, de Hazlehoufe, Arm. & SARÆ uxoris ejus felicis natu maximæ

nec non

MARIÆ fororis prædictæ ESTHERÆ minimæ natu illa animam meliora fperans Deo reddidit die 25° Decembris, 1775. Hæc vitam ærumnofam cum beafa immortalitate commutavit die 11° Augufti, 1782.

Et

hoc monumentum fororiæ Caritatis erigi juffit.

IN THE CHURCH-YARD.

ON TOMBS.

HEARE WEARE BURIED THE BODYS OF ANTHONY OCKHOVLD AND TACEY HIS WIFE WHICH ANTHONY DECEASED THE 24 OF MAY, 1605, AND TACEY THE 15 OF JANUARY, 1612.

HERE LYETH THE BODY OF JOHN GIBBINS, BURIED THE 10 DAY OF DECEMB. ANNO DOM. 1659.

In Memory of ANTHONY GIBBINS, Yeoman, who was buried the 1 Day of Nov. 1707, aged 77.

Alfo of ANN his Wife, who was buried the 16 of Sept. 1719, aged 78.

To the Memory of WILLIAM COATES, of this Parifh, Yeoman, who departed this Life May the 4, anno Dom. 1764, aged 79 Years.

ANN, Relict of WILLIAM COATES, died Dec. 15, 1772, aged 86 Years.

In Memory of WILLIAM COATES, late of the Parifh of Winfton, Yeoman, who departed this Life the 23d Day of Auguft, 1764, aged 45 Years.

Here refteth the Body of THOMAS MUGGLETON, who deceafed the 29 Day of May, 1659.

In Memory of ELIZABETH BARKSDALE, of Cirencefter, who departed this Life Novem. the 14, A. D. 1744, aged 76 Years.

In Memory of Mrs. MARY BARBARA BARKSDALE, Spinfter, Daughter of JOHN and ELIZABETH BARKSDALE. She departed this Life Nov. the 22, A. D. 1758, aged 55 Years.

Here lies the Body of ELIZABETH, Daughter of Mr. JOHN BARKSDALE, and of ELIZABETH his Wife, who died . . . . . 17 . . aged 30 Years.

Here refteth the Body of Mrs. ANNE WARNEFORD, who departed this Life Dec. the 12, Anno Dom. 1755, aged 95 Years.

Beneath refteth the Remains of JOHN PARTRIDGE, Gent. of Wifhanger, who, after a tedious and painful Illnefs, exchanged this Life for a State of Immortality Jan. 5, 1785, aged 71 Years.

Alfo in Memory of ANNE, the Wife of JOHN PARTRIDGE, Gent. who was interred at Bifley in June 1768, aged 56 Years.

SARAH his fecond Wife was near this Tomb interred in the Year 1787.

In Memory of Mr. JOHN HALE, Member of the Corporation of Surgeons in London. He departed this Life the 9 Day of January, 1788, aged 49.

This Tomb was erected by JOHN STEPHENS, Native of Hullhavington, in the County of Wilts, and MARGARET his Wife, Daughter of PETER and MARGARET HERBERT, of this Parifh.

Beneath this Tomb is interred the Remains of JOHN STEPHENS. He departed this Life September the 8, 1791, aged 64 Years.

WILLIAM, only Son of JOHN and MARGARET STEPHENS, died Jan. 13, 1790, aged 17 Years.

ON FLAT STONES.

To the Memory of DANIEL GIBBINS, fen. of this Parifh, and SARAH his Wife. She died 15 Oct. 1773, aged 70 Years. He the 27 Nov. 1783, aged 81 Years.

Here lyeth the Body of SAMUEL MILLS, of this Parifh, who departed this Life . . February, 1717, aged 45.

Here refteth the Body of WILLIAM, the Son of DANIEL and SARAH MILLS, of this Parifh, who died the 29 Sept. 1741, aged 12 Years.

In Memory of JOHN HILL, of Sutgrove, who departed this Life February 13, 1782, aged 36 Years.

In Memory of ELIZABETH, the Wife of JOHN HILL, of Sutgrove, who died May 13, 1737, aged 36 Years.

JOHN HILL, fen. departed this Life Sept. 25, 1774, aged 76 Years.

Near this Place lyeth the Body of MARY, the Wife of JOHN HILL, who died Feb. 17, 1781, aged 81.

Here

Here lyeth the Remains of JOHN WELLS, who died the 11 May, 1785, in the 63 Year of his Age.

In Memory of SARAH, the Wife of JOHN PERKINS, of this Parish, who died March 15, 1773, aged near 70 Years.

To the Memory of SARAH, the Wife of THOMAS MOUSTO, and first the Wife of CHRISTO. NAISH, who died May the 22, 1720, aged 58 Years.

HENRY CLEMENTS, of this Parish, died July the 12, 1762, aged 91 Years.

SARAH his Wife died Dec. 25, 1720, aged 31 Years.

JOHN PINCHIN, of this Parish, died the 28 Day of January, 1727, aged 75 Years.

MARY, Wife of JOHN PINCHIN, of this Parish, died Feb. 13, 1748-9, aged 79 Years.

To the pious Memory of ANNE, the Wife of JOHN COATES, of this Parish, Yeoman. She died Dec. 11, 1772, aged 39 Years.

To the Memory of MARY, Relict of THOMAS DOWDIN, of Cirencester, Innholder, and Daughter of JOHN COATES, of this Parish, Yeoman. She departed this Life the 1st of April, 1783, aged 26 Years.

In Memory of JOHN, Son of WILLIAM and MARTHA PAINTER, of this Parish. He departed this Life the 30 Jan. 1765, aged 18.

Also MARTHA, Wife of WILLIAM PAINTER, who departed this Life the 19 Sept. 1782, aged 78 Years.

THOMAS HUNT, of Hampton, died November the 13, 1746, aged 61 Years.

ON HEAD-STONES.

	Died	Aged
Thomas Clements	—— 1706	70
Elizabeth his Wife	17 July, 1705	71
Richard Soul	11 Nov. 1767	88
Sarah his Wife	30 Dec. 1764	79
Richard their Son	28 June, 1783	60
Jane Westbury	—— 1722	76
John Bryan	31 May, 1735	70
Benjamin Sheppard	18 Mar. 1764	73
Selena, Wife of Thomas Russell	29 July, 1749	49
John Halling	9 Jan. 1727	51
Elizabeth his Wife	30 Sept. 1735	51
Mary, Wife of John Bryan	10 May, 1712	35
Henry Mace	19 May, 1744	56
Margaret his Wife	28 Mar. 1749	—
Thomas Mace	24 Mar. 1696	—
Sarah, Wife of Thomas Allen	27 Nov. 1733	25
Elizabeth, Wife of Jarvis Sayer	6 Mar. 1777	68
Peter Herbert	6 Aug. 1727	69
Jane his Wife	17 Oct. 1724	52
Peter Herbert	23 Sept. 1776	72
Margaret his Wife	31 Mar. 1770	70
Sarah his Wife	29 May, 1777	37
George Wilkins	3 Mar. 1731	—
Ann, Wife of John Burrows	12 July, 1779	55

CLXXVII. MORETON

CLXXVII. MORETON HENMARSH;

O R, as it is fometimes written, *MORETON IN THE MARSH*, received its name of *Moor Town* from its low and damp Situation. The additional Title of *Henmarfh* has been confidered as fynonymous, and explained in fignifying the *Old Marfh*; but it is with great Probability derived by Sir ROBERT ATKYNS from Þen, *Old*, and Ꝏeapc, a *Boundary*, as an ornamented Pillar is placed on a Spot of Ground near the Village to mark the Boundaries of four adjoining Counties, *Oxfordfhire* lying on the Eaft, *Gloucefterfhire* on the Weft, *Warwickfhire* on the North-eaft, and a detached Part of the County of *Worcefter* running up to this Point on the South.

It is a Parifh of inconfiderable Extent, fituated on the *Roman* Fofs Road from *Cirencefter*, and comprifed within the upper Part of *Weftminfter* Hundred, is diftant four Miles North from *Stowr*, five South-eaft from *Campden*, and twenty-nine North-eaft from GLOUCESTER.

In the Reign of HENRY III. a Charter was granted to this Place for a Market and Fair, but they have long fince been difufed.

The Church is a fmall Fabric, dedicated to *St. David*, the Patron of the *Welfh* Nation, confifting of one Aifle, and an embattled Tower at the Weft End. It is a Chapel of Eafe to *Bourton on the Hill*, and being under the peculiar Jurifdiction of *Blockley*, where the Inhabitants formerly had a Right of Sepulture, it pays Mortuaries to the Vicar of that Parifh.

Pope JULIUS II. by a Bull, dated 1512, 15 kal. Feb. pontificat anno 10, permitted the Parifhioners of *Morton Hemmerfche* to bury their Dead at *Morton* " propter interpofita montium Juga præcipuè bru-" mali tempore," as it is therein expreffed.

The Lands are chiefly Pafture, and the Soil varies from Clay to Stonebrafh.

There is a Place called *Dorn*, about a Mile North of the Village, in *Worcefterfhire*, where large Quantities of *Roman* Coins have been difcovered, and near to which are two confiderable Barrows, whence we may infer that it was a fmall *Roman* Poft or Station.

The Manor was held by two Thanes * in the Reign of King EDWARD the CONFESSOR, but at the Time of the general Survey no mention is made of it as a diftinct Manor; and, as it antiently formed Part of the Parifh of *Bourton on the Hill*, a probable Conjecture may be allowed, that it was included in the eight Hides which the Church of *Weftminfter* had there, dependent on the Manor of *Deerhurft*. At the Diffolution of the Abbey it was granted to the Dean and Chapter of *Weftminfter*, 34 HEN. VIII. but in the 4th Year of the Reign of Queen MARY, the Abbey was reftored, and the Manor re-granted to it.

In the 2d Year of ELIZABETH's Reign it was again confirmed to the Dean and Chapter, under whom WILLIAM BATESON, Efq. is the prefent Leffee, and holds a Court Leet.

RICHARD DALBY and his Wife levied a Fine of Lands in *Moreton Henmarfh*, 9 HEN. VII. †

No Benefactions to the Poor.

The Lift of INCUMBENTS the fame as *BOURTON ON THE HILL.*

PRESENT LORD OF THE MANOR.

The Perfons fummoned from this Place by the Heralds, in 1682 and 1683, were

Samuel Crefwick, Efq.	Mr. Dyer.
Mr. Fines.	Mr. Batefon.
Mr. Beeke.	Mr. Meredith.

---

* Saxon Barons, or Nobles, a Title to which no one was raifed, except ffrom noble Birth, and the Poffeffion of Lands.
HUME's Hiftory of *England*, Appendix 1.

† ATKYNS, Hiftory of *Gloucefterfhire*, p. 295.

VOL. II.   N n n   At

At the Election in 1776 Fifteen Freeholders polled from this Parish.

The first Date of the Register is in 1643.

ANNUAL ACCOUNT OF MARRIAGES, BIRTHS, AND BURIALS, IN THIS PARISH.

A. D.	Mar.	Bir.	Bur.	A.D.	Mar.	Bir.	Bur.	A.D.	Mar.	Bir.	Bur.	A.D.	Mar.	Bir.	Bur.
1781	1	24	14	1786	5			1791				1796			
1782	3	15	7	1787	9			1792				1797			
1783	6	26	13	1788	4			1793				1798			
1784	4	24	10	1789	5			1794				1799			
1785	10	20	9	1790	8			1795				1800			

INSCRIPTIONS IN THE CHURCH.

IN THE CHANCEL.

ON FLAT STONES.

Arms; on an Atchievement; a Lion rampant, for CRESWICKE.

SAMUEL CRESWICK died the 24 of April, 17 · ·

HENRY, Son of SAMUEL CRESWICK, was buried 12 March, 1731.

ANNE, Daughter of SAMUEL CRESWICK, was interred March the 10, 1757.

HENRY CRESWICKE, of the Custom-house, London, was buried here 17 October, 1773.

GEORGE GREENWOOD, Son of Mr. THOMAS GREENWOOD, of Chafelton, was interred Febr. 18, 1685.

JOHANNES HAMMOND, natus 25 die Junii, A. D. 1682, denatus 25 die Julii, A. D. 1683.

IN THE NAVE.

Arms; on an Atchievement; quarterly, 1st and 4th, three Owls; 2d and 3d, six Annulets, 3, 2, and 1, for LODER.

Here lyeth the Body of BEEKE LODER, Gent. who departed this Life August the 16, 1728, aged 55.

In Memory of Mrs. MARY LODER, who lyeth here under her own Pew. She departed this Life December 10, 1735, aged 86 Years.

Here lyeth the Body of MARY THEOBALD, Widow, Relict of THOMAS THEOBALD, of Barking, in the County of Suffolk, and only Daughter of the abovesaid MARY LODER, who died on the 1st of June, in the Year of our Lord 1744, aged 66 Years.

HERE LYETH THE BODY OF MR. BENJAMIN COLES, JUN. WHO DIED THE 11 OF NOV. 1692, HAVING JUST ENTERED THE 30TH YEAR OF HIS AGE.

ALSO THE BODY OF BENJAMIN COLES, SEN. IS HERE INTERRED. HE DIED MAY 3, 1703, AGED 74.

In Memory of THOMAS DAVIS, who died Nov. 7, 1783, aged 61 Years.

Also of ELIZABETH his Wife, who died the 11 of June, 1784, aged 56 Years.

Here lyeth interred the Body of RICHARD ALLBERT, who departed this Life Dec. 20, An. Dom. 1722. aged 80 Years.

IN THE NORTH AISLE.

ON FLAT STONES.

Here lyeth the Body of MARY, the Wife of JOSEPH CLAYDON. She died July the 22, 1744, aged 42.

Near this Place lyeth the Body of Mrs. HESTER WINSLOW, Relict of Mr. JOHN WINSLOW, who died January the 30, 1758, aged 64.

Also the Body of the Rev. THOMAS WINSLOW, Son of JOHN and HESTER WINSLOW, who departed this Life January 27, 1766, aged 41.

In hopes of a joyful Refurrection here lyeth the Body of JOHN WINSLOW, of this Town, who departed this Life the 1st Day of August, 1714, ætat. suæ 76.

Beyond this Stone also lyeth the Body of ANNE, the Wife of JOHN WINSLOW, who departed this Life Sept. 5, Anno Dni 1727, aged 77 Years.

Also the Body of JOHN WINSLOW, the Son of JOHN and ANNE WINSLOW, who departed this Life Sept. 19, 1737, aged 56.

IN THE CHURCH-YARD.

AGAINST THE CHURCH, ON A MONUMENT:

In Memory of NICHOLAS DYER, who died Sept. 22, 1713, aged 57 Years.

Also the Body of FRANCES READE, the Daughter of NICHOLAS and ELIZABETH DYER, who departed this Life Dec. 28, 1720, aged 19.

ON A TOMB:

In Memory of RICHARD PARR, of Dorn. He departed this Life January the 28th, 1691, aged 84.

Also EDWARD, the Son of RICHARD PARR, died Nov. the 4th, 1697, aged 48.

In Memory of MARY, the Wife of NICHOLAS FLETCHER, of Dorn, who departed this Life Dec. 10, 1738, aged 78.

Here lyeth the Body of NICHOLAS, the Son of NICHOLAS and MARY FLETCHER, of Dorn, who departed this Life Feb. 14, 1719, aged 15 Years.

O N

ON HEAD-STONES.

Name	Died	Aged
Anthony Gueſt	1 Oct. 1766	60
John Proctor	16 Aug. 1779	68
Thomas Bryan	10 Jan. 1780	82
Thomas Fifield	29 Nov. 1759	25
Mary his Wife	26 Aug. 1761	25
Robert Hawes	11 Jan. 1767	76
Sarah his Wife	4 Sept. 1765	67
Thomas Monnington	28 Mar. 1789	73
Phebe his Wife	30 June, 1788	62
John Powers	20 Jan. 1789	54
Mary his Wife	6 Jan. 1784	46
Robert Triſtram	7 Oct. 1716	88
Alice his Wife	11 Nov. 1713	87
Sarah, Wife of Charles Triſtram	18 Mar. 1764	45
Charles Kitſon Triſtram	31 Mar. 1775	59
Thomas Morris	19 Oct. 1790	66
William Townſend	10 July, 1675	—
Thomas Page	9 Sept. 1724	74
Thomas Horne	7 Mar. 1765	27
Stephen Morley	23 Sept. 1729	69
Alice his Wife	28 Mar. 1730	62
Sarah, Wife of William Dyer	4 Dec. 1777	31
Martha Smith	4 May, 1733	91
Mary, Wife of James Smith	25 Mar. 1742	39
Thomas, Son of William Smith	21 Mar. 1732	—
Elizabeth, Wife of Henry Smith	16 Aug. 1779	26
Sarah, Wife of John Luckett	24 Sept. 1783	40
Mary, Wife of William Driver	14 Nov. 1760	45
William Driver	7 Apr. 1770	75
Mary his Wife	14 Nov. 1760	45
Henry Goodear	24 Dec. 1752	56
Martha his Wife	17 Oct. 1771	84
Mary, Wife of Benjamin Buſby	7 Nov. 1791	65
Robert Jane	—— 1646	—
William Sanders	7 May 1716	89
Anne his Wife	21 Feb. 1714	82
James Procter	4 Oct. 1778	39
Anne his Wife	29 Sept. 1766	27
John Mayo	25 Apr. 1781	70
Elizabeth his Wife	24 Aug. 1755	39
Francis Miles	26 June, 1771	28
Mary, Wife of Robert Miles	24 Mar. 1789	65
John Horſeley	18 Nov. 1774	81
Joan his Wife	7 May 1775	84
Elizabeth, Wife of Thomas Horſeley	2 Aug. 1778	58
Mary, Wife of Richard Collet	20 Feb. 1699	—
Elizabeth, Daughter of John Collet	24 Oct. 1737	27
Francis Tyms	2 Jan. 1695	83
Thomas Roſe	21 June, 1685	—
Margaret Roſe	10 July, 1685	—
Philip Baldwin	6 May, 1745	33
Roſe his Wife	2 Aug. 1780	77
Rachel, Wife of Richard Hopkins	10 June, 1748	22
Richard Beckett	30 Apr. 1775	82
Elizabeth his Wife	27 June, 1745	57
Joſeph, Son of Joſeph Percy	7 May, 1737	20
Mary, Wife of John Herbert	8 Nov. 1770	71
John their Son	10 July, 1765	20
Ann Sanders	—— 1707	56
Grace, Wife of Arthur Dyer	25 Jan. 1715	89
John Dyer	4 Mar. 1725	75
Frances, Wife of Thomas Dyer	10 July, 1695	—
Elizabeth, Wife of John Hine	11 Oct. 1699	75
John their Son	8 Oct. 1699	—
Thomas Bryan	10 Jan. 1780	82
Elizabeth his Wife	26 May, 1755	52
George Bryan	18 June, 1789	50
Elizabeth his Wife	7 May, 1786	51
Elizabeth Procter	31 Aug. 1726	53
Thomas, Son of Thomas and Elizabeth Procter	8 May, 1740	33
John Procter	16 Aug. 1779	68
Robert Brunett	— Sept. 1727	52
William Hyate	27 Feb. 1725	26
Elizabeth, Wife of James Hyatt	10 Feb. 1791	71
William Poole	14 Nov. 1693	—
Mary Poole	4 —— 1701	—
Iſaac Poole	21 Nov. 1778	62
John Phipes	14 Apr. 1678	—
Robert Phipes	6 Mar. 1708	—
Lawrence Ratcliffe	29 July, 1695	—
William Whatcat	5 Nov. 1684	—
Ann his Wife	—— 1702	—
Iſaac Snow	17 Feb. 1720	80
Mary his Wife	28 May, 1726	82
Thomas Snow	10 July, 1733	60
Joane, Wife of John Charlet	15 Feb. 1707	24
Lydia, Daughter of Thomas Broadway	28 Sept. 1739	19
Joſeph Townſend	24 May, 1704	—
Hodges Wood	20 Sept. 1737	24
Anthony Gueſt	4 May, 1680	—
Anthony Gueſt	1 Oct. 1766	60
Thomas Browne	20 Apr. 1723	74
John, Son of William and Lucy Perey	—— 1715	31
Sarah, Daughter of Joſeph Townſend	25 Apr. 1685	—
Robert Read	26 July, 1667	—
Elizabeth his Wife	10 Oct. 1706	102
Jone, Daughter of John and Mary Carter	24 Nov. 1667	—
Thomas Blizard	24 July, 1747	—
Dorothy his Wife	3 May, 1754	61
Nicholas Izod	1 May, 1758	66
Thomas Morris	8 July, 1769	81
Mary, Daughter of Charles Parker	23 Mar. 1768	39
John Berry	18 May, 1762	38
John Croſs	23 Dec. 1729	61
Thomas Archar	27 Apr. 1721	80
Sarah his Wife	24 —— 1709	—
Sarah Archar	9 Feb. 1738	54
Rachel, Wife of Thomas Minchin	9 Jan. 1764	42
Thomas Minchin	16 Apr. 1788	67
William Curtis	22 Jan. 1756	71
Mary his Wife	22 Aug. 1760	73
John Callow	1 June, 1769	52
Ann, Wife of Samuel Callow	28 May, 1781	59
Robert Shirley	15 Jan. 1745	49
Sarah his Wife	5 June, 1748	47
Edward Parr	4 Nov. 1697	48
Mary, Wife of Thomas Eechnam	— Sept. 1664	—
Frances, Wife of Abel Bennet	29 June, 1666	—
John Mayo	19 Dec. 1695	37
Frances Mayo	13 Dec. 1695	—
Alice, Wife of William Kearby	8 Mar. 1717	—

CLXXVIII. MORETON

CLXXVIII. MORETON VALENCE;

S O denominated from its antient Poffeffors the VALENTIAS Earls of PEMBROKE, in the Reign of EDWARD the Firft and EDWARD the Second.

This Village is fituated in the great Vale of *Severn*, which River bounds it on the Weft, and in the Hundred of *Whitftone*. It is diftant Seven Miles Weft from *Durfley*, and fix South from the City of GLOUCESTER.

Of the Soil, which is a ftrong Clay, the greater Part is Pafture and Meadow Land, with a fmall Portion of Arable, and its Orchards are particularly luxurious and productive.

The Living is a perpetual Curacy, the Stipend of which has been augmented by Queen ANNE's Bounty. The impropriate Tithes belong to one of the Prebends of the Cathedral Church of *Hereford*, whofe Leffee is Patron.

The Church, which is dedicated to *St. Stephen*, has a large Aifle on the South Side, and at the Weft End an embattled Tower.

From the Difcovery of an antient Foundation of hewn Stones in a Field near the Church, which appears to have been encircled by a Moat, it has been thought to be the Site of the manerial Manfion Houfe of the VALENCES, or fome of their Succeffors.

Domefday Book recites " DURAND of GLOWEC" to have held *Mortune* in *Witeftan* Hundred in the Reign of WILLIAM the CONQUEROR; and in the 3cth Year of HENRY III. ROBERT DE PONT DE LARCH conveyed this Manor to WILLIAM DE VALENTIA, half Brother to King HENRY III. afterwards created Earl of PEMBROKE, who married JOAN, the Daughter of WARINE DE MONTCHENSY, a great Baron, called the Craffus of *England*, his Will amounting to 200,000 Marks. This Manor was appendant to *Whaddon*, in the 23d of EDWARD the Firft, and in the 17th EDWARD the Second, AUDOMARE, or AYMER DE VALENCIA, died feized of it, who granted two Acres and a Half in *Moreton* to the Abbey of *Gloucefter* 10 EDWARD II. In the fame Reign, JOHN COMYN, one of the Competitors for the Crown of *Scotland*, married JOAN, the youngeft Sifter and Coheirefs of the above AUDOMARE; and their Daughter ELIZABETH being married to RICHARD TALBOT, Anceftor to the Earls of *Shrewfbury*, he was in her Right feized of a third Part of this Manor, 20 EDW. II. JOHN Earl of SHREWSBURY, and THOMAS Vifcount LISLE, joined in levying a Fine of the Manor of *Moreton Valence* to Sir RICHARD BINGHAM, and others, 9 EDW. IV. and ELIZABETH Countefs of SHREWSBURY died feized of it 11 HENRY VIII. when ARTHUR PLANTAGENET and ELIZABETH his Wife had Livery granted them. It foon afterwards became vefted in the Crown, and was granted to THOMAS CROMWEL, Earl of *Effex*, upon whofe Attainder it was given to Sir WILLIAM KINGSTON, to whofe Son and Heir, Sir ANTHONY KINGSTON, Livery was granted of it 32 H. VIII. At a fubfequent Period it was purchafed by the JERNINGHAMS of *Norfolk*, the Proprietors of the Manor of *Painfwick*; and early in the prefent Century Sir RALPH DUTTON was Lord of it, whofe Defcendant JAMES DUTTON, Efq. created Baron SHERBORNE in 1784, is the prefent Lord.

This Parifh contains four

H A M L E T S.

1. *Horfe Marley*, wherein are feveral Eftates belonging to THOMAS SKIPP, Efq. 2. *Little Moreton.* 3. *Epney*, in which Lands were granted to Sir WILLIAM KINGSTON. 4. Part of *Framilode*.

Proprietors of Lands in this Parifh, and the feveral Hamlets, and WILDEY, REMINGTON, DANGERFIELD, FRYER, PALMER, HOWELL, BARON, WILKINS, OWEN, CAMBRIDGE, CHAMBERLAINE, &c.

B E N E F A C T I O N.

WILLIAM HOWE, by Will, dated 1666, gave a Rent Charge of 1*l.* annually to poor Houfeholders not receiving Relief of the Parifh.

4

Moreton

Moreton Valence and *Whaddon* are perpetual Curacies, and are Impropriations, the Tithes whereof, in 1704, were valued at 70*l.* *per annum*, out of which the Sum of 25*l.* *per annum* is paid to the Curate. The Curates are nominated by the Leſſee of the Tithes, who holds the ſame under a Canon of the Cathedral Church of *Hereford.*

Incumbents.	Patrons.	Incumbents.	Patrons.
1683 Henry Abbot, licenſed.	———————	1760 J. Bach, A. M.	———————
Daniel Capel, M. A.	———————	1763 John James, Clerk,	Nominated by James Ballard, Eſq.
1712 Daniel Bond, A. B.	———————		
1730 V. Rice, Clerk,	———————		Nominated by Samuel Remington,
1734 J. Somers, Clerk,	———————	1782 Joſeph Cheſter, D. D.	Gent. Leſſee of the
1740 H. Deane, Clerk,	———————	1784 Benjamin Jones, Clerk.	Great Tithes.
1754 H. Dimock, A. M.	———————		

Present Lords of the Manor,

Benjamin Hyett, Eſq. Lord Sherborn.

No Perſon was ſummoned from this Place by the Heralds, in 1682 and 1683.

At the Election in 1776 Twenty-two Freeholders polled from this Pariſh.

The earlieſt Date in the Regiſter occurs in 1684.

Annual Account of Marriages, Births, and Burials, in this Parish.

A.D.	Mar.	Bir.	Bur.	A.D.	Mar.	Bir.	Bur.	A.D.	Mar.	Bir.	Bur.	A.D.	Mar.	Bir.	Bur.
1781	2	4	1	1786	2	5	5	1791	6	6	3	1796			
1782	2	4	3	1787	3	11	2	1792	1	11	1	1797			
1783	3	4	3	1788	1	8	3	1793	1	9	6	1798			
1784	3	10	4	1789	2	6	1	1794	3	7	4	1799			
1785	1	10	7	1790	1	9	2	1795				1800			

INSCRIPTIONS IN THE CHURCH.

IN THE CHANCEL.
On a Monument :

To the
Memory of
John Harriss, of
this Pariſh, Yeoman. He
deceaſed Sept. 1, 1727,
aged 39.

Alſo in Memory of
Benjamin Harris, of this
Pariſh, Yeoman, who died
.. December, 1764, aged
68 Years.

Alſo Anne, the Wife of Benjamin
Harriss, of this Pariſh, Yeoman,
departed this Life January the
25, A. D. 1767, aged near
66 Years.

ON FLAT STONES.

HERE LYETH THE
BODY OF ANN, THE
WIFE OF JOHN
HARRIS, WHO DEPART-
ED THIS LIFE THE 6
DAY OF MAY, 1665,
AGED 81.

In Memory of Elizabeth,
the Wife of John Harris,
of this Pariſh, Yeoman, who
departed this Life the 12 Day
of March, Anno Domini 1725-6,
aged 35 Years.

In Memory of Benjamin Harris,
of Matſon, Yeoman, who
died May 30, 1722, aged
58 Years.

Elizabeth his Wife died
May 12, 1748, aged 88.

IN MEMORY OF
THOMAS SYMES, WHO
DECEASED THE 8TH OF
JULY, 1569.

John Symes, of this
Pariſh, departed this Life
June the 25, 1713.

In Memory of Elizabeth,
Wife of John Partridge, and
eldeſt Daughter of Henry Allin.
She died the 21ſt Day of October,
Anno Domini 1681, aged 61 Years.

In Memory of two Daughters of
George Barron, by Ann his Wife.
Anne died 7 Day of Auguſt,
A. D. 1724.
Mary died the 20 of Sept.
A. D. 1725.

In Memory of
Hannah, the Wife of George
Barron, who departed this Life
March 7, 1738,
in the 42 Year of her Age.

John Barron, eldeſt Son of
George Barron, by Hannah his
Wife, departed this Life Feb.
the 28, Anno Domini 1750-1,
aged 25 Years,

In Memory of
Hester, Daughter of George
Barron, Gent. by Anne his Wife,
who died the 8 Day of Novemb.
Anno Domini 1740, in the
31ſt Year of her Age.

Arms ; on a Chief two Creſcents.

In Memory of Mary, the
beloved Wife of George Barron,
jun. and Daughter of Mr.
John Smith, of Podgmead.
She departed this Life the 28
Jan. 1754, in the 24 Year of
her Age.

Arms as before.

To the Memory of
George Barron, ſen. of
this Pariſh, Son of
Mr. George Barron, of Little Dean,
by Anne his Wife. He departed
this Life the 13 Day of October, 1770,
aged 71.

Arms as above.

To the Memory of
Anne, Wife of Mr. George Barron,
of Little Dean,
and Daughter of Mr. John Brayne,
of the ſame Place, Gent.
by Mary his Wife.

She

She departed this Life
the 2 Day of Sept. 1754,
aged near 80 Years.

Also to the Memory of
ELIZABETH, second Wife of
GEORGE BARRON, jun.
the only Daughter of
Mr. THOMAS ASTMAN,
of Longney, by MARY his Wife.

She departed this Life
the 23 Day of Sept. 1770, aged
near 35 Years.

Underneath
are deposited the Remains
of the Rev. JOHN JONES,
twenty Years Minister of

this Parish,
during which Time he
discharged the several
Duties of his Office with
the greatest Assiduity.
He died
on the 8th of February, 1782,
aged 64 Years.

I N   T H E   C H U R C H - Y A R D.

ON TOMBS.

In Memory of THOMAS HARRIS, late of
Epney, who died April the 12, 1768,
aged 59 Years.

In Memory of
MARY, the Wife of THOMAS HARRIS,
of Epney, in this Parish, who died
Sept. 12, 1753, aged 24.

In Memory of JOSEPH TYKELL,
of the Town of Newnham, Mariner,
who departed this Life the 9 Day of
Aug. Anno Domini 1721,
aged 45 Years.

Also of WILLIAM, Brother to the
said JOSEPH TYKELL, who was
buried at Frampton on Severn,
the 6 Nov. 1758, aged near 80 Years.

In Memory
of ANNE TYKELL, the Wife of
JOZEPH TYKELL, Mariner.
She died the 14 Day of Oct.
Anno Domini 1721, aged 63 Years.

In Memory of THOMAS HUMPHRIS,
of Epney, who died the 27 Feb, 1714,
aged 79 Years.

Here resteth the Body of WILLIAM,
Son of THOMAS HUMPHRIS,
of this Parish,
who departed this Life the 6 Sept.
Anno Dom. 1676, aged 29.

In Memory of SAMUEL GREENING,
of the Parish of Saul, Yeoman, who
died Jan. 3, Anno Domini 1743,
aged 67.

In Memory of MARY, the Wife
of DANIEL WILY, Daughter of
THOMAS HUMPHRIS,
who died the 10 Feb. 1744,
aged 58 Years.

In Memory of RICHARD WILY,
of this Parish, Yeoman, who died
July the 10, 1757, aged 40 Years.

THOMAS, eldest Son of DANIEL
and MARY WILY, died August
1728.

ON A BRASS PLATE:

In Memory of MARY, the Wife
of WILLIAM BAILEY, of this Parish,
who departed this Life the 24th Day
of Dec. 1766, aged 42 Years.

ON FLAT STONES.

Here resteth tne Body
of SAMUEL HARRIS, who
departed this Life the 24
Day of June, Anno Dom. 1689,
ætatis suæ 32.

SAMUEL HOLDER departed
this Life the 16 Day of Dec.
Anno Domini 1674.

Here lyeth the Body
of WILLIAM HANDMAN, Mariner,
who departed this Life
Jan. 25, 1686.

Here lyeth also the Body of
HESTER, the Wife of WILLIAM
HANDMAN, who departed this
Life October the 31, 16..
aged 79 Years.

Here lyeth the
Body of ELIZABETH, the Daughter
of JEREMIAH GREENING, who
deceased . . . . 1678.

Here lyeth interred the
Body of ELIZABETH, the Daughter
of JEREMIAH GREENING, and of
EDBOROUGH his Wife, who de-
parted this Life the 29 of
September, 1689.

Here resteth the Body
of WILLIAM PALMER, of this
Parish, who departed this
Life November the 26, 1728,
aged 48 Years.

Here resteth the Body of
MARY, the Wife of WILLIAM
PALMER, Yeoman, who left
this Life January the 29, 1722,
aged 39 Years.

Here resteth the Body of
HANNAH, the Wife of WILLIAM
PALMER, of this Parish, Yeoman,
the eldest Daughter of BENJAMIN
and ELIZABETH HARRIS, of Matson,
who died May the 5, 1727
aged 42 Years.

In Memory of JOHN PALMER,
of this Parish, Yeoman. He
died May the 12, 1789,
aged 75 Years.

In Memory of
MARY, the Wife
of JOHN PALMER, of this
Parish, who died January the 20,
1777, aged near 63 Years.

In Memory of
MARY, the Wife of ANTHONY
ROGERS, who departed this
Life February the 25, 174..

O N   H E A D   S T O N E S.

	Died	Aged
Thomas, Son of William Palmer	24 June, 1683	—
Judith, Wife of Giles Palmer	12 Dec. 1692	39
Judith their Daughter -	23 July, 1683	—
Thomas, Son of William and Mary Palmer - -	13 June, 1737	18
Giles Palmer - -	28 Aug. 1759	48
William, Son of William Martin	28 Nov. 1729	—
Esther Wade - -	28 Mar. 1784	—
Sarah, Wife of Edmund Beard	15 Oct. 1673	63
Mary, Daughter of Samuel and Mary Beard - -	24 Jan. 1755	—
Ann, Wife of Anselm Fowler	17 May, 1672	—
Sarah their Daughter -	10 Nov. 1671	—
John Moody - -	9 Feb. 1779	59
Elizabeth his Wife -	29 Jan. 1779	49
Rachel Wells - -	27 Aug. 1783	80
Samuel Humphris -	23 Apr. 1693	—
Elizabeth his Wife -	4 Sept. 1685	—
Susannah, Wife of John Etheridge	22 Nov. 1721	43
James Birt - -	2 June, 1733	53
Elizabeth his Wife -	23 Apr. 1733	47
James Birt - -	24 Nov. 1751	45
Mary his Wife - -	3 Dec. 1770	60
Richard their Son -	7 Nov. 1766	25
William Birt - -	3 Mar. 1768	41
John Birt - -	27 Oct. 1787	48
Elizabeth Merrett - -	14 July, 1784	39
Elizabeth, Wife of Thomas Kedd	30 Oct. 1724	48
Peter Fry - -	—— —— 1700	—
Henry Gingell - -	26 Mar. 1731	67
Margaret his Wife -	7 Oct. 1718	—
Thomas Gregory -	—— —— 1710	—
Katharine his Wife -	24 Jan. 1718	71
Mary their Daughter -	9 Jan. 1707	—

2

DEERHURST   DEYNTON   DIDBROKE   DIDMARTON   DODINGTON   DOWDESWELL
Lane   Powell   Langton   Tracey   Codrington   Codrington   Rogers   Rich

DOWNE AMPNEY   DOWNE HATHERLEY   DUMBLEDON   DURSLEY
Villars   Hungerford   Porteredge   Gibbes   Brett   Peraye   Cockes   Wallington

DURSLEY   DYMOCK   DYRHAM
Phelps   Purnell New House   Capel   Wynter   Lye   De la Riviere   Rufsell   Dennis

DYRHAM   EASTINGTON   EAST LECHE St Martin   EAST LECHE Turville
Wynter   Blathwayte   Stephens   Stafford   Knevet   Clutterbuck   Parsons   Saunders

EBRINGTON   ELKSTONE   ELMORE   FAIRFORD
Keyte   Fortescue   Horton   Bowyer   Guise   Tame   Lygon   Tracey

FAIRFORD   FLAXLEY
Oldisworth   Huntington   Morgan   Barker   Colston   Ready   Boevey   Lloyd

FLAXLEY   FORTHAMPTON   FRAMPTON Cotterell
Clarke   Dowdeswell   Hayward   Kemys   Browne   Biss   Milborn   Simes

FRAMPTON upon Severn   FROCESTER   GUITING Power   GUITING Temple
Clifford   Codrington   Clutterbuck   Winchcombe   Wilkins   Bigland   Stratford   Talbot

END OF PART 2